WATERFOWL
ECOLOGY
AND
MANAGEMENT
Second Edition

WATERFOWL ECOLOGY AND MANAGEMENT
Second Edition

Guy A. Baldassarre
Eric G. Bolen

Illustrated by
Tamara R. Sayre

KRIEGER PUBLISHING COMPANY
Malabar, Florida
2006

Cover photo, background: Snow Geese field-feeding near Prime Hook National Wildlife Refuge, Delaware.
Photograph by Guy A. Baldassarre.
Cover photo, insert: A Mallard–American Black Duck pair in the Adirondacks, New York.
Photograph by Chris P. Dwyer

Original Edition 1994
Second Edition 2006

Printed and Published by
KRIEGER PUBLISHING COMPANY
KRIEGER DRIVE
MALABAR, FLORIDA 32950

**FROM A DECLARATION OF PRINCIPLES JOINTLY ADOPTED BY A COMMITTEE OF THE AMERI-
CAN BAR ASSOCIATION AND A COMMITTEE OF PUBLISHERS:**
This publication is designed to provide accurate and authoritative information in regard to the subject matter
covered. It is sold with the understanding that the publisher is not engaged in rendering legal, accounting, or other
professional service. If legal advice or other expert assistance is required, the services of a competent professional
person should be sought.

Library of Congress Cataloging-in-Publication Data

Baldassarre, Guy A.
    Waterfowl ecology and management / Guy A. Baldassarre, Eric G. Bolen—2nd ed.
        p. cm.
    Includes bibliographical references (p.) and index.
    ISBN 1-57524-260-5 (alk. paper)
    1. Waterfowl—Ecology—North America. 2. Waterfowl management—North America. I. Bolen, Eric G. II. Title.

QL696.A52B335   2006
639.9'7841'097—dc22

2005044485

10 9 8 7 6 5 4 3 2

CONTENTS

DEDICATION

We take great honor in dedicating the second edition of *Waterfowl Ecology and Management* to

THE LATE
FRANK C. BELLROSE

who by any standard was the dean of waterfowl biologists in North America. His many contributions to wildlife science and commitment to waterfowl and wetland conservation could by themselves fill several volumes. He inspired all who knew him with his knowledge, humility, and gentle strength, and we are proud to acknowledge his long-standing collegiality and friendship.

FOREWORD

In 1994, Guy A. Baldassarre and Eric G. Bolen published *Waterfowl Ecology and Management*, thereby completing their mission to provide a contemporary textbook designed to deal forthrightly with waterfowl ecology and management. This daunting task provided a text for advanced students and practicing biologists. What a job Baldassarre and Bolen did! The first edition of *Waterfowl Ecology and Management* was a splendid compendium of more than 1,600 citations tailored into 12 chapters covering virtually every important aspect of waterfowl ecology and management, especially in North America. Those of us who deal with research, management and policy associated with waterfowl and wetlands understand why the task was so challenging — primarily the synthesis and thorough presentation of an overwhelming deluge of scientific and popular literature generated in recent decades. Their efforts were well received by colleagues and peers who realized that the book filled an essential niche in the state of knowledge of waterfowl biology.

The authors are uniquely qualified to pursue the first and second editions of *Waterfowl Ecology and Management*. Both authors have had extensive careers in the waterfowl arenas of research and education. Their extensive experience is obvious from the thoroughness, presentation and clarity of the book's content. Bolen's career, since 1965, has been embellished by tenures at Texas A & M University at Kingsville, Texas Tech University, and the Rob and Bessie Welder Wildlife Foundation in Sinton, Texas. After becoming Associate Dean of the Graduate School at Texas Tech, he became Dean of the Graduate School and Professor of Biology at the University of North Carolina at Wilmington, where he is today Professor Emeritus. In addition to Bolen's administrative and teaching responsibilities over the years, he has continued to author and coauthor nu-

merous scientific articles and other books, including *Mississippi Kite: Portrait of a Southern Hawk*, and five editions of *Wildlife Ecology and Management*, as well as mentoring graduate students. Fortunately, one of his doctoral students at Texas Tech University was Guy Baldassarre.

After completing his doctoral program at Tech, Baldassarre was hired by Auburn University where he further developed his skills in teaching and research in waterfowl and wildlife ecology. In 1987, he assumed responsibilities for a noteworthy teaching and research career at the State University of New York, College of Environmental Science and Forestry where he now holds the rank of Distinguished Teaching Professor. Fortunately, Baldassarre, like his mentor, Bolen, has been a prolific publisher of scientific investigations and an instructor of a variety of waterfowl and wetland ecology classes. Both scientists delivered a wealth of knowledge, experience and passion to those undergraduate and graduate students lucky enough to study under their guidance. Now once again, these two talented investigators and instructors have teemed up to provide another litany of information for those interested in the management, biology, policy, welfare and future of our waterfowl and wetland resources throughout the world.

What could further enhance the impressive first edition of *Waterfowl Ecology and Management*? Leave it to Baldassarre and Bolen to find the ways. Principally, the burgeoning amount of new information available since the first edition has been digested for incorporation; now some 2,800 citations form the basis of this text providing a terrific benchmark in our current knowledge regarding many important aspects of waterfowl. Additionally, the authors have broadened their scope of coverage from primarily on the North American continent in the first edition to an international level. For example, in this edition there is a section on wetlands elsewhere in the world, including the Ouse Washes and Martin Mere in the United Kingdom, Okavango in Africa, the Volga Delta, and Doñana in Europe, plus wetlands in South America, Australia, and Asia. Also incorporated in the new edition are summary data from the Ramsar Convention, descriptions of selected sites, and discussions of many general waterfowl ecology issues from Europe, Africa, and Australia — all timely additions in our modern globally connected world.

The authors also provide a classy and instructive series of "infoboxes," which are stand-alone inserts in the various chapters. Infoboxes were previously used by Bolen in his *Wildlife Ecology and Management* text and were well received. The infoboxes present information on important waterfowl people (e.g., Bellrose, Cottam, Darling, Delacour, Hochbaum, Kear, McKinney, and Scott), places (e.g., Delta, Patuxent, and the Wildfowl and Wetlands Trust), and issues (e.g., Mute Swans and resident Canada Geese in North America, hybridization between the Ruddy Duck and White-headed Duck in Europe, and the plight and restoration of Campbell Island Teal).

This second edition, like the first, contains twelve chapters — Introduction; Waterfowl Classification; Courtship Behavior, Mating Systems, and Pair-Bond Formation; Reproductive Ecology; Feeding Ecology; Nesting, Brood Rearing, and Molting; Winter; Mortality and Harvest Management; Major Waterfowl Habitats; Wetlands and Wetland Management; Waterfowl Policy and Administration; and the Conclusion. A very thorough and helpful Index is also provided.

Some chapters include minor revisions, such as the Introduction which already provided a complete and interesting history of waterfowl science, management and people. Other chapters incorporate major and important revisions. Chapter 2 — Waterfowl Classification — integrates an exhaustive review of the taxonomy of the world's waterfowl and features the work of Brad Livezey, who identified 171 species of Anatidae while addressing all the major groups of waterfowl in a very comprehensive and authoritative treatise. Along with this major upgrade, recently extinct species and extinctions since the Holocene, such as the moa-nalos of Hawaii, are discussed.

In Chapter 3 — Courtship, Mating Systems, and Pair-Bond Formation — new information on re-formation of pair bonds in Harlequin Ducks and on perennial monogamy among Southern Hemisphere

waterfowl (e.g., White-checked Pintails in the Bahamas, Speckled Teal in Argentina, and long-term data from Barnacle Geese) are presented. Also included in the revision of this chapter are new examples of territoriality in ducks exhibited by river specialists (the African Black Duck and the Blue Duck of New Zealand), as well as recent knowledge of mate choice in Mallards, such as the importance of soft body parts (i.e., bill color), which can be an indicator of more immediate condition of males rather than body plumage.

The Reproductive Ecology chapter (4) incorporates an entirely new section on the evolution of clutch size, clutch size limitation, and incubation, along with recent material on extra-pair copulations, including a discussion on White-checked Pintails and the ability of males to assess the fertility of females. New nutritional information has been integrated in the Feeding Ecology chapter (5), thus elevating the chapter to the state of our current knowledge.

The largest update in this edition occurs in the Nesting, Brood Rearing, and Molting chapter (6), topics for which a wealth of new research findings have become available. Approximately 450 references have been assimilated in the chapter. Topics include predator management, brood survival, and the beneficial effects of the Conservation Reserve Program in the Prairie Pothole Region. The chapter has new sections describing methods to calculate nest success, renesting, brood parasitism and amalgamation (creching), and habitat use by goslings, as well as incorporation of recent information on breeding propensity and the effects of habitat on brood survival. The Harvest and Mortality chapter (8) provides informative additions on the Harvest Information Program and Adaptive Harvest Management, a program that becomes more important every year for setting harvest regulations. Current information on waterfowl diseases nicely rounds out the chapter.

The most notable change in the chapter of Major Waterfowl Habitats (9) is a review of The Ramsar Convention, along with a summary table of sites by continent and a brief treatment of selected sites. The Wetlands and Management chapter (10) also has significant new sections, including an update on the status of wetlands in the United States, Integrated Wetland Management, and incorporation of the major findings from the Marsh Ecology Research Program completed at the Delta Waterfowl and Wetlands Research Station.

The final chapter, Conclusion (11), provides updated information and an outlook regarding global warming and hunting. A significant addition for those of us associated with the training and collaboration of professional waterfowl enthusiasts is a section regarding our concerns with the future production and training of waterfowl biologists at universities. There is an unfortunate and worrisome paucity of new instructors devoted to the teaching, training, and research supervision of students wanting to pursue a career in waterfowl and wetlands as the older generations of instructors move further down the flyways to their eventual wintering areas.

Overall, Baldassarre and Bolen have provided us with a thorough and well-presented compendium of timely, useful, and necessary information for the advanced students, practicing biologists, and managers facing the challenges of a new century. The knowledge presented in *Waterfowl Ecology and Management* is desirable because of the enormous pressure exerted on waterfowl populations and their

habitats worldwide by our burgeoning human population, the increasing development of rural lands, often unfavorable agricultural policies and practices, and waning conservation ethics. The concerns of the education and training of future waterfowl students and professionals so aptly discussed in the final chapter are well-founded. The best efforts to maintain and enhance our waterfowl populations, their habitats, their future, and our passion must be based upon the transfer of knowledge acquired from those before and beside us. *Waterfowl Ecology and Management* offers us a means to a brighter future for waterfowl and their admirers.

STEPHEN P. HAVERA, Emeritus
Illinois Natural History Survey
Havana, Illinois
January 2005

PREFACE TO THE SECOND EDITION

Concerns for the welfare of North America's waterfowl populations have not diminished since the first edition of *Waterfowl Ecology and Management* appeared in 1994. Indeed, during the intervening decade the North American Waterfowl Management Plan has been twice updated and expanded because of continuing interest in the future of waterfowl. During this same period, more than 16 million Duck Stamps were purchased and hunters in the United States reaped a harvest of nearly 140 million ducks. In contrast, the IUCN Red Data Book now lists 26 species of waterfowl as either critically endangered, endangered, or vulnerable. The U.S. Fish and Wildlife Service lists five threatened or endangered species of waterfowl, two of which also are listed by the IUCN. Less than 100 Campbell Island Teal persist on two small islands off the coast of New Zealand at the same time excessive numbers — in the millions — of Snow Geese destroy their own nesting grounds in the Canadian Arctic. The extent of these circumstances — overabundance to extreme scarcity — obviously presents biologists with a range of challenges.

Protection for wetlands continues to roll forward, but the extent and pace of the programs involved have increased dramatically since the first edition of *Waterfowl Ecology and Management*. The Conservation Reserve Program now enrolls about 14.2 million ha of idled cropland, much of it suitable as habitat for waterfowl and other wildlife. Likewise, the somewhat newer Wetland Reserve Program currently includes nearly 405,000 ha of wetland habitat, and the Partners for Wildlife program has protected nearly 300,000 ha more. The breadth and associated achievements under the North American Waterfowl Management Plan are nearly unrivaled in the history of waterfowl and wetland conservation.

Nor has the output of waterfowl and wetland research lessened, as evidenced by a continuous flow of new papers and other publications—this edition accordingly includes some 1,200 more citations than the previous edition (2,800 total). Significantly, some of the newer research now identifies *"why"* as well as *"how"* things happen. For example, mink (*Mustela vison*) depend on permanent water, so their influence as nest predators in prairie areas diminishes during droughts. Thus on landscapes lacking permanent water, nesting success soars when precipitation again creates seasonal, but not permanent, wetlands (see Chapter 6). These circumstances, in other words, are *why* seasonal wetlands increase duck production, as well as *why* seasonal wetlands are a prime target for protection and management. Our present effort is the product of incorporating these new findings — and new events — into the framework followed in the first edition. Our goal, however, remains unchanged: to produce a comprehensive textbook for those students, practicing professionals, and others who recognize waterfowl and their habitat as one of our planet's important natural resources.

The bulk of waterfowl research still originates in North America, but the coverage in this edition was expanded to include more examples and information from Europe and other regions of the world. We believe a global view will better enable our readers to grasp that many of the same issues — diseases, habitat loss, and invasive species, among others — face waterfowl wherever they may occur. Some key wetlands in Europe, Asia, and elsewhere in the world also are described, as are important ecological and management activities for several nations.

All told, we believe *Waterfowl Ecology and Management* offers a degree of coverage and depth not otherwise available in a single volume.

HISTORY

Various parts of *Waterfowl Ecology and Management* were begun as early as 1968, when EGB began teaching a course entitled Waterfowl Management at Texas Tech University. The chapters were little more than mimeographed handouts, which at times were bound together for easier handling, but certainly never published formally or subject to more than casual external review. There matters rested until an esteemed colleague — Frank C. Bellrose — urged EGB to renew the work, but by then it was clear that the task of preparing a truly comprehensive text would require additional expertise. At that time, two esteemed waterfowl ecologists — Dennis Raveling and Leigh Fredrickson — joined EGB as coauthors, but progress was slow and that partnership dissolved amicably. Fortunately, Leigh Fredrickson later published the contributions of the late Dennis Raveling (1939–1991) as *Waterfowl of the World — a Comparative Perspective*, which appeared in 2004 through the Gaylord Memorial Laboratory at the University of Missouri.

In the meantime, GAB joined the project with EGB, which was quickly revitalized with the steady appearance of revised and entirely new material. Indeed, because GAB was able to devote the time and energy demanded by the task, he assumed the leading role, and in 1994 the first edition of *Waterfowl Ecology and Management* became a reality. GAB likewise continued as the primary contributor to the second edition. We also should mention that we formed a team once before, as mentor and graduate student, studying waterfowl on the playa wetlands of west Texas. In the interim, our student–teacher relationship steadily evolved into an association of friendship and collaboration, of which both editions of this book bear testament.

MAKING CHOICES

Several choices confront the authors of most textbooks. In our case, these included decisions concerning taxonomic matters — to which we devote considerable attention in Chapter 2 — as well as format and organization. We decided to follow the designations of Brad Livezey because his extensive work uses a modern phylogenetic approach. Nonetheless,

we made a serious attempt to note some of the more controversial issues concerning taxonomy in hope of advising our readers of other opinions and choices. Our major themes, however, are (1) that waterfowl taxonomy is a dynamic topic, which constantly seeks to discover true relatedness, and hence new information necessarily obliges updated classifications; and (2) that what might otherwise appear as an arcane subject in fact has valuable application to management actions. In this edition, as before, we provide a list of scientific names for waterfowl at the end of Chapter 2, but we otherwise refer to ducks, geese, and swans only by what are widely recognized common names (although here, too, some might challenge our choices). The scientific names for plants and other organisms, however, are presented throughout the text, and are those used by the authors of the associated references. Each chapter ends with a section of literature citations. We chose this format to facilitate our readers' quick entry into the literature addressing a single subject or closely related subjects, instead of diffusing these among a single, much longer listing for all topics at the end of the book.

We also had to make decisions regarding the ordering of chapters within the text, which remains unchanged from the first edition. These begin with a brief historical perspective (Chapter 1) and then moves through the taxonomy and biology of the Anseriformes (Chapters 2-8), before addressing matters of important waterfowl habitats (Chapter 9), wetland management (Chapter 10), and policy (Chapter 11). Readers not acquainted with the wetlands of North America may wish to include Chapter 9, along with Chapters 1 and 2, in their preliminary reading, thereby gaining some familiarity with wetland resources such as the prairie potholes, playa lakes, and California Valley marshes, among others.

The literature on waterfowl spans many decades. During this period scientific standards changed considerably, including a shifting emphasis from descriptive to often highly statistical treatments of extensive data. Wildlife science also changed from English units to metric, hence we faced a choice of citing older works as originally published (i.e., using acres, inches, and pounds) or converting these to metric units; we chose the latter. Throughout the text we also converted values such as calories and kilocalories to joules and kilojoules, respectively, using the International System of Units (abbreviated SI). We do not believe that the implications of the original data have been altered by these transformations.

Finally, we identified locations in one of two ways. We did not further identify sites in the United States or Canada and instead simply noted the place and/or state or province name (e.g., Bear River Refuge, Utah, or Delta, Manitoba), whereas national identities accompanied all other locations.

ACKNOWLEDGMENTS

This project has obviously — we should say "visibly" — benefited from the skilled artwork of Tamara R. Sayre. Her drawings are informative and esthetically pleasing yet maintain the highest standards of technical accuracy, and our text is richly enhanced by her work. We thank Tamara for unfailingly, as well as cheerfully, meeting our needs and schedules.

We continue our indebtedness to those many colleagues who assisted in various ways with the first edition, and we a pleased to again acknowledge Dave Ankney, Barry Grand, Rick Kaminski, Brad Livzey, Rich Malecki, Frank McKinney, Tom Moorman, Jim Nichols, Roy Norton, John Thompson, and Milt Weller, as well as Ray Alisauskas, Dick Banks, Bruce Batt, Judy Bladen, Bob Blohm, Columbus Brown, M. Ralph Browning, Vern Byrd, Don Delnicki, Dirk Derksen, Craig Ely, Mike Haramis, Tom Heberlein, Tom Hess, Gene Hocutt, Debbie Jones, Paul Keywood, Woody Martin, Kim Miller, Janice Nicholls, Dan Pennington, Ken Reinecke, Clyde Schnack, Jim Sedinger, Bill Shields, Don Tiller, and David Weaver. Mike Losito, Marc Romano, Suni Edson, Steve Campbell, and Alda Ingram helped us with proofreading, verifying literature citations, and typing.

The second edition likewise benefited from the contributions, some for a second time, of many colleagues, and we accordingly thank Alan Afton, Ray Alisauskas, Jennifer Amie, Dan Baldassarre, Eileen Baldassarre, Shane Bapista, Bruce Batt, Allison Beard, Montserrat Carbonell, Sandra Caziani, Bob Clark, Jaime Collazo, Bobby Cox, Dennis Daly, Tim Davis, Dirk Derksen, Kathy Dickson, John Dini, Sandie Doran, Paul Flint, Fred Greenslade, Mary Gustafson, Siu-Ling Han, Mike Haramis, Gary Hepp, Jan Herr, Robin Holevinski, Baz Hughes, Amy Deller Jacobs, Wendy Jensen, Fred Johnson, Mike Johnson, Rex Johnson, Tim Jones, Matt Kaminski, Rick Kaminski, Ron Kokel, C. D. "Kip" Koss, Scott Lanyon, Dale Lockwood, Jerry Longcore, Tom Maher, Rich Malecki, Mark Mallory, Pete McClelland, Rhona McDougal, Bob McLandress, Cathy McNassor, Kimberli Miller, Tommy Michot, Doug Mock, Seth Mott, Tom Nudds, Bridget Olson, Storrs Olson, Dwight Peck, Paul Padding, Margaret Petersen, Mark Petrie, Scott Petrie, Pam Pietz, Jeff Port, Evan Rehm, Elizabeth Reif, Ken Reinecke, Neil Ringler, Lissette Ross, Doug Ryan, Tobias Salathe, Carl Schwartz, Kim Scribner, Phillip Seddon, Jim Sedinger, Jerry Serie, Sue Shaeffer, Kevin Shaw, Ruth Shea, Loren Smith, Mike Sorenson, Christine Sousa, Carolyn Spilman, Sonya Taylor-Jones, Francisco Vilella, Marilyn Whitehead, Richard Whyte, Khristi Wilkins, Murray Williams, and Robert Williams. We are indebted to all for their time, effort, and expertise, although we alone are responsible for whatever flaws remain in the pages that follow.

Steve Havera, whose own book – *Waterfowl of Illinois* – stands as a landmark, kindly consented to write the Foreword. We thank him for his generous remarks and overview of the new edition.

Finally, a work of this sort does not reach fruition without the support and nurturing of another kind. Our wives — Eileen and Elizabeth — encouraged our efforts every step of the way. In many ways, they once again are genuine coauthors of this book.

GAB Syracuse, New York
EGB Wilmington, North Carolina
15 February 2005

Chapter 1
INTRODUCTION AND HISTORICAL OVERVIEW

History does not favor us with a tangible record of the first encounter between waterfowl and our ancestors, but hunger no doubt prompted an affiliation sometime during the dawn of human development. Still later, when skin-clad hunters wielded crude weapons, waterfowl became a dietary staple. We cannot precisely recount these events, but they nonetheless set in motion an age-old association that continues today.

Waterfowl appear early in the archives of recorded history. Indeed, etchings of swans date to Ice Age times in northern Eurasia (Maringer and Bandi 1953), and a goose is among the Paleolithic artwork appearing in French caves (Ucko and Rosenfeld 1967). Egyptian hieroglyphics clearly depict several species of ducks and geese, and Moses and Abraham undoubtedly were familiar with the waterfowl they encountered while traveling along the Nile (Parmelee 1959). A wall painting (circa 1900 B.C.) in the tomb of Khum-Hotpe shows an Egyptian netting swimming ducks with a clever trap operated from a blind (Fig. 1-1). Early Romans forecast the severity of the forthcoming winter based on the thickness of a goose's breastbone, and both Roman and Greek seers viewed the appearance of swans as omens of fair weather and good sailing (Barker 1966). Representations of Muscovy Ducks (for scientific names of waterfowl, see Appendix A in Chapter 2) appear in the Mochica culture, which flourished in Peru between 200 and 700 A.D. (Donkin 1989). Swans are especially common in ancient art and mythology and figure prominently in the history of many cultures (Evans and Dawnay 1972). In all, Alison (1978) traced waterfowl hunting through 21 civilizations — spanning some 6,000 years — including Egyptian, Greek, Etruscan, Persian, and Aztec cultures.

Native Americans understood the gregarious habits of waterfowl and used replicas of ducks as a means of bringing flocks into range of their arrows. Indeed, decoys constructed of reeds and decorated with feathers lured ducks at least a millennium ago (Fig. 1-2). In 1924, 11 such decoys — some clearly mimicking Canvasbacks — were discovered in Lovelock Cave, Nevada, among artifacts attributed to a vanished Indian civilization known as Tule Eaters (Loud and Harrington 1929). The Indian's ingenious replicas thus established the artificial decoy as an effective means of attracting waterfowl into killing range. Wooden decoys later became an American art form, as witnessed by the skilled carvings of turn-of-the-century waterfowlers (Fig. 1-3; also see Barber 1954, Fleckenstein 1979).

The impact of subsistence hunting by Native Americans apparently was substantial at some locations. Broughton (2004) analyzed an extensive deposit of vertebrate bones and other remains as a means of determining the hunting pressure exerted by humans living on the eastern shore of San Francisco Bay 700 to 2,600 years ago. The materials included the remains of 15 species of ducks and geese distributed over 10 strata. In the oldest strata, large-bodied geese were well represented, but the smaller species of geese steadily became more common in the younger strata. Ducks likewise occurred more frequently as evidence of the larger geese dimin-

Figure 1-1. A wall painting (circa 1900 B.C.) in the tomb of Khum-Hotpe depicts an Egyptian netting swimming ducks with a clever trap operated from a blind. Photo courtesy of The Metropolitan Museum of Art.

Figure 1-2. American Indians in Nevada crafted these decoys from reeds and feathers perhaps a thousand years ago. Photo courtesy of the University of California.

Figure 1-3. Wooden decoys, originally designed expressly for duck hunting, later established an American art form. Collectors pay large sums for the works of prominent decoy carvers, among them Henry Shourdes, Joseph Lincoln, Charles "Shang" Wheeler, Elmer Crowell (*top*), and the Ward brothers — Lem and Steve (*bottom*). Photos courtesy of the Heritage Museums and Gardens and the Ward Museum of Wildfowl Art, Salisbury, Maryland.

ished. Moreover, the remains of Mallards and other ducks that frequent shoreline areas gave way over time to sea ducks, which live well off shore and thus are relatively more difficult to capture. These trends provide strong evidence for human-induced depressions in waterfowl populations. Namely, as populations of the various kinds of ducks and geese were progressively exploited for food, Native Americans switched from one kind of waterfowl to another (i.e., overhunting made it necessary thereafter to seek birds that were of smaller size and greater difficulty to secure).

Waterfowl remains also suggest that bones from the larger species served as tools. Parmalee (1961) described the polished appearance of bones cut from the wing of a Trumpeter Swan and suggested they may have been used as gouges or handles; the site containing the swan bones and other Indian cultural debris dates to 1500 A.D. Interestingly, these artifacts were discovered in Pennsylvania, indicating that the former distribution of Trumpeter Swans possibly extended farther eastward than once supposed. A midden in Illinois also contained swan bones, some of which were manufactured into ornaments (Parmalee 1958).

Waterfowl also were domesticated early in the course of civilization. Delacour (1964) noted that two species of geese and another two of ducks formed the nucleus of waterfowl domesticated for meat, eggs, and down. These were the Greylag Goose, Swan Goose, Mallard, and Muscovy Duck. Of these, the Greylag Goose probably is the oldest domestic bird, having been tamed by Egyptians some 4,000 years ago. Records of domestic Swan Geese date back 2,000 years in China (Fig. 1-4), and Mallards probably were

tamed during the Middle Ages although they earlier were held in captivity at the time of the Roman Empire. Spanish conquistadors invading Peru and Columbia in the 16th century found Native Americans with domestic Muscovy Ducks, but it remains uncertain how long these birds had been held under human control prior to the European incursion (Crosby 2003). In fact, as a result of Columbus's second voyage to the New World in 1494, Muscovy Ducks first came to the attention of the Western world when Diego Alverez Chanca noted that "no kind of domestic fowl has been found here, with the exception of some ducks . . . with flat crests, most of them white as snow, but some black" living in the houses of the indigenous people (Donkin 1989:59). All told, domestication caused these species of waterfowl to adapt to new environmental conditions, often in lands well beyond their original distribution, and undergo

Figure 1-4. Centuries of domestication may produce remarkable increases in the body mass of waterfowl. Swan Geese weigh about 3.5 kg in the wild, whereas a domestic form of this species (the "African Goose," shown here) reaches 10 kg. Except for a white form, the color of Swan Geese remains essentially unchanged between the wild and domestic birds, but in other species, domestication often significantly increases the amount of white plumage. Photo courtesy of D. Andrew Saunders.

marked changes in size, coloration, body proportions, and biological cycles (Delacour 1964).

As might be expected, domestication of plants and animals had far-reaching consequences — domestication was the genesis of agriculture, and agriculture became the cornerstone of civilization. And with agriculture, the uncertainties of nomadic living gave way to more stable lifestyles. Men and women settled in villages, thereby initiating a new way of life for people weary of wandering for food and fiber. Architecture and other forms of culture gradually blossomed as town sites formed in the midst of new attachments to a civilized landscape. We emphasize these developments because they largely freed developing societies from hunting as a means of subsistence. Hunting henceforth became a sport in many of the world's civilizations, largely evolving from a form of subsistence to the adventure of recreation.

At first, sport hunting remained primarily the domain of the privileged classes. During the dynasty of Tutmosis IV, for example, the office of "Overseer of the Swamps of Enjoyment" was established; later in Egyptian history, the duties of the "Chief Treasurer" also included those of the "Chief Fowler"

(Alison 1978). Ducks were among the prizes seized by falcons set awing by the princes of eastern empires. In medieval times, the kings of Europe also adopted falconry and took measures to assure the abundance of waterfowl for their sport. Henry VIII decreed protection for waterfowl and their eggs between 31 May and 31 August each year, and by 1631 Mallards were propagated for the swift falcons of English royalty (Leopold 1933).

Ownership of waterfowl and other wildlife also was restricted steadfastly to the royal court. A particular case concerns Mute Swans of the River Thames. Swans were a delicacy jealously reserved for important royal banquets, giving further credence to the culinary description "food fit for a king." Late in the 15th century, however, two trade guilds were granted a royal charter for owning swans, thereby requiring specific identification of each bird in the Thames flock; ownership meant hefty profits for those selling swans for the royal table. Thus began the annual ritual of "swan upping," wherein representatives of the two guilds and the crown captured and marked the bill of each cygnet in keeping with which group owned the young bird's parents (Kear 1990). Swan upping continues along the Thames today as a colorful tradition heralding the ancient custom, replete with costumes and bannered skiffs (Fig. 1-5).

With the development of shotguns, however, waterfowl hunting reached a new zenith. Indeed, the history of modern waterfowl hunting essentially parallels the evolution of the shotgun — neither falcons nor longbows matched the efficiency of weapons that propelled a blanket of shot toward an elusive, fast-flying quarry. Muzzle-loading, black-powder guns were first in the parade of weaponry, and by 1855 double-barreled hammer breechloaders were in use, followed in 1871 by hammerless varieties (Walsh 1971). Around 1900, John M. Browning developed the automatic shotgun, which along with the availability of fast-burning smokeless powder, catapulted the harvest of waterfowl by a growing army of hunters.

Other developments compounded the effects of the improved weaponry: Railroads crossed the northern prairies during the mid-1880s (Wilgus 1970). Cooke (1906:11) accordingly wrote of the tracks cutting across Minnesota and North Dakota, but " . . . the final doom of the ducks was apparent when the Canadian Pacific Railroad crossed between Winnipeg and the Rocky Mountains." Thus, by the end of the 19th century, shotguns — coupled with the opening of the prairies to settlement — became a means of

Figure 1-5. The rich tradition of "swan upping" originated centuries ago in England and continues today on the River Thames. Cygnets and their parents are caught (*top*) and marked to identify their ownership among two guilds (*left*) and the crown. Photos courtesy of the British Travel Authority.

killing waterfowl in numbers never before possible (Fig. 1-6).

Repeating shotguns could hold six shells and, given the seemingly limitless flocks of ducks and geese, waterfowl hunting flourished with only the most meager restrictions. Indeed, prior to passage of the Migratory Bird Treaty Act in 1918, no restrictions governed bag limits, hunting hours, gun size, or the number of shots each gun could hold. Spring hunting was allowed as was the use of live ducks as decoys, and the sale of harvested ducks was legal. Accordingly, harvests often were large (Fig. 1-7)

So armed with weapons, few restrictions, and an abundance of waterfowl, market hunting began to flourish late in the 19th century (see Chapter 11). With market hunting came the development of weapons that were capable of killing scores of ducks with a single discharge. Some punt guns weighed more than the men who fired them, and their huge barrels — often with bores the size of steam pipes! — could hurl a cupful of shot into a flock of ducks (Fig. 1-8). Perhaps 100 such guns once operated on Chesapeake Bay, where the blast of several of these reportedly killed more than 400 Redheads at one time (Walsh 1971). In the winter of 1893-94, one market hunter at Big Lake, Arkansas, sold 8,000 Mallards, with a total of 120,000 ducks sent to market from this one place (Cooke 1906). Ducks indeed seemed plentiful, but hard times were

Figure 1-6. Settlement of the North American prairies heralded hard times for waterfowl and their habitat. Railroads crossed the continent's heartland in the years following the Civil War; note the freshly turned prairie sod in the foreground (*top*). A generation later, automobiles brought new opportunities for the exploitation of waterfowl as shown here by a bag of ducks shot in North Dakota in the early 1900s (*bottom*). Photos courtesy of the Archives of Canadian Pacific Ltd. and the North Dakota Game and Fish Department.

Figure 1-7. Women hunters (circa 1930) at the Wright Brothers' Hunting Lodge, Currituck Sound, North Carolina, with a day's harvest of ducks and geese. Photo courtesy of J. A. "Archie" Johnson.

Figure 1-8. Market hunters often fired large-bore weapons — punt guns — capable of killing dozens of ducks with one shot. The gun shown here was manufactured by the Hall Rifle Company, Baltimore, Maryland, about 1860. Photo courtesy of J. A. "Archie" Johnson.

coming — and with them waterfowl management gained its birthright.

A MANAGEMENT DILEMMA

The waterfowl resource in North America is both a heritage from the past and a legacy for the future. That blessing remains marred, however, by long-standing dilemmas still facing waterfowl managers. On one hand, in no other region of the world are so many hunters engaged in shooting waterfowl as in North America. The demand for waterfowl hunting grew steadily in the years following World War II, and by 1976 the annual kill of waterfowl by some 2.5

million licensed hunters totaled 20 million ducks and 2.5 million geese in the United States and Canada (Cooch and Boyd 1980). The demand continues. Data compiled by the U.S. Fish and Wildlife Service reveal that hunters in the United States harvested 13.4 million ducks and 3.8 million geese in 2003.

Associated with this heavy gunning pressure is the highly vocal demand for an abundant, yet managed waterfowl population year after year. Duck hunters are a hardy clan who willingly brave the cold and often wet discomfort of a winter's dawn for outdoor recreation, and they seldom fail to comment — sometimes harshly — on the shooting regulations governing their chosen sport. Thus, hunting clubs

Figure 1-9. Dark clouds of soil blew across the heartland of North America in the 1930s after years of drought. The Dust Bowl coincided with a wrecked economy and drastic reductions in waterfowl populations as marshes dried during the long drought. Photo courtesy of the USDA Natural Resources Conservation Service.

and other organizations often exert heavy pressure on those persons and agencies responsible for waterfowl management and policy. Nonhunters, too, voice strong opinions about waterfowl populations, but unlike hunters, their concerns are for greater protection and smaller bag limits. Yet another group — antihunters — regard sport hunting as inhumane and call for complete cessation of what for others is valued as a cultural heritage. Each of these groups, however, typically shares a common interest in the conservation of waterfowl habitat.

Regardless of the varied perspectives about hunting, the regrettable fact remains that waterfowl habitat has dwindled dramatically from its former abundance — and continues to decrease. The most recent report estimated that only 42.7 million ha of wetland habitat remain in the lower 48 states (Dahl 2000), which is less than half of the original 89.5 million ha once found in this part of North America (Dahl 1990). Fortunately, the rate of loss — although still nearly 24,000 ha per year — has diminished

significantly (Dahl 2000). Habitat quality, too, is less than it was in the past. These trends began with the colonization of North America and the quest for productive land, and steadily increased as technology improved and human populations expanded. Wetlands, it seemed, were "useless" obstacles in the march of civilization toward its vision of "progress" in fulfillment of the nation's Manifest Destiny. Every hectare of drained marsh was a hectare available for economic expansion.

Natural phenomena at times joined forces with people and machines in the devastation of wetland environments. Hence, the great drought of the 1930s wrecked farm economics and wetlands alike (Fig. 1-9). Waterfowl populations plunged to their lowest ebb in memory when rainfall failed year after year in much of North America. Today, the Dust Bowl is history now dimmed by the return of more or less good times, but the difficult years of the 1930s did spawn two new forces aimed directly at the improvement of habitat conditions for waterfowl. In 1934, the first "Duck Stamps" were sold by mandate of the federal government and, in the private sector, Ducks Unlimited started its work in 1937. Nonetheless, the regrettable loss of potholes and marshes continued unabated in the heart of the breeding grounds, as drainage claimed some 405,000 ha of prairie potholes in the United States from 1943 to 1961 alone (Briggs 1964; see also Jahn 1961). This same region of North America, although containing only about 10% of the continent's breeding habitat, nonetheless once produced about 50% of North America's ducks (Smith et al. 1964). And, as we shall see in Chapter 9, other wetland habitats have fared little better in recent years. Unfortunately, the obvious difficulty of producing more birds from less habitat increases in proportion to expanding human populations.

In sum, waterfowl managers face a two-fold logistical problem: more ducks for the public — hunters, nonhunters, and antihunters alike — and more habitats for ducks. The two, of course, are not unrelated.

GAINING MOMENTUM

The following chapters contain many references to studies of waterfowl. Indeed, waterfowl are among the most studied groups of wildlife in the world. Here, however, some of the earlier works are highlighted from an era (circa 1910–55) when far less was known about waterfowl or their management. They mark a winding pathway to the present and delineate milestones for the future (see Bolen 2000).

The first serious attempt at field research concerned investigations of diseased waterfowl. Wetmore (1915, 1918) studied a then unknown malady killing thousands of ducks and geese in the marshes bordering Great Salt Lake, Utah (Fig. 1-10). The disease later would be identified as botulism caused by the toxin of *Clostridium botulinum* (Kalmbach 1930). Bowles (1908), McAtee (1908), and Wetmore (1919) also pinpointed lead poisoning as another killer of waterfowl, a malady whose source — expended lead shot — would not be eliminated completely from waterfowl hunting until 1991. In 1934, a form of avian malaria was discovered in waterfowl (O'Roke 1934). These parasitic infections are particularly severe in young birds and at times may limit recruitment in some duck and goose populations. In 1944, the first known outbreak of avian cholera was confirmed among wild waterfowl in North America (Quortrup et al. 1946), but like many other diseases, avian cholera has yet to be controlled effectively.

Literature about the life histories of waterfowl

Figure 1-10. Among the earliest field studies of wildlife were those of a "duck sickness" conducted by Alexander Wetmore for the U.S. Bureau of Biological Survey. Thousands of dead waterfowl littered the Bear River marshes of Utah when the 27-year-old Wetmore began his work there in 1913. By 1918, the young assistant biologist had concluded that alkali salts were poisoning the birds. Years later, other research identified the disease as botulism, but Wetmore went on to a brilliant career as one of the world's premier ornithologists. Photo courtesy of the U.S. Fish and Wildlife Service.

began with the four volumes of *A Natural History of the Ducks* (Phillips 1922-26). Almost concurrently, Bent (1923, 1925) continued his landmark series of life histories of North American birds with two volumes devoted to waterfowl. These sources brought together large amounts of information, much of which was anecdotal or based on unpublished observations from field and aviary; each represented a major contribution for its time and undoubtedly served as models for Delacour's (1954–64) magnificent four-volume set covering the waterfowl of the

Figure 1-11. Studies of food habits were among the initial thrusts in the development of waterfowl ecology and management, reaching a peak in the late 1930s. Thousands of stomachs were collected, usually from hunters, and tediously examined for seeds, invertebrates, and other types of food, as shown underway here by W. L. McAtee of the U.S. Bureau of Biological Survey in the early 1900s. These pioneering efforts established the fall diets for many species, but insights into the energetics and nutritional requirements of waterfowl did not follow until many decades thereafter. Photo courtesy of the American Ornithologists' Union and Smithsonian Institution Archives.

world. Kortright (1942) published *The Ducks, Geese & Swans of North America* in which species-by-species accounts of waterfowl were complemented by color plates, range maps, and up-to-date coverage of the then-available literature. That book, perhaps as no other, stimulated broad interest in waterfowl and waterfowl management; it remained the "bible" for a wide audience for more than 30 years, until significantly updated and expanded by Bellrose (1976, revised in 1980).

In its infancy, waterfowl management placed considerable emphasis on the kinds of foods waterfowl consumed (McAtee 1911, 1914, and later). Detailed analyses of stomach contents largely represented the immediate approach to management, and a section of the Bureau of Biological Survey — predecessor to the U.S. Fish and Wildlife Service — was assigned these tasks for waterfowl and other wildlife (Fig. 1-11). Thousands of duck stomachs were

collected and examined, eventually producing major studies of food habits (Cottam 1939, Martin and Uhler 1939). Nearly 40 years would pass before these and other data were related to the bioenergetics of waterfowl.

Pirnie (1935) focused on one state's waterfowl "problems" in *Michigan Waterfowl Management*. Much of that book was devoted to food habits and the propagation of marsh and aquatic vegetation as a means of improving waterfowl habitat — a significant turning point in the growing concern for wetland management and conservation in the overall picture of waterfowl management. Other milestones in these early years stemmed from wide-ranging surveys of waterfowl populations. The history of these efforts appears in *Flyways*, a chronicle richly endowed with photos of the biologists and machines of another era (Hawkins et al. 1984). The flyway concept itself developed from the studies of Frederick

C. Lincoln whose analyses of thousands of banding records (e.g., McIlhenny 1934) indicated the existence of four major north-south routes across North America: the Atlantic, Mississippi, Central, and Pacific Flyways (Lincoln 1935, 1939). These units were formally adopted as the administrative basis for waterfowl management in 1948, following discussions of their usefulness in this regard (Gabrielson 1944, Lincoln 1945; see Chapter 11).

Studies of nesting ecology began in earnest, some of which included hundreds of records (e.g., Williams and Marshall 1938). Much was being learned about nesting habitat, and together with the accumulation of food habits information, management programs began enhancing waterfowl habitat (e.g., Addy and MacNamara 1948). As one prominent example, the effectiveness of nest boxes as substitutes for natural cavities was demonstrated for Wood Ducks in the years following World War II (McLaughlin and Grice 1952, Bellrose 1955).

Research aimed at the ecology and management of individual species began with the publication of *The Blue-winged Teal: its Ecology and Management* (Bennett 1938) and continued for other species in the following decades (e.g., Girard 1941, Soper 1942, Low 1945, Hanson and Smith 1950, Wright 1954). In 1944, another book produced even greater impact on the emerging interest in waterfowl ecology. *The Canvasback on a Prairie Marsh* described, in eloquent prose and skilled artwork, the breeding activities of a major game bird (Hochbaum 1944; see Chapter 3). Perhaps for the first time, serious attention was paid to courtship behavior as a component of the annual nesting cycle. Hochbaum (1955) followed this work with *Travels and Traditions of Waterfowl*, which remains a benchmark in our understanding of waterfowl migration. Hochbaum's works also confirmed the scientific merit for founding the Delta Waterfowl Research Station on the southern shores of Lake Manitoba in 1937. Now known as the Delta Waterfowl and Wetlands Research Station, "Delta" would steadily produce major research, but perhaps more importantly, soon became a major center for training students in waterfowl and wetland ecology. In England, the Severn Wildfowl Trust (later The Wildfowl and Wetlands Trust) was initiated in 1946 by the talented artist and conservationist, Peter Scott; funds gained from the sales of his paintings provided part of the financial backing for the Trust's mission of research and conservation (see Infoboxes 1-1, 1-2).

A two-fold thrust aimed at developing fundamental knowledge about waterfowl populations across the breadth of North America included large-scale surveys of waterfowl populations on their breeding grounds (Hochbaum *in* Sowls 1955). Experience gained by the military in World War II now was turned to aerial reconnaissance over vast areas of nesting habitat from the northern prairies to the high Arctic. The U.S. Fish and Wildlife Service also began surveys of wintering waterfowl populations in the United States, and expanded that work to include waterfowl wintering in Mexico (Saunders and Saunders 1981). The second approach focused on interpreting these surveys in terms of the behavior and ecology of waterfowl in their nesting environment. Research of this type led to *Prairie Ducks*, in which there is firm evidence for homing behavior, the contribution of second-nesting efforts to annual production, and the spatial relationships between female ducks and their nests (Sowls 1955).

These landmarks, to be sure, only highlight an era when momentum gathered for the acquisition of new knowledge but, with them, waterfowl management was coming of age. A capstone for this era was the appearance of *Waterfowl Tomorrow*, an informative and nontechnical book in which 103 authors summarized existing knowledge and the art of waterfowl management as it stood by the early 1960s (Linduska 1964).

In the years that followed, more species-by-species compendia appeared for North American waterfowl (Bellrose 1976, Palmer 1976, and Johnsgard 1975), as well as state (Havera 1999) and global coverage (Johnsgard 1978; Kear 2005). Frith (1967) described the waterfowl of Australia, the home of Freckled Ducks and several other unusual species; Owen (1980) and Ogilvie (1982) covered the waterfowl of Europe. Numerous other sources of crucial information surfaced for selected topics, among them waterfowl behavior (Johnsgard 1965), diseases (Wobeser 1981; second edition in 1997), and human interactions with the waterfowl resource (Kear 1990). Individual species, of course, still received detailed attention, including monographs for the Giant Canada Goose (Hanson 1965), Hawaiian Goose (Kear and Berger 1980), Ring-necked Duck (Mendall 1958), Bufflehead (Erskine 1972), and many more. A compilation of papers selected from the *Journal of Wildlife Management* and other sources also provides a major source of information (Ratti et al. 1982), as do those treatments of groups of waterfowl such as swans (Scott 1972) and geese (Owen 1980) or special geographical situations such as island-dwelling waterfowl (Weller 1980) — even an entire volume devoted exclusively to downy waterfowl (Nelson 1993).

Infobox 1-1

Sir Peter Scott
Founder, The Wildfowl and Wetlands Trust
1909–1989

A complete description of Peter Scott would also include artist, naturalist, author, explorer, figure skater, glider pilot, radio and TV personality, and yachtsman, as well as the son of the ill-fated Antarctic explorer, Robert Falcon Scott.

Peter Scott's early interest in waterfowl stemmed from sport hunting, which quickly spilled over into his

artwork and eventually into a long career associated with wildlife conservation. He subsidized his many interests and activities with funds derived from the sales of his striking paintings of waterfowl, which usually were completed in oils on large canvases. He painted waterfowl around the world, as well as in his native England. Scott also launched several explorations associated with waterfowl, including a successful search in Iceland for the nesting grounds of Pink-footed Geese and described in his book, *A Thousand Geese* (1954, with J. Fisher).

Scott achieved success in virtually all of his endeavors. He was a nationally competitive ice skater, won the British championship as a glider pilot, a bronze medal for single-sailing in the 1936 Olympics, and three times won the Prince of Wales' Cup. He also skippered the British yacht in competition for the America's Cup. After distinguished service in the Royal Navy in World War II, Scott dedicated much of his energies to conservation, at first by founding (in 1946) The Wildfowl Trust (later renamed as The Wildfowl and Wetlands Trust) with its headquarters at Slimbridge in Gloucestershire and later as a founder of the World Wildlife Fund. He served as the Fund's first president (1961–1967) and designed the organization's familiar panda logo. He also hosted a long series of popular radio and televison broadcasts designed to introduce the British public to the marvels of natural history. Among his several books are *Wild Geese and Eskimos* (1951), *A Coloured Key to the Wildfowl of the World* (1961a), an autobiography entitled *The Eye of the Wind* (1961b), and *The Swans* (1972). He also painted the plates appearing in Delacour's four-volume treatise, *Waterfowl of the World* (1954-1964). For biographies, see Courtney (1989) and especially Huxley (1993). Copyrighted photo courtesy of Philippa Scott.

Weller (1988) organized a symposium that initiated a long-overdue focus on the ecology of wintering waterfowl, soon followed by Smith et al. (1989) who brought together an array of work addressing op-

tions for managing the migrating and wintering habitat for waterfowl in each of the North American flyways. Batt et al. (1992) similarly edited a volume appraising the breeding biology of waterfowl; the

Infobox 1-2

The Wildfowl and Wetlands Trust
European Center for Waterfowl Conservation

In 1946, artist-naturalist Peter Scott's growing concern for the future of waterfowl was transformed into action when he founded The Severn Wildfowl Trust at Slimbridge, Gloustershire, in the United Kingdom. Research, conservation, and education underpin the Trust's mission. Scott selected the site — on the estuary of the Severn River – because it served as a major wintering area for several species of waterfowl, including what was likely his favorite: Bewick's Swan, the European counterpart of the North American Tundra Swan. The organization's name was changed to The Wildfowl Trust in 1955 when another center was opened, and again in 1989 to The Wildfowl and Wetlands Trust in recognition of an expanding interest in wetland environments. The Trust currently administers nine centers, all open to the public, throughout the United Kingdom and employs 18 full-time research scientists.

The Trust's facilities include housing for a large collection of captive waterfowl that represents 151 species and subspecies. These offered unique opportunities for the comparative study of waterfowl behavior (Newton 1997), which indeed was among the first areas of research undertaken by the Trust's scientific staff and prominent visitors (e.g., Konrad Lorenz and Niko Tinbergen, each later to become Nobel Laureates). The usefulness of courtship behavior as a taxonomic tool for waterfowl classification in large part was developed at Slimbridge (see Johnsgard 1965). The Trust's avicultural facilities also were instrumental in the successful effort to restore the once highly endangered population of Hawaiian Geese ("Nene"), now again secure in its native habitat. The conservation program currently emphasizes the restoration of White-headed and White-winged Duck populations

throughout their respective distributions.

Population studies were another early focus, which included banding — "ringing" to the English — waterfowl and other waterbirds gathering in season at stations maintained by the Trust. Initially, traditional means — some centuries old — were used to trap waterfowl, but the Trust soon adopted newer methods, including rocket-propelled nets first used at Slimbridge in 1948. Thousands of Pink-footed, Greylag, and Barnacle Geese and three species of swans have been banded by the Trust, as well as even larger numbers of ducks. Special efforts were made to catch and mark family groups of swans to learn more about site fidelity, natal dispersal, survival rates for cygnets, and recruitment to breeding populations. In all, the Trust accounts for the vast majority of waterfowl banded in Great Britain (Mitchell and Ogilvie 1997), and its scientific staff provides important population analyses based on data accumulating from this work.

Pathology represented another thrust in the Trust's research program. Postmortem examinations included both wild birds and those housed in the collection; for the latter, the information aided the management of captive waterfowl elsewhere in the world. Habitat studies at first centered on crop damage allegedly caused by geese, then turned to broader studies of wetland ecology and management. Among these were the development of methods to create wetlands of value for wildlife from treated wastewater and on lands devoted to industrial uses. See Newton (1997) for an overview of the Trust's first 50 years of research activities, whose results often appear in its own scientific journal, *Wildfowl*. Photo courtesy of Richard Taylor-Jones, Wildfowl and Wetlands Trust.

---

latter volume commemorated the 50th anniversary of the Delta Waterfowl and Wetlands Research Station.

THE STAGE IS SET

The span of the 20th century witnessed a great movement, one in which people of every stripe awakened to their role as stewards of the land and its biota. For waterfowl, that movement touched many areas that we describe more fully later, particularly in Chapter 11. These include ground-breaking treaties, the end of market hunting, the development of a national wildlife refuge system, "Duck Stamps" and other new sources of revenue, overdue attention to endangered species, and new appreciation for wetlands and the goods and services they provide to human societies everywhere.

In the United States, tangible gains occurred when the Food Security Act of 1985 provided farmers with strong incentives for leaving wetlands intact — a provision popularly known as "Swampbuster." The Act also encouraged farmers to remove highly erodible croplands from production and instead protect their fields with various types of cover, some of which provide ducks with excellent nesting habitat ("Sodbuster"). Significantly, both programs continue today, supplemented by the Wetlands Reserve Program.

The North American Waterfowl Management Plan, begun in 1986, is a signal agreement among the United States, Canada, and Mexico. And, after two updates, the plan continues into another century as the rallying point for the conservation of wetlands and waterfowl populations across the breadth of the continent. Similarly, the number of locations listed as Wetlands of International Importance continues to grow under the aegis of the Ramsar Convention. Indeed, Mexico listed 34 new sites — the largest number ever declared at one time — on World Wetlands Day 2004. Among these were Laguna San Ignacio, the main wintering area for Black Brant, and the lower reaches of the Laguna Madre, where tens of thousands of Redheads and Northern Pintails winter each year. Collectively, these efforts translate into a wetland and waterfowl conservation program that is moving ahead at a pace and scale never before seen. Moreover, these activities are happening at local, state/provincial, national, and international levels, and we are optimistic about their successes.

All told, a legacy goes forward to another generation, as it did to ours, perhaps with a footnote that the 20th century marked waterfowl conservation's finest hour. The 21st century awaits to challenge that claim.

LITERATURE CITED

Addy, C. E., and L. G. MacNamara. 1948. Waterfowl management on small areas. Wildlife Management Institute, Washington, D.C.

Alison, R. M. 1978. The earliest records of water-fowl hunting. Wildlife Society Bulletin 6:196–199.

Barber, J. 1954. Wild fowl decoys. Dover Publications, New York.

Barker, W. 1966. Tales once told. Pages 49–57 *in* A. Stefferud, editor. Birds in our lives. U.S. Fish and Wildlife Service, Washington, D.C.

Batt, B. D. J., A. D. Afton, M. G. Anderson, C. D. Ankney, D. H. Johnson, J. A. Kadlec, and G. L. Krapu, editors. 1992. Ecology and management of breeding waterfowl. University of Minnesota Press, Minneapolis.

Bellrose, F. C. 1955. Housing for Wood Ducks. Illinois Natural History Survey Circular 45.

Bellrose, F. C. 1976. Ducks, geese and swans of North America. Stackpole Books, Harrisburg, Pennsylvania.

Bennett, L. J. 1938. The Blue-winged Teal: its ecology and management. Collegiate Press, Ames, Iowa.

Bent. A. C. 1923. Life histories of North American wild fowl, Part I. Smithsonian Institution, U.S. National Museum Bulletin 126.

Bent, A. C. 1925. Life histories of North American wild fowl, Part II. Smithsonian Institution, U.S. National Museum Bulletin 130.

Bolen, E. G. 2000. Waterfowl management: yesterday and tomorrow. Journal of Wildlife Management 64:323–335.

Bowles, J. H. 1908. Lead poisoning in ducks. Auk 25:312–313.

Briggs, F. P. 1964. Waterfowl in a changing continent. Pages 3–11 *in* J. P. Linduska, editor. Waterfowl tomorrow. U.S. Government Printing Office, Washington, D.C.

Broughton, J. M. 2004. Prehistoric human impacts on California birds: evidence from the Emeryville shellmounds. Ornithological Monographs 56.

Cooch, F. G., and H. Boyd. 1980. Waterfowl conservation in North America. International Ornithological Congress 17:912–917.

Cooke, W. W. 1906. Distribution and migration of North American ducks, geese, and swans. U.S. Biological Survey Bulletin 26.

Cottam, C. 1939. Food habits of North American diving ducks. U.S. Department of Agriculture Technical Bulletin 643.

Courtney, J. 1989. Sir Peter Scott: champion for the environment and founder of the World Wildlife Fund. G. Stevens, Milwaukee, Wisconsin.

Crosby, A. W. 2003. The Columbian exchange, biological and cultural consequences of 1492. Praeger, Westport, Connecticut.

Dahl, T. E. 1990. Wetlands losses in the United States, 1780's to 1980's. U.S. Fish and Wildlife Service, Washington, D.C.

Dahl, T. E. 2000. Status and trends of wetlands in the conterminous Unite States, 1986 to 1997. U.S. Fish and Wildlife Service, Washington, D.C.

Delacour, J. 1954–64. The waterfowl of the world. Volumes. 1-4. Country Life, London.

Donkin, R. A. 1989. The Muscovy Duck, *Cairina moschata domestica*, origins, dispersal and associated aspects of the geography of domestication. A. A. Balkema, Brookfield, Vermont.

Erskine, A. J. 1972. Buffleheads. Canadian Wildlife Service Monograph Series 4.

Evans, M., and A. Dawnay. 1972. The swan in mythology and art. Pages 143–166 *in* P. Scott, editor. The swans. Houghton Mifflin, Boston.

Fleckenstein, H. A., Jr. 1979. Decoys of the mid-Atlantic region. Schiffer Publishing, Exton, Pennsylvania.

Frith, H. J. 1967. Waterfowl in Australia. Angus & Robertson, Sydney.

Gabrielson, I. N. 1944. Managing the waterfowl. Transactions of the North American Wildlife Conference 9:264–269.

Girard, G. L. 1941. The Mallard: its management in western Montana. Journal of Wildlife Management 5:233–259.

Hanson, H. C. 1965. The Giant Canada Goose. Southern Illinois University Press, Carbondale.

Hanson, H. C., and R. H. Smith. 1950. Canada Geese of the Mississippi Flyway, with special reference to an Illinois flock. Illinois Natural History Survey Bulletin 25 (Article 3):67–210.

Havera, S. P. 1999. Waterfowl of Illinois: status and management. Illinois Natural History Survey Special Publication 21.

Hawkins, A. S., R. C. Hanson, H. K. Nelson, and H. M. Reeves, editors. 1984. Flyways. U.S. Fish and Wildlife Service, Washington, D.C.

Hochbaum, H. A. 1944. The Canvasback on a prairie marsh. Stackpole Books, Harrisburg, Pennsylvania, and the Wildlife Management Institute, Washington, D.C.

Hochbaum, H. A. 1955. Travels and traditions of waterfowl. Charles T. Branford, Newton, Massachusetts.

Huxley, E. 1993. Peter Scott, painter and naturalist. Faber and Faber, London.

Jahn, L. R. 1961. The status of waterfowl conservation. Wilson Bulletin 73:96–106.

Johnsgard, P. A. 1965. Handbook of waterfowl behavior. Cornell University Press, Ithaca, New York.

Johnsgard, P. A. 1975. Waterfowl of North America. Indiana University Press, Bloomington.

Johnsgard, P. A. 1978. Ducks, geese, and swans of the world. University of Nebraska Press, Lincoln.

Kalmbach, E. R. 1930. Western duck sickness produced experimentally. Science 72:658–660.

Kear, J. 1990. Man and wildfowl. T & A D Poyser, London.

Kear, J., editor. 2005. Ducks, geese and swans. Oxford University Press, Cambridge.

Kear, J., and A. J. Berger. 1980. The Hawaiian Goose: an experiment in conservation. Buteo Books, Vermillion, South Dakota.

Kortright, F. H. 1942. The ducks, geese & swans of North America. American Wildlife Institute, Washington, D.C.

Leopold, A. 1933. Game management. Charles Scribner's Sons, New York.

Lincoln, F. C. 1935. The waterfowl flyways of North America. U.S. Department of Agriculture Circular 342.

Lincoln, F. C. 1939. The migration of American birds. Doubleday, Doran & Company, New York.

Lincoln, F. C. 1945. Flyway regulations. Transactions of the North American Wildlife Conference 10:50–51.

Linduska, J. P., editor. 1964. Waterfowl tomorrow. U.S. Government Printing Office, Washington, D.C.

Loud, L. L., and M. R. Harrington. 1929. Lovelock Cave. Pages 1–183 in A. L. Kroeber and R. H. Lowie, editors. University of California Publications in American Archaeology and Ethnology. Volume 25. (reprinted 1965).

Low, J. B. 1945. Ecology and management of the Redhead, Nyroca americana, in Iowa. Ecological Monographs 15:35–69.

Maringer, J., and H-G. Bandi. 1953. Art in the ice age. Frederick A. Praeger, New York.

Martin, A. C., and F. M. Uhler. 1939. Food of game ducks in the United States and Canada. U.S. Department of Agriculture Technical Bulletin 634.

McAtee, W. L. 1908. Lead poisoning in ducks. Auk 25:472.

McAtee, W. L. 1911. Three important wild duck foods. U.S. Bureau of Biological Survey Circular 81.

McAtee, W. L. 1914. Five important wild-duck foods. U.S. Department of Agriculture Bulletin 58.

McIlhenny, E. A. 1934. Twenty-two years of banding migratory wild fowl at Avery Island, Louisiana. Auk 51:328–337.

McLaughlin, C. L., and D. Grice. 1952. The effectiveness of large-scale erection of Wood Duck boxes as a management procedure. Transactions of the North American Wildlife Conference 17:242–259.

Mendall, H. L. 1958. The Ring-necked Duck in the Northeast. University of Maine Studies, second series, number 73.

Mitchell, C., and M. Oglivie. 1997. Fifty years of wildfowl ringing by the Wildfowl & Wetlands Trust. Wildfowl 47:241–247.

Nelson, C. H. 1993. The downy waterfowl of North America. Delta Station Press, Deerfield, Illinois.

Newton, I. 1997. Fifty years of scientific research by the Waterfowl & Wetlands Trust. Wildfowl 47: 1–8.

Ogilvie, M. 1982. The wildfowl of Britain and Europe. Oxford University Press, Oxford.

O'Roke, E. C. 1934. A malaria-like disease of ducks caused by Leucocytozoon anatis Wickware. University of Michigan School of Forestry Conservation Bulletin 4.

Owen, M. 1980. Wild geese of the world: their life history and ecology. B T Batsford, London.

Palmer, R. S., editor. 1976. Handbook of North American birds. Waterfowl. Volumes 2–3. Yale University Press, New Haven, Connecticut.

Parmelee, A. 1959. All the birds of the Bible, their stories, identification and meaning. Harper and Brothers, New York.

Parmalee, P. W. 1958. Remains of rare and extinct birds from Illinois Indian sites. Auk 75:169–176.

Parmalee, P. W. 1961. A prehistoric record of the Trumpeter Swan from central Pennsylvania. Wilson Bulletin 73:212–213.

Phillips, J. C. 1922-26. A natural history of the ducks. Volumes. 1–4. Houghton Mifflin, Boston. (reprinted by Dover Books).

Pirnie, M. D. 1935. Michigan waterfowl management. Michigan Department of Conservation, Lansing.

Quortrup, E. R., F. B. Queen, and L. J. Merovka. 1946. An outbreak of pasteurellosis in wild ducks. Journal of the American Veterinary Medical Association 108:94–100.

Ratti, J. T., L. D. Flake, and W. A. Wentz, compilers. 1982. Waterfowl ecology and management: selected readings. The Wildlife Society, Bethesda, Maryland.

Saunders, G. B., and D. C. Saunders. 1981. Waterfowl and their wintering grounds in Mexico, 1937-64. U.S. Fish and Wildlife Service Resource Publication 138.

Scott, P. 1951. Wild geese and Eskimos: a journal of the Perry River Expedition of 1949. Country Life, London.

Scott, P., and J. Fisher. 1954. A thousand geese. Houghton Mifflin, Boston.

Scott, P. 1961a. A coloured key to the wildfowl of the world. Revised edition, Charles Scribner's Sons, New York.

Scott, P. 1961b. The eye of the wind. Houghton Mifflin, Boston.

Scott, P. 1972. The swans. Houghton Mifflin, Boston.

Smith, A. G., J. H. Stoudt, and J. B. Gollop. 1964. Prairie potholes and marshes. Pages 39–50 in J. P. Linduska, editor. Waterfowl tomorrow. U.S. Government Printing Office, Washington, D.C.

Smith, L. M., R. L. Pederson, and R. M. Kaminski, editors. 1989. Habitat management for migrating and wintering waterfowl in North America. Texas Tech University Press, Lubbock.

Soper, J. D. 1942. Life history of the Blue Goose, *Chen caerulescens* (Linneaus). Boston Society of Natural History 42:121–225.

Sowls, L. K. 1955. Prairie ducks: a study of their behavior, ecology and management. Stackpole Books, Harrisburg, Pennsylvania, and the Wildlife Management Institute, Washington, D.C.

Ucko, P. J., and A. Rosenfeld. 1967. Palaeolithic cave art. McGraw-Hill, New York.

Walsh, H. M. 1971. The outlaw gunner. Tidewater Publications, Centreville, Maryland.

Weller, M. W. 1980. The island waterfowl. Iowa State University Press, Ames.

Weller, M. W., editor. 1988. Waterfowl in winter. University of Minnesota Press, Minneapolis.

Wetmore, A. 1915. Mortality among waterfowl around Great Salt Lake, Utah. U.S. Department of Agriculture Bulletin 217.

Wetmore, A. 1918. The duck sickness in Utah. U.S. Department of Agriculture Bulletin 672.

Wetmore, A. 1919. Lead poisoning in waterfowl. U.S. Department of Agriculture Bulletin 793.

Wilgus, W. J. 1970. The railway interrelations of the United States and Canada. Russell & Russell, New York.

Williams, C. S., and W. H. Marshall. 1938. Duck nesting studies, Bear River Migratory Bird Refuge, Utah, 1937. Journal of Wildlife Management 2:29–48.

Wobeser, G. A. 1981. Diseases of wild waterfowl. Plenum Press, New York (second edition 1997).

Wright, B. S. 1954. High tide and an east wind, the story of the Black Duck. Stackpole Books, Harrisburg, Pennsylvania, and the Wildlife Management Institute, Washington, D.C.

Chapter 2
WATERFOWL CLASSIFICATION

All classification systems currently place waterfowl into the order Anseriformes, with all but three species assigned to the family Anatidae — the ducks, geese, and swans. However, several well-known classifications recognize various numbers of anatid species, ranging from 141 (Phillips 1922–26) to 144 (Delacour and Mayr 1945) to 148 (Johnsgard 1978). Livezey (1986, 1991) listed 162 species in Anatidae, but Livezey (1997a) later listed 171, including two recently extinct species (Labrador Duck and Auckland Islands Merganser) and three provisional species (two are extinct), as well as phylogenetic placement of 30 well-known fossil species (Table 2-1). Overall, despite different opinions on the designation of "species," about 90% were discovered by 1849, and nearly all were known by 1945. The most recently described extant species, the White-headed Flightless Steamer-Duck, was discovered on the coast of Argentina in 1981 (Humphrey and Thompson 1981).

Some of the early attempts to classify the Anseriformes were remarkably thorough, given the information then at hand. These include the works of Eyton (1838), Sclater (1880), Salvadori (1895), and Peters (1931); see Livezey (1997a) for a succinct summary of the early history of waterfowl classification. Nonetheless, early data were strictly morphological, although behavioral characteristics later were incorporated into waterfowl taxonomy. Indeed, following the classic treatise by Delacour and Mayr (1945), important studies by Lorenz (1951–53), McKinney (1953), and Johnsgard (1961a, 1961b, 1961c, 1965) significantly increased the body of knowledge about waterfowl behavior, which in turn greatly influenced the classifications developed after 1945 (see Woolfenden 1961; Johnsgard 1965, 1978).

Livezey (1986, 1997a) listed many of the specialized studies of waterfowl taxonomy. Some of the features highlighted in these works included the plumage patterns of downy young (Kear 1967, 1970), tracheal anatomy (Johnsgard 1961b), osteology (Woolfenden 1961), cytogenetics (Yamashina 1952), egg-white proteins (Sibley and Ahlquist 1972), lipids from the uropygial gland (Jacob and Glaser 1975), mitochondrial DNA (mtDNA; Kessler and Avise 1984), and even parasitic feather lice (Timmermann 1963). Most newer systems recognize the extensive revision proposed by Delacour and Mayr (1945), who added "tribes" to the taxonomic hierarchy of Anatidae (see Infobox 2-1). Tribes, identified with the suffix

Table 2-1. The family Anatidae according to the classification of Livezey (1997a)[a]. See Appendix A for a complete list of species and common names, including recently extinct species and selected fossil species.

Subfamily	Tribe	Number of genera	Number of species	Common name
Dendrocygninae	Dendrocygnini	1	8	Whistling-Ducks
	Thalassornithini	1	1	White-backed Duck
Anserinae	Cereopsini	1	1	Cape Barren Goose
	Anserini	2	16	True Geese
	Cygnini	2	8	Swans
Stictonettinae	None	1	1	Freckled Duck
Tadorninae	Merganettini	3	6	Torrent Ducks and Allies
	Plectropterini	2	3	Pied Shelducks
	Tadornini	6	15	True Sheldgeese and Shelducks
Anatinae	Malacorhynchini[b]	2	2	Salvadori's and Pink-eared Duck
	Anatini	11	62	Surface-feeding Ducks
	Aythyini	5	17	Pochards
	Mergini	10	22	Sea Ducks
	Oxyurini	4	9	Stiff-tailed Ducks

[a]Note: the order Anseriformes also includes three species in the family Anhimidae (screamers) and one in the family Anseranatidae (Magpie Goose).
[b]Composition of the tribe and inclusion in Anatinae are provisional (Livezey 1996c).

Infobox 2-1

Jean Delacour
Aviculturist and Systematist
(1890–1985)

Born in Paris but reared on family estates elsewhere in France, Jean Delacour quickly developed a keen interest in nature. While still a boy he maintained a sizable collection of captive birds, which in turn triggered his academic interests in ornithology. He subsequently earned a doctorate in biology at the University of Lille and began a long and distinguished career devoted to aviculture, conservation, and avian systematics. In 1920, Delacour founded *L'Oiseau*, France's leading ornithological journal.

Unfortunately, the Delacour estate became a battle ground in World War I, and his beloved aviaries were destroyed. After the war, he built new aviaries as part of an exceptional private zoo at Chateau Cleres in Normandy, only to have these destroyed once more, shortly before World War II. In 1940, Delacour fled war-torn France for New York where he began associations with the Bronx Zoo and the American Museum of Natural History. He later served as director of what is now known as the Natural History Museum of Los Angeles County until his retirement in 1960. By then, he again

had restored his private zoo at Cleres and regularly traveled between France and the United States as he continued his activities.

Delacour's systematic revisions dealt with diverse groups of birds, many of which he had maintained in his aviaries. He also explored widely, especially tropical areas in South America and what was then Indochina, where his work added considerably to the ornithology of these regions. Besides his many journal papers, Delacour also produced major volumes, including *Pheasants of the World* (1951, with J. C. Harrison), *Wild Pigeons and Doves* (1959), and *Curassows and Related Birds* (1973, with D. Amadon).

Delacour held a long-standing interest in the systematics of the family Anatidae, no doubt because waterfowl are relatively easy to maintain in captivity where he could closely observe their daily activities. His extensive knowledge and passion for waterfowl resulted in a seminal taxonomic work, *The Family Anatidae* (1945, with E. Mayr), in which such misleading characters as bill shape were discarded in favor of more con-

servative features such as tarsal pattern, plumages, behavior, and syrinx structure. Many small taxa (e.g., *Spatula* and *Dafila*) therefore were eliminated and united with larger genera (e.g., *Anas*). Anatids also were separated into subfamilies, which in turn were divided into tribes (a taxon ending with -ini), each consisting of related genera. Even with later refinements, the revision remains a landmark in waterfowl classification. Delcaour's devotion to waterfowl resulted in the four-

volume series, *The Waterfowl of the World* (1951–1964), a magnificent work that included taxonomy, life history, range maps, care in captivity, and color plates by Peter Scott. He bequeathed his estate and zoological park at Cleres to the people of France. See Mayr (1986) for a full tribute to Jean Delacour. Photo courtesy of the Museum Archives, Natural History Museum of Los Angeles County.

"ini," united related genera and, in large measure, replaced many of the subfamily designations proposed in earlier systems.

Although these studies provided useful information, they nevertheless remain quite different from the phylogenetic approaches used by modern systematists. Livezey (1986, 1991) was the first to apply such a completely modern phylogenetic analysis to waterfowl. He began by analyzing 120 morphological characters to develop a phylogeny of the Recent genera within Anseriformes (Livezey 1986), and later used 157 morphological characters to study the phylogeny of species within the Anatini (surface-feeding or dabbling ducks; Livezey 1991).

Livezey subsequently produced phylogenetic analyses of the remaining major subfamilies and tribes of Anseriformes: Dendrocygninae or whistling-ducks and allies (Livezey (1995a), Oxyurini or stiff-tailed ducks (Livezey 1995b), Mergini or sea ducks (Livezey 1995c), Aythyini or pochards (Livezey 1996a), Anserinae or geese and swans (Livezey 1996b), Tadornini or sheldgeese and shelducks (Livezey 1996c, 1997b), as well as other important topics related to the phylogeny of Anseriformes (Livezey 1997c, Zusi and Livezey 2000). Livezey (1997a) later summarized these works into a seminal paper on the phylogenetic classification of Anseriformes.

Molecular data also were used to develop waterfowl classifications (Kessler and Avise 1984, Sibley and Ahlquist 1990, among others), but most of these systems did not use a phylogenetic approach (for a review, see Livezey 1997a). However, Johnson and Sorenson (1999) used DNA sequences of two mtDNA protein-coding genes to develop a phylogenetic analysis of dabbling ducks in the genus *Anas*.

We have adopted Livezey's (1997a) classification of Anseriformes as the basis of this chapter; it represents the most complete and recent analysis, and it uses a phylogenetic approach, which offers distinct

advantages over older methodologies (see below). Some of the terminal taxa in his proposed phylogeny correspond to conventional subspecies, especially for the Common Eider, Canada Goose, and Torrent Duck, but Livezey did not recommend that such lineages be elevated to species status in checklists, field guides, and popular books. Our checklist includes these taxa to offer readers a perspective that better depicts the diversity of Anatidae (see Appendix A at end of chapter). Common names also follow Livezey (1997a), although we noted a few departures where we selected a more widely used common name. For species occurring in North America, we used the common name recommended by the American Ornithologists' Union (1983) in the few instances where discrepancies occurred with Livezey's names. We also review the fossil history of Anseriformes and incorporated into Appendix A those species mentioned in the text. We then review general characteristics of the families, subfamilies, tribes, and genera of Anseriformes. We include some details about the natural history of selected species, especially those that are rare, unique, or recently extinct or endangered.

For more about the identification and life histories of waterfowl throughout the world, see Madge and Burn (1988) for excellent color plates and life-history information on all species, and Soothill and Whitehead (1978) for a useful guide. Johnsgard (1978) offers a succinct source of detailed species accounts, whereas Todd (1996) provides a more general approach accompanied by beautiful photographs. Phillips's (1922–26) classic work was reprinted in two volumes in 1986. The four-volume treatise by Delacour (1954–64), long a standard reference, but now out-of-print, is available in many libraries. Bellrose (1980) completely revised Kortright's (1942) renowned *Ducks, Geese, and Swans of North America,* which many regard as a bible for life-history information. The most recent and authorita-

Infobox 2-2

Janet Kear
England's Preeminent Waterfowl Biologist
(1933–2004)

After completing her studies of ethology for a Ph.D. at Cambridge University in 1959, Janet Kear began her career as a research scientist at what is now The Wildfowl and Wetlands Trust. She eventually attained the position of Director for the Trust's eight centers located throughout the United Kingdom.

Her research activities culminated in about 100 journal papers and other publications concerned with many aspects of waterfowl ecology and management. Her early work concerned the feeding behavior of waterfowl, especially in the context of crop damage from the increasing numbers of geese wintering in the United Kingdom and how it might be prevented. Later her research turned to the parental care of waterfowl and the behavioral inputs required for producing eggs and young. Her several books include *The Hawaiian Goose: An Experiment in Conservation* (1980, with A. J. Berger), *The Mute Swan* (1988), *Man and Waterfowl* (1990), which won the Natural World's Book of the Year Award, and *Ducks of the World* (1991). She also edited *Ducks, Geese, and Swans* (2005) for the Oxford University Series, Bird Families of the World. Kear traveled in Australia and North America as well as in Europe while pursuing her interests in waterfowl and wetland habitat. She also investigated the impacts of Pink-footed and Greylag Geese on agricultural lands in Iceland, studied the unique feeding ecology of Blue Ducks in New Zealand, and worked on Salvadori's Ducks in New Guinea.

Kear was an advisor to organizations such as English Nature, Durrell Wildlife Conservation Trust, and the Royal Society for the Protection of Birds. She also served as president of the British Ornithologists' Union and as editor of the Union's scientific journal, *Ibis,* and was the first woman to hold either of these positions. She subsequently received the Union Medal in recognition of her service and contributions to British ornithology. In 1993, the Queen bestowed the Order of the British Empire to Janet Kear for her many contributions to waterfowl conservation. She formally retired from her director's position after a 34-year career with the Wildfowl and Wetlands Trust and, until her death, continued to write and advise on issues of concern to the welfare of waterfowl and their habitat. Photo courtesy of Janet Kear.

tive treatise dealing with waterfowl on a global basis is *Ducks, Geese and Swans* by Janet Kear (2005), formerly an administrator–biologist with the Wildfowl and Wetlands Trust (see Infobox 2-2).

MODERN PHYLOGENETIC
SYSTEMATICS

The basic quest of phylogenetic systematics is to use empirical methods and evolutionary principles to reconstruct monophyletic groups, which means the group includes an ancestral species and all the descendants of that species (Hennig 1966, Cracraft 1981, Wiley 1981, Avers 1989). Indeed, the discovery of these monophyletic groups forms the core endeavor of phylogenetic systematics, resulting in a classification that contains only monophyletic groups that truly reflect the historical development of each lineage. In contrast, traditional approaches to systematics often relied on intuition and expert opinion, which were impossible to question empirically and often created artificial groups with no evolutionary significance. Indeed, we agree with Livezey 1997c:399) that, ". . . phylogenetic (cladistic) analy-sis of morphological and molecular data remains the only rigorous and philosophically grounded tool available for the reconstruction of higher-order relationships of birds." Nonetheless, because the phylogenetic approach is comparatively new for systematics in general and waterfowl systematics in particular, we review the basis of this approach and its advantages over older methods (see Table 2-2 for useful definitions).

Evolution deals with two basic concepts: descent with modification (anagenesis) and speciation (cladogenesis). Thereafter follows the corollary that all organisms (extinct and living) are related, although the degree of relatedness varies markedly. Evidence for relatedness is seen in shared phylogenetic patterns, which reflect the appearance of new intrinsic features, each the result of one or more genes and producing observable traits such as morphological structures and behavior. Importantly, however, some

Table 2-2. Definitions of some important terms used in phylogenetic systematics. Modified from Schuh (2000).

Apomorphy	a derived character; group-defining character
Autapomorphy	a derived character unique to a taxon
Clade	synonymous with a monophyletic group; whole branch of a tree
Cladogram	a branching diagram used to depict a phylogeny
Consistency	a measure of the fit of a given character index to a cladogram
Derived	a character state modified from the primitive (ancestral) state. Apomorphic
Homology	similarity among taxa due to common evolutionary origin
Monophyletic group	a group of species that contains a common ancestor and all its descendents (a natural taxon)
Paraphyletic group	a set of species containing an ancestral species and some, but not all descendents
Parsimony	a method to choose among all possible cladograms wherein the cladogram selected contains the fewest character changes
Phylogenetics	the study of evolutionary relationships within and between groups
Plesiomorphy	an ancestral character state
Polyphyletic group	an artificial grouping of taxa because of superficial resemblances; also lacks the most recent common ancestor
Primitive	a character state present in the common ancestor of a monophyetic group
Sister-groups	a pair of taxa united by one or more unique characters
Synapomorphy	an apomorphy shared by two or terminal taxa

of these features appear earlier than others in the course of evolutionary development.

Hence, an ordered, nested arrangement of taxa exists whose similarities can be established hierarchically. Phylogenetics then recognizes taxa according to empirical criteria that delineate membership within natural (monophyletic) groups that reflect true relatedness (Cracraft 1981). The science of systematics seeks to capture this orderliness, which has resulted from patterns of phylogenetic ancestry and descent (Eldredge and Cracraft 1980). In essence, a systematist records the path of evolution by looking at "footprints" (i.e., the intrinsic features), with the goal of developing a classification that represents the true ancestry (i.e., historical "traits") and relatedness of organisms. Such a classification reflects a degree of relatedness familiar to all biologists: Species within a genus are more closely related to each other than those assigned to another genus, family, or order. Phylogenies also can be used to analyze additional evolutionary patterns exhibited by ecomorphological characteristics such as body mass, clutch size, sexual dimorphism, diet, and nest-site selection, among others.

Nonetheless, the numbers of species recognized within any taxon and the inferred relationships among them are subject to continuing flux. New information and the ever-changing concepts about "what is a species?" steadily produce alternative proposals and debatable interpretations. Of special importance, however, has been the development of new analytical methods. Early classifications were scenarios of phylogenetic history and evolutionary relationships among various taxa and, although these often sounded reasonable, they could not be subjected to the critical analysis inherent in phylogenetic systematics (Eldredge and Cracraft 1980). In short, there were no numerical data to analyze — and no formal methods for analysis — hence the systems instead relied on comparative descriptions of features such as anatomy or plumage. In many cases, these assessments led to polyphyletic or paraphyletic groupings that were formed by unnatural and unnecessary "splitting" of closely related taxa, thereby obscuring informative taxonomic distinctions. Excessive grouping of taxa also obscures information about evolutionary relationships and ancestry.

In contrast with these older systems, modern phylogenetic systematists use cladograms to develop empirical hypotheses, which then may be objectively rejected or accepted in keeping with the data at hand. These techniques — reviewed by Eldredge and Cracraft (1980) — develop "parsimonious" cladograms

that estimate evolutionary trees. The cladograms are constructed using highly restricted and presumably homologous characters (i.e., of similar ancestry), the states of which fall into two groups: ancestral (plesiomorphic) and derived (apomorphic). Derived states represent evolutionary novelties and, because they occur in smaller subsets of taxa, they are useful as well as necessary for determining true relationships (Wiley 1981, Avers 1989). For example, molt of the remiges (flight feathers) evolved from asynchronous (the ancestral state) to an annual synchronous molt, then to a twice-annual synchronous molt. The reticulate pattern on the tarsus is the ancestral character state, whereas a scutellate pattern is derived (Fig. 2-1). Synapomorphies thus are derived character states shared by a group of taxa; hence synapomorphies are especially important in determining relatedness, which then aids in the identification of taxonomic groups.

A phylogenetic systematist then uses these data to construct a cladogram, which portrays in graphic form the relationships among taxa. In appearance, cladograms are trees whose branches represent groups that share derived characters (i.e., they possess synapomorphies). Modern systematists thus group taxa by hierarchically nested, derived characters as a means of developing a classification system that accurately represents the true phylogeny of the group in question. Thus, the phylogenetic trees developed by Livezey (1986, 1991) and Johnson and Sorenson (1999) used synapomorphies to unite taxonomic units into monophyletic branches (clades).

In reality, classifications for Anseriformes and other organisms are themselves still "evolving" because of *what* and *how* characters are analyzed. For example, while phylogenetic studies already use most of the morphological traits that are feasible to analyze with current methods (Livezey and Zusi 2001), tens of thousands of genes and vast amounts of other DNA characters remain untapped. However, molecular data are not themselves superior to morphological data (see Hillis et al. 1996, Wiens and Hillis 1996). Lastly, computer algorithms and theoretical approaches are constantly improving.

The debate on what constitutes a "good" species also continues in full force. Not only do many biologists have reservations about the "species concept," but modern phylogenetic systematists also question the *rank* assigned to the terminal units on a phylogenetic tree. For example, the taxa of northern swans, all of which are white, may represent either (1) two species, each with two subspecies; or (2) four species. In either case, a cladogram of the northern

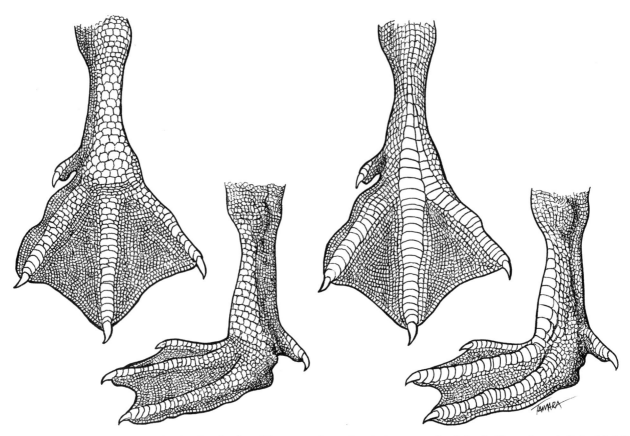

Figure 2-1. Tarsal patterns in the family Anatidae are of two basic types: reticulate (left) and scutellate (right). Whistling-ducks (subfamily Dendrocygninae), true geese and swans (subfamily Anserinae), and the Freckled Duck (subfamily Stictonettinae) have reticulate tarsi (ancestral trait), whereas the tarsi of all other waterfowl are scutellate (derived trait).

swans might show four terminal points. Herein lies the difference between phylogenetics and classification (i.e., pure taxonomy). The phylogeneticist is most interested in retaining the differences leading to the terminal points and might thus regard each as a "species" (a phylogenetic species concept), whereas a descriptive taxonomist/biologist seeks to assign taxonomic rankings to the nested subgroups and thus might recognize only one or two "species." Approaches to the classification of Anseriformes therefore vary according to purpose, and no single approach is "best." See Livezey (1997a) for more about this issue relative to waterfowl classification.

While modern approaches have supplanted previous attempts to classify waterfowl, difficulties such as those for the northern swans nonetheless remain unresolved to full satisfaction of the scientific community. Students thus should expect continuing debate about some taxonomic relationships. Indeed, a universally accepted species-level classification is as unlikely for Anseriformes as it might be for any other

major group of vertebrates. Accordingly, the classification presented in this book represents a snapshot of an ever-changing stream of knowledge, and new information will trigger appropriate revisions. Still, much is known about waterfowl classification, and a review of this information represents more than an academic exercise — phylogenetic relationships bear directly on waterfowl management.

Problem Genera and Species

Several genera in Anseriformes present special problems for systematists. Livezey (1996c) analyzed eight such "problematic" genera; except for the steamer-ducks of South America and the Falkland Islands, the Gray-sided Comb Duck of Africa and Asia (Fig. 2-2), and the Black-sided Comb Duck of Central and South America, all are monotypic genera (i.e., contain only one species). These include the Freckled Duck of Australia, Torrent Duck of South America, Pink-eared Duck of Australia, Blue Duck of New

Figure 2-2. The Gray-sided Comb Duck of Africa and Asia is among eight "problem" genera that have long perplexed waterfowl taxonomists. The sexes share similar iridescent plumage, but males are somewhat larger and have an enlarged and distinctive caruncle atop their bills. Photo courtesy of Frank McKinney and the Bell Museum of Natural History.

Zealand, Salvadori's Duck of New Guinea, and Spur-winged Goose of Africa. In fact, Livezey (1996c) described a century-long struggle with the taxonomy of these species, which will remain a challenge until new data can resolve their phylogenetic placement. Here we present the current thinking with regard to the classification of these and other enigmatic taxa, as well as problems and management issues associated with subspecies and populations.

Subspecies and Populations

Recognition of infraspecific groups (e.g., subspecies or "races") presents taxonomic dilemmas, some of which remain hotly disputed. In particular, the racial distinctions among some populations of Canada Geese in North America have perplexed systematists for some time (Hanson 1965, 1997). In the past, taxonomists recognized subtle differences in body size and plumage shading as the basis for subspecific designations, most notably for Canada Geese in North America (Fig. 2-3). Recently, molecular genetic markers also have proven useful. For example, mtDNA analysis revealed that large and small-bodied Canada Geese in western North America were highly divergent and represented monophyletic groups (Scribner

et al. 2003). Indeed, all 11 populations examined in this study were genetically divergent, albeit to varying degrees. Van Wagner and Baker (1990) estimated a divergence time of 700,000 years for the development of large and small-bodied forms from a common ancestor, and 100,000 years for the divergence of subspecies within the large and small forms. Similarly, Pierson et al. (2000) used molecular techniques to compare the genetics of two populations of Aleutian Canada Geese, a small-bodied goose of the Aleutian Islands of Alaska, and a small-bodied mainland form, the Cackling Canada Goose. The two widely separated populations of Aleutian Canada Geese were genetically far more similar to each other than to the Cackling Canada Goose on the mainland. In 2004 — based on these and other genetic studies — the American Ornithologists' Union divided *Branta canadensis* by recognizing a set of smaller-bodied forms as the Cackling Canada Goose (*Branta hutchinsii*), noting that further splitting may result after additional analyses (Banks et al. 2004). Indeed, Livezey (1997a) recognized six potential species within the complex known collectively as Canada Geese (Appendix A). Molecular techniques also identified Canada Geese from eastern Canada as the source of the population now breeding in Greenland,

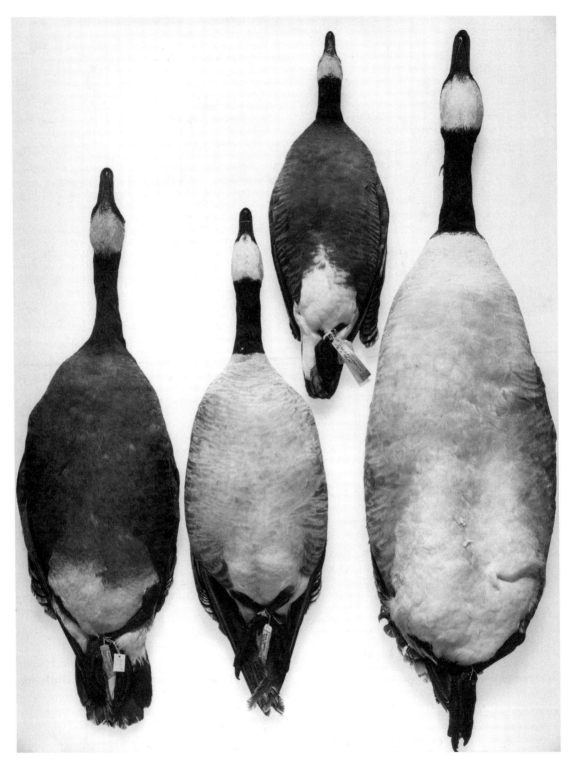

Figure 2-3. Authorities have long recognized different races and subspecies of the Canada Goose. Each is distinguished by variation in geographical range, coloration, structural size, and body mass. Such variation is readily seen in these specimens, which from left to right are the Vancouver Canada Goose, Lesser Canada Goose (2.77 kg), Cackling Canada Goose (1.55 kg), and Giant Canada Goose (5.68 kg). The number in parentheses is the average body mass of adult males as reported in Bellrose (1980); data were not available for the Vancouver Canada Goose. Photo courtesy of Victor E. Krantz, U.S. National Museum of Natural History.

where they apparently arrived only about 50 years ago (Scribner et al. 2003, see also Fox et al. 1996).

Subspecies also occupy different geographical areas within the total range of a species. For example, the stricture of the Isthmus of Panama apparently provided enough geographical separation so that, in time, easily distinguishable subspecies of the Black-bellied Whistling-Duck evolved on either side of the isthmus; the breast plumage of the southern form is clearly gray, whereas northern subspecies lack such coloration (Bolen and Rylander 1983). On the other hand, Wood Ducks in the eastern United States appear the same as those in the Pacific Northwest, but these widely separated populations are not regarded as subspecies. Elsewhere in North America, King Eiders are delineated into widely separated breeding populations in the western and eastern Arctic, yet genetic differences within this vast range are virtually nonexistent (Pearce et al. 2004). An even more pronounced example is the lack of differentiation among populations of the Fulvous Whistling-Duck. This species occurs in parts of the Nearctic, Neotropical, Ethiopian, and Oriental realms, yet birds from each of these locations are so similar that no subspecies or forms are recognized by modern taxonomists (Johnsgard 1978, Livezey 1997a).

Overall, molecular analyses provide increasingly useful insights about goose populations in North America (see Cathey et al. 1998, Talbot et al. 2003), as well as for species such as the Spectacled Eider (Scribner et al. 2001), Northern Pintail (Cronin et al. 1996), and Mottled Duck (Williams et al. 2002). To illustrate, mtDNA analyses of Northern Pintails breeding in Alaska, California, and the midcontinent prairies of North America revealed 20 genotypes but no significant genetic differences among these populations, a result perhaps not unexpected because of frequent gene exchange among populations of this highly nomadic species (Cronin et al. 1996).

Mallards and Mallard-like ducks present a particular set of taxonomic difficulties, of which three examples (of several) amply illustrate the complexity of the situation. First, the Gray Duck, along with various other Mallard-like ducks in New Zealand, Australia, and several islands of the South Pacific Ocean, has been subject to a dizzying array of taxonomic designations — species to subspecies to species again (see Johnsgard 1978, Livezey 1991). Similarly, the endangered Laysan Duck — once known as the Laysan Teal — of the Hawaiian Archipelago is clearly a Mallard derivative, but debate continues

regarding its status as a species or subspecies (Weller 1980a, American Ornithologists' Union 1983, Moulton and Weller 1984, Livezey 1991). All systematists agree that the American Black Duck of eastern North America is closely related to the Mallard and probably is a recent evolutionary derivative of a Mallard-like ancestor (Johnsgard 1961d, Ankney et al. 1986, Avise et al. 1990, Livezey 1991). However, whereas Livezey (1991) regards the Mallard and American Black Duck as closely related but separate species based on a phylogenetic analysis of morphological data, genetic evidence suggests these two forms in fact may be so genetically alike as to preclude their separation even as subspecies (Avise et al. 1990).

In Australasia, five extant species of teal provide an interesting example of speciation in the Southern Hemisphere. The taxonomy of this group has always been subject to debate (Dumbell 1986, Williams and Robertson 1996, Johnson and Sorenson 1999), but recent DNA work has provided some resolution of the issue (Kennedy and Spencer 2000). In the resultant phylogeny, the Gray Teal and Chestnut Teal of Australia were grouped together as sister taxa, whereas the New Zealand teal were considered a monophyletic taxon, which agreed with earlier genetic work (Daugherty et al. 1999). Members of the New Zealand group were each accorded species status as the Auckland Islands Teal, the Campbell Island Teal, and the Brown Teal. Only the latter retains the ability to fly — the other species are flightless. Kennedy and Spencer (2000) also argued for separate conservation strategies for each of these species, particularly for the Campbell Island Teal (see Infobox 6-1). The Madagascan Teal, an endangered endemic of Madagascar, also is related to this group, particularly to the Gray Teal (Young et al. 1997). Many other examples might be cited of unresolved taxonomic issues — whether for species, subspecies, and populations — but all are significant because taxonomy forms the foundation for management and conservation strategies (see Avise 1989, Daugherty et al. 1990, Hazevoet 1996).

Hybridization and Waterfowl Conservation

Hybridization is rare in birds, with an interspecific hybrid occurring only in about one of 50,000 individuals (Mayr 1970). In Anseriformes, however, the frequency of both interspecific and intergeneric hybridization is among highest in all orders of birds, and may reach 30–40% (Johnsgard 1960a, Grant and Grant 1992). Indeed, Gray (1958) listed about 400 hybrid combinations in waterfowl, thereby showing the limited nature of genetic barriers within the family Anatidae. Wood Ducks alone hybridize with 26 species, including 5 pochards and 16 dabbling ducks, among others (Dilger and Johnsgard 1959). Abnormally high rates of hybridization may develop when otherwise allopatric taxa become artificially sympatric. Species recognition falters under such conditions, as suggested by the common occurrence of hybrid waterfowl in zoo collections. Further, and perhaps more significantly for managers, some 20% of hybrids may be fertile (Scherer and Hilsberg 1982). Rhymer and Simberloff (1996), in reviewing the effects of hybridization and introgression on plants and animals, noted that morphological observations alone may underestimate the problem. Introgressive gene flow between populations is especially serious because the hybrids can backcross with one or both of the parent populations, and hybrid swarms may occur at locations where introgression is especially prevalent.

Among the best-known examples of hybridization in birds concerns crosses between the sexually dimorphic Mallard and closely related nondimorphic species in the Mallard complex. The effects of the genetic dominance of Mallards are well documented in the United States where hybridization has been implicated in the decline of the American Black Duck (Johnsgard 1961e, Johnsgard 1967b, Johnsgard and DiSilvestro 1976, Rogers and Patterson 1984, Ankney et al. 1987, Mank et al. 2004) and the Mexican Duck (Hubbard 1977); increasing numbers of Mallard × Mottled Duck hybrids are reported from Florida (Mazourek and Gray 1994). Indeed, Mallard × Mexican Duck hybridization is so pervasive that the American Ornithologists' Union (1983) declared the Mexican Duck as conspecific with the Mallard!

Unfortunately, releases of game-farm Mallards have occurred on major wintering areas of American Black Ducks. In 1988–89 alone, a single privately owned hunting facility released about 240,000 Mallards (Heusmann 1991). These circumstances are particularly significant because pair formation in American Black Ducks and Mallards begins during winter (Stotts 1958, Stotts and Davis 1960, Brodsky and Weatherhead 1984), and the releases thereby promote further opportunities for hybridization. Hence, beyond their academic interest in the classification of Mallards and American Black Ducks as either species or subspecies, phylogenetic systematists could have predicted the troubling prospect of hybridization and, on that basis, opposed the releases.

In New Zealand, introduced Mallards have hybridized extensively with the native Gray Duck (Braithwaite and Miller 1975, Rhymer et al. 1994). Game-stock Mallards from Europe were introduced to South Island in 1867, and North American stock was introduced to the North Island in the 1930s (Thomson 1922, Williams 1981). The impact of these introductions was stunning: Hybridization had reached 51% on South Island by 1980–81, and the proportion of pure Gray Ducks dropped to a meager 4.5% (Gillespie 1985). More recent genetic data revealed widespread introgression of mtDNA from Mallards to Gray Ducks throughout New Zealand, leading to the conclusion that the process of speciation is undergoing reversal (Rhymer et al. 1994). Mallard reproductive rates also exceed those of Gray Ducks, perhaps hastening the already evident decline of the native species (Caithness et al. 1991). New Zealand apparently is doomed to harbor a hybrid swarm of Mallards × Gray Ducks and the eventual loss of its endemic species. In Australia, releases of Mallards long ago produced similar effects in Gray Duck populations (Frith 1967).

Mallards were also involved in hybridization issues with the Marianas Duck, an endemic but recently extinct duck on the western Pacific islands of Guam, Tinian, and Saipan (see Reichel and Lemke 1994). Meller's Duck, a Mallard-like endemic of Madagascar, certainly would become highly vulnerable to hybridization if Mallards ever arrive on the island (see Young and Rhymer 1998). Similarly, Mallards likely would hybridize readily with the endemic Philippine Duck of the Philippine Archipelago (see Ripley 1951, Johnsgard 1978). In a somewhat reversed situation, the Chinese Spot-billed Duck expanded its breeding range in the last 60-70 years from East Asia into eastern Siberia, where they contacted and then hybridized with Mallards (Kulikova et al. 2004).

Regrettably, significant conservation issues concerning hybridization continue on a world-wide basis. In Hawaii, for example, an array of studies have documented that Mallards introduced for hunting are hybridizing with the endemic Hawaiian Duck (Browne et al. 1993, Rhymer 2001, Engilis et al. 2002). Similarly, in the United Kingdom and mainland Europe, Ruddy Ducks introduced from North America are hybridizing with the White-headed Duck, an endemic species already endangered by other causes (see Infobox 2-3). These and similar issues emphasize the importance of a well-grounded understanding of genetic relationships, including ancestry, as a tool in waterfowl management.

Infobox 2-3

**Invasion of an Exotic Species
The White-headed Duck at Risk: A Case History**

The introduction, whether accidental or intentional, of exotic species may pose threats for native organisms by bringing into play such agents as disease, competition, predation, and habitat alteration. In other cases, hybridization followed by introgression (i.e., the process of hybrids backcrossing with the parental stock) results in the continued introduction of foreign genes into the gene pool of the native species. As its genetic integrity diminishes, the native species becomes progressively threatened with extinction.

Ruddy Ducks are native to North America, but when some escaped from an aviary in England, a powerful new threat was introduced for the White-headed Duck — a Palearctic species already in dire straits. Disjunct populations of White-headed Ducks are scattered in western Asia, but a nonmigratory population also per-

sists in Spain. Current estimates suggest a global population of about 10,000 White-headed Ducks — down from some 100,000 — which reflects the impacts of widespread habitat loss and unregulated hunting during the last century. By 1979, the resident population in Spain plummeted to just 22 birds, but legal protection and habitat management had increased their numbers to about 2,600 by 2002. Conservation plans elsewhere in the species' former range (e.g., Hungary) concern releases of stock from captive-breeding programs.

After escaping in 1953, Ruddy Ducks soon established a viable breeding population in the United Kingdom, where they initially increased at the astonishing rate of 30% per year (the rate later slowed considerably). By 2002, with a total population of 6,000, they were reported at locations in England, Wales, Scotland,

and Northern Ireland. Meanwhile, Ruddy Ducks invaded mainland Europe, where sightings were recorded in 19 nations between 1965 and 1996. Some flocks migrate each year between the United Kingdom and northern France, but others remain on the European mainland throughout the year. The first Ruddy Duck × White-headed Duck hybrids were recorded in 1991, and hunters shot 57 in 2000. Breeding experiments confirmed that male hybrids can be backcrossed with female White-headed Ducks though at least the third generation, thereby proving the unchecked introgression of Ruddy Duck DNA into the genome of White-headed Ducks. Recent mtDNA analyses indicate that hybridization also can result from crossings between male White-backed Ducks and female Ruddy Ducks.

The challenge of this new threat will require effective control of Ruddy Ducks wherever they occur in Europe (further assault on White-headed Ducks surely will arise if Ruddy Ducks reach western Asia). Based on field trials conducted in the United Kingdom, shooting before and after the breeding season repre-

sents the most effective means of culling Ruddy Ducks; trapping was ineffective. A model indicted an 80% certainty of reducing Ruddy Duck numbers in the United Kingdom to less than 175 birds within 4–6 years. Control efforts also are underway in 12 countries in mainland Europe.

Public support is necessary to implement programs designed to cull wildlife, and some groups indeed have opposed removing Ruddy Ducks in favor of White-headed Ducks. Some claim that culling will thwart natural selection (i.e., leave the birds alone and let the fittest species survive). Others believe that the European Ruddy Ducks have themselves undergone genetic differentiation after they escaped and now are unlike those in North America; hence they are also rare and should be preserved. See Brunner and Andreotti (2001), Munoz et al. (2003), Hughes (2003), Bajomi (2003), Torres (2003), and Li and Mundkur (2003). For more about threats from hybridization and introgression, see Rhymer and Simberloff (1996). Photo courtesy of Richard Taylor-Jones, the Wildfowl and Wetlands Trust.

Other Management Implications of Taxonomy

Real-world, on-the-ground management decisions and operations must move forward regardless of the often perplexing status of certain taxonomic designations. For example, although systematists might endlessly debate the taxonomic rank of the Laysan Duck, the stark fact remains that a small, distinct population of "a duck" remains isolated on Laysan Island, a 415-ha dot in the Hawaiian Archipelago, and only careful management will protect the continued existence of these birds (Moulton and Weller 1984, Reynolds 2004). Indeed, the U.S. Endangered Species Act (1973) recognizes subpopulations, and when these are in jeopardy, the full weight of federal protection comes into play. The U.S. Fish and Wildlife Service lists the Laysan Duck as endangered; only six birds apparently remained in 1911, and the entire adult population in 2000 still numbers only about 300 (see Brock 1951, Reynolds 2000). Recent radiotelemetry studies revealed that Laysan Teal spend 88% of their time in terrestrial vegetation and apparently make no effort to disperse from Laysan Island (Reynolds 2004).

An example concerning the management of two closely related species involves the Ross's Goose and Snow Goose. Indeed, these species are so closely

related that the divergence of mtDNA between the two registers only 0.80 (Shields and Wilson 1987), considerably less than the peak of 2.54 recorded among subspecies of Canada Geese (Van Wagner and Baker 1986, 1990). Both species are white and, although different in size, hunters find the two species almost impossible to distinguish in the field. This situation was particularly troublesome when the winter population of Ross's Geese declined to only 5,000–6,000 birds in 1931 (see Ryder and Alisauskas 1995, Moser 2001), which prompted a closed hunting season in the United States from 1931 to 1962. In fact, the two species are so similar that waterfowl managers overlooked a threefold increase in the numbers of Ross's Geese when the latter mixed with Snow Geese wintering in California (McLandress 1979). Fortunately, the current harvest of Ross's Geese appears to pose little threat to the population, which has exceeded 800,000 in recent years (Moser 2001, Moser and Duncan 2001, U.S. Fish and Wildlife Service 2003). However, these species hybridize (Trauger et al. 1971), and the eastward expansion of the winter range of Ross's Geese has increased their contact with Snow Geese and opportunities for hybridization (Weckstein et al. 2002).

Perhaps an even more complex management dilemma concerns Dusky Canada Geese, which breed primarily on the Copper River Delta of Alaska.

However, the population of Dusky Canada Geese declined from 20,000–25,000 in the 1970s to 16,700 in 2002–03 (U.S. Fish and Wildlife Service 2003, Bromley and Rothey 2003). These birds winter in western Washington and Oregon, where the population mixes with 250,000 birds from five other subspecies of Canada Goose, each more abundant than the Dusky Canada Geese. Hence the management challenge is to protect the Dusky Canada Goose — whose annual harvest is limited to 250 birds — yet allow suitable harvests of the other subspecies, some of which cause crop depredations. Management is also hampered by dramatic changes in breeding habitat on the Copper River Delta, which was only 130 km from the epicenter of the disastrous 1964 earthquake. The powerful tremor uplifted the delta by 1.8–3.4 m and subsequently changed the habitat from marsh to scrub-shrub, which in turn allowed an influx of previously uncommon predators (e.g., coyotes, *Canis latrans*) and reduced nest success in some years to no more than 4% (see Bromley and Rothey 2003). Further, Bald Eagles (*Haliaeetus leucocephalus*), a threatened species, concentrating on the delta are important predators of goslings and adults.

A final example — and a genuine success story in waterfowl conservation — involves the largest subspecies of the Canada Goose. For many years, the subspecies known as the Giant Canada Goose was considered extinct, but its rediscovery in 1962 prompted an immediate call for management specifically designed for this component of the North American goose flock (Hanson 1965, 1997). Biologists soon realized that regional hunting regulations governing harvests for the more numerous subspecies of Canada Goose might produce unrecognized or unintended impacts on the distribution and abundance of less common or unrecognized subspecies sharing the same hunting zone (Raveling 1978). The first step required recognition of the morphological differences for each of the numerous subspecies of Canada Geese in North America (see Thompson et al. 1999), which then permitted assessments of the migration patterns and hunting vulnerability peculiar to each subspecies (see Raveling and Dixon 1981). As mentioned previously, sophisticated genetic techniques now aid taxonomic refinements and, in fact, may prove the only feasible way to accurately identify subpopulations and subspecies of Canada Geese (Ely and Scribner 1994, Pearce et al. 2000, Talbot et al. 2003). Hence, armed with the appropriate taxonomic information, waterfowl managers can make informed decisions about specific habitat require-

ments, promulgate better regulations, and establish priorities for additional research. Once again we highlight the important role of systematics in the practice of waterfowl management.

FOSSIL HISTORY AND PHYLOGENY OF EARLY ANSERIFORMES

Compared to most other avian orders, Anseriformes is well represented in the fossil record (Brodkorb 1964, Livezey 1997a). Nonetheless, fossils of waterfowl are seldom represented by complete skeletons, and instead often consist of no more than a few disarticulated bones. The assignment of taxa based on such fragmentary material often leads to incorrect phylogenetic inferences (Livezey and Martin 1988). Moreover, fossils usually do not provide good data for identifying either synapomorphy or a sequence of ancestral to derived characters simply because the fossil record is often too incomplete for such a purpose (Eldredge and Cracraft 1980). Despite these shortcomings, fossils offer insights about the minimum ages for the branch points of evolutionary trees, and dated fossils for living taxa provide minimum ages of those taxa. A thorough treatment of fossil Anseriformes lies beyond our scope, but we nonetheless shall outline some major points and review the phylogenetic relationships of early Anseriformes (Livezey 1997a).

Based on fossil evidence, Howard (1964) speculated that waterfowl probably originated in the early Eocene of the Cenozoic Era about 54 million years ago. Current data and the analysis of Livezey (1997c, 1998) now indicate Anseriformes arose in the late Mesozoic (about 65 million years ago), followed by diversification of Anhimae and Anseres during the Paleocene (55–65 million years ago). Suggestions that waterfowl arose in the early Cretaceous (100–135 million years ago) seem doubtful; they rely solely on two bone fragments upon which the species *Gallornis straeleni* was proposed, but the characters described for *Gallornis* are very different from those used to define Anseriformes.

The earliest taxon assigned to Anatidae is the late Eocene fossil *Eonessa anaticula* from the United States (Wetmore 1938), but subsequent review regarded the specimen as too poorly preserved to make a definitive assignment (Olson and Feduccia 1980). The earliest fossil currently assigned to the Anatidae is the goose-size *Romainvillia stehlini* from the early Oligocene (about 37 million years ago) of France (Lebedinsky 1927, Olson and Feduccia 1980). Other early fossil anseriforms include the swan-like

Cygnopterus affinis from the middle Oligocene of Belgium (Lambrecht 1931) and *Mionetta* from the early Miocene (about 26 million years ago) of France (Livezey and Martin 1988).

Paleontologists subsequently uncovered fossils from the late Oligocene–early Miocene that are representative of present-day subfamilies: Anserinae (swans and geese) and Anatinae (true ducks). *Paranyroca magna* from the early Miocene of the United States apparently was highly specialized for diving in ways similar to modern pochards (Miller and Compton 1939). The modern genera *Dendrocygna*, *Branta*, and *Anser* also were established firmly in the fossil record by the mid-Miocene (Howard 1950, 1964). Howard (1964) also believed *Anas* appeared during the late Oligocene and early Miocene, but her specimens probably were misclassified, as were those regarded as *Aythya* (Livezey and Martin 1988). The duck-like fossils from those periods more likely were earlier forms of Anseriformes instead of representatives of modern genera in Anatinae (Livezey and Martin 1988). *Anas* and *Aythya* probably did not appear until the Miocene was well underway.

By the Pliocene (2–5 million years ago), at least 10 anseriforms, including the Mallard, Gadwall, and Bufflehead, existed in a form indistinguishable from modern species (Howard 1964). Other specimens assignable to the Tadornini (sheldgeese and shelducks) and Mergini (sea ducks) also were uncovered in Pliocene deposits. With the advent of the Pleistocene, many living species of Anseriformes are represented in the fossil record, as well as many species that are now extinct.

Holocene (Recent) Extinctions

Young et al. (1997) provided accounts of 54 waterfowl taxa (species and subspecies) lost to extinction during the Holocene Period (last 10,000 years), mostly as a result of direct or indirect contact with humans. For the most part, these extinctions occurred on four island areas: (1) the Hawaiian Islands, (2) New Zealand, (3) Madagascar and other islands of the western Indian Ocean, and (4) other Pacific Ocean islands. In contrast to the greater vulnerability of island waterfowl to human influences, extinction has claimed only four taxa on continental areas, as shown by Young et al. (1997) and Fuller (2000).

The Hawaiian Islands once were inhabited by four species of large, flightless goose-like birds, the moa-nalos ("lost fowl"). Several extinct goose species also are known from Hawaii, including the

Greater Nene or Nene-nui, for which a surviving relative is the endangered Hawaiian Goose or Lesser Nene. These extinctions rapidly followed colonization of the islands by Polynesians some 1,500 years ago (Olson and James 1984). Indeed, expansion of the Polynesians across the Pacific Islands may have exterminated more than 2,000 bird species, some 20% of the world's total (Steadman 1995). In the Hawaiian Archipelago, the first 2000 years of human occupation likely exterminated 50% of the native avifauna (Olson and James 1982, Engilis and Pratt 1993). However, three endemic taxa survive on Hawaii — the Hawaiian Goose, the Hawaiian Duck or Koloa Maoli ("native duck"), and the Laysan Duck — but each requires intensive conservation efforts.

In New Zealand, 11 species of now extinct moas (Dinornithidae) were the dominant herbivores (Bell 1991), but waterfowl evolved to fill vacant niches. Indeed, New Zealand once harbored 13 species of waterfowl in 10 genera, but 8 became extinct following human settlement. Extinct species include the New Zealand Swan (similar to the Black Swan), the South Island Goose, the North Island Goose, and at least five species of ducks, including the Chatham Island Shelduck and Finsch's Duck. Finsch's Duck was not included in Livezey's 1997 phylogeny, but he earlier had placed this unique duck in a separate subfamily, Euryanatinae (Livezey 1989). Finsch's Duck was a small (2.2–2.3 kg), flightless duck common on both North and South Island, with a short bill that probably was an adaptation to feed on terrestrial vegetation. The geese also were flightless, large herbivores (15–18 kg) exploiting grazing niches not occupied by the moas (Worthy and Holdaway 2002). Colonization of New Zealand by the Polynesians some 1,000–1,200 years ago precipitated the extinction of these waterfowl species as well as the moas and other fauna (Cassels 1984, Flannery 1994, Worthy and Holdaway 2002). The most recent extinction concerns the Auckland Islands Merganser. Discovered in 1840, this small, nearly flightless merganser became extinct in 1902 (see Kear and Scarlett 1970). Subsequently, remains of yet another extinct species of merganser were discovered on the Chatham Islands, New Zealand (Millener 1999). However, New Zealand retains eight endemic taxa, including an endemic genus represented solely by the Blue Duck.

Humans colonized Madagascar about 1,500 years ago (Dewar 1984), and the Mascarene Islands of the western Indian Ocean were settled some time in the 16th century (Cheke 1987). The result was predictable and catastrophic for the fauna: extinction of all large mammals, birds, and reptiles, except the giant tortoise (*Geochelone elephantine*) on Aldabra Island. Six waterfowl taxa were lost from the region, consisting of four sheldgeese similar to the Egyptian Sheldgoose of sub-Saharan Africa, and two ducks. Recent extinctions (i.e., since 1600 A.D.) include the Mauritius Sheldgoose (1698), the Mauritius Duck (1710), and the Réunion Island Sheldgoose (1710). Young et al. (1997) also list the recently described the Amsterdam Island Duck, a small, teal-size duck from the Amsterdam Islands in the Indian Ocean (see Olson and Jouventin 1996). The Amsterdam Island Duck had a strikingly short, pointed bill suggestive of wigeon ancestry, but this duck probably was exterminated around 1800 by humans or human-introduced mammals. However, five endemic taxa survive in the western Indian Ocean, three of which are endemic to Madagascar: Meller's Duck, Madagascan Teal, and Madagascan White-eyed Pochard.

On other Pacific Ocean islands, Young et al. (1997) reported only four taxa that became extinct during the Holocene. The Bering Canada Goose, extinct since about 1900, bred on the Kuril and Commander Islands off northeastern Siberia. The Rennell Island Teal, found only on Rennell Island in the Solomon Islands of the central Pacific, was described in 1942 but has not been seen reliably since 1959 (see Kear and Williams 1978, Fuller 2000). The Washington Island or Coues' Gadwall of Washington and New York Islands in the Fanning (now Tabuaeran) Archipelago of the central Pacific probably succumbed to extinction soon after its discovery in 1874; only one pair of birds was ever collected to substantiate existence of this species (see Fuller 2000). The last Marianas Duck from the northern Marianas Islands of the western Pacific died sometime in the late 1980s, although this species may have originated as a hybrid (see Reichel and Lemke 1994).

Endangered Species

Regrettably, waterfowl are not exceptions to the world's avifauna in avoiding appearance on global lists of threatened and endangered species. We used the *Red List of Threatened Species* (IUCN 2004) and *Threatened Birds of the World* (BirdLife International 2000) to develop a list that yielded six species extinct since 1600, as well as six critically endangered species, nine endangered species, and 11 vulnerable species (Table 2-3). IUCN also recognizes eight species as near-threatened. In the United States, the U.S. Fish and Wildlife Service lists the Hawaiian

Duck, Laysan Duck, and Hawaiian Goose as endangered, and the Spectacled and Steller's Eiders as threatened. Callaghan and Green (1993) reviewed 50 species and other taxa of waterfowl then listed by the IUCN, and Green (1992) provided information on the status and conservation of island waterfowl still surviving the imminent threat of extinction; Weller (1980a) likewise provides life-history and ecological information for waterfowl inhabiting the world's islands. Among the extant island forms, the Campbell Island Teal is critically endangered and is the focus of a major conservation effort by the New Zealand government (see Infobox 6-1)

The Threatened Waterfowl Specialist Group (TWSG), which is coordinated from The Wildfowl and Wetlands Trust, has produced an as yet unpublished list that includes the species in Table 2-3 but also addresses subspecies, listing five as extinct, eight as endangered or critically endangered, 10 as vulnerable, and eight as near-threatened. TWSG, established in 1990, now includes about 900 members from 143 countries with the goal of determining which taxa of waterfowl are globally threatened, and thereafter to produce and implement action plans designed for their conservation.

Phylogenetic Relationships of Anseriformes

The dominant hypothesis proposes that gallinaceous birds (Galliformes) were the ancestors of Anseriformes (Beddard 1898, Delacour 1954, Johnsgard 1965, Johnsgard 1968). However, Olson and Feduccia (1980) questioned this hypothesis, claiming waterfowl were derived from the shorebirds (Charadriiformes). They based their proposal on the fossil *Presbyornis,* which they interpreted as having the head of a duck with the postcranial skeleton of a shorebird (Fig. 2-4). Cracraft (1981) immediately criticized this idea, noting serious flaws in their reasoning and methodology, especially in the context of modern phylogenetic systematics (see also Olson 1982). Furthermore, an extensive analysis of morphological characters (Livezey 1997c, 1998), along with an examination of important cranial and associated adductor musculature of galliforms and anseriforms (Zusi and Livezey 2000), conclusively support a sister-group relationship for the two orders.

Prager and Wilson (1976, 1980) also uncovered a close relationships between these two orders based on the immunological patterns of various proteins. Anseriformes and Galliformes also share similar stereotypic displays not shared with other orders of birds (see Cracraft 1981). Moreover, Anseriformes and

Table 2-3. Recently extinct (since 1600 A.D.) and currently globally endangered, threatened, and vulnerable species of waterfowl as listed by IUCN (2004). Data on population status are from BirdLife International (2000). Scientific nomenclature and common names follow Livezey (1997a; see Appendix A).

Status	Distribution	Population
Extinct since 1600 A.D.		
Mauritius Sheldgoose	Mauritius Islands	Extinct (1698)
Réunion Island Sheldgoose[a]	Réunion Island	Extinct (1710)
Mauritius Duck	Mauritius Island	Extinct (1710)
Amsterdam Island Duck	Amsterdam Island	Extinct (about 1800)
Labrador Duck	Northeastern North America	Extinct (1875)
Auckland Island Merganser	Auckland Islands, New Zealand	Extinct (1902)
Critically Endangered		
Laysan Duck	Laysan Island, Hawaii	375
Crested Shelduck	Russia and South Korea	Possibly extinct
Campbell Island Teal	Dent Island, New Zealand	60–100
Pink-headed Duck	India, Myanmar, and Bangladesh	Probably extinct
Madagascan White-eyed Pochard	Madagascar	Near extinct
Brazilian Merganser	south-central Brazil	250
Endangered		
White-headed Duck	Europe and Asia	<10,000
Swan Goose	Russia, Mongolia, China	30,000–50,000
White-winged Duck	Southeast Asia, Indonesia	450
Hawaiian Duck	Hawaiian Islands	2,500
Meller's Duck	Madagascar	500
Madagascan Teal	Madagascar	500–1,000
Brown Teal	New Zealand	1,300–1,800
Blue Duck	New Zealand	1,200
Scaly-sided Merganser	Far East (scattered locations)	3,600–4,500
Vulnerable		
West Indian Whistling-Duck	Caribbean Islands	15,500
Lesser White-fronted Goose	Europe and Asia	25,000–30,000
Hawaiian Goose	Hawaiian Islands	1,000
Red-breasted Goose	Russia	88,000
Salvadori's Duck	New Guinea and Papua New Guinea	2,500–20,000
Eaton's Pintail	Kerguelen and Crozet Islands, Indian Ocean	15,000–21,000
Philippine Duck	Phillipine Islands	10,000–100,000
Auckland Islands Teal	Auckland Islands	2,000
Baikal Teal	East Asia	210,000
Marbled Duck	western Mediterranean and Northern Africa	9,000–19,000
Baer's Pochard	Russia, China	10,000–20,000

[a]Réunion Island Sheldgoose (*Mascarenachen kervazoi*) not in Livezey (1997a).

Galliformes each have a malate dehydrogenase mobility of 100 (Kitto and Wilson 1966). In contrast, this same characteristic is only 55 in Charadriiformes, thereby casting doubt on an ancestral relationship between waterfowl and shorebirds.

Another concept proposes that waterfowl are related to herons, storks, and their allies

Figure 2-4. A reconstruction of the early Eocene fossil *Presbyornis*, an early anseriform in the monotypic family Presybornithidae. The unique filter-feeding apparatus of *Presbyornis* indicates that ancestral anseriforms sieved and strained for food. Most modern species also filter-feed — a behavior highly developed in Northern Shovelers — but geese (e.g., grazers and grubbers) and mergansers (e.g., graspers) are among the waterfowl whose feeding behavior is derived from the ancestral condition suggested by *Presbyornis*.

(Ciconiiformes) through ancestors of the modern flamingo family (Phoenicopteridae). A flamingo-like fossil *Telmabates* from the Eocene of Patagonia suggested such a relationship to Howard (1955), which together with *Presbyornis* later suggested to Feduccia (1978) a close phylogenetic link between Phoenicopteriformes (flamingos) and Charadriiformes (shorebirds). However, Sibley et al. (1969) compared the egg-white proteins of modern flamingos with other birds and found patterns with greater resemblance to Ciconiiformes than to Anseriformes.

Livezey (1997c) used 123 morphological characters in a phylogenetic analysis of early Anseriformes, as well as other avian orders to develop a topology of early anseriform phylogeny. Within Anseriformes, his analysis confirmed the Anhimidae (screamers) as a monophyletic sister-group of other waterfowl (Anseres), and the Magpie Goose in the family Anseranatidae as the sister-group of modern waterfowl exclusive of the screamers (Anhimidae). *Presbyornis* was deemed a sister-group of Anatidae and relegated to a monotypic family, Presbyornithidae, which refutes the earlier claim of Olson and Feduccia (1980) that Anseriformes were derived from Charadriiformes: *Presbyornis* and Anatidae probably diverged from other Anseriformes in the early Eocene. Livezey's (1997c, 1998) analysis also strongly refuted the suggestion of Hagey et al. (1990) that flamingos be placed in Anseriformes. Livezey's (1997c) proposal of a new rank for the superorder, Galloanserimorphae (fowl), within which are Galliformes and Anseriformes, agrees with a molecular analysis that proposes three major clades: the paleognaths or tinamous (Tinamidae) and Ostrich (*Struthio camelus*), (2) the duck and chicken-like taxa, and (3) all other birds (Groth and Barrowclough 1999).

Livezey's (1997c) analysis of Anseriformes and work on the filter-feeding mechanism of flamingos by Zweers et al. (1995) also permit important insights into the evolution of filter-feeding in waterfowl, a key adaptation for exploitation of aquatic habitats. The proposed sequence is (1) the pecking structure of *Gallus* represents the primitive stage of the Galliformes–Anseriformes clade, (2) this state gave rise to the initial "through pump" of *Presbyornis* and the anseriform clade, and then came (3) the "grasp pump" of *Anser* (the geese) followed by the true "through pump" of *Anas* (Livezey 1997). See Zweers et al. (1995) for detailed discussion on the evolution of filter-feeding in birds.

The location and geological age of fossil anseriforms have traditionally suggested that waterfowl originated and developed in the Northern Hemisphere, probably the Palearctic, and later spread to other continents (Howard 1950, Weller 1964a). However, given the Neotropical distribution of the Anhimidae, the Australian distribution of the Magpie Goose, and the location of many endemic genera, Livezey (1986, 1997c) argues that anseriforms originated in the Southern Hemisphere. In Anatini, for example, 8 of the 11 genera are limited to the Southern Hemisphere, whereas only 4 groups of subgeneric rank or higher are limited to the Northern Hemisphere (Livezey 1991; see also Cracraft 1980). Cracraft (1973) also proposed a Southern Hemisphere origin for the Galliformes. However, the phylogenetic position of *Presbyornis* indicates that anseriform ancestors paraphyletic to modern Anatidae existed in the Northern Hemisphere by the early Eocene.

Either way, radiation of Anatidae thereafter proceeded more rapidly in Europe than in North America, as judged by discoveries of fossils and the diversity in modern taxa, and assuming that taxonomic designations are viewed equitably (i.e., grouping vs. grouping of genera). For example, modern genera of waterfowl are well represented as fossils from the Oligocene of Europe, whereas only fossils of extinct genera are known for the same epoch in North America. Only later, in the Pliocene, did most modern waterfowl genera appear in the fossil record for North America. Indeed, fossils from the Miocene and the Pleistocene in North America include extinct genera of shelducks (e.g., *Brantadorna*) but North America lacks any modern species of shelducks (Brodkorb 1964, Alvarez and Olson 1978).

THE ORDER ANSERIFORMES

The following synopsis presents an overview of the taxonomic organization along with some brief comments on the natural history of living Anseriformes. The modern species are organized into 3 families, 5 subfamilies, and 13 tribes. A full list of species appears in Appendix A, at the end of this chapter. As mentioned earlier, we have adopted the phylogenetic sequence and species names proposed by Livezey (1997a), which summarized and updated his earlier taxonomic work, as cited throughout this section. Livezey used five categories of morphological characters to develop the phylogenies we discuss: (1) adult plumage, (2) natal plumage (Fig. 2-5), (3) soft parts such as the bill and feet, (4) the trachea, and (5) the syrinx (Fig. 2-6), and the skeleton exclusive of the trachea.

Family Anhimidae — Screamers

This family contains three species of rather strange birds known as screamers, which are among the loudest birds in the world, hence their name. Screamers are restricted to South America, where the IUCN (2004) lists the Northern Crested Screamer as near threatened, with a total population of only 3,000–5,000 (Fig. 2-7). Screamers are large birds about the size of geese, but otherwise bear little resemblance to other anseriforms. Of the three species, the Southern Crested Screamer and Northern Crested Screamer have crests, whereas the Horned Screamer

Figure 2-5. Features in the plumage of downy waterfowl offer useful characteristics for assessing the phylogeny of Anseriformes and assigning species to genera and tribes. With few exceptions, the patterns are quite uniform for the species within each group. Swans and geese, for example, lack distinctive markings, whereas downy whistling-ducks have a well-defined pattern. Shown here is a selection of patterns representing some of the more familiar tribes of waterfowl. Left column, from top to bottom: Canvasback, Mallard, Canada Goose, Tundra Swan. Right column, from top to bottom: Ruddy Duck, Common Eider, Snow Goose, Black-bellied Whistling-Duck.

has a long, thin, horn-like frontal projection. Screamers feed largely on plant materials using a chicken-like bill, and their broad wings have sharp spurs near the alula. The legs of screamers are long and robust; their feet are also large, with long toes connected by semipalmate webbing. Screamers can swim, and they also perch and walk on floating mats of aquatic vegetation. Other characteristics include a single annual molt of body plumage in which the wing feathers (primaries) are molted sequentially (the ancestral condition in anseriforms); hence, there is no flightless period. Their plumage is sexually

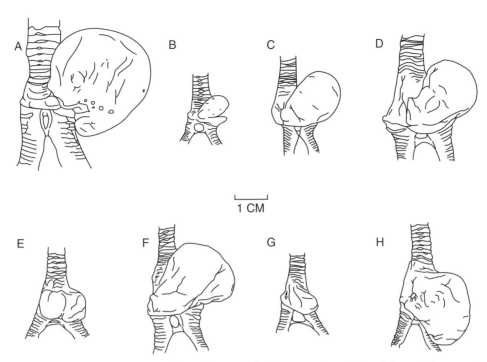

Figure 2-6. Tracheal structure has long offered a useful character for determining phylogenetic relationships among the Anseriformes. Shown here are ventral views of the syringeal bullae associated with the trachea of eight species of adult male dabbling ducks (Anatini): (A) Muscovy Duck, (B) Ringed Teal, (C) Eurasian Wigeon, (D) American Black Duck, (E) Red Shoveler, (F) Red-billed Pintail, (G) Baikal Teal, and (H) Puna Teal. From Livezey (1991:497). With permission from the American Ornithologists' Union.

Figure 2-7. Three species of screamers comprise the unique family Anhimidae within the Anseriformes; all are endemic to the marshes and wet grasslands of South America. Shown here are the Southern Crested Screamer (*left*) and Northern Crested Screamer (*right*). Note bill and foot structure. Photos courtesy of Frank McKinney and the Bell Museum of Natural History *(left)*, and Guy A. Baldassarre *(right)*.

monomorphic. Unique, bubbly air sacs lie under their skin and produce a rumbling sound when their bodies are disturbed. Screamers lack an uncinate process on their ribs, their feathers are soft, and their feather tracts are nearly continuous.

Screamers are not migratory and occur in the marshes and wet grasslands of South America. They are slow flyers, but they often soar high above the ground for long periods of time. Screamers nest on the ground in semiaquatic habitats where their clutches of two to six eggs are incubated by both sexes for 42–44 days. Both sexes also build the nest and accompany the brood. They have not been well studied, however, except for work with the Horned Screamer in southwestern Columbia (Naranjo 1986). Stonor (1939) long ago described the breeding habits of the Southern Crested Screamer.

Family Anseranatidae — Magpie Goose

This family is monotypic (Livezey 1986, Livezey 1997c), represented only by the unusual Magpie Goose, an endemic of Australia and southern New Guinea where it is common to abundant within its preferred habitats on the floodplains of tropical rivers (Wilson 1997; Fig. 2-8). Magpie Geese are large, stork-like birds weighing about 2,500 g and lacking much similarity to other waterfowl (Frith 1967). They are unique among the waterfowl (except the aberrant Freckled Duck) in having an extremely long (e.g., 150 cm) coiled trachea lying, in part, external to the breast musculature (Johnsgard 1978). Also, its mallophagan ectoparasites include the host-specific genus *Heteroproctus*, and the pattern of their egg-white proteins are separable from those of all other anseriforms (Sibley 1960). Magpie Geese also have heavily clawed, long toes with semipalmate webbing; the fourth toe is opposable. They frequent semiaquatic and terrestrial habitats and frequently perch on convenient limbs. Like the screamers, Magpie Geese molt their flight feathers sequentially, and together these birds are the only anseriforms without a flightless period during molt.

Magpie Geese are colonial nesters that probably breed at 3 years of age. They mate for life, but males usually mate with two females. Copulation is on land (unique in Anseriformes), and the male does not grasp the female by the nape of the neck as occurs with most other waterfowl. Both females lay in the same nest, with the total clutch size averaging 9.4 eggs (Frith 1967). Based on a molecular analysis, the females are highly related (Horn et al. 1996). The gray-colored goslings, in addition to foraging in-

Figure 2-8. The Magpie Goose — endemic to northern Australia and southern New Guinea and Papua New Guinea — exhibits curious morphological and behavioral characteristics unlike any other species of Anatidae and accordingly is placed in the monotypic family Anseranatidae. Photo courtesy of Ederic Slater, Division of Wildlife and Rangelands Research, CSIRO, Australia.

dependently, also are fed bill-to-bill by their parents in response to begging behavior (unique) and rest on a "brood nest" prepared by the adults (Johnsgard 1961f, 1978). The Musk Duck, also endemic to Australia, is the only other anseriform species that directly feeds its young (Frith 1967). Frith and Davies (1961) and Davies (1963) studied many of the interesting behavioral and ecological features of Magpie Geese, and Davies and Frith (1964) commented on the significance of these characteristics in relation to the taxonomic position of this unusual bird.

Family Anatidae — Typical Waterfowl (Ducks, Geese, and Swans)

This family contains the ducks, geese, and swans, which are collectively known as "waterfowl" in the

United States and Canada, but are usually called "wildfowl" in Europe. Livezey (1997a) organized the Anatidae into 5 subfamilies, 13 tribes, 51 genera, and 171 species (Table 2-1, Appendix A). Anatids have more or less flattened bills equipped with lamellae and tipped by a nail (the dertrum), although the bills of some, such as the mergansers, are modified greatly. The forward three toes of waterfowl are webbed, but perching, walking, and swimming habits vary considerably among species. Plumage also varies within the family; patterns may be colorful or drab, molts normally occur either once or twice per year (more often in some species), and the sexes are monomorphic and monochromatic in some species but not others. Some species have metallic-colored wing patches (the speculum), whereas others lack this or other highly distinctive markings. All species undergo at least one flightless period annually in association with the wing molt. Nesting habits are variable and include sites on uplands or tundra or in tree cavities or marsh vegetation over water.

Many waterfowl are strongly migratory, but movements of others are quite limited or are responsive to unpredictable changes in rainfall or other environmental conditions. Some species or subspecies are limited to islands, such as the Hawaiian Goose and Laysan Duck in the Hawaiian Archipelago (Weller 1980a). In all, waterfowl have radiated widely into a variety of niches on all continents except Antarctica and, in doing so, have acquired a broad array of anatomical and behavioral features reflecting the varied ecological conditions they encounter.

Subfamily Dendrocygninae — Whistling-Ducks and Allies

This subfamily consists of two tribes: Dendrocygnini (whistling-ducks), which contains eight species in a single genus, *Dendrocygna*, and Thalassornithini, represented by a single species, the White-backed Duck. Whistling-ducks are medium-size waterfowl, averaging about 600–1,000 g (see Johnsgard 1978). Some or all of the whistling-ducks once were known as "tree ducks," although only a few species actually have arboreal habits. Further, because all eight species indeed whistle, the newer name is more appropriate and now widely accepted. Whistling-ducks are primarily vegetarians with a pantropical distribution.

Livezey (1995a) used 68 morphological characters to perform a phylogenetic analysis of the whistling-ducks and the White-backed Duck. The analy-

sis produced three shortest trees with a length of 91 and a consistency index of 0.766 (Fig. 2-9). Monophyly of *Dendrocygna* and *Thalassornis* was supported by three unambiguous synapomorphies, and monophyly of *Dendrocygna* by eight. The trees supported two major clades within the *Dendrocygna*: (1) the Black-bellied Whistling-Duck and the White-faced Whistling Duck, and (2) the other six species of *Dendrocygna*. All species of *Dendrocygna* and, especially, *Thalassornis* were highly autapomorphic, the latter with 22 autapomorphies. Madsen et al. (1988) considered Dendrocygninae as an isolated group not closely related to the Anserinae (swans and geese).

The sexes are similar in plumage and voice, and precopulatory and postcopulatory displays are nearly identical (see Meanley and Meanley 1958, Johnsgard 1962). Both sexes share incubation and brood-rearing duties (Flickinger 1975, Bolen and Smith 1979). Whistling-ducks do not exhibit a defeathered incubation patch, however, but the lower abdomen of both sexes in at least the Black-bellied Whistling-Duck becomes highly vascularized during the incubation period (Rylander et al. 1980). Whistling-ducks also are unique in not adding down to their nests, likely because incubation proceeds more or less continuously under the alternate care of the adults. The syrinx is symmetrical but somewhat larger in males than females, and the tarsus is reticulate. Whistling-ducks mature at 1 year of age and nest in various settings, including nest boxes and tree cavities far from water (Bolen 1967).

The downy young are distinctively patterned in comparison with other waterfowl, as a dark T-shaped stripe marks the rear of the head and neck of most species (Delacour and Mayr 1945; see Fig. 2-5). Subspecies rarely occur among whistling-ducks despite the wide distribution of some species on two or more continents, of which the Fulvous Whistling-duck is the most notable example. Bolen and Rylander (1983) summarized the ecological information available for whistling-ducks.

The White-backed Duck is endemic to Africa and nearby Madagascar. Clark (1969) studied the social behavior of White-backed Ducks, and Kear (1967) described their eggs and downy young, but other aspects of these unusual birds remain poorly known. Their escape behavior is remarkably grebe-like wherein they lower themselves into the water and prefer to swim rather than fly from intruders. The male guards the nest and does much, and perhaps all, of the incubation (Johnsgard 1978). The species exhibits many adaptations for diving and, like

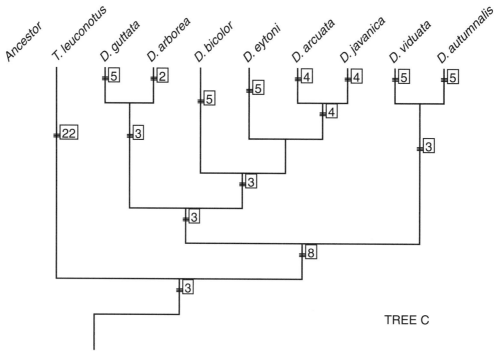

Figure 2-9. An example of a phylogenetic tree for the whistling-ducks (subfamily Dendrocygninae) based on analysis of 68 morphological characteristics. Numbers in boxes depict unambiguous character changes used to develop the tree. From Livezey (1995a:71). With permission from the Carnegie Museum.

whistling-ducks, probably diverged from other anseriforms near the Anserinae (Livezey 1986). Taxonomically, the White-backed Duck represents a "problem species" that Johnsgard (1967a) regarded as an aberrant whistling-duck (see also Raikow 1971). Livezey (1986) originally placed the White-backed Duck into a monotypic subfamily of Anatidae, Thalassorninae.

Subfamily Anserinae — Geese and Swans

This subfamily contains the largest species of waterfowl (see Scott 1972) organized into three tribes: Cereopsini (Cape Barrren Goose), Anserini (true geese), and Cygnini (swans). Geese are primarily terrestrial grazers, whereas swans submerge their heads to feed on aquatic plants (Johnsgard 1978). Most species are highly social at least for part of the year and exhibit a distinctive "*triumph ceremony*" in their behavioral profile (see Chapter 3). The *triumph ceremony* is a key display of the Anserinae that is performed by mated pairs (or all members of a family) after spatial or temporal separation, often before vigorous aggressive encounters, and after such encounters by the victors. Functions of the *triumph ceremony* include redirection of aggression between

mates and threatening of conspecifics (see Lorenz 1957, Fischer 1965, Raveling 1970). Plumage and vocalizations are similar between the sexes. Unlike the Dendrocygninae, however, the plumage patterns of downy young lack strong markings (except for the Cape Barren Goose of Australia), and the adult plumage of most species is not colorful, although the Red-breasted Goose of Siberia is a stunning exception. The syrinx is symmetrical but lacks an enlarged bulla and is little different in either sex. Anserinae mate for life but do not sexually mature until 2–3 years old. The female builds the nest, which the male helps guard, but only the female incubates, except in the Black Swan. Both sexes rear the brood, and family members often migrate and winter together. There is a single annual molt during which the birds undergo a flightless period. The tarsus pattern is reticulate.

Livezey (1996b) used 165 morphological characters to develop a phylogenetic analysis of the modern Anserinae and selected fossil species. This analysis produced five shortest trees with a total length of 318 and a consistency index of 0.634; the trees differed only in details for three species of geese (*Branta*). The trees supported (1) *Cnemiornis*, the large, extinct flightless geese of New Zealand, as a

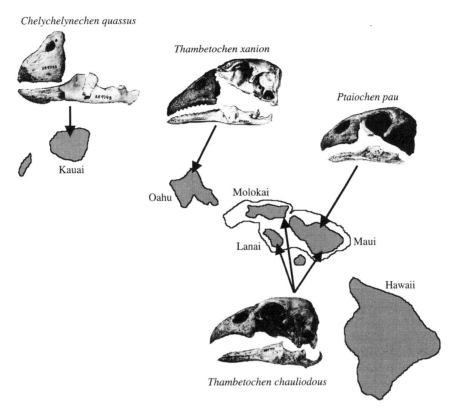

Chelychelynechen quassus

Thambetochen xanion

Ptaiochen pau

Kauai

Oahu

Molokai

Lanai

Maui

Hawaii

Thambetochen chauliodous

Figure 2-10. In an example of island speciation, the four known species of moa-nalos evolved to fill different grazing niches on the Hawaiian Islands. The line around Maui, Molokai, and Lanai depicts the extent of the Pleistocene Island Maui Nui. Moa-nalos did not occur on Hawaii, which was occupied by another herbivore, the Giant Hawaiian Goose. From Paxinos et al. (2002:1400). With permission from the Royal Society of London.

sister-group of all other taxa and placement of the genus in a separate family, Cnemiornithidae; (2) a sister-group relationship between the extinct flightless moa-nalos of Hawaii (Fig. 2-10) and all other geese and swans; (3) Cape Barren Goose as a sister-group of *Anser, Branta, Coscoroba,* and *Cygnus* (thus differing from Livezey 1986); (4) monophyly of *Anser, Branta,* and the extinct Giant Hawaiian Goose, which is as yet undescribed (see Olson and James 1991); and (5) Coscoroba Swan as a sister group to *Cygnus.* The entire group was supported by 10 unambiguous synapomorphies. This analysis also led to a conclusion that the Anserinae likely evolved in the Southern Hemisphere, but *Anser, Branta,* and *Cygnus* later radiated to the Northern Hemisphere.

On the other hand, a phylogenetic analysis of fragmentary, "ancient" DNA supports the surface-feeding or dabbling ducks (Anatini) as a sister group of the moa-nalos (*Thambetochen* spp., *Ptaiochen, Chelchelynechen*); the four known species of moa-nalos likely evolved from a relatively small duck that arrived early in the history of the Hawaiian Islands

(Sorenson et al. 1999). Livezey (1996b) placed the moa-nalos in a separate tribe, Thambetochenini, within the Anserinae. DNA analysis also convincingly argues that the Hawaiian Goose, and the extinct Nene-nui and Giant Hawaiian Goose, were derived from a large-bodied ancestor of a Canada Goose; phylogenetically, these species thus should be nested within the *Branta canadensis* group (Paxinos et al. 2002).

The moa-nalos ranged in size from 4.0 to 7.5 kg (Campbell and Toni 1983) and, along with the Nene-nui and Giant Hawaiian Goose, likely were the grazing equivalents of the giant tortoises on other oceanic islands that lacked terrestrial mammals. Indeed, an analysis of fossilized feces (coprolites) concluded that the hindguts of moa-nalos were specialized for the digestion of plant fibers (James and Burney 1997). The Turtle-billed Moa-nalo or Large Kauai Goose, known only from the island of Kauai, was the most divergent of the group; its bill resembled the jaws of a tortoise, perhaps reflecting an adaptation for feeding on ferns (Fig. 2-11). The Gi-

Figure 2-11. The Turtle-billed Moa-nalo or Large Kauai Goose — known only from the island of Kauai — was among a group of large birds in the Hawaiian archipelago that apparently filled the grazing niche but became extinct after arrival of the Polynesians.

ant Hawaiian Goose, limited only to the island of Hawaii — where moa-nalos were absent — was much larger than either the moa-nalos or other species of *Branta*, and likely was the largest of all land animals in the archipelago. Paxinos et al. (2002) estimated its mass at 8.6 kg. Unfortunately, the Giant Hawaiian Goose, Nene-nui, and other Hawaiian avifauna became extinct some time after the islands were settled by Polynesians, about 1,600 years ago.

Tribe Cereopsini — Cape Barren Goose: In the past, the Cape Barren Goose (Fig. 2-12) was regarded as a primitive, enigmatic goose (Livezey 1986), an enigmatic shelduck (Delacour and Mayr 1945), or the only member of a separate tribe (Johnsgard 1978). In contrast to his earlier work that placed the Cape Barren Goose in Anserini (Livezey 1986),

Figure 2-12. The Cape Barren Goose is endemic to Australia. These geese are prized by hunters, but the birds also are heavily persecuted by ranchers who believe the geese foul pastures and compete with sheep for forage. Intensive conservation efforts have increased the population to about 17,000. Photo courtesy of Ederic Slater, Division of Wildlife and Rangelands Research, CSIRO, Australia.

Livezey (1996b) later placed this species in a monotypic tribe, as designated here. Nonetheless, this species remains as enigmatic as ever. The male assists with nest building and fiercely defends the nest (Frith 1967); copulation occurs on land (Johnsgard 1978), a trait only shared with the Magpie Goose. Large birds of 3.7–5.1 kg, Cape Barren Geese are endemic to the southern coast of Australia, where they are most abundant in the Furneaux Islands off the northeast coast of Tasmania, and to the west in the Recherché Archipelago (Frith 1967, Johnsgard 1978). Humans have persecuted these geese almost since their discovery in 1797 (Frith 1967). They are highly prized as food, but they also are regarded as competitors of sheep for pastureland and thus are shot by farmers (Dorward et al. 1980). Cape Barren Geese numbered only about 1,000 in the 1960s, but later estimates place the population at 17,000 birds (Marchant and Higgins 1990). The population is most vulnerable in the Recherché Archipelago

Tribe Anserini — True Geese: The tribe Anserini consists of two genera (*Anser*, *Branta*) and 16 species. Subspecies are especially common in Canada Geese of the Nearctic and in Bean Geese and Greylag Geese of the Palearctic, several of which are proposed for species status (see Livezey 1997a). In particular, Livezey (1996b) recognized the Pink-footed Goose as a separate species, whereas Johnsgard (1978) considered this form as a subspecies of Bean Goose. Livezey (1997a) also recognized two species of brant: the Dark-bellied (Black) Brant and Pale-bellied (Atlantic) Brant. The extensive speciation (and subspeciation) in true geese is the result of long pair bonds, strong family associations, and traditional migratory habits, each of which promotes reproductive isolation (Mayr 1945, 1951; see also Cushing 1941, Hochbaum 1955, Raveling 1979). As mentioned earlier, in 2004 the American Ornithologists' Union recognized one group of small-bodied Canada Geese as a separate species — the Cackling Canada Goose — and similar changes for other "subspecies" seem likely to follow as more evidence accumulates (Banks et al. 2004). Members of this tribe are large (males easily reach 3,000–4,000 g; see Johnsgard 1978) and, except for the Cape Barren Goose, they are restricted to the Northern Hemisphere. *Branta* dominates in the Nearctic, whereas *Anser* dominates in the Palearctic.

Tribe Cygnini — Swans: The tribe Cygnini consists of two genera (*Coscoroba* and *Cygnus*) and eight

species. In the past, the genus *Olor* was applied to the four northern white swans (Livezey 1996b), but Livezey (1997a) now assigns this group to *Cygnus*. The Cygnini are the largest waterfowl, with males ranging in average body mass from 5.4 to 11.9 kg (see Scott 1972, Johnsgard 1978). The Trumpeter Swan of North America is the largest species. Three species occur in the Southern Hemisphere; five in the Northern Hemisphere. The Coscoroba Swan is especially interesting and enigmatic; the species exhibits characteristics of swans, geese, and whistling-ducks (Johnsgard 1978), thereby being particularly difficult to classify (Livezey 1996b).

All species are white or largely white, except the Black Swan, which is endemic to Australia and introduced into New Zealand. The predominance of white plumage appears related to territorial spacing on their arctic breeding grounds, where the open habitat makes visibility possible for some distance. Unlike others in this tribe, the male Black Swan assists with incubation. The population of Black Swans in New Zealand has greatly increased in numbers (especially on Lake Ellesmere), whereby commercial egg collecting is allowed in an effort to control their numbers (Johnsgard 1978). Other species of swans are protected over much of their range, but carefully regulated harvests of Tundra Swans are permitted in some parts of North America.

Subfamily Stictonettinae — Freckled Duck

This monotypic subfamily is represented by the enigmatic Freckled Duck, another species endemic to Australia, where it occurs in the southeast and extreme southwest (Fig. 2-13). Livezey (1986) considered the Freckled Duck as the last branch in the lineage of waterfowl with a reticulate tarsus and erected a subfamily for the species. Livezey (1996c) also considered the Freckled Duck as a sister taxon to a clade comprising the Tadorninae (shelducks and allies) and Anatinae (true ducks). In contrast, Johnsgard (1978) believed the Freckled Duck is closely allied with the subfamily Anserinae, within which he placed the species in a monotypic tribe, Stictonettini (see also Frith 1964a). In the past, the Freckled Duck also was regarded as an aberrant shelduck (Peters 1931) or dabbling duck (Delacour and Mayr 1945). DNA analysis (Madsen et al. 1988) supports earlier work that the Freckled Duck is only distantly related to other Anatidae and likely diverged very early from the main lineage leading to other anseriforms.

The swan and goose-like features of Freckled

Figure 2-13. The Freckled Duck is another atypical species endemic to Australia. Unfortunately, Freckled Ducks are not numerous, apparently because of wetland drainage and irrigation projects. Many aspects of their behavior and ecology remain poorly known. Photo courtesy of Ederic Slater, Division of Wildlife and Rangelands Research, CSIRO, Australia.

Ducks include an undifferentiated syrinx and lack of a pattern in either the downy young or the adult plumage. Similarly, Frith (1964a) noted strong similarities in downy plumage between Freckled Ducks and swans, and Johnsgard (1978) observed a display that was similar to the *triumph ceremony* of some swans. Olson and Feduccia (1980) noted the similarities in the skull and mandible of the Freckled Duck with the fossil *Presbyornis*; they also noted that only the Freckled Duck, along with the Pink-eared Duck of Australia and the Torrent Duck of South America, have never been known to hybridize with other ducks. Male Freckled Ducks have a sharply curved trachea lying outside the sternum, a feature otherwise present only in Magpie Geese (Frith 1964b). Swans have convoluted trachea, but these remain inside the sternum. In a unique series of biochemical analyses, Edkins and Hansen (1972) and Jacob and Glaser (1975) determined that the waxy secretions from the uropygial glands of Freckled Ducks resemble those of some swans (e.g., Mute Swan).

Unfortunately, the Freckled Duck is still poorly studied in the wild (Frith 1965, Johnsgard 1965). Only a few nests have been found; these were placed

in dense cover over water. Clutch size typically numbers seven eggs, and only females incubate for up to 36 days (Braithwaite 1976). Freckled Ducks depend on permanent swamps for breeding habitat, and protection of these wetland systems remains an important step in the conservation of this unique species, which had dwindled to only 8,000–13,000 birds in 1983 (Madge and Burn 1988). Whereas they are protected from hunting throughout Australia, some are shot when they are mistaken for Gray Ducks. Populations of Freckled Ducks and other Australian waterfowl may fluctuate in keeping with patterns of the Southern Oscillation (Kingsford et al. 1999).

Subfamily Tadorninae — Shelducks and Allies

This subfamily is distributed worldwide except for the Nearctic. The group has been extensively studied by Livezey (1996c, 1997a, 1997c) who recognized 11 genera and 24 species arranged into 3 tribes: Merganettini, Plecopterini, and Tadornini.

Tribe Merganettini — Blue Duck, Steamer-Ducks, Torrent Duck: This tribe consists of three groups: (1) the Blue Duck, (2) four species of steamer-ducks, and (3) the Torrent Duck. However, based on their molecular analysis and subsequent phylogeny, Johnson and Sorenson (1999) placed *Tachyeres* (steamer-ducks) in the tribe Anatini (dabbling ducks). Regardless, both sexes of all three genera are extremely territorial and pugnacious, and territorial combat often involves physical blows from carpal wing spurs (see Livezey and Humphrey 1985, Eldridge 1986a).

The Blue Duck or Whio is a small (750–900 g), monomorphic, gray duck endemic to New Zealand where it inhabits swift-flowing mountain streams in wooded areas (Fig. 2-14). Williams (1991) studied the demographics and social behavior of Blue Ducks, noting that they mate for life and are highly territorial in their defense of riverine habitat. Genetic analyses support observations that Blue Ducks have limited dispersal ability (Triggs et al. 1991). They nest in burrows and produce an average of 5.4 eggs per clutch; only the female incubates, although both parents care for the ducklings (see Kear 1972, Williams 1991). Blue Ducks have unique flexible lobes on their upper mandibles, which aid in probing for invertebrates, their principal food. Blue Ducks were once widely distributed throughout New Zealand, but the steady loss of habitat has created a patchy distribution in the mountainous regions of western South Island and parts of North Island (Madge and

Figure 2-14. The Blue Duck is endemic to New Zealand where it inhabits fast-flowing rivers and streams but is globally endangered. Populations are severely fragmented, with none thought to be more than 250 individuals (IUCN 2004). Photo courtesy of Alan Reith.

Burn 1988). Short-tailed weasels or stoats (*Mustela erminea*), introduced from North America, prey on ducklings, and introduced trout may compete with Blue Ducks for invertebrates (Kear 1972). The Blue Duck is listed as endangered by IUCN (2004), with perhaps only 1,200 individuals remaining in the wild, a response to the loss of its specialized habitat of clear, clean, fast-flowing streams.

The four species of steamer-ducks are united in a single genus, *Tachyeres*, whose taxonomy was studied by Livezey and Humphrey 1992, Livezey 1996c, Livezey 1997b (Fig. 2-15). Steamer-ducks occur along the coasts of southern South America and in the Falkland Islands, where they are especially adapted for marine environments; the Flying Steamer-Duck also occurs on inland waters. The name "steamer-duck" originates from their habit of rapidly paddling over the water with their wings and feet when disturbed or pursued (Livezey and Humphrey 1983).

All species are large (males weigh 3,000–6,000 g) and have heavy bills adapted for grabbing and crushing mollusks, insect larvae, and other invertebrates. Weller (1976) suggested that steamer-ducks are the most specialized of all the diving species of waterfowl; they seemingly represent the southern ecological equivalents of eiders. Only three species were known until Humphrey and Thompson (1981) described the White-headed Flightless Steamer-Duck

from the coast of Argentina. Except for the Flying Steamer-Duck, the three other species are flightless (Livezey and Humphrey 1986). However, even the Flying Steamer-Duck is not always capable of flight, and large males may be incapable of flying as adults (Humphrey and Livezey 1982).

Steamer-ducks are more or less slate gray and lack chromatic colors, but their wings have white patches. Plumage is similar among the species, making their identification difficult, although head color serves as a key mark to observe under field conditions (Madge and Burn 1988). Distribution can help identify the flightless species because each occurs in a separate range; the distribution of the Flying Steamer-Duck overlaps the others in most areas.

Like most shelducks and sheldgeese, steamer-ducks have wing spurs, long pair bonds, and other similarities, but the downy plumage of young steamer-ducks shows less spotting and contrasting coloration (Humphrey and Livezey 1985). The sexes differ slightly in plumage and voice, but sex-specific coloration of their bills is more obvious. Considerable sexual dimorphism also occurs in the larger size and body mass of the males. The robust nature of males in the three flightless species may reflect, at least in part, structural refinements for combat (Livezey and Humphrey 1984).

Flying Steamer-Ducks breed in both freshwater

Figure 2-15. The four species of steamer-ducks are endemic to the southern tip of South America, where they largely occur in marine environments. Identification of each species is often difficult. Shown here is the Falkland Flightless Steamer-Duck. Photo courtesy of Milton W. Weller.

and marine habitats, but the flightless species are limited to marine environments. Steamer-ducks are particularly aggressive and frequently attack and sometimes kill other species of waterbirds (Nuechterlein and Storer 1985). Livezey and Humphrey (1985), in discussing the pugnacity of steamer-ducks, found an inordinate number of fractures in the skeletons they examined and suggested that most of that damage resulted from combat associated with territorial and interspecific aggression (see also Moynihan 1958 for behavioral features of Flying Steamer-Ducks).

The Torrent Duck may grade into as many as seven distinct taxa within their distribution, which stretches the length of the Andes Mountains in South America; they most often occur between 1,000 and 4,000 m above sea level (see Callaghan 1997). Early taxonomists at times recognized three, five, or six full species (Salvadori 1895, Phillips 1922–26, Conover 1943), but Delacour and Mayr (1945) combined these into a single species. Livezey (1997a) argues for five species. Regardless, each population is resident, occupying turbulent mountain streams throughout the year. The white heads and necks of males are marked with an unusual pattern of striping and, except for the wings, the plumage is strongly dimorphic (Weller 1968c). Both sexes have wing spurs, which are somewhat larger in males. Weller (1968c) determined that the length, dark coloration, and sharpness of the spurs increase with age. Downy Torrent Ducks are light gray with white undersides; their flanks have a strong pattern of bars.

Torrent Ducks forage in rapidly moving water for aquatic insects and possibly small fish; they commonly dive from perches on large rocks (Johnsgard 1966a). Courtship behavior is unlike most other ducks. A bowing display maintains the pair bond and also is used when defending territories along a 1–2 km length of river (Callaghan 1997). Johnson (1963), Wright (1965), Johnsgard (1966a), Moffett (1970), and Eldridge (1979, 1986b) each described various components of Torrent Duck behavior. Nests occur in crevices on ledges bordering streams, or sometimes in cavities of various types; only three to four eggs are laid over an extended period of time, and these apparently are incubated by the female for as long as 44 days (Moffett 1970). Males do not incubate, but they apparently share brooding duties with their mates.

Torrent ducks are threatened by degradation of rivers, but census data are virtually nonexistent. Nonetheless, Callaghan (1997) estimated 20,000–35,000 remain in a population that is declining slowly.

Two of the taxa may be globally threatened, but further knowledge of the group's systematics and population boundaries remains an urgent requirement for effective conservation (Callaghan 1997).

Tribe Plectropterini — Spur-winged Goose and Comb Ducks: This tribe is represented by three species: (1) the Spur-winged Goose, an endemic to sub-Saharan Africa; and (2) two species of Comb Duck — the Gray-sided Comb Duck of the Old World (Africa and Madagascar, India, Myanmar, Thailand, Laos, southeastern China (see Fig. 2-2), and the Black-sided Comb Duck in the New World (South America). In the past, both the Spur-winged Goose and the Comb Duck were placed in Cairinini, but Livezey (1986) has rejected Cairinini as an unnatural, polyphyletic assemblage of genera and species, a finding held by others as well (e.g., Woolfenden 1961, Johnsgard 1978). Livezey (1996c) considers the Plectropterini as the sister-group of the Tadornini (shelducks and sheldgeese).

The Spur-winged Goose is among the most common species of waterfowl in Africa, where it ranges widely along rivers, swamps, and lakesides. However, this species is poorly studied, despite its widespread range and large population. Spur-winged Geese are large birds ranging from 5.4–6.8 kg in males to as much as 10 kg (Johnsgard 1978). The birds are largely vegetarian and frequently feed in fields of agricultural crops. Little is known about their courtship behavior, but the nest is aggressively defended. Clutch size can reach some 14 to 15 eggs, and only the female incubates (32 days); no evidence indicates that males participate in rearing broods (see Johnsgard 1978, Brown et al. 1982, Kear 2005).

Comb Ducks are large (males weigh 1,300–2,610 g), and the male features a large fleshy caruncle at the base of the bill (see Fig. 2-2; Johnsgard 1978). The breeding season seems associated with rainy periods. Nests are located in cavities and on the ground; only the female incubates. Johnsgard (1978) remarks that pair bonds are quite weak and may be lacking altogether; breeding males often acquire a "harem" of two or more females. Although both species of Comb Ducks have wide distributions, they occur somewhat locally, especially in South America (Madge and Burn 1988). Comb Ducks, because of their poor palatability, are not avidly sought by hunters (Johnsgard 1978).

Tribe Tadornini — Shelducks and Sheldgeese: This tribe of 6 genera and 15 species includes the shelducks, which Livezey (1997a) differentiated into the banded shelducks (*Tadorna*) and reddish shelducks (*Casarca*), and the sheldgeese (*Cyanochen, Alopochen, Neochen, Chloephaga*). The extant group is distributed worldwide, except for North America and most oceanic islands, although Livezey (1997a) lists the Chatham Island Shelduck, a species that disappeared after Polynesians arrived on the Chatham Islands. Sheldgeese are restricted to the Southern Hemisphere and apparently are the ecological equivalents of true geese; all are grazers (Johnsgard 1978). In contrast, shelducks are primarily waders and dabblers. Livezey (1986) originally placed the steamer-ducks, the Blue Duck, the Torrent Duck, the Salvadori's Duck, and the Pink-eared Duck in Tadornini. Most members of this tribe generally have brightly colored feathers, and the sexes have similar plumage in all but five species. Shelducks and sheldgeese use their wings for fighting, wherein most species are equipped with blunt wing spurs.

Livezey (1997c) considers the Tadornini a basal, monophyletic complex of genera intermediate between true geese (Anserinae) and true ducks (Anatinae) in anatomy and behavior. Livezey's (1997c) phylogenetic analysis of 64 morphological characters produced three shortest trees with a consistency index of 0.764 and retention index of 0.810. Monophyly of the Tadornini was supported by five synapomorphies and divided into two groups: (1) the sheldgeese, supported by four synapomorphies; and (2) the shelducks, supported by seven synapomorphies. There are three monotypic genera within the sheldgeese group: the Egyptian Sheldgoose of Africa, the Orinoco Sheldgoose of the Amazon Basin, and the Blue-winged Sheldgoose of Ethiopia. The latter has the most restricted range of any of the continental anatids, being restricted to highland rivers of Ethiopia where its ecology is not well known (Johnsgard 1978).

Most shelducks have white wing plumage and a greenish speculum formed by the secondaries and/or secondary coverts. Syrinx structure and voice differ between the sexes of all species. Shelducks mature at 2 years of age, and most species, if not all, are monogamous and probably pair for life (Siegfried 1976). Females exhibit *inciting* displays and undertake incubation duties without assistance from males; males, however, often guard nests and/or their mates during incubation. Nesting sites are variable among species, but most select sheltered sites in tussocks, crevices, tree cavities, or burrows. The Cape Shelduck of southern Africa often nests in the burrows of aardvarks (*Orycteropus afer*), and because these unique mammals are threatened in South Africa, the implication arises that the future of these birds may be closely linked to the status of a highly vulnerable mammal (Geldenhuys 1980). The plumage of both downy shelducks and sheldgeese typically shows a well-marked black-and-white pattern.

Most species of shelducks and sheldgeese are vegetarians and, in particular, sheldgeese graze in grassy uplands. In Argentina, herders believe that sheldgeese in the *Chloephaga* group compete with sheep for forage, with the result that the birds often are persecuted (Weller 1968b). Indeed, Ruddy-headed Sheldgeese have been subjected to a massive nest destruction campaign under a bounty system, poisoning programs, and predation from Patagonian gray foxes (*Dusicyon griseus*) released on Tierra del Fuego (King 1981). The Crested Shelduck probably is extinct throughout its former range in eastern Asia (see Greenway 1967), although three birds were reported near Vladivostok, Russia, in 1964 (Fisher et al. 1969). IUCN (2004) still lists this species as critically endangered. Hori (1964, 1969) and Riggert (1977) studied the Australian Shelduck, and Patterson (1982) published a monograph on the Common Shelduck.

Subfamily Anatinae — True Ducks

The Anatinae represent the largest subfamily within Anseriformes, containing 32 genera and 112 species of true ducks organized into five tribes. This subfamily contains the genus *Anas*, which by far includes more species (42) than any other genus of waterfowl. The subfamily is distributed worldwide except Antarctica, and the species therein occupy nearly all types of wetland habitats and exhibit a wide array of morphological and behavioral characteristics (Fig. 2-16).

The true ducks normally have two annual molts, a scutellate pattern on the front of the tarsus, elaborate sex-specific courtship behavior and, with some exceptions, sexually dimorphic plumage, voice, and syrinx structure. A third feather generation occurring between the Basic and Alternate plumages — the Supplemental Plumage (Palmer 1972) — occurs in the Long-tailed Duck, a member of the tribe Mergini (see Chapter 6).

Tribe Malacorhynchini — Pink-eared Duck and Salvadori's Duck: Livezey (1996c) proposed a new tribe for two species: (1) the Pink-eared Duck; and

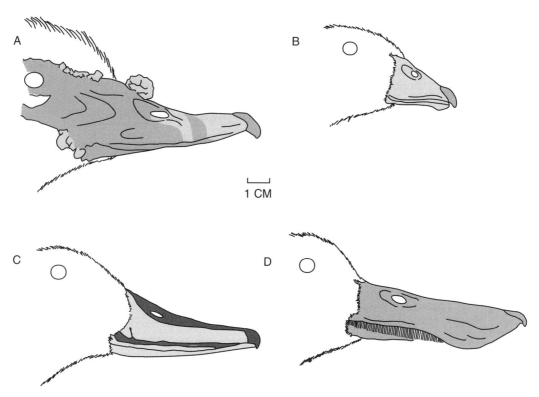

Figure 2-16. Bill structure illustrates the degree of morphological variation occurring within the dabbling ducks (Anatini). Shown here are the Muscovy Duck (A), African Pygmy-Goose (B), Northern Pintail (C), and Northern Shoveler (D). From Livezey (1991:496). With permission from the American Ornithologists' Union.

(2) Salvadori's Duck, each of which were formerly placed in other tribes. Both species were grouped into the Tadornini by (Livezey 1986, 1991), and the Anatini by Johnsgard (1978).

The Pink-eared Duck is endemic to Australia where it is widespread and common (Morcombe 2000). These unique ducks live on temporary saline ponds in Australia's dry interior where rainfall instead of photoperiod triggers its breeding cycle; thus they may breed at any time of the year (Frith 1967). Their bills are highly modified for straining small aquatic invertebrates, and their foraging behavior resembles that of shovelers; the birds forage socially, each following and feeding in the wake of the preceding bird (Johnsgard 1978). The taxonomic position of this species has been unclear for some time (see Johnsgard 1978, Livezey 1996c).

Salvadori's Duck is endemic to the mountainous areas of New Guinea where it is common at elevations of 4,000 m (Johnsgard 1978). Salvadori's Duck is a specialist of fast-moving streams and rivers, not unlike the Blue Duck of New Zealand or Torrent Duck of South America (Kear 1975). Pairs occupy territories, and males likely use their wing spurs in territorial defense. Males remain with their females during the brood-rearing period (Kear 1975, Johnsgard 1978). Except for Kear (1975), the species has not been well studied, but introduced trout apparently compete with Salvadori's Ducks for invertebrates.

Tribe Anatini — Surface-Feeding or Dabbling Ducks: The Anatini contains 11 genera and 62 species, which is by far the largest tribe in Anatinae. Livezey (1986) initially considered the typical surface-feeding or "dabbling ducks" (e.g., *Anas*), as well as some of the genera in the tribe Cairinini or perching ducks (e.g., *Pteronetta*, *Cairina*, *Aix*, *Nettapus*, *Callonetta*, *Chenonetta*, *Amazonetta*), as a poorly resolved grade of taxonomic entities. Livezey (1986) also justified eliminating the tribe Cairinini, noting the group was paraphyletic and lacking a single character to distinguish it from other tribes. Woolfenden (1961) agreed, based on osteology. Livezey (1986) also resurrected the genus *Mareca* for the wigeon, and *Speculanas* as the genus for the Bronze-winged Duck of South America. Livezey (1991, 1997a) later provided the phylogenetic analysis of the Anatini followed here, together with some contrasting designations based on the molecular phylogeny developed by Johnson and Sorenson (1999). See Livezey (1991) for a comprehensive review of the taxonomic history for the Anatini.

Livezey's (1991) phylogeny addressed 157 morphological characters of 59 species that yielded a tree with a consistency index of 0.71. Monophyly of the tribe was weakly supported, and the analysis revealed three subtribes: (1) the Cairinina , composed of the genera *Cairina*, *Pteronetta*, and *Aix*; (2) the Nettapodina, with the genera *Chenonetta* and *Nettapus*; and (3) the Anatini, which included all other genera. The large *Anas* genus included two weakly supported subgroups: (1) Mallards and blue-winged ducks; and (2) Australasian teal, pintails, Holarctic teal, and spotted teal. In contrast, Johnson and Sorenson (1999) divided the dabbling ducks into four groups: (1) four South American genera of *Amazonetta*, *Lophonetta*, *Speculanas*, and *Tachyeres*; (2) the Baikal Teal; (3) the blue-winged ducks and allies; and (4) a large clade that included the wigeons, pintails, Mallards, and several teal lineages, of which the wigeons were considered the basal and sister-group. Interestingly, the molecular analysis revealed an extremely high genetic divergence (5.8%) between the Eurasian Green-winged Teal and the American Green-winged Teal, despite their nearly identical plumage. Such divergence is similar to the genetic distance (5.7%) between the Mallard and Northern Pintail. Hence, molecular analysis led Johnson and Sorenson (1999) to recognized two separate species of Green-winged Teal, which agrees with the morphologically based conclusion of Livezey (1991). Relative to the blue-winged ducks, the molecular analysis revealed very low divergence and paraphyly between the Blue-winged Teal and the Cinnamon Teal. Hence, several different haplotypes of Cinnamon Teal may be intermixed with the Blue-winged Teal (Johnson and Sorenson 1999), which casts some doubt on mtDNA inferences.

Livezey (1991) considered the four species of shovelers as a monophyletic group; he also resurrected the genus *Mareca* for six species, including the wigeons. Most (96%) bootstrap replicates of the molecular data of Johnson and Sorenson (1999) strongly supported monophyly of a dabbling duck clade that included all species of *Anas* and taxa Livezey (1991) placed in *Mareca*. Placement of the wigeon as a sister-group to all other species of *Anas*, as suggested by Livezey (1991), would require 36 additional steps with the molecular data set used; hence, Johnson and Sorenson (1999) did not elevate

Mareca to generic status. Johnson and Sorenson (1999) also strongly supported monophyly of the pintails, with some indication of the Cape Teal as the sister-group to the pintail clade, and not the wigeons as proposed by Livezey (1991).

Within the ever-confusing "Mallard Group," Johnson and Sorenson (1999) recognized the paraphyly of the group (see Avise et al. 1990, Cooper et al. 1996, Rhymer 2001), noting a sequence divergence in haplotypes as only 0.58%. Johnson and Sorenson (1999) subsequently advocated three biogeographic groups for the mallards: (1) a basal clade in Africa, (2) a clade in North America, and (3) a clade of eastern Asia–Pacific Island birds. In North America, there are no base pair substitutions over the 2,147 base pairs between three of four taxa, and the fourth, the Mottled Duck, differs from the others by only two positions. They also discuss scenarios for speciation in the Mallard Group. Livezey (1991) considered the African mallards — Yellow-billed Duck and Meller's Duck — as one of two clades included as a sister-group to the Northern Hemisphere mallards, the other group being the four species of South Pacific mallards (the Philippine Duck, Gray Duck, and two species of spot-billed ducks — the Indonesian Spot-billed Duck and Chinese Spot-billed Duck). However, Livezey (1991:108) noted that several previous authorities regarded the continental forms as conspecific, and most of the Pacific forms as a polytypic group of the Mallard. Overall, Johnson and Sorenson (1999:804) discussed how the high dispersal ability of dabbling ducks may lead to such rapid species radiation that "reconstruction of the phylogenetic relationships among species or lineages that radiated in this way may be essentially intractable."

The dabbling ducks are ecologically diverse, and the widespread distribution of *Anas* on all continents except Antarctica is a rare occurrence for any genus of birds. As the name "dabbling duck" implies, they generally feed in shallow water, either by skimming the surface for food or by tipping ("dabbling") their heads and necks underwater. Most species of Anatini in North America dabble at depths of less than 25 cm (Fredrickson and Taylor 1982). Dabbling ducks can dive, but their legs are situated more or less under the body and hence provide minimal underwater propulsion compared to other tribes in the Anatinae. The hallux (hind toe) is not strongly lobed, probably reflecting the infrequent occurrence of underwater activities (but see Miller 1983). Most dabbling ducks are associated with freshwater habitats, particularly in the breeding season, but many species winter on coastal bays or brackish marshes. Nesting occurs near wetlands, but the nest itself often is placed in an upland setting on the ground or in a cavity.

The Anatini generally undergo two annual molts of the body feathers (a derived characteristic), of which the Prebasic includes the wing feathers (remiges). Hence, there is a pronounced Basic (nonbreeding or eclipse) Plumage in the molting sequence of many species that coincides with a short period of flightlessness at the end of the breeding season (see Chapter 6); this drab plumage occurs in both sexes of North American dabbling ducks, although it is more obvious in males than females. However, these and other features in the molting patterns of *Anas* are complex and vary (at least superficially) among species and by hemispheric distribution (Weller 1980b).

The downy plumage may be distinctively patterned in some species, with the downy young of *Anas* characterized by a dark eye-stripe. As adults, the sexes are usually distinguished by highly dimorphic plumage, especially within the genus *Aix* where the plumage of the males is spectacularly colored. Within the largest genus (*Anas*), the adult plumage of most species includes an iridescent speculum on the secondaries.

Voices differ between the sexes, and the syrinx in male *Anas* is comparatively elaborate, having an enlarged, partially ossified bulla located asymmetrically on the left side of the trachea (see Fig. 2-6). In females, the syrinx is not enlarged, but females are more vocal than males ("quacking" is typically a female vocalization, but other types of calls characterize the females of some species). Males do not incubate but may assist in brood rearing. The tarsus is scutellate.

Dabbling ducks reach maturity at 1 year of age, although the Greenland Mallard apparently does not breed until approaching 2 years of age (Palmer 1976). Species in the Northern Hemisphere usually pair seasonally and display a complex sequence of courtship behavior, but pair bonds may be much longer for species in the Southern Hemisphere (see Chapter 3). Relatively few subspecies are recognized except on oceanic islands (see Weller 1980a), but, as mentioned previously, several forms of Nearctic Mallards and a group of "southern Mallards" have been variably recognized as either species or as subspecies (see Johnsgard 1961d, Huey 1961, Aldrich and Baer 1970, Hubbard 1977, Scott and Reynolds 1984). Livezey (1991) "split" the "Mallard Group" by recognizing the American Black Duck, Gray Duck,

Laysan Duck, Mexican Duck, Hawaiian Duck, and Marianas Duck as distinct species, whereas Johnsgard (1978) considered each a subspecies of the Mallard or close relative.

Tribe Aythyini — Pochards: The pochards comprise five genera and 17 species, 12 of which are in the genus *Aythya*. Livezey (1997a) elevated *Aristonetta* from subgeneric to generic rank to better represent phylogenetic relationships in the classification for the red-headed pochards (Canvasback, Redhead, Eurasian Pochard) but, because *Aythya* is widely recognized, we retained *Aythya* in parentheses (Appendix A) for our summary here. Systematists have supported the Aythyini as a natural group for more than a century, and Livezey (1996a) used 99 morphological characters to develop three parsimonious trees for the tribe. Members of the Aythyini, except the Marbled Duck, were deemed monophyletic based on 20 unambiguous synapomorphies. Summary statistics for these trees were a length of 148, a consistency index of 0.750, and a retention index of 0.684. Differences among the three trees were limited to one clade involving three species or species groups: Madagascan White-eyed Pochard, Australian White-eyed Pochard, and the couplet of the Ferruginous White-eyed Pochard and Baer's Pochard.

Within the tribe, the Marbled Duck was the sister-group of all other members of the tribe. The remaining large clade comprised two monophyletic subgroups. The first, a subgroup of four "stem" pochards, was composed of two couplets of sister species: (1) the Pink-headed Duck and the Red-crested Pochard, and (2) the Rosy-billed Pochard and Southern Pochard. The second subgroup contained all other Aythyini. This group consisted of three clades: the redheads (three species), the white-eyed pochards (four species), and the scaup (five species), although relationships within the white-eyed pochards remained unresolved. Several species in the tribe were highly autapomorphic: Red-crested Pochard (eight autapomorphies), Pink-headed Duck (seven), Ring-necked Duck (seven), and Rosy-billed Pochard (seven).

Pochards occur in both the Northern (12 species) and Southern Hemispheres (5 species). One species, the Pink-headed Duck of northeast India, central Nepal, and northern Myanmar (Burma) is listed as extinct by Green (1992) and probably extinct by IUCN (2004). Prestwitch (1974) gives 1935 as the last date of a reliable sighting in the wild, but BirdLife International (2000) gives 1949. Since then, however, there are reports of Pink-headed Ducks from Nepal, and much of Myanmar has not been surveyed (also see Ali 1960, Nugent 1991, Collar et al. 1994). The Madagascan White-eyed Pochard is also listed by IUCN (2004) as near extinct. Endemic to Lake Alaotra, the largest lake in Madagascar, none were seen in 1989–90 surveys (Wilmé 1994). Serious declines also are reported for the Marbled Duck of the western Mediterranean, southern Spain, Morocco, and Turkey east to central Asia (Green 1993), the Ferruginous White-eyed Pochard of southern Europe and Asia, and the Siberian White-eyed or Baer's Pochard of eastern Asia (Tucker and Heath 1994).

Pochards have stout, heavy bodies with large heads and are strong divers with large feet set back on the body. Unlike the dabbling ducks, the hallux of pochards is variably lobed. Pochards also have a higher wing loading than most Anatini and must run across water for some distance before lifting off. They are medium-size waterfowl, with the group ranging in size from the Marbled Duck with a body mass of 500-600 g to the Canvasback at about 1,200 g (Johnsgard 1978).

All pochards have sexually dimorphic plumage, except the Marbled Duck of the Mediterranean and western Asia, although dimorphism is not pronounced in every species (especially the white-eyed pochards), and the males of most species are not especially colorful. Wing plumage lacks a distinctive iridescent speculum and instead usually is marked with a wash of white or gray on the upper surface. Metallic-colored plumage is uncommon and found sparingly on the heads of a few species. Downy plumage is usually yellow and without a distinct eye line or other head stripes. The syrinx is highly developed, with a large, asymmetrical bulla in males that is less rounded and more angular than in dabbling ducks; the bulla also has membranous fenestrae ("windows") on the outer wall (Johnsgard 1961b).

Courtship behavior in males is well developed and similar in most details among the species. For most species, there has been loss or a great reduction of the *"decrescendo"* call of females (Johnsgard 1961a). The head-pumping precopulatory display characteristic of dabbling ducks is lost or rudimentary in the pochards (Johnsgard 1965). Other homogenous displays within the Aythyini include the *kinked-neck call* of males, as well as *turn-the-back-of-the-head, head-throw, sneaking,* and *neck-stretching.* Females exhibit *inciting calls,* and both sexes exhibit the *preen-behind-the-wing* display (see Johnsgard 1965, Chapter 3).

Pochards usually mature at 1 year, as shown by McKnight and Buss (1962) who found that 12 of 16

Lesser Scaup ovulated as yearlings. However, despite their apparent physiological abilities to do so, as few as 15% of the yearling Lesser Scaup studied by Trauger (1971) produced broods. Pochards usually nest over water in emergent vegetation, although Lesser Scaup and Redheads also may choose dry-land sites (Low 1945, McKnight 1974, Bellrose 1980). Pochards generally are associated with freshwater environments, but large concentrations of some species overwinter on coastal bays and lagoons. For example, about 78% of the Redhead population winters in the Laguna Madre on the western edge of the Gulf of Mexico (Weller 1964b, Baldassarre et al. 1989).

Livezey (1996a) noted that a vegetative diet was a primitive character except for the three most derived species of scaup (Lesser Scaup, Greater Scaup, and Tufted Duck), which prefer invertebrates. Pochards dive expertly, searching for much of their food in water 1.5 m or more in depth.

Tribe Mergini — Typical Sea Ducks: This tribe contains 22 species in 10 genera collectively known as sea ducks. Two species are extinct: the Labrador Duck of North America (1875) and the Auckland Islands Merganser (1902). The Labrador Duck was endemic to the northeastern coast of North America where apparently it was never common, although it did appear in the meat markets of Baltimore and New York in the first half of the 19th century (see Fuller 2000). The Labrador Duck was known to science only for about 100 years, and only 31 museum specimens exist. No convincing evidence has emerged to explain the disappearance of Labrador Ducks, but their highly specialized diet and the introduction of mammalian predators to nesting islands may have been involved, and they were apparently sought by market hunters. Auckland Islands Mergansers once occurred on mainland New Zealand where they were likely exterminated by Polynesians, but others (perhaps just 200) survived on the Auckland Islands, which lie about 300 km south of New Zealand. The subsequent introduction of several species of mammals to the Auckland Islands likely posed additional threats (Johnsgard 1978), but the final blow apparently occurred in 1901–02 when museum collectors shot remnants of the population. Nonetheless, only 26 skins exist in the world's museums (Kear and Scarlett 1970, Flannery and Schouten 2001).

Livezey's (1995c) phylogenetic analysis examined 137 morphological characteristics and produced a single, completely dichotomous tree with a total length of 223, a consistency index of 0.692, and a retention index of 0.894. Monophyly of the tribe was supported by 13 synapomorphies. The analysis produced strong support for a goldeneye – Smew – merganser clade (17 synapomorphies) and an eider (*Somateria*) clade (13). Nine branches of the final tree were preserved in over 90% of bootstrap replications, but there was weaker support for other branches (58–68% preservation). The eiders (*Polysticta* and *Somateria*) were monophyletic and deemed the sister-group to all other Mergini. Within the latter group, the Harlequin Duck was the sister-group of the remaining genera. Exclusive of the eiders and Harlequin Duck, there were two major clades for Mergini: (1) a clade where the extinct Labrador Duck was the sister-group of the scoters (*Melanitta*); and (2) a clade where the Long-tailed Duck was the sister-group of the goldeneyes (*Bucephala*), Smew, and the mergansers (*Mergus* and *Lophodytes*). Several species were marked by pronounced autapomorphies: the Harlequin Duck (11), Long-tailed Duck (10), Steller's Eider (8), Labrador Duck (8), and Smew (8). Livezey (1995c) also recommended phylogenetic species status for several taxa in the eider and scoter groups, and he later differentiated the Eurasian Black Scoter from the American Black Scoter, and the Velvet Scoter of Eurasia from the White-winged Scoter of North America. Earlier but significant taxonomic studies of Mergini include Humphrey (1958) and Johnsgard (1960b, 1964).

Sea ducks are large birds (eiders exceed 2,500 g) with a distribution largely limited to the Northern Hemisphere, although the extinct Auckland Islands Merganser and the critically endangered Brazilian Merganser — each from the Southern Hemisphere — are intriguing exceptions (Kear and Scarlett 1970, Livezey 1989, Livezey 1995c). These also are the only two species in the tribe that are nonmigratory and lack sexual dimorphism.

IUCN (2004) lists the Brazilian Merganser as critically endangered, with a remaining population of less than 250 birds. This merganser inhabits swift, clear rivers and streams in remote areas of southern Brazil, Paraguay, and northern Argentina (Bartmann 1988, Antas 1996). Apparently always rare, the Brazilian Merganser was declared extinct in 1924 but was rediscovered in 1948 (Partridge 1956). Fortunately, Brazilian Mergansers occur in three national parks in Brazil, where various national and international conservation groups are working for its protection. The Scaly-sided Merganser inhabits fast-flowing rivers in mountain forests,

with major breeding areas located in northeastern China and parts of the Russian Far East (Hughes and Bocharnikov 1992). The current population numbers 3,600–4,500 individuals, and IUCN (2004) classifies the species as endangered.

Sea ducks are accomplished divers but are otherwise not closely related to Aythyini or other tribes with the same behavior. Indeed, foraging Long-tailed Ducks have been entrapped in fish nets as deep as 55 m and regularly at depths greater than 23 m (Cottam 1939). Bill structure differs among the genera, reflecting their respective food habits, and features the strongly serrated lamellae of the fish-eating mergansers. All sea ducks feed principally on animal matter. Sea ducks also lack metallic plumage coloration, except for an iridescent gloss on the heads of males in the goldeneye group and on the wings of eiders and a few other species. Features of the downy plumage vary considerably within the tribe: Some have strong black-and-white patterns (e.g., goldeneyes and scoters), whereas others are brownish and lack clear markings (e.g., eiders). Few species of sea ducks other than eiders emit vocalizations, but male courtship behavior generally is elaborate and showy.

Syringeal anatomy varies greatly within the tribe, and a general description is not presented here, but Beard (1951) and Johnsgard (1961b) showed the taxonomic affinities between Hooded Mergansers and three species of *Bucephala* based on the structure of the male syrinx and trachea. Humphrey (1958) and others proposed that, in part, the *Anas*-like syrinx anatomy of eiders — now considered an ancestral trait in eiders (Livezey 1986) — warranted their placement in the separate tribe Somaterini, but that suggestion was rejected on other grounds by Johnsgard (1960b, 1964), Woolfenden (1961), and Livezey (1986). Nonetheless, an analysis of feather proteins indicated differences between eiders and other sea ducks (Brush 1976).

Sea ducks mature at 2–3 years of age and often nest in sites offering some type of shelter, including crevices in rocks and tree cavities. Most species seem to pair annually, although the pair bond in Barrow's Goldeneyes sometimes persists from one breeding season to the next in spite of long periods of separation (Savard 1985). Molting patterns are complex, and females may undergo two or more at least partial molts during the annual cycle. Juveniles of either sex retain female-like plumage well into their second year, which makes certain population features difficult to determine (but see Bolen and Chapman 1981).

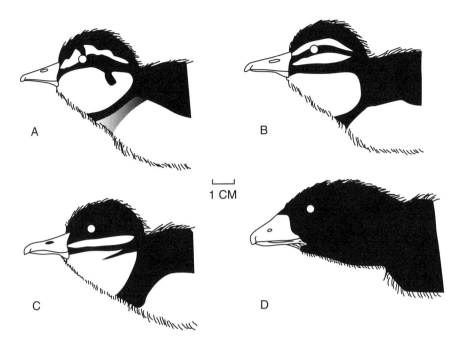

Figure 2-17. Plumage patterns of the downy young are very distinctive among the four genera of stuff-tailed ducks the tribe Oxyurini. (A) Black-headed Duck, (B) Masked Duck, (C) Ruddy Duck, and (D) Musk Duck. From Livezey (1995b:228). With permission from the Wilson Ornithological Society.

Livezey (1995c) proposed that Mergini originated in the Northern Hemisphere. The distributional patterns for a number of species as well as the presence of fossil Mergini (*Chendytes*) in California (Livezey 1995c) underscore the importance of the Pacific Basin and adjacent continental regions for speciation within the group.

Tribe Oxyurini — Still-tailed Ducks: The final tribe in the subfamily of true ducks contains nine species known as stiff-tailed ducks. This tribe is organized into four genera: *Oxyura* with six species, and three somewhat aberrant genera of a single species each, *Heteronetta*, *Biziura*, and *Nomonyx* (Fig. 2-17). Livezey (1995b) analyzed 92 morphological characters to propose a single, completely dichotomous tree for the Oxyurini, the monophyly of which was supported by 17 unambiguous synapomorphies. The tree had a total length of 127, a retention index of 0.81, and a consistency index of 0.71. The Black-headed Duck of southern South America was the sister-group of all other Oxyurini. The Musk Duck of Australia had the highest number of autapomorphies (28), a number that exceeds all other species of Anseriformes. The branches defining the tribe, exclusive of the Black-headed Duck, were retained in 100% of bootstrap replicates. The taxonomic status of the Peruvian Ruddy Duck pro-

visionally included the Columbian Rudy Duck — the later may represent a hybrid swarm between the Ruddy Duck (Northern) and the Peruvian Ruddy Duck (Livezey (1995b, 1997a).

Stiff-tailed ducks occur in freshwater marshes worldwide where they typically construct nests over water. Incubation and brood rearing vary somewhat, and one species, the Black-headed Duck, is an obligate nest parasite, the only such species among the Anseriformes. Some 18 host species have been reported, especially the Red-fronted Coot (*Fulica rufifrons*) and Red-gartered Coot (*F. armillata*), but also gulls, ibises, and even birds of prey (Weller 1968a). In Argentina, nest parasitism was common: 29.3% of 1,927 nests of 11 species were parasitized by Black-headed Ducks, but 80% of their eggs were laid in the nests of the two aforementioned species of coots (Lyon and Eadie 2004). Rees and Hillgarth (1984) speculated that *Heteronetta* might be assigned to a monotypic tribe.

The Musk Duck (Fig. 2-18), another unique species in the group, is an endemic to Australia where it inhabits permanent marshes and swamps. The name derives from a powerful musky odor of unknown function that exudes from the uropygial (oil) gland. Indeed, the smell is so powerful that Captain George Vancouver of the H.M.S. *Discovery*, while traveling in Western Australia in 1791 remarked, "A

Figure 2-18. The Musk Duck is another endemic from Australia. The Musk Duck is widespread in permanent water habitats throughout its primary range in southern Australia, where it is unimportant as a game species because of its musky odor. Photo courtesy of Frank McKinney and the Bell Museum of Natural History.

very peculiar one [duck] was shot, of a dark grayish plumage, . . . which smelt so intolerably that it scented nearly the whole ship" (Frith 1967:308). Musk Ducks are dark, gray-brown and virtually monochromatic, but males are much larger than the females. Indeed, the ratio of male:female body mass exceeds 3:1, which is among the highest reported for birds (McCraken et al. 2000a). Musk Ducks display in leks, yet another unique feature for waterfowl. Beneath the bill of males is a pendulous lobe that enlarges and becomes turgid during the breeding season (Frith 1967), and males are especially noisy when establishing territories in which more than one female may nest (Lowe 1966, Johnsgard 1966b). Clutch size is small (one to three eggs), and females feed their young — a particularly unique feature in Anatidae (Frith 1967, McCraken et al. 2000b).

Stiff-tailed ducks feature rigid retrices and short tail coverts; their wings are small in proportion to their bodies, and their feet are large. Stiff-tailed ducks walk with difficulty on land because their legs are situated well to the rear of their squat bodies; they are adept divers, but not strong fliers. Stiff-tails have

unusually small feathers that give a distinctive sheen to the body plumage, and except for the Black-headed Duck and Musk Duck, they have sexually dimorphic plumage that generally lacks any metallic coloration. Curiously, a double wing molt occurs in at least the Maccoa Duck and the Ruddy Duck, a feature that makes these two species quite unlike other waterfowl (Siegfried 1970). Further investigation may well reveal a double wing molt in all species of *Oxyura*. The downy plumage of some stiff-tailed ducks is not conspicuously marked.

Except for the Musk Duck, adult stiff-tailed ducks have broad, flat, often bluish bills tipped with sharp nails. The bills of most species undergo seasonal changes in color, turning from black in autumn and winter to blue in spring and summer. The blue coloration is a structural phenomenon associated with the distribution of melanin and, similar to the coloration of blue feathers, is not the result of blue pigmentation (Hays and Habermann 1969). All species have short, thick necks. In at least the Masked Duck and all species of *Oxyura,*, the males perform unique courtship displays by slapping their bills against their inflated throat (sacs) and puffed-out breasts, but vocalizations are apparently uncommon or absent. The eggs of stiff-tailed ducks are the largest of all ducks and are laid in elaborate nests constructed in emergent vegetation (see Low 1941).

The phylogenetic analysis of Livezey (1995b) strongly supports a Southern Hemisphere origin for the stiff-tailed ducks. Oxyurini do not occur on islands, which suggests the species in this group are among the poorest dispersers of all waterfowl. Also see Johnsgard and Carbonell (1996) for information on the Oxyurini.

CONCLUDING REMARKS

This chapter reviewed the organization of the order Anseriformes and its three extant families: Anhimidae (screamers), Anseranatidae (Magpie Goose), and Anatidae (ducks, geese, and swans). All but four of the species in the order occur in the family Anatidae. Based on Livezey (1986, 1991, 1997a), the classification of Anatidae recognizes 5 subfamilies, 13 tribes, 51 genera, and 171 recent species. The fossil history of Anseriformes extends at least to the early Oligocene, and possibly earlier in the paleontological record. Anseriformes likely evolved from ancestors related to Galliformes, and originated in the Southern Hemisphere.

The taxonomic relationships of waterfowl undoubtedly will undergo further refinement — and, in doing so, is sure to stimulate additional debate, as witnessed by the plethora of changes and disagreements marking the past. Nonetheless, armed with the current understanding of the basic associations within the family, we can now turn our attention to the biology, ecology, and management of waterfowl.

LITERATURE CITED

Aldrich, J. W., and K. P. Baer. 1970. Status and speciation in the Mexican Duck (*Anas diazi*). Wilson Bulletin 82:63–73.

Ali, S. 1960. The Pink-headed Duck *Rhodonessa caryophyllacea* (Latham). Wildfowl Trust Annual Report 11:55–60.

Alvarez, R., and S. L. Olson. 1978. A new merganser from the Miocene of Virginia (Aves: Anatidae). Proceedings of the Biological Society of Washington 91:522–532.

American Ornithologist's Union (AOU). 1983. Check list of North American birds, sixth edition. American Ornithologist's Union, Washington, D.C.

Ankney, C. D., D. G. Dennis, and R. C. Bailey. 1987. Increasing Mallards, decreasing Black Ducks: coincidence or cause and effect? Journal of Wildlife Management 51:523–529.

Ankney, C. D., D. G. Dennis, L. N. Wishard, and J. E. Seeb. 1986. Low genic variation between Black Ducks and Mallards. Auk 103:701–709.

Antas, P. T. Z. 1996. The Brazilian Merganser (*Mergus octosetaceous*), the most threatened duck in South America. Gibier Faune Sauvage 13:799–800.

Avers, C. J. 1989. Process and pattern in evolution. Oxford University Press, New York.

Avise, J. C. 1989. A role for molecular genetics in the recognition and conservation of endangered species. Tree 4:279–281.

Avise, J. C., C. D. Ankney, and W. S. Nelson. 1990. Mitochondrial gene trees and the evolutionary relationship of Mallard and Black Ducks. Evolution 44:1109–1119.

Bajomi, B. 2003. White-headed Duck breeding and reintroduction programme in Hungary, 1982–1992. Threatened Waterfowl Specialist Group News 14:73–76.

Baldassarre, G. A., A. R. Brazda, and E. Rangel Woodyard. 1989. The east coast of Mexico. Pages 407–425 *in* L. M. Smith, R. L. Pederson, and R. M. Kaminski, editors. Habitat management for migrating and wintering waterfowl in North America. Texas Tech University Press, Lubbock.

Banks, R. C., C. Cicero, J. L. Dunn, A. W. Kratter, P. C. Rasmussen, J. V. Remsen, Jr., J. D. Rising, and D. F. Stotz. 2004. Forty-fifth supplement to the American Ornithologists' Union Check-List of North American Birds. Auk 121:985–995.

Bartmann, W. 1988. New observations on the Brazilian Merganser. Wildfowl 39:7–14.

Beard, E. B. 1951. The trachea of the Hooded Merganser. Wilson Bulletin 63:296–301.

Beddard, F. E. 1898. The structure and classification of birds. Longmans, Green & Company, London.

Bell, B. D. 1991. Recent avifaunal changes and the history of ornithology in New Zealand. International Ornithological Congress 20:195–230.

Bellrose, F. C. 1980. Ducks, geese and swans of North America. Stackpole Books, Harrisburg, Pennsylvania.

BirdLife International. 2000. Threatened birds of the world. Lynx Edicions, Barcelona.

Bolen, E. G. 1967. Nesting boxes for Black-bellied Tree Ducks. Journal of Wildlife Management 31:794–797.

Bolen, E. G., and B. R. Chapman. 1981. Estimating winter sex ratios for Buffleheads. Southwestern Naturalist 26:425–428.

Bolen, E. G., and M. K. Rylander. 1983. Whistling-ducks: zoogeography, ecology, anatomy. Special Publication 20, The Museum, Texas Tech University, Lubbock.

Bolen, E. G., and E. N. Smith. 1979. Notes on the incubation behavior of Black-bellied Whistling Ducks. Prairie Naturalist 11:119–123.

Braithwaite, L. W. 1976. Notes on the breeding of the Freckled Duck in the Lachlan River Valley. Emu 76:127–132.

Braithwaite, L. W., and B. Miller. 1975. The Mallard, *Anas platyrhynchos*, and Mallard-Black Duck, *Anas superciliosa rogersi*, hybridization. Australian Wildlife Research 2:47–61.

Brock, V. E. 1951. Some observations on the Laysan Duck, *Anas wyvilliana laysanensis*. Auk 68:371–372.

Brodkorb, P. 1964. Catalogue of fossil birds, Part 2. Bulletin of the Florida State Museum 8:195–335.

Brodsky, L. M., and P. J. Weatherhead. 1984. Behavioral and ecological factors contributing to American Black Duck-Mallard hybridization. Journal of Wildlife Management 48:846–852.

Bromley, R. G., and T. C. Rothey. 2003. Conservation assessment for the Dusky Canada Goose (*Branta canadensis occidentalis* Baird). U.S. Forest Service General Technical Report PNW-GTR-591.

Brown, L. H., E. K. Urban, and K. Newman. 1982. The birds of Africa. Volume 1. Academic Press, London.

Browne, R. A., C. R. Griffin, P. R. Chang, M. Hubley, and A. E. Martin. 1993. Genetic divergence among populations of the Hawaiian Duck, Laysan Duck, and Mallard. Auk 110:49–56.

Brunner, A., and A. Andreotti. 2001. White-headed Duck reintroduction in Europe. Threatened Waterfowl Specialist Group News 13: 33–36.

Brush, A. H. 1976. Waterfowl feather proteins: analysis of use in taxonomic studies. Journal of Zoology (London) 179:467–498.

Caithness, T., M. Williams, and J. D. Nichols. 1991. Survival and band recovery rates of sympatric Grey Ducks and Mallards in New Zealand. Journal of Wildlife Management 55:111–118.

Callaghan, D. A. 1997. Conservation status of the Torrent Ducks *Merganetta*. Wildfowl 48:166–173.

Callaghan, D. A., and A. J. Green. 1993. Wildfowl at risk, 1993. Wildfowl 44:149–169.

Campbell, K. E., and E. P. Toni. 1983. Size and locomotion in teratorns (Aves: Teratornithidae). Auk 100:390–403.

Cassels, R. 1984. The role of prehistoric man in the faunal extinctions of New Zealand and other Pacific islands. Pages 741–767 *in* P. S. Martin and R. G. Klein, editors. Quaternary extinctions: a prehistoric revolution. University of Arizona Press, Tucson.

Cathey, J. C., J. A. DeWoody, and L. M. Smith. 1998. Microsatellite markers in Canada Geese (*Branta Canadensis*). Journal of Heredity 89:173–175.

Cheke, A. S. 1987. An ecological history of the Mascarene Islands, with particular reference to extinctions and introductions of land vertebrates. Pages 5–89 *in* A. W. Diamond, editor. Studies of Mascarene Island birds. Cambridge University Press, Cambridge.

Clark, A. 1969. The behavior of the White-backed Duck. Wildfowl 20:71–74.

Collar, N. J., M. J. Crosby, and A. J. Stattersfield. 1994. Birds to watch 2. The world list of threatened birds. BirdLife International, Cambridge.

Conover, B. 1943. A study of the Torrent Ducks. Field Museum of Natural History Zoological Series 24:345–356.

Cooper, A., J. M. Rhymer, H. F. James, S. L. Olson, C. E. McIntosh, M. D. Sorenson, and R. C. Fleischer. 1996. Ancient DNA and island endemics. Nature 381:484.

Cottam, C. 1939. Food habits of North American diving ducks. USDA Technical Bulletin 643.

Cracraft, J. 1973. Continental drift, paleoclimatology, and the evolution and biogeography of birds. Journal of Zoology (London) 169:455–545.

Cracraft, J. 1980. Avian phylogeny and intercontinental biogeographic patterns. International Ornithological Congress 17:1302–1308.

Cracraft, J. 1981. Toward a phylogenetic classification of the recent birds of the world (Class Aves). Auk 98:681–714.

Cronin, M. A., J. B. Grand, D. Esler, D. V. Derksen, and K. T. Scribner. 1996. Breeding populations of Northern Pintails have similar mitochondrial DNA. Canadian Journal of Zoology 74:992–999.

Cushing, J. E., Jr. 1941. Non-genetic mating preference as a factor in evolution. Condor 43:233–236.

Daugherty, C. H., A. Cree, J. H. Hay, and M. B. Thompson. 1990. Neglected taxonomy and continuing extinctions of tuatara (Sphenedon). Nature 347:177–179.

Daugherty, C. H., M. Williams, and J. M. Hay. 1999. Genetic differentiation, taxonomy and conservation of the Australasian teals *Anas* spp. Bird Conservation International 9:29–42.

Davies, S. J. J. F. 1963. Aspects of the behaviour of the Magpie Goose, *Anseranas semipalmata*. Ibis 105:76–98.

Davies, S. J. J. F., and H. J. Frith. 1964. Some comments on the taxonomic position of the Magpie Goose *Anseranas semipalmata* (Latham). Emu 63:265–272.

Delacour, J. 1954–64. The waterfowl of the world. Volumes 1–4. Country Life, London.

Delacour, J. 1959. Wild pigeons and doves. All-Pets Books, Fond du Lac, Wisconsin.

Delacour, J., and D. Amadon. 1973. Curassows and related birds. American Museum of Natural History, New York.

Delacour, J., and J. C. Harrison. 1951. Pheasants of the world. Country Life, London.

Delacour, J., and E. Mayr. 1945. The family Anatidae. Wilson Bulletin 57:3–55.

Dewar, R. E. 1984. Extinctions in Madagascar: the loss of the subfossil fauna. Pages 574–593 *in* P. S. Martin and R. G. Klein, editors. Quaternary extinctions: a prehistoric revolution. University of Arizona Press, Tucson.

Dilger, W. C., and P. A. Johnsgard. 1959. Comments on "species recognition" with special reference to the Wood Duck and the Mandarin Duck. Wilson Bulletin 71:46–53.

Dorward, D. F., F. I. Norman, and S. J. Cowling. 1980. The Cape Barren Goose in Victoria, Australia: management related to agriculture. Wildfowl 31:144–150.

Dumbell, G. S. 1986. The New Zealand Brown Teal: 1845–1985. Wildfowl 37:71–87.

Edkins, D., and I. A. Hansen. 1972. Wax esters secreted by the uropygial gland of some Australian waterfowl, including the Magpie Goose. Comparative Biochemistry and Physiology 41B:105–112.

Eldredge, N., and J. Cracraft. 1980. Phylogenetic patterns and the evolutionary process. Columbia University Press, New York.

Eldridge, J. L. 1979. Display inventory of the Torrent Duck. Wildfowl 30:5–15.

Eldridge, J. L. 1986a. Territoriality in a river specialist: the Blue Duck. Wildfowl 37:123–135.

Eldridge, J. L. 1986b. Observations of a pair of Torrent Ducks. Wildfowl 37:113–122.

Ely, C. R., and K. T. Scribner. 1994. Genetic diversity in arctic-nesting geese: implications for management and conservation. Transactions of the North American Wildlife and Natural Resources Conference 59:91–110.

Engliss, A., Jr., and T. K. Pratt. 1993. Status and population trends of Hawaii's native waterbirds, 1977–1987. Wilson Bulletin 105:142–158.

Engilis, A., Jr., K. J. Uyehara, and J. G. Griffin. 2002. Hawaiian Duck (*Anas wyvilliana*). The birds of North America, 694. The American Ornithologists' Union, Washington, D.C., and The Academy of Natural Sciences, Philadelphia.

Eyton, T. C. 1838. A monograph on the Anatidae, or duck tribe. Longman, Orme Brown, Green, Longman, Paternoster-Row, Eddowes, Shrewsbury, London.

Feduccia, A. 1978. *Presbyornis* and the evolution of ducks and flamingos. American Scientist 66:298–304.

Fischer, H. 1965. The triumph ceremony of the Grey-Lag Goose (*Anser anser*). Zeitschrift für Tierpsychologie 22:247–304.

Fisher, J., N. Simon, and J. Vincent. 1969. Wildlife in danger. Viking Press, New York.

Flannery, T. F. 1994. The future eaters: an ecological history of the Australasian Islands and people. Reed Books, Port Melbourne, Victoria, Australia.

Flannery, T., and P. Schouten. 2001. A gap in nature: discovering the world's extinct animals. Atlantic Monthly Press, New York.

Flickinger, E. L. 1975. Incubation by a male Fulvous Tree Duck. Wilson Bulletin 87:106–107.

Fox, A. D., C. Glahder, C. R. Mitchell, D. A. Stroud, H. Boyd, and J. Frikke. 1996. North American Canada Geese (*Branta canadensis*) in west Greenland. Auk 113:231–233.

Fredrickson, L. H., and T. S. Taylor. 1982. Management of seasonally flooded impoundments for wildlife. U.S Fish and Wildlife Service Resource Publication 148.

Frith, H. J. 1964a. The downy young of the Freckled Duck *Stictonetta naevosa*. Emu 64:42–47.

Frith, H. J. 1964b. Taxonomic relationships of *Stictonetta naevosa* (Gould). Nature 202:1352–1353.

Frith, H. J. 1965. Ecology of the Freckled Duck, *Stictonetta naevosa* (Gould). CSIRO, Wildlife Research 10:125–139.

Frith, H. J. 1967. Waterfowl in Australia. Angus & Robertson, Sydney.

Frith, H. J., and Davies, S. J. J. F. 1961. Ecology of the Magpie Goose, *Anseranas semipalmata* Latham (Anatidae). CSIRO Wildlife Research 6:91–141.

Fuller, E. 2000. Extinct birds. Oxford University Press, Oxford.

Geldenhuys, J.N. 1980. Breeding ecology of the South African Shelduck in the southern Orange Free State. South African Journal of Wildlife Research 10:94–111.

Gillespie, G. D. 1985. Hybridization, introgression, and morphometric differentiation between Mallard (*Anas platyrhynchos*) and Grey Duck (*Anas superciliosa*) in Otago, New Zealand. Auk 102:459–469.

Grant, P. R., and B. R. Grant. 1992. Hybridization of bird species. Science 256:193–197.

Gray, A. P. 1958. Bird hybrids, a check-list with bibliography. Technical Communication 13, Commonwealth Agricultural Bureaux, Farnham Royal, Bucks, United Kingdom.

Green, A. J. 1992. Wildfowl at risk, 1992. Wildfowl 43:160–184.

Green, A. J., editor. 1993. The status and conservation of the Marbled Teal *Marmaronetta angustirostris*. International Waterfowl and Wetlands Research Bureau Special Publication 23.

Greenway, J. C., Jr. 1967. Extinct and vanishing birds of the world. Second edition. Dover Publications, New York.

Groth, J. G., and G. F. Barrowclough. 1999. Basal divergences in birds and phylogenetic utility of the nuclear RAG-1 gene. Molecular Phylogenetics and Evolution 12:115–123.

Hagey, L. R., C. D. Schteingart, H-T. Ton-Nu., S. S. Rossi, D. Odell, and A. F. Hofmann. 1990. â-phocacholic acid in bile: biochecmical evidence that the Flamingo is related to an ancient goose. Condor 92:593–597.

Hanson, H. C. 1965. The Giant Canada Goose. Southern Illinois University Press, Carbondale.

Hanson, H. C. 1997. The Giant Canada Goose, revised edition. Southern Illinois University Press, Carbondale.

Hays, H., and H. M. Habermann. 1969. Note on bill color of the Ruddy Duck, *Oxyura jamaicensis rubida*. Auk 86:765–766.

Hazevoet, C. J. 1996. Conservation and species lists: taxonomic neglect promotes the extinction of endemic birds, as exemplified by taxa from eastern Atlantic islands. Bird Conservation International 6:191–196.

Hennig, W. 1966. Phylogenetic systematics. University of Illinois Press, Urbana.

Heusmann, H. W. 1991. The history and status of the Mallard in the Atlantic Flyway. Wildlife Society Bulletin 19:14–22.

Hillis, D. M., B. K. Mable, and C. Moritz. 1996. Applications of molecular systematics: the state of the field and a look to the future. Pages 515–543 *in* D. M. Hillis, C. Moritz, and B. K. Mable, editors. Molecular systematics. Second edition. Sinauer Associates, Sunderland, Massachusetts.

Hochbaum, H. A. 1955. Travels and traditions of waterfowl. Charles T. Branford Company, Newton, Massachusetts.

Hori, J. 1964. The breeding biology of the Shelduck, *Tadorna tadorna*. Ibis 106:333–360.

Hori, J. 1969. Social and population studies in the Shelduck. Wildfowl 20:5–22.

Horn, P. L., J. A. Rafalski, and P. J. Whitehead. 1996. Molecular genetic (RAPD) analysis of breeding Magpie Geese. Auk 113:552–557.

Howard, H. 1950. Fossil evidence of avian evolution. Ibis 92:1–21.

Howard, H. 1955. A new wading bird from the Eocene of Patagonia. American Museum Novitates 1710:1–25.

Howard, H. 1964. Fossil Anseriformes. Pages 233–248 *in* J. Delacour, editor. Waterfowl of the world. Volume 4. Country Life, London.

Hubbard, J. P. 1977. The biological and taxonomic status of the Mexican Duck. New Mexico Department of Game and Fish Bulletin 16.

Huey, W. S. 1961. Comparison of female Mallard with female New Mexican Duck. Auk 78:428–431.

Hughes, B. 2003. Ruddy Duck control in Europe and North Africa. Threatened Waterfowl Specialist Group News 14:70–72.

Hughes, B., and V. N. Bocharnikov. 1992. Status of the Scaly-sided Merganser *Mergus squamatus* in the Far East of Russia. Wildfowl 43:193–199.

Humphrey, P. S. 1958. Classification and systematic position of the eiders. Condor 60:129–135.

Humphrey, P. S., and B. C. Livezey. 1982. Flightlessness in Flying Steamer-Ducks. Auk 99:368–372.

Humphrey, P. S., and B. C. Livezey. 1985. Nest, eggs, and downy young of the White-headed Flightless Steamer-Duck. Ornithological Monographs 36:944–953.

Humphrey, P. S., and M. C. Thompson. 1981. A new species of steamer-duck (*Tachyeres*) from Argentina. University of Kansas Museum Natural History Occasional Paper 95.

International Union for the Conservation of Nature and Natural Resources (IUCN). 2004. IUCN Red List of threatened species. Gland, Switzerland.

Jacob, J., and A. Glaser. 1975. Chemotaxonomy of Anseriformes. Biochemical Systematics and Ecology 2:215–219.

James, H. F., and D. A. Burney. 1997. The diet and ecology of Hawaii's extinct flightless waterfowl: evidence from coprolites. Biological Journal of the Linnean Society 62:279–297.

Johnsgard, P. A. 1960a. Hybridization in the Anatidae and its taxonomic implications. Condor 62:25–33.

Johnsgard, P. A. 1960b. Classification and evolutionary relationships of the sea ducks. Condor 62:426–433.

Johnsgard, P. A. 1961a. The taxonomy of the Anatidae — a behavioural analysis. Ibis 103a:71–85.

Johnsgard, P. A. 1961b. Tracheal anatomy of the Anatidae and its taxonomic significance. Wildfowl Trust Annual Report 12:58–69.

Johnsgard, P. A. 1961c. The sexual behavior and systematic position of the Hooded Merganser. Wilson Bulletin 73:226–236.

Johnsgard, P. A. 1961d. Evolutionary relationships among the North American Mallards. Auk 78:3–43.

Johnsgard, P. A. 1961e. Wintering distribution changes in Mallards and Black Ducks. American Midland Naturalist 66:477–484.

Johnsgard, P. A. 1961f. Breeding biology of the Magpie Goose. Wildfowl Trust Annual Report 12:92–103.

Johnsgard, P. A. 1962. Evolutionary trends in the behavior and morphology of the Anatidae. Wildfowl 13:130–148.

Johnsgard, P. A. 1964. Comparative behavior and relationships of the eiders. Condor 66:113–129.

Johnsgard, P. A. 1965. Handbook of waterfowl behavior. Cornell University Press, Ithaca, New York.

Johnsgard, P. A. 1966a. The biology and relationships of the Torrent Duck. Wildfowl Trust Annual Report 17:66–74.

Johnsgard, P. A. 1966b. Behavior of the Australian Musk Duck and Blue-billed Duck. Auk 83:98-110.

Johnsgard, P. A. 1967a. Observations on the behaviour and relationships of the White-backed Duck and the stiff-tailed ducks. Wildfowl 18:98–107.

Johnsgard, P. A. 1967b. Sympatry changes and hybridization incidence in Mallards and Black Ducks. American Midland Naturalist 77:51–63.

Johnsgard, P. A. 1968. Waterfowl: their biology and natural history. University of Nebraska Press, Lincoln.

Johnsgard, P. A. 1978. Ducks, geese, and swans of the world. University of Nebraska Press, Lincoln.

Johnsgard, P. A., and M. Carbonell. 1996. Ruddy Ducks and other stifftails. University of Oklahoma Press, Norman.

Johnsgard, P. A., and R. DiSilvestro. 1976. Seventy-five years of changes in Mallard-Black Duck ratios in eastern North America. American Birds 30:904–908.

Johnson, A. W. 1963. Notes on the distribution, reproduction and display of the Andean Torrent Duck, *Merganetta armata*. Ibis 105:114–116.

Johnson, K. P., and M. D. Sorenson. 1999. Phylogeny and biogeography of dabbling ducks (Genus: *Anas*): a comparison of molecular and morphological evidence. Auk 116:792–805.

Kear, J. 1967. Notes of the eggs and downy young of *Thalassornis leuconotus*. Ostrich 38:227–229.

Kear, J. 1970. The adaptive radiation of parental care in waterfowl. Pages 357–92 *in* J. H. Crook, editor. Social behaviour in birds and mammals. Academic Press, New York.

Kear, J. 1972. The Blue Duck of New Zealand. Living Bird 11:175–192.

Kear, J. 1975. Salvadori's Duck of New Guinea. Wildfowl 26:104–111.

Kear, J. 1988. The Mute Swan. Shire Publications, Princes Risborough, United Kingdom.

Kear, J. 1990. Man and waterfowl. T & A D Poyser. London.

Kear, J. 1991. Ducks of the world. Mallard Press, New York.

Kear, J., editor. 2005. Ducks, geese and swans. Oxford University Press, Cambridge.

Kear, J., and A. J. Berger. 1980. The Hawaiian Goose: an experiment in conservation. Buteo Books, Vermillion, South Dakota.

Kear, J., and R. J. Scarlett. 1970. The Auckland Islands Merganser. Wildfowl 21:78–86.

Kear, J., and G. Williams. 1978. Waterfowl at risk. Wildfowl 29:5–21.

Kennedy, M., and H. G. Spencer. 2000. Phylogeny, biogeography, and taxonomy of Australasian teals. Auk 117:154–163.

Kessler, L. G., and J. C. Avise. 1984. Systematic relationships among waterfowl (Anatidae) inferred from restriction endonuclease analysis of mitochondrial DNA. Systematic Zoology 33:370–380.

King, W. B., (compiler.). 1981. Endangered birds of the world, the ICBP Bird Red Data Book. Smithsonian Institution Press, Washington, D.C.

Kingsford, R. T., P. S. Wong, L. W. Braithwaite, M. T. Maher. 1999. Waterbird abundance in eastern Australia, 1983–92. Wildlife Research 26:351–366.

Kitto, G. B., and A. C. Wilson. 1966. Evolution of malate dehydrogenase in birds. Science 153:1408–1410.

Kortright, F. H. 1942. The ducks, geese & swans of North America. The Stackpole Company, Harrisburg, Pennsylvania.

Kulikova, I. V., Y. N. Zhuravelev, and K. G. McCracken. 2004. Asymmetric hybridization and sex-biased gene flow between Eastern Spot-billed Ducks (*Anas zonorhyncha*) and Mallards (*A. platyrhynchos*) in the Russian Far East. Auk 121:930–949.

Lambrecht, K. 1931. *Cygnopterus* und *Cygnavus*, zwei fossile Schwäne aus dem Tertiär Europas. Bulletin du Musée Royal d'Histoire Naturelle de Belgique 7:1–6

Lebedinsky, N. G. 1927. *Romainvillia stehlini* n. g. n. sp. canard eocène provenant des marnes blanches du basin de Paris. Memoires de la Société Paléontologique Suisse 47:1–8.

Li, Z. W. D., and T. Mundkur. 2003. Status overview and recommendations for conservation of the White-headed Duck *Oxyura leucocephala* in Central Asia. Wetlands International Global Series 15.

Livezey, B. C. 1986. A phylogenetic analysis of Recent anseriform genera using morphological characters. Auk 103:737–754.

Livezey, B. C. 1989. Phylogenetic relationships and incipient flightlessness in the extinct Auckland Islands Merganser. Wilson Bulletin 101:410–435.

Livezey, B. C. 1991. A phylogenetic analysis and classification of Recent dabbling ducks (Tribe Anatini) based on comparative morphology. Auk 108:471–507.

Livezey, B. C. 1995a. A phylogenetic analysis of whistling and white-backed ducks (Anatidae: Dendrocygninae) using morphological characters. Annals of Carnegie Museum 64:65–97.

Livezey, B. C. 1995b. Phylogeny and comparative ecology of stiff-tailed ducks (Anatidae: Oxyurini). Wilson Bulletin 107:214–234.

Livezey, B. C. 1995c. Phylogeny and evolutionary ecology of modern seaducks (Anatidae: Mergini). Condor 97:233–255.

Livezey, B. C. 1996a. A phylogenetic analysis of modern pochards (Anatidae: Aythyini). Auk 113:74–93.

Livezey, B. C. 1996b. A phylogenetic analysis of geese and swans (Anseriformes: Anserinae), including selected fossil species. Systematic Biology 45:415–450.

Livezey, B. C. 1996c. A phylogenetic reassessment of the Tadornine — Anatine divergence (Aves: Anseriformes: Anatidae). Annals of Carnegie Museum 65:27–88.

Livezey, B. C. 1997a. A phylogenetic classification of waterfowl (Aves: Anseriformes), including selected fossil species. Annals of the Carnegie Museum 66:457–496.

Livezey, B. C. 1997b. A phylogenetic analysis of modern sheldgeese and shelducks (Anatidae: Tadornini). Ibis 139:51–66.

Livezey, B. C. 1997c. A phylogenetic analysis of basal Anseriformes, the fossil *Presbyornis*, and the interordinal relationships of waterfowl. Zoological Journal of the Linnean Society 121:361–428.

Livezey, B. C. 1998. A phylogenetic analysis of the Gruiformes (Aves) based on morphological characters, with emphasis on the rails (Rallidae). Philosophical Transactions of the Royal Society of London (Series B) 353:2077–2151.

Livezey, B. C., and P. S. Humphrey. 1983. Mechanics of steaming in steamer-ducks. Auk 100:485–488.

Livezey, B. C., and P. S. Humphrey. 1984. Sexual dimorphism in continental steamer-ducks. Condor 86:368–377.

Livezey, B. C., and P. S. Humphrey. 1985. Territoriality and interspecific aggression in steamer-ducks. Condor 87:154–157.

Livezey, B. C., and P. S. Humphrey. 1986. Flightlessness in steamer-ducks (Anatidae: *Tachyeres*): its morphological bases and probable evolution. Evolution 40:540–558.

Livezey, B. C., and P. S. Humphrey. 1992. Taxonomy and identification of steamer-ducks (Anatidae: *Tachyeres*). University of Kansas Museum of Natural History Monograph 8.

Livezey, B. C., and L. D. Martin. 1988. The systematic position of the Miocene anatid *Anas* [?] *blanchardi* Milne-Edwards. Journal of Vertebrate Paleontology 8:196–211.

Livezey, B. C., and R. L. Zusi. 2001. Higher-order phylogenetics of modern Aves based on comparative anatomy. Netherlands Journal of Zoology 51:179–205.

Lorenz, K. Z. 1951–53. Comparative studies on the behavior of the Anatinae. Avicultural Magazine 57:157–182; 58:8–17, 61–72, 86–94, 172–184; 59:24–34, 80–91.

Lorenz, K. Z. 1957. The role of aggression in group formation. Pages 181–252 *in* B. Schaffner, editor. Group processes: transactions of the fourth conference. Josiah Macy Jr. Foundation, New York.

Low, J. B. 1941. Nesting of the Ruddy Duck in Iowa. Auk 58:506–517.

Low, J. B. 1945. Ecology and management of the Redhead, *Nyroca americana*, in Iowa. Ecological Monographs 15:35–69.

Lowe, V. T. 1966. Notes on the Musk-Duck *Biziura lobata*. Emu 65:279–290.

Lyon, B. E., and J. M. Eadie. 2004. An obligate brood parasite trapped in the intraspecific arms race of its hosts. Nature 432:390–393.

Madge, S., and H. Burn. 1988. Waterfowl: an identification guide to the ducks, geese and swans of the world. Houghton Mifflin, Boston.

Madsen, C. S., K. P. McHugh, and S. deKloet. 1988. A partial classification of waterfowl (Anatidae) based on single-copy DNA. Auk 105:452–459.

Marchant, S., and P. J. Higgins. 1990. *Cereopsis novaehollandiae*. Cape Barren Goose. Pages 1194–1200 *in* Handbook of Australian, New Zealand & Antarctic birds. Volume 1b. Oxford University Press, Melbourne.

Mayr, E. 1945. Systematics and the origin of species from the viewpoint of a zoologist. Columbia University Press, New York.

Mayr, E. 1951. Speciation in birds. Progress report on the years 1938–1950. International Ornithological Congress 10:91–131.

Mayr, E. 1970. Populations, species and evolution: an abridgment of animal species and evolution. Belknap Press, Cambridge, Massachusetts.

Mayr, E. 1986. In memoriam: Jean (Theodore) Delacour. Auk 103:603–605.

Mazourek, J. C., and P. N. Gray. 1994. The Florida Duck or the Mallard. Florida Wildlife 48:29–31.

McCraken, K. G., D. C. Paton, and A. D. Afton. 2000a. Sexual dimorphism of the Musk Duck. Wilson Bulletin 112:457–466.

McCraken, K. G., A. D. Afton, and D. C. Paton. 2000b. Nests and eggs of Musk Ducks (*Biziura lobata*) at Murray Lagoon, Cape Gantheaume Conservation Park, Kangaroo Island, South Australia. South Australian Ornithologist 33:65–70.

McKinney, F. 1953. Studies on the behaviour of the Anatidae. Dissertation, University of Bristol, Bristol, United Kingdom.

McKnight, D. E. 1974. Dry-land nesting by Redheads and Ruddy Ducks. Journal of Wildlife Management 38:112–119.

McKnight, D. E., and I. O. Buss. 1962. Evidence of breeding in yearling female Lesser Scaup. Journal of Wildlife Management 26:328–329.

McLandress, M. R. 1979. Status of Ross' Goose in California. Pages 255-265 *in* R. L. Jarvis and J. C. Bartonek, editors. Management and biology of Pacific Flyway geese. OSU Book Stores, Corvallis, Oregon.

Meanley, B., and A. G. Meanley. 1958. Post-copulatory display in Fulvous and Black-bellied Tree Ducks. Auk 75:96.

Millener, P. R. 1999. The history of the Chatham Islands bird fauna of the last 7000 years — a chronicle of change and extinction. Smithsonian Contributions to Paleobiology 89:85–109.

Miller, A. H., and L. V. Compton. 1939. Two fossil birds from the Lower Miocene of South Dakota. Condor 41:153–156.

Miller, M. 1983. Foraging dives by post-breeding Northern Pintails. Wilson Bulletin 95:294–296.

Moffett, G. M., Jr. 1970. A study of nesting Torrent Ducks in the Andes. Living Bird 9:4–27.

Morcombe, M. 2000. Field guide to Australian birds. Steve Parish Publishing, Archerfield, Queensland, Australia.

Moser, T. J. 2001. The status of Ross' Geese. Arctic Goose Joint Venture, special publication. U.S. Fish and Wildlife Service, Washington, D.C., and Canadian Wildlife Service, Ottawa.

Moser, T. J., and D. C. Duncan. 2001. Harvest of Ross' Geese. Pages 43–54 *in* T. J. Moser, editor. The status of Ross' Geese. Arctic Goose Joint Venture, special publication. U.S. Fish and Wildlife Service, Washington, D.C., and Canadian Wildlife Service, Ottawa.

Moulton, D. W., and M. W. Weller. 1984. Biology and conservation of the Laysan Duck (*Anas laysanensis*). Condor 86:105–117.

Moynihan, M. 1958. Notes on the behavior of the Flying Steamer-Duck. Auk 75:183–202.

Munoz, V., A. J. Green, J. J. Negro, and M. D. Sorenson. 2003. Population genetics of White-headed Ducks and North American Ruddy Ducks. Threatened Waterfowl Specialist Group News 14:55–58.

Naranjo, L. 1986. Aspects of the biology of the Horned Screamer in southwestern Colombia. Wilson Bulletin 98:243–256.

Nuechterlein, G. L., and R. W. Storer. 1985. Aggressive behavior and interspecific killing by Flying Steamer-Ducks in Argentina. Condor 87:87–91.

Nugent, R. 1991. The search for the Pink-headed Duck. Houghton Mifflin, Boston.

Olson, S. L. 1982. A critique of Cracraft's classification of birds. Auk 99:733–739.

Olson, S. L., and A. Feduccia 1980. *Presbyornis* and the origin of the Anseriformes (Aves: Charadriomorphae). Smithsonian Contributions to Zoology 323.

Olson, S. L., and H. F. James. 1982. Fossil birds from the Hawaiian Islands: evidence for wholesale extinction by man before western contact. Science 217:633–635.

Olson, S. L., and H. F. James. 1984. The role of the Polynesians in the extinction of the avifauna of the Hawaiian Islands. Pages 768-780 *in* P. S. Martin and R. G. Klein, editors. Quaternary extinctions: a prehistoric revolution. University of Arizona Press, Tucson.

Olson, S. L., and H. F. James. 1991. Descriptions of thirty-two species of birds from the Hawaiian Islands: Part I. Non-passeriforms. Ornithological Monographs 45.

Olson, S. L., and P. Jouventin. 1996. A new species of flightless duck from Amsterdam Island, southern Indian Ocean (Anatidae: *Anas*). Condor 98: 1–9.

Palmer, R. S. 1972. Patterns of molting. Avian biology 2:65–102.

Palmer, R. S., editor. 1976. Handbook of North American birds. Volume 2. Yale University Press, New Haven, Connecticut.

Partridge, W. H. 1956. Notes on the Brazilian Merganser in Argentina. Auk 73:473–488.

Patterson, I. J. 1982. The Shelduck: a study in behavioural ecology. Cambridge University Press, Cambridge.

Paxinos, E. E., H. F. James, S. L. Olson, M. D. Sorenson, J. Jackson, and R. C. Fleischer. 2002. mtDNA from fossils reveals a radiation of Hawaiian geese recently derived from a Canada Goose (*Branta canadensis*). Proceedings of the National Academy of Sciences of the United States of America 99:1399–1404.

Pearce, J. M., B. J. Pierson, S. L. Talbot, D. V. Derksen, D. Kraege, and K. T. Scribner. 2000. A genetic evaluation of morphology used to identify harvested Canada Geese. Journal of Wildlife Management 64:863–874.

Pearce, J. M., S. L. Talbot, B. J. Pierson, M. R. Petersen, K. T. Scribner, D. L. Dickson, and A. Mosbech. 2004. Lack of spatial genetic structure among nesting and wintering King Eiders. Condor 106:229–240.

Peters, J. L. 1931. Check-list of birds of the world. Volume 1. Harvard University Press, Cambridge, Massachusetts.

Phillips, J. C. 1922–26. A natural history of the ducks. Volumes 1–4. Houghton Mifflin, Boston. (Reprinted by Dover Publications).

Pierson, B. J., J. M. Pearce, and S. L. Talbot. 2000. Molecular genetic status of Aleutian Canada Geese from Buldir and Semidi Islands, Alaska. Condor 102:172–180.

Prager, E. M., and A. C. Wilson. 1976. Congruency of phylogenies derived from different proteins. Journal of Molecular Evolution 9:45–47.

Prager, E. M., and A. C. Wilson. 1980. Phylogenetic relationships and rates of evolution in birds. International Ornithological Congress 17:1209–1214.

Prestwich, A. A. 1974. The Pink-headed Duck (*Rhodonessa caryophyllacea*) in the wild and in captivity. Avicultural Magazine 80:47–52.

Raikow, R. J. 1971. The osteology and taxonomic position of the White-backed Duck, *Thalassornis leuconotus*. Wilson Bulletin 83:270–277.

Raveling, D. G. 1970. Dominance relationships and agonistic behavior of Canada Geese in winter. Behaviour 37:291–319.

Raveling, D. G. 1978. Dynamics of distribution of Canada Geese in winter. Transactions of the North American Wildlife and Natural Resources Conference 43:206–225.

Raveling, D. G. 1979. Traditional use of migration and winter roost sites by Canada Geese. Journal of Wildlife Management 43:229–235.

Raveling, D. G., and C. C. Dixon. 1981. Distribution and harvest of Canada geese (*Branta canadensis*) in southern Manitoba prior to development of Oak Hammock Marsh. Canadian Field-Naturalist 95:276–280.

Rees, E. C., and N. Hillgarth. 1984. The breeding biology of captive Black-headed Ducks and the behavior of their young. Condor 86:242–250.

Reichel, J. D., and T. O. Lemke. 1994. Ecology and extinction of the Mariana Mallard. Journal of Wildlife Management 58:199–205.

Reynolds, M. H. 2000. Rescuing island castaways. Endangered Species Bulletin 25:8–9.

Reynolds, M. H. 2004. Habitat use and home range - of the Laysan Teal on Laysan Island, Hawaii. Waterbirds 27:183–192.

Rhymer, J. M. 2001. Evolutionary relationships and conservation of Hawaiian anatids. Studies in Avian Biology 22:61–67.

Rhymer, J. M., and D. Simberloff. 1996. Extinction by hybridization and introgression. Annual Review of Ecology and Systematics 27:83–109.

Rhymer, J. M., M. J. Williams, and M. J. Braun. 1994. Mitochondrial analyses of gene flow between New Zealand Mallards (*Anas platyrhynchos*) and Grey Ducks (*A. superciliosa*). Auk 111:970–978.

Riggert, T. L. 1977. The biology of the Mountain Duck on Rottnest Island, Western Australia. Wildlife Monographs 52.

Ripley, S. D. 1951. Remarks on the Philippine Mallard. Wilson Bulletin 63:181–191.

Rogers, J. P., and J. H. Patterson. 1984. The Black Duck population and its management. Transactions of the North American Wildlife and Natural Resources Conference 49:527–534.

Ryder, J. P., and R. T. Alisauskas. 1995. Ross' Goose (*Chen rossii*). The birds of North America, 162. The American Ornithologists' Union, Washington, D.C., and The Academy of Natural Sciences, Philadelphia.

Rylander, M. K., E. G. Bolen, and R. E. McCamant. 1980. Evidence of incubation patches in whistling-ducks. Southwestern Naturalist 25:126-128.

Salvadori, T. 1895. Catalogue of the Chenomorphae (Palamedeae, Phoenicopteri, Anseres), Crypturi and Ratitae in the collection of the British Museum. Longmans, London.

Savard, J-P. L. 1985. Evidence of long-term pair bonds in Barrow's Goldeneye (*Bucephala islandica*). Auk 102:389–391.

Scherer, S., and T. Hilsberg. 1982. Hybridisierung und Verwandtschaftsgrade innerhalb der Anatidae — eine systematische und evolutionstheoretische Betrachtung. Journal für Ornithologie 123:357–380.

Schuh, R. T. 2000. Biological systematics: principles and applications. Cornell University Press, Ithaca, New York.

Sclater, P. L. 1880. List of the certainly known species of Anatidae, with notes on such as have been introduced into the zoological gardens of Europe, and remarks on their distribution. Proceedings of the Zoological Society of London, 1880: 496–536.

Scott, N. J., Jr., and R. P. Reynolds. 1984. Phenotypic variation of the Mexican Duck (*Anas platyrhynchos diazi*) in Mexico. Condor 86:266–274.

Scott, P. 1972. The swans. Houghton Mifflin, Boston.

Scribner, K. T., R. A. Malecki, B. D. J. Batt, R. L. Inman, S. Libants, and H. H. Prince. 2003. Identification of source population for Greenland Canada Geese: genetic assessment of a recent colonization. Condor 105:771–782.

Scribner, K. T., M. R. Petersen, R. L. Fields, S. L. Talbot, J. M. Pearce, and R. K. Chesser. 2001. Sex-biased gene flow in Spectacled Eiders (*Somateria fischeri*): influences from molecular markers with contrasting modes of inheritance. Evolution 55:2105–2115.

Shields, G. F., and A. C. Wilson. 1987. Calibration of mitochondrial DNA evolution in geese. Journal of Molecular Evolution 24:212–217.

Sibley, C. G. 1960. The electrophoretic patterns of avian egg-white proteins as taxonomic characters. Ibis 102:215–284.

Sibley, C. G., and J. E. Ahlquist. 1972. A comparative study of the egg-white proteins of non-passerine birds. Peabody Museum of Natural History, Yale University Bulletin 39.

Sibley, C. G., and J. E. Ahlquist. 1990. Phylogeny and classification of birds: a study in molecular evolution. Yale University Press, New Haven, Connecticut.

Sibley, C. G., K. W. Corbin, and J. H. Haavie. 1969. The relationships of the flamingos as indicated by the egg-white proteins and hemoglobins. Condor 71:155–179.

Siegfried, W. R. 1970. Double wing-moult in the Maccoa Duck. Wildfowl 21:122.

Siegfried, W. R. 1976. Sex ratio in the Cape Shelduck. Ostrich 47:113–116.

Soothill, E., and P. Whitehead. 1978. Wildfowl of the world. Blandford Press, Poole, Dorset, United Kingdom.

Sorenson, M. D., A. Cooper, E. E. Paxinos, T. W. Quinn, H. F. James, S. L. Olson, and R. C. Fleischer. 1999. Relationships of the extinct moanalos, flightless Hawaiian waterfowl, based on ancient DNA. Proceedings of the Royal Society of London (B): 266:2187–2193.

Steadman, D. W. 1995. Prehistoric extinctions of Pacific island birds: biodiversity meets zooarchaeology. Science 267:1123–1131.

Stonor, C. R. 1939. Notes on the breeding habits of the Common Screamer (*Chauna torquata*). Ibis 14:45–49.

Stotts, V. D. 1958. The time of formation of pairs in Black Ducks. Transactions of the North American Wildlife Conference 23:192–197.

Stotts, V. D., and D. E. Davis. 1960. The Black Duck in the Chesapeake Bay of Maryland: breeding behavior and biology. Chesapeake Science 1:127–154.

Talbot, S. L., J. M. Pearce, B. J. Pierson, D. V. Derksen, and K. T. Scribner. 2003. Molecular status of the Dusky Canada Goose (*Branta canadensis occidentalis*): a genetic assessment of translocation effort. Conservation Genetics 4:367–381.

Thompson, J. E., M. R. J. Hill, M. T. Merendino, and C. D. Ankney. 1999. Improving use of morphometric discrimination to identify Canada Goose subspecies. Wildlife Society Bulletin 27:274–280.

Thomson, G. M. 1922. The naturalization of animals and plants in New Zealand. Cambridge University Press, Cambridge.

Timmermann, G. 1963. Fragen der Anatidensystematik in parasitologischer Sicht. International Ornithological Congress 13:189–197.

Todd, F. S. 1996. Natural history of the waterfowl. Ibis Publishing, Vista, California.

Torres, J. 2003. White-headed Ducks in Spain in 2002. Threatened Waterfowl Specialist Group News 14:62–63.

Trauger, D. L. 1971. Population ecology of Lesser Scaup *Aythya affinis* in subarctic taiga. Dissertation, Iowa State University, Ames.

Trauger, D. L., A. Dzubin, and J. P. Ryder. 1971. White geese intermediate between Ross' Geese and Lesser Snow Geese. Auk 88:856–875.

Triggs, S., M. Williams, S. Marshall, and G. Chambers. 1991. Genetic relationships within a population of Blue Duck *Hymenolaimus malacorhynchos*.

Tucker, G. M., and M. F. Heath. 1994. Birds in Europe: their conservation status. Birdlife Conservation Series 3. Birdlife International, Cambridge.

U.S. Fish and Wildlife Service. 2003. Waterfowl population status, 2003. U.S. Department of Interior, Washington, D.C.

Van Wagner, C. E., and A. J. Baker. 1986. Genetic differentiation in populations of Canada Geese (*Branta canadensis*). Canadian Journal of Zoology 64:940–947.

Van Wagner, C. E., and A. J. Baker. 1990. Association between mitochondrial DNA and morphological evolution in Canada Geese. Journal of Molecular Evolution 31:373–382.

Weckstein, J. D., A. D. Afton, R. M. Zink, and R. T. Alisauskas. 2002. Hybridization and population subdivision within and between Ross's Geese and Lesser Snow Geese: a molecular perspective. Condor 104:432–436.

Weller, M. W. 1964a. Distribution and species relationships. Pages 108–120 *in* J. Delacour, editor. The waterfowl of the world. Volume 4. Country Life, London.

Weller, M. W. 1964b. Distribution and migration of the Redhead. Journal of Wildlife Management 28:64–103.

Weller, M. W. 1968a. The breeding biology of the parasitic Black-headed Duck. Living Bird 7:169–207.

Weller, M. W. 1968b. Notes on some Argentine anatids. Wilson Bulletin 80:189–212.

Weller, M. W. 1968c. Plumages and wing spurs of Torrent Ducks *Merganetta armata*. Wildfowl 19:33–40.

Weller, M. W. 1976. Ecology and behaviour of steamer ducks. Wildfowl 27:45–53.

Weller, M. W. 1980a. The island waterfowl. Iowa State University Press, Ames.

Weller, M. W. 1980b. Molts and plumages of waterfowl. Pages 34–38 *in* F. C. Bellrose. Ducks, geese and swans of North America. Stackpole Books, Harrisburg, Pennsylvania.

Wetmore, A. 1938. A fossil duck from the Eocene of Utah. Journal of Paleontology 12:280–283.

Wiens, J. J., and D. M. Hillis. 1996. Accuracy of parsimony analysis using morphological data: a reappraisal. Systematic Botany 21:237–243.

Wiley, E. O. 1981. Phylogenetics. John Wiley & Sons, New York.

Williams, C. L., R. C. Brust, and O. E. Rhodes, Jr. 2002. Microsatellite polymorphism and genetic structure of Florida Mottled Duck populations. Condor 104:424–431.

Williams, M. 1981. The duckshooter's bag. Wetland Press, Wellington, New Zealand.

Williams, M. 1991. Social and demographic characteristics of Blue Duck *Hymenolaimus malacorhynchos*. Wildfowl 42:65–86.

Williams, M., and C. J. R. Robertson. 1996. The Campbell Island Teal *Anas aucklandica nesiotis*: history and review. Wildfowl 47: 134–165.

Wilmé, L. 1994. Status, distribution and conservation of two Madagascar bird species endemic to Lake Alaotra: Delacour's Grebe *Tachybaptus rufolavatus* and Madagascar Pochard *Aythya innotata*. Biological Conservation 69:15–21.

Wilson, R. 1997. Temporal and spatial variation in the distribution and abundance of the Magpie Goose, *Anseranas semipalmata*, in the Rockhampton region of Queensland. Wildlife Research 24:347–357.

Woolfenden, G. E. 1961. Postcranial osteology of the waterfowl. Bulletin of the Florida State Museum 6.

Worthy, T. H., and R. N. Holdaway. 2002. The lost world of the moa: prehistoric life of New Zealand. Indiana University Press, Bloomington.

Wright, J. K. 1965. Observations of behavior of the Andean Torrent Duck. Condor 67:535.

Yamashina, Y. 1952. Classification of the Anatidae based on cytogenetics. Papers from the Coordinating Committee, Research Genetics 3:1–24.

Young, H. G., and J. M. Rhymer. 1998. Meller's Duck: a threatened species receives recognition at last. Biodiversity and Conservation 7:1313–1323.

Young, H. G., M. D. Sorenson, and K. P. Johnson. 1997. A description of the Madagascar Teal *Anas bernieri* and an examination of its relationships with the Grey Teal *A. gracilis*. Wildfowl 48:174–180.

Zusi, R. L., and B. C. Livezey. 2000. Homology and phylogenetic implications of some enigmatic cranial features in Galliform and Anseriform birds. Annals of Carnegie Museum 69:157–193.

Zweers, G. A., F. deJong, and H. Berkhoudt. 1995. Filter feeding in Flamingos (*Phoenicopterus ruber*). Condor 97:297–324.

APPENDIX A
RECENT CLASSIFICATION OF THE ANSERIFORMES[a]

Family **Anhimidae** — **Screamers**
    Anhima cornuta — Horned Screamer
    Chauna chavaria — Northern Crested Screamer
    Chauna torquata — Southern Crested Screamer

Family **Anseranatidae**
    Anseranas semipalmata — Magpie Goose

†Family **Presbyornithidae**[b]
    Presbyornis pervetus

†Family **Cnemiornithidae**
    Cnemiornis calcitrans — South Island Goose
    Cnemiornis gracilis — North Island Goose

Family **Anatidae** — **Typical Waterfowl (Ducks, Geese, and Swans)**
  Subfamily   **Dendrocygninae** — **Whistling-Ducks and Allies**
    Tribe **Dendrocygnini**
        Dendrocygna viduata — White-faced Whistling-Duck
        Dendrocygna autumnalis — Black-bellied Whistling-Duck
        Dendrocygna guttata — Spotted Whistling-Duck
        Dendrocygna arborea — West Indian Whistling-Duck
        Dendrocygna bicolor — Fulvous Whistling-Duck
        Dendrocygna eytoni — Plumed Whistling-Duck
        Dendrocygna arcuata — Wandering Whistling-Duck
        Dendrocygna javanica — Lesser Whistling-Duck
    Tribe **Thalassornithini**
        Thalassornis leuconotus — White-backed Duck
  Subfamily **Anserinae** — **Geese and Swans**
    Tribe **Cereopsini**
        Cereopsis novaehollandiae — Cape Barren Goose
    Tribe **Anserini** — **True Geese**
        Anser cygnoides — Swan Goose
        Anser fabalis — Bean Goose (partition is provisional)
          Anser (f.) fabilis[c] — Taiga Bean Goose
          Anser (f.) serrirostris — Tundra Bean Goose
        Anser brachyrhynchus — Pink-footed Goose
        Anser anser — Greylag Goose
          Anser (a.) anser — Western Greylag Goose
          Anser (a.) rubrirostris — Eastern Greylag Goose
        Anser albifrons — Greater White-fronted Goose
          (includes *frontalis*, the Pacific White-fronted Goose
          and *elgasi*, the Tule White-fronted Goose and
          flavirostris, the Greenland While-fronted Goose)
        Anser erythropus — Lesser White Fronted Goose
        Anser indicus — Bar-headed Goose
        Anser (Chen) canagicus — Emperor Goose
        Anser (Chen) caerulescens — (Lesser) Snow Goose
          (includes *atlanticus*, the Greater Snow Goose)
        Anser (Chen) rossi — Ross's Goose

Branta canadensis	Canada Goose
Branta (c.) canadensis	Atlantic Canada Goose
(includes *interior*, the Interior Canada Goose)	
Branta (c.) moffitti	Giant and Great Basin Canada Goose
(includes *maxima*)	
Branta (c.) leucopareia	Aleutian Canada Goose
(includes *asiatica*, the Bering Canada Goose)	
Branta (c.) hutchinsii	Lesser Canada Goose
(includes *parvipes*)	
Branta (c.) occidentalis	Dusky Canada Goose
(includes *fulva*, the Vancouver Canada Goose)	
Branta (c.) minima	Cackling Canada Goose
(includes *taverneri*)	
†*Branta hylobadistes*	Greater Nene (Nene-nui)
Branta sandvicensis	Lesser Nene (Hawaiian Goose)
Branta bernicla	Dark-bellied (Black) Brant
Branta hrota	Pale-bellied (Atlantic) Brant
Branta leucopsis	Barnacle Goose
Branta ruficollis	Red-breasted Goose

Tribe **Cygnini — Swans**

Coscoroba coscoroba	Coscoroba Swan
Cygnus atratus	Black Swan
†*Cygnus sumnerensis*	New Zealand Swan (provisional placement)
Cygnus melancoryphus	Black-necked Swan
Cygnus olor	Mute Swan
Cygnus buccinator	Trumpeter Swan
Cygnus columbianus	Whistling (Tundra) Swan
Cygnus bewickii	Bewick's Swan
Cygnus cygnus	Whooper Swan

†Tribe **Thambetochenini — Moa-nalos** (position of tribe provisional)

Chelychelynechen quassus	Turtle-billed Moa-nalo (Large Kauai Goose)
Ptaiochen pau	Short-billed Moa-nalo
Thambetochen chauliodus	Greater Moa-nalo
Thambetochen xanion	Oahu Moa-nalo

Subfamily **Stictonettinae**

Stictonetta naevosa	Freckled Duck

Subfamily **Tadorninae — Shelducks and Allies**

Tribe **Merganettini — Torrent Ducks and Allies**

Hymenolaimus malacorhynchos	Blue Duck
Tachyeres patachonicus	Flying Steamer-Duck
Tachyeres pteneres	Magellanic Flightless Steamer-Duck
Tachyeres brachypterus	Falkland Flightless Steamer-Duck
Tachyeres leucocephalus	White-headed Flightless Steamer-Duck
Merganetta armata	Torrent Duck
Merganetta (a.) armata	Southern Torrent-Duck
Merganetta (a.) turneri	Turner's Torrent-Duck
Merganetta (a.) garleppi	Bolivian Torrent-Duck
Merganetta (a.) leucogenis	Peruvian Torrent Duck
Merganetta (a.) colombiana	Columbian Torrent-Duck

Tribe **Plectropterini — Pied Shelducks**

Plectropterus gambensis	Spur-winged Goose
Sarkidiornis melanotos	Gray-sided Comb Duck

Sarkidiornis sylvicola	Black-sided Comb Duck

Tribe **Tadornini — True Shelducks and Sheldgeese**

Cyanochen cyanopterus	Blue-winged Sheldgoose
Alopochen aegyptiacus	African (Egyptian) Sheldgoose
†*Alopochen mauritianus*	Mauritius Sheldgoose
Neochen jubata	Orinoco Sheldgoose
Chloephaga melanoptera	Andean Sheldgoose
Chloephaga picta	Upland Sheldgoose
Chloephaga hybrida	Kelp Sheldgoose
Chloephaga poliocephalus	Ashy-headed Sheldgoose
Chloephaga rubidiceps	Ruddy-headed Sheldgoose
†*Pachyanas chathamica*	Chatham Island Shelduck
Tadorna tadorna	Red-billed (Common) Shelduck
Tadorna radjah	Radjah Shelduck
Casarca ferruginea	Ruddy Shelduck
Casarca cana	Cape Shelduck
Casarca tadornoides	Australian Shelduck
Casarca variegata	Paradise (New Zealand) Shelduck
Casarca cristata	Crested Shelduck (probably extinct)

Subfamily **Anatinae — True Ducks**

Tribe **Malacorhynchini**

Malacorhynchus membranaceous	Australian Pink-eared Duck (Pink-eared Duck)
Salvadorina waigiuensis	Salvadori's Duck

Tribe **Anatini — Surface-feeding Ducks (Dabbling Ducks)**

Cairina moschata	Muscovy Duck
Cairina scutulata	White-winged Duck
Pteronetta hartlaubi	Hartlaub's Duck
Aix sponsa	American Wood Duck (Wood Duck)
Aix galericulata	Mandarin Duck
Chenonetta jubata	Maned Duck
Nettapus auritus	African Pygmy-Goose
Nettapus coromandelianus	Cotton Pygmy-Goose
Nettapus pulchellus	Green Pygmy-Goose
Amazonetta brasiliensis	Brazilian Teal
Callonetta leucophrys	Ringed Teal
Lophonetta specularioides	Crested Duck
Speculanas specularis	Bronze-winged Duck
†*Anas theodori*	Mauritius Duck
†*Anas marecula*	Amsterdam Island Duck
Mareca capensis	Cape Teal
Mareca (Anas) strepera	Common Gadwall (Gadwall)
†*Mareca couesi*	Washington Island (Coues') Gadwall (provisional)
Mareca falcata	Falcated Duck
Mareca sibilatrix	Chiloé Wigeon
Mareca (Anas) penelope	Eurasian Wigeon
Mareca (Anas) americana	American Wigeon
Anas sparsa	African Black Duck
Anas rubripes	American Black Duck
Anas platyrhynchos	Mallard
(includes *conboschas*, the Greenland Mallard)	
Anas fulvigula	Mottled Duck
Anas diazi	Mexican Duck
Anas wyvilliana	Hawaiian Duck

Anas laysanensis	Laysan Duck
†*Anas oustaleti*	Marianas Duck (possibly a hybrid)
Anas luzonica	Philippine Duck
Anas superciliosa	Pacific Gray Duck (Gray Duck)
(includes *pelewensis* and rogersi)	
Anas poecilorhyncha	Indonesian Spot-billed Duck
Anas zonorhyncha	Chinese Spot-billed Duck
Anas undulata	Yellow-billed Duck
Anas melleri	Meller's Duck
Anas discors	Blue-winged Teal
Anas cyanoptera	Cinnamon Teal
Anas smithii	Cape Shoveler
Anas platalea	Red Shoveler
Anas rhynchotis	Australasian Shoveler
Anas clypeata	Northern Shoveler
Anas bernieri	Madagascan Teal
Anas gibberifrons	Indonesian Gray Teal
Anas gracilis	Australasian Gray Teal (Gray Teal)
(includes *remissa*, the †Rennell Island Teal)	
Anas albogularis	Andaman Teal
Anas castanea	Chestnut Teal
Anas chlorotis	Brown Teal
Anas aucklandica	Auckland Islands Teal
Anas nesiotis	Campbell Island Teal
Anas bahamensis	White-cheeked Pintail
Anas erythrorhyncha	Red-billed Pintail
Anas flavirostris	Yellow-billed (Speckled) Teal
Anas andium	Andean Teal
Anas georgica	Brown Pintail
Anas acuta	Northern Pintail
Anas eatoni	Eaton's Pintail
Anas querquedula	Garganey Teal (Garganey)
Anas formosa	Baikal Teal
Anas crecca	Eurasian Green-winged Teal
Anas carolinensis	American Green-winged Teal (Green-winged Teal)
Anas versicolor	Silver Teal
Anas puna	Puna Teal
Anas hottentota	Hottentot Teal

Tribe **Aythini — Pochards (Diving Ducks)**

Marmaronetta angustirostris	Marbled Duck
Netta rufina	Red-crested Pochard
Netta (Rhodonessa) caryophyllacea	Pink-headed (Duck) Pochard (probably extinct)
Metopiana peposaca	Rosy-billed Pochard
Metopiana erythrophthalma	Southern Pochard
Aristonetta (Aythya) valisineria	Canvasback
Aristonetta (Aythya) americana	Redhead
Aristonetta (Aythya) ferina	Eurasian (Common) Pochard
Aythya australis	Australian White-eyed Pochard
Aythya innotata	Madagascan White-eyed Pochard
Aythya nyroca	Ferruginous White-eyed Pochard
Aythya baeri	Siberian White-eyed Pochard (Baer's Pochard)
Aythya novaeseelandiae	New Zealand Scaup

Aythya collaris	Ring-necked Duck
Aythya fuligula	Tufted Scaup (Tufted Duck)
Aythya marila	Greater Scaup
Aythya affinis	Lesser Scaup

Tribe Mergini — Sea Ducks

Polysticta stelleri	Steller's Eider
Somateria fischeri	Spectacled Eider
Somateria spectabilis	King Eider
Somateria mollissima	Common Eider
Somateria (m.) v-nigrum	Pacific Eider
Somateria (m.) borealis	Northern Eider
Somateria (m.) dresseri	Canada Eider
(includes *sedentaria*)	
Somateria (m.) mollissima	European Eider
(includes *islandica*)	
Histrionicus histrionicus	Harlequin Duck
†*Camptorhynchus labradorius*	Labrador Duck (extinct 1875)
Melanitta perspicillata	Surf Scoter
Melanitta fusca	Velvet Scoter
Melanitta deglandi	White-winged Scoter
Melanitta nigra	Eurasian Black Scoter
Melanitta americana	American Black Scoter (Black Scoter)
Clangula hyemalis	Long-tailed Duck (Oldsquaw)
Bucephala albeola	Bufflehead
Bucephala clangula	Common Goldeneye
Bucephala islandica	Barrow's Goldeneye
Mergellus albellus	Smew
Lophodytes cucullatus	Hooded Merganser
†*Mergus australis*	Auckland Island Merganser (extinct 1902)
Mergus octosetaceus	Brazilian Merganser
Mergus merganser	Common Merganser
Mergus serrator	Red-breasted Merganser
Mergus squamatus	Chinese (Scaly-sided) Merganser

Tribe Oxyurini — Stiff-tailed Ducks

Heteronetta atricapilla	Black-headed Duck
Nomonyx dominicus	Masked Duck
Oxyura jamaicensis	Northern Ruddy Duck (Ruddy Duck)
Oxyura ferruginea	Peruvian Ruddy Duck
(includes *andina*, the Columbian Ruddy Duck)	
Oxyura vittata	Argentine Blue-billed (Ruddy) Duck
Oxyura australis	Australian Blue-billed Duck
Oxyura maccoa	Maccoa Duck
Oxyura leucocephala	White-headed Duck
Biziura lobata	Musk Duck

---

[a]Sequence, nomenclature, and common names follow Livezey (1997a). Common names in parentheses follow the American Ornithologists' Union (AOU) Checklist, 6th Edition (1983), or are otherwise in wide use and are the common names used throughout the text. Genus names in parentheses follow the AOU checklist. Finsch's Duck (*Euryanas finshi*) was not included in Livezey (1997a) but was treated in an earlier publication (Livezey 1989).

[b]† Denotes an extinct or fossil taxa.

[c]Scientific names containing a single letter in parentheses denote potential species as identified by Livezey (1997a).

Chapter 3
COURTSHIP BEHAVIOR, MATING SYSTEMS, AND PAIR-BOND FORMATION

Reproduction is a critical component of fitness wherein individuals seek to maximize their probability of leaving descendants. Reproduction obviously cannot proceed successfully unless the sexes unite and sperm are transferred, but this union is not easily accomplished; potential mates must be recognized, assessed, and chosen. Indeed, pair formation entails at least four complicated tasks for the individuals involved: (1) demonstrating interest in a particular individual, (2) attracting and holding that individual's attention, (3) establishing a pair bond, and (4) countering interference from rivals (McKinney 1992). Courtship behavior is the major signaling mechanism for accomplishing these tasks.

Courtship behaviors operate within the mating systems of monogamy, polygamy, and promiscuity, and variations therein, and each system entails costs and benefits for both males and females (see Alcock 2001). Ultimately, mate acquisition is affected primarily by (1) the availability and distribution of resources needed for breeding, and (2) the ability of an individual to control those resources (see Oring and Sayler 1992). The mating systems of waterfowl have resulted from the interaction of these factors.

There is, however, much variation within these mating systems as seen in the timing of pair-bond formation, which varies among species both interspecifically as well as intraspecifically (Rohwer and Anderson 1988). To illustrate an interspecific difference, Mallards and other dabbling ducks form pairs earlier than Ring-necked Ducks and other pochards (Weller 1965, 1967; Soutiere et al. 1972). Intraspecifically, older birds tend to establish pair bonds earlier than younger birds (McKinney 1965a, Cowardin et al. 1985, Hepp 1986), and those individuals that first acquire their Alternate (i.e., breeding) Plumage often are first to form pairs during a given breeding season (Weller 1965). Time and energy constraints related to physical condition also affect pairing chronology (Wishart 1983, Brodsky and Weatherhead 1985). In fact, because so many factors affect pair formation, several months may pass before all eligible birds in the population are paired.

Importantly, these spatial and temporal aspects of pair formation have meaningful management implications. In temperate areas, for example, paired males of both pochards and dabbling ducks establish regular "waiting areas," which are sites that males use while their females are laying or incubating eggs. By tallying these "waiting males" or "lone drakes," biologists gained an indirect measure of the size of the breeding population (Dzubin 1969). Brasher et al. (2002) later evaluated this technique by radiomarking paired and unpaired Mallards in prairie habitats in Manitoba. Paired males occurred with their mates 54–77% of the time and as lone males only 17–33% of the time, whereas unpaired males occurred alone or in small groups of two to four as much as 80% of the time. They concluded that tallies of waiting males could underestimate the spring breeding population by about 7%. Serie and Cowardin (1990) tallied pairs, unpaired single males, and groups of male Canvasbacks breeding in Manitoba. These observations then were used to calculate a "social index," which was highly correlated ($r^2 = 0.69$–0.93) with nest success.

In this chapter, we review the basic mating systems of waterfowl, factors affecting the evolution and operation of those systems, and the temporal patterns of pair formation. We also present the basic courtship displays of geese and ducks and discuss their context in the pair-formation process.

WATERFOWL MATING SYSTEMS

General Patterns

There are three major characteristics associated with the breeding of waterfowl that are uncommon among birds. First, although the mating system itself is primarily monogamous, ducklings and goslings are highly precocial, which should permit evolution of a polygynous mating system (see Lack 1968). Second, the pair formation process largely occurs away from breeding areas, often during fall and winter; among ducks in the Northern Hemisphere, these pair bonds only persist for one breeding season. Lastly, waterfowl apparently are the only group of birds where females are more philopatric (i.e., return to natal areas) than males (Rohwer and Anderson 1988). In this section, we discuss the factors leading to the evolution of these three uncommon traits of waterfowl as the basis for understanding their mating system, review the fitness benefits of monogamy, and compare and contrast seasonal with perennial monogamy.

Evolution of Monogamy and Aspects of Parental Care

Among the Anatidae, 93% of species are monogamous (Oring and Sayler 1992), which means that neither sex can monopolize more than one member of the opposite sex (Emlen and Oring 1977). Thus, one male usually mates with only one female during a given reproductive season, although there is an important distinction between social monogamy and actual genetic monogamy (see Alcock 2001). Monogamy is the dominant mating system in birds, occurring in more than 90% of all species (Lack 1968), and contrasts with two forms of polygamy: (1) polygyny, in which males control access to more than one female; and (2) polyandry, which is a much rarer mating system in which females control access to more than one male. Polygyny is uncommon in waterfowl and polyandry is unknown (Table 3-1).

However, although most waterfowl are monogamous, the reasons for the evolution of this mating system in waterfowl are different from those lending to monogamy in other avian taxa. First, except for the Magpie Goose, whistling-ducks, and the Black Swan, male waterfowl do not share incubation duties with their mates. Instead, as seen in all species of ducks in the Northern Hemisphere, the males abandon their females some time during the incubation period. Oring and Sayler (1992) argued that such female-biased parental care was the primary selection characteristic that affected the evolution of waterfowl mating systems. In the Southern Hemisphere, males of at least nine species of dabbling ducks do exhibit some parental care, but none incubate (Brewer 1989, Buitron and Nuechterlein 1989, McKinney and Brewer 1989, McKinney 1991, Sorenson 1991).

The pattern of parental care is different in the swans and geese (Anserinae) and the shelducks and sheldgeese (Tadornini), where males extensively participate in rearing the young, yet species in these groups also are primarily monogamous. However, male geese and swans (except the Black Swan) also do not incubate, although they do lead the brood and are the primary providers of vigilance and predator defense, as was well documented for the Pink-footed Goose in Iceland (Lazarus and Inglis 1978). Such shared parental care as seen here in geese and swans is the primitive condition among waterfowl (Kear 1970). Among ducks in the Northern Hemisphere, however, the pattern of parental care is quite clear: Only females incubate, and highly precocial young leave the nest and procure their own food within 24 hr after hatching; no males participate in brood rearing, and none participate in incubation. Males are thus emancipated from those duties whereby mating-system theory would otherwise predict that waterfowl should have evolved a polygynous mating system wherein males would be "free" to breed with more than one female. Polygyny is not the case, however, and only occurs in about 7% of waterfowl species (Oring and Sayler 1992). Hence, the first difference to highlight about the evolution of the monogamous mating system of waterfowl is the paradox that polygyny would be expected, not monogamy (Orians 1969, Rohwer and Anderson 1988, Oring and Sayler 1992).

In ducks, polygyny often cannot develop because each female requires the support of a male during critical segments of the annual cycle (e.g., egg production), whereby the attention of a single male cannot be shared among several females (McKinney 1986). Further, because pairing in ducks occurs during fall and winter and females are philopatric to breeding areas (see below), polygyny cannot develop, because males obviously cannot follow more than one female to separate breeding areas. In geese and swans, young birds may not be full grown at departure from the breeding area, so parental care during the nonbreeding season is needed to assist their growth and survival. For example, Bewick's Swan cygnets won 75% of aggressive encounters when close to their parents but only 33% when more than

Table 3-1. Mating systems of the major groups of waterfowl. Adapted from Oring and Sayler (1992:194). Most data are from Johnsgard (1978).

Tribe	Common name	Mating system
Dendrocygnini	Whistling-ducks	Long-term monogamy
Anserini	Geese and swans	Long-term monogamy
Merganettini	Torrent Duck	Long-term monogamy
Tadornini	Shelducks and sheldgeese	Seasonal and long-term monogamy
Anatini	Dabbling ducks	Seasonal monogamy, some long-term monogamy
Aythyini	Pochards	Seasonal monogamy
Mergini	Sea ducks	Seasonal monogamy, some re-pairing
Oxyurini	Stiff-tailed ducks	Polygynous, some seasonal monogamy

four "swan lengths" away, and parents protected cygnets by intervening in encounters on their behalf (Scott 1980a, 1980b). Barnacle Goose goslings attended by parents during winter in southwest Scotland acquired better foraging opportunities and higher dominance status (Siriwardena and Black 1998). In Pink-footed Geese, agonistic encounters between parents and nonbreeding birds were both initiated and won by parents (Lazarus and Inglis 1978).

Among the exceptions to the monogamous mating system of waterfowl, one of the few and most notable occurs in Magpie Geese. These unusual birds mate in trios of one male and two females, with all three birds cooperatively rearing a combined brood (Frith 1967). Siegfried (1978) reported a polygynous system of "harems" in the Gray-sided Comb Duck of Africa, and mixtures of polygyny, monogamy, and promiscuity have been reported in various populations of the Ruddy Duck of North America (Gray 1980). The Maccoa Duck of Africa is polygynous (Siegfried 1976), and the Musk Duck of Australia (Frith 1967) and probably the Muscovy Duck of the Neotropics are promiscuous (Johnsgard 1978). In Africa, unmated female Gray-sided Comb Ducks approach dominant males occupying quality breeding habitat within which males may vigorously defend at least two or three females (Siegfried 1978). Oring and Sayler (1992) reviewed the mating systems of these species and the overall mating systems of waterfowl.

Pairing Chronology

A second major characteristic associated with waterfowl mating systems is that pairing takes place during fall and winter, many months before nesting actually occurs. There is also much inter- and intraspecific variation in the timing of pair formation (Table 3-2). Among temperate species, for example, Mallards and Gadwalls form pairs by October and November, whereas Green-winged Teal and Lesser Scaup do not pair until late January, February, and even March. Most Red-breasted Mergansers wintering in the Fraser River Estuary in southwestern Canada do not begin pair formation until late March (Kahlert et al. 1998)

Pairing also represents a continuum within each species. Thus, Harlequin Ducks in Alberta first formed pairs in early October; 60–80% were paired by mid-December, and 100% were paired by March–April (Robertson et al. 1998). In Saskatchewan, pairing of American Wigeon increased

steadily from 10–15% in December to 81% by March (Wishart 1983, see also Soutiere et al. 1972). Pairing chronology also varied annually within this population; during a 2-year study, 50% of the female wigeon were paired by early January of the first year, but only 20% were paired by early January in the second year. All females were paired by April. For Wood Ducks in Missouri, the percentage of paired females was 45–46% in January and February but reached 83% by March (Armbruster 1982).

Various hypotheses have been advanced to explain interspecific variation in the timing of pair formation in waterfowl. Weller (1965) was among the first to address this question and, based on his studies of seven species of North American ducks, proposed that species breeding early were also the first to form pairs. He also concluded that pochards generally pair later in the season than dabbling ducks. However, these relationships were not strongly supported by subsequent analysis. Statistical tests yielded a weak correlation ($r = 0.34$) between average pairing time and breeding dates (Rohwer and Anderson 1988).

Paulus (1983) proposed that waterfowl experiencing poor-quality diets might form pairs earlier because pairs socially dominate unpaired birds; thus paired birds would have greater access to high-quality feeding areas. Rohwer and Anderson (1988) criticized this hypothesis because it assumed that early pairing benefits *both* sexes (i.e., if true, early pairing would be expected for waterfowl of all species). Thus, while diet may affect the pairing process for some species but not others, the "diet-quality hypothesis" nonetheless may explain differential pairing within a species.

Competition between males may offer another explanation for interspecific variation in pairing chronology. This hypothesis predicts that those species with a sex ratio heavily skewed toward males should pair earliest. However, supporting correlations are not apparent in either *Anas* or *Aythya*. Another scenario suggests that pairs form just before females start accumulating the nutrient reserves needed for nesting (Milne 1974, Ashcroft 1976). However, this idea is not supported, because many dabbling ducks pair in early fall and winter and yet do not gain body mass until several months later (i.e., pairing occurs well before there is evidence of nutrient storage; see Rohwer and Anderson 1988).

However, there is a relationship between the timing of pair formation and body mass — an association likely resulting from the known ability of larger-bodied species of birds to store greater abso-

Table 3-2. Examples of interspecific, intraspecific, and geographic variation in pairing chronology of ducks in North America.

Species	Percentage paired										Site	Source[a]
	Aug	Sep	Oct	Nov	Dec	Jan	Feb	Mar	Apr	May		
American Wigeon					10	30	79	81	100		British Columbia	A
American Wigeon				27	21	45	67	81			Texas	B
American Wigeon			0	0	6	11	22	32			Yucatan	C
Wood Duck	0	18	67	60	—[b]	46	45	83	91	95	Missouri	D
Northern Shoveler				9	42	68	97				North Carolina	E
Northern Shoveler			0	0	0	0	0	0			Yucatan	C
Northern Pintail				0	11	84	100				North Carolina	E
Northern Pintail				0	0	0	3				Yucatan	C
Green-winged Teal				2	0	34	80				North Carolina	E
Green-winged Teal						7	35	59			Louisiana	F

[a]Sources: A, Wishart (1983); B, Soutiere et al. (1972); C, Thompson and Baldassarre (1992); D, Armbruster (1982); E, Hepp and Hair (1984); F, Rave and Baldassarre (1989).
[b]Pairs were not distinguishable in December due to field conditions.

lute amounts of lipids than smaller species (Blem 1973). As shown in Table 3-3, the pairing chronologies of North American dabbling ducks indicate that small-bodied species pair later than larger species. Baldassarre and Bolen (1986) were first to recognize this relationship, which was confirmed by a strong correlation ($r = 0.96$) in dabbling ducks (Rohwer and Anderson 1988). The underlying basis involves the costs, in both energy and time, associated with courtship (Ricklefs 1974). Hence, the demands of courtship may require an accumulation of endogenous energy reserves before pairing activity is actually initiated (Afton and Sayler 1982). Conversely, those birds that do not accumulate reserves may have less time and energy available to begin courtship and/or may have difficulty maintaining a previously established pair bond. Unlike the larger species, small-bodied species may not be able to accumulate the necessary reserves during late fall-early winter while, at the same time, preparing for the rigors of mid- and late winter (Baldassarre and Bolen 1986, Rohwer and Anderson 1988).

Pochards and the Mergini show a similar trend, but they all pair in spring, regardless of body size.

Their diets are usually high in protein, however, which does not facilitate the acquisition of lipid reserves in comparison with the high-carbohydrate diets typical of dabbling ducks. Also, their primary means of feeding (diving) may make it difficult for pochards to attend their mates or economically defend a food source. Diving is also energetically costly (Sayler and Afton 1981); thus, because of diet and/or the energetic and behavioral costs of diving, pochards (regardless of size) may delay pairing until the arrival of less severe weather (Baldassarre and Bolen 1986, Rohwer and Anderson 1988).

An exception to this pattern in small-bodied ducks that dive occurs in the Harlequin Duck, which forms pairs from early fall onward (Robertson et al. 1998). This exception may occur because Harlequin Ducks feed in relatively shallow water, which is an inexpensive foraging methodology for diving ducks (Goudie and Ankney 1988). Also, Harlequin Ducks reunite established pair bonds in winter (see Smith et al. 2000).

Intraspecific differences in pairing chronology undoubtedly result from striking a balance between the benefits and costs to each sex. Hence, if females

Table 3-3. Body mass and pairing chronology of some North American Anatinae. Data are from Bellrose (1980) except as noted. Table is from Baldassarre and Bolen (1986:365).

Species	Average body mass (g)		Pair-formation period
	Adult male	Adult female	
Green-winged Teal	350	326	late February–March
Blue-winged Teal	463	377	March–May
Cinnamon Teal	341	354	March–May
American Wigeon	822	767	December–February
Gadwall[a]	967	835	October–November
Northern Pintail	1026	867	December–January
Mallard	1249	1108	late October–December
American Black Duck	1253	1112	October–December
Canvasback	1253	1158	April–May
Redhead	1108	972	March–April
Lesser Scaup	826	749	March–April
Ring-necked Duck	745	672	April–May
Bufflehead	518	309	April

[a]Paulus (1983).

benefit from pairing, they should pair as early as possible, but males may seek to delay pairing to the point where the benefits of obtaining a quality mate outweigh the costs of securing and maintaining a pair bond. For example, paired male Harlequin Ducks engaged in more interactions than did unpaired males, and the interactions usually involve guarding their mates (see Torres et al. 2002). Generally, intraspecific variation in pairing chronology arises from several causes, including age (Spurr and Milne 1976), plumage color (Cooke et al. 1972), resource availability (Paulus 1983, Brodsky and Weatherhead 1985, Hepp 1986), physical condition (Wishart 1983, Hepp 1986), winter temperature (Jonsson and Gardarsson 2001), and cross-seasonal effects within the annual cycle (Weller 1965), as follows.

Males in good physical condition pair earlier than conspecifics. For example, the peak winter body mass of American Black Ducks maintained on an ad libitum diet was on average 22% greater than their initial body mass, whereas the increase was only 7% for individuals fed the same food in restricted amounts (Hepp 1986). Individuals on the ad libitum diet also paired earlier — and their pair bonds were stronger. Significantly, 75% of the females on the ad libitum diet were paired by the end of October compared

with 50% of the females on the restricted diet. Supporting data were obtained for Lesser Scaup; when paired, males were in better physical condition than those pairing later or not pairing at all (Afton and Ankney 1991). These results suggest a means whereby the pairing chronology of wild birds might be influenced, because ducks experiencing food shortages may not readily allocate time and energy to pairing activities (Hepp 1986).

Brodsky and Weatherhead (1985) witnessed these relationships in wild American Black Ducks wintering at three sites in Ontario where food varied in quality. Those Black Ducks at the site where the diet was most nutritious were the first to begin courtship, again indicating that ducks wintering in high-quality (i.e., energy-rich) habitats are better prepared for courtship and pair formation. These results emphasize yet another cross-seasonal effect, namely that events during one segment of the annual cycle strongly influence those of another. Quite simply, the quality of winter habitat in Louisiana may influence events occurring weeks later and half a continent away.

For American Wigeon in early winter, paired males were structurally larger and heavier than unpaired males, but the larger birds had lower lipid and energy reserves (Wishart 1983). However, in late winter and after arriving early on their breeding areas, paired males had larger reserves than unpaired birds. The occurrence of larger reserves on arrival in the paired birds may be the result of having spent more time feeding and less time locomoting than unpaired birds. Such findings indicate that males must attain some "threshold" of condition before they can expend time and energy for pair formation, and thus balance the benefits of early pair formation with the energetic costs of maintaining a pair bond afterward. Wishart (1983) concluded that habitat quality on nonbreeding areas regulated the overall condition of American Wigeon. However, factors such as experience and competitiveness also affected each bird's individual condition within the broader constraint of habitat quality, and therefore influenced the chronology of pair formation in American Wigeon and probably other species.

Male dominance and age also appear to affect mate choice and pairing chronology. For example, dominant males were first to form pair bonds among Mallards and American Black Ducks (Brodsky et al. 1988). Older, more experienced males also have decided advantages over yearlings in terms of competing for mates, which is supported by studies documenting high numbers of yearling male dabbling ducks that do not obtain mates during their first breeding season (see McKinney 1992).

One also needs to consider the importance of quality of courtship displays relative to the probability that a displaying male ultimately will attract a mate and form a lasting pair bond. For example, among Wood Ducks, yearling males do not exhibit the same quality of courtship behavior as do older males, and thus females more likely pair with older individuals (Korschgen and Fredrickson 1976).

Philopatry

Philopatry is the third issue keenly related to a discussion of waterfowl mating systems. Early studies demonstrated that females of seasonally monogamous species (e.g., ducks) and pairs of perennially monogamous species (e.g., swans and geese) exhibited high rates of philopatry (Table 3-4). Indeed, as already mentioned, waterfowl are unique among birds in that females exhibit greater philopatry for their breeding areas than do males (Rohwer and Anderson 1988, Anderson et al. 1992, Oring and Sayler 1992). In contrast, the males of most other species of birds (e.g., passerines) return to breeding areas and establish territories from which they attract females as mates (Lack 1968). Whereas both sexes might benefit by returning to familiar breeding areas, females invest more in reproduction (Trivers 1972) and experience greater mortality during the breeding season (Sargeant et al. 1984; see Chapters 6 and 8). Hence, for waterfowl, female-based philopatry likely (1) increases feeding efficiency (Anderson 1985a), (2) increases the probability of nest success in the current season if nesting was successful in the previous year (Doty and Lee 1974, Dow and Fredga 1983), and (3) provides a familiar area for rearing broods (Lokemoen et al. 1990). Because these benefits are clearly of major importance to an

Table 3-4. Philopatry rates of North American waterfowl to breeding areas. Modified from Rohwer and Anderson (1988:196). Additional data from Doherty et al. (2002).

Species/age	Percentage returning	
	Females	Males
Canada Goose[a]		
Adults	47.1	50.0
Young	79.4	40.0
Northern Shoveler[b]		
Adults	25.0	10.5
Young	4.3	0.7
Gadwall[c]		
Adults	40.7	9.5
Young	6.4	2.4
Mallard[d]		
Adults	50.0	3.3
Mallard[e]		
Adults	85.0	76.0
Young	40.0	24.0
American Black Duck[f]		
Adults	36.0	27.3
Young	17.9	10.0
Lesser Scaup[g]		
Adults	20.0	5.9
Young	12.0	0.0
Canvasback[h]		
Adults	74.5	9.6
Young	26.8	1.5
Barrow's Goldeneye[i]		
Adult	69.6	63.3

[a]Lessells (1985); [b]Poston (1974); [c]Blohm (1979); [d]Titman (1983); [e]Doherty et al. (2002); [f]Seymour (1991); [g]Trauger (1971); [h]Anderson (1985b); [i]Savard (1985).

individual's fitness, it is not surprising that philopatry is so well developed in female waterfowl (McKinney 1986, Anderson et al. 1992).

However, recent analysis of both male and female philopatry to breeding areas in Canada revealed that male Mallards were much more philopatric than previously thought (Doherty et al. 2002). Specifically, adult males in Alberta returned with an estimated probability of 0.76 compared with 0.85 for adult females, and return rates in Saskatchewan were 0.87 for adult males and 0.85 for adult females. Fidelity estimates for juvenile males were 0.24–0.37 and 0.40–0.99 for juvenile females. These estimates were not confounded by survival and recapture issues that affected earlier studies, and these analyses occurred over a large area. Hence, at least for Mallards, this study questions the generalization that males are not highly philopatric to breeding areas.

Nonetheless, Rohwer and Anderson (1988) discuss several reasons why a mating system in which male ducks arrive on breeding areas, establish territories, and then attract females has not evolved in waterfowl. Foremost among these may be the benefits, described above, that females gain from obtaining a mate early in the annual cycle. Females thus seem at a disadvantage if they pair on breeding areas instead of their wintering grounds (i.e., late instead of early in relation to nesting). Also, given the strong selection for early breeding in waterfowl, a territorial system would require that males assess highly seasonal and thus unpredictable resources. In the Arctic, time spent establishing a territory would sacrifice time from an already short breeding season. Hence, the reluctance of females to mate with territorial males may be a prime reason that has eliminated, in evolutionary terms, waterfowl from adopting an otherwise common strategy of breeding birds.

Females also affect the mating system of waterfowl because, although the sex ratio is nearly 50:50 at hatching, females subsequently experience greater mortality because of their greater investment in parental care (i.e., risks associated with incubation and rearing broods). Males therefore predominate in virtually all waterfowl populations (see Chapter 8), which results in a surplus of unpaired males during the breeding season when, concurrently, essentially all females are paired. Several studies have documented that some males, even experienced breeders, arrive on the breeding grounds without mates (Poston 1974, Blohm 1978, Seymour and Titman 1978, Brasher et al. 2002). Hence, given the excess of males, the odds of each male securing

a mate are less than certain, and a segment of the male population likely fails to breed each year.

Furthermore, the predominance of males designates females as the limiting sex, which means that females can be "choosy" in selecting their mates. Among the potential benefits of this arrangement is that females can select mates well before the nesting season begins, thereby gaining the advantage of having a male in attendance at a time when she can forage and accumulate crucial nutrient reserves without harassment from other males (Spurr and Milne 1976, Afton and Sayler 1982, Paulus 1983). The resulting increase in foraging efficiency occurs because paired birds enjoy a higher social ranking and thus dominate other social groups (e.g., unpaired birds), as shown for Gadwalls wintering in Louisiana (Paulus 1983) and Canvasbacks on Lake Erie and the upper Mississippi River (Lovvorn 1990). Lovvorn (1990), Sorenson and Derrickson (1994), Johnson and Rohwer (1998), and others have suggested that pairing itself leads to dominance rather than the reverse (i.e., dominance leading to pairing), a finding later supported by observational and experimental work with Mallards. Omland (1996a, 1996b) experimentally manipulated male Mallards into four groups: (1) dark (black) bills; (2) shaved head, neck ring, and breast; (3) wing-patch (speculum) clipping; and (4) bill yellowing. None of the treatments affected male dominance. Males benefit from monogamy by gaining mates from the limited pool of females and, once mates are secured, by protecting their genetic investment — if they can prevent extra-pair copulations by other males (see Chapter 4). However, although dominance of pairs is well established, this pattern may result from early pairing by dominant individuals (Johnson and Rohwer 1998).

Perennial and Seasonal Monogamy

Although monogamy is the dominant mating system of waterfowl, it occurs in two major forms: (1) perennial monogamy, which is essentially life-long; and (2) seasonal monogamy, wherein pair bonds are formed anew each year, usually with a different mate. Perennial monogamy is common in birds, occurring in at least 50% of all orders and 21% of all families (Black 1996). Among anseriforms, perennial monogamy is best known in the geese and swans breeding in the Arctic where the nesting season is short; hence, one benefit of perennial monogamy is the ability to begin nesting without incurring delays associated with pairing behavior (Akesson and Raveling 1982). Further, because the breeding season is short at high latitudes, opportunities for renesting are often restricted or even precluded. Males in these settings have little opportunity to breed with more than one female, but instead are subject to a strong selective force for assisting with brood-rearing activities that help their mates succeed during the brief "window" available for reproduction (Rohwer and Anderson 1988).

Insights about the fitness consequences of long-term pair bonds in geese stem from long-term studies of individually marked Barnacle Geese breeding in Svalbard (Black and Owen 1995, Black 1996, Black et al. 1996, Black 2001). In particular, long-term reproductive success was clearly influenced by the number of years pair bonds persisted (Black 2001). Long-term pair bonds may be selected for in goose populations because of the constant (i.e., annual) need for male–female cooperation that includes male defense of the female from competitors (Black and Owen 1988), pairs acting together to maintain territories within a colony (Inglis 1977), and pairs cooperating during brood-rearing on the breeding grounds (Black and Owen 1989a, Sedinger and Raveling 1990). Barnacle Geese also have a high fidelity to breeding sites (95%); thus, a continuous partnership acting through a "social feedback loop" (Black 2001) allows pairs to learn and capitalize on the subtleties of habitats, a process that may take years to achieve (Black 1998).

Young geese and swans also are not fully grown when migrating from their nesting areas; thus, perennial monogamy provides the benefits of parental assistance during the offspring's first winter (Scott 1980a, 1980b). By maintaining their unity, for example, families of Canada Geese gained higher dominance in the social order of winter flocks, which likely increases the survival rates for the young birds in each family group (Raveling 1970; see also Gregoire and Ankney 1990). Further, parent Canada Geese wintering in the Midwest region of the United States spent more time on alert than nonparents during fall, winter, and spring, which likely allowed their broods greater access to food (Caithamer et al. 1996). Wintering families of Barnacle Geese defend a foraging space at the outer edge of feeding flocks where they obtain better food than conspecifics (Black and Owen 1989b, Black et al. 1992). Conversely, orphaned juvenile geese are highly subordinate within the social systems of geese and thus easily displaced from prime feeding sites (Raveling 1970).

Bioenergetics may also influence the evolution of perennial monogamy in geese and swans, which commonly breed in the Arctic. Females in these species transport large amounts of stored energy to breeding areas, where these reserves are mobilized to produce and incubate eggs (Ankney and MacInnes 1978, Raveling 1979; see Chapter 4). The presence of males at nest sites ensures that females may incubate for long periods without interference, although females are emaciated when the clutch hatches. After egg hatch, however, the male assumes principal guardianship of the brood, which frees the female for feeding and recovery of lost body mass. Indeed, experimental removal of males from nesting pairs of Ross's and Lesser Snow Geese did not affect nesting success, which suggested that male attendance in arctic-nesting geese was more important during the brood-rearing period (LeSchack et al. 1998). Hence, selection mitigates against a system in which males are absent at this crucial time: Lacking the assistance of males, females alone would face full-time vigilance over their broods while concurrently recovering from acute starvation — predictably, brood mortality would increase and fitness of adults of both sexes would decline.

Finally, note that male and female geese usually molt at this time, which at first glance might imply a period of greater predation. Males, it would seem, might be better off as bachelors molting elsewhere without sharing the demands of brood-rearing duties. At high latitudes, however, relatively few predators are capable of attacking adult-size birds — even those that are flightless — which offsets the implied risk to males that remain with their families during the molting period (Rohwer and Anderson 1988).

Swans and geese are large birds, and their large size also may be of importance in that males can defend their nests and broods against most predators. A pair can form a formidable nest defense. For example, Lesser Snow Goose nests attended only by the female suffered higher rates of egg loss by arctic foxes (*Alopex lagopus*) compared to nests attended by pairs (Samelius and Alisauskas 2001). Indeed, paired geese were avoided by the foxes and also exhibited greater resistance to foxes. In contrast, most species of ducks are much smaller and thus cannot use their physical presence to deter predators. Female ducks instead avoid predators, in large measure by concealing their nests in the best available cover and by leading their broods to rearing areas with similar protection. Thus, in terms of thwarting predators, virtually no benefits accrue if male ducks were to remain with their females much beyond the egg-laying period. In fact, the brightly colored plumage of males (most species) might be more detectable by predators and thus actually increase nest and brood losses if males remained with their mates throughout the nesting season (Rohwer and Anderson 1988).

Further, because breeding male ducks often attempt copulations with more than one female (see Chapter 4), a period of extended companionship might limit these opportunities, although extended pair bonds in the White-cheeked Pintail did not limit attempts at extrapair copulations (Sorenson 1994). Indeed, male White-cheeked Pintails pursued extrapair copulations primarily when their own females were fertile. But, a brief pair bond can free males for activities that increase their survival, especially those associated with an early molt and readiness for migration (McKinney 1986), or opportunities to re-pair with other females. For example, male Harlequin Ducks in Alberta depart for molting areas on the Pacific Coast by late June while females remain on the breeding area with their broods (Smith et al. 2000). Male White-cheeked Pintails at times may engage in serial monogamy, with one male fathering two broods in succession with two different females (Sorenson et al. 1992). Williams (1991) proposed that perennial pair bonds in the Blue Duck, a habitat specialist of fast-flowing steams and rivers in New Zealand, stemmed from the need of males to attend broods in dangerous habitats, and thus close cooperation between males and females throughout the breeding effort. Pairs remained together up to 81 months, and changes of mates largely resulted only from death of one member of the pair. Perennial pair bonds also occur in the other three anatid river specialists: the Torrent Duck of South America, Salvadori's Duck of New Guinea, and the African Black Duck of sub-Saharan Africa.

Whistling-ducks also exhibit perennial monogamy but breed in tropical and semitropical areas where the breeding season is not restricted by unfavorable temperatures. Elsewhere in the tropics, 43% of marked pairs of White-cheeked Pintails in the Bahamas remained together for two or more breeding seasons, and 4–9% of males were polygynous, despite a preponderance of males (1.45:1.00) in the population (Sorenson 1992). The term "male-quality polygyny" was coined to describe this form of polygyny. Sorenson (1992) believed that such a variable mating system evolved in the White-cheeked Pintail because timing of breeding seasons in the tropics varies with the occurrence of rainfall, the species is sedentary, and the breeding season is prolonged. Hence, a long-term pair bond enhances opportunities to breed quickly when suitable conditions

arrive (e.g., rainfall). Similarly, long-term pair bonds in the Gray Teal and Pink-eared Duck, both Australian endemics, may be adaptations for breeding in highly variable environments (Braithwaite 1976). Gray Teal in the dry interior of Australia breed at any time of year, doing so in response to rainfall. Indeed, sexually inactive birds initiate courtship displays immediately after rainfall and lay eggs within 10 days (Frith 1967). Long-term pair bonds are of great advantage under these circumstances.

Some temperate species of ducks, especially the Mergini, also exhibit long-term monogamy, although the pair may break-up at the end of the breeding season. Such behavior has been reported for at least four species of Mergini, including the goldeneyes (Savard 1985, Gauthier 1987a), the Common Eider (Ashcroft 1976), and the Harlequin Duck (Smith et al. 2000). For example, paired Common Eiders spent less time in aggressive interactions and more time feeding than did unpaired birds; hence, paired females accumulated more nutrient reserves for producing and incubating a clutch (Ashcroft 1976). Pairs of Harlequin Ducks in Alberta return to breeding streams in late April and early May, but males depart for molting areas on the Pacific Coast by late June. However, in all 37 cases where pairs from a prior year returned (separately) to a wintering area, they reunited (Smith et al. 2000). Both males and females were highly philopatric to wintering sites (62% for females, 77% for males; Robertson et al. 2000), which obviously enhances the opportunities for the same individuals to re-pair. Females benefit by reuniting with a mate of known quality (Savard 1985) and can be protected from harassment by other males (Torres et al. 2002). Males who re-pair benefit by conserving energy, by avoiding competition with unpaired males, and avoiding the possibility of going unpaired. Pairs that reunite also exhibited little courtship display (Gowans et al. 1997). All told, re-pairing provides both sexes with advantages and potentially improves their reproductive output (Robertson et al. 1998). However, a study of costs and benefits of pairing in Harlequin Ducks revealed no significant difference in overall feeding time (6–7 hr/day) spent by paired or unpaired birds of either sex (6–7 hr/day), although paired males engaged in more interactions than unpaired males (2.0 vs. 0.6) and spent 4% less time under water (Torres et al. 2002). Thus, although the pair bond was costly to males, it did not benefit females in terms of increased feeding time. Early pairing in Harlequin Ducks therefore may result from other factors, such as the benefits of pair reunion.

In rare cases, temperate dabbling ducks may maintain long-term pair bonds. For example, Mallards sometimes extend their pair bonds beyond one season (Dwyer et al. 1973, Blohm and Mackenzie 1994), including a rare report of a marked pair observed on the same breeding wetland for three seasons (Losito and Baldassarre 1996). Otherwise, seasonal monogamy is the dominant pattern in temperate-breeding ducks. Pair bonds break in early to midincubation, as recorded for Mallards (Gilmer et al. 1977, Losito and Baldassarre 1996), and re-form with new mates early in the following fall, depending on species. Such short-term pair bonds are characteristic of migratory species that exploit seasonally productive environments in temperate latitudes where breeding time is somewhat restricted and resources may be unpredictable (see Oring and Sayler 1992).

Patterns in Perennial Monogamy

Behavioral patterns associated with perennial monogamy are nicely exemplified in swans and geese, and ducks. One example stems from long-term studies of about 119 individually marked Barnacle Geese in Svalbard (Black and Owen 1995, Black 2001), and another comes from a study of 337 individually marked Speckled Teal in Argentina (Port 1998).

In the Barnacle Goose, individuals took 1–5 years to establish pair bonds, and on average remained unpaired for a third of their lifespan. The majority of geese chose mates of the same age. Some 40% of geese had more than one mate during their lifespan (range = 1–4 mates). Pair-bond duration averaged 4.70 years; 17 pairs were together for more than 10 years, and three were together for 19 years. Very few geese divorced and then re-paired with new partners (less than 2% annually). Overall reproductive rates increased with age, peaked in years 10–11, and declined moderately thereafter. In contrast, a 15-year study of Greylag Geese recorded an annual divorce rate of 10.5%, with 29.7% of all pairs ending in divorce (Nilsson and Persson 2001).

The Speckled Teal inhabits open wetlands and Andean lakes in South America outside the Amazon, where they sometimes nest in the large, compound nests erected by Monk Parakeets (*Myiopsitta monachus*). During a study in Argentina by Port (1998), pair bonds averaged 2.24 years and lasted 4–6 years in some pairs. Mate fidelity was high (89.4%) and divorce was low (10.6%). Most mate changes (66.6%) followed disappearance of one member of the pair. Mate changes among pairs together for two or

more consecutive breeding seasons usually occurred following the death of one member of the pair (7 of 8). However, no significant difference in reproductive success occurred between divorced and nondivorced pairs, and no general relationship existed between reproductive success and length of the pair bond. Interestingly, eight of nine males failed to re-pair following loss of mates, and most males unpaired at the beginning of the study were unpaired at the end (16 of 21). Such fierce competition among males for mates may have been a key factor leading to the perennial monogamy of this species; biparental care of the ducklings, particularly because of the long overland journey from nest site to water, also likely played a role (see Port 1998).

To summarize this section, monogamy is the basic mating system in waterfowl, the benefits of which extend to species with seasonal pair bonds as well as to those whose pair bonds remain intact for a lifetime. However, variations of this mating system occur across taxa (geese, swans, ducks), habitats (Arctic vs. tropics), and body sizes (Barnacle Goose vs. Harlequin Duck). As an adaptation to specific environmental conditions, natural selection produced perennial monogamy (Barnacle Goose and Harlequin Duck), whereas seasonal monogamy emerged in others (e.g., temperate ducks). Perennial monogamy is the pattern for swans and geese in both the Northern and Southern Hemispheres. For temperate-nesting, migratory ducks, however, seasonal monogamy is nearly unavoidable because females benefit by returning to previous breeding sites. Thus, given that pair formation does not occur on the breeding area, polygyny cannot develop because males cannot individually follow more than one female to its respective nesting area. However, paired and unpaired males may breed by forcefully copulating with females on the breeding grounds (Chapter 4) or by breeding with renesting females no longer attended by their former mates.

HOME RANGE, TERRITORY, AND SPACING

"Home range" is commonly defined as the area within which an animal conducts its normal activities and contrasts with "territory," which is a smaller area within the home range that is defended from conspecifics for the exclusive use of the occupants (Grier and Burk 1992). Brown and Orians (1970) listed the essential attributes of territory as follows: (1) a fixed area, (2) defensive behavior in the fixed area, and (3) exclusive use of the area. Territoriality in waterfowl is not unexpected because selection favors those males whose behavior increases their probability of reproductive success (Gauthier 1988). Females likewise benefit by pairing with such males. In the latter case, females profit because they are (1) defended from harassment, (2) protected from unwanted matings or attempted matings with other males, and (3) provided with undisturbed feeding times and places during the breeding period (Stewart and Titman 1980, Titman 1983). Additionally, McKinney (1965a) suggested that territorial behavior helps to disperse nests, which may reduce predation, and Amat (1983) proposed that aggression may regulate populations by dispersing the birds within the available habitat. However, observations of territorial behavior can be misleading and actually represent mate defense, not defense of a particular site. Male waterfowl become highly aggressive toward conspecifics during the breeding season; such aggression can lead to exclusive use of space and subsequently provide benefits for females associating with those males, namely her defense and not defense of a space per se. For example, Robertson et al. (2000) observed that a several pairs of wintering Harlequin Ducks used the same sections of habitat, and these pairs were aggressive only toward unpaired males that approached to court their mates (Gowans et al. 1997). The conclusion: Harlequin Ducks exhibit a mate-defense system, not defense of a territory (Robertson et al. 2000).

Dzubin (1955:293) perhaps was the first to offer specific definitions for the activities of breeding ducks, defining home range as "the area in which the pair is most active during the prenesting, nesting and incubation periods," and territory as "the defended portion of the home range from which a male attacks another pair, drake or female, of his own species." A more complete discussion of territory and home range appeared in the classic work of Margaret Morse Nice (1941). She based the system on *how* and *when* an area is defended, noting that these attributes varied among and within species. Nice originally recognized three types of territories that she termed "A," "B," and "C." However, because many waterfowl did not fit these categories, Anderson and Titman (1992) modified her approach to accommodate waterfowl (Table 3-5).

The advantages of a territory or mate defense are obvious — an individual remaining in a given locality soon becomes familiar with that area's food and cover resources, potential mates, opportunities for rearing young, and similar assets (see Anderson and Titman 1992, Huntingford and Turner 1987).

Conversely, individuals must weigh these features against the energy, time, and risk of injury expended defending a specific site.

Geese and Swans — Anserinae: In geese, males accompany females to their nest sites, around which the male exhibits aggressive behavior toward other geese. Because such sites are defended, these areas represent territories, but their exact function is unclear because territory size varies among and within species (Owen 1980). Ryder (1975), for instance, proposed that territories in colonially nesting geese (Type 6) evolved to a size large enough to protect their owners from nonsexual harassment by other males and, additionally, to provide some food resources so that the defending male did not have to leave the site for long periods. However, nonsexual harassment has not been witnessed in other species of geese (Mineau and Cooke 1979); hence, what appears to be defense of a "territory" might actually be mate defense.

Mineau and Cooke (1979) argued that the territories maintained by breeding Snow Geese cannot serve to protect food resources, because the defended areas overlap. Moreover, other Snow Geese, including nonneighboring males, enter these areas without challenge during the latter stages of incubation. They argued that territorial behavior guards against unwanted copulations by other males and keeps nests free of eggs laid by unfamiliar females. Aggressive behavior in the case of Snow Geese thus seems unrelated to protecting space per se. Owen and Wells (1979) also proposed that territorial behavior in Barnacle Geese serves to protect the nest instead of defending space. Pink-footed Geese nesting in Iceland also do not exhibit nonsexual harassment, and territorial/aggressive behavior declined markedly after incubation began (Inglis 1976).

Canada Geese do not nest colonially, but harassment of nesting females by intruding males is especially significant as a cause of nest failure. For example, successful pairs of Canada Geese nesting at Dowling Lake, Manitoba, won most of their aggressive interactions with intruding males, largely because the territorial male was present more often than not (Ewaschuk and Boag 1972). In a captive flock of Giant Canada Geese, the frequency of aggressive displays by breeding males increased during egg-laying and remained high throughout incubation, and these males rarely retreated from aggressive behaviors of other geese (Akesson and Raveling 1982). "Territories" were well established by the egg-laying period, but such exclusive space

Table 3-5. Classification of territorial systems as proposed by Nice (1941) and modified by Anderson and Titman (1992:258-259).

Type and definition of territory	Species/group examples
Type 1 — A typical Type A territory in which occurs mating, nesting, and foraging by adults and young. Aggression often intense, and occupants often perennially monogamous. However, courtship and pair formation may occur elsewhere.	Mute Swan, steamer-ducks, Salvadori's Duck, Blue Duck, Torrent Duck, African Black Duck
Type 2 — A Type A territory that is exclusive and defended vigorously for the breeding season only. Used for copulations, nesting, brood rearing, and foraging by adults and young.	Trumpeter Swan, Whooper Swan, Tundra Swan, Bewick's Swan
Type 3 — A Type B territory defended for the breeding season. Used for copulation and foraging by adults.	Northern Shoveler, Blue-winged Teal
Type 4 — A Type B territory defended for the breeding season where boundaries frequently overlap but areas occupied are temporally exclusive. Used for mating and some foraging by adults; nests built within or close by territory.	Mallard
Type 5 — Breeding pairs dispersed; moving area around female and nest site (sometimes) defended. Often little evidence of aggression.	Northern Pintail, scoters
Type 6 — A Type C colonial-breeding situation where female and a restricted area around the nest are defended.	Snow Goose

clearly could be the byproduct of male aggression and mate defense, not defense of space per se.

The white swans are all strongly territorial, but there are poor data for the other species such as the Black-necked Swan and Coscoroba Swan from South America. In most locations, Mute Swans vigorously defend Type I territories year-round, and the "northern swans" defend Type 2 territories (see Anderson and Titman 1992). As in geese, however, territorial defense is usually most intense during egg-laying and incubation (Kear 1972). Mute Swans can be especially aggressive as evidenced when they actually kill encroaching conspecifics (Birkhead and Perrins 1986).

Among the northern white swans, territories are large, reaching 320 ha per pair in Tundra Swans (Kear 1972). In Russia, pairs of Bewick's Swans may breed at a density of one pair per 2,000 ha (Dementiev and Gladkov 1952). Territories are defended before nest-site selection well until after cygnets hatch, as Banko (1960) observed in the Trumpeter Swan of North America. In contrast to the white swans, the Black Swan of Australia and New Zealand breeds in colonies and is nonterritorial — nests may be less then 1 m apart (Guiler 1966).

True Ducks — Anatinae: For ducks, home ranges vary considerably in size and type both within and among species, within and among habitats (Table 3-6), and by reproductive status. For example, Derrickson (1978) reported that the home range of Northern Pintails using prairie pothole habitat in Manitoba was 579 ha for unpaired males, 896 ha for paired males, and 480 ha for paired females (also see Anderson and Titman 1992). For north-temperate ducks in general, however, Nudds and Ankney (1982) explain variation in home range size in terms of differences in (1) body size, and (2) the spatial and

Table 3-6. Examples of home range sizes for dabbling ducks in North America.

Species	Home range Size (ha)	Type	Habitat type	Source
Mallard	468	4	Prairie potholes	Dwyer et al. (1979)
Mallard	106	4	Forested wetlands	Dwyer and Baldassarre (1994)
Mallard	210–240	4	Mixed forest	Gilmer et al. (1975)
American Black Duck	119	4	Forested wetlands	Ringelman et al. (1982)
American Black Duck	152	4	Forested wetlands	Dwyer and Baldassarre (1994)
Gadwall	28	3	Managed marshes	Gates (1962)
Northern Pintail	509	5	Prairie potholes	Derrickson (1978)
Northern Shoveler	20	3	Prairie potholes	Poston (1974)

temporal distribution of food resources. However, habitat structure, quality, and energy expenditures also exert considerable influence (Godfrey et al. 2003). Larger home range and/or territory size was correlated ($r = 0.44$) with increasing body size in eight species. Larger areas also occurred in "patchy" habitats such as prairie potholes when compared with large marshes and other more homogeneous sites. These data reflect familiar concepts in ecology, namely that larger species generally require larger home ranges and that home-range size generally varies inversely with habitat quality. Thus, concepts concerning the home range of ducks are neither new nor uncontroversial — much in concert with ideas about the functions of territory.

Major credit for the concept of territoriality in ducks goes to Hochbaum (1944) for his studies of Mallards, Canvasbacks, and other ducks on the Delta Marsh in Manitoba (see Infobox 3-1). He contended that paired males defend certain water areas from conspecifics, thereby preventing interruption of paired birds "during the copulation link of the reproductive cycle." Subsequent work questioned Hochbaum's concepts; these studies indicated that home ranges of the same species overlapped broadly and that rigid territorial behavior often was lacking (Sowls 1955, Dzubin 1955). In spite of the conflicting evidence resulting from these early studies, however, it is now widely accepted that ducks exhibit a considerable diversity of territorial/spacing systems (Anderson and Titman 1992), which should not be unexpected given the size and diversity of the group. Nonetheless, beginning in the 1960s and continuing today, waterfowl biologists debate the cause and function of territories in ducks.

Most information concerning interactions among breeding pairs of ducks stems from observations of species in the genus *Anas*, mostly in the Northern Hemisphere but with some notable exceptions (e.g., Williams 1991, Brewer 1997, Port and McKinney 2001). In the north-temperate species, "pursuit flights" represent the most visible feature of territorial encounters, and they have been recorded in nearly all species of *Anas* (McKinney 1965a, Stewart and Titman 1980). Pursuit flights were first observed by Heinroth (1910, 1911) and since have been classified into two major types: (1) three-bird flights; and (2) attempted rape flights, which are now called "forced copulation" instead of "rape." Three-bird flights feature an interloping male pursuing a paired female; the third bird in the group is the pursued female's mate (Hori 1963, Titman 1983).

In Mallards, Titman (1983) recorded several features of three-bird flights: (1) most (60%) originate on the territory of the chasing male; (2) three birds usually (86%) but not always take part; (3) flights last less then 30 sec (60%); and (4) the flights cover less than 400 m (77%). In contrast, forced-copulation flights involve a female pursued by several males; these flights usually extend far beyond the starting point and often terminate when the female is forced to the ground and subjected to repeated copulations (McKinney 1965a, McKinney et al. 1983).

Despite the extensive literature on the subject, the debate remains unresolved as to the function of these flights in relation to territorial behavior in breeding ducks. For example, during 14 years of observation involving about 200 flights, Hori (1963) never recorded aerial attacks of lone male Mallards in ways suggestive of a territorial defense, and only

Infobox 3-1

H. [Hans] Albert Hochbaum
Founding Director, Delta Waterfowl Research Station
(1911–1988)

Hochbaum (at right in photo) attended graduate school at the University of Wisconsin under the tutelage of Aldo Leopold (at left), who arranged for him to study waterfowl on the Delta marsh at the southern end of Lake Manitoba (years later, at Leopold's request, Hochbaum critiqued many of the essays that subsequently appeared as the classic *A Sand County Almanac*). The site included a hunting lodge and other facilities; in 1938, these became the nucleus of the Delta Waterfowl Research Station. Hochbaum served as the station's first director — a position he held until 1970, when he assumed a new role as writer and artist in residence at Delta. Hochbaum's thesis later became the basis for *Canvasback on a Prairie Marsh* (1944), a

book that reflected his keen observations of waterfowl behavior and included his own pen-and-ink artwork. The success of the book — it won prestigious awards from the American Ornithologists' Union and The Wildlife Society — established both Hochbaum and Delta as major forces in the field of waterfowl ecology. It also offered a new generation of fledgling biologists a benchmark on which to base their own studies.

In 1955, Hochbaum published his second book, *Travels and Traditions of Waterfowl*, which provided unique insights into the infant field of behavior and its relationship to several aspects of management. The book drew heavily from his own observations on the Delta marshes and once again included skilled pen-and-ink sketches; for a second time, he received a publication award from The Wildlife Society. His capstone work — nearly three dozen technical papers were sandwiched between his books — was *To Ride the Wind* (1973), a collection of paintings (in color) and sketches of waterfowl in and near the Delta marshes. He worked in oil, watercolor, and egg tempera, which were exhibited in a dozen one-man shows. Among other places, his paintings hang in the Smithsonian Institution in Washington and in the National Museum of Natural Sciences in Ottawa. In 1970, Queen Elizabeth was presented with one of his paintings.

H. Albert Hochbaum's talents as an artist were fully matched by his abilities as a writer, and his words frequently bore a touch not often equaled in biological literature: *The Delta Marsh [is] a wilderness in a land of wheat fields. The conquests of man have pressed hard upon its borders, but deep within its screen of tules there still exists a solitude as wild and clean and fresh as the peak of an unscaled mountain.*

Hochbaum achieved success in art, writing, and science, each of which were recognized by numerous awards and honors (e.g., Manitoba Medal of Honor), as well by as an honorary LL.D. degree. In 1980, Hochbaum received the Leopold Award from The Wildlife Society for his contributions to waterfowl and wetland conservation. Also see Houston (1988). Photo courtesy of the Delta Waterfowl Foundation.

in rare cases did three-bird flights seem associated with specific areas on the ground (i.e., territories). Based on this study, three-bird flights apparently are sexual (mate defense) in nature and do not represent the defense of territories. Lebret (1961) also concluded that Mallards are not a territorial species. In contrast, Titman (1983) recorded that individually marked birds ($n = 6$) returned to specific sites following 80 of the 82 three-bird flights he witnessed. Evidence of this behavior (Type 4) was most pronounced during the brief period (13–22 days) between nest-site selection and early incubation. Titman (1983) thus concluded that Mallards indeed elicit territorial behavior, but his observations are still compatible with a mate-defense system.

However, after comparisons among species, it appears that dabbling ducks exhibit a continuum of social organization, ranging from rigid territoriality to a system much less so (Anderson and Titman 1992, Oring and Sayler 1992). For example, male Blue-winged Teal and Northern Shovelers aggressively defend definite areas (Type 3) to which they return regardless of whether their mates are present (see Seymour 1974a, 1974b; Stewart and Titman 1980; Titman and Seymour 1981). In contrast, male Northern Pintails lack attachments to discrete areas (Derrickson 1978); whereas they chase females during pursuit flights, they may not return to the females with which they seem paired, and they often attempt to copulate with the female they chase (Type 5). This type of territorial defense is also characteristic of many pochards as well as scoters (Anderson and Titman 1992). Thus, in their comparison of six North American species of dabbling ducks, Titman and Seymour (1981) recorded a gradient of territorial behavior from strong territoriality in the Northern Shoveler and Blue-winged Teal to weak territoriality (but strong defense of mates) in the Northern Pintail. Mallards, American Black Ducks, and Gadwalls represent an intermediate position (Type 3 or 4). Pursuit flights of Northern Shovelers and Blue-winged Teal commonly focus only on males, which bears witness to the strong territoriality in these species. In contrast, pursuit flights almost always focus on females in the less territorial species such as Northern Pintails, Mallards, and American Black Ducks.

The diversity represented in these spacing systems may reflect characteristics of the breeding habitat such as the heterogeneity of resources in space and time, which strongly affects the probability that such resources can be defended for exclusive use of a territory's occupants without costs ex-

ceeding benefits (McKinney 1965a, Nudds and Ankney 1982). Among temperate species, Northern Shovelers illustrate a classic model of territoriality because their food resources are relatively easy to defend, whereas the food resources for Northern Pintails are distributed more patchily (Nudds and Ankney 1982).

In the Southern Hemisphere, the four anatid riverine specialists (Blue Duck, African Black Duck, Torrent Duck, Salvadori's Duck) are all highly territorial. Two species, the Blue Duck and African Black Duck, are fairly well studied, and both exhibit classical territorial behaviors (Type I). Blue Ducks form perennial pairs and establish year-round territories from 470 to 640 m in length along fast-flowing rivers and streams (Eldridge 1986). The pair defends the territory and can remain in these territories for life (Williams 1991). The males are particularly aggressive, and fights between males can last 2–4 min. Territories are centered around food resources associated with rapids, and large areas between territories usually are shared. Energetic costs of territorial defense vary with territory size, length, and habitat type (Godfrey et al. 2003).

The African Black Duck features territories about 700 m in length that are vigorously defended by pairs, with only a 10.4% overlap in the territories used by neighboring pairs (see Ball et al. 1978). Pairs are perennially monogamous and, except for the molting period, rarely separated by more than 10 m. The comparative stability of river habitats in comparison to ephemeral marshes seems especially important in the evolution of this type of territorial behavior in African Black Ducks (see Ball et al. 1978, McKinney et al. 1978). Thus, habitats can be occupied and defended year-round, with benefits accruing to the pair in the form of intimate knowledge of resources, competitors and predators, and reduced energetic costs. In great contrast to riverine specialists, Gray Teal of Australia are nomadic and exhibit no territorial behavior whatsoever (Frith 1967), most likely because they breed in arid habitats where the availability of water is extremely unpredictable and thus undefendable.

Among pochards, male Canvasbacks and some other species establish large home ranges (525 ha), but they defend only a small "moving territory" about 3 m in diameter around the female (Dzubin 1955). Canvasbacks may not defend a large area because they forage on patchily distributed benthic foods; hence the costs of defense likely outweigh the benefits (Anderson and Titman 1992). Other waterfowl exhibiting strong territorial behavior include shelducks and sheldgeese (Tadornini; Young 1970, Williams 1979) and steamer-ducks (Weller 1976, Summers 1983).

Most Mergini (eiders, scoters, some mergansers) nest colonially or exhibit Type 5 territorial behavior (Anderson and Titman 1992), but the goldeneyes and Buffleheads are strongly territorial both intra- and interspecifically (Savard 1984, Gauthier 1987b). These species defend Type 3 territories from spring arrival until late incubation. Territorial males vigorously exclude conspecifics and most other species with a variety of threat displays, aerial pursuits, and actual fights.

Territorial behavior is less well studied in the Oxyurini, but male Ruddy Ducks and probably Whiteheaded Ducks defend the female (Siegfried 1976; also see Johnsgard and Carbonell 1996). For a more detailed review of the territory and spacing systems of waterfowl, consult the review by Anderson and Titman (1992).

Overall, territorial behavior and mate defense are shaped by myriad environmental conditions acting as selective pressures; thus, the diversity of these systems found in waterfowl is not surprising. Nevertheless, this topic remains an area for fruitful research given the still-true remarks of Anderson and Titman (1992:270): "The clearest conclusion from our search for general patterns is that we still do not have sufficient information to allow many generalizations about the evolution of spacing systems." Future studies, especially those with a comparative approach among species and long-term study of marked individuals, undoubtedly will reveal much more about the function of these behaviors.

COURTSHIP DISPLAYS

Waterfowl usually court in groups. This behavior, often referred to as "social courtship" or "pair courtship," most likely evolved as a consequence of competition among males for potential mates. McKinney (1992:226) pointed out the problems with these terms, however, and used the inclusive term "courtship," which he defined as "activities associated with the formation, testing, and maintenance of pair bonds or liaisons" (see Infobox 3-2).

Courtship serves different functions in males and females: Males engage in competition, and females engage in mate choice (Trivers 1972). Male courtship functions to (1) attract the attention of females, (2) specify which female is being courted, (3) hold that female's attention, (4) lead that female away from the courting group, and (5) compete with other

males (McKinney 1975). Females, in turn, evaluate potential mates based on (1) vigor, skill, and persistence in courtship; (2) physical condition as potentially reflected by plumage; (3) attentiveness, compatibility, and constancy in reaffirming the pair bond; (4) success in competition with other males; and (5) efficiency in copulation. Overall, courtship displays should be regarded as signals that have evolved in those individuals that gained crucial advantages — mates and the transmission of genes — from performing these behavioral patterns (McKinney 1975, McKinney 1992). However, to identify and evaluate the function of a particular display is not easy, although McKinney (1992) recommended considering (1) the situation in which the display is performed, (2) the characteristics of the display, (3) the spatial orientation of the display, and (4) the effect of the display in terms of behavioral changes of the receiver. Displays also reflect evolution and thus have been used to develop phylogenetic perspectives (see Johnson et al. 2000).

A review of the exhaustive and often detailed literature addressing courtship display in waterfowl lies beyond the scope of this book, but numerous in-depth treatments address this topic (Heinroth 1911, Lorenz 1951–53, McKinney 1953, Johnsgard 1965, McKinney 1992). Further, *The Birds of North America* series provides in-depth treatment of courtship and pair formation for each species of waterfowl in North America. We also omit consideration of comfort movements in waterfowl: shaking, preening, bathing, and similar behaviors are self-descriptive and of almost universal occurrence (see McKinney 1965b). Instead, we will examine the more prominent displays of representative species, because little knowledge can be gained in the broader area of mating systems and pair formation unless the displays themselves are recognized correctly and their potential meaning assessed.

Courtship Displays of Geese and Swans — Anserinae

Pair formation in geese generally begins in winter, but the displays are not easily observed in the large flocks characteristic of winter aggregations. In the following section, we have relied on Owen (1980:76–96), who provides an excellent summary of the courtship behavior of geese, and we have highlighted several additional studies that provide good examples of the pair formation process in Anserini.

Black and Owen (1988) aptly describe pair formation of Barnacle Geese, based on their studies of

Infobox 3-2

Frank McKinney
Waterfowl Behaviorist
(1928–2001)

Knowledge about the social behavior of dabbling ducks reached new heights under the keen eye and interpretive insight of Frank McKinney. His studies, which included both comparative and experimental approaches, often were conducted in special flight pens he designed and built at a natural history area operated by the University of Minnesota. Other work took place in the field where he spent long hours observing the behavior of free-ranging ducks in Canada, South Africa, Australia, New Zealand, and the Bahamas. Among other contributions, McKinney determined some of the important selective pressures that apparently shaped the patterns of social behavior in dabbling ducks. Most of his work focused on species of *Anas,* but he also delved into the behavior of other taxa such as the Blue Duck of New Zealand (see Fig. 2-14).

A native of Northern Ireland, McKinney attended

Oxford and Bristol Universities and later completed a postdoctorate at the Wildfowl and Wetlands Trust in Slimbridge where he studied under the future Nobel laureate Niko Tinbergen. He then left for Canada to begin a 12-year tenure as Assistant Director of the Delta Waterfowl Research Station in Manitoba. In 1963, McKinney joined the faculty in the Department of Ecology, Evolution, and Behavior at the University of Minnesota, remaining there until he retired in 2000.

Central to his research were the evolutionary aspects of social signals displayed by dabbling ducks and later, the sexual conflicts that may result from the differing interests of males and females in regard to fitness. So-called "three-bird chases" (also known as "pursuit flights"), which typically include two males and one female in such species as Northern Pintails, were among the latter. McKinney had previously interpreted these as territorial disputes, but when new ideas emerged regarding sperm competition and other forms of sex-specific fitness, McKinney quickly realized that new interpretations — for example, the implications of forced copulations and extrapair matings — were needed to explain these behaviors. In addition to his focus on North American species, especially the Green-winged Teal, he and his students also studied the behavior of the White-cheeked Pintail, the African Black Duck, and South American dabbling ducks. These studies revealed patterns of long-term monogamy in ducks and the behavioral aspects associated with mixed reproductive strategies. He championed the comparative approach when deciphering his observations of the movements, displays, and vocalizations of ducks.

McKinney's papers, which were often coauthored with students and colleagues, appeared as reviews (e.g., McKinney et al. 1983) or reported original research (e.g., Cheng et al. 1983). In 1994, the American Ornithologists' Union presented the Brewster Award — its highest honor — to McKinney for his contributions to waterfowl social behavior. He was working on a book about waterfowl behavior at the time of his death. See Mock (2002) for more about Frank McKinney. Photo courtesy of Meryl McKinney.

Figure 3-1. Geese exhibit two main threat postures, the *erect threat*, and the *forward threat* shown here in an Atlantic Brant. Threats are often accompanied by hissing and can lead to an attack of the intruder.

a wintering population in Scotland. They identified four chronological stages in the process: (1) *mate searching*, (2) *herding*, (3) *mock attacks* (including wing displays), and (4) prolonged *triumph ceremonies*. *Mate searching* occurs when males walk through flocks and display a variety of forward neck extensions, head pumping, and erect postures accompanied by vocalizations similar to those used during *triumph ceremonies*. *Herding* or "*sheparding*" (Owen 1980) occurs when a male locates a particular female and unceasingly attempts to separate her from the flock. *Mock attack* occurs when a male runs up to 15 m from the female and exhibits threat postures (Fig. 3-1) toward "imaginary aggressors," although these attacks rarely elicit a response from other birds. The male then runs back toward the female, who often responds with display accompanied by wing-flicking and biting. Black and Owen (1988) believed *mock attack* signified the initiation of a trial liaison that could lead to a long-term bond. Among captive Barnacle Geese allowed to mate in large social groups for 2 years, males sampled one to six potential mates in temporary "trial liaisons" (Choudhury and Black 1993). Males often exhibited a "partner-hold strategy" where they maintained a liaison with one female while sampling another, ul-

timately making a choice between the two. Alternatively, males exhibited a "one-step strategy" and accept or reject a single female before soliciting another.

The last phase of pair formation occurs when pairs exhibited the *triumph ceremony* and aggressive displays toward neighboring birds in the flock (Fig. 3-2). The *triumph ceremony* is a diagnostic and significant display in geese and swans, serving to strengthen or maintain pair bonds and aid the pair in asserting their dominance in aggressive interactions (see Lorenz 1966, Fischer 1965, Lorenz 1979). The *triumph ceremony* occurs throughout the year and also may be performed by family members. The posture of the *triumph ceremony* is similar to the aggressive displays of geese, but both male and female birds participate and orient themselves laterally instead of head-on as occurs during aggressive encounters. Both birds then stretch out their necks and call simultaneously. The *triumph ceremony* also is displayed when a pair reunites, especially after an aggressive interaction with a rival. A *greeting ceremony,* in which a wheezy call is accompanied by a horizontally stretched neck, represents the low-intensity, normal greeting between the members of a pair in the absence of conflict (Balham 1954). See

Figure 3-2. The *triumph ceremony* characterizes the true geese and swans (Anserinae), as exhibited here in Canada Geese. Paired birds display this behavior (1) when mates rejoin each other after periods of spatial or temporal separation, (2) often before aggressive encounters with other birds, and (3) when emerging as "victors" after such encounters. The display is accompanied by loud vocalizations.

Black and Owen (1988) for illustrations of major displays such as *herding, mock attack*, and the *triumph ceremony*.

In Canada Geese, males increase their threatening and aggressive activities with displays that are largely self-descriptive: *bent-neck, forward, erect*, and *head-pumping* postures (Blurton Jones 1960). Generally, each male defends the area around his chosen female, who in turn closely follows her chosen male. Male aggression often includes loud vocalizations accompanying *herding*, which leads to *mock attack,* then *triumph ceremony*. Akesson and Raveling (1982) provide a good description of the behaviors of breeding Canada Geese, including *aggressive approach, retreat, triumph ceremony, calling, head-tossing*, and *head-pumping*.

Just before copulation, both sexes exhibit a precopulatory display characterized by mutual and synchronized *head-dipping*, in which water may run off the bill and over the back in a fashion somewhat resembling bathing movements. As the display

progresses, the female lowers herself into the water in preparation for mounting by the male. Both sexes join in a postcopulatory display, which involves the male lifting his wings and both sexes calling loudly (also see Collias and Jahn 1959).

The Mute Swan provides a good example of courtship display among the swans. During courtship, the mates face each other with raised upper neck feathers and bills pointed downward, almost touching the breast; the secondaries are also sometimes raised, and there is mutual *head-turning* (see Johnsgard 1965, Kear 1972, Ciaranca et al. 1997). *Head-turning* is accompanied by dipping the neck, and vocalizations accompany the entire courtship display. Courtship display is generally brief but can be prolonged when leading to actual copulation. During precopulation, both sexes become synchronized in dipping their heads and preening back and flank feathers, with necks held upright and close together. Copulation occurs shortly after this synchronized display. The postcopulatory display is quite dramatic as the pair rises out of the water, breast to breast with necks extended, eventually subsiding into the water, after which both birds bathe and preen.

Courtship Displays of Dabbling Ducks — Anatini

Dabbling ducks are by far the largest group of waterfowl, and their courtship displays have been well studied in some species. Most species of Anatini, especially those in *Anas*, show homologous movements (i.e., of similar ancestry) in their courtship displays (Ramsay 1956, Johnsgard 1965, Lorenz 1971). With few exceptions, the major displays of males in Northern Hemisphere dabbling ducks fall into three categories: (1) displays directed at a specific female, (2) displays directed at rival males, and (3) displays directed simultaneously at the female and another male (McKinney et al. 1990).

The number of displays varies among species, which reflects courtship habitat and the intensity of sexual selection (Johnson 2000). Specifically, the display repertoire is larger for species that display only on water, as well as for species with dimorphic plumage. Several significant studies address the courtship displays of dabbling ducks: the Chiloé Wigeon (Brewer 1997), the Garganey (Pearce 2000), and the Ringed Teal (Brewer 2001). Within the group, however, the courtship displays of the Mallard have been studied most intensively and therefore provide a sound basis for understanding behavior representative of other dabbling ducks, and the complexities of courtship behavior. We relied on Lorenz (1951–53), Johnsgard (1960), Lebret (1961), Weidmann and Darley 1971), Cramp (1977), and Drilling et al. (2002) for our summary.

For Mallards and many other Anatini, males gather in groups on open water for courtship displays, which Lorenz (1951–53) called "social play." Males in these groups perform a number of differentiated movements, most of which are accompanied by vocalizations. Males begin with a courtship-intent posture where the head is lowered between the shoulders and, with head feathers erect, use ritualized shaking to exhibit interest in a particular female. These displays (*head-shake, head-flick, swimming-shake*) occur while the male is oriented broadside to the female. Males also use *jump flights* to attract the attention of females. Courtship "bouts" last up to 15 min and sometimes longer, and the displays of the males are usually highly synchronized.

Initial displays may also involve *drinking*. In this display, two ducks encountering each other "drink," which Lorenz interpreted as a "sign of peace." Thus, this display represents reduced aggression and may initiate further behavioral interactions. However, *drinking* is also simply a reaction between two ducks encountering each other and, although frequently true, it is not necessarily confined to male–female associations. *Drinking* is often followed by *mock-preening*, which almost always occurs after a male "drinks" in front of a potential mate. *Mock-preening* involves the male moving his bill behind his wing, but instead of actually preening, the nail of the bill is rubbed against the underside of the wing to produce a "*Rrr*" sound that can be heard several meters away. Males also exhibit *mock-preening* when encountering other males.

Preliminary shaking commonly occurs once courtship behavior intensifies. In this display, males first withdraw their heads toward their shoulders, ruffle their underfeathers, and elevate their bodies on the water's surface. This posturing is quickly followed by a thrusting upward of the head and body in a series of shakes, the first of which is usually followed by a second and third, each with increasing intensity. *Preliminary shaking* apparently attracts a female's attention and likely indicates that more elaborate displays will follow: *grunt-whistle, down-up,* or *head-up-tail-up.*

The *head-up-tail-up* complex forms the major social display of male Mallards and usually consists of four displays given in quick succession: (1) *head-up-tail-up,* (2) *turn-head-to-female,* (3) *nod-swimming,* and (4) *leading* (see below). The *head-up-tail-up* display itself is perhaps the most complicated and appears as the courtship process intensifies. It begins with a simultaneous drawing of the head backwards and upwards and curving of the rump upward, which gives the appearance of sitting short but high on the water. The wings also are uplifted so that the curl feathers on the tail can be seen easily from the side. The "burp," which is a single sharp whistle, accompanies this display and only occurs at this time. This display lasts about 1 sec after which the body returns to normal position, but the head may remain high with the bill pointed toward a particular female. Importantly, the male directs this display while broadside to the female, which serves to signal the intended receiver. Indeed, orientation and accompanying vocalizations are vital components of courtship display, critical to understanding their ultimate function in the courtship process.

Head-up-tail-up is often immediately followed by *turn-head-to-female* and *nod-swimming* where the

Figure 3-3. The *grunt-whistle* as seen here in a Green-winged Teal is a common display in the courtship repertoire of dabbling ducks (Anatini). This display — often given by groups of males — is easily observed and indicates intensification of the courtship process.

male lowers his outstretched head and neck to the waterline and swims away from the female or moves in a circle around her. At the end of the *nod-swimming* bout, the male returns to normal position but *leads* the female from the group with the *turn-the-back-of-the-head* display. During *turn-the-back-of-the-head*, the male exposes the feathers on the back of the head in such a way as to present a stiffly raised central line of neck feathers; this posture presents a striking dark line of black on green to the female.

Lorenz (1951–53) assigned "equal value" to the *grunt-whistle*, *head-up-tail-up*, and *down-up* in the repertoire of courtship displays. However, Johnsgard (1960) considered the *grunt-whistle* as a low-intensity display, the *down-up* as most intense and the *head-up-tail-up* as intermediate. The *grunt-whistle* may be displayed more frequently early in the period of courtship, with the *down-up* increasing in frequency and eventually comprising about half of all male displays at the peak of pair formation.

The *grunt-whistle* is displayed by a lone male or, more frequently, by a group of males and heralds growing intensification of the courtship process (Fig. 3-3). The *grunt-whistle* appears directed toward a particular female (Simmons and Weidmann 1973).

In this display, the bill is lowered into the water and shaken slightly from side to side. The body then is arched upward while the bill is still held low and often extended into the water. The bird's windpipe may be stretched in this bent position, for the male emits a loud, sharp whistle followed by a deep grunt just before the peak of the body's arch is attained. The bird's head then straightens and the body settles back onto the water. At the peak of the arch, the bill touches the water and often is accompanied by tossing a fine stream of droplets in the direction of the female.

The *down-up* movement involves the male quickly lowering the bill into the water and then jerking the head quickly upward without lifting the breast. A whistle is emitted when the head is highest and the bill lowest. A stream of water often rises when the bill is lifted, at which time the male utters the "raebraeb" call. The *down-up* is especially associated with strong hostility and the proximity of males to one another. Mallards also exhibit *courtship flights*, where a female takes flight, followed by as many as 5–15 males and lasting 5–10 min (Dzubin 1957). These flights are generally slow and erratic, and the female will exhibit the *inciting* display (see below).

Figure 3-4. All waterfowl normally copulate on the water with the male grasping the back of the female's head in the posture shown here in a pair of Northern Shovelers. After Todd (1996:40).

Females stimulate the males to display with *nod-swimming* (Weidmann and Darley 1971), where the female nods while extending her head flatly near the water as she swims among males, or by *steaming* with head held low over the water. This display is usually exhibited in the presence of several males, whose own displays have signaled their readiness for courtship. In function, this behavior appears to stimulate the males into further courtship displays, and its occurrence usually indicates that courtship will intensify.

Inciting is the most distinctive posture in the courtship behavior of female Mallards, and is basically the same display in all dabbling ducks and several other groups of ducks as well (Lorenz 1951–53). In this display, the female swims after her mate (or mate-to-be) and at the same time "threatens" another male by flicking her head over her shoulder. *Inciting* also can be given in flight, and is accompanied by a specific call described as "queggegge'ggeggeggeggegg," which is accented mostly on the third syllable. The male's response to *inciting* may be to attack the individual designated by the female or to exhibit *leading* (Johnsgard 1960), where the male attempts to lead her away from the courtship group by exhibiting *turn-the-back-of-the-*

head. Turn-the-back-of-the-head in this context involves the male turning his head toward the *inciting* female as he swims rapidly away from her. Importantly, males and females involved with *inciting* displays often have formed pair bonds, but *inciting* also can reflect temporary liaisons formed early in the pairing process.

Another major display for females is *pumping*, which occurs as a prelude to actual copulation in many species of Anatini. In this display, the head is rapidly jerked downward and then more slowly returned upward. *Pumping* often is displayed simultaneously by both members of the pair, but because males often initiate copulatory behavior, they generally exhibit more intensive *pumping* than females. *Pumping* provides good evidence that copulation is imminent.

Copulation in Mallards and all other ducks normally occurs on the water and is characterized by the female assuming a low posture, with the male then climbing onto the female's back and grabbing her head (Fig. 3-4). Waterfowl are among the few birds of any kind in which the male has a penis for introducing sperm. In other birds, sperm are transferred when the cloacas of the two birds come into contact without intromission of a penis or other

Figure 3-5. Postcopulatory behavior in many species of waterfowl often involves displays derived from bathing movements. In some species of whistling-ducks (Dendrocygninae), however, the postcopulatory display is quite distinctive, as shown here by a pair of Fulvous Whistling-Ducks. Photo courtesy of Brooke Meanley.

specialized organ.

Postcopulatory displays almost always involve bathing by the female (as in all waterfowl), while the male performs *bridling* (and accompanying call) where the head is drawn in and the chest lifted out of the water (Fig. 3-5). Postcopulatory displays are quite elaborate in some groups of ducks and likely serve to maintain pair bonds, individual identification, and signaling of successful copulation (see Johnson et al. 2000).

Female Mallards and other species of *Anas* also exhibit a vocalization known as the "decrescendo call," which varies from one to more than 20 syllables (Johnsgard 1965). This vocalization is the familiar six-syllable "*quaegaegaegaegaegaegaeg*" in which the strongest accent is on the second syllable, after which the sound decreases (Lorenz 1951–53). The decrescendo call is a feature of unpaired females, which are stimulated by another bird flying nearby. The call also is emitted by females separated from their mates (Lockner and Phillips 1969).

Courtship Displays of Pochards —Aythyini

The pochards are not a particularly large group of waterfowl, but they are commonly encountered;

hence we address their courtship displays here. Male pochards share some displays with dabbling ducks (e.g., *turn-the-back-of-the-head*), but males are generally silent except during courtship, and the vocalizations of females do not include the decrescendo call of the dabbling ducks. Among the males of most species, courtship displays include the *kinked-neck*, *head-throw*, *sneak*, *turn-the-back-of-the-head*, and *preening-behind-the-wing* (Johnsgard 1965). "*Coughing*" is a major vocalization of many pochards, although infrequent and not conspicuous in Canvasbacks. *Bill-dipping* and *preening-dorsally* are the precopulatory displays of males, but unlike dabbling ducks, only rudimentary *pumping* is present in just a few species of pochards and altogether absent in females (Johnsgard 1965). Here we review the basic displays of the Canvasback as our model, using as sources the classic work of Hochbaum (1944), as well as Johnsgard (1965), Cramp (1977), and especially Mowbray (2002).

The major courtship displays of male Canvasbacks are the *neck-stretch*, *head-throw*, *kinked-neck*, *sneak*, and *turn-the-back-of-the head*. As in dabbling ducks, male pochards typically perform in groups, with "courting parties" consisting of one female and three to eight males. The *neck-stretch* is the most common display and features the male's head being held as high as the neck can extend for at least a minute, while the performing bird swims back and forth or remains stationary. The male may also perform a very soft, repeated one-syllable "*rrr*" along with this display. The *neck-stretch* usually occurs early in the courtship sequence and probably serves as a synchronizing mechanism for birds at, or near, the same stage of reproduction. For this reason, this behavior is common in late winter and early spring. Females may respond by also exhibiting a *neck-stretch* accompanied by a low-pitched "*kuck-kuck*," whereas pairs may perform this display during aggressive interactions with conspecifics.

Displays that follow *neck-stretch* include *head-throw*, in which the head is extended backward over the body, with the bill pointed upward and toward a preferred female. There is an associated "*ick-ick-cooo*" call, the first two notes given as the head is brought back and the last while the head is brought forward; the "*coo*" at times is given without the *head-throw*. The *head-throw* has been reported for all species of *Aythya*, but the posture and notes vary among each. The display is most often performed by unpaired males during social courtship and by paired males when other males interact with their females.

Sneak and *turn-the-back-of-the head* are two

other major displays of male Canvasbacks. During *sneak*, the head and neck are extended forward on the water's surface while swimming around the female, or in a stationary position nearby. This display is common among males displaying to a given female, and in aggressive interactions between pairs. In *turn-the-back-of-the head*, the male swims ahead of the female while slowly turning the head toward the female. This display is common early in the pair-formation process but rarely occurs in established pairs.

Inciting among the pochards, as in dabbling ducks, is the primary display of the female. This display is directed toward the preferred male and consists of threatening movements and *neck-stretching* accompanied by a soft "*krrr-krrr*." Males respond to inciting by swimming in front of the female and displaying *turn-the-back-of-the-head*. As in the Anatini, *inciting* indicates at least a temporary liaison.

Precopulatory behavior in males consists of alternately displaying the self-descriptive *bill-dipping*, *arch*, and *preening-dorsally* postures. The female may respond with the same displays, but there is no *pumping* as occurs in the dabbling ducks. Copulation takes place in the water, after which the male gives the *kinked-neck call* and swims away in the *bill-down* posture. The *kinked-neck* vocalization — the courtship call of Hochbaum (1944) — is given with the neck held in a characteristic posture. After copulation, the female bathes, but she may assume the *bill-down* posture briefly beforehand. The pair also may swim parallel to each other or in tight circles. Other species of Aythyini typically exhibit the same postcopulatory displays as described here.

Courtship Displays of Sea Ducks — Mergini

Sea ducks also are not a large group of waterfowl, but they are widely distributed and frequently encountered. Courtship patterns of males are diverse, but common displays within the tribe include *shake* and *wing-flapping*; the females in most species *incite*, but this behavior is displayed in variable fashion (Johnsgard 1965). Precopulatory behavior also is quite variable among species but generally provides the best behavioral evidence for homogeneity of membership within the tribe. We have chosen the Common Goldeneye as our model for the Mergini because this species is widespread and encountered in a variety of habitats in both the Nearctic and Palearctic. Moreover, the behavior of the Common Goldeneye is well studied (Dane et al.

1959, Lind 1959, Dane and van der Kloot 1964). Our terminology largely follows Johnsgard (1965), and we also have relied on the summary provided by Eadie et al. (1995).

Courtship behavior occurs in small groups averaging 4.4 males and 1.2 females (Afton and Sayler 1982) and occurs from December through April. Males exhibit a large number of major displays, of which *bowsprit-pumping* is probably the most commonplace. *Bowsprit-pumping*, much like *head-pumping* in females, features a diagonally extended neck, which then is withdrawn to its normal position. *Head-turning* also is frequently displayed, most often by the male-of-choice in association with an inciting female. During *head-turning*, the neck is extended upward, the bill is held horizontally, and the head is turned rigidly from side to side.

Several types of head-throws are the most distinctive displays of male Common Goldeneyes, but the most common is the simple *head-throw* in which the head is quickly tossed back with a call of "*rrrt*." Another is a *fast head-throw-kick*, which lasts about 1 sec, during which the head is thrown back and both feet concurrently are kicked rearward; a loud "*zeee-zeee*" accompanies these movements (Fig. 3-6). A *slow head-throw-kick* is nearly identical, but less commonly displayed. A final major display is the *masthead*, which starts with the head held low to the water, much like *bowsprit-pumping*, but the head is rapidly elevated upward, then thrust downward without bending the neck. A soft "*rrrrt*" accompanies *bowsprit-pumping*. Common Goldeneye males also engage in short display flights, which may function as a means of encouraging females to follow and, at the same time, separating a potential mate from the courtship of other males (Afton and Sayler 1982).

The most frequent display of the female is *head-pumping*, during which the head is pumped up and down in a diagonal movement. Another frequent display of females is the *head-up*, which is an indication of general excitement to the courtship process. *Neck-dipping* is another common display, during which the neck is lowered into the water and a weak call is given. *Inciting* commonly involves the female and two males whereby the female swims behind the preferred male, alternately turning her head over each shoulder.

Female copulatory behavior can begin with *drinking*, *head-lifting*, or *bathing*, which is often rapidly followed by the female assuming a prone posture. Males perform two major precopulatory dis-

Figure 3-6. The sea ducks (Mergini) exhibit an array of head-throws in their courtship displays, as depicted here in the Common Goldeneye. An array of other displays round out the courtship repertoire, but the postcopulatory *bill-down* is also unique to this tribe (McKinney 1992).

plays, *drinking* and the *wing-and-leg-stretch*. After a series of jabs, the male *preens-dorsally* on the side facing the female and *steams* to her while issuing a soft "*bzzzzt.*" The male then mounts the female while displaying *preens-dorsally* one or more times. Copulation itself averages 8.3 sec. After copulation, the male continues holding the female and the pair *rotates* in small circles. After release, the male *steams* away and performs *head-turning*, after which the pair bathes and flaps their wings; less often, Common Goldeneyes dive after copulation.

FACTORS AFFECTING MATE CHOICE

In addition to display repertoires, other factors can influence choice of mates among waterfowl. In ducks, for example, female Northern Pintails prefer to mate with males with the whitest breast color and longest scapular feathers (Sorenson and Derrickson 1994). Females also preferred 2-year-old males instead of yearlings. In comparison to yearlings, the older males were more colorful and attentive, and courted more aggressively. The study concluded that female choice played a significant role in the evolution of secondary sexual characteristics of male Northern Pintails (see also Cunningham 2003).

Omland (1996a, 1996b) studied mate choice by female Mallards, which assess male ornaments such as bill color, tail curls, neck rings, maroon breasts,

and more. Only bill color significantly affected the pairing process, explaining 24% of the variation in male pairing success: Males with more yellow, unblemished bills consistently had higher pairing success. Bill color coupled with molt intensity explained 39% of the variation in pairing success. Potentially, fleshy ornaments such as bills better reflect short-term body condition (and hence male quality) than plumage. A second experiment darkened (black) male bills, shaved the head, neck ring, and breast (anterior shaving), clipped the wing-patch (speculum), and yellowed the bill. Anterior shaving caused 15 of 16 males to lower pairing success, and bill blackening lowered success in 15 of 19. However, because the bill covers a much smaller area than the anterior plumage, it is comparatively much more important in mate assessment. In fowl, comb size is strongly correlated with blood testosterone, which reflects current physical condition. Hence, characteristics of fleshy ornaments such as the bill can provide females with significant signals of potential mate quality (see Ligon et al. 1990). Interestingly, Johnson (1999) reported that all species of dabbling ducks with bill coloration also possess monomorphic plumage, which led to the conclusion that bill color was a less costly male ornament than bright plumage and is thus a derived condition among dabbling ducks.

However, females still may assess plumage quality as an "honest signal" of male condition. For example, plumage "immaculateness" is a novel measure of plumage quality that assesses feather wear and damage. In the Severn River estuary, United Kingdom, Common Shelducks with immaculate plumage were in better body condition, tended to mate assortatively at preferred feeding sites, and were more likely to produce a brood (Ferns and Lang 2003). Hence, immaculateness was deemed a potential honest signal of parental quality and therefore mate choice.

In another study with captive Mallards, male plumage status was an important factor affecting mate choice by females, although male courtship remained the most important factor (Holmberg et al. 1989), a finding supported by other studies as well (Bossema and Kruijt 1982, Klint et al. 1989). Interestingly, body weight of males was not a significant factor in female choice, perhaps because body weight is the most difficult factor to assess visually. Females did, however, exclusively incite males fed on an ad libitum regime, perhaps because those males might exhibit better survival following pair formation and thereafter.

Among geese, assortative mating with respect to plumage color is especially well known in the dimorphic Lesser Snow Goose, which is characterized by white and blue color phases. Assortative mating occurs when individuals mate nonrandomly with respect to a phenotypic attribute such as plumage color; such behavior was first described for the Lesser Snow Goose by Cooch and Beardmore (1959). Subsequent work verified a hypothesis that mate selection in Snow Geese reflected imprinting of the goslings on the parental color type as well as on sibling color (see Cooke et al. 1972, Cooke and McNally 1975, Cooke et al. 1976, Cooke 1978). Indeed, birds from nests with adults and goslings of the same color tended to choose mates of that color, whereas birds from families of mixed colors tended to choose mates of either color, which led to a prediction that mixed pairs would eventually disappear from the population. However, long-term studies of Snow Geese at La Perouse Bay in northern Manitoba by Cooke and his colleagues revealed that the assortative system was not perfect. Over 15 years, the frequency of mixed pairs was 14–19% annually. Indeed, 9.7% of goslings from white parents chose blue mates, and 21.8% of goslings from blue parents chose white mates (see Cooke 1987). Hence, mixed pairs persist in the population. Findlay et al. (1985) subsequently documented few differences between pure and mixed pairs in several components of reproductive success. However, higher recruitment rates occurred among

mixed pairs for two of seven cohorts, and nest failure was also consistently lower. Such results predict an advantage in mixed matings, yet positive assortment occurs, probably because the color phases were allopatric until the early part of the 20th century; hence, cues for species (color phase) recognition may still act as an isolating mechanism against mixed pairs (see Cooke 1987).

In Barnacle Geese, mate selection is influenced by vigilance, facial patterns, and female body mass (Choudhury and Black 1993), as well as by male body size and dominance status (Choudhury and Black 1994). Barnacle Geese also preferentially paired with familiar individuals from their own breeding grounds, which may provide advantages such as earlier pairing and local adaptation of the pair to the breeding area (Choudhury and Black 1994). Similar re-pairing behavior has been recorded during a 15-year study of Greylag Geese wintering in the Guadalquivir marshes of southwestern Spain and the Dutch Delta (Nilsson and Persson 2001).

OTHER FUNCTIONS OF COURTSHIP DISPLAY

McKinney et al. (1990) recognized that major displays of dabbling ducks (Anatini) were used in contexts of *both* male–female courtship and agonistic male–male encounters; hence displays serve multiple functions. For example, the *down-up* display of captive male Green-winged Teal signaled interest in a female but also threatened rival males (McKinney and Stolen 1982). In the Bahamas, 51% of *down-up* displays of White-cheeked Pintails were directed toward males (see McKinney et al. 1990). In captive Speckled Teal, 47% of *grunt-whistle* and 44% of *bridling* displays were directed at males (see McKinney et al. 1990). The Speckled Teal of South America also uses displays for both courtship and aggression (Port and McKinney 2001). The orientation of displays (e.g., broadside, facing) was deemed especially significant when determining display context. For example, in many major male–female displays such as *grunt-whistle*, *head-up-tail-up*, and *bridling*, the male orients broadside to the female, whereas others are pointed directly away from the female (e.g., *turn-the-back-of-the-head*).

McKinney et al. (1990) proposed that multiple uses of courtship displays may develop where males have an opportunity to develop intense rivalry such as the island-based White-cheeked Pintail or in species with long-term pair bonds. In both situations, individuals may interact for several years, which could lead to development of complex dominance hierarchies. However, the Garganey, a common migratory species of Europe and Asia, uses several courtship displays in male–male interactions (Pearce 2000), but these observations were made from captive birds, which may have facilitated development of intense male rivalries. Observations of wild Mallards nevertheless demonstrated that a major Mallard display, *down-up*, often served different functions (Davis 1997). *Down-up* displays given early in courtship bouts were directed toward a particular female (broadside), whereas *down-up* displayed later was directed toward the first male to display in the bout (head-on). Overall, multiple use of courtship displays is an important area for behavioral research of waterfowl and should consider orientation of displays as well as the species involved.

SOME FINAL THOUGHTS

As noted earlier, much additional information is available on the courtship, pairing, and mating systems in waterfowl than we can present here, and much remains to be discovered in this exciting area of waterfowl ecology. Yet significant work has come forward in recent years. For example, detailed studies on the breeding displays of the Chiloé Wigeon of South America revealed a year-round *triumph ceremony,* absence of two major displays (*head-and-tail-up* and *down-up*), absence of the female decrescendo call, and courtship of ducklings by unpaired, adult males (Brewer 1997). Display behavior (some previously undescribed) and accompanying vocalizations have been described for the Ringed Teal, also from South America (Brewer 2001), along with advertising displays of the Musk Duck of Australia (McCracken et al. 2002). Courtship behavior ultimately unites the sexes, which begins the physiological processes and reproductive strategies associated with producing and hatching a clutch of eggs, the topics for the next chapter.

LITERATURE CITED

Afton, A. D., and C. D. Ankney. 1991. Nutrient-reserve dynamics of breeding Lesser Scaup: a test of competing hypotheses. Condor 93:89–97.

Afton, A. D., and R. D. Sayler. 1982. Social courtship and pairbonding of Common Goldeneyes, (*Bucephala clangula*), wintering in Minnesota. Canadian Field-Naturalist 96:295–300.

Akesson, T. R., and D. G. Raveling. 1982. Behaviors associated with seasonal reproduction and long-term monogamy in Canada Geese. Condor 84:188–196.

Alcock, J. 2001. Animal behavior: an evolutionary approach. Seventh edition. Sunderland Associates, Sunderland, Massachusetts.

Amat, J. A. 1983. Pursuit flights of Mallard and Gadwall under different environmental conditions. Wildfowl 34:14–19.

Anderson, M. G. 1985a. Social behavior of breeding Canvasbacks (*Aythya valisineria*): male and female strategies of reproduction. Dissertation, University of Minnesota, Minneapolis.

Anderson, M. G. 1985b. Variations on monogamy in Canvasbacks (*Aythya valisineria*). Ornithological Monographs 37:57–67.

Anderson, M. G., J. M. Rhymer, and F. C. Rohwer. 1992. Philopatry, dispersal, and the genetic structure of waterfowl populations. Pages 365–395 *in* B. D. J. Batt, A. D. Afton, M. G. Anderson, C. D. Ankney, D. H. Johnson, J. A. Kadlec, and G. L. Krapu, editors. Ecology and management of breeding waterfowl. University of Minnesota Press, Minneapolis.

Anderson, M. G., and R. D. Titman. 1992. Spacing patterns. Pages 251–289 *in* B. D. J. Batt, A. D. Afton, M. G. Anderson, C. D. Ankney, D. H. Johnson, J. A. Kadlec, and G. L. Krapu, editors. Ecology and management of breeding waterfowl. University of Minnesota Press, Minneapolis.

Ankney, C. D., and C. D. MacInnes. 1978. Nutrient reserves and reproductive performance of female Lesser Snow Geese. Auk 95:459–471.

Armbruster, J. S. 1982. Wood Duck displays and pairing chronology. Auk 99:116–122.

Ashcroft, R. E. 1976. A function of the pairbond in the Common Eider. Wildfowl 27:101–105.

Baldassarre, G. A., and E. G. Bolen. 1986. Body weight and aspects of pairing chronology of Green-winged Teal and Northern Pintails wintering on the Southern High Plains of Texas. Southwestern Naturalist 31:361–366.

Balham, R. W. 1954. The behavior of the Canada Goose *Branta canadensis* in Manitoba. Dissertation, University of Montana, Missoula.

Ball, I. J., P. G. H. Frost, W. R. Siegfried, and F. McKinney. 1978. Territories and local movements of African Black Ducks. Wildfowl 29:61–79.

Banko, W. E. 1960. The Trumpeter Swan. U.S. Fish and Wildlife Service North America Fauna Series 63.

Bellrose, F. C. 1980. Ducks, geese and swans of North America. Stackpole Books, Harrisburg, Pennsylvania.

Birkhead, M., and C. M. Perrins. 1986. The Mute Swan. Croom Helm Publishing, London.

Black, J. M. 1996. Introduction: pair bonds and partnerships. Pages 3–20 *in* J. M. Black, editor. Partnerships in birds. The study of monogamy. Oxford University Press, Oxford.

Black, J. M. 1998. Movement of Barnacle Geese between colonies in Svalbard and the colonization process. Norsk Polarinst Skrifter 200:115–127.

Black, J. M. 2001. Fitness consequences of long-term pair bonds in Barnacle Geese: monogamy in the extreme. Behavioral Ecology 12:640–645.

Black, J. M., C. Carbone, M. Owen, and R. Wells. 1992. Foraging dynamics in goose flocks: the cost of living on the edge. Animal Behaviour 44:41–50.

Black, J. M., S. Choudhury, and M. Owen. 1996. Do geese benefit from lifelong monogamy? Pages 91–117 *in* Partnerships in birds. The study of monogamy. J. M. Black, editor. Oxford University Press, Oxford.

Black, J. M., and M. Owen. 1988. Variation in pairbond and agonistic behaviors in Barnacle Geese on the wintering grounds. Pages 39–57 *in* M. W. Weller, editor. Waterfowl in Winter. University of Minnesota Press, Minneapolis.

Black, J. M., and M. Owen. 1989a. Parent–offspring relationships in wintering Barnacle Geese. Animal Behaviour 37:187–198.

Black, J. M., and M. Owen. 1989b. Agonistic behaviour in goose flocks: assessment, investment and reproductive success. Animal Behaviour 37:199–209.

Black, J. M., and M. Owen. 1995. Reproductive performance and assortative pairing in relation to age in Barnacle Geese. Journal of Animal Ecology 64:234–244.

Blem, C. R. 1973. Geographic variation in the bioenergetics of the House Sparrow. Ornithological Monographs 14:96–121.

Blohm, R. J. 1978. Migrational homing of male Gadwalls to breeding grounds. Auk 95:763–766.

Blohm, R. J. 1979. The breeding ecology of the Gadwall in southern Manitoba. Dissertation, University of Wisconsin, Madison.

Blohm, R. J., and K. A. Mackenzie. 1994. Additional evidence of migrational homing by a pair of Mallards. Journal of Field Ornithology 65:476–478.

Blurton Jones, N. G. 1960. Experiments on the causation of the threat postures of Canada Geese. Wildfowl Trust Annual Report 11:46–52.

Bossema, I., and J. P. Kruijt. 1982. Male activity and female mate acceptance in the Mallards (*Anas platyrhynchos*). Behaviour 79:313–324.

Braithwaite, L. W. 1976. Breeding seasons of waterfowl in Australia. International Ornithological Congress 16:235–247.

Brasher, M. G., R. M. Kaminski, and L. W. Burger. 2002. Evaluation of indicated breeding pair criteria to estimate Mallard breeding populations. Journal of Wildlife Management 66:985–992.

Brewer, G. 1989. Biparental care behavior of captive Ringed Teal *Callonetta leucophrys*. Wildfowl 40:7–13.

Brewer, G. L. 1997. Displays and breeding behaviours of the Chiloe Wigeon *Anas sibilatrix*. Wildfowl 47:97–125.

Brewer, G. L. 2001. Displays and breeding behaviour of captive Ringed Teal *Callonetta leucophrys*. Wildfowl 52:97–125.

Brodsky, L. M., C. D. Ankney, and D. G. Dennis. 1988. The influence of male dominance on social interactions in Black Ducks and Mallards. Animal Behaviour 36:1371–1378.

Brodsky, L. M., and P. J. Weatherhead. 1985. Time and energy constraints on courtship in wintering American Black Ducks. Condor 87:33–36.

Brown, J. L., and G. H. Orians. 1970. Spacing patterns in mobile animals. Annual Review of Ecology and Systematics 1:239–262.

Buitron, D., and G. L. Nuechterlein. 1989. Male parental care of Patagonian Crested Ducks *Anas (Lophonetta) specularioides*. Wildfowl 40:14–21.

Caithamer, D. F., R. J. Gates, and T. C. Tacha. 1996. A comparison of diurnal time budgets from paired interior Canada Geese with and without offspring. Journal of Field Ornithology 67:105–113.

Cheng, K. M., J. T. Burns, and F. McKinney. 1983. Forced copulation in captive Mallards III. Sperm competition. Auk 100:302–310.

Choudhury, S., and J. M. Black. 1993. Mate selection behaviour and sampling strategies in geese. Animal Behaviour 46:747–757.

Choudhury, S., and J. M. Black. 1994. Barnacle Geese preferentially pair with familiar associates from early life. Animal Behaviour 48:81–88.

Ciaranca, M. A., C. C. Allin, and G. S. Jones. 1997. Mute Swan (*Cygnus olor*). The birds of North America, 273. The American Ornithologists' Union, Washington, D.C., and The Academy of Natural Sciences, Philadelphia.

Collias, N. E., and L. R. Jahn. 1959. Social behavior and breeding success in Canada Geese (*Branta canadensis*) confined under semi-natural conditions. Auk 76:478–509.

Cooch, F. G., and J. A. Beardmore. 1959. Assortative mating and reciprocal differences in the Blue–Snow Goose complex. Nature 183:1833–1834.

Cooke, F. 1978. Early learning and its effect on population structure. Studies of a wild population of Snow Geese. Zeitschrift fur Tierpsychologie 46:344–358.

Cooke, F. 1987. Lesser Snow Goose: a long-term population study. Pages 407–432 *in* F. Cooke and P. A. Buckley, editors. Avian genetics: a population and ecological approach. Academic Press, London.

Cooke, F., G. H. Finney, and R. F. Rockwell. 1976. Assortative mating in Lesser Snow Geese (*Anser caerulescens*). Behavior Genetics 6:127–140.

Cooke, F., and C. M. McNally. 1975. Mate selection and colour preferences in Lesser Snow Geese. Behaviour 53:151–170.

Cooke, F., P. J. Mirsky, and M. B. Seiger. 1972. Color preferences in the Lesser Snow Goose and their possible role in mate selection. Canadian Journal of Zoology 50:529–536.

Cowardin, L. M., D. S. Gilmer, and C. W. Shaffer. 1985. Mallard recruitment in the agricultural environment of North Dakota. Wildlife Monographs 92.

Cramp, S., editor. 1977. Handbook of the birds of Europe, the Middle East, and North Africa. The birds of the western Palearctic. Volume 1. Ostrich to ducks. Oxford University Press, Oxford.

Cunningham, E. J. A. 2003. Female mate preference and subsequent resistance to copulation by the Mallard. Behavioral Ecology 14: 326–333.

Dane, B., and W. G. van der Kloot. 1964. An analysis of the display of the goldeneye duck (*Bucephala clangula* L.). Behaviour 22:282-328.

Dane, B., C. Walcott, and W. H. Drury. 1959. The form and duration of the display actions of the Goldeneye (*Bucephala clangula*).Behaviour 14:265–281.

Davis, E. S. 1997. The down-up display of the Mallard: one display, two orientations. Animal Behaviour 53:1025–1034.

Dementiev, G. P., and N. A. Gladkov. 1952. The birds of the Soviet Union, Volume 4. Moscow, Soviet Union (in Russian).

Derrickson, S. R. 1978. The mobility of breeding Pintails. Auk 95:104–114.

Doherty, P. F., Jr, J.D. Nichols, and 15 other authors. 2002. Sources of variation in breeding-ground fidelity of Mallards (*Anas platyrhynchos*). Behavioral Ecology 13:543–550.

Doty, H. A., and F. B. Lee. 1974. Homing to nest baskets by wild female Mallards. Journal of Wildlife Management 38:714–719.

Dow, H., and S. Fredga. 1983. Breeding and natal dispersal of the Goldeneye, *Bucephala clangula*. Journal of Animal Ecology 52:681–695.

Drilling, N., R. Titman, and F. McKinney. 2002. Mallard (*Anas platyrhynchos*). The birds of North America, 658. The American Ornithologists' Union, Washington, D.C., and The Academy of Natural Sciences, Philadelphia.

Dwyer, C. P., and G. A. Baldassarre. 1994. Habitat use by sympatric female Mallards and American Black Ducks breeding in a forested environment. Canadian Journal of Zoology 72:1538–1542.

Dwyer, T. J., S. R. Derrickson, and D. S. Gilmer. 1973. Migrational homing by a pair of Mallards. Auk 90:687.

Dwyer, T. J., G. L. Krapu, and D. M. Janke. 1979. Use of prairie pothole habitat by breeding Mallards. Journal of Wildlife Management 43: 526–531.

Dzubin, A. 1955. Some evidences of home range in waterfowl. Transactions of the North American Wildlife Conference 20:278–298.

Dzubin, A. 1957. Pairing display and spring and summer flights of the Mallard. Blue Jay 15:10–13.

Dzubin, A. 1969. Assessing breeding populations of ducks by ground counts. Pages 178–230 *in* Saskatoon wetlands seminar. Canadian Wildlife Service Report Series 6.

Eadie, J. M., M. L. Mallory, and H. G. Lumsden. 1995. Common Goldeneye (*Bucephala clangula*). The birds of North America, 170. The American Ornithologists' Union, Washington, D.C., and The Academy of Natural Sciences, Philadelphia.

Eldridge, J. L. 1986. Territoriality in a river specialist: the Blue Duck. Wildfowl 37:1213–135.

Emlen, S. T., and L. W. Oring. 1977. Ecology, sexual selection, and the evolution of mating systems. Science 197:215–233.

Ewaschuk, E., and D. A. Boag. 1972. Factors affecting hatching success of densely nesting Canada Geese. Journal of Wildlife Management 36:1097–1106.

Ferns, P. N., and A. Lang. 2003. The value of immaculate mates: relationships between plumage quality and breeding in shelducks. Ethology 109:521–532.

Findlay, C. S., R. F. Rockwell, J. A. Smith, and F. Cooke. 1985. Life-history studies of the Lesser Snow Goose (*Anser caerulescens caerulsecens*). VI. Plumage polymorphism, assortative mating and fitness. Evolution 39:904–914.

Fischer, H. 1965. Das triumphgeschrei der Graugans. Zeitschrift fur Tierpsychologie 22:247–304.

Frith, H. J. 1967. Waterfowl in Australia. Angus & Robertson, Sydney.

Gates, J. M. 1962. Breeding biology of the Gadwall in northern Utah. Wilson Bulletin 74:43–67.

Gauthier, G. 1987a. Further evidence of long-term pair bonds in the ducks of the genus *Bucephala*. Auk 104:521–522.

Gauthier, G. 1987b. The adaptive significance of territorial behavior in breeding Buffleheads: a test of three hypotheses. Animal Behaviour 35:348–360.

Gauthier, G. 1988. Territorial behaviour, forced copulations and mixed reproductive strategy in ducks. Wildfowl 39:102–114.

Gilmer, D. S., I. J. Ball, L. M. Cowardin, H. H. Riechmann, and J. R. Tester. 1975. Habitat use and home range of Mallards breeding in Minnesota. Journal of Wildlife Management 39:781–789.

Gilmer, D. S., I. J. Ball, and J. H. Riechmann. 1977. Post-breeding activities of Mallards and Wood Ducks in north-central Minnesota. Journal of Wildlife Management 41:345–359.

Godfrey, J. D., D. M. Bryant, and M. Williams. 2003. Energetics of Blue Ducks in rivers of differing physical and biological characteristics. Science for Conservation (Wellington) 214:35–68.

Goudie, R. I., and C. D. Ankney. 1988. Patterns of habitat use by sea ducks wintering in southeastern Newfoundland. Ornis Scandinavica 19:249–256.

Gowans, B., G. J. Robertson, and F. Cooke. 1997. Behaviour and chronology of pair formation by Harlequin Ducks (*Histrionicus histrionicus*). Wildfowl 48:135–146.

Gray, B. J. 1980. Reproduction, energetics and social structure of the Ruddy Duck. Dissertation, University of California, Davis.

Gregoire, P. E., and C. D. Ankney. 1990. Agonistic behavior and dominance relationships among Lesser Snow Geese during winter and migration. Auk 107:550–560.

Grier, J. W., and T. Burk. 1992. Biology of animal behavior. Second Edition. Mosby-Year Book, St. Louis.

Guiler, E. R. 1966. The breeding of Black Swan (*Cygnus atrata*) in Tasmania with special reference to some management problems. Proceedings of the Royal Society of Tasmania 100:31–52.

Heinroth, O. 1910. Beobachtungen bei einem Einburgerungsversuch mit der Brautente (*Lampronessa sponsa* [L.]). Journal für Ornithologie 1:101–156.

Heinroth, O. 1911. Beiträge zur Biologie, namentlich Ethologie und Psychologie der Anatiden. International Ornithological Congress 5:589–702.

Hepp, G. R. 1986. Effects of body weight and age on the time of pairing of American Black Ducks. Auk 103:477–484.

Hepp, G. R., and J. D. Hair. 1984. Dominance in wintering waterfowl (Anatini): effects on distribution of sexes. Condor 86:251–257.

Hochbaum, H. A. 1944. The Canvasback on a prairie marsh. Stackpole Books, Harrisburg, Pennsylvania, and the Wildlife Management Institute, Washington, D.C.

Hochbaum, H. A. 1955. Travels and traditions of waterfowl. Charles T. Branford, Newton, Massachusetts.

Hochbaum, H. A. 1973. To ride the wind. Harlequin Enterprises, Toronto.

Holmberg, K., L. Edsman, and T. Klint. 1989. Female preferences and male attributes in Mallard ducks *Anas platyrhynchos* Animal Behaviour 38:1–7.

Hori, J. 1963. Three-bird flights in the Mallard. Wildfowl Trust Annual Report 14:124–132.

Houston, C. S. 1988. In memoriam: Hans Albert Hochbaum. Auk 105:767–770.

Huntingford, F. A., and A. K. Turner. 1987. Animal conflict. Chapman & Hall, London.

Inglis, I. R. 1976. Agonistic behaviour of breeding Pink-footed Geese with reference to Ryder's hypotheses. Wildfowl 27:95–99.

Inglis, I. R. 1977. The breeding behaviour of the Pink-footed Goose: behavioral correlates of nesting success. Animal Behaviour 25:747–764.

Johnsgard, P. A. 1960. A quantitative study of sexual behavior of Mallards and Black Ducks. Wilson Bulletin 72:133–155.

Johnsgard, P. A. 1965. Handbook of waterfowl behavior. Cornell University Press, Ithaca, New York.

Johnsgard, P. A. 1978. Ducks, geese, and swans of the world. University of Nebraska Press, Lincoln.

Johnsgard, P. A., and M. Carbonell. 1996. Ruddy Ducks and other stifftails. University of Oklahoma Press, Norman.

Johnson, K. P. 1999. The evolution of bill coloration and plumage dimorphism supports the transference hypothesis in dabbling ducks. Behavioral Ecology 10:63–67.

Johnson, K. P. 2000. The evolution of courtship display repertoire in the dabbling ducks (Anatini). Journal of Evolutionary Biology 13:634–644.

Johnson, K. P., F. McKinney, R. Wilson, and M. D. Sorenson. 2000. The evolution of postcopulatory displays in dabbling ducks (Anatini): a phylogenetic perspective. Animal Behaviour 59:953–963.

Johnson, W. P., and F. C. Rohwer. 1998. Pairing chronology and agonistic behaviors of wintering Green-winged Teal and Mallards. Wilson Bulletin 110:311–315.

Jonsson, J. E., and A. Gardarsson. 2001. Pair formation in relation to climate: Mallard, Eurasian Wigeon and Eurasian Teal wintering in Iceland. Wildfowl 52:55–68.

Kahlert, J., M. Coupe, and F. Cooke. 1998. Winter segregation and timing of pair formation in Red-breasted Merganser Mergus serrator. Wildfowl 49:161–172.

Kear, J. 1970. The adaptive radiation of parental care in waterfowl. Pagers 357-392 in J. H. Crook, editor. Social behavior in birds and mammals. Academic Press, London.

Kear, J. 1972. Reproduction and family life. Pages 79–124 in P. Scott, editor. The swans. Houghton Mifflin, Boston.

Klint, T., L. Edsman, K. Holmberg, and B. Silverin. 1989. Hormonal correlates of male attractiveness during mate selection in the Mallard ducks (Anas platyrhynchos). Hormones and Behavior 23:83–91.

Korschgen, C., and L. H. Fredrickson. 1976. Comparative displays of yearling and adult male Wood Ducks. Auk 93:793–807.

Lack, D. 1968. Ecological adaptations for breeding in birds. Methuen & Company, London.

Lazarus, J., and I. R. Inglis. 1978. The breeding behaviour of the Pink-footed Goose: parental care and vigilant behaviour during the fledging period. Behaviour 65:62–88.

Lebret, T. 1961. The pair formation in the annual cycle of the Mallard, Anas platyrhynchos L. Ardea 49:97–158.

LeSchack, C. R., A. D. Afton, and R. T. Alisauskas. 1998. Effects of male removal on female reproductive success in Ross' and Lesser Snow Geese. Wilson Bulletin 110:56–64.

Lessells, C. M. 1985. Natal and breeding dispersal of Canada Geese Branta canadensis. Ibis 127:31–41.

Ligon, J. D., R. Thornhill, M. Zuk, and K. Johnson. 1990. Male–male competition, ornamentation and the role of testosterone in sexual selection in Red Jungle Fowl. Animal Behaviour 40:367–373.

Lind, H. 1959. Studies on courtship and copulatory behavior in the Goldeneye (Bucephala clangula L.). Dansk Ornithologisk Forenings Tidsskrift 53:177–219.

Lockner, F. R., and R. E. Phillips. 1969. A preliminary analysis of the decrescendo call in female Mallards (Anas platyrhynchos L.). Behaviour 35:281–287.

Lokemoen, J. T., H. F. Duebbert, and D. E. Sharp. 1990. Homing and reproductive habits of Mallards, Gadwalls, and Blue-winged Teal. Wildlife Monographs 106.

Lorenz, K. Z. 1951–53. Comparative studies on the behavior of the Anatinae. Avicultural Magazine 57:157–182; 58:8–17, 61–72, 86–94, 172–184; 59:24–34, 80–91.

Lorenz, K. 1966. On aggression. Harcourt, New York.

Lorenz, K. 1971. Comparative studies of the motor patterns of Anatinae. Pages 14–114 in Studies in animal and human behavior. Volume 2. (translated by R. Martin). Methuen, London.

Lorenz, K. 1979. The year of the Greylag Goose. Harcourt Brace Jovanovich, London.

Losito, M. P., and G. A. Baldassarre. 1996. Pair-bond dissolution in Mallards. Auk 113:692–695.

Lovvorn, J. R. 1990. Courtship and aggression in Canvasbacks: influence of sex and pair-bonding. Condor 92:369–378.

Mank, J. E., J. E. Carlson, and M. C. Brittingham. 2004. A century of hybridization: decreasing genetic distance between American Black Ducks and Mallards. Conservation Genetics 5:395–403.

McCracken, K. G., P. J. Fullagar, E. C. Slater, D. C. Patton, and A. D. Afton. 2002. Advertising displays of male Musk Ducks indicate population subdivision across the Nullarbor Plain of Australia. Wildfowl 53:137–154.

McKinney, F. 1953. Studies on the behaviour of the Anatidae. Dissertation, University of Bristol, United Kingdom.

McKinney, F. 1965a. Spacing and chasing in breeding ducks. Wildfowl Trust Annual Report 16: 92–106.

McKinney, F. 1965b. The comfort movements of Anatidae. Behaviour 25:120–209.

McKinney, F. 1975. The evolution of duck displays. Pages 331-357 *in* G. Baerends, C. Beer, and A. Manning, editors. Function and Evolution in Behaviour. Clarendon Press, Oxford.

McKinney, F. 1986. Ecological factors influencing the social systems of migratory dabbling ducks. Pages 153–174 *in* D. I. Rubenstein and R. W. Wrangham, editors. Ecological aspects of social evolution — birds and mammals. Princeton University Press, Princeton, New Jersey.

McKinney, F. 1991. Male parental care in Southern Hemisphere dabbling ducks. International Ornithological Congress 20:868–875.

McKinney, F. 1992. Courtship, pair formation, and signal systems. Pages 214–250 *in* B. D. J. Batt, A. D. Afton, M. G. Anderson, C. D. Ankney, D. H. Johnson, J. A. Kadlec, and G. L. Krapu, editors. Ecology and management of breeding waterfowl. University of Minnesota Press, Minneapolis.

McKinney, F., and G. Brewer. 1989. Parental attendance and brood care in four Argentine dabbling ducks. Condor 91:131–138.

McKinney, F., S. R. Derrickson, and P. Mineau. 1983. Forced copulation in waterfowl. Behaviour 86:250-294.

McKinney, F., W. R. Siegfried, I. J. Ball, and P. G. H. Frost. 1978. Behavioral specializations for river life in the African Black Duck (*Anas sparsa* Eyton). Zeitschrift fur Tierpsychologie 48:349–400.

McKinney, F., L. G. Sorenson, and M. Hart. 1990. Multiple functions of courtship displays in dabbling ducks (Anatini). Auk 107:188–191.

McKinney, F., and P. Stolen. 1982. Extra-pair-bond courtship and forced copulation among captive Green-winged Teal (*Anas crecca carolinensis*). Animal Behaviour 30:461–474.

Milne, H. 1974. Breeding numbers and reproductive rate of eiders at the sands of Forvie National Nature Reserve, Scotland. Ibis 116:135–154.

Mineau, P., and F. Cooke. 1979. Territoriality in Snow Geese or the protection of parenthood–Ryder's and Inglis's hypotheses re-assessed. Wildfowl 30:16–19.

Mock, D. W. 2002. In memoriam: Frank McKinney, 1928–2001. Auk 119:507–509.

Mowbray, T. B. 2002. Canvasback (*Aythya valisineria*). The birds of North America, 659. The American Ornithologists' Union, Washington, D.C., and The Academy of Natural Sciences, Philadelphia.

Nice, M. M. 1941. The role of territory in bird life. American Midland Naturalist 26:441–487.

Nilsson, L., and H. Persson. 2001. Change of mate in a Greylag Goose *Anser anser* population: effects of timing on reproductive success. Wildfowl 52:31–40.

Nudds, T. D., and C. D. Ankney. 1982. Ecological correlates of territory and home range size in North American dabbling ducks. Wildfowl 33: 58–62.

Omland, K. E. 1996a. Female Mallard mating preferences for multiple male ornaments I. Natural variation. Behavioral Ecology and Sociobiology 39:353–360.

Omland, K. E. 1996b. Female Mallard mating preferences for multiple male ornaments II. Experimental variation. Behavioral Ecology and Sociobiology 39:361–366.

Orians, G. H. 1969. On the evolution of mating systems in birds and mammals. American Naturalist 103:589–603.

Oring, L. W., and R. D. Sayler. 1992. The mating systems of waterfowl. Pages 190–213 *in* B. D. J. Batt, A. D. Afton, M. G. Anderson, C. D. Ankney, D. H. Johnson, J. A. Kadlec, and G. L. Krapu, editors. Ecology and management of breeding waterfowl. University of Minnesota Press, Minneapolis.

Owen, M. 1980. Wild geese of the world, their life history and ecology. B T Batsford, London.

Owen, M., and R. Wells. 1979. Territorial behaviour in breeding geese — a re-examination of Ryder's hypothesis. Wildfowl 30:20–26.

Paulus, S. L. 1983. Dominance relations, resource use, and pairing chronology of Gadwalls in winter. Auk 100:947–952.

Pearce, A. N. 2000. Displays of the Garganey *Anas querquedula*: evidence of multiple functions. Wildfowl 51:83–101.

Port, J. L. 1998. Long-term pair bonds and male parental care in Speckled Teal *Anas flavirostris* in eastern Argentina. Wildfowl 49:139–149.

Port, J. L., and F. McKinney. 2001. Behavioral adaptations for breeding in arboreal-nesting Speckled Teal. Wilson Bulletin 113:177–188.

Poston, H. J. 1974. Home range and breeding biology of the Shoveler. Canadian Wildlife Service Report Series 25.

Ramsay, A. O. 1956. Seasonal patterns in the epigamic displays of some surface-feeding ducks. Wilson Bulletin 68:275–281.

Rave, D. P., and G. A. Baldassarre. 1989. Activity budget of Green-winged Teal wintering in coastal wetlands of Louisiana. Journal of Wildlife Management 53:753–759.

Raveling, D. G. 1970. Dominance relationships and agonistic behavior of Canada Geese in winter. Behaviour 37:291–317.

Raveling, D. G. 1979. The annual cycle of body composition of Canada Geese with special reference to control of reproduction. Auk 96:234–252.

Ricklefs, R. E. 1974. Energetics of reproduction in birds. Pages 152–292 in R. A. Paynter, Jr., editor. Avian energetics. Nuttall Ornithological Club Publication 15.

Ringelman, J. K., J. R. Longcore, and R. B. Owen, Jr. 1982. Breeding habitat selection and home range of radio-marked Black Ducks (Anas rubripes) in Maine. Canadian Journal of Zoology 60:241–248.

Robertson, G. J., F. Cooke, R. I. Goudie, and W. S. Boyd. 1998. The timing of pair formation in Harlequin Ducks. Condor 100:551–555.

Robertson, G. J., F. Cooke, R. I. Goudie, and W. S. Boyd. 2000. Spacing patterns, mating systems, and winter philopatry in Harlequin Ducks. Auk 117:299–307.

Rohwer, F. C., and M. G. Anderson. 1988. Female biased philopatry, monogamy, and the timing of pair formation in migratory waterfowl. Current Ornithology 5:187–221.

Ryder, J. P. 1975. The significance of territory size in colonial nesting geese — an hypothesis. Wildfowl 26:114–116.

Samelius, G., and R. T. Alisauskas. 2001. Deterring arctic fox predation: the role of parental nest attendance by Lesser Snow Geese. Canadian Journal of Zoology 79:861–866.

Sargeant, A. B., S. H. Allen, and R. T. Eberhardt. 1984. Red fox predation on breeding ducks in midcontinent North America. Wildlife Monographs 89.

Savard, J-P. L. 1984. Territorial behaviour of Common Goldeneye, Barrow's Goldeneye, and Bufflehead in areas of sympatry. Ornis Scandinavica 15:211–216.

Savard, J-P. L. 1985. Evidence of long-term pair bonds in Barrow's Goldeneye (Bucephala islandica). Auk 102:389–391.

Sayler, R. D., and A. D. Afton. 1981. Ecological aspects of Common Goldeneyes Bucephala clangula wintering on the upper Mississippi River. Ornis Scandinavica 12:99–108.

Scott, D. K. 1980a. Functional aspects of the pair bond in winter in Bewick's Swans (Cygnus columbianus bewickii). Behavioral Ecology and Sociobiology 7:323–327.

Scott, D. K. 1980b. Functional aspects of prolonged parental care in Bewick's Swans. Animal Behaviour 28:938–952.

Sedinger, J. S., and D. G. Raveling. 1990. Parental behavior of Cackling Canada Geese during brood rearing: division of labor within pairs. Condor 92:174–181.

Serie, J. R., and L. M. Cowardin. 1990. Use of social indices to predict reproductive success in Canvasbacks. Journal of Wildlife Management 54:66–72.

Seymour, N. R. 1974a. Territorial behaviour of wild Shovelers at Delta, Manitoba. Wildfowl 25:49–55.

Seymour, N. R. 1974b. Site attachment in the Northern Shoveler. Auk 91:423–427.

Seymour, N. R. 1991. Philopatry in male and female American Black Ducks. Condor 91:189–191.

Seymour, N. R., and R. D. Titman. 1978. Changes in activity patterns, agonistic behavior, and territoriality of Black Ducks (Anas rubripes) during the breeding season in a Nova Scotia tidal marsh. Canadian Journal of Zoology 56:1773–1785.

Siegfried, W. R. 1976. Social organization in Ruddy and Maccoa Ducks. Auk 93:560–570.

Siegfried, W. R. 1978. Social behavior of the African Comb Duck. Living Bird 17:85–104.

Simmons, K. E. L., and U. Weidmann. 1973. Directional bias as a component of social behaviour with special reference to the Mallard, Anas platyrhynchos. Journal of Zoology 170:49–62.

Siriwardena, G. M., and J. M. Black. 1998. Parent and gosling strategies in wintering Barnacle Geese Branta leucopsis. Wildfowl 49:18–26.

Smith, C. M., F. Cooke, and G. J. Robertson. 2000. Long-tern pair bonds in Harlequin Ducks, Condor 102:201–205.

Sorenson, L. G. 1991. Mating systems of tropical and Southern Hemisphere dabbling ducks. International Ornithological Congress 20:851–859.

Sorenson, L. G. 1992. Variable mating systems of a sedentary tropical duck: the White-cheeked Pintail (Anas bahamensis bahamensis). Auk 109:277–292.

Sorenson, L. G. 1994. Forced extra-pair copulation and mate guarding in the White-cheeked Pintail: timing and trade-offs in an asynchronously breeding duck. Animal Behaviour 48:519–533.

Sorenson, L. G., and S. R. Derrickson. 1994. Sexual selection in the Northern Pintail (*Anas acuta*): the importance of female choice versus male-male competition in the evolution of sexually selected traits. Behavioral Ecology and Sociobiology 35:389–400.

Sorenson, L. G., B. L. Woodworth, L. M. Ruttan, and F. McKinney. 1992. Serial monogamy and double brooding in the White-cheeked (Bahama)Pintail *Anas bahamensis*. Wildfowl 43:156–159.

Soutiere, E. C., H. S. Myrick, and E. G. Bolen. 1972. Chronology and behavior of American Widgeon wintering in Texas. Journal of Wildlife Management 36:752–758.

Sowls, L. K. 1955. Prairie ducks: a study of their behavior, ecology and management. Stackpole, Harrisburg, Pennsylvania, and the Wildlife Management Institute, Washington, D.C.

Spurr, E. B., and H. Milne. 1976. Adaptive significance of autumn pair formation in the Common Eider *Somateria mollissima* (L.). Ornis Scandinavica 7:85–89.

Stewart, G. R., and R. D. Titman. 1980. Territorial behaviour by prairie pothole Blue-winged Teal. Canadian Journal of Zoology 58:639–649.

Summers, R. W. 1983. The life cycle of the Upland Goose *Chloephaga picta* in the Falkland Islands. Ibis 125:524–544.

Thompson, J. D., and G. A. Baldassarre. 1992. Dominance relationships of dabbling ducks wintering in Yucatan, Mexico. Wilson Bulletin 104:529–536.

Titman, R. D. 1983. Spacing and three-bird flights of Mallards breeding in pothole habitat. Canadian Journal of Zoology 61:839–847.

Titman, R. D., and N. R. Seymour. 1981. A comparison of pursuit flights by six North American ducks of the genus *Anas*. Wildfowl 32:11–18.

Todd, F. S. 1996. Natural history of the waterfowl. Ibis Publishing, Vista, California.

Torres, R., F. Cooke, G. J. Robertson, and W. S. Boyd. 2002. Pairing decisions in the Harlequin Duck: costs and benefits. Waterbirds 25:340–347.

Trauger, D. L. 1971. Population ecology of Lesser Scaup (*Aythya affinis*) in subarctic taiga. Dissertation, Iowa State University, Ames.

Trivers, R. L. 1972. Parental investment and sexual selection. Pages 136-179 *in* B. G. Campbell, editor. Sexual selection and the descent of man, 1871–1971. Aldine Publishing, Chicago.

Weidmann, U., and J. Darley. 1971. The role of the female in the social display of Mallards. Animal Behaviour 19:287–298.

Weller, M. W. 1965. Chronology of pair formation in some Nearctic *Aythya* (Anatidae). Auk 82: 227–235.

Weller, M. W. 1967. Courtship of the Redhead (*Aythya americana*). Auk 84:544–559.

Weller, M. W. 1976. Ecology and behaviour of steamer ducks. Wildfowl 27:45–53.

Williams, M. 1979. The social structure, breeding and population dynamics of Paradise Shelduck in the Gisborne—east coast district. Notornis 26:213–272.

Williams, M. 1991. Social and demographic characteristics of Blue Duck *Hymenolaimus malacorhynchos*. Wildfowl 42:65–86.

Wishart, R. A. 1983. Pairing chronology and mate selection in the American Wigeon (*Anas americana*). Canadian Journal of Zoology 61:1733–1743.

Young, C. M. 1970. Territoriality in the Common Shelduck *Tadorna tadorna*. Ibis 112:330–335.

Chapter 4
REPRODUCTIVE ECOLOGY

Once courtship is finished and a pair is formed, the process of gamete transfer, fertilization, and egg production begins. As with pair formation, however, the transfer of sperm is not as simple as it initially appears. Paired waterfowl mate frequently, but males in many species also forcibly copulate with other females; both behaviors influence which eggs are fertilized, when they are fertilized, and who fertilizes them. Regardless, once sperm are transferred and eggs fertilized, females build the nests, produce their clutches, and (with some exceptions) begin incubation.

The energetic costs of producing a clutch of eggs are high for waterfowl relative to other groups of birds, as is the cost of incubation (Hepp et al. 1990). King (1973) estimated the maximum daily costs of egg production for waterfowl as 52–70% of the daily energy intake at a constant body mass. Waterfowl also store energy, which plays a prominent role in the reproductive process. Geese and swans primarily rely on stored energy to meet their reproductive demands, whereas ducks use various combinations of stored energy and energy acquired during the breeding season. Further, the temporal considerations related to energy acquisition are an especially important aspect of waterfowl reproduction.

Another matter concerns breeding opportunities if the first clutch is destroyed (i.e., renesting). In ducks, males often desert their mates some time after incubation begins; hence, if their first nests later fail, how do these abandoned females find new males with whom to pair again and begin second nests? For most species of geese and swans, such options are often quite limited — the short growing season characteristic of their nesting areas in the Arctic usually does not allow time for renesting efforts. However, because swans and geese are perennially monogamous, attempts to renest normally occur with the original partners.

Various ecological features also affect breeding, but climate, hydroperiod, length of the growing season, photoperiod, and the temporal availability of suitable food are among the more obvious. Waterfowl also nest across an immense geographical area ranging in latitude from the Arctic to the tropics. Hence, waterfowl nesting in temperate zones deal with various combinations of ecological features, whereas those breeding in the tropics face still another set of ecological circumstances.

In an extensive review of the literature, Laurila (1988) found that body size, geographic location, and phylogenetic relationship (i.e., tribal association) had the greatest overall influence on reproductive strategy. Considering these traits, and especially body size, the reproductive strategy for a given species is largely predetermined (Tables 4-1, 4-2). Hence, reproductive strategies have evolved in keeping with the selective pressures associated with each of these many environments where waterfowl breed. For example, geese nesting in the Arctic benefit from the long days and an abundant food supply, but the nesting season is brief. In contrast, ducks breeding at lower latitudes in temperate areas enjoy a longer nesting season, but the unpredictable nature of precipitation produces volatile changes in the availability of wetland habitat. Climate also influences waterfowl reproduction, particularly for species breeding over a broad geographical range. For example, because of mild temperatures in the southern United States, Wood Ducks begin nesting in late January, and up to 11.5% of the females may produce two broods in a single nesting season compared with less than 1% for those breeding farther north (Moorman and Baldassarre 1988).

Overall, these reproductive events, together with the associated temporal and spatial aspects of habitat, represent a critical part in the annual cycle of waterfowl; hence, a wealth of research has addressed these topics. We begin with a review of the basic reproductive systems of male and female waterfowl, and the behaviors associated with sperm transfer. We then summarize aspects of avian energetics as a prelude to examining the costs of egg production and activities such as incubation. These concepts, along with the general reproductive strategies used by waterfowl, provide the requisite foundation for effective management. On one hand, life-history attributes such as the timing of reproduction, clutch size, incubation period, and so forth are relatively fixed and unchanging events that cannot be affected by management. On the other hand, the temporal and spatial availability of habitat exert a profound influence on how or even if these life-history attributes can be expressed — and habitat can be stunningly affected by management. To illustrate, fall age ratios (i.e., indicators of reproductive success) for arctic-nesting Lesser Snow Geese are related to the body mass and stored lipids of adults during the preceding spring at staging areas in North and South Dakota and southern Manitoba. Hence, management of these food resources — primarily agricultural grains — at spring staging areas influences the growth of goose populations (Alisauskas 2002). This example is one of many that demonstrates why habitat management,

Table 4-1. Relationships between phylogeny (e.g., subfamily or tribe) and various reproductive attributes of female waterfowl. Modified from Laurila (1988:52).

Attribute (means)	Dendrocygninae (n = 9)	Anserinae (n = 22)	Tadorninae[a] (n = 14)	Anatini (n = 37)	Aythyini (n = 16)	Mergini (n = 16)	Oxyurini (n = 8)
Body mass (g)	764	3,870	1,724	620	824	986	694
Clutch size	10	5	8	8	9	8	5
Egg mass (g)	49	181	93	45	56	67	85
Incubation period (days)	29	30	30	26	26	28	25
Age at maturity (years)	1	3	2	1	2	2	1
Fledging age (days)	59	66	70	53	58	57	56
Breeding latitude	41	20	24	39	24	27	42

[a]Does not include the steamer-ducks.

Table 4-2. Relationships between geographic locations of breeding range and reproductive parameters of waterfowl. Modified from Laurila (1988:54).

Attribute (means)	Breeding Range		
	Tropical (n = 18)	Temperate (n = 76)	Arctic (n = 48)
Body mass (g)	994	866	1,269
Clutch size	8.4	7.6[a]	6.9
Egg mass (g)	59	64	77
Incubation period (days)	29	28	28

[a]n = 75.

whether by preservation or enhancement, must match the fixed biological demands of waterfowl, thereby assuring that requisite resources (e.g., food, nesting cover, brood habitat) are present and available when and where needed, in this case for reproduction.

THE MALE REPRODUCTIVE SYSTEM

An understanding of the reproductive strategy of any species involves some knowledge of endocrinology and anatomy. Circadian and circannual rhythms also affect the reproductive cycles of birds, but these aspects of reproduction are reviewed elsewhere (see Gwinner 1973, 1975; Gwinner and Brandstätter 2001, and Dunlap et al. 2004). The basic mechanics and structures of male (and female) reproductive systems are fixed, which dictates when and what behavior occurs in the successful transfer of sperm. Our brief review largely draws from Welty (1982), Sturkie (1986), Gill (1990), and Bluhm (1988, 1992).

Photoperiod is clearly the major environmental cue that controls spermatogenesis in birds in temperate zones; 12–14 hr of light are required to stimulate maximum testes growth, which begins when lengthening daylight stimulates the hypothalamus (see Johnson 1986a). The testes occur in pairs and, when compared with other times of the year, may increase 400–500 times in size during the breeding season (Gill 1990). These changes are rapid; domestic ducks subjected to a photoperiod of 15 hr of light and 9 hr of darkness develop mature testes in 12–15 days. If conditions are optimal, the testes may increase in volume as much as 10 times in 10 days, and 80 times in 20 days (Welty 1982). Note that lengthening photoperiods also stimulate other activities such as molting into breeding plumage and courtship behavior.

Using domestic Mallards, Benoit and Assenmacher (1955) established that the hypothalamus is the critical link in the brain between the central nervous system (CNS) and the anterior pituitary gland, which produces many of the hormones regulating reproductive activity. The complex neural systems of the hypothalamus and CNS control gonadotropin releasing factor and other releasing factors such as luteinizing hormone (Bluhm 1988).

These releasing factors stimulate the pituitary to produce hormones such as follicle-stimulating hormone (FSH), luteinizing hormone (LH), thyrotropin (TSH), and prolactin; collectively, these hormones are known as gonadotropins. FSH regulates the formation of gametes in both males and females, whereas LH regulates secretion of hormones from the testes (e.g., testosterone) and maturation of eggs in the ovary.

In wild Mallards, the endocrinology of male reproduction begins in early autumn with an increase in the production of LH from the pituitary; this action immediately stimulates a concurrent increase in testosterone from the testes. Testosterone, the primary steroid hormone of males, largely activates courtship behavior and initiates development of secondary sexual characteristics (e.g., the acquisition of breeding plumage). Testosterone is produced within the cells of Leydig, which are located in the testes between the seminiferous tubules. For males, the increases in LH and testosterone in autumn usually coincide with increased courtship behavior. Castration, which removes the site of testosterone production, terminates courtship displays (see Balthazart 1983). However, because some individuals escalate their courtship activities but show no corresponding increase in LH or testosterone, the link between sexual activity and hormonal activity in the autumn requires further study in waterfowl (Haase 1983, John et al. 1983, Bluhm 1988). Perhaps photorefractoriness — the failure to elevate gonadotropins under suitable conditions of day length — may explain variations in gonadal recrudescence (see Bluhm 1988). In any event, the testes grow smaller in autumn and complete their regression by November. Later, when the photoperiod lengthens in late winter–early spring, plasma gonadotropins are generated, thereby stimulating production of testosterone and the growth of testes mass.

The increases in gonadotropins and testosterone eventually lead to the production of gametes. By the end of January, the spermatogonia in the testes are undergoing meiosis. Temperature, however, is probably the major modifier of the testicular cycle at this stage of development. For example, low temperatures may delay the onset of reproduction in Mute Swans by 6–8 weeks. The complete process of gamete production usually occurs from February through May in both Mallards (Hohn 1947) and Mute Swans (Breucker 1982). Overall, the environmental factors of photoperiod and temperature are the primary regulators of spermatogenesis in the annual cycle of male waterfowl (see Bluhm 1988, 1992).

Seminiferous tubules in the testes produce spermatozoa, which develop in three stages. First, small cells known as spermatogonia line the wall of each seminiferous tubule, where they multiply by mitosis to form millions of cells within the tubules. The older spermatogonia then move toward the central cavity of each tubule and begin a period of growth in which they approximately double their diameter; at this second stage, the cells are called spermatocytes. Finally, after undergoing meiosis, the cells become spermatozoa, each with a vibrating tail and carrying a halved load of genetic material. The vas deferens also increases greatly in size, especially near the cloaca, during the breeding season. The spermatozoa, propelled by their tails, move from the testes and accumulate in the ciliated vas deferens until ejaculated.

The penis of male waterfowl is erectile and grooved, formed by an "out-pocketing" of the ventral wall of the cloaca; it guides sperm into the female during copulation. In adults, the penis is encased by a large sheath, whereas it is unsheathed in juveniles. These features are easily observed and therefore are useful for aging individuals (females also can be aged by cloacal examination; Fig. 4-1). However, well-developed copulatory male organs are uncommon in birds — a phallus occurs in only 3% of all species (Briskie and Montgomerie 1997) — and a truly intromittent organ occurs only in ratites, tinamous (Tinamidae), cracids (Cracidae), screamers, and waterfowl. The well-developed penis in ducks may reflect their habit of copulating in the water: An intromittent organ prevents damage to the sperm (Lake 1981). Other evidence, however, suggests a functional penis may bear greater association with the mating systems of waterfowl, especially in relation to extrapair copulations and sperm competition (see below).

Based on work with domestic birds (see Johnson 1986a), chickens produce 0.5–1.0 ml of ejaculate that contains some 1.7–3.5 billion spermatozoa, although counts for Brown Leghorns may reach 8 billion. In domestic ducks, the volume of ejaculate varies from 0.18 to 0.41 ml, with a concentration of spermatozoa ranging from 2.10 to 9.33 million/ml. Similar data, however, are not available for wild birds. Once in a female, a single dose of sperm can remain viable for about 2 weeks. Nonetheless, experiments with captive Mallards revealed that egg fertility declined rapidly from 64% during the first week to 37% in the second week, and was less than 3% by the third week; hence, more than one copulation is required for efficient fertilization (Elder and Weller 1954).

FEMALE | MALE

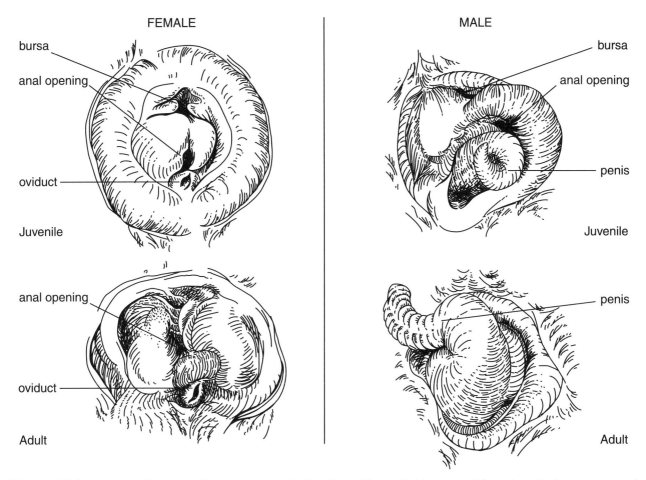

Figure 4-1. Features in the cloacal structure of waterfowl provide a reliable method for aging ducks, geese, and swans. The exposed cloaca of the adult male (*bottom right*) shows the large, sheathed penis, whereas the penis of juvenile males (*top right*) is unsheathed and the bursa of Fabricius opens into the cloaca (*top*). The adult female (*bottom left*) shows the opening to the oviduct and the anus (*in the center*). In juvenile females (*top left*), the opening to the oviduct is visible and the bursa of Fabricius still opens into the cloaca (*top*).

THE FEMALE REPRODUCTIVE SYSTEM

The ovary is the primary reproductive organ of the female and is responsible for the production of eggs. Only the left ovary normally develops in most groups of birds; the right ovary is vestigial, likely because two functional ovaries would permit simultaneous egg development and thus increase the chances of cracking one or both eggs lying side by side in the body cavity of the female.

The ovary enlarges enormously during the breeding season, but it remains barely visible at other times of the year. The mature ovary of a domestic chicken weighs 20–30 g (Gill 1990), and at maximum size resembles a bunch of grapes, with each "grape" forming the yolk of a complete egg (Fig. 4-2). The yolk is actually the ovum, which is a cell greatly

enlarged by stored food; yolks mature in about 6–8 days in ducks (King 1973). Each ovum of a developing egg is encapsulated by a layer of supporting cells known collectively as the follicle. The ova initially develop from smaller follicles located in the outer layer (cortex) of the ovary. There are thousands of these smaller follicles, but only 200–500 will mature and be ovulated during the life span of most domestic birds, fewer still in wild birds (Gill 1990).

The endocrinology of follicle growth begins with release of FSH from the anterior pituitary, which is followed by release of LH. The latter hormone stimulates both growth of the interstitial cells within the ovary and discharge of the ovum from the follicle; LH levels peak with egg laying. Later in the breeding cycle, the pituitary secretes prolactin, which reduces production of both FSH

Figure 4-2. Developing follicles from the reproductive tract of a female Lesser Snow Goose. The size of the follicles is proportional to their age, with the largest being the oldest. Photo courtesy of C. Davison Ankney, University of Western Ontario.

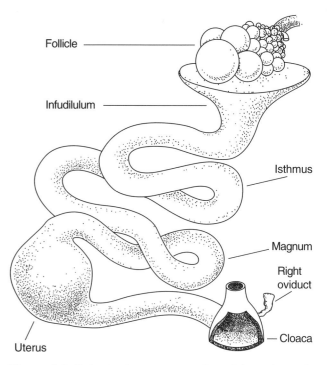

Figure 4-3. Schematic representation of the avian oviduct. After Gill (1990:329).

and LH and initiates incubation behavior. Thus, prolactin is an important hormone for terminating reproduction. Changes in photoperiod and hormone activity from the thyroid gland also are important in terminating the reproductive effort of both females and males.

When the ovum matures (i.e., all the yolk is deposited), the enveloping follicle ruptures and the ovum falls into the trumpet-like upper end of the oviduct, the infundibulum (Fig, 4–3). This process, of course, is ovulation, which in ducks and many other birds occurs within 15–75 min after the previous egg is laid. The ovum remains in the infundibulum for about 18 min, which is the only time it can be fertilized (Sturkie 1986).

The ovum then moves to the magnum, where it remains for about 4 hr in the domestic chicken while acquiring albumen or egg white, which is deposited around the yolk. The albumen is largely water (90%), but the rest is protein (10%). The primary functions of albumen are to supply water for the embryo and to cushion the inner components of the egg. Some albumen proteins also inhibit microbial activity, which serves to protect the yolk and enhance the

lifespan of the egg (Freeman and Vince 1974). Indeed, the central location of the yolk likely contributes to its defense by the albumen (Board and Hornsey 1978).

The next sequence of movements begins with passage of the ovum into the isthmus, where it remains for about 15 min while acquiring shell membranes, which function to shield the embryo, to conserve food and water, and to facilitate gas exchange (Gill 1990). The ovum then moves to the uterus, where it acquires a shell, and hence spends the most time (18–20 hr). The egg shell comprises about 11–15% of the egg's mass and provides protection and structural support for the egg's contents. Shell formation is initiated immediately after the ovum enters the uterus and ends with addition of the pigment. The egg finally moves into the vagina, where mucous glands and a strong muscular wall aid its deposition into the nest.

The actual laying rate for waterfowl varies from about 0.5 eggs/day in swans and 0.75/day in geese, to 0.62–0.75/day in sea ducks and eiders, to 1.00/day in dabbling ducks, pochards, whistling-ducks, and stiff-tailed ducks (Alisauskas and Ankney 1992). The timing of actual ovulation is strongly correlated with the timing of egg laying (Alisauskas and Ankney 1994a), which can be important in birds because laying eggs at a particular time of day can affect fitness. For example, many passerines lay eggs around sunrise, which presumably reduces the likelihood of damaging eggs still in the oviduct when the female is active, as well as reduce the energy costs of transporting the egg (Oppenheimer et al. 1996). Based on the nest attentiveness behavior of females, most species of ducks are assumed to lay their eggs in the morning (Gloutney et al. 1993). In subarctic Alaska, however, Esler (1999) observed that both Northern Pintails and American Wigeon usually ovulated throughout the day, which suggests that fitness is more related to egg-laying interval and not to egg-laying time. Specifically, the egg-laying interval may provide a selective advantage in waterfowl by (1) reducing the period of nest exposure (Clark and Wilson 1981), (2) causing earlier hatching dates and thus increase fecundity (Rohwer 1992), (3) reducing hatch asynchrony (Flint et al. 1994), and (4) improving viability of early-laid eggs (Arnold et al. 1987). Esler (1999) concluded that selection in ducks favored short ovulation and egg-laying intervals, but there was no adaptive significance to the time of day these events occurred.

MATING, GAMETE TRANSFER, AND EXTRAPAIR COPULATIONS

Waterfowl primarily exhibit a monogamous mating system; hence pair bonds occur in nearly all species. However, social monogamy does not guarantee genetic monogamy (i.e., paternity), because paired males often mate with females other than their partners in what is known as extrapair copulation (EPC). EPC is defined as the "grasping and mounting of a female by a male other than her mate, followed by intromission in spite of her resistance" (McKinney et al. 1983:255); this behavior has been documented in 55 species of waterfowl in 17 genera (McKinney and Evarts 1998). EPC is unlike pair-bond behavior in several respects: (1) precopulatory displays are absent; (2) males aggressively pursue the females; (3) copulation may occur on land instead of in the water; and (4) postcopulatory displays are almost always absent, especially when the female's mate chases away the intruding male. EPC apparently is absent in swans, shelducks, and most geese (but see Dunn et al. 1999), probably because it is not compatible with the roles that males in these groups play in the defense of territories, mates, nest sites, and broods (McKinney et al. 1983, McKinney and Evarts 1998).

EPC may be an artifact of crowding, thwarted

male sex drive, territorial defense, or an alternative reproductive strategy of unpaired males, but these explanations are not supported in the literature (see McKinney et al. 1983, McKinney and Evarts 1998). However, Trivers (1972), in his reexamination of a hypothesis proposed long ago by Heinroth (1911), suggested that the occurrence of EPC in monogamous species may function from the standpoint of natural selection. More specifically, because sperm are energetically much less costly to produce than eggs, a "mixed reproductive strategy" may represent the optimal form of male reproduction. This occurs when an individual male supplements his primary parental investment in a single mate with additional transfers of sperm to other females. Accordingly, with EPC, a male makes virtually no additional investment, yet potentially realizes the same genetic benefits as does copulation with a mate — both types of copulation result in offspring with his genes. Studies of EPC in waterfowl began in earnest during the1980s and, along with more recent research, is providing new and fascinating insights into the mating behavior of waterfowl.

To begin, if EPC is indeed favored by natural selection in the form of a mixed reproductive strategy for males, then this behavior should occur at a time when males can successfully inseminate females. This opportunity occurs at or near ovulation when females are either already laying or about to lay their eggs, and early research demonstrated just how this scenario might be realized. First, females can retain inseminated sperm in specialized sperm storage tubules located at the junction of the uterus and the vagina (see Briskie and Montgomerie 1993). Thus, although EPC largely occurs during the laying or prelaying period, the sperm deposited by an EPC will be overlaid by additional sperm originating from the subsequent and more frequent copulations occurring in the regular course of pair-bond maintenance. In Lesser Scaup, for example, paired males copulated with their mates 4.1 times more often than EPC, *and* pair-bond copulations were far more successful than EPC (96.5 % vs. 19.6%; Afton 1985). Nonetheless, sperm from each of these two types of copulations actually may "compete" for the opportunity to fertilize eggs.

Timing is therefore crucial if an EPC is to have any chance of success, as shown experimentally by Cheng et al. (1983). Namely, when a female was artificially inseminated with two competing doses of sperm, the proportion of progeny resulting from either the first and second inseminations was no different when the inseminations occurred simultaneously or were 1–3 hr apart. In these instances, the sperm probably mixed before entering a sperm storage tubule, and thereby produced an equal probability that sperm from either dose will fertilize the ova. When inseminations were 6 hr apart, however, 70% of the progeny were from the *second* insemination. In this case, the sperm probably filled the sperm storage tubules sequentially rather than concurrently; hence sperm from the most recent insemination — the second — remained on top and were released first (DeMerritt 1979). As mentioned above, sperm from an EPC competes with sperm originating from more than one pair-bond copulation, and therefore the progeny resulting from an EPC is unlikely to reach 70%. However, sperm originating from an EPC gain a better chance of successful fertilization *if* insemination can occur near the time of ovulation. Recall that a freshly ovulated ovum can be fertilized only during a period of about 18 min, after which albumen is deposited around the yolk and sperm are thereafter denied access. Indeed, in experiments where females were inseminated more than 1 hr after laying their eggs, only one of 179 eggs laid the next day was fertile (Cheng et al. 1983).

But, if EPC can be timed to coincide closely with ovulation, the freshly inseminated sperm can bypass the uterovaginal junction and reach the site of fertilization — the infundibulum — in minutes (Howarth 1971), just at the time when sperm transport will not be inhibited by the presence of an egg in the oviduct (Morzenti et al. 1978). As demonstrated in domestic turkeys, sperm can reach the infundibulum within 15 min (Howarth 1971), and this period may be even shorter in waterfowl because the males have intromittent penises. Therefore, sperm intro-

duced from an EPC within 1 hr after an egg is laid experience the best chance of competing with sperm deposited by the female's mate for the opportunity of fertilizing the next egg.

In fact, Cheng et al. (1983) found that 9 of 36 (25%) artificial inseminations occurring within 1 hr after an egg was laid indeed fertilized the next ovum in the laying sequence. Hence, there is a "window" of opportunity where sperm from an EPC have some chance of competing either with previously deposited sperm or with those from subsequent inseminations. Cheng and his colleagues thus established the physiological and mechanical basis by which the EPC phenomenon evolved as an effective component in the mixed reproductive strategy of male ducks. Observations on captive Mallards (Cheng et al. 1982) confirmed this prediction, as males attempted significantly more EPCs with females during egg laying in comparison with other periods. Moreover, few EPCs occurred after the last egg of a clutch was laid. In captive White-cheeked Pintails, 73.5% of all EPC attempts were directed at females in laying or prelaying condition (McKinney et al. 1983). These observations were compelling, but they required corroboration under field conditions.

Such results were forthcoming from Manitoba, where a field study of Lesser Scaup documented that EPC occurred most often in late-prelaying, laying, and premolting females (Afton 1985; Table 4-3). Further, rates of EPC were greatest in early morning (0500) when the chances of successful fertilization also were greatest (i.e., females had just laid their eggs). Thus, both experimental and field data confirmed that males somehow could assess the reproductive status of females and thereby attempt EPC

Table 4-3. The frequency of extrapair copulation (EPC) and EPC attempts by marked pairs of Lesser Scaup in Manitoba. Rate is the combined frequency of EPC and EPC attempts per hour. Modified from Afton (1985:151).

Reproductive condition	Hours observed	On the female			On the male		
		EPC	Attempt	Rate	EPC	Attempt	Rate
Early prelaying	404	0	10	0.03	0	6	0.02
Late prelaying	462	7	30	0.09	1	10	0.03
Laying	440	6	17	0.08	3	21	0.06
Incubation	160	0	4	0.06	0	2	0.03
Nonbreeding	190	0	5	0.03	2	2	0.02

at times when ova were indeed available for fertilization.

These studies were further corroborated in an extensive investigation of wild White-cheeked Pintails in the Bahama Islands, where EPC peaked during the fertile period of females (prelaying, laying, postfailed nest) and represented 23.1% of all successful copulations with laying females (Sorenson 1994a). The number of attempted EPC on fertile females was 7.2 times greater than occurred on nonfertile females, which strongly implied that males could assess the reproductive status of target females. However, the success rate of EPC was 19% compared to 80% for pairs, probably because males guarded their females from attempted EPC. Indeed, males guarded their paternity vigorously by escorting their mates to nests and by defending a territory; hence, EPC occurred 3.4 times more often with an unattended female than with a female accompanied by her mate. Males also vigorously attacked intruding males attempting EPC, and they also forcefully copulated with their mates after a successful EPC occurred. Contrary to predictions, males engaged in guarding their mates themselves attempted EPC, but they probably did so only when their own mates were less at risk to EPC attack (e.g., absent, usually on the nest).

Nonetheless, although field data demonstrated that males were timing EPC to maximize the probability of successful fertilization, the mechanisms used by males to assess the reproductive status of females remained unknown until Sorenson (1994b) determined that male White-cheeked Pintails used a variety of tactics for that purpose. Specifically, males apparently monitor the behavior of neighboring birds, because 44% of EPC were directed at females residing on the same pond. Males likely assessed the aggressive behavior of neighboring males as a cue, because the mates of nonbreeding females did not defend territories, and their females were not subject to EPC. Males also gathered information when they chased females, particularly in flight, with the chase rate 5.4 times higher for fertile females compared with nonfertile females. Chases were also significantly longer when a fertile female was pursued. Males may have assessed the reproductive status of females during these flights as a female carrying an egg in her oviduct exhibited a distinct "drooped" profile. Finally, males appeared to directly observe females during the laying process. Armed with these cues, males become especially sophisticated and aggressive when chasing females, and may ambush females leaving their nests,

approach females surreptitiously by swimming nearly submerged or sneaking through shoreline vegetation, and capture and mount females underwater. Indeed, in 27% of EPC attempts, the male captured the female underwater and came to the surface mounted on her back!

Lastly, the penis of males in some species seems especially modified to engage in EPC. Specifically, large penises and testes develop in those species of ducks where EPC is commonplace, and their penises have a proportionally large surface area covered with knobs, ridges, or both (Coker et al. 2002). Penis size is comparatively smaller among geese, which tend to copulate on land and engage in fewer EPC (but see Dunn et al. 1999). Coker et al. (2002) concluded that penis size and morphological complexity were related to sperm competition because a large penis with various knobs and ridges would make it more difficult for a female to disengage or for the female's partner to dislodge the intruding male. The knobs and ridges also point backwards toward the base of the penis and thus might be an adaptation to scrape sperm of other males from the oviduct when the penis is withdrawn. Remarkably, the penis of the Argentine Ruddy Duck is exceptionally long and spiny and, with an average length of 22.3 cm, is nearly half the length of the body (McCracken 2000; Fig. 4-4). The penis of one specimen measured 32.5 cm, which is truly remarkable for a bird that weighs about 640 g (McCracken et al. 2001); the penis was about the same size as those of the Ostrich (*Struthio camelus*). Such a large penis in the Argentine Ruddy Duck may be an adaptation to the promiscuous mating systems that characterize this species and other Oxyurini, which also have large penises.

Female White-cheeked Pintails did not solicit EPC, which they strongly resisted, usually by diving (57%). Sorenson (1994b) argued that such behavior may act to preserve the pair bond and the investment of her mate, which would in turn protect her investment. For example, Afton (1985) noted that male Lesser Scaup reduced and eventually ceased defending mates that were repeatedly subjected to EPC. Also, White-cheeked Pintails subjected to frequent EPC and associated harassment often abandoned their nests. Other studies likewise concluded that female waterfowl do not solicit EPC (see McKinney and Evarts 1998). Cunningham (2003) suggested that EPC increased the risk of sexually transmitted diseases and therefore was a major reason why females preferred a particular male and resisted intruders. In fact, the prevalence of pathogens in domestic waterfowl increases with the fre-

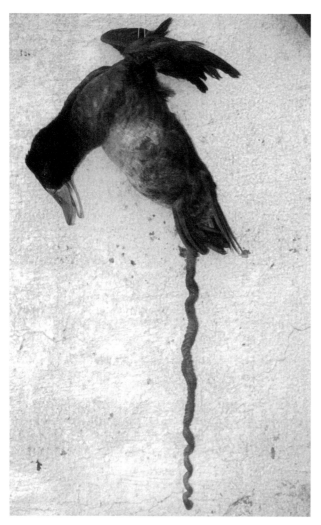

Figure 4-4. The extraordinary penis of the Argentine Ruddy Duck likely evolved with the promiscuous mating system of this species. Photo courtesy of Kevin G. McCracken, University of Alaska.

quency of copulation (Stipkovits et al. 1986), and the sublethal effects of sexually transmitted diseases are common and more detrimental to females than males (see Wobeser 1997). Hence, the costly resistance of females to EPC persists instead of passive acceptance of a behavior that clearly benefits males.

Further understanding of EPC and waterfowl mating systems came from a study of Gadwalls in which microsatellite DNA fingerprinting determined the ultimate result of extrapair paternity (EPP; Peters et al. 2003). Eleven of 261 ducklings (4.2%) from 8 of 29 broods (27.6%) resulted from EPC, and EPP was not correlated with breeding synchrony. These data are consistent with EPP rates reported for other waterfowl: 3% in Mallards (Evarts and Williams 1987),

2–5% in Lesser Snow Geese (Lank et al. 1989), and 2% in the Ross's Geese; Dunn et al. 1999). In contrast, EPP seems absent in the highly territorial Blue Duck (Triggs et al. 1991). In comparison with waterfowl, EPP is far more common in passerines, where about 18% of the offspring may result from EPC; however, female passerines often solicit and may benefit from EPC (see Westneat et al. 1990, Wink and Dyrcz 1999).

Dunn et al. (1999) studied EPC and paternity in Ross's and Lesser Snow Geese nesting at the Karrk Lake colony in Nunavut, Canada, which, with nearly 300,000 birds of each species, is the largest known goose nesting colony in the world. As with ducks, EPC was observed only during laying and incubation, mostly when females were on their nests. Further, EPC represented 46–56% of all copulations, which is perhaps the highest percentage yet reported for waterfowl. EPC likewise represented 33–38% of all successful copulations, but they were relatively inefficient at fertilizing eggs (2.4–5.0%). The paired male always returned and attacked the intruding male, but in contrast to ducks, most male Ross's and Lesser Snow Geese also guarded their fertile females, but later engaged in EPC after their own mates had completed egg laying, Hence, most of the offspring produced by EPC originated from the last eggs in a clutch. This study was one of the few examples were EPC was negatively related to breeding synchrony. Mineau and Cooke (1979) observed that male Lesser Snow Geese partitioned EPC and mate-guarding, attempting EPC when their own females were nonfertile. Dunn et al. (1999) concluded that EPC was inefficient as an alternative reproductive strategy in these species of geese.

A final topic relative to EPC concerns the reproductive strategy for unpaired males. Males dominate the sex ratios for many species of ducks (see Chapter 8), and thus some males are unpaired during the breeding season. In Lesser Scaup, paired males engaged in EPC 4.6 times more often than unpaired males, which led Afton (1985) to argue that pair formation is a better strategy for males rather than to remain unpaired and rely solely on EPC for breeding. Afton listed four factors to support his argument: (1) mate-switches occur frequently after birds arrive on their breeding areas, so an unpaired male still has opportunities to find a mate; (2) most unpaired males are probably yearlings with little experience at copulating; (3) yearling males probably do not assess the reproductive status of females as well as adult males; and (4) a paired male often successfully thwarts EPC directed toward his mate. In White-cheeked Pintails, 87% of all EPC attempts were by older, paired males (Sorenson 1994b). Unpaired males were mostly yearlings and thus may have had difficulty successfully identifying fertile females and completing EPC. However, Sorenson (1994b) reported EPC in two unpaired White-cheeked Pintails that were at least 3–4 years old. The behavior of these two males differed markedly from other unpaired males — they repeatedly moved among ponds (often together), intruding on territories, chasing females, and attempting EPC. The frequency of EPC rate for the 4-year-old male was 1.9 times greater than the average for paired males, and third highest among all males. In contrast, other unpaired males did intrude on territories and instead engaged in social courtship, but not EPC. Of seven unpaired yearling males under observation, six were unpaired and did not attempt EPC.

In summary, the transfer of sperm in waterfowl is not a simple event. Instead, the process is a complex strategy in which two methods of mating behavior have evolved to maximize the reproductive output of males. Paired males, however, must constantly assess the benefits of engaging in EPC against the costs of leaving their own females unguarded, but some males maintain a mate and engage in EPC. Female White-cheeked Pintails paired to males with the highest EPC rates were themselves rarely subject to EPC (Sorenson 1994a). Still, EPC offers no apparent benefits for female ducks, which may actually be killed during these episodes (see McKinney et al. 1983).

MANAGEMENT IMPLICATIONS OF A MIXED REPRODUCTIVE STRATEGY

The male-dominated sex ratio so prevalent in waterfowl, especially ducks, exerts a major influence on mating systems but also offered a cornerstone for harvest management. The underlying premise held that excess males could be removed from the population without adversely affecting the probability that all females would find mates. The imbalanced sex ratio indeed formed the basis for experimental seasons in which only males were harvested legally (Grieb et al. 1970), as well as the "point system" in which males usually were assigned fewer points than females (Mikula et al. 1972, Geis and Crissey 1973; see Chapter 8). However, these systems of harvest management were designated without fully understanding the potential function of excess males in breeding populations, and more important, the effects of their removal. Decades ago, Elder and Weller

(1954) speculated that the excess males formed a pool to supply renesting females with mates late in the nesting season, but more recent studies have provided greater insight into this issue.

Ohde et al. (1983) individually marked 89 male and 47 female Mallards in central Iowa, and then attempted to equalize the sex ratio by removing 117 males and adding 45 females. The results provide quantitative information on the role of excess males in breeding duck populations. For 32 males whose mating activities were recorded, five (16%) established regular associations with a second female at the same time their original mates were laying eggs or beginning incubation, a result not in conflict with a mixed reproductive strategy. However, each of the five males apparently maintained simultaneous pair bonds with two females.

At least 8 (25%) of the 32 males mated with 2–3 different females during the breeding season. Also, of 14 marked females that lost nests, 9 rejoined their original mates. An earlier study in Iowa also identified 11 cases of females remating, eight of which were with their original males (Humburg et al. 1978). According to Ohde et al. (1983), the males breeding earliest in the season also remained sexually active the longest. Nine of the last 10 males still active on the breeding area were among the first 12 males marked in the study; the nine males averaged 78 ± 4 days of breeding activity. In marked contrast to these results, Dzubin (1969) reported that male Mallards deserted their mates during incubation and joined other males on molting areas.

Overall, Ohde et al. (1983) concluded that a Mallard population with an excess of males was not essential to ensure the successful renesting efforts of females, because females renested with their original mates or with other, already paired males still active on the breeding area. Therefore, increasing the harvest of males during the hunting season, at least up to a point, likely exerts little effect on breeding success — a conclusion supported by the mixed reproductive strategy of males.

Ohde et al. (1983) removed unpaired males, which were likely yearlings, so their role in the reproductive effort in this population could not be assessed. However, recall that both Sorenson (1994b) and Afton (1985) determined that unpaired males, although active in social courtship, were seldom successful in forming pairs and did not engage in EPC. In a captive population, Cunningham (2003) reported that six of seven unpaired males also remained unpaired for the following two seasons, a finding that demonstrates the difficulty for an unpaired male to break an existing pair bond. Thus, the mating strategy of unpaired males appears to be one of gaining experience and waiting to form pairs in the years ahead.

ANIMAL ENERGETICS AND NUTRITION

In this section, we highlight the basic concepts of energetics and nutrition and introduce the associated terminology. This review provides the foundation for discussions of waterfowl reproduction in this chapter, as well as topics presented in Chapters 5 (Feeding Ecology) and 7 (Winter), among others. We have converted values from older literature (e.g., kcal) using the International System of Units (abbreviated SI), which has been adopted by all the major industrial nations. These conversions are not an academic exercise; the SI system takes advantage of the equivalence of work and heat, and thereby offers real advantages over older terminology. For instance, the definition of a calorie as the amount of energy required to raise 1 g of water 1 °C is familiar, but this quantity varies with temperature. However, when the calorie is redefined as work (1 cal = 4.1868 joules), this source of variation is eliminated. Hence, like the advantages of the metric system over the English system of measurements, the SI system also is of greater scientific value than those units of measurement that have persisted more because of tradition than utility.

To begin, energy is required for all life processes. Birds thus extract energy as well as minerals and other nutrients from their environment. These constituents of food are either exhausted relatively quickly or stored for use later. Stored nutrients (e.g., lipid and protein reserves) are referred to as "endogenous," whereas nutrients that are not stored are considered as "exogenous." The study of energetics is thus the acquisition, use, storage, and conservation of energy, all of which are central to an understanding of vertebrate ecology. For example, the energy required just to keep an organism alive is clearly less than the total energy needed by that same organism during its reproductive cycle. Similarly, the amount of energy an endotherm needs to maintain a core body temperature is less at warm than cold ambient temperatures. Animals also exhibit adaptations for conserving energy and thereby reduce the time they spend foraging and exposed to predators and the elements. The behavioral means that animals use to conserve energy is often overlooked; animals in fact constantly assess their needs and react by acquiring energy, using stored energy,

conserving energy, or by engaging in combinations of these three strategies.

Basal Metabolic Rate (BMR)

Central to any study of energetics is the understanding that energy is required for normal cellular function and the replacement of worn tissue. In birds, for instance, the average daily turnover of body protein — the most abundant component of tissue — averages 4.4%, which is why BMR is so strongly influenced by body size (Gordon 1977, Morowitz 1978). Temperature, of course, also affects BMR, but BMR is basically a measure of little else than the energetic requirements for tissue maintenance. More formally, BMR is "the rate of energy utilization by animal organs and tissues at complete rest, unstimulated by the digestion and assimilation of food or by low temperature" (Kendeigh et al. 1977:129). This relationship is represented mathematically using the general equation $BMR = aW^{0.73}$, where a is the height of the curve that relates BMR in watts to 1 kg of body mass, and W is the body mass. For waterfowl, a general value for a is 4.64 watts (Zar 1968). Among larger birds (i.e., 500 g or larger), the measurement of BMR is 10–25% higher during the day than at night (Kendeigh et al. 1977). Thus, for nonpasserines at night a general equation is $BMR = 3.56W^{0.73}$, whereas $BMR = 4.40W^{0.73}$ during the day.

Existence Metabolic Rate (EMR)

According to Kendeigh et al. (1977:140), "existence metabolism" is "the rate at which energy is used by caged birds maintaining a constant mass ($\pm$ 1–2%) over a period of days when not undergoing reproduction, molting, migratory unrest, growth, or fat deposition." Their equation for the calculation of the EMR in nonpasserines at 30 °C and a $\pm$ 10-hr photoperiod is $EMR \text{ (watts)} = 0.070W^{0.6256}$; at 0 °C, $EMR = 0.201W^{0.5316}$.

Heat/Work Increment of Feeding

When animals are assimilating food, they experience a higher rate of metabolism than when at rest. This difference in heat production is called the "thermic effect of food," "specific dynamic action," or "heat increment of feeding" (HIF). Basically, HIF is the release of heat that accompanies digestion, assimilation, and nutrient interconversion; HIF occurs with all food types (Brody 1945). The importance of HIF in avian energetics concerns the substitution of the heat produced from thermogenesis and thus a reduction in thermoregulatory costs. Indeed, HIF can reach 40–50% of the metabolizable energy of food, depending on the type and amount of food consumed (see Ricklefs 1974, McDonald et al. 1995, Kaseloo and Lovvorn 2003). At high ambient temperatures, HIF is lost from the body, but it is retained at lower ambient temperatures, thereby supplementing the heat required by metabolism for the maintenance of body temperature (thermogenesis). HIF is generally highest for protein foods, but birds using low-protein foods can substitute HIF for thermoregulatory costs. HIF substitution is also likely to be higher for large meals or high protein foods. After feeding Mallards cereal grains, in which HIF substitution for thermogenesis did not occur, Kaseloo and Lovvorn (2003) concluded that little HIF substitution occurs when meals are small, low in protein, and the intake is below that required for maintenance. When HIF is much greater (large meals, high protein foods) or heat loss high because of cold temperatures or high activity, HIF substitution can be complete, which is especially important for waterfowl wintering in cold regions as they seek to maintain homeostasis (see Chapter 7).

Productive Energy (PE)

Productive energy is the amount of energy that a bird uses above and beyond that required for EMR (Kendeigh et al. 1977). At its lower limits of temperature tolerance, a bird thus musters all of its energy simply for existence. But as the ambient temperature rises, EMR decreases and more energy becomes available as PE. The amount of PE available to a bird is important because it is the source of energy used to meet the demands of reproduction, molting, migration, and other essential activities.

Daily Energy Expenditure (DEE)

DEE is the energy expended by wild birds not involved with reproduction, molt, migration, or similar activities. In the wild, birds undergo a variety of activities (e.g., flying, swimming, or preening), each of which requires various amounts of energy (Wooley and Owen 1978). Thus, DEE for a given species is estimated by determining a time budget, which is the proportion of time spent in sundry activities throughout the day as determined by behavioral observations (Altmann 1974, Baldassarre et al. 1988). The proportions

Table 4-4. The energetic costs of various activities as determined for a male American Black Duck. Modified from Wooley and Owen (1978:742).

Activity	Energetic cost		
	kJ/bird/hr	Watts	Multiple of BMR
Resting	19.7	5.5	1.4
Preening	25.5	7.1	1.8
Walking	24.7	6.9	1.7
Feeding	25.5	7.1	1.8
Swimming	32.2	9.0	2.3
Flying	178.7	50.0	12.5

of time spent per activity then are multiplied by the energetic costs of each activity; when summed, the products provide an estimate of DEE (Table 4-4). Whereas this approach yields a reasonable estimate of DEE, the energetic costs of these activities still must be corrected to account for energy-demanding phenomena such as low ambient temperatures (Wooley and Owen 1977) and high winds (Weathers et al. 1984); such conditions demand more energy than is otherwise required to perform the same activity in a less environmentally stressful setting.

DEE also may be estimated using doubly-labeled water, which is water composed of deuterium and oxygen-18 isotopes. Doubly-labeled water is injected in a sample bird, which is recaptured at a later date. A blood sample then is taken from which the rate of CO_2 production is estimated by calculating the difference between the turnover rates of the two isotopes (Nagy 1975). This technique is expensive, however, so most studies using doubly-labeled water thus far have been restricted to small birds (e.g., passerines). Further, estimates of DEE from time-activity data yield results largely comparable with those obtained from the doubly-labeled water technique (Weathers et al. 1984).

Thermoregulation

Endotherms enjoy a zone of thermoneutrality, which is the range of ambient temperatures within which an organism can maintain a core body temperature primarily by changing the effectiveness of its insulation (e.g., fluffing feathers). However, as ambient temperatures drop, a point is reached where the core body temperature cannot be maintained without actually increasing heat production. This point is known as the "lower critical temperature" (LCT). Conversely, when ambient temperatures increase, endotherms reach a point known as the "upper critical temperature" (UCT), and excess heat must be dissipated. For nonpasserines and expressed in degrees centigrade, $LCT = 47.17W^{-0.1809}$, where W is body mass in grams (Kendeigh et al. 1977).

LCT varies inversely with body mass because (1) smaller birds have a larger ratio of surface area to body mass, and thus must produce more heat per unit mass than larger birds (Calder and King 1974); and (2) plumage mass is nearly a linear function of body mass, so that larger birds have more plumage and hence greater insulation capacities. Thus, on a per unit basis of body mass, larger birds are metabolically able to withstand cold temperatures better than smaller birds, but smaller birds require less total energy from the environment. LCT thus confers a physiological advantage to larger birds but an ecological advantage to smaller birds (Kendeigh 1969).

Energy Conservation

Animals engage in thermal exchanges with their environment by means of radiation, conduction, convection, and evaporation. Birds accordingly respond to the environment with a variety of energy-conserving behaviors (see Calder and King 1974). These are extremely important because energy conservation lowers EMR requirements and raises the amount of PE.

Heat losses resulting from radiation occur when the ambient temperature is lower than the bird's surface temperature. In light of the similar measurements recorded by Best (1981) for Canada Geese and Snow Geese, radiant heat loss seems unaffected by plumage coloration. However, in comparing dark-colored (blue phase) with light-colored (white phase) goslings of Lesser Snow Geese, those with the darker plumage absorbed more visible and near-infrared radiation than did goslings with the lighter plumage (Beasley and Ankney 1988). Goslings reduced heat loss by selecting thermally favorable microclimates where their coloration ultimately exerted little influence on energy budgets.

Birds also may gain heat from surrounding objects with higher temperatures than their own surface temperature, which means that birds can absorb heat from solar radiation. Most animals, except for those that are white, dorsally absorb about 70–90% of the available solar energy under the most favorable conditions; the rest is reflected. To illustrate, swans with white plumage absorb just 35% of the sun's radiation, whereas Pileated Woodpeckers (*Dryocopus pileatus*) absorb 84% (Kendeigh et al. 1977).

Birds accordingly position themselves in sunlight as a means of conserving energy. Note, however, that heat absorbed from the sun cannot power a bird's activities. Instead, the value of solar radiation lies in reducing thermoregulatory costs, so that energy otherwise needed for thermoregulation is conserved and therefore becomes available for power-demanding activities. Hence, the EMR of a Northern Cardinal (*Cardinalis cardinalis*) is 1.11 watts in still air at -5 °C, but when the same bird is exposed to full sunlight, its EMR is reduced 53% to 0.59 watts (Kendeigh et al. 1977). In White-crowned Sparrows (*Zonotrichia leucophrys*), birds exposed to just 3 hr of full sunlight at low temperatures during the early morning subsequently reduced their energy intake for that day by 12.6% (Morton 1967). These circumstances obviously diminish the length of time birds spend foraging, which concurrently reduces their exposure to predators.

Fluffing is another effective energy-conserving behavior wherein the expanded volume of the plumage increases its insulatory capacity. In experiments conducted with the Chaffinch (*Fringilla coelebs*), birds at 0 °C with fully fluffed feathers lost 0.61 watts of heat. The loss increased to 0.83 watts when the birds were prevented from fluffing their feathers and reached 1.15 watts when their feathers were removed (Gavrilov et al. 1970). Because the short feathers on the heads of birds and their exposed bills are sources of heat loss, birds adopt postures that cover these parts of their bodies (Kendeigh et al. 1977). Heat lost through the bills of domestic Mallards exposed to an ambient temperature of 0 °C can be as high as 85–117% of BMR, but this is reduced to only 5–6% when the bill is vasoconstricted (Hagan and Heath 1980) — and even less when the bill is hidden under the body plumage.

Birds select thermally favorable microhabitats as another strategy for conserving energy; these are usually sites where heat losses associated with convection are reduced. Wind greatly accelerates thermal convection, as shown by Birkebak (1966) who calculated that heat loss increased at the rate of 10%/m/sec increase in wind speed. Meteorologists accordingly report winter temperatures in terms of the "wind-chill factor." In experiments with American

Kestrels (*Falco sparverius*), combinations of cold temperatures and wind caused peak metabolic rates, although larger raptors such as the Red-tailed Hawk (*Buteo jamaicensis*) were less affected (Hayes and Gessaman 1980). To avoid the detrimental effects of wind on heat loss, birds commonly face into the wind and select wind-protected sites. Huddling behavior also is a beneficial means of conserving energy, whereby birds often roost at sites where they enjoy thermal advantages. Birds also may lose or gain heat through conduction, in which heat moves — hot to cold — by contact across thermally different surfaces. Thus, a duck standing on ice loses heat through its feet by conduction.

Animals may behave in ways that achieve effective heat conservation by reducing losses from one or more factors while gaining heat from another. When animals huddle in a cavity, for example, heat losses from both radiation and convection are reduced while heat is gained from conduction. See Chapter 7 for a treatment of avian energetics in relation to wintering waterfowl.

THE AVIAN EGG AND ENERGETICS OF EGG PRODUCTION

The avian egg is "one of the most complex and highly differentiated reproductive cells achieved in the evolution of animal sexuality" (Gill 1990:325; for additional details see also Romanoff and Romanoff 1949, Johnson 1986b). Here we review clutch size and as-

pects of the energy requirements for egg production, which provide a basis for understanding the various strategies used by nesting waterfowl.

Egg Mass and Composition

Alisauskas and Ankney (1992) summarized available data on egg mass and composition in waterfowl, which in general consist of 14.9% yolk lipids, 6.3% yolk proteins, and 9.2% albumens. Egg lipids as a percentage of dry egg mass averages 38% for waterfowl compared to 21–36% for birds in general (Gill 1990). In comparison to other birds, waterfowl lay large eggs relative to the body mass of females. Waterfowl eggs also have a high energy density (kJ of proteins and lipids/fresh egg mass) that is relatively constant among species (9.5 kJ/g).

Egg mass in waterfowl increases with the size of the female, generally varying at about two-thirds the power of body mass (Rahn et al. 1975); this value varies from an average of 43 g in dabbling ducks to 283 g in swans (Table 4-5). However, egg mass as a proportion of body mass increases from a low of about 2.5% in the White-winged Duck of Southeast Asia to more than 20% in the Maccoa Duck of Africa and the Masked Duck of South America; the Ruddy Duck of North America lays a clutch about equal in mass to body mass (Lack 1967).

Because of their relatively large size, the eggs of waterfowl contain an abundance of yolk, some of which is retained in the abdomens of newly hatched

Table 4-5. Summary characteristics (means) associated with egg production by waterfowl. Modified from Alisauskas and Ankney (1992:37).

Taxonomic group	Body mass (g)	Egg mass (g)	Eggs laid per day	RFG (days)	Clutch size
Dendrocygnini	788	47	1.00	6	10
Cygnini	6,500	283	0.52	12	5
Anserini	2,518	127	0.75	12	5
Cairinini	565	43	1.00	7	11
Anatini	673	43	1.00	6	9
Aythyini	831	58	1.00	6	9
Somaterini	1,846	96	0.75	6	4
Mergini	835	64	0.62	8	9
Oxyurini	653	88	1.00	12	7

downy young to provide an immediate source of nourishment. According to Lack (1967), this source of yolk (1) provides newly hatched young with the energy necessary to travel overland from nest to water, (2) acts as a layer of insulation in arctic-nesting species, and (3) offers an advantage to those species whose young do not easily obtain food (i.e., species that dive). After hatching, for instance, Mallard ducklings survived 4.9–6.3 days without food (Krapu 1979), and Lesser Snow Goose goslings survived 3.9–4.1 days (Ankney 1980).

Waterfowl also produce abnormally small or "runt" eggs in their clutches. Such unusually small eggs have a volume at least 25% less than average, often lack egg yolks or some embryonic membranes, and do not hatch (Koenig 1980a). Mallory et al. (2004) surveyed the occurrence of runt eggs in wild and domestic birds, including waterfowl. Of 551,632 eggs examined, only 215 (0.039%) were runt eggs, and they occurred about equally across all taxonomic groups of birds. For waterfowl, the frequency of runt eggs fell within the range reported for most wild birds (0.02–0.6%; Koenig 1980b). The results supported the hypothesis that runt eggs result from some temporary impairment of the reproductive tract and are not associated with heredity, nest-site location, geographic location, or productivity.

Rapid Follicle Growth and Costs of Egg Production

In reviewing the costs of egg laying in waterfowl and its relationship to nutrient reserves, Alisauskas and Ankney (1992) determined that energy density of eggs was remarkably consistent among species. They began by calculating the average constituents of dry egg mass, which as already stated were 14.9% yolk lipids, 6.3% yolk proteins, and 9.2% albumen. Weighting these proportions — using the energy equivalents of 39.57 kJ/g for lipids and 23.66 kJ/g for protein (Brody 1945) — yields an average energy density of 9.55 kJ/g of fresh egg mass. This figure is high, and in terms of percent BMR, means that waterfowl expend more daily energy than other birds in the production of their clutches (King 1973, 1974).

Most of the energy costs associated with egg production concern the manufacture of yolk, which contains the energy supplies required by the developing embryo. Yolk production does not occur simultaneously in all of the developing follicles that ultimately form the clutch; instead, yolk is deposited in a lesser number of follicles over a period of days. Before each egg is laid, an important physiological

event occurs; "rapid follicle growth" (RFG) begins when a follicle starts to rapidly accumulate yolk and ends when that follicle is ovulated (Alisauskas and Ankney 1992). RFG can also refer to the period between the growth for the first follicle until ovulation of the last follicle in a clutch, but the first definition is more prevalent.

Females experiencing RFG undergo a period when their energy demands reach a maximum. This period begins on the day before the first egg is laid and extends throughout the period when the maximum number of follicles are simultaneously receiving yolk (Fig. 4-5). The maximum number of developing follicles, when multiplied by the laying interval, represents the time needed for RFG of a single follicle. Recall that laying rate per days varies from about 0.5 egg in swans to 1.0 in dabbling ducks. RFG for a single follicle thus varies from about 12 days in Cygnini and Anserini to 5–7 days in Anatini, Aythyini, and Mergini, to a high of 12 days in Oxyurini (Table 4-5). For waterfowl, there also is a general relationship between the duration of RFG and grams of egg mass (E), which is expressed as RFG = $1.273E^{0.43}$, and for which the r^2 was 0.71 (see Alisauskas and Ankney 1992).

One way of estimating the energetic costs of egg production is to measure the cost of producing a whole clutch, which is determined by multiplying the mass of each constituent in an egg by the energy equivalent of that constituent, multiplied by the number of eggs in the clutch (Alisauskas and Ankney 1992). Drobney (1980) thereby calculated the cost of producing a 12-egg clutch in Wood Ducks as 5,996 kJ. However, as Alisauskas and Ankney (1992) point out, the daily cost — especially the *maximum* daily cost — of egg production is especially critical because waterfowl can reduce total daily costs by increasing the number of days used to produce a clutch. For example, species whose clutch size is equal to, or greater than, the duration of RFG for each follicle and whose laying rate is 1/day (e.g., *Anas* and *Aythya*), reach a maximum daily cost of the energy per nutrients in one egg (King 1973, Alisauskas and Ankney 1992). Conversely, species whose clutch size is less than the duration of RFG for each follicle (e.g., Oxyurini, Anserini, Cygnini) never reach the daily maximum of energy per nutrients in one egg.

If the mass of developing follicles is separated by the laying interval, the results depict the pattern of yolk deposition (and other constituents) over the period of RFG (Fig. 4-6). A slow rate of RFG has the effect of lengthening the time required to develop

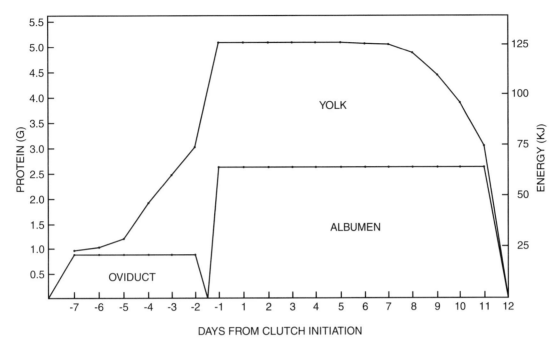

Figure 4-5. Partitioning of the daily energy and protein components necessary to produce a 12-egg clutch in the Wood Duck. From Drobney (1980:482). With permission from the American Ornithologists' Union.

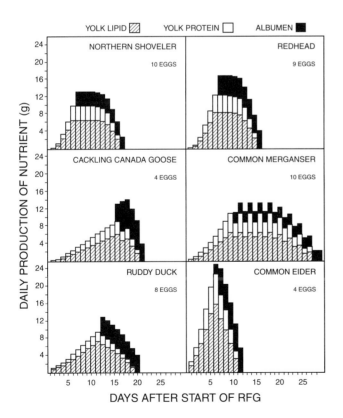

Figure 4-6. The daily allocation of nutrients for the production of a clutch varies among the taxa of waterfowl. Body size, breeding habitat, and predation are among the factors influencing the apportionment of the nutrients. RFG = rapid follicle growth. From Alisauskas and Ankney (1992:39). With permission from the University of Minnesota Press.

effect of this strategy is to reduce the number of days when the maximum energy costs will be incurred (e.g., the contents of one egg), and thus a species can spread out the costs of producing a clutch (Alisauskas and Ankney 1992). Hence, prairie-nesting waterfowl exhibit a rapid rate of RFG, which may be an adaptation for exploiting productive habitats where predation is high. In contrast, cavity-nesting species such as the Wood Duck do not experience predation rates as high as ground-nesting waterfowl, and although they have the same rate of RFG as dabbling ducks (6–7 days), they can spread out the costs of egg production without incurring additional risks of predation (Alisauskas and Ankney 1992). Drobney (1980) thus showed that Wood Ducks require 18 days to produce a 12-egg clutch, but they incur maximum costs for only 6 days. Swans, geese, and stiff-tailed ducks also produce eggs in a regime

the clutch but does not reduce the total commitment of energy for producing the clutch. The theoretical of reduced maximum daily costs by increasing the time for RFG and reducing their clutch size.

REPRODUCTIVE STRATEGIES AND THE ROLE OF NUTRIENT RESERVES

The daily, total, and maximum daily costs of producing a clutch of eggs are high for waterfowl. These costs also vary by species, depending on clutch size, laying rates, duration of RFG, and habitat quality. Therefore, it is not surprising that waterfowl exhibit several ecological and physiological adaptations for meeting the costs associated with reproduction—the costs for both laying and incubating a clutch of eggs.

Many studies have evaluated the relative importance of endogenous and exogenous reserves in waterfowl reproduction, and two major patterns have emerged. The first — used by arctic-nesting geese and eiders — involves using large amounts of endogenous (stored) reserves of lipid, protein, and other nutrients during egg laying and incubation. The second — used by temperate-nesting ducks — also depends on some endogenous lipids during laying, but concurrently relies on exogenous protein and minerals; the remaining lipid reserves are mobilized during incubation. A third strategy was documented in the White-winged Scoter, which does not use any reserves for egg production. Apparently because of their low laying rate (0.7/day; Brown 1981), large body size, and proportionately small eggs, White-winged Scoters obtain enough exogenous nutrients for egg production without relying on endogenous sources (Ankney and Alisauskas 1991a). This anomaly aside, we can turn to specific examples of the two major reproductive strategies.

Arctic-Nesting Geese (Anserini) and Eiders (Mergini)

Studies of the Lesser Snow Goose (Ankney and MacInnes 1978) and the Cackling Canada Goose (Raveling 1979a) revealed that the reproductive effort of these species depends largely on nutrient stores acquired prior to their arrival in the Arctic (i.e., endogenous reserves). Female Snow Geese, for example, arrived at their breeding colonies along the McConnell River in the Northwest Territories with an average body mass of 2,950 g, of which 228 g were protein, 492 g were lipid, and 41 g were calcium (Table 4-6). During laying, their average body mass decreased 420 g (14%), protein decreased 34 g (15%), lipid decreased 122 g (25%), and calcium decreased 7 g (17%). These losses were relatively modest, and thus after laying their clutches, Lesser Snow Geese still retained significant energy reserves with which to begin incubation. Late in the incubation period, however, females had lost 42% of their original body mass, and large amounts of lipids (89%) and protein (35%) had been exhausted. Some females indeed lost so much body mass that they starved to death on their nests. Alisauskas (2002) later determined that most of the stored lipid reserves used by these Lesser Snow Geese were acquired in the northern prairies to the south, but accumulation of these reserves had a dramatic effect on young produced that year.

Two ecological conditions are important here: (1) Lesser Snow Geese (and other arctic-nesting geese) arrive on their breeding grounds at a time when food is largely unavailable, and (2) unattended nests often are lost to predators if females take recesses during incubation (Samelius and Alisauskas 2001). Given these circumstances, the most adap-

Table 4-6. Changes in body mass and nutrient reserve indices of breeding female Lesser Snow Geese on the McConnell River Delta, Northwest Territories. For each parameter, means in adjacent columns were significantly different ($P < 0.01$). Modified from Ankney and MacInnes (1978:463).

Parameter means (g)	Arrival ($n = 78$)	Laying ($n = 44$)	Early Incubation ($n = 33$)	Late Incubation ($n = 41$)	Post Hatching ($n = 35$)
Body mass	2,950	2,530	2,040	1,710	1,900
Protein index	228	194	180	148	163
Lipid index	492	370	177	56	0
Calcium index[a]	41	34			

[a]Sample size was 48 for arrival and 27 for laying females.

Table 4-7. The annual cycle of body composition (means, g) of Cackling Canada Geese, the smallest of the Canada Goose complex, whose principal breeding area is the Yukon-Kuskokwim Delta in Alaska. Modified from Raveling (1979a:237–238).

Event	Body mass Male	Female	Water Male	Female	Protein Male	Female	Lipid Male	Female
Fall migration	1,540	1,287	832	721	328	276	230	182
Midwinter	1,398	1,205	835	719	325	280	70	57
Spring migration	1,487	1,295	844	738	331	290	205	172
Prelaying	1,871	1,890	971	861	382	352	386	532
First day of incubation	1,530	1,387	974	781	370	272	56	171
Midincubation	1,455	1,195	937	734	356	269	46	73
Hatch day	1,460	1,095	917	702	343	249	53	33

Note: Sample sizes ranged from 1 to 11 for any particular sex/time period category.

tive strategy is for the females to transport to the breeding site all the reserves necessary for both production of the clutch *and* incubation (Ankney and MacInnes 1978).

Ankney (1977) determined that male Lesser Snow Geese also deplete their lipid stores during the breeding cycle, although only 14% of their protein reserves were expended compared with 35% for females. Males likely mobilize lipids for territorial behavior, a cost that probably is high because Lesser Snow Geese nest in colonies where conflicts between males are common. However, because males do feed on their territories, they maintain better body condition than the nest-bound females (Ankney 1977). This strategy in turn allows the males to protect their females during incubation. To illustrate, egg losses to arctic foxes ((*Alopex lagopus*) were greater in unattended nests and nests attended only by the female compared to nests attended by paired geese (Samelius and Alisauskas 2001). The male also guards the family after hatching, which allows females to resume feeding and regain body condition.

The strength of Raveling's (1979a) work lies in its coverage of the entire annual cycle of Cackling Canada Geese (Table 4-7). His study accordingly pinpointed *when* and *where* reserves were acquired. When Cackling Canada Geese arrived at their breeding area on the Yukon-Kuskokwim Delta of Alaska in May and June, for example, average body mass had increased 26% (384 g) for males

and 46% (595 g) for females over average body masses in April at staging areas in California. Lipid reserves had increased 88% (181 g) in males and 209% (360 g) in females. Protein had increased 15% (51 g) in males and 21% (62 g) in females. Overall, females gained 1.8 times more body mass, 2.4 times more lipid, and 1.4 times more protein than did males.

By the end of incubation, the females were emaciated, having lost 42% (795 g) of the body mass they carried at the time of their arrival 43 days earlier. Lipid levels were nearly exhausted during this time, decreasing from 532 g upon arrival to 33 g, and protein was at its lowest level (249 g) of the annual cycle. The energy for incubation came from lipid metabolism (85%) and protein metabolism (15%; Raveling 1979b). In contrast, the body mass of males had not decreased significantly between the laying period and the end of incubation, although the lipid levels of males were at their lowest level of the annual cycle (53 g compared with 386 g at arrival). As with Lesser Snow Geese, a similar pattern emerges for the posthatching behavior of Cackling Canada Geese: Males become the primary caretakers of the goslings, while the females feed almost continuously to recover their body condition.

However, not all geese rely totally on endogenous energy reserves for reproduction. For Black Brant nesting on Southampton Island in the Northwest Territories, only 70% of the protein needed for egg production came from reserves, which was not enough for the females to fast during incubation (Ankney 1984). Unlike other geese, the Black Brant in this study nested successfully even though the females took recesses during incubation; they nested in habitats (high-tide line in salt marshes) where new growth was available as food immediately around the nest site.

The Greater Snow Goose breeds farther north than any other goose in North America. Hence, it seemed unusual when a study on Bylot Island (73 °N latitude) revealed that after their arrival, these birds delayed nesting for 16–18 days, during which the females spent 75% of their time feeding (Gauthier and Tardif 1991). This behavior may be necessary to replenish the lipid reserves depleted during their long northward flight from the St. Lawrence River estuary. Similarly, Greater White-fronted Geese increased their endogenous reserves after arriving on the Yukon-Kuskokwim Delta in Alaska (Budeau et al. 1991). Before nesting, these geese spent considerable time feeding, primarily on shoots of pendent grass (*Arctophila fulva*), crowberries (*Empetrum nigrum*), and bulbs of arrowgrass (*Triglochin palustris*). Because the larger species of waterfowl may store relatively larger amounts of reserves in comparison with the smaller species, some authorities believe there may be a minimum size below which females are too small to carry reserves for both egg laying and incubation (Ankney 1984).

Weather conditions on breeding areas also may exert powerful effects on reproductive output of both geese and ducks. For geese, late spring snows and cold temperatures may delay nesting, increase nest failures, or even cause complete reproductive failure for the year (Barry 1962, Ryder 1972, Raveling 1978, Petersen 1992). Fall age ratios for Lesser Snow Geese accordingly were inversely related to the severity of arctic weather (Alisauskas 2002). In ducks, clutch sizes may be reduced when weather limits the food supplies available to females (Bengtson 1971), and when weather produces unusually poor habitat conditions, ducks may forgo breeding altogether (Krapu et al. 1983).

Common Eiders nesting on islands in Penobscot Bay, Maine, and in Norway show a variation of the strategy adopted by arctic-nesting geese. In contrast to geese, female Common Eiders accumulate large reserves of protein and lipids during a 4–6 week period *after* arrival to breeding sites. Maximum body mass is reached just before egg laying, after which females fast during laying and incubation. In Maine, females weighed 1,830 g at the start of incubation and 1,290 g — about 30% less — when their duck-

lings hatched (Korschgen 1977). In Norway, the daily energy expenditure of laying females was 2,528 kJ, which was 5.2 times greater than the daily rate during incubation (Parker and Holm 1990). From prelaying to hatching, body mass of the eiders in Norway declined 46.4%, lipids by 81.4%, and protein by 36.8%. Of the total energy reserve at hand before laying began, 33.8% was used during laying, 34.6% during incubation, and 31.6% remained at hatching. This pattern of reproduction most likely evolved in response to the severe egg losses resulting from gull (*Larus* spp.) predation when female eiders leave their nests during incubation (Milne 1976, Korschgen 1977). The pattern also may reflect selection of small nesting islands that, although free of mammalian predators such as arctic foxes, are also far removed from optimal feeding areas (Parker and Holm 1990).

Temperate-Nesting Dabbling Ducks —Anatini

Patterns for the use of nutrient reserves during reproduction are now well documented for several species of dabbling ducks. We selected examples that include species with different life histories and geographical distributions (e.g., cavity or ground nesting, herbivorous or animal diets, subarctic or temperate nesting). See also Alisauskas and Ankney (1992) for a more extensive review of nutrient reserves required by waterfowl breeding in temperate North America. Regrettably, similar studies are lacking for dabbling ducks nesting in temperate latitudes elsewhere. Nonetheless, the studies at hand provide exciting insights into the life-history strategies of waterfowl.

Wood Duck: Drobney (1980) was the first to examine the nutrient reserves used by female dabbling ducks in his study of Wood Ducks nesting in bottom-land hardwood forests in the United States. Wood Duck eggs averaged 42.6 g and were composed of 22.8 g of albumen (53.5%), 15.2 g of yolk (35.8%), and 4.6 g of shell (10.7%). Major components of the egg were water (69.5%), lipid (14.1%), and protein (13.5%), and small amounts of ash (1.7%) and carbohydrates (1.2%). Total energy costs for a 12-egg clutch were 5,996 kJ, which included 2,969 kJ for carbohydrates and lipids, 1,595 kJ for protein, and 1,432 kJ for biosynthesis (the energetic cost of producing tissue and eggs). However, the equivalent costs for a single egg are incurred only for 6 days during the breeding cycle because the costs of clutch production are spread over an 18-day period and not just the 12 days required for laying (see Fig. 4–5).

During laying, females used endogenous lipids to meet 88% of the costs of clutch production and other types of biosynthesis (e.g., the nonprotein fraction of the oviduct). Overall, the lipid reserves of females decreased from 134 to 31 g. Females acquired protein and minerals exogenously from aquatic invertebrates, which required substantial foraging efforts. In fact, estimates indicated that females must forage for 8 hr and ingest over 300 invertebrates per hour to obtain the protein required for one egg. Drobney (1980) thus argued that the use of lipid reserves ensured that females had enough time to forage on invertebrates. Indeed, female Wood Ducks underwent a period of hyperphagia in spring when they deposited large quantities of lipids prior to laying.

Another study of Wood Ducks nesting in the southeastern United States focused on the nutrient reserves of males (Hipes and Hepp 1995). Males lost 79% of their lipid reserves during reproduction, an amount nearly identical to that of females. Most of the loss (86%) occurred between pair formation and egg laying. Protein reserves also declined 23 g during this period. These losses likely reflect the reduced feeding time of males (34% compared with 73% for females) as they spend more time in alert behavior and guarding their females. This study was the first to demonstrate that male dabbling ducks use substantial nutrient reserves to cope with the time and energy constraints of reproduction.

Mallard: Although Mallards are among the most intensively studied birds in the world (Anderson et al. 1974), the role of nutrient reserves in the reproduction of this species was not known until the late 1970s. The distribution of Mallards extends across the Northern Hemisphere, but their principal range lies in the Prairie Pothole Region (PPR) of midcontinental North America, where Krapu (1981) demonstrated a major strategy of temperate-nesting dabbling ducks: concurrent dependence on exogenous sources of protein and on an endogenous reserve of lipids acquired prior to arriving on breeding areas. In the heart of this range — North Dakota — Mallards arrive from their wintering areas between late March and early April. The body mass of both males and females is high on arrival, but from mid-April to late May, males lost an average of 94 g and females lost 217 g. Lipid reserves on arrival averaged 86 g in males and 109 g in females. Females relied heavily on these lipid reserves, and used an average of 57% (63 g) between

Table 4-8. Carcass composition of breeding female Mallards in North Dakota. This pattern is typical for north-temperate dabbling ducks. Modified from Krapu (1981:31).

Mass (g)	Prelaying	Laying	Incubation
Body	1,200	1,301	967
Total lipids	109	80	17
Protein reserves			
Flight muscle	65	65	58
Leg muscle	27	27	25
Gizzard	34	29	22
Heart	13	14	11
Liver	30	31	27
Ovary	6	32	2
Oviduct	14	32	7

Note: Sample size was 14–19 for prelaying birds, 5–11 for laying, and 3 for incubation.

the initiation of laying and the 6th day of incubation; all of their lipids probably are exhausted by the time hatching occurs (Table 4-8). The accumulation of lipids at hand on arrival correlated positively with the clutch size of the initial nest, and because of the substantial contribution of stored lipids, the energy costs of egg formation in wild Mallards proved less than the maximum estimates (King 1973, 1974). Late in the incubation period, the body mass of female Mallards averaged 900 g, which was 25% less than during the prelaying period (Krapu 1981). In contrast to endogenous lipids, the proteins required for breeding were contained in the invertebrate foods female Mallards secured on their breeding area. So, by relying on lipid reserves to meet their energy requirements, females can instead focus on acquiring the more scarce invertebrates to meet their needs for protein. Indeed, female Mallards in North Dakota foraged for 55% of daylight hours (Dwyer et al. 1979). The closely related American Black Duck follows a similar reproductive strategy (Owen and Reinecke 1979).

Gadwall and American Wigeon: In contrast to Mallards, Gadwalls breeding on the PPR (southwestern Manitoba) exhibit a different pattern of nutrient use during reproduction (Ankney and Alisauskas 1991b). Gadwalls were chosen for study because they are among the more herbivorous dabbling ducks, possibly excepting the American Wigeon. Lipid reserves declined 0.78 g for each gram deposited in eggs, and protein reserves declined 0.16 g. In other words, about 78% of the lipids deposited in eggs came from endogenous reserves compared with about 16% of the protein. American Wigeon use protein reserves for 44% of egg production (Alisauskas and Ankney 1992). Thus, unlike Mallards, American Wigeon and Gadwall use some stored protein to meet the costs of egg production.

Northern Shoveler: This species is an invertebrate specialist, consuming more animal matter than any other puddle duck, and thus offers an interesting example. Once again, the research originated on the PPR (southern Manitoba). The lipid reserves of females declined 0.72 g for every gram deposited in eggs, and protein increased 0.1 g for every gram deposited in eggs (Ankney and Afton 1988). The protein to lipid ratio in the diet of Northern Shovelers was about 14 to 1, and protein was arguably easy to obtain during spring from the highly productive wetlands characteristic of PPR wetlands. Hence, the study concluded that lipids, and not proteins, limited egg production.

Other research, in this case for Northern Shovelers breeding in subarctic Alaska, contrasted with the PPR study (MacCluskie and Sedinger 2000). As in Manitoba, Northern Shovelers in Alaska did not use stored protein for egg production, but in marked contrast they did not use stored lipids. One explanation for this difference is that the high rates of invertebrate productivity in Alaska, and 22 hr of daylight, enable Northern Shovelers there to ingest greater quantities of nutrients, and thereby maintain energy and nutrient balance during egg production. Overall, this study revealed how Northern Shovelers adapt their reproductive strategies in keeping with the environmental conditions peculiar to different geographical regions.

Northern Pintail: Elsewhere in subarctic Alaska, two studies of Northern Pintails again contrast with studies of dabbling ducks from the midcontinent prairies. In one study, the lipids of breeding females declined 2.58 g per gram committed to reproduction, and protein declined 0.20 g (Esler and Grand 1994). The commitment of lipids varied from a high of 3.35 g at the earliest date of nest initiation to 0 g some 40 days later. Hence, females used their lipid reserves in excess of the costs needed for egg production — some lipids also were used for maintenance. Such a strategy is intermediate in comparison with those

of the other temperate-nesting puddle ducks studied thus far, which use lipid reserves in amounts equal to or less than requirements for the clutch (also see Mann and Sedinger 1993).

Temperate-Nesting Pochards — Aythyini

Ring-necked Ducks, one of the few pochards studied in regard to reproductive strategy, exhibit a reproductive pattern similar to that of dabbling ducks (Alisauskas et al. 1990). Body lipids declined 0.48 g per gram of egg produced. Protein declined 1.7 g on the first day of clutch production, but females increased protein reserves from mid- to late RFG. This study concluded that the strategy of Ring-necked Ducks, and perhaps other temperate-nesting ducks as well, evolved in a way that matches the lipid supply for clutches with the effort required to procure dietary protein (invertebrates); the ducks typically met their protein requirements by nesting near wetlands with a seasonal flush of invertebrates. Studies of breeding Ringed-necked Ducks also showed that yearling females were lighter than adults on arrival, and thus younger birds probably depend heavily on the food resources available on their breeding areas (Hohman 1986).

Females of another pochard, the Lesser Scaup, accumulated protein and mineral reserves on their breeding areas in Manitoba (Afton and Ankney 1991). Most of their lipid reserves likely were acquired before the scaup arrived, and these reserves were expended in egg production. Lipids stored in females declined 0.5 g for every 1.0 g of lipid deposited in their eggs. In subarctic Alaska, 68% of the clutch lipids used by Lesser Scaup were derived from stored reserves, along with a small reserve (up to 7%) of proteins (Esler et al. 2001). In general, use of nutrient reserves by Lesser Scaup did not differ between Alaskan and midcontinent birds, except that subarctic birds used a small amount of protein reserves.

Temperate-Nesting Stiff-tailed Ducks — Oxyurini

Among waterfowl, stiff-tailed ducks lay the largest eggs in proportion to their body size, and their reproductive strategy accordingly is interesting. Indeed, maximum daily cost of egg production (584 kJ) is among the highest (280% of BMR) reported for waterfowl (Alisauskas and Ankney 1994a). The lipid reserves of females declined 0.49 g for every gram committed to egg production, protein declined 0.41

g, and minerals declined 0.08 g in early nesters. In contrast, late nesters also relied on endogenous lipids for about half the cost of egg production, but protein and minerals were acquired exogenously. Further, during RFG early nesters began laying with 23 g more lipids and 5 g more protein than females not experiencing RFG. Thus, the onset of breeding appears related to reaching a threshold of nutrient reserves, as first hypothesized for waterfowl by Reynolds (1972). Although they did not immediately sample Ruddy Ducks, Alisauskas and Ankney (1994b) speculate that Ruddy Ducks, like pochards, acquire their reserves after they arrive on their breeding areas.

Ruddy Ducks lay small clutches (avg. 6.73 eggs), and RFG averages 5–6 days. Thus, because there are never more than 5–6 developing follicles in any female and the average clutch is completed in 13 days, the maximum cost of egg production (584 kJ/day) was only incurred for 1 day. Nonetheless, as Alisauskas and Ankney (1994a:17) conclude, "The ability of these small ducks to produce clutches of six or more large eggs at intervals of one per day is remarkable."

Southern Hemisphere
Whistling Ducks — Dendrocygninae

White-faced Whistling-Duck: Almost nothing is known about the dynamics of nutrient reserves for waterfowl breeding outside the temperate environments of North America. Hence, the work of Petrie and Rogers (2004) with the White-faced Whistling-Duck in South Africa helps fill a significant void and provides a basis for comparisons with waterfowl breeding in north-temperate areas. The study took place in the Nyl River floodplain, which is a semiarid area of South Africa characterized by high temperatures and low rainfall. Female whistling-ducks arrived on their breeding wetlands with large reserves of lipids (75 g) and did not store additional lipids after arriving. The reserves allowed females to initiate egg laying shortly after they arrived, which is likely a key adaptation to breeding in semiarid environments. The females catabolized 37 g of lipids and 27 g of protein during rapid follicle growth, which amounted to 87% of the total lipid and 60% of the total protein requirements for egg laying.

Petrie and Rogers (2004) then contrasted temperate areas (i.e., where pronounced seasonality leads to predictable food supplies and thus more options for ducks to acquire nutrients after reaching their breeding areas) with semiarid areas (i.e., where

rainfall varies greatly in both its occurrence and intensity). In semiarid habitats, females that acquire their reserves prior to arriving at breeding areas can begin nesting as soon as habitat becomes available, which is a key adaptation to sites with unpredictable rainfall. Both male and female whistling-ducks also incubate the clutch, so females have less need for nutrient reserves after egg laying, which allows greater allocation to actual egg production. In contrast, loss of body mass is substantial in species where only the female incubates (see Afton and Paulus 1992). Petrie and Rogers (2004) also note that the large size of arctic-nesting geese allows them to store enough nutrient reserves to satisfy the needs of incubating females. However, the comparatively small size of whistling-ducks probably precludes this tactic, which is further exacerbated by the unpredictable supplies of food available in semiarid habitats. For whistling-ducks, biparental care is a particularly significant life-history strategy for this phase of reproduction. Petrie and Rogers (2004) in fact noted that shared incubation occurs in only 12 of the 144 waterfowl species included in their review, and all of these occur in semiarid environments.

CLUTCH SIZE

Evolution of Clutch Size

The evolution of clutch size is another aspect central to understanding the life history and ecology of waterfowl (for review, see Rohwer 1992, Loos and Rohwer 2004). Currently, two hypotheses explain the evolution of clutch size in waterfowl: the nutrient reserve hypothesis, and the egg viability–predation hypothesis. David Lack, the noted British ornithologist, described a broad inverse relationship between clutch size and individual egg mass. In other words, species producing small clutches tend to lay relatively large eggs (Lack 1967, 1968). Lack accordingly proposed the "egg production hypothesis" — now known as the "nutrient reserve hypothesis" — which suggests clutch size in waterfowl evolved in relation to the quantity of food available to the female at the time of laying. Ryder (1970) later modified the nutrient reserve hypothesis to account for arctic-nesting geese, which do not acquire their nutrient reserves at nesting time. Instead, Ryder proposed that clutch size in arctic-nesting geese was limited by the amount of endogenous reserves the female could transport to the breeding area. Rohwer (1988) questioned the nutrient reserve hypothesis, but his results in turn were challenged by Blackburn

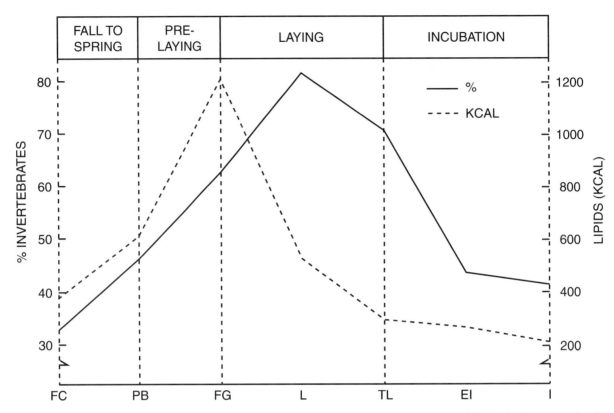

Figure 4-7. A clear pattern marks the consumption of invertebrates and the storage of lipids during reproduction in Wood Ducks. Invertebrate consumption is especially high during laying, and body lipids are stored and then used throughout the laying and incubation periods. FC = fall courtship, PB = prebreeding, FG = follicle growth, L = laying, TL = terminal laying, EI = early incubation, and I = incubation. From Drobney and Fredrickson (1985:124). With permission from the Wildfowl and Wetlands Trust.

(1991), whose analysis showed clutch size explained 29% of the variation in egg size compared with 13% reported by Rohwer (1988). Clutch size therefore may reflect an evolutionary trade-off in which a species laying large eggs is constrained by food availability and produces a small clutch, yet produces an egg size that maximizes the survival of both the female and her offspring. However, the food availability referred to by Lack (1967, 1968) obviously involves both proteins and lipids, and researchers thereafter argued about which nutrients limit clutch size in waterfowl.

Protein is unquestionably important to breeding dabbling ducks, as was demonstrated in controlled feeding experiments with captive female Mallards (Krapu 1979). In these tests, females maintained on a diet high (29%) in protein produced 31 eggs/pair compared with 17 eggs/pair for females on a 14% protein diet; the latter group also did not lay eggs at the usual rate of 1/day. Also, when food was removed for 3 days from pairs on the high-protein

diet, their egg production was reduced by 45%. The scenario emerges that endogenous lipid reserves for egg production and/or maintenance allows females the time necessary to forage for the presumably scarce protein resources required for egg production. For example, although the protein content of an egg was only 5.2 g, Drobney (1980) estimated that a female Wood Ducks must forage 8 hr/day for about 300 invertebrates/hr to meet the requirements of egg laying. Moreover, as shown in Figure 4–7, the greatest consumption of invertebrates occurs during the egg-laying period (Drobney and Fredrickson 1985). As we noted in Reproductive Strategies, Drobney (1980) and others (Krapu 1981, Drobney 1982, Hohman 1986) argued that if ducks acquired lipid stores on their breeding areas, scarce reserves of protein would not have to be allocated for maintenance and instead could be used for egg production. The ability of the female to acquire protein therefore became a major proximate factor limiting the clutch size of ducks (Drobney and

Fredrickson 1985). Ankney and Afton (1988) coined the "protein limitation hypothesis" to describe this scenario.

However, based on work with the Northern Shoveler (Ankney and Afton 1988), Gadwall (Ankney and Alisauskas 1991b), Lesser Scaup (Afton and Ankney 1991), and Ring-necked Duck (Alisauskas et al. 1990), a contrary opinion arose (Ankney et al. 1991). In this scenario, lipid storage apparently evolved to meet the nutritional demands associated with RFG in temperate-nesting ducks. Lipids represent the major nutrients limiting clutch size, and the "lipid limitation hypothesis" followed. Ankney and Afton (1988) reached this conclusion because (1) some species (e.g., Northern Shoveler) ingested more protein than required for maintenance and egg production; (2) if protein was limited, it would be stored and then used for egg production, but this was not the case except in Gadwalls and American Wigeon (protein reserves actually increased in Northern Shovelers); and (3) in spring, temperate-nesting ducks forage in wetlands where protein is more easily obtained than lipids. As noted, Gadwall and American Wigeon are largely herbivorous (Ankney and Alisauskas 1991b) and both species used *protein* reserves during egg production and thereby apparently represent interesting exceptions to the lipid limitation hypothesis. Nonetheless, Ankney and Alisauskas (1991b) still argued in favor of lipids as a limiting factor. However, captive Canada Geese fed ad libitum still exhibited a pattern of declining egg size (Leblanc 1987). Flint and Sedinger (1992) also argued against the egg production (nutrient limitation) hypothesis in their study of Black Brant; they did not find trade-offs among females between clutch size and egg size.

More recently, Arnold et al. (2002) found that continuously laying Mallards — females continuing to produce eggs after loss of a nest, but without interruption of the laying sequence — could produce three to four additional eggs without adverse effects, which they believed refuted the nutritional limitation hypothesis. However, because lipids are a more efficient form of energy storage than proteins — and more efficiently catabolized — Petrie and Rogers (2004) believe that these advantages alone might explain why most species of ducks studied to date rely heavily on stored lipids during reproduction.

Regardless, Arnold et al. (1987) had developed a competitive "egg viability–nest predation hypothesis" or "viability–predation hypothesis" to explain the evolution of clutch sizes in waterfowl. This hypothesis assumes that (1) the viability of eggs declines as

laying progresses if incubation is delayed until the last egg is laid, and (2) eggs face increased risk of predation if incubation does not begin until the last egg is laid (i.e., increased exposure to predators). Arnold et al. (1987) then combined egg viability with predation risk in a model, which they believe explains most of the selective pressure determining clutch size — up to about 14 eggs — in prairie nesting ducks in North America. Nest attendance during the laying period can initiate incubation of the oldest eggs in the clutch (i.e., those laid first) yet still assure a synchronous hatch, which is obviously adaptive for species with precocial young (Arnold et al. 1987, Kennamer et al. 1990, Flint et al. 1994). Early incubation is well known; by the time the last egg is laid in the nests of temperate-nesting ducks, the oldest eggs will have developed to a stage equivalent to 2–3 days of continuous incubation (Prince et al. 1969, Kennamer et al. 1990). In later work, Loos and Rohwer (2004) used microprocessor data loggers to monitor nest attendance and egg temperatures of ducks nesting in southwestern Manitoba; by the time when the second egg was laid, the maximum hollow-egg temperature may be more than 30 °C, which is above the 25–27 °C minimum temperature required for embryonic development (see Haftorn 1978). These data conclusively demonstrated that all species involved began incubation during the laying cycle, not at the end.

Early initiation of incubation is consistent with the viability–predation hypothesis; warming maintains the viability of previously laid eggs, which in turn allows more eggs to hatch (Loos and Rohwer 2004). Further, Loos and Rohwer (2004) noted that the time spent at the nest increased more rapidly for Blue-winged Teal and Northern Shovelers that laid smaller clutches compared with females of the same species that laid larger clutches. By the end of the shorter laying period incurred by small-clutch, these females had spent as much time at the nest as females laying a larger clutch. These results also contradict the nutrient limitation hypothesis, which predicts that females laying small clutches would spend less time at the nest because they are nutritionally stressed.

A third hypothesis proposed that clutch size may be limited by the ability to rear broods. However, experimental manipulation of brood size in Blue-winged Teal (Rohwer 1985), Canada Geese (Lessells 1986, and Wood Ducks (Clawson et al. 1979) all found that the survival rates for offspring from hatching to flying stage were independent of brood size.

The search for factors controlling clutch size in

waterfowl has sparked debate and controversy (Drobney 1991, Ankney et al. 1991, Arnold and Rohwer 1991) and still requires further resolution, although Loos and Rohwer (2004) have helped narrow the focus. Nonetheless, several factors undoubtedly influence the number of eggs forming the optimal clutch, and it seems likely that future evaluations of just one factor will prove inadequate. Instead, an integrated approach, as shown by Arnold et al. (1987), seems necessary to explain the adaptive nature of clutch size (also see Johnsgard 1973, Yoshimura and Shields 1992). Nonetheless, it seems clear that nutrient dynamics (lipids and proteins) act as proximate factors in their affect on clutch size (see Esler and Grand 1994), whereas predation risk, egg viability, and hatching asynchrony likely act as ultimate factors (Arnold et al. 1987).

Inter- and Intraclutch Variation

Rohwer (1988) argued that the nutrient reserve hypothesis should apply within species and predicted that a trade-off exists between clutch size and egg size. In other words, for a given female there is a negative correlation between clutch size and egg size. However, field studies have not detected such a relationship (Rohwer 1988, Lessels et al. 1989, Flint and Grand 1996). See Rohwer (1988) for a useful list of egg mass, the mass of females, and the clutch sizes for all species of waterfowl.

In general, egg size in birds varies within and between populations, but most variation occurs among females. Variation in egg size also can occur within a clutch, but these variations are much less than those occurring among females (Ricklefs 1984, Alisauskas 1986). Egg size is strongly heritable (see Van Noordwik et al. 1980), but egg size is also affected by proximate factors such as age, laying date, and food supply (see Hepp et al. 1987). Younger females also tend to lay smaller eggs, and egg size tends to decline with laying date and position in the clutch (see Rohwer 1992).

In addition to egg size, egg composition also varies among females. For example, differences among females explained 52–82% of the variation in mass and composition of Wood Duck eggs (Hepp et al. 1987). The body mass of females was positively related to mean egg mass, egg composition, energy content of eggs, and clutch mass, but not clutch size or the time of nesting. In general, heavy females laid significantly heavier eggs with more yolk, albumen, and shell components, but clutch size was not greater than that of light females. However, optimal egg-size theory predicts little variation in egg size, and that females with more available energy should lay larger clutches but not larger eggs. For Wood Ducks, Hepp et al. (1987) concluded that adjustments in clutch size are slight and occur secondarily to adjustment in egg size.

Kennamer et al. (1997) expanded the work with Wood Ducks by examining individual variation in egg composition in relation to egg size and laying sequence. Egg size increased during the first half of the laying period but decreased thereafter. Further, absolute lipid levels of each egg were near average until about 75% of the clutch was laid and then declined, but a fat index (egg lipid/lean dry-egg content) tended to be highest in the first 40% of the clutch. Indeed, first-laid eggs, regardless of their size, contained about 2.5 kJ more energy per gram of lean dry-egg content than the largest eggs in the clutch. Such intraclutch variations may be an adaptation that allows embryos in early eggs to delay hatching until incubation is completed for the last eggs. Larger lipid reserves in first-laid eggs allows females to initiate incubation before the clutch is completed yet still ensure synchronous hatching without losing the first-laid eggs. Reduction in egg size later in the clutch is particularly adaptive because smaller eggs require less incubation (Martin and Arnold 1991). Female Wood Ducks also often skipped a day between the next to last and last egg they lay, which tended to increase yolk mass, a likely benefit for ducklings hatching from these later eggs.

However, for this adaptation to occur, the value of each egg in the clutch should be equal because there are limits to the amount of hatching asynchrony that can be accommodated during incubation so that all eggs hatch synchronously (Davies and Cooke 1983). Significantly, Hepp et al. (1989) found that the body mass of hatching Wood Ducks was related to recruitment into the subsequent breeding population in only 1 year of 6. Hence, the occurrence of ducklings of various sizes in a clutch as a means of synchronizing hatch appears to outweigh any disadvantages that may accrue to smaller hatchlings (Kennamer et al. 1997), which supports the egg viability ideas of Arnold et al. (1987).

Flint and Sedinger (1992) observed similar patterns in the trade-off between clutch size and egg size for Black Brant breeding in Alaska — egg size decreased with position in the laying sequence. A substantial overlap occurred in the total volume of all eggs in clutches of different sizes, and clutch size explained 92% of the variation in total clutch volume. The range of average egg sizes was nearly identical for clutches of three, four, and five eggs, and trade-offs therefore occurred among individual females with comparable investments in their clutches. However, because Flint and Sedinger (1992) did not observe increased variation in egg size in keeping with clutch size (particularly for the last egg laid), they concluded that egg size declined not because nutrients were limiting but, as with Wood Ducks, that it represented an adaptation for synchronized hatching.

Overall, although variations in clutch size remain an interesting part of waterfowl life histories, they probably play a minor role in explaining the recruitment rates of waterfowl. Recruitment instead seems more influenced by the propensity for breeding, which is governed by the acquisition of nutrient reserves both on and away from breeding areas.

INCUBATION

Among waterfowl, only females incubate eggs, except for the Magpie Goose, Black Swan, and whistling-ducks (Dendrocygninae). Afton and Paulus (1992) reviewed the incubation requirements in waterfowl, addressing such topics as the thermal environment at the nest, the gaseous environment in the egg, female rotation of eggs in the nest, and incubation rhythms of parents, much of which applies to birds in general. We briefly review those topics here, while providing more detail for incubation rhythms and the role of lipid reserves in meeting the energetic costs of incubation.

Incubation is the process by which the heat nec-essary for embryonic development is applied to an egg. The internal egg temperature for 22 waterfowl species averaged 35.6 °C (Afton and Paulus 1992), which is similar to temperatures recorded for other species. Like other birds, waterfowl achieve this relatively narrow range of egg temperatures, despite a wide range of environmental temperatures, by varying (1) the amount of time they spend on the nest (incubation rhythm) and (2) the amount of heat transferred to their eggs from a highly vascularized abdominal area known as a brood patch. Incubating birds also rotate eggs in their clutches to promote the even distribution of heat to each egg (see Drent 1975, Afton 1979, Afton and Paulus 1992).

Afton and Paulus (1992) summarized the incubation rhythms for 34 species of waterfowl. For these species, incubation constancy — the percentage of time during the incubation period that eggs are warmed by a parent — ranged from 72.6% to 99.5% and averaged 88.1%. Total recess time per day averaged 171 min and ranged from 3 to 395 min. The average length of each recess lasted for 59 min, with a frequency of 3.0 recesses per day. In general, geese maintain higher incubation constancy than ducks (Table 4-9). Various factors influence incubation rhythm, but weather exerts the most influence as determined by the inverse relationship between incubation constancy and ambient temperature (see Afton and Paulus 1992).

Loos and Rohwer (2004) used microprocessor data loggers to acquire new data on incubation rhythms at duck nests in southwestern Manitoba. Females of all species increased their nest attendance as laying progressed (Fig. 4-8). The total time

Table 4-9. Summary (mean) of incubation-rhythm components in various groups of waterfowl. Modified from Afton and Paulus (1992:76).

Group	Incubation constancy (%)	Recess time/day (min)	Recess frequency/day	Recess duration (min)
Swans	84.3	226	4.5	54
Geese	95.1	70	3.0	19
Ducks	85.4	210	2.7	80
Anas spp.	86.0	202	2.2	88
Diving Ducks[a]	84.2	227	3.5	70
Aythyini	84.1	229	4.2	55
Mergini	86.7	191	2.4	97

[a] Includes Aythyini, Mergini, and Oxyurini.

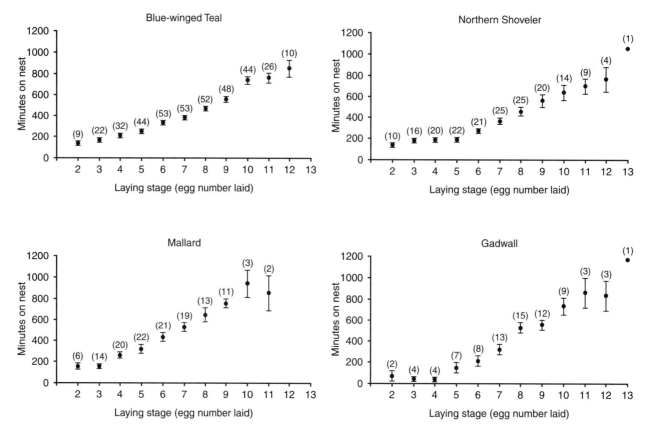

Figure 4-8. Examples of nest attendance (mean ± SE) by incubating dabbling ducks in relation to stage of egg laying. Sample sizes at each laying stage are in parentheses. From Loos and Rohwer (2004:592). With permission from the American Ornithologists' Unioin.

females spent on their nests during the laying period averaged 3,242 min for Blue-winged Teal, 4,057 for Mallards, 3,283 for Gadwalls, 3,520 for Northern Shovelers, and 2,508 for Northern Pintails. Interestingly, and unlike previous studies, this study did not confirm that nest attendance was influenced by precipitation or low ambient temperatures. Also, species nesting late in the season attended their nests less often early in the laying sequence than did early-nesting species, perhaps because early-nesting species needed more time to warm their eggs.

The strong commitment of females to nest attendance places a heavy reliance on their lipid reserves to meet the costs of incubation — foraging time diminishes as incubation progresses — and females eventually spend about 50% of the day in incubation once the clutch is 80–90% complete (Caldwell and Cornwell 1975, Afton 1980, Kennamer et al. 1990). Thereafter, female ducks take only short daily recesses from their nests for the remainder of the incubation period. As a result, the energy intake of incubating females is proportionately

reduced, sometimes even below the levels needed to sustain BMR (Drent et al. 1985), and body mass accordingly declines as incubation progresses. But if too much energy is allocated to egg production, then successful incubation and/or brood-rearing may be jeopardized. Hence, in terms of reproductive strategy, a clear interaction exists between the energetic costs of producing eggs and those associated with incubation — the interaction occurs because females of most species of waterfowl use lipid reserves to accomplish both tasks. However, females in poor condition during incubation may abandon their nests, as Korschgen (1977) noted among Common Eiders during a 3-year study in Maine. Some 11% of all nesting attempts failed from abandonment, and all but one female in this group had lower than average body mass. Long-lived species like the sea ducks (Mergini) may abandon their nests during incubation in an attempt to increase their future reproductive success, whereas species with shorter life spans (e.g., the Anatini) are less likely to do so (Forbes et al. 1994).

For dabbling ducks (Anatini), endogenous reserves account for about 25% of incubation costs in Mallards, 16% in Northern Shovelers, and 11% in Blue-winged Teal (see Gloutney and Clark 1991) but increases to about 80% in Lesser Snow Geese and Common Eiders. Overall, use of endogenous lipids during incubation averaged 29.8% for 14 waterfowl species where only females incubated (Afton and Paulus 1992). Weight loss during incubation averages 17.5% (range = 3–33%) for 24 species of waterfowl in which only the female incubates (Afton and Paulus 1992). King Eiders lost about 30% of their preincubation body mass during incubation (Kellett and Alisauskas 2000), and Spectacled Eiders lost 26%, with an average loss of 16.6 g/day (Flint and Grand 1999). Generally, larger species such as swans and geese accumulate larger absolute reserves and thus maintain a greater degree of incubation constancy, although this results in less time for feeding — these species rely more on endogenous lipids and therefore lose proportionately more weight than smaller species. See Afton and Paulus (1992:78–79) for a summary of the energetic costs incurred by waterfowl during incubation.

The time waterfowl spend feeding per day during incubation recesses averaged 104 min, but ranged from 0 to 239 min (Afton and Paulus 1992). Generally, the larger species spend more time on their nests, and these species therefore rely more heavily on endogenous energy reserves during incubation. As a cost of reproduction, females necessarily balance the benefits of expending their energy reserves for the proper thermal environment for their clutches against those required for maintaining their own body condition at a level where their survival is not impaired. In captive Canada Geese, for example, the amount of time devoted to nest recesses increased dramatically once the body mass of females fell to 3,200–3,300 g (Aldrich and Raveling 1983). The additional periods of inattentiveness also prolonged their incubation period, a liability that increases the risk of nest predation in the wild. Conversely, the survival of incubating females may be jeopardized when their body mass becomes too low. Female Lesser Snow Geese sometimes die by the end of the incubation period as a result of severely depleted energy reserves (Ankney and MacInnes 1978).

The body mass of female Wood Ducks, a cavity-nesting species, declined from 578 g early in the incubation period to 553 g in late incubation, and those females that were the heaviest at the end of incubation had a higher probability of surviving to the next breeding season than did lighter females (Hepp et al. 1990). Body mass of female Common Goldeneyes, another cavity-nesting species, declined 10–11% during incubation, but most of the lost mass was regained by the time females abandoned their broods (Zicus and Riggs 1996). A relationship may exist between absolute body size and the amount of energy stored for incubation. Namely, because the large-bodied species store proportionately — and absolutely — more lipids than small-bodied species, the larger species may rely on stored reserves as part of their incubation strategy, whereas heat loading or egg cooling may be important in determining the incubation strategies of smaller species (Gloutney and Clark 1991). Finally, cool temperatures and other environmental factors may increase the risk of chilling developing embryos and thus require more attendance at the nest, although waterfowl eggs can survive short-term exposure to ambient temperatures as low at 0 °C (Batt and Cornwell 1972). However, incubating females may lose more body mass while incubating during periods of cold weather, as Mallory and Weatherhead (1993) documented for Common Goldeneyes. Conversely, incubating females may increase their recesses during periods of favorable weather when chilling is unlikely (Afton 1980), and the additional feeding time may help offset the nutritional demands associated with incubation.

CONCLUDING COMMENTS

In this chapter, we reviewed the energetic demands of clutch formation and the major strategies used by waterfowl to meet those demands (i.e., the relationships between exogenous and endogenous energy reserves), as well as the costs of egg production and incubation, and the factors (both proximate and ultimate) affecting clutch size. Still, the acquisition of energy for reproductive (and other) activities requires that waterfowl interact with their environment to obtain the necessary foods. Choices must be made because food varies both in abundance and quality, as well as in its availability. Habitats also vary in the temporal and spatial ways they produce food — and waterfowl vary in the ways they exploit food resources. The next chapter discusses these topics.

LITERATURE CITED

Afton, A. D. 1979. Incubation temperatures of the Northern Shoveler. Canadian Journal of Zoology 57:1052–1056.

Afton, A. D. 1980. Factors affecting incubation rhythms of Northern Shovelers. Condor 82:132–137.

Afton, A. D. 1985. Forced copulation as a reproductive strategy of male Lesser Scaup: a field test of some predictions. Behaviour 92:146–167.

Afton, A. D., and C. D. Ankney. 1991. Nutrient-reserve dynamics of breeding Lesser Scaup: a test of competing hypotheses. Condor 93:89–97.

Afton, A. D., and S. L. Paulus. 1992. Incubation and brood care. Pages 62–108 *in* B. D. J. Batt, A. D. Afton, M. G. Anderson, C. D. Ankney, D. H. Johnson, J. A. Kadlec, and G. L. Krapu, editors. Ecology and management of breeding waterfowl. University of Minnesota Press, Minneapolis.

Aldrich, T. W., and D. G. Raveling. 1983. Effects of experience and body weight on incubation behavior of Canada Geese. Auk 100:670–679.

Alisauskas, R. T. 1986. Variation in the composition of the eggs and chicks of American Coots. Condor 88:84–90.

Alisauskas, R. T. 2002. Arctic climate, spring nutrition, and recruitment in midcontinent Lesser Snow Geese. Journal of Wildlife Management 66:181–193.

Alisauskas, R. T., and C. D. Ankney. 1992. The cost of egg laying and its relationship to nutrient reserves in waterfowl. Pages 30–61 *in* B. D. J. Batt, A. D. Afton, M. G. Anderson, C. D. Ankney, D. H. Johnson, J. A. Kadlec, and G. L. Krapu, editors. Ecology and management of breeding waterfowl. University of Minnesota Press, Minneapolis.

Alisauskas, R. T., and C. D. Ankney. 1994a. Costs and rates of egg formation in Ruddy Ducks. Condor 96:11–18.

Alisauskas, R. T., and C. D. Ankney. 1994b. Nutrition of breeding female Ruddy Ducks: the role of nutrient reserves. Condor 96:878–897.

Alisauskas, R. T., R. T. Eberhardt, and C. D. Ankney. 1990. Nutrient reserves of breeding Ring-necked Ducks (*Aythya collaris*). Canadian Journal of Zoology 68:2524–2530.

Altmann, J. 1974. Observational study of behavior: sampling methods. Behaviour 49:227–267.

Anderson, D. R., P. A. Skaptason, K. G. Fahey, and C. J. Henny. 1974. Population ecology of the Mallard III. Bibliography of published research and management findings. U.S. Fish and Wildlife Service Resource Publication 119.

Ankney, C. D. 1977. The use of nutrient reserves by breeding male Lesser Snow Geese (*Chen caerulescens caerulescens*). Canadian Journal of Zoology 55:1984–1987.

Ankney, C. D. 1980. Egg weight, survival, and growth of Lesser Snow Goose goslings. Journal of Wildlife Management 44:174–182.

Ankney, C. D. 1984. Nutrient reserve dynamics of breeding and molting Brant. Auk 101:361–370.

Ankney, C. D., and A. D. Afton. 1988. Bioenergetics of breeding Northern Shovelers: diet, nutrient reserves, clutch size, and incubation. Condor 90:459–472.

Ankney, C. D., A. D. Afton, and R. T. Alisauskas. 1991. The role of nutrient reserves in limiting waterfowl reproduction. Condor 93:1029–1032.

Ankney, C. D., and R. T. Alisauskas. 1991a. The use of nutrient reserves by breeding waterfowl. International Ornithological Congress 20:2170–2176.

Ankney, C. D., and R. T. Alisauskas. 1991b. Nutrient-reserve dynamics and diet of breeding female Gadwalls. Condor 93:799–810.

Ankney, C. D., and C. D. MacInnes. 1978. Nutrient reserves and reproductive performance of female Lesser Snow Geese. Auk 95:459–471.

Arnold, T. W., D. W. Howerter, J. H. Devries, B. L. Joynt, R. B. Emery, and M. G. Anderson. 2002. Continuous laying and clutch-size limitation in Mallards. Auk 119:261–266.

Arnold, T. W., and F. C. Rohwer. 1991. Do egg formation costs limit clutch size in waterfowl? A skeptical view. Condor 93:1032–1038.

Arnold, T. W., F. C. Rohwer, and T. Armstrong. 1987. Egg viability, nest predation, and the adaptive significance of clutch size in prairie ducks. American Naturalist 130:643–653.

Baldassarre, G. A., S. L. Paulus, A. Tamisier, and R. D. Titman. 1988. Workshop summary: techniques for timing activity of wintering waterfowl. Pages 181–188 *in* M. W. Weller, editor. Waterfowl in winter. University of Minnesota Press, Minneapolis.

Balthazart, J. 1983. Hormonal correlates of behavior. Avian Biology 7:221–365.

Barry, T. W. 1962. Effect of late seasons on Atlantic Brant reproduction. Journal of Wildlife Management 26:19–26.

Batt, B. D. J., and G. W. Cornwell. 1972. The effects of cold on Mallard embryos. Journal of Wildlife Management 36:745–751.

Beasley, B. A., and C. D. Ankney. 1988. The effect of plumage color on the thermoregulatory abilities of Lesser Snow Goose goslings. Canadian Journal of Zoology 66:1352–1358.

Bengtson, S. A. 1971. Variations in clutch-size in ducks in relation to the food supply. Ibis 113:523–526.

Benoit, J., and I. Assenmacher. 1955. Le controle hypothalamique de l'activite prehypophysaire gonadotrope. Journal of Physiology (Paris) 47:427–567.

Best, R. G. 1981. Infrared emissivity and radiant surface temperatures of Canada and Snow Geese. Journal of Wildlife Management 45:1026–1029.

Birkebak, R. C. 1966. Heat transfer in biological systems. International Review of General and Experimental Zoology 2:269–344.

Blackburn, T. M. 1991. The interspecific relationship between egg size and clutch size in waterfowl. Auk 108:209–211.

Bluhm, C. K. 1988. Temporal patterns of pair formation and reproduction in annual cycles and associated endocrinology in waterfowl. Current Ornithology 5:123–185.

Bluhm, C. K. 1992. Environmental and endocrine control of waterfowl reproduction. Pages 323–364 in B. D. J. Batt, A. D. Afton, M. G. Anderson, C. D. Ankney, D. H. Johnson, J. A. Kadlec, and G. L. Krapu, editors. Ecology and management of breeding waterfowl. University of Minnesota Press, Minneapolis.

Board, R. G., and D. J. Hornsey. 1978. Plasma and egg white proteins. Pages 47–74 in M. Florkin and B. T. Scheer, editors. Chemical zoology, volume X. Aves. Academic Press, New York.

Breucker, H. 1982. Seasonal spermatogenesis in the Mute Swan (Cygnus olor). Pages 1–94 in F. Beck, W. Hild, J. van Limborgh et al., editors. Advances in anatomy, embryology and cell biology. Volume 72. Springer-Verlag, New York.

Briskie, J. V., and R. Montgomerie. 1993. Patterns of sperm storage in relation to sperm competition in passerine birds. Condor 95:442–454.

Briskie, J. V., and R. Montgomerie. 1997. Sexual selection and the intromittent organ in birds. Journal of Avian Biology 28:73–86.

Brody, S. 1945. Bioenergetics and growth. Reinhold, New York.

Brown, P. W. 1981. Nesting biology of the White-winged Scoter. Journal of Wildlife Management 45:38-45.

Budeau, D. A., J. T. Ratti, and C. R. Ely. 1991. Energy dynamics, foraging ecology, and behavior of prenesting Greater White-fronted Geese. Journal of Wildlife Management 55:556–563.

Calder, W. A., and J. R. King. 1974. Thermal and caloric relations of birds. Avian Biology 4:259–413.

Caldwell, P. J., and G. W. Cornwell. 1975. Incubation behavior and temperatures of the Mallard duck. Auk 92:706–731.

Cheng, K. M., J. T. Burns, and F. McKinney. 1982. Forced copulation in captive Mallards (Anas platyrhynchos): II. Temporal factors. Animal Behaviour 30:695–699.

Cheng, K. M., J. T. Burns, and F. McKinney. 1983. Forced copulation in captive Mallards III. Sperm competition. Auk 100:302–310.

Clark, A. B., and D. S. Wilson. 1981. Avian breeding adaptations: hatching asynchrony, brood reduction, and nest failure. Quarterly Review of Biology 56:253–277.

Clawson, R. L., G. W. Hartman, and L. H. Fredrickson. 1979. Dump nesting in a Missouri Wood Duck population. Journal of Wildlife Management 43:347–355.

Coker, C. R., F. McKinney, H. Hays, S. V. Briggs, and K. M. Cheng. 2002. Intromittent organ morphology and testes size in relation to mating system in waterfowl. Auk 119:403–413.

Cunningham, E. J. A. 2003. Female mate preferences and subsequent resistance to copulation in the Mallard. Behavioral Ecology 14:326–333.

Davies, J. C., and F. Cooke. 1983. Annual nesting productivity in Snow Geese: prairie droughts and arctic springs. Journal of Wildlife Management 47:291–296.

DeMerritt, R. J. 1979. The role of the uterovaginal junction in sperm cell storage and release in the domestic fowl. Poultry Science 58:1048–1049.

Drent, R. H. 1975. Incubation. Avian Biology 5:333–420.

Drent, R., J. M. Tinbergen, and H. Biebach. 1985. Incubation in the Starling, Sturnus vulgaris: resolution of the conflict between egg care and foraging. Netherlands Journal of Zoology 35:103–123.

Drobney, R. D. 1980. Reproductive bioenergetics of Wood Ducks. Auk 97:480–490.

Drobney, R. D. 1982. Body weight and composition changes and adaptations for breeding in Wood Ducks. Condor 84:300–305.

Drobney, R. D. 1991. Nutrient limitation of clutch size in waterfowl: is there a universal hypothesis? Condor 93:1026–1028.

Drobney, R. D., and L. H. Fredrickson. 1985. Protein acquisition: a possible proximate factor limiting clutch size in Wood Ducks. Wildfowl 36:122–128.

Dunlap, J. C., J. J. Loros, and P. J. DeCoursey. 2004. Chronobiology: biological timekeeping. Sinauer Associates, Sunderland, Massachusetts.

Dunn, P. O., A. D. Afton, M. L. Gloutney, and R. T. Alisauskas. 1999. Forced copulation results in few extrapair fertilizations in Ross's and Lesser Snow Geese. Animal Behaviour 57:1071–1081.

Dwyer, T. J., G. L. Krapu, and D. M. Janke. 1979. Use of prairie pothole habitat by breeding Mallards. Journal of Wildlife Management 43:526–531.

Dzubin, A. 1969. Comments on carrying capacity of small ponds for ducks and possible effects of density on Mallard production. Pages 138–160 in Saskatoon Wetlands Seminar. Canadian Wildlife Service Report Series 6.

Elder, W. H., and M. W. Weller. 1954. Duration of fertility in the domestic Mallard hen after isolation from the drake. Journal of Wildlife Management 18:495–502.

Esler, D. 1999. Time of day of ovulation by three duck species in subarctic Alaska. Condor 101:422–425.

Esler, D., and J. B. Grand. 1994. The role of nutrient reserves for clutch formation by Northern Pintails in Alaska. Condor 96:422–432.

Esler, D., J. B. Grand, and A. D. Afton. 2001. Intraspecific variation in nutrient reserve use during clutch formation by Lesser Scaup. Condor 103:810–820.

Evarts, S., and C. J. Williams. 1987. Multiple paternity in a wild population of Mallards. Auk 104:597–602.

Flint, P. L., and J. B. Grand. 1996. Variation in egg size of the Northern Pintail. Condor 98:162–165.

Flint, P. L., and J. B. Grand. 1999. Incubation behavior of Spectacled Eiders on the Yukon-Kuskokwim Delta, Alaska. Condor 101:413–416.

Flint, P. L., M. S. Lindberg, M. C. MacCluskie, and J. S. Sedinger. 1994. The adaptive significance of hatching synchrony of waterfowl eggs. Wildfowl 45:248–254.

Flint, P. L., and J. S. Sedinger. 1992. Reproductive implications of egg-size variation in Black Brant. Auk 109:896–903.

Forbes, M. R. L., R. G. Clark, P. J. Weatherhead, and T. Armstrong. 1994. Risk-taking by female ducks: intra- and interspecific tests of nest defense theory. Behavioral Ecology and Sociobiology 34:79–85.

Freeman, B. M., and M. A. Vince. 1974. Development of the avian embryo. Chapman and Hall, London.

Gauthier, G., and J. Tardif. 1991. Female feeding and male vigilance during nesting in Greater Snow Geese. Condor 93:701–711.

Gavrilov, V. M., V. R. Dol'nik, and Y. E. Kespaik. 1970. The winter energy metabolism in the Chaffinch. Eesti NSV Teaduste Akadeemia Toimetised, Biologia 19:211–218.

Geis, A. D., and W. F. Crissey. 1973. 1970 test of the point system for regulating duck harvests. Wildlife Society Bulletin 1:1–21.

Gill, F. B. 1990. Ornithology. W. H. Freeman, New York.

Gloutney, M. L., and R. G. Clark. 1991. The significance of body mass to female dabbling ducks during late incubation. Condor 93:811–816.

Gloutney, M. L., R. G. Clark, A. D. Afton, and G. J. Huff. 1993. Timing of nest searches for upland nesting waterfowl. Journal of Wildlife Management 57:597–601.

Gordon, M. S. 1977. Animal physiology: principles and adaptations. Third edition. Macmillan, New York.

Grieb, J. R., H. D. Funk, R. M. Hopper, G. F. Wrakestraw, and D. Witt. 1970. Evaluation of the 1968–1969 experimental Mallard drake season in Montana, Wyoming and Colorado. Transactions of the North American Wildlife and Natural Resources Conference 35:336–348.

Gwinner, E. 1973. Circannual rhythms in birds: their interaction with circadian rhythms and environmental photoperiod. Journal of Reproduction and Fertility Supplements 19:51–65.

Gwinner, E. 1975. Circadian and circannual rhythms in birds. Avian Biology 5:221–285.

Gwinner, E., and R. Brandstätter. 2001. Complex bird clocks. Philosophical Transactions of the Royal Society of London 356:1801–1810.

Haase, E. 1983. The annual reproductive cycle in Mallards. Journal of Steroid Biochemistry 19:731–737.

Haftorn, S. 1978. Egg laying and regulation of egg temperature during incubation of Goldcrest (*Regulus regulus*). Ornis Scandinavia 9:2–21.

Hagan, A. A., and J. E. Heath. 1980. Regulation of heat loss in the duck by vasomotion in the bill. Journal of Thermal Biology 5:95–101.

Hayes, S. R., and J. A. Gessaman. 1980. The combined effects of air temperature, wind and radiation on the resting metabolism of avian raptors. Journal of Thermal Biology 5:119–125.

Heinroth, O. 1911. Beiträge zur Biologie, namentlich Ethologie und Psychologie der Anatiden. International Ornithological Congress 5:589–702.

Hepp, G. R., R. A. Kennamer, and W. F. Harvey IV. 1989. Recruitment and natal philopatry of Wood Ducks. Ecology 70:897–903.

Hepp, G. R., R. A. Kennamer, and W. F. Harvey IV. 1990. Incubation as a reproductive cost in female Wood Ducks. Auk 107:756–764.

Hepp, G. R., D. J. Stangohr, L. A. Baker, and R. A. Kennamer. 1987. Factors affecting variation in the egg and duckling components of Wood Ducks. Auk 104:435–443.

Hipes, D. L., and G. R. Hepp. 1995. Nutrient-reserve dynamics of breeding male Wood Ducks. Condor 97:451–460.

Hohman, W. L. 1986. Changes in body weight and body composition of breeding Ring-necked Ducks (*Aythya collaris*). Auk 103: 181–188.

Hohn, E. O. 1947. Sexual behaviour and seasonal changes in the gonads and adrenals of the Mallard. Proceedings of the Zoological Society of London 117:281–304.

Howarth, B., Jr. 1971. Transport of spermatozoa in the reproductive tract of turkey hens. Poultry Science 50:84–89.

Humburg, D. D., H. H. Prince, and R. A. Bishop. 1978. The social organization of a Mallard population in northern Iowa. Journal of Wildlife Management 42:72–80.

John, T. M., J. C. George, and C. G. Scanes. 1983. Seasonal changes in circulating levels of luteinizing hormone and growth hormone in the migratory Canada Goose. General and Comparative Endocrinology 51:44–49.

Johnsgard, P. A. 1973. Proximate and ultimate determinants of clutch size in Anatidae. Wildfowl 24:144–149.

Johnson, A. L. 1986a. Reproduction in the male. Pages 432–451 *in* P. D. Sturkie, editor. Avian physiology. Springer-Verlag, New York.

Johnson, A. L. 1986b. Reproduction in the female. Pages 403–431 *in* P. D. Sturkie, editor. Avian physiology. Springer-Verlag, New York.

Kaseloo, P. A., and J. R. Lovvorn. 2003. Heat increment of feeding and thermal substitution in Mallard ducks feeing voluntarily on grain. Journal of Comparative Physiology B:173:207–213.

Kellett, D. K., and R. T. Alisauskas. 2000. Body-mass dynamics of King Eiders during incubation. Auk 117:812–817.

Kendeigh, S. C. 1969. Tolerance of cold and Bergmann's rule. Auk 86:13–25.

Kendeigh, S. C., V. R. Dol'nik, and V. M. Gavrilov. 1977. Avian energetics. Pages 127–204 *in* J. Pinowski and S. C. Kendeigh, editors. Granivorous birds in ecosystems. Cambridge University Press, New York.

Kennamer, R. A., S. K. Alsum, and S. V. Colwell. 1997. Composition of Wood Duck eggs in relation to egg size, laying sequence, and skipped days of laying. Auk 114:479–487.

Kennamer, R. A., W. F. Harvey IV, and G. R. Hepp. 1990. Embryonic development and nest attentiveness of Wood Ducks during egg laying. Condor 92:587–592.

King, J. R. 1973. Energetics of reproduction in birds. Pages 78–107 *in* D. S. Farner, editor. Breeding biology of birds. National Academy of Science, Washington, D.C.

King, J. R. 1974. Energetics of reproduction in birds. Pages 152–292 *in* R. A. Paynter, Jr., editor. Avian energetics. Nuttall Ornithological Club Publication 15.

Koenig, W. D. 1980a. The determination of runt eggs in birds. Wilson Bulletin 92:103–107.

Koenig, W. D. 1980b. The incidence of runt eggs in woodpeckers. Wilson Bulletin 92:169–176.

Korschgen, C. E. 1977. Breeding stress of female eiders in Maine. Journal of Wildlife Management 41:360–373.

Krapu, G. L. 1979. Nutrition of female dabbling ducks during reproduction. Pages 59–70 *in* T. A. Bookhout, editor. Waterfowl and wetlands–an integrated review. La Crosse Printing, La Crosse, Wisconsin.

Krapu, G. L. 1981. The role of nutrient reserves in Mallard reproduction. Auk 98:29–38.

Krapu, G. L., A. T. Klett, and D. G. Jorde. 1983. The effect of variable spring water conditions on Mallard reproduction. Auk 100:689–698.

Lack, D. 1967. The significance of clutch-size in waterfowl. Wildfowl 18:125–128.

Lack, D. 1968. Ecological adaptations for breeding in birds. Methuen, London.

Lake, P. E. 1981. Male genital organs. Pages 1–61 *in* A. S. King and J. McClelland, editors. Form and function in birds. Academic Press, New York.

Lank, D. B., P. Mineau, R. F. Rockwell, and F. Cooke. 1989. Intraspecific nest parasitism and extrapair copulation in Lesser Snow Geese. Animal Behaviour 37:74–89.

Laurila, T. 1988. Reproductive strategies in waterfowl: the effect of ultimate environmental factors, size and phylogeny. Ornis Fennica 65:49–64.

Leblanc, Y. 1987. Intraclutch variation in egg size of Canada Geese. Canadian Journal of Zoology 65:3044–3047.

Lessells, C. M. 1986. Brood size in Canada Geese: a manipulation experiment. Journal of Animal Ecology 55:669–689.

Lessells, C. M., F. Cooke, and R. F. Rockwell. 1989. Is there a trade-off between egg weight and clutch size in wild Lesser Snow Geese (*Anser caerulescens caerulescens*)? Journal of Evolutionary Biology 2:457–472.

Loos, E. R., and F. C. Rohwer. 2004. Laying-stage nest attendance and onset of incubation in prairie nesting ducks. Auk 121:587–599.

MacCluskie, M. C., and J. S. Sedinger. 2000. Nutrient reserves and clutch-size regulation of Northern Shovelers in Alaska. Auk 117:971–979.

Mallory, M. L., L. Kiff, R. G. Clark, T. Bowman, P. Blums, A. Mednis, and R. T. Alisauskas. 2004. The occurrence of runt eggs in waterfowl clutches. Journal of Field Ornithology 75:209–217.

Mallory, M. L., and P. J. Weatherhead. 1993. Incubation rhythms and mass loss of Common Goldeneyes. Condor 95:849–859.

Mann, F. E., and J. S. Sedinger. 1993. Nutrient-reserve dynamics and control of clutch size in Northern Pintails breeding in Alaska. Auk 110:264–278.

Martin, P. A., and T. W. Arnold. 1991. Relationships among fresh mass, incubation time, and water loss in Japanese Quail eggs. Condor 93:28–37.

McCracken, K. G. 2000. The 20-cm spiny penis of the Argentine Lake Duck (*Oxyura vittata*). Auk 117:820–825.

McCracken, K. G., R. E. Wilson, P. J. McCracken, and K. P. Johnson. 2001. Are ducks impressed by drakes' display? Nature 413:128.

McDonald, P., R. A. Edwards, J. F. D. Greenhalgh. and C. A. Morgan. 1995. Animal nutrition. Fifth edition. John Wiley & Sons, New York.

McKinney, F., S. R. Derrickson, and P. Mineau. 1983. Forced copulation in waterfowl. Behaviour 86:250–294.

McKinney, F., and S. Evarts. 1998. Sexual coercion in waterfowl and other birds. Ornithological Monographs 49:163–195.

Mikula, E. J., G. F. Martz, and C. L. Bennett, Jr. 1972. Field evaluation of three types of waterfowl hunting regulations. Journal of Wildlife Management 36:441–459.

Milne, H. 1976. Body weights and carcass composition of the Common Eider. Wildfowl 27:115–122.

Mineau, P., and F. Cooke. 1979. Rape in the Lesser Snow Goose. Behaviour 70:280–291.

Moorman, T. E., and G. A. Baldassarre. 1988. Incidence of second broods by Wood Ducks in Alabama and Georgia. Journal of Wildlife Management 52:426–431.

Morowitz, H. J. 1978. Foundations of bioenergetics. Academic Press, New York.

Morton, M. L. 1967. The effects of isolation on the diurnal feeding pattern of White-crowned Sparrows (*Zonotrichia leucophrysc gambelii*). Ecology 48:690-694.

Morzenti, A., F. X. Ogasawara, and C. L. Fuqua. 1978. The relationship of infundibular fluid to the avian sperm transport mechanism. Poultry Science 57:1173.

Nagy, K. A. 1975. Water and energy budgets of free-living animals: measurement using isotopically labeled water. Pages 227–245 *in* N. F. Hadley, editor. Environmental physiology of desert organisms. Dowden, Hutchinson, and Ross, Stroudsburg, Pennsylvania.

Ohde, B. R., R. A. Bishop, and J. J. Dinsmore. 1983. Mallard reproduction in relation to sex ratios. Journal of Wildlife Management 47:118–126.

Oppenheimer, S. D., M. E. Pereyra, and M. L. Morton. 1996. Egg laying in Dusky Flycatchers and White-crowned Sparrows. Condor 98:428–430.

Owen, R. B., Jr., and K. J. Reinecke. 1979. Bioenergetics of breeding dabbling ducks. Pages 71–93 *in* T. A. Bookhout, editor. Waterfowl and wetlands — an integrated review. La Crosse Printing, La Crosse, Wisconsin.

Parker, H., and H. Holm. 1990. Patterns of nutrient and energy expenditure in female Common Eiders nesting in the high Arctic. Auk 107:660–668.

Peters, J. L., G. L. Brewer, and L. M. Bowe. 2003. Extrapair paternity and breeding synchrony in Gadwalls (*Anas strepera*) in North Dakota. Auk 120:883–888.

Petersen, M. R. 1992. Reproductive ecology of Emperor Geese: annual and individual variation in nesting. Condor 94:383–397.

Petrie, S. A., and K. H. Rogers. 2004. Nutrient-reserve dynamics of semiarid-breeding White-faced Whistling Ducks: a north-temperate contrast. Canadian Journal of Zoology 82:1082–1090.

Prince, H. H., P. B. Siegel, and G. W. Cornwell. 1969. Hatchability, clutch position, and hatching sequence in Mallards. Auk 86:762–763.

Rahn, H., C. V. Paganelli, and A. Ar. 1975. Relation of avian egg weight to body weight. Auk 92:750–765.

Raveling, D. G. 1978. The timing of egg laying by northern geese. Auk 95:294–303.

Raveling, D. G. 1979a. The annual cycle of body composition of Canada Geese with special reference to control of reproduction. Auk 96:234–252.

Raveling, D. G. 1979b. The annual energy cycle in the Cackling Canada Goose. Pages 81–93 *in* R. L. Jarvis and J. C. Bartonek, editors. Management and biology of Pacific Flyway geese. OSU Book Stores, Corvallis, Oregon.

Reynolds, C. M. 1972. Mute Swan weights in relation to breeding. Wildfowl 23:111–118.

Ricklefs, R. E. 1974. Energetics of reproduction in birds. Pages 152–292 *in* R. A. Paynter, Jr., editor. Avian energetics. Nuttall Ornithological Club Publication 15.

Ricklefs, R. E. 1984. Variation in the size and composition of eggs of the European Starling. Condor 86:1–6.

Rohwer, F. C. 1985. The adaptive significance of clutch size in prairie ducks. Auk 102:354–361.

Rohwer, F. C. 1988. Inter- and intraspecific relationships between egg size and clutch size in waterfowl. Auk 105:161–176.

Rohwer, F. C. 1992. The evolution of reproductive patterns in waterfowl. Pages 486–539 *in* B. D. J. Batt, A. D. Afton, M. G. Anderson, C. D. Ankney, D. H. Johnson, J. A. Kadlec, and G. L. Krapu, editors. Ecology and management of breeding waterfowl. University of Minnesota Press, Minneapolis.

Romanoff, A. L., and A. J. Romanoff. 1949. The avian egg. John Wiley & Sons, New York.

Ryder, J. P. 1970. A possible factor in the evolution of clutch size in Ross' Goose. Wilson Bulletin 82:5–13.

Ryder, J. P. 1972. Biology of nesting Ross's Geese. Ardea 60:185–215.

Samelius, G., and R. T. Alisauskas. 2001. Deterring arctic fox predation: the role of parental nest attendance by Lesser Snow Geese. Canadian Journal of Zoology 79:861–866.

Sorenson, L. G. 1994a. Forced extra-pair copulation and mate guarding in the White-cheeked Pintail: timing and trade-offs in an asynchronously breeding duck. Animal Behaviour 48:519–533.

Sorenson, L. G. 1994b. Forced extra-pair copulation in the White-cheeked Pintail: male tactics and female responses. Condor 96:400–410.

Stipkovits, L., Z. Varga, G. Czifra, and M. Dobos Kovacs. 1986. Occurrence of mycoplasmas in geese infected with inflammation of the cloaca and phallus. Avian Pathology 15:289–299.

Sturkie, P. D., editor. 1986. Avian physiology. Fourth edition. Springer-Verlag, New York.

Triggs, S. M., M. Williams, S. Marshall, and G. Chambers. 1991. Genetic relationships within a population of Blue Duck *Hymenolaimus malacorhynchos*. Wildfowl 42:87–93.

Trivers, R. L. 1972. Parental investment and sexual selection. Pages 136–179 *in* B. G. Campbell, editor. Sexual selection and the descent of man, 1871–1971. Aldine Publishing, Chicago.

Van Noordwijk, A. J., J. H. Van Balen, and W. Scharloo. 1980. Heritability of ecologically important traits in the Great Tit. Ardea 68:193–203.

Weathers, W. W., W. A. Buttemer, A. M. Hayworth, and K. A. Nagy. 1984. An evaluation of time-budget estimates of daily energy expenditure in birds. Auk 101:459–472.

Welty, J. C. 1982. The life of birds. Third editon. Saunders College Publishing, New York.

Westneat, D. F., P. W. Sherman, and M. L. Morton. 1990. The ecology and evolution of extrapair copulations in birds. Current Ornithology 7:331–369.

Wink, M., and A. Dyrcz. 1999. Mating systems in birds: a review of molecular studies. Acta Ornithologica 34:91–109.

Wobeser, G. 1997. Diseases of wild waterfowl. Second edition. Plenum Press, New York.

Wooley, J. B., Jr., and R. B. Owen, Jr. 1977. Metabolic rates and heart rate-metabolism relationships in the Black Duck (*Anas rubripes*). Comparative Biochemistry and Physiology 57:363–367.

Wooley, J. B., Jr., and R. B. Owen, Jr. 1978. Energy costs of activity and daily energy expenditure in the Black Duck. Journal of Wildlife Management 42:739–745.

Yoshimura, J., and W. M. Shields. 1992. Components of uncertainty in clutch-size optimization. Bulletin of Mathematical Biology 54:445–464.

Zar, J. H. 1968. Standard metabolism comparisons between orders of birds. Condor 70:278.

Zicus, M. C., and M. R. Riggs. 1996. Change in body mass of female Common Goldeneyes during nesting and brood rearing. Wilson Bulletin 108:61–71.

Chapter 5
FEEDING ECOLOGY

The foods and feeding behavior of waterfowl are important aspects of their life history and represent an essential ingredient of habitat management. Many species of waterfowl feed on a somewhat broad spectrum of foods, whereas others are more exclusive. For example, Canada Geese graze on leafy vegetation, Blue-winged Teal often select seeds, and Northern Shovelers strain minute invertebrates. The plant foods sought by waterfowl can be subdivided into two groups: those growing naturally in wetland habitats (e.g., tubers of submerged vegetation) or those produced by agriculture (e.g., corn). Management strategies and habitat values accordingly differ markedly in each case.

Biologists also distinguish between food habits and feeding ecology. The former provides basic information on the type and quantity of food in the diet, whereas feeding ecology concerns relationships between food and its quality and availability in regard to specific nutritional requirements or the physiological condition of waterfowl at certain times of the year. Accordingly, the most useful studies of feeding ecology consider food habitats in relation to a defined aspect of the life history of waterfowl. To illustrate, some species seek foods rich in carbohydrates during cold winter months when demands for energy are high, whereas birds wintering in the Neotropics or other places with mild climates may eat much less food because of lower thermoregulatory needs. The diet of many species shifts dramatically to other foods during the breeding season, when protein is needed for egg production. Because of these crucial features, this chapter emphasizes the feeding ecology of waterfowl from the perspective of their annual cycle.

HISTORY OF WATERFOWL
FOOD HABITS STUDIES

Studies of waterfowl food habits took root early in the 20th century with a series of small bulletins published by the U.S. Bureau of Biological Survey, forerunner of the U.S. Fish and Wildlife Service (McAtee 1911, 1914, 1915). A few other studies were completed in the 1920s (e.g., Mabbott 1920, Wetmore 1921), but the first truly comprehensive research did not appear until 1939 (e.g., Cottam 1939; see Infobox 5-1). In particular, the work of Martin and Uhler (1939) provided an index to preferred duck foods based on an analysis of 7,998 stomachs collected from 18 species throughout the United States and Canada. They also described some 200 species of plants important as duck foods, and included drawings, range maps, and notes on the life history and propagation of the more prominent species.

These early studies were invaluable because of their broad geographical coverage and large sample sizes; they also provide a useful historical backdrop. However, most of the samples were obtained in fall and winter (i.e., hunting season), and the foods from gizzards and esophagi were combined for analysis, which we now know may substantially bias the results. Regional differences in food habits were acknowledged, but otherwise no supplemental data were reported; hence, the information could not be related to sex, age, or reproductive status of each species. Nevertheless, these early studies identified important foods for waterfowl, thereby guiding management and habitat protection for many years thereafter — and they are not without influence on such efforts today.

Techniques for the Analysis of
Waterfowl Food Habits

Collection of Specimens: Techniques for investigating food habits have varied over the years and, as might be expected, the methods of collecting and presenting the data may influence the results. We review these techniques here to help readers interpret the results of food-habits studies, particularly those published before the 1970s.

To begin, the digestive system in waterfowl consists of the esophagus (gullet or "crop"), below which are a glandular stomach known as the "proventriculus," then a muscular ventriculus ("gizzard"), followed by the intestines (Fig. 5-1). Food is ground in the gizzard before passing into the small intestine. Thus, any examination of food collected exclusively from gizzards may present a strong bias because soft-bodied foods (e.g., many invertebrates), if present, often become unrecognizable after only a short period in the gizzard. Feeding trials with Blue-winged Teal, for example, revealed just how rapidly food passes from the esophagus to the gizzard: After only 10 min, all of the scuds (*Hyalella azteca*), 82% of the snails (Gastropoda), and 24% of the fly larvae (Diptera) were digested beyond recognition (Swanson and Bartonek 1970). In contrast, hard seeds were retained in the digestive tract for days, and some were even excreted fully intact.

This research clearly demonstrated how much disparity might result in a diet determined only from gizzard contents in comparison with a diet based solely on esophageal samples. Bartonek (1968) highlighted the significance of this bias: Fully 95% of 125

Infobox 5-1

Clarence Cottam
Biologist, Administrator, and Conservationist
(1899–1974)

Clarence Cottam's distinguished career can be divided into three parts: first as an investigator specializing in the food habits of birds, particularly waterfowl, then as an intrepid administrator in the U.S. Fish and Wildlife Service, and finally as the first director of the Rob and Bessie Welder Wildlife Foundation, a privately endowed research facility in Sinton, Texas. Whatever his position, however, Cottam remained a stalwart conservationist who fearlessly championed the inherent value and careful husbandry of natural resources, whether wildlife or fisheries, forest or prairie, national park or refuge.

In 1929, Cottam joined the U.S. Bureau of Biological Survey, later to become the U.S. Fish and Wildlife Service, in the entry-level position of junior biologist. His primary task concerned the identification and analysis of foods consumed by birds. Cottam's abilities gained the attention of the bureau's new director, Jay N. "Ding" Darling, who quickly advanced him to senior biologist and head of the Section of Food Habits. In 1936, he earned a Ph.D. while working full time, using job-related data for his dissertation, which appeared as

a government publication in 1939, *Food Habits of North American Diving Ducks* — the work immediately became a benchmark of its genre. Darling also gave Cottam responsibilities for handling the annual regulations governing waterfowl hunting, a task that often involved face-to-face dealings with duck hunters who typically wanted more liberal bag limits than those proposed. He quickly gained a reputation as a skilled — and fearless — troubleshooter and often represented the government on missions fraught with controversy (e.g., baiting waterfowl during the hunting season). Cottam became the Chief of the Division of Wildlife Research in 1945 and a year later was appointed Assistant Director of the U.S. Fish and Wildlife Service, a position he held until retiring from government service in 1954.

After a year as a dean at Brigham Young University, Cottam accepted the position of director at the newly established Welder Wildlife Foundation, where he served for nearly 20 years (1955–74). During his tenure at Welder, nearly 150 students earned graduate degrees under the foundation's sponsorship, many of whom studied waterfowl and other birds either on site or at study areas across North America.

Cottam was an early supporter of Rachel Carson in the fight against the indiscriminate application of pesticides, and he was an outspoken watchdog whenever wetlands were endangered (e.g., the Cache River in Arkansas, where a federal refuge now protects critical winter habitat for waterfowl). He served on several "blue ribbon committees" for the Secretary of the Interior that addressed difficult issues such as predator control, wildlife management on national parks, and the function and administration of national wildlife refuges. He also served as president for The Wildlife Society and the National Parks Association, and as a trustee or board member for numerous conservation organizations (e.g., National Audubon Society). During his career, he was the author, coauthor, or editor of some 250 publications. In 1955, Clarence Cottam received the Aldo Leopold Medal from The Wildlife Society. See Bolen (1975) for more details. Photo courtesy of the Welder Wildlife Foundation.

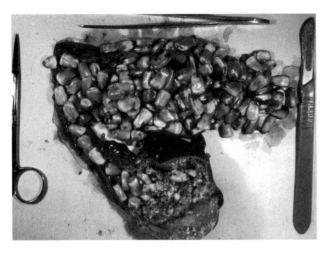

Figure 5-1. The lower digestive tract of a Mallard. The proventriculus ("glandular stomach") connects the esophagus (not shown) with the ventriculus (gizzard, or "muscular stomach"), where waterfowl pulverize corn and other hard foods. Photo courtesy of Richard L. Moore.

waterfowl food habits studies published before 1965 were based largely on the analysis of gizzard contents. Thus, the primary conclusion reached by the studies conducted prior to the 1970s, and especially the comprehensive work of the 1930s, is not surprising — ducks depended primarily on plants for most of their food.

Swanson and Bartonek (1970) recommended reducing the bias associated with food-habits analysis by (1) observing and then collecting actively feeding birds for samples; (2) restricting examination to esophageal contents; and (3) avoiding postmortem digestion by immediately removing and preserving food items or, under some field conditions, by flooding the upper digestive tract of freshly killed birds with preservative. These recommendations are now widely accepted and, for the most part, guided food-habits research conducted after 1970. Keep in mind, however, that the biases associated with gizzard samples do not invalidate the results of earlier studies, but one should understand the limitations of those data.

Presentation of Data: Food habits are usually reported in at least one of three ways: (1) frequency of occurrence, (2) aggregate volume, or (3) aggregate percentage. Frequency of occurrence is determined simply by dividing the number of birds in the sample that contain each food item by the total number in the sample, multiplied by 100; the result is expressed as a percentage. Frequency of occurrence indicates the availability of a food and its utilization, but does not necessarily provide a measure of preference.

A brief example helps illustrate differences between the two calculations for volume; each method has advantages and disadvantages (Swanson et al. 1974). Using the data shown in Table 5-1, the aggregate volume of a given food item (e.g., A) equals the total volume of that item in a sample of N birds (50 ml in our example), divided by the total volume of all foods in the sample (170 ml in our example), multiplied by 100%. Thus, the aggregate volume of food A in our example is 29%, which is the way most food-habits data were presented before 1975. Two biases are associated with this method: (1) an overemphasis of foods occurring in a few individuals, but present in great volume; and (2) no sample size is available on which to base statistical tests (i.e., the calculations are based on grand totals for each food item).

Both biases, above, are removed using the aggregate percentage method, which is now the most common way to present food-habits data. The major difference between the two methods is that the aggregate percentage gives equal weight to each bird in the sample. In other words, aggregate percentage equals the aggregate (average) volume of each food item calculated for *each bird*, which then is averaged over all birds. Returning to Table 5-1, first the aggregate volume of food A in Bird 1 is again calculated, but this time the volume of food A in Bird 1 is divided by the total volume of food removed from the same bird (60 ml), and *not* the total removed from all birds (170 ml). In this example, the aggregate volume of food A in Bird 1 is 40/60 × 100% = 67%. This calculation is repeated for each item and each bird, with the resulting totals averaged per bird to yield the aggregate percentage.

We also should consider the concept of "preference," which indicates the degree to which waterfowl select each of their foods from whatever choices may be available. A food may be consumed because of its inherent qualities or because little else is available, and the difference in these alternatives is of clear importance to waterfowl ecology and management. An appraisal of preference requires that some measurement of food abundance can be obtained in the field. Rollo and Bolen (1969), for example, employed a simple step-point method for determining the abundance of seed-producing vegetation on the margins of playa lakes, whereas more sophisticated methods of sampling may be used, as needed, in other instances. In any case, these data are analyzed in

Table 5-1. Sample calculations of aggregate volume and aggregate percentage from hypothetical food habits data.

Specimen	Food items (volume in ml)				
	A[a]	B	C	D	Total
Bird 1	40	5	10	5	60
Bird 2	5	5	15	0	25
Bird 3	0	0	10	30	40
Bird 4	5	5	5	30	45
Totals	50	15	40	65	170

[a] Aggregate volume of item A = 50/170 × 100% = 29%. Aggregate percentage of item A is determined by first dividing the volume of item A in Bird 1 by the total volume of food in that bird (e.g., 40/60 × 100% = 67). Repeating that procedure for each bird yields values of 20%, 0%, and 11% for Birds 2, 3 and 4, respectively. Averaging these four values yields an aggregate percentage of 25% for food item A, and a frequency of occurrence of 75%.

conjunction with the utilization of each food (i.e., volumetric data, described above). Bellrose and Anderson (1943) were among the first to calculate a preference rating (% volume in diet/% abundance in habitat = preference index).

A perfect relationship between utilization and abundance yields an index of 1.0, which means the food in question is selected in direct proportion to its abundance. Higher values indicate a stronger preference — that is, a food consumed in greater proportion in relation to its abundance — whereas ratings below 1.0 characterize foods of lesser desirability. Other and perhaps more sophisticated preference indices have been developed (see Ivlev 1961, Johnson 1980), but the goal remains unchanged: to measure dietary choices. Ideally, information produced by an appraisal of preferences should be complemented by nutritional analyses of the same foods to achieve a fuller picture of feeding ecology. Moreover, conclusions about the abundance of each food must be tempered in light of the actual availability of the same food to waterfowl (see following).

The most recent advance in methods to determine waterfowl food habits uses stable isotopes, which identify the isotopic "signatures" of each food in searches of whole blood collected from the target species (see Rundel et al. 1989). Haramis et al. (2001) used this approach to assess the diets of Canvas-backs wintering on Chesapeake Bay in the United States; the analysis revealed that corn from feeding stations was more important than submerged aquatic vegetation, previously the traditional food of Canvasbacks before the beds declined in abundance. Alisauskas and Hobson (1993) likewise used stable-isotope analysis to determine the diets of wintering Lesser Snow Geese.

GENERAL PROPERTIES OF FOOD

Basic Components

Central to understanding the nature of animal diets is some knowledge of each food's nutritional value. Accordingly, a food may be divided into two major components: (1) water, and (2) dry matter. Dry matter can be further subdivided into inorganic mineral components and organic components of protein, carbohydrate, fat, and fiber (Fig. 5-2). Each component offers different nutritional "values" relative to the needs of an organism at any particular time and place.

Proteins, which consist of amino acid chains, are essential for formation, growth, and maintenance of all animal tissues. Indeed, the average daily turnover of protein in body tissue of birds is 4.4% (Morowitz 1978). All proteins are not alike, however, because of various combinations of their amino acids. Further, from the standpoint of feeding ecology, some amino acids can be synthesized by the body (nonessential amino acids), whereas others must be obtained from dietary sources (essential amino acids). Examples of nonessential amino acids include the ketogenic amino acids (e.g., leucine, isoleucine, lysine, tyrosine, phenylalanine), whereas examples of essential amino acids are methionine, cystine, tryptophan, and threonine. Several waterfowl foods have been analyzed for amino acid content (see Sugden 1973a, Driver et al. 1974, Krapu 1974, Alisauskas and Ankney 1992).

Hence, the composition of each protein's amino acids is an important consideration when evaluating the quality of food. Corn contains about 9.7% protein (Baldassarre et al. 1983), for instance, but corn lacks lysine, tryptophan, and methionine, each of which is required for body maintenance in higher vertebrates (Schaible 1970, Sturkie 1976). In contrast, aquatic invertebrates such as midge larvae (Chironomidae), water boatmen (Corixidae), and scuds (*Gammarus* spp.) are rich in protein content (56%, 72%, and 47%, respectively); these foods also provide the most complete array of amino acids based on requirements of domestic poultry chicks (Sugden

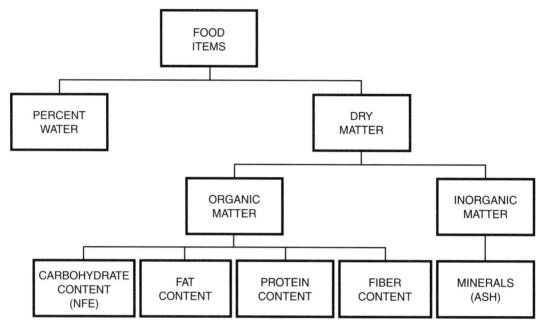

Figure 5-2. Schematic representation of the basic constituents of food. Percentages of these constituents vary with each kind of food; hence, some foods are more important at certain times of the year than others (e.g., protein-rich foods for nesting females).

1973a). Amino acid composition is especially important for egg production because dietary protein is not efficiently assimilated into egg proteins if even a single essential amino acid is limiting; hence, such amino acids can be considered rate-limiting in the process of egg production (Sedinger 1984). Cystine is a particularly limiting amino acid during egg production (Alisauskas and Ankney 1992).

Protein does not provide a store of energy, however, because its breakdown is complex, inefficient, and produces toxic by-products (Blem 1990). Protein therefore is not mobilized for energy until both glycogen and lipid reserves have been nearly exhausted. The energy contained in protein is also comparatively small, yielding only 18.0 kJ/g (Schmidt-Nielsen 1979). Excess amino acids can be deaminated and metabolized for energy or converted to fatty acids, but production of energy (ATP) from amino acids is about 20% less than would occur from sugars (Krebs 1964).

Carbohydrates provide most of the energy requirements for birds, except during periods of stress or intensive activity. Most carbohydrates are stored as glycogen in the liver and muscle tissues. This reserve is small, however, representing about 3% of the wet liver mass in small birds — and the reserve can be 90% depleted in less than 36 hr when inactive birds are deprived of food (see Blem 1990). Thus,

while carbohydrate (glycogen) stores are physiologically important, they are useful only on the occasion of short-term demands. Those excess carbohydrates not stored as glycogen usually accumulate as lipids; hence, a high-carbohydrate diet facilitates lipid storage.

Lipids themselves occur in both plant and animal tissues; these include fats, phospholipids, and glycolipids, which represent the primary form of energy storage in birds. Lipids represent a particularly labile form of energy, which can be accumulated rapidly under good feeding conditions and, on the other hand, used rapidly when conditions demand (e.g., harsh weather or reproduction). To illustrate, migrating Sandhill Cranes (*Grus canadensis*) staging in spring on the Platte River of Nebraska in the United States stored fat at the rate of 13–18 g/day (Krapu et al. 1985). When catabolized, lipids yield about 37.7–39.8 kJ/g or about twice that of a similar amount of protein (Schmidt-Nielsen 1979).

Fiber comprises the bulk of green plants and is also a component of seeds, rhizomes, and tubers. Fiber, because of its cellulose, hemicellulose, and lignin content, is generally the most difficult component of food to digest, yet about half the gross energy contained in green plants occurs as structural carbohydrates and lignin of plant cell walls (see

Robbins 1993, Van Soest 1994). Animal nutritionists have long sought analytical methods like proximate analysis, neutral detergent fiber, and acid detergent fiber to assess the components of fiber (e.g., cellulose, hemicellulose, and lignin), or methods to separate digestible from indigestible components (see Van Soest 1994). Such methodologies lie beyond our scope, but the nutritive availability of fiber can be separated into three components. The first group is highly digestible (more than 90%) and composed of soluble carbohydrates, starch, organic acids, protein, and pectin, compared with a second group that is indigestible (lignin, cutin, silica, tannins; see Van Soest 1994). The digestibility of a third group, cellulose and hemicellulose, is variable and the subject of intense research relative to geese.

Biologists long thought that much of the energy contained in fiber was largely unavailable to waterfowl because — unlike cattle or other ruminants — most vertebrates cannot break down cellulose and hemicellulose. However, geese, swans, and some ducks are herbivorous, and cell walls represent nearly 50% of the biomass of green leaves (Sedinger and Raveling 1984); hence, it is not surprising that some waterfowl, especially swans and geese, can digest these plant components (see also Sedinger 1997).

Minerals occur in tissues throughout the body, where they prove essential for the proper function of nearly all systems and physiological processes in higher vertebrates. For birds, calcium and phosphorus are especially important for eggshell production. Calcium requirements for breeding ducks represent 2.25–2.75% of the diet, with the phosphorus requirement being about 25% that for calcium (National Research Council 1977). Selenium and vitamin E are especially important because ducks appear quite sensitive to deficiencies of either in their diets.

Energetic and Nutritional Properties

The dietary benefits of each food largely depend on its constituent amounts of protein, carbohydrate, fat, fiber, vitamins, and minerals. All foods also contain gross energy (GE), which is measured in kilojoules per gram. However, an energy budget must consider the amount of GE actually metabolized, because not all GE is liberated for use during digestion and assimilation. Some GE is excreted in the feces, but this amount of unused energy can be measured (Sibbald 1976). Metabolizable energy (ME) thus represents the energy available to birds from their diets. ME can be expressed as apparent metabolizable energy (AME), which represents the difference between a food's energy value before ingestion (GE) and after digestion. However, because other by-products of metabolism are contained in the feces, ME values can be corrected for fecal energy production (Sibbald 1976, Sibbald and Morse 1983). When corrected, the appropriate biological term is "true metabolizable energy" (TME). Miller and Reinecke (1984) reviewed metabolizable energy and its expression in avian energetics.

The difference between GE and ME or TME can be large for some foods, especially some seeds difficult to digest. For example, the GE of Walter's millet (*Echinochloa walteri*) is 19.3 kJ/g, whereas the TME is only 11.7–12.1 kJ/g, or about 37% less (Hoffman and Bookhout 1985). Hard-shelled mollusks provide low TME because of their high ash content (i.e., inorganic content). For example, the GE of periwinkles (*Littorina* spp.) fed to American Black Ducks was 14.7 kJ/g compared to a TME of only about 1.6 kJ/g (Jorde and Owen 1988). Soft-shelled clams (*Mya arenaria*) and blue mussels (*Mytilus edulis*) also had low TME values (1.1–5.1 kJ/g). In contrast, the GE of gammarus (*Gammarus oceanicus*) — a soft-bodied invertebrate — was 14.7 kJ/g and TME averaged 9.3 kJ/g. The GE of four species of acorns averaged 23.0 kJ/g compared to 11.5 kJ/g for TME (Kaminski et al. 2003). Checkett et al. (2002) reported that TME values for 10 species of plant seeds fed to Mallards ranged from 6.4 kJ/g for nodding smartweed (*Polygonum lapathifolium*) to 13.0 kJ/g for little hairy crabgrass (*Digitaria ischaemum*). Kaminski et al. (2003:547) provided a summary of TME estimates for four species of waterfowl, reporting values for 21 plant seeds, tubers, and acorns. Most data were available for Mallards, for which TME values for 14 plant seeds ranged from 5.5 kJ/g for Pennsylvania smartweed (*Polygonum pensylvanicum*) to 13.0 kJ/g for smooth crabgrass (*Digitaria sanguinalis*), and averaged 10.3. TME values for agricultural foods were 15.4 kJ/g for corn, 16.6 for milo (sorghum), 14.0 for rice, 11.1 for soybeans, and 14.1 for wheat. TME for a commercial ration was 11.5 kJ/g. Few studies have determined TME estimates for invertebrates, although we report a sample of the available estimates in Table 5-2, along with data from the nutritional analyses of an array of waterfowl foods (see also Fredrickson and Reid 1988, Euliss et al. 1997, Anderson and Smith 1998, Petrie et al. 1998).

We note that the basic nutritional components of waterfowl foods (protein, fat, fiber, NFE) are determined from proximate analysis, which assumes

Table 5-2. Examples of nutritional analysis of waterfowl foods as reported in the literature.

Food item	Protein (%)	Fat (%)	Fiber (%)	NFE (%)	Ash (%)	GE (kJ/g)	TME (kJ/g)	Source[a]
Agricultural Foods								
Corn	8.7	3.3	7.1	84.8	1.1	4.41	16.3	13
Hard wheat	18.5	1.9	4.1	73.7	1.8	18.4	13.0	3
Winter wheat	23.3	7.8	11.9	53.9	10.9	4.35	10.0	13
Soybeans	34.8	10.9	17.6	23.0	5.6		11.3	5
Rice	8.1	2.7	10.4	61.5	6.1		13.8	5
Millet	10.9	5.7	12.0	56.7	4.1			5
Invertebrate Foods								
Cladocera	31.7	2.1	13.8	1.7	50.7	10.9	3.3	3
Chironomidae	66.4	5.8	0.0	14.9	13.1			6
Anostraca	71.9	8.6	3.9	1.5	14.0			6
Gammarus (freshwater)	47.8	7.7	9.6	12.1	22.8	15.9	9.6	3
Gammarus (marine)	47.0	3.6	9.7	10.0	29.7	16.7	10.0	12
Lymnaeidae	16.1	1.3	0.9	5.7	76.0	22.6	2.5	3
Mulinia lateralis (dwarf surf clam)	4.0	0.2	1.2	0.3	94.3	0.9	0.0	12
Gastropoda	9.4	0.6	2.2	0.0	87.8	17.4	2.5	12
Littorina spp. (periwinkle)	9.4	0.6		2.2	87.8	1.1	1.1	14
Mytilus edulis (blue mussel)	15.6	1.1		3.3	80.0	2.2	1.8	14
Plant Foods								
Echinochloa crusgalli	12.5	5.0	22.2	51.4	8.9			1
Echinochloa walteri	16.3	3.6	14.2	61.4	4.4			9
Polygonum lapathifolium	11.8	3.5	23.6	58.1	2.9	19.7		1
Polygonum pensylvanicum						19.3	5.0	4
Scirpus validus (nutlets)	6.7	3.5	39.7	47.0	3.1	20.5	2.1	3
Ruppia maritima (seeds)	7.8	2.9	35.2	51.0	3.1		5.9	12
Myriophyllum spicatum	16.9		50.1		3.2			7
Ceratophyllum demersum	18.0		36.2		4.1			7
Algae	14.4		17.8		3.2			7
Halodule wrightii (rhizomes)	7.7	0.6	11.5	51.1	29.1	12.1	3.9	12
Halodule wrightii (foliage)	18.8	0.6	15.6	49.4	15.6	15.4	3.4	12
Spartina patens	11.1		31.9	43.2	11.4			8
Spartina patens (tubers)	6.5		12.1	73.0	4.7			8
Scirpus (rhizomes)	3.9		28.2	62.7	3.0			8
Sagittaria graminea (tubers)	15.9	1.5	16.1	54.9	6.8			9
Quercus nigra (acorns)	3.8	14.6	17.2	48.7	1.6	5.45		9, 11
Panicum verrucosum	18.1	1.1	12.6	51.7	7.1			9
Potamogeton spp. (leaves)	15.9	2.8	25.3	43.1	10.0			9
Leersia oryzoides	13.8	1.9	9.3	57.8	7.6			9
Bidens fondosa	26.6	11.9	18.5	27.5	8.8			9
Cyperus iria	8.9	3.9	14.5	65.0	7.6			10
Scirpus robustus	8.3	3.2	16.2	65.8	6.4			10

[a]Sources: 1, Baldassarre et al. (1983); 2, Sibbald (1976); 3, Sugden (1973b); 4, Hoffman and Bookhout (1985); 5, Loesch and Kaminski (1989); 6, Krapu and Swanson (1975); 7, Paulus (1982); 8, Alisauskas et al. (1988); 9, Landers et al. (1977); 10, Bardwell et al. (1962); 11, Kaminski et al. (2003); 12, Ballard et al. (2004); 13, Petrie et al. (1998); 14, Jorde and Owen (1988).

nitrogen-free extract—highly digestible

that fiber is indigestible and that NFE represents highly digestible carbohydrates. However, proximate analysis cannot separate fiber into its structural components such as lignin, cellulose, and hemicellulose, some of which can be digestible (see Haukos and Smith 1995). Nonetheless, the data at-hand from proximate analysis are valid estimates and serve as an important guide for waterfowl managers. For example, the high TME, fat, and protein content of gammarus accentuates their importance in the diet of wintering American Black Ducks compared to the poor nutritional properties of mollusks (Jorde and Owen 1988). Indeed, wintering American Black Ducks lost body mass when restricted to a diet composed primarily of mollusks (Albright et al. 1983). AME and TME estimates also can provide effective and accurate assessment of habitat needs for waterfowl, assessments that would be otherwise underestimated by the GE values resulting from proximate analysis. For example, Reinecke et al. (1989) used TME values of natural and agricultural foods to determine the habitat needs of waterfowl wintering in the Mississippi Alluvial Valley. Similarly, Miller and Newton (1999) used AME values of waterfowl foods to assess habitat needs for Northern Pintails wintering in the Sacramento Valley of California (see below). On the Southern High Plains of Texas, Anderson and Smith (1998) estimated that 160,000 ha of playa lake wetlands produced about 24.3 million kg of seeds and invertebrates, 9.2 million kg of protein, and 454.4 billion kJ of energy. These estimates were enough to support 3 million ducks for 3 months, assuming the playa lakes filled with water.

Ecological Considerations

Three general categories of waterfowl foods appear in Table 5-2: (1) agricultural plants, (2) wetland plants,

and (3) animal matter. Native plants can be further subdivided into categories of seeds, tubers, bulbs and rhizomes, and leafy vegetation. Compared with agricultural grains, native plant foods are generally lower in carbohydrate content. Leafy aquatic vegetation is generally the lowest in quality because of its high water content and high fiber content. Animal matter is highest in protein content and a good source of amino acids. Green plants provide a good balance of amino acids but contain proportionately less protein than animal foods and are less digestible (Alisauskas and Ankney 1992). Carbohydrate values for animal foods are comparatively lower than plants, but their energy values are nearly equivalent.

These nutritional attributes, coupled with the abundance and availability of each food, generate very real costs and benefits relative to the feeding ecology for each species of waterfowl (Table 5-3). Of primary importance is the ecological difference between food abundance and availability — the two should not be confused. To illustrate, the biomass of seeds produced on managed moist-soil impoundments may reach 1,629 kg/ha (Fredrickson and Taylor 1982). However, foraging waterfowl must contend with water depth, debris, water turbidity, and other factors that will restrict their access to seeds and other foods. These conditions increase foraging time, an effect exacerbated by the steady reduction in abundance as the foods are consumed. Moreover, because waterfowl generally rely on tactile cues when feeding in water, their foraging efficiency in aquatic habitats may be much less than occurs at drier sites where birds use visual cues. In the Mississippi Alluvial Valley of the south-central United States, Reinecke et al. (1989) thus estimated that ducks feeding in wetlands probably cannot exploit foods with densities much less than 50 kg/ha, which

Table 5-3. The relationships among food quality, availability, and feeding ecology of waterfowl.

Food Source	Energy (kJ/g)	Protein (%)	Carbohydrate (%)	Availability	Feeding Time
Seeds	18.8	9–15	35–60	Variable	Moderate
Agricultural grains	20.9	9–25	35–80	High	Low
Animal	20.9	40–75	1–20	Low	High
Leafy vegetation	16.6	15–20	15–50	Variable	High
Tubers	16.7	15	75	Moderate–high	Low

in effect represents a point of diminishing returns in foraging efficiency.

In contrast, agricultural foods provide high levels of carbohydrates and often occur in both great abundance *and* availability. On a major waterfowl wintering area in Texas, for example, Baldassarre et al. (1983) recorded an average of 364 ± 12 kg/ha of waste corn remaining in fields after harvest. In this case, field-feeding ducks often could satisfy their food requirements in about 23 min — and remove almost all of the corn present (Baldassarre and Bolen 1984). Even at low levels of abundance, agricultural foods may be so readily available as to attract large numbers of waterfowl. Conversely, when foraging on poor-quality leafy aquatic vegetation, Gadwalls wintering in Louisiana spent up to 75% of their time engaged in feeding activities (Paulus 1982, 1984). Grazing geese also forage on leafy vegetation and thus can easily spend 7–8 hr/day foraging for food, especially during winter (Owen 1980), but foraging is greatly reduced if geese feed on agricultural foods. In North America, for example, wintering Cackling Canada Geese satisfied their daily energy requirements in about 2 hr when feeding on agricultural grains, but their foraging time increased to 8–9 hr (80% of the day) when feeding on poor-quality green leaves (Raveling 1979). In Europe, Lesser White-fronted Geese spent 90% of the day foraging during winter (Owen 1980).

We thus emphasize the interactions existing among foods, their energy and nutritional content, abundance and availability, and feeding and processing times. All of these factors interact to shape the feeding ecology for each species of waterfowl at a given time and place.

Some Final Thoughts

Waterfowl display a wide diversity of morphological attributes and capabilities (e.g., body size, bill structure, neck length, and diving ability); thus, we find great variability in the foods consumed by the constituent species. Moreover, to obtain their food, waterfowl exploit a tremendous array of wetland and nonwetland habitats over an immense geographical area, which further increases their choice of foods. However, the nutritional requirements of waterfowl are relatively fixed, the result of the biological demands peculiar to each species. As shown in Chapter 4, for example, the protein and lipid requirements of producing an egg are identified rather precisely — individuals obtaining those requirements will produce a clutch, whereas those lacking them will not.

However, much variation exists between and within habitats in terms of the quantity, quality, abundance, and availability of food resources. Accordingly, an interaction forged between habitat variability and nutritional requirements largely determines the selection of food.

Note, however, that waterfowl select their foods on the basis of nutritional and energetic values and not by taxa per se. For example, a demand for protein might be satisfied by any one of several protein-rich foods (e.g., midge larvae, water boatmen, scuds), but the food actually selected will depend on its spatial and temporal abundance and availability. Hence, managers might well evaluate waterfowl habitats in terms of the abundance and availability of protein, carbohydrate, and energy, and not the presence of particular taxonomic groups of plant and animal foods. Habitats then might be manipulated in ways that synchronize the abundance and availability of protein and other components of food to the current physiological (annual cycle) demands of waterfowl — a strategy that lets local conditions dictate which taxa offer the best opportunities for management.

At Montezuma National Wildlife Refuge in central New York, for example, the same management that encourages desirable seed-producing emergent vegetation also favors an undesirable plant, purple loosestrife (*Lythrum salicaria*). Refuge managers raised water levels in response to these conditions, which discouraged purple loosestrife as well as desirable emergent vegetation, but provided optimal conditions for sago pondweed (*Potamogeton pectinatus*), a submergent species. The objective — in this case, to provide an abundance of carbohydrate-rich seeds for postbreeding waterfowl — was achieved by using an alternative management strategy to substitute one type of vegetation for another.

WATERFOWL FOOD HABITS

Dabbling Ducks and Pochards — Anatini and Aythyini

Breeding: Prior to 1969, few detailed studies addressed the food habits of breeding waterfowl. Earlier studies typically relied on materials collected by hunters during the fall and winter, which reflected a diet of seeds and other plant matter but included few invertebrates. Not surprising, therefore, was the conclusion that the overall diet of common game ducks included 73% plant materials and 27% animal matter (Martin and Uhler 1939). Such data thereafter shaped the management for most species of ducks for many years.

Ideas about the food habits of ducks changed dramatically in the early 1970s when biologists stationed at the Northern Prairie Wildlife Research Center in North Dakota began examining the feeding ecology of breeding ducks. Not only were ducks collected in spring, but — as already discussd — the samples were handled in ways that reduced those biases associated with analyses of gizzard contents (Swanson and Bartonek 1970). The results revealed that invertebrates comprised 76% of the diet for several species of female dabbling ducks and 92% for female pochards (Swanson and Meyer 1973).

Indeed, a notable shift occurs in the diet of ducks, especially females, when spring foods consumed on breeding areas are compared with those selected at other times of the year. For example, animal matter comprised only 11% of the winter food diet of Wood Ducks compared to 89% plant foods (Delnicki and Reinecke 1986), but diets of egg-laying females were 76% animal matter (Drobney and Fredrickson 1979). Generally, the fall–winter diet of dabbling ducks, highlighted by plant materials (= carbohydrates), switches to a dietary regime dominated by protein-rich foods. In particular, female dabbling ducks increase their intake of animal matter from the prelaying period into the egg-laying period. For species studied thus far, the proportion of animal matter in the diet during the prelaying period ranges from 32% in American Wigeon (Wishart 1983) to 56% for Northern Pintails (Krapu 1974). During egg laying, the proportion of animal matter has ranged from 41% in American Wigeon (Wishart 1983) and 72% in Mallards (Swanson et al. 1985), to 99% in Blue-winged Teal (Swanson and Meyer 1977) and Northern Shovelers (Swanson et al. 1979). Animal matter ingested by egg-laying pochards in Nevada amounted to 78% of the diet for Canvasbacks and 77% for Redheads (Noyes and Jarvis 1985). In contrast, female Redheads at Horicon Marsh in Wisconsin consumed only 16–17% animal matter during egg-laying and incubation, but agricultural activities at the time may have diminished the abundance of invertebrate populations (Kenow and Rusch 1996). Before then, females consumed nearly 100% plant matter, largely seeds from emergent vegetation.

We emphasize again that (1) the demand for protein during reproduction is relatively fixed; and (2) this requirement is not tied to specific foods, which may vary by species and location. Teal breeding in Minnesota thus may consume midge larvae, whereas those in Alberta might meet the same demand for protein by foraging on quite another group of insects. Nevertheless, some invertebrate groups dominate the foods selected by breeding female ducks; primary among these are the classes Insecta, Crustacea, and Gastropoda. For Insecta, major taxa are represented by Diptera (flies, midges, and mosquitoes), Coleoptera (adult and larval beetles), Odonata (damselfly and dragonfly larvae), Trichoptera (caddisfly larvae), Hemiptera (larvae and adults of true bugs), and Ephemeroptera (mayfly larvae). Cladocera (water fleas), Anostraca (fairy shrimp), Amphipoda (amphipods), Ostracoda (seed shrimp), Isopoda (isopods), Conchostraca (clam shrimp), and Copepoda (copepods) are important crustaceans. For snails, the families Lymnaeidae, Planorbidae, and Physidae are often included (Table 5-4).

As might be imagined, the availability and the abundance of aquatic macroinvertebrates are strongly influenced by environmental conditions such as water permanence and water levels. Seasonal and temporary wetlands in the Prairie Pothole Region of North America, for example, usually retain water for just a few weeks. In spring, however, the shallow water in these same wetlands is the first to thaw. Thus, because of their short "life span," these wetlands harbor invertebrates that complete their life cycles rapidly. In their egg stage, for instance, fairy shrimp are capable of surviving both the drying and freezing conditions common to prairie wetlands, but when water becomes available in early spring, the eggs develop into adults — and a major food source — in just 2–3 weeks (Pennak 1989). Seasonal wetlands accordingly may abound with fairy shrimp, as well as mosquitoes, water fleas, and other invertebrates, thereby providing key feeding sites for breeding waterfowl during the spring and early summer. Similarly, Krapu (1974) noticed that the saturated soil associated with the spring flooding of potholes in North Dakota also forced large numbers of earthworms (Annelida) to the soil surface, where they became a ready source of protein for early-arriving female Northern Pintails.

The availability of invertebrates, in fact, may be a major proximate factor governing the onset of egg laying in Northern Pintails and other ducks (Krapu 1974). Temporary and seasonal wetlands served as major foraging habitats for both male and female Mallards using prairie habitats prior to the nesting season in south-central North Dakota (Dwyer et al. 1979). Indeed, in spring, the overall density of Mallards breeding in the North Dakota study was correlated ($r = 0.54$) with the abundance of potholes, but

Table 5-4. Invertebrate foods important in the diet of breeding North American ducks.

Food item	Aggregate percentage	Percent occurrence	Location	Species
Gastropods	36	79	North Dakota	Blue-winged Teal[a]
Crustacea	16	72	North Dakota	Blue-winged Teal[a]
Chironomidae	9	61	North Dakota	Blue-winged Teal[a]
Oligochaeta	10	13	North Dakota	Northern Pintail[b]
Anostraca	11	21	North Dakota	Northern Pintail[b]
Diptera	28	64	North Dakota	Northern Pintail[b]
Gastropoda	23	62	North Dakota	Northern Pintail[b]
Coleoptera	32	80	Missouri	Wood Duck[c]
Diptera	10	45	Missouri	Wood Duck[c]

[a]Swanson et al. (1974).
[b]Krapu (1974).
[c]Drobney and Fredrickson (1979).
Note: Crustacea included Amphipoda, Ostracoda, Copepoda, Cladocera, Conchostraca, Anostraca. Diptera largely included Chironomidac.

it was the type, frequency, and duration of flooding of these wetlands that markedly influenced food supplies, and in turn Mallard nesting (Krapu et al. 1983). In normal years, these wetlands dry by early summer, and waterfowl move to more permanent ponds and lakes where aquatic insects — especially midge larvae — dominate the invertebrate fauna (Swanson et al. 1974, Swanson and Meyer 1977). In drought years, however, prelaying Mallards must feed in deeper water where invertebrate foods persist at low densities; these conditions resulted in fewer nests, a shorter nesting period, and a shorter period of nest initiation. Specifically, eight radiomarked females produced 14 nests during wet years when wetland density averaged 5.3–7.4/km² and stayed for an average of 44 days. In contrast, when drought reduced wetland density to 1.5/km², eight radiomarked females produced just one nest and remained in the area for only 16 days (Krapu et al. 1983). In the case of severe drought, Northern Pintails and other prairie-nesting ducks may not breed at all, or initiate drought-displaced migrations to northern areas (Smith 1969, Smith 1970).

Foods of Ducklings: The diet of ducklings changes as the young birds grow and plumage develops from Natal Down to Juvenal Plumage at fledging. Details of these age-related changes in plumage characteristics are presented in Chapter 6, but we note here

that these changes are used to identify three primary age classes of ducklings: I, II, and III, with the first two classes further subdivided into Ia, Ib, Ic, and IIa, IIb, IIc (Southwick 1953, Gollop and Marshall 1954; see Table 6-8). The diets of ducklings change as they develop through these plumage-identified age classes.

As they develop, most of the weight gain in ducklings stems from tissue growth. Thus, because the proteins available in invertebrates provide the building blocks for body tissue, insects and crustaceans are among the animal foods forming the major part of the young birds' diets. Based on feeding trials, captive-reared ducklings achieved maximum growth rates on diets of 16–19% protein (Holm and Scott 1954, Scott et al. 1959). In the wild, the diets of young American Black Ducks averaged 95% invertebrates for Class I ducklings (1–18 days) and 84% for Class II (19–43 days), but decreased to 34% for fully-feathered young (Class III; Reinecke 1979). The protein content in the diets of the young Black Ducks at first glance may seem much higher than the requirements determined for domestic ducklings, as noted above. However, invertebrates are about 85% water, and a great variety of types may be required to obtain a full complement of the amino acids necessary for normal growth and development. Few of the 21 duckling foods Sugden (1973a) examined individually contained adequate proportions of the required nutrients. In contrast, a commercially prepared diet, normally used for rearing domestic ducklings, is fortified with specific amino acids in exact proportions.

One of the first field studies of feeding ecology of ducklings concerned Mallards at the Bear River Migratory Bird Refuge in Utah (Chura 1961). The diets of ducklings in this study contained invertebrates in the following proportions: Class Ia, 97%; Class Ib, 90%; and Class Ic, 75%. By the time the ducklings reached Class IIa, the proportion was about 50% invertebrates and 50% plant materials, most of which were seeds. Adult and larval midges, water boatmen, and adult water scavenger beetles (Hydrophilidae) were key invertebrate foods. Terrestrial forms of aquatic invertebrates, especially adult midges, dominated (59–87%) the diet of Class I ducklings, but the percentage of terrestrial forms diminished as the ducklings matured (i.e., as their down was replaced by Juvenal Plumage, the ducklings began tipping underwater, thereby acquiring more aquatic species as food). Collias and Collias (1963) noted that downy young Mallards, Blue-winged Teal, and to a lesser extent Gadwalls, American Wigeon, and Northern Shovelers, were adept at catching flying insects, and Swanson and Sargeant (1972) recorded ducklings of several species feeding at night on emerging mayflies and midges.

In southern Alberta, Sugden (1973a) conducted an extensive 5-year study of the feeding ecology of ducklings of several species, including Northern Pintails, Gadwalls, American Wigeon, and Lesser Scaup. His work revealed that ducklings of all species relied heavily on invertebrates during their first 2–3 weeks of life. The proportion of plant matter increased thereafter, except for Lesser Scaup, which continued to consume large amounts of animal matter throughout the duckling period. Generally, ducklings selected the most available invertebrates based on each species' characteristic feeding behavior. Thus, ducklings of all species except Lesser Scaup selected surface invertebrates (41–79% of the diet) during the first week after hatching. After the first week, Northern Pintails started dabbling for benthic organisms, whereas Gadwalls and American Wigeon dabbled for foods from within the water column instead of from the bottom. After 1 week, virtually all of the Lesser Scaup ducklings were diving for food. Snails, midges, water fleas, water boatmen, beetles, and scuds represented the important foods for all of the species in this study.

At the Ruby Lake National Wildlife Refuge in Nevada, invertebrates similarly dominated the di-

ets of Canvasback and Redhead ducklings (Jarvis and Noyes 1986). Downy young (Class I) and partially feathered (Class II) Canvasbacks consumed 85% and 90% invertebrates, respectively; snails, caddisfly larvae, and damselfly larvae were especially prominent foods. In contrast, Class I Redhead ducklings consumed 47% invertebrates, but for Class II ducklings the proportion of invertebrates dropped to just 9%. Water boatmen were important invertebrate foods for the young Redheads. Overall, the diets of Class I and II Canvasback ducklings were 50–51% protein and 27–30% carbohydrates, whereas the Redhead diet was 35% protein and 32% carbohydrates for Class I ducklings, but changed to 9% protein and 48% carbohydrates for Class II ducklings. In Manitoba, juvenile Canvasbacks (Ia to III, inclusive) consumed 94% animal matter, whereas the diet of juvenile Redheads from 2 weeks age to flying stage included 43% animal matter (Bartonek and Hickey 1969). Caddisflies, midges, water fleas, scuds, water boatmen, and snails were important foods for both species.

These and other studies clearly reveal the crucial importance of invertebrates in the diets of ducklings. Indeed, hatching peaks for ducks often coincide with the periods when invertebrates are especially abundant (Bartonek and Hickey 1969). The relationship between invertebrates and duckling food habits nonetheless will vary with the availability of invertebrates and the physical and behavioral adaptations of each species of waterfowl (e.g., whether ducklings dabble or dive to secure food). Here we again see the importance of habitat diversity on breeding areas, this time in terms of conditions that promote invertebrate production. Snails, insect larvae, and other wetland invertebrates thus become a focus of management (see Chapter 10) for the needs of breeding ducks, as does management of nesting cover (see Chapter 6).

Postbreeding and Winter: The nutritional requirements of ducks during the postbreeding and wintering periods largely concern the energy demands associated with the rigors of migration and winter survival; in some species, the availability of energy at this time also serves as a precursor for attaining breeding condition the following spring. As with breeding waterfowl, nonbreeding waterfowl also have fixed physiological demands, which are satisfied only when the birds systematically exploit the requisite resources in both time and space. Thus, an examination of feeding ecology in nonbreeding waterfowl again reveals the interaction between time-constrained physiological needs and the availability of suitable food resources.

The physiological demands for lipid accumulation prior to fall migration and again before the onset of cold winter weather offer a good illustration. Waterfowl during this segment of their annual cycle accordingly seek foods laden with carbohydrates instead of those rich in protein. In fact, Mallards wintering in Louisiana selected foods with an average carbohydrate content of 52.4% and only 14.8% protein (Junca et al. 1962). Important foods included brownseed paspalum (*Paspalum plicatulum*), Walter's millet, Japanese millet (*Echinochloa crusgalli*), domestic rice, and fall panicum (*Panicum dichotomiflorum*). Similarly, the diet of Northern Pintails wintering in Louisiana averaged 52.2% carbohydrates (Bardwell et al. 1962). The winter diets of Blue-winged Teal and Green-winged Teal examined in the same study averaged 54.1% carbohydrates. In California, the diet of wintering Northern Pintails averaged 23–38% carbohydrates and 14–38% protein (Euliss et al. 1997).

However, diets and nutrition are affected by several factors. Ballard et al. (2004), for example, discussed the nutritional aspects for the winter diets of Northern Pintails during a 2-year study on the Gulf Coast of Texas (Laguna Madre), a major wintering ground in the Central Flyway. The diet included 11 plant taxa and 23 animal taxa, but five foods comprised more than 70% of the aggregate dry mass: shoalgrass (*Halodule wrightii*), the rhizomes, foliage, and seeds from widgeongrass (*Ruppia maritima*), and *Gammarus* spp., as well as dwarf surf clams (*Mulinia lateralis*). The proximate composition of the diet was 7.03–17.78% protein, 11.13–42.88% NFE (carbohydrate), 0.59–2.19% fat, 6.23–23.75% fiber, and 21.59–74.84% ash. TME ranged from 1.84 kJ/g for males in late winter of a dry year to 5.02 kJ/g for females during early winter of a wet year (Table 5-5). Overall, the diets in coastal areas contained less protein and fat, more ash, and only about half the TME when compared to Northern Pintail diets in freshwater habitats. Hence, to maintain their body mass, Northern Pintails needed to ingest 226–527 g dry mass of food per day during a dry winter compared to 156–288 g/day during a wet winter — nearly a three-fold difference. In contrast, wintering Northern Pintails required only 83–148 g/day when feeding on rice and less than 94 g/day when feeding on waste corn. Hence, reductions in rice acreage along the Texas coast may adversely affect Northern Pintails in this important wintering area if they instead must rely on saline habitats for food.

In contrast to the Texas coast, Miller and Newton (1999) studied the feeding ecology of Northern Pintails in the Sacramento Valley of California, another major wintering area for this species in North America. This 2-year study is significant because it focused on energetic requirements at the population level. The daily existence energy requirements needed between mid-August and mid-March were calculated as 794 to 1,180 kJ/day for males and from 700 to 1,044 kJ/day for females. Each bird met this requirement by consuming 49–82 g of food per day from ricefields and wetlands, an amount that equaled 5.9–8.3% of male body mass and 6.0–8.1% of female body mass. In a year with a large Pintail population, total food consumption reached 11.4 million kg from ricefields and 2.89 million kg from wetlands. Pintails accordingly required 41,500 ha (18.6%) of the harvested ricefields and 9.0% of the wetlands in the Sacramento Valley to obtain this amount of food. At the management level, the study predicated that about 10,000 ha of additional wetlands would be needed to satisfy the winter energy requirements of Pintails in the absence of commercially grown rice.

Food availability obviously affects the acquisition of a suitable diet, and this factor in large measure reflects the types of habitat accessible to wintering waterfowl. At the Rockefeller Wildlife Refuge in coastal Louisiana, for example, Green-winged Teal spent most of their time feeding in impounded marshes — those of intermediate salinity — where natural foods were abundant and readily available (Rave and Baldassarre 1989). However, when 40 cm of rain rapidly increased water depth, most foods in the impoundments were no longer available, and the teal then fed in flooded pastures about 25 km from the refuge — new habitat whose availability was created by the same rainfall.

Within habitats, waterfowl can shift their use of food resources, as seen for nonbreeding Northern Pintails using ricefields on refuges in California (Miller 1987). Rice represented the dominant food (100% frequency of occurrence and 94% aggregate volume) in August and September. Thereafter, birds in this same habitat shifted to seeds from wetland plants through January, when the volume of rice in the diet diminished to only 1.1%. By February and March, Pintails again foraged on rice (17.6%), but their diet at this time also included a large percentage of aquatic invertebrates (40%).

In addition to nutritional values and environmental conditions (e.g., water depth), other factors — some rather subtle — influence the food ducks select. For example, because of their high content

Table 5-5. Proximate composition (% dry matter) and true metabolizable energy (TME; kJ/g) of the diet of Northern Pintails collected during fall and winter along the Texas Gulf Coast, 1997–99. From Ballard et al. (2004:377).

	Protein	Fat	Fiber	Ash	NFE[a]	TME[b]
Wet winter (1997–98)						
Females						
Early winter	9.88	1.90	23.75	21.59	42.88	5.02
Midwinter	9.41	1.07	13.95	35.04	40.53	3.47
Late winter	17.78	2.19	17.63	30.39	32.09	5.78
Males						
Early winter	11.08	1.90	20.13	24.65	42.24	4.90
Midwinter	8.84	1.21	13.96	41.01	34.98	3.85
Late winter	11.07	1.53	16.49	32.28	38.63	4.60
Dry winter (1998–99)						
Females						
Early winter	12.24	1.45	13.51	39.91	32.89	4.27
Midwinter	8.79	1.36	15.28	39.66	34.91	3.56
Late winter	7.49	1.23	14.70	45.56	31.02	3.10
Males						
Early winter	9.70	1.53	16.82	33.46	38.49	4.23
Midwinter	9.16	0.59	7.89	52.94	29.42	2.93
Late winter	7.03	0.77	6.23	74.84	11.13	1.84

[a]Nitrogen-free extract (NFE) = 100% − (protein + fat + fiber + ash).
[b]TME corrected for nitrogen (Sibbald and Morse 1983).

of carbohydrates, acorns (*Quercus* spp.) are well established in the diets of dabbling ducks wintering in bottomland hardwood habitats of the lower Mississippi Valley. In feeding trials, captive Wood Ducks nonetheless preferred acorns from willow oaks (*Quercus phellos*) over those from three other species of oaks, even though willow oak acorns contained less fat and carbohydrate (Barras et al. 1996). However, compared with the others, willow oak acorns also had small widths, thin shells, and the greatest ratio of meat-to-shell mass. These conditions likely facilitated their ingestion as well as in the assimilation of nutrients, as shown by their higher yield of true metabolizable energy in comparison with the other species tested. Similarly, several species of diving ducks preying on zebra mussels (*Dreissena polymorpha*) preferred those 11–21 mm in size, perhaps because larger mussels are more difficult to ingest and crush and smaller mussels required too much foraging time (Hamilton et al. 1994).

Waterfowl readily respond to the availability of new foods when these provide the requisite nutri-

tional needs. Such a response occurred in the 1980s following the invasion of zebra mussels into the Great Lakes of North America. By 1993, the biomass of zebra mussels averaged 1,270 g/m² on the near-shore areas of western Lake Erie, where on average they covered 17% of the lake bottom — but as much as 70% at some locations (Custer and Custer 1997). Zebra mussels exceed densities of 700,000/m² at power plants on Lake Erie (Kovalak et al. 1993) and reach 342,000/m² on fish-spawning reefs (Leach 1993). Diving ducks quickly exploited the remarkable abundance of zebra mussels, which soon comprised 99% of the diet of Lesser Scaup, 79% of the diet of Common Goldeneyes, and were important foods for four other species of diving ducks (Custer and Custer 1996). In Europe, Tufted Ducks, Greater Scaup, Common Pochards, and Common Goldeneyes frequently feed on zebra mussels (Olney 1963, de Vaate 1991).

Diving is the primary means of foraging for pochards as well as sea ducks. For Tufted Ducks feeding in 0.6 m of water at a temperature of 7.4 °C, the diving cost was 18.9 W/kg or 1.7 times the energetic cost of resting on the surface (Bevan and Butler 1992). Lovvorn et al. (1991) and Lovvorn and Jones (1991) calculated the mechanical costs for pochards diving to various depths for different durations. For most pochards, buoyancy was far more significant than body drag in the locomotor costs associated with shallow dives. For example, in the dives of Canvasbacks, Redheads, and Lesser Scaup, work against drag amounted to 10–12% but reached 36–38% against buoyancy; and work to accelerate during stroking of feet amounted to 49–54% of all work involved in diving (Lovvorn et al. 1991). If the effects of acceleration are removed, the work against buoyancy represents at least 82% of all work during descent and 95% of the work associated with an entire dive (Stephenson et al. 1989). Smaller ducks are favored with greater plumage volume per unit of body mass than larger species, which reduces their buoyancy as pressures increase (body tissues, in comparison with air, are essentially incompressible), and smaller birds thus become negatively buoyant at relatively shallow depths. Hence, the comparatively small Long-tailed Duck, which has dived to depths of 60 m (Schorger 1947, 1951), must ascend by active propulsion — they are the only species of duck that relies on wing propulsion underwater (see Snell 1985). Larger ducks such as eiders, which weigh more than 1,200g, can ascend passively (Lovvorn and Jones 1991). Lastly, when body lipids increase, as occurs during winter in many species, the energy cost of descent increases in response to the greater accumulation of mass, as Lovvorn and Jones (1991) demonstrated in Lesser Scaup. At the same time, foraging costs on the bottom are reduced by 20%, the result of the increased resistance to the buoyant force exceeding the actual increase in buoyancy of the birds.

In a subsequent study, Lovvorn and Gillingham (1996) examined the energetics of foraging Canvasbacks in relation to the density of food resources at Lake Mattamuskeet, North Carolina. At this location, Canvasbacks feed exclusively on the belowground winter buds of the submergent plant, wild celery (*Vallisneria americana*). The size of these buds and the locomoter costs of diving determined the energetic profits for Canvasbacks, whereas factors such as water temperature, bud dispersion, and search and handling time exerted little influence. The study concluded that water depth, which directly affects the energetic demands of diving, and food size seem more important than food density in sustaining diving ducks.

Agricultural foods — corn, rice, and soybeans —

occur in the diets of some species of ducks, especially Mallards, Northern Pintails, American Wigeon, and Green-winged Teal (Bellrose 1980). Nonetheless, the degree with which waterfowl feed on agricultural grains is affected by the abundance and availability of food in natural habitats. On the Southern High Plains of Texas, Mallards, Northern Pintails, American Wigeon, Green-winged Teal, and even Blue-winged Teal field-feed on waste corn, but each species also foraged on natural foods available in playa lakes (Baldassarre and Bolen 1984). The time Green-winged Teal spent feeding on playa lakes peaked at 23% in September–October and thereafter averaged about 10% until March (Quinlan and Baldassarre 1984). This feeding regime likely occurred because corn and other agricultural foods represent a nutritionally incomplete diet for wintering waterfowl (see Baldassarre et al. 1983). Indeed, as shown experimentally by Loesch and Kaminiski (1989), captive female Mallards lost significant amounts of body mass when their diets were restricted to corn and other agricultural foods. In California, wintering Northern Pintails feed extensively on rice available in nearby agricultural fields, but they also relied on natural foods in wetlands, likely because rice is low in protein content (Miller 1987).

Because waste grains are so readily available, waterfowl usually expend less time feeding on corn and other agricultural grains in comparison to the time they forage for natural foods. Hence, Green-winged Teal wintering in Louisiana spent 33% of their time foraging for natural foods, whereas this figure dropped to 20% for teal feeding on waste corn in Texas (Rave and Baldassarre 1989).

Winter feeding ecology thus is a complex interaction of nutritional needs, resource availability, habitat quality, and waterfowl behavior. Consider once more the Southern High Plains of Texas, where only 6.0 cm of rain fell during September–October 1980; as a result, playa wetlands contained little water, and waterfowl began field-feeding immediately after arriving in late August. The following year, however, 17.7 cm of rain fell and flooded playas during the same time period; waterfowl subsequently fed on natural vegetation and did not begin extensive field-feeding until mid-October (Baldassarre and Bolen 1984). Hence, field-feeding may begin when it minimizes overall feeding time and other costs (e.g., exposure to predators and extra energy for the flights) weighed against foraging exclusively in wetlands where diets are nutritionally complete.

Before the advent of agriculture, wintering waterfowl foraged exclusively in natural wetlands where nutritionally complete diets presumably were available. Today, the matter may be more complex. Whereas agricultural foods now provide waterfowl with ready sources of carbohydrates, the diminishing presence of wetlands — and the natural foods therein — may lessen the sources of a balanced diet for wintering birds. The field-feeding behavior of ducks, in fact, may reflect the decreasing availability of natural foods — and we might speculate that this behavior has occurred, at least in part, in response to the degradation and loss of wetland habitats around the world.

Sea Ducks and Mergansers — Mergini

The diets of sea ducks consist almost entirely of animal matter, especially mollusks (see Bellrose 1980). Sea ducks often do not select mollusks that provide the maximum return of energy, which may be explained by two hypotheses: (1) to minimize shell ingestion (see Bustness and Erikstad 1990) or salt ingestion (see Nyström et al. 1991); and (2) to avoid large prey, which increase handling time and resist crushing (see DeLeeuw and Van Eerden 1992). These hypotheses were examined in studies of the Common Eider, a Holarctic species and the most intensively studied sea duck.

In waters of high salinity, Common Eiders select foods containing less salt (e.g., certain crustaceans and gastropods instead of mollusks). When feeding on their primary prey, blue mussels, eiders selected smaller individuals, which contain less salt than those of larger size, but eiders did not avoid larger mussels in areas of low salinity (Nyström and Pehrsson 1988). Osmoregualting vertebrates avoid excess salt because its excretion imposes an energetic cost that may affect growth (Schmidt-Nielsen and Kim 1964). In Scandanavia, Common Eiders consume more blue mussels in the Baltic Sea than in areas elsewhere with higher salinities. A morphometric study of 1,000-year-old bones revealed a decline in the body size of Common Eiders in the Baltic compared with those on the west coast of Sweden — a result that implies an adaptation to higher salinity (see Nyström et al. 1991).

In regard to prey size, ducks may select mussels of suboptimal sizes to avoid the cost of obtaining food too large to ingest (Draulans 1982, 1984). Hamilton et al. (1999) tested this hypothesis by placing blue mussels of four sizes classes on ceramic tiles, which then were offered year-round to Common Eiders foraging on the coast of New Brunswick. For most of the year, eiders preferred mussels in the two smaller

size classes (10–19 mm and 19–28 mm) and avoided the two larger sizes (28–37 mm and 37–50 mm). In winter, however, the trend was reversed: Smaller mussels were avoided, and larger mussels were preferred. In general, eiders would have to consume 15–20 small mussels in less time than needed to ingest just one large mussel to obtain an equal amount of energy, so the seasonal shift in prey size is an interesting phenomenon. The bill tips of sea ducks have robust "nails," which together with their strong grasping action, enables easy removal of even the largest mussels from the substrate (Meire 1993). Accordingly, large prey would seemingly represent the most energetically profitable food. However, by selecting smaller mollusks, eiders might ingest fewer shell fragments and thereby create more room in the gut for digestible tissues. During most of the year, eiders thus foraged on smaller mussels but, during winter, it became more profitable to select larger mussels that maximized the birds' short-term energy intake — apparently a response to seasonal differences in shell mass, which was least variable in winter and much greater at other times.

The Harlequin Duck provides another interesting example of feeding ecology. This species is a river specialist during the breeding season, but in winter forages along rocky shores in coastal areas. In Canada, Robert and Cloutier (2001) used fecal analysis to determine the foods Harlequin Ducks consume during the breeding season. Insects were the dominant (99.7%) food; based on frequency of occurrence, midge larvae (Simuliidae) were most common (87.2%), followed by Trichoptera (83%), Ephemeroptera (64%), Diptera (62%), Plecotptera (33%), Coleoptera (12%), and Heteroptera (10%). Harlequin Ducks in Iceland also relied heavily on Simuliidae (larvae and pupae), which comprised 96% of the summer diet (Bengston 1972). These results support observations of Harlequin Ducks feeding during the breeding season in the beds of fast-flowing rivers, which are the preferred habitat of Simuliidae larvae. In Price William Sound, Alaska, Harlequin Ducks opportunistically foraged on the drifting roe of spawning salmon (Dzinbal and Jarvis 1982).

Harlequin Ducks dramatically shift their diet in winter, when they typically feed on mollusks (Gastropoda, Polyplacophora, Pelecypoda) and crustaceans (Deapoda, Amphipoda, Isopoda, Cirripedia). In the Aleutian Islands of Alaska, for example, gastropods (mainly *Littorina sitkana*), crustaceans, and dipteran larvae comprised 83% of the diet (Fischer and Griffin 2000). However, although their foods changed in winter, diet energy density did not (i.e., kJ/g dry mass). Harlequin ducks were generalists, consuming prey of 45 taxa and replacing dipteran larvae with crustaceans as winter progressed. In this case, the occurrence of dipteran larvae in the winter diet was unusual and may reflect environmental conditions specific to the Aleutian Islands. In Puget Sound, Washington, wintering Harlequin Ducks selected prey characteristic of rocky areas (67%) and seaweeds (20%), but only 13% was associated with sandy habitats (Gaines and Fitzner 1987).

A final example concerns the winter food habits of the Spectacled Eider, a species whose winter distribution was discovered only recently — in the Bering Sea south of St. Lawrence Island, where at least 333,000 birds occur in single-species flocks (Petersen et al. 1999). The core wintering area covers about 2,900 km^2 in a basin with water depths ranging between 40 and 90 m (Petersen and Douglas 2004). The diet of birds collected in this area during May and June, expressed in terms of frequency of occurrence, included gastropods (20%), bivalves (80%; predominately clams, *Macoma* spp.), and crustaceans (31%). All of the prey species typically occur in water 25–60 m deep (Petersen et al. 1998).

In addition to harsh winter conditions, sea ducks wintering in northern environments must cope with short periods of daylight. Systad et al. (2000) thus examined the influence of decreasing day length on wintering sea ducks in Norway at about 70°N, where the sun remains below the horizon for 2 months and daylight decreases to 5 hr of twilight by late December. Eiders extended their feeding periods as day length decreased and light intensities diminished, and they also spent more time diving. Despite these adjustments, the birds still foraged less in midwinter. Specifically, time spent underwater during the shortest days was less than half that spent on the longest days. Hence, their ability to survive the short days of midwinter likely relies on stored lipid reserves, nighttime feeding, or the increased availability of food.

Mergansers, included with sea ducks in Mergini, are specialists whose bills have lamellae modified to grasp and hold fish (hence they are sometimes called "sawbills"). The feeding ecology of mergansers has received considerable research attention because they sometimes prey on commercially important fish, namely salmonids. Common Mergansers or Goosanders can consume 18–27% of their body mass daily (Latta and Sharkey 1966) and thus may render a substantial impact on fish populations. In the United

Kingdom, mergansers are regarded as significant predators of young salmon, and permits may be issued to kill birds that damage highly prized salmon fisheries. In Scotland, for example, Feltham (1995) estimated that Common Mergansers consumed 480–522 g of fish per day to satisfy an existence energy requirement of 1,939 kJ/day. About two-thirds of this demand was met by consuming juvenile salmon, an intake equivalent to 10–11 smolts (32%) and 48–52 parr (68%). Hence, Common Mergansers might remove 8,000 to 15,000 smolts annually, or 3–16% of the total salmon production on the River North Esk.

Sjöberg (1988) studied food searching and selection behavior using captive-reared Common Mergansers and Red-breasted Mergansers. When combinations of two species of prey fish were presented to hungry birds in a small trough (i.e., readily available prey), neither species of merganser exhibited any preference. However, when the same combinations were presented to satiated birds, both species of mergansers exhibited definite preferences: Baltic salmon (*Salmo salar*) and brown trout (*S. trutta*). Hungry birds selected larger fish, regardless of species, whereas satiated birds preferred smaller fish. However, when the fish were placed in troughs with adequate cover, grayling (*Thymallus thymallus*) dominated the diet, followed by minnows (*Phoxinus phoxinus*), but only two of 30 brown trout were eaten because they hid well in the cover of stones and gravel. The mergansers also differed in the way they searched for prey. Common Mergansers searched for prey from the surface, whereas Red-breasted Mergansers dived more frequently and searched for prey along the bottom of the experimental troughs.

In an experiment with Common Mergansers in natural streams, smolts and fry of coho salmon (*Oncorhynchus kisutch*) proved less vulnerable in streams with undercut banks and other kinds of escape cover (Wood and Hand 1985). In general, the birds' daily energy gains were constrained more by handling food and digestion time than by their hunting performance. About 1 hr was required to ingest a 43-g smolt; hence, each bird could consume about 500 g of fish during an average 12-hr day. Wood and Hand (1985) concluded that mergansers could satisfy a daily food requirement of 400 g in streams with low densities of fish (less than 0.33 smolts/m^2). Because the smolts of wild coho salmon attain densities of 0.17–0.67/m^2 in productive streams, mergansers feeding exclusively on juvenile salmon could satisfy their food requirements in most streams.

Swans and Geese — Cygnini and Anserini

Swans are vegetarians, as is clear from the diets determined from the Mute Swan, Tundra Swan, Trumpeter Swan, and Black Swan. Mute Swans in England selected roots and stolons (45%), sprouts and other new growth (15%), and agricultural grains (40%; Owen and Cadbury 1975). On a major wintering area in Chesapeake Bay on the east coast of the United States, Tundra Swans once fed primarily on widgeongrass, pondweeds, and wild celery (Stewart 1962). When the quantity of aquatic vegetation in the bay began declining, however, Tundra Swans started feeding in fields to exploit the availability of waste corn, soybeans, and shoots of winter wheat (Bellrose 1980). Tundra Swans also field-feed on waste corn during their spring migration, especially where shallow flooding increases the availability of this food (Nagel 1965). The stomach contents of 617 Black Swans examined in New South Wales, Australia, consisted entirely of vegetation (Frith 1967). Cumbungi or narrow-leaved cattail (*Typha angustifolia*) occurred in 37% of the stomachs and comprised 19% of total food volume, followed by algae (Chlorophyceae) at 31% occurrence and 20% volume. When water levels were high, Black Swans fed at the edge of marshes where 90% of the food volume then consisted of pasture plants. See Owen and Kear (1972) for a summary of food habits for each of the seven species of swans.

Grant et al. (1994, 1997) studied the feeding ecology of Trumpeter Swans breeding on the Copper River Delta, Alaska, where they tallied 1,295 hr of observations and 7,574 feeding events. During the prenesting period, females fed 42% of the time and males 31%, but during incubation this declined to 8% for females and remained little different for males (37%). Posthatch feeding averaged 32% for both females and males. Adult swans fed on submerged aquatics (about 90% of all feeding observations) during prelaying, but their diets shifted to emergent horsetails (*Equisetum fluviatile* and *E. arvense*) and sedge (*Carex lyngbyaei*) during incubation (23–43% of all feeding observations). Compared with the adults, cygnets spent more time feeding on horsetails and less time on submergents.

Swans, as the largest of waterfowl, consume large quantities of aquatic vegetation. Mathiasson (1973), for example, calculated that about 45 Mute Swans consumed 8,635 kg of sea lettuce (*Ulva lactuca*) during a 45-day period in which they virtually eliminated a 0.8-ha bed of this large marine alga! In pens, molting Mute Swans consumed an average of 7.69 kg/bird/day of sea lettuce and eelgrass (*Zostera marina*). Because plants serve as a vital substrate for many aquatic invertebrates (see Chapter 9), the extensive removal of aquatic vegetation by swans also may adversely affect the integrity of food chains in wetland ecosystems. Indeed, large concentrations of swans may be inimical to the welfare of other species of waterfowl and wildlife, as witnessed by the expanding population of feral Mute Swans along the Atlantic Coast of the United States in general, and Chesapeake Bay in particular (Allin et al. 1987); by 2003, a population of some 14,300 Mute Swans occurred on the Atlantic Coast. This situation created an interesting management dilemma because Mute Swans are now degrading aquatic habitats, yet the birds remain popular with the public (see Infobox 5-2).

Geese are also herbivores and forage primarily during daylight hours. Species in the genus *Branta* generally have bills adapted for feeding on the above-ground parts of plants, whereas the bills of those in *Anser* are adapted to feed on tubers, rhizomes, and other belowground plant parts (Goodman and Fisher 1962; Fig. 5-3). However, there are subtleties that allow some species to exploit different feeding niches. For instance, the short bill of the Red-breasted Goose facilitates precise control of pecking, which may have been especially useful when feeding on glasswort (*Salicornia*) during winter, although they now largely use agricultural foods (Owen 1977). In contrast, the Giant Canada Goose has a long, narrow bill adapted for stripping seeds and shearing vegetation. The intermediate bill length of the Hawaiian Goose facilitates a varied diet, which includes at least 31 plant species (Black et al. 1994). The bill of the Lesser Snow Goose is perhaps the most specialized of all, having a horny area along the edge of each mandible (the "grinning patch"); this adaptation produces a vice-like grip for extracting the underground tubers and rhizomes of marsh plants (Bolen and Rylander 1978, Owen 1980). Indeed, subtle variations in bill morphology and feeding methods likely allowed five species of geese to co-exist in the preagricultural British Isles, which at that time (4,000 years ago) were 95% forested (Owen 1976). Thus, the Greylag Goose, a resident of southern fens and tidal marshes, fed on roots and tubers. The Pink-footed Goose likely sought estuaries along the west coast where they grazed on saltmarsh grasses, whereas the Greenland White-fronted Goose frequented acidic bogs in western Scotland, Ireland, and Wales, probing for tubers and roots of sedges (*Carex*

Infobox 5-2

Mute Swans
A Graceful, Beautiful, But Troublesome Exotic

Mute Swans, native to parts of Eurasia, were almost certain to be released in North America. They are large, attractive birds of story and verse that adapt readily to zoos, parks, and aviaries. The first introductions thus occurred early in the last century (e.g., in New York in 1910 and in New Jersey in 1912). By 1954, however, enough Mute Swans had escaped confinement to be included in the annual Midwinter Waterfowl Surveys. Their numbers increased slowly at first, but then expanded exponentially. By 2003, the survey estimated that 21,400 feral swans were free-ranging in the United States. Of these, about 14,300 occurred in the Atlantic Flyway, particularly in the Chesapeake Bay area of Maryland. For waterfowl biologists, the birds' charm began to erode concurrently with their increasing numbers and growing impacts on native wildlife and their habitats.

Mute Swans consume large amounts of food per day, notably submerged aquatic vegetation (SAV), although they also graze in upland settings and, when food is scarce, beg handouts from humans. In Chesa-

peake Bay, SAV underpins much of the marine ecosystem by providing food and cover for a number of animals, including those of economic and ecological importance (e.g., shellfish) as well as native waterfowl of several species (e.g., American Black Ducks, Canvasbacks, and Redheads). SAV is involved with nutrient cycling and helps reduce sedimentation and shoreline erosion. Unfortunately, the growing numbers of Mute Swans may be damaging SAV beds, which in turn imperils the food chain in Chesapeake Bay. The birds are destructive feeders, tearing up more vegetation than they actually consume and killing plants by exposing their roots and other underground parts. Large areas of aquatic vegetation are accessible to Mute Swans, whose long necks and upending feeding behavior enable them to forage in water up to 1 m in depth. Moreover, because few Mute Swans migrate, their impact on local vegetation continues year-round.

During the breeding season — March to October — Mute Swans are highly territorial and, while not always physically harmful, often become aggressive toward con-

specifics and other waterfowl. Their large size — males average about 12 kg with a wingspan reaching 238 cm — makes them formidable adversaries. They at times have displaced or even killed ducks and geese (and their broods), as well as destroyed their nests. In Maryland, wildlife officials removed 250 Mute Swans after they trampled the nesting colonies of Black Skimmers (*Rynchops niger*) and Least Terns (*Sterna antillarum*). While not proven, Mute Swans also may be involved in the relocation of Tundra Swans, many of which at one time overwintered in Chesapeake Bay but now have declined in Maryland and increased in North Carolina. The aggressive behavior of Mute Swans extends to humans and their pets, each of which have been vigorously attacked; other accounts report the birds attacking small boats and even capsizing canoes.

Mute Swans currently do not cause major agricultural damage to field crops in the United States (as they do in England), but they have damaged cranberry crops in Massachusetts and New Jersey. Their role, if any, either as vectors or reservoirs of avian diseases remains unknown.

Management options for controlling Mute Swans often face public opposition. The birds are popular with many segments of society, who often disregard the harmful aspects of their growing numbers, and methods such as shooting, destroying eggs, and relocation are not always deemed acceptable, or even necessary. Nonetheless, because they are an introduced species, Mute Swans seemed excluded from the Migratory Bird Treaty Act; hence, the states alone assumed legal authority for dealing with the birds. However, a court decision in 2001 ruled otherwise, and Mute Swans thereafter fell under federal jurisdiction. In response, Congress amended the Act in 2004 to exclude nonnative birds, including the Mute Swan; hence, the states again have primary authority to control Mute Swans. Meanwhile, the member states established the Atlantic Flyway Mute Swan Task Force, which issued a management plan in 2003, as did the Maryland Department of Natural Resources. Both plans focus on protecting native wildlife and their habitats by controlling the Mute Swan population. See also Allin et al. (1987), Conover and McIvor (1993), Conover and Kania (1994), Naylor (2004), and Perry (2004). Photo courtesy of Frank McKinney and the Bell Museum of Natural History.

spp.) and cotton grass (*Eriophorum* spp.). In contrast, the European Greater White-fronted Goose may have colonized the British Isles only after the Pink-footed Goose moved northward to forage on newly available pastures and open land. Today, all geese in the British Isles depend heavily on agricultural foods (see below).

Buchsbaum et al. (1986) demonstrated that Atlantic Canada Geese feeding on smooth cordgrass (*Spartina alterniflora*) absorbed only 28% of the dry matter contained in cellulose, and 25% of the hemicellulose. In a controlled experiment, Lesser Snow Geese retained 45% of the cellulose and thus 46% of the energy in alfalfa pellets, which represents the greatest metabolic use of cell walls yet reported for birds (Sedinger et al. 1995). In contrast, neither Black Brant nor Cape Barren Geese obtained energy from cellulose (Marriott and Forbes 1970, Sedinger et al. 1989). Instead, Black Brant metabolized about 41% of the hemicellulose and protein available in cell walls. Overall, fiber digested by Black Brant represented only 19% of the total organic matter metabolized. Cellulose digestion thus appears associated with the length of time food is retained in the gut, which may be limited in Black Brant and other small species of geese (see Sedinger et al. 1989).

Snow Geese retained more energy than the smaller-bodied Black Brant, but they also lost more of this energy as heat (33%), which suggests an interesting relationship between size and energy processing in herbivorous birds.

In general, geese retain food for short periods of time (1.4 hr in Snow Geese; Hupp et al. 1996) and instead process large amounts of forage. For example, Lesser Snow Geese staging in fall on the coastal plain of the Beaufort Sea in Alaska consumed 662 g/bird of tall cotton-grass (*Eriophorum angustifolium*), which equals 29% of the body mass of a 2.3-kg goose (Hupp et al. 1996). During a 21-day staging period prior to migration, some 300,000 geese likely consumed more than 900,000 kg of food. In further experiments at this site, human-imprinted Snow Geese reduced the aerial coverage of cotton-grass by 60% after 1 year of feeding and 39% after the second year (Hupp et al. 2000). The foraging effect, simulated by hand removal, reduced the underground biomass (stem bases and rhizomes) by 80% after 2 years and by 62% after 4 years. Overall, the foraging activities of Snow Geese affected plants for the following 2–4 years but probably did not alter plant community composition. Nonetheless, a large staging area is probably needed so that geese can

Figure 5-3. The bills of geese reflect their foraging strategies. Those of some species of *Anser* (*left*) are heavy and strong with hard, horny lamellae for digging and extracting roots and tubers (*top*, Greylag Goose, Snow Goose, and Bean Goose). In contrast, the short bill of the Red-breasted Goose (*top right*) reflects rapid and precise pecking. The long, narrow bill of the Giant Canada Goose (*middle left*) shears vegetation and strips seeds from stalks. The bill of the Hawaiian Goose (*bottom left*) is intermediate and indicative of a more varied diet (After Owen 1980).

exploit new feeding locations while the previously used sites recover.

During the spring and summer, geese select actively growing green leaves that are high in crude protein content but low in fiber (Sedinger and Raveling 1984, Gauthier 1993). Hence, the birds produce essentially all of their lean tissue in these time periods (McLandress and Raveling 1981, Hobaugh 1985). In Alaska, for example, Cackling Canada Geese selected leaves of arrowgrass (*Triglochin palustris*), which contained more protein and less fiber than other available plant foods (Sedinger and Raveling 1984). In general, geese select forage high in nonstructural carbohydrates, especially during periods of lipid deposition (Thomas and Prevett 1980, Sedinger and Raveling 1984). We described the ability of geese to digest cellulose in our previous discussion of fiber as a component of plant foods (see above).

Raveling (1979) coupled changes in body mass and time spent foraging during much of the annual cycle of Cackling Canada Geese. During winter in California, the geese lost weight and relied on stored lipids to meet 6–7% of their daily energy needs. Daily food intake was satisfied with 80–90 g of seeds, which required about 2 hr of foraging time. Later in winter, the birds met their energy requirements by grazing on green leaves, of which about 200 g were consumed daily during an 8–9-hr period. Body weights during this period increased 26% for males and 45% for females; these gains coincided with new growth of grasses and sedges, which the birds exploited while migrating northward. In early May, the foraging time lengthened to an average of 13–16 hr, which represented 70–85% of the available daylight, and the lipids accumulating at this time satisfied about 50% of energy demands the geese needed from their arrival to the onset of incubation.

During fall and winter, geese, more than other species of waterfowl, have adapted their feeding behavior to the availability of cereal grains. Indeed, Linnaeus ascribed the very name of the Bean Goose to reflect its use of the field bean (*Vicia faba*), which was widely grown throughout Europe before the advent of nitrogen fertilizers. In North America, reports dating to the early 1880s mention geese feeding in the first grain fields established in the Whitewater Lake region of southeastern Manitoba (Bossenmaier and Marshall 1958). Geese feed on agricultural grains during fall and winter when these foods are richer in carbohydrates than green plants; carbohydrates are needed to form lipid reserves for fall migration and to maintain homeostasis during the winter months. A variety of agricultural crops attract geese. In Europe, geese readily forage on root crops such as turnips, carrots, potatoes, and sugar beets, as well as on beans and peas (Owen 1980). In North America, geese more commonly eat corn, wheat, and rice. Regardless of geographical location, however, the attraction of geese to agricultural crops shares a common cause — an abundant and readily available source of energy-rich food.

Geese also forage on the vegetative parts of wetland vegetation. For the latter, the roots, tubers, rhizomes, stems, and leaves of such plants as marsh hay cordgrass (*Spartina patens*) and various bulrushes (*Scirpus* spp.) represent desirable foods. In the central United States (e.g., Missouri), corn, soybeans, and winter wheat made up only 15% of the diet of Canada Geese, whereas 36% wild millet (*Echinochloa muricata*), 10% smartweed (*Polygonum* spp.), 10% cut-grasses (*Leersia* spp.), and 8% spike rushes (*Eleocharis* spp.) formed the bulk of the remaining foods. These foraging activities are capable of removing large amounts of aquatic vegetation. For example, Black Brant grazing during fall and winter in Boundary Bay, British Columbia, were largely responsible for removing 50% (262 tons) of aboveground biomass and 43% (100 tons) of belowground biomass of the exotic seagrass *Zostera japonica* (Baldwin and Lovvorn 1994).

Giant Canada Geese wintering at Silver Lake in Rochester, Minnesota, fed primarily on waste corn in nearby fields (McLandress and Raveling 1981). However, in spring the same geese shifted to bluegrass (*Poa pratensis*) and a generally more diverse diet. This shift, occurring just before the breeding season, more than likely reflects the crude protein content (26.2%) and essential amino acids available to the birds in the spring growth of bluegrass leaves.

Lesser Snow Geese wintering on converted prairie in southeastern Texas also shifted their diet from rice in October and November to green vegetation by January (Hobaugh 1985). These data again demonstrate the linkages between food habits, biological demands, and food availability.

Alisauskas et al. (1988) provided an important study of the feeding ecology of Lesser Snow Geese wintering in midcontinental North America. The feeding ecology for these birds depends strongly on features of the habitat, of which three different types were investigated: (1) coastal marshes of Louisiana; (2) inland prairies developed for rice in Texas and Louisiana; and (3) agricultural land in Iowa, Missouri, and Kansas, where waste corn was available. In coastal Louisiana, the January–February diet was dominated (61–80% dry mass) by rhizomes of marsh hay cordgrass and tubers of bulrushes (*Scirpus olneyi* and *S. robustus*). In contrast, geese feeding in rice stubble favored grasses (28%) and forbs (70%), but when winter rains loosened the soil, the birds began grubbing for rhizomes. As might be expected, corn formed 88% of the winter diet in those agricultural areas where cornfields were commonplace, although winter wheat and other grasses supplemented the diet (Fig. 5-4). Alisauskas et al. (1988) then compared the nutritional values of these diets; those from ricefields were highest in protein, whereas fiber content was greatest in the foods obtained in the coastal marshes (Table 5-6). Thus, to meet their requirements for existence energy, the geese in this study would have had to eat 2.4 times more food in coastal Louisiana and 4.3 times more in the ricefields to match the energy available in cornfields, all else being equal (e.g., weather conditions).

These data formed the basis of some specific management recommendations. In natural marshes of coastal Louisiana, the long-standing practices of setting cool burns and grazing cattle should continue; these disturbances increase the availability of tubers and rhizomes. Indeed, Alisauskas et al. (1988) did not observe any Lesser Snow Geese feeding where marsh hay cordgrass remained undisturbed by either of these influences. More recent studies with this population revealed linkages between recruitment in the Arctic and nutrition available on migration areas in the spring, which may provide management opportunities to reduce the burgeoning Lesser Snow Goose population in North America (Alisauskas 2002). Recommendations called for increased attention to the management of agricultural areas because of the importance of waste grain to

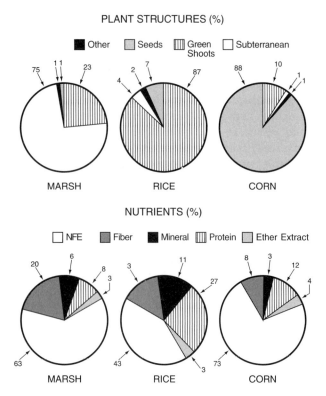

PLANT STRUCTURES (%)

■ Other   ▨ Seeds   ▥ Green   □ Subterranean
                        Shoots

MARSH   RICE   CORN

NUTRIENTS (%)

□ NFE   ▨ Fiber   ■ Mineral   ▥ Protein   ▨ Ether Extract

MARSH   RICE   CORN

Figure 5-4. Comparison of diets for Lesser Snow Geese wintering in three types of habitat: (1) coastal marsh in Louisiana (MARSH), (2) rice prairies in Louisiana and Texas (RICE), and (3) agricultural areas near the Missouri River Valley (CORN). As shown, the birds consume not only different plants, but different parts of plants, in each habitat (*top*), and the nutrient composition varies accordingly (*bottom*). NFE = carbohydrate; ether extract = fat. From Alisauskas et al. (1988:410–411). With permission from The Wildlife Society.

the nutritional status of geese. The latter subject, including the often serious problem of crop damage, is discussed more fully in the next section.

AGRICULTURAL FOODS

The association between waterfowl and crops is as old as agriculture itself. Indeed, Egyptian writings 3,000 years ago speak of Egyptian Sheldgeese destroying crops of wheat and dates (Kear 1990). Today, as in the past, the ready availability and high energy content of agricultural crops make corn and other grains attractive to a variety of waterfowl.

Farmers may gain some benefits from field-feeding waterfowl. In Europe, for example, geese of several species remove waste potatoes, which harbor the cysts of the potato root elworm (*Heterodera rostochiensis*), thereby lessening damage to the next year's crop (Owen 1980). Field-feeding waterfowl also remove weed seeds and enrich the soil with their droppings. In many parts of the United States, goslings effectively remove weeds from cotton, onions, asparagus, and other crops (Kear 1990). The geese relish many of the weeds, but fortunately find the crop itself relatively unpalatable. Apparently the young birds were so effective that 250,000 "working geese" cultivated croplands in California as recently as the early 1960s; 68 goslings controlled the weeds on about 1 ha at 20% less cost than either pesticides or laborers! On the Southern High Plains of Texas, field-feeding waterfowl removed as much as 98% of the waste corn remaining after the crops were harvested, which markedly reduces the amount of unwanted sprouting the following growing season (Baldassarre and Bolen 1987). This activity reduces the fuel and other operating costs because farmers need not plow under a "volunteer crop" of corn. In California, waterfowl foraging in ricefields flooded after harvest increased decomposition of surface straw by 78% (Bird et al. 2000). Such an effect is significant because recent legislation in California has restricted traditional open-field burning of rice straw residues. Indeed, farmers who encourage wa-

Table 5-6. Nutritional characteristics of three composite diets consumed by Lesser Snow Geese on major wintering habitats in North America. From Alisauskas et al. (1988:412).

Habitat[a]	Dry matter (%)	True metabolizable energy (kJ)	Daily requirement (g dry mass)
Marsh	17.4	10.3	88.8
Rice	9.0	11.4	82.7
Corn	31.8	13.3	67.6

[a]Marsh habitat was at the Rockefeller Wildlife Refuge in southwestern Louisiana. Rice habitats were the Garwood Prairie in Texas, and the Calcasieu Prairie in Louisiana. Corn habitats were in Missouri, Iowa, and Kansas.

Figure 5-5. Large amounts of corn remain in fields after harvest (*top*), but burning the overlying stalks and leaves markedly increases the availability of waste corn as a winter food for waterfowl (*bottom*). When available, burned cornfields most consistently attracted field-feeding ducks during winter on the Southern High Plains of Texas. Photos courtesy of Guy A. Baldassarre.

terfowl use of harvested ricefields with shallow flooding could attract enough birds to alleviate any need of autumn tillage. Overall, the general pattern of waterfowl feeding on waste grain in postharvested fields causes little, if any, agricultural damage, and in many circumstances benefits farming operations.

Waste grains also provide good opportunities for the management of field-feeding waterfowl. Ducks field-feeding on waste corn in Texas preferred fields where farmers had burned the stubble, thereby removing the debris and improving access to the corn (Fig. 5-5). If, however, farmers plowed under the fall stubble, up to 97% of the waste corn was buried and no longer available as waterfowl food (Baldassarre et al. 1983). In the Mississippi Alluvial Valley and

the Central Valley in California, managers regularly reflood ricefields after harvest to attract large numbers of ducks and geese (Reinecke et al. 1989, Heitmeyer et al. 1989; see Chapter 10). On private lands in the Mississippi Alluvial Valley, flooding of harvested rice and soybean fields attracted large numbers of waterfowl as well as shorebirds (Twedt and Nelms 1999, Twedt et al. 1998). Flooding ricefields also makes seeds from other wetland plants available, as well as a variety of invertebrates, as shown in the diets of Northern Pintails wintering in the Sacramento Valley (Miller 1987). In parts of Texas, the postharvest management of ricefields to attract wintering Lesser Snow Geese provides farmers with a significant economic incentive — fees paid by hunters — and now is a practice influenced by federal agricultural policies (see Musacchio and Coulson 2001).

The high energy content and tremendous area planted in agricultural grains cannot be ignored by waterfowl managers, but agricultural crops are not a stable resource. For example, in the Midwest and Great Plains regions of the United States — principal agricultural areas — harvested cropland area in corn has remained relatively stable for the past half-century, whereas soybeans increased 600% and wheat declined by 43% (see Krapu et al. 2004). A more significant concern relative to waste grain is the increasing efficiency of harvest. Under ideal conditions, modern farm machinery can achieve corn harvests approaching 99% efficiency. Krapu et al. (2004) documented the effect of increased harvest efficiency by comparing the postharvest biomass of waste corn from fields in central Nebraska in 1978 with comparable data for 1997 and 1998. Waste corn averaged 254 kg/ha in 1997 (an unusually high year) and 177 kg/ha in 1998 compared with 333 kg/ha in 1978. After accounting for a 20% increase in yield, the biomass of waste corn in 1997 and 1998 was reduced 24% and 47%, respectively, from 1978 as harvest efficiency increased from 96 to 98%. In response, fat storage decreased by 46% in Greater Sandhill Cranes (*Grus canadensis tabida*) and likewise declined in White-fronted Geese from 14 g/day in 1978–79 to 0 g/day in 1998–99 (see Krapu et al. 2004). Such findings are alarming because corn comprises more than 90% of the diet of Sandhill Cranes (Reinecke and Krapu 1986) and White-fronted Geese (Krapu et al. 1985) feeding on spring staging areas in Nebraska.

In the Mississippi Alluvial Valley, ricefields have long provided important food for migrating and wintering waterfowl, with waste rice averaging as much as 491 kg/ha or about 8.7% of the average yield

(Manley et al. 2004). However, 79–99% of the waste had disappeared between harvest in August and September and early winter, largely as a result of changing agricultural practices such as harvest efficiency and planting dates. In particular, the planting of early-maturating varieties of rice now allows as many as 90 days to elapse between harvest and flooding of fields in winter, during which time substantial amounts of waste can deteriorate or germinate and thus not be available as food for waterfowl (see Manley et al. 2004). The common practice of burning rice stubble after harvest also can destroy up to 30% of the residual rice (Miller et al. 1989). Indeed, subsequent studies of waste rice dynamics in the Mississippi Alluvial Valley concluded that prior estimates of carrying capacity for waterfowl were overestimated by 52–83% (Stafford et al. 2006).

In other areas, the replacement of corn with soybeans is also significant: Soybean waste (48–63 kg/ha; Warner et al. 1985) is much less than corn, soybeans deteriorate rapidly when flooded (Nelms and Twedt 1996), and soybeans are poorly suited to meet the nutritional needs of waterfowl (see Loesch and Kaminski 1989). In Nebraska, waterfowl and cranes do not feed in soybean fields when corn is available (see Krapu et al. 2004). Nonetheless, soybean acreage is dramatically increasing in the United States and now occupies nearly 25% of the Nation's cropland. Further, some 75% of this crop was planted in genetically modified soybeans, which has increased the efficacy of weed control —glyphosate herbicides applied to genetically modified crops target all other types of vegetation (see Krapu et al. 2004). Federal farm policies have encouraged these changes with a proliferation of subsidies that favor reduced production of the same high-energy foods that occur in waterfowl diets.

Regardless of its abundance and availability as waterfowl food, waste grains generally lack many of the nutrients found in natural foods occurring in wetland habitats (Baldassarre et al. 1983). To offset these nutritional deficiencies, comprehensive management programs accordingly should provide waterfowl with sources of natural foods by ensuring the presence of good quality, natural wetlands. Management focused entirely on agricultural crops usually benefits only a few species of waterfowl. Indeed, Fredrickson and Taylor (1982) recorded 80% more species visiting managed moist-soil wetlands in comparison with nearby fields of row crops; the array of species in these wetlands included mammals, herons, rails, small passerines, and upland game birds. Overall, management of waterfowl and other wetland wildlife in agricultural settings depends on striking a balance between food available as waste grains and food available in wetlands; for managers, this includes issues of species diversity and ecology, as well as government policies related to agriculture.

Waterfowl managers also must remain sensitive to situations where field-feeding waterfowl may damage agricultural crops. Waterfowl depredations at times may be severe, especially to ripening grain or growing wheat (Knittle and Porter 1988, Patterson 1992). If such crop depredations are ignored, farmers and other landowners understandably may withdraw their support for any number of desirable conservation programs (e.g., wetland preservation). In North America, crop damage may be especially serious in the Canadian prairies where wheat and barley are major crops. These are cut and then left to dry and ripen in the fields (Fig. 5-6); most damage occurs at this particularly vulnerable stage in the harvest (i.e., when the grain is on the ground in swathes). Ducks not only eat the grain, but they also trample and foul the ripening crop, thereby causing losses estimated at $10 million each year in Alberta, Saskatchewan, and Manitoba (Sugden 1976). Damage tends to be most severe when rains delay the harvest and the crops remain in fields longer to dry.

In Europe, which was settled long before North America, forest cover has been reduced from more than 80% to about 33%. About 42% of Europe is now classified as agricultural and exceeds 70% in the United Kingdom and other mid-latitude countries (see Newton 1998). Conflicts with waterfowl increased in keeping with the proportion of arable land in cultivation, and for the most part these involve geese feeding on waste potatoes, sugar beets, carrots, and sprouting wheat (see Owen 1980, Kear 1990).

Crop damage by waterfowl has been well documented in Europe and the United States, but fewer reports originate elsewhere. In the Far East, Japan is an important wintering area for migratory waterfowl in northeast Asia, with a midwinter survey in 1996 tallying nearly 2 million birds (see Lane et al. 1998). Because about 5 million ha of farmland also occur in Japan, conflicts with waterfowl were inevitable. Lane et al. (1998) summarized these events, which involve the damage Spot-billed Ducks and Mallards inflict on transplanted and seeded rice; fortunately, these depredations are local in nature and have not been extensive at the national level. White-fronted Geese and Bean Geese have damaged harvested rice around Lake Izunuma, but the losses again were slight. Other incidents concern damage to vegetables such as cabbage.

Figure 5-6. Wheat and barley are among the cereal grains commonly dried in swathes on the Canadian prairies, but this cultural practice predisposes these crops to the depredations of postbreeding waterfowl. Photo courtesy of Guy A. Baldassarre.

Figure 5-7. Acetylene exploders are among the tools both farmers and biologists can use for frightening field-feeding waterfowl from croplands. The "guns" are quite loud and can be fired randomly or at timed intervals, but waterfowl often habituate to the explosions. This necessitates frequently changing the location of the exploders to maximize their effectiveness. Photo courtesy of U.S. Fish and Wildlife Service.

Currently, biologists recommend several methods to cope with waterfowl depredations: (1) deploying acetylene exploders, "scare crows," and other devices that frighten the birds; (2) paying farmers a government subsidy to compensate for their losses; (3) planting crops that are less attractive to waterfowl and/or adopting alternate harvest methods; and (4) planting "lure crops" or establishing feeding stations designed to attract birds away from fields where damage might be severe (see Knittle and Porter 1988).

Acetylene exploders equipped with automatic timers are among the best devices for frightening waterfowl (Fig. 5-7). This equipment is reasonably effective in keeping waterfowl from crops, and its operation is relatively inexpensive and requires little maintenance (Sugden 1976). In Wisconsin, mylar flagging and human effigies significantly reduced use of agricultural fields by Canada Geese (Heinrich and Craven 1990). No government-approved repellents are currently available to protect crops from waterfowl depredations, but research has addressed repellents to discourage Canada Geese at urban lawns, airports, and golf courses (Dolbeer et al.1998, Blackwell et al. 1999).

To summarize this section, waste grains resulting from harvest of agricultural crops have long provided important food sources for migrating and wintering waterfowl. However, the availability of agricultural foods can be undependable. Thus, although managers should manage agricultural food sources for waterfowl, such food sources are no substitute for the long-term benefits of foods provided in natural wetland habitats.

LITERATURE CITED

Albright, J. J., R. B. Owen, Jr., and P. O. Corr. 1983. The effects of winter weather on the behavior and energy reserves of Black Ducks in Maine. Transactions of the Northeast Fish and Wildlife Conference 40:118–128.

Alisauskas, R. T. 2002. Arctic climate, spring nutrition, and recruitment in mid-continent Lesser Snow Geese. Journal of Wildlife Management 66:181–193.

Alisauskas, R. T., and C. D. Ankney. 1992. The cost of egg laying and its relationship to nutrient reserves in waterfowl. Pages 30–61 in B. D. J. Batt, A. D. Afton, M. G. Anderson, C. D. Ankney, D. H.Johnson, J. A. Kadlec, and G. L. Krapu, editors. Ecology and management of breeding waterfowl. University of Minnesota Press, Minneapolis.

Alisauskas, R. T., C. D. Ankney, and E. E. Klaas. 1988. Winter diets and nutrition of midcontinental Lesser Snow Geese. Journal of Wildlife Management 52:403–414.

Alisauskas, R. T., and K. A. Hobson. 1993. Determination of Lesser Snow Goose diets and winter distribution using stable isotope analysis. Journal of Wildlife Management 57:49–54.

Allin, C. C., G. G. Chasko, and T. P. Husband. 1987. Mute Swans in the Atlantic Flyway: a review of the history, population growth and management needs. Transactions of the Northeast Section of the Wildlife Society 44:32–47.

Anderson, J. T., and L. M. Smith. 1998. Protein and energy production in playa lakes: implications for management. Wetlands 18:437–446.

Baldassarre, G. A., and E. G. Bolen. 1984. Field-feeding ecology of waterfowl wintering on the Southern High Plains of Texas. Journal of Wildlife Management 48:63–71.

Baldassarre, G. A., and E. G. Bolen. 1987. Management of waste corn for waterfowl wintering on the Texas High Plains. Texas Tech University Range and Wildlife Management Note 13.

Baldassarre, G. A., R. J. Whyte, E. E. Quinlan, and E. G. Bolen. 1983. Dynamics and quality of waste corn available to postbreeding waterfowl in Texas. Wildlife Society Bulletin 11:25–31.

Baldwin, J. R., and J. R. Lovvorn. 1994. Expansion of seagrass habitat by the exotic *Zostera japonica*, and its use by dabbling ducks and Brant in Boundary Bay, British Columbia. Marine Ecology Progress Series 103:119–127.

Ballard, B. M., J. E. Thompson, M. J. Petrie, M. Chekett, and D. G. Hewitt. 2004. Diet and nutrition of Northern Pintails wintering along the southern coast of Texas. Journal of Wildlife Management 68:371–382.

Bardwell, J. L., L. L. Glasgow, and E. A. Epps, Jr. 1962. Nutritional analyses of foods eaten by Pintail and teal in south Louisiana. Proceedings of the Southeastern Association of Game and Fish Commissioners 16:209–217.

Barras, S. C., R. M. Kaminski, and L. A. Brennan. 1996. Acorn selection by female Wood Ducks. Journal of Wildlife Management 60:592–602.

Bartonek, J. C. 1968. Summer foods and feeding habits of diving ducks in Manitoba. Dissertation, University of Wisconsin, Madison.

Bartonek, J. C., and J. J. Hickey. 1969. Selective feeding by juvenile diving ducks in summer. Auk 86:443–457.

Bellrose, F. C. 1980. Ducks, geese and swans of North America. Stackpole Books, Harrisburg, Pennsylvania.

Bellrose, F. C., and H. G. Anderson. 1943. Preferential rating of duck food plants. Illinois Natural History Survey Bulletin 22:417–433.

Bengston, S. A. 1972. Breeding ecology of the Harlequin Duck *Histrionicus histrionicus* (L.) in Iceland. Ornis Scandinavica 3:1–19.

Bevan, R. M., and P. J. Butler. 1992. The effects of temperature and oxygen consumption, heart rate and deep body temperature during diving in the Tufted Duck *Aythya fuligula*. Journal of Experimental Biology 163:139–151.

Bird, J. A., G. S. Pettygrove, and J. M. Eadie. 2000. The impact of waterfowl foraging on the decomposition of rice straw: mutual benefits for rice growers and waterfowl. Journal of Applied Ecology 37:728–741.

Black, J. M., J. Prop, J. M. Hunter, F. Woog, A. P. Marshall, and J. M. Bowler. 1994. Foraging behavior and energetics of the Hawaiian Goose *Branta sandvicensis*. Wildfowl 45:65–109.

Blackwell, B. F., T. W. Seamans, and R. A. Dolbeer. 1999. Plant growth regulator (Stringhold) enhances repellency of anthraquinone formulation (Flight Control) to Canada Geese. Journal of Wildlife Management 63:1336–1343.

Blem, C. R. 1990. Avian energy storage. Current Ornithology 7:59–113.

Bolen, E. G. 1975. In memoriam: Clarence Cottam. Auk 92:118–125.

Bolen, E. G., and M. K. Rylander. 1978. Feeding adaptations in the Lesser Snow Goose *Anser caerulescens*. Southwestern Naturalist 23:158–161.

Bossenmaier, E. F., and W. H. Marshall. 1958. Field-feeding by waterfowl in southwestern Manitoba. Wildlife Monographs 1.

Buchsbaum, R., J. Wilson, and I. Valiela. 1986. Digestibility of plant constituents by Canada Geese and Atlantic Brant. Ecology 67:386–393.

Bustness, J. O., and K. E. Erikstad. 1990. Size selection of common mussels, *Mytilus edulis*, by Common Eiders, *Somateria mollissima*: energy maximization or shell weight minimization? Canadian Journal of Zoology 68:2280–2283.

Checkett, J. M., R. D. Drobney, M. J. Petrie, and D. A. Graber. 2002. True metabolizable energy of moist-soil seeds. Wildlife Society Bulletin 30:1113–1119.

Chura, N. J. 1961. Food availability and preferences of juvenile Mallards. Transactions of the North American Wildlife and Natural Resources Conference 26:121–133.

Collias, N. E., and E. C. Collias. 1963. Selective feeding by wild ducklings of different species. Wilson Bulletin 75:6–14.

Conover, M. R., and G. S. Kania. 1994. Impact of interspecific aggression and herbivory by Mute Swans on native waterfowl and aquatic vegetation in New England. Auk 111:744–748.

Conover, M. R., and D. E. McIvor. 1993. Exotic species in urban environments: lessons from New England's Mute Swans. Transactions of the North American Wildlife and Natural Resources Conference 58:87–91.

Cottam, C. 1939. Food habits of North American diving ducks. U.S. Department of Agriculture Technical Bulletin 634.

Custer, C. M., and T. W. Custer. 1996. Food habits of diving ducks in the Great Lakes after the zebra mussel invasion. Journal of Field Ornithology 67:86–99.

Custer, C. M., and T. W. Custer. 1997. Occurrence of zebra mussels in near-shore areas of western Lake Erie. Journal of Great Lakes Research 23:108–115.

DeLeeuw, J. J., and M. R. VanEeerden. 1992. Size selection in diving Tufted Ducks *Aythya fuligula* explained by differential handling of small and large mussels *Dreissena polymorpha*. Ardea 80:353–362.

Delnicki, D., and K. J. Reinecke. 1986. Mid-winter food use and body weights of Mallards and Wood Ducks in Mississippi. Journal of Wildlife Management 50:43–51.

de Vaate, A. B. 1991. Distribution and aspects of population dynamics of the zebra mussel *Dreissena polymorpha* (Pallas, 1771), in the Lake Ijsselmeer area (the Netherlands). Oecologia 86:40–50.

Dolbeer, R. A., T. W. Seamans, B. F. Blackwell, and J. L. Belant. 1998. Anthraquinone formulation (Flight Control) shows promise as avian feeding repellent. Journal of Wildlife Management 62:1558–1564.

Draulans, D. 1982. Foraging and size selection of mussels by the Tufted Duck, *Aythya fuligula*. Journal of Animal Ecology 51:943–956.

Draulans, D. 1984. Sub-optimal mussel selection by Tufted Ducks *Aythya fuligula*: test of a hypothesis. Animal Behaviour 32:1192–1196.

Driver, E. A., L. G. Sugden, and R. J. Kovach. 1974. Calorific, chemical and physical values of potential duck foods. Freshwater Biology 4:281–292.

Drobney, R. D., and L. H. Fredrickson. 1979. Food selection by Wood Ducks in relation to breeding status. Journal of Wildlife Management 43:109–120.

Dwyer, T. J., G. L. Krapu, and D. M. Janke. 1979. Use of prairie pothole habitat by breeding Mallards. Journal of Wildlife Management 43:526–531.

Dzinbal, K. A., and R. L. Jarvis. 1982. Coastal feeding ecology of Harlequin Ducks in Prince William Sound, Alaska, during summer. Pages 6–10 *in* D. N. Nettleship, G. A. Sanger, and P. F. Springer, editors. Marine birds: their feeding ecology and commercial fisheries relationships. Canadian Wildlife Service Special Publication, Ottawa.

Euliss, N. H., Jr., R. L. Jarvis, and D. S. Gilmer. 1997. Relationship between waterfowl nutrition and condition on agricultural drainwater ponds in the Tulare Basin, California: waterfowl body condition. Wetlands 17:106–115.

Feltham, M. J. 1995. Consumption of Atlantic salmon smolts and parr by Gooseanders: estimates from doubly-labelled water measurements of captive birds released on two Scottish rivers. Journal of Fish Biology 46:273–281.

Fischer, J. B., and C. R. Griffin. 2000. Feeding behavior and food habits of wintering Harlequin Ducks at Shemya Island, Alaska. Wilson Bulletin 112:318–325.

Fredrickson, L. H., and F. A. Reid. 1988. Nutritional values of waterfowl foods. U.S. Fish and Wild life Service, Fish and Wildlife Leaflet 13.1.1.

Fredrickson, L. H., and T. S. Taylor. 1982. Management of seasonally flooded impoundments for wildlife. U.S. Fish and Wildlife Service Resource Publication 148.

Frith, H. J. 1967. Waterfowl in Australia. Angus & Robertson, Sydney.

Gaines, W. L., and R. E. Fitzner. 1987. Winter diet of Harlequin Duck at Sequim Bay, Puget Sound, Washington. Northwest Science 61:213–215.

Gauthier, G. 1993. Feeding ecology of nesting Greater Snow Geese. Journal of Wildlife Management 57:216–223.

Gollop, J. B., and W. H. Marshall. 1954. A guide for aging duck broods in the field. Mississippi Flyway Council Technical Section (unpublished mimeo).

Goodman, D. C., and H. I. Fisher. 1962. Functional anatomy of the feeding apparatus in waterfowl (Aves: Anatidae). Southern Illinois University Press, Carbondale.

Grant, T. A., P. Hensen, and J. A. Cooper. 1994. Feeding ecology of Trumpeter Swans breeding on south central Alaska. Journal of Wildlife Management 58:774–780.

Grant, T. A., P. Hensen, and J. A. Cooper. 1997. Feeding behavior of Trumpeter Swans *Cygnus buccinator*. Wildfowl 48:6–15.

Hamilton, D. J., C. D. Ankney, and R. C. Bailey. 1994. Predation of zebra mussels by diving ducks: an exclosure study. Ecology 75:521–531.

Hamilton, D. J., T. D. Nudds, and J. Neate. 1999. Size-selective predation of blue mussels (*Mytilus edulis*) by Common Eiders (*Somateria mollissima*) under controlled field conditions. Auk 116:403–416.

Haramis, G. M., D. G. Jorde, S. A. Macko, and J. L. Walker. 2001. Stable-isotope analysis of Canvasback winter diet in upper Chesapeake Bay. Auk 118:1008–1017.

Haukos, D. A., and L. M. Smith. 1995. Chemical composition of seeds from plants in playa wetlands. Wildlife Society Bulletin 23:514–519.

Heinrich, J. W., and S. R. Craven. 1990. Evaluation of three damage abatement techniques for Canada Geese. Wildlife Society Bulletin 18:405–410.

Heitmeyer, M. E., D. P. Connelly, and R. L. Pederson. 1989. The Central, Imperial, and Coachella Valleys of California. Pages 475–505 *in* L. M. Smith, R. L. Pederson, and R. M. Kaminski, editors. Habitat management for migrating and wintering waterfowl in North America. Texas Tech University Press, Lubbock.

Hobaugh, W. C. 1985. Body condition and nutrition of Snow Geese wintering in southeastern Texas. Journal of Wildlife Management 49:1028–1037.

Hoffman, R. D., and T. A. Bookhout. 1985. Metabolizable energy of seeds consumed by ducks in Lake Erie marshes. Transactions of the North American Wildlife and Natural Resources Conference 50:557–565.

Holm, E. R., and M. L. Scott. 1954. Studies on the nutrition of wild waterfowl. New York Fish and Game Journal 1:171–187.

Hupp, J. W., D. G. Robertson, and J. A. Schmutz. 2000. Recovery of tall cotton-grass following real and simulated feeding by Snow Geese. Ecogeography 23:367–373.

Hupp, J. W., R. G. White, J. S. Sedinger, and D. G. Robertson. 1996. Forage digestibility and intake by Lesser Snow Geese: effects of dominance and resource heterogeneity. Oecologia 108:232–240.

Ivlev, V. S. 1961. Experimental ecology of the feeding of fishes. Yale University Press, New Haven, Connecticut.

Jarvis, R. L., and J. H. Noyes. 1986. Foods of Canvasbacks and Redheads in Nevada: paired males and ducklings. Journal of Wildlife Management 50:199–203.

Johnson, D. H. 1980. The comparison of usage and availability measurements for calculating food preference. Ecology 61:65–71.

Jorde, D. G., and R. B. Owen, Jr. 1988. Efficiency of nutrient use by American Black Ducks wintering in Maine. Journal of Wildlife Management 52:209–214.

Junca, H. A., E. A. Epps, and L. L. Glasgow. 1962. A quantitative study of the nutrient content of food removed from the crops of wild Mallards in Louisiana. Transactions of the North American Wildlife and Natural Resources Conference 27:114–121.

Kaminski, R. M., J. B. Davis, H. W. Essig, P. D. Gerard, and K. J. Reinecke. 2003. True metabolizable energy for Wood Ducks from acorns compared to other waterfowl foods. Journal of Wildlife Management 67:542–550.

Kear, J. 1990. Man and waterfowl. T & A D Poyser, London.

Kenow, K. P., and D. H. Rusch. 1996. Food habits of Redheads at the Horicon Marsh, Wisconsin. Journal of Field Ornithology 67:649–659.

Knittle, C. E., and R. D. Porter. 1988. Waterfowl damage and control methods in ripening grain: an overview. U.S. Fish and Wildlife Service Technical Report 14.

Kovalak, W. P., G. D. Longton, and R. D. Smithee. 1993. Infestation of power plant water systems by the zebra mussel (Dreissena polymorpha). Pages 359–380 in T. F. Nalepa and D. W. Schloesser, editors. Zebra mussels biology, impacts, and control. Lewis Publishers, Boca Raton, Florida.

Krapu, G. L. 1974. Feeding ecology of Pintail hens during reproduction. Auk 91:278–290.

Krapu, G. L., D. A. Brandt, and R. R. Cox, Jr. 2004. Less waste corn, more land in soybeans, and the switch to genetically modified crops: trends with important implications for wildlife management. Wildlife Society Bulletin 32:127–136.

Krapu, G. L., G. C. Iverson, K. J. Reinecke, and C. M. Boise. 1985. Fat deposition and usage by arctic-nesting Sandhill Cranes during spring. Auk 102:362–368.

Krapu, G. L., A. T. Klett, and D. G. Jorde. 1983. The effect of variable spring water conditions on Mallard reproduction. Auk 100:689–698.

Krapu, G. L., and G. A. Swanson. 1975. Some nutritional aspects of reproduction in prairie nesting Pintails. Journal of Wildlife Management 39:156–162.

Krebs, H. A. 1964. Metabolic fate of amino acids. Pages 125-176 in H. N. Munro and J. Alison, editors. Mammalian protein metabolism. Academic Press, New York.

Landers, J. L., T. T. Fendley, and A. S. Johnson. 1977. Feeding ecology of Wood Ducks in South Carolina. Journal of Wildlife Management 41:118–127.

Lane, S. J., A. Azuma, and H. Higuchi. 1998. Wildfowl damage to agriculture in Japan. Agriculture, Ecosystems & Environment 70:69–77.

Latta, W. C., and R. F. Sharkey. 1966. Feeding behavior of the American Merganser in captivity. Journal of Wildlife Management 30:17–23.

Leach, J. H. 1993. Impacts of the zebra mussel (Dreissena polymorpha) on water quality and fish spawning reefs in the western Lake Erie. Pages 381–397 in T. F. Nalepa and D. W. Schloesser, editors. Zebra mussels biology, impacts, and control. Lewis Publishers, Boca Raton, Florida.

Loesch, C. R., and R. M. Kaminski. 1989. Winter body-weight patterns of female Mallards fed agricultural seeds. Journal of Wildlife Management 53:1081–1087.

Lovvorn, J. R., and M. P. Gillingham. 1996. Food dispersion and foraging energetics: a mechanistic synthesis for field studies of avian benthivores. Ecology 77:435–451.

Lovvorn, J. R., and D. R. Jones. 1991. Effects of body size, body fat, and change in pressure with depth on buoyancy and costs of diving in ducks (Aythya spp.). Canadian Journal of Zoology 69:2879–2887.

Lovvorn, J. R., D. R. Jones, and R. W. Blake. 1991. Mechanics of underwater locomotion in diving ducks: drag, buoyancy and acceleration in a size gradient of species. Journal of Experimental Biology 159:89–108.

Mabbott, D. C. 1920. Food habits of seven species of American shoal-water ducks. U.S. Department of Agriculture Bulletin 862.

Manley, S. W., R. M. Kaminski, K. J. Reinecke, and P. D. Gerard. 2004. Waterbird foods in winter-managed ricefields in Mississippi. Journal of Wildlife Management 68:74–83.

Marriott, R. W., and D. K. Forbes. 1970. The digestion of Lucerne chaff by Cape Barren Geese, Cereopsis novaehollandiae Latham. Australian Journal of Zoology 18:257–263.

Martin, A. C., and F. M. Uhler. 1939. Food of game ducks in the United States and Canada. U.S. Department of Agriculture Technical Bulletin 634.

Mathiasson, S. 1973. A moulting population of non-breeding Mute Swans with special reference to flight-feather moult, feeding ecology and habitat selection. Wildfowl 24:43–53.

McAtee, W. L. 1911. Three important wild duck foods. U.S. Bureau of Biological Survey Circular 81.

McAtee, W. L. 1914. Five important wild-duck foods. U.S. Department of Agriculture Bulletin 58.

McAtee, W. L. 1915. Eleven important wild-duck foods. U.S. Department of Agriculture Bulletin 205.

McLandress, M. R., and D. G. Raveling. 1981. Changes in diet and body composition of Canada Geese before spring migration. Auk 98:65–79.

Meire, P. M. 1993. The impact of bird predation on marine and estuarine bivalve populations: a selective review of patterns and underlying causes. Pages 197–243 in R. F. Dame, editor. Bivalve filter feeders in estuarine and coastal ecosystem processes. NATO ASI Series G: Ecological Sciences, Volume 33.

Miller, M. R. 1987. Fall and winter foods of Northern Pintails in the Sacramento Valley, California. Journal of Wildlife Management 51:405–414.

Miller, M. R., and W. E. Newton. 1999. Population energetics of Northern Pintails wintering in the Sacramento Valley, California. Journal of Wildlife Management 63:1222–1238.

Miller, M. R., and K. J. Reinecke. 1984. Proper expression of metabolizable energy in avian energetics. Condor 86:396–400.

Miller, M. R., D. E. Sharp, D. S. Gilmer, and W. R. Mulvaney. 1989. Rice available to waterfowl in harvested fields in the Sacramento Valley, California. California Fish and Game 75:113–123.

Morowitz, H. J. 1978. Foundations of bioenergetics. Academic Press, New York.

Musacchio, L. R., and R. N. Coulson. 2001. Landscape ecological planning processes for wetland, waterfowl, and farmland conservation. Landscape and Urban Planning 56:125–147.

Nagel, J. 1965. Field feeding of Whistling Swans in northern Utah. Condor 67:446–447.

National Research Council. 1977. Nutrient requirements of poultry. National Academy of Sciences, Washington, D.C.

Naylor, M. 2004. Potential impacts of Mute Swans to SAV in Chesapeake Bay. Pages 36–37 in M. C. Perry, editor. Mute Swans and their Chesapeake Bay habitats: proceedings of a symposium. U.S. Geological Survey Information and Technology Report USGS/BRD/ITR — 2004–0005.

Nelms, C. O., and D. J. Twedt. 1996. Seed deterioration in flooded agricultural fields during winter. Wildlife Society Bulletin 24:85–88.

Newton, I. 1998. Bird conservation problems resulting from agricultural intensification in Europe. Pages 307–322 in J. M. Marzluff and R. Sallabanks, editors. Avian conservation: research and management. Island Press, Washington, D.C.

Noyes, J. H., and R. L. Jarvis. 1985. Diet and nutrition of breeding female Redhead and Canvasback ducks in Nevada. Journal of Wildlife Management 49:203–211.

Nyström, K. G., and O. Pehrsson. 1988. Salinity as a constraint affecting food and habitat choice in mussel-feeding diving ducks. Ibis 130:94–110.

Nyström, K. G., O. Pehrsson, and D. Broman. 1991. Food of juvenile Common Eiders (Somateria mollissima) in areas of high and low salinity. Auk 108:250–256.

Olney, P. J. S. 1963. The food and feeding habits of Tufted Duck Aythya fuligula. Ibis 105:55–62.

Owen, M. 1976. Factors affecting the distribution of geese in the British Isles. Wildfowl 27:143–147.

Owen, M. 1977. The role of wildfowl refuges on agricultural land in lessening the conflict between farmers and geese in Britain. Biological Conservation 11:209–222.

Owen, M. 1980. Wild geese of the world: their life history and ecology. B T Batsford, London.

Owen, M., and C. J. Cadbury. 1975. The ecology and mortality of swans at the Ouse Washes, England. Wildfowl 26:31–42.

Owen, M., and J. Kear. 1972. Food and feeding habits. Pages 57–87 in P. Scott, editor. The swans. Houghton Mifflin, Boston.

Patterson, J. H. 1992. The need for crop damage mitigation in North American waterfowl conservation. International Waterfowl and Wetlands Research Bureau Special Publication 21:53–58.

Paulus, S. L. 1982. Feeding ecology of Gadwalls in Louisiana in winter. Journal of Wildlife Management 46:71–79.

Paulus, S. L. 1984. Activity budgets of nonbreeding Gadwalls in Louisiana. Journal of Wildlife Management 48:371–380.

Pennak, R. W. 1989. Fresh-water invertebrates of the United States: protozoa to mollusca. Third edition. John Wiley & Sons, New York.

Perry, M. C., editor. 2004. Mute Swans and their Chesapeake Bay habitats: proceedings of a symposium. U.S. Geological Survey Information and Technology Report USGS/BRD/ITR — 2004–0005.

Petersen, M. R., and D. C. Douglas. 2004. Winter ecology of Spectacled Eiders: environmental characteristics and population change. Condor 106:79–94.

Petersen, M. R., W. W. Larned, and D. C. Douglas. 1999. At-sea distribution of Spectacled Eiders: a 120-year-old mystery resolved. Auk 116:1009–1020.

Petersen, M. R., J. F. Piatt, and K. A. Trust. 1998. Foods of Spectacled Eiders *Somateria fischeri* in the Bering Sea, Alaska. Wildfowl 49:124–128.

Petrie, M. J., R. D. Drobney, and D. A. Graber. 1998. True metabolizable energy estimates of Canada Goose foods. Journal of Wildlife Management 62:1147–1152.

Quinlan, E. E., and G. A. Baldassarre. 1984. Activity budgets of nonbreeding Green-winged Teal on playa lakes in Texas. Journal of Wildlife Management 48:838–845.

Rave, D. P., and G. A. Baldassarre. 1989. Activity budget of Green-winged Teal wintering in coastal wetlands of Louisiana. Journal of Wildlife Management 53:753–759.

Raveling, D. G. 1979. The annual energy cycle of the Cackling Canada Goose. Pages 81–93 *in* R. I. Jarvis and J. C. Bartonek, editors. Management and biology of Pacific Flyway geese. OSU Book Stores, Corvallis, Oregon.

Reinecke, K. J. 1979. Feeding ecology and development of juvenile Black Ducks in Maine. Auk 96:737–745.

Reinecke, K. J., R. M. Kaminski, D. J. Moorhead, J. D. Hodges, and J. R. Nassar. 1989. Mississippi Alluvial Valley. Pages 203–247 *in* L. M. Smith, R. L. Pederson, and R. M. Kaminski, editors. Habitat management for migrating and wintering waterfowl in North America. Texas Tech University Press, Lubbock.

Reinecke, K. J., and G. L. Krapu. 1986. Feeding ecology of Sandhill Cranes during spring migration in Nebraska. Journal of Wildlife Management 50:71–79.

Robbins, C. T. 1993. Wildlife feeding and nutrition. Second edition. Academic Press, New York.

Robert, M., and L. Cloutier 2001. Summer food habits of Harlequin Ducks in eastern North America. Wilson Bulletin 113:78–84.

Rollo, J. D., and E. G. Bolen. 1969. Ecological relationships of Blue and Green-winged Teal on the High Plains of Texas in early fall. Southwestern Naturalist 14:171–188.

Rundel, P. W., J. R. Ehleringer, and K. A. Nagy. 1989. Stable isotopes in ecological research. Springer-Verlag, New York.

Schaible, P. 1970. Poultry: feeds and nutrition. Avi Publishing, Westport, Connecticut.

Schmidt-Nielsen, K. 1979. Animal physiology: adaptation and environment. Cambridge University Press, Cambridge.

Schmidt-Nielsen, K., and Y. T. Kim. 1964. The effect of salt intake on the size and function of the salt gland of ducks. Auk 81:160–172.

Schorger, A. W. 1947. The deep diving of the loon and Old-Squaw and its mechanism. Wilson Bulletin 59:151–159.

Schorger, A. W. 1951. Deep diving of the Old-Squaw. Wilson Bulletin 63:112.

Scott, M. L., F. W. Hill, E. H. Parson, Jr., and J. H. Bruchner. 1959. Studies on duck nutrition 7. Effect of dietary energy: protein relationships upon growth, feed utilization and carcass composition in market ducklings. Poultry Science 38:497–507.

Sedinger, J. S. 1984. Protein and amino acid composition of tundra vegetation in relation to nutritional requirements of geese. Journal of Wildlife Management 48:1128–1136.

Sedinger, J. S. 1997. Adaptations to and consequences of an herbivorous diet in grouse and waterfowl. Condor 99:314–326.

Sedinger, J. S., and D. G. Raveling. 1984. Dietary selectivity in relation to availability and quality of food for goslings of Cackling Geese. Auk 101:295–306.

Sedinger, J. S., R. G. White, and J. Hupp. 1995. Metabolizability and portioning of energy and protein in green plants by yearling Lesser Snow Geese. Condor 97:116–122.

Sedinger, J. S., R. G. White, F. E. Mann, F. A. Burris, and R. A. Kedrowski. 1989. Apparent metabolizability of alfalfa components by yearling Pacific Black Brant. Journal of Wildlife Management 53:726–734.

Sibbald, I. R. 1976. A bioassay for true metabolizable energy in feedingstuffs. Poultry Science 55:303–308.

Sibbald, I. R., and P. M. Morse. 1983. Provision of supplemental feed and the application of a nitrogen correction in bioassays for true metabolizable energy. Poultry Science 62:1587–1605.

Sjöberg, K. 1988. Food selection, food-seeking patterns and hunting success of captive Gooseanders *Mergus merganser* and Red breasted Mergansers *M. serrator* in relation to behaviour of their prey. Ibis 130:79–93.

Smith, A. G. 1969. Waterfowl–habitat relationships on the Lousana, Alberta, waterfowl study area. Pages 116-122 *in* Saskatoon wetlands seminar. Canadian Wildlife Service Report Series 6.

Smith, R. I. 1970. Response of Pintail breeding populations to drought. Journal of Wildlife Management 34:943–946.

Snell, R. R. 1985. Underwater flight of Long-tailed Duck (Oldsquaw) *Clangula hyemalis.* Ibis 127:267.

Southwick, C. 1953. A system of age classification for field studies of waterfowl broods. Journal of Wildlife Management 17:1–8.

Stafford, J. D., R. M. Kaminski, K. J. Reinecke, and S. W. Manley. 2006. Waste rice for waterfowl in the Mississippi Alluvial Valley. Journal of Wildlife Management 70:61–69.

Stephenson, R., J. R. Lovvorn, M. R. A. Heieis, D. R. Jones, and R. W. Blake. 1989. A hydromechanical estimate of the power requirements of diving and surface swimming in Lesser Scaup (*Aythya affinis*). Journal of Experimental Biology 147:507–519.

Stewart, R. E. 1962. Waterfowl populations in the upper Chesapeake region. U.S. Fish and Wildlife Service Special Scientific Report Wildlife 65.

Sturkie, P. D., editor. 1976. Avian physiology. Third edition. Springer-Verlag, New York.

Sugden, L. G. 1973a. Feeding ecology of Pintail, Gadwall, Amcrican Wigeon and Lesser Scaup ducklings. Canadian Wildlife Service Report Series 24.

Sugden, L. G. 1973b. Metabolizable energy of wild duck foods. Canadian Wildlife Service Progress Notes 35.

Sugden, L. G. 1976. Waterfowl damage to Canadian grain. Canadian Wildlife Service Occasional Paper 24.

Swanson, G. A., and J. C. Bartonek. 1970. Bias associated with food analysis in gizzards of Blue-winged Teal. Journal of Wildlife Management 34:739–746.

Swanson, G. A., G. L. Krapu, J. C. Bartonek, J. R. Serie, and D. H. Johnson. 1974. Advantages in mathematically weighting waterfowl food habits data. Journal of Wildlife Management 38: 302–307.

Swanson, G. A., G. L. Krapu, and J. R. Serie. 1979. Foods of laying female dabbling ducks on the breeding grounds. Pages 47-57 *in* T. A. Bookhout, editor. Waterfowl and wetlands — an integrated review. La Crosse Printing, La Crosse, Wisconsin.

Swanson, G. A., and M. I. Meyer. 1973. The role of invertebrates in the feeding ecology of Anatinae during the breeding season. Pages 143–177 *in* The waterfowl habitat management symposium. Moncton, New Brunswick.

Swanson, G. A., and M. I. Meyer. 1977. Impact of fluctuating water levels on feeding ecology of breeding Blue-winged Teal. Journal of Wildlife Management 41:426–433.

Swanson, G. A., M. I. Meyer, and V. A. Adomaitis. 1985. Foods consumed by breeding Mallards on wetlands of south-central North Dakota. Journal of Wildlife Management 49:197–203.

Swanson, G. A., and A. B. Sargeant. 1972. Observation of nighttime feeding behavior of ducks. Journal of Wildlife Management 36:959–961.

Systad, G. H., J. O. Bustness, and K. E. Erikstad. 2000. Behavioral responses to decreasing day length in wintering sea ducks. Auk 117:33–40.

Thomas, V. G., and J. P. Prevett. 1980. The nutritional value of arrow grasses to geese at James Bay. Journal of Wildlife Management 44:830-836.

Twedt, D. J., and C. O. Nelms. 1999. Waterfowl density on agricultural fields managed to retain water in winter. Wildlife Society Bulletin 27: 924–930.

Twedt, D. J., C. O. Nelms, V. E. Rettig, and S. R. Aycock. 1998. Shorebird use of managed wetlands in the Mississippi Alluvial Valley. American Midland Naturalist 140:140–152.

Van Soest, P. J. 1994. Nutritional ecology of the ruminant. Second edition. Comstock Publishing, Ithaca, New York.

Warner, R. E., S. P. Havera, and L. M. David. 1985. Effects of autumn tillage systems on corn and soybean harvest residues in Illinois. Journal of Wildlife Management 49:185–190.

Wetmore, A. 1921. Wild ducks and duck foods of the Bear River marshes, Utah. U.S. Department of Agriculture Bulletin 936.

Wishart, R. A. 1983. The behavioral ecology of the American Wigeon (*Anas americana*) over its annual cycle. Dissertation, University of Manitoba, Winnipeg.

Wood, C. C., and C. M. Hand. 1985. Food-searching behaviour of the Common Merganser (*Mergus merganser*) I: functional responses to prey and predator density. Canadian Journal of Zoology 63:1260–1270.

Chapter 6
NESTING, BROOD REARING, AND MOLTING

Waterfowl managers have long recognized that quality nesting cover is an essential component of waterfowl habitat. Waterfowl are a product of the land, however, which means the best populations are produced on the most productive landscapes, and those landscapes usually are endowed with the most productive soils. Unfortunately for waterfowl and other wildlife, humans compete for those same productive landscapes and soils, wherein prime habitat often has been usurped for agriculture. Consider a stunning example from the midwestern United States: In eastern Illinois and adjacent parts of Indiana, the original tallgrass, black-soil prairie once covered 5.3 million ha — today only 8 ha remain undisturbed, with the remainder converted to agriculture (Saunders et al. 1987). Indeed, the total area (162 million ha) of tallgrass prairie has declined in some areas by 99.9% since European settlement, which represents the greatest loss for any ecosystem in North America (Samson and Knopf 1994). Mixed prairie has fared little better, having also lost 99% of its former area in some locations; 85% of the shortgrass prairie no longer exists in its original form. Only 23% of historic native grassland remains in Canada's three prairie provinces — a key region for waterfowl production in North America — and less than 0.1% remains within those areas highly suited for agriculture (Samson and Knopf 1994). Overall, grassland ecosystems elsewhere around the globe have experienced similar losses to agricultural development. Regrettably, the conversion from native grasslands to agriculture usually includes draining wetland habitats (e.g., prairie potholes and sloughs), which for waterfowl results in the concurrent loss of both nesting and feeding habitat.

Management programs designed to provide nesting cover are varied, ranging from intensive manipulation of vegetation to policy-making decisions that affect regional or national land-use practices. Similar efforts have been directed to wetland habitat, which managers must consider in tandem with nesting cover in order to provide suitable breeding habitat. Considerable time, effort, and money also have been expended on programs that provide artificial nesting structures. In North America, for example, man-made boxes have played a critical role in the recovery of Wood Duck populations and illustrate one of the most notable success stories in wildlife management. Wood Ducks faced extinction early in the 20th century but have since returned to abundance, in large measure as a result of the thousands of nest boxes erected to replace natural cavities lost to logging and other habitat alterations (Bellrose 1990).

However, in contrast to the optimistic picture for Wood Ducks and a few other species that successfully nest in artificial structures, other ducks — especially those breeding in grassland habitats like the Prairie Pothole Region (PPR) of the United States and Canada — currently face severe losses of suitable nesting cover. With favorable conditions, the PPR produces about 50% of the annual fall flight of ducks, yet the area represents just 10% of the breeding habitat in North America (Smith et al. 1964). Still, the vast reduction of grasslands in the prairie states and provinces has become a major limiting factor for duck production in North America

A successfully hatched nest, however, is only the first step in the annual recruitment of waterfowl. Next comes the brood-rearing period, when young waterfowl run a gamut of demands ranging from avoiding predators to obtaining the high-protein foods necessary for rapid growth. Prior to attaining flight and their first breeding plumage, ducklings also undergo several molts that require specific nutritional needs. During the same period, adult waterfowl likewise face the energetic demands and ecological risks of molting. In this chapter we examine the basic ecology of nesting, rearing broods, and molting by waterfowl.

WATERFOWL NESTING ECOLOGY

As might be expected, the many species of waterfowl vary in their selection of nesting habitat, nesting chronology, minimum age for breeding, and renesting potential. Neither space nor our intent warrants a review of these features for each species; readers should consult other sources for species-specific information: for North America, Johnsgard (1975) and Bellrose (1980); for Europe, Owen (1980) and Ogilve (1982); for Australia, Frith (1967); life-history accounts of all species of anatids appear in Johnsgard (1978) and Kear (2005). Instead, we highlight some of the general principles concerning these events in the life history and life cycle of waterfowl.

Nest Sites of Waterfowl

Nesting habitat for waterfowl can be divided into three broad categories: (1) tree cavities, including nest boxes; (2) uplands such as grasslands, brushlands, or agricultural lands; and (3) vegetation over water (e.g., cattails, *Typha* spp.; bulrushes, *Scirpus* spp.). Generally, species restrict their choices to a single category, but some may select two or more of these types. The Black-bellied Whistling-Duck, for example, commonly nests both in cavities and on the ground in uplands (Bolen 1967, Markum and Baldassarre 1989). Mallards typically nest in upland communities but also readily nest in emergent vegetation (Krapu et al. 1979) and artificial structures (Doty and Lee 1974). In Australia, the Gray Duck nests on the ground, in tree cavities, and even in the deserted nests of ibises and other waterbirds (Frith 1967). Wood Ducks typically nest in natural or artificial cavities, but there are rare records of Wood Ducks nesting on the ground (Mason and Dusi 1983, Zipko and Kennington 1977, McIlquham and Bacon 1989).

The Common Shelduck exhibits one of the most unique choices of nest site among waterfowl. On the island of Sheppy in northern Kent, United Kingdom, Hori (1964) reported that Common Shelducks chose "any site with a hole or space beneath it." Some 25% of all nests were in European rabbit (*Oryctolagus*

cuniculus) burrows, and rabbits and Shelducks commonly competed for burrows; concurrent use of single burrow by two female Shelducks was not uncommon. The Normans introduced rabbits to England in the 12th century as a source of meat and fur. The Cape Shelduck, an endemic of semiarid regions of southern Africa (e.g., the Karoo), is even more unique in its choice of nest sites. This species almost always nests in a burrow, frequently those of the aardvark (*Orycteropus afer*) or another mammal, and far from water. Within the burrow, the nest itself may be as far as 8 m from the entrance hole (Clancey 1967).

Canada Geese are among the species having a broad range in their selection of nest sites, especially within the general category "upland." In wetland settings, Canada Geese often select islands or lodges built by muskrats (*Ondatra zibethicus*) because of the good visibility of the surrounding terrain afforded by these sites (Kaminski and Prince 1977; Fig. 6-1), but Canada Geese also build nests over water in emergent vegetation and readily use

Figure 6-1. Canada Geese often select nest sites where clear visibility of the surrounding terrain aids in the detection of approaching predators. This Canada Goose is nesting atop a muskrat house at the Montezuma National Wildlife Refuge in New York. Photo courtesy of the Montezuma National Wildlife Refuge.

artificial structures (Naylor and Hunt 1954). Regardless of intra- and interspecific variation, however, the first step of management is to understand the general pattern used by waterfowl to select their nest locations. Obviously, little is accomplished by managing grassland habitats if the target species nests over water.

Upland Nesting Sites: Most dabbling ducks and many pochards nest in upland habitats of grassland, shrub, or forest. The numerous studies of upland-nesting waterfowl in North America reveal wide variations in the selection of cover in relation to local conditions. In central North Dakota, for example, 42% of Mallard nests and 35% of Gadwall nests were located in patches of western snowberry (*Symphoricarpos occidentalis*) and/or Wood's rose (*Rosa woodsii*), yet these plants made up only 2% of the available cover (Duebbert et al. 1986). In contrast, Mallards in southeastern Alberta preferred rush (*Juncus* spp.) communities for nesting cover (Keith 1961). In still further contrast, fully 66% of the Mallards nesting in the Missouri Coteau of south-central North Dakota selected wetland sites in stands of dense emergent vegetation as opposed to upland sites (Krapu et al. 1979).

Despite such variability, however, a few general principles emerge as guides for management. Perhaps foremost is that waterfowl nesting in grassland habitats experience the best nesting success where the cover presents the greatest physical barrier to the movements of predators (Duebbert 1969). A study in South Dakota dramatically illustrates the point: 71% of the duck nests hatched in heavy cover, whereas only 45% success occurred in light cover (Schranck 1972; Fig. 6-2). During a 3-year study in southern Saskatchewan, nesting success for four species of ducks was compared between plots of dense nesting cover and unmanaged plots (McKinnon and Duncan 1999). Nest success was twice as great (15%) in dense nesting cover than in the unmanaged plots (7%). Overall, these and other studies document that better cover improves nest success. We emphasize here that vegetative structure — community physiognomy — is of greater importance than the actual species of plants as an agent for reducing the effects of predators. Nesting success also improves in habitats where spatial heterogeneity is increased, because predators must expend more time searching for nests (Bowman and Harris 1980). Moreover, management that improves spatial heterogeneity enriches diversity within the local wildlife community — butterflies, songbirds, and many other spe-

Figure 6-2. An example of dense nesting cover (DNC), measured here with a Robel cover board. The dominant plants are intermediate wheatgrass (*Agropyron intermedium*) and tall wheatgrass (*A. elongatum*). Photo courtesy of the U.S. Fish and Wildlife Service.

cies — a result with social as well as ecological benefits.

Nest success also generally increases with an increase in patch size. For example, Duncan (1987) reported a 64% nest success rate for Northern Pintails on unbroken, grazed prairie in Alberta. However, the relationship between patch size and nesting success is complex and can be confounded with the effects of other factors such as predator communities, nest density, and matrix of wetlands and uplands surrounding a given patch (see Clark and Nudds 1991). Further, patch size may have to reach some threshold before an increase in nest success becomes apparent. For example, Clark and Nudds (1991) doubled the area of dense nesting cover from 100 to 200 ha on a study site in Saskatchewan, but duck nest success did not increase. In a reanalysis of data presented by Duebbert and Lokemoen (1976), Clark and Nudds (1991) found no correlation between patch size and nesting success for patches of 12–54 ha.

Sovada et al. (2000) addressed the question of patch size and duck nest success with a well-designed, spatially and temporally replicated study that spanned 3 years (1993–95) and three states in the PPR, but the results demonstrated the difficulties of providing answers. Patches of nesting cover on lands enrolled in the Conservation Reserve Program were selected from 141 41.4 km²-areas and grouped into three size categories: (1) 32 ha or less, (2) 33–130 ha, and (3) more than 130 ha. In addition, indices of activity were calculated for major nest predators, and nest-initiation times were categorized as early or late. Resultant daily survival rates of duck nests were significantly greater for nests in large patches for one of six possible year × patch size comparisons, and the trend was similar for the remaining five. Success also depended on nest-initiation date and year. However, Sovada et al. (2000) also agreed with Clark and Nudds (1991) in that it was impractical to conduct the experiment needed to overcome environmental variation and thus conclusively test the patch-size hypothesis. For example, habitat conditions during the Sovada study rapidly transitioned from extremely dry to extremely wet, which affected predator populations as well as ducks. In some localities, rabies sharply reduced striped skunk (*Mephitis mephitis*) populations. Nonetheless, they suggested that landscapes with a mix of wetlands and grasslands configured in relatively large tracts are the most productive for nesting ducks, whereas small, isolated tracts of nesting habitat provide only marginal value, unless concerted efforts are undertaken to reduce predator populations.

However, the effect of patch size on nest success can also be influenced by the composition of the landscape. For example, Phillips et al. (2003) used radiotelemetry to evaluate habitat preferences of two major predators of duck nests — the red fox (*Vulpes vulpes*) and striped skunk — to determine how their choices might affect nest success in grassland cover. The study selected two 42.4-km² areas in North Dakota containing either low amounts of perennial grassland cover (15–20%) or high amounts of perennial grassland cover (45–55%). In either landscape, striped skunks usually selected wetland edges surrounded by agriculture. In contrast, red foxes generally preferred the more isolated patches of cover in low grassland landscapes. In the high grassland landscape, however, red foxes frequently selected the edges of the planted cover and less often visited the interior. Red foxes also selected core areas of planted cover more frequently in the low grassland landscape compared with the high grassland landscape, where they selected pastureland more frequently. Overall, nesting success was greater in the high grassland landscape, perhaps because the foraging efficiency of red foxes for duck nests was reduced by the increased amount of interior cover associated with larger patch sizes and the greater use of pastureland as alternate foraging sites. These results thus were important in supporting efforts to restore large blocks of nesting cover, but also demonstrated the potential effects of alternative cover types (i.e., pastureland) as a factor that might mitigate nest predation. Hence, the effects of grassland restoration efforts may be greatest when focused on areas already characterized by a high percentage of grasslands, including pastures.

Overall, the relationship between patch size and nest success is especially important in the PPR of North America because intensive agriculture has reduced both the quality and quantity of nesting cover over large areas. Indeed, as early as the mid-1950s, an estimated 72% of all uplands in the PPR of Canada had been converted to cereal grain production, and nearly all the remainder was grazed by livestock (Lynch et al. 1963). Much of this habitat loss was fueled by government programs in both Canada and the United States that provided subsidies for tillage and wetland drainage as well as by price supports for crops. Regardless of the ultimate cause, the proximate effect of practices that lead to "clean farming" spawns severe consequences for duck production. The PPR of North America provides, by far, the best documented example of the effects of agricultural development on waterfowl populations in general and nesting populations of ducks in particular, which is the topic of the following discussion.

Historically, Kalmbach (1939) reported an average nesting success of 60% based on 22 studies conducted across the United Sates in the early 1900s. For ducks nesting on two national wildlife refuges in the Pacific Flyway, nesting success reached 85% (Rienecker and Anderson 1960), which was well above the low nesting success now observed across the PPR. Between 1966 and 1984, for example, overall nesting success for Mallards and four other species of dabbling ducks in the PPR areas of North Dakota, South Dakota, and Minnesota was less than 20% in many areas and less than 5% in some areas (Table 6-1; Klett et al. 1988). Over the 18-year period, nest success averaged 11.5% and never exceeded 19%. These studies must be compared with caution, however, because different methods were used to estimate nest success (see Analysis of Nest Success below).

Beauchamp et al. (1996a) adjusted for these differences in their assessment of whether nest success had actually declined over time across a large area of PPR in Canada and the United States. They compared 37 studies conducted at 67 sites between 1935 and 1992, which revealed that nest success had indeed declined during this period at all sites. Estimated mean nest success was 33% in 1935 (the first

Table 6-1. The estimated percent nest success of five species of dabbling ducks over a broad range of the Prairie Pothole Region from 1966 to 1984. Modified from Klett et al. (1988:436).

Region	Mallard	Gadwall	Blue-winged Teal	Northern Shoveler	Northern Pintail
Western Minnesota	5	10	16	1	6
Eastern North Dakota	5	11	12	5	7
Central North Dakota	10	18	16	19	13
Eastern South Dakota	10	23	27	15	5
Central South Dakota	19	25	29	36	19

year of analysis), 21% in 1955 (the first year of population surveys for breeding waterfowl), 15% in 1970 (beginning of a decade of high duck populations), and 10% in 1992 (the last year of analysis). Subsequent analysis (Drever et al. 2004) demonstrated that average nest success was more variable per year than originally reported, but the general pattern nonetheless still exhibited a decline from about 40% in the 1930s to 20% between 1950 and 1970, and then leveled-off in the early 1980s.

Other individual studies with large sample sizes and rigorous statistical designs continue to document low nest success in the PPR. In Saskatchewan, Alberta, and Manitoba, for example, a survey of 17 areas from 1982 to 1985 revealed a 12% (range = 2–29%) nest success per year for Mallards and, alarmingly, only 7 of 31 annual estimates of nest success on individual study areas reached 15% or more (Greenwood et al. 1987). Estimated recruitment — defined as the number of females fledged into the fall population divided by the number of females in the previous spring population — ranged from 0.04 to 0.94 on all study areas. Recruitment per year was 0.60 in 1982, 0.53 in 1983, 0.23 in 1984, and 0.46 in 1985. Overall numbers of young ducks produced on individual study areas ranged from 8 to 356 and, for all areas combined, averaged 166 in 1982, 231 in 1983, 50 in 1984, and 80 in 1985. Nest success rates also were low for other species examined during the study.

All told, these trends are especially alarming in light of population simulation models, which indicate that a 15% nest success is necessary to maintain Mallard populations in agricultural regions (Cowardin et al. 1985). Mammalian predators were the major cause of nest failure (54–85%), but farming operations destroyed 37% of the nests in crop-

lands and 27% of those in haylands. Generally, late-nesting species such as Blue-winged Teal and Northern Shovelers were more successful than early-nesting species such as Mallards and Northern Pintails; late-nesting species can take advantage of both residual and new plant growth for nesting cover, whereas only residual vegetation from the previous growing is season is available as cover for early-nesting species. This difference in nest success between early- and late-nesting species appears repeatedly in the literature (Greenwood et al. 1995; Beauchamp et al. 1996a, 1996b; McKinnon and Duncan 1999).

A broader study in the PPR of Canada recorded similar results for five species of dabbling ducks (Greenwood et al. 1995). Pooled annual nest success was 17% in 1982, 15% in 1983, 7% in 1984, and 14% in 1985; for individual species, nesting success was Mallard (11%), Gadwall (14%), Blue-winged Teal (15%), Northern Shoveler (12%), and Northern Pintail (7%). Overall, approximately 77% of all nests failed because of predation. Nest success decreased about 4% for each 10% increase in area of cropland, and local populations of ducks probably were not stable when cropland exceeded about 56% of the landscape. Despite temporal and spatial variations in these data, the trend was clear — large areas of the PPR in Canada are not producing sustainable populations of dabbling ducks.

Hoekman et al. (2002) revealed new insights about the role of nesting success as a factor affecting the growth rate for Mallard populations in the PPR. Nest success explained most (43%) of the population growth, followed by the survival of adult females during the breeding season (19%), and the survival of ducklings (14%). Survival at other times of the year accounted for only 9% of the variation in population growth. In contrast, Beauchamp et al.

(1996a) found that populations of Gadwalls and Northern Shovelers did not decline over time, despite a concurrent decline in nest success. Thus, for those species, nest success may not be causally related to population changes, which instead may be more affected by brood survival and annual survival rates.

The current situation in the PPR is perhaps best summarized by Greenwood et al. (1987), who agreed with Boyd (1985) that "marginal farming practices" probably represent the greatest threat to duck nesting habitat, the best of which — native grassland — was converted to cropland long ago. Their data showed that large native pastures containing brush provide the best nesting habitat remaining throughout much of Prairie Canada. Nevertheless, Greenwood et al. (1987) recognized that recruitment over a broad area of prairie Canada was too low to maintain current Mallard populations.

These reports of low nest success, however, are only a symptom — the underlying "disease" remains the massive destruction of habitat throughout the breeding range of most species. One only needs to consider a study that monitored 10,000 wetlands across the PPR of Canada from 1981 to 1985 (Turner et al. 1987). Initially, 57% of the basins and 74% of the margins were already degraded. During the study, however, the degradation of wetland margins increased to 82% in parkland habitat and to 89% in grasslands. Overall, the impact on basins increased to 59%, but peaked at 78% on ephemeral wetlands. In 1982, an even more extensive survey across the major duck-producing areas in Canada revealed that cultivation had claimed 83% of the tallgrass prairie, 84% of the shortgrass prairie, 78% of the mixed-grass prairie, and 80% of the aspen parklands (Millar 1986). Obviously, large duck populations cannot be sustained in the face of this onslaught to nesting habitat.

In the United States, conditions for nesting habitat are even worse in much of the PPR. Higgins (1977) reported that 84% of the landscape in parts of North Dakota is cultivated; this impact, when coupled with the nest failures caused by predators and farm machinery, suggested that nesting success was not high enough to maintain duck populations, much less produce increases. Cowardin et al. (1985) supported this contention, based on an intensive study of Mallard recruitment in North Dakota from 1977 to 1980. They marked 235 female Mallards with radio transmitters and found that overall nest success was only 8%; individual females averaged only 15% success (for the latter, success was defined as the probability that a female would produce one successful nest in one or more attempts in a given year). On average,

the recruitment rate was only 0.27 females entering the fall population, which, based on population models, predicted an annual population decline of 20%! For comparison, a stable population would require an estimated nest success of 15% and, for individual females, success of 31%.

Nesting success for ducks in the Yukon Flats in central Alaska, where habitats are virtually pristine in comparison with the PPR, was still low and varied from almost 0 to only 12% (Grand 1995). These data suggested that nest predation severely limited duck production on the Yukon Flats just as it did in much of the PPR. Similarly, during a 3-year study on the Yukon-Kuskokwim Delta in Alaska — another virtually pristine environment — nest success for Northern Pintails was low in 1992 (18%) and 1993 (11%), but not 1991 (43%); overall success was 24%. Predation accounted for most of the lost nests (36–70%), followed by flooding, which destroyed a high of 15% in 1991 (Flint and Grand 1996).

Overall, the results — poor nest success and substantial female mortality — from the PPR of North America are not too surprising, given the staggering alteration of habitat that has occurred in this ecosystem. Still, marked spatial and temporal variations occur in the data for nest success and female survival across the huge PPR. Drever et al. (2004) noted that duck nest success is affected by many variables, including the quality of upland and wetland habitat, climate, and duck and predator densities. Certainly these parameters might interact in ways that create variable results, wherein nest success fluctuates in metapopulation fashion (sources and sinks; Pulliam 1988). Duck populations therefore persist and even increase, even though nest success and survival may be very low at local scales. Flint and Grand (1996) postulated just such a scenario based on their work with Northern Pintails in Alaska, where their study area covered only a miniscule (27.4 km^2) part of the Yukon-Kuskokwim Delta. They accordingly proposed that nest success could vary greatly within geographic areas wherein much of the annual production might originate from localized "hot spots." In North Dakota, for example, nest success was merely 2% at a study area predominately occupied by red foxes compared with 32% in an area where coyotes (*Canis latrans*) were the dominate predator— the two areas were 5 km apart (Sovada et al. 1995).

Overwater Nests: Because only a few kinds of emergent plants form dense cover, waterfowl that construct their nests over water have somewhat fewer sites to choose from in comparison with those species that nest in upland habitats. Among pochards, Canvasbacks generally choose hardstem bulrush (*Scirpus acutus*), cattails, burreed (*Sparganium* spp.), or sedges (*Carex* spp.) that extend 15–61 cm above water (see Bellrose 1980). Redheads also typically select stands of hardstem bulrush, cattails, and sedges (Low 1945).

Dabbling ducks at times also readily nest over water. In North Dakota, 66% of 53 Mallard nests located by following radiomarked females were situated in wetland vegetation, where nest success was higher (54%) than nests in upland areas (14%; Krapu et al. 1979). Similarly, wetland vegetation ranked second in the nesting habitat selected by 142 female Mallards marked with radios in North Dakota (Cowardin et al. 1985). These data challenge traditional ideas by demonstrating that wetland habitats are important nesting sites for many species of waterfowl — not just pochards — and thus should be considered in management programs, especially given the massive loss and deterioration of upland nesting habitat. Indeed, nest success of overwater Mallard nests in Manitoba (44%) was three times greater than the threshold of 15% needed for annual population stability (Cowardin et al. 1985), whereas the rate in uplands (12%) was slightly below this level (Arnold et al. 1993). Further, because about 50% of all nests were placed over water, this habitat can be providing a disproportionate amount of the Mallard productivity in a given year. The nest success rate for Mallards nesting overwater was similar to pochards (Canvasback and Redhead) nesting in the same study area (Sorenson 1991), which again underscores the importance of emergent vegetation as nesting cover in highly altered grassland habitats like the PPR.

These findings raise the question of whether the pressures of habitat loss in uplands, poor nesting success, and high female mortality might cause dabbling ducks to favor nesting sites in wetland habitats. Hence, in the relative safety of wetland habitats, nest densities may increase steadily because female ducks "home" to areas where they were previously successful (see Chapter 3). During a 7-year study in Poland, the homing rate of successfully nesting female Mallards was 34%, compared with just 16% for unsuccessful females (Majewski and Beszterda 1990). In North Dakota, more successfully nesting female Mallards and Gadwalls returned the following year to the same nesting area than did unsuccessful females (Lokemoen et al. 1990).

Cavity Nests: Although most studies of cavity-nesting waterfowl concern management opportunities with constructed boxes, a wealth of information also addresses the ecology of natural cavities as nesting habitat. Generally, nesting success is higher for species using cavities in comparison with those waterfowl nesting in other settings (e.g., uplands) and, indeed, often approaches 100% in nest boxes equipped with predator guards. In Illinois, nest success of Wood Ducks using natural cavities was 64% (note contrast with the PPR), which was higher than reported elsewhere (40%), but less than the success in nest boxes (see Ryan et al. 1998). Soulliere's (1990a) review of nest-cavity characteristics for Wood Ducks forms the basis for much of the information presented here.

Most (90%) suitable cavities occur in living trees, with 60% or more of all cavities originating from broken branches or heart rot. Completely dead trees, although sometimes replete with cavities, seldom remain erect long enough to provide dependable nesting sites year after year, but a few species with particularly durable wood may be unusually persistent (e.g., baldcypress, *Taxodium distichum*). Trees containing suitable cavities usually are more than 30 cm dbh (diameter at breast height), and commonly near 60 cm dbh. Densities of suitable cavities in hardwood forests have ranged from 0.11 to 5.50/ha. Trees important for cavity formation vary from north to south and include aspen (*Populus* spp.), maple (*Acer* spp.), American basswood (*Tilia americana*), elm (*Ulmus* spp.), sycamore (*Platanus occidentalis*), American beech (*Fagus grandifolia*), oak (*Quercus* spp.), willow (*Salix* spp.), tupelo (*Nyssa* spp.), and baldcypress. In Indiana, American beech, red maple, and sycamore produced 72% of the suitable cavities but composed only 28% of the total basal area of trees; Wood Ducks nested in only 7–9% of the suitable cavities (Robb and Bookhout 1995).

Cavities are generally of two major types. Typical cavities have a side entrance, whereas bucket cavities have a top entrance; the former are more commonplace. Wood Ducks select cavities that are 2–17 m above the ground and seem to prefer the higher sites. Wood Ducks used cavities with entrances ranging in size from 6 × 10 cm (Haramis 1975) to as large as 30 × 60 cm (Bellrose et al. 1964), but females most often select the smallest entrance through which they can move easily. In Minnesota, 26% of the cavity nests were located at least 1.0 km from water (Gilmer et al. 1978); in Indiana, Wood Ducks used cavities that were 0.0–1.2 km from brood habitat (Robb and Bookhout 1995); in Illinois, Wood

Ducks used cavities at upland sites that averaged 1.41 km from water (Ryan et al. 1998). In Indiana, distance to water was greater for successful nests (122 m) compared with unsuccessful nests (50 m; Robb and Bookhout 1995). Fox squirrels (*Sciurus niger*) and raccoons (*Procyon lotor*) were important competitors for cavities, and nest success (22%) was limited by raccoon predation.

Although the number of suitable cavities seems low at first glance, hardwood forests cover about 97 million ha in the eastern United States. Thus, using this area and an estimate of 0.6 cavities/ha — as determined from several studies — Soulliere (1990a) calculated that some 60 million cavities potentially suitable as nest sites occur in the eastern United States. The highest reported cavity density (5.5/ha) was from virgin hardwoods in a floodplain forest in New Brunswick, where the average cavity tree was 230 years old (Prince 1968). In contrast, cavity density in second growth forest in Wisconsin was only 0.65/ha (Soulliere 1988). In two mature bottomland hardwood forests of Mississippi, the density of natural cavities ranged from 0.19 to 0.23/ha; at one site, sycamore and American beech contained 60% of the cavities but comprised only 2.6% of the available trees (Lowney and Hill 1989). In Illinois, natural cavities averaged 2.12/ha (Yetter et al. 1999), many of which were excavated by Pileated Woodpeckers (*Dryocopus pileatus*). Pileated Woodpeckers are the only species in North America that regularly excavate large (more than 45 cm deep) cavities for nest or roost sites (Bull and Jackson 1995). Wood Ducks are secondary users of these cavities and aggressively compete with Pileated Woodpeckers for their use (Conner et al. 2001).

The geographical range of studies for cavity-nesting waterfowl extends from Common Goldeneyes in New Brunswick (Prince 1968) to Black-bellied Whistling-Ducks in southern Texas (Delnicki and Bolen 1975). In the latter study, 30% of the nests were located in cavities at least 500 m from water and, because the study concerned nesting habitat in Texas, the density of suitable cavities (1/7.8 ha) permits a comparison with cavity density in nesting areas farther north.

Analysis of Nest Success: We briefly interject here that biologists have used various techniques and calculations for determining nest success; hence, results among studies are not always strictly comparable. Nonetheless, estimates of nest success are clearly essential to any understanding of avian demographics, and they are an excellent indicator of the effects of habitat on avian reproduction.

Early studies simply reported nest success as the proportion of nests that eventually hatched (i.e., all nests were treated as being at equal risk). This method is usually referred to as "apparent nest success" or "the traditional method" (Johnson 1979). However, the nests in a sample are not all located at the same time and, if the developmental history of each nest is not considered in the calculations, the results may bias estimates of predation. To illustrate, a nest located in midincubation has a greater probability of hatching compared with a nest located after only one egg is laid. Because such differences are of both biological and statistical significance, most studies now report nest success using what is known as the Mayfield Method, which takes into account the length of time each nest is exposed to predation (Mayfield 1961, 1975).

The Mayfield Method uses the time a nest is under observation (exposure days) as a key factor in calculating a daily survival rate (DSR), wherein

$$DSR = \frac{\text{number of failed nests}}{\text{number of exposure days.}}$$

The estimate of nest survival over the entire nesting period is calculated by raising the DSR to the power equivalent of the average number of days (d) in the nesting period. Thus, nest survival = $(DSR)^d$. Green (1989) later developed a method to transform the results from early studies of nest success for comparison with Mayfield estimates.

The Mayfield Method represented a major advance in the analysis of nest-success data, and the method has been refined since its introduction, particularly to address the assumption that daily survival rates remain constant throughout the nesting period. Dinsmore et al. (2002) developed program MARK (White and Burnham 1999) to evaluate nest survival in relation to biologically meaningful factors such as nest age and weather conditions. Jehle et al. (2004) provide a thorough review of alternatives to the Mayfield Method and compare the Mayfield Method with program MARK. Shaffer (2004) proposed a new way to analyze nesting data. His approach uses a general linear model that yields results similar to the methods of Mayfield and Dinsmore et al. (2002), but the model allows much greater flexibility for assessing the importance of predictors of nest success.

Methods have also been developed to estimate nest initiation attempts, which may be underreported in radiotelemetry studies. For example, McPherson et al. (2003) estimated that female Mallards nesting in Alberta initiated 1.91 nests/female compared with an observed rate of 1.41 (about 25% less).

Nesting Chronology

Nesting chronology varies intraspecifically wherein each species at a particular latitude generally can be categorized as either an "early" or "late" nester. For example, Canada Geese are among the earliest of all birds to nest in the spring; nesting begins in mid-March in Missouri (Brakhage 1965), yet may not start until early April in southern Wisconsin (Collias and Jahn 1959). Still farther north, on the McConnell River in northern Manitoba, Canada Geese may not initiate nesting until June (MacInnes et al. 1974). Nevertheless, at each site, the Canada Goose is an "early nester" relative to other waterfowl nesting at the same latitude. Other early-nesting species include Mallards and Northern Pintails, whereas Lesser Scaup and Gadwall represent late-nesting species. However, weather conditions can cause intraspecific variation in nesting chronology at a particular latitude, as Sowls (1955) found during his pioneering studies of dabbling ducks nesting in Manitoba. An abnormally cold spring delayed nesting by about 2 weeks compared with a spring when temperatures were near normal, a finding widely supported in subsequent literature on nesting dabbling ducks and pochards (see Langford and Driver 1979).

Many studies have investigated the effects of the spring environment on the nesting phenology of northern nesting geese (Raveling 1978). Raveling proposed that geese nesting at high latitudes, as well as species with periods of long incubation and gosling development, actually begin egg development (rapid follicle growth; see Chapter 4) during spring migration and can therefore initiate nesting soon after arriving on their breeding areas. For example, Ross's Geese nesting in the Perry River areas of the Northwest Territories (67°22′N, 102°10′W) and Lesser Snow Geese nesting at Southampton Island in Hudson Bay begin nesting soon (3 days) after arrival to breeding areas (see Raveling 1978). However, this strategy can greatly reduce reproduction during unusually late springs if nest sites are not available by the time follicle development is completed, and for this reason massive nest failures have occurred in Lesser Snow Geese (see Cooch 1961, Raveling 1978).

In contrast, geese nesting at lower latitudes, or requiring less time for incubation and gosling growth,

demonstrate a more conservative approach by delaying rapid follicle development until after departing from the final spring staging area or just after arrival to the breeding area. For example, Atlantic Brant nesting on Southampton Island in the Northwest Territories arrive in early June, regardless of the snow cover and progress of the spring thaw, and the period of peak nest initiation generally begins 10 days later, which was about the time needed for rapid follicle growth (Barry 1962). However, nesting was delayed 16 days during an unusually late spring, atretic (reabsorbed) follicles were detected in many geese, and clutch sizes were reduced for those Brant that did nest. Hence, snow cover may be a major proximate cue on the breeding area that affects reproductive output in some years. For example, temperature and snowfall conditions in May, which determine the timing of snow melt, were the best predictors of breeding success for Canada Geese in the Atlantic Population, which largely nests on the Ungava Peninsula in Quebec (Sheaffer and Malecki 1996). Black Brant nesting on the Yukon-Kuskokwim Delta in Alaska also initiated their nests 6–12 days after the date of peak arrival, regardless of spring weather conditions (Lindberg et al. 1997). However, Black Brant are unable to take full advantage of early springs, which reflects a cost of their strategy for follicle development. Similarly, Cackling Canada Geese nesting on the Yukon-Kuskokwim Delta also delayed nesting for 10–12 days after arrival, which is again about the time required for rapid follicle growth (see Raveling 1978).

During an 8-year study of Greylag Geese breeding in southern Sweden, marked pairs first appeared on the study area as late as 15 March in years with cold winters and as early as 6 February when the winters were mild (Nilsson and Persson 1994). Greylags initiated breeding 5–8 days after arrival, but the variation in arrival dates produced similar variations in the timing of reproduction. Specifically, the time between arrival on the breeding grounds and appearance of the first broods ranged from 52 to 65 days.

During a 13-year study of Tundra Swans nesting near the Kashunuk River in the Yukon-Kuskokwim Delta of Alaska, initiation of egg laying ranged from 1 to 27 May, and hatching dates ranged from 12 June to 4 July (Babcock et al. 2002). Both nest-initiation date and hatch date were highly correlated with the date when 90% of the uplands were snow-free (r = 0.95–0.96). Peak arrival was highly correlated (r = 0.89) with the date of ice break-up on the Kashunuk River.

Minimum Breeding Age and Breeding Propensity

The age at which females first breed is another feature that varies among species and in response to habitat conditions (e.g., wet or dry). Breeding ages influence reproductive performance and the lifetime output of each female. The general pattern is as follows: Dabbling ducks (Anatini) breed as yearlings (i.e., the first spring after hatching), most pochards (Aythyini) breed as 1- or 2-year-olds, sea ducks (Mergini) breed at 2 or 3 years, and swans and geese (Anserinae) also breed when 2 or 3 years old. However, there are many subtleties within these general patterns, and some exceptions.

Dabbling ducks, as noted, generally breed as yearlings, but several studies have discovered nonbreeding yearlings and, for those yearlings that do breed, reduced reproductive output in comparison to adult birds. Calverley and Boag (1977) examined reproductive tracts of Mallards and Northern Pintails (ages pooled) and reported nonbreeding rates of 5% in Alberta and 17% in the Northwest Territories. Yearlings likely comprised most of the nonbreeders. Among 90 female Wood Ducks marked as ducklings, 70 (78%) began reproduction as yearlings, 15 (17%) as 2-year-olds, and 5 (6%) as 3-year-olds (Oli et al. 2002). However, females that began reproduction as yearlings had shorter lifespans (2.54 years) than those delaying reproduction until at least their second year (4.25 years). In a study of radiomarked Mallards, only 44% of the yearlings were discovered on nests compared with 86% of the adults, again indicating that some yearlings likely did not breed (Losito et al. 1995). In North Dakota, the reproductive effort of radiomarked yearling Mallards was significantly different from adult birds: Yearling hens produced 0.92 nests/hen compared with 2.26 for adults, and hen success was 10.3% for yearlings against 18.6% for adults (Cowardin et al. 1985). Captive Mallards did not exhibit any age-related differences in reproductive performance, but captive birds are not subject to the same behavioral interactions or breeding experiences that accrue to wild birds (Batt and Prince 1978).

Among pochards, Afton (1984) reported 29% of yearlings and 10% of 2-year-old Lesser Scaup did not nest during a 4-year study in southeast Manitoba, but these rates varied in response to water conditions and ranged from 2.3 to 28.0% (Table 6-2). Reproductive performance generally increased with female age and water conditions. In contrast, Ring-necked Ducks regularly breed as yearlings (Mendall 1958). For other pochards, including Canvasbacks and Redheads, most yearlings likely breed, but the proportion of breeding yearlings declines when poor habitat conditions prevail. For example, during a 7-year study of Canvasbacks in southwestern Manitoba, yearling females did not nest during dry years, whereas all but one female nested during wet and moderately wet years (Serie et al. 1992). Yearling females achieved 52% nesting success compared with

Table 6-2. The relationship of age and reproductive parameters in ducks based on data from a study of Lesser Scaup in southwestern Manitoba. Modified from Afton (1984:258).

Parameter (means)	Female age (years)			
	1	2	3	4
Arrival date	129.1	127.0	132.2	122.8
Rate of nonbreeding (%)	29.3	9.6	0.0	0.0
Prelaying period	36.6	39.3	29.9	37.4
Nest-initiation date	171.1	165.5	162.8	163.4
Clutch size	9.0	10.0	10.9	12.1
Nest success (%)	26.3	22.2	45.5	41.7
Rate of renesting (%)	8.7	17.9	27.3	18.2
Brood survival	0.693	0.672	0.575	0.751

59% for adult females, but nest success was lower in dry years (17%) compared to moderately wet (54%) or wet years (60%). In another study, Anderson et al. (2001) recorded breeding probabilities of 0.54–0.94 for juvenile female Canvasbacks compared with 0.74–0.95 for adults, but breeding probabilities of juveniles were low during dry years.

In the Mergini, female Common Eiders delay nesting until they are at least 3 years old (Mendall 1968), whereas scoters and mergansers generally do not breed until 2 years old (see Bellrose 1980). Few data are available for shelducks and sheldgeese (Tadornini), but they appear to delay breeding until 2–3 years of age (see Johnsgard 1978).

For geese, the proportion of breeding females increases with age, but females normally do not nest until at least 2 years old; most individuals do not nest until 3–4 years of age or older (Owen 1980). A good example of age-specific reproduction was documented for Interior Canada Geese near Cape Churchill, Manitoba, where breeding effort was 7, 15, 40, 100, 95, and 94%, respectively, for 2-, 3-, 4-, 5-, 6-, and 7- or more year-old females (Moser and Rusch 1989). In the Flathead Valley of Montana, Canada Geese did not breed until 3 years of age (Craighead and Stockstad 1964).

As with ducks, geese exhibit a relationship between age and reproductive performance. In Giant Canada Geese nesting along the southeast shore of Lake Manitoba, Canada, 25% of the 2-year-old females raised broods averaging 2.3 young, whereas about 31% of 3–4-year olds raised broods averaging 2.9 young (Raveling 1981). In contrast, 58% of the older geese — those 4 or more years old — raised broods averaging 3.7 young. Overall, the older geese comprised just 26% of the potential breeding population but produced 50% of the young; the older birds also where twice as likely to raise at least one gosling to flying age than were younger age classes. Regardless of age, however, individuals successfully raising a brood were more than twice as likely to successfully raise a brood in ensuing years.

During a study of the lifetime reproductive success of Barnacle Geese at Svalbard, 3–40% of the pairs were successful in any given year; in this case, Owen and Black (1989a) defined successful breeding as marked adults accompanied by offspring on wintering areas. Only two females and six males raised more than five young in their lifetimes, and birds with proven reproductive success had a higher probability of continued success in the future than did unsuccessful breeders. Overall, the prob-

ability of a goose breeding over its lifetime was only 15.8%.

Blums and Clark (2004) studied the effect of female age and other factors on the lifetime reproductive success of three species of European ducks — Tufted Duck, Eurasian or Common Pochard, and Northern Shoveler — by examining a 22-year dataset of 1,279 individually marked ducks and their offspring. Late-hatched female Tufted Ducks and Common Pochards tended to delay nesting until 2-years old, but few females produced offspring that reached breeding age (Tufted Duck, 26%; Common Pochard, 29%; Northern Shoveler, 41%). Female Common Pochards that delayed nesting until 2-years old gained a slight advantage in lifetime reproductive success when compared with yearlings, but the other species did not show the same relationship. Overall, the number of breeding attempts was most strongly correlated with lifetime reproductive success, which was highest for early-nesting females, regardless of age. Interestingly, the number of fledged ducklings and lifetime reproductive success were related in the Tufted Duck, but weakly related in the Common Pochard, and not related in the Northern Shoveler. This finding led to a conclusion that the number of times a female produces ducklings is more important to lifetime reproductive success than the total number of ducklings a female produces because multiple production events increase the probability of encountering conditions suitable for duckling survival.

Renesting

Renesting occurs when a female initiates a new nest after an earlier clutch or brood (occasionally) is abandoned or destroyed — an aspect of waterfowl ecology that is fundamental to an understanding of waterfowl production. Bennett (1938) and Low (1945) were among the first to document renesting in waterfowl during their work with Blue-winged Teal and Redheads in Iowa. Sowls (1949, 1955) later studied renesting in prairie-nesting ducks on the Delta Marsh in Manitoba. These early studies noted that renests generally were characterized by a smaller clutch size than initial nests and often contained less down. Sowls (1955) also calculated that the renesting interval — the time period between loss of the first nest and laying the first egg in the second — increased by 0.62 days for each day that the initial nest had been incubated. Since these early studies, researchers have continued to produce information on renesting, from which we now summarize major findings.

To begin, waterfowl exhibit a high propensity to renest, which is a key adaptation in response to the high nest predation rates ducks often experience. Near Minnedosa, Manitoba, 58% of marked Canvasbacks renested, with an average interval of 9.8 days between termination of the first nest and initiation of the second (Doty et al. 1984). Keith (1961) estimated that renesting occurred among all unsuccessful Mallards on his study areas in Prairie Canada, and that 63% attempted third nests if the second nest was destroyed. On the Yukon-Kuskokwim Delta in Alaska, 56% of unsuccessful Northern Pintails renested at least once, and three renested a third time (Grand and Flint 1996a). Renesting in captive, wild-strain Mallards was studied experimentally by removing first clutches during a 3-year period where females were provided unlimited food while held on experimental wetlands (Swanson et al. 1986). All yearling females renested, and two of four produced three clutches. All eight 2 year-olds in the study produced three clutches, and three produced four clutches; all eight 3-year-olds produced four clutches, and three produced five. These studies thus documented the strong persistence to continue nesting after an earlier failure.

Renesting intervals averaged 7 days and increased 0.18 days for each day of incubation, which was considerably less than the 0.62 reported by Sowls (1955). However, most of his observations were from females incubating 10 days or less, which is when the variation is greatest, as Coulter and Miller (1968) determined for American Black Ducks and Mallards. Hence, the results from the experimental work on Mallards probably more accurately represent the relationship between renesting interval and incubation. The interval is strongly influenced by the nutritional and physiological status of the female. For example, whereas the renesting interval averaged 7 days for females provided with unlimited food, those with limited sources of food renested in 6 to 24 days; 42% exceeded the maximum of 10 days that was recorded for females on unlimited food (Swanson et al. 1986). Captive female Mallards fed a reduced diet (wheat) initiated fewer renesting attempts, laid at a slower rate, produced smaller eggs, and laid fewer eggs than females fed an enriched diet (Eldridge and Krapu 1988). In Alaska, the renesting interval for Northern Pintails averaged 11.4 days between first and second nests, and 11.3 days between second and third nests (Grand and Flint 1996a).

In summary, renesting intervals generally increase with time spent incubating the previous clutch, are longer for females in poor physical condition, and are more frequently attempted by adults. From an ecological viewpoint, the length of the breeding also season influences the ability to renest. To illustrate, the ability of female Mallards to produce eggs extends over an average period of 44 days (Eldridge and Krapu 1988) — ample time to begin second or third nests — but geese nesting in the Arctic generally do not renest, because cold weather shortens the breeding season.

Continuous laying, also relevant to a discussion of renesting, occurs when a female loses a nest during egg laying but continues to produce eggs in a new nest without interruption (i.e., renesting interval = 0). Arnold et al. (2002) documented continuous laying in 278 (9.1%) of 3,064 radiomarked Mallards nesting in the PPR of Canada. Females laying continuously produced an average of 12.1 total eggs compared with 8.9 for other females; on average, those females also were 25 g heavier.

As determined in earlier studies, clutch size also generally declines in renests, but the difference is least pronounced between the first and second nests. Coulter and Miller (1968) reported no decrease in clutch size between 46% of the renesting attempts made by American Black Ducks. Based on experimental studies with Mallards, clutch size averaged 10.36 for first clutches, 9.97 for second, 9.59 for third, 8.47 for fourth, and 8.50 for fifth. Further, 16% of second clutches were larger than first clutches and 39% did not change (Swanson et al. 1986). Renests usually are located near initial nests. Coulter and Miller (1968) reported that 50% of Mallard and American Black Duck renests were within 92 m of first nests, and 67% were within 183 m. In Alaska, distance between first and second nests of Northern Pintails averaged 276 m (Grand and Flint 1996a).

Most explanations for the decline in clutch size in renests have focused on poorer nutrition of the females as the breeding season progresses, but the smaller clutches also may reflect a reduced reproductive effort because of poorer survival of late-hatching ducklings (see Rohwer 1992). Most dabbling ducks (five species of *Anas*) in North and South Dakota terminated their nesting efforts by the summer solstice, which presumably represents an adaptation that deters continued breeding at a time (i.e., late summer) when few ducklings will survive (Krapu 2000). Nesting efforts ended sooner for early-nesting species like Northern Shovelers and Northern Pintails, likely because they evolved to breed in response to habitat conditions that are optimal in early spring but thereafter decline rapidly.

Brood Parasitism

Brood parasitism occurs when two or more females contribute eggs to a single clutch (Bellrose and Holm 1994). Brood parasitism is widespread among waterfowl, occurring in some 50–70% of all species, although much more commonly in some than others (Sayler 1992). In general, brood parasitism occurs more frequently in cavity-nesting species and pochards than in other groups — it is uncommon in dabbling ducks, except in species using nest cavities or when they crowd together on nesting islands. We address brood parasitism here, particularly aspects that affect management decisions, but refer readers to Sayler (1992) for a more thorough treatment. We have, however, also reviewed some key additional studies since Sayler's summary paper appeared.

Conspecific brood parasitism occurs much more commonly in waterfowl than does interspecific brood parasitism, and the rate can be especially high. For example, McCamant and Bolen (1979) reported that 70% of all Black-bellied Whistling-Duck nests were conspecifically parasitized over a 12-year period in south Texas. Among pochards, 36% of Canvasback nests were conspecifically parasitized, and at least 9.7% of all Canvasback eggs were laid parasitically during a 3-year study in southwestern Manitoba (Sorenson 1993). Among Wood Ducks using nest boxes in Massachusetts, at least 57% of all nests contained eggs from other females (Grice and Rogers 1965), and 95% of Wood Duck nests in boxes were conspecifically parasitized on a study site in Missouri (Semel and Sherman 1986). These high rates of brood parasitism at times produce extremely large clutch sizes: 101 in Black-bellied Whistling-Ducks and 41 in Wood Ducks.

Although less common, interspecific brood parasitism is well documented in waterfowl, particularly between Redheads and Canvasbacks. Indeed, Redheads parasitized more than 50% of the Canvasback nests in some areas, usually laying three or more parasitic eggs per nest; as many as 75% of their eggs may be laid parasitically (Weller 1959, Bouffard 1983, Sorenson 1991). In a classic study of Redhead and Canvasback brood parasitism on marshes in Utah and Manitoba, Weller (1959) reported that Redheads parasitized the nests of other Canvasbacks before starting their own nests and continued parasitism throughout the nesting period; parasitic Redheads laid an average of 10.8 eggs in the nests of Canvasbacks. As many as 13 females were trapped at a host's nest, although three or four was more common, and

parasitized nests contained as many as 30 eggs. However, more than 50% of all parasitic eggs were laid after the host female began incubation, and thus were not likely to hatch.

Sayler (1992) discussed the evolutionary explanations for brood parasitism in waterfowl, which he grouped into three major categories: (1) nonadaptive responses that are either a reproductive error or accidental; (2) a salvage or conditional strategy wherein females attempt to achieve some reproductive success when faced with poor environmental conditions such as drought, and (3) an alternative strategy, which includes spreading eggs among different nests so as to reduce the risk of predation, and by increasing fecundity (i.e., laying more eggs than a single female can hatch alone). In his study of interspecific nest parasitism between Redheads and Canvasbacks, Sorenson (1991) used time-lapse photography to compile nesting histories of individual Redhead females. In years of favorable environmental conditions, many adult females laid parasitic eggs prior to initiation of their own nests. In contrast, females either laid parasitic eggs or nested, but did not do both during a drought year. Hence, in an effort to interpret the adaptive significance of parasitic nesting, Sorenson (1991) suggested that Redheads used a flexible, conditional reproductive strategy with four options for increasing their reproductive effort: (1) nonbreeding, (2) parasitic egg laying, (3) typical nesting, and (4) a dual strategy of parasitic laying prior to nesting. Thus, when environmental conditions are favorable, the dual strategy enabled Redheads to increase their reproductive output above the size of a normal clutch.

Brood parasitism also has obvious consequences for the host, likewise summarized by Sayler (1992); these include lower egg success, higher duckling mortality, and even host mortality. In general, host success is reduced by egg displacement, breakage, and nest desertion — as well as by fewer eggs being laid by the host — but the severity of these effects may depend on the intensity of parasitism. Weller (1959) reported that Redhead parasitism reduced the number of eggs laid by host Canvasbacks by 20%, and reduced both egg and nest success of hosts. However, these effects were not apparent until 60–70% of nests were parasitized and four to six eggs were added per nest. In more recent work, Dugger and Blums (2001) added eggs to nests of Tufted Ducks and Common Pochards to examine the costs paid by hosts. An additional three eggs produced no effects on the host's clutch size, hatching success, or nest success of either species. Recruitment probability also did not differ between parasitized and nonparasitized nests, and parasitism did not affect adult survival. Hence, moderate levels of parasitism did not negatively affect hosts for these two species.

In contrast, Amat (1985) reported lower hatching success for Common Pochard nests parasitized by Red-crested Pochards, because large clutches were not efficiently incubated. Some of the pochard nests contained as many as nine parasitic eggs as opposed to the three eggs Dugger and Blums (2001) added in their experiments. In their studies of Wood Ducks, Semel and Sherman (1986) and Semel et al. (1990) reported that many parasitized clutches in nest boxes were abandoned without any attempt at incubation, and in others only the top layer of eggs received enough incubation to actually hatch. Semel et al. (1990) calculated that 31% fewer ducklings would be produced from parasitized nests with 20 eggs than from the 11-egg clutches normally produced by a single female. Semel et al. (1988, 1990) recommended placing nest boxes in visually occluded sites and in densities approximating those for natural cavities (i.e., duplicating conditions under which Wood Ducks evolved), which presumably applies to other cavity-nesting species as well. In contrast, there is little evidence to suggest that conspecific brood parasitism of nests in natural cavities reduces hatching success and production, probably because clutch size usually does not exceed 16 eggs (Bellrose and Holm 1994).

NEST PREDATION

Predation is a natural component of waterfowl population biology. Accordingly, waterfowl exhibit a variety of adaptations to reduce nest predation, all of which are influenced by habitat and the associated guilds of predators. In the Arctic, for example, waterfowl are exposed to a comparatively small predator group, largely the arctic fox (*Alpoex lagopus*; see Ely et al. 1994), the large species of gulls (*Larus* spp.), and the jaegers (*Stercorarius* spp.; see Grand and Flint 1997, Tremblay et al. 1997). The arctic fox, however, is the most common predator of arctic-nesting birds (Larson 1960), and the impact of arctic fox predation can be severe. Near Churchill, Manitoba, Common Eiders nest extensively on islands, but arctic foxes nonetheless can access those islands within 25–50 m of the mainland after which they destroyed every nest in 1–2 days (Robertson 1995). Introduction of arctic foxes to the Aleutian Islands precipitated the near extinction of the Aleutian Canada

Goose (Bailey 1993). This subspecies of Canada Goose once nested throughout most of the Aleutian Islands, the Commander Islands, and the Kuril Islands of nearby Russia. However, trappers introduced arctic foxes on most of the islands in these archipelagos and, by the late 1970s, the only known breeding population of Aleutian Canada Geese was on the Aleutian Island of Buldir, where foxes had not been introduced (see Byrd and Woolington 1983). For swans and the larger species of geese, however, both males and females defend the nest and effectively deter arctic foxes (see Scott 1972, Owen 1980).

To avoid arctic fox predation, Common Eiders often nest on islands, as mentioned earlier. Common Eiders are also very attentive to their nests, taking few recesses and only for short durations, which are adaptations against avian predators (Milne 1974, Korschgen 1977). In Alaska, female Common Eiders effectively defend their eggs from Glaucous Gulls (*Larus hyperboreus*), but they could not defend against arctic foxes (Schamel 1977). However, when flushed from their nests, Common Eiders eject foul-smelling excreta onto their clutches (as do other species of ducks), which may make the eggs less palatable to mammalian predators (Swennon 1968).

Many arctic-nesting geese nest colonially, which may be an adaptation to minimize losses to predators by "swamping," wherein the risk to each nest is proportionally less as colony size increases (Wittenberger and Hunt 1985). For example, on the Yukon-Kuskokwim Delta in Alaska, nest loss to predators (largely arctic foxes) in Black Brant colonies was 55 and 85% in two small colonies in comparison with 31–32% in two large colonies (Raveling 1989). Colonial-nesting geese also initiate their nests with considerable synchrony, which minimizes the time period that eggs are available to predators. Synchronized hatching likewise produces a "swamping" effect against predators (see Ryder 1967, Cooke et al. 1995).

Geese, like eiders, also are highly attentive to their nests and thereby reduce the risk of avian predation. In Alaska, Emperor Geese attended their nests for 99.5% of the incubation period. On average, recesses occurred at a frequency of less than once per day and lasted for only 13 min. Overall, the incubation constancy (average time spent on nests per day) among geese ranges from 90 to 94% for the comparatively small Black Brant and Cackling Canada Goose, to 98–99% for the larger subspecies of Canada Geese (see Thompson and Raveling 1987). Emperor Geese can defend their nests from arctic foxes, but are less capable of defending nests from avian predators than are the smaller species of geese. In contrast, the smaller species are more vulnerable to arctic foxes but more agile and effective in defending against aerial predators. Thompson and Raveling (1987) thus concluded that incubation constancy in geese reflects an interaction that involves the risk of nest predation, body size, and defense capabilities.

Smaller species of geese and even some species of ducks will nest in association with raptors or among colonies of larger species of geese, which can afford some protection from predators. For example, Common Eiders nesting on islands in association with nesting Lesser Snow Geese experienced greater nest success than Common Eiders nesting elsewhere (Robertson 1995). Greater Snow Geese on Bylot Island, Northwest Territories, improve their nesting success when nesting near Snowy Owls (*Nyctea scandiaca*), which maintain a predator-free environment around their own nest sites (Tremblay et al. 1997). Overall nest success at the colony was 90% when Snowy Owls nested in the area, but only 23–42% when owls were absent. Black Brant and King Eiders on the Taimyr Peninsula, Russia, experienced 100% nest success when Snowy Owls nested abundantly in the area during a year of peak lemming populations (*Lemmus sibiricus* and *Dicrostonyx torquatus*; Summers et al. 1994).

In contrast to the Arctic, the more complex grassland ecosystems of the PPR harbor a much larger guild of waterfowl nest predators. Sargeant et al. (1993) identified 20 avian and mammalian predators, of which 9 species of mammals and 7 species of birds commonly preyed on nests and/or adults and ducklings. The interactions between nesting waterfowl and their predators have been studied more extensively in the PPR than anywhere else in the world; hence this region is emphasized here.

To begin, adaptations that reduce the effects of predation include breeding as yearlings, large clutch sizes, and the ability to renest if the first nest is destroyed (see Bellrose 1980). In contrast to swans, geese, and some species of ducks nesting in the Arctic, ducks in the PPR and elsewhere conceal their nests in dense cover and spend comparatively less time attending their nests. In their summary of nest attentiveness, Afton and Paulus (1992) reported an incubation constancy of 80–90% for dabbling ducks compared with 95% or more in swans and geese. For ducks, the greater frequency of nest recesses allows females to feed more often and thus limits reductions in body mass that in turn facilitates renesting (see Thompson and Ravel-

ing 1987). Moreover, the continued presence of the female at a nest would do little to deter most predators.

Current rates of predation in the PPR are related to massive habitat alterations and changes in the predator community (Sovada et al. 2001). Mammals are especially significant as predators in most areas, but birds and reptiles also destroy large numbers of duck nests in certain areas and situations. Predators also occur at high densities in the PPR, averaging 12.2 for 33 study areas ranging in size from 23 to 26 km^2 (Sargeant et al. 1993); the number of egg-eating predators averaged 4.6/study area. See Greenwood and Sovada (1996) and especially Sargeant et al. (1993) for reviews of waterfowl predation on the PPR.

Among mammals, the striped skunk, raccoon, Franklin's ground squirrel (*Spermophilus franklinii*), and red fox are the major predators of waterfowl nests in the PPR as well as in many other areas in North America. Raccoons are especially important predators of overwater nests, whereas skunks, coyotes, and red foxes are more important predators of upland nests. In North Dakota, nest success averaged 15% on areas where striped skunks were removed compared with 5% success elsewhere (Greenwood 1986). Franklin's ground squirrels were implicated as predators of more than 27% of the nests in the study. Unfortunately, management that promotes dense nesting cover for ducks also provides quality habitat for Franklin's ground squirrels (Choromanski-Norris et al. 1989). At the Horicon Marsh in Wisconsin, striped skunks and raccoons together destroyed 81% of about 700 duck nests (Livezey 1981).

Nonetheless, no mammal currently causes more serious and widespread damage than the red fox — a result of its ability to prey on both nesting females and their eggs. Indeed, red foxes may kill 900,000 adult ducks in midcontinental North America each year. In reporting these data, Sargeant et al. (1984) also noted that dabbling ducks were far more vulnerable than pochards to red foxes (Fig. 6-3). More importantly, females comprised 76% of the dabbling ducks killed by foxes, which further distorts the sex ratio for Mallards breeding in the PPR (Table 6-3; see Chapter 8). In pristine times, the ratio was calculated as 110 or fewer males per 100 females, but that disparity expanded to 117:100 from 1939 to 1964 and reached 129:100 from 1959 to 1964 (Johnson and Sargeant 1977).

During their extensive study in North Dakota, Sargeant et al. (1984) estimated that a single red fox

Figure 6-3. Red foxes are major predators affecting nest success and survival of female dabbling ducks in the Prairie Pothole Region. This red fox (*left*) is carrying a female Northern Pintail to feed her pups (*right*). Photos courtesy of Alan B. Sargeant, U.S. Fish and Wildlife Service, and Chris P. Dwyer, Ohio Divison of Wildlife.

female killed 16.1–65.9 ducks/yr. The composition of dabbling duck remains ($n = 1,798$) discovered at fox dens consisted of 27% Blue-winged Teal, 23% Mallards, 20% Northern Pintails, 9% Northern Shovelers, 8% Gadwalls, 3% Green-winged Teal, 2% American Wigeon, and 10% unidentified. Foxes annually removed 13.5% of the females and 4.5% of the males present on an intensively studied area. Similar findings occurred in Minnesota where nesting females comprised 84% of the duck remains at fox dens, but the sample included no pochards (Sargeant 1972).

Importantly, the increase in red fox numbers across the PPR was a direct result of human activities: intensive cultivation that created suitable habitat for foxes and systematic removal of the gray wolf (*Canis lupus*) and coyote, the principal competitors of the red fox (Johnson and Sargeant 1977, Sargeant 1982). Indeed, the perpetual changes wrought by human settlement have continually altered the abundance and distribution of predators on the prairie landscape (Sargeant et al. 1993). Generally, population levels, distribution, or both have changed since settlement began for nearly all species of predators in the PPR. Some species changed because of human exploitation, whereas others increased due to

Table 6-3. The percentage female dabbling ducks found at red fox dens in North Dakota during the early and late nesting seasons in North Dakota. Modified from Sargeant et al. (1984:20).

	22 April–11 June (early)		12 June–20 July (late)	
Species	Total	% females	Total	% females
Mallard	113	80	62	82
Northern Pintail	119	70	123	74
Northern Shoveler	32	88	33	94
Blue-winged Teal	146	74	114	77
Gadwall	34	50	63	65

newly created habitats, absence of competitors, or both. Canid populations especially have changed because of human-induced mortality and interspecific interactions (Sargeant 1982). Specifically, gray wolves suppress coyote numbers (Mech 1970, Mech and Boitani 2003), and coyotes suppress red foxes (Sargeant 1982). Thus, extirpation of the gray wolf in the early 1900s was a major factor facilitating expansion of other canids in the PPR. Coyotes were widely distributed throughout the PPR before settlement, but populations were low. In contrast, the red fox was sparsely distributed in the PPR before settlement, but expanded greatly in the 1930s and 1950s, following heavy control of coyote populations (see Sargeant 1982, Sargeant et al. 1993). Unlike red foxes, coyotes prey on livestock and various game species; thus, coyotes were heavily persecuted throughout the PPR and elsewhere (see Andelt 1987). For example, some 250,000 coyotes were killed in Alberta from 1951 to 1956 (Ballantyne 1958), and loss of coyotes facilitated population increases and range expansion of red foxes. However, coyote populations have increased since the 1970s, the result of restrictions placed on the harvest methods (aerial hunting and poisons) and lower commercial value of their fur. Concurrently, the abundance of red foxes has declined in areas reoccupied by coyotes (see Sovada et al. 1995). During their 1983–88 studies of predator populations across the PPR of North America, Sargeant et al. (1993) noted that red foxes were most abundant on study areas with the fewest coyotes. Coyotes also may suppress populations of raccoons (Sargeant et al. 1993). Such changes in predator communities can affect nesting success, as noted by Sovada et al. (1995) during a 3-year study in North and South Dakota. Overall nest success for ducks on 36 study areas averaged 32% where coyotes were the principal canid compared with 17% where red foxes were more abundant.

Such predator–prey interactions are complex, however, as Devries et al. (2003) documented during a 6-year (1993–98) study that radiotracked 2,249 breeding female Mallards at 19 different 54–78-km²-sites in the Aspen Parkland and Mixed-grass Prairie Ecoregions of the PPR of Canada. Female survival ranged from 0.62 to 0.84 and averaged 0.76 during the 90-day breeding season; survival rates were lowest when females were nesting. However, survival was lower in western compared to eastern sites, yet predator indices in the west were higher for coyotes and Red-tailed Hawks (*Buteo jamaicensis*) and lower for red foxes and mink (*Mustela vison*). Hence, predators other than red foxes are important sources of mortality for waterfowl nesting in the western portion of the PPR of Canada wherein management efforts to protect coyotes as a means of suppressing red foxes may only be a valid management option where red foxes are common.

The raccoon is another major nest predator in the PPR, and their numbers expanded with agricultural development (Sargeant et al. 1993) and the availability of buildings suitable as denning sites (Fritzell 1978). Because they prefer to forage in and around wetlands, raccoons often prey on overwater nests, whereas they seldom damage nests in upland habitats such as pasture, haylands, or idle upland cover (Fritzell 1978). Hence, rates of raccoon predation on overwater nests increase with decreasing water depth (Jobin and Picman 1997).

The striped skunk also preys on duck nests in the PPR, especially in upland areas where Greenwood et al. (1999) recorded shell fragments from duck eggs in 40% of 1,248 scats examined in North Dakota; 32% contained shells from passerine eggs. Female striped skunks likely cause more damage because they outnumber males and travel more extensively than males within their home ranges (Larivière and Messier 1998). Further, when rearing young, female skunks concentrate their foraging activities around their dens, which increases nest losses at these locations (Shields and Parnell 1986). Thus, efforts to control female skunks at den sites may be the best approach to reduce nest predation (Larivière and Messier 1998).

Among birds, American Crows (*Corvus brachyrhynchos*) prey on waterfowl nests across a broad geographical area of North America (Kalmbach 1937, Picozzi 1975, Johnson et al. 1989). Crows generally are more effective predators on nests in uplands, and especially on nests located within their home ranges (Sullivan and Dinsmore 1990), but dense nesting cover serves as a deterrent (Sugden and Beyersbergen 1987). California Gulls (*Larus californicus*) also are effective predators of waterfowl nests. In Utah, for instance, California Gulls destroyed 317 — or nearly 11% — of 2,997 waterfowl nests and attacked many newly hatched ducklings (Odin 1957). All told, California Gulls likely destroyed 30% of the eggs and young produced on the Utah study area. Ring-billed Gulls (*L. delawarensis*) preyed on the eggs of ducks nesting in elevated baskets in North Dakota (Doty et al. 1975).

Although not important nest predators in the PPR, reptiles can be important nest predators elsewhere. Black rat snakes (*Elaphe obsoleta obsoleta*) preyed effectively on Wood Duck nests in Missouri

Figure 6-4. Snakes adept at climbing often are effective nest predators of cavity-nesting waterfowl. Here a gray rat snake (*Elaphe obsoleta spiloides*) is consuming Wood Duck eggs after bypassing a predator guard on a nest box at the Eufaula National Wildlife Refuge in Alabama. Photo courtesy of Thomas E. Moorman, Ducks Unlimited.

(Hansen 1971) and on Canada Goose nests in Oklahoma (Aldrich and Endicott 1984; Fig. 6-4). Fox snakes (*E. vulpina*) are recorded as nest predators in Wisconsin (Wheeler 1984). In Nebraska, bullsnakes (*Pituophis melanoleucus*) destroyed 42% of 274 duck nests under observation in 1938, and an analysis of 111 stomachs revealed that duck eggs comprised fully 29% of the bullsnake's spring and summer diet (Imler 1945).

Overall, Sargeant et al. (1993) concluded that more data are needed to clarify interactions between predator populations and duck production in the PPR. In particular, the composition and abundance of predators across space and time — particularly where nesting cover is of marginal quality — likely will emerge as a major factor affecting duck production, In the interim, Sargeant et al. (1984:39) concluded that "Effective management to increase duck production will necessitate coping with the predation problem."

PREDATOR MANAGEMENT

Predator control is a highly controversial subject, especially in an era when strong concerns for the welfare of virtually all species — not just for game animals — permeates across a wide spectrum of so-

ciety (Goodrich and Buskirk 1995). Managers thus can expect that predator management will continue to be a complex and often emotional topic for which there will not be easy solutions or answers (see Berryman 1972). Nonetheless, predator control can be an extremely effective means of improving the nesting success of waterfowl (Duebbert and Kantrud 1974, Beauchamp et al. 1996b, Clark et al. 1996, Greenwood and Sovada 1996, Drever et al. 2004). Predator management itself involves various approaches, which fall into three general categories: (1) restoration and protection of good cover at important nesting habitats, (2) isolation of nests from predators, and (3) removal of predators by lethal methods (Sovada et al. 2001). These approaches also can be viewed as either intensive (applied to small areas) or extensive (applied to large areas), as well as lethal and nonlethal. The clear challenge to managers lies in selecting the best approach, if any, to apply in a given situation.

Landscape Management

Removal of predators across broad areas will increase nest success, as shown at Agassiz National Wildlife Refuge in northwestern Minnesota, where nest predators were killed by several methods from 1959 to 1964 (Balser et al. 1968). During this 6-year study, 1,342 predators were removed, including 444 raccoons, 761 striped skunks, and 137 red foxes. Nest success ranged from 35 to 76%, and 60% more Class I ducklings (i.e., about 1–20 days old) were produced on units where predators were removed compared with those units without predator control.

In north-central South Dakota, a 51-ha field of undisturbed grass-legume cover and the surrounding 8.13 km² area were studied relative to removal of mammalian predators within a 259-km² zone (Duebbert and Lokemoen 1980). During the 6-year study, seven species of dabbling ducks produced 1,062 nests in the field, of which 81% hatched and produced at least 7,250 ducklings. Hatching success reached 94% during the years when predator control was most successful. A maximum density of 631 nests/100 ha occurred in 1972, and the highest hatching success was 96% in 1971. Also, Mallard pairs increased from 2.8/km² to 16.8/km² during the study period. The authors pointed out that the successful recruitment of ducklings resulted from a combination of factors: the complex of 74 high-quality wetlands in the area, the 51-ha field of dense nesting cover, and the rigid control of predators. One worker was able to control the predators over the 259-km² area, but this occurred before the application of strychnine — the most successful control method — was outlawed on federal lands in 1972. Although this study documents a positive response to predator control, care must be exercised in extrapolating the results because the treatments were not replicated and there were no control plots (see Johnson 1999).

More recently, predator control was implemented for 3 years on eight 41.5-km² blocks of habitat in the PPR of south-central North Dakota (Garrettson and Rohwer 2001). Trappers removed 2,404 predators from the study sites (41% were raccoons, 26% were red foxes). Nest success was higher on trapped sites (mean success of 42%; range 37–46%) in comparison with control sites where predators were not removed (23%; 19–25%).

Although effective at times, predator control is not always appreciated by some sectors of the public; favorable attitudes toward hunting and trapping are more prevalent in rural areas (Kellert 1985). Nonetheless, animal rights groups vehemently oppose predator control, which is often debated among professional biologists as well. Furthermore, predator control will never be a panacea for improving nesting success, if for no other reason than it cannot be conducted — physically, financially, politically, or ethically — across areas large enough to offset the tremendous loss of nesting habitat. Effort and costs of predator control on large areas are particular management concerns. For example, predator control efforts on just six Waterfowl Production Areas in the PPR involved 30,872 trap-days to remove 611 adult predators at a cost of $1,661/area, which did not include transportation, equipment, and other costs (Sargeant et al. 1995). In response, the hatching rate reached 13.5% compared with 5.6% on untrapped areas. Also, in contrast to habitat management, predator control does not produce long-term benefits; without repeated efforts, dispersal and compensatory reproduction will replenish the predator population that was depleted the year before (Sovada et al. 2001).

Furthermore, although nest success is generally higher on areas with predator management, this relationship is complex and may vary with climatic conditions and interrelationships among duck species, their predators, and their prey. For example, Drever et al. (2004) noted a negative relationship between nest success and wet conditions at unmanaged sites compared to a positive relationship between the same variables at sites where predators were excluded. Hence, predator management might be less effective at increasing nest suc-

cess during drought years (i.e., any effect of predator control is minimized by poor habitat conditions). Increased nest success during dry years also might be offset by lower brood survival and the propensity to renest.

Beauchamp et al. (1996a) further documented the complex relationship between predation and nest success. For example, they determined that nest success and its rate of decline did not differ between major geographical regions of the PPR (e.g., parkland and grassland), despite differences in predator communities. Instead, large-scale agent(s) likely caused the observed patterns. They then suggested that extensive management efforts (e.g., recovery of marginal farmland or better faming practices) at the regional scale may be more cost effective for improving nest success than intensive, site-specific programs such as predator control.

Islands, Peninsulas, Colonies, Endangered Species

Predator control may be more defendable in certain situations or on areas intensively managed for waterfowl production (e.g., endangered species, colony-nesting species, islands, peninsulas), or where wetlands are abundant but upland cover is lacking (Reynolds et al. 1996). As noted earlier, the endangered Aleutian Canada Goose likely escaped extinction because arctic foxes were removed from islands in the Aleutian Archipelago (Bailey 1993, Boylan 1998). Similarly, the endangered Campbell Island Teal also survived, in part, because rats were controlled (see Infobox 6-1).

Arctic foxes also have interfered with the Black Brant breeding on the Yukon-Kuskokwim Delta of Alaska, where nesting colonies have declined in both size and abundance since the 1970s. From 1986 to 1989, however, foxes were removed near the vicinity of a large nesting colony, resulting in an average nest success of about 82% during the 4-year period of predator control (Anthony et al. 1991). Arctic foxes occupy exclusive areas during the spring, and managers thus can target and remove specific individuals during the nesting season (Anthony 1997). Overall, removing foxes in local areas proved a feasible and successful way to increase the nesting success of Black Brant. At a colony of Spectacled Eiders on the Yukon-Kuskokwim Delta in Alaska, nest success increased from 18 to 76% one year after Mew Gulls (*Larus canus*) were controlled (Grand and Flint 1997).

Islands can provide unusually secure nesting

Infobox 6-1

Island Waterfowl: Conservation of an Endangered Species
Campbell Island Teal: A Case Study

Species endemic to insular ecosystems often suffer from the introduction of alien species. The newcomers may effectively compete for existing niches, inimically alter essential habitat, or carry diseases to which native species have no resistance. Predation is another potent threat for which insular species often are without either behavioral or physical defenses. In sum, insular biota have evolved in isolation and therefore may lack those adaptations necessary to cope with the arrival of alien organisms. Moreover, many insular species have limited distributions and were not abundant even before external threats arrived, and they are likewise at risk from the random occurrence of catastrophic events such as hurricanes.

An invasion of rats was responsible for the precipitous decline in Campbell Island Teal (CIT), a small brown duck that today is likely the rarest and most isolated of the world's waterfowl. Like some other species of island-dwelling waterfowl, these small birds are flightless, a clear indication that predation was not part of their evolutionary history. They formerly ranged in tussock grasslands on the bleak islands of the subantarctic region of New Zealand. Rats appeared in early in the 1800s

when whaling and sealing vessels visited the area. They soon became a local scourge and, in fact, rat densities on Campbell Island are the highest ever recorded. The rats eliminated CIT (among other birds) from all but Dent Island, a 23-ha islet where about 25 pairs persisted. Because of these dire circumstances, the New Zealand Department of Conservation listed (in 1975) the species as critically endangered and thereafter initiated a management plan to prevent its extinction.

A captive breeding program was begun in 1984 with the capture of 11 adults from which offspring could be propagated and released in suitable areas. The first releases took place on another small island (Codfish Island, after it was declared rat-free) in 1999 as part of a two-fold mission: first, to establish a second population of wild birds as a form of conservation "insurance" and, second, to establish a temporary source of wild birds for capture and release on Campbell Island when it was again rat-free. At 11,300 ha, Campbell Island is the largest of the subantarctic islands in southern New Zealand and before 1800 likely supported a sizable population of CIT. Before releasing the birds — all genetically representative of wild stock — each was screened for dis-

eases, acclimated to local conditions in on-site aviaries for up to 2 weeks, and fitted with radio transmitters to which they already had been habituated. Within months the birds produced at least one nest. Eventually, 24 birds were released on Codfish Island. By March 2004, the population numbered at least 21 birds, but others, including a brood, were observed; hence a total of 35–40 is more likely representative.

Meanwhile, Campbell Island was declared rat-free in 2003, 2 years after baits containing a lethal, rodent-specific anticoagulant had been distributed from helicopters. These results triggered the next phase of the plan, namely to release breeding stock on Campbell Island itself, where no CIT had survived for nearly 200 years. The first release — 25 birds from captive stock and 25 from the wild population on Codfish Island — occurred in 2004, and 55 more were released in 2005. The 5-year objective of the recovery plan is to establish and maintain at least two self-sustaining populations of CIT on Campbell Island — a goal that now seems within grasp. If successful, the plan surely will stand as a working model for adoption wherever island waterfowl are endangered. For a fuller discussion, see Williams and Robertson (1996), Gummer and Williams (1999), Seddon and Maloney (2003), and Williams (2004). Photo courtesy of Gary Norman.

---

habitat for waterfowl, a circumstance appreciated for many years (Hammond and Mann 1956). In northwestern North Dakota, for instance, Mallards and Gadwalls nest on a natural 4.5-ha island within 385-ha Miller Lake. During a 5-year study, 2,561 nests of nine species were found on the island, with densities for Mallards reaching 241–389 nests/ha and 139–237 nests/ha for Gadwalls (Duebbert et al. 1983). In one study site, a single 0.59-ha clump of thick shrubs contained 225 simultaneously active Mallard nests (Lokemoen et al. 1984). The average hatching rate for these nests was 85%, which produced a minimum of 15,960 ducklings during the 5 years. Islands in Lake Champlain provided secure nesting habitat for American Black Ducks and Mallards (Coulter and Miller 1968). In Tamaulipas, Mexico, Black-bellied Whistling-Ducks built ground nests on three natural islands 4.3–15.8 ha in size, achieving an overall density of 15.7 nests/ha and a nest success of 28.3–41.7% (Markum and Baldassarre 1989). In North Dakota, South Dakota, and northeastern Montana, waterfowl nest success on 209 islands surveyed averaged 60% on islands without predator control (Lokemoen and Woodward 1992). As suggested earlier, high nest densities on islands probably occur because more females survive predators and thereafter return each year (home) to the security of these nesting sites.

Predator removal from islands can be very effective and warranted. Further, in comparison to upland areas, predator populations are much smaller and may not need control every year. In these cases, predator control may yield large benefits, and the time and effort required to live-trap individual animals for transport elsewhere may be justified. Nearly all mammalian nest predators (except canids) are relatively easy to live-trap — a method more acceptable to the public than lethal measures. We emphasize here that "predator control" does not always equate with killing unwanted animals. Instead, the operative term is predator management, which considers a full array of approaches for dealing with the legitimate problem of nest predation.

Peninsulas also offer secure nesting sites for waterfowl, and they have been managed to exclude predators by constructing electric fences, moats, or other physical barriers (see Lokemoen and Messmer 1994). Lokemoen and Woodward (1993) evaluated use of electric fences and moats to enhance peninsulas as waterfowl nesting sites in North Dakota. Their study selected 10 pairs of peninsulas, with one of each pair then randomly selected to receive a fence or moat (managed sites) and removal of predators. The other sites served as controls on which predators were not managed. Nest success over a 5-year study period averaged 75% on peninsulas with moats, 16% on peninsulas without moats, 54% on peninsulas with electric fences, and 17% on peninsulas without electric fences. Fence construction averaged $23/m compared with $328/m for moats, and translated into $12 per fledged duckling on fenced sites and $62 on sites with moats. Even so, managing peninsulas with fences and moats was deemed more cost effective than building islands, which can cost $10,000–20,000/acre (0.4 ha) to construct.

Nonetheless, properly constructed islands located in suitable habitat can receive considerable use by breeding ducks, although the results may vary. Nesting on artificial islands ranged from 1.4 nests/ha in Quebec (Belanger and Tremblay 1989) to 136 nests/ha in North Dakota (Johnson et al. 1978), and

300 nests/ha in Arizona (Piest and Sowls 1985). A "model" island, as proposed by Jones (1975), is at least 0.02 ha in area and 30 m from the mainland, with the intervening channel 0.5–0.6 m in depth. Duebbert et al. (1983) recommended that islands be located 150–200 m from shore and surrounded by water 2–3 m deep; nests on islands too close to shore can suffer high rates of predation (Getz and Smith 1989). Belanger and Tremblay (1989) determined that artificial islands 0.2 ha or larger in area were most attractive to breeding ducks.

Construction of artificial nesting islands involves more than just haphazardly piling soil, as shown by an evaluation in North Dakota (Higgins 1986). In this study, nesting declined over time as a result of habitat deterioration on the islands; hence, production during the first 15 years averaged only 0.8 ducklings/island at an estimated cost of $31.25/duckling. In Quebec, only 8–14% of the artificial islands were used by waterfowl, and the cost per duck produced was estimated at $166 (Belanger and Tremblay 1989). Accordingly, Higgins (1986) suggested that the best method of reducing the cost per duckling was to construct taller, more durable islands and to carefully

locate the islands within impoundments. Islands also should be constructed where there are high densities of breeding ducks (see Lokemoen and Messmer 1993).

In Pennsylvania, floating Styrofoam rafts were tested as nesting structures for dabbling ducks breeding on surface-mine pools, where water levels often fluctuated dramatically during the nesting season (Brenner and Mondok 1979). In a 3-year period, Mallards, Blue-winged Teal, and Canada Geese increased their utilization of the rafts by 62%, and nest success averaged 79%. Construction and installation costs averaged $9.75/raft, or $0.85/duckling. After 5 years, assuming the same level of production, the estimated cost dropped to just $0.05/duckling. American Black Ducks and Mallards also nested on rafts constructed in the forested areas of northern Ontario (Young 1971).

Electric fencing also has been used to surround quality nesting habitat (Fig. 6-5); once predators inside are removed, few others can gain access to the protected area (Sargeant et al. 1974). Pietz and Krapu (1994) modified these fences to include exits for broods. In North Dakota and Minnesota, nest suc-

Figure 6-5. Electric fencing powered by solar batteries offers an effective means for increasing nest success in the Prairie Pothole Region. Duck production is enhanced considerably where relatively small areas of protected nesting habitat occur within a complex of wetlands. Photo courtesy of John T. Lokemoen, U.S. Fish and Wildlife Service.

cess reached 55–65% inside electric-fence exclosures compared to 12–45% on unfenced areas (Lokemoen et al. 1982). The exclosures produced 127% more ducklings at a cost of $0.65–0.87/duckling. This technique seems most effective where ducks nest in high densities (i.e., abundant wetlands) and where good cover is lacking outside the fenced area (Reynolds et al. 1996).

Other Predator Management Methods

Several other types of predator control have produced limited or no success. For example, Greenwood et al. (1998) provided supplemental food for striped skunks in North Dakota; the 2-year study concluded that the extra food was of limited value to deter nest predation because so many other kinds of nest predators occurred in the same area (i.e., a complex predator community in which predation continues unabated even if one species no longer destroys nests). In the 1960s, reproductive inhibitors were proposed as a means to limit carnivore populations (Balser 1964), and a variety of immunocontraceptives were considered (Kirkpatrick and Turner 1985). However, their widespread use on the PPR does not seem feasible (see Greenwood and Sovada 1996).

Conditioned taste aversion (CTA) seeks to deter predation by placing chemically treated eggs in nesting areas, where predators thereafter associate all eggs with an unpalatable taste and no longer destroy duck nests for food (Conover 1989, 1990). However, the response to CTA varies by species of predator, so it seems unlikely that a single agent can be developed to deal effectively with a complex predator community consisting of both birds and mammals.

Final Comments on Predator Management

The PPR is an extremely dynamic area where myriad factors interact to affect duck production, of which predator populations are only one component; hence a single approach to predator management likely will not succeed. We have reviewed the major tools of predator management, but the challenge for managers is to select and implement the correct tool for a given situation. Long ago, Balser et al. (1968) recommended that predator control should be evaluated on a case-by-case basis after addressing the following: (1) determine if predation rates are high enough to warrant predator control, (2) find a means of controlling the entire predator complex, (3) use a combination of control measures, (4) explore other means of reducing predation, and (5) consider the public response. These suggestions are as appropriate today as they were in the 1960s. Further, decisions concerning predator control should include both spatial and temporal considerations. For example, Reynolds et al. (1996) suggests focusing management on those landscapes with the greatest potential for duck production (e.g., areas with numerous wetlands). Garrettson and Rohwer (2001) likewise argued that predator removal would be most effective where habitat management attracted high densities of nesting ducks, but an abundance of predators limited nest success. We believe that long-term studies will be needed to assess the effects of predator control on both target and nontarget species. For example, suppression of foxes and other mesopredators might lead to dramatic increases in small rodent populations, which might eventually affect waterfowl and other birds nesting in grasslands.

Overall, predator management is a legitimate concern of wildlife managers, and we have detailed examples here where action was clearly warranted, effective, and defensible. However, we agree with Sovada et al. (2001:12-13) who state, "Strategies must be tailored to each situation, but ultimately integrated with long-term conservation of waterfowl. This means that predator management, even at a local scale, is *usually* (emphasis added) not a substitute for proper habitat management."

MANAGEMENT OF GRASSLAND NESTING HABITAT AND NESTING STRUCTURES

Manipulation of Nesting Cover

Less than 5% of the total land base in the PPR is devoted primarily to wildlife management (Duebbert et al. 1981). Such a finding underlies the fact that management — no matter how intensive — can only provide a small part of the solution to the problem of nesting habitat loss. Nevertheless, on much of this remaining area, seeded grasslands are established to promote what is known as dense nesting cover (DNC; see Fig. 6-2). These man-made upland communities of mixed grasses and legumes furnish quality nesting habitat for waterfowl as well as cover for other species of prairie wildlife such as the Great Plains toad (*Bufo cognatus*), prairie vole (*Microtus ochrogaster*), and an array of grassland nesting birds (Reynolds et al. 1994).

The DNC technique was pioneered many years ago in the United States in response to federally sponsored programs aimed at removing agricultural land from production at a time when farms produced huge surpluses of cereal grains. To participate, farmers where required to plant their idled land with perennial grasses, which could not be grazed or hayed. In turn, techniques were developed to establish a protective cover of grasses on the retired croplands (Cooper 1957, Bement et al. 1965, Lavin 1967, and others). DNC thus emerged as a management tool, which was enhanced and refined in subsequent years (see Duebbert et al. 1981).

The Soil Bank Act of 1956, administered by the Department of Agriculture (USDA), was the first of these programs and converted about 11.6 million ha of cropland to perennial grass cover from 1956 to 1972. The USDA then continued to sponsor programs that retired croplands after the Soil Bank Act expired, with the Food and Agriculture Act of 1965 establishing the Cropland Adjustment Program (CAP), which set a national goal to retire 16 million ha. The effect on waterfowl was spectacular. For example, hatching success of waterfowl nests at nine DNC sites enrolled in the CAP program in South Dakota averaged 31–75% for a 3-year period (Duebbert and Lokemoen 1976; also see Jaenke 1966, Duebbert 1969). Fields managed with DNC also provided nesting habitat for other birds, among them American Bitterns (*Botaurus lentiginosus*), Northern Harriers (*Circus cyaneus*), Short-eared Owls (*Asio flammeus*), Ring-necked Pheasants (*Phasianus colchicus*), and many species of passerines (Duebbert and Lokemoen 1977). The latest federal program is the Conservation Reserve Program (CRP), which was authorized as part of the Food Security Act of 1985 and has continued under renewals of the original legislation. Enrollment in the program began in 1986 and had affected about 14 million ha by 2004. Such land retirement programs likely will continue to be a component of federal conservation efforts (see Chapter 11).

Areas seeded to DNC generally fall into three major categories: (1) introduced cool-season grasses and legumes; (2) tall, warm-season native grasses; and (3) mixed-grass prairie grasses (Duebbert et al. 1981). Among the cool-season grasses and legumes are tall wheatgrass (*Agropyron elongatum*), intermediate wheatgrass (*A. intermedium*), alfalfa (*Medicago sativa*), and sweetclover (*Melilotus* spp.). Big bluestem (*Andropogon gerardii*), Indiangrass (*Sorghastrum nutans*), and switchgrass (*Panicum virgatum*) represent primary species of warm-season native grasses, whereas mixed-grass prairie is established with green needlegrass (*Stipa viridula*), little bluestem (*Schizachyrium scoparium*), western

wheatgrass (*Agropyron smithii*), and sideoats gramma (*Bouteloua curtipendula*). Generally, tall, warm-season grasses can be established where annual precipitation reaches or exceeds 50 cm, whereas cool-season grasses do well where precipitation is 40 cm or less (Klett et al. 1984).

Establishing DNC is expensive and, to keep the areas in optimal condition, rejuvenation is required at 5–10-year intervals (e.g., burning or light grazing, mechanical disturbance, fertilization, reseeding). The consequences of idling grasslands and suppressing fire for long periods may produce various states of plant succession, but they emphasize the need for continued management (Johnson et al. 1994). Hence the expense of establishing and maintaining DNC underscores the importance of choosing sites carefully so as to achieve maximum benefits. Furthermore, after a location is selected, additional management decisions await, including those concerning clearing the site, seedbed preparation, seed sources, planting equipment and methodology, rates and dates of seeding, and maintenance schedules. Duebbert et al. (1981) address these factors, to which we refer readers for appropriate details. However, some basic principles are addressed here.

Generally, greater nest densities and hatching success occur in fields greater than 16 ha in size that do not include crops, wetlands, or other habitat types (Duebbert et al. 1981). The response of nesting females also increases if the DNC fields are located within 3–5 km of a complex of temporary, seasonal, and semipermanent wetlands (Stewart and Kantrud 1971; also see Cowardin et al. 1995, Reynolds et al. 1996). An ideal setting results when the residual cover available in mid-April provides 100% effective screening up to a height of 20 cm or more, which can be determined with a cover board (Robel et al. 1970; see Fig. 6-2).

Cowardin et al. (1995) used simulation models to demonstrate cost–benefit ratios for proposed habitat management scenarios relative to Mallard production in the PPR. As the amount of nesting cover increased in a landscape, production rose and then leveled off. Interestingly, competition for nesting habitat produced unexpected results when nesting Mallards were lured away from cover where nest success was already high (e.g., areas fenced to exclude predators). Hens thus moved from sites with 54% nest success to cover with success of 20%. Overall, their models provided some valuable guidelines. Specifically, on areas where recruitment is inadequate (e.g., poor nesting cover), management to increase recruitment should preclude management

efforts to attract breeding pairs (e.g., by adding wetlands). Conversely, managers should strive to attract
pairs to areas where existing recruitment rates are
high.

Artificial Nest Structures

Nest baskets and nesting platforms (Fig. 6-6) are
readily used by waterfowl, especially Mallards and
Canada Geese, respectively. Mallards, American
Black Ducks, and Canada Geese also nest in dead
stubs and snags, as occurred at Montezuma National
Wildlife Refuge in New York after flooding killed
large tracts of timber (Cowardin et al. 1967). These
observations prompted the development of a proto-
type chicken-wire basket lined with hay; nesting
ducks quickly responded to the availability of these
structures. In Iowa, 222 cone-shaped baskets were
monitored for a 6-year period at selected state-owned
management areas (Bishop and Barratt 1970). Use,
almost entirely by Mallards, averaged 33%, and
hatching success averaged 87%.

A larger-scale study of open-top nest baskets was
conducted in North Dakota, South Dakota, Minnesota, and Wisconsin (Doty et al. 1975). From 1966 to
1968, the study monitored 1,038 baskets of which
38% were used, and hatching success was 83%, once
again mostly by Mallards (98%). However, in North
Dakota, avian predation increased after the first 3
years from only 2 to 23%, which probably reflects a
learned response by the predators — primarily Ring-
billed Gulls — to availability of the nests. Furthermore, in areas of high basket density, nest predation averaged 49% between 1971 and 1973. The study
suggested that nest baskets could be maintained for
up to 20 years at an average annual cost of $3.85/
basket; ducklings were produced at a cost of $1.48
each. Doty and Lee (1974) also determined that 46%
of the female Mallards nesting in these baskets returned to nest at least one more time. Thus, similar
to the results for nesting islands, baskets may be a
highly effective technique for building nesting populations.

Because avian predators began to recognize nest
baskets, Doty (1979) conducted further research to
compare nesting in three different designs: open
baskets, covered cones, and covered cylinders. From
1974 to 1977, Mallards used 25% of the baskets, 46%
of the covered cones, and 14% of the cylinders. Overall nesting success was 79% and did not vary significantly among the designs. However, tests with simulated clutches showed that avian predators destroyed
four "nests" in open baskets, two in covered cones
and none in cylinders. The two sets of data — utili-

Figure 6-6. Some species of ducks readily nest in artificial structures. Shown here are a Mallard using an
open cylinder (*top*) and a Canada Goose using a floating platform (bottom). Photos courtesy of George V.
Burger and R. A. Montgomery, Max McGraw Wildlife
Foundation.

zation and avian predation — indicate that covered
cones are the best structures for this type of management. These structures benefit only a few species and a few individuals because they are usually
erected over small areas. In contrast, improved nesting cover enhances habitat for a greater variety and
number of waterfowl as well as for other birds, mammals, and plants.

Chouinard (2005) evaluated the effects of different numbers of overwater nest structures per wetland (1, 2, or 4) and wetland size (less than 0.4 ha or 0.45–1.5 ha). Most (more than 98%) nests were made by Mallards, and use increased an average of 28% between years. By the second year, the number of structures per wetland was not a significant factor influencing utilization, and overall use reached 78%. Nest success averaged 99% across treatments in the first year but declined to 48% the second year, largely because of egg predation by corvids (61%) but also mammals (23%). The numbers of ducklings departing wetlands with one or two structures were similar and twice that from wetlands with four structures, where nest success was poor. Wetland area had no effect. Hence, two structures per wetland proved cost-effective ($2.16/fledged duck). The study concluded that artificial nest structures could be an effective management tool where suitable brood habitat exists but secure nesting habitat does not. However, nesting structures were not considered a suitable means to replace the restoration and management of habitats suitable for nesting ducks.

In a study of duckling survival from overwater nest structures used by Mallards in South Dakota, Stafford et al. (2002) reported high survival rates (0.42–1.00) from sites characterized by good brood cover. However, they did not recommend use of overwater nest structures on small wetlands surrounded by trees or lacking emergent cover.

Nest Boxes

Perhaps no species of duck has benefited more from the management of nesting habitat than the Wood Duck (Fig. 6-7). Literally thousands upon thousands of nest boxes have been erected throughout the range of the Wood Duck; either wooden or metal boxes are suitable (Bellrose 1955). Bellrose (1980) summarized the basics for constructing and placing nest boxes, noting first and foremost that the structures should be protected with predator guards. This form of protection is essential, as nests in boxes lacking predator guards may fare no better than nests in tree cavities (see Bolen 1967). Predators soon learn that nest boxes often contain easily obtained food and, if not protected, the boxes are regularly entered by raccoons and other nest predators. In fact, because each successful raid acts as reinforcement for additional visits, predators eventually may destroy more nests in unprotected boxes than if no boxes were present at all. Hence, this form of management

Figure 6-7. Frank Bellrose, the acknowledged dean of Wood Duck management, checks a nest box early in his more-than-50-year career as a distinguished waterfowl biologist. Bottom photo shows a Wood Duck incubating her clutch in the safety of a wooden nest box protected with a predator guard. Top photo courtesy of the Illinois Natural History Survey; bottom photo courtesy of Thomas E. Moorman, Ducks Unlimited.

should not be initiated unless the nest boxes are adequately protected and maintained. Other work determined that temperatures inside metal boxes — especially those erected at southern latitudes — can become high enough to kill embryos and even nesting females (Hartley and Hill 1990). See Fredrickson et al. (1990) and Bellrose and Holm (1994) for more about nest-box management for Wood Ducks.

Nest boxes also have been used successfully with other cavity-nesting waterfowl, especially Black-bellied Whistling-Ducks (McCamant and Bolen 1979) and Hooded Mergansers (Morse et al. 1969), but also Common Goldeneyes (Johnson 1967), Barrow's Goldeneyes (Savard 1988), Common Mergansers (Bellrose 1980), and Buffleheads (Erskine 1972). Thus, where nest sites are limiting, erection of artificial cavities may represent a significant management program. For example, boxes erected for Barrow's Goldeneyes in British Columbia increased the number of breeding pairs from 212 in 1980 to 322 in 1984 (Savard 1988), and a nest-box program designed for Muscovy Ducks holds promise in Mexico, where large areas of riparian woodlands have been destroyed (Rangel-Woodyard and Bolen 1984).

Some biologists have questioned whether nest boxes are needed for species such as the Wood Duck, arguing that the birds would nest in the ample supply of natural cavities if boxes were not available. For example, Soulliere (1986) calculated that nest boxes in Wisconsin increased Wood Duck production by only 20%. Soulliere (1990b) later suggested that although boxes could increase local production, they were much less important at a regional scale. At a landscape level, however, Wood Duck production from state-maintained nest box programs in Massachusetts fledged an estimated 4,300 birds in comparison to a state harvest of 5,500 (Heusmann 2000). Furthermore, when state-sponsored and privately maintained boxes were considered together, Wood Ducks produced in boxes may exceed the total state harvest.

BROOD REARING

Hatching is only the first step toward successful reproduction. Thereafter comes the brood-rearing period, which we define as lasting from the time of hatching to the time young waterfowl attain flight (fledge). This part of the annual cycle, once poorly studied, is now better known and includes a number of species. In this section, we review the basic patterns of duckling/gosling growth, feeding ecology, survival, and habitat use, all in relation to the population growth of waterfowl.

General Patterns of Duckling and Gosling Growth

In general, young waterfowl grow more rapidly than other precocial birds of similar size (Ricklefs 1973), most likely because of high seasonal food availability and short breeding seasons (Lesage and Gauthier 1997). For example, ducklings grow at an exponential rate from the time of hatching, as seen in Redheads (Weller 1957) and Gadwalls (Oring 1968). Males generally weigh more than females by the second week after hatching, and remain heavier thereafter. In Redheads, the greatest increase in body mass occurs at 4–6 weeks.

More explicitly, Lightbody (1985) used the Gompertz equation (Ricklefs 1967) to describe the growth of Redhead ducklings, which grew from 10 to 90% of asymptotic size in 53 days (Fig. 6-8). Ducklings fledged at 93% of the estimated asymptotic mass, which they reached in 75 days. However, the ducklings of related species do not necessary grow at the same rate. For example, Lesser Scaup — a late-nesting species — fledged 6 days earlier than Canvasbacks, an early-nesting species, which led Lightbody and Ankney (1984) to conclude that the pattern of duckling growth may be influenced by the timing of nesting.

In a study of growth and development of semi-captive Northern Pintails, ducklings averaged 28 g at hatching and grew most rapidly between the first and fourth weeks; after 7 weeks, the ducklings were 24 times heavier than at hatching (Blais et al. 2001). Adult size was reached in 117 days. At hatching, bill length was more developed than bill width and height, but bill growth was very rapid during the first 3 weeks and nearly completed after 40 days (Table 6-4). The first feather sheaths appeared at about 12 days, and the juvenal plumage was fully developed at about 110 days. At 52 days, the young birds were capable of short flights.

Reinecke (1979) analyzed the growth rates for ducklings of American Black Ducks. The legs of ducklings were relatively large at hatching — almost 50% of adult size — but grew slowly thereafter. In contrast, the flight muscles were relatively small at hatching; these grew slowly until 4 weeks before fledging, then increased rapidly at 4.75 the power of body mass. The delayed maturity of the wing musculature permitted an increase in the overall growth

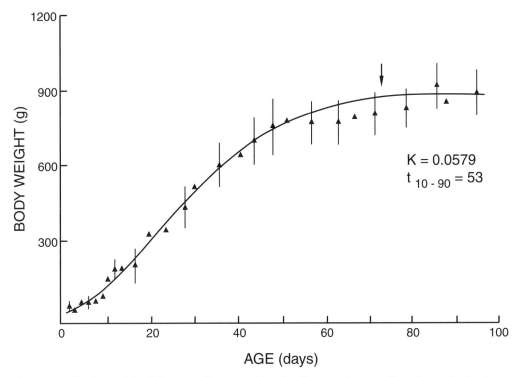

Figure 6-8. Growth of Redhead ducklings as illustrated by the Gompertz equation. Arrow indicates mean age at fledging. From Lightbody (1985:555). With permission from the Wilson Ornithological Society.

rate, a clear advantage for birds at an especially vulnerable stage of life.

Lesage et al. (1997) studied plumage growth and development in wild Surf Scoters in Quebec. The ducklings averaged 43.8 g at hatching, grew rapidly, and were difficult to distinguish from their parents in only 29–34 days. The ducklings were fully feathered in 42–55 days, when body mass had increased 19 times from hatching. In contrast, White-winged Scoters averaged 54.5 g at hatching (Brown and Fredrickson 1983).

Sedinger (1986) studied gosling growth and development of the Cackling Canada Goose, the smallest taxon of goose in North America. Growth rates were well described by the Gompertz equation, with growth rate constants (k) of 0.082 for males and 0.072 for females. Goslings fledged at 87–89% of their adult weights. The weight of leg muscles increased rapidly until goslings were 30–35 days old, and reached 71–72% of adult levels after 34 days. In contrast, breast muscles did not begin substantial growth until 15 days, and the most rapid growth occurred near fledging (after 40 days). The mass of breast muscles at fledging was 62% of adult values for male goslings and 74% for females. The gizzard was the largest muscle at hatching, comprising 11–

12% of body mass, compared with 4% for leg muscles and 0.5% for breast muscles. Lipid levels in 2-day-old goslings could only meet energy requirements for one additional day.

In contrast to the Cackling Canada Goose, the growth and development for goslings of Greater Snow Geese is of particular interest because these geese are considerably larger. Moreover, they nest in one of the northernmost breeding areas in North America (Bylot Island, Northwest Territories) and thus experience a very short brood-rearing season (Lesage and Gauthier 1997). The goslings grow rapidly: Mean body mass increased from 80 g at hatching to 2,332 g in the St. Lawrence Estuary, 110 days later. The growth constant ($k = 0.093$) for these goslings is among the highest reported for precocial birds. Leg muscles grew especially rapidly, reaching 50% of asymptotic mass 11 days before body mass reaches the same point, and 95% of asymptotic mass at fledging (Table 6-5). Lipid accumulation is delayed, more so than all other body constituents. At hatching, the vitellum, which is 85% lipid, comprised at least 4% of gosling body mass. This lipid reserve is quickly mobilized, however, wherein goslings remain lean during most of the growing period. Indeed, the lipid reserve at fledging was only about 1% of body mass. The over-

Table 6-4. Measurements (means) of Northern Pintail ducklings at hatching, fledging, postfledging, and juvenile stages. $n = 4$ for males and females, except for bill length in females at day 98 ($n = 3$). Modified from Blais et al. (2001:74).

	Hatching (day 0)	Fledging (day 53)	Postfledging (day 98)	Juvenile (10 months)
Body mass (g)				
Males	28.2	711.7	702.0	742.8
Females	27.8	642.5	686.8	714.3
Tarsus (mm)				
Males	27.9	53.0	54.9	
Females	28.2	50.3	51.9	
Wing (mm)				
Males	32.7	274.3	273.5	
Females	32.3	259.8	262.0	
Bill length (mm)				
Males	15.5	50.1	50.9	
Females	15.6	46.8	48.1	
Bill width (mm)				
Males	8.5	18.0	18.6	
Females	8.6	17.4	18.0	
Bill height (mm)				
Males	8.3	19.8	20.3	
Females	8.6	18.8	19.8	

Table 6-5. Timing of growth constituents and organs in Greater Snow Goose goslings. Fledging is estimated at 43 days of age. From Lesage and Gauthier (1997:233).

	% asymptotic value at fledging	Age (days) at 50% of asymptotic value
Body Constituents		
Body mass	76	30
Body protein	71	33
Body ash	69	37
Body water	87	27
Body Organs		
Breast muscles	41	44
Leg muscles	95	19
Esophagus	97	18
Gizzard	100	13
Intestine	97	18
Liver	88	24
Carcass	76	34

Figure 6-9. Goslings grow rapidly in the Arctic because of long periods of daylight during the summer months and the concurrent flush of new plant growth. Shown here are several broods of young White-fronted Geese and accompanying adults foraging on the Yukon-Kuskokwim Delta in Alaska. Such brood aggregations appear to be an anti-predator strategy and may also facilitate food acquisition. Photo courtesy of Craig R. Ely, U.S. Geological Survey, Alaska Science Center.

all growth rate was similar to smaller species of geese. However, Greater Snow Geese fledged at about the same age as species of smaller geese; they fledge at 68% of adult body mass compared with 79% for Lesser Snow Geese and 89% for the Cackling Canada Goose (Sedinger 1986). Overall, the authors concluded that selection for rapid growth is exceptionally strong in arctic-nesting geese because short summers force goslings to grow quickly and thereby prepare for an early departure (Fig. 6-9). These rapid growth rates likely are facilitated by the 24-hr daylight characteristic of arctic summers (i.e., extended feeding time).

To achieve such rapid growth rates, developing ducklings and goslings require a protein intake of 16–18% (Holm and Scott 1954, Scott et al. 1959), and feed for an average of about 62% of the daylight hours (Sedinger 1992). In an experimental study of Mallard ducklings, mean body mass at day 17 after hatching and mean growth ratio of ducklings per brood (i.e., proportion of body mass relative to predicated mass for wild ducklings) were positively correlated

to the numbers of aquatic invertebrates present in experimental ponds (Cox et al. 1998). Street (1978) also reported higher growth rates for Mallard ducklings that were fed large amounts of insect larvae. However, ducklings must spend considerable time obtaining macroinvertebrates. During their first 2 weeks of life, Mallard ducklings using man-made ponds in southern Britain spent more than 80% of their time foraging for aquatic insects (Robinson et al. 2002). The goslings of Cackling Canada Geese spent 63% of 20-hr days feeding on plants averaging 26% protein (Sedinger 1986, Sedinger and Raveling 1986, Sedinger and Raveling 1988).

Overall, the rate of growth (k) for downy waterfowl is inversely related to adult body mass, as described by the equation, $k = 0.27M^{-0.20}$. Thus, ducks have the highest and swans the lowest relative growth rates among waterfowl (Ricklefs 1968). See Sedinger (1992) for information regarding growth rates of young waterfowl, and Nelson (1993) for a superbly illustrated treatment of the downy waterfowl of North America.

Effects of Egg Size and Hatching Date
(Anserini — True Geese)

Characteristics associated with the growth of ducklings and goslings also vary with egg size; these attributes can affect fitness (Williams 1994), a topic that has been especially studied in geese. For example, waterfowl hatching from large eggs have a greater body mass and grow rapidly (e.g., Lesser Snow Goose; Ankney 1980), have greater thermal resistance (e.g., Northern Pintail; Duncan 1988), and have higher survival rates as seen in Lesser Scaup (Dawson and Clark 1996) and Emperor Geese (Schmutz 1993). Despite these findings, however, research only recently has started to identify the specific mechanisms by which the advantages of egg size may lead to higher survival of hatchlings.

Lesser Snow Geese hatching from the heaviest eggs survived starvation longer, suffered much lower mortality, and hatched at a greater body mass than those hatching from lighter eggs (Ankney 1980). However, the relationship and potential advantage between egg mass and body mass decreased as the goslings grew, so that the body mass of goslings was not different at fledging. Similarly, Sedinger and Flint (1991) also noted that egg size was only weakly correlated with the size of Black Brant goslings 1 month after they hatched. Nonetheless, the advantages of large size may be especially relevant for young goslings, when they are most vulnerable to hypothermia. For example, the lower critical temperature of 3–4-day-old Barnacle Geese is 21°C (Steen and Gabrielsen 1986), and the energy expenditure of Snow Goose goslings increased more than 7% for each degree below 21 °C (Beasley and Ankney 1992). These findings are significant for young goslings, which have small lipid reserves (Lesage and Gauthier 1997).

However, as goslings age, it is clear that body mass at or near fledging has important implications for their subsequent survival. For example, body mass just before fledging was positively related to winter survival in Barnacle Geese (Owen and Black 1989b). Prefledging body mass also affected first-year survival in Lesser Snow Geese (Francis et al. 1992). In Emperor Geese, goslings banded near fledging were more likely to be resighted on their fall staging areas; they averaged 2–3% heavier at banding than birds not later resighted (Schmutz 1993). Further, because this study involved resighting of geese on their primary fall staging area, the results indicate that body mass affected the ability of Emperor Goose goslings

to leave the nesting grounds and/or affected their survival during the first stage of fall migration.

A subsequent study of Black Brant in Alaska supported the observations for Emperor Geese and also provided new insights about the patterns of goose survival (Ward et al. 2004). Brant goslings were captured from three breeding sites in Alaska about 1 month after hatching peaked at each location. First-year survival was lower in the early fall (15 Jul–1 Oct) when goslings fledged and migrated to their primary staging areas in comparison with survival later in the fall and early winter (1 Oct–15 Feb), despite the fact Black Brant had completed a substantial flight of more than 5,000 km to their primary wintering areas in Baja California, Mexico. Overall, most juvenile mortality occurred during the first 2 months after banding as fledglings on the breeding grounds, but survival varied during this period in response to environmental conditions. Specifically, monthly survival during early fall was 20–24% lower during the year of latest hatch rates and slowest gosling growth.

Interestingly, egg size in geese, and presumably ducks, is a highly heritable, repeatable trait (Larsson and Forslund 1992), whereas clutch size is not (Findaly and Cooke 1983). Hence, theory predicts that egg size should respond to natural selection, if egg size is correlated with gosling survival. Directional selection should then act to favor larger eggs and reduce variations in egg sizes. However, egg size is highly variable in many species of geese, yet the mechanism(s) maintaining this variability remains unknown. In Lesser Snow Geese, Ankney and Bissett (1976) proposed that egg size was adapted to cope with the average environmental conditions encountered by the birds; thus, selection favors large eggs in some years and small eggs in others (i.e., variability). In contrast, Williams et al. (1994) suggested that physiological constraints on egg production and the effects of pleiotropic genes freed egg size from direct selection. Hence, although offspring from larger eggs appear to have some advantages — especially in thermogenesis — the benefits may only be short-term and offset by parental care and/or become muddled by mortality factors expressed later in the brood-rearing period (see Williams 1994).

Hatching date and its effect on growth and survival is another topic of importance for arctic-nesting geese, which are confronted with a short growing season. Goslings depend almost entirely on plant nutrients for their growth and development, but the nutritional quality of arctic plants declines as summer progresses (Sedinger and Raveling 1986,

Manseau and Gauthier 1993). The colonial-nesting habits of many species of geese also can lead to over-grazed habitat, which can affect forage availability for late-hatching goslings (Sedinger and Raveling 1986, Sedinger and Flint 1991). Various studies thus have documented the negative effects associated with late-hatched goslings. For example, late-hatching Lesser Snow Geese often grow more slowly than their early-hatching counterparts (Cooch et al. 1991), and they are recruited more slowly into the breeding population (Cooke et al. 1984). In Black Brant, body mass, tarsus length, and culmen length were all negatively correlated with hatching date (Sedinger and Flint 1991).

In a study of the effects of hatching date on Greater Snow Goose nesting on Bylot Island, Northwest Territories, early-hatched goslings grew faster, were heavier and larger at 40 days (near fledging), and survived better than late-hatched goslings (Lindholm et al. 1994). The steep decline in food quality during the summer likely accounts for the poor growth of late-hatched goslings; the fiber content in food plants increases while nitrogen decreases as the season progresses. Specifically, the nitrogen content of the preferred food, cotton-grass (*Eriophorum* spp.) reaches a maximum of 4.4% about 2 weeks before hatching peaks, but the nitrogen content declines up to 40% during the next 5 weeks (Manseau and Gauthier 1993). Thus, late-hatched goslings cannot maintain their intake of nitrogen, which is the key limiting factor for growth. Other factors may include the lower ambient temperatures and more rain that late-hatching goslings experience during their first 3 weeks of life, whereas these conditions are not in play for early-hatched birds. Thus, a strong selective pressure is placed on arctic-nesting geese to initiate their nests as early as possible, wherein differences in hatching dates of only 5–7 days may affect their fitness (Lindholm et al. 1994).

However, a subsequent study of this same population of Greater Snow Geese revealed that late-hatched goslings may adapt to reduced food availability (Lesage and Gauthier 1998). Specifically, although early-hatched goslings had more body protein than late-hatched goslings, the mass of organs associated with food acquisition (legs, esophagus, intestine, liver) was similar between the two groups. In contrast, late-hatched goslings had much smaller breast muscles. Hence, in an attempt to maintain a high nutrient intake, late-hatched goslings appear to favor the development of organs associated with food acquisition at the expense of other organs.

Lastly, population density can affect growth of goslings, as documented by Sedinger et al. (1998) during a long-term study of Black Brant nesting on the Yukon-Kuskokwim Delta in Alaska. During the study, this population increased from 1,100 to more than 5,000 nesting pairs. Subsequent mass of goslings at 30 days of age declined from 764 g for males and 723 g for females in 1986 to 665 g for males and 579 g for females in 1994. Cooch et al. (1991) and Francis et al. (1992) reported a similar pattern in Lesser Snow Geese. In sum, these studies demonstrated that the growth rate of goslings was directly linked to survival during the first year and thus the principal mechanism of density-dependent population regulation in arctic-nesting geese.

Subsequent study of Black Brant revealed that the often substantial *geographic* difference in growth rates of goslings is strongly related to food availability (Sedinger et al. 2001). The study compared growth rates of Black Brant nesting at two colonies on the Yukon-Kuskokwim Delta and another at the Colville River Delta on the Arctic Coastal Plain. Goslings from Colville River were nearly 30% larger (211–286 g) at 4–5 weeks of age than goslings on the Yukon-Kuskokwim Delta, likely because the standing crop of *Carex subspathacea*, the principal food of goslings, was two-times greater on the Arctic Coastal Plain. Interestingly, Black Brant do not disperse to breeding sites with better food supplies, and instead remain highly philopatric to their breeding locations, as do other species of geese (Lindberg et al. 1998). Hence, lack of a response to large-scale variations in habitat quality suggests that any increase in fitness by breeding at a better site would be offset by risks associated with postbreeding dispersal. The Colville River colony is also more than 2,000 km from the Yukon-Kuskokwim colony; thus, Black Brant on the Yukon-Kuskokwim Delta presumably could not assess habitat conditions at Colville River. However, given that the Colville River colony contains less than 4% of the Black Brant population nesting in Alaska and is not limited by density-depended feedbacks, the entire population may be held below maximum size because it does not distribute itself in response to habitat conditions (see Lindberg et al. 1998).

In addition to geese, studies of King Eiders in the Canadian Arctic revealed the effects of egg size on ducklings (Anderson and Alisauskas 2001, 2002). Hatchlings from larger eggs were relatively smaller in structural size compared with those from smaller eggs. However, larger eggs consistently produced ducklings that were absolutely heavier and had absolutely greater lipid and protein reserves, larger breast and leg muscles, higher functional maturity for breast, leg, and whole body musculature, and higher growth rates for tarsal and body mass. These differences in body composition and growth rates may affect survival in several ways: by improving thermogenesis, by reducing the time spent as optimal prey size for avian predators, and by enhancing motor development and thereby improving foraging efficiency. In particular, larger ducklings had better sprint speed, endurance, and feeding rates, which represent advantages for escaping aerial predators and for efficient foraging. Further, this relationship held until the ducklings were at least 16 days of age.

Although these studies demonstrated that large egg size enhances the survival of offspring, the results are confounded by maternal influences (i.e., "good" mothers rear more offspring successfully, regardless of egg size). In a novel approach to this issue, Pelayo and Clark (2003) switched day-old broods of Ruddy Ducks to foster mothers. The results again exhibited that offspring survival increased with egg size, which, unlike other studies, is unequivocal in this case (i.e., no maternal influence). The increase in survival likely occurred because ducklings hatching from large eggs were larger, heavier, and had more energy reserves than ducklings hatching from smaller eggs. Survival declined for ducklings hatched later in the season, despite the fact that neither egg size nor duckling condition exhibited corresponding changes with hatching date or habitat conditions. Pelayo and Clark (2003) speculated that duckling survival declined in response to a seasonal increase in the occurrence of parasites and diseases.

Brood Survival (Anatinae — True Ducks)

In their study of Mallards nesting in the PPR of Canada, Dzubin and Gollop (1972:135) concluded that brood survival was ". . . the single most important proximate factor controlling fall population size," and yet brood survival has remained among the least understood components of recruitment (Johnson et al. 1992). However, recent studies have used miniature radiotransmitters to monitor the survival and habitat use of individual goslings and ducklings; the technique provides significant information about waterfowl ecology during this important period in the annual cycle. These studies reveal that brood survival is a complex topic, subject to spatial, temporal, and interspecific differences and influenced by variables such as habitat conditions, distance from nest to water, hatching date, weather, and preda-

tion. In this section, we review these aspects of brood-survival, particularly for ducks, for which survival rates vary greatly. For example, survival rates of Mallard ducklings range from 0.16 on reservoirs in North Dakota (Sayler and Willms 1997) to 0.59 in aspen parkland habitat in Saskatchewan (Gendron and Clark 2002) and from 0.22 in highly cultivated landscapes in Montana (Rotella and Ratti 1992) to 0.35 on agricultural areas in central North Dakota. We note that most studies report survival rates for either broods or individual ducklings at 30 days of age.

General Patterns and Causes of Duckling Mortality: The greatest loss of ducklings occurs during the first 2 weeks after hatching, and the loss of the entire brood during this period is not uncommon. Two reasons explain why mortality rates are high at this time. First, young ducklings are vulnerable to adverse weather, especially cold and rainfall that cause direct mortality from hypothermia or cause indirect mortality by increasing their vulnerability to predation (Johnson et al. 1992). Second, because of their small size, young ducklings are suitable as prey for most predators and are susceptible to environmental hazards (see below).

The magnitude of early mortality of ducklings is illustrated in studies conducted across a broad area of North America. McGilvrey (1969), for example, recorded a 4-year average of 47% mortality for Wood Duck ducklings in Maryland, where 90% of all duckling mortality occurred during the first 2 weeks. In Minnesota, brood mortality during the first 2 weeks after hatching was 86% for Wood Ducks and 70% for Mallards (Ball et al. 1975). In North Dakota, 13 females Mallards lost entire broods, 11 (85%) of which occurred during the first 2 weeks after hatching (Talent et al. 1983). In California, 93% of all Mallard mortality occurred during the first 10 days (Mauser et al. 1994). For Spectacled Eiders breeding on the Yukon-Kuskokwim Delta in Alaska, 74% of the duckling mortality occurred in the first 10 days, and 49% of the females lost their entire broods (Flint and Grand 1997). For Canvasback ducklings in Minnesota, duckling mortality was greatest during the first 10 days after hatching (Korschgen et al. 1996), as occurred with Northern Pintails in both Alberta (Guyn and Clark 1999) and the Yukon-Kuskokwim Delta (Grand and Flint 1996b). During a 3-year study of Mallard brood survival at four sites in southern Ontario, overall 30-day duckling survival was 0.40 but ranged from 0.07 to 0.50 (Hoekman et al. 2004). However, the odds of daily survival were 8.8 times greater for older ducklings (more than 7 days) compared to younger ducklings (7 days old or less), and 1.7 times greater for early-hatched ducklings (before 1 June) compared to late-hatched ducklings (1 June or later). These data suggested that early nests contributed 61% of recruitment at 30 days posthatching.

Losses of entire broods usually account for a higher proportion of the total loss of ducklings than attrition within broods where at least some survive. For example, total brood loss accounted for 298 of 550 (54%) Mallard ducklings lost during a study in Manitoba (Rotella and Ratti 1992). Because of this loss, production estimates based on the average number of ducklings fledged per female will be biased sharply upward if the zero-size brood class is not included in the analysis (see also Ball et al. 1975, Ringelman and Longcore 1982, Duncan 1986).

Ducklings and goslings fall victim to an array of predators. Indeed, during their study of Mottled Ducks in Florida (the "Florida Duck"), LaHart and Cornwell (1970:120) remarked that "a list of possible duckling predators would include most of the carnivorous, terrestrial and aquatic vertebrates in Florida." In many key nesting areas, mink are by far the major predators of ducklings (Sargeant et al. 1973, Ball et al. 1975, Talent et al. 1983). For example, during a 4-year study of Canvasback broods, mink accounted for 39–100% of all known losses of ducklings (Korschgen et al. 1996). Other predators of ducklings include snapping turtles (*Chelydra serpentina*; Coulter 1957), northern pike (*Esox lucius*; Solman 1945, Lagler 1956), bullfrogs (*Rana catesbeiana*; Stewart 1967a), Northern Harriers and other raptors (Dzubin and Gollop 1972, Duncan 1983), and various species of gulls (*Larus* spp.; Duncan 1986, Milne 1974). Fire ants (*Solenopsis invicta*; Ridlehuber 1982) and blue crabs (*Callinectes sapidus*; Milne 1965) are among the invertebrates preying on ducklings. Vegetation, too, may cause the drowning deaths of ducklings, especially when very young birds dive to escape predators. Stewart (1967b) rescued Wood Duck ducklings fatally entangled in a filamentous algae (e.g., *Spirogyra* spp.); he also cited heavy losses of Lesser Scaup broods to the same cause and mentioned that fewer ducklings may survive where ponds are choked with bladderwort (*Utricularia* spp.).

In the only study to evaluate the effects of predator removal on duckling survival, Pearse and Ratti (2004) radiomarked 686 ducklings from 78 broods in south-central Saskatchewan in 2000 and 2001. Overall, duckling survival was greater (0.573) on sites where predators were removed in comparison with untreated areas (0.357). Broods also hatched earlier on predator removal sites compared to controls. Hence, predator removal obviously affected duckling survival by removing predators that likely caused total brood loss. However, earlier hatching dates caused by predator removal can also affect duckling survival because early-hatching ducklings generally have better survival rates that late-hatching ducklings (see Rotella and Ratti 1992, Sayler and Willms 1997, Stafford et al. 2002). Although this study demonstrated that brood survival responded to predator removal, control efforts nonetheless were focused on nest predators, not brood predators — of 509 predators removed, only four were mink.

Effects of Habitat Conditions and Hatching Dates: Many studies of brood survival were conducted in the PPR of North America, and the collective results revealed some general patterns. In particular, brood survival is highest where and when wetland habitats contain abundant water during the brood-rearing period, and early-hatched broods tend to have higher survival rates than late-hatched broods. In southwestern Manitoba, brood survival of 69 radiomarked female Mallards (an early-nesting species) averaged 0.49 during a 3-year study and was greatest (70%) during the wettest year and lowest in the driest (34%). Survival also was highest for broods that hatched early and in areas of greatest wetland density within 0.8 km of the nest site (Rotella and Ratti 1992). Based on a study of 56 radiomarked Mallard broods in North Dakota, total brood loss during the first 30 days of exposure was 11.2 times more likely for broods hatched in areas where the percentage of seasonal basins with water was less than 17% compared with areas where more than 59% of the basins were water filled (Krapu et al. 2000). Overall brood survival averaged 0.914 in wet years and 0.381 in dry years. A fitted model of brood survival considered the influences of seasonal basins with water, hatching date, and rainfall. Total brood loss occurred for 16 of 56 broods (28.5%) and was 5.2 times more likely during rainy instead of dry conditions; mortality increased 5% for each 1-day delay in hatching. On the Yukon-Kuskokwim Delta, Alaska, survival rates of Northern Pintail ducklings declined with hatching date at a rate of 0.6%/day (Grand and Flint 1996b).

Seasonal ponds were an especially important factor affecting brood survival because they are avoided by mink, the major predator of ducklings and other young waterbirds in the PPR (Sargeant et al. 1973, Arnold and Fritzell 1990). Mink instead require permanent water to survive drought (Sargeant et al. 1993). Krapu et al. (2000) concluded that areas lacking permanent water will have low mink populations and thus higher brood survival if seasonal wetlands are abundant. Krapu et al. (2004) subsequently reported that the permanent water resulting from construction of a 125-km canal in North Dakota provided optimal habitat for mink, which in turn affected survival of Mallard and Gadwall ducklings and broods over a broad area of surrounding landscape. Indeed, mink caused at least 65% of the identifiable predation in this area, and the 30-day survival rates for Gadwall and Mallard ducklings declined markedly after water filled the canal. The recruitment rate (females fledged per hen) for Gadwalls declined by more than 50%.

Krapu et al. (2000) proposed that the higher survival of early-hatched broods likely resulted from the greater availability of seasonal wetlands in late spring and early summer, as seasonal wetlands provide excellent habitat for aquatic invertebrates, which are the preferred foods of young ducklings. However, despite the better survival rate of early-hatched broods, the poor nest success of early-nesting waterfowl in the PPR (e.g., Mallards) causes more late-hatched broods to appear on the landscape. Hence, there is a trade-off between nesting early (low nest success but high brood survival) versus nesting late (high nest success, low brood survival), a trade-off that has intensified across the PPR over the past 60 years due to agricultural development (see Krapu et al. 2000).

In contrast to Mallards, the late-nesting Gadwall exhibits different patterns of duckling survival, as determined by a concurrent study on the same study area (Pietz et al. 2003). The 30-day survival rate of broods was 0.84, and only 9 of 58 (15.5%) radiomarked females lost their entire broods; duckling survival was 0.438. Ultimately, brood size proved a better predicator of survival than any environmental variable included in the model. Specifically, the risk of brood loss decreased 24% with each additional duckling in the brood. Unlike Mallards, however, the survival of Gadwall ducklings was not affected by rainfall during the first 7 days. Indeed, rainfall and temperature variables were not strongly associated with brood survival, probably because Gadwalls are late nesters and their broods are reared in relatively mild weather in comparison with the early-nesting Mallard. In contrast, rainfall earlier in the season is more likely to be accompanied by cold temperatures and thus greater need for females to protect young ducklings against exposure. However, the increased brooding time reduces feeding time, which further depletes a duckling's limited energy reserves and thus may increase the probability of hypothermia, predation, or starvation (see Krapu et al. 2000, Pietz et al. 2003). As with Mallards, however, mink were the principal predators of Gadwall ducklings, accounting for 68% or more of all deaths in those instances where the predator could be determined. All told, predation accounted for 86% of deaths and exposure to weather accounted for 12–13%. In comparison with Mallards, Gadwalls also may lose fewer broods because they are less cohesive and often spread out over wide areas of a wetland. This behavior, coupled with their greater preference for open water, and not shoreline, likely reduces the chances for predators to encounter and destroy entire broods of Gadwalls (Pietz et al. 2003).

The survival of Gadwall ducklings varied considerably during the 5-year study (0.13–0.60), which demonstrates the influence of environmental heterogeneity (Table 6-6). For example, survival risk for individual ducklings was twice as high when seasonal wetlands were scarce compared with times when they were abundant, likely because mink and Gadwall broods were concentrated. Poor water conditions also likely reduced the availability of aquatic invertebrates. Ducklings were exposed to very cool temperatures in those years when survival was poor. In contrast, years of high survival were characterized by an increase in seasonal wetlands and warmer temperatures. However, although survival more than doubled in successive years of this study, the number of seasonal wetlands and temperature gradients were only marginally different. Hence, other factors as yet unknown may also influence brood survival of Gadwalls (see Pietz et al. 2003).

These patterns of brood survival also help explain the seasonal decline in the clutch size of waterfowl, for which the adaptive significance is debated (see Rohwer 1992). The seasonal decline in brood survival may be an important ultimate factor influencing clutch-size decline because selection should reduce clutch size when the probability of recruitment is lowest. Thus, at least for Mallards, the selective advantage of early nesting is an adaptation to a decline in duckling survival, which appears most associated with decreasing wetland density (see Dzus and Clark 1998).

Distance Traveled to Water: Females often move

Table. 6-6. Kaplan-Meier survival rates[a] and average environmental conditions experienced by radiomarked Gadwall ducklings in each of 5 years on study areas in North Dakota. From Pietz et al. (2003:571).

Year	30-day survival	% seasonal basins wet[b]	Minimum daily temperature (°C)[c]	% exposure days with rain[d]
1990	0.28	2.0	12.6	61.6
1991	0.60	7.0	13.6	72.6
1992	0.13	2.8	8.9	51.9
1993	0.60	62.2	11.6	80.0
1994	0.52	63.9	13.0	70.0

[a] Measured from the time ducklings reached their first wetland until 30 days old.

[b] Percent of seasonal wetland basins containing water, averaged across duckling exposure days.

[c] Mean minimum daily temperature on current and previous 2 days, averaged across duckling exposure days.

[d] Presence of rain on current or 2 previous exposure days.

their broods long distances from the nest site to suitable habitat. In prairie pothole habitat at Kinderseley, Saskatchewan, Mallards frequently traveled overland with their broods, in two cases moving a straight-line distance of 4.8 km (Dzubin and Gollop 1972). Some research suggests that brood mortality may be extensive during these overland movements (Ball et al. 1975, Rotella and Ratti 1992, Mauser et al. 1994), whereas other studies have not (Evans and Black 1956, Talent et al. 1983, Dzus and Clark 1997, Guyn and Clark 1999). For example, in North Dakota, total brood loss always occurred while the ducklings were in wetland habitat and not while traveling overland; mink were the principal predators of ducklings (Talent et al. 1983). In California, 18% of the mortality experienced by Mallard ducklings occurred as broods moved from nest to water, despite the short travel distance (avg. 32 m); long-tailed weasels (*Mustela frenata*) and avian predators caused most of this mortality (Mauser et al. 1994). In Prairie Canada, Dzubin and Gollop (1972) estimated that 52% of all Mallard broods were lost during their initial journey from nest to water. In Redheads, Yerkes (2000) reported that the distance of the first move *between* wetlands accounted for the most variation associated with brood success. Female body mass, but not age, also was related to brood and duckling survival, as well as the number of surviving ducklings.

Effects of Salinity: Saline water can affect growth and condition of both adult and juvenile ducks, but effects are especially acute on young ducklings (Windingstad et al. 1987, Tietje and Teer 1988). Indeed, ducklings, especially those less than 6 days old, are particularly intolerant of saline water because their salt glands are poorly developed (Schmidt-Nielsen and Kim 1964, Riggert 1977). Mallard ducklings using natural wetlands in Saskatchewan suffered reduced growth, a variety of sublethal physiological abnormalities, and mortality when exposed to high concentrations of sodium sulphate, magnesium sulphate, and saline water (Mitcham and Wobeser 1988a, 1988b).

In experiments with Mottled Ducks in coastal Louisiana, duckling mortality varied with water salinity: 100% at 18 ppt, 90% at 15 ppt, and 10% at 12 ppt (Moorman et al. 1991). No ducklings died when exposed to salinities less than 12 ppt, but their growth rates were reduced. Further, ducklings exposed to salinities of 12 ppt and then exercised to simulate brood movements in the wild likely experienced 70% mortality (the experiment was terminated once the ducklings could not keep pace with researchers). Northern Pintail females nesting on the Yukon-Kuskokwim Delta in Alaska moved their broods to less saline habitats, whereas those nesting in nonsaline areas never moved their broods to more saline habitats. Ducklings reared in saline wetlands in North Dakota concentrated their feeding around freshwater seepages (Swanson et al. 1984). Hence, the lethal and sublethal effects of salinity significantly influence the kinds of habitat that are suitable for duck broods.

Geographic Variation: Rates of brood survival also vary geographically. During a 3-year study of Northern Pintail broods in southern Alberta, brood survival did not vary among years, ranging from 72.2 to 88.2%, although the survival of individual ducklings was more variable, ranging from 42.4 to 65.2% (Guyn and Clark 1999). In contrast, the survival rates for broods of the same species on the Yukon-Kuskokwim Delta, Alaska, were much lower, ranging from 17.7 to 45.5% during a 3-year period. Survival rates for individual ducklings also were lower, ranging from 4.0 to 14.5% (Grand and Flint 1996b). Both of these studies noted a decrease in survival as the season progressed. However, while Grand and Flint (1996b) proposed that decreased duckling survival in Alaska was related to increased predation, survival in Alberta (the prairies) may be more related to habitat quality (i.e., wetlands containing water).

Patterns and Causes of Gosling Mortality (Anserini — True Geese)

As with ducks, the majority of brood and gosling mortality occurs within the first 2 weeks. More than 82% of gosling mortality in Black Brant observed on the Yukon-Kuskokwim Delta in Alaska occurred in the first 15 days, and little mortality occurred thereafter (Flint et al. 1995). Overall, mortality rates of prefledged geese range from 0.15 to 0.40, which are generally lower than those reported for ducks (see Sargeant and Raveling 1992). As with ducks, survival rates for goslings vary considerably among years, as seen in Black Brant in Alaska, where gosling mortality ranged from 56 to 79% over a 3-year study period (Flint et al. 1995).

In the Arctic, the principal predators of ducklings and goslings are the same as those preying on nests: arctic foxes and various species of gulls and jaegers. However, predation by these groups can be severe. In the Yukon-Kuskokwim Delta in Alaska, for example, Glaucous Gulls annually may remove a minimum of 21,000 goslings of Emperor Geese, 34,000 Cackling Canada Geese, and 16,000 Greater White-fronted Geese (Bowman et al. 2004). These estimates represent 33% of the Cackling Canada Geese, 47% of the Emperor Geese, and 39% of the White-fronted Geese hatching in the area. In another study on the Yukon-Kuskokwim Delta, the survival of Emperor Goose goslings to 30 days of age varied from 0.332 to 0.708 over a 4-year period (Schmutz et al. 2001). Survival was lowest during years when Glaucous Gulls frequently disturbed the goslings. Rainfall occurring early in the brood-rearing period also caused considerable mortality.

Waterfowl Brood Habitat

The nature of duck brood habitat varies by species, as might be expected, but two generalities are apparent for ducks: Females rearing broods generally select habitats with (1) abundant invertebrate populations and (2) dense vegetative cover (pochards, however, often select open water). The availability of the former is especially necessary for the nutritional needs of ducklings, particularly during their first 2 weeks of life (see Chapter 5).

The broods of many species of dabbling ducks often spend most of the daytime secluded in dense emergent cover and reserve most of their activities for the early morning and late evening hours (Ringelman and Flake 1980). In contrast, broods of Lesser Scaup raised in forested areas of the Northwest Territories frequent large, deep wetlands where high populations of amphipods (*Gammarus lacustris, Hyalella azteca*) are available as food (Fast et al. 2004). After sunset, both dabbling and diving duck ducklings may seek open water where they actively feed on emerging insects (Swanson and Sargeant 1972).

Loafing sites, where ducklings can leave the water to preen and dry their plumage, are another important feature of brood-rearing habitat. Muskrat houses provide important loafing sites for Wood Duck broods in Massachusetts (Grice and Rogers 1965). In Minnesota, broods of Ring-necked Ducks frequented exposed mudflats 16% of the time, although these sites occupied only 0.3% of the available habitat (Maxson and Pace 1992). While on the mudflats, the ducklings spent most of their time either resting (65.8%) or engaging in comfort and preening movements (28.4%).

Prairie Potholes: Krapu et al. (2001) surveyed duck broods for 3 years in a 3,735-km² area in North Dakota and recorded the following brood numbers and wetland types along 18 transects: temporary, 1,116 (241 ha); seasonal, 1,265 (746 ha); seimipermanent, 228 (421 ha); and lake, 12 (66 ha). Blue-winged Teal and Mallard broods used seasonal wetlands (67%), whereas semipermanent wetlands were used by Gadwall (50%), Redhead (56%), and Ruddy Ducks (59%). In the PPR of Saskatchewan, Mallard broods also occurred most frequently (69–95% of days) on semipermanent wetlands (Dzus and Clark 1997). Females and their broods visited one to five wetlands during the first week after hatching, but most females remained on one wetland by the second week. In California, 12 of 27 Mallard broods moved up to six times, selecting seasonally flooded wetlands with cover instead of open or permanently flooded areas (Mauser et al. 1994). In North Dakota, Mallard broods used seasonal wetlands where whitetop rivergrass (*Scolochloa festucacea*) provided cover and high densities of invertebrates were available as food (Swanson and Meyer 1973). Broods, in fact, moved from wetlands with sparse numbers of midge larvae (Chironomidae) to those where the larvae densities were greater (Talent et al. 1982). Generally, the size of a brood's home range stabilized by the end of the second week after hatching, and ranged from 4.0 to 20.2 ha (avg. 11.0 ± 4.7 ha). With favorable water conditions, 12 of 16 broods traveled overland, eventually visiting 2–10 different wetlands during the brood-rearing period, but most (89%) moves occurred before the broods were 2 weeks old. In the prairie potholes of Montana, females led their ducklings overland to the best brood-rearing habitats (Berg 1956). Talent et al. (1982) concluded that wetland complexes with a large component of seasonal wetlands provided the optimal brood-rearing habitat for prairie-nesting Mallards, and stressed that the productivity of Mallards is greatly enhanced when management protects entire complexes of wetland types (e.g., seasonal, semipermanent, and permanent wetlands). These findings and recommendations are supported by other studies of brood survival in the PPR (Krapu et al. 2000, Pietz et al. 2003).

In another study, 4,370 broods of 14 species were observed on prairie potholes in North and South Dakota (Duebbert and Frank 1984). Considering all species, 58% of the observations occurred on semipermanent wetlands and another 24% involved seasonal wetlands. Stewart and Kantrud (1971) also reported the strong association of breeding activities with seasonal and semipermanent wetlands, which further underscores the importance of these two types of wetland habitats in the PPR. Despite the significance of these findings, wetland acquisition and protection programs often limit their focus to permanent and semipermanent wetlands, thereby overlooking seasonal wetlands except when they happen to occur in a larger complex of managed wetlands. Because of their importance to broods, seasonal wetlands warrant more attention in wetland preservation and management (Duebbert and Frank 1984).

An extensive study of brood habitat was conducted in Washington, where 320 broods of nine species were analyzed in relationship to 12 niche di-

mensions (Monda and Ratti 1988). Niche overlaps (maximum = 1.0) for 36 possible species pairs ranged from 0.62 to 0.94, with the greatest separation occurring for the dimensions of hatching date and water depth at feeding sites. For example, overlap was high for Blue-winged Teal, Gadwalls, and Cinnamon Teal because these species had similar midseason hatching peaks and also fed over dense beds of submergent vegetation. Mallard broods were isolated from other dabbling ducks because they fed in shallow water dominated by emergent vegetation. Pochard broods, in comparison with dabbling ducks, generally feed farther from shore in deeper water where the vegetation is sparse.

Stoudt (1969) described similar habitat for Canvasback broods, which preferred ponds larger than 0.4 ha with less than 10% coverage of emergent vegetation. Broods of Ring-necked Ducks in Minnesota spent 82.6% of their time in open water, where feeding was the dominant (50.9%) activity (Maxson and Pace 1992). For management, Monda and Ratti (1988) recommended a variety of water depths, which promotes greater diversity in the composition and amount of vegetative cover, and therefore benefits more species of wildlife (see also Weller and Spatcher 1965).

Forested Wetlands: In forested areas, waters impounded by beaver (*Castor canadensis*) often furnish high-quality brood habitat, especially for species such as American Black Ducks and Wood Ducks. In South Carolina, Wood Duck broods made extensive use of beaver ponds and used other kinds of wetlands primarily as travel lanes (Hepp and Hair 1977). Wood Duck broods favored larger beaver ponds (1.5–3.8 ha), especially those with a mixture of emergents and overhead shrub cover. Some 30% of the females under observation moved their broods an average of 3.2 km from small, deep-water beaver ponds to those that were well vegetated, shallow, and of larger size. Home ranges for these broods varied greatly (0.8–29.6 ha), which probably reflected the sizes of the available sites. Generally, most females and their broods initially ranged over a large area, presumably searching for suitable brood-rearing habitat, then remained relatively sedentary once a favorable site was located.

Man-made Habitats: Man-made wetlands also provide important habitat for duck broods. In Quebec, broods made extensive use of sewage lagoons where benthic invertebrate populations were five times greater than those occurring on sand-pit or excavated ponds (Belanger and Couture 1988). The attractiveness of sewage lagoons to broods in Arizona also was attributed to high densities of macroinvertebrates (Piest and Sowls 1985). Sewage ponds located near natural wetlands of good quality enhance the attractiveness of the former to duck broods (Swanson 1977). For all types of man-made ponds, more broods used those with highly irregular shorelines and at least 30% cover of emergent vegetation with a density of 30 or more stems/m²; these features are useful management guidelines for constructing ponds suitable for duck broods. For the management of brood habitat for Wood Ducks, McGilvrey (1968) recommended 25% open water and 75% vegetation, with an ideal combination of 0–10% trees, 30–50% shrubs, and 40–70% emergents.

Waterfowl broods make extensive use of stock ponds in South Dakota, where the construction of thousands of such ponds, although intended for watering livestock, have significantly contributed to waterfowl production (Bue et al. 1952, Ruwaldt et al. 1979, Mack and Flake 1980; see Chapter 9). Because most stock ponds hold water throughout the summer, they can be especially important habitat whenever natural wetlands dry up. Several factors increase the occurrence of broods on stock ponds: (1) large size, (2) large areas of shallow water with submergent vegetation, (3) presence of natural wetlands within a 1.6-km radius, and (4) the composition of emergent vegetation (Rumble and Flake 1983). Moreover, grazing must be maintained at levels conducive to preserving shoreline and emergent vegetation.

Gosling Habitat: In contrast to ducklings, goslings prefer upland habitats where they can graze on the nutritious new growth of grasses and sedges as well as consume some terrestrial invertebrates. On the Yukon-Kuskokwim Delta in Alaska, goslings of Black Brant, Cackling Canada Geese, and Emperor Geese all used a grass-sedge community dominated by *Carex subspathacea* and *Puccinellia phryganodes* (Sedinger and Raveling 1984, Sedinger 1992). Nonetheless, each species showed individual preferences (e.g., Emperor Geese strongly favored saline ponds, mudflats, and meadows dominated by *Carex ramensk*; Schmutz 2001).

Hughes et al. (1994) studied the movements and spatial differences for Greater Snow Geese breeding on Bylot Island, Northwest Territories. They identified three types, based on space, of goose families: sedentary, shifters, and wanderers. Home ranges averaged 680 ha for sedentary families, 1,660 ha for shifters, and 1,820 ha for wanderers, and initial movements from the nest to brood-rearing areas varied from less than 1 to 5 km. The home ranges of sedentary families included more ponds and lakes, whereas shifters and wanders included more upland habitat. Sedentary families also nested earlier, which indicated they were the more experienced breeders. In contrast, Lindberg and Sedinger (1998) did not find a relationship between hatching date and the type of brood-rearing areas selected by Black Brant.

Brood Amalgamation

Posthatch brood amalgamation occurs when offspring are reared by adults other than their genetic parents, a behavior broadly categorized as alloparental care (Eadie et al. 1988). Two or more adults and offspring thus "amalgamate" into a crèche, which is defined as a group consisting of any number of parentally unrelated adult females and young (Munro and Bédard 1977a). Amalgamation is particularly common among waterfowl, having been recorded for at least 28 species and appearing commonly in 14 (Eadie et al. 1988).

Brood amalgamation often occurs in Mergini, in which it has been well studied in the Common Eider. The Common Eider, the largest duck in the Northern Hemisphere, is closely associated with marine habitats. Clutch size averages three to five eggs, and incubation lasts 26 days; after their broods hatch, one or more female eiders commonly form crèches. Lone females breeding in the St. Lawrence Estuary are accompanied by an average of 14 ducklings (Beauchamp 2000). Broods amalgamate when they are about 1 week old, and the amalgamation persists until they reach fledging age (Munro and Bédard 1977a). Ducklings less than 10 days old are readily adopted into crèches, but the rate of acceptance drops for older ducklings. The final crèche size is variable but often reaches 20–30 ducklings and has exceeded 150 (Goudie et al. 2000).

Crèches may include females ranked in a hierarchy; Munro and Bédard (1977a, 1977b) accordingly recognized four categories of female Common Eiders: broody, associate, visiting, and neutral. Broody females assume leadership of the crèche, produce most vocalizations, watch for predators, occupy a central position in the group, and do not abandon the crèche. Associates do not exhibit brood behavior, but they will defend against predators, and they will remain with the crèche for days at a time. Visiting females are temporarily attracted to a crèche and, when disturbed even slightly, may depart. Lastly, neutral females are not attracted to a crèche. Together, the associate, visiting, and neutral females have been referred to as "aunts" in the crèche system (Robertson 1929, Gorman and Milne 1972, Schmutz et al. 1982).

The significance of brood amalgamation in waterfowl is hotly debated (Bustness and Erikstad 1991, Pöysä 1995, Eadie and Lyon 1998), and two hypotheses have emerged to explain this behavior. The first, the "accidental mixing hypothesis," proposes that crowded conditions and various disturbances promote accidental mixing of broods, which occurs before development of strong female–duckling bonds (Munro and Bédard 1977a, 1977b; Patterson et al. 1982, Savard et al. 1998). Offspring can mix accidentally during encounters between broods (Bustness and Erikstad 1991) or mix as the result of intraspecific aggression and territoriality (Savard 1987). Gull predation also may force broods together and thus be a major proximate factor causing amalgamation (Munro and Bédard 1977b). Colonial-nesting behavior or high nest densities likewise may be a proximate factor predisposing a species to brood amalgamation (Beauchamp 1997).

The second hypothesis incorporates several arguments, but basically proposes that brood amalgamation is adaptive and benefits the donating and/or receiving female and her ducklings (Eadie et al. 1988, Pöysä 1995, Öst 1999, Öst et al. 2000). For example, the "salvage strategy hypothesis," developed during a study of Common Eiders in Norway, proposes that females in poor condition are more likely to abandon their broods (Bustness and Erikstad 1991). During a 3-year period, 42% of females abandoned their broods, and abandonment was correlated with small clutch sizes and females with low body mass at the time their eggs hatch. These females thus appeared to sacrifice the current year's nesting effort in order to increase their own survival. However, abandonment rates as well as the formation of crèches attended by one or more females varies greatly from year to year (Öst 1999).

Female Common Eiders in crèches also gain benefits in their time budgets compared with females tending broods alone. Öst et al. (2000) reported that crèche-tending females in groups of three or more spent 80% more time feeding and 27% less time in vigilance than females tending broods alone. Further, the collective vigilance of females in crèches was at least 20% greater than lone females. Shared parental care also may provide females with access to better food, because they can make more of the long dives needed to gain access to their preferred food (blue mussels; *Mytilus edulis*) in comparison with surface feeding for other foods (Öst and Kilpi 1999, 2000).

Brood success may be enhanced in crèches because several females are available to defend against gull attacks; the large size of a crèche lowers the probability of predation for each duckling, whereas mortality rates for lone ducklings are extremely high (Munro and Bédard 1977b). Nonetheless, gull predation on Common Eider crèches can be substantial. In the St. Lawrence Estuary, Munro and Bédard (1977b) documented 906 gull attacks on 2,485 ducklings, 37% of which were successful. Larger crèches suffered more attacks, but the survival of individual ducklings within a crèche increased when the attacks involved only one gull. However, entire crèches were lost when groups of 5–40 gulls attacked.

All told, brood amalgamation represents an interesting phenomenon in the behavioral ecology of waterfowl reproduction. At this juncture, it seems of adaptive significance for the survival of eider ducklings. Nonetheless, much remains to be learned, and the current hypotheses and mechanisms associated with brood amalgamation will continue to stimulate research.

MOLTING

Molting in adult waterfowl is not restricted to the breeding season, but all species indeed replace all or most of their feathers at least once during this portion of the annual cycle. Ducklings and goslings likewise are developing and replacing various sets of feathers at this time. Thus, we include our discussion of molting in this chapter as a logical component in the progression of events during the breeding season.

Molting is an essential process in the life history of birds because the replacement of worn feathers assures the best plumage for insulation, protection from the elements, and flight. Molt also functions in other ways, including the acquisition of plumages adapted for courtship, camouflage, and signaling, and as a means of regularly lessening the load of feather lice (Amadon 1966, Gill 1990, Hohman et al. 1992, Rohwer 1999).

Despite these advantages, the molting period produces major physiological stresses. For birds in general, plumage mass is related to body size, averaging about 6.3% of ingesta-free body mass (Turcek 1966), and up to 25% of a bird's lean dry body mass may be shed and regenerated in the form of new feathers (King 1980). Also, because their primary and secondary feathers are shed in one simultaneous wing molt each year, most waterfowl experience a flightless period in which their susceptibility to predation may increase. The same condition — flightlessness — also means that molting waterfowl necessarily forage in limited areas for several weeks. Thus, the flightlessness associated with molting intricately involves such diverse matters as habitat selection, feeding ecology, predator avoidance, and energetics. In this section, we review the terminology, patterns, energetics, and strategies for molting as a basis for understanding the significance and ecology of molting in the annual cycle of waterfowl.

Terminology and Definitions

The topic of molts and plumages often seems tedious, a situation not at all helped by the plethora of synonymous terms associated with these phenomena. For instance, the dull, female-like plumage acquired in late summer by otherwise brightly colored male ducks has been termed variously as "eclipse," "nonbreeding," and "basic plumage!" To correct this confusion, Humphrey and Parkes (1959) presented a standardized terminology for all birds (the H-P system), noting the pitfalls of the previous terms that relied on seasonal or other designations (e.g., winter plumage, breeding plumage). For example, "nonbreeding or immature plumage" is confusing in regard to birds such as hawks, which often breed in just such plumages. Among its major tenets, the H-P system regards the molt of adults as homologous (common origin) and hence comparable among species. The plumage shared by all species is termed Basic, which is acquired by a complete or near-complete molt of body, wing (remiges), and tail (retrices) feathers. Any additional plumages are termed Alternate, but these plumages only involve molt of head and body feathers. As we will see below, the adult plumage usually repeats itself on an annual cycle. Amadon (1966) presented an alternative system to describe molt, but the H-P system has prevailed for waterfowl (Palmer 1976a, 1976b; Hohman et al. 1992). Howell et al. (2003) provided the most recent modification to the H-P system, which we incorporate at the end of this section, but we have focused on the H-P system because of its widespread use and acceptance.

To begin, Humphrey and Parkes (1959:6) define molting as "the normal shedding of feathers and the replacement of most or all of these by a new generation of feathers." Any single molt produces only one new generation of feathers; the term "plumage" denotes each generation. However, a feather generation often does not involve replacement of a bird's entire feather coat — a feather coat being the aggregate of feathers worn by a bird regardless of when they were acquired; in other words, regardless of origin. Thus, a given feather coat can consist of one, two, or even three generations (plumages) of feathers. Also, because each specific generation is prompted by a specific molt, the H-P system equates the number of plumages with the same number of molts. A plumage cycle refers to the time elapsing between the occurrence of a given plumage or molt until the next occurrence of that plumage or molt.

This terminology may seem confusing at first, but the system is simple because it recognizes that molts and plumages occur in a successional sequence whereby the feathers shed during a given molt may belong to more than one generation (plumage) that has survived one or more previous molts. In summary, a molt leads to a new generation of feathers, each named as a characteristic plumage, although that plumage can occur as part of a feather coat containing other generations (plumages). "*Plumage*" is the operative descriptive term in this system.

The H-P system recognizes five major plumages: (1) Natal, (2) Juvenal, (3) Basic, (4) Alternate, and (5) Supplemental, for which there are synonymously named molts. Humphrey and Parkes (1959) used the term "Basic" to describe the plumage of birds that as adults have one plumage per cycle that is replaced by a complete molt (the prebasic molt). For species that as adults have two plumages per cycle, the complete molt (prebasic) results in Basic Plumage and the prealternate molt results in Alternate Plumage, which replaces only part of the feather coat (usually other than tail and wing feathers). Prior to the H-P system, Alternate Plumage was often referred to as breeding plumage. Some species such as the Long-tailed Duck or Oldsquaw have three plumages per cycle, with the third known as the Supplemental Plumage.

For first-year swans, geese, and some species of ducks, the initial Basic and Alternate Plumages are recognizably different from the Basic and Alternate Plumages of adults. These one-time plumages were referred to as Basic I and Alternate I, after which a predictable pattern is established in which plumages do not change further with age. In other words, in contrast to juveniles and subadults, an adult bird repeatedly replaces the same plumage using the same molt; such repetitive plumages are identified with the term "definitive." In those cases where subsequent Basic or Alternate Plumages are still different from definitive (e.g., hawks, as noted earlier), they can be sequentially numbered Basic II, Basic III, and so on, although for many species of birds the additional numbering is unnecessary (i.e., definitive status is reached immediately after Basic I and Alternate I). The H-P system recognizes that plumages such as the Natal and Juvenal are worn just once in a lifetime.

We noted above, however, that Howell et al. (2003) identified some inconsistencies in use of the H-P system, which they believe stems from its use of the highly variable molt that replaces Juvenal Plumage with Basic I Plumage as the starting point of cyclic plumage succession. This approach can lead to an arbitrary first plumage cycle, which a given species or even individual could start at any point in their first 1–2 years of life. Indeed, the first prebasic molt can range from complete to absent among species; hence, it cannot be homologous among or even within species. Accordingly, plumages known as "First Basic" under the H-P system might best be considered a novel first-cycle plumage lacking any homologous counterparts in subsequent plumage cycles. Hence, the Juvenal Plumage should be considered an unambiguous starting point of the first plumage cycle because Juvenal Plumage is shared by all birds and thus homologous among species, and it also is the first true covering of feathers. Traditional Juvenal Plumage would still be named as such but should be considered synonymous with Basic I in the H-P system (see also Howell and Corben 2000). Howell et al. (2003) also proposed the term "Formative Plumage" as any plumage present in the first cycle that is not a Basic Plumage and not present in subsequent cycles. Thus under their proposed changes to the H-P system, Juvenal Plumage in puddle ducks (Anatini) and pochards (Aythyini) is succeeded by a "Formative Plumage" that is very limited in many species but is a more-or-less continuous transition to the next molt that produces the bright Alternate I Plumage of the H-P system. In summary, Howell et al. (2003) suggested the H-P system could be improved by (1) establishing the Juvenal Plumage as the starting point for molt and plumage nomenclature, (2) defining a consistent first plumage cycle, and (3) recognizing the existence of formative plumages. However, because these proposed changes are not in widespread use, and because the H-P system has long been used to describe molts and plumages of waterfowl without much ambiguity, we have used the latter system in our presentation below, but insert insights from these new ideas where appropriate. These proposed changes also were refuted by Thompson (2004).

General Patterns of Molts and Plumages

Palmer (1976a, 1976b) presents the basic patterns of waterfowl molts and plumages for each species, using the terminology of Humphrey and Parks (1959). Detailed and in-depth discussions of avian molt also can be found in Palmer (1972) and Payne (1972); the latter focuses heavily on hormonal activity during molt. Here we have drawn from Bellrose (1980), Palmer (1976a, 1976b), Oring (1968), Weller (1957), and Pyle (2005) for our summary of the major patterns.

The ancestral pattern of molt in waterfowl is one molt per cycle. Howell et al. (2003) named this pattern a "Simple Basic Strategy," noting that molts seen here are the only molts that should be considered homologous across all species of birds. This pattern is exhibited by geese, swans, and whistling-ducks wherein a complete body and wing molt (the prebasic molt) results in the Basic Plumage. Thus, adults of these species molt repeatedly from Basic Plumage to Basic Plumage. Unlike ducks, the Juvenal Plumage in swans, geese, and whistling-ducks is retained well into fall and sometimes winter, during which this plumage is molted (first prebasic molt) into the Basic I Plumage. Pyle (2005) noted that this molt extended from 22 September to 6 March in 124 specimens examined. During this time period, however, the resultant feather coat is readily recognized as distinct from the definitive Basic Plumage of adults. Hence, the number of young per family group (reproductive effort) can be determined under field conditions without actually handling the birds (Lynch and Singleton 1964). The ability to use plumage patterns to assess reproductive effort is especially important for species nesting in inaccessible areas (e.g., the Arctic) because biologists still can easily assess productivity of these species on migration routes or wintering areas.

In contrast to geese, swans, and whistling-ducks, most ducks undergo two molts per year, whereby the Basic Plumage is completely molted in the prealternate molt to produce the Alternate Plumage. Note, however, that the feather coat of a bird in Alternate Plumage contains a new generation of most body feathers but retains the wing and tail feathers of the preceding Basic Plumage. Hence, ducks in the north-temperate zone undergo two molts of their body plumage per year, but only molt the wing feathers once (see below). Another important difference among the taxa of waterfowl is that adult swans, geese, and whistling-ducks lack obvious sexual differences in their plumages. Conversely, sexual dimorphism prevails in most ducks, wherein males and females are characterized by markedly different plumage.

Wing Molt

Nearly all waterfowl display a synchronous wing molt, which means that all flight feathers (remiges) are shed simultaneously. Such a molting pattern occurs only in 11 families of birds in eight orders (King 1974). Among Anseriformes, the Magpie Goose is the only known exception, although asynchronous molting also may occur in the Ruddy-headed Sheldgoose, and the Upland Sheldgoose may skip a wing molt in some years (Summers 1982, 1983).

Waterfowl apparently must molt their remiges in synchrony to accommodate the wing loading produced by their heavy bodies and small wings; otherwise, given their high ratio of wing loading, waterfowl losing only one or two primaries would experience greatly reduced or even a total loss of flight (Woolfenden 1967, Welty 1982). Consequently, molting all of the remiges in synchrony completes the wing molt faster, which reduces the total period of flightlessness. Hohman et al. (1992) proposed an alternate, albeit not mutually exclusive, explanation that suggested synchronous molting evolved — with a few exceptions — only in wetland-dwelling birds (e.g., loons, grebes, waterfowl). They argue that waterbirds can afford to be flightless either because they can hide effectively (e.g., waterfowl) or because they do not use flight as their

primary means of escape (e.g., loons and grebes dive). Many species of male ducks, especially in the Northern Hemisphere, also acquire a dull, female-like body plumage during the flightless period, which likely represents an adaptation for reducing the risk of predation.

Flightless Period

For North American waterfowl, the period of flightlessness resulting from the wing molt varies by species from about 3 to 5 weeks. The flightless period lasts 30–40 days for swans (Scott 1972), about 25 days in geese (except for the large subspecies of Canada Geese), and about 30 days for Mallards and other ducks (Owen and King 1979; Table 6-7). Generally, geese molt during the brood-rearing period, whereas ducks molt differentially according to sex during the postbreeding period: males, when the pair-bond ends, or soon thereafter; females molt soon after their broods fledge or the brood is lost.

Patterns of Feather Replacement

Natal and Juvenal Plumage: All species of waterfowl are precocial and hatch well feathered with Natal Plumage popularly known as "down." Nelson (1993) is an excellent source for plumage descriptions for downy waterfowl and comparisons among tribes, but we review general aspects here. To begin, each downy feather originates in a specific feather follicle from which the feathers of later plumages eventually will arise. According to species, the downy Natal Plumage is replaced in about 2.5 to 16 weeks by the Juvenal Plumage, which is the first covering of true feathers. Importantly, the characteristics associated with this progression of plumage development can

Table 6-7. The duration of the flightless period in North American waterfowl resulting from the wing molt.

Subfamily or tribe	Species	Flightless period (days)	Source
Dendrocygninae	Black-bellied Whistling-Duck	20	Cain (1970)
Cygnini	Tundra Swan	35–40	Palmer (1976a)
Anserini	Canada Goose	32	Hanson (1962)
Anatini	Mallard	29–33	Owen and King (1979)
Aythyini	Canvasback	21–28	Hochbaum (1944)
Mergini	Common Merganser	28	Erskine (1971)

Table 6-8. Characteristics of plumage development have long been used to age ducklings, which is an essential technique for assessment of mortality and recruitment. From Gollop and Marshall (1954).

Plumage class	Plumage subclass	Description	Midpoint duckling age (days)	
			Anas[a]	Aythya[b]
I "Downy young" No feathers visible	a	"Bright ball of fluff." Down bright. Patterns distinct (except diving ducks). Body rounded; neck and tail not prominent.	3–4	3–5
	b	"Fading ball of fluff." Down color fading, patterns less distinct. Body still rounded; neck and tail not prominent.	8–11	8–14
	c	"Gawky-downy." Down color and patterns faded. Neck and tail prominent. Body long and oval.	12–17	14–22
II "Partly feathered as viewed from side"	a	"First feathers." First feathers show on the side under ideal field conditions. Stays in this class until side view shows one-half of side and flank feathered.	18–23	21–29
	b	"Mostly feathered." Side view shows one-half of the side and flank feathered. Primaries break from sheaths. Stays in this class until side view shows down in one or two areas only (nape, back, or upper rump).	22–38	25–45
	c	"Last down." Side view shows down in one or two areas only (nape, back, upper rump). Sheaths visible on erupted primaries through this class. Stays in this class until profile shows no down.	26–33	28–39
III "Fully Featherd in profile"		"Feathered-flightless." No down visible. Primaries completely out of sheaths but not fully developed. Stays in this class until capable of flight.	39–52	47–58

[a]Species of *Anas*: Mallard, American Black Duck, Gadwall, American Wigeon, Northern Pintail, Blue-winged Teal, Northern Shoveler.
[b]Species of *Aythya*: Redhead, Ring-necked Duck, Canvasback, Lesser Scaup.

be used to accurately determine age of ducklings as they mature to flight age (Table 6-8; Southwick 1953, Gollop and Marshall 1954). In captive Northern Pintails, for example, the first feather sheaths appeared at about 12 days and where those of the scapulars and underwing coverts (Blais et al. 2001). As these juvenal feathers arise and push the downy feathers outward, some of the latter remain temporarily attached to the tips of the new feathers (i.e., both down and juvenal feathers arise on the same, continuously emerging shafts). On the tail feathers (retrices) this pattern of plumage replacement commonly produces a notched feather, which occurs when the fragile down breaks off from the tip of the shaft. This biological feature has management value: When banding ducks late in the summer and early fall, biologists can definitively age birds with notched retrices as less than 1 year old (Fig. 6-10). The same technique may be used when checking birds killed by hunters, although, by late fall, the juvenal retrices are replaced with

Figure 6-10. Age-related appearance of waterfowl tail feathers. The two feathers on the left illustrate the retrices of juvenile birds (i.e., downy plume still intact at tip, *far left*, and after the plume has broken off to create a notched appearance). The two retrices on the right are from older birds.

feathers lacking a notch; thus, young birds can no longer be identified reliably using this criterion. Nonetheless, for the early part of the postbreeding season, young ducks in hand — dead or alive — can be rapidly separated from older birds on the basis of their tail plumage. Hence, the technique provides an easy and accurate means of determining age ratios as an index to annual production.

Young waterfowl can begin flying when their Juvenal Plumage has fully replaced their Natal

Table 6-9. Time required from hatching to flight for various species of North American waterfowl. Data are from Bellrose (1980) and references cited within.

Subfamily or tribe	Species	Time from hatching to flight (days)
Dendrocygninae	Black-bellied Whistling-Duck	53–63
Cygnini	Tundra Swan	60–70
Anserini	Canada Goose	40–70[a]
Anatini	Mallard	42–60
Anatini	Blue-winged Teal	35–44
Aythyini	Canvasback	56–68
Mergini	Common Merganser	65–70
Oxyurini	Ruddy Duck	42–49

[a]Wide range reflects variability among subspecies.

Plumage. For ducks, this process varies from about 5–6 weeks in Blue-winged Teal to 8–10 weeks in Canvasbacks (Table 6-9). Juvenile geese start flying in 6–10 weeks, and swans take even longer, requiring up to 14–16 weeks (Weller 1980). Some of the Juvenal Plumage, along with Basic I, — especially in swans, geese, and whistling-ducks — is retained well into winter and even into spring. Juvenal wing feathers in all species will not be molted until the following summer, a feature representing another useful management tool. Namely, differences in the wing feathers are used to determine the ratio of adult to juvenile birds harvested by hunters, which becomes a means for assessing populations and for guiding future harvest regulations. Similarly, sex ratios are determined from the wings collected and analyzed in each flyway (see Chapter 8).

Dendrocygninae and Anserini — Whistling-Ducks and Geese and Swans: Among whistling-ducks, geese, and swans, adult plumage is similar between the sexes, and there is one complete molt per cycle (prebasic) that results in Basic Plumage. In whistling-ducks, the Juvenal Plumage is not fully developed until about 9–14 weeks; it develops in about 9–18 weeks in swans (Palmer 1976a). In Canada Geese, the Juvenal Plumage is acquired when goslings are 5–6 weeks old, but is not fully developed until about 8 weeks (Palmer 1976a). By early fall (October) into winter, the Juvenal Plumage is gradually replaced by Basic I Plumage within the whistling-ducks and swans (see Cain 1970). Howell et al. (2003) termed the associated molt as "preformative." This Basic I Plumage is molted late the following summer — via the prebasic II molt — into the Basic II Plumage, which is considered the definitive plumage, as also is the case for geese (Palmer 1976a).

Gates et al. (1993) described the molts of Canada Geese. The wing molt was most intense in late July, about 35–40 days after goslings hatched. By late July, primary growth was 50% complete in adults and 40% complete in juveniles. The intensity of wing molt declined markedly between late July and early September, and was largely complete by early September. The body molt of both adults and juveniles increased from July to September and then declined through February. Overall, nearly all the wing molt and about 50% of the body molt occurred before the birds migrated in late September. In specimens examined by Pyle (2005), the wing molt of geese occurred from 30 June to 22 August.

Anatini — Dabbling Ducks: Most species of ducks molt the Juvenal Plumage in late summer with the prebasic molt, which results in the Basic I Plumage or the "immature plumage" recognized by Weller (1980). This molt is usually partial and may vary somewhat with each sex, but the juvenal wing feathers are retained in all species. Basic I Plumage may involve only the replacement of a few head or body feathers; in female Mallards, for example, the tail, wing, and some dorsal areas are not molted (Palmer 1976a). Indeed, Pyle (2005) noted that this molt in specimens of *Anas* that he examined (n =19) only involved 8–19% of the head, neck, upper back, breast, and sides. However, other specimens (n = 22) exhibited no evidence of molt, but instead retained the Juvenal Plumage. Thus, Pyle (2005) argues that the traditional prebasic molt does not exist in *Anas* and other genera of Anatinae as well, likely because of confusion between actual molt and pigment deposition. During the protracted molt that occurs at this time, feathers renewed early in the juvenile period appear to be cryptic (July–August), whereas those renewed later are more brightly colored, yet *all* can be part of the same molt as a given feather follicle is only activated once during this time period.

By fall and early winter, the prealternate molt in dabbling ducks begins and replaces all plumage except the wing feathers. Pyle (2005) reported that this molt in *Anas* occurred from 2 September to 16 November in most species, but was significantly later (15 Oct–18 Jan) in Blue-winged Teal, Cinnamon Teal, and Northern Shovelers. Regardless, the resulting plumage is known as the Alternate I Plumage, which is the first time "breeding plumage" is acquired. Note that the terminology identifies these plumages as Basic I and Alternate I, respectively, which along with the Juvenal Plumage are worn only once during the life of a bird. For males, the Alternate Plumage is colorful (except in a few species) and is retained until the end of the following breeding season, when the prebasic molt produces the Basic Plumage. Males are flightless at this time, and their plumage resembles that of females. Pyle (2005) reported the wing molt occurred from 6 July to 4 September. In late summer–fall, male ducks then experience the prealternate molt and again acquire their colorful Alternate Plumage. Thus, by the second year of life, the molting pattern for males in most species of dabbling ducks is established: A repeating cycle in which they enter the breeding season in Alternate Plumage, which is molted in late summer into Basic Plumage, and then quickly returns to Alternate Plumage in late fall–early winter.

For a dabbling duck hatched in a given year, that individual will undergo three molts and acquire three plumages by or during fall migration. The pattern would be as follows: (1) natal down is quickly molted (via the juvenal molt) into the Juvenal Plumage, (2) the Juvenal Plumage is molted (via the prebasic molt) during the summer into Basic I Plumage, (3) Basic I is molted (via the prealternate molt) into Alternate I by late summer early fall.

Females follow the same pattern, except they undergo a prebasic molt in late winter–early spring; the resulting Basic II Plumage is retained until late summer. In the female *Anas* specimens examined by Pyle (2005), this molt occurred from 5 February to 19 April but did not involve all the body feathers. Males underwent this molt from 13 May to 1 July. Conventional wisdom suggests that the more dull-colored Basic II Plumage gives females the advantage of camouflage during the nesting period. After breeding, a repeating cycle is established in which females molt their remiges and part of the body plumage during the prealternate molt and usually acquire the Alternate Plumage sometime during the fall, except that juvenal wing feathers are retained in first-year birds. All subsequent molting cycles thereafter follow this sequence, which establishes the definitive pattern in adult females: Basic to Alternate Plumage and back again.

Aythyini — Pochards: For pochards, the sequence is similar to dabbling ducks except that the Basic I (immature) Plumage replaces more of the Juvenal Plumage and lasts longer. Weller (1957) and Dzubin (1959) described the plumage sequences for Redheads and Canvasbacks, respectively, much of which follows. After the downy Natal Plumage, the first Juvenal Plumage appears on the tail at 12–14 days. The Juvenal Plumage is otherwise nearly complete in 5 weeks and fully complete at 8 weeks. The Basic I Plumage of both sexes begins to appear in the late summer and early fall, but this plumage is confusing to identify because it appears in a continuum and thus usually cannot be seen entirely at a given time on an individual bird (Palmer 1976b). Indeed, as with species of *Anas*, Pyle (2005) believes that Basic I Plumage does not exist in species of *Aythya*. Regardless, the first feathers of this plumage (Basic I) are visible at about 9 weeks of age, but the last feathers may not be acquired until 28 weeks of age. In both sexes, feathers of the Alternate I Plumage appear before the primaries of the Juvenal Plumage

harden. Alternate I Plumage is complete by January or February, when individuals are 6.5–8.0 months old, and rarely is as bright as subsequent Alternate Plumages. Females undergo prebasic molt in April, May, and June, and acquire Basic II Plumage, which involves the crown, cheeks, and neck; also acquired is the down used during nesting, which is longer and coarser than ordinary down. Yearling males begin prebasic molt from late June to early July, and by September are in Alternate I Plumage. Adult males begin prebasic molt in late June after leaving their mates. The resulting Basic Plumage, which is worn briefly in late summer, starts the repeating cycle; thereafter follows the prealternate molt and Alternate Plumage. Adult females undergo a prealternate molt in late summer, which leads to the Alternate Plumage.

Mergini — Sea ducks: Sea ducks, which are not usually sexually mature until their second year, do not acquire their Alternate Plumage until their second fall prior to the period of winter courtship. Thus, the immature male component of the population is easily identifiable from mature males, but they may resemble both mature and immature females (see Bolen and Chapman 1981). Long-tailed Ducks are an interesting exception as they have three plumages per cycle (Salomonsen 1949); recall that this extra generation is termed the Supplemental Plumage (Humphrey and Parkes 1959, Palmer 1972). In essence, both sexes acquire a plumage during winter that is equivalent to Alternate Plumage in other species, but in spring the birds undergo a partial molt into a duller summer plumage in which they breed. Overall, less is known about molting in sea ducks than in many of the other tribes of waterfowl.

Oxyurini — Stiff-tailed Ducks: Molting in Ruddy Ducks, and perhaps in other species of Oxyurini, is unlike other waterfowl taxa. In this case, adults of both sexes retain the Basic Plumage from late summer through to the following spring, after which they molt into Alternate Plumage. In first-year birds, the Juvenal Plumage is retained through the first winter and into early spring (Pyle 2005). The first prebasic molt into Basic I Plumage occurred from 19 October to 18 February in the 19 specimens examined by Pyle (2005).

The definitive Alternate Plumage of adults is acquired in winter and early spring, but is partial: Cryptic feathers of males are replaced with bright feathers, and most retrices are replaced (Pyle 2005).

Adults of both sexes undergo the wing molt in late summer and early autumn (Pyle 2005), but a second wing molt — as assumed by previous workers — is very rare (Jehl and Johnson 2004). However, the retrices are molted twice annually but gradually, so that two generations of full-length feathers are present at any time. This pattern assures that a functional tail is always present, which is important because the tail is used in the foraging behavior of the Ruddy Duck (see Jehl and Johnson 2004).

Energetics of Molt

The molting process involves the synthesis of new feathers as well as the replacement of other keratinized structures such as scales, claws, and horny parts of the bill. The resulting increase in keratin synthesis involves intensification of amino acid metabolism, modification of water balance, increase in blood volume, and a cyclic osteoporosis (see King 1974, 1980). Molting is thus nutritionally costly; hence, it is somewhat surprising that the energy efficiency of feather synthesis is low compared with reproduction and other events in the annual cycle of birds. King (1980) also noted that the energy invested in actual keratin synthesis is only about 7% of the total cost of molting, which indicates that molting involves nutritional costs above and beyond simple growth of feathers.

The cost of producing new feathers averages about 448 kJ/g (Kendeigh et al. 1977). The amino acids cystine and cysteine also are more concentrated in feathers than in the animal proteins (0.0–6.3 g/100 g) or the plant proteins (0.0–2.9 g/100 g) that birds ingest (Newton 1968). Molting birds therefore must consume food in excess of their other nutritional requirements in order to obtain essential amino acids. Other studies, however, indicate that overall nitrogen retention beyond the necessary range of amino acids is a more important constraint on feather synthesis than specific sulfur amino acids (Murphy and King 1984a, 1984b).

Some of the most detailed work on molting waterfowl concerns female Mallards during the prebasic molt (Heitmeyer 1987, 1988a). The mean dry mass of the Basic Plumage of adult female Mallards was 72.7 g. Moreover, during the prebasic molt, females replaced all but the wing feathers, and the dry mass of the new Basic Plumage was 53.7 g, which consisted of about 46 g of protein. This feather synthesis required ingestion of 84 g of protein, assuming a 55% conversion efficiency of ingested protein to feathers. This conversion may be an overestimate, how-

ever, considering that about 80% of the protein ingested by molting White-crowned Sparrows (*Zonotrichia leucophrys*) was either oxidized or converted to nonprotein compounds such as fat or carbohydrate (Murphy and King 1984b).

Heitmeyer (1988a) also determined that protein costs were higher during the middle stages of the molt, when the largest proportion of the plumage was being replaced (Fig. 6-11). Using data reported

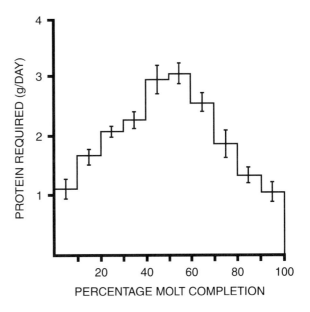

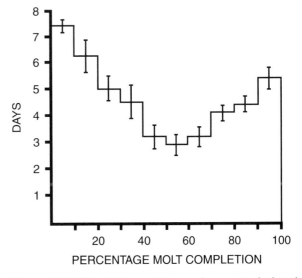

Figure 6-11. The daily protein requirements during the prebasic molt of female Mallards can exceed 3 g/day during mid-molt (*top*), but this demand is reduced because completion of the molt is staggered over many days (*bottom*). From Heitmeyer (1988a:264–265). With permission from the Cooper Ornithologocal Society.

by Swanson et al. (1979), Krapu (1981), and Drobney (1980), Heitmeyer (1988a) calculated that female Mallards require 125 g of exogenous protein to produce a clutch of 11 eggs, whereas 84 g is required for the prebasic molt. However, protein costs associated with egg production extend for about 18 days, whereas the protein demands for the prebasic molt extend for 46 days. Even so, the protein costs of 3 g/day during mid-molt approach those associated with reproduction (i.e., about 5 g/day, the highest in the annual cycle).

Hohman et al. (1997) examined the relative costs of the prebasic and prealternate molt in male Blue-winged Teal. Alternate body plumage was about 10% more than Basic Plumage (14.8 compared with 13.3 g). Although the potential of molt-induced stress might be greatest in small-bodied waterfowl like teal, Hohman et al. (1997) concluded that molting male Blue-winged Teal were not nutritionally stressed because the length of the remiges was correlated with structural size. Nonetheless, the sum of the energy demands during molt obviously requires changes in a bird's energy budget and adaptations to reduce predation, especially during the flightless period. Thus, waterfowl exhibit a variety of ecological and physiological strategies to cope with the demands of molting. Waterfowl biologists only recently have begun to determine the nature of these strategies.

Strategies for Molting

Food and Habitat Selection: Foraging for the protein-rich foods — especially invertebrates — necessary for feather production is time-consuming (Drobney and Fredrickson 1979), and birds must concurrently seek and obtain foods to meet their daily energy requirements (e.g., carbohydrates). During fall and winter on the Southern High Plains of Texas, invertebrates were selected by molting Green-winged Teal (Anderson et al. 2000) and Northern Pintails (Smith and Sheeley 1993). For Green-winged Teal, invertebrates comprised 8–31% of the overall diet from October through December.

On the breeding grounds, the nutritional demands of molt occur concurrently with flightlessness, wherein birds are at a greater risk of predation. Hence, given the necessity of heightened foraging activities at this crucial time, flightless waterfowl usually seek habitats with dense cover or, in some cases, large expanses of open water (see Bailey 1983). Concurrently, however, such habitats must provide the requisite food resources without unnecessarily

lengthening the flightless period (Pehrsson 1987). Alternatively, waterfowl may adopt other strategies to offset these restrictions (i.e., protective cover) yet still replace their wing feathers as quickly as possible.

Dynamics of Body Reserves: As an example, at the Rockefeller Wildlife Refuge in coastal Louisiana, Moorman et al. (1993) studied the carcass mass and composition of molting male and female Mottled Ducks. Both sexes entered the flightless period with equal reserves of lipids, which had increased over the previous period (i.e., late brood-rearing for females and breeding for males); but these reserves were enough to satisfy only 33% (9 days) of the existence energy required during the 27-day flightless period. By relying on stored lipids during the flightless period, Mottled Ducks can reduce their activities somewhat (e.g., feeding time), which probably decreases their exposure to predators and increases the probability of surviving the flightless period. Mallards also experience decreased body mass during the flightless period (Panek and Majewski 1990), a response that may be typical of dabbling ducks (i.e., the birds temporarily forego their usual behavior of foraging in shallow water, presumably because of the increased risk of predation in such areas). Other dabbling ducks increase their body mass before the wing molt but then experience a 10–24% decrease in body mass during the flightless period (see Panek and Majewski 1990).

Declining body mass also may be adaptive because it presumably represents the mobilization of stored lipids to meet everyday energy requirements, whereas most of the proteins acquired in the diet at this time can be allocated to feather synthesis. This is similar to the pattern reported for female Mallards undergoing prebasic molt during late winter in the Mingo Basin of southeastern Missouri (Heitmeyer 1988b). In Canada, Young and Boag (1982) similarly noted the mobilization of lipid reserves of male Mallards during their flightless period, after which lipid stores were replenished, probably in preparation for fall migration.

The mobilization of lipid reserves during the molt represents an additional adaptation: Because of the associated loss of body mass, wing loading also is reduced, which in turn shortens the time before at least limited flight is regained (i.e., brief escape flights become possible). For example, although Balát (1970) and Owen and King (1979) recorded the flightless period of Mallards as lasting 29–36 days, Pehrsson (1987) observed that Mallards were capable of short escape flights 19–26 days into the flightless period. Similarly, captive Gadwalls completely renewed their flight feathers in 35–40 days, but could fly on about day 25 (Oring 1968). Black Brant made short flights when the ninth primary averaged 62% of its final mean length, and sustained flight was possible at about 70% (Taylor 1995).

Overall, molting waterfowl are capable of flight when their remiges reach approximately 70% of their final length (Hohman et al. 1992). Panek and Majewski (1990) measured the growth of flight feathers in male Mallards as 5.5–6.7 mm/day, which occurred independent of body mass, even though the latter declined 12% in both sexes during the flightless period. The average daily growth rate of remiges in most molting waterfowl is 2–3% of their final length (Hohman et al. 1992).

Ducks probably do not increase their lipid reserves to levels that would allow little or no feeding during the flightless period because the increased body mass would affect wing loading, the length of the flightless period and, ultimately, survival (Pehrsson 1987). Moorman et al. (1993) concluded that Mottled Ducks — and perhaps other ducks as well — strike a balance whereby their levels of lipid reserves permit some reduction in those activities that lessen their exposure to predators, but not to the point where wing loading and the length of the flightless period are increased significantly. Thus, the selective pressure of predation may be the ultimate factor regulating body mass and lipid reserves of molting Mottled Ducks. In any case, mobilization of lipid reserves for energy, together with reduced foraging and other activities, may represent an effective strategy in light of the high survival rate (0.89) recorded for male American Black Ducks molting in Labrador (Bowman and Longcore 1989).

Nutritional Stress: Although the protein requirement for molt is substantial at times, it may not be "stressful" in an evolutionary sense if such a requirement does not affect fitness (Ankney 1979). In White-crowned Sparrows, for example, the process of feather replacement spans 54 days; hence, the rate at which amino acids are required actually might be slight (Murphy and King 1984b).

Hanson (1962) long ago argued that Canada Geese could not meet the nutritional demands of their wing molt with increased food consumption, and therefore catabolized pectoral muscle and leg bone for the nutrients required for feather synthesis. He subsequently proposed that the molt was the most stressful period in the annual cycle of water-

fowl, especially for females. However, Ankney (1979) showed that there was no overall protein deficit during the molt of Lesser Snow Geese. Instead, he asserted that the catabolization of pectoral muscles noted by Hanson was better explained by a "use-disuse" hypothesis. The study concluded that Lesser Snow Geese met the nutritional demands of the wing molt by increasing nutrient intake — and suggested that other waterfowl behaved similarly. In the case of Lesser Snow Geese, entire families walk to feeding areas up to 50 km distant from their breeding colonies; thus, their leg muscles undergo hypertrophy *before* the geese experience flightlessness. Also, because undisturbed geese are behaviorally flightless during the brood-rearing period, it hardly seems surprising that the pectoral muscles experience atrophy. Indeed, Ankney (1979) determined that an increase in protein in either the leg or pectoral musculature was always at least partially compensated by a decrease in the other.

Similarly, Gates et al. (1993) did not find significant catabolism of protein reserves by molting Canada Geese, even during the flightless portion of the wing molt. As with Lesser Snow Geese, protein mass declined because breast muscles atrophied during the flightless period. Gadwalls (Hay 1974) and Mallards (Young and Boag 1982) also reduce their pectoral muscle mass during the wing molt, but concurrently experience an increase of leg muscle mass, apparently the result of their increased swimming activities during the flightless period.

Most biologists now accept that waterfowl and other molting birds do not rely on catabolism of their body tissues for protein and other nutrients necessary for new feather growth (Heitmeyer 1988a), although it remains possible that small amounts of body protein may be catabolized for feather synthesis (Dol'nik and Gavrilov 1979, Hartman 1985). Experiments conducted by Murphy and King (1984b) demonstrated that molting White-crowned Sparrows fulfill the demands for protein and sulphur amino acids by adjusting their dietary intake, and not by depleting tissue proteins. Their study further elucidated sulphur amino acids as especially important to molting birds.

Chronology and Intensity of Molting: A major strategy for meeting the demands of molting is to spread the cost over a long period, particularly in response to variation in habitat conditions. Heitmeyer (1987), for example, recorded seasonal and annual variations in the timing of the prebasic molt for female Mallards, and related these variations to differences in age, pairing status, habitat, and weather conditions. Specifically, when habitat conditions were poor, Mallards initiated and completed molting later when compared to years with good habitat conditions. On the Southern High Plains of Texas, the intensity of feather molt in Green-winged Teal was greater (11.6%) during wet years than in dry years (3.6%; Anderson et al. 2000), as likewise occurred for molting Northern Pintails (Smith and Sheeley 1993). Similarly, Gates et al. (1993) reported annual differences in molting intensity for Canada Geese in response to variations in food energy. In a controlled experiment, captive female Mallards fed a commercial duck food ad libitum began prebasic molt 27–35 days before females on a restricted diet (Richardson and Kaminski 1992).

Because female Mallards probably complete the prebasic molt before the stress of spring migration, these two energetically demanding events likely did not overlap. Conversely, Bluhm (1988) believed the prebasic molt of females may overlap with fall migration, and Lovvorn and Barzen (1988) suggested that — except for laying, incubation, and wing molt — the energetic costs of molting in Canvasbacks are not great enough to separate molting from other activities (e.g., nutrient storage, migration, courtship, or even the early stages of rapid follicle growth). Heitmeyer (1987) found that feather replacement is staggered in Mallards, whereby the two largest areas of feathering (neck and belly) are not molted at the same time.

According to Gates et al. (1993), the prebasic molt in Canada Geese spanned at least 5–6 months for both adults (July to December) and juveniles (August to December), but molt intensity was greatest before fall migration. Specifically, primary growth was about 50% complete in adults and 40% complete in juveniles by late July, and most of the body molt occurred after geese regained their flight capabilities. Final wing molt was nearly complete by early September. Overall, nearly all of the wing molt and about half the body molt was completed before fall migration, which began in late September. However, more than 60% of the geese showed some indication of molt through at least March; hence, molt in these birds required at least 8 months. Only the nesting season (May to June) was entirely free of molt activity. Adults also concentrate energy and nutrients after completing the wing molt and before intensifying the body molt, which likely reduced their flightless period. Hence, the apparent "best" strategy is to complete the wing molt and most of the body molt during late summer and early fall, when weather conditions are favorable, but geese can still complete molt in fall and winter, if necessary. Thus, the molting pattern in this subspecies of Canada Goose appears to minimize nutritional conflicts because the molt process itself is spread out over 8 or more months in some individuals. Further, the simple, single annual molt in geese maximizes their flexibility in adjusting to environmental conditions.

Male Canvasbacks provide a final example of strategies used by molting waterfowl, in this case for a pochard. Canvasbacks are primarily herbivores, but their diets were not altered during postreproductive molts — plant material never comprised less than 93% of their diet, although protein intake was slightly higher during the preflightless period (Thompson and Drobney 1997). Canvasbacks did not catabolize body protein during molt, but they did enhance amino acid acquisition by modifications in gut morphology and by improved efficiency of protein assimilation (Thompson and Drobney 1996). Postreproductive molts were extended over a 6-month period, which reduced daily protein costs; this likely represented the key adaptation that allowed Canvasbacks to meet the nutritional demands of molt despite a primarily herbivorous diet.

Overall, ecological adaptations such as these, coupled with those adaptations associated with habitat selection and the dynamics of body reserves, support the conclusions of Murphy and King (1984b:331): ". . . these considerations begin to explain how and why molting birds do, in fact, succeed in nature and are much less susceptible to nutritional constraints than has been imagined."

Molting Patterns and Strategies Outside the Temperate Zone

Research on waterfowl ecology is markedly skewed toward north-temperate species. However, patterns identified from studies of north-temperate species may not pertain to species elsewhere and, in fact, may be quite different. A look at tropical species or those from arid zones helps understand the full scope of molting strategies adopted by waterfowl.

Consider, for example, the molting patterns of the White-faced Whistling-Duck in the Nyl River floodplain of South Africa, an arid zone in the Southern Hemisphere (Petrie 1998a, 1998b). Both sexes are molting in most feather areas when (December and January) they arrive on their breeding areas and continued to molt through the period of rapid follicle growth, but molting essentially ended during egg laying and incubation. Replacement of contour (body) feathers peaked during brood-rearing and before the wing molt, and was followed by the loss of primaries and secondaries. Thus, White-faced Whistling Ducks extended the prebasic molt over the 5 months they spent on breeding areas, and it continued throughout the time birds were on wintering areas. In contrast, female Mallards in the temperate zone complete prebasic molt in as little as 7 weeks (Heitmeyer 1987).

Unlike temperate ducks, which always replace remiges on their breeding areas, White-faced Whistling-Ducks undergo wing molts in early winter (10%), late winter (3%), or spring (34%; Petrie 1998a). At least four other species of South African waterfowl also do not exhibit distinct periods of remige replacement (Dean 1978). Waterfowl breeding in semi-arid environments may retain their flight capabilities during the brood-rearing period, which enables them (1) to search for new habitat as current areas begin to dry, (2) to escape predators during overland brood movements, and (3) even to desert their broods during periods of extreme drought (see Petrie 1998b). However, even the occurrence of good quality molting habitat can be ephemeral in semiarid areas; thus, timing of the remigial molt is likely influenced by completion of reproduction and by persistence of suitable postbreeding habitat. For example, White-faced Whistling-Ducks could not complete their wing molt on the Nyl River floodplain in years when flooding did not occur (Petrie 1998b).

In sum, the molting patterns of White-faced Whistling-Ducks likely reflect adaptations to the unpredictability of habitat conditions in semiarid environments that occur in South Africa and elsewhere (Alexander 1985). Hence, they are distinctly unlike north-temperate and arctic species that experience comparatively very predictable but dramatic climactic changes associated with their breeding seasons — a virtual "climatic trumpet" (Flannery 2001) — and instead respond with temporal and spatial adjustments to the annual cycle of events. Thus, White-faced Whistling-Ducks are characterized by only one molt per year, spread over a long time period, which permits much greater flexibility in adjusting molt intensity and chronology than is possible for species that molt twice annually. White-faced Whistling-Ducks simply interrupt prebasic molt whenever breeding habitats become available, and interrupt molt for a short period (egg laying and incubation). Intense molt of contour feathers also occurs while both sexes are cooperatively rearing broods, which is likely permitted because whistling-ducks exhibit biparental care. In contrast, temper-

ate species of ducks, because their habitat conditions are predictable, can completely separate two plumage replacements (Basic and Alternate) with an intervening period devoted to reproduction.

White-faced Whistling-Ducks are also monomorphic; thus, extension of the molting period may be possible because they are not constrained by acquisition and replacement of a second (Alternate) Plumage, as occurs in temperate species of ducks. Further, extended molting spreads protein costs of feather production over a long period, which may be very important for White-faced Whistling-Ducks because they are primarily herbivores (Petrie and Rogers 1996) and thus may have difficulty satisfying the amino acid (protein) requirements needed for feather replacement. Most all species of waterfowl that undergo a second or third molt per cycle are omnivores or carnivores. In contrast, herbivorous species (swans, geese, whistling-ducks) retain the ancestral pattern of one molt per cycle, perhaps because low dietary protein and/or deficiencies of specific amino acids have precluded the evolution of a second annual replacement of feathers (Petrie 1998b). These species also spread the cost of molting over a long period, such as Gates et al. (1993) reported for Canada Geese (8 or more months) and Eoin and Petrie (2003) described for Tundra Swans. Geese and swans therefore may be able to overlap nutritionally costly events like molt and migration because they molt at low intensity and migrate slowly; thus, daily costs of molting are low, which permit an overlap of two important life-history events (see Eoin and Petrie 2003).

Molt Migration

If the habitat requirements necessary for successfully completing the wing molt are not available near the nesting area, waterfowl often undergo a "molt migration" to more suitable locations (Salomonsen 1968). This behavior is particularly well developed in waterfowl and can result in concentrations of many thousands of individuals on molting areas (Fig. 6-12). Ideal molting areas have shallow water, abundant food, good cover, and are free from disturbance; waterfowl often travel great distances to find these conditions. Canada Geese from midcontinent North America undergo a molt migration of at least 1,000 km to the Thelon River area of the Northwest Territories (Sterling and Dzubin 1967). Canada Geese breeding at the Crex Meadows Wildlife Management Area in northwest Wisconsin undergo a molt migration to northern Manitoba; some geese travel 1,300

Figure 6-12. Many species of waterfowl often undergo a "molt migration" from the breeding area to large, remote lakes where the wing molt is undertaken, such as the lakes shown here on the Arctic Coastal Plain of Alaska. The flightless Black Brant (*left*) was captured near Teshekpuk Lake, Alaska, an especially important molting site for Black Brant and several species of geese. Photos courtesy of Dirk V. Derksen (*top*), and Karen S. Bollinger (*left*), U.S. Geological Survey, Alaska Science Center.

km for this purpose (Zicus 1981). Canada Geese originating from populations in 26 states and 6 Canadian provinces undergo molt migrations to James Bay and Hudson Bay (Abraham et al. 1999).

Two features characterize the molt migration of geese: (1) The flight is composed of unsuccessful breeders and nonbreeding birds, and (2) the route is nearly always northerly in direction. A northward migration at this time apparently offers two advantages: (1) The birds arrive just when the production of new food has peaked (Owen and Ogilvie 1979); and (2) because of the longer day lengths, there is more time in which to forage (Derksen et al. 1982). The individuals undertaking a molt migration also may increase their probability of survival by avoiding competition with those birds that have successfully produced offspring (Sterling and Dzubin 1967).

Among ducks, males often leave their females

sometime after the onset of incubation and gather to molt on large bodies of water. Males are accompanied by nonbreeding females or failed breeders, whereas successfully breeding females tend to molt in the vicinity of brood-rearing wetlands (Hohman et al. 1992). However, 32 of 34 radiomarked female Mallards (including successful breeders) left their breeding marshes in California for molting areas 12–536 km distant (Yarris et al. 1994). Female Mallards also exhibited site fidelity to molting areas, which were permanent, emergent marshes associated with shallow lakes or rivers or managed wetlands flooded in summer.

The molt migrations of sea ducks often involve spectacular concentrations of individuals traveling long distances. One of these involves about 100,000 King Eiders that gather on Disko Bay on the west coast of Greenland after leaving breeding areas in the eastern Canadian Arctic (Salomonsen 1968, Frimer 1994). Some 10,000 sea ducks and pochards annually gather to complete their wing molt at Takslesluk Lake on the Yukon Delta in Alaska (King 1973), and 10,000–30,000 Long-tailed Ducks traditionally gather to molt in the near-shore lagoons along the Beaufort Sea in Alaska (Flint et al. 2004). Molt migrations also occur in most species of shelducks (Williams 1979); more than 90% of the European population of Common Shelducks molt together on the Wadden Sea mudflats in Germany (Salomonsen 1968).

Postbreeding pochards from the Canadian prairies move northward to the numerous lakes in the southern boreal forests of Manitoba and Saskatchewan (Bailey 1983). The four species in this study segregated their use of habitats within this area based on food choice and foraging behavior. They also formed large concentrations while molting and staging, including 300,000 Lesser Scaup on MacCallum Lake in Saskatchewan and 80,000 Redheads in Long Island Bay in Lake Winnipegosis, Manitoba. Molt migrations are less prevalent in populations breeding in more southerly areas and are unknown in tropical waterfowl (Owen and Black 1990).

Waterfowl often gather at traditional molting sites year after year and, for some areas, continuously for nearly a century (Kumari 1979). An individual's fidelity to molting areas is less well known, although a recent study of male American Black Ducks molting in Labrador revealed that 52% returned to the same pond where they molted the previous year (Bowman and Brown 1992). More than 67% of molting Gadwalls were recaptured on the same wetland in subsequent years (Szymczak and Rexstad 1991). Black Brant from 10 different colonies in Alaska and Canada converge at a traditional molting site in the Teshekpuk Lake area on the Arctic Coastal Plain, where the birds displayed high (95%) rates of fidelity to specific sites (Bollinger and Derksen (1996). Steller's Eiders also exhibited high fidelity rates to traditional molting areas in Alaska (Flint et al. 2000). These findings underscore the importance of protecting molting areas from degradation and disturbances with the same zeal that managers guard nesting or other habitat crucial to each stage in the life cycle of waterfowl.

LITERATURE CITED

Abraham, K. F., J. O. Leafloor, and D. H. Rusch. 1999. Molt migration Canada Geese in northern Ontario and western James Bay. Journal of Wildlife Management 63:649–655.

Afton, A. D. 1984. Influence of age and time of reproductive performance of female Lesser Scaup. Auk 101:255–265.

Afton, A. D., and S. L. Paulus. 1992. Incubation and brood care. Pages 62–108 in B. D. J. Batt, A. D. Afton, M. G. Anderson, C. D. Ankney, D. H. Johnson, J. A. Kadlec, and G. L. Krapu, editors. Ecology and management of breeding waterfowl. University of Minnesota Press, Minneapolis.

Aldrich, J. W., and C. G. Endicott. 1984. Black rat snake predation on Giant Canada Goose eggs. Wildlife Society Bulletin 12:263–264.

Alexander, W. J. R. 1985. Hydrology of low latitude Southern Hemisphere land masses. Hydrobiologia 125:75–83.

Amadon, D. 1966. Avian plumages and molts. Condor 68:263–278.

Amat, J. A. 1985. Nest parasitism of Pochard Aythya ferina by Red-crested Pochard Netta rufina. Ibis 127:255–262.

Andelt, W. F. 1987. Coyote predation. Pages 128–140 in M. Novak, J. A. Barker, M. E. Obbard, and B. Mallloch, editors. Wild furbearer management and conservation in North America. Ontario Trappers Association, North Bay, Ontario.

Anderson, J. T., L. M. Smith, and D. A. Haukos. 2000. Food selection and feather molt by nonbreeding American Green-winged Teal in Texas playas. Journal of Wildlife Management 64:222–230.

Anderson, M. R., M. S. Lindberg, and R. B. Emery. 2001. Probability of survival and breeding for juvenile female Canvasbacks. Journal of Wildlife Management 65:385–397.

Anderson, V. R., and R. T. Alisauskas. 2001. Egg size, body size, locomotion, and feeding performance in captive King Eider ducklings. Condor 103:195–199.

Anderson, V. R., and R. T. Alisauskas. 2002. Composition and growth of King Eider ducklings in relation to egg size. Auk 119:62–70.

Ankney, C. D. 1979. Does the wing molt cause nutritional stress in Lesser Snow Geese? Auk 96:68–72.

Ankney, C. D. 1980. Egg weight, survival, and growth of Lesser Snow Goose goslings. Journal of Wildlife Management 44:174–182.

Ankney, C. D., and A. R. Bissett. 1976. An explanation of egg-weight variability in the Lesser Snow Goose. Journal of Wildlife Management 40:729–734.

Anthony, R. M. 1997. Home ranges and movements of arctic fox (Alopex lagopus) in western Alaska. Arctic 50:147–157.

Anthony, R. M., P. L. Flint, and J. S. Sedinger. 1991. Arctic fox removal improves nest success of Black Brant. Wildlife Society Bulletin 19:176–184.

Arnold, T. W., and E. K. Fritzell. 1990. Habitat use by male mink in relation to wetland characteristics and prey abundances. Canadian Journal of Zoology 68:2205–2208.

Arnold, T. W., D. W. Howerter, J. H. Devries, B. L. Joynt, R. B. Emery, and M. G. Anderson. 2002. Continuous laying and clutch-size limitation in Mallards. Auk 119:261–266.

Arnold, T. W., M. D. Sorenson, and J. J. Rotella. 1993. Relative success of overwater and upland Mallard nests in southwestern Manitoba. Journal of Wildlife Management 57:578–581.

Babcock, C. A., A. C. Fowler, and C. R. Ely. 2002. Nesting ecology of Tundra Swans on the coastal Yukon-Kuskokwim Delta, Alaska. Waterbirds 25 (Special Publication 1):236–240.

Bailey, E. P. 1993. Introduction of foxes to Alaskan islands — history, effects on avifauna, and eradication. U.S. Fish and Wildlife Service Resource Publication 193.

Bailey, R. O. 1983. Use of southern boreal lakes by moulting and staging diving ducks. International Waterfowl Research Bureau Symposium 28:54–59.

Balát, F. 1970. On the wing-moult in the Mallard, Anas platyrhynchos, in Czechoslovakia. Zoologicke Listy 19:135–144.

Ball, I. J., D. S. Gilmer, L. M. Cowardin, and J. H. Riechmann. 1975. Survival of Wood Duck and Mallard broods in north-central Minnesota. Journal of Wildlife Management 39:776–780.

Ballantyne, E. E. 1958. Rabies control in Alberta wildlife. Veterinarni Medicina 53:87–91.

Balser, D. S. 1964. Management of predator populations with antifertility agents. Journal of Wildlife Management 28:352–358.

Balser, D. S., H. H. Dill, and H. K. Nelson. 1968. Effect of predator reduction on waterfowl nesting success. Journal of Wildlife Management 32:669–682.

Barry, T. W. 1962. Effect of late seasons on Atlantic Brant reproduction. Journal of Wildlife Management 26:19–26.

Batt, B. D. J., and H. H. Prince. 1978. Some reproductive parameters of Mallards in relation to age, captivity, and geographic origin. Journal of Wildlife Management 42:834–842.

Beasley, B. A., and C. D. Ankney. 1992. Physiological responses of cold-stressed blue and snow phase Lesser Snow Goose goslings. Canadian Journal of Zoology 70:549–552.

Beauchamp, G. 1997. Determinants of intraspecific brood amalgamation in waterfowl. Auk 114:11–21.

Beauchamp, G. 2000. Parental behaviour and brood integrity in amalgamated broods of the Common Eider. Wildfowl 51:169–179.

Beauchamp, W. D., R. R. Koford, T. D. Nudds, R. G. Clark, and D. H. Johnson. 1996a. Long-term declines in nest success of prairie ducks. Journal of Wildlife Management 60:247–257.

Beauchamp, W. D., T. D. Nudds, and R. G. Clark. 1996b. Duck nest success declines with and without predator management. Journal of Wildlife Management 60:258–264.

Belanger, L., and R. Couture. 1988. Use of man-made ponds by dabbling duck broods. Journal of Wildlife Management 52:718–723.

Belanger, L., and S. Tremblay. 1989. Ducks nesting on artificial islands in Quebec. Wildlife Society Bulletin 17:233–236.

Bellrose, F. C. 1955. Housing for Wood Ducks. Illinois Natural History Survey Circular 45.

Bellrose, F. C. 1980. Ducks, geese and swans of North America. Stackpole Books, Harrisburg, Pennsylvania.

Bellrose, F. C. 1990. The history of Wood Duck management. Pages 13–20 in L. H. Fredrickson, G. V. Burger, S. P. Havera, D. A. Graber, R. E. Kirby, and T. S. Taylor, editors. Proceedings of the 1988 North American Wood Duck Symposium, St. Louis.

Bellrose, F. C., and D. J. Holm. 1994. Ecology and management of the Wood Duck. Stackpole Books, Mechanicsburg, Pennsylvania.

Bellrose, F. C., K. L. Johnson, and T. U. Meyers. 1964. Relative value of natural cavities and nesting houses for Wood Ducks. Journal of Wildlife Management 28:661–676.

Bement, R. E., R. D. Barmington, A. C. Everson, L. O. Hylton, Jr., and E. E. Remenga. 1965. Seeding of abandoned croplands in the central Great Plains. Journal of Range Management 18:53–58.

Bennett, L. J. 1938. The Blue-winged Teal: its ecology and management. Collegiate Press, Ames, Iowa.

Berg, P. F. 1956. A study of waterfowl broods in eastern Montana with special reference to movements and the relationship of reservoir fencing to production. Journal of Wildlife Management 20:253–262.

Berryman, J. H. 1972. The principles of predator control. Journal of Wildlife Management 36:395–400.

Bishop, R. A., and R. Barratt. 1970. Use of artificial nest baskets by Mallards. Journal of Wildlife Management 34:734–738.

Blais, S., M. Guillemain, D. Durant, H. Fritz, and N. Guillon. 2001. Growth and development of Pintail ducklings. Wildfowl 52:69–86.

Bluhm, C. K. 1988. Temporal patterns of pair formation and reproduction in annual cycles and associated endocrinology in waterfowl. Current Ornithology 5:123–185.

Blums, P., and R. G. Clark 2004. Correlates of lifetime reproductive success in three species of European ducks. Oecologia 140:61–67.

Bolen, E. G. 1967. Nesting boxes for Black-bellied Tree Ducks. Journal of Wildlife Management 31:794–797.

Bolen, E. G., and B. R. Chapman. 1981. Estimating winter sex ratios for Buffleheads. Southwestern Naturalist 26:49–52.

Bollinger, K. S., and D. V. Derksen. 1996. Demographic characteristics of molting Black Brant near Teshekpuk Lake, Alasjka. Journal of Field Ornithology 67:141–158.

Bouffard, S. H. 1983. Redhead egg parasitism of Canvasback nests. Journal of Wildlife Management 47:213–216.

Bowman, G. B., and L. D. Harris. 1980. Effect of spatial heterogeneity on ground-nest depredation. Journal of Wildlife Management 44:806–813.

Bowman, T. D., and P. W. Brown. 1992. Site fidelity of male Black Ducks to a molting area in Labrador. Journal of Field Ornithology 63:32–34.

Bowman, T. D., and J. R. Longcore. 1989. Survival and movements of molting male Black Ducks in Labrador. Journal of Wildlife Management 53:1057–1061.

Bowman, T. D., R. A. Stehn, and K. T. Scribner. 2004. Glaucous Gull predation on goslings on the Yukon-Kuskokwim Delta, Alaska. Condor 106:288–298.

Boyd, H. 1985. The large-scale impact of agriculture on ducks in the Prairie Provinces, 1956–81. Canadian Wildlife Service Progress Notes 149.

Boylan, K. 1998. Outfoxing the fox. Endangered Species Bulletin 23:18.

Brakhage, G. K. 1965. Biology and behavior of tub-nesting Canada Geese. Journal of Wildlife Management 29:751–771.

Brenner, F. J., and J. J. Mondok. 1979. Waterfowl nesting rafts designed for fluctuating water levels. Journal of Wildlife Management 43:979–982.

Brown, P. W., and L. H. Fredrickson. 1983. Growth and moult progression of White-winged Scoter ducklings. Wildfowl 34:115–119.

Bue, I. G., L. Blankenship, and W. H. Marshall. 1952. The relationship of grazing practices to waterfowl breeding populations and production on stock ponds in western South Dakota. Transactions of the North American Wildlife Conference 17:396–414.

Bull, E. L., and J. A. Jackson. 1995. Pileated Woodpecker. (Dryocopus pileatus). The birds of North America, 148. The American Ornithologists' Union, Washington, D.C., and The Academy of Natural Sciences, Philadelphia.

Bustness, J. O., and K. E. Erikstad. 1991. Parental care in the Common Eider (Somateria mollissima): factors affecting abandonment and adoption of young. Canadian Journal of Zoology 69:1538–1545.

Byrd, G. V., and D. W. Woolington. 1983. Ecology of Aleutian Canada Geese at Buldir Island, Alaska. U.S. Fish and Wildlife Service Special Scientific Report Wildlife 253.

Cain, B. W. 1970. Growth and plumage development of the Black-bellied Tree Duck, *Dendrocygna autumnalis* (Linnaeus). Texas A & I University Studies 3:25–48.

Calverley, B. K., and D. A. Boag. 1977. Reproductive potential in parkland- and arctic-nesting populations of Mallards and Pintails. Canadian Journal of Zoology 55:1242–1251.

Choromanski-Norris, J., E. K. Fritzell, and A. B. Sargeant. 1989. Movements and habitat use of Franklin's ground squirrels in duck-nesting habitat. Journal of Wildlife Management 53:324–331.

Chouinard, M. D., R. M. Kaminski, P. D. Gerard, and S. J. Dinsmore. 2005. Experimental evaluation of duck nesting structures in praire–parkland Canada. Wildlife Society Bullitin 33:in press.

Clancey, P. A. 1967. Gamebirds of southern Africa. Purnell & Sons, Cape Town, South Africa.

Clark, R. G., K. L. Guyn, R. C. N. Penner, and B. Semel. 1996. Altering predator foraging behavior to reduce predation of ground-nesting birds. Transactions of the North American Wildlife and Natural Resources Conference 61:118–126.

Clark, R. G., and T. D. Nudds. 1991. Habitat patch size and duck nesting success: the crucial experiments have not been performed. Wildlife Society Bulletin 19:534–543.

Collias, N. E., and L. R. Jahn. 1959. Social behavior and breeding success in Canada Geese (*Branta canadensis*) confined under semi-natural conditions. Auk 76:478–509.

Conner, R. N., C. E. Shackelford, D. Saenz, and R. R. Schaefer. 2001. Interactions between nesting Pileated Woodpeckers and Wood Ducks. Wilson Bulletin 113:250–253.

Conover, M. R. 1989. Potential compounds for establishing conditioned food aversions in raccoons. Wildlife Society Bulletin 17:430–435.

Conover, M. R. 1990. Reducing mammalian predation on eggs by using conditioned taste aversion to deceive predators. Journal of Wildlife Management 54:360–365.

Cooch, E. G., D. B. Lank, A. Dzubin, R. F. Rockwell, and F. Cooke. 1991. Body size variation in Lesser Snow Geese: environmental plasticity in gosling growth rates. Ecology 72:503–512.

Cooch, F. G. 1961. Ecological aspects of the Blue–Snow Goose complex. Auk 78:72–89.

Cooke, F., C. S. Findlay, and R. F. Rockwell. 1984. Recruitment and timing of reproduction in Lesser Snow Geese (*Chen caerulescens caerulescens*). Auk 101:451–458.

Cooke, F., R. F. Rockwell, and D. B. Lank. 1995. The Snow Geese of La Perouse Bay: natural selection in the wild. Oxford University Press, New York.

Cooper, H. W. 1957. Some plant materials and improved techniques used in soil and water conservation in the Great Plains. Journal of Soil and Water Conservation 12:163–168.

Coulter, M. W. 1957. Predation by snapping turtles upon aquatic birds in Maine marshes. Journal of Wildlife Management 21:17–21.

Coulter, M. W., and W. R. Miller. 1968. Nesting biology of Black Ducks and Mallards in northern New England. Vermont Fish and Game Department Bulletin 68–2.

Cowardin, L. M., G. E. Cummings, and P. B. Reed. 1967. Stump and tree nesting by Mallards and Black Ducks. Journal of Wildlife Management 31:229–235.

Cowardin, L. M., D. S. Gilmer, and C. W. Shaiffer. 1985. Mallard recruitment in the agricultural environment of North Dakota. Wildlife Monographs 92.

Cowardin, L. M., T. L. Shaffer, and K. M. Kraft. 1995. How much habitat management is needed to meet Mallard production objectives? Wildlife Society Bulletin 23:48–55.

Cox, R. R., Jr., M. A. Hanson, C. C. Roy, N. H. Euliss, Jr., D. H. Johnson, and M. G. Butler. 1998. Mallard duckling growth and survival in relation to aquatic invertebrates. Journal of Wildlife Management 62:124–133.

Craighead, J. J., and D. S. Stockstad. 1964. Breeding age of Canada Geese. Journal of Wildlife Management 28:57–64.

Dawson, R., and R. Clark. 1996. Effects of variation in egg size and hatching date on survival of Lesser Scaup (*Aythya affinis*) ducklings. Ibis 138:693–699.

Dean, W. R. 1978. Moult seasons of some Anatidae in the western Transvaal. Ostrich 49:76–84.

Delnicki, D., and E. G. Bolen. 1975. Natural nest site availability for Black-bellied Whistling Ducks in South Texas. Southwestern Naturalist 20:371–378.

Derksen, D. V., W. D. Eldridge, and M. W. Weller. 1982. Habitat ecology of Pacific Black Brant and other geese moulting near Teshekpuk Lake, Alaska. Wildfowl 33:39–57.

Devries, J. H., J. J. Citta, M. S. Linberg, D. W. Howerter, and M. G. Anderson. 2003. Breeding-season survival of Mallard females in the Prairie Pothole Region of Canada. Journal of Wildlife Management 67:551–563.

Dinsmore, S. J., G. C. White, and F. L. Knopf. 2002. Advanced techniques for modeling avian nest survival. Ecology 83:3476–3488.

Dol'nik, V. R., and V. M. Gavrilov. 1979. Bioenergetics of molt in the Chaffinch (*Fringilla coelebs*). Auk 96:253–264.

Doty, H. A. 1979. Duck nest structure evaluations in prairie wetlands. Journal of Wildlife Management 43:976–979.

Doty, H. A., and F. B. Lee. 1974. Homing to nest baskets by Mallards. Journal of Wildlife Management 38:714–719.

Doty, H. A., F. B. Lee, and A. D. Kruse. 1975. Use of elevated nest baskets by ducks. Wildlife Society Bulletin 3:68–73.

Doty, H. A., D. L. Trauger, and J. R. Serie. 1984. Renesting by Canvasbacks in southwestern Manitoba. Journal of Wildlife Management 48:581–584.

Drever, M. C., A. Wins-Purdy, T. D. Nudds, and R. G. Clark. 2004. Decline of duck nest success revisited: relationships with predators and wetlands in dynamic prairie environments. Auk 121:497–508.

Drobney, R. D. 1980. Reproductive bioenergetics of Wood Ducks. Auk 97:480–490.

Drobney, R. D., and L. H. Fredrickson. 1979. Food selection by Wood Ducks in relation to breeding status. Journal of Wildlife Management 43:109–120.

Duebbert, H. F. 1969. High nest density and hatching success of ducks on South Dakota CAP land. Transactions of the North American Wildlife and Natural Resources Conference 34:218–228.

Duebbert, H. F., and A. M. Frank. 1984. Value of prairie wetlands to duck broods. Wildlife Society Bulletin 12:27–34.

Duebbert, H. F., E. T. Jacobson, K. F. Higgins, and E. B. Podoll. 1981. Establishment of seeded grasslands for wildlife habitat in the Prairie Pothole Region. U.S. Fish and Wildlife Service Special Scientific Report Wildlife 234.

Duebbert, H. F., and H. A. Kantrud. 1974. Upland duck nesting related to land use and predator reduction. Journal of Wildlife Management 38:257–265.

Duebbert, H. F., and J. T. Lokemoen. 1976. Duck nesting in fields of undisturbed grass–legume cover. Journal of Wildlife Management 40:39–49.

Duebbert, H. F., and J. T. Lokemoen. 1977. Upland nesting of American Bitterns, Marsh Hawks and Short-eared Owls. Prairie Naturalist 9:33–40.

Duebbert, H. F., and J. T. Lokemoen. 1980. High duck nesting success in a predator-reduced environment. Journal of Wildlife Management 44:428–437.

Duebbert, H. F., J. T. Lokemoen, and D. E. Sharp. 1983. Concentrated nesting of Mallards and Gadwalls on Miller Lake Island, North Dakota. Journal of Wildlife Management 47:729–740.

Duebbert, H. F., J. T. Lokemoen, and D. E. Sharp. 1986. Nest sites of ducks in grazed mixed-grass prairie in North Dakota. Prairie Naturalist 18:99–108.

Dugger, B. D., and P. Blums. 2001. Effect of conspecific brood parasitism on host fitness for Tufted Duck and Common Pochard. Auk 118:717–726.

Duncan, D. C. 1983. Extensive overland movement of Pintail, *Anas acuta*, brood and attempted predation by hawks. Canadian Field-Naturalist 97:216–217.

Duncan, D. C. 1986. Survival of dabbling duck broods on prairie impoundments in southeastern Alberta. Canadian Field-Naturalist 100:110–113.

Duncan, D. C. 1987. Nesting of Northern Pintails in Alberta: laying date, clutch size, and renesting. Canadian Journal of Zoology 65:234–246.

Duncan, D. C. 1988. Body reserves of neonate Northern Pintails (*Anas acuta*). Canadian Journal of Zoology 66:811–816.

Dzubin, A. 1959. Growth and plumage development of wild-trapped juvenile Canvasback (*Aythya valisineria*). Journal of Wildlife Management 23:279–290.

Dzubin, A., and J. B. Gollop. 1972. Aspects of Mallard breeding ecology in Canadian parkland and grassland. Pages 113–152 *in* Population ecology of migratory birds. U.S. Fish and Wildlife Service Wildlife Research Report 2.

Dzus, E. H., and R. G. Clark. 1997. Brood size manipulation in Mallard ducks: effects on duckling survival and brooding efficiency. Ecoscience 4:437–445.

Dzus, E. H., and R. G. Clark. 1998. Brood survival and recruitment of Mallards in relation to wetland density and hatching date. Auk 115:311–318.

Eadie, J. M., F. P. Kehoe, and T. D. Nudds. 1988. Pre-hatch and post-hatch brood amalgamation in North American Anatidae: a review of hypotheses. Canadian Journal of Zoology 66:1709–1721.

Eadie, J. M., and B. E. Lyon. 1998. Cooperation, conflict, and crèching behaviour in goldeneye ducks. American Naturalist 151:397–408.

Eldridge, J. L., and G. L. Krapu. 1988. The influence of diet quality on clutch size and laying pattern in Mallards. Auk 105:102–110.

Ely, C. R., P. Dau, and C. A. Babcock. 1994. Decline in a population of Spectacled Eiders on the Yukon-Kuskokwim Delta, Alaska. Northwestern Naturalist 75:81–87.

Eoin, C. G., and S. A. Petrie. 2003. Moult intensity and chronology of Tundra Swans during spring and fall migration at Long Point, Lake Erie, Ontario. Canadian Journal of Zoology 81:1057–1062.

Erskine, A. J. 1971. Growth, and annual cycles in weights, plumages and reproductive organs of Goosanders in eastern Canada. Ibis 113:42–58.

Erskine, A. J. 1972. Buffleheads. Canadian Wildlife Service Monograph Series 4.

Evans, C. D., and K. E. Black. 1956. Duck production studies on the prairie potholes of South Dakota. U.S. Fish and Wildlife Service Special Scientific Report Wildlife 32.

Fast, P. L. F., R. G. Clark, R. W. Brook, and J. E. Hines. 2004. Patterns of wetland use by brood-rearing Lesser Scaup in northern boreal forest of Canada. Waterbirds 27:177–182.

Findlay, C. S., and F. Cooke. 1983. Genetic and environmental components of clutch size variance in a wild population of Lesser Snow Geese (*Anser caerulescens caerulescens*). Evolution 37:724–734.

Flannery, T. 2001. The eternal frontier: an ecological history of North America and its peoples. Atlantic Monthly Press, New York.

Flint, P. L., and J. B. Grand. 1996. Nesting success of Northern Pintails on the coastal Yukon-Kuskokwim Delta, Alaska. Condor 98:54–60.

Flint, P. L., and J. B. Grand. 1997. Survival of Spectacled Eider adult females and ducklings during brood rearing. Journal of Wildlife Management 61:217–221.

Flint, P. L., D. L. Lacroix, J. A. Reed, and R. B. Lanctot. 2004. Movements of flightless Long-tailed Ducks during wing molt. Waterbirds 27:35–40.

Flint, P. L., M. R. Petersen, C. P. Dau, J. E. Hines, and J. D. Nichols. 2000. Annual survival and site fidelity of Steller's Eiders molting along the Alaska Peninsula. Journal of Wildlife Management 64:261–268.

Flint, P. L., J. S. Sedinger, and K. H. Pollock. 1995. Survival of juvenile Black Brant during brood rearing. Journal of Wildlife Management 59:455–463.

Francis, C. M., M. H. Richards, F. Cooke, and R. F. Rockwell. 1992. Long-term changes in survival rates of Lesser Snow Geese. Ecology 73:1346–1362.

Fredrickson, L. H., G. V. Burger, S. P. Havera, D. A. Graber, R. E. Kirby, and T. S. Taylor, editors. 1990. Proceedings of the 1988 North American Wood Duck Symposium, St. Louis.

Frimer, O. 1994. Occurrence and distribution of King Eiders *Somateria spectabilis* and Common Eiders *S. mollissima* at Disko, West Greenland. Polar Research 12:111–116.

Frith, H. J. 1967. Waterfowl in Australia. Angus & Robertson, Sydney, Australia.

Fritzell, E. K. 1978. Habitat use by prairie raccoons during the waterfowl breeding season. Journal of Wildlife Management 42:118–127.

Garrettson, P. R., and F. C. Rohwer. 2001. Effects of mammalian predator removal on production of upland-nesting ducks in North Dakota. Journal of Wildlife Management 65:398–405.

Gates, R. J., D. F. Caithamer, T. C. Tacha, and C. R. Paine. 1993. The annual molt cycle of *Branta canadensis interior* in relation to nutrient reserve dynamics. Condor 95:680–693.

Gendron, M., and R. G. Clark. 2002. Survival of Gadwall and Mallard ducklings in southcentral Saskatchewan. Journal of Wildlife Management 66:170–180.

Getz, V. K., and J. R. Smith. 1989. Waterfowl production on artificial islands in Mountain Meadows Reservoir. California Fish and Game 75:132–140.

Gill, F. B. 1990. Ornithology. W. H. Freeman, New York.

Gilmer, D. S., I. J. Ball, L. M. Cowardin, J. E. Mathisen, and J. H. Riechmann. 1978. Natural cavities used by Wood Ducks in north-central Minnesota. Journal of Wildlife Management 42:288–298.

Gollop, J. B., and W. H. Marshall. 1954. A guide for again duck broods in the field. Mississippi Flyway Council Technical Section (unpublished mimeo).

Goodrich, J. M., and S. W. Buskirk. 1995. Control of abundant native vertebrates for conservation of endangered species. Conservation Biology 9:1357–1364.

Gorman, M. J., and H. Milne. 1972. Crèche behaviour in the Common Eider *Somateria m. mollissima* L. Ornis Scandinavica 3:21–25.

Goudie, R. I., G. J. Robertson, and A. Reed. 2000. Common Eider, *Somateria mollissima*. The birds of North America, 546. The American Ornithologists' Union, Washington, D.C., and The Academy of Natural Sciences, Philadelphia.

Grand, J. B. 1995. Nesting success of ducks on the central Yukon Flats, Alaska. Canadian Journal of Zoology 73:260–265.

Grand, J. B., and P. L. Flint. 1996a. Renesting ecology of Northern Pintails on the Yukon-Kuskokwim Delta, Alaska. Condor 98:820–824.

Grand, J. B., and P. L. Flint. 1996b. Survival of Northern Pintail ducklings on the Yukon-Kuskokwim Delta, Alaska. Condor 98:48–53.

Grand, J. B., and P. L. Flint. 1997. Productivity of nesting Spectacled Eiders on the lower Kashunuk River, Alaska. Condor 99:926–932.

Green, R. E. 1989. Transformation of crude proportions of nests that are successful for comparison with Mayfield estimates of nest success. Ibis 131:305–306.

Greenwood, R. J. 1986. Influence of striped skunk removal on upland duck nest success in North Dakota. Wildlife Society Bulletin 14:6–11.

Greenwood, R. J., D. G. Pietruszewski, and R. D. Crawford. 1998. Effects of food supplementation on depredation of duck nests in upland habitat. Wildlife Society Bulletin 26:219–226.

Greenwood, R. J., A. B. Sargeant, D. H. Johnson, L. M. Cowardin, and T. L. Shaffer. 1987. Mallard nest success and recruitment in Prairie Canada. Transactions of the North American Wildlife and Natural Resources Conference 52:298–309.

Greenwood, R. J., A. B. Sargeant, D. H. Johnson, L. M. Cowardin, and T. L. Shaffer. 1995. Factors associated with duck nest success in the Prairie Pothole Region of Canada. Wildlife Monographs 128.

Greenwood, R. J., A. B. Sargeant, J. L. Piehl, D. A. Buhl, and B. A. Hanson. 1999. Foods and foraging of prairie striped skunks during the avian nesting season. Wildlife Society Bulletin 27:823–832.

Greenwood, R. J., and M. A. Sovada. 1996. Prairie duck populations and predation management. Transactions of the North American Wildlife and Natural Resources Conference 61:31–42.

Grice, D., and J. P. Rogers. 1965. The Wood Duck in Massachusetts. Pittman-Robertson Project Report W-19-R, Massachusetts Division of Fish and Game, Westboro.

Gummer, H., and M. Williams. 1999. Campbell Island Teal: conservation update. Wildfowl 50:133–138.

Guyn, K. L., and R. G. Clark. 1999. Factors affecting survival of Northern Pintail ducklings in Alberta. Condor 101:369–377.

Hammond, M. C., and G. E. Mann. 1956. Waterfowl nesting islands. Journal of Wildlife Management 20:345–352.

Hansen, J. L. 1971. The role of nest boxes in management of the Wood Duck on Mingo National Wildlife Refuge. Thesis, University of Missouri, Columbia.

Hanson, H. C. 1962. The dynamics of condition factors in Canada Geese and their relation to seasonal stresses. Arctic Institute of North America Technical Paper 12.

Haramis, G. M. 1975. Wood Duck (*Aix sponsa*) ecology and management within the green-timber impoundments at Montezuma National Wildlife Refuge. Thesis, Cornell University, Ithaca, New York.

Hartley, D. R., and E. P. Hill. 1990. Effect of heat in plastic nest boxes for Wood Ducks. Pages 247–250 *in* L. H. Fredrickson, G. V. Burger, S. P. Havera, D. A. Graber, R. E. Kirby, and T. S. Taylor, editors. Proceedings of the 1988 North American Wood Duck Symposium, St. Louis.

Hartman, G. 1985. Foods of male Mallard, before and during moult, as determined by faecal analysis. Wildfowl 36:65–71.

Hay, R. L. 1974. Molting biology of male Gadwalls at Delta, Manitoba. Thesis, University of Wisconsin, Madison.

Heitmeyer, M. E. 1987. The prebasic moult and basic plumage of female Mallards (*Anas platyrhynchos*). Canadian Journal of Zoology 65:2248–2261.

Heitmeyer, M. E. 1988a. Protein costs of the prebasic molt of female Mallards. Condor 90:263–266.

Heitmeyer, M. E. 1988b. Body composition of female Mallards in winter in relation to annual cycle events. Condor 90:669–680.

Hepp, G. R., and J. D. Hair. 1977. Wood Duck brood mobility and utilization of beaver habitats. Proceedings of the Southeastern Association of Fish and Wildlife Agencies 31:216–225.

Heusmann, H W. 2000. Production from Wood Duck nest boxes as a proportion of the harvest in Massachusetts. Wildlife Society Bulletin 28:1046–1049.

Higgins, K. F. 1977. Duck nesting in intensively farmed areas of North Dakota. Journal of Wildlife Management 41:232–242.

Higgins, K. F. 1986. Further evaluation of duck nesting on small man-made islands in North Dakota. Wildlife Society Bulletin 14:155–157.

Hochbaum, H. A. 1944. The Canvasback on a prairie marsh. Stackpole Books, Harrisburg, Pennsylvania, and the Wildlife Management Institute, Washington, D.C.

Hoekman, S. T., T. S. Gaber, R. Gabor, R. Maher, H. R. Murkin, and L. M. Armstrong. 2004. Factors affecting survival of Mallard ducklings in southern Ontario. Condor 106:485–495.

Hoekman, S. T., L. S. Mills, D. W. Howerter, J. H. Devries, and I. J. Ball. 2002. Sensitivity analyses of the life cycle of midcontinent Mallards. Journal of Wildlife Management 66:883–900.

Hohman, W. L., C. D. Ankney, and D. H. Gordon. 1992. Ecology and management of postbreeding waterfowl. Pages 128–189 in B. D. J. Batt, A. D. Afton, M. G. Anderson, C. D. Ankney, D. H. Johnson, J. A. Kadlec, and G. L. Krapu, editors. Ecology and management of breeding waterfowl. University of Minnesota Press, Minneapolis.

Hohman, W. L., S. W. Manley, and D. Ricahrd. 1997. Relative costs of prebasic and prealternate molts for male Blue-winged Teal. Condor 99:543–548.

Holm, E. R., and M. L. Scott. 1954. Studies on the nutrition of wild waterfowl. New York Fish and Game Journal 1:171–187.

Hori, J. 1964. The breeding biology of the Shelduck Tadorna tadorna. Ibis 106:333–360.

Howell, S. N. G., and C. Corben. 2000. A commentary on molt and plumage terminology: implications from the Western Gull. Western Birds 31:50–56.

Howell, S. N. G., C. Corben, P. Pyle, and D. I. Rogers. 2003. The first basic problem: a review of molt and plumage homologies. Condor 105:635–653.

Hughes, R. J., A. Reed, and G. Gauthier. 1994. Space and habitat use by Greater Snow Goose broods on Bylot Island, Northwest Territories. Journal of Wildlife Management 58:536–545.

Humphrey, P. S., and K. C. Parkes. 1959. An approach to the study of molts and plumages. Auk 76:1–31.

Imler, R. H. 1945. Bullsnakes and their control on a Nebraska wildlife refuge. Journal of Wildlife Management 9:265–273.

Jaenke, E. A. 1966. Opportunities under the Cropland Adjustment Program. Transactions of the North American Wildlife and Natural Resources Conference 31:323–327.

Jehle, G., A. A. Yackel Adams, J. A. Savidge, and S. K. Skagen. 2004. Nest survival estimation: a review of alternatives to the Mayfield estimator. Condor 106:472–484.

Jehl, J. R., and E. Johnson. 2004. Wing and tail molts of the Ruddy Duck. Waterbirds 27:54–99.

Jobin, B., and J. Picman. 1997. Factors affecting predation on artificial nests in marshes. Journal of Wildlife Management 61:792–800.

Johnsgard, P. A. 1975. Waterfowl of North America. Indiana University Press, Bloomington.

Johnsgard, P. A. 1978. Ducks, geese, and swans of the world. University of Nebraska Press, Lincoln.

Johnson, D. H. 1979. Estimating nest success: the Mayfield Method and an alternative. Auk 96:651–661.

Johnson, D. H. 1999. The insignificance of statistical significance testing. Journal of Wildlife Management 63:763–772.

Johnson, D. H., R. L. Kreil, G. B. Berkey, R. D. Crawford, D. O. Lambeth, and S. F. Galipeau. 1994. Influences of waterfowl management on nongame birds: the North Dakota experience. Transactions of the North American Wildlife and Natural Resources Conference 59:293–302.

Johnson, D. H., J. D. Nichols, and M. D. Schwartz. 1992. Population dynamics of breeding waterfowl. Pages 446–485 in B. D. J. Batt, A. D. Afton, M. G. Anderson, C. D. Ankney, D. H. Johnson, J. A. Kadlec, and G. L. Krapu, editors. Ecology and management of breeding waterfowl. University of Minnesota Press, Minneapolis.

Johnson, D. H., and A. B. Sargeant. 1977. Impact of red fox predation on the sex ratio of prairie Mallards. U.S. Fish and Wildlife Service Wildlife Research Report 6.

Johnson, D. H., A. B. Sargeant, and R. J. Greenwood. 1989. Importance of individual species of predators on nesting success of ducks in the Canadian Prairie Pothole Region. Canadian Journal of Zoology 67:291–297.

Johnson, L. L. 1967. The Common Goldeneye duck and the role of nesting boxes in its management in north-central Minnesota. Journal of the Minnesota Academy of Science 34:110–113.

Johnson, R. F., Jr., R. O. Woodward, and L. M. Kirsch. 1978. Waterfowl nesting on small man-made islands in prairie wetlands. Wildlife Society Bulletin 6:240–243.

Jones, J. D. 1975. Waterfowl nesting island development. U.S. Department of Interior, Bureau of Land Management Technical Note 260.

Kalmbach, E. R. 1937. Crow–waterfowl relationships based on preliminary studies on Canadian breeding grounds. U.S. Department of Agriculture Circular 433.

Kalmbach, E. R. 1939. Nesting success: its significance in waterfowl reproduction. Transactions of the North American Wildlife Conference 4:591–604.

Kaminski, R. M., and H. H. Prince. 1977. Nesting habitat of Canada Geese in southeastern Michigan. Wilson Bulletin 89:523–531.

Kear, J., editor. 2005. Ducks, geese and swans. Oxford University Press, Cambridge.

Keith, L. B. 1961. A study of waterfowl ecology on small impoundments in southeastern Alberta. Wildlife Monographs 6.

Kellert, S. R. 1985. Public perception of predators, particularly the wolf and coyote. Biological Conservation 31:167–189.

Kendeigh, S. C., V. R. Dol'nik, and V. M. Gavrilov. 1977. Avian energetics. Pages 127–204 in J. Pinowski and S. C. Kendeigh, editors. Granivorous birds in ecosystems. Cambridge Press, New York.

King, J. G. 1973. A cosmopolitan duck moulting resort; Takslesluk Lake, Alaska. Wildfowl 24:103–109.

King, J. R. 1974. Seasonal allocation of time and energy resources in birds. Pages 4–70 in R. A. Paynter, Jr., editor. Avian energetics. Nuttall Ornithological Club Publication 15.

King, J. R. 1980. Energetics of avian moult. International Ornithological Congress 17:312–317.

Kirkpatrick, J. F., and J. W. Turner. 1985. Chemical fertility and control in wildlife management. BioScience 35:485–491.

Klett, A. T., H. F. Duebbert, and G. L. Heismeyer. 1984. Use of seeded native grasses as nesting cover by ducks. Wildlife Society Bulletin 12:134–138.

Klett, A. T., T. L. Shaffer, and D. H. Johnson. 1988. Duck nesting success in the Prairie Pothole Region. Journal of Wildlife Management 52:431–440.

Korschgen, C. E. 1977. Breeding stress of female eiders in Maine. Journal of Wildlife Management 41:360–373.

Korschgen, C. E., K. P. Kenow, W. L. Green, D. H. Johnson, M. D. Samuel, and L. Sielo. 1996. Survival of radiomarked Canvasback ducklings in northwestern Minnesota. Journal of Wildlife Management 60:120–132.

Krapu, G. L. 1981. The role of nutrient reserves in Mallard reproduction. Auk 98:29–38.

Krapu, G. L. 2000. Temporal flexibility of reproduction in temperate-breeding dabbling ducks. Auk 117:640–650.

Krapu, G. L., D. A. Brandt, and J. A. Beiser. 2001. Factors associated with autumn rearing of duck broods in temperate North America. Wildfowl 52:143–156.

Krapu, G. L., P. J. Pietz, D. A. Brandt, and R. R. Cox, Jr. 2000. Factors limiting Mallard brood survival in prairie pothole landscapes. Journal of Wildlife Management 64:553–561.

Krapu, G. L., P. J. Pietz, D. A. Brandt, and R. R. Cox, Jr. 2004. Does presence of permanent fresh water affect recruitment in prairie-nesting dabbling ducks? Journal of Wildlife Management 68:332–341.

Krapu, G. L., L. G. Talent, and T. J. Dwyer. 1979. Marsh nesting by Mallards. Wildlife Society Bulletin 7:104–110.

Kumari, E. 1979. Moult and moult migration of waterfowl in Estonia. Wildfowl 30:90–98.

Lagler, K. F. 1956. The pike, *Esox lucius* Linnaeus, in relation to waterfowl on the Seney National Wildlife Refuge, Michigan. Journal of Wildlife Management 20:114–124.

LaHart, D. E., and G. W. Cornwell. 1970. Habitat preference and survival of Florida Duck broods. Proceedings of the Southeastern Association of Fish and Wildlife Agencies 24:117–120.

Langford, W. A., and E. A. Driver. 1979. Quantification of the relationship between Mallard nest initiation and temperature. Wildfowl 30:31–34.

Larivière, S., and F. Messier. 1998. Spatial organization of a prairie striped skunk population during the waterfowl breeding season. Journal of Wildlife Management 62:199–204.

Larson, S. 1960. On the influence of the arctic fox *Alopex lagopus* on the distribution of arctic birds. Oikos 11:276–305.

Larsson, K., and P. Forslund. 1992. Genetic and social inheritance of body and egg size in the Barnacle Goose (*Branta leucopsis*). Evolution 46:235–244.

Lavin, F. 1967. Fall fertilization of intermediate wheatgrass in the southwestern ponderosa pine zone. Journal of Range Management 20:16–21.

Lesage, L., and G. Gauthier. 1997. Growth and development in Greater Snow Goose goslings. Auk 114:229–241.

Lesage, L., and G. Gauthier. 1998. Effect of hatching date on body and organ development in Greater Snow Goose goslings. Condor 100:316–325.

Lesage, L., A. Reed, and J-P. L. Savard. 1997. Plumage development and growth of wild Surf Scoter *Melanitta perspicillata* ducklings. Wildfowl 47:198–203.

Lightbody, J. P. 1985. Growth rates and development of Redhead ducklings. Wilson Bulletin 97:555–559.

Lightbody, J. P., and C. D. Ankney. 1984. Seasonal influence on the strategies of growth and development of Canvasback and Lesser Scaup ducklings. Auk 101:121–133.

Lindberg, M. S., and J. S. Sedinger. 1998. Ecological significance of brood-site fidelity in Black Brant: spatial, annual, and age-related variation. Auk 115:436–446.

Lindberg, M. S., J. S. Sedinger, D. V. Derksen, and R. F. Rockwell. 1998. Natal and breeding philopatry in a Black Brant, *Branta bernicla nigricans*, metapopulation. Ecology 79:1893–1904.

Lindberg, M. S., J. S. Sedinger, and P. L. Flint. 1997. Effects of spring environment on nesting phenology and clutch size of Black Brant. Condor 99:381–388.

Lindholm, A., G. Gauthier, and A. Desrochers. 1994. Effects of hatch date and food supply on gosling growth in arctic-nesting Greater Snow Geese. Condor 96:898–908.

Livezey, B. C. 1981. Duck nesting in retired croplands at Horicon National Wildlife Refuge, Wisconsin. Journal of Wildlife Management 45:27–37.

Lokemoen, J. T., H. A. Doty, D. E. Sharp, and J. E. Neaville. 1982. Electric fences to reduce mammalian predation on waterfowl nests. Wildlife Society Bulletin 10:318–323.

Lokemoen, J. T., H. F. Duebbert, and D. E. Sharp. 1984. Nest spacing, habitat selection, and behavior of waterfowl on Miller Lake Island, North Dakota. Journal of Wildlife Management 48:309–321.

Lokemoen, J. T., H. F. Duebbert, and D. E. Sharp. 1990. Homing and reproductive habits of Mallards, Gadwalls, and Blue-winged Teal. Wildlife Monographs 106.

Lokemoen, J. T., and T. A. Messmer. 1993. Locating, constructing, and managing islands for nesting waterfowl. U.S. Fish and Wildlife Service, Branch of Extension and Publications, Arlington, Virginia, and the Berryman Institute, Logan, Utah.

Lokemoen, J. T., and T. A. Messmer. 1994. Locating and managing peninsulas for nesting ducks. U.S. Fish and Wildlife Service, Branch of Extension and Publications, Arlington, Virginia, and the Berryman Institute, Logan, Utah.

Lokemoen, J. T., and R. O. Woodward. 1992. Nesting waterfowl and water birds on natural islands in the Dakotas an Montana. Wildlife Society Bulletin 20:163–171.

Lokemoen, J. T., and R. O. Woodward. 1993. An assessment of predator barriers and predator control to enhance duck nest success on peninsulas. Wildlife Society Bulletin 21:275–282.

Losito, M. P., G. A. Baldassarre, and J. H. Smith. 1995. Reproduction and survival of female Mallards in the St. Lawrence River Valley, New York. Journal of Wildlife Management 59:23–30.

Lovvorn, J. R., and J. A. Barzen. 1988. Molt in the annual cycle of Canvasbacks. Auk 105:543–552.

Low, J. B. 1945. Ecology and management of the Redhead, *Nyroca americana*, in Iowa. Ecological Monographs 15:35–69.

Lowney, M. S., and E. P. Hill. 1989. Wood Duck nest sites in bottomland hardwood forests of Mississippi. Journal of Wildlife Management 53:378–382.

Lynch, J. J., C. D. Evans, and V. C. Conover. 1963. Inventory of waterfowl environments of Prairie Canada. Transactions of the North American Wildlife and Natural Resources Conference 28:93–109.

Lynch, J. J., and J. R. Singleton. 1964. Winter appraisals of annual productivity in geese and other water birds. Wildfowl Trust Annual Report 15:114–126.

MacInnes, C. D., R. A. Davis, R. N. Jones, B. C. Lieff, and A. J. Pakulak. 1974. Reproductive efficiency of McConnell River small Canada Geese. Journal of Wildlife Management 38:686–707.

Mack, G. D., and L. D. Flake. 1980. Habitat relationships of waterfowl broods on South Dakota stock ponds. Journal of Wildlife Management 44:695–700.

Majewski, P., and P. Beszterda. 1990. Influence of nesting success on female homing in the Mallard. Journal of Wildlife Management 54:459–462.

Manseau, M., and G. Gauthier. 1993. Interactions between Greater Snow Geese and their rearing habitat. Ecology 74:2045–2055.

Markum, D. E., and G. A. Baldassarre. 1989. Ground nesting by Black-bellied Whistling Ducks on islands in Mexico. Journal of Wildlife Management 53:707–713.

Mason, P. J., and J. L. Dusi. 1983. A ground nesting Wood Duck. Auk 100:506.

Mauser, D. M., R. L. Jarvis, and D. S. Gilmer. 1994. Survival of radio-marked Mallard ducklings in northeastern California. Journal of Wildlife Management 58:82–87.

Maxson, S. J., and R. M. Pace, III. 1992. Diurnal time-activity budgets and habitat use of Ring-necked Duck ducklings in northcentral Minnesota. Wilson Bulletin 104:472–484.

Mayfield, H. 1961. Nesting success calculated from exposure. Wilson Bulletin 73:255–261.

Mayfield, H. 1975. Suggestions for calculating nest success. Wilson Bulletin 87:456–466.

McCamant, R. E., and E. G. Bolen. 1979. A 12-year study of nest box utilization by Black-bellied Whistling Ducks. Journal of Wildlife Management 43:936–943.

McGilvrey, F. B. 1968. A guide to Wood Duck production habitat requirements. U.S. Fish and Wildlife Service Resource Publication 60.

McGilvrey, F. B. 1969. Survival in Wood Duck broods. Journal of Wildlife Management 33:73–76.

McIlquham, C. J., and B. R. Bacon. 1989. Wood Duck nest on a muskrat house. Journal of Field Ornithology 60:84–85.

McKinnon, D. T., and D. C. Duncan. 1999. Effectiveness of dense nesting cover for increasing duck production in Saskatchewan. Journal of Wildlife Management 63:382-389.

McPherson, R. J., T. W. Arnold, L. M. Armstrong, and C. J. Schwarz. 2003. Estimating the nest-success rate and the number of nests initiated by radiomarked Mallards. Journal of Wildlife Management 67:843–851.

Mech, L. D. 1970. The wolf: the ecology and behavior of an endangered species. Natural History Press, Garden City, New York.

Mech, L. D., and L. Boitani. 2003. Wolves: behavior, ecology, and conservation. University of Chicago Press, Chicago.

Mendall, H. L. 1958. The Ring-necked Duck in the northeast. University of Maine Studies, Second Series Number 73.

Mendall, H. L. 1968. An inventory of Maine's breeding eider ducks. Transactions of the Northeast Section of the Wildlife Society 25:95–104.

Millar, J. B. 1986. Estimates of habitat distribution in the settled portions of the prairie provinces in 1982. Canadian Wildlife Service, Saskatoon, Saskatchewan (unpublished report).

Milne, H. 1974. Breeding numbers and reproductive rate of eiders at the Sands of Forvie National Nature Reserve, Scotland. Ibis 116:135–154.

Milne, R. C. 1965. Crab predation on a duckling. Journal of Wildlife Management 29:645.

Mitcham, S. A., and G. Wobeser. 1988a. Effects of sodium and magnesium sulfate in drinking water on Mallard ducklings. Journal of Wildlife Diseases 24:30–44.

Mitcham, S. A., and G. Wobeser. 1988b. Toxic effects of natural saline waters on Mallard ducklings. Journal of Wildlife Diseases 24:45–50.

Monda, M. J., and J. T. Ratti. 1988. Niche overlap and habitat use by sympatric duck broods in eastern Washington. Journal of Wildlife Management 52:95–103.

Moorman, A. M., T. E. Moorman, G. A. Baldassarre, and D. M. Richard. 1991. Effects of saline water on growth and survival of Mottled Duck ducklings in Louisiana. Journal of Wildlife Management 55:471-476.

Moorman, T. E., G. A. Baldassarre, and T. J. Hess, Jr. 1993. Carcass mass and nutrient dynamics of Mottled Ducks during remigial molt. Journal of Wildlife Management 57:224–228.

Morse, T. E., J. L. Jakabosky, and V. P. McCrow. 1969. Some aspects of the breeding biology of the Hooded Merganser. Journal of Wildlife Management 33:596–604.

Moser, T. J., and D. H. Rusch. 1989. Age-specific breeding rates of female Interior Canada Geese. Journal of Wildlife Management 53:734–740.

Munro, J., and J. Bédard. 1977a. Crèche formation in the Common Eider. Auk 94:759–771.

Munro, J., and J. Bédard. 1977b. Gull predation and crèching behaviour in the Common Eider. Journal of Animal Ecology 46:799–810.

Murphy, M. E., and J. R. King. 1984a. Sulfur amino acid nutrition during molt in the White-crowned Sparrow. 1. Does dietary sulfur amino acid concentration affect the energetics of molt as assayed by metabolized energy? Condor 86:314–323.

Murphy, M. E., and J. R. King. 1984b. Sulfur amino acid nutrition during molt in the White-crowned Sparrow. 2. Nitrogen and sulfur balance in birds fed graded levels of the sulfur-containing amino acids. Condor 86:324–332.

Naylor, A. E., and E. G. Hunt. 1954. A nesting study and population survey of Canada Geese on the Susan River, Lassen County, California. California Fish and Game 40:5–16.

Nelson, C. H. 1993. The downy waterfowl of North America. Delta Station Press, Deerfield, Illinois.

Newton, I. 1968. The temperatures, weights, and body composition of molting Bullfinches. Condor 70:323–332.

Nilsson, L., and H. Persson. 1994. Factors affecting the breeding performance of a marked Greylag Goose *Anser anser* population in south Sweden. Wildfowl 45:33–48.

Odin, C. R. 1957. California Gull predation on waterfowl. Auk 74:185–202.

Ogilvie, M. 1982. Wildfowl of Britain and Europe. Oxford University Press, Oxford.

Oli, M. K., G. R. Hepp, and R. A. Kennamer. 2002. Fitness consequences of delayed maturity in female Wood Ducks. Evolutionary Ecology Research 4:563–576.

Oring, L. W. 1968. Growth, molts, and plumages of the Gadwall. Auk 85:355–380.

Öst, M. 1999. Within-season and between-year variation in the structure of Common Eider broods. Condor 101:598–606.

Öst, M., and M. Kilpi. 1999. Parental care influences the feeding behaviour of female eiders *Somateria mollissima*. Annales Zoologici Fennici 36:195–204.

Öst, M., and M. Kilpi. 2000. Eider females and broods from neighboring colonies use segregated local feeding areas. Waterbirds 23:24–32.

Öst, M., L. Mantila, and M Kilpi. 2000. Shared care provides time-budgeting advantages for female eiders. Animal Behaviour 64:223–231.

Owen, M. 1980. Wild geese of the world: their life history and ecology. B T Batsford, London.

Owen, M., and J. M. Black. 1989a. Barnacle Goose. Pages 349–362 *in* I. Newton, editor. Lifetime reproduction in birds. Academic Press, New York.

Owen, M., and J. M. Black. 1989b. Factors affecting the survival of Barnacle Geese on migration from the breeding grounds. Journal of Animal Ecology 58:603–617.

Owen, M., and J. M. Black. 1990. Waterfowl ecology. Chapman & Hall, New York.

Owen, M., and R. King. 1979. The duration of the flightless period in free-living Mallard. Bird Study 26:267–269.

Owen, M., and M. A. Ogilvie. 1979. Wing molt and weights of Barnacle Geese in Spitsbergen. Condor 81:42–52.

Palmer, R. S. 1972. Patterns of molting. Avian Biology 2:65–102

Palmer, R. S. 1976a. Handbook of North American birds. Volume 2. Yale University Press, New Haven, Connecticut.

Palmer, R. S. 1976b. Handbook of North American birds. Volume 3. Yale University Press, New Haven, Connecticut.

Panek, M., and P. Majewski. 1990. Remex growth and body mass of Mallards during wing molt. Auk 107:255–259.

Patterson, I. J., A. Gilboa, and D. J. Tozer. 1982. Rearing other people's young: brood mixing in the Shelduck *Tadorna tadorna*. Animal Behaviour 30:199–202.

Payne, R. B. 1972. Mechanisms and control of molt. Avian Biology 2:103–155.

Pearse, A. T., and J. T. Ratti. 2004. Effects of predator removal on Mallard duckling survival. Journal of Wildlife Management 68:342-350.

Pehrsson, O. 1987. Effects of body condition on molting in Mallards. Condor 89:329–339.

Pelayo, J. T., and R. G. Clark. 2003. Consequences of egg size for offspring survival: a cross-fostering experiment in Ruddy Ducks (*Oxyura jamaicensis*). Auk 120:384–393.

Petrie, S. A. 1998a. Molt patterns of nonbreeding White-faced Whistling-Ducks in South Africa. Auk 115:774–780.

Petrie, S. A. 1998b. Intensity and chronology of prebreeding and post-breeding moult in White-faced Whistling-Ducks *Dendrocygna viduata*. Wildfowl 49:207–218.

Petrie, S. A., and K. H. Rogers. 1996. Foods consumed by breeding White-faced Whistling Ducks on the Nyl River floodplain, South Africa. Gibier Faune Sauvage 13:755–771.

Phillips, M. L., W. R. Clark, M. A. Sovada, D. J. Horn, R. R. Koford, and R. J. Greenwood. 2003. Predator selection of prairie landscape features and its relation to duck nest success. Journal of Wildlife Management 67:104–114.

Picozzi, N. 1975. Crow predation on marked nests. Journal of Wildlife Management 39:151–155.

Piest, L. A., and L. K. Sowls. 1985. Breeding duck use of a sewage marsh in Arizona. Journal of Wildlife Management 49:580–585.

Pietz, P. J., and G. L. Krapu. 1994. Effects of predator exclosure design on duck brood movements. Wildlife Society Bulletin 22:26–33.

Pietz, P. J., G. L. Krapu, D. A. Brandt, and R. R. Cox, Jr. 2003. Factors affecting Gadwall brood and duckling survival in prairie pothole landscapes. Journal of Wildlife Management 67:564–575.

Pöysä, H. 1995. Factors affecting abandonment and adoption of young in Common Eiders. Canadian Journal of Zoology 73:1575–1577.

Prince, H. H. 1968. Nest sites used by Wood Ducks and Common Goldeneyes in New Brunswick. Journal of Wildlife Management 32:489–500.

Pulliam, H. R. 1988. Sources, sinks, and population regulation. American Naturalist 132:652–661.

Pyle, P. 2005. Molts and plumages of ducks (Anatinae). Waterbirds 28:208–219.

Rangel-Woodyard, E., and E. G. Bolen. 1984. Ecological studies of Muscovy Ducks in Mexico. Southwestern Naturalist 29:453–461.

Raveling, D. G. 1978. The timing of egg laying by northern geese. Auk 95:294–303.

Raveling, D. G. 1981. Survival, experience, and age in relation to breeding success of Canada Geese. Journal of Wildlife Management 45:817–829.

Raveling, D. G. 1989. Nest-predation rates in relation to colony size of Black Brant. Journal of Wildlife Management 53:87–90.

Reinecke, K. J. 1979. Feeding ecology and development of juvenile Black Ducks in Maine. Auk 96:737–745.

Reynolds, R. E., D. R. Cohan, and M. A. Johnson. 1996. Using landscape information approaches to increase duck recruitment in the Prairie Pothole Region. Transactions of the North American Wildlife and Natural Resources Conference 61:86–93.

Reynolds, R. E., T. L. Shaffer, J. R. Sauer, and B. G. Peterjohn. 1994. Conservation Reserve Program: benefit for grassland birds in the Northern Plains. Transactions of the North American Wildlife and Natural Resources Conference 59:328–336.

Richardson, D. M., and R. M. Kaminski. 1992. Diet restrictions, diet quality, and prebasic molt in female Mallards. Journal of Wildlife Management 56:531–539.

Ricklefs, R. E. 1967. A graphical method of fitting equations to growth curves. Ecology 48:978–983.

Ricklefs, R. E. 1968. Patterns of growth in birds. Ibis 110:419–451.

Ricklefs, R. E. 1973. Patterns of growth in birds. II. Growth rate and mode of development. Ibis 115:177–201.

Ridlehuber, K. T. 1982. Fire ant predation on Wood Duck ducklings and pipped eggs. Southwestern Naturalist 27:222.

Rienecker, W. C., and W. Anderson. 1960. A waterfowl nesting study on Tule Lake and Lower Klamath National Wildlife Refuges, 1957. California Fish and Game 46:481–506.

Riggert, T. L. 1977. The biology of the Mountain Duck on Rottnest Island, Western Australia. Wildlife Monographs 52.

Ringelman, J. K., and L. D. Flake. 1980. Diurnal visibility and activity of Blue-winged Teal and Mallard broods. Journal of Wildlife Management 44:822–829.

Ringelman, J. K., and J. R. Longcore. 1982. Survival of juvenile Black Ducks during brood rearing. Journal of Wildlife Management 46:622–628.

Robb, J. R., and T. A. Bookhout. 1995. Factors influencing Wood Duck use of natural cavities. Journal of Wildlife Management 59:372–383.

Robel, R. J., J. N. Briggs, A. D. Dayton, and L. C. Hurlert. 1970. Relationships between visual obstruction measurements and weight of grassland vegetation. Journal of Range Management 23:295–297.

Robertson, D. J. 1929. Notes on the breeding habits of the eiders in the Orkneys. British Birds 23:26–30.

Robertson, G. J. 1995. Factors affecting nest site selection and nesting success in the Common Eider Somateria mollissima. Ibis 137:109–115.

Robinson, J. A., L. G. Culzac, and N. S. Aldridge. 2002. Age-related changes in the habitat use and behaviour of Mallard Anas platyrhynchos broods at artificially created lakes in southern Britain. Wildfowl 53:107–118.

Rohwer, F. C. 1992. The evolution of reproductive patterns in waterfowl. Pages 486–539 in B. D. J. Batt, A. D. Afton, M. G. Anderson, C. D. Ankney, D. H. Johnson, J. A. Kadlec, and G. L. Krapu, editors. Ecology and management of breeding waterfowl. University of Minnesota Press, Minneapolis.

Rohwer, F. C. 1999. Time constraints and moult-breeding tradeoffs in large birds. International Ornithological Congress 22:568–581.

Rotella, J. J., and J. T. Ratti. 1992. Mallard brood survival and wetland habitat conditions in south-western Manitoba. Journal of Wildlife Management 56:499–507.

Rumble, M. A., and L. D. Flake. 1983. Management considerations to enhance use of stock ponds by waterfowl broods. Journal of Range Management 36:691–694.

Ruwaldt, J. J., Jr., L. D. Flake, and J. M. Gates. 1979. Waterfowl pair use of natural and man-made wetlands in South Dakota. Journal of Wildlife Management 43:375–383.

Ryan, D. C., R. J. Kawula, and R. J. Gates. 1998. Breeding biology of Wood Ducks using natural cavities in southern Illinois. Journal of Wildlife Management 62:112–123.

Ryder, J. P. 1967. The breeding biology of Ross' Goose in the Perry River region, Northwest Territories. Canadian Wildlife Service Report Series 3.

Salomonsen, F. 1949. Some notes on the molt of the Long-tailed Duck (Clangula hyemalis). Avicultural Magazine 55:59–62.

Salomonsen, F. 1968. The moult migration. Wildfowl 19:5–24.

Samson, F. B., and F. L. Knopf. 1994. Prairie conservation in North America. BioScience 44:418–421.

Sargeant, A. B. 1972. Red fox spatial characteristics in relation to waterfowl predation. Journal of Wildlife Management 36:225–236.

Sargeant, A. B. 1982. A case history of a dynamic resource — the red fox. Pages 121–137 in G. C. Sanderson, editor. Midwest furbearer management. Proceedings of the 43th Midwest Fish and Wild-life Conference.

Sargeant, A. B., S. H. Allen, and R. T. Eberhardt. 1984. Red fox predation on breeding ducks in midcontinent North America. Wildlife Monographs 89.

Sargeant, A. B., R. J. Greenwood, M. A. Sovada, and T. L. Shaffer. 1993. Distribution and abundance of predators that affect duck production — Prairie Pothole Region. U.S. Fish and Wildlife Service Resource Publication 194.

Sargeant, A. B., A. D. Kruse, and A. D. Afton. 1974. Use of small fences to protect ground bird nests from mammalian predators. Prairie Naturalist 6:60–63.

Sargeant, A. B., and D. G. Raveling. 1992. Mortality during the breeding season. Pages 396–422 in B. D. J. Batt, A. D. Afton, M. G. Anderson, C. D. Ankney, D. H. Johnson, J. A. Kadlec, and G. L. Krapu, editors. Ecology and management of breeding waterfowl. University of Minnesota Press, Minneapolis.

Sargeant, A. B., M. A. Sovada, and T. L. Shaffer. 1995. Seasonal predator removal relative to hatch rate of duck nests in Waterfowl Production Areas. Wildlife Society Bulletin 23:507–513.

Sargeant, A. B., G. A. Swanson, and H. A. Doty. 1973. Selective predation by mink, Mustela vison, on waterfowl. American Midland Naturalist 89:208–214.

Saunders, D., G. Arnold, A. Burbidge, and A. Hopkins. 1987. The role of remnants of native vegetation in nature conservation: future directions. Pages 259–268 in D. Saunders, G. Arnold, A. Burbidge, and A. Hopkins, editors. Nature conservation: the role of remnants of native vegetation. Surrey Beatty and Sons, New South Wales, Australia.

Savard, J-P. L. 1987. Causes and functions of brood amalgamation in Barrow's Goldeneye and Bufflehead. Canadian Journal of Zoology 65:1548–1553.

Savard, J-P. L. 1988. Use of nest boxes by Barrow's Goldeneyes: nesting success and effect on the breeding population. Wildlife Society Bulletin. 16:125–132.

Savard, J-P. L., A. Reed, and L. Lesage. 1998. Brood amalgamation in Surf Scoters Melanitta perspicillata and other Mergini. Wildfowl 49:129–138.

Sayler, R. D. 1992. Ecology and evolution of brood parasitism in waterfowl. Pages 290–322 in B. D. J. Batt, A. D. Afton, M. G. Anderson, C. D. Ankney, D. H. Johnson, J. A. Kadlec, and G. L. Krapu, editors. Ecology and management of breeding waterfowl. University of Minnesota Press, Minneapolis.

Sayler, R. D., and M. A. Willms. 1997. Brood ecology of Mallards and Gadwalls nesting on islands in large reservoirs. Journal of Wildlife Management 61:808–815.

Schamel, D. 1977. Breeding of the Common Eider (*Somateria mollissima*) on the Beaufort Sea coast of Alaska. Condor 79:478–485.

Schmidt-Nielsen, K., and Y. T. Kim. 1964. The effect of salt intake on the size and function of the salt gland of ducks. Auk 81:160–172.

Schmutz, J. A. 1993. Survival and pre-fledging body mass in juvenile Emperor Geese. Condor 95:222–225.

Schmutz, J. A. 2001. Selection of habitats by Emperor Geese during brood rearing. Waterbirds 24:394–401.

Schmutz, J. A., B. F. J. Manly, and C. P. Dau. 2001. Effects of gull predation and weather on survival of Emperor Goose goslings. Journal of Wildlife Management 65:248–257.

Schmutz, J. K., R. J. Robertson, and F. Cooke. 1982. Female sociality in the Common Eider duck during brood rearing. Canadian Journal of Zoology 60:3326–3331.

Schranck, B. W. 1972. Waterfowl nest cover and some relationships. Journal of Wildlife Management 36:182–186.

Scott, M. L., F. W. Hill, E. H. Parsons, Jr., J. H. Bruckner, and E. Dougherty, III. 1959. Studies on duck nutrition — 7. Effect of dietary energy: protein relationships upon growth, feed utilization and carcass composition in market ducklings. Poultry Science 38:497–507.

Scott, P. 1972. The swans. Houghton Mifflin, Boston.

Seddon, P. J., and R. F. Maloney. 2003. Campbell Island Teal re-introduction plan. New Zealand Department of Conservation, DOC Internal Series 154.

Sedinger, J. S. 1986. Growth and development of Canada Goose goslings. Condor 88:169–180.

Sedinger, J. S. 1992. Ecology of prefledging water fowl. Pages 109–127 *in* B. D. J. Batt, A. D. Afton, M. G. Anderson, C. D. Ankney, D. H. Johnson, J. A. Kadlec, and G. L. Krapu, editors. Ecology and management of breeding waterfowl. University of Minnesota Press, Minneapolis.

Sedinger, J. S., and P. L. Flint. 1991. Growth rate is negatively correlated with hatch date in Black Brant. Ecology 72:496–502.

Sedinger, J. S., M. P. Hezog, B. T. Person, M. T. Kirk, T. Obritchkewitch, P. P. Martin, and A. A. Stickney. 2001. Large-scale variation in growth of Black Brant goslings related to food availability. Auk 118:1088–1095.

Sedinger, J. S., M. S. Lindberg, B. T. Person, M. E. Eichholz, M. P. Herzog, and P. L. Flint. 1998. Density-dependent effects on growth, body size, and clutch size in Black Brant. Auk 115:613–620.

Sedinger, J. S., and D. G. Raveling. 1984. Dietary selectivity in relation to availability and quality of food for goslings of Cackling Geese. Auk 101:295–306.

Sedinger, J. S., and D. G. Raveling. 1986. Timing of nesting by Canada Geese in relation to the phenology and availability of their food plants. Journal of Animal Ecology 55:1083–1102.

Sedinger, J. S., and D. G. Raveling. 1988. Foraging behavior of Cackling Canada Goose goslings: implications for the roles of food availability and processing rate. Oecologia 75:119–124.

Semel, B., and P. W. Sherman. 1986. Dynamics of nest parasitism in Wood Ducks. Auk 103:813–816.

Semel, B., P. W. Sherman, and S. M. Byers. 1988. Effects of brood parasitism and nest-box placement on Wood Duck breeding ecology. Condor 90:920–930.

Semel, B., P. W. Sherman, and S. M. Byers. 1990. Nest boxes and brood parasitism in Wood Ducks: a management dilemma. Pages 163–170 *in* L. H. Fredrickson, G. V. Burger, S. P. Havera, D. A. Graber, R. E. Kirby, and T. S. Taylor, editors. Proceedings of the 1988 North American Wood Duck Symposium, St. Louis.

Serie, J. R., D. L. Trauger, and J. E. Austin. 1992. Influence of age and selected environmental factors on reproductive performance of Canvasbacks. Journal of Wildlife Management 56:546–556.

Shaffer, T. L. 2004. A unified approach to analyzing nest success. Auk 121:526–540.

Sheaffer, S. E., and R. A. Malceki. 1996. Predicting breeding success of Atlantic population Canada Geese from meteorological variables. Journal of Wildlife Management 60:882–890.

Shields, M. A., and J. F. Parnell. 1986. Fish Crow predation on eggs of the White Ibis at Battery Island, North Carolina. Auk 103:531–539.

Smith, A. G., J. H. Stoudt, and J. B. Gollop. 1964. Prairie potholes and marshes. Pages 39–50 in J. P. Linduska, editor. Waterfowl tomorrow. U.S. Government Printing Office, Washington, D.C.

Smith, L. M., and D. G. Sheeley. 1993. Molt patterns of wintering Northern Pintails in the Southern High Plains. Journal of Wildlife Management 57:229–238.

Solman, V. E. F. 1945. The ecological relations of pike, *Esox lucius* L., and waterfowl. Ecology 26:157–170.

Sorenson, M. D. 1991. The functional significance of parasitic egg laying and typical nesting in Redhead ducks: an analysis of individual behavior. Animal Behaviour 42:771–796.

Sorenson, M. D. 1993. Parasitic egg laying in Canvasbacks: frequency, success, and individual behavior. Auk 110:57–69.

Soulliere, G. J. 1986. Cost and significance of a Wood Duck nest-house program in Wisconsin: an evaluation. Wildlife Society Bulletin 14:391–395.

Soulliere, G. J. 1988. Density of suitable Wood Duck nest cavities in a northern hardwood Forest. Journal of Wildlife Management 52:86–89.

Soulliere, G. J. 1990a. Review of Wood Duck nest-cavity characteristics. Pages 153–162 in L. H. Fredrickson, G. V. Burger, S. P. Havera, D. A. Graber, R. E. Kirby, and T. S. Taylor, editors. Proceedings of the 1988 North. American Wood Duck Symposium, St. Louis.

Soulliere, G. J. 1990b. Regional and site-specific trends in Wood Duck use of nest boxes. Pages 235–244 in L. H. Fredrickson, G. V. Burger, S. P. Havera, D. A. Graber, R. E. Kirby, and T. S. Taylor, editors. Proceedings of the 1988 North. American Wood Duck Symposium, St. Louis.

Southwick, C. 1953. A system of age classification for field studies of waterfowl broods. Journal of Wildlife Management 17:1–8.

Sovada, M. A., R. M. Anthony, and B. D. J. Batt. 2001. Predation on waterfowl in arctic tundra and prairie breeding areas: a review. Wildlife Society Bulletin 29:6–15.

Sovada, M. A., A. B. Sargeant, and J. W. Grier. 1995. Differential effects of coyotes and red foxes on duck nest success. Journal of Wildlife Management 59:1–9.

Sovada, M. A., M. C. Zicus, R. J. Greenwood, D. P. Rave, W. E. Newton, R. O. Woodward, and J. A. Beiser. 2000. Relationship of habitat patch size to predator community and survival of duck nests. Journal of Wildlife Management 64:820–831.

Sowls, L. K. 1949. A preliminary report on renesting in waterfowl. Transactions of the North American Wildlife Conference 14:260–275.

Sowls, L. K. 1955. Prairie ducks: a study of their behavior, ecology and management. Stackpole Company, Harrisburg, Pennsylvania, and the Wildlife Management Institute, Washington, D.C.

Stafford, J. D., L. D. Flake, and P. W. Mammenga. 2002. Survival of Mallard broods and ducklings departing overwater nesting structures in eastern South Dakota. Wildlife Society Bulletin 30:327–336.

Steen, J. B., and G. W. Gabrielson. 1986. Thermogenesis in newly hatched eider (*Somateria mollissima*) and Long-tailed Duck (*Clangula hyemalis*) ducklings and Barnacle Goose (*Branta leucopsis*) goslings. Polar Research 4:181–186.

Sterling, T., and A. Dzubin. 1967. Canada Goose molt migrations to the Northwest Territories. Transactions of the North American Wildlife and Natural Resources Conference 32:355–373.

Stewart, P. A. 1967a. Wood Duck ducklings captured by bullfrogs. Wilson Bulletin 79:237–238.

Stewart, P. A. 1967b. Diving Wood Duck ducklings entangled in filamentous algae. Condor 69:531.

Stewart, R. E., and H. A. Kantrud. 1971. Classification of natural ponds and lakes in the glaciated prairie region. U.S. Fish and Wildlife Service Resource Publication 92.

Stoudt, J. H. 1969. Relationships between waterfowl areas on the Redvers Waterfowl Study Area. Pages 123–131 in Saskatoon Wetlands Seminar. Canadian Wildlife Service Report Series 6.

Street, M. 1978. The role of insects in the diet of Mallard ducklings — an experimental approach. Wildfowl 28:113–125.

Sugden, L. G., and G. W. Beyersbergen. 1987. Effect of nesting cover density on American Crow predation of simulated duck nests. Journal of Wildlife Management 51:481–485.

Sullivan, B. D., and J. J. Dinsmore. 1990. Factors affecting egg predation by American Crows. Journal of Wildlife Management 54:433–437.

Summers, R. W. 1982. The absence of flightless molt in the Ruddy-headed Goose in Argentina and Chile. Wildfowl 33:5–6.

Summers, R. W. 1983. Moult-skipping by Upland Geese *Chloephaga picta* in the Falkland Islands. Ibis 125:262–266.

Summers, R. W., L. G. Underhill, E. E. Syroechkovski, Jr., H. G. Lappo, R. P. Prys-Jones, and V. Karpov. 1994. The breeding biology of Dark-bellied Brent Geese *Branta b. bernicla* and King Eiders *Somateria spectabilis* on the northeastern Taimyr Peninsula, especially in relation to Snowy Owl *Nyctea scandiaca* nests. Wildfowl 45:110–118.

Swanson, G. A. 1977. Diel food selection by Anatinae on a waste-stabilization system. Journal of Wildlife Management 41:226–231.

Swanson, G. A., V. A. Adomaitis, F. B. Lee, J. R. Serie, and J. A. Shoesmith. 1984. Limnological conditions influencing duckling use of saline lakes in south-central North Dakota. Journal of Wildlife Management 48:340–349.

Swanson, G. A., G. L. Krapu, and J. R. Serie. 1979. Foods of laying female dabbling ducks on the breeding grounds. Pages 47–57 *in* T. A. Bookhout, editor. Waterfowl and wetlands-an integrated review. La Crosse Printing, La Crosse, Wisconsin.

Swanson, G. A., and M. I. Meyer. 1973. The role of invertebrates in the feeding ecology of Anatinae during the breeding season. Pages 143–177 *in* The waterfowl habitat management symposium. Moncton, New Brunswick.

Swanson, G. A., and A. B. Sargeant. 1972. Observation of nighttime feeding behavior of ducks. Journal of Wildlife Management 36:959–961.

Swanson, G. A., T. L. Shaffer, J. F. Wolf, and F. B. Lee. 1986. Renesting characteristics of captive Mallards in experimental ponds Journal of Wildlife Management 50:32–38.

Swennon, C. 1968. Nest protection of eider ducks and shovelers by means of feces. Ardea 56:249–258.

Szymczak, M. R., and E. A. Rexstad. 1991. Harvest distribution and survival of a Gadwall population. Journal of Wildlife Management 55:592–600.

Talent, L. G., G. L. Krapu, and R. L. Jarvis. 1982. Habitat use by Mallard broods in south central North Dakota. Journal of Wildlife Management 46:629–635.

Talent, L. G., R. L. Jarvis, and G. L. Krapu. 1983. Survival of Mallard broods in south-central North Dakota. Condor 85:74–78.

Taylor, E. J. 1995. Molt of Black Brant (*Branta bernicla nigricans*) on the Arctic Coastal Plain, Alaska. Auk 112:904–919.

Thompson, C. W. 2004. Determining evolutionary homologies of molts and plumages: a commentary on Howell et al. (2003). Condor 106:199–206.

Thompson, J. E., and R. D. Drobney. 1996. Nutritional implications of molt in male Canvasbacks: variation in nutrient reserves and digestive tract morphololgy. Condor 98:512–526.

Thompson, J. E., and R. D. Drobney. 1997. Diet and nutrition of male Canvasbacks during reproductive molts. Journal of Wildlife Management 61:426–434.

Thompson, S. C., and D. G. Raveling. 1987. Incubation behavior of Emperor Geese compared with other geese: interactions of predation, body size, and energetics. Auk 104:707–716.

Tietje, W. D., and J. G. Teer. 1988. Winter body condition of Northern Shovelers on freshwater and saline habitats. Pages 353–376 *in* M. W. Weller, editor. Waterfowl in winter. University of Minnesota Press, Minneapolis.

Tremblay, J. P., P. G. Gauthier, D. Lepage, and A. Desrochers. 1997. Factors affecting nest success in Greater Snow Geese: effects of habitat and association with Snowy Owls. Wilson Bulletin 109:449–461.

Turcek, F. J. 1966. On plumage quality of birds. Ekologia Polska, Series A 14:617–634.

Turner, B. C., G. S. Hochbaum, F. D. Caswell, and D. J. Nieman. 1987. Agricultural impacts on wetland habitats on the Canadian prairies, 1981–85. Transactions of the North American Wildlife and Natural Resources Conference 52:206–215.

Ward, D. H., J. A. Schmutz, J. S. Sedinger, K. S. Bollinger, P. D. Martin, and B. A. Anderson. 2004. Temporal and geographic variation in survival of juvenile Black Brant. Condor 106:263–274.

Weller, M. W. 1957. Growth, weights, and plumages of the Redhead, *Aythya americana*. Wilson Bulletin 69:5–38.

Weller, M. W. 1959. Parasitic egg laying in the Redhead (*Aythya americana*) and other North American Anitadae. Ecological Monographs 29:333–365.

Weller, M. W. 1980. Molts and plumages of waterfowl. Pages 34-38 *in* F. C. Bellrose. Ducks, geese and swans of North America. Stackpole Books, Harrisburg, Pennsylvania.

Weller, M. W., and C. S. Spatcher. 1965. Role of habitat in the distribution and abundance of marsh birds. Iowa State University Agricultural and Home Economics Experiment Station Special Report 43.

Welty, J. C. 1982. The life of birds. Third edition Saunders College Publishing, New York.

Wheeler, W. E. 1984. Duck egg predation by fox snakes in Wisconsin. Wildlife Society Bulletin 12:77–78.

White, G. C., and K. P. Burnham. 1999. Program MARK: survival estimation from populations of marked animals. Bird Study 46 (Supplement):120–139.

Williams, A. J., D. B. Lank, F. C. Cooke, and R. F. Rockwell. 1993. Fitness consequences of egg size variation in the Lesser Snow Goose. Oecologia 96:331–338.

Williams, M. 1979. The moult gatherings of Paradise Shelduck in the Gisborne–East Coast District. Notornis 26:369–390.

Williams, M. 2004. Rats vs. Campbell Island Teal . . . and the winner is? Birdscapes, fall issue.

Williams, M., and C. J. R. Robertson. 1996. The Campbell Island Teal *Anas aucklandica nesiotis*: history and review. Wildfowl 47:134–165.

Williams, T. D. 1994. Intraspecific variation in egg size and egg composition in birds: effects on offspring fitness. Biological Reviews 68:35–59.

Windingstad, R. M., F. X. Kartch, R. K. Stroud, and M. R. Smith. 1987. Salt toxicosis in waterfowl in North Dakota. Journal of Wildlife Diseases 23:443–446.

Wittenberger, J. F., and G. L. Hunt, Jr. 1985. The adaptive significance of coloniality in birds. Avian Biology 8:1–78.

Woolfenden, G. E. 1967. Selection for a delayed simultaneous wing molt in Loons (Gaviidae). Wilson Bulletin 79:416–420.

Yarris, G. S., M. R. McLandress, and A. E. H. Perkins. 1994. Molt migration of postbreeding female Mallards from Suisun Marsh, California. Condor 96:36–45.

Yerkes, T. 2000. Influence of female age and body mass on brood and duckling survival, number of surviving ducklings, and brood movements in Redheads. Condor 102:926–929.

Yetter, A. P., S. P. Havera, and C. S. Hine. 1999. Natural-Cavity use by nesting Wood Ducks in Illinois. Journal of Wildlife Management 63:630–638.

Young, C. M. 1971. A nesting raft for ducks. 1971. Canadian Field-Naturalist 85:179–181.

Young, D. A., and D. A. Boag. 1982. Changes in physical condition of male Mallards (*Anas platyrhynchos*) during moult. Canadian Journal of Zoology 60:3220–3226.

Zicus, M. C. 1981. Molt migration of Canada Geese from Crex Meadows, Wisconsin. Journal of Wildlife Management 45:54–63.

Zipko, S. J., and J. Kennington. 1977. A ground-nesting Wood Duck. Auk 94:159.

Chapter 7
WINTER

In North America and elsewhere, most scientific investigations of waterfowl began with field studies of breeding birds. This narrow focus continued for some time, largely because biologists believed that conditions and events during the breeding season were almost solely responsible for the abundance of waterfowl (Weller and Batt 1988). Moreover, the breeding areas of many species were reasonably accessible to biologists, and logistical considerations thus were not major barriers for conducting field research. The early domination of breeding studies perhaps is best illustrated by the literature cited in the classic *Ducks, Geese and Swans of North America* (Bellrose 1980), which reviewed nearly all of the waterfowl research published by the 1970s — but only 50 (5.5%) of about 900 citations dealt with any aspect of waterfowl ecology outside the breeding period. This situation gains significance considering that most species of North American waterfowl spend several months each year far removed from their breeding grounds at sites where courtship and other important events often occur. At the time, much was known about habitat management designed to attract migrating and wintering waterfowl, but most of this work was local in scope and not reported in published literature (Weller and Batt 1988).

By the late 1970s, however, the number of published studies on wintering waterfowl began to increase dramatically as biologists turned their research and management efforts to this segment of the annual cycle. This effort was stimulated, in part, from basic research on birds in general where arguments emerged that food resources during the nonbreeding period regulated bird populations (Lack 1966). Still another study indicated that food and environmental conditions during winter regulated the numbers of several species of North American grassland birds (Fretwell 1972). Nonetheless, in comparison to breeding waterfowl, interest in wintering waterfowl remained limited, as noted Fredrickson and Drobney (1979:119): ". . . information on the nutritional and energy requirements of molting, migrating, and wintering waterfowl is minimal." By the late 1970s, only a few studies had appeared, among them White and James (1978) who examined the factors affecting habitat use by 14 species of waterfowl wintering at the Welder Wildlife Refuge in Texas. Then, with the work of Fredrickson and Drobney (1979), a new thrust began in earnest.

These efforts coalesced in April 1982 when the Delta Waterfowl and Wetlands Research Station convened a 3-day workshop on the ecology of wintering waterfowl at the Gaylord Memorial Laboratory in Missouri (Anderson and Batt 1983). Many of the 40 invited participants were actively engaged in major studies of wintering waterfowl ecology, and 26 speakers presented results and ideas. The participants then divided into groups to discuss research needs relative to habitat selection, social behavior, habitat ecology, and bioenergetics. The report from the workshop did much to guide and stimulate research on wintering waterfowl into the new millennium.

The terms "wintering," "nonbreeding," and "postbreeding" are often used interchangeably, and we make no major attempt to define each here. As a term, "nonbreeding" clearly encompasses postbreeding, wintering, and migrating, but the latter terms may never become well defined because they usually overlap at least partially in time and space. "Migration," in particular, grades into both the postbreeding and wintering periods. Further, all individuals of a population are not necessarily engaged simultaneously in the same activities in the annual cycle. For example, a successful, early-nesting female may have completed rearing her brood and started postbreeding activities at the very time a renesting female is still incubating. Spatial considerations also color these terms; thus, for a Mallard remaining in bottomland hardwood habitat in Missouri from September through February, the site may function as wintering habitat, but for a Mallard moving northward from Texas, the same habitat serves as staging or resting site. Finally, the nonbreeding period covers much of the annual cycle, and thus some events are better treated elsewhere (e.g., Courtship and Pair Formation in Chapter 3, Feeding Ecology in Chapter 5, and Molting in Chapter 6). This chapter instead places its focus on those events that affect winter survival and the forthcoming period of reproduction.

THE ROLE OF WINTER IN THE ANNUAL CYCLE OF WATERFOWL

Research has confirmed that habitat conditions and events occurring during the nonbreeding period affect both the survival and reproduction of waterfowl. As we have seen (Chapter 4), arctic-nesting geese accumulate substantial lipid and protein reserves in late winter and early spring that are mobilized later for the production and incubation of eggs (Ankney and MacInnes 1978, Raveling 1979, Alisauskas 2002). In this case, the critical, cross-seasonal effect of winter–early spring conditions on the subsequent reproductive performance of geese can be demonstrated because geese generally breed, migrate, and winter as distinct subpopulations (Raveling 1978, Bellrose 1980, Tacha et al. 1988, Ely and Scribner 1994). Biologists therefore could sample these subpopulations in time and space to pinpoint not only when and where nutrient reserves were acquired, but when and where these reserves were mobilized.

Heitmeyer and Fredrickson (1981), later confirmed by Kaminski and Gluesing (1987), first suggested a relationship between winter habitat conditions and recruitment for ducks in the following breeding season. Their study considered Mallards wintering in bottomland hardwood habitats along the Mississippi River and revealed a small but statistically significant correlation ($r = 0.46$) between increased winter precipitation (i.e., better habitat conditions) and Mallard age ratios the following year. Heitmeyer (1988) later noted that changes in the carcass composition of female Mallards wintering in Missouri were influenced by pairing and other events in the annual cycle; he concluded that Mallards completing these events early in winter may realize increased reproductive advantages, especially following wet winters. Raveling and Heitmeyer (1989) also

linked increases in Northern Pintail populations to the quality of winter habitat conditions.

Overall, the impact of winter habitat conditions on reproductive success should be viewed as a continuum — a progression from winter habitat to migration habitat to breeding habitat. Theoretically, the highest populations might be expected when habitat conditions are optimal within all three types of habitats, lowest when conditions are poor within all three, and somewhere in between for other combinations of quality among the three (Fig. 7-1). This scenario is suggested by the data analyzed for Mallards (Heitmeyer and Fredrickson 1981, Kaminski and Gluesing 1987) and Northern Pintails (Raveling and Heitmeyer 1989). Other studies have shown, however, that the effects of poor winter conditions on recruitment may be offset when high-quality habitats are available during the spring and late summer (Leitch and Kaminski 1985). Thus, those stopover areas located near breeding areas represent crucial habitat for ensuring that female Mallards acquire adequate nutrient reserves (LaGrange and Dinsmore 1988).

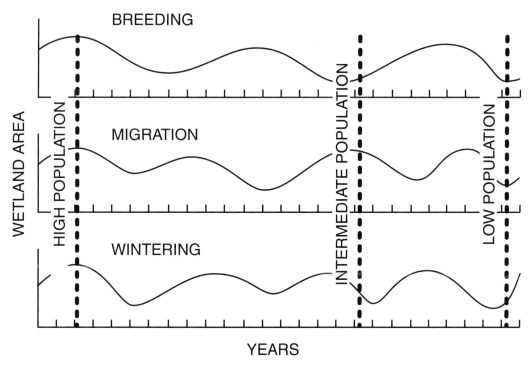

Figure 7-1. Fluctuations in the status of wetland areas that waterfowl use for breeding, migration, and wintering potentially produce corresponding changes in Mallard populations, as shown in this theoretical model. The Mallard population peaks when habitat conditions are optimal over all parts of the annual cycle (*left*) and is lowest when conditions are simultaneously poor (*right*). A population of intermediate size results when habitat conditions lie between these extremes (*middle*). From Heitmeyer and Fredrickson (1981:55). With permission from, The Wildlife Management Institute.

In addition to the probable relationship between winter habitat conditions and reproductive success, a similar relationship clearly exists between winter conditions and survival rates for waterfowl. Reinecke et al. (1982) suggested such a relationship for female American Black Ducks wintering in Maine, but Haramis et al. (1986) later provided direct evidence that linked winter body mass and the probability of survival. Their analysis of mass and the recapture histories for 6,000 Canvasbacks banded on Chesapeake Bay revealed that adult males with large body mass realized greater probabilities of overwinter and annual survival than individuals with less mass. This relationship did not hold for adult females, but the sample sizes were small. In contrast, no sex or age class of American Black Ducks along the coast of Maine showed a relationship between late-winter body mass and annual survival (Krementz et al. 1989). The authors cautioned against accepting the general conclusion that body mass during winter is related to annual survival; instead, they suggest that annual survival rates are probably the product of survival probabilities associated with smaller periods of time (e.g., seasons). For example, during a 3-year study of female Northern Pintails in the Sacramento Valley of California, nonwintering survival (annual survival/winter survival) was lower than winter survival (0.748 vs. 0.874). Thus, significant mortality of female Northern Pintails occurs during late fall and early winter (Miller et al. 1995), as has been documented for other species of ducks (see Johnson et al. 1992). The next section examines the factors affecting waterfowl survival during winter in more detail, for which recent studies of radiomarked birds have provided significant insight.

FACTORS AFFECING WINTER SURVIVAL

Age Class and Hunting

Surprisingly, research addressing age-related winter survival of ducks has produced equivocal results, whereas analyses of band-recovery data unequivocally reveal that immatures experience higher *annual* mortality rates than adults (see Bellrose 1980). In southwestern Louisiana, winter (Oct–Feb) survival rates of radiomarked female Northern Pintails during a 3-year study were 0.714 for adults compared with 0.550 for immatures, primarily because immatures experienced higher hunting mortality (0.287) than adults (0.139; Cox et al. 1998). In the San Joaquin Valley of California, the cumulative September to March survival rate for female North-

ern Pintails during a 4-year study also was higher for adults (0.756) than immatures (0.654; Fleskes et al. 2002). In contrast, Migoya and Baldassarre (1995) detected no difference in survival between adult and immature female Northern Pintails wintering farther south in Sinaloa, Mexico, probably because hunting pressure was low and quality habitat was abundant. Survival rates for female Canvasbacks wintering in coastal Louisiana during a 4-year study were high and did not differ between age classes, averaging 0.946 for adults and 0.952 for immatures (Hohman et al. 1993), likely because the birds had access to an abundant food supply (Hohman 1993).

Body Condition

As we have seen (Chapter 4), lipids are the major form of energy storage in birds. Hence, the amount of stored lipids relative to body mass is an indicator of body condition, which has been defined as the ability of an individual to meet present or future energy needs (Owen and Cook 1977), or the nutritional status of an individual relative to its energetic needs at a given time (Weatherhead and Ankney 1984). Body condition itself generally refers to energy stored in the form of lipids (Johnson et al. 1985).

Lipid storage becomes significant to wintering waterfowl because the birds predictably face cold weather and periodic food shortages, each of which necessitates a reliance on stored energy. The increase storage of lipids in anticipation of the energy demands of winter can be dramatic: Green-winged Teal wintering on the Southern High Plains of Texas increased their lipid reserves by as much as 219% between September and January (Baldassarre et al. 1986). However, the relationship between body condition of ducks and their winter survival is not necessarily firm. Many studies have documented reduced winter survival for individuals whose body mass was low at the time they were initially captured or marked (Greenwood et al. 1986, Haramis et al. 1986, Hepp et al. 1986, Conroy et al. 1989, Dufour et al. 1993), whereas other studies have not (Migoya and Baldassarre 1995, Dugger et al. 1994, Jeske et al. 1994, Krementz et al. 1989, Haramis et al. 1993, Miller et al. 1995, Cox et al. 1998). For example, winter survival of female Mallards in the Playa Lakes Region of Texas was high (0.888) for individuals in good body condition but less (0.661) for those that were not (Bergan and Smith 1993). In contrast, body condition did not affect winter survival of female Northern Pintails in Louisiana (Cox et al. 1998).

The effect of body condition on winter survival might not be detected if individuals in the poorest condition arrive later to wintering areas, or fail to arrive at all because of greater mortality during migration, including being harvested by hunters in more northern areas (Cox et al. 1998). In a 3-year study of adult female Northern Pintails radiomarked in the Sacramento Valley of California, Miller et al. (1995) reported that nonwinter annual survival (0.748) was lower than winter survival, indicating that the breeding–migration period was a period of significant mortality.

Many studies of winter survival also capture birds early in winter, and these individuals may be in good body condition, certainly above a threshold that might predispose them to differential mortality. Further, with favorable habitat conditions, body condition can increase rapidly after arrival to winter areas (Miller 1986a), which again might lead to a biased sample (i.e., birds outfitted with radios are captured early in winter). For example, carcass mass and body lipids did not differ between adult and immature Northern Pintails collected on the Southern High Plains of Texas from October through March (Smith and Sheeley 1993). Tamisier et al. (1995) proposed that the first and/or heaviest birds to arrive at winter sites are also the first to form pairs, and they thus have the best chance of reproducing successfully the following spring. Hence, although body condition can influence survival as well as reproduction, the issue is complex and interacts with hunting pressure, age, habitat abundance and quality, and time of arrival to winter areas.

In Louisiana, immature Northern Pintails were in poorer condition than adults, but winter survival did not vary with body condition (Cox et al. 1998), and habitat use did not differ by age class (Cox and Afton 1997). These studies concluded that immature female Northern Pintails were more vulnerable than adults because they were less wary of hunters, and not because they were in poorer condition per se. Hepp et al. (1986) found that all sex and age classes of Mallards in poor condition when banded had a higher probability of being shot during the hunting season compared with those in good condition. This result implied that individuals in poor condition may search more for food and thereby increase their exposure to hunters.

Fleskes et al. (2002) provided support for an interaction of age and body condition during their studies of female Northern Pintails in the San Joaquin Valley of California, where survival was best explained by two models, one of which was age × body

mass. They speculated that individuals in poor condition were more focused on feeding than on avoiding predators and hunters, were more readily attracted to decoys (hunting caused 83% of all mortality), and were more susceptible to diseases. Body condition during the fall also may be more related to the survival of immatures than it is for adults; the body condition of immatures changed less before the hunting season started, perhaps because immatures were less adept than adults at finding or competing for food resources.

Temporal and Spatial Variation: Collectively, survival studies of wintering waterfowl reveal significant degrees of spatial and temporal variation. Examples of spatial differences are nicely illustrated in studies of Northern Pintails; they exhibit high fidelity to wintering areas (Hestbeck 1993a), and winter survival has been investigated at several of these locations. In the San Joaquin Valley of California, survival of female Northern Pintails was 0.756 for adults and 0.654 for immatures (Fleskes et al. 2002), but was much higher (0.974) for adults in the Sacramento Valley of California to the north (Miller et al. 1995). In this instance, the results were attributed to differences in the availability of refuges and other sanctuaries, types of feeding habitats, waterfowl populations, and hunting pressure (Fleskes et al. 2002). About 25% of the wetland habitat on wildlife areas and national wildlife refuges in the Sacramento Valley was closed to hunting compared with only 6% in the San Joaquin Valley. Pintails in the Sacramento Valley also had access to ricefields, which fulfilled their energetic requirements and provided some refuge from hunters. The high survival rates for female Northern Pintails in Sinaloa, Mexico, likewise were attributed to low hunting pressure (Migoya and Baldassarre 1995).

Rates of hunting mortality were high for female Northern Pintails in southwestern Louisiana, averaging 16.5% for adults and 31.5% for immatures (Cox et al. 1998). Unlike other areas, hunting mortality in Louisiana remained consistently high throughout the hunting season, which reflected the knowledge and experience of hunters with a long-standing tradition for hunting Northern Pintails. Also, because Northern Pintails arrived in Louisiana closer to the beginning of the hunting season, they did not become as familiar with refuge areas as did Northern Pintails in California. Indeed, prior to the hunting season, Northern Pintails in Louisiana made more (67%) daytime use of nonrefuge habitats than refuges (33%; Cox and Afton 1997).

At a continental scale, Hestbeck (1993b) examined annual survival rates of Northern Pintails banded during the winter from 1950 through 1988, when their breeding population varied from 2.0 to 9.9 million. Overall survival rates ranged from 0.632 to 0.806 for males and from 0.421 to 0.769 for females. Geographic variation was limited in the survival rates for males and did not occur for females — males had lower survival rates in the Imperial Valley of California in comparison with higher rates in the Central Valley or the Gulf Coast (Texas and Louisiana). Temporally, however, survival rates for males were higher in the Pacific Flyway during 1959–61, a period of drought, declining breeding populations, and restrictive hunting regulations, and lower in 1950–58, a period marked by larger breeding populations and liberal harvest regulations.

Condition Indices: Most of the fluctuations in body mass during winter are attributable to changes in lipid reserves; protein, water, and ash do not fluctuate appreciably. Accordingly, researchers quickly realized that lipid reserves are highly correlated with body mass. Measurements of body mass therefore could provide an indicator of winter body condition and did not require either sacrificing birds or costly and time-consuming laboratory analyses (Table 7-1). However, inferring condition solely from body mass may produce biased information because the heaviest individual is not necessarily in best condition. Wishart (1979) found that skeletal mass was highly correlated with structural size in American Wigeon, but determining structural size is not practical when large numbers of birds are sampled, and

again requires sacrificing individuals. However, body mass can be corrected for structural size by measurements of more readily obtainable body components that correlate with structural size (e.g., wing, keel, bill, or body length). Consequently, "condition indices" have been developed for many species of wintering waterfowl, including the Redhead (Bailey 1979), Greater Snow Goose (Gauthier and Bédard 1984), Spur-winged Goose (Halse and Skead 1983), Ring-necked Duck (Hohman and Taylor 1986), Mallard (Owen and Cook 1977, Robb et al. 2001), American Black Duck (Robb et al. 2001), American Wigeon (Wishart 1979, DeVault et al. 2003), and many others.

However, Moser and Rusch (1988) cautioned that researchers should carefully choose measurements to represent structural size; wing and culmen length correlated poorly with skeletal volume in their study of Canada Geese. Instead, they used skeletal volume as a measure of structural size in developing a condition index for Canada Geese because skeletal volume remains constant once geese are full-grown. On the other hand, Owen and Cook (1977) and Ringelman and Szymczak (1985) recommended dividing body mass by wing length to determine condition indices for ducks. During winter, the abdominal profiles of geese also provide a useful, nondestructive index of fat reserves (Owen 1981). Omental fat is highly correlated with total body fat and thus represents another useful condition index (Woodall 1978, DeVault et al. 2003). However, despite the development of many types of condition indices, they have not been widely used in research on wintering waterfowl, likely because traditional analysis of carcass composition provides more accu-

Table 7-1. Correlation coefficients (r) of body mass and total lipid reserves for various species of waterfowl during winter.

Species	Correlation coefficient	Source
Red-billed Pintail	0.75	Woodall (1978)
Redhead	0.80	Bailey (1979)
American Wigeon	0.96	Wishart (1979)
American Black Duck	0.90	Reinecke et al. (1982)
White-fronted Goose	0.70	Johnson et al. (1985)
Mallard	0.70	Whyte and Bolen (1984)
Northern Pintail	0.79	Miller (1989)

rate and precise data (but see Robb et al. 2001; also see Johnson et al. 1985 for a review).

WINTER BODY MASS AND CARCASS COMPOSITION

Nonbreeding ducks of several species studied over a broad geographical range generally show a pattern of increasing body mass from late summer and early fall to late fall (i.e., Aug–Sep to Nov), a decrease in winter (i.e., Dec–Jan), and another increase in late winter–early spring (Feb–Mar). Such a pattern has been reported for Mallards in Czechoslovakia (Folk et al. 1966), England (Owen and Cook 1977), and Texas (Whyte et al. 1986), female American Black Ducks in Maine (Reinecke et al. 1982), Northern Pintails in California (Miller 1986a), Gadwalls in Louisiana (Paulus 1980), Long-tailed Ducks on Lake Michigan (Peterson and Ellarson 1979), Canvasbacks and Redheads on Seneca Lake in New York (Ryan 1972, Kaminsky and Ryan 1981), and Green-winged Teal in Texas (Baldassarre et al. 1986). Based on the winter body mass of 2,973 Tufted Ducks and 1,335 Common Pochards studied in Switzerland, males were heavier than females in both adult and first-year age classes, and adults were heavier than first-winter individuals of the same sex; age-related differences continued throughout the winter (Kestenholz 1994). An exception to the general pattern noted above was recorded for Ring-necked Ducks wintering on freshwater ponds in central Florida, where body mass increased steadily from November through February (Hohman et al. 1988). In this case, the increase was attributed to a high carbohydrate diet and few energy-demanding activities such as courtship and aggression.

Green-winged Teal wintering on the Southern High Plains of Texas offer an example of the usual pattern (Baldassarre et al. 1986). The birds arrived in September and steadily increased body mass through December; increases were 5% (19 g) for adult males, 12% (37 g) for adult females, 10% (31 g) for juvenile males, and 6% (17 g) for juvenile females (Fig. 7-2). Body mass then decreased to their lowest levels in February; decreases averaged 14% (50 g) for adult males, 16% (54 g) for adult females, 11% (40 g) for juvenile males, and 14% (46 g) for juvenile females. Body mass then increased 3–10% from February to March. Most of these changes reflected increased lipid mass, which increased most from September to December: 29 g (67%) for adult males, 39–57 g (150–219%) for adult females, 45 g (161%) for

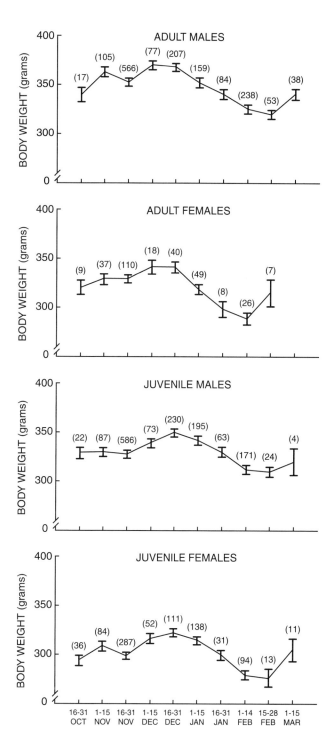

Figure 7-2. Changes in the mean body mass of Green-winged Teal wintering on the Southern High Plains of Texas are typical of many species of ducks wintering in temperate climates. Vertical bars indicate standard error; sample sizes appear in parentheses. From Baldassarre et al. (1986:421). With permission from The Wildlife Society.

juvenile males, and 27 g (73%) for juvenile females (Fig. 7-3).

Data from studies of geese have not always paralleled the general pattern seen in ducks. For example, body mass of adult male and female Lesser Snow Geese wintering in southeastern Texas did not change from October through March (Hobaugh 1985). In contrast, Greater White-fronted Geese wintering in the Klamath Basin of California exhibited a pattern more like ducks: Geese gained or maintained body mass in fall, lost mass from early winter into early spring, and then gained mass through the remainder of the spring before migrating to their breeding grounds in Alaska (Ely and Raveling 1989). Raveling (1968) determined that adult male and female Interior Canada Geese wintering in Illinois lost significant body mass between November–December and February (93 g for males, 140 g for females), despite sufficient food supplies. However, yearlings and immatures did not exhibit changes in body mass from October through February and March. All sex and age classes of Canada Geese wintering at the Horseshoe Lake Refuge in Illinois lost significant body mass during winter (Elder 1946, Hanson 1962). Experimentally, Joyner et al. (1984) found that captive Canada Geese fed unlimited food gained body mass from January through April.

Ankney (1982) used data from an array of studies to report the annual cycle of body weight for the Lesser Snow Goose. Interestingly, Lesser Snow Geese wintering on the Gulf Coast of Texas lost mass throughout the winter, whereas those wintering in Louisiana did not. The differences where so great that birds wintering in Texas would have to gain twice as much weight during spring migration compared to those in Louisiana if they were to arrive on breeding areas in James Bay in similar body condition. These data are especially important because they represent one of the few complete datasets for the annual cycle of body mass for any species of waterfowl. To date, the only other species for which the annual cycle of body mass has been determined are Mallards in Czechoslovakia (Folk et al. 1966) and Ring-necked Ducks in North America (Hohman et al. 1988).

Fluctuations in Winter Body Mass and Composition

Some studies of both wild and captive waterfowl suggest that declines in body mass and lipid reserves during winter are primarily controlled by an endogenous mechanism (Reinecke et al. 1982, Baldassarre

et al. 1986, Perry et al. 1986, Loesch et al. 1992). Others, however, argue that these patterns are caused by environmental conditions such as declining food supplies, temperatures, and winter courtship activities (Elder 1946, Ryan 1972, Kaminsky and Ryan 1981, Joyner et al. 1984, Miller 1986a, Lovvorn 1994).

Support for the endogenous rhythm hypothesis is shown in the case of captive Canvasbacks where birds fed unlimited food still showed decreased body mass, food intake, and activity during midwinter (Perry et al. 1986). Similarly, the body mass of captive Mallards provided with unlimited food also declined over winter (Loesch et al. 1992; Fig. 7-3). The average mass loss was 3–7%, which is comparable to the 3–8% reported for wild Mallards and Green-winged Teal wintering on the Southern High Plains of Texas (Whyte and Bolen 1984, Baldassarre et al. 1986). Additionally, free-ranging Canada Geese wintering at the Crab Orchard National Wildlife Refuge in Illinois decreased winter body mass despite sufficient food supplies (Raveling 1968). Overall, these studies indicate the likelihood that waterfowl have an endogenous rhythm of decreasing body mass and lipid reserves that serves as an adaptation to winter conditions (Fig. 7-4). Nonetheless, this rhythm can be upset by severe weather or food shortage, wherein wintering birds continually assess energy needs and food availability.

Such an explanation was supported by studies of body mass for wintering Green-winged Teal on the Southern High Plains of Texas (Baldassarre et al. 1986). The value of this study was enhanced by concurrent estimates of abundance, availability, and use of food resources (Baldassarre and Bolen 1984), time budgets (Quinlan and Baldassarre 1984), and movements (Baldassarre et al. 1988a). Miller (1985, 1986a, 1986b) provided similarly valuable data relative to the wintering ecology of Northern Pintails in the California Valley, but we review the Green-winged Teal data here.

Green-winged Teal wintering on the Southern High Plains of Texas arrive in September when their body and lipid mass are at their lowest levels. Their

Figure 7-3. Changes in the carcass composition of adult male and female Green-winged Teal wintering on the Southern High Plains of Texas. Means (vertical bars denote standard error) denoted by the same letter are not different (*P* > 0.05). Annual effects of weather on lipid content are especially evident in mid- and late winter. From Baldassarre et al. (1986:422). With permission from The Wildlife Society.

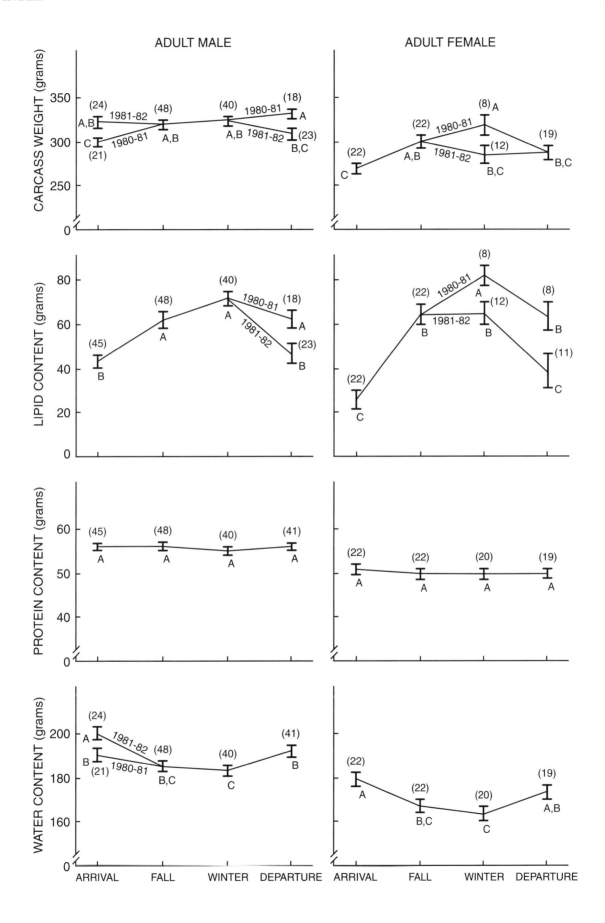

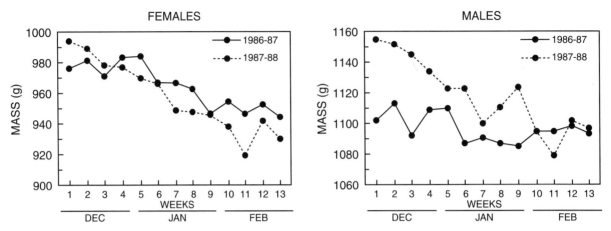

Figure 7-4. Mean loss of body mass for Mallards maintained on ad libitum food in an outdoor aviary. These are among the data indicating that body condition of wintering waterfowl is controlled by an endogenous rhythm. From Loesch et al. (1992:737). With permission from The Wildlife Society.

body mass and lipids then increased to their highest levels in December and January. Peak lipid levels in January did not differ among sex and age classes, and these ranged from 21.7 to 23.4% of carcass mass. Thereafter the lipid content for each sex and age class declined steadily through the winter (Fig. 7-3). Throughout winter, however, Green-winged Teal and other waterfowl usually field-feed twice daily (early morning and early evening) on waste corn that is both abundant and available throughout the winter months; total field-feeding time is about 1 hr/day (Baldassarre and Bolen 1984). Although waste corn declined in abundance over a 50-km² study area, corn-fields in January and February averaging 20–100 kg/ha waste corn still covered 28% of the area in 1981 and 40% in 1982; teal and other waterfowl continued to feed in those fields where corn was most abundant and available. Green-winged Teal also foraged for natural foods in playa lakes (Quinlan and Baldassarre 1984).

Baldassarre et al. (1986) calculated that Green-winged Teal require about 414–439 kJ/day for existence energy in January. The birds met this requirement by field-feeding; they obtained about 15 g of corn/flight (30 g/day), which yields a true metabolizable intake of about 502 kJ/day. Teal could have easily increased their energy intake by engaging in midday feeding flights (i.e., corn obtained in the morning was digested by 0900 and the evening flight did not begin until after sunset), but midday feeding flights were never observed. Thus, midwinter declines in lipids and body mass occurred even though food and time to exploit that food were available to Green-winged Teal.

Baldassarre et al. (1986) argued that because the teal arrived on the Southern High Plains in September when the weather was still warm, the birds were seldom exposed to a regime of critical temperatures (see Chapter 4). Thus, large lipid reserves are unnecessary at this time because the birds' thermoregulatory needs are essentially nil, and the probability of encountering a food or energy shortage is low. Additionally, accumulating lipids this early in the fall would incur metabolic costs associated with carrying and maintaining the extra mass for a longer period of time than necessary. An adaptive advantage therefore is gained to accumulate lipids in late fall when food is abundant and thermoregulatory costs are still low. Maximum energy storage is achieved immediately before the period (i.e., late Dec through Jan and Feb) when the probability of encountering a food shortage or energy deficit is highest. This strategy of lipid accumulation thus minimizes both foraging time and the energy costs of storing and maintaining lipid reserves. It therefore becomes an adaptive advantage to use these reserves progressively throughout winter. Otherwise, efforts to maintain high levels of stored energy would increase (1) foraging time, (2) exposure to weather and predation, (3) energy costs of searching for food, (4) metabolic costs of maintaining extra mass, and (5) the flight costs of transporting extra mass. Also, the probability of encountering an energy deficit and its duration *decreases* as cold weather wanes and spring approaches. Hence, all the costs of maintaining high levels of lipids, coupled with increasingly better weather conditions, make it adaptive for teal to progressively use their energy reserves — or at least maintain low levels of lipids — throughout the winter. The decline in lipid reserves and body mass during the winter therefore more likely reflects an adaptation to, rather than a consequence of, winter conditions.

In contrast, Lovvorn (1994) studied body mass and lipid reserves of Canvasbacks wintering at northern and southern latitudes in the United States; he found little evidence that endogenous schedules of nutrient reserves could be effectively tuned to the occurrence and duration of cold spells at a particular latitude. Cold spells indeed were more probable at northern latitudes, but their duration was unpredictable; hence, there was little basis for specific timing in the regulation of endogenous reserves. The mating and migration systems of Canvasbacks and other pochards also may disrupt any genetic adaptation to wintering conditions (see Lovvorn 1994). Further, if reserves were a function of need, they should increase with latitude, but Canvasbacks wintering in Louisiana —where food is abundant and the weather is mild — carried greater reserves than those collected farther north in North Carolina (Hohman et al. 1990). Lovvorn concluded that his arguments did not preclude the existence of an endogenous rhythm in the regulation of winter energy reserves, but only that such control could not be tuned effectively to the month-by-month probabilities of winter cold spells.

Seasonal Variation: Although the general pattern of winter body mass and lipid declines may be adaptive for wintering Green-winged Teal, this pattern nonetheless can be influenced by yearly differences in weather conditions. For example, lipid levels were higher in spring of 1981 than in 1982, but a 4-cm snowfall on 25 February and an average wind speed in late winter of 31 km/hr in 1982 compared with 16 km/hr in 1981 probably contributed to the differences in lipid reserves. Bennett and Bolen (1978) measured a variety of stress-indicating blood parameters for Green-winged Teal wintering on the Southern High Plains of Texas and found that the onset of cold weather, especially when accompanied by high winds, caused increased stress. Similarly, Dugan et al. (1981) determined that body mass of wintering Grey Plovers (*Pluvialis squatarola*) on the Tees Estuary in northeast England was internally programmed, but this condition was temporarily depressed by severe weather. Notably, wind chill and wind speed produced greater effects than temperature alone on body and lipid mass of species that forage in open habitats (e.g., Grey Plovers).

Cold temperatures, high winds, and snowfall are not the only factors that can cause annual variations in the lipid reserves and body mass of wintering waterfowl. In the Central Valley of California, for example, wintering Northern Pintails studied over three winters (1979–82) exhibited greater losses of body and lipid mass during a dry winter, probably because of food shortages exacerbated by limited wetland habitat and the reduced availability of ricefields (Miller 1986a). Indeed, carcass mass during January of the dry year was 60–70 g less than during the wet winters. Further, carcass mass in January of the dry winter was 16.4% less than carcass mass in November for males and 15.7% less for females. In contrast, losses during the two comparatively wet winters were only 3.2–3.6% in one and 8.2–9.2% in the other (Fig. 7-5). Northern Pintails

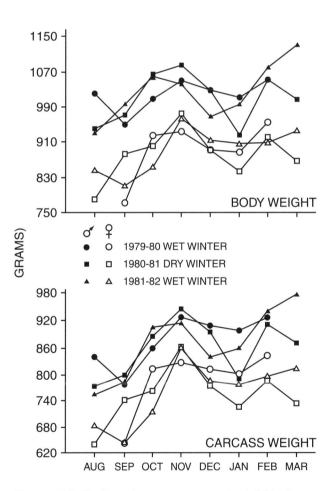

Figure 7-5. Body and carcass mass of adult Northern Pintails in the Sacramento Valley of California during two wet and one dry winter exhibit the effects of habitat availability on body condition. From Miller (1986a:192). With permission from The Wildlife Society.

apparently responded to these poor conditions by adjusting their behavioral and physiological activities whereby loafing and diurnal feeding increased but courtship decreased (Miller 1985) and the prebasic molt of females was delayed (Miller 1986b). Male Northern Pintails wintering on the Southern High Plains of Texas had higher body mass (8.9%) and more lipids during a winter that was 70% wetter than normal, which increased the availability of wetland feeding areas (Smith and Sheeley 1993). There was no difference between years for females.

Geographic Variation

The "typical pattern" of body mass and composition of wintering ducks originates from studies at northerly wintering sites but has not been shown for conspecifics wintering at more southerly latitudes. In the Yucatan Peninsula of Mexico, the body-mass cycle of nonbreeding female Blue-winged Teal remained unchanged from October through March, although males exhibited slight fluctuations (Thompson and Baldassarre 1990). Northern Pintails exhibited a similar pattern but nonetheless were 5–22% lighter than Northern Pintails wintering in California (Miller 1986a). Thompson and Baldassarre (1990) believed these data argue for an endogenous control mechanism, but that proximate cues such as temperature influence the amplitude of these fluctuations and cause intraspecific geographic variation. Intraspecifc geographic variation in body and lipid mass also has been documented in birds such as Starlings (*Sturnis vulgaris*; Blem 1981) and Dark-eyed Juncos (*Junco hyemalis*; Nolan and Ketterson 1983); both studies identified temperature as a proximate cause of winter cycles in the body and lipid mass in birds. For Canvasbacks wintering in Louisiana, those in the Mississippi River Delta were generally fatter than those wintering at Catahoula Lake (Hohman 1993), but the body mass of birds at both sites was greater than for Canvasbacks wintering elsewhere.

Rave and Baldassarre (1991) compared body mass and composition of Green-winged Teal wintering in natural wetland habitats in Louisiana with Green-winged Teal wintering on the Southern High Plains of Texas. Unlike teal in Texas, the carcass mass and lipid reserves of all sex and age classes of teal examined in Louisiana did not change between fall and winter, and winter lipid levels of teal in Louisiana were 26–50% lower in comparison with birds on the Southern High Plains. Winter body mass was not different between the two sites.

These patterns were best explained by the temperature hypothesis: Winter temperatures in Louisiana are considerably milder than on the Southern High Plains of Texas, and cold spells in Louisiana normally do not last for more than a few days. Teal wintering in Louisiana accordingly have less need for acquiring large reserves of lipids. However, differences in winter diets also may have contributed to the variations in lipid reserves recorded for the two areas. Teal in Texas had constant access to high-energy food in the form of waste corn, whereas teal in Louisiana fed on protein-rich foods available in natural wetlands. Thus, diet may be a significant proximate influence on lipid reserves. Rave and Baldassarre (1991) concluded that habitat conditions in coastal Louisiana may be similar to the historic conditions encountered by wintering Green-winged Teal inasmuch as their diet consisted of natural foods instead of the agricultural grains used in Texas. Thus, the lipid patterns seen in Louisiana may better reflect the evolutionary adaptations to winter conditions, whereas the lipid levels of teal (and presumably other species of waterfowl) wintering farther north represent responses to human-induced changes in the landscape (i.e., agriculture). Such changes now allow waterfowl to winter well north of their traditional ranges, even in areas that regularly experience severe cold, as shown by Mallards wintering along the Platte River in Nebraska (Jorde et al. 1984).

Most of these studies did not identify causes for the patterns that were revealed — an endogenous mechanism may indeed control body mass and energy reserves during winter, but severe temperatures and reduced food availability still may be important proximate factors responsible for the amplitude of these changes (King and Farner 1966). Hence, a threshold may exist for body mass and lipid loss below which survival is impaired or life-cycle events (e.g., pairing) are affected, which subsequently reduce fitness (Loesch et al. 1992). King (1972) and Blem (1990) believed that temperature was the most significant factor controlling lipid stores in birds because of the strong inverse relationship between temperature and body mass.

We end this section with the conclusion that an endogenous rhythm apparently controls the basic pattern of body-mass cycles shown in wintering waterfowl. However, temperature, diet, and other environmental factors are major proximate causes that affect the amplitude of these cycles. Temperature is perhaps the most significant factor. These circumstances thus may reduce body mass and lipid reserves in some areas and not in others. Body mass and lipid reserves may reach a threshold where fitness is reduced.

TIME BUDGETS OF NONBREEDING WATERFOWL

A time or activity budget is a quantitative description of how animals apportion their time for feeding, resting, and other activities (Altmann 1974, Baldassarre et al.1988b). Waterfowl, like other animals, have relatively fixed physiological and energetic requirements, but the ways an individual allocates time toward meeting those demands may be highly variable. In terms of evolutionary biology, selection should favor those individuals that optimally allocate their time in meeting these needs. Time budgets provide insight into such topics as feeding ecology, habitat selection, and courtship behavior. Time budgets are especially useful in determining the functional role of habitats for waterfowl and for evaluating the responses of waterfowl to environmental factors (e.g., low temperatures), hunting pressure, and habitat changes.

Time budgets vary by species for waterfowl studied thus far during the nonbreeding period, although comparisons are somewhat difficult because techniques may differ. Moreover, few studies include nocturnal data, which are especially important because waterfowl may be active at night (Table 7-2). Nevertheless, the available data (largely diurnal) indicate that nonbreeding waterfowl spend most of their time feeding and resting. These two activities are related inversely because time budgets reflect a "zero sums" game — increased time spent in one

activity results from a decrease in time spent in another activity. As an example, during a 3-year study of female Northern Pintails wintering in Sinaloa, Mexico, the dominant daytime activities were resting (47%), feeding (20%), preening (17%), and locomotion (13%; Migoya et al. 1994). In Florida, a 24-hr time budget for wintering Ring-necked Ducks revealed that foraging (30–40%) and resting (39–42%) were the dominant activities (Jeske and Percival 1995). The time allocated to feeding and resting does vary both within and between taxa, however, with Anserinae (geese and swans) averaging 30–90% feeding compared with 20–60% for Anatinae (ducks); for both ducks and geese, resting averages 10–50%, preening and locomotion averages less than 20%, and the combined time spent in alert, aggressive, and courtship displays averages less than 5% (Table 7-3). Time budgets also are strongly influenced by habitat conditions, diets and food availability, environmental factors (e.g., temperature, ice, snowfall, rainfall, and tides), the physical condition of individuals, and pair status.

Generally, time budgets for nonbreeding Anatinae reveal a pattern dominated by feeding time in late summer and early fall (Aug–Nov), which declines in winter (Dec–Jan), and increases again in early spring (Paulus 1988). Feeding rates may be high in autumn when waterfowl begin to accumulate lipid reserves necessary as energy sources later in winter. Molting birds also may increase feeding rates at this time to acquire the specific nutrients and energy needed for feather replacement. By winter, however, most individuals probably have acquired lipid reserves and completed the prealternate molt

Table 7-2. A comparison of diurnal and nocturnal activity budgets of waterfowl during winter.

Species	Period	Percent of time spent per activity			
		Feeding	Locomotion	Resting	Preening
Green-winged Teal[a]	Day	5	33	60	2
	Night	90	5	4	1
Mallard[b]	Day	30	13	30	13
	Night	20	9	39	23
Gadwall[c]	Day	61	13	8	7
	Night	69	7	18	3
Mottled Duck[d]	Day	39	8	37	9
	Night	51	3	34	8

[a] Tamisier (1976); [b] Jorde (1981) [c] Paulus (1984a); [d] Paulus (1984b).

Table 7-3. Examples of diurnal activity budgets for wintering waterfowl. Note the higher proportion of time spent feeding where birds primarily exploit natural wetland foods compared to agricultural seeds.

Species	Diet[a]	Percent of time spent per activity						
		Feeding	Resting	Locomotion	Preening	Courtship	Alert	Agonistic
Barnacle Goose[b]	NAT	83	1		1		15	<1
White-fronted Goose[c]	NAT	90	3		2		3	
Canada Goose[d]	AGR	13						
Northern Pintail[e]	AGR	18	48	13	13	4		
Northern Pintail[f]	NAT	61	29	5	3	1		<1
American Black Duck[f]	NAT	43	40	9	7	1		<1
Green-winged Teal[f]	NAT	56	35	4	3	2		<1
Green-winged Teal[g]	AGR	14	72	7	6			
Green-winged Teal[h]	NAT	33	45	9	11	<1	<1	<1
Ring-necked Duck[i]	NAT	35	24	17	15	<1	10	<1

[a] The major foods consumed during the period of observation were either agricultural grains (AGR) or natural wetland foods (NAT).
[b] Ebbinge et al. (1975), [c] Owen (1972), [d] Raveling et al. (1972), [e] Miller (1985), [f] Hepp (1982), [g] Quinlan and Baldassarre (1984), [h] Rave and Baldassarre (1989), [i] Hohman (1984). See also Paulus (1988).

(or moved farther south; Jorde et al. 1984). By late winter, feeding activities usually increase, probably to acquire lipids for the spring migration.

Relative to diet choices and food availability, species feeding on foods of low water content, high energy content (i.e., carbohydrates), and high availability spend the least amount of time feeding. For example, Green-winged Teal feeding on readily available, high energy waste corn in Texas expended 15–20% of their diurnal time budget on feeding activities (Quinlan and Baldassarre 1984), whereas Green-winged Teal feeding on natural foods in the coastal wetlands of Louisiana averaged 33% (Rave and Baldassarre 1989). Green-winged Teal feeding on natural foods in the Camargue, France, expended 40–50% of their time feeding (Tamisier 1976). Similarly, Lesser Snow Geese gleaning waste corn in Iowa averaged 13% feeding time (Frederick and Klaas 1982), whereas Snow Geese feeding on natural plants in British Columbia averaged 30% (Burton and Hudson 1978). Baldassarre and Bolen (1984) discussed the idea that the ready availability and high energy content of agricultural foods (e.g., corn) decreased the time necessary for feeding, whereas waterfowl

selecting the seeds of natural plants require more feeding time because these foods contain less energy per gram. Moreover, the seeds of wetland plants are generally small as well as less available because of fluctuating water levels and the overburden of sediment and debris — factors that affect feeding efficiency.

In contrast to species feeding on natural plant seeds or agricultural foods, waterfowl that graze (e.g., geese) or prefer leafy aquatic vegetation (e.g., American Wigeon and Gadwalls) generally feed for lengthy periods. This is a behavioral response to the high water and fiber content and the comparatively low nutritional content of the foods preferred by these species. For example, Gadwalls wintering in coastal Louisiana spent more than 50% of their diurnal time in feeding activities (Paulus 1984a). In Alabama, wintering American Wigeon foraging on leafy aquatic vegetation such as water milfoil (*Myriophyllum spicatum*) spent 45–71% of their time feeding (Turnbull and Baldassarre 1987). Paulus (1984a) also noted intraspecific variation among Gadwalls whereby feeding time was 70–75% when foods were of poor quality (e. g., water milfoil and algae) but

Table 7-4. The relationship between the percentage of time spent in various activities and the food choice of Gadwalls wintering in coastal Louisiana. Modified from Paulus (1984a:377).

Activity	*Myriophyllum spicatum*	Algae	*Eleocharis parvula*
Feeding	75	68	46
Locomotion	3	10	14
Resting	13	7	25
Preening	4	4	7
Other	5	11	18

decreased to 46% when Gadwalls fed on higher quality foods such as dwarf spikerush (*Eleocharis parvula*; Table 7-4). Greater White-fronted Geese and Barnacle Geese may feed for more than 80% of the daylight hours, consuming up to 25% of their body mass in grass/day (Owen 1972, Ebbinge et al. 1975). As a physical adaptation for feeding on foods of poor quality, Gadwalls and other species have elongated and enlarged intestines, which allows greater food consumption and nutrient extraction than might otherwise occur (Paulus 1982).

Research has shown that feeding time increases in response to declining temperatures. Below 0 °C, however, the energetic costs of foraging may exceed the benefits of additional food consumption, and the birds thus reduce their activity and/or seek thermally favorable sites (Sayler and Afton 1981). For example, American Black Ducks wintering along the coast of Maine sought protective roost sites and rested for most of the day when temperatures dropped below -20 °C (Albright et al. 1983). At temperatures below 10 °C, Green-winged Teal wintering on the Southern High Plains of Texas also spent all of their time resting (Quinlan and Baldassarre 1984). Canada Geese wintering in Illinois continued their field-feeding flights as long as temperatures remained above -7 °C, but they stopped when temperatures dropped below -9 °C (Raveling et al. 1972). In contrast, Mottled Ducks wintering in Louisiana spent more time feeding (52%) at temperatures below their lower critical temperature (14 °C) than above (39%; Paulus 1988). However, Mottled Ducks did not feed when temperatures were extremely cold (-8 to -15 °C).

The responses of American Black Ducks to cold temperatures were studied at three wintering sites near Ottawa, Ontario (Brodsky and Weatherhead 1985a, 1985b). Each site was rated according to an energetic profile as (1) a high-energy site, where

Black Ducks fed on cracked corn provided by a local resident; (2) a moderate-energy site where the birds "tipped up" for aquatic vegetation growing in a shallow, ice-free lagoon receiving sewage effluent; and (3) a low-energy site where ice in shallow areas forced Black Ducks to dive for food in deeper water. At low temperatures, high-energy activities such as swimming and courtship were reduced at all three sites, but feeding increased at the moderate-energy site, remained the same at the high-energy site (until all food was consumed), and was reduced at the low-energy site. The study concluded that if the intake of food can increase in proportion to feeding time — as occurred at the moderate-energy site — and if energy gains exceed costs, then ducks respond to environmental stresses by adjusting their time budgets to increase feeding time. Conversely, when the costs of foraging exceed the energetic gains, as occurred at the low-energy site, then ducks either decrease or cease feeding and instead assume a less costly behavior (e.g., resting). In response to cold weather in Nebraska, Mallards reduced energetically costly activities such as courtship and aggression, but increased the intensity of field-feeding and selected thermally favorable microhabitats (Jorde et al. 1984).

High winds may affect waterfowl time budgets, especially when accompanied by cold temperatures. Bennett and Bolen (1978) found that high winds produced stressful conditions for Green-winged Teal wintering on the Southern High Plains of Texas, where wind breaks may offer a management tool to reduce weather-induced stress on wintering waterfowl. Strong winds also may make it difficult for birds to feed, especially in open water habitats (Paulus 1984a). High tides likewise reduce feeding time, and abnormally high tides may even prohibit feeding for several days (Thompson and Baldassarre 1991). Tidal cycles also may affect the feeding cycles of wintering waterfowl, as occurred on the Maine coast where American Black Ducks foraged extensively at night when low tides exposed food resources (Jorde and Owen 1988).

Hunting pressure and other forms of human disturbance often affect the time budgets of wintering waterfowl, thereby producing potentially dramatic effects on energy budgets (Fredrickson and Drobney 1979). On the Keokuk Pool in the upper Mississippi River, pochards altered their diurnal activity budgets in response to hunting pressure (Thornburg 1973). Gadwalls (Paulus 1984a) and Mottled Ducks (Paulus 1984b) in Louisiana spent more time in alert behavior and locomotion on areas where hunting was permitted than where it was not. However, other studies have not revealed any effect of hunting pressure on the time budgets of wintering waterfowl (Tamisier 1976, Burton and Hudson 1978, Miller 1985).

Boat traffic is another major cause of disturbance to migrating and wintering waterfowl. For instance, on Lake Onalaska, a major navigational pool on the upper Mississippi River, migrating Canvasbacks were disturbed by recreational boaters; a daily average of 17.2 boats resulted in 5.2 disturbances/day (Korschgen et al. 1985). Large numbers of birds were involved; on average, boaters disturbed flocks of 12,474 Canvasbacks with a minimum flight time of 4.4 min per event. Overall, these disturbances may have caused about 1 hr/day of additional flight time, whereby Canvasbacks and other pochards left the area an estimated 19 times. In some areas of Switzerland, wintering Tufted Ducks decreased in numbers and/or began feeding at night in response to extensive boating disturbances (Pedroli 1982). Brant wintering in Essex, England, increased their flight time 7-fold and lost about 12% of their feeding time as a result of human disturbances (Owens 1977). On a national wildlife refuge in Oklahoma, recreational activities during the spring migration of waterbirds, including waterfowl, accounted for 87% of all disturbances occurring on an open-water pool used heavily by fishermen (Schummer and Eddleman 2003). However, the rates of disturbance varied by species and appeared related to foraging strategies, habitat requirements, and the type of disturbance. Thus, when scheduling boating and other recreational activities, managers should consider the habits and migration chronologies of waterbirds.

Sex, age, and social status also influence the time budgets of nonbreeding waterfowl. Few studies have recorded large differences in the time budgets for male and female waterfowl; in the case of feeding time, such results suggest that nutritional requirements for each sex are largely similar during this period of the annual cycle. Where sexual differences have occurred, however, males tend to move more often, which may indicate juvenile males searching for unpaired females (Turnbull and Baldassarre 1987). Jorde et al. (1984) recorded that unpaired Mallards devoted more time to social display than did paired birds. Conversely, adults may spend more time aggressively protecting their mates.

PATTERNS AND FUNCTIONS OF HABITAT USE IN WINTER

Studies of habitat use by wintering waterfowl reveal three major patterns: (1) use of habitat complexes, (2) use of habitats that provide refuge from hunting, and (3) use of habitats where food is abundant. Food abundance and availability were addressed in Chapter 5, but we review the two other patterns here.

Habitat Complexes

Several studies demonstrate how waterfowl use winter habitat, but the work of Anderson et al. (2000) along the coast of Texas is especially revealing and provided results for 25 species of ducks observed on 1,201 types of wetlands (Table 7-5). For dabbling ducks, 10 species used 47 wetland types that represented 91.5% of the study area; overall density for all ducks was greatest in lacustrine littoral emergent, nonpersistent wetlands. Four species of pochards used 36 wetland types that represented 42.4% of the study area. Their density ranking was highest in permanently flooded lacustrine littoral wetlands with beds of aquatic vegetation and fresh water. Whistling-ducks used 27 wetland types representing 47.0% of the study area, where their density ranking was highest in natural freshwater wetlands, especially those that were permanently flooded and characterized by beds of aquatic vegetation and emergent vegetation interspersed with open water. Overall, ducks used 48 of 82 available subtypes, of which natural wetlands seemed of the greatest value.

In Sinaloa, Mexico, radiomarked female Northern Pintails primarily used four major habitat types during the day (mangrove mudflat, ephemeral pond, fresh-brackish marsh, and reservoir), but the results varied among and within winters (Migoya et al. 1994; Fig. 7-6). Pintails, for example, heavily used ephem-

Table 7-5. Nonbreeding waterfowl readily use complexes of wetlands as seen here from survey data on the coastal plain of Texas, where waterfowl were observed on 65-ha study plots during fall and winter, 1991–93. From Anderson et al. (2000:196).

Species	No. birds	No. flocks	No. wetland types
Dendrocygnini	4,575	124	34
Black-bellied Whistling-Duck	3,538	101	29
Fulvous Whistling-Duck	1,037	33	11
Anatini[a]	159,207	823	47
American Wigeon	22,902	137	28
Blue-winged Teal	23,838	302	36
Gadwall	5,509	143	29
Green-winged Teal	49,207	200	39
Mottled Duck	6,295	504	40
Northern Pintail	39,149	164	35
Northern Shoveler	9,373	244	37
Aythyini[b]	9,883	146	36
Lesser Scaup	1,539	75	28
Redhead	7,407	42	20
Ruddy Duck	4,401	70	25
Total Ducks[c]	178,958	975	48

[a]Anatini also includes American Black Duck, Mallard, and Cinnamon Teal.
[b]Aythyini also includes Canvasback and Ring-necked Duck.
[c]Total ducks include all species shown in the table, plus eight others that were not recorded in high numbers.

eral ponds created by 9.2 cm of rainfall in 1991–92 but not at all in 1989–90 when rainfall dropped to only 3.4 cm.

The functional role of each habitat helps fulfill the specific life-history needs of wintering waterfowl. In Sinaloa, for instance, Northern Pintails fed most often (6–39%) on fresh-brackish marshes, whereas mangrove mudflats primarily (68%) served as resting and loafing sites (Migoya et al. 1994). Ephemeral ponds also functioned as resting sites (62%) as well as for feeding (14%) and preening (15%). Overall, Northern Pintails wintering in Sinaloa spent most (38–55%) of the day resting, because at night an abundant source of food was readily available in nearby ricefields. In contrast, Northern Pintails wintering in the Yucatan Peninsula of Mexico depended solely on mangrove habitats in which feeding represented the dominant activity (42–48%) followed by resting (19–23%; Thompson and Baldassarre 1991).

In coastal Louisiana, the feeding time of wintering Green-winged Teal was lowest (17%) in brackish impounded marsh, moderate (35%) in fresh unimpounded marsh, and highest (41%) in interme-

diate impounded marsh where food was more abundant and available (Rave and Baldassarre 1989). In contrast, resting ranged from 35 to 40% in intermediate impounded marsh, brackish tidal flat, and unimpounded fresh marsh, but was 50–60% in other habitats where structural features such as clumps of vegetation and small islands provided teal with sites to loaf, preen, and sleep (Table 7-6). At the Eufaula National Wildlife Refuge in Alabama, Mallards fed more (36%) in managed waterfowl impoundments compared with 18% in open-water habitats along the adjacent Chattahoochee River (Turnbull and Baldassarre 1987). Courtship behavior also was much higher (7%) in managed impoundments where the structural diversity provided by willows (*Salix* spp.) allowed the isolation of paired birds; elsewhere courtship activities were reduced to 2%.

In coastal South Carolina, time budgets for seven species of dabbling ducks revealed that feeding activities were greatest in open water and saltmarsh–bulrush habitats and lowest in salt grass habitat (Gray et al. 1996). Resting was greatest in salt marshes and lowest in open water. In general, the

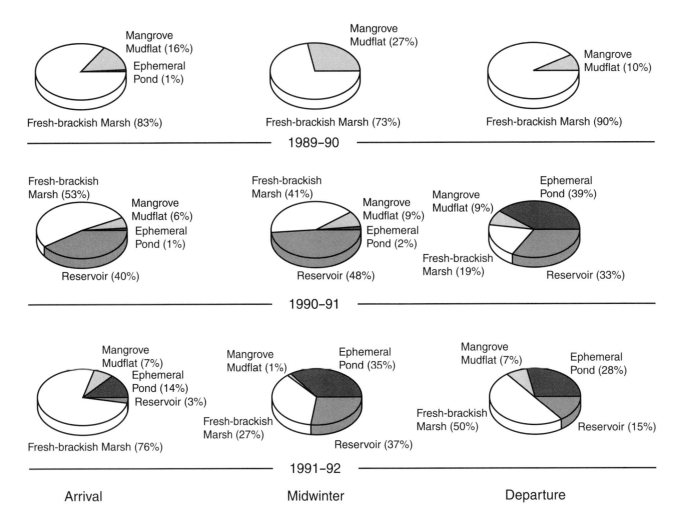

Figure 7-6. Habitat use by female Northern Pintails wintering in Sinaloa, Mexico, demonstrate the variability that occurs both within and among winters. Use of ephemeral ponds was especially high in 1991–92. From Migoya et al. (1994:139). With permission from the Wildfowl and Wetlands Trust.

birds preferred managed wetlands in these areas (Gordon et al. 1998). Overall, this study further demonstrated the flexibility of dabbling ducks in allocating their time in response to regional habitat and

climactic conditions — again underscoring that wintering waterfowl require a complex of wetland types to satisfy their life-history needs.

Anderson et al. (1999) reported that geese win-

Table 7-6. The relationship between the percentage of time spent in various activities and habitat types used by wintering Green-winged Teal in coastal Louisiana. Modified from Rave and Baldassarre (1989:756).

Habitat type	% Feeding	% Locomotion	% Resting	% Preening
Intermediate impounded marsh	41	7	38	13
Brackish weired marsh	21	5	62	11
Brackish impounded marsh	17	9	63	11
Fresh impounded marsh	35	6	35	23

tering in the Coastal Plains and Rice Prairie Regions of Texas used 16 of 82 available wetland types. Greater White-fronted Geese were most abundant in wetlands described as lacustrine littoral aquatic-bed floating vascular and unconsolidated shore organic, whereas Ross's Geese and Lesser Snow Geese were most abundant on estuarine intertidal aquatic-bed algal wetlands. In Scotland, Pink-footed Geese spent most of their time foraging in grasslands and cereal-grain stubble (Giroux and Patterson 1995). On a daily basis, most geese concentrated their activities in a 1-km² area located within 5 km of their roost site.

Avoidance of Hunting

Waterfowl obviously will select habitats that provide sanctuary from hunting; thus, refuges have long been an integral component of waterfowl management. Northern Pintails wintering in Louisiana made significantly greater (46–60%) diurnal use of refuges during the hunting season than immediately before or after the season (22–33%; Cox and Afton 1997). At night, refuges were less used (3–13%), but Northern Pintails continued (86–96%) feeding at night in nearby fields during both hunting and nonhunting periods, mostly (68–93%) in ricefields. In Sinaloa, Mexico, wintering Northern Pintails shifted their diurnal activities from hunted marshes to ricefields, reservoirs, and ephemeral ponds that were not hunted (Migoya et al. 1994; see also Migoya and Baldassarre 1993). Lesser Snow Geese wintering in Iowa made extensive use of refuges and foraged in nearby agricultural fields (Frederick et al. 1987). These studies demonstrate the importance of refuges where waterfowl can find sanctuary during the hunting season.

BEHAVIORAL DOMINANCE

A significant number of aggressive interactions occur among wintering waterfowl, leading to the dominance of one individual or pair of individuals. Behavioral dominance deserves attention because it may bear on the population dynamics of a species, as well as explain differences in habitat selection and geographical distribution during winter (Gauthreaux 1978). Dominant birds also gain greater access to food and mates (Paulus 1983, Rohwer and Anderson 1988), which can affect individual survival (Caraco 1979) and reproduction (Hepp 1989). Generally, males dominate females and pairs dominate unpaired individuals, although paired females remain

subordinate to unpaired males (Hepp and Hair 1984). In Chapter 3, we discussed the role of dominance as a factor in pair formation, so here we turn to some aspects of dominance in relation to the winter ecology of waterfowl.

Most aggressive interactions in waterfowl are intraspecific and occur while one or both of the interacting parties are feeding. For example, of 1,266 aggressive interactions recorded for six species of ducks wintering in North Carolina, 89% were intraspecific (Hepp and Hair 1984). Likewise, 87% of 1,543 aggressive interactions observed for four species of ducks wintering on the Yucatan Peninsula of Mexico were intraspecific (Thompson and Baldassarre 1992). Generally, when the social status of each bird is similar, the individual initiating the encounter usually wins the conflict, such as occurred in Yucatan where initiators won 92% of the interactions. Aggressive interactions may accelerate in intensity, from supplanting, to threatening, to chasing and, eventually, to actual fighting. Hepp and Hair (1984) suggest that aggression is not arbitrary; instead, individual birds recognize the rank order of dominance within a flock and initiate aggressive encounters against other individuals when there is a high probability of achieving success. Wintering Gadwalls were more likely to threaten birds of similar social status (Paulus 1983). Generally, less intensive forms of aggression typically occur with greater frequency because individuals often assess the likelihood of winning an encounter before the bout accelerates to a greater level of intensity. When a pair initiates an aggressive interaction with an unpaired individual, for example, the unpaired bird may quickly reveal its subordinate status by moving away (i.e., the subordinate bird recognizes the likelihood of losing a more intensive encounter). Conversely, if two individuals of equal social status (i.e., two unpaired males) interact and all else is equal (e.g., size, plumage), then the intensity of the encounter is more likely to increase because neither individual can assess the likely outcome of the encounter.

Hepp and Hair (1984) suggested that the behavioral dominance of unpaired males and pairs over unpaired females may be a major factor producing a sex-specific winter distribution in some waterfowl (especially species pairing late in winter). Large numbers of unpaired females thus may overwinter farther south because dominant males exclude the females from the better feeding areas in the northern part of the species' winter range, a pattern especially true for Green-winged Teal.

ASPECTS OF MIGRATION ECOLOGY

Migration has long fascinated many ornithologists, who in turn produced numerous publications dealing with the mechanics of migration. In this section, we review a few of the studies that address the ecology of waterfowl migration. Our focus falls on those aspects of when, where, and why habitats are used during migration and the functional role of these sites in relation to the annual cycle of waterfowl. Additional topics associated with waterfowl migration appear elsewhere (e.g., molt migration in Chapter 6).

Migration Corridors and Routes

In the mid-1930s, Frederick Lincoln proposed the idea that migratory waterfowl followed four geographical flyways during their spring and fall migrations across North America: East to west, these are the Atlantic, Mississippi, Central, and Pacific Flyways (Lincoln 1935; see Fig. 11-4). These broad boundaries soon formed the geopolitical basis for many types of management activities, especially those concerning harvest (see Chapter 8). For the most part, the flyways represent fairly accurate indicators of biological pathways; waterfowl populations generally remain within a single flyway. Then, some 30 years later, Frank Bellrose refined the flyway concept. Using radar surveillance, banding data, and other information, he described the presence of migration corridors within the flyways (Bellrose 1968). He defined a corridor as a narrow strip of airspace used by waterfowl as they migrated between their breeding and wintering grounds. For Mallards, the corridors were perhaps only 80–240 km wide (Bellrose 1972), but in other cases, the corridors may be little more than 16 km wide (Bellrose 1980).

The location and description of migration corridors was significant: Biologists now could focus their attention on important habitats lying within each corridor. On a larger scale, many of the older national wildlife refuges in the United States were designed to provide habitat along the major pathways followed by migrating waterfowl, even though the functional role of these habitats (e.g., nutritional content of natural foods) was still largely unknown at the time. Today, with the finer scale provided by migration corridors, biologists can better coordinate habitat management with the specific needs of waterfowl during migratory periods. Still, much remains to be learned about these important periods in the annual cycle of waterfowl.

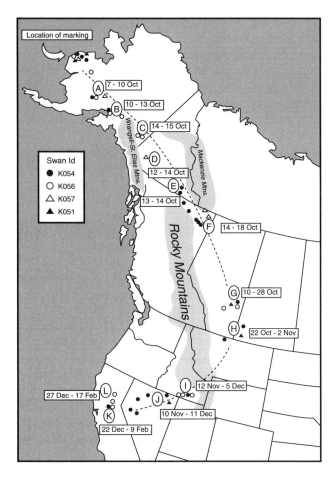

Figure 7-7. The autumn migration route of Tundra Swans marked with satellite radiotransmitters on the Yukon-Kuskokwim Delta in Alaska. Letters identify locations such as the Cook Inlet of Alaska (A), the Snake River in Idaho (I), and the Sacramento–San Joaquin Delta in California (K). From Ely et al. (1997:685). With permission from the Wilson Ornithological Society.

New techniques are revealing detailed information about waterfowl migrations, as shown by a study of Tundra Swans outfitted with satellite transmitters (Ely et al. 1997). The swans left their breeding grounds on the outer coast of the Yukon-Kuskokwim Delta in August, moved eastward across the Delta in late September and stopped in wetlands on the west side of the Alaska Range in early October. The swans then crossed the Alaska Range, stopped briefly on the Upper Cook Inlet, and continued east into the Yukon of Canada before turning south parallel to the Wrangell Mountains to a staging area in northwestern British Columbia. The swans then gradually continued southward to a staging area in southeastern Idaho, where they remained from mid-November until early December before moving to their final destination — the Sacramento-San Joaquin Delta of California (Fig. 7-7). The spring migration route essentially retraced the same route. Bewick's Swans in Europe also were tracked with satellite transmitters (Nowak 1990); this equipment likewise pinpointed the breeding grounds of Bewick's Swans in Asia (Higuchi et al. 1991). Because of such studies, major habitats can be identified and targeted for protection and management.

Malecki et al. (2001) tracked Canada Geese from the Atlantic Population in northern Quebec with satellite transmitters; the goal was to determine where and when these geese occurred during the fall and winter months in the United States. This goose population had experienced declines severe enough to stop hunting from 1995 to 1999, or even longer in some areas. However, satellite tracking revealed that the geese did not arrive in those areas (e.g., New York) in time to be included in special hunting seasons designed to manage a burgeoning population of resident Canada Geese. Hence, the special hunts could continue without harming another population of geese in need of protection.

Habitat Use and Staging Areas

As detailed here and in other chapters, waterfowl generally select habitats that are safe from predation — including hunting — and provide those resources necessary to satisfy their needs for survival and reproduction. During fall migration to wintering areas, however, birds may be moving from familiar sites to those where habitat quality is comparatively unknown. In spring, migrating Mallards in Iowa made extensive use of 455 seasonally flooded farm basins (sheetwater wetlands) and 16 small emergent wetlands (LaGrange and Dinsmore 1989). Sheetwater wetlands are extremely ephemeral, with some 5-ha sites drying completely in as little as 2 days. Mallards preferred the larger sheetwater wetlands where they fed 40% of the time. Such data highlight the characteristics of spring habitats used by migrating waterfowl and emphasize the importance of managing and protecting wetland complexes even though, as in this case, some may be highly ephemeral. Diets during migration also appear to be highly variable, as shown in northwest Missouri where female Mallards selected a variety of plant foods during spring migration (Gruenhagen and Fredrickson 1990). Elsewhere in Missouri, Blue-winged Teal migrating northward through Mingo National Wildlife Refuge made extensive use of sea-

sonally flooded impoundments where they consumed both plant (35%) and animal (65%) foods (Taylor 1978).

With good weather, Canada Geese migrating from a breeding area at Marshy Point, Manitoba, to their wintering grounds in Rochester, Minnesota, made nonstop flights in fall (Wege and Raveling 1983). In contrast, the spring migration included shorter segments that followed the advancing edge of snow melt, where patches of open water likely served as routing cues and indicated suitable habitat. On the Cook Inlet of Alaska, migrating Lesser Snow Geese selected spring habitats with 10–50% snow cover. Snow Geese avoided areas with no snow cover, probably because the large number of Snow Geese migrating through this area already had exploited the available forage; snow-free soils are dry, which also made it difficult for geese to extract underground forage (Hupp et al. 2001).

Prior to fall migration, postbreeding ducks and geese concentrate on larger wetlands (see Bellrose 1980). By this time, most of the smaller, ephemeral wetlands are dry; hence, the larger sites provide available food and space where large flocks can assemble before beginning their fall migration. Such sites — "staging areas" — are important habitats that waterfowl use each year during both spring and fall migration. For example, Cackling Canada Geese remained strongly attached to staging areas in Alaska (Gill et al. 1997). Lesser Snow Geese of the Western Canadian Arctic Population annually stage each fall for 2–4 weeks on the coastal plain of the Beaufort Sea before continuing their southward migration (Hupp and Robertson 1998). Virtually the entire population of Black Brant gathers each fall at Izembeck Lagoon in the Aleutian Islands of Alaska before migrating to wintering areas in the Pacific Northwest and Baja California (Bellrose 1980, Reed et al. 1989, Dau 1992) where eelgrass (Zostera marina) provides food (Wilson and Atkinson 1995). Based on data from satellite transmitters, Lesser White-fronted Geese stopped at 11 staging areas during their spring migration from Ireland to West Greenland (Glahder et al. 2002). The birds stayed at a staging area for an average minimum of 11.2 days, but the length of their stay shortened to 7.2 days (instead of 13.3 days) during a spring when May temperatures were 4 °C warmer than usual.

Unlike geese, the winter distributions and movements of ducks may be quite fluid. For example, only 12% of 1,067 Green-winged Teal marked with patagial tags were resighted during the winter on the Southern High Plains of Texas, and females passed through the area before December

(Baldassarre et al. 1988a). Mallards wintering in the Mississippi Alluvial Valley also were widely distributed in succeeding years, depending on climatic factors such as rainfall (Nichols et al. 1983). Thus, sampling a population is difficult because the group of individuals present at one time period may be quite different both temporally and biologically from a group sampled during a subsequent period. These conditions make it difficult to pinpoint the exact time and place wintering waterfowl acquire nutrient reserves. In comparison with geese, the seasonal events (e.g., molting, pairing, migrating) in the annual cycle of ducks are generally less synchronized. Nevertheless, those general patterns that have emerged thus far amply highlight the interseasonal linkages that play on the year-round fitness of both ducks and geese.

LITERATURE CITED

Albright, J. J., R. B. Owen, Jr., and P. O. Corr. 1983. The effects of winter weather on the behavior and energy reserves of Black Ducks in Maine. Transactions of the Northeast Section of The Wildlife Society 40:118–128.

Alisauskas, R. T. 2002. Arctic climate, spring nutrition, and recruitment in midcontinent Lesser Snow Geese. Journal of Wildlife Management 66:181–193.

Altmann, J. 1974. Observational study of animal behavior: sampling methods. Behaviour 49:227–267.

Anderson, J. T., G. T. Muehl, and T. C. Tacha. 1999. Wetland use by wintering geese in the Gulf Coast Plains and Rice Prairie Region of Texas, USA. Wildfowl 50:45–56.

Anderson, J. T., G. T. Muehl, T. C. Tacha, and D. S. Lobpries. 2000. Wetland use by non-breeding ducks in coastal Texas, U.S.A. Wildfowl 51:191–214.

Anderson, M. G., and B. D. J. Batt. 1983. Workshop on the ecology of wintering waterfowl. Wildlife Society Bulletin 11:22–24.

Ankney, C. D. 1982. Annual cycle of body weight in Lesser Snow Geese. Wildlife Society Bulletin 10:60–64.

Ankney, C. D., and C. D. MacInnes. 1978. Nutrient reserves and reproductive performance of female Lesser Snow Geese. Auk 95:459–471.

Bailey, R. O. 1979. Methods of estimating total lipid content in the Redhead duck (*Aythya americana*) and an evaluation of condition indices. Canadian Journal of Zoology 57:1830–1833.

Baldassarre, G. A., and E. G. Bolen. 1984. Field-feeding ecology of waterfowl wintering on the Southern High Plains of Texas. Journal of Wildlife Management 48:63–71.

Baldassarre, G. A., S. L. Paulus, A. Tamisier, and R. D. Titman. 1988a. Workshop summary: techniques for timing activity of wintering waterfowl. Pages 181–188 *in* M.W. Weller, editor. Waterfowl in winter. University of Minnesota Press, Minneapolis.

Baldassarre, G. A., E. E. Quinlan, and E. G. Bolen. 1988b. Mobility and site fidelity of Green-winged Teal wintering on the Southern High Plains of Texas. Pages 483–493 *in* M.W. Weller, editor. Waterfowl in winter. University of Minnesota Press, Minneapolis.

Baldassarre, G. A., R. J. Whyte, and E. G. Bolen. 1986. Body weight and carcass composition of nonbreeding Green-winged Teal on the Southern High Plains of Texas. Journal of Wildlife Management 50:420–426.

Bellrose, F. C. 1968. Waterfowl migration corridors east of the Rocky Mountains in the United States. Illinois Natural History Survey Biological Notes 61.

Bellrose, F. C. 1972. Mallard migration corridors as revealed by population distribution, banding, and radar. Pages 3–26 *in* Population ecology of migratory birds. Bureau of Sport Fish and Wildlife Research Report 2.

Bellrose, F. C. 1980. Ducks, geese and swans of North America. Stackpole Books, Harrisburg, Pennsylvania.

Bennett, J. W., and E. G. Bolen. 1978. Stress response in wintering Green-winged Teal. Journal of Wildlife Management 42:81–86.

Bergan, J. F., and L. M. Smith. 1993. Survival rates of female Mallards wintering in the Playa Lakes Region. Journal of Wildlife Management 57:570–577.

Blem, C. R. 1981. Geographic variation in midwinter body composition of Starlings. Condor 83:370–376.

Blem, C. R. 1990. Avian energy storage. Current Ornithology 7:59–113.

Brodsky, L. M., and P. J. Weatherhead. 1985a. Time and energy constraints on courtship in wintering American Black Ducks. Condor 87:33–36.

Brodsky, L. M., and P. J. Weatherhead. 1985b. Variability in behavioural response of wintering Black Ducks to increased energy demands. Canadian Journal of Zoology 63:1657–1662.

Burton, B. A., and R. J. Hudson. 1978. Activity budgets of Lesser Snow Geese wintering on the Fraser River Estuary, British Columbia. Wildfowl 29:111–117.

Caraco, T. 1979. Time budgeting and group size: a theory. Ecology 60:618–627.

Conroy, M. J., G. R. Costanzo, and D. B. Stotts. 1989. Winter survival of female American Black Ducks on the Atlantic Coast. Journal of Wildlife Management 53:99–109.

Cox, R. R., Jr., and A. D. Afton. 1997. Use of habitats by female Northern Pintails wintering in southwestern Louisiana. Journal of Wildlife Management 61:435–443.

Cox, R. R., Jr., A. D. Afton, and R. M. Pace, III. 1998. Survival of female Northern Pintails wintering in southwestern Louisiana. Journal of Wildlife Management 62:1512-1521.

Dau, C. P. 1992. The fall migration of Pacific Brent *Branta bernicla* in relation to climatic conditions. Wildfowl 43:80-95.

DeVault, T. L., L. M. Smith, and O. E. Rhodes, Jr. 2003. Condition indices for wintering American Wigeon. Wildlife Society Bulletin 31:1132-1137.

Dufour, K. W., C. D. Ankney, and P. J. Weatherhead. 1993. Condition and vulnerability to hunting among Mallards staging at Lake St. Clair, Ontario. Journal of Wildlife Management 57: 209-215.

Dugan, P. J., P. R. Evans, L. R. Goodyer, and N. C. Davidson. 1981. Winter fat reserves in shorebirds: disturbance of regulated levels by severe weather conditions. Ibis 123:359-363.

Dugger, B. D., K. J. Reinecke, and L. H. Fredrickson. 1994. Late winter survival of female Mallards in Arkansas. Journal of Wildlife Management 58:94–99.

Ebbinge, B., K. Canters, and R., Drent. 1975. Foraging routines and estimated daily food intake in Barnacle Geese wintering in the northern Netherlands. Wildfowl 26:5-19.

Elder, W. H. 1946. Age and sex criteria and weights of Canada Geese. Journal of Wildlife Management 10:93-111.

Ely, C. R., D. C. Douglas, A. C. Fowler, C. A. Babcock, D. V. Derksen, and J. Y. Takekawa. 1997. Migration behavior of Tundra Swans from the Yukon-Kuskokwim Delta, Alaska. Wilson Bulletin 109:679-692.

Ely, C. R., and D. G. Raveling. 1989. Body composition and weight dynamics of wintering Greater White-fronted Geese. Journal of Wildlife Management 53:80-87.

Ely, C. R., and K. T. Scribner. 1994. Genetic diversity in arctic-nesting geese: implications for management and conservation. Transactions of the North American Wildlife and Natural Resources Conference 59:91–110.

Fleskes, J. P., R. L. Jarvis, and D. S. Gilmer. 2002. September–March survival of female Northern Pintails radiotagged in the San Joaquin Valley, California. Journal of Wildlife Management 66:901–911.

Folk, C., K. Hudec, and J. Toufar. 1966. The weight of the Mallard, *Anas platyrhynchos* and its changes in the course of the year. Zoologicke Listy 15:249–260.

Frederick, R. B., W. R. Clark, and E. E. Klaas. 1987. Behavior, energetics, and management of refuging waterfowl: a simulation model. Wildlife Monographs 96.

Frederick, R. B., and E. E. Klaas. 1982. Resource use and behavior of migrating Snow Geese. Journal of Wildlife Management 46:601–614.

Fredrickson, L. H., and R. D. Drobney. 1979. Habitat utilization by postbreeding waterfowl. Pages 119–131 *in* T. A. Bookhout, editor. Waterfowl and wetlands-an integrated review. La Crosse Printing, La Crosse, Wisconsin.

Fretwell, S. D. 1972. Populations in a seasonal environment. Monograph in Population Biology 5. Princeton University Press, Princeton, New Jersey.

Gauthier, G., and J. Bédard. 1984. Fat reserves and condition indices in Greater Snow Geese. Canadian Journal of Zoology 63:331–333.

Gauthreaux, S. A., Jr. 1978. The ecological significance of behavioral dominance. Pages 17–54 *in* P. P. G. Bateson and P. H. Klopfer, editors. Perspectives in ethology. Plenum Press, New York.

Gill, R. E., C. A. Babcock, C. M. Handel, W. R. Butler, Jr., and D. G. Raveling. 1997. Migration, fidelity, and use of autumn staging grounds in Alaska by Cackling Canada Geese *Branta canadensis mimima*. Wildfowl 47:42–61.

Giroux, J-F., and I. J. Patterson. 1995. Daily movements and habitat use by radio-tagged Pink-footed Geese *Anser brachyrhynchus* in northeast Scotland. Wildfowl 46:31–44.

Glahder, C. M., A. D. Fox, and A. J. Walsh. 2002. Spring staging areas of White-fronted Geese in West Greenland; results from aerial survey and satellite telemetry. Wildfowl 53:35–52.

Gordon, D. H., B. T. Gray, and R. M. Kaminski. 1998. Dabbling duck–habitat associations during winter in coastal South Carolina. Journal of Wildlife Management 62:569–580.

Gray, B. T., D. H. Gordan, and R. M. Kaminski. 1996. Activity patterns of dabbling ducks wintering in coastal South Carolina. Proceedings of the Southeastern Association of Fish and Wildlife Agencies 50:475–495.

Greenwood, H., R. G. Clark, and P. J. Weatherhead. 1986. Condition bias of hunter-shot Mallards (*Anas platyrhynchos*). Canadian Journal of Zoology 64:599–601.

Gruenhagen, N. M., and L. H. Fredrickson. 1990. Food use by migratory female Mallards in Northwest Missouri. Journal of Wildlife Management 54:622–626.

Halse, S. A., and D. M. Skead. 1983. Wing moult, body measurements and condition indices of Spur-winged Geese. Wildfowl 34:108–114.

Hanson, H. C. 1962. The dynamics of condition factors in Canada Geese and their relation to seasonal stresses. Arctic Institute of North America Technical Paper 12.

Haramis, G. M., D. G. Jorde, and C. M. Bunck. 1993. Survival of hatching-year female Canvasbacks wintering on Chesapeake Bay. Journal of Wildlife Management 57:763–771.

Haramis, G. M., J. D. Nichols, K. H. Pollock, and J. E. Hines. 1986. The relationship between body mass and survival of wintering Canvasbacks. Auk 103:506–514.

Heitmeyer, M. E. 1988. Body composition of female Mallards in winter in relation to annual cycle events. Condor 90:669–680.

Heitmeyer, M. E., and L. H. Fredrickson. 1981. Do wetland conditions in the Mississippi Delta hardwoods influence Mallard recruitment? Transactions of the North American Wildlife and Natural Resources Conference 46:44–57.

Hepp, G. R. 1982. Behavioral ecology of waterfowl (Anatini) wintering in coastal North Carolina. Dissertation, North Carolina State University, Raleigh.

Hepp, G. R. 1989. Benefits, costs, and determinants of dominance in American Black Ducks. Behaviour 109:222–234.

Hepp, G. R., R. J. Blohm, R. E. Reynolds, J. E. Hines, and J. D. Nichols. 1986. Physiological condition of autumn-banded Mallards and its relationship to hunting vulnerability. Journal of Wildlife Management 50:177–183.

Hepp, G. R., and J. D. Hair. 1984. Dominance in wintering waterfowl (Anatini): effects on distribution of sexes. Condor 86:251–257.

Hestbeck, J. B. 1993a. Overwinter distribution of Northern Pintail populations in North America. Journal of Wildlife Management 57:582–589.

Hestbeck, J. B. 1993b. Survival of Northern Pintails banded during winter in North America, 1950–88. Journal of Wildlife Management 57:590–597.

Higuchi, H., F. Sata, S. Matsu, M. Soma, and N. Kanmuri. 1991. Satellite tracking of the migration routes of Whistling Swans *Cygnus columbianus*. Journal of the Yamashina Institute of Ornithology 23:6–12.

Hobaugh, W. C. 1985. Body condition and nutrition of Snow Geese wintering in southeastern Texas. Journal of Wildlife Management 49:1028–1037.

Hohman, W. L. 1984. Diurnal time-activity budgets for Ring-necked Ducks wintering in central Florida. Proceedings of the Southeastern Association of Fish and Game Commissioners 38:158–164.

Hohman, W. L. 1993. Body composition dynamics of wintering Canvasbacks in Louisiana: dominance and survival implications. Condor 95:377–387.

Hohman, W. L., R. D. Pritchert, J. L. Moore, and D. O. Schaeffer. 1993. Survival of female Canvasbacks wintering in coastal Louisiana. Journal of Wildlife Management 57:758–762.

Hohman, W. L., and T. S. Taylor. 1986. Indices of fat and protein for Ring-necked Ducks. Journal of Wildlife Management 50:209–211.

Hohman, W. L., T. S. Taylor, and M. W. Weller. 1988. Annual body weight change in Ring-necked Ducks (*Aythya collaris*). Pages 257–269 *in* M.W. Weller, editor. Waterfowl in winter. University of Minnesota Press, Minneapolis.

Hohman, W. L., D. W. Woolington, and J. H. DeVries. 1990. Food habits of wintering Canvasbacks in Louisiana. Canadian Journal of Zoology 68:2605–2609.

Hupp, J. W., and D. G. Robertson. 1998. Forage site selection by Lesser Snow Geese during autumn staging on the Arctic National Wildlife Refuge, Alaska. Wildlife Monographs 138.

Hupp, J. W., A. B. Zacheis, R. M. Anthony, D. G. Robertson, W. P. Erickson, and K. C. Palacios. 2001. Snow cover and Snow Goose *Anser caerulescens caerulescens* distribution during spring migration. Wildlife Biology 7:65–76.

Jeske, C. W., and H. F. Percival. 1995. Time and energy budgets of wintering Ring-necked Ducks *Aythya collaris* in Florida, USA. Wildfowl 46: 109–118.

Jeske, C. W., M. R. Szymczak, D. R. Anderson, J. K. Ringelman, and J. A. Armstrong. 1994. Relationship of body condition to survival of Mallards in San Luis Valley, Colorado. Journal of Wildlife Management 58:787–793.

Johnson, D. H., G. L. Krapu, K. J. Reinecke, and D. G. Jorde. 1985. An evaluation of condition indices for birds. Journal of Wildlife Management 49:569–575.

Johnson, D. H., J. D. Nichols, and M. D. Schwartz. 1992. Population dynamics of breeding waterfowl. Pages 446–485 *in* B. D. J. Batt, A. D. Afton, M. G. Anderson, C. D. Ankney, D. H. Johnson, J. A. Kadlec, and G. L. Krapu, editors. Ecology and management of breeding waterfowl. University of Minnesota Press, Minneapolis.

Jorde, D. G. 1981. Wintering and spring staging ecology of Mallards in south central Nebraska. Thesis, University of North Dakota, Grand Forks.

Jorde, D. G., G. L. Krapu, R. D. Crawford, and M. A. Day. 1984. Effects of weather on habitat selection and behavior of Mallards wintering in Nebraska. Condor 86:258–265.

Jorde, D. G., and R. B. Owen, Jr. 1988. The need for nocturnal activity and energy budgets of waterfowl. Pages 169–180 *in* M. W. Weller, editor. Waterfowl in winter. University of Minnesota Press, Minneapolis.

Joyner, D. E., R. D. Arthur, and B. N. Jacobson. 1984. Winter weight dynamics, grain consumption and reproductive potential in Canada Geese. Condor 86:275–280.

Kaminski, R. M., and E. A. Gluesing. 1987. Density- and habitat-related recruitment in Mallards. Journal of Wildlife Management 51:141–148.

Kaminsky, S., and R. A. Ryan. 1981. Weight changes in Redheads and Canvasbacks during the winter. New York Fish and Game Journal 28:215–222.

Kestenholz, M. 1994. Body mass dynamics of wintering Tufted Duck *Aythya fuligula* and Pochard *A. ferina* in Switzerland. Wildfowl 45:147–158.

King, J. R. 1972. Adaptive periodic fat storage in birds. International Ornithological Congress 15:200–217.

King, J. R., and D. S. Farner. 1966. The adaptive role of winter fattening in the White-crowned Sparrow with comments on its regulation. American Naturalist 100:403–418.

Korschgen, C. E., L. S. George, and W. L. Green. 1985. Disturbance of diving ducks by boaters on a migrational staging area. Wildlife Society Bulletin 13:290–296.

Krementz, D. G., J. E. Hines, P. O. Corr, and R. B. Owen, Jr. 1989. The relationship between body mass and annual survival in American Black Ducks. Ornis Scandinavica 20:81–85.

Lack, D. 1966. Population studies of birds. Clarendon Press, Oxford.

LaGrange, T. G., and J. J. Dinsmore. 1988. Nutrient reserve dynamics of female Mallards during spring migration through central Iowa. Pages 287–297 *in* M. W. Weller, editor. Waterfowl in winter. University of Minnesota Press, Minneapolis.

LaGrange, T. G., and J. J. Dinsmore. 1989. Habitat use by Mallards during spring migration through central Iowa. Journal of Wildlife Management 53:1076–1081.

Leitch, W. G., and R. M. Kaminski. 1985. Long-term wetland-waterfowl trends in Saskatchewan grassland. Journal of Wildlife Management 49:212–222.

Lincoln, F. C. 1935. The waterfowl flyways of North America. U.S. Department of Agriculture Circular 342.

Loesch, C. R., R. M. Kaminski, and D. M. Richardson. 1992. Endogenous loss of body mass by Mallards in winter. Journal of Wildlife Management 56:735–739.

Lovvorn, J. R. 1994. Nutrient reserves, probability of cold spells and the question of reserve regulation in wintering Canvasbacks. Journal of Animal Ecology 63:11–23.

Malecki, R. A., B. D. J. Batt, and S. E. Sheaffer. 2001. Spatial and temporal distribution of Atlantic Population Canada Geese. Journal of Wildlife Management 65:242–247.

Migoya, R., and G. A. Baldassarre. 1993. Harvest and food habits of waterfowl wintering in Sinaloa, Mexico. Southwestern Naturalist 38:168–171.

Migoya, R., and G. A. Baldassarre. 1995. Winter survival of female Northern Pintails in Sinaloa, Mexico. Journal of Wildlife Management 59:16–22.

Migoya, R., G. A. Baldassarre, and M. P. Losito. 1994. Diurnal activity budgets and habitat functions of Northern Pintail *Anas acuta* wintering in Sinaloa, Mexico. Wildfowl 45:134–146.

Miller, M. R. 1985. Time budgets of Northern Pintails wintering in the Sacramento Valley, California. Wildfowl 36:53–64.

Miller, M. R. 1986a. Northern Pintail body condition during wet and dry winters in the Sacramento Valley, California. Journal of Wildlife Management 50:189–198.

Miller, M. R. 1986b. Molt chronology of Northern Pintails in California. Journal of Wildlife Management 50:57–64.

Miller, M. R. 1989. Estimating carcass fat and protein in Northern Pintails during the nonbreeding season. Journal of Wildlife Management 53:123–129.

Miller, M. R., J. P. Fleskes, D. L. Orthmeyer, W. E. Newton, and D. S. Gilmer. 1995. Survival of adult female Northern Pintails in Sacramento Valley, California. Journal of Wildlife Management 59:478–486.

Moser, T. J., and D. H. Rusch. 1988. Indices of structural size and condition of Canada Geese. Journal of Wildlife Management 52:202–208.

Nichols, J. D., K. J. Reinecke, and J. E. Hines. 1983. Factors affecting the distribution of Mallards wintering in the Mississippi Alluvial Valley. Auk 100:932–946.

Nolan, V., Jr., and E. D. Ketterson. 1983. An analysis of body mass, wing length, and visible fat deposits of Dark-eyed Juncos wintering at different latitudes. Wilson Bulletin 95:603–620.

Nowak, E. 1990. Satellite tracking of migrating Bewick's Swans. Naturwissenschaften 77:549–550.

Owen, M. 1972. Some factors affecting food intake and selection in White-fronted Geese. Journal of Animal Ecology 41:79–92.

Owen, M. 1981. Abdominal profile — a condition index for wild geese in the field. Journal of Wildlife Management 45:227–230.

Owen, M., and W. A. Cook. 1977. Variations in body weight, wing length and condition of Mallard *Anas platyrhynchos platyrhynchos* and their relationship to environmental changes. Journal of Zoology, London 183:377–395.

Owens, N. W. 1977. Responses of wintering Brent Geese to human disturbance. Wildfowl 28:5–14.

Paulus, S. L. 1980. The winter ecology of the Gadwall in Louisiana. Thesis, University of North Dakota, Grand Forks.

Paulus, S. L. 1982. Gut morphology of Gadwalls in Louisiana in winter. Journal of Wildlife Management 46:483–489.

Paulus, S. L. 1983. Dominance relations, resource use, and pairing chronology of Gadwalls in winter. Auk 100:947–952.

Paulus, S. L. 1984a. Activity budgets of nonbreeding Gadwalls in Louisiana. Journal of Wildlife Management 48:371–380.

Paulus, S. L. 1984b. Behavioral ecology of Mottled Ducks in Louisiana. Dissertation, Auburn University, Auburn, Alabama.

Paulus, S. L. 1988. Time-activity budgets of nonbreeding Anatidae: a review. Pages 135–152 *in* M.W. Weller, editor. Waterfowl in winter. University of Minnesota Press, Minneapolis.

Pedroli, J. C. 1982. Activity and time budget of Tufted Ducks on Swiss lakes during winter. Wildfowl 33:105–112.

Perry, M. C., W. J. Kuenzel, B. K. Williams, and J. A. Serafin. 1986. Influence of nutrients on feed intake and condition of captive Canvasbacks in winter. Journal of Wildlife Management 50:427–434.

Peterson, S. R., and R. S. Ellarson. 1979. Changes in Oldsquaw carcass weight. Wilson Bulletin 91:288–300.

Quinlan, E. E., and G. A. Baldassarre. 1984. Activity budgets of nonbreeding Green-winged Teal on playa lakes in Texas. Journal of Wildlife Management 48:838–845.

Rave, D. P., and G. A. Baldassarre. 1989. Activity budget of Green-winged Teal wintering in coastal wetlands of Louisiana. Journal of Wildlife Management 53:753–759.

Rave, D. P., and G. A. Baldassarre. 1991. Carcass mass and composition of Green-winged Teal wintering in Louisiana and Texas. Journal of Wildlife Management 55:457–461.

Raveling, D. G. 1968. Weights of *Branta canadensis* during winter. Journal of Wildlife Management 32:412–414.

Raveling, D. G. 1978. Dynamics of distribution of Canada Geese in winter. Transactions of the North American Wildlife and Natural Resources Conference 43:206–225.

Raveling, D. G. 1979. The annual cycle of body composition of Canada Geese with special reference to control of reproduction. Auk 96:234–252.

Raveling, D. G., W. E. Crews, and W. D. Klimstra. 1972. Activity patterns of Canada Geese during winter. Wilson Bulletin 84:278–295.

Raveling, D. G., and M. E. Heitmeyer. 1989. Relationships of population size and recruitment of Pintails to habitat conditions and harvest. Journal of Wildlife Management 53:1088–1103.

Reed, A., M. A. Davison, and D. K. Kraege. 1989. Segregation of Brent Geese *Branta bernicla* wintering and staging in Puget Sound and the Strait of Georgia. Wildfowl 40:22–31.

Reinecke, K. J., T. L. Stone, and R. B. Owen, Jr. 1982. Seasonal carcass composition and energy balance of female Black Ducks in Maine. Condor 84:420–426.

Ringelman, J. K., and M. R. Szymczak. 1985. A physiological condition index for wintering Mallards. Journal of Wildlife Management 49:564–568.

Robb, J. R., G. M. Tori, and R. W. Kroll. 2001. Condition indices of live-trapped American Black Ducks and Mallards. Journal of Wildlife Management 65:755–764.

Rohwer, F. C., and M. G. Anderson. 1988. Female-biased philopatry, monogamy, and the timing of pair formation in migratory waterfowl. Current Ornithology 5:187–221.

Ryan, R. A. 1972. Body weight and weight changes of wintering diving ducks. Journal of Wildlife Management 36:759–765.

Sayler, R. D., and A. D. Afton. 1981. Ecological aspects of Common Goldeneyes *Bucephala clangula* wintering on the upper Mississippi River. Ornis Scandinavica 12:99–108.

Schummer, M. L., and W. R. Eddleman. 2003. Effects of disturbance on activity and energy budgets of migrating waterbirds in south-central Oklahoma. Journal of Wildlife Management 67:789–795.

Smith, L. M., and D. G. Sheeley. 1993. Factors affecting condition of Northern Pintails wintering in the Southern High Plains. Journal of Wildlife Management 57:62–71.

Tacha, T. C., A. Woolf, and W. D. Klimstra. 1988. Breeding distribution and subpopulations of the Mississippi Valley population of Canada Geese. Journal of Wildlife Management 52:689–693.

Tamisier, A. 1976. Diurnal activities of Green-winged Teal and Pintail wintering in Louisiana. Wildfowl 27:19–31.

Tamisier, A., L. Allouche, F. Aubry, and O. Dehorter. 1995. Wintering strategies and breeding success: hypothesis for trade-off in some waterfowl species. Wildfowl 46:76–88.

Taylor, T. S. 1978. Spring foods of migrating Blue-winged Teals on seasonally flooded impoundments. Journal of Wildlife Management 42:900–903.

Thompson, J. D., and G. A. Baldassarre. 1990. Carcass composition of nonbreeding Blue-winged Teal and Northern Pintails in Yucatan, Mexico. Condor 92:1057–1065.

Thompson, J. D., and G. A. Baldassarre. 1991. Activity patterns of Nearctic dabbling ducks wintering in Yucatan, Mexico. Auk 108:934–941.

Thompson, J. D., and G. A. Baldassarre. 1992. Dominance relationships of dabbling ducks wintering in Yucatan, Mexico. Wilson Bulletin 104:529–536.

Thornburg, D. D. 1973. Diving duck movements on Keokuk Pool, Mississippi River. Journal of Wildlife Management 37:382–389.

Turnbull, R. E., and G. A. Baldassarre. 1987. Activity budgets of Mallards and American Wigeon wintering in east-central Alabama. Wilson Bulletin 99:457–464.

Weatherhead, P. J., and C. D. Ankney. 1984. A critical assumption of band-recovery models may often be violated. Wildlife Society Bulletin 12:198–199.

Wege, M. L., and D. G. Raveling. 1983. Factors influencing the timing, distance, and path of migrations of Canada Geese. Wilson Bulletin 95:209–221.

Weller, M. W., and B. D. J. Batt. 1988. Waterfowl in winter: past, present, and future. Pages 3–8 *in* M. W. Weller, editor. Waterfowl in winter. University of Minnesota Press, Minneapolis.

White, D. H., and D. James. 1978. Differential use of fresh water environments by wintering waterfowl of coastal Texas. Wilson Bulletin 90:99–111.

Whyte, R. J., G. A. Baldassarre, and E. G. Bolen. 1986. Winter condition of Mallards on the Southern High Plains of Texas. Journal of Wildlife Management 50:52–57.

Whyte, R. J., and E. G. Bolen. 1984. Variation in winter fat depots and condition indices of Mallards. Journal of Wildlife Management 48:1370–1373.

Wilson, U. W., and J. B. Atkinson. 1995. Black Brant winter and spring-staging use at two Washington coastal areas in relation to eelgrass abundance. Condor 97:91–98.

Wishart, R. A. 1979. Indices of structural size and condition of American Wigeon (*Anas americana*). Canadian Journal of Zoology 57:2369–2374.

Woodall, P. F. 1978. Omental fat: a condition index for Redbilled Teal. Journal of Wildlife Management 42:188–190.

Chapter 8
MORTALITY AND HARVEST MANAGEMENT

A population is a group of organisms of the same species that occupies a defined area at a given time. However, animal populations seldom exist as static entities in time or space and instead may change — sometimes rapidly — because of mortality, natality, immigration, and emigration. Population dynamics is the study of these processes in animal populations, which remain important to waterfowl managers because of their influences on how, when, and where populations adjust in numbers during the annual cycle. Management actions thereafter may be focused on the factors and circumstances that will yield the greatest benefits. For waterfowl, natality and mortality appear to have the greatest effect on population size, and these topics accordingly have received a great deal of study.

The analytical tools used to estimate waterfowl mortality must be sensitive enough to detect signs warning of unfavorable circumstances. These "red flags" are not just estimates of declining numbers; they also include signs such as imbalanced sex and age ratios, inadequate food and cover, outbreaks of diseases, excessive predation, and overharvest. These same tools also gauge the recovery of diminished populations. Finally, and not unrelated to the foregoing, biologists must have rational arguments for justifying the year-to-year harvests of game species. Hunting remains a powerful influence on mortality and, of all factors affecting game populations, only hunting is directly subject to human regulation. Habitat management ultimately bears longer lasting effects on wildlife populations, but regulated hunting represents the primary tool for immediate application — and therefore, the one most subject to controversy both inside and outside the hunting community.

Avian mortality can result from an array of causes, but these can be divided into two major categories: natural and human-related, with hunting mortality representing the major form of the latter. For waterfowl, hunting mortality is highly seasonal and, for the most part, well controlled and measurable. In contrast, natural mortality occurs throughout the year, and although analyses of banding data may indicate its magnitude, the timing, extent, and specific causes of natural mortality are less well known. This chapter first reviews the ways waterfowl populations are estimated and then turns to the various aspects of natural mortality that affect waterfowl once they have attained flight (see Chapter 6 for mortality associated with the breeding season). Lastly, we review hunter harvest from the standpoint of establishing hunting regulations and

methodologies, and then discuss the extent and magnitude of the harvest

ESTIMATING THE SIZE OF WATERFOWL POPULATIONS

Since 1955, the U.S. Fish and Wildlife Service and the Canadian Wildlife Service annually have conducted surveys of breeding duck populations in May and again in July to assess habitat conditions, population sizes, and production of waterfowl in North America. The first survey is called the Breeding Waterfowl and Habitat Survey, or May Survey, and normally covers about 5.2 million km^2 of principal waterfowl breeding habitat (Fig. 8-1). These surveys occur in two primary areas of the continent. The Traditional Survey Area (Strata 1–18, 20–50, 75–77), long known as some of the most productive waterfowl habitat in the world, has been assessed since 1955 and covers about 3.4 million km^2 across parts of Alaska, Canada, and the north-central United States. An Eastern Survey Area (Strata 51–56, 62–69) has been assessed only since 1990 and encompasses about 1.8 million km^2 across parts of Ontario, Quebec, and the Maritime Provinces, and parts of the states of New York and Maine. All strata were not surveyed until 1996 (see U.S. Fish and Wildlife Service 2004a). The Eastern Survey is especially noteworthy because a significant portion of the continental Mallard population occurs outside the Traditional Survey Area, and the area also includes a significant portion of the continental population of Wood Ducks and almost all the American Black Ducks (Trost 1987).

The May Survey began in 1946, but the methods were not standardized until 1955, which therefore marks the benchmark year from which long-term trends are now evaluated. The survey consists of aerial transects on an east to west axis; transects are up to 241 km long and broken into 29-km segments. Some 71,000 km of transects are flown across the north-central United States, western and northern Canada, and Alaska (Smith et al. 1989). Transects are spaced within specific strata; the length and density of transects vary according to the quantity and quality of habitat. Thus, transects are 22.5 km apart in good habitat on the prairie potholes, whereas they are 48–97 km apart in the poorer habitats of the boreal forest (Henny et al. 1972). Transects are surveyed from light aircraft flying about 170 km/hr (105 mph) at a height of about 45 m (150 ft) above ground; the pilot counts ducks observed within 0.40 km (0.25 miles) on one side of the plane while an observer simultaneously counts both ducks and wetlands

Figure 8-1. Locations of transects and strata in both the traditional and eastern survey areas that are assessed annually by the U.S. Fish and Wildlife Service during the Breeding Waterfowl and Habitat Survey (May Survey). Map courtesy of the U.S. Fish and Wildlife Service.

('ponds') on the other side. Because even trained observers will not see all the ducks present, concurrent ground surveys are conducted to develop a correction factor for calibrating the number of ducks seen from the air with those counted on the ground. The ground-to-air corrections range from about 10:1 for the diminutive Green-winged Teal to 3:1 for the more conspicuous Mallard.

Those species with more restrictive ranges or whose distribution occurs largely outside the survey areas are not a primary concern. Accordingly, few data are collected for arctic-nesting ducks (e.g., Long-tailed Duck, among others). Nevertheless, when viewed over a long span of years, the May Survey is invaluable for assessing changes in breeding duck populations and habitat conditions over a broad area of North America. Indeed, at a landscape level, the May Survey represents the longest-running dataset on the status of any group of wildlife species in the world, which is an invaluable tool in the management of harvested wildlife (see Gibbs 1999).

When completed, the May Survey provides an estimate of the breeding population of the 10 most common species of ducks in North America. The 2005 May Survey data tallied 31.7 million ducks in the Traditional Survey Area, which was similar to 2004 (32.2 million) but 5% below the long-term (1955–2004) average (Table 8-1). Mallards are always the most abundant duck tallied in the Traditional Survey Area — 6.8 million were counted in 2005, which was 9% below 2004 and 10% below the long-term average. In contrast, only 2.6 million Northern Pintails were counted, but that tally was 17% above 2004 albeit 38% below the long-term average. Relative to habitat conditions for breeding waterfowl, 5.4 million "ponds" were tallied during the 2005 May Survey for Prairie Canada and the north-central United States combined, which was 37% higher than the 3.9 million tallied in 2004 and 12% higher than the long-term average of 4.8 million ponds (U.S. Fish and Wildlife Service 2005). In the Eastern Survey Area (2004 data), some 3.9 million ducks were tallied, which was 7% greater than 2003 and 17% greater

Table 8-1. The 2005 duck breeding population estimates (thousands) from the Traditional Survey Area in North America in comparison to 2004 and the long-term average (LTA) from 1955 to 2004. Data are from U.S. Fish and Wildlife Service (2005).

Species	2004	2005	% change	LTA	% change from LTA
Mallard	7,425	6,755	-9	7,510	-10
Gadwall	2,590	2,179	-16	1,683	+30
American Wigeon	1,981	2,225	+12	2,624	-15
Green-winged Teal	2,461	2,157	-12	1,861	+16
Blue-winged Teal	4,073	4,586	+13	4,499	+2
Northern Shoveler	2,810	3,591	+28	2,149	+67
Northern Pintail	2,185	2,561	+17	4,142	-38
Redhead	605	592	-2	625	-5
Canvasback	617	521	-16	563	-8
Scaup	3,807	3,387	-11	5,220	-35
Total	32,164	31,735	-1	33,281	-5

than the long-term (1996–2003) average. The American Black Duck was the most abundant species (730,000). We have reported the 2004 data from the Eastern Survey Area because new analytical methods used in 2005 preclude direct comparison of the data with previous surveys (see U.S. Fish and Wildlife Service 2005).

The July Survey, formally known as the Waterfowl Production and Habitat Survey, is less extensive than the May Survey, only covering about 2.1 million km² in North and South Dakota, Montana, Manitoba, Saskatchewan, and Alberta (Strata 20–49, 75–77; see U.S. Fish and Wildlife Service 2004a). The July Survey is conducted in a similar fashion to the May Survey but records the number, age, and size of broods, the number of pairs still involved with breeding, and the number of ponds still containing water. The July Survey was not conducted in 2004, but the 2003 survey recorded 1.5 million ponds in Prairie Canada and 1.1 million in the north-central United States (U.S. Fish and Wildlife Service 2004a). The number of broods recorded in 2003 was 142% above the long-term average for Prairie Canada, and 18% above that average for the north-central United States.

Data from the July Survey are then combined with the May Survey to estimate the size of the continental duck population in September (the Fall-Flight Index). For example, the Mallard Fall-Flight Index is based on models used for Adaptive Harvest Management (see this chapter), which considers the breeding population size as determined during the May Survey, habitat conditions, adult summer survival, and a projected fall age ratio (young/adult; U.S. Fish and Wildlife Service 2004b). Data are considered from the Traditional Survey Area as well as Michigan, Minnesota, and Wisconsin, wherein the fall-flight of Mallards was estimated as 9.4 million in 2004 versus 10.3 million in 2003. Data from the various waterfowl surveys have been summarized to depict continental duck populations and trends (Table 8-2).

In addition to the May and July surveys on the breeding grounds, a widespread survey of wintering waterfowl is conducted in December or January, largely in the United States but also in Mexico. This is known as the Midwinter Survey, and although it does not yield a reliable measure of the total size of the duck population, the survey provides valuable information on the winter distribution of ducks as well as a means of assessing the condition of winter habitats. The Midwinter Survey also remains a primary means of assessing swan, goose, and brant numbers (Blohm 1989). The Midwinter Survey has been conducted since the 1930s.

Among swans and geese, some 26 populations are assessed by the Midwinter Survey and other data, and some highlights are worthy of mention

Table. 8-2. Breeding duck populations and trends in North America (in thousands). Table modified from U.S. Fish and Wildlife Service (2004c:Table 2).

Species/Subspecies/Population	1994–2003 Mean population estimates			Long-term trend (1970–2003)
	Continental[a]	Traditional survey area	Other survey areas	
Mallard	13,000	8,640	3,380	No trend
Northern Pintail	3,600	2,815	169	Decreasing
American Black Duck	910	31	625	Decreasing
Mottled Duck	660	Not Applicable	11	No trend
Gadwall	3,900	2,963	456	Increasing
American Wigeon	3,100	2,628	382	No trend
Green-winged Teal	3,900	2,485	633	Increasing
Blue-winged Teal/Cinnamon teal	7,500	5,875	798	No trend
Blue-winged Teal	7,240	Not Differentiated	543	No trend
Cinnamon Teal	260	Not Differentiated	30	No trend
Northern Shoveler	3,800	3,318	284	Increasing
Wood Duck	4,600	Not Applicable	653	Increasing
Whistling-Ducks	215	Not Applicable	Not Applicable	Increasing
Redhead	1,200	811	216	No trend
Canvasback	740	657	51	No trend
Lesser Scaup	4,400	3,502	535	Decreasing
Greater Scaup	800	515	Not Applicable	No trend
Ring-necked Duck	2,000	1,101	683	Increasing
Ruddy Duck	1,100	566	192	Increasing
Harlequin Duck	254	Not Applicable	25	No trend
Long-tailed Duck	1,000	170	112	Decreasing
King Eider	575	Not Differentiated	Not Applicable	Decreasing
Common Eider	1,050	Not Differentiated	Not Applicable	Decreasing
Steller's Eider	1	Not Differentiated	1	Decreasing
Spectacled Eider	17	Not Differentiated	17	Decreasing
Black Scoter	400	Not Differentiated	Not Applicable	Decreasing
Surf Scoter	600	Not Differentiated	1	Decreasing
White-winged Scoter	600	Not Differentiated	14	Decreasing
Common Goldeneye	1,345	Not Differentiated	610	No trend
Barrow's Goldeneye	255	Not Differentiated	184	No trend
Bufflehead	1,400	953	359	Increasing
Hooded Merganser	350	Not Differentiated	241	Increasing
Red-breasted Merganser	250	Not Differentiated	10	Increasing
Common Merganser	1,000	Not Differentiated	257	Increasing

[a]Continental estimates include the surveyed area estimates as well as approximate estimates of populations outside surveyed areas as based on harvest derivation studies, expert opinion, winter surveys, or other special surveys.

here (see U.S. Fish and Wildlife Service 2004a). For example, the Atlantic Population of Canada Geese was 174,800 pairs in 2004, up from a low of only 29,000 pairs as recently as 1995. The Atlantic Flyway population of resident Canada Geese was 980,400, and has been increasing at about 2%/year for the last decade, with resultant problems in urban areas throughout its range (see Infobox 8-1). The population of the Dusky Canada Goose, a species that nests almost entirely on the Copper River Delta in Alaska, was only 14,900 in 2003–04, an 11% decrease from 2002–03. White or "light" geese are comprised of various Snow Goose and Ross's Goose populations, many of which have increased to levels that damage breeding habitat to a point where population control measures appear warranted (see this chapter).

OVERVIEW OF WATERFOWL MORTALITY

An extensive study conducted in the early 1970s by the U.S. Fish and Wildlife Service estimated that humans caused the deaths of 196 million birds per year, or about 1.9% of the total bird population in the continental United States (Banks 1979). Hunting represented the largest mortality factor (61%), followed by collisions with man-made objects such as buildings and TV towers (32%), and pollution (2%); several miscellaneous categories accounted for less than 1%. Obviously, hunting disproportionately affects game species, but other factors — those not associated with hunting — cause the largest percentage of mortality in most wild bird populations.

Any estimate of waterfowl mortality resulting from hunting, as measured by retrieved birds, is beset with sampling difficulties, but estimates concerning the extent, causes, and temporal distribution of nonhunting mortality are even more difficult to determine. To illustrate, 4,165 waterfowl carcasses were discovered during an intensive study of nonhunting mortality at three wildlife refuges in Missouri, but only 934 (22.4%) were still intact (Humburg et al. 1983). Scavengers, as might be expected, accounted for the majority of those carcasses that disappeared, as shown by the fates of 62 intact carcasses that were monitored daily: 44% disappeared after day 1, 68% by day 2, 79% by day 3, and 82% by day 4.

Even when intact carcasses are located, the cause of death may still be difficult to determine. In the Missouri study, for instance, 675 duck and goose carcasses were examined, but the exact cause of death was determined for only 82%. Importantly, losses

due to predation were undetected in this study. These data revealed that 47% of the deaths resulted from crippling loss, 34% from lead poisoning, 11% from avian cholera, 7% from aspergillosis, and 1% from esophageal impactions. Thus, in many instances, what initially seemed to be nonhunting mortality actually was related to hunting.

In general, however, total annual mortality among waterfowl seems roughly divided equally between deaths from hunting and nonhunting (Bellrose 1980). Stout and Cornwell (1976) presented a 34-year summary of nonhunting mortality in waterfowl based on 25,817 band recoveries and 2,108,880 records garnered from published literature, unpublished federal reports, and questionnaires. Most (88%) mortalities resulted from diseases, of which botulism was the major cause (90%), followed by avian cholera (5%) and lead poisoning (4%). However, deaths from predation would be much underrepresented in such a dataset because predation is not commonly observed, and recovery of bands would be less likely because consumption of the carcass by a predator leaves few, if any, remains to be noticed by humans. Nonetheless, nonhunting mortality is a critical factor affecting waterfowl populations, wherein we begin our discussion of mortality with a focus on nonhunting mortality in general, and the role of diseases in particular.

NONHUNTING MORTALITY

Role and Scope of Waterfowl Diseases

Disease can be defined as any impairment of health or any condition of abnormal functioning. Diseases have long killed waterfowl and other wildlife, but ecologists were slow to recognize disease as a significant factor affecting bird populations (Price 1991), and biologists were even slower to seek remedial action (Friend et al. 2001). In the early years of waterfowl management, diseases were dismissed as regrettable — and unmanageable — "acts of God" (Friend 1981a). Managers later began expressing their concerns about the consequences of diseases, but knowledge remained inadequate for effective action. Eventually, waterfowl dying in major epizootics were buried and/or incinerated, but these measures failed to address the underlying causes of outbreaks. Meanwhile, evidence mounted that diseases imposed serious impacts on waterfowl populations.

In 1975, the U.S. Fish and Wildlife Service acknowledged the severity of wildlife diseases by establishing the National Wildlife Health Center at

Infobox 8-1

Canada Geese
Waterfowl in the All the Wrong Places

The spectacular increase in Canada Geese represents one of the great success stories of wildlife management, and one subspecies, previously believed extinct, was discovered thriving in suburban Rochester, Minnesota. About 1 million resident Canada Geese flourish in the Atlantic Flyway alone, where they perhaps outnumber their migratory counterparts. Therein lies the crux of an issue: Canada Geese of several subspecies today prosper in urban and suburban environments where, as year-round residents, they become nuisances. For managers, the issue is sociological as much as biological.

Several factors play on the increasing numbers of urban Canada Geese: predation and hunting exert little or no influence; nesting conditions are often optimal; supplemental foods are available; and the birds are long-

lived and tolerate human and other disturbances. These conditions prevail at city parks, golf courses, airports, and corporate office complexes where ponds and extensive lawns dominate the landscape. In these and other settings (e.g., residential areas, shopping malls, and academic campuses) the birds damage turf, interfere with traffic, endanger aircraft, contaminate soil and water with accumulations of their feces, pose concerns for public heath, and, when breeding, may be aggressive.

In response to these problems, resident geese at first were captured and moved to rural locations (but many often returned), and those that escaped relocation continued increasing. At best, relocation was expensive and labor intensive. Moreover, refuges and other sites soon were saturated and transfers were no

longer accepted. Other techniques, including treating eggs with oil (which killed the embryos but kept adults tied to their clutches, thereby precluding second nesting attempts) and other lethal methods often provoke public outrage, including cries from children who "befriend" the birds with handouts of food. Managers also tried hazing, treating turf with chemical repellants, surgical sterilization, and habitat modifications (e.g., reducing access to water). Hazing with noise makers or sonic devices, along with taped alarm and distress calls produce no long-term benefits, as the geese become habituated or return when the hazing ends. Dogs, particularly border collies, drive off nuisance geese but, while publicly accepted, they must be deployed 24-hr/day year-round for effective results and require costly training, housing, and care. Such methods also simply send the problem elsewhere.

Development of a food-ingested agent that reduces fertility may offer some help. Nicarbizan (NCZ), currently approved to treat chickens for coccidosis, also decreases both egg production and embryonic development. Preliminary research produced similar results in captive geese — only 20% of the eggs remain viable — and trials continue to develop ways to administer

NCZ under field conditions. In terms of population dynamics, however, techniques that reduce the survival rates of adult geese are many times more efficient in altering population growth than those that reduce reproductive success.

Canada Geese fall under jurisdiction of the Migratory Bird Treaty Act, and federal approval is required for most management activities (habitat modification is among the few exceptions). In 1999, a Special Canada Goose Permit was authorized specifically for the control of resident Canada Geese. The permits, issued directly to state wildlife agencies, allow local managers to deal with nuisance geese without lengthy case-by-case reviews by federal authorities. Currently (2004), an Environmental Impact Statement is in preparation that will examine alternative methods for controlling troublesome Canada Geese.

This issue has produced a wealth of literature, only a few of which are cited here: Converse and Kennelly (1994), Christens et al. (1995), Cooper and Keefe (1997), Smith et al. (1999), Castelli and Sleggs (2000), York et al. (2000), and U.S. Department of Interior (2002). Photo courtesy of Bryan L. Swift, New York State Department of Environmental Conservation.

Madison, Wisconsin, in part because of an epizootic in 1973 at a national wildlife refuge. The Center subsequently recorded numerous epizootics that killed 25,000–100,000 waterfowl, and epizootics killing 5,000–10,000 birds were commonplace. Indeed, an annual average of about 200 epizootics (mostly waterfowl) was reported to the Center during the 1980s; hence, diseases likely kill millions of birds each year (Friend 1992). Epizootics continued through the 1990s, most dramatically in 1997 with the loss of one million waterfowl at Old Wives Lake in Saskatchewan and 500,000 waterfowl at the Bear River Marshes near Great Salt Lake in Utah. Unfortunately, such outbreaks are likely to continue.

Regrettably, waterfowl diseases also have expanded in both geography and severity in the past 25 years in North American and elsewhere in the world (e.g., botulism killed an estimated one million waterfowl on the Caspian Sea in Kazachstan in 1982). Indeed, the threat of disease has clearly emerged as a major global threat to bird populations in the 21st century (see Friend et al. 2001). In noting the significance of these trends, Friend et al. (2001:290) stated, " . . . failure to adequately address disease emergence in free-ranging wildlife is result-

ing in a diminished capacity to achieve and sustain desired geographic distributions and population abundance for species of wild birds, including some threatened and endangered avifauna." For example, because of juvenile mortality, populations of Common Eiders in the Baltic Sea near the Gulf of Finland have declined 6–10%/year during the 1990s, and as much as 50% in some areas (Hario 1998). Duckling mortality was 95–99% in some areas. Infectious bursal disease virus (IBDV) may be responsible, as antibodies to the virus occurred in 75% of a combined sample of Common Eiders from Finland and Spectacled Eiders in Alaska (Hollmén et al. 2000), and reached 96% at some locations. IBDV is especially serious in Spectacled Eiders, which were listed as a threatened species in the United States in 1993. Indeed, Spectacled Eider populations in western Alaska in the early 1990s were less than 4% of the numbers estimated in the 1970s (Stehn et al. 1993; also see Petersen and Douglas 2004). IBDV attacks the developing lymphoid tissue of young birds, primarily in the bursa of Fabricius, and thereby compromises the ability of the immune system to fight infections from secondary pathogens (see Hollmén et al. 2000).

Disease has possibly affected Northern Pintails in North America, where their breeding population numbered 10 million in 1956 but, despite intensive management, plummeted to 2.2 million in 2004. Friend et al. (2001) hypothesized that continued suppression of Northern Pintails was not surprising, because Northern Pintails are often the dominant species affected in major epizootics of avian botulism and cholera (see also Ball et al. 1998). For example, three outbreaks of avian botulism in 1997 likely killed more than 350,000 Northern Pintails (see Miller and Duncan 1999). Austin and Miller (1995) also noted the importance of avian cholera and botulism as a mortality factor of Northern Pintails. On the Texas High Plains, for example, 2,345 waterfowl carcasses were collected on just 16 playa lakes during an outbreak of botulism and avian cholera in the winter of 1977–78; 40% of the dead birds were Northern Pintails, and the seasonal die-off was projected to be 33,000–35,000 birds (Moore and Simpson 1981).

In general, diseases today are especially prevalent because of invasive diseases (e.g., West Nile virus), new and emerging diseases (e.g., IBDV, duck plague), and re-emerging diseases (e.g., cholera and botulism). Further, reductions in habitat quantity and quality, as well as rapid global movement of people, pets and domestic animals, and pathogens, now increase opportunities to seriously threaten wildlife populations (see Friend et al. 2001, McLean 2002a). To combat this serious threat, diseases must be seen as an outcome, rather than a cause. Friend et al. (2001) thus note that continued human-wrought changes in the landscape will in turn alter the distribution and aggregation of avifauna in ways that will likely facilitate the emergence and spread of diseases. These changes decrease the likelihood that avian populations can recover from epizootics wherein some species may descend to population levels that can no longer provide society with values such as hunting. Friend et al. (2001:298) concluded that, ". . . neither the avian nor greater conservation communities are responding to disease emergence in a manner consistent with the biological significance of that threat, or with the ecological understanding of how to approach the problem." They cite two major barriers that must be overcome if managers are to reverse this situation: (1) persistence of the idea that disease is not a significant mortality factor in wild bird populations, and (2) tendency to focus on the affected species or causative agent instead of the affected environment.

Nonetheless, progress is underway, largely in the form of new information available to managers. Three significant contributions are the new editions of *Field Manual of Wildlife Diseases* (Friend and Franson 1999), *Diseases of Wild Waterfowl* (Wobeser 1997a), and *Infectious and Parasitic Diseases of Wild Birds* (Thomas et al. 2007). These publication provided much of the basis for our review of the major diseases of waterfowl, in which we emphasize epizootiology (the ecology of diseases) and, when known, methods of control.

WATERFOWL SUSCEPTIBILITY TO DISEASES

Although diseases are a significant and increasing threat to birds in general, four general factors render waterfowl especially susceptible to diseases. First, many species of waterfowl are gregarious at some time of the year. Waterfowl thus are predisposed to transmitting infectious pathogens, especially during the nonbreeding period when the birds are migrating or overwintering in large flocks. Second, although waterfowl have been stricken by diseases for millennia, the percentage of disease-killed birds has increased substantially in recent decades. A major cause of this increased disease mortality is diminished habitat availability, as large numbers of ducks and geese today remain for several months each year at a smaller number of suitable sites, thereby increasing exposure to pathogens. Such concentrations of birds are indeed spectacular and pleasing to the public, but these situations are often alarming to professional biologists — overcrowding leaves little question about whether an epizootic will occur. Indeed, one might instead ask when will disease strike, what pathogens will be involved, and how many birds will perish. Droughts also accentuate crowding, given the diminished base of suitable habitat. For example, outbreaks of avian cholera and botulism in the Texas Panhandle often follow late-summer droughts, which shrink the size and number of playa lakes available as habitat for a large population of wintering waterfowl (Petrides and Byrant 1951).

Waterfowl concentrated on refuges seem unusually susceptible to infectious diseases. In fact, the first known episodes of two virulent diseases in wild waterfowl in North America occurred on refuges. The management implications are clear, but sometimes these have been overshadowed by the faulty notion that managers somehow are doing a "better job" if they build and retain ever larger waterfowl populations on their refuges. For instance, large numbers of wintering ducks and geese were killed by avian cholera when pumps were used to maintain small pools of ice-free water at Squaw Creek National Wildlife Refuge in Missouri (Vaught et al. 1967). The birds concentrated on the pools, and an epizootic ensued. On the other hand, refuges are among the few places where it is often possible to alter habitat conditions for the prevention and control of diseases. Most waterfowl refuges, for example, have some means for manipulating water levels; hence, disease-prone habitat conditions may be avoided. In sum, management objectives on refuges must be considered carefully, balancing the health and welfare of waterfowl populations against the numbers of birds offered sanctuary by other conditions on the refuge.

A third predisposing factor is the migratory nature of most species, which can potentially spread diseases over large areas, thereby introducing pathogenic agents into flocks far removed from the original sources of infection. Diseases, just like waterfowl, heed no boundaries between states or nations, although some diseases are more common in some areas than others. Nonetheless, poor or no management of diseases at any site may produce disaster elsewhere. The long-range mobility of waterfowl also means they visit many places and experience numerous environmental conditions during their travels. These sites include ponds in city parks, contaminated waters of several kinds, and exposure to domestic fowl as well as a variety of more natural settings and associations. Each situation may offer a greater or lesser opportunity for infection. For example, because of their exposure to poultry waste, gulls (Laridae) may carry IBDV, a virus that has infected Common Eiders in Finland (Hollmén et al. 2000). In Michigan, the severity of avian malaria differed considerably between two groups of Canada Geese located just 40 km apart (Dresser et al. 1978).

Fourth, some species of waterfowl seem inherently more disposed to certain diseases than others. We have already discussed the apparent increased susceptibility of Northern Pintails to botulism and avian cholera, but they were least susceptible to duck plague in assays conducted by Spieker et al. (1996).

In summary, we cannot overemphasize that avian diseases represent an increasingly severe factor depressing waterfowl populations, thereby becoming a serious issue for waterfowl and wetland management. Three factors are associated with dis-

eases: (1) a susceptible host, (2) a pathogen, and (3) conditions that create contact between the two. New research and thoughtful management must address these topics as a means of reaching the ultimate goal of disease *prevention* as a component in the restoration of waterfowl populations in North America (Friend 1981a, 1992). The initial costs of prevention may be high, but the long-term benefits are far more cost-effective than disposing of dead waterfowl after the fact (Fig. 8-2). This approach strives not only to prevent diseases before they occur but also to integrate disease-related concepts into the full spectrum of waterfowl management. We turn now to several of the more important diseases of waterfowl in North America. Some of these diseases have affected waterfowl for many years (e.g., botulism and avian cholera), whereas others are new, emerging threats (e.g., West Nile virus). The group, however, represents a full range in the state of the art of disease management — from near helplessness to near prevention.

Botulism

Avian botulism is caused by the ingestion of a potent neurotoxin produced by the bacterium *Clostridium botulinum*; hence, the disease is a biotoxin, which Friend and Franson (1999:260) define as, "poisons that are produced by and derived from the cells or secretions of living organisms." We have addressed avian botulism first and in some detail, because botulism is probably the most infamous disease of waterfowl and likely represents the most critical disease affecting migratory birds worldwide (Friend and Franson 1999; Fig. 8-3). The total annual mortality caused by botulism is unknown, but major epizootics have been reported for more than a century (Kalmbach 1968; see also Jensen and Williams 1964, Rosen 1971a, Allen and Wilson 1977, Wilson and Locke 1982). In 1910, for example, botulism killed "millions" of waterfowl in California and Utah, and a 1952 epizootic killed 4–5 million waterfowl across the western United States (Locke and Friend 1987). An epizootic in the Central Valley of California killed an estimated 250,000 waterfowl in 1968–69 (Hunter et al. 1970), and we have already mentioned the 1997 epizootic at Old Wives Lake in Saskatchewan that claimed one million birds. During the latter half of the 1990s, Rocke et al. (1999) examined records from the National Wildlife Health Research Center and subsequently estimated that millions of waterfowl in the United States and Canada had died from botulism during this period. At the Bear River Migratory Bird Refuge in Utah, waterfowl mortality from botu-

Figure 8-2. Disposal of waterfowl carcasses following an epizootic of avian cholera in Nebraska. Carcasses are collected and then incinerated to control the spread of this highly contagious disease. Photo courtesy of Milton Friend, U.S. Geological Survey, National Wildlife Health Center.

Figure 8-3. The devastation of avian botulism is readily apparent in the aftermath of this epizootic in Utah. Botulism may strike in wetlands across North America, but the disease has a long-standing association with the marshes bordering Great Salt Lake. Photo courtesy of the Utah Division of Wildlife Resources.

lism has exceeded hunting mortality since 1950 (Barras and Kadlec 2000). Indeed, a 1997 outbreak at the refuge killed an estimated 400,000 birds (see Kadlec 2002).

Before the causative agent was determined, botulism was known as "western duck sickness" and "alkali disease" (as well as "limberneck" and "duck disease"). In the early days, toxicosis was attributed to alkaline salts in the waters of Great Salt Lake and other western wetlands (Wetmore 1915, 1918). Research later determined that the toxin produced by the bacterium *Clostridium botulinum* (Type C) was the lethal pathogen (Kalmbach 1930, Giltner and Couch 1930, Kalmbach and Gunderson 1934).

There are seven strains of *C. botulinum* (types A–G), but biologists now know that the Type C strain causes nearly all of the epizootics of botulism in waterfowl (Wobeser 1997a). Subsequent outbreaks of Type C and resultant death of waterfowl have occurred on every continent except Antarctica and probably is the most important disease affecting migratory birds (Friend and Franson 1999). The toxin from Type C does not harm people, but Types A, B, E, and at times F cause serious food poisoning and sometimes death in humans.

Type E botulism has caused sporadic mortality among fish-eating birds such as mergansers (*Mergus* spp.), gulls (*Larus* spp.), and loons (Gaviidae). Type E outbreaks are much less frequent than Type C, and, within the United States, have been restricted to the Great Lakes (Brand et al. 1988, Friend and Franson 1999). Kaufmann and Fay (1964) and Fay (1966) first reported Type E among fish-eating birds along the southern shore of Lake Michigan. Mortality (mostly gulls and loons) was 7,720 birds in 1963 and 4,920 in 1964 (Fay et al. 1965). These outbreaks have continued on the Great Lakes — 8,000 gulls and mergansers were killed on Lake Erie in November 2000 (Thill 2001). Dead fish apparently were sources of the toxin for the gulls, but sources of Type E toxin for the other species remained less well known.

Avian botulism affects the peripheral nerves; thus, signs suggesting botulism include varying degrees of paralysis, listlessness, sagging heads ("limber neck"), and drooping wings, although affected individuals often remain in good body condition because botulism kills quickly. Botulism produces no specific internal lesions, but death may occur within 24 hr. Many birds drown because they cannot hold their heads upright; otherwise, death results from respiratory failure caused by the toxin. Windrows of carcasses, which coincide with receding water levels, often mark the aftermath of large-scale epizootics.

Laboratory confirmation is necessary for conclusive evidence of botulism toxicosis. For many years, the mouse protection test was the standard assessment (Quortrup and Sudheimer 1943). This test involves injecting three mice with antitoxin, while three others act as controls — all six are then inoculated with serum from sick birds. (Dead birds cannot be used because of the possibility of postmortem toxigenesis.) A positive diagnosis of botulism is concluded if the protected mice survive and the controls die within 5 days. Recently, however, a promising new test has been developed to assess the presence of botulism toxicosis. The enzyme-linked immunosorbent assay (ELISA) costs about 50% less than the mouse test and can be preformed in the field (Rocke et al. 1998). The ELISA test can replace the mouse tests given adequate sample volumes, and holds promise as the future standard. There is also a polymerase chain reaction (PCR) assay that can detect Type C botulism in wetland sediments (Williamson et al. 1999).

Epizootiology and Management of Botulism: Conditions leading to an epizootic of botulism generally have included declining water levels, high pH (optimum of 5.7–6.2), warm water (optimum 25–40 °C), reduced oxygen, and an appropriate organic medium for toxin production (Friend and Franson 1999). *C. botulinum* itself is almost ubiquitous in nature, persisting in wetlands in a spore form resistant to heat and drought and capable of maintaining viability for years (Smith et al. 1982, Sandler et al. 1993, Wobeser 1997b). In the Bear River marshes, *C. botulinum* may reach densities of 10^9 cells per gram of mud (Kadlec 2002). Large-scale epizootics typically occur in the western United States from July through September, although episodes have occurred in most states and at other times of the year.

C. botulinum can occur in a range of substrates, but decaying plant matter seems a poor substrate for toxin production, whereas decaying animal tissue is highly suitable (see Wobeser 1997a, Friend and Franson 1999, Wobeser and Bollinger 2002). *C. botulinum* cannot synthesize several essential amino acids; hence, the substrate must contain a protein source (Friend and Franson 1999). Bell et al. (1955) proposed the "microenvironmental concept" to explain the production and transfer of the toxin to waterfowl based, in part, on experiments that separately exposed plant and animal tissues in a botulism-prone environment. Only the animal tissues yielded toxin; hence, the following conclusion: *C. botulinum* produces toxin in the bodies of macroinvertebrates — the microenvironment — in which the metabolic activities of the bacterium can proceed without dependence on the external environment. Moreover, the mechanics of the microenvironmental concept explain how waterfowl become intoxicated: They ingest toxin-laden bacteria in the bodies of macroinvertebrates and not from exposure to toxin freely diffused in the soil, water, or mats of vegetation. For an outbreak to occur, birds must ingest the toxin. A competing "sludge-bed" hypothesis proposed that aerobic bacteria exhaust oxygen supplies in the litter, and anaerobic bacteria such as *C. botulinum* then proliferate and secrete toxin (Bell et al. 1955). However, this hypothesis offered no explanation of how the toxin was transferred from the litter to the birds, and subsequent research demonstrated that decaying plant material is not a good substrate for toxin production (see Wobeser and Bollinger 2002).

Further research emphasized the importance of macroinvertebrates in the epizootiology of botulism (Hunter et al. 1970, Duncan and Jensen 1976). As suggested, the carcasses of macroinvertebrates killed by declining water levels are one medium for toxin production. More recent work that exposed caged Mallards to wetland conditions reported a higher probability of botulism with increasing invertebrate abundance (Rocke et al. 1999). Kadlec (2002) believed that living macroinvertebrates can bioaccumulate the toxin and thus might be an important but previously overlooked mechanism leading to an outbreak. Maggots (i.e., larvae of Diptera) living on dead animals also are suitable microenvironments for toxin production, and waterfowl are poisoned when they ingest the toxin-laden larvae. (The maggots themselves are immune to the toxin.) Hence, a single animal dying of any cause, when infected with maggots, may initiate an epizootic of botulism (see Malcolm 1982). Indeed, the potential of the carcass–maggot cycle to spread botulism is staggering. For example, a single Northern Shoveler carcass can contain 9,000–10,000 maggots, and a single maggot can contain enough toxin to kill a single duck (see Wobeser and Bollinger 2002). Once started, the carcasses of waterfowl dying of botulism themselves become hosts for more maggots and perpetuate the epizootic (Fig. 8-4). Just 1 g of maggots (*n* = 42 larvae) collected from botulism-killed birds may contain more than 400,000 mouse units (LD_{50}) of toxin.

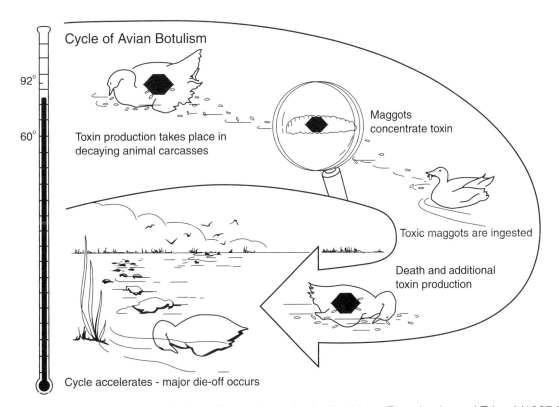

Figure 8-4. Maggots play a key role in the epizootiology of avian botulism. From Locke and Friend (1987:84).

At that level of concentration, about 50% of the ducks ingesting 0.05–0.25 g of toxic maggots may die from botulism (Duncan and Jensen 1976).

Several studies recently attempted to identify factors that might predict the occurrence of a botulism outbreak. On the Bear River marshes in Utah, an area long subject to botulism epizootics, Barras and Kadlec (2000) reported that high precipitation and increased water flow in the Bear River were associated with botulism outbreaks, but there was no correlation between waterfowl use-days and the magnitude of outbreaks that had occurred over a 25-year period. More detailed work by Rocke et al. (1999) examined 22 environmental variables associated with the probability of botulism occurrence in caged Mallards placed at the Sacramento National Wildlife Refuge in California, another area with a long history of botulism outbreaks. The probability of botulism in the caged Mallards was associated with increasing water temperature, higher abundance of invertebrates, and lower water turbidity, but these factors were not consistently different between wetlands with and without botulism outbreaks. However, redox potential was lower in wetlands without outbreaks and explained the largest portion (23%) of the 22 environmental variables. However, low redox potential apparently does not limit growth of *C. botulinum* in the laboratory (Smoot and Pierson 1979); thus, redox may interact with other factors such as pH and salinity (see Rocke et al. 1999). Cooch (1964) demonstrated that sublethal doses of *C. botulinum* may cause death for those waterfowl drinking salt water because the toxin impairs the function of the salt glands whereby the osmolarity of the blood plasma cannot be regulated, and death follows. Nonetheless, a subsequent study examined environmental variables in 32 pairs of wetlands in nine different states over a 9-year period (Rocke and Samuel 1999). Regression models showed that botulism risk increased when water temperature was greater than 20 °C, pH was between 7.5 and 9.0, and redox potential was negative. Risk declined when water temperature was 10–15 °C, redox potential was greater than 100, pH was less than 7.5 or greater than 9.0, and salinity was less than 2 ppt . These risk models provide a significant new method to identify wetlands prone to botulism outbreaks. However, no single factor has been identified to predict an outbreak (Wobeser and Bollinger 2002).

Botulism is a unique waterfowl disease, however, because production of the toxin in victims leads to secondary poisoning of healthy individuals. Hence, Wobeser (1997b) proposed that because botulism and

subsequent toxin production likely occur at low levels in many marshes, factors affecting the reproductive rate of the bacteria will determine when the disease will develop into a major epizootic, spread by secondary poisoning. The cycle begins when botulism spores are ingested by animals feeding in a given wetland (see Reed and Rocke 1992). When this animal dies, however, the tissues are invaded by *C. botulinum* present in the gut, and toxin is subsequently produced and available for spread to healthy birds. Maggots then appear on dead carcasses, and the maggots contain large amounts of toxin, although not all carcasses contain toxin-bearing maggots. For example, during experiments with Mallards at the Sacramento National Wildlife Refuge in California, Reed and Rocke (1992) found that maggots appeared on some carcasses in 2–4 days, and on most carcasses within 5–6 days. However, toxin-bearing maggots occurred on only 41% of the birds. Wobeser (1997b) then used these and other data in a model designed to predict the extent of an epizootic and guide future research. The four major factors in the model were (1) the number of vertebrate carcasses in a given wetland, (2) the probability that a carcass contains spores of *C. botulinum*, (3) the probability that a carcass persists until toxin-bearing maggots emerge and are thus available for ingestion, (4) the probability of contact between healthy birds and the toxin.

Left alone, epizootics of botulism apparently run their course (1) when temperatures cool, although winter outbreaks may occur from the persistence of residual toxin or where water is warmed artificially; (2) when waterfowl leave the site or switch to other foods; (3) when flies stop breeding and pupation begins in the current cohort of maggots; and/or (4) when water levels are stabilized (Wobeser 1997a). Intoxicated birds can be treated directly either by placing them in shaded pens with clean water or with injections of antitoxin; such measures may save 75–90% of the affected individuals (Friend and Franson 1999). However, these measures are costly and treat only a fraction of the victims in most epizootics.

Prevention and control are effective forms of management, but most of the suggested approaches are limited to sites where the wetland environment can be manipulated (e.g., waterfowl refuges). Reflooding of managed wetlands is not recommended in summer, for example, because it promotes decay of organic matter. Summer drawdowns are not recommended, because they can kill fish and invertebrates, which provide an optimal medium for toxin production (see Friend and Franson 1999). Sandler et al. (1993) found that the prevalence of botulism in substrate samples was lower in wetlands drained over summer compared with those with permanent water (31 vs. 62%). However, prompt removal and proper disposal of vertebrate carcasses (waterfowl, fish, mammals) is the only technique with proven effectiveness for reducing botulism losses, and this approach cannot be overemphasized (Friend and Franson 1999). For example, healthy Mallards placed in enclosures with a duck carcass were 4.5 times more likely to contract botulism than a control group in enclosures without carcasses (Reed and Rocke 1992). Hence, outbreaks of botulism can be theoretically prevented with early surveillance to detect initial mortalities, followed by removal of carcasses (Wobeser and Bollinger 2002). Further, because botulism tends to recur in the same wetlands, and outbreaks can occur at "hotspots" within those wetlands, this approach seems especially worthy for managers responsible for such sites.

Avian Cholera

The bacterium *Pasteurella multocida* causes avian cholera, also referred to as "fowl cholera" or "avian pasteurellosis," and has received considerable attention (see Wilson 1979, Botzler 1991). The generic name honors the famous French microbiologist Louis Pasteur, who produced the first vaccine, and the species epithet recognizes the broad range of hosts for the pathogen. The disease has been reported in more than 180 species of wild birds, but waterfowl remain its most obvious victims.

Some 16 different serotypes of *P. multocida* are recognized (Rimler et al. 1984), with Type 1 the predominant cause of waterfowl mortality in the western and central United States, and Types 3 and 4 predominating in the east (Brogden and Rhoades 1983, Windingstad et al. 1983). Avian cholera is a virulent, highly infectious disease capable of killing exposed birds in 6–12 hr, although 24–48 hr is more common (Friend and Franson 1999). Losses vary, but some estimates indicate that no less than 70,000 and perhaps 100,000 waterfowl have died in the more devastating epizootics in North America (see Friend 1981b, Botzler 1991, Friend and Franson 1999). On Banks Island, Northwest Territories, Canada, avian cholera killed 5–9% of a breeding colony of Lesser Snow Geese (Samuel et al. 1999). Avian cholera is unrelated to the dysenteric cholera infecting humans and therefore represents no known hazard to duck hunters or other persons contacting infected birds.

Avian cholera may have appeared as early as

1600 (in Italy), but the disease was first confirmed in France in 1780–82 (see Gray 1913), and since 1867 has emerged as an important source of mortality in domestic poultry. However, the first documented occurrence in wild waterfowl likely occurred in 1940 on Lake Nakuru, Kenya, where it infected about 40 Egyptian Sheldgeese and Spur-winged Geese (see Botzler 1991). Avian cholera now occurs on most major land masses around the world, but the disease currently is a significant threat to waterfowl mainly in North America, where it represents a relatively new concern for management (Friend 1981a, Botzler 1991). Nonetheless, in 2000, an outbreak of avian cholera in South Korea killed 13,228 Baikal Teal at Cheonsoo Bay (about 13% of the birds present), which is the foremost wintering site for Baikal Teal in the world (Kwon and Kang 2003).

Avian cholera likely was introduced into the United States in 1880–82 (Gray 1913), but the disease was unknown in waterfowl until the winter of 1943–44, when an epizootic struck waterfowl wintering at the Muleshoe National Wildlife Refuge and other areas in the Texas Panhandle (Quortrup et al. 1946), as well as in south San Francisco Bay, California (Rosen and Bischoff 1949). Presumptive evidence suggests that diseased poultry, which often were discarded indiscriminately, transmitted avian cholera to waterfowl during the initial outbreaks of the 1940s (Friend 1981b). Nonetheless, avian cholera did not emerge as a significant disease of waterfowl in North America until the 1970s (Friend 1981a, Friend and Franson 1999). Since then, many thousands of waterfowl have died in each of several epizootics, with major focal points in the Central Valley of California, Tule Lake and Klamath Basin in northern California and southern Oregon, the Texas Panhandle, and the Rainwater Basin in Nebraska. More recently, epizootics in Missouri, Maine, parts of Chesapeake Bay, and other locations in all flyways and in Canada, now confirm a continental-wide distribution of avian cholera.

An important consideration in the epizootiology of avian cholera is the identification of the "reservoir" of the disease, which Botzler (1991:379) defined as, "a dependable, nonclinical source of a pathogen; a place where the infective agent can survive on a year-round basis." To date, most studies do not support the hypothesis that either soil or water represents an important reservoir for *P. multocida* (see Botzler 1991), whereas surviving birds are verified carriers and thus major sources of infection (Botzler 1991, Wobeser 1992, Samuel et al. 1999). Indeed, the chronological and geographical sequence of epizootics between 1970 and 1980 suggests that waterfowl have transmitted avian cholera along their migratory routes from several locations where the disease was enzootic (Brand 1984). The bacteria can persist in the environment, however, as Samuel et al. (2003) determined from their assays of wetlands across the Pacific and Central Flyways during 1996–99. They documented isolates (mostly Serotype 1) of *P. multocida* from 20 (46%) of 44 wetlands with outbreaks, and in 7% of the water and 4.5% of the sediment samples taken during or shortly after epizootics. Bredy and Botzler (1989) reported that *P. multocida* could survive in water for more than 1 year under certain conditions such as high calcium and magnesium concentrations (Price et al. 1992). Later, however, Samuel et al. (2004) were not able to isolate *P. multocida* from fall samples collected at 44 wetlands that experienced outbreaks the previous winter or spring. These studies provide the strongest evidence that wetlands are not the primary reservoir of *P. multocida*

Avian cholera epizootics are explosive and may strike at anytime during the year, but losses tend to be greater when large numbers of birds concentrate during winter or spring migration. Remarkably, external signs of avian cholera are virtually absent; hence, the disease can appear with little if any warning. Infected birds die suddenly, often without showing gross abnormalities in behavior, thereby testifying to the disease's virulence. Indeed, incubating Common Eiders died on or near their nests during an epizootic in Maine (Korschgen et al. 1978). Many infected birds continue feeding normally; hence the esophagi of dead birds regularly contain ample amounts of food. Vaught et al. (1967) found 1,100 apparently healthy Lesser Snow Geese dying overnight after feeding flights the previous evening. In other instances, infected birds may show signs of weakness, abnormal flight, and poor balance (Klukas and Locke 1970, Rosen 1971b, Friend and Franson 1999). However, managers should suspect avian cholera if large numbers of dead birds in good physical condition appear in a short time. Avian cholera also may differentially affect various species of waterbirds (Rosen 1969, Friend and Franson 1999).

Internal signs include pinpoint lesions on the liver, heart, and sometimes the gizzard and other organs. Small white-to-yellowish spots often occur on the liver. The intestinal tract typically contains viscous globules of clear mucus; the intestines often are turgid and may show hemorrhages. Overall, however, avian cholera produces rather unremarkable signs of infection and may be confused with other

infectious diseases, especially duck plague; hence the need for a laboratory diagnosis (Hunter and Wobeser 1980, Wobeser 1997a, Friend and Franson 1999). A complete diagnosis typically involves obtaining a complete carcass. Blood smears from infected birds (either dead or dying) show huge numbers of bacteria; presumptive evidence of avian cholera is possible when these show bipolar staining, but conclusive diagnosis must be based upon isolation and identification of *P. multocida* from heart blood, liver, bone marrow, or other tissues (Wobeser 1997a). However, Rocke et al. (2002) recently developed a serotype-specific PCR test for avian cholera. Further, properly obtained and stored (in liquid nitrogen) swab samples from the cloaca, eye, leg joint, or nasal and oral cavities of recently dead birds could detect carrier birds up to 14 weeks postinfection, a technique preferable to transporting whole carcasses for laboratory analysis (Samuel et al. 2003).

Epizootiology and Management of Avian Cholera: Despite decades of research, the epizootiology of cholera is still poorly known, which hampers management efforts. Biologists do know, however, that the disease is highly contagious and transmittable within wetland environments; both factors render containment difficult. As we have already discussed, the disease also kills quickly; hence, control must be implemented promptly to have any hope of thwarting an initial infection and thus averting an epizootic.

Environmental contamination from diseased birds is a major source of infection because an epizootic contaminates the water. A single infected Snow Goose, for example, can shed "massive" amounts of *P. multocida* in as little as 15 ml of nasal discharge (Friend and Franson 1999), and ingestion of contaminated water then becomes a mode of transmission. Quortrup et al. (1946), for example, found that healthy ducks placed near infected individuals died within 28 hr, when they had access to the same water. The bacteria also concentrate at the water's surface wherein air bubbles breaking at the air-water interface eject the bacteria into the atmosphere. These ejected droplets can harbor bacterial concentrations 10 to 10,000 times greater than those at the surface. Thus, concentrated waterfowl splashing at the surface may create bacteria-rich aerosols wherein the pathogen enters healthy birds through the mucous membranes of the pharynx or upper air passages (see Rosen and Morse 1959, Blanchard and Syzdek 1970, Friend and Franson 1999). The carcasses themselves are another source of *P. multocida* in the water (Price and Brand 1984). The disease also is transmitted by direct contact between infected and noninfected birds, or between carcasses and noninfected birds (Friend and Franson 1999). Hence, the close contact produced when large numbers of birds concentrate in small areas becomes a significant factor in spreading avian cholera. Smith and Higgins (1990) thus noted that loss of nearly 90% of the original wetlands in the Rainwater Basin of Nebraska contributed to the chronic presence of avian cholera in an area annually used by millions of waterfowl.

The role of "carrier" individuals is also significant in the transmission of avian cholera. Few tissue samples or nasal swabs taken from otherwise healthy but susceptible waterfowl yield positive indications of the pathogen, but perhaps a single carrier may ignite an epizootic under favorable conditions, such as winter concentrations of large flocks of waterfowl (Donahue and Olson 1969, Korschgen et al. 1978, Botzler 1991). Several species of wild and domestic mammals are carriers of cholera, but the serological types found in mammals do not commonly cause the disease in birds (Windingstad et al. 1988, Friend and Franson 1999, Wobeser 1997a). Scavenging birds, especially crows (*Corvus* spp.) and gulls, also have been suggested as carriers or reservoirs of avian cholera, as have American Coots (*Fulica americana*), but the role, if any, of these and other associates of waterfowl in the epizootiology of the disease remains uncertain (Vaught et al. 1967, Rosen 1971b, Zinkl et al. 1977, Taylor and Pence 1981).

Birds dying of avian cholera probably are a major source of new infections, and therefore early and vigorous collection and sanitary disposal of the carcasses offer the best opportunities to prevent an epizootic (Botzler 1991, Friend and Franson 1999). Ideally, carcasses are destroyed by burning, either in pits or portable incinerators (see Fig. 8-2). Carcasses that are buried without burning may harbor viable bacteria for long periods; Rosen and Bischoff (1950) reported that *P. multocida* survived in soil for as long as 4 months, although the bacteria in this instance had lost their virulence.

Other management practices are not specific for avian cholera. These include dispersing birds from areas where the disease has an enzootic history, either by harassment or by making the habitat unattractive (e.g., drawdown). Price et al. (1992) determined that the survival of *P. multocida* was enhanced where calcium and/or magnesium concentrations were high; hence, these chemicals might be monitored at sites with histories of avian cholera as a means of assessing the potential for future epizoot-

ics. There is evidence that nutritional stress may predispose birds to cholera, and that precipitation was related to outbreaks in California (see Botzler 1991). Smith et al. (1991) proposed that mycotoxins acquired by waterfowl feeding on waste corn predisposed birds to cholera by suppressing their immune systems during spring migration through the Rainwater Basin of Nebraska. However, none of the many causes proposed to trigger or predict a cholera outbreak have proven conclusive (see Botzler 1991, Friend and Franson 1999). Blanchong et al. (2006) found no association between water conditions and the risk of an avian cholera outbreak when they compared wetlands with and without histories of epizootics. However, where avian cholera did occur, concentrations of eutrophic nutrients (K, NO_3, PO_3) were positively correlated with the amount of *P. multocida* in the sediment and water column. Nonetheless, this study provided further support that wetland environments are not closely correlated with outbreaks of avian cholera (see Samuel et al. 2004).

At times, managers may consider eradicating waterfowl exposed to avian cholera, but this approach can be effective only on small numbers of birds in well-defined areas. Such measures have been attempted twice: once at Common Eider colonies and again on a flock of American Coots (Gershman et al. 1964, Pursglove et al. 1976). However, even this extreme response certainly does not guarantee containment of the disease. Moreover, wholesale elimination of local bird populations may seem indefensible or even irresponsible in the eyes of an emotional public, perhaps weakening broader support for other forms of waterfowl management. Finally, managers should avoid producing conditions (e.g., artificial feeding or maintaining ice-free water) that concentrate waterfowl unnaturally (e.g., Vaught et al. 1967); such practices are clearly questionable where avian cholera or other contagious diseases are enzootic. Despite such precautions, however, managers still lack effective means for preventing epizootics in the full range of situations where avian cholera strikes waterfowl. An effective vaccine for *P. multocida*, Serotype 1, is of limited utility for inoculating large numbers of wild birds, but it could prove useful when applied to local populations or endangered species (see Price 1985).

Duck Virus Enteritis (Duck Plague)

This infection, caused by a herpesvirus, is among the more recent diseases invading wild waterfowl in North America. Duck plague attacks the vascular system, causing hemorrhaging and death within 14 days of exposure. The disease is aptly named, as only ducks, geese, and swans are affected (American Coots, shorebirds, and other waterbirds are immune). Hence, duck plague should be suspected where only waterfowl exhibit mortality. The disease also differentially affects waterfowl. In an experimental study, for example, 300,000 times more virus was needed to infect Northern Pintails than Blue-winged Teal, which are the most susceptible species (see Wobeser 1997a, Friend and Franson 1999). Another study determined that duck plague virus, particularly the Lake Andes strain, was especially virulent to Blue-winged Teal, Wood Ducks, and Redheads, moderately virulent to Gadwalls but less so to Mallards, and least virulent to Northern Pintails (Spieker et al. 1996). Overall, the disease has been reported in some 40 species of waterfowl, 23 of which occur in North America (see Converse and Kidd 2001).

Figure 8-5. Waterfowl carcasses gathered for disposal following the first known epizootic of duck virus enteritis (or duck plague) in wild waterfowl in the United States. The outbreak occurred in 1973 at Lake Andes National Wildlife Refuge in South Dakota. Photo courtesy of Milton Friend, U.S. Geological Survey, National Wildlife Health Center.

Originally recognized in the Netherlands in 1923, and also occurring elsewhere in Europe and Asia (Jansen 1968), duck plague was first confirmed in North America in 1967 at a commercial Pekin Duck farm near Eastport, Long Island, New York, where efforts to contain the disease were unsuccessful (Leibovitz and Hwang 1968). The disease eventually killed about 1,100 commercial ducks and 100 wild ducks in Flanders Bay (mostly Mallards and American Black Ducks). The virus likely was imported into the United States in exotic ducks and geese. Since the initial outbreak, waterfowl deaths from duck plague have occurred across the United States and Canada, although most outbreaks still occur in domestic or captive flocks (Brand and Docherty 1984, Converse and Kidd 2001). From 1967 to 1995, for instance, 120 epizootics of duck plague were reported in the United States, but only five cases involved migratory waterfowl; the cumulative mortality during this 29-year period was <50,000 birds (Converse and Kidd 2001). Most deaths occurred during a 1973 epizootic among wild waterfowl at Lake Andes National Wildlife Refuge in South Dakota, where some 40,000 of 100,000 Mallards died, along with 350 Canada Geese — some 18–26% of the birds at risk (Fig. 8-5; Friend and Pearson 1974, Pearson and Cassidy 1997). Duck plague next reappeared as a substantial epizootic in wild waterfowl during February 1994 and killed about 1,200 Mallards and American Black Ducks on the Finger Lakes in central New York (Friend and Cross 1995). Hence, except for these two events, epizootics have involved small numbers of birds.

Waterfowl surviving initial duck plague infections may become carriers of the disease. Indeed, because of the persistency of the herpesvirus, otherwise healthy carrier birds can periodically shed pathogens in cloacal or oral discharges for as long as 4 years (Burgess et al. 1979). Unfortunately, the factors influencing either the shedding of the virus or the reactivation of the latent infections remain unknown. The disease occurs throughout the year, but most outbreaks take place from March through June (Converse and Kidd 2001).

Since the initial outbreak in 1967, several surveys searched for duck plague in resident and migratory waterfowl populations. The first was conducted in 1968 and did not detect duck plague antibodies in more than 3,000 waterfowl sampled from migratory and commercial flocks at 14 sites in 12 states (Walker et al. 1969). A second survey in 1982–83 sampled 3,169 migratory waterfowl from sites across the United States, as well as 1,033 birds from sites with recurrent duck plague outbreaks, and 590 from the Lake Andes National Wildlife Refuge, site of the largest epizootic — no duck plague was detected (Brand and Docherty 1984). These and other studies led to the conclusion that duck plague is not established as an enzootic (i.e., present) in North America. Nonetheless, during the Lake Andes epizootic, some 13–31% of 395 otherwise healthy Mallards tested positive for duck plague antibodies, which extrapolated to 14,000–34,000 carriers leaving the refuge (Pearson and Cassidy 1997). However, given only one epizootic (i.e., Finger Lakes in New York) since that time, many carriers apparently can be present in wild populations without prompting an epizootic. Still, duck plague persists in captive and domesticated flocks of ducks, especially Muscovy Ducks, Mallards, and American Black Ducks, which led Converse and Kidd (2001) to conclude that these populations represent a reservoir of the duck plague virus; hence, the disease still represents a dangerous threat to wild waterfowl that contact these flocks (Friend 1981b).

Waterfowl do not exhibit specific indications of duck plague infections. In general, signs of the disease include drooped wings accompanied by little or no flight, a discharge from the eyes that eventually may close the eyelids, reduced wariness, and diarrhea that may be bloody and stain the plumage about the cloaca. Blood commonly drips from the nares and mouths of infected birds. The penis of dead males, especially Mallards, may protrude from the cloaca. Dead birds often are found in grotesque positions, including those with arched necks so that their heads point downward; others have raised tails, with their heads and necks extended backward over their bodies, a posture indicating convulsions at the time of death (see Friend and Franson 1999).

Internal lesions vary according to the period of infection and among species; several birds thus should be examined for a presumptive diagnosis of duck plague. In general, the liver is marked by white, pinpoint lesions and may be enlarged. The spleen, often darkened, sometimes shows similar lesions. Hemorrhages are characteristic of duck plague infections; these may occur widely in the viscera, including the liver, heart, pancreas, bursa of Fabricius, esophagus, and intestines. Bloody fluid commonly accumulates inside the esophagus and intestines, which are the sources of drainage from the mouth, nares, and cloaca. In Mallards, hemorrhages in the lymphatic tissues characteristically produce dark bands around the intestines, whereas in Canada Geese the intestinal hemorrhages are associated with small disks of lymphoid tissues. Of all the lesions associated with duck plague, those of most diagnostic value are hemorrhagic or necrotic bands or disks within the intestines, copious blood in the digestive tract, and cheesy plaques in the esophagus and cloaca. Conclusive diagnosis requires isolation and identification of the herpesvirus under highly controlled laboratory conditions (Wobeser 1997a, Friend and Franson 1999).

Epizootiology and Management of Duck Plague: The occurrence of duck plague in North America follows the pattern of an emerging disease — the number of outbreaks is increasing each decade since the 1970s (Friend and Franson 1999, Converse and Kidd 2001). Control of duck plague must be aggressive. Birds that are otherwise healthy are the major reservoirs for the virus; hence, prompt and complete destruction of infected flocks, including eggs, is essential because survivors will become carriers (Friend and Franson 1999). Carcasses should be incinerated and the infected area decontaminated (e.g., by chlorination). A low-virulence vaccine has been developed for use in the domestic Pekin Duck, but has yet to prove reliable for other species of ducks and geese (Shawky and Sandhu 1997, Friend and Franson 1999). Feare (1998) recommended use of the vaccine as a preventative and to treat a developing epizootic. Lastly, because duck plague occurs in captive waterfowl such as Mallards, stocking programs should not release birds from flocks with a history of the disease. New techniques may allow detection of carriers in a given flock, which can then lead to prompt and aggressive control (see Hansen et al. 1999).

Lead Poisoning

Lead poisoning is a unique disease of waterfowl in being the only major affliction caused entirely by humans. The disease occurs when feeding waterfowl ingest lead pellets expended from shotgun shells. However, waterfowl managers were unusually slow to react to lead poisoning because, unlike the epizootics associated with avian cholera or botulism, lead poisoning often goes unnoticed. Afflicted individuals often take several weeks to succumb and, because individuals become weaker as the disease progresses, they often seek dense cover or are removed by predators and scavengers. Hence, lead-poisoned birds die singly or in small numbers, and few carcasses remain in evidence. At Catahoula Lake in Louisiana, Zwank et al. (1985) examined 854 moribund Mallards and Northern Pintails for the presence of lead shot in their gizzards and lead residues in their tissues (Zwank et al. 1985). The incidence of ingested lead shot was 69% for Mallards and 75% for Northern Pintails, and lead in liver samples for both species ranged from 86 to 131 ppm (20–30 ppm is suggestive of lead poisoning; Friend and Franson 1999). Moreover, the probability of death from lead poisoning was 76% for Mallards and 81% for Pintails, *yet no dead birds were reported.*

Hunters also may remove potentially lead-poisoned birds from the population. For example, Mallards experimentally dosed with one lead pellet were 1.5–2.3 times more vulnerable to hunters than lead-free birds (Bellrose 1959). In Missouri, Heitmeyer et al. (1993) reported that the proportion of hunter-killed Mallards containing ingested lead shot was 3.8 times greater than in Mallards collected by researchers. In Missouri and Minnesota, hunter-killed Canada Geese had elevated blood levels of lead compared with live-captured geese (DeStefano et al. 1995).

The first documented report of lead-poisoned ducks in the United States occurred in Texas in 1874, (Bowles 1908, McAtee 1908), but it remained for Bellrose (1959) to highlight the severity of the disease (see Infobox 8-2). He examined nearly 40,000 gizzards of waterfowl collected throughout the United States and in British Columbia for ingested lead pellets. The results were shocking: Lead occurred in 6.7% of the gizzards, which suggested the deaths of 1.6–2.4 million waterfowl, or 2–3% of the fall population, *each year*. Sanderson and Bellrose (1986) later updated these figures for ducks collected across North America between 1973 and 1984. Fully 8.9% of 171,697 gizzards contained lead shot, which indicated that up to *one-third* of the continental duck population may consume lead in a given year. Moreover, because many of these gizzards were examined manually, these results may underestimate the presence of pellets by 20–25% (Anderson and Havera 1985); later studies used X-rays, which were more accurate.

Bellrose (1959) also estimated that no less than 3,000 tons of lead shot were deposited in the wetlands of North America each year, and the number of spent pellets in some wetlands averaged 69,847/ha. A heavily hunted area on the Texas coast contained 1.6 million pellets/ha (Fisher et al. 1986). Ingestion of only a few pellets can cause death, and in some cases a single pellet proves lethal. However, because of species-specific variation in feeding ecology, not all waterfowl are equally vulnerable: The disease's frequency decreases with increasing specialization in food habits. Generally, bottom-feeding species such as Redheads, Canvasbacks, and Lesser Scaup have the highest rates of ingestion (12–28%), whereas Mallards, American Black Ducks, and Northern Pintails are intermediate (7–12%); most other ducks range from 1–3% (Bellrose 1959, Sanderson and Bellrose 1986). Several other factors influence the threat of lead poisoning. These include water depth, firmness of the bottom substrate, size of the pellets, ice cover, and time of year (Bellrose 1959).

Hunting pressure also is a significant local factor, especially on those wetlands with a history of shooting from long-established duck blinds. Blinds often are located near feeding areas and, after years of shooting, pellets may accumulate exactly where they are most likely to be ingested. In any case, many areas have become "hot spots" for lead poisoning because of long-standing hunting pressure.

Lead poisoning also can occur when waterfowl ingest lead sinkers used on fishing lines, as has long occurred among Mute Swans on the River Thames in England (see Simpson et al. 1979, Sears 1988). Lead caused 24% of all mortality among swans on the Thames in 1987 and 16% in 1988; however, the 1983–88 mortality rate was reduced by 70% following a 1987 ban on the larger lead sinkers (see Sears 1989). Elevated blood lead levels were reduced from occurring in 84–89% of swans sampled from 1983 to 1986, to 44% in 1987, to 24% in 1988, although elevated levels still occur in many swans (Perrins et al. 2003). In the western United States, lead sinkers have killed Trumpeter Swans (Blus et al. 1989). Lead sinkers are also a significant mortality factor of Common Loons (*Gavia immer*). For example, lead sinkers caused 21% of the deaths of Common Loons necropsied between 1972 and 1999 in New York State (Stone and Okoniewski 2001). Such mortality among loons has produced a call for nontoxic substitutes (see Pokras and Chafel 1992, Twiss and Thomas 1998).

Lead-poisoned waterfowl also can cause secondary poisoning in birds of prey that scavenge dead birds or prey on weakened birds, and location of such individuals can be very rapid. In the Fraser River Delta of British Columbia, for instance, all but 2 of 54 Mallard carcasses experimentally placed in agricultural fields were discovered by scavenging birds, especially Bald Eagles (*Haliaeetus leucocephalus*) and Northwestern Crows (*Corvus caurinus*), and 78% were discovered within 24 hr (Peterson et al. 2001). Indeed, secondary lead poisoning in Bald Eagles is well known in North America and was a major factor leading to the ban of lead shot for waterfowl hunting in the United States (see Pattee and Hennes 1983, Feierabend and Myers 1984, Cohn 1985). However, despite the ban, lead is still present in the tissues of Bald Eagles and causes mortality, although the incidence is slowly declining (see Wayland et al. 1999, 2003). In Spain, secondary lead poisoning has impacted the globally endangered Spanish Imperial Eagle (*Aquila adalberti*), as evidenced by lead shot

Infobox 8-2

Frank C. Bellrose
Eminent Waterfowl Biologist
(1916–2005)

Beginning in 1938, Bellrose spent his long career entirely with the Illinois Natural History Survey. Essentially all of his research was devoted to a better understanding of waterfowl and to the conservation and management of wetland habitat. Few others, if any, were better known or more respected as a waterfowl biologist — and as a kind and genteel human — than Frank Bellrose.

Wood ducks were his primary focus from his earliest days on the job and resulted in the development of nest boxes to overcome the loss of natural cavities where the birds otherwise nested. Because of these efforts, thousands of nest boxes eventually were erected throughout the breeding range of wood ducks — a pro-

gram crucial to stemming their declining numbers and the mainstay of their eventual recovery. During the early years of his career, Bellrose also studied the ecology of important waterfowl food plants and, with J. B. Low, he initiated the concepts and applications of moist-soil management. Meanwhile, his expert testimony was instrumental in halting dam and drainage projects that would ruin prime waterfowl habitat in the Illinois River Valley; this was the first of many other challenges to wetland destruction in which Bellrose would participate in the decades to follow.

Bellrose was among the first to conduct serious studies of lead poisoning, and these led to a land-mark publication on the subject in 1959. From his earliest

days in the field, Bellrose and his colleagues banded thousands of ducks and examined thousands more bagged by hunters and dead from disease. In 1961, these data resulted in another major publication, *Sex Ratios and Age Ratios in North American Ducks*. He also conducted pioneering studies of waterfowl migrations using radar, which allowed accurate tracking around-the-clock. This research produced important refinements of waterfowl movements within and between flyways and established migration corridors as a new concept for management.

In 1976 (revised in 1980), Bellrose completed a new version of the classic, *Ducks, Geese, and Swans of North America,* which remains a primary source of life-history information; he was completing a newer edition at the time of his death. A monumental work, *The Ecology and Management of the Wood Duck* (1994, with D. J. Holm), provided a capstone for his half century of experience with the species. When he retired after 53 years of service, the Illinois Natural History Survey named a research center in his honor, as were wetland conservation areas in the United States and Canada. He was the recipient of two honorary doctorates. Frank Bellrose received the Leopold Award from The Wildlife Society in 1985. Photo courtesy of the Illinois Natural History Survey.

---

in 11% of regurgitated pellets (Mateo et al. 2001). In 1991, as many as 52 Greater Flamingos (*Phoenicopterus ruber roseus*) succumbed to lead poisoning at the Doñana National Park in southwest Spain (Ramo et al. 1992). In eastern Spain during fall and winter 1992–93 and 1993–94, 106 lead-poisoned Greater Flamingos were found dead or moribund in the wetlands of El Fondo and the Salinas de Santa Pola (Mateo et al. 1997). The effects of lead poisoning also can be sublethal yet predispose birds to other forms of mortality. In Great Britain, for example, Perrins and Sears (1991) hypothesized that the large number of Mute Swan collisions with overhead wires may be linked to high levels of lead poisoning and the subsequent impairment of the neuro-muscular system. Body mass of lead-poisoned pochards was lighter than that of unexposed birds, which has clear ramifications for survival (Hohman et al. 1985, Havera et al. 1992). For example, winter survival estimates for immature Canvasbacks in Louisiana were lower among those exposed to lead (0.569–0.747) compared to unexposed birds (0.815–0.923; Hohman et al. 1985). On the Yukon-Kuskokwim Delta in Alaska, female Spectacled Eiders (federally listed as a threatened species) exposed to lead survived at a much lower rate (0.44) than unexposed females (0.78), wherein Grand et al. (1998) suggested that lead poisoning was prohibiting recovery of some local populations. Some 20% of females sampled had blood lead levels at or exceeding 0.5 ppm wet weight (Franson et al. 1998).

In waterfowl, diet is probably the single most significant factor affecting the level of toxicity from ingested lead pellets (Jordan and Bellrose 1951); lead does not become toxic until it erodes in the gizzard and then enters the bloodstream. Hence, waterfowl feeding on hard foods, particularly corn, experience the highest levels of toxicity; such foods require increased grinding in the gizzard wherein lead pellets are crushed efficiently when mixed with corn or other hard seeds. Conversely, the risk of lead poisoning is reduced when waterfowl feed on softer foods or those high in protein and calcium (Jordan and Bellrose 1951, Longcore et al. 1974). Protein and calcium apparently reduce the absorption of lead in the gastrointestinal tract and also lower the toxicity of lead that is absorbed into the bloodstream (see Sanderson and Bellrose 1986).

The field signs of lead poisoning include birds that are reluctant to fly when approached and later develop drooped wings. An abundance of bile-stained droppings in an area is also a warning sign of lead poisoning (Friend and Franson 1999). As the disease advances, infected individuals become severely emaciated, and the vent is stained with bright green diarrhea; impacted food in the esophagus or proventriculus occurs in about 20–30% of the infected birds. Internally, lead-poisoned birds have enlarged dark or bright green gall bladders often filled with bile, a green-stained gizzard, severely reduced breast muscles which expose the sternum ("hatchet-breast"), and reduced or absent visceral fat (Friend and Franson 1999; Fig. 8-6).

Positive diagnosis of lead poisoning involves these clinical signs as well as laboratory analysis. To begin with, soluble lead is quickly absorbed into the bloodstream where it appears almost immediately in bones, the liver, and kidneys. A blood level of 0.5 ppm lead is considered toxic but sublethal (Sanderson and Bellrose 1986); 40 ppm protoporphyrin in the blood is another indicator of lead poisoning (Roscoe et al. 1979; see also Sanderson and Bellrose 1986 for

Figure 8-6. Waterfowl suffering from lead poisoning typically experience starvation prior to death. Hence, an exposed sternum as shown here — known as "hatchet breast" — often is associated with lead poisoning. Photo courtesy of Milton Friend, U.S. Geological Survey, National Wildlife Health Center.

other diagnostic techniques). A lead level of 20–30 ppm dry weight in the liver is suggestive of lead poisoning when other signs are present (Friend and Franson 1999).

Epizootiology and Management of Lead Poisoning: Lead poisoning may be managed in some situations by tilling the soil in front of duck blinds. Fredrickson et al. (1977) decreased the number of pellets in the top 5 cm of soil by 21% with a tractor-drawn disk. In Louisiana, tillage of experimental plots seeded with size 4 lead shot resulted in movement of 60–75% of shot to depths below 20 cm and 95–97% below 10 cm (Peters 1992). However, disking is possible only where wetlands can be drained sufficiently to allow access of farm machinery.

In severely affected areas, waterfowl can be discouraged with scare devices or by draining wetlands during times of large concentrations. At Catahoula Lake in Louisiana, drawdowns are conducted during summer to encourage production of moist-soil plants attractive to wintering waterfowl. However, to reduce the availability of lead shot, the area is not usually flooded until about 10 days before the hunting season. Dead birds should be promptly removed, if for no other reason than to help prevent botulism epizootics and reduce secondary poisoning of raptors (see above). Overall, however, habitat management has not been effective in reducing lead poisoning.

The substitution of steel or other kinds of nontoxic shot for lead seemed to be the long-term solution to lead poisoning. Initial proposals by the U.S. Fish and Wildlife Service to require steel shot for waterfowl hunting were met with strong and often emotional rebuttals (U.S. Fish and Wildlife Service 1976). These arguments largely focused on the idea that steel would cripple more ducks than lead because steel is less dense, but this shortcoming — if indeed real — can be negated when hunters use a larger size of steel shot (e.g., use size 4 steel instead of size 6 lead). In 15 subsequent studies comparing steel with lead shot, there were no statistically significant differences in crippling rates in all but three tests (Sanderson and Bellrose 1986). Most of these were "blind" tests (i.e., hunters in the tests did not know whether they were shooting lead or steel shot). Thus, Sanderson and Bellrose (1986) concluded that crippling losses will not increase given the proper use of steel shot by responsible hunters who accordingly adjust their shot size and shooting habits (i.e., shoot within reasonable ranges).

Overall, any increases in crippling loss from steel are much less harmful than the combined damage of crippling losses and lead poisoning resulting from the continued use of lead shot. In response, several states declared lead shot illegal for waterfowl hunting at selected locations; others adopted statewide prohibition. Nebraska was the first to do so, requiring the statewide use of steel shot beginning with the 1985 waterfowl season. The Secretary of the Interior subsequently announced that lead shot would be illegal for all waterfowl hunting in the United States starting with the 1991 season. This decision, although long overdue, nonetheless represented a major initiative for controlling a devastating disease — and a decisive step in waterfowl conservation. Steel shot has been the lead substitute of choice among manufacturers and waterfowl hunters, but other nontoxic substitutes are also in use, such as bismuth-tin, tungsten-nickel-iron (e.g., Heavi Shot TM, Ecomas), and several others with tungsten as a major component. Toxicity tests of these substitutes did not detect any adverse effects on experimentally dosed Mallards (see Mitchell et al. 2001, Brewer et al. 2003).

Since the 1991 ban, studies designed to evaluate the exposure of waterfowl to residual lead shot have yielded encouraging results. For example, at Catahoula Lake in Louisiana, a site with a long history of lead poisoning, the incidence of shot (lead or steel) in the gizzards of Canvasbacks and

Lesser Scaup was similar (34 and 38%) during the winters of 1987–88 compared with 1992–93, but the incidence of birds with lead was just 6% in 1992–93 compared with 27% in 1987–88 (Moore et al. 1998). Experiments with the settlement rates of lead shot in tundra wetlands led Flint (1998) to conclude that exposure to lead poisoning likely would occur for more than 3 years after lead shot was banned, but the studies in Louisiana and elsewhere nevertheless indicate occurrence of a clear decline in exposure.

At Lac Qui Parle Wildlife Management Area in Minnesota, where steel shot zones were established in 1980, the incidence of steel shot in the gizzards of Canada Geese increased from 38% in 1981–83 to 81% in 1986–88. Steel shot zones were established in 1978 at Swan Lake National Wildlife Refuge in Missouri, where the incidence of steel in Canada Goose gizzards was 19% in 1974, 46% in 1978–81, and 60% in 1986–88 (see DeStefano et al. 1995). DeStefano et al. (1995:505) thus concluded that, "use of nontoxic shot for hunting waterfowl is reducing the number of birds that would otherwise suffer lead poisoning," and that "with continued use of nontoxic shot, the incidence of lead poisoning should continue to decline with time." Samuel and Bowers (2000) reached the same conclusion during a study of lead exposure in American Black Ducks in Tennessee where the incidence of elevated blood lead had declined 44% from before (11.7%) to after (6.5%) the ban (1997–99). Lead exposure in adults was particularly reduced, from 14.3 to 5.3%.

In the most extensive study to date, Anderson et al. (2000) examined gizzards of 16,651 ducks harvested in the Mississippi Flyway and found dramatic reductions in the incidence of lead shot. The incidence of ingested pellets (lead or nontoxic) was 8.9% for Mallards, 12.7% for Ring-necked Ducks, 4.3% for scaups (*Aythya* spp.), and 9.7% for Canvasbacks. For those gizzards containing pellets, however, nontoxic shot comprised as much as 68% of all pellets in Mallards, 45% in Ring-necked Ducks, 44% in scaup, and 71% in Canvasbacks; the ingestion of two or more lead pellets declined by as much as 78%! The authors also estimated that nontoxic shot reduced Mallard mortality in the Mississippi Flyway by as much as 64%. Lastly, when these findings were extrapolated to all flyways in North America for the 1997 season, the authors estimated that 1.4 million ducks may have been spared fatal lead poisoning. Hence, after more than a century, the scourge of lead poisoning may no longer pose a significant threat to waterfowl in North America.

The International Situation and Lead Shot: Elsewhere in North America, Canada had established steel shot zones in selected areas (Wendt and Kennedy 1991) and instituted a total ban on hunting waterfowl with lead shot in 1999. However, lead shot is still widely used to hunt waterfowl in Mexico. The only exception occurs on the Yucatan Peninsula, where a high incidence of lead shot in wintering waterfowl and a lead-induced die-off of Caribbean Flamingos (*Phoenicopterus ruber ruber*; Thompson et al. 1989, Schmitz et al. 1990) prompted a 1992 declaration of a steel shot zone for waterfowl hunting, the first such area in Mexico. Nonetheless, lead poisoning has been documented elsewhere in Mexico (Estabrooks 1987); hence needless death of waterfowl continues.

Lead shot in waterfowl is especially severe in areas of northern Europe and along the Mediterranean, where the incidence of lead in both wetlands and waterfowl is as high or higher than in the United States. At the Ebro Delta, a Ramsar site on the Mediterranean coast of Spain, lead shot in the upper 20 cm of sediments ranged from 8,900 to a high of 2,661,000 pellets/ha; the latter number is perhaps the highest incidence of lead pellets recorded in the world (Mateo et al. 1997). The incidence of lead shot in the gizzards of waterfowl was especially high in Tufted Ducks (80%), Northern Pintails (71%), and Common Pochards (69%). From these and other data, Mateo et al. (1997) estimated that some 16,270 ducks succumbed to lead poisoning, more than half the number harvested legally. Elsewhere in Spain, lead poisoning has affected two globally endangered species of waterfowl, the Marbled Duck and the White-headed Duck (Mateo et al. 2001). The incidence of ingested lead was 38% in Marbled Ducks and 50% in the White-headed Duck, while elevated lead levels in the liver (>5 ppm) occurred in 33% of the Marbled Teal and 50% of the White-headed Ducks. On 1 June 2001, however, Spain banned use of lead shot at all of its Ramsar sites.

In France, the Camargue is an important wintering site for waterfowl on the Rhone River Delta, but lead densities in the substrate can exceed 2 million/ha. Furthermore, more than 97% of the pellets remained in the first 6 cm of sediment and thus are available to waterfowl (Pain 1991). Ingestion rates of 10 species of wintering waterfowl averaged 27% and were highest for Common Pochard (60%), Mallards (45%), and Northern Shovelers (23%; Pain 1990). A high incidence of ingested lead also was reported in shorebirds and rails. The French government has proposed phasing out lead shot for waterfowl hunting by 2010.

In the United Kingdom, Mudge (1983) examined 2,683 gizzards from 24 species of waterfowl. The overall incidence of lead shot averaged 3.2%, with highest levels recorded for Tufted Duck (12%), Gadwall (12%), Common Pochard (10%), and Greylag Goose (7%). Potentially, 2.3% of the Mallard population died annually from lead poisoning. Liver lead levels were especially high in Bewick's Swans (91.5 ppm) and Greylag Geese (60.1 ppm).

Basically, lead and lead poisoning occur wherever waterfowl have been hunted with lead shot. In Italy, for example, lead occurred in the blood samples taken from every Mallard sampled during winter at Orbetello Lagoon in Tuscany (Tirelli et al. 1996). Several studies have documented lead poisoning among waterfowl in Japan (Ochiai et al. 1993, Ochiai et al. 1999), and elevated lead levels in waterfowl were recorded in Australia (Norman et al. 1993).

However, the global issue of lead poisoning in waterfowl and other waterbirds is clearly improving, and the future looks promising given the positive results of the lead shot ban in the United States. In an extensive review, Beintema (2001) determined the international scope of lead poisoning in waterbirds with a questionnaire sent to 137 countries, of which 74 responded. As of 2000, seven countries had instituted a total ban on lead shot (Canada, Denmark, Finland, The Netherlands, Norway, Switzerland, United States). Twelve countries have instituted partial bans (Australia, Belgium, Cyprus, Ghana, Israel, Japan, Latvia, Malaysia, Spain, Sweden, Russian Federation, South Africa); England has also banned lead shot but its use continues elsewhere in the United Kingdom (Wales, Scotland, Ireland).

Oil and Oil Spills

In the United States alone, some 53 million liters of oil from more than 10,000 accidental spills are released annually into aquatic habitats (Friend and Franson 1999). Oil spills have occurred in all 50 states and represent a potentially serious source of waterfowl mortality. Oil destroys the insulation properties of the plumage, thus death is usually caused by hypothermia (Fig. 8-7). Hunt (1961) determined that a single application of less than 1 g of oil per bird is enough to cause death from exposure. Oil-soaked waterfowl also die from the toxic effects of oil ingested when the birds preen their fouled plumage. Ducks oiled with 7.0 g of oil ingested about 1.5 g the first day, and after 8 days of preening consumed about

Figure 8-7. This King Eider was killed during an oil spill from the *M/V Citrus*, near St. Paul Island, Alaska, in 1996. Photo courtesy of Paul L. Flint, U.S. Geological Survey, Alaska Science Center.

half of all the oil on their plumage (Hartung and Hunt 1966). Maladies developing thereafter vary with the type of oil but include pancreatic atrophy, toxic nephrosis, lipid pneumonia, adrenocortical hyperplasia, and neural disruptions. Cold ambient temperatures, of course, magnify these effects, but oil spills cause mortality even in warmer regimes. Oiled ducks also usually stop feeding, which coupled with rapid increases in their metabolic rates to combat heat loss causes the birds to quickly exhaust their energy reserves so that starvation is accelerated (Hartung 1967). Thus, any oil spill may have some environmental consequences, but fortunately many spills are small and often do not kill numbers of waterfowl or attract much public fanfare. Nonetheless, the number of birds exposed to oil pollution is not necessarily correlated with the size of the spill; instead, the kill is more closely associated with the time of the year and the location of the oil spill (Perry et al. 1978).

Whereas oil-soaked birds most often are associated with grounded tankers (see following), other sources of oil may inflict serious damage. During winter, about 12,000 oil-soaked ducks died on the Detroit River where more than 60,500 liters of oil were dumped as industrial waste each day (Hunt and Cowan 1963). Drainage pits in oil fields also claim large numbers of ducks and other waterbirds that fatally mistake the sheen of the oil for water (Flickinger 1981). Such losses may be staggering, although they usually remain unheralded in the public media. For example, at a single pit in Texas, Flickinger and Bunck (1987) counted nearly 300 carcasses of birds, mostly ducks. These authors also cited work based on samples from 361 pits in southeastern New Mexico, which led to an estimated mortality of 225,000 birds per year on some 5,600 pits in the region. These estimates are conservative because carcasses sink, whereby only birds dead for 1–3 weeks remain visible long enough for counting. For waterfowl visiting arid regions where oil fields occur, these pits seemingly represent readily available wetlands; thus, birds in western flyways are especially vulnerable to this form of oiling.

Large spills in areas where waterfowl are concentrated can be disastrous. In 1967, tons of crude oil spilled when the *Torrey Canyon* sank off the Cornish coast of England, killing large numbers of aquatic birds, including waterfowl. That mishap initiated worldwide attention to the danger of large oil spills in aquatic environments, which was tragically relived when the *Exxon Valdez* — a supertanker laden with 1.26 million barrels of crude oil — ran aground in Prince William Sound, Alaska, on 24 March 1989 and spilled more than 260,000 barrels of oil (Piatt et al. 1990).

The *Exxon Valdez* spill has been extensively studied, which ironically provided biologists with significant information about the immediate and long-term effects of a major oil spill on aquatic birds. The overall spill eventually drifted over 300,000 km² of coastal and offshore water occupied by some one million marine birds, with the immediate impact of killing more than 30,000 birds of 90 species, 5.3% of which were sea ducks (Piatt et al. 1990). The total kill was extrapolated to be 100,000 to 300,000 birds. Long-term, some 40% of the oil was deposited in nearshore areas (Galt et al. 1991, Wolfe et al. 1994) and has continued to affect waterbirds, especially waterfowl. By 1995–98, for example, the population of Harlequin Ducks in the area of the spill still had not fully recovered, based in part on elevated cytochrome P450 levels, which indicated continued exposure to oil (Esler et al. 2002). Harlequin Ducks may be especially vulnerable because their benthic, nearshore foraging ecology exposed them to oil long after the initial spill. Adult female Harlequin Ducks in the same area experienced lower survival rates

(78%) in comparison with birds using non-oiled areas (84%; Esler et al. 2000). Recovery of Harlequin Duck populations in the Prince William Sound area is expected to take many years (Lanctot et al. 1999). Scoters, mergansers, and goldeneyes also recovered slowly from the spill, again likely because they use nearshore habitats for feeding activities (Lance et al. 2001).

Well-intentioned rescue efforts following oil spills receive considerable publicity, but in truth only a few birds are recovered for treatment, and of these, even fewer survive (Hay 1975). Although cleaning individual birds usually cannot be justified from the standpoint of population ecology, such efforts are desired by the public and may be warranted when threatened or endangered species are involved (Gullett 1987). Chemical dispersants often are used to manage oil spills, but chemically treated oil may decrease plumage insulation (Jenssen and Ekker 1991). Persons discovering oil spills should call the National Response Center at its 24-hr, toll-free number: (800) 424-8802.

Other Diseases, Parasites, and Chemical Toxins Affecting Waterfowl

Our intent has been to address diseases of waterfowl that are major causes of mortality, but there are many others. Further, an array of parasites and chemical toxins also affect waterfowl. We briefly mention these factors here, but readers should refer to Wobeser (1997a) and Friend and Franson (1999) for more details.

Friend and Franson (1999) categorized diseases affecting waterfowl into seven major groups: (1) bacterial, (2) fungal, (3) viral, (4) parasitic, (5) biotoxins, (6) chemical toxins, and (7) miscellaneous diseases. We have already mentioned two major bacterial diseases, botulism and cholera. However, because mortality from botulism is actually produced by the toxin produced by the bacteria, the disease is considered a biotoxin. Other bacterial diseases affecting waterfowl are avian tuberculosis and salmonellosis, although neither has caused significant mortality. Avian tuberculosis is caused by the bacterium *Mycobacterium avium*, of which only 3 of 20 types cause mortality in birds, but all avian species are susceptible to infection. Avian salmonellosis is caused by several bacteria in the genus *Salmonella*, and the resultant disease can also affect all species of birds.

Aspergillosis is a respiratory tract infection caused by fungi in the genus *Aspergillus*, of which *A. fumigatus* causes most infections in birds. The disease was described in 1813 and has caused serious losses of domestic birds in hatcheries, but aspergillosis also affects wild waterfowl, especially when they consume moldy grains such as corn. For example, aspergillosis killed about 1,000 Mallards in Colorado after they fed on moldy ensilage scattered on the snow (Neff 1955).

Among the viral diseases, we have discussed duck plague in depth, but avian influenza is another viral disease that commonly afflicts wild waterfowl, especially Mallards. The disease is caused by a group of viruses collectively known as Type A influenzas. Avian influenza is spread and maintained by fecal and oral routes. Avian influenza has not caused epizootics, but the disease is of long-standing concern to the poultry industry, which views wild birds as the source of infection. Type A influenzas do not infect humans, but managers should be aware of this disease to respond to public concerns.

Another viral disease of concern is the emergence of West Nile virus, which was introduced to the United States in New York City in 1999. By 2001, just 2 years after introduction, the disease had spread to 27 states and Ontario (McLean 2002b), and the disease is now as far west as Montana (Aune et al. 2003). West Nile virus is in the genus *Flavivirus*, for which birds are the principal vertebrate host. Maintenance of the virus requires transmission from infected mosquitoes to birds, although some bird species are not competent hosts for the virus. By 2003, the disease had been detected in at least 208 native and exotic species of birds in North America (see Marra et al. 2004). American Crows (*Corvus brachyrhynchos*) are especially affected and are also a competent reservoir for the virus; about 40,000 died in New York state alone from 2001 to 2002 (McLean 2002b). West Nile virus has been reported from at least 33 native and exotic species of waterfowl in North America (Center for Disease Control and Wildlife Health Lab) but the extent of mortality is unknown.

A long list of parasites and parasitic diseases affect waterfowl, several of which we mention here, but most can be placed into five general categories: (1) nematodes or roundworms, (2) cestodes or tapeworms, (3) trematodes or flukes, (4) acanthocephalans or thorny-headed worms, and (5) protozoans such as coccidians, malarias, trichomonads, and others (see Friend and Franson 1999:189).

Lastly, an impressive array of chemical toxins affect waterfowl and other birds. We earlier addressed lead shot and oil, but other important toxins include selenium, mercury, and cyanide, as well as the organophosphorus and carbamate pesticides. The effects of selenium are well documented in aquatic birds, causing malformations in both adults and embryos (Hoffman et al. 1988). Chlorinated hydrocarbon insecticides also can cause mortality or morbidity in waterfowl; of these, DDT is probably the most infamous. DDT and its sister compounds are no longer applied legally in the United States, but huge amounts are still manufactured for application in other countries. However, many other legally used herbicides and insecticides in this group are highly toxic to waterfowl and aquatic invertebrates (see Grue et al. 1989).

We present a few of the examples documenting the effects of toxins on waterfowl, but there are many in the literature. Aldrin-treated rice seed, for instance, killed more than 300 Lesser Snow Geese wintering on the Garwood Prairie in Texas (Flickinger 1979). In Missouri and elsewhere in the United States, Canada Geese, Brant, and other waterfowl have died after grazing on the turf of golf courses sprayed with the insecticide Diazinon (Zinkl et al. 1978, Vangilder et al. 1986). In the Ebro Delta of Spain, massive use of herbicides within the watershed likely eliminated macrophytes in the delta, and use of organophosphorus and carbamate pesticides has killed waterfowl directly and indirectly affected other organisms (Mañosa et al. 2001).

Other pesticides or herbicides, while not necessarily fatal for adult birds, may cause the death of embryos if the eggs are sufficiently exposed to these chemicals. Paraquat, for example, caused high mortality in Mallard embryos, even when this herbicide was applied at half the recommended rate (Hoffman and Eastin 1982). Overall, agricultural chemicals are so widely used that most waterfowl probably experience some degree of exposure. Indeed, the U.S. Fish and Wildlife Service lists toxicity estimates for more than 200 different pesticides that pose some risk to wildlife (Hudson et al. 1984). Waterfowl also have been contaminated with numerous kinds of industrial pollutants such as heavy metals (e.g., mercury), polychlorinated biphenyls (PCBs), and detergents (Krapu et al. 1973, Heinz 1976, Choules et al. 1978). Wood Duck reproduction was impaired in individuals using a wetland in Arkansas that had been contaminated by dioxins and furans (White and Seginak 1994).

Concluding Comments on Diseases

Diseases have long affected waterfowl populations, but diseases bring new challenges to managers in the 21st century: New pathogens emerge while old ones recur with increasing frequency and severity (Friend et al. 2001). Hence, diseases *must* weigh heavily in the framework of waterfowl management. As with human disease, early detection and action are often essential, especially in thwarting epizootics of botulism and avian cholera. Managers have successfully reduced lead poisoning, but new threats (e.g., IBDV) have emerged to cause significant mortality, with no known control measures. Worse yet are the unknown causes of mortality such as occurred during the winter of 2000–01 in New Jersey, when about 1,500 Atlantic Brant died from exposure to a pathogen that has remained unidentified, despite extensive investigation. These examples, coupled with recurring epizootics of well-known diseases, emphasize the challenges now facing managers and clearly call for monitoring and research that will enhance early detection and abatement.

Predation

Predation is among the more difficult sources of mortality to quantify and is clouded further by the fact that predators often take significant numbers of ducks that have been crippled by hunters. Hence, where studies of predation are conducted concurrently with hunting seasons, it can be difficult to assign an exact cause of death. However, recent studies using radiotelemetry or intensive observations now provide new information. We have addressed brood predation in Chapter 6; hence, our discussion here focuses on predation of postfledging birds.

On the Maine–New Brunswick border, for instance, 21 of 106 (20%) juvenile female American Black Ducks marked with radiotransmitters were killed by predators from late August to mid-December in 1985–87, of which 14 were killed by mammals or unknown predators, and seven by raptors (Longcore et al. 1991). The predators responsible were difficult to determine, but river otter (*Lutra canadensis*) and, especially, mink (*Mustela vison*) were the most likely mammalian predators, whereas the Great Horned Owl (*Bubo virginianus*) was the most frequent avian predator. Along the coast of Maine, American Black Ducks comprised 15% of the winter diets of Bald Eagles (*Haliaeetus leucocephalus*; Todd et al. 1982).

At the Wheeler National Wildlife Refuge in Alabama, only 2 of 82 radiomarked Wood Ducks were killed by predators during a 108-day postbreeding period between 15 August and 30 November (Th-

ompson and Baldassarre 1988). In Virginia and New Jersey, 38 of 227 (17%) female American Black Ducks radiomarked during winter were killed by nonhunting agents, but the probable cause could be determined in only 21 cases, of which 12 apparently were killed by raccoons (*Procyon lotor*) and red foxes (*Vulpes vulpes*; Conroy et al. 1989). However, much of the monitoring in this study occurred during the hunting season, wherein some deaths may have resulted when wounded, unretrieved birds later were killed by predators.

In the lower Mississippi River Valley, only 10 (4.5%) nonhunting mortalities occurred among 223 female Mallards radiomarked between 1980 and 1985 (Reinecke et al. 1987). Mammals were the most likely predators, but because six of the mortalities occurred during the hunting season, hunting (i.e., unretrieved cripples) again could not be ruled out as a contributing factor. Overall, the hunting mortality rate for all females (adults and immatures) was 5.4 times the rate of natural mortality during the hunting season and 2.4 times the natural mortality rate for the full duration of the winter period.

Predation by large fish such as northern pike (*Esox lucius*) and reptiles such as snapping turtles (*Chelydra serpentina*) does not seem important for fledged waterfowl, but on occasion these predators may claim significant numbers of ducklings (Solman 1945, Lagler 1956, Coulter 1957).

The Peregrine Falcon (*Falco peregrinus*) is widely regarded as a predator of ducks; hence, "duck hawk" has been a long-standing common name for the species. However, populations of Peregrine Falcons are small, and their overall impact on the mortality of fledged ducks is correspondingly small. For example, Peregrine Falcons migrating through Alberta successfully attacked only 25 ducks in more than 778 days of observations between 1969 and 1986 (Dekker 1987).

Bald Eagles commonly associate with winter concentrations of waterfowl, especially Canada Geese and Mallards. However, wintering eagles seldom prey on healthy waterfowl but instead feed mostly on dead or crippled birds (Griffin et al. 1982). The Northern Harrier (*Circus cyaneus*), while another potential avian predator of fledged ducks, seldom preys on healthy waterfowl (Tamisier 1976, Wishart et al. 1981).

Other Forms of Nonhunting Mortality

Disease and predation are the major nonhunting mortality factors affecting waterfowl populations.

However, other causes of mortality at times may produce significant losses, some of which may be controlled with management. Others are clearly "accidents" over which management has few options, and such accidents vary from the bizarre to those occurring more frequently.

In 1908, for example, what became locally known as the "swan disaster" occurred during a fog when about 100 Tundra Swans were swept over Niagara Falls (Fleming 1908); more recently, about 4,000 Common Mergansers and other ducks suffered the same fate (Bonfatti 1984). Waterfowl also become ensnared in monofilament lines discarded by fishermen or fatally entangled in the plastic loops from packages of canned beverages.

More frequently, power lines and even barbed wire in or near wetland habitat may kill or cripple significant numbers of waterfowl and other aquatic birds (Cornwell and Hochbaum 1971, Siegfried 1972, Krueger and Whyte 1978). For example, between May 1980 and September 1981, 1,804 ducks of 14 species were killed by striking a power transmission line extending over a single wetland in south-central Montana (Malcolm 1982). In England, overhead wires were the single most important cause of mortality (44%) for Mute Swans (Ogilvie 1967). Elsewhere in England, about 30% of a 90-bird flock of Mute Swans was electrocuted in just 2 months on a 0.4-km stretch of power line crossing their flight path (Harrison 1963). Perrins and Sears (1991) reported that collisions with wires were the cause of death in 22% of 11,105 Mute Swan band recoveries reported to the British Trust for Ornithology from 1958 to 1988. Using postmortem data from 366 dead swans recovered in Britain between 1951 and 1989, Brown et al. (1992) also reported that flying accidents were a major source of mortality among Mute, Bewick's, and Whooper Swans in Great Britain, causing 22% of deaths in adults and 23% in juveniles. At a power plant in Illinois, transmission lines crossing habitats used by thousands of waterfowl killed about 200 birds each year based on actual counts of carcasses; however, these probably represented only about half of the total mortality from collisions at the site (Anderson 1978).

In all, studies of waterfowl collisions implicate several factors: (1) poor visibility, either from inclement weather or darkness; (2) number of birds present; (3) behavior, either during migration, along daily flight paths, or during courtship flights; (4) familiarity of the birds with the area; and (5) disturbance, as when resting waterfowl are flushed suddenly by machinery or hunters. Some evidence also suggests

that certain species are more vulnerable to collisions; for example, on the same area, Blue-winged Teal experienced 0.549 casualties per 1000 bird-days of exposure to overhead wires, whereas the rate for Mallards was only 0.026 (Anderson 1978).

Management recommendations include (1) removing unused fences in waterfowl habitat, (2) planning less hazardous routes for new power lines that avoid wetlands where waterfowl concentrate or migrate, and (3) increasing the visibility of existing lines while also reducing disturbances of waterfowl near these areas. Control of these situations is important because the dead birds may initiate the maggot cycle associated with botulism (Malcolm 1982). Hence, regularly scheduled removal of carcasses may reduce the risk of epizootics in botulism-prone habitats crossed by power lines.

Waterfowl are also killed from collisions with vehicles, although the losses seem insignificant when compared with other causes of mortality. During a 1969–78 study in North Dakota, Sargeant (1981) estimated that 4,500 adult ducks were killed annually, which was less than 0.2% of the breeding population in the area.

Commercial fishing operations also cause mortality of waterfowl. McMahan and Fritz (1967) calculated that fishhooks on trotlines in the Laguna Madre of Texas might catch nearly 22,000 Redheads during a 3-month period each winter; of these, about 3,200 would die and another 7,400 would have poor chances of survival following their release. On Lake Okeechobee in Florida, commercial trotlines killed an estimated 7,458 Lesser Scaup, or about 8% of the average winter population present between November 1985 and March 1986; most (81%) were hooked in body parts other than the mouth (Turnbull et al. 1986; Fig. 8-8). Ducks also drown accidentally in gill nets set by commercial fishermen and, as might be expected, diving species are most susceptible. Mortality of this type has occurred in Canvasbacks and Redheads on Lake Winnipegosis in Manitoba (Bartonek 1965) and in Long-tailed Ducks or Oldsquaws on Lake Michigan (Peterson and Ellarson 1977).

Leghold traps set for furbearers also may claim waterfowl. During spring in the northeast United States, for example, traps set for muskrats (Ondatra zibethicus) may be an especially important cause of mortality for breeding American Black Ducks and Ring-necked Ducks (Wright 1954, Mendall 1958). In Maine, Gashwiler (1949) estimated that nearly 2,000 ducks were killed in muskrat traps during one season. During an extended muskrat trapping season

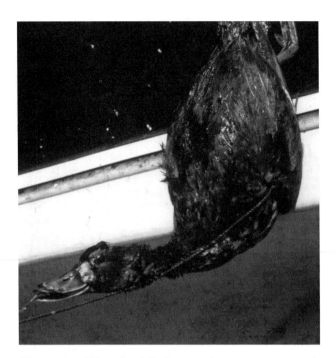

Figure 8-8. Waterfowl die from various causes associated with human activities. This Lesser Scaup was hooked on a trotline set by commercial fishermen on Lake Okeechobee, Florida. Photo courtesy of Richard E. Turnbull, Florida Game and Freshwater Fish Commission.

in Manitoba, Bailey and Jones (1976) recorded a loss of 3.8 female Mallards per 2.6 km², or 10.4% of the breeding population.

Soybeans sometimes cause fatal impactions in the esophagi of Canada Geese; the birds may die suddenly when the impactions are acute or slowly starve from chronic impactions (Durant 1956). These conditions occur when waterfowl eat dry soybeans, which then enlarge internally to more than twice their original size. Losses can be severe in some instances; Jarvis (1976) recorded an episode where nearly 20% of a local population of 3,100 Canada Geese succumbed from soybean impactions. Factors associated with soybean impaction included (1) the amount of precipitation falling before and during the feeding period; (2) availability of alternate, more preferred foods; and (3) migration schedules (Jarvis 1976).

The adversities of weather — drought, floods, storms, and unseasonable temperatures — also may cause mortality. In the north-central states, for example, the hail that often accompanies severe thunderstorms commonly kills waterfowl and other birds. Stout and Cornwell (1976) noted that inclement weather accounted for 7.4% of the nonhunting mortality experienced by waterfowl, with hail causing 93% of these losses. Most mortality from hail, however, befalls young birds still unable to fly; two hailstorms in July killed an estimated 64,120–148,360 waterfowl in Alberta (Smith and Webster 1955). Hochbaum (1955), however, reported an incident in which hail killed flying waterfowl, and a September storm accompanied by golf-ball-sized hail and 145 km/hr winds at the Chase Lake National Wildlife Refuge in North Dakota killed 36 ducks as well as 151 American White Pelicans (*Pelecanus erythrorhynchos*; Higgins and Johnson 1978). At times high winds also may kill waterfowl, but this is a comparatively rare event (Wooten 1954, Rate 1957). No less an observer than John James Audubon (1840) reported occasions when Canada Geese collided with lighthouses during snowstorms.

HUNTING MORTALITY

Humans have harvested waterfowl for more than 6,000 years (Alison 1978), but waterfowl hunting in the United States and Canada was not well regulated until passage of the Migratory Bird Treaty in 1916 (see Chapter 11). Not until 1952, however, did systematic efforts begin to determine the extent of the annual waterfowl harvest in North America. Today, hunting accounts for about 50% of the mortality waterfowl experience each year in North America (Bellrose 1980). Since 1952, the retrieved kill of ducks in the United States has ranged from a low of 4.3 million in 1962, to a high of 16.9 million in 1998 (U.S. Fish and Wildlife Service, unpublished data). Harvests generally vary in response to habitat conditions and population sizes in the Prairie Pothole Region because poor conditions result in low populations, which lead to restrictive harvest regulations and lower hunter participation. Hence, harvests (retrieved kill) were low during the drought years of the late 1950s and early 1960s (4.3–8.8 million), but — except for 1968 — increased from 1965 through 1984 (11.9–15.9 million). Harvest was again low in the late 1980s and early 1990s (5.0–8.6 million), but again increased from 1995 though 2003 (13.0–16.9 million). In 2003, the preliminary estimate of duck harvest in the United States reached 13.4 million, of which 5 million (37%) were Mallards. However, these and other harvest data do not include unretrieved kill or crippling loss, which averaged 18% from 1952 to 2001. Mallards by far comprise the bulk of the annual harvest (about 33%), followed by Wood Ducks (about 10%) and Green-winged Teal (about 10%). Total goose harvest in 2003 was 3.8 million, of which 2.9 million (76%) were Canada Geese. The harvest in Canada is always less than in the United States, and in 2001 was 1.4 million ducks and 1 million geese.

Estimating the Harvest

Traditional Surveys: Since 1952, the U.S. Fish and Wildlife Service estimated hunting mortality in the United States from an annual Waterfowl Harvest Survey. The survey consists of two separate parts, the first of which was, until recently, the Mail Questionnaire Survey. This survey selected a stratified random sample of U.S. post offices — about 4,000 of some 16,000 eligible sites — which issued a standard name and address form to each person who purchased a Duck Stamp. These persons were asked to send the completed form to the U.S Fish and Wildlife Service. The Service then contacted those returning the forms and sent them a questionnaire asking them to report on their hunting activity and success. Average harvest, unretrieved harvest (crippling loss), and number of hunts were estimated from these data. The response to this request has declined to about 30,000 in recent years, but response had averaged about 70,000. The U.S. Fish and Wildlife Service uses the data from the Mail Questionnaire Survey (provided by the U.S. Postal Service) to estimate total duck and goose harvest for each state and flyway. More details on these surveys are found in Martin and Carney (1977), Blohm (1989), and Trost (1989). In 2002, however, the Mail Questionnaire was replaced by the Harvest Information Program (see below).

The second part of the Waterfowl Harvest Survey is known as the Cooperative Parts Collection Survey, which began in 1961. This survey randomly selects a sample of successful hunters responding to the Mail Questionnaire Survey; these persons then are sent envelopes in which to return one wing from each duck harvested and the tail feathers from each goose harvested. Once received, the wings and tails are examined at "wing bees" — one for each flyway — in which the parts are categorized by species, sex, and age (Fig. 8-9). These data then are used in conjunction with the Mail Questionnaire Survey to determine the composition of the waterfowl harvest. In all, this part of the survey currently samples about 12,000 hunters who provide about 100,000 wings and tail feathers each year.

The Canadian Wildlife Service conducts similar surveys, but these did not begin until 1966, when a

Figure 8-9. Each year a cross section of hunters provides biologists with duck wings and goose tails which in part provide estimates of the annual waterfowl harvest. State and federal biologists in each flyway hold "wing bees" to identify the species, sex, and age of the samples. Photo courtesy of the U.S. Fish and Wildlife Service.

federal permit (also sold at post offices) was required for hunting migratory birds (Cooch et al. 1978). No formal surveys are conducted in Mexico, but other data indicate that the proportion of the continental waterfowl harvest occurring in Mexico is very small (Gustafson 1989, Migoya and Baldassarre 1993).

Migratory Bird Harvest Information Program (HIP): The HIP program was proposed by the International Association of Fish and Wildlife Agencies in 1990 as means to provide accurate and reliable information of hunter activity and harvest at both regional and national scales than was obtainable from the traditional harvest surveys. Previous federal surveys of migratory bird harvest only sampled hunters required to purchase a Duck Stamp; hence, those surveys could not obtain any data from the approximately 2 million hunters who only hunted nonwaterfowl species such as doves and American Woodcock (*Scolopax minor*), because these hunters were not required to purchase a duck stamp. In contrast, HIP requires registration to hunt *all* migratory birds: ducks, geese, swans, coots, brant, doves, American Woodcock, rails and gallinules (Rallidae), Wilson's Snipe (*Gallinago delicata*), Sandhill Cranes (*Grus canadensis*), and Band-tailed Pigeons (*Patagioenas fasciata*). Thus, HIP is a truly comprehensive approach toward assessing harvest of migratory birds at a national level.

HIP is a cooperative state–federal program. The state agencies collect the name, address, and other basic information from hunters registering to hunt, from which the U.S. Fish and Wildlife Service randomly selects a sample to whom they send a form to record the kind and number of migratory birds harvested during the current hunting season. A complete list of hunters in each state improves statistical validity of the data because it ensures sampling of all segments of the hunting population. These reports are then used by the U.S. Fish and Wildlife Service to develop estimates of total harvest of all migratory birds. Thus, the HIP waterfowl harvest survey serves the same function as the Mail Questionnaire Survey that HIP replaced in 2002.

To estimate waterfowl harvest, the U.S. Fish and Wildlife Service combines the total harvest estimated from the HIP surveys with the results of the Cooperative Parts Collection Survey. A simple example illustrates the process. Assume that HIP data determine the total duck harvest in a given state as 10,000 birds, and 30% of the wings from the Cooperative Parts Collection Survey are male Mallards and 20% are female Mallards. Total Mallard harvest for that state would thus be 3,000 males and 2,000 females, which could further by categorized by age classes (adult, immature).

The HIP program became fully operational in 1999, with all states participating, except Hawaii. HIP surveys were conducted concurrently with the Mail Questionnaire Survey from 1999 to 2001, after which the Mail Questionnaire Survey was discontinued. The HIP survey samples about 70,000 of the 1.5 million waterfowl hunters, 40,000 of 2 million dove hunters, 15,000 of 200,000 American Woodcock hunters, and about 15,000 hunters of coots, snipe, and rails. Ver Steeg and Elden (2002) contain an array of papers relative to the HIP program, and Richkus (2004) provides a good overall review.

Illegal Harvest

The harvest surveys conducted in the United States and Canada do not account for the illegal harvest of waterfowl, yet the numbers of birds involved in the latter may be substantial (Hall 1987). Gray and Kaminski (1989), after reviewing several studies of illegal waterfowl hunting, concluded that the incidence of violations among hunters ranged from about 14 to 66%. In descending order, the most common violations were (1) shooting outside legal hunting hours, (2) exceeding or attempting to exceed daily bag limits, (3) discarding harvested birds, (4) shoot-ing protected or nongame species, and (5) failing to retrieve downed birds. According to this review, the incidence of overharvest and other illegal hunting behavior was highly related to the opportunity to do so. Hence, among hunting parties presented with an opportunity to violate, 31% or more attempted to overharvest after reaching the legal bag limit. In Wisconsin, Jackson et al. (1979) interviewed 442 waterfowl hunters, of which 46% admitted to committing some form of violation. Again, the incidence of violations was greatest given the opportunity. For example, among hunters shooting no ducks during the hunting season, the violation rate was 12% compared to 28% for those shooting more than 20 ducks per season. Overall, violators shot an average of 18 ducks per season compared to 14 for nonviolators.

An extensive survey of conservation officers in Louisiana, Minnesota, and Wisconsin revealed hunting before or after hours, followed by bag-limit violations, as the two most serious violations out of a potential list of 19 (Hall et al. 1989). In Wisconsin, Jackson et al. (1979) linked waterfowl hunting violations to five major factors: (1) opportunity to violate, (2) hunting methods and intensity, (3) hunting conditions, (4) demographic relationships, and (5) hunter attitudes and ethics.

An extensive study of hunter behavior was conducted at the Delta Marsh in Manitoba, where Hochbaum and Walters (1984) used "spy blinds" to observe 61 parties of hunters. They found that hunters passed-up the opportunity to harvest ducks in 39 of 267 opportunities (14.6%) and rejected smaller species such as teal more often than larger species such as the Mallard ($r = 0.77$). Mean crippling loss was 36.7%. They also found, however, that the vulnerability of ducks to harvest was not related to the cumulative hunting effort but rather reflected the current hunting effort. Basically, harvest increased up to a point, but it stabilized and then declined as the addition of more hunters caused too much interference (e.g., shooting beyond an effective killing range, or "sky busting") and/or drove waterfowl from the area.

Overall, in a society where the role of sport hunting is coming under increased scrutiny, the policies associated with harvest of any species must be founded on the best scientific evidence currently available (see Heberlein 1991). The ethical and moral considerations of hunting are another matter and lie beyond our scope here, but biologists nonetheless must demonstrate that animal populations can withstand reasonable harvest if hunting is to continue as a legitimate use of the wildlife resource.

The "bookends" enclosing the issue of hunting mark points where, at one end, some animals will die each year regardless of whether the population is hunted, and at another end, where unregulated hunting inflicts disastrous slaughter. Regulated hunting and debate lie in the middle ground, however, where we shall focus our attention.

COMPENSATORY AND ADDITIVE MORTALITY

General Concepts

The concepts of compensatory and additive mortality are critical to discussion of waterfowl population dynamics. To begin, recall that wildlife management holds to the fundamental theory that most animal populations annually produce a "harvestable surplus," which can be intelligently harvested without adversely affecting the residual population. Underlying this theory is the premise that each species has an inherent rate of natural or nonhunting mortality, which means — assuming stable habitat conditions and other environmental factors — that the population will suffer annual losses of the same average magnitude regardless of *how* the deaths occur. Mortality resulting from hunting therefore is offset by a corresponding decrease in deaths from nonhunting mortality, wherein total mortality accordingly remains unchanged; hence, the term "compensatory mortality" (Fig. 8-10).

However, the hypothesis of compensatory mortality explicitly acknowledges presence of a threshold point where additional hunting mortality indeed begins to increase total mortality. At the extreme, hunting mortality equals total mortality. In summary, compensatory mortality proposes that hunting deaths — up to some point — replace deaths from other causes; hence, total mortality does not increase beyond the losses that would occur in the absence of hunting.

Errington (1945) — among the first to investigate the compensatory mortality hypothesis — studied Northern Bobwhite (*Colinus virginianus*) in habitats where winter conditions affected survival. Thus, when autumn populations exceeded the winter "carrying capacity," many birds died before spring from predation, diseases, and other natural causes. These individuals represented a "doomed surplus," which suggested that autumn hunting merely removed those animals that would have died anyway. Errington's work also revealed an inverse relationship between spring population density and recruit-

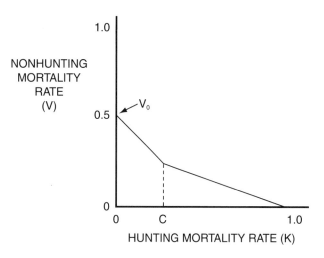

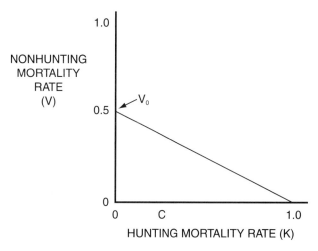

Figure 8-10. Diagrammatic representations between the rates of nonhunting mortality and hunting mortality where the relationship is compensatory (*top*) and additive (*bottom*). C = the threshold point where hunting mortality becomes additive, V_0 = the nonhunting mortality rate when the hunting mortality rate is 0. From Anderson and Burnham (1976:6, 9).

ment; hence, losses during winter also were compensated by increased natality during the breeding season. Many other studies have since provided evidence for compensatory mortality and natality in a variety of vertebrate populations.

Relative to waterfowl, Geis (1963) proposed that hunting mortality did not replace any proportion of nonhunting mortality —that is, hunting *increased* total mortality — and thus represented "additive mortality." This argument was based on features particular to hunting a resident species in comparison to hunting a migratory species such as waterfowl. First, unlike resident species, waterfowl experience several months of continuous hunting pressure as they migrate southward. Moreover, as waterfowl move southward across state and provincial borders, they encounter new habitat conditions and several opening days — times when the zeal and numbers of hunters typically produce the highest harvest. Hence, the point of diminishing returns, where harvesting a resident species is no longer profitable in terms of hunter effort, does not operate as a self-regulating process in the case of waterfowl hunting. Secondly, waterfowl are relatively more vulnerable to hunting because they concentrate in specific types of habitat. Hunters therefore may locate and harvest waterfowl effectively even when populations are at diminished levels.

These arguments were complemented with analyses of banding data, which further indicated that hunting added to the other forms of mortality experienced by waterfowl. Geis (1963) thus inferred that hunting was a direct means of regulating the size of waterfowl populations. Other studies also suggested that hunting represented additive mortality (e.g., Martinson et al. 1968, Geis and Crissey 1969; Geis et al. 1969, 1971; Geis 1972a, 1972b), wherein the concept of additive mortality guided the management of waterfowl harvests in North America until the mid-1970s.

In 1976, however, a benchmark analysis of nearly 700,000 band recoveries from Mallards concluded that hunting mortality, at least *up to a threshold point*, indeed was compensatory and not additive to total mortality (Anderson and Burnham 1976; see Fig. 8-10). Additive mortality, according to this research, had been based on invalid methodologies associated with certain types of life tables (Hickey 1952) and the relative recovery rate used in the analysis of banding data (Geis et al. 1971). Anderson and Burnham (1976:43) thus concluded ". . . that the past 'evidence' for additive hunting mortalities in waterfowl is unsubstantiated." This work, although mathematically complex, produced a strong body of statistical evidence in support of compensatory mortality, and stimulated a substantial research effort into the compensatory mortality hypothesis.

Compensatory Mortality and Waterfowl (additional studies)

One way of examining the hypothesis was to compare the survival rates for ducks between years when hunting regulations were liberal compared with restrictive. If hunting mortality is indeed additive, the underlying idea of this approach is that survival rates will decrease in years when hunters are allowed to harvest more birds. Anderson and Burnham (1978) accordingly discovered that survival rates for Mallards differed by no more than 0.04% between years with restrictive compared to liberal hunting regulations. This finding then led to their conclusion that Mallards could not be "stockpiled," which means that restrictive hunting regulations would not increase the size of the breeding population of Mallards the following year.

Rogers et al. (1979) provided additional information in support of compensatory mortality with their comparison of Mallard survival rates during 3 years of restrictive regulations (1962, 1965, 1968) and 3 years of liberal regulations (1970, 1974, 1975). They too found that survival rates of Mallards, while varying, showed no evidence of being higher in years with restrictive regulations as reflected by lower harvest rates. In addition, the correlation between survival rate and harvest rate was not statistically significant for males ($r^2 = 0.009$) or females ($r^2 = 0.019$). These low correlations also clearly implied that other factors such as population size and habitat conditions — especially on breeding areas — affected mortality and natality (see Kaminski and Gluesing 1987, Raveling and Heitmeyer 1989). Several other studies were summarized by Nichols et al. (1984), who concluded that the bulk of the evidence for Mallards supported the compensatory mortality hypothesis, although the evidence was not as conclusive for females as for males. For example, Nichols and Hines (1983) determined that juvenile female Mallards experienced lower survival in years of high harvest, but this relationship did not occur for other sex and age classes.

In contrast, however, later work by Smith and Reynolds (1992) was the first analysis to thoroughly reject the compensatory mortality model for Mallards after comparing years of liberal harvest regulations (1979–84) compared with more restrictive regulations (1985–88). Indeed, their analysis suggested that harvest was additive for all sex and age classes in nearly all reference areas they examined, which led to the conclusion that harvest was additive some time during the 1979–89 period. Their results likely differed from pervious studies (i.e., Anderson and Burnham 1976), however, because each study examined different groups of years. Population levels, weather and habitat conditions, recruitment, regulations, and other factors differed between these time periods; hence, harvest may have been largely compensatory in the 1960s and 1970s, but not during the 1980s. Overall, the findings of Smith and Reynolds (1992) suggested that restrictive regulations may best benefit Mallard populations during years of low recruitment and population size.

These findings were refuted by Sedinger and Rexstad (1994), however, who reexamined the data for relationships between survival rates and both harvest and population size. Their analysis reported that a model relating Mallard survival to population size performed almost as well as one relating survival to harvest, which suggested that density-related mortality was as viable a hypothesis as hunting mortality for explaining temporal patterns in survival. In other words, because Mallard populations declined between 1979 and 1988, fewer birds were available to use existing habitat, which may have enhanced physiological condition and survival; hence, the potential cause of higher survival rates observed by Smith and Reynolds (1992). However, Smith and Reynolds (1994) countered that the hunting model was a better fit to the historical data available and thus the most appropriate approach.

Other important datasets in the compensatory mortality debate stem from studies of the American Black Duck, which is largely restricted to northeastern North America. Krementz et al. (1988) recorded higher survival rates for males and immature female American Black Ducks in years with restrictive regulations, after examining data from 1950 to 1983, and suggested that hunting mortality was additive for immature males and adult females. Francis et al. (1998) also addressed the effect of restrictive harvest regulations on survival and recovery of American Black Ducks by comparing data among three periods of increasingly restrictive harvest regulations (1950–56, 1967–82, and 1983–93) implemented in response to the then long-term decline of the American Black Duck population. Between the first and second period, direct recovery rates declined for at least one age class within four of six reference banding areas, with a mean decline of 14% for adults and 7% for immatures. Between the second and third periods, however, direct recovery rates declined in all six reference areas — 37% for adults and 27% for immatures. Estimated mean survival rates especially increased between the first and second periods, which was consistent with a model of additive mortality. However, there was limited evidence for increased survival between the second and third periods, despite a much greater decrease in recovery rates. Indeed, the analysis of adults rejected the hypothesis of additive mortality, which suggests that harvest was not associated with survival rate, perhaps because harvest rates had declined over time.

Hence, hunting mortality rate may have dropped below a threshold point which then permitted compensatory mortality to operate, but shortcomings in the dataset rendered explanatory conclusions equivocal. In particular, banding data are observational compared with experimental, which can provide only limited information to guide management (see also Nichols 1991).

Survival rates for other species have been similarly compared, but the results were inconclusive for Wood Ducks (Johnson et al. 1986), Canvasbacks (Nichols and Haramis 1980a), and Ring-necked Ducks (Conroy and Eberhardt 1983), largely because sample sizes were too small for powerful statistical inferences. Other examinations of compensatory mortality in waterfowl populations (e.g., Nichols and Hines 1983, Burnham and Anderson 1984, Trost 1987) have not produced consistent results. Accordingly, the question lingers as to whether harvest can reduce waterfowl populations below levels that would occur under less hunting pressure.

Hence, despite major research efforts spanning some 30 years, most biologists admit that the relationships among hunting regulations, hunting mortality, and population size are still not well understood. Even when survival rates for waterfowl are higher during years of restrictive regulations, just how — or if — the harvest is related to population dynamics is much less clear. Part of this difficulty occurs because most studies of compensatory mortality have necessarily tested only the relationship between total annual mortality and hunting mortality (Krementz et al. 1988), whereas myriad factors such as breeding population size, habitat conditions, and recruitment all interact with harvest to determine subsequent population size in a given year.

Still another difficulty surrounding the hypothesis of compensatory mortality in waterfowl concerns the premise that nonhunting mortality functions in a density-dependent manner (at least during some part of the year), wherein mortality rate increases with population size. However, Murray (1979, 1982) has suggested that nonhunting mortality rates of vertebrates in general *are not* a direct function of population densities (Fig. 8-11). Instead, individuals may survive at a constant rate when the population is at some low or intermediate density relative to habitat conditions, although survival rates will decline at higher densities when resources become limiting. If this relationship is true, compensatory mortality might not occur until the population reaches some upper level of density relative to current habitat conditions.

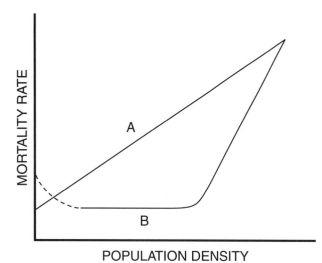

Figure 8-11. A hypothetical explanation of population mortality, which assumes that density-dependent mortality is the cause of compensatory mortality. If so, nonhunting mortality would increase directly with increasing population density (line A). Alternatively, nonhunting mortality may be constant until some point is reached in population density, and thereafter increases rapidly (line B). From Murray (1982) as redrawn by Kautz and Malecki (1990:14).

As noted earlier, animal populations also may experience density-dependent natality. Based on immature-adult age ratios in the harvest, Kaminski and Gluesing (1987) concluded that the Mallard recruitment rate in south-central Saskatchewan was correlated negatively ($r = -0.59$) with the population size in May, thus suggesting density-dependent natality. Recruitment rate also was correlated positively ($r = 0.51$) to mean numbers of May and July ponds present, which indicated that habitat conditions on breeding areas were more important to Mallard recruitment than winter habitat conditions. In the case of Northern Pintails, however, recruitment proved uncorrelated with the number of July ponds present when populations were above average, although the correlation proved positive ($r = 0.72$) when populations were low (Raveling and Heitmeyer 1989). From these studies, it would appear that compensation is likely at certain levels of population density and habitat conditions. Conversely, compensatory natality may not occur (or be limited) at high population densities, when high rates of harvest prevail, or when habitat conditions are poor, especially on breeding areas. Such conclusions, however, are based on correlations, which do not allow strong inferences of cause and effect, but the results do provide useful

perspectives on the complexity of population dynamics in general and the issue of compensatory mortality in particular.

In New York, an experimental study of four populations of feral Rock Doves (*Columbia livia*), each harvested at different rates, offered some interesting insights into the question of compensation (Kautz and Malecki 1990). The study found that at various rates of harvest (18–39%), increased natality was the main mechanism for recovery of population size. Overall, however, the population declined once harvest exceeded 35%. Relative to the continental population of Mallards, hunters have removed about 25% of the fall population in some years, although the fraction of deaths associated with hunting varies from year to year, area to area, and by sex and age (Martin and Carney 1977). At the upper extreme, hunting may account for nearly 50% of all Mallard deaths. Hence, with such high levels of harvest, the threshold point may be exceeded and hunting mortality then may be additive (Anderson and Burnham 1976). However, despite their exhaustive analysis of the largest set of banding data available for any migratory bird, Anderson and Burnham (1976:41) remarked, "We can barely speculate regarding the threshold point for Mallards," and "Whatever this point is, it may be easy to exceed on the breeding grounds or on areas where the birds may be particularly vulnerable." Thus, although some biologists may accept compensatory mortality as fact, the issue remains highly complex, especially in relation to the threshold point where hunting mortality becomes additive.

These ambiguities suggested to Conroy and Krementz (1990) that completely compensatory and additive mortality represented two extremes, and that density-dependent mortality might be so weakly developed in waterfowl that complete compensation of hunting losses was unlikely. Remember, the compensatory hypothesis states that, at least up to a threshold point, deaths from hunting are offset, *one for one*, by a reduction in deaths from nonhunting mortality. Thus, a partially compensatory hypothesis might better describe the actual situation.

From the discussions above, it seems clear that various segments of the Mallard population may experience compensatory mortality, whereas additive mortality occurs in others. The results vary by time and location. As noted earlier, an analysis of data collected after the work of Anderson and Burnham (1976) was completed thoroughly rejected the influence of compensatory mortality in Mallard populations, likely because other factors such as population size, recruitment, and hunting regulations differed between the years covered by the two studies (Smith and Reynolds 1992). Thus, a population may at times lack much ability to compensate for hunting mortality (Conroy and Krementz 1990).

Conroy and Krementz (1990) proposed that waterfowl biologists may be no closer to reaching conclusions about compensatory mortality after nearly 30 years of investigation, in part because they may be asking the wrong questions. As presented above, population size interacts with several mortality factors and complex habitat conditions, all of which may vary each year; hence, the threshold point where hunting mortality becomes additive also is not fixed. Indeed, as Anderson and Burnham (1976) pointed out in their pioneering research, the threshold where hunting mortality becomes additive is probably less a point on a graph than it is a region. What subsequent research may have revealed is that the region is broad and varies temporally, spatially, and by subpopulations as well as by sex and age classes. Thus, when habitat conditions are poor and recruitment is low, populations may exhibit little ability for compensation, and hunting mortality quickly may become additive. Conversely, when populations are high and habitat conditions are excellent, compensation may be high and the threshold point reached much later. Lynch (1984) presents a colorful and perceptive viewpoint on these relationships.

Hence, after reviewing the effects of hunting on American Black Ducks, Conroy and Krementz (1990) raised two key questions regarding compensatory mortality: (1) How resilient is a given species to changes in hunting pressure; and (2) to what degree is that resilience subject to temporal, spatial, and demographic factors. As Krementz et al. (1988:225) summarized the issue, ". . . managing Black Ducks under the assumption that compensatory mortality occurs for all sex–age classes, at all times, and in all locations *may lead to over-harvest of populations in certain major reference areas*" (emphasis added). Caswell et al. (1985) similarly concluded that it was unwise to manage the continental Mallard population under the assumption of compensatory mortality. Furthermore, until additional data are available, it is unsafe to assume that populations of other species behave in the same fashion as Mallards with respect to compensation (Nichols et al. 1984). Canada Geese, for example, exhibit rather low rates of natural mortality and accordingly lack much leeway for the influence of compensatory mortality (Rexstad 1992).

Spatial and Temporal Variation

Compensatory mortality may be especially absent in local duck populations in which heavy hunting mortality occurs before the onset of autumn migration. If mortality of this kind regularly occurs over a broad area, duck populations will decline as hunting steadily eliminates those females that would otherwise return to the same breeding areas the following year (see Chapter 3). For example, on the 980-ha Shepody National Wildlife Area in New Brunswick, survival rates of juvenile American Black Ducks declined 43–54% over the first 2 weeks of the hunting season; some 81–85% of all hunting mortality occurred on opening day (Parker 1991). Caswell et al. (1985) determined that survival rates of Mallards increased 12.5% for adult males and 24.1% for adult females on local hunting areas in southern Manitoba during years of restrictive compared to liberal harvest regulations, but there were no differences for juveniles of either sex. The increase in female survival was attributed to the delayed opening of the hunting season, which allowed adult females to disperse from natal areas and/or attain better body condition. These females then can return to natal areas, which supports the idea that ducks could indeed be "stockpiled," at least locally. In Minnesota, an analysis of band recoveries during the 1950s indicated that hunting harvested 54–64% of the locally reared Mallards (Jessen 1970). Hochbaum (1947) argued this point nearly 40 years ago, referring to the consequences of excessive, early-season shooting as "burned out marshes" — an allusion not to fire-charred wetlands but to local overharvest. On a more widespread basis, Trauger and Stoudt (1978) argued that liberalized hunting regulations had restricted the recovery of Mallard populations in parts of Prairie Canada.

On yet a larger scale, an analysis of data originating from an area of more than 3,000,000 km^2 also indicated underutilized or vacant habitat; the area harbored some 78–84% of the breeding population of Mallards in North America, but use of the habitat was less in 1971–85 than in 1955–70 (Johnson and Shaffer 1987). Specifically, the mean correlation between Mallard numbers and May ponds for selected breeding areas was 0.47 from 1955 to 1970 but fell to 0.27 for 1971–85. However, the study did not address whether the decline resulted from increased mortality, decreased natality, or both. Nudds and Cole (1991), based on studies of waterfowl breeding in boreal forest habitat, concluded that the loss of breeding habitat was the major factor causing the decline of continental Mallard populations; the results for Lesser Scaup, however, were less clear.

Concluding Comments on Compensatory Mortality

The data available regarding compensatory mortality provide only a guide to harvest management. In essence, the answer to the question of whether hunting has reduced populations of Mallards and other waterfowl appears to be "no" most of the time, for most places, and with most populations. But the answer also has been "yes" at some times, and in some places and with some populations, especially local populations.

However, although waterfowl biologists have learned much from these research efforts, by the 1990s managers became increasingly frustrated by the uncertainty associated with biological processes and an inability to reach consensus on an appropriate harvest strategy in the face of that uncertainly (Williams et al. 2001:667). A new approach was needed, which arrived in the form of Adaptive Harvest Management, our next topic.

ADAPTIVE HARVEST MANAGEMENT (AHM)

AHM emerged from a broader concept — adaptive resource management — developed by Walters (1986) that can be defined a management in the face of uncertainty, with a focus on its reduction (Nichols et al. 1995, Williams and Johnson 1995). In brief, adaptive resource management acknowledges that the response of environmental systems to management actions cannot be predicted with certainty, and it provides a framework for making objective decisions in the face of that uncertainty. Adaptive resource management is based on an iterative cycle of monitoring, assessment, and decision-making to clarify the relationships between management actions and environmental responses. In 1995, the U.S. Fish and Wildlife Service applied this concept to the regulation of duck harvests in the United States using a process known as AHM, which is designed to account for the uncertainties in the response of waterfowl populations to various harvest regulations.

Prior to 1995, each year's harvest regulations were based primarily on current estimates of waterfowl numbers, so that legal harvests were liberal in those years when ducks and geese seemed abun-

dant, but were restrictive in years when populations dropped. Restrictive regulations might reduce the bag limit to, say, two Mallards per day during a 40-day season, whereas liberal regulations might allow a daily bag limit of four Mallards during a 55-day season. In effect, the regulations "chased" the yearly changes in population sizes (Williams and Johnson 1995). Despite the good intentions of these efforts, the process was filled with shortcomings, which are reflected in four sources of uncertainty that limit the ability of waterfowl managers to predict the impact of hunting on duck populations (Nichols 2000):

(1) *Environmental variation.* The uncertainty posed by yearly variations in the environmental conditions that influence waterfowl populations (e.g., yearly changes in the numbers of water-filled basins in the Prairie Pothole Region, which influences reproductive success).

(2) *Partial controllability.* The uncertainty resulting from the inability of managers to precisely predict or control harvest rates. Factors such as hunter effort (i.e., how many people will duck hunt each season and how often), the timing of migration, and weather, all affect harvest rates but cannot be regulated.

(3) *Partial observability.* The uncertainty resulting from the limited precision available from current methods used to estimate key attributes such as population size, reproduction, and harvest (i.e., sampling limitations and analytical biases limit precision).

(4) *Structural uncertainty.* The uncertainty resulting from the incomplete understanding by managers about the ways biological systems actually work and, in turn, respond to management. Structural uncertainties produce the most controversy among biologists, duck hunters, and others concerned with waterfowl conservation. The degree to which harvest mortality is additive or compensatory is a particularly nettlesome issue.

Instead of ignoring these uncertainties, AHM explicitly recognizes their existence and potential influences as part of the framework for making objective decisions about hunting regulations (Williams and Johnson 1995). Williams and Johnson (1995) list the major components of AHM:

(1) A limited number of regulatory alternatives for managing the annual waterfowl harvest in

each flyway. These are season lengths, bag limits, and framework dates, which delimit the beginning and ending dates within which hunting will be allowed (see below).

(2) A set of population models that describe each of the competing hypotheses about the effects of harvest and environmental conditions on waterfowl abundance.

(3) A measure of reliability ("weight") for each model.

(4) A mathematical description for the objective(s) of harvest management that allows comparisons of alternative regulatory strategies.

Since its implementation in the 1995–96 hunting season, AHM has focused on Mallard populations, which are test subjects for four competing models based on combinations of (1) additive versus compensatory harvest mortality, and (2) weak versus strong density-dependent reproductive success. Of the four combinations, the model reflecting the most conservative harvest strategy (leading to highly restrictive regulations) is represented by additive mortality coupled with weak density-dependent reproduction, whereas the most model reflecting the most liberal harvest strategy (leading to generous bag limits and season lengths) is represented by pairing compensatory mortality and strong density-dependent reproduction. The other two combinations lie between these extremes.

AHM is implemented by a three-step process (Johnson and Case 2000):

(1) Each year, managers select one regulatory alternative, which is optimal based on current environmental conditions (e.g., wetland conditions in the Prairie Pothole Region), the status of Mallard populations (e.g., estimated size of the spring breeding population), and the relative probability (model weight) currently assigned to each of the four models.

(2) Model-specific predictions then are determined for the size of the breeding population the following year (in effect, the population surviving the hunting season).

(3) In the following year, when current estimates of the breeding population size are available, the weight assigned to each model is updated, either increased or decreased, to reflect the relative ability of each to predict the estimated change in population size from the previous year (i.e., the extent of agreement between the predictions and population size). The new

weights are used to begin another iteration of the process, which is repeated annually as new survey data are added to the historical base.

Initially, each of the four models received equal weight (25%) and thereafter steadily evolves, as intended, to account for new knowledge. Those models that yield better predictions receive ever-larger weights. By 2003, the model weights for midcontinent Mallards strongly favored (91%) the weakly density-dependent reproductive hypothesis, whereas the evidence for additive mortality in this population remained more equivocal at 58% (U.S. Fish and Wildlife Service 2004b).

AHM is "adaptive" because the harvest strategy evolves to account for new knowledge produced by the comparisons of predicted and observed size of the breeding population. Managers in fact learn by following a structured testing process, instead of by trial and error, and then adjust each year's regulations accordingly, which should produce ever-better decisions (i.e., uncertainties are progressively lessened by repeated feedback). The process establishes a quantitative link between population data and hunting regulations, and it integrates research because more is learned about the workings of biological systems. Indeed, AHM encourages the integration of management and research into a single coordinated effort that reduces uncertainty and improves predictions (Lancia et al. 1996; see also Williams et al. 1996, Johnson et al. 2002).

AHM is still in its early stages of development. Midcontinent Mallards were selected initially because they are a heavily harvested population that is closely monitored, but managers also have developed interim models for the eastern and western segments of the North American Mallard population as well as for Northern Pintails, Canvasbacks, American Black Ducks, Wood Ducks, and a regional population of Canada Geese. Conversely, because adequate monitoring data are sparse, models for such species as scaup will require a different approach and thus are not yet available. In sum, AHM represents an objective means for setting hunting regulations that is designed to reduce uncertainty and thereby improve management performance.

WATERFOWL HARVEST MAMAGEMENT STRATEGIES

AHM provides the general guidance for harvest scenarios, ranging from very restrictive to very liberal, but specific techniques and tools bring about the objective of choice. Generally, harvest management uses a variety of specific techniques, each seeking to control the size, distribution, and composition of the harvest, but other objectives also are associated with hunting regulations (Table 8-3).

The legal authority of federal and provincial governments to regulate hunting of migratory birds in North America is rooted in the Migratory Bird Treaty of 1916 (see Chapter 11). Provisions in the Treaty empower the federal governments of Canada and the United States to establish national harvest regulations each year. In the United States, as a result of the Migratory Bird Treaty Act of 1918, the regulations serve as guidelines to state governments, which may adopt the federal guidelines without change or introduce changes that are more restrictive (e.g., a shorter season), but not more liberal. These regulations are established annually and fall into two basic categories: (1) framework regulations, and (2) special regulations.

Framework regulations form the backbone of the annual regulations; they include the beginning and ending dates for the hunting season, the season length within those dates, and the daily bag limit. They represent the oldest type of regulations; they also are commonly changed in response to the current needs of management. In contrast, special regulations are specific — in terms of species, location, or situation — and developed for unique management opportunities. Some special regulations, for example, attempt to spread hunting pressure to otherwise underharvested species. However, much of our current knowledge concerning the effects of various hunting regulations is not infallible, in part because of the difficulty to conduct spatially replicated, manipulative experiments (Nichols and Johnson 1989). Still, much is known regarding some specific regulatory options and the impact of each on waterfowl harvests.

Framework Dates

Framework regulations establish the earliest and latest dates for waterfowl hunting each year. As initially specified by the Migratory Bird Treaty, nearly all of these dates fall between 1 September and 10 March, and for waterfowl these usually occur between 1 October and 20 January. Framework dates are set for each of the four Flyways, with the individual states in each Flyway thereafter selecting dates that coincide with the period when waterfowl will be most abundant.

Season Length

Season length is the number of hunting days that may occur annually as prescribed by the U.S. Fish and Wildlife Service, based on a maximum of 107 days as set by the Migratory Bird Treaty Act. Season lengths vary among the Flyways as a reflection of species differences and population levels, numbers of hunters, harvest rates, and other factors. In general, season length is longest in the Pacific Flyway and shortest in the Atlantic Flyway, but season length is uniform within a given Flyway. Since the 1960s, season lengths generally have ranged from 30 to 60 days in the Atlantic and Mississippi Flyways (25 in the Mississippi Flyway in 1962), 39 to 74 days in the Central Flyway (25 in 1962, and longer in the High

Table 8-3. Objectives of hunting regulations for migratory birds. From Blohm (1989:125–126).

Provide an opportunity to harvest a portion of certain migratory game bird populations by establishing legal hunting seasons.

Limit harvest of migratory game birds to levels compatible with their ability to maintain their populations.

Avoid taking of threatened or endangered species.

Limit taking of other protected species where there is a reasonable possibility that hunting is likely to adversely affect their populations.

Provide equitable hunting opportunity in various parts of the country within limits imposed by abundance, migration, and distribution of migratory game birds.

Prevent depredations on agricultural crops by migratory game birds.

Plains region), and from 59 to 107 days in the Pacific Flyway.

Adjusting the season length remains an effective way to reduce the annual harvest; hence, waterfowl biologists spend considerable time deliberating this dimension of hunting regulations. In Tennessee, for example, lengthening the season from 35 to 40 days increased the harvest of Mallards by 18%, whereas shortening the season from 40 to 35 days decreased the harvest by 15% (Martin and Carney 1977). Nonetheless, determining the impact of this parameter is extremely difficult because population size and daily bag limit each interact with season length relative to the total annual harvest (Nichols and Johnson 1989).

Studies of Wood Ducks and American Black Ducks also reveal effects of season length on harvest. In the Atlantic and Mississippi Flyways, for example, the proportional share of the Wood Duck harvest among parts of the flyways did not increase appreciably until season length changed from 40 to 60 days (Heusmann and McDonald 2002). Harvest of Wood Ducks also experienced a spatial shift in relation to season length, with hunters in southern areas harvesting a disproportionate share in relation to the number of hunters. Hunters in southern states probably benefited more from the increased season length because onset of cold weather in northern-latitude states shortens the availability of Wood Ducks. In a study of American Black Ducks, Longcore et al. (2000) radiomarked 397 juveniles in Canada (Quebec and Nova Scotia) and Vermont prior to the 1990 and 1991 hunting seasons. Overall kill was greatest for birds marked on the Vermont–Quebec border (94 of 149). However, 73% were shot in Quebec, where season length was 103 days, compared with 26% in Vermont, where season length was 30 days.

Relative to starting date of the hunting season, American Black Ducks survived at nearly twice the rate (0.885 against 0.465) when the opening was delayed (15 Nov) in Maine as when the season opened earlier (1 Oct) in adjacent New Brunswick (Longcore et al. 1991). Parker (1991) reported that 81–85% of juvenile American Black Ducks harvested on a wildlife management area in New Brunswick were shot on opening day, and Longcore et al. (2000) determined that most juvenile mortality occurred during the first 2 weeks of the hunting season. Survival of American Black Ducks was also greater in isolated, unmanaged forested areas in comparison with managed impoundments near the coast, where hunters were concentrated (Longcore et al. 2000).

Daily Bag Limit

The last of the framework regulations, bag limit, represents an effective means for controlling the annual harvest. Indeed, season length and bag limit are viewed as the cornerstones for managing the hunting of waterfowl and other migratory birds. Boyd (1983) accordingly developed a "regulation index" — season length × bag limit — which correlated positively with Duck Stamp sales in the United States (r = 0.86). Hence, waterfowl hunters are more likely to stay home in years of restrictive regulations. Daily bag limits are modified nearly every year in response to estimates of populations and harvest objectives. Bag limits generally tend to be liberal in the Pacific Flyway and conservative in the Atlantic Flyway, a reflection of differences in the abundance of waterfowl as well as the number of hunters in each of these units.

An increase of one bird in the bag limit generally has a greater effect on the total harvest when the bag limit is low than when the bag limit is high. In Idaho, for example, increasing the bag limit of ducks from two to three escalated the total harvest by 28%, whereas an increase from five to six expanded the harvest by only 4% (Martin and Carney 1977). In Minnesota, a daily bag limit of one Mallard reduced the direct recovery rate — an indication of hunting pressure — to 8%, whereas it increased to 14% when the limit was two or more Mallards (Jessen 1970). Obviously, changes in the bag limit for a given species will affect the total harvest only when that species comprises a significant proportion of the harvest.

The Point System

Bag limits inherently require that hunters correctly identify waterfowl on the wing (i.e., *before* shooting). After field testing, however, Evrard (1970) concluded that most hunters could not identify waterfowl to the degree required by regulations in effect at the time (late 1960s). Another method was needed to achieve species-specific waterfowl harvests — a way that offered hunters a reasonable means of compliance while concurrently meeting the objectives of harvest and species management. Hence, the Point System began, which hoped to fulfill two major objectives: (1) to direct the harvest toward certain species and sexes and away from others, and (2) to reduce bag-limit violations by eliminating the need to identify birds in flight.

The Point System assigned "points" to ducks, by

species, *after* they were shot; with birds in-hand, hunters presumably were better able to identify the species correctly (Mikula et al. 1972). High point values could be assigned to species requiring protection, whereas lower values were assigned more liberally to other species. The range varied from 10 to 100 points per bird per species, and the system considered sex as well (i.e., females often carried more points than males of the same species). Hunters thus kept a running tally on their bag until a total of 100 points was reached or exceeded by the last duck they bagged. Low point values (10) were assigned to abundant and/or lightly harvested species (e.g., Blue-winged Teal), whereas high point values (100) were assigned less abundant species in need of protection (e.g., Canvasback); other species were assigned intermediate values.

The Point System was field tested in 1968 and 1969 (Mikula et al. 1972, Hopper et al. 1975), then was offered to a small number of states in 1970, and by 1973 became an alternative to the conventional bag limit in all flyways. Assessments revealed that the Point System successfully shifted hunting pressure among species and between sexes but did not increase the harvest beyond the conventional system (Geis and Crissey 1973, Nelson and Low 1977). However, subsequent analyses revealed little change in the recovery rates of male and female Mallards under the Point System in comparison with conventional bag limits, even though male Mallards were assigned much lower point values and were preferentially selected by hunters (Rexstad and Anderson 1988, Rexstad et al. 1991, Metz and Ankney 1991). Further, the potential for "reordering" under the Point System emerged as a significant issue for law enforcement. Reordering is the illegal practice of adding up points in a sequence other than that in which the birds are shot and therefore allows a larger daily bag; wardens thus could seldom enforce compliance with the Point System unless they actually observed hunters retrieving each bird they shot.

The Point System was widely used from 1970 to 1987 by states in all except the Pacific Flyway, but it was suspended in 1988 in response to declining populations of prairie-nesting ducks. In 1990, the U.S. Fish and Wildlife Service again offered the Point System to the states, but the restrictions were so great that states instead chose a bag limit based solely on a fixed number of birds, irrespective of species and sex. In 1994, after extensive review, the U.S. Fish and Wildlife Service once more eliminated the Point System as a harvest option because of concerns about compliance and a lack of evidence that

the system indeed redirected harvest pressure as originally intended (see Smith and Dubovsky 1998).

Shooting Hours

The Migratory Bird Treaty Act generally set shooting hours to begin 30 min before sunrise and end at sunset, although exceptions have been made for special seasons (e.g., for teal) and for the 1988 general season (sunrise opening). A sunrise opening presumably increases the probability that hunters might better identify waterfowl, as well as other birds, but a study of this issue concluded that protected species were not affected by the earlier shooting hour (U.S. Fish and Wildlife Service 1977). In one of these tests, even experienced hunters correctly identified only 58% of the Wood Ducks they encountered. However, because duck hunting is generally better in the early morning — and few protected species are killed — hunting continues to begin at 30 min before sunrise. In the Pacific Flyway, as determined from the Cooperative Parts Collection Survey, about 10% of the harvest occurred before sunrise, 65% between sunrise and noon, and 25% after noon (Martin and Carney 1977).

Average and total hunter success are reduced when the waterfowl season opens on a weekday and the starting time was noon. Conversely, extending shooting hours until 30 min after sunset increased the duck harvest by nearly 6% (Martin and Carney 1977). In Minnesota, recovery rates of Mallards were lower when hunting seasons closed in late afternoon instead of sunset — although survival rates remained unchanged — but the sample sizes were too small for powerful statistical tests of these data (Kirby et al. 1983). This study also demonstrated that restrictive regulations in one state produced detectable, flyway-wide effects on the recovery and harvest rates of Mallards.

Zoning and Split Seasons

At times, some states have split their waterfowl seasons into two and sometimes three nonconsecutive segments as a means of increasing hunting opportunities; the intent is to synchronize each segment with the migration schedules of the various species. Thus, a common practice of a mid-latitude state is to designate an early but short "split" to harvest early migrants like Blue-winged Teal, and take a longer split when the bulk of migrants arrive. Some biologists believe split seasons afford states a greater overall harvest, but analyses are inconclusive and, in any case, splits remain subject to the vagaries of migration (Martin and Carney 1977). Even so, about half the states adopted split seasons by the mid-1980s.

Zoning is the allowable practice whereby two or more areas can be designated in the same state but have different seasons. The primary purpose of zoning is to provide hunters with more equitable opportunities for harvesting waterfowl. For example, in a large and habitat-diverse state like New York, a single season without zones may offer hunters good harvest opportunities in the western part of the state but not along the coastal areas of Long Island. Accordingly, New York has five designated zones and a special sea duck area. In 1975, Louisiana was divided into an eastern zone where birds were harvested from the Mississippi Flyway and a western zone where the harvest was derived from the Central Flyway.

As with split seasons, the effect of zoning is difficult to evaluate. Split seasons and zoning were authorized with the intent to increase harvest opportunities, but such is not always achieved. Nevertheless, zoning is a common practice in about 25 states. For many states, a major objective is to arrange their hunting zones and split seasons in ways that produce as many opening days per year as possible and yet keep within the limits of the framework season.

Special Seasons

North American waterfowl populations plummeted during the late 1950s and early 1960s —the result of prolonged drought in the Prairie Pothole Region — as did the number of duck hunters. In response, the U.S. Fish and Wildlife Service focused on underharvested species in an attempt to increase recreational opportunities for hunters (see Gottschalk and Studholme 1970). The approaches included special seasons, bonus bag limits, special management units, zoning and split seasons, and the Point System (see Ladd et al. 1989), some of which we already have addressed. Here we review selected special seasons, management units, and other means designed to achieve harvest objectives. These approaches usually were in addition to changes in the framework regulations (e.g., season lengths and bag limits).

September Teal Season: The special season best known to hunters in the United States is the September Teal Season; it was initiated experimentally in 1965–67 in the Mississippi and Central Flyways,

then became a regular option for the states in 1969 (see Ladd et al. 1989). The season was designed to harvest Blue-winged Teal, which are early migrants and hence escaped hunting pressure in most states during the regular season. Moreover, few Blue-winged Teal winter in the continental United States — their primary winter range is Mexico, Central America, and northern South America (see Botero and Rusch 1988). A bag limit of four per day was authorized for the special season, which included Green-winged Teal and Cinnamon Teal. The harvest during the first year was about 400,000 Blue-winged Teal, 39,000 Green-winged Teal, and 34,000 ducks of other species, which was not considered harmful to the continental population of any species (Martinson et al. 1966). The Special Teal Season ran for up to 9 days in 13 states, but the program was altered in 1969 and 1970 in response to evidence of increased harvests of non-teal species. The U.S. Fish and Wildlife Service then offered those states designated as "waterfowl production states" the option of a bonus bag limit of Blue-winged Teal in lieu of the special September season. The option provided a "bonus" bag of Blue-winged Teal during 9 consecutive days of the regular duck season, provided the Point System was not used. Overall, the program was successful: Between 1970 and 1987, 35–46% of the total Blue-winged Teal harvest in the Mississippi and Central Flyways occurred during the special September seasons (see Ladd et al. 1989). The September Teal Season and most other special seasons were eliminated in 1988 in response to the diminished continental populations of waterfowl. When waterfowl populations recovered during the 1990s, however, Special Teal Seasons were reinstituted experimentally in the Atlantic Flyway in 1998; they now are authorized in several states in the Mississippi and Central Flyways as well. The season generally runs for 16 consecutive days in September, with a daily bag limit of four birds. In 2003, 62,000 Green-winged Teal and 461,000 Blue-winged Teal were harvested during the special September season (U.S. Fish and Wildlife Service, unpublished data).

Early Wood Duck Seasons: In 1977, several southeastern states requested a special season to harvest resident Wood Ducks (see Johnson et al. 1986). The special season, set to precede the arrival of northern migrants, directed hunting pressure to comparatively lightly harvested local populations of Wood Ducks (Bowers and Martin 1975). The option allowed these states to split their regular season to provide no more than 9 consecutive days of hunting during

1–15 October, with a bag limit of four or five birds. Florida held an experimental 5-day season in September. By 1981, all southern states had liberalized bag limits for Wood Ducks. Adjustments were made in some states to include Blue-winged Teal and no more than one bird of any other species. By 1988, however, the harvest included only Wood Ducks. Johnson et al. (1986), in an evaluation of special Wood Duck seasons, concluded that liberalized regulations did not adversely affect the survival rates for either northern populations or southern populations. However, local populations contributed substantially to these early harvests (Thul 1990), which could inflict adverse effects (i.e., overharvest of resident breeders). For example, of 62 radiomarked Wood Ducks on breeding areas in northern Alabama, only four left the study area before 1 November; hence local populations remained in the area during the special harvest seasons. Further, of 57 direct recoveries of 1,136 Wood Ducks, only one occurred more than 30 km from the banding site (Thompson and Baldassarre 1989). These results emphasize the importance of evaluating special harvest regulations at several spatial and temporal scales.

Special Scaup Seasons and Bonus Bag Limits: A bonus bag limit for both species of scaup was first offered to all but the Pacific Flyway in 1962. The new regulations allowed the harvest of two additional Greater or Lesser Scaup, singly or in aggregate, in designated areas. Areas with concentrations of Canvasbacks, American Black Ducks, Redheads, and Mallards were excluded (see Ladd et al. 1989). In 1966, a Special Scaup Season of 15 days replaced the scaup bonus. The bag limit was five birds, including the similarly looking Ring-necked Duck, but harvest of the latter species was prohibited in 1967. By 1968, 19 states in the Atlantic, Mississippi, and Central Flyways were participating in the Bonus Scaup Season, which ran for 16 consecutive days outside the season for other species, except sea ducks. The Bonus Scaup Season was discontinued in 1988 in response to declining population levels, which still continue from an unknown cause (see Austin et al. 2000, Afton and Anderson 2001).

Other Special Seasons: A special 107-day season for sea ducks in the Atlantic Flyway is the oldest of all special seasons; it was first authorized in 1938 with limits of 7–10 birds/day (see Ladd et al. 1989). Special seasons also permit harvests of resident populations of Canada Geese. Quotas have been authorized in circumstances where waterfowl populations are discrete and hunters are easily monitored. In these instances, the harvest is controlled either by issuing hunters a set number of tags or permits — as in the case of some swan hunts — or by ending hunting when a certain number of birds have been removed. Canada Geese in the Mississippi Valley Population are commonly harvested under a quota system. However, after extensive review, the U.S. Fish and Wildlife Service cancelled bonus bag limits in 1990. On the other hand, special seasons are still available; these remain sound management options if they are carefully designed, periodically evaluated, and refined.

Special Management Units: These units focus on geographical locations with unique harvest opportunities. The Columbia Basin Special Mallard Area was established in 1961 in response to high Mallard populations in the Pacific Northwest. Between 1971 to 1975, hunters in the unit were allowed two to four additional Mallards in their daily bag limit and 10–17 days of additional hunting. Similarly, a lightly harvested Mallard population in the Central Flyway initiated the High Plains Mallard Management Unit in 1968, which authorized a special 23-day season for the exclusive harvest of male Mallards (see Ladd et al. 1989).

Youth Waterfowl Hunt Day: Beginning with the 1996–97 season, the U.S. Fish and Wildlife Service offered states an opportunity for a 1-day addition to the regular hunting season that could be reserved as a special youth hunting day. The Youth Hunt was expanded to 2 days in 2000–01. Only hunters aged <15 years old can participate, but they must be accompanied by a licensed adult who is not allowed to hunt. In 2001, Canada instituted a similar program known as Waterfowler Heritage Days.

Summary Comments on Waterfowl Harvests

Overall, regulations governing waterfowl harvests are difficult to design because different species, populations, and sex and age classes are included, often at the same time and place. Thus, managers are continually directing hunting efforts to maximize harvests for different groups (stocks). As with the Point System, however, the desired results may not materialize. Johnson and Moore (1996), after analyzing direct recovery rates of ducks banded between 1976 and 1991, found little evidence that regulatory changes differentially affected duck populations from three major banding areas, despite years of widely different regulations. Nonetheless, their analysis provided some support that regulatory changes were effective on an area and age-specific basis. Nichols and Johnson (1989) also summarized the effects of harvest management strategies, noting that inferences from the analyses at hand where not as strong as possible, because studies lacked replications with adequate controls. Johnson and Moore (1996) concluded that the optimal harvest of duck stocks requires an ability to harvest selectively, which in turn necessitates an understanding each stock's dynamics and interdependence, if any, with other stocks. However, the ability to observe the effects of regulations on harvest, and the effects of harvest on abundance, clearly varies spatially and temporally. For example, special Wood Duck seasons in the southern states might not have a detrimental impact on regional or state populations (e.g., Johnson et al. 1986), but the local effect can be substantial (e.g., Thompson and Baldassarre 1989). Longcore et al. (2000:250) recognized these relationships during their studies of harvest mortality in American Black Ducks when they stated, "Depleted local and regional breeding populations can be restored only by allowing sufficient numbers of adults breeders and progeny to return to natal habitats," and further that "Recognizing that these local and regional populations make up the continental population is fundamental to increasing this population." Nonetheless, new ideas and approaches to harvest management are constantly evolving (e.g., AHM), which continually improves an imperfect system.

Arctic Geese: Strategies for Reducing Their Numbers

A special case associated with waterfowl harvest concerns some populations of Lesser Snow Geese, which along with those of Greater Snow Geese and Ross's Geese — species known collectively as either "white" or "light" geese — have increased dramatically for nearly 35 years. Indeed, what might at first be considered as an example of successful management soon became "an embarrassment of riches" (Ankney 1996). In particular, the numbers of Lesser Snow Geese climbed to some 3 million birds, which represented a 300% increase since 1969 (Batt 1997). At the root of this spectacular growth are the high annual survival rates of adults and juveniles, which is the result of a nutrient subsidy provided by the availability of corn and other agricultural crops remaining in fields as postharvest waste. Fortified by these foods, white geese no longer faced the historical limi-

tations of winter food shortages and therefore experienced corresponding increases in survival rates. Moreover, because of their enhanced physical condition at the end of winter, the birds no doubt benefit from improved breeding success after returning to their nesting areas in northern Canada. Additional food resources available at National Wildlife Refuges further supplemented the waste grain left by farming operations on privately owned lands. In effect, the abundant food supply no longer restricted the limits that winter carrying capacity once placed on white geese.

Whereas conditions improved on the wintering grounds, the burgeoning numbers of white geese eventually overwhelmed the carrying capacity of their nesting areas, particularly along the western edge of Hudson Bay. When foraging, white geese "grub" to extract tubers and roots, and the disturbance accordingly damages not only the vegetation but also disrupts the thin layer of soil above permafrost. With ever larger numbers of foraging geese, the feeding areas that once supported the nesting colonies become denuded mudflats known as "eat outs," and the exposed soils, already naturally thin, steadily erode into wastelands with little chance of regaining the original vegetation (Fig. 8-12; see Kerbes et al. 1990, Kotanen and Jefferies 1997, and especially Jefferies et al. 2003). Additionally, the chances of recovery are lessened even more because evaporation leaves a salty crust on the mudflats and, even if new vegetation somehow should appear in such a hostile environment, it is immediately consumed (i.e., the geese are present during the brief summer growing season). At one site, La Pérouse Bay in Manitoba, LANDSAT imagery indicates that about 2,400 ha of habitat was severely damaged or destroyed between 1973 and 1993, and ground transects monitored since 1985 reveal enough damage at the same area to render two-thirds of the inter-tidal marsh as nonproductive (Abraham and Jefferies 1997). The deteriorating habitat has been likened to a "snow goose ghetto," with such habitat damage dramatically depicted in the video *Snow Geese in Peril*, developed by Ducks Unlimited, along with an accompanying book, *Snow Geese — Grandeur and Calamity on an Arctic Landscape* (Batt 1998).

These conditions have set the stage for what may become an ecological disaster in which the population of white geese crashes concurrently with irreversible habitat degradation. In response, longer hunting seasons and larger bag limits were authorized to curtail the numbers of white geese, but

Figure 8-12. The impact of Snow Goose grazing is readily apparent at this site on the shore of La Pérouse Bay in northern Manitoba, Canada. With their heavy grubbing, the geese have removed nearly all the vegetation in the light areas outside the enclosure, whereas the few dark areas still contain the dominant plants (*Puccinellia phryganodes* and *Carex subspathacea*). Photo courtesy of Robert L. Jefferies, University of Toronto.

these did not keep pace with the spectacular growth of the goose population. Additional measures were enacted, which included those that contradicted the orthodox view of migratory bird management. A special Conservation Order, designed exclusively for white geese, thus began in 1998–99 that legalized unplugged shotguns (i.e., removed restrictions on the shell-holding capacity of repeating shotguns) and electronic calling devices (see Olson and Afton 2000) and further extended the season length and daily bag limit (no limit in some cases). The regulations allowed by the Conservation Order became an option available in 24 states in the Central and Mississippi Flyways in the United States and in Canada. In its first year of operation, the combined harvest of the regular and conservation seasons was 1.29 million white geese, which increased to 1.46 million in 1999–2000. In comparison, the annual

harvest averaged 602,000 in each of the five preceding seasons. By 2003–04, almost 58% of the total harvest of 1.38 million white geese resulted from provisions of the Conservation Order (U.S. Fish and Wildlife Service and Canadian Wildlife Service, unpublished data). The impact of these increased harvests has not been assessed, but it appears that the rapid growth of the midcontinent population of white geese has been halted.

The additional hunting pressure occurring during the spring conservation hunt in Canada between 15 April and 31 May also affected those Greater Snow Geese that were not harvested. At a staging area in southern Quebec, an analysis of females surviving the special hunt recorded 5–11% less breast muscle — an indicator of protein reserves — and 29–48% less abdominal fat than occurred in females in years before the special hunt was in force (Feret et al.

2003). Hunting disturbance, which decreased the birds' feeding activities and increased flying time, likely explains these reductions in nutrient storage. Thus, the surviving birds continued migrating northward to their arctic nesting areas in poor body condition, which in turn likely reduced their fecundity and therefore increased the impact of the spring hunt. While this added effect is desirable in terms of further controlling an overabundant species, care must be exercised that other waterfowl (e.g., Canada Geese) concurrently feeding at the same staging area are not similarly affected.

Biologists also examined direct control, which is defined as the purposeful removal of large numbers of white geese from a target population in a short period of time (Johnson and Ankney 2003). Such measures represent a "last resort" and may never be required, but they were studied as alternatives to resolve a human-induced ecological dilemma that continues to affect valuable natural resources. A summary of these strategies follows.

(1) *Increase the harvest of white geese in the United States and Canada* (Johnson 2003). These actions go beyond the changes already enacted to improve hunting success: hunting with live decoys, baiting, shooting at night, hazing and herding (perhaps with model airplanes), using rifles, removing restrictions on the gauge of shotguns, and suppressing firearm noise with silencers. Managers of state and federal refuges should encourage goose hunting by adding blinds, improving access trails, roads, and parking facilities, and increasing success with the placement of bait, live decoys, and water-level and other forms of habitat management. More white geese might be harvested if processing locations were established where hunters could donate birds for charitable uses ("food banks"), thereby encouraging bags beyond the limitations of their own freezer space (see also Maier et al. 2003). Tax incentives (e.g., deductions of hunting expenses), awards, or even bounties might be authorized to encourage additional hunting.

(2) *Direct methods of reducing the population* (Alisauskas and Malecki 2003). Removing adults from their breeding grounds seems the most efficient means of reducing the numbers of a long-lived species such as white geese. In this case, control — primarily by hunting with rifles or helicopter-assisted mass capture — is enhanced because the birds nest in colonies and are isolated by species, sex, and age (e.g., nesting pairs are discernible from immature birds and, during the postbreeding molt, flightless adults and their broods can be herded). The primary

disadvantage of these methods concerns handling of the carcasses for human consumption in remote areas of the Arctic, although some benefits may accrue if the carcasses are instead left on site as a source of nutrients to accelerate recovery of the vegetation.

(3) *Trapping and shooting ~~light~~ white geese on migration and wintering areas* (Cox and Ankney 2003). In addition to hunting by the general public, these proposals consider hunting (and trapping with rocket nets) conducted by management agencies at a time of year when the birds are concentrated in large flocks in areas close to centers of human population (i.e., distribution and processing the carcasses for meat is facilitated in comparison with birds killed in the Arctic). However, the birds also are more wary and mobile at this time, which reduces opportunities for significant control.

(4) *Administration of lethal chemicals at key locations* (Cummings and Poulos 2003). Avicides offer, at least potentially, a means of rapidly reducing large numbers of white geese at both wintering and staging areas on their migratory routes (i.e., before reaching nesting locations). An effective avicide — three compounds are currently registered but not explicitly approved for killing geese — could treat flocks of up to 20,000 birds with one application. To do so will require determination of the baits best suited for each location, their rates of consumption, and the potential for attracting nontarget species. The goal is to develop a single-dose bait that will cause more than 90% mortality. However, carcasses of the poisoned birds would not be suitable as human food, and they would have to be disposed of by other means (e.g., incineration). While potentially effective, applications of lethal chemicals undoubtedly would face significant — and heated — opposition from many segments of the general public.

As Ankney and Johnson (2003) emphasized, biologists examining the current situation remain convinced that increasing the harvest by hunters (item 1, above) offers the most desirable solution for reducing the overabundant population of white geese. Unlike other proposals (e.g., item 4), hunting incurs relatively little cost to the agencies responsible for natural resources and ensures that humans use the birds properly. Indeed, a major reason why governments began managing migratory birds nearly a century ago was to ensure a sustainable harvest for hunters. Today, however, waterfowl managers face a unique situation: helping hunters *increase* their harvest in ways that keep goose populations at optimal levels to the same degree that managers once *restricted* harvests to accomplish the same purpose. Nonetheless, other, more drastic means may be necessary before a desirable balance is restored.

WATERFOWL BANDING

Birds have been banded for centuries in Europe, the earliest of which often were falcons marked by their royal keepers as a means to determine ownership; some species — herons, for example — were identified with metal leg bands (Rydzewski 1951). As far as is known, birds were first banded in North America by John James Audubon who attached silver wires to the legs of nestling Eastern Phoebes (*Sayornis phoebe*) at Mill Grove Plantation near Philadelphia in 1804 (Rhodes 2004) — two of the nestlings Audubon banded returned as adults the following year.

In 1909, Jack Miner began identifying large numbers of waterfowl on a private refuge at Kingsville, Ontario, with bands bearing his address, and often a short verse of scripture (e.g., "God is able"), but not otherwise marked with individual numbers (Miner 1931; see also Miner 1925). Nonetheless, in January 1910, the first of Miner's banded ducks was recovered in South Carolina, and in 1915 the first of a large number of Canada Geese bearing one of his bands was recovered in northern Ontario. (Because of the scriptures, Inuit and other native peoples often brought bands to missionaries for interpretation.)

The first fully scientific use of bird bands was initiated about 1890 by the Danish ornithologist H. C. C. Mortensen (Dorst 1962). At first, Mortensen used zinc bands, but he later switched to aluminum, the metal still widely used today. Mortensen also was the first to use numbered bands, thereby permitting recognition of individual birds. In the United States, Paul Bartsch of the Smithsonian Institution used serially numbered bands in 1902 to mark Black-crowned Night Herons (*Nycticorax nycticorax*) in the Washington, D.C. area (Bartsch 1952). He attached bands inscribed with "Return to Smithsonian Institution."

North American bird banding developed rapidly in the following decades, stimulated in large part by Frederick C. Lincoln. In 1920, Lincoln joined the then U.S. Biological Survey and took charge of the bird-banding program, a position he held until 1946. In addition to co-authoring *Manual for Bird Banders* in 1929, Lincoln produced some 250 publications, many of which concerned bird banding. In 1935, based largely on band returns from waterfowl, Lincoln cre-

ated the flyway concept that remains the administrative cornerstone for waterfowl management.

Today, tens of thousands of waterfowl and other birds are banded each year (Fig. 8-13), which yields significant information (Table 8-4). Nonmigratory birds are banded under state authority, whereas waterfowl and other migratory birds (and all endangered species of birds) require federal authorization. Federal permits, bands, and banding records for migratory birds are administered by the Bird Banding Laboratory of the U.S. Geological Survey (the facility formerly was part of the U.S. Fish and Wildlife Service) and is housed at the Patuxent Wildlife Research Center in Laurel, Maryland (see Infobox 8-3). Analyses of banding data can be mathematically complex, but detailed computer programs and algorithms are available to estimate survival rates and other population parameters as well as to test hypotheses about population ecology (Brownie et al. 1985).

For purposes of standardizing banding data in North America, Canada adopted the same reporting system used in the United States. Records for migratory birds banded in either nation are maintained by the U.S. Geological Survey, but these, of course, are equally accessible to all parties. The U.S. Geological Survey also issues bands to workers in Canada and, in certain instances, for studies in Mexico. In addition to the band number, each band carries the notation, "Avise Bird Band, Washington, D.C., U.S.A." or a similar inscription for reporting a banded bird. "Avise" in Spanish is near enough to its English counterpart, advise, to be useful in all of the languages commonly used in North and South America. In 1995, experimental bands with the inscription "Call 1-800-327 BAND" and "Write Bird Band Laurel MD 20708 USA" were used on Mallards and are now required for all waterfowl banding. Thus, waterfowl and other migratory birds in North America are basically banded in uniform fashion, including a centrally located depository for all data. By 2004, some 58 million birds had been banded, which have yielded 3.5 million recoveries.

Bands are manufactured in several sizes, each of which is based on the leg size of one or more species of birds. *The North American Bird Banding Manual*, issued by the U.S. Geological Survey to licensed banders, lists the appropriate band size for each species. Most species of ducks require size 4–7 bands, geese sizes 7–8, and swans size 9. Bands for waterfowl are issued in strings of 100, with each band in the string bearing the same 3- or 4-digit prefix. The prefix is followed by a 5-digit number that indi-

Figure 8-13. Waterfowl are captured for banding using a variety of traps and other methods. Common techniques include using a rocket net (*top*) and corralling flightless waterfowl such as Black Brant. Photos courtesy of Guy A. Baldassarre (*top*) and Paul L. Flint, U.S. Geological Survey, Alaska Science Center (*bottom*).

vidually identifies each band, and the last digit in the prefix indicates the band size (e.g., 746-12345 is a size 6 band).

Banding is a critical component of waterfowl management in North America. Banding data provide essential information on survival and harvest rates, as well as relationships between breeding populations and where those populations are harvested (see Smith et al. 1989). More Mallards have been

banded than any other species of waterfowl (6.2 million by 2004), which alone has resulted in nearly 1 million recoveries.

SEX RATIOS

Sex ratios of waterfowl populations usually are expressed as the proportion of males to females. Sex ratios may change within populations because

Table 8-4. Definitions of some common terms and associated information obtained from waterfowl banding and analyses. Note, the term "year" in these definitions usually means the duration of a given hunting season. Modified from Anderson and Burnham (1976), and U.S. Fish and Wildlife Service and Canadian Wildlife Service (1991).

Banding terms

Local (L): a young bird incapable of sustained flight.

Hatching Year (HY): a bird capable of flight and known to have hatched during the calendar year when banded.

After Hatching Year (AHY): a bird known to have hatched before the calendar year of banding.

Second Year (SY): a bird known to have hatched in the calendar year preceding the year of banding and thus in its second calendar year of life.

Banding analysis terms

Direct recovery: a bird killed or found dead during the first hunting season after banding.

Indirect recovery: a bird killed or found dead after the first hunting season within which it was banded.

Harvest rate: the proportion of the population alive at the start of the year that is harvested in that year.

Band reporting rate: the proportion of banded birds taken by hunters and reported to the Bird Banding Laboratory.

Recovery rate: the probability that a banded bird alive at the start of the year is shot and reported to the Bird Banding Laboratory.

Mortality rate: the proportion of the population alive at the start of the year that dies during that year due to all causes. Mortality rate is the complement of survival rate.

Hunting mortality rate: the proportion of the population alive at the start of the year that dies due to hunting that year. The hunting mortality rate is synonymous with kill rate.

Nonhunting mortality rate: the proportion of the population alive at the start of the year that dies due to causes other than hunting.

of sex-specific mortality patterns that may result from external forces such as hunting or the vulnerability of breeding females to predators. Bellrose et al. (1961) recognized these differences in the sex ratios of waterfowl populations with the following four categories. (1) Primary sex ratio: the sex ratio at fertilization; normally 50:50 based on simple genetic probability. (2) Secondary sex ratio: the sex ratio at hatching; usually approximates 50:50, but may show the first indication of sex-specific mortality with a slight preponderance of females (e.g., 49:51). (3) Tertiary sex ratio: the sex ratio of juveniles (e.g., 1-year-olds); important because it indicates the proportion of each sex later entering the breeding population. Hunting becomes an external influence for the first time; some inherent species-specific differences also may be present. (4) Quaternary sex ratio: the sex ratio of the adult population,

which is often skewed in favor of one sex, usually males.

Little is known about primary sex ratios because of the obvious difficulty to find and reliably identify sexual characteristics in embryos (besides looking for gonads, which often are barely visible, sexual differences in syrinx structure may offer another means to determine the sex of embryos in many species). Because of this shortcoming, sex-specific mortality that might occur early in embryonic development remains undetected, thereby adding another albeit unavoidable bias. Nonetheless, primary sex ratios are estimated by combining data from embryos with ducklings that hatch. Hochbaum (1944) thus reported a 50:50 primary sex ratio for Canvasbacks, and Bellrose et al. (1961) similarly found a 51:49 ratio for Wood Ducks. A slight preponderance of males (52%) occurred in the primary sex

Infobox 8-3

Patuxent Wildlife Research Center
The First Experiment Station for Wildlife Management

This facility was established near Laurel, Maryland, in 1936, thereby becoming the first of its kind in the United States — an experiment station akin to those devoted to agricultural research. Acquisition of Patuxent — the name of a local river — is another monument in the legacy of J. N. "Ding" Darling. Once administered by the U.S. Fish and Wildlife Service, the center today is part of the U.S. Geological Survey and maintains a core of 70 scientists, supported by a staff of more than 100. The Merriam Laboratory (photo), one of the center's original buildings, was named for the first chief — C. Hart Merriam — of what was eventually to become the U.S. Fish and Wildlife Service. The center is situated on the 5,160-ha Patuxent Research Refuge, which is a unit of the National Refuge System; the area includes wetland and other habitats suitable for experimental manipulations designed to improve conditions for a variety of wildlife.

The center maintains facilities for the study and propagation of endangered species (e.g., Whooping Cranes; *Grus americana*). The center also conducted much of the original research concerning the impacts of DDT and other pesticides on wildlife, and the influences of environmental contaminants on wildlife are still actively studied at Patuxent. In addition to its headquarters in Maryland, the center is responsible for research work at eight field stations.

The thrust of the Migratory Bird Treaty Act often shapes the research mission at Patuxent, which in turn directs a good deal of work toward the management of

waterfowl populations and their habitat. For example, increasing hunting pressure on sea ducks triggered an on-going investigation designed to locate the breeding and molting areas of Black Scoters and other sea ducks overwintering on Chesapeake Bay. The project relies on satellite tracking to monitor the birds' movements along the northeastern coast of North America. Other projects address the changing nature of Canada Goose populations (i.e., decreasing numbers of those that migrate and increasing numbers of resident geese, which too often become urban pests); evaluation of models used in the management strategies governing Mallard harvests; and the role of ricefields as foraging habitat for waterfowl wintering in the Lower Mississippi Valley. The annual Breeding Bird Survey, started in 1966, is directed from the center, which also is the focal point for sophisticated analyses of waterfowl and other bird populations.

The center also manages the Bird Banding Laboratory (BBL), which issues permits and bands and acts as the clearing house for data for birds banded in both Canada and the United States. All told, BBL handles records for about 1.2 million migratory birds banded each year, and annually receives about 95,000 recoveries, often including those from locations in Central and South America, Europe, and eastern Asia. Whereas waterfowl and other migratory game birds comprise only about 25% of all birds banded each year, they nonetheless represent the vast majority — about 75% — of all band recoveries. Hence, the availability of such a large volume of banding data for waterfowl presents unique opportunities for extensive population analyses, including yearly updates for Adaptive Harvest Management. Photo courtesy of Michael G. Haramis, Patuxent Wildlife Research Center.

---

ratio of Black-bellied Whistling-Ducks, but the difference was not statistically significant from 50:50; in a sample of 183 eggs from clutches where all eggs hatched, thereby including all embryos, the sex ratio was exactly 50:50 (Bolen 1970).

Data on the secondary sex ratio of ducks (at hatching) largely stem from ducklings hatched in an incubator from eggs collected from wild, free-ranging females; these studies reported 50:50 sex ratios (Sowls 1955, Mendall 1958, Bellrose et al. 1961, Swennen et al. 1979). In the wild, Blums and Mednis (1996) determined the sex of 2,425 Northern Shovelers and 3,035 Tufted Ducks immediately after hatching, and the sex ratio did not differ from 50:50. Secondary sex ratios also did not differ in response to clutch size, duckling mass, or mass of the female.

As adults, most species of ducks exhibit a sex ratio with a preponderance of males, with the sex ratios of pochards usually more skewed than those of dabbling ducks (Table 8-5). For example, the sex ratio of Ring-necked Ducks was the most imbalanced (77:23) of the nine species studied by McIlhenny (1940). Similarly, sex ratios for Redhead, Canvasbacks, and other pochards are heavily skewed in favor of males, often by a factor of two or three. On the mid-Atlantic Coast, aerial surveys of more than 95,000 wintering Canvasbacks in 165 flocks revealed a sex ratio of 2.91 males per female (Haramis et al. 1985). In Great Britain, a sample of some 24,000 Common Pochards at 114 sites consisted of only 29.5% females (Owen and Dix 1986). The disparity in sex

ratios for ducks in North America was discussed decades ago in a paper cleverly entitled, *Do Drakes Outnumber Susies?* (Lincoln 1932).

Several subsequent ideas have been proposed to explain why there are proportionately more males than females in duck populations. Blums and Mednis (1996) concluded that their data, along with their evaluations of published sources, provided no evidence of nonrandom processes affecting the secondary sex ratio of at least 10 species of Anatinae. Hence, the disparate sex ratios recorded in adult populations are clearly a result of sex-specific mortality that occurs after hatching.

One explanation suggests that sex ratio data obtained in winter may mistakenly favor males simply because the samples originate from areas where males predominate; females may be equally numerous elsewhere but remain unsampled (Petrides 1944). For Ring-necked Ducks, the proportion of males in winter populations at various locations ranged from 66 to 91% (Mendall 1958). For wintering Canvasbacks on the mid-Atlantic Coast, sex ratio (males to females) varied from 3.98 in Maryland and 3.71 in Virginia, to 1.70 in North Carolina (Haramis et al. 1985). Sex ratios for Canvasbacks in these areas also were influenced by flock sizes and locations (Haramis et al. 1994).

Geographically, the more northerly parts of wintering range often harbor more males than females, and data collected in those areas clearly reflect such disparities (Lebret 1950, Nilsson 1970, Anderson and

Table 8-5. Sex ratios of some North American waterfowl. Ratios reported are for adults.

Species	% males	Reference
Black-bellied Whistling-Duck	51.8	Bolen (1970)
Lesser Snow Goose	52.2	Hanson et al. 1972
Canada Goose	53.5	Vaught and Kirsch (1966)
Mallard	62.3	Bellrose (1980)
Green-winged Teal	56.6	Bellrose (1980)
Blue-winged Teal	59.3	Bellrose et al. (1961)
Northern Pintail	59.4	Bellrose et al. (1961)
Canvasback	66.4	Bellrose et al. (1961)
Redhead	60.2	Bellrose et al. (1961)
Lesser Scaup	70.0	Bellrose et al. (1961)
Common Eider	51.0	Mendall (1968)
Long-tailed Duck	52.3	Ellarson (1956)
Hooded Merganser	64.9	Bellrose (1980)
Ruddy Duck	62.0	Bellrose et al. (1961)

Timken 1972, Bennett and Bolen 1978). In Great Britain, for example, the sex ratio of Common Pochards was 150 males/100 females below 51° latitude, but 840/100 north of 58° latitude (Owen and Dix 1986). However, even after accounting for geographic differences, sex ratios remain skewed in favor of males; hence, other factors must be causing the imbalance.

Johnson and Sargeant (1977) proposed that red foxes kill enough incubating females to distort quaternary sex ratios in prairie-nesting Mallards. Their model yielded a male–female sex ratio of 52:48 for pristine times, but when fox populations increased because of agricultural developments and elimination of coyote (*Canis latrans*) populations, the disparity reached 58:42 (see Chapter 6). In the absence of hunting, which places heavier shooting pressure on male Mallards, the sex ratio might reach an imbalance of as much as 61:39 as a direct result of fox predation. Reductions in the availability of prime nesting cover presumably increase the vulnerability of incubating females, especially if the limited habitat forms "predator lanes." However, these relationships for species nesting in upland habitat do not fully explain the imbalanced sex ratios typical of Canvasbacks and other pochards nesting in somewhat more secure cover over water (but see Nichols and Haramis 1980a).

The effects of hunting on sex ratios of adult ducks have yielded equivocal results. Olson (1965) demonstrated that female Canvasbacks decoy more readily than males, which suggested that sex ratios were distorted because of hunting pressure. Nichols and Haramis (1980a) also found band recovery rates at some locations were higher for female Canvasbacks, and that overall mortality rates were significantly higher for females than for males. However, in Northern Pintails, males were more vulnerable to decoys set in various combinations according to "sex" (Alford and Bolen 1977). Metz and Ankney (1991) reported that hunters generally select brightly colored males, but Owen and Dix (1986) did not detect sex-specific differences to hunting vulnerability for ducks in Great Britain.

Thus, if hunting indeed is a major factor, then the Point System should have helped reduce the imbalance but, as already discussed, that does not appear to be the case (Rexstad and Anderson 1988, Rexstad et al. 1991). Conversely, if other factors are responsible (e.g., higher predation of females on breeding areas), then the Point System treated only the symptoms and not the cause of disparate sex ratios. Waterfowl diseases do not seem sex-specific; hence, sex ratios determined from carcasses apparently reflect the correct proportion of each sex in local populations (Bellrose et al. 1961). However, because of some sex-specific differences in migration schedules or preferred winter habitat, sex ratios based on dead or moribund waterfowl may favor either sex in ways that are not representative of the overall population.

Intraspecific encounters between males and females also may influence the sex ratios of wintering waterfowl. An analysis of band recoveries for Canvasbacks suggested sex-specific differences in winter distributions, possibly because of competition between males and females (Nichols and Haramis 1980b). The dominance of males over females, especially when competing for food, seems important in this respect. Canvasbacks defended individual foraging sites on a wintering area in South Carolina, and when heterosexual encounters occurred, adult males normally dominated females; males thus comprised 74% of the Canvasback flock where food resources were concentrated, but they made up only 48% elsewhere (Alexander and Hair 1977). Based on the aggressive behavior of six species of dabbling ducks, Hepp and Hair (1984) reported that unpaired females of late-pairing species (e.g., Green-winged Teal) often are excluded from preferred feeding sites and therefore may move to other areas (see Chapter 7). These and other studies indicated that male dominance in winter may cause higher overwinter mortality of females (see Nichols and Haramis 1980a, 1980b; Owen and Dix 1986, Alexander 1987). Overall, it seems that the disparate sex ratios commonly observed in ducks are caused by a combination of higher female mortality during nesting and, to a lesser extent, higher mortality during winter, although hunting cannot be dismissed entirely.

For geese, sex ratios of adults are much closer to 50:50. However, here the sexes do not differ greatly in their respective life-history events. Geese pair for life and hence each sex is exposed to the same risk factors in time and space, especially during the breeding season when the male remains in attendance near the nest site. Further, because the plumages of geese are similar between the sexes, hunters cannot select males over females, as often occurs in ducks where males are often brightly colored but females are not (see Metz and Ankney 1991).

The adult plumage of whistling-ducks, like swans and geese, does not differ by sex, but whistling-ducks are unlike almost all other waterfowl in that both sexes share incubation duties (Bolen and Smith 1979, Flickinger 1975). A sample of 631 adult Black-bellied Whistling-Ducks caught in Texas with a cannon-net revealed a quaternary sex ratio of 52:48, or 1.08 males per female, which statistically represents an equal distribution (Bolen 1970). These results suggest that the risks (e.g., predation) associated with incubation, which are typically assigned only to females in other species, are spread evenly between male and female Black-bellied Whistling-Ducks (Johnson and Sargeant 1977). Additionally, because Black-bellied Whistling-Ducks were not legally hunted in the United States

at the time, the adult sex ratio indicated that neither sex was differentially harvested in Mexico where they were legal game (cf. Olson 1965).

AGE RATIOS

The proportion of juveniles in fall waterfowl populations is a prime indicator of annual production. Nesting studies require considerable effort, and while these offer valuable ecological information in their own right, the resulting data do not necessarily reflect annual recruitment (and, in fact, may increase predation when humans leave their scent while checking active nests). A large percentage of nests may hatch but, because of subsequent brood mortality, nesting data alone typically overestimates annual production. Hence, fall age ratios remain the best direct measure of annual production. Ideally, the age structure in waterfowl populations should be determined after fledging is complete, but obtained before autumn migration begins. Such data help managers set annual hunting regulations, but in practice, age ratios often are determined from bag checks or other means long after the seasons are set.

Four age categories are recognized for postfledgling waterfowl: (1) juvenile, (2) yearling, (3) subadult, and (4) adult. However, the identification and/or biological importance of each group varies by taxa. For most species of dabbling ducks, only the juvenile and adult categories are important or identifiable, whereas those categories, as well as subadults in both yearling and 2-year old birds, are important distinctions in assessing the age structure of goose, swan, and brant populations. Over a series of years, age ratios are about equally composed of adults and immatures, but these proportions in a population can vary widely from year to year (Bellrose 1980).

HAND-REARED WATERFOWL AND WATERFOWL MANAGEMENT

Releases of hand-reared waterfowl — stocking — was a focus of waterfowl management for many years (Pirnie 1935, Benson 1939). Hand-reared Mallards, in particular, were released in attempts to increase breeding populations, an idea that often gains currency when duck populations are low (Burger 1975). Duck hunters and others in the private sector — as well as federal and state governments — all have been attracted to stocking as a management technique, in no small measure because the act of releasing birds provides such positive feedback. Photos in newspapers and other media showing the release of several hundred caged birds indeed is an impressive sight. Such events seemingly represent wildlife management "in action." Despite the popularity of stocking, however, hand-reared ducks must survive and reproduce at rates near those of wild birds before the technique can be considered a successful management tool. Fortunately, a considerable body of literature is available to evaluate the survival rates of hand-reared ducks, and a review of this information offers significant insight into the value of stocking as a means of increasing breeding populations.

It has long been known that semi-domesticated or game-farm birds survived poorly in the wild (Foley 1954, Bailey 1979, Burger 1975). Hence, most data pertain to "pure" or "wild-strain" stocks, which are individuals less than two generations removed from the wild (Batt and Nelson 1990). Brakhage (1953) was among the first to study the fate of such ducks by comparing migration and mortality between 6,623 hand-reared ducks of four species and 6,284 wild-trapped ducks at the Delta Marsh in Manitoba from 1932 to 1951. The study demonstrated that wild-strain, hand-reared birds migrated and returned to breeding sites in a manner similar to wild ducks. However, the hand-reared birds were so much more vulnerable to hunting mortality that Brakhage (1953:476) concluded: ". . . the release of ducks hand-reared from wild eggs cannot be recommended as a practical management technique." Hickey (1952) constructed life tables comparing wild and hand-reared Mallards, and these also underscored the high mortality rate for stocked birds in their first 2 years of life. Only by their third year did the stocked birds attain a mortality rate similar to wild Mallards, but by then only 5% of the original cohort remained alive compared with 16% of the wild Mallards.

Hunt et al. (1958) studied the release of more than 10,000 hand-reared Mallards in Wisconsin, which permitted still another large-scale evaluation of stocking programs. The hand-reared birds, because of their relative tameness, proved far more vulnerable to hunting than their wild counterparts — for every 100 Mallards released, 47 were harvested by hunters. Crippling losses and other mortality claimed the balance. Moreover, about 155,800 Mallards would have to be stocked in most years to increase the state-wide duck harvest by just 10%. Hence, the conclusion was reached that habitat improvements instead of stocking represented the best means of increasing waterfowl harvests.

Schladweiler and Tester (1972) reported similar results and conclusions following their evaluation of releasing hand-reared Mallards. Note also that if only half the released birds actually enter the hunter's bag, then the rearing cost per harvested bird is doubled.

Nonetheless, Heusmann (1991) reported that large numbers of Mallards are still released as part of Maryland's waterfowl management program; more than 300,000 were released between 1974 and 1988, with an additional 240,000 released by private sources. Maryland continued this program, which combined with releases by private interests, reached 140,000 Mallards/year at the peak of this effort in the late 1980s (Smith and Rohwer 1997). Hindman et al. (1992) determined that about 16% of the Mallards released in Maryland enter the hunter's bag, each of which incurred an average cost of $43.87. Moreover, the overall harvest of captive-reared Mallards likely did not exceed 5–6% of Maryland's total duck harvest. During 1991–93, 6–30% of the harvest on state wildlife management areas were captive-reared Mallards compared to 4–10% on regulated shooting areas (Smith 2000). Hence, releases of captive Mallards for harvest is a costly endeavor, and released birds can hybridize with American Black Ducks and increase the ever present risk of introducing duck virus enteritis into wild flocks of waterfowl (see Chapter 8).

In a large study of the release of hand-reared female Mallards in Manitoba, breeding populations indeed increased from 19.3 to 24.5 pairs/km^2. However, only 9–12% of the released Mallards produced broods despite good breeding habitat, and the population subsequently declined because of low nesting success (Sellers 1973). Such evidence suggested that hand-released birds do not reproduce well even if they survived and homed to the release area. This suggestion was later substantiated at the Delta Marsh in Manitoba, where only 0–11% of the hand-reared Mallards ever produced broods, thereby prompting Bailey (1979:61) to conclude that "Mallard stocking is of questionable value . . ."

Yerkes and Bluhm (1998) evaluated release of 5–6-week-old Mallard ducklings into prairie pothole habitat in southwestern Manitoba during 1992–93. A total of 1,766 ducks was released during the study, but low direct recovery rates (less than 2% compared to 3.4% for wild birds) indicated poor prefledging or premigratory survival. Average annual return rates also were low (5.8–8.5%), which led to the conclusion that, "attempting to increase local breeding populations by releasing captive-reared Mallards is not a viable management technique" (Yerkes and Bluhm 1998:197).

Indeed, in their extensive review of the literature on releases of hand-reared, wild-strain Mallards as a technique to bolster breeding populations, Batt and Nelson (1990:560) stated that, "Hand-reared birds have been shown, in every recruitment and survival parameter measured, to be inferior to wild birds," and they thus seriously questioned how stocking could possibly work, especially where natural populations were unable to sustain themselves. These authors emphatically highlighted the implications of virtually every study of stocking: The long-term density of Mallard populations was driven by improved habitat conditions leading to enhanced recruitment. Additionally, because of their pioneering behavior, Mallards will readily seek those new or restored habitats that management efforts provide. Indeed, using a population model developed by Cowardin and Johnson (1979), Batt and Nelson (1990) demonstrated that, once habitat conditions are improved and the Mallard population accordingly increases, the total size of the population receives little additional boost from the release of hand-reared birds. In other words, the recovery potential of wild Mallards is so great that it overshadows the influx of poorly surviving hand-reared birds. For example, the model demonstrates that releasing 100,000 Mallards per year into an increasing population *for 15 years* accounted for only a 5% gain in a population that already had increased by 39%.

Such arguments clearly underscore that habitat protection and enhancement remain the key factors to the welfare of waterfowl populations — as well as fostering a more holistic approach to wetland conservation in general. Hence, we strongly support the conclusion that hand-reared birds "have no potential of contributing to the broader goals of waterfowl and wetlands conservation" (Batt and Nelson 1990:567). Nevertheless, attempts continue in both the United States and Canada to augment the numbers and production of wild Mallards by releasing hand-reared birds.

In some cases, stocking has proven a reliable technique to locally reestablish waterfowl populations. Wood Ducks and other cavity-nesting ducks are especially well suited to restoration because the females of these species have exceptionally high homing rates (Bellrose 1980). However, even where habitats have been improved by the addition of nest boxes or by the formation of natural cavities, nest-searching females may take several years to move into the area. In these situations, stocking may es-

tablish new populations. Wild birds usually are used in these efforts, although hand-reared stocks also may be successful (Lee and Nelson 1966).

Capen et al. (1974) captured wild female Wood Ducks and their newly hatched broods in nests on established breeding sites in Maine and relocated these family units into nest boxes elsewhere. The translocated females usually returned to the initial capture sites, but about 9% of the ducklings subsequently returned to the release site, a rate comparing favorably to the normal homing of yearling Wood Ducks (Grice and Rogers 1965, McGilvrey 1969). Similarly, Coulter et al. (1979) established Common Goldeneyes at the edge of their breeding range in northern New England. Of 43 ducklings initially translocated, 58% survived to flying age and, of these, three females later produced 103 ducklings in nest boxes at the release site.

Doty and Kruse (1972) released 253 hand-reared Wood Ducks on a refuge in North Dakota where no Wood Ducks had nested previously, although the area was within the general range of the species. Nest boxes were installed the next year; in the two nesting seasons thereafter, the boxes contained 50 Wood Duck nests of which 40 successfully produced 486 ducklings. Conversely, hand-reared Wood Ducks released by Hunt and Smith (1966) did not increase production from nest boxes erected in Wisconsin.

Canada Geese also have been stocked for many years, usually to reestablish depleted or extirpated breeding populations. In one of the earliest reports, Johnson (1947) estimated that 2,000 goslings were released in a 10-year period at Seney National Wildlife Refuge in Michigan. Stocking seems especially successful for reestablishing Canada Geese because of their precise homing patterns (Surrendi 1970). Nelson (1963) presented a full summary of stocking programs for Canada Geese, which have been widely successful in restoring this species, especially the Giant Canada Goose.

EXOTIC AND FERAL WATERFOWL

For centuries, wildlife of all kinds has been introduced into environments far removed from their native distributions. Many introductions were accidental escapees from captive collections, but others were intentional releases designed to "improve" the endemic fauna with species of sporting or other values. Regrettably, many exotics later became pests or threats to native species (Greig 1980), or even worse, disrupted the integrity of entire communities (Laycock 1966).

Whereas exotic wildlife is often regarded as species transported from foreign lands, *any* species released outside its normal geographical distribution also represents a *fait accompli* of an exotic introduction. Mallards stocked in southern Texas were well outside their breeding range in North America (Kiel 1970), but the release took place well *inside* the native range of the closely related Mottled Duck. In 1966, 97 Muscovy Ducks from Venezuela and four from Paraguay were liberated in Florida. Predators likely claimed all of these birds shortly after their release, but plans thereafter called for additional efforts (Palmer 1976). Fortunately, however, interest in stocking exotic waterfowl was never widespread in North America.

Weller (1969) raised biological and ethical questions concerning introductions of exotic waterfowl, a few of which are mentioned here (see also Bolen 1971). First is the matter of hybridization, for unlike many avian taxa, crosses in waterfowl involve both intergeneric and intertribal hybrids. Indeed, more hybrids are known among waterfowl than in any other family of birds (Johnsgard 1960). We discussed the issue of waterfowl hybridization in Chapter 2, but note here that escaped or deliberately introduced exotics are the precursors to the conservation problems created by hybridizations.

Diseases and parasites represent a second concern. In recent years, however, potentials for infecting native waterfowl with pathogens carried by exotics have been lessened somewhat by stricter controls. Legally imported wildlife must remain quarantined, and only the offspring of the imported stocks may be released. Even so, much remains unknown about wildlife diseases and the complex situations arising when biological communities are infused with foreign species. These shortcomings often are learned too late. For example, Warner (1968) described how the introduction of mosquitoes (*Culex pipiens fatigans*) into Hawaii provided the vector necessary for the transmission of avian malaria, which thereafter initiated deadly epizootics in the island's avifauna. The same mosquitoes apparently transmit a pox-like disease to Hawaiian Geese, perhaps further limiting the geese to breeding habitat above 1,000 m, where mosquitoes are absent (Kear and Brown 1976, Kear and Berger 1980).

Mute Swans have been stocked widely throughout the world because of their attractiveness as ornamentals in city parks and private collections (see Ogilvie 1972). Some of these, however, have established feral populations that move freely or even show migratory tendencies. Such a population visits Lake Musconetcong in northern New Jersey, where about 250 died of ulcerative hemorrhagic enteritis between 1970 and 1980 (Roscoe and Huffman 1982). The malady stems from acute infections of a trematode (*Sphaeridiotrema globulus*) whose intermediate host at Lake Musconetcong is a snail (*Goniobasis virginica*; Huffman and Fried 1983). At least one Tundra Swan died of the same infection at Lake Musconetcong (Roscoe and Huffman 1983), presumably because of similar food habits and contact with the feral population of Mute Swans. Wider transmission to Tundra Swans elsewhere in the Atlantic Flyway remains a possibility. Fortunately, the intensity of *S. globulus* infections seems somewhat host-specific and some birds may develop resistance (Macy et al. 1968, Macy 1973), perhaps lessening mortalities in other species of North American waterfowl currently sharing environments with Mute Swans. However, free-ranging Mute Swan populations have caused concern in North America because of their competition with native species of waterfowl and damage to habitat (see Infobox 5-2).

LITERATURE CITED

Abraham, K. F., and R. L. Jefferies. 1997. High goose populations: causes, impacts, and implications. Pages 7–71 *in* B. D. J. Batt, editor. Arctic ecosystems in peril: report of the Arctic Goose Habitat Working Group. Arctic Goose Joint Venture Special Publication. U.S. Fish and Wildlife Service, Washington, D.C., and Canadian Wildlife Service, Ottawa.

Afton, A. D., and M. G. Anderson. 2001. Declining scaup populations: a retrospective analysis of long-term population and harvest survey data. Journal of Wildlife Management 65:781–796.

Alexander, W. C. 1987. Aggressive behavior of wintering diving ducks (Aythyini). Wilson Bulletin 9:38–49.

Alexander, W. C., and J. D. Hair. 1977. Winter foraging behavior and aggression of diving ducks in South Carolina. Proceedings of the Southeastern Association of Fish and Wildlife Agencies 31:226–232.

Alford, J. R., III, and E. G. Bolen. 1977. Differential response of male and female Pintail ducks to decoys. Journal of Wildlife Management 41:657–661.

Alisauskas, R., and R. Malecki. 2003. Direct control methods for population reduction of light geese in the Arctic. Pages 43–86 *in* M. A. Johnson and C. D. Ankney, editors. Direct control and alternative harvest strategies for North American light geese. Report of the Direct Control and Alternative Harvest Measures Working Group. Arctic Goose Joint Venture Special Publication. U.S. Fish and Wildlife Service, Washington, D.C., and Canadian Wildlife Service, Ottawa.

Alison, R. M. 1978. The earliest records of waterfowl hunting. Wildlife Society Bulletin 6:196–199.

Allen, J. P., and S. S. Wilson. 1977. A bibliography of references to avian botulism. U.S. Fish and Wildlife Service Special Scientific Report Wildlife 204.

Anderson, B. W., and R. L. Timken. 1972. Sex and age ratios and weights of Common Mergansers. Journal of Wildlife Management 36:1127–1133.

Anderson, D. R., and K. P. Burnham. 1976. Population ecology of the Mallard. VI. The effect of exploitation on survival. U.S. Fish and Wildlife Service Resource Publication 128.

Anderson, D. R., and K. P. Burnham. 1978. Effect of restrictive and liberal hunting regulations on annual survival rates of the Mallard in North America. Transactions of the North American Wildlife and Natural Resources Conference 43:181–186.

Anderson, W. L. 1978. Waterfowl collisions with power lines at a coal-fired power plant. Wildlife Society Bulletin 6:77–83.

Anderson, W. L., and S. P. Havera. 1985. Blood lead, protoporphyrin, and ingested shot for detecting lead poisoning in waterfowl. Wildlife Society Bulletin 13:26–31.

Anderson, W. L., S. P. Havera, and B. W. Zercher. 2000. Ingestion of lead and nontoxic shotgun pellets by ducks in the Mississippi Flyway. Journal of Wildlife Management 64:848–857.

Ankney, C. D. 1996. An embarrassment of riches: too many geese. Journal of Wildlife Management 60:217–223.

Ankney, C. D., and M. A. Johnson. 2003. Discussion and conclusions. Pages 119–124 *in* M. A. Johnson and C. D. Ankney, editors. Direct control and alternative harvest strategies for North American light geese: report of the Direct Control and Alternative Harvest Measures Working Group. Arctic Goose Joint Venture Special Publication. U.S. Fish and Wildlife Service, Washington, D.C., and Canadian Wildlife Service, Ottawa.

Audubon, J. J. 1840. The birds of America. J. B. Chevalier, Philadelphia.

Aune, K., N. Anderson, T. Linfield, and T. Damrow. 2003. West Nile virus emergence in Montana, 2002. Intermountain Journal of Sciences 9:130.

Austin, J. E., A. D. Afton, M. G. Anderson, R. G. Clark, C. M. Custer, J. S. Lawrence, J. B. Polalrd, and J. K. Ringelman. 2000. Declining scaup populations: issues, hypotheses, and research needs. Wildlife Society Bulletin 28:254–263.

Austin, J. E., and M. R. Miller. 1995. Northern Pintail (*Anas acuta*). The birds of North America, 163. The American Ornithologists' Union, Washington, D.C., and The Academy of Natural Sciences, Philadelphia.

Bailey, R. O. 1979. Wild Mallard stocking in a large marsh habitat. Canadian Field-Naturalist 93:55–62.

Bailey, R. O., and R. E. Jones. 1976. Mallard mortality in Manitoba's extended spring muskrat-trapping season. Wildlife Society Bulletin 4:26–28.

Ball, G., T. Bollinger, M. Conly, J. Kadlec, B. MacFarlane, H. Murkin, T. Murphy, M. Pybus, T. Rocke, M. Samuel, D. Sharp, and G. Wobeser. 1998. Report to the Prairie Habitat Joint Venture by the working group on avian botulism. Canadian Cooperative Wildlife Health Centre, Saskatoon, Saskatchewan.

Banks, R. C. 1979. Human related mortality of birds in the United States. U.S. Fish and Wildlife Service Special Scientific Report Wildlife 215.

Barras, S. C., and J. A. Kadlec. 2000. Abiotic predictors of avian botulism outbreaks in Utah. Wildlife Society Bulletin 28:724–729.

Bartonek, J. C. 1965. Mortality of diving ducks on Lake Winnipegosis through commercial fishing. Canadian Field-Naturalist 79:15–20.

Bartsch, P. 1952. A note on the first bird-banding in America. Bird-Banding 23:59–60.

Batt, B. D. J., editor. 1997. Arctic ecosystems in peril: report of the Arctic Goose Habitat Working Group, Arctic Goose Joint Venture Special Publication, U.S. Fish and Wildlife Service, Washington, D.C., and Canadian Wildlife Service, Ottawa.

Batt, B. D. J. 1998. Snow geese, grandeur and calamity on an arctic landscape. Ducks Unlimited, Memphis, Tennessee.

Batt, B. D. J., and J. W. Nelson. 1990. The role of hand-reared Mallards in breeding waterfowl conservation. Transactions of the North American Wildlife and Natural Resources Conference 55:558–568.

Beintema, N., compiler. 2001. Lead poisoning in waterbirds — international update report 2000. Wetlands International, Wageningen, The Netherlands.

Bell, J. F., G. W. Sciple, and A. A. Hubert. 1955. A microenvironment concept of the epizoology of avian botulism. Journal of Wildlife Management 19:352–357.

Bellrose, F. C. 1959. Lead poisoning as a mortality factor in waterfowl populations. Bulletin of the Illinois Natural History Survey 27:235–288.

Bellrose, F. C. 1980. Ducks, geese and swans of North America. Stackpole Books, Harrisburg, Pennsylvania.

Bellrose, F. C., and D. J. Holm. 1994. Ecology and management of the Wood Duck. Stackpole Books, Mechanicsburg, Pennsylvania.

Bellrose, F. C., T. G. Scott, A. S. Hawkins, and J. B. Low. 1961. Sex ratios and age ratios in North American ducks. Bulletin of the Illinois Natural History Survey 27:391–474.

Bennett, J. W., and E. G. Bolen 1978. Stress response in wintering Green–winged Teal. Journal of Wildlife Management 42:81–86.

Benson, D. 1939. Survival studies of Mallards liberated in New York State. Transactions of the North American Wildlife Conference 4:411–415.

Blanchard, D. C., and L. Syzdek. 1970. Mechanism for water-to-air transfer and concentration of bacteria. Science 170:626–628.

Blanchong, J. A., M. D. Samuel, D. R. Goldberg, D. J. Shadduck, and L. H. Creekmore. 2006. Wetland environmental conditions associated with the risk of avian cholera outbreaks and the abundance of *Pasturella multocida*. Journal of Wildlife Management 70:54–60.

Blohm, R. J. 1989. Introduction to harvest: understanding surveys and season settings. International Waterfowl Symposium 6:118–129.

Blums, P., and A. Mednis. 1996. Secondary sex ratio in Anatinae. Auk 113:505–511.

Blus, L. J., R. K. Stroud, B. Reiswig, and T. McEneaneu. 1989. Lead poisoning and other mortality factors in Trumpeter Swans. Environmental Toxicology and Chemistry 8:263–271.

Bolen, E. G. 1970. Sex ratios in the Black-bellied Tree Duck. Journal of Wildlife Management 34:68–73.

Bolen, E. G. 1971. Some views on exotic waterfowl. Wilson Bulletin 83:430–434.

Bolen, E. G., and E. N. Smith. 1979. Notes on the incubation behavior of Black-bellied Whistling-Ducks. Prairie Naturalist 11:119–123.

Bonfatti, J. F. 1984. 10,000 ducks swept over Niagara Falls. Associated Press newscopy, 17 January 1984. Niagara Falls, New York.

Botero, J. E., and D. H. Rusch. 1988. Recoveries of North American waterfowl in the Neotropics. Pages 469–482 *in* M. W. Weller, editor. Waterfowl in winter. University of Minnesota Press, Minneapolis.

Botzler, R. G. 1991. Epizootiology of avian cholera in waterfowl. Journal of Wildlife Diseases 27:367–395.

Bowers, E. F., and F. W. Martin. 1975. Managing Wood Ducks by population units. Transactions of the North American Wildlife and Natural Resources Conference 40:300–324.

Bowles, J. H. 1908. Lead poisoning in ducks. Auk 25:312–313.

Boyd, H. 1983. Intensive regulation of duck hunting in North America: its purposes and achievements. Canadian Wildlife Service Occasional Paper 50.

Brakhage, G. K. 1953. Migration and mortality of ducks hand-reared and wild-trapped at Delta, Manitoba. Journal of Wildlife Management 17:465–477.

Brand, C. J. 1984. Avian cholera in the Central and Mississippi Flyways during 1979–80. Journal of Wildlife Management 48:399–406.

Brand, C. J., and D. E. Docherty. 1984. A survey of North American migratory waterfowl for duck plague (duck virus enteritis) virus. Journal of Wildlife Diseases 20:261–266.

Brand, C. J., S. M. Schmitt, R. M. Duncan, and T. M. Cooley. 1988. An outbreak of Type E botulism among Common Loons (*Gavia immer*) in Michigan's upper peninsula. Journal of Wildlife Diseases 24:471–476.

Bredy, J., and R. G. Botzler. 1989. The effects of six environmental variables on the survival of *Pasturella multocida* in water. Journal of Wildlife Diseases 25:232–239.

Brewer, L., A. Fairbrother, J. Clark, and D. Amick. 2003. Acute toxicity of lead, steel, and an iron-tungsten-nickel shot to Mallard ducks (*Anas platyrhynchos*). Journal of Wildlife Diseases 39:638–648.

Brogden, K. A., and K. R. Rhodes. 1983. Prevalence of serological types of *Pasturella multocida* from 57 species of birds and mammals in the United States. Journal of Wildlife Diseases 19:315–320.

Brown, M. J., E. Linton, and E. C. Rees. 1992. Causes of mortality among wild swans in Britain. Wildfowl 43:70–79.

Brownie, C., D. R. Anderson, K. P. Burnham, and D. S. Robson. 1985. Statistical inference from band recovery data — a handbook. Second edition. U.S. Fish and Wildlife Service Resource Publication 156.

Burger, G. V. 1975. The role of artificial propagation in waterfowl management. International Waterfowl Symposium 1:104–109.

Burgess, E. C., J. Ossa, and T. M. Yuill. 1979. Duck plague: a carrier state in waterfowl. Avian Diseases 23:940–949.

Burnham, K. P., and D. R. Anderson. 1984. Tests of compensatory vs. additive hypotheses of mortality in Mallards. Ecology 64:105–112.

Capen, D. E., W. J. Crenshaw, and M. W. Coulter. 1974. Establishing breeding populations of Wood Ducks by relocating wild broods. Journal of Wildlife Management 38:253–256.

Castelli, P. M., and S. E. Sleggs. 2000. Efficacy of border collies to control nuisance Canada Geese. Wildlife Society Bulletin 28:385–392.

Caswell, F. D., G. S. Hochbaum, and R. K. Brace. 1985. The effect of restrictive regulations on survival rates and local harvests of southern Manitoba Mallards. Transactions of the North American Wildlife and Natural Resources Conference 50:549–556.

Choules, G. L., W. C. Russell, and D. A. Gauthier. 1978. Duck mortality from detergent-polluted water. Journal of Wildlife Management 42:410–414.

Christens, E., H. Blokpoel, G. Ranson, and S. W. D. Jarvie. 1995. Spraying white mineral oil on Canada Goose eggs to prevent hatching. Wildlife Society Bulletin 23:228–230.

Cohn, J. P. 1985. Lead shot poisons Bald Eagles. BioScience 35:474–476.

Conroy, M. J., and R. T. Eberhardt. 1983. Variation in survival and recovery rates of Ring-necked Ducks. Journal of Wildlife Management 47:127–137.

Conroy, M. J., G. R. Costanzo, and D. B. Stotts. 1989. Winter survival of female American Black Ducks on the Atlantic Coast. Journal of Wildlife Management 53:99–109.

Conroy, M. J., and D. G. Krementz. 1990. A review of the evidence for the effects of hunting on American Black Duck populations. Transactions of the North American Wildlife and Natural Resources Conference 55:501–517.

Converse, K. A., and J. J. Kennelly. 1994. Evaluation of Canada Goose sterilization for population control. Wildlife Society Bulletin 22:265–269.

Converse, K. A., and G. A. Kidd. 2001. Duck plague epizootics in the United States, 1967–1995. Journal of Wildlife Diseases 37:347–357.

Cooch, F. G. 1964. A preliminary study of the survival value of a functional salt gland in prairie Anatidae. Auk 81:380–393.

Cooch, F. G., S. Wendt, G. E. J. Smith, and G. Butler. 1978. The Canadian migratory gamebird hunting permit and associated surveys. Pages 8–39 *in* H. Boyd and G. H. Finney, editors. Migratory game bird hunting in Canada. Canadian Wildlife Service Report Series 43.

Cooper, J. A., and T. Keefe. 1997. Urban Canada Goose management: policies and procedures. Transactions of the North American Wildlife and Natural Resources Conference 62:412–430.

Cornwell, G., and H. A. Hochbaum. 1971. Collisions with wires — a source of anatid mortality. Wilson Bulletin 83:305–306.

Coulter, M. W. 1957. Predation by snapping turtles upon aquatic birds in Maine marshes. Journal of Wildlife Management 21:17–21.

Coulter, M. W., W. Crenshaw, G. Donovan, and J. Dorso. 1979. An experiment to establish a Goldeneye population. Wildlife Society Bulletin 7:116–118.

Cowardin, L. M., and D. H. Johnson. 1979. Mathematics and Mallard management. Journal of Wildlife Management 43:18–35.

Cox, R. R., Jr., and C. D. Ankney. 2003. Trapping and shooting light geese on migration and wintering areas. Pages 87–94 *in* M. A. Johnson and C. D. Ankney, editors. 2003. Direct control and alternative harvest strategies for North American light geese: report of the Direct Control and Alternative Harvest Measures Working Group, Arctic Goose Joint Venture Special Publication. U.S. Fish and Wildlife Service, Washington, D.C., and Canadian Wildlife Service, Ottawa.

Cummings, J., and P. Poulos. 2003. Potential chemicals to manage light goose populations. Pages 95–104 *in* M. A. Johnson and C. D. Ankney, editors. 2003. Direct control and alternative harvest strategies for North American light geese: report of the Direct Control and Alternative Harvest Measures Working Group, Arctic Goose Joint Venture Special Publication. U.S. Fish and Wildlife Service, Washington, D.C., and Canadian Wildlife Service, Ottawa.

Dekker, D. 1987. Peregrine Falcon predation on ducks in Alberta and British Columbia. Journal of Wildlife Management 51:156–159.

DeStefano, S., C. J. Brand, and M. D. Samuel. 1995. Seasonal ingestion of toxic and nontoxic shot by Canada Geese. Wildlife Society Bulletin 23:502–506.

Donahue, J. M., and L. D. Olson. 1969. Survey of wild ducks and geese for *Pasteurella* spp. Bulletin of the Wildlife Diseases Society 5:201–205.

Dorst, J. 1962. The migrations of birds. Houghton Mifflin, Boston.

Doty, H. A., and A. D. Kruse. 1972. Techniques for establishing local breeding populations of Wood Ducks. Journal of Wildlife Management 36:428–435.

Dresser, S. S., J. Stuht, and A. M. Fallis. 1978. Leucocytozoonosis in Canada Geese in upper Michigan. I. Strain differences among geese from different localities. Journal of Wildlife Diseases 14:124–131.

Duncan, R. M., and W. I. Jensen 1976. A relationship between avian carcasses and living invertebrates in the epizootiology of avian botulism. Journal of Wildlife Diseases 12:116–126.

Durant, A. J. 1956. Impaction and pressure necrosis in Canada Geese due to eating dry hulled soybeans. Journal of Wildlife Management 20:399–404.

Ellarson, R. S. 1956. A study of the Oldsquaw Duck on Lake Michigan. Dissertation, University of Wisconsin, Madison.

Errington, P. L. 1945. Some contributions of a fifteen-year local study of the Northern Bobwhite to acknowledge of population phenomena. Ecological Monographs 15:1–34.

Esler, D., T. D. Bowman, K. A. Trust, B. E. Ballachey, T. A. Dean, S. C. Stephen, and C. E. O'Clair. 2002. Harlequin Duck population recovery following the "*Exxon Valdez*" oil spill: progress, process and constraints. Marine Ecology Progress Series 241:271–286.

Esler, D., J. A. Schmutz, R. L. Jarvis, and D. M. Mulcahy. 2000. Winter survival of adult female Harlequin Ducks in relation to history of contamination by the *Exxon Valdez* oil spill. Journal of Wildlife Management 64:839–847.

Estabrooks, S. R. 1987. Ingested lead shot in Northern Red-billed Whistling Ducks (*Dendrocygna autumnalis*) and Northern Pintails (*Anas acuta*) in Sinaloa, Mexico. Journal of Wildlife Diseases 23:169.

Evrard, J. O. 1970. Assessing and improving the ability of hunters to identify flying waterfowl. Journal of Wildlife Management 34:114–126.

Fay, L. D. 1966. Type E botulism in Great Lakes water birds. Transactions of the North American Wildlife and Natural Resources Conference 31:139–149.

Fay, L. D., O. W. Kaufmann, and L. A. Ryel. 1965. Mass mortality of water birds in Lake Michigan, 1963–1964. University of Michigan Great Lakes Research Division Publication 13:36–46

Feare, D. D. 1998. Duck plague: analysis of the disease of waterfowl and perspective on the effective response to an epizootic. Proceedings of the International Rehabilitation Council Conference 21:91–98.

Feierabend, J. S., and O. Myers. 1984. A national summary of lead poisoning in Bald Eagles and waterfowl. National Wildlife Federation, Washington, D.C.

Feret, M., G. Gauthier, A. Bechet, J-F. Giroux, and K. A. Hobson. 2003. Effect of a spring hunt on nutrient storage by Greater Snow Geese in southern Quebec. Journal of Wildlife Management 67:796–807.

Fisher, F. M., Jr., S. L. Hall, W. R. Wilder, B. C. Robinson, and D. S. Lopries. 1986. An analysis of spent shot in upper Texas coastal waterfowl wintering habitat. Pages 50–54 *in* J. S. Fierabend and A. B. Russell, editors. Lead poisoning in wild waterfowl: a workshop. National Wildlife Federation, Washington, D.C.

Fleming, J. H. 1908. The destruction of Whistling Swans (*Olor columbianus*) at Niagara Falls. Auk 25:306–309.

Flickinger, E. L. 1979. Effects of aldrin exposure on Snow Geese in Texas rice fields. Journal of Wildlife Management 43:94–101.

Flickinger, E. L. 1975. Incubation by a male Fulvous Tree Duck. Wilson Bulletin 87:106–107.

Flickinger, E. L. 1981. Wildlife mortality at petroleum pits in Texas. Journal of Wildlife Management 45:560–564.

Flickinger, E. L., and C. M. Bunck. 1987. Number of oil-killed birds and fate of bird carcasses at crude oil pits in Texas. Southwestern Naturalist 32:377–381.

Flint, P. L. 1998. Settlement rate of lead shot in tundra wetlands. Journal of Wildlife Management 62:1099–1102.

Foley, D. 1954. Studies on survival of three strains of Mallard ducklings in New York State. New York Fish and Game Journal 1:75–83.

Francis, C. M., J. R. Sauer, and J. R. Serie. 1998. Effect of restrictive harvest regulations on survival and recovery rates of American Black Ducks. Journal of Wildlife Management 62:1544–1557.

Franson, J. C., M. R. Petersen, L. H. Creekmore, P. L. Flint, and M. R. Smith. 1998. Blood lead concentrations of Spectacled Eiders near Kashunuk River, Yukon Delta National Wildlife Refuge, Alaska. Ecotoxicology 7:175–181.

Fredrickson, L. H., T. S. Baskett, G. K. Brakhage, and V. C. Cravens. 1977. Evaluating cultivation near duck blinds to reduce lead poisoning hazard. Journal of Wildlife Management 41:624–631.

Friend, M. 1981a. Waterfowl management and waterfowl disease: independent or cause and effect relationships? Transactions of the North American Wildlife and Natural Resources Conference 46:94–103.

Friend, M. 1981b. Waterfowl disease — changing perspectives for the future. International Waterfowl Symposium 4:189–196.

Friend, M. 1992. Environmental influences on major waterfowl diseases. Transactions of the North American Wildlife and Natural Resources Conference 57:517–525.

Friend, M., and D. H. Cross. 1995. Waterfowl diseases: causes, prevention, and control. Waterfowl Management Handbook 13. U.S. Department of the Interior, National Biological Service, Washington, D.C.

Friend, M., and J. C. Franson, editors. 1999. Field manual of wildlife diseases. U.S. Geological Survey, Biological Resources Division Information and Technology Report 1999-001.

Friend, M., R. G. McLean, and F. J. Dein. 2001. Disease emergence in birds: challenges for the twenty-first century. Auk 118:290–303.

Friend, M., and G. L. Pearson. 1974. Duck plague: the present situation. Proceedings of the Western Association of Game and Fish Commissioners 53:315–325.

Galt, J. A., W. J. Lehr, and D. L. Payton. 1991. Fate and transport of the Exxon Valdez oil spill. Environmental Science and Technology 25:202–209.

Gashwiler, J. S. 1949. The effect of spring muskrat trapping on waterfowl in Maine. Journal of Wildlife Management 13:183–188.

Geis, A. D. 1963. Role of hunting regulations in migratory bird management. Transactions of the North American Wildlife and Natural Resources Conference 28:164–171.

Geis, A. D. 1972a. Use of banding data in migratory game bird research and management. U.S. Fish and Wildlife Service Special Scientific Report Wildlife 154.

Geis, A. D. 1972b. Role of banding data in migratory bird population studies. Pages 213–228 in Population ecology of migratory birds. U.S. Fish and Wildlife Service Wildlife Research Report 2.

Geis, A. D., and W. F. Crissey. 1969. Effect of restrictive hunting regulations on Canvasback and Redhead harvest rates and survival. Journal of Wildlife Management 33:860–866.

Geis, A. D., and W. F. Crissey. 1973. 1970 test of the point system for regulating duck harvests. Wildlife Society Bulletin 1:1–21.

Geis, A. D., R. K. Martinson, and D. R. Anderson. 1969. Establishing hunting regulations and allowable harvest of Mallards in the United States. Journal of Wildlife Management 33:848–859.

Geis, A. D., R. I. Smith, and J. P. Rogers. 1971. Black Duck distribution, harvest characteristics, and survival. U.S. Fish and Wildlife Service Special Scientific Report Wildlife 139.

Gershman, M., J. F. Witter, H. E. Spencer, Jr., and A. Kalvaitis. 1964. Case report: epizootic of fowl cholera in the Common Eider duck. Journal of Wildlife Management 28:587–589.

Gibbs, J. P. 1999. Effective monitoring for adaptive management: lessons from the Galápagos Islands. Journal of Wildlife Management 63:1055–1065.

Giltner, L. T., and J. F. Couch. 1930. Western duck sickness and botulism. Science 72:660.

Gottschalk, J. S., and A. T. Studholme. 1970. Waterfowl management in the seventies. Transactions of the North American Wildlife and Natural Resources Conference 35:297–304.

Grand, J. B., P. L. Flint, M. R. Petersen, and C. L. Moran. 1998. Effect of lead poisoning on Spectacled Eider survival rates. Journal of Wildlife Management 62:1103–1109.

Gray, B. T., and R. M. Kaminski. 1989. Illegal harvest of waterfowl: what do we know? Transactions of the North American Wildlife and Natural Resources Conference 54:333–340.

Gray, H. 1913. Avian cholera. Pages 420–432 *in* E. W. Hoare, editor. A system of veterinary medicine. Volume 1. Alexander Eger, Chicago.

Greig, J. C. 1980. Duck hybridization: a threat to species integrity. Bokmakierie 32:88–89.

Grice, D., and J. P. Rogers. 1965. The Wood Duck in Massachusetts. Massachusetts Division of Fish and Wildlife, Federal Aid in Wildlife Restoration Project Report W-19-R.

Griffin, C. R., T. S. Basket, and R. D. Sparrow. 1982. Ecology of Bald Eagles wintering near a waterfowl concentration. U.S. Fish and Wildlife Service Special Scientific Report Wildlife 247.

Grue, C. E., M. W. Tome, T. A. Messmer, D. B. Henry, G. A. Swanson, and L. R. DeWeese. 1989. Agricultural chemicals and prairie pothole wetlands: meeting the needs of the resources and the Farmer — U.S. Perspective. Transactions of the North American Wildlife and Natural Resources Conference 54:43–58.

Gullett, P. A. 1987. Oil toxicosis. Pages 191–196 *in* M. Friend, editor. Field guide to wildlife diseases. Volume 1. General field procedures and diseases of migratory birds. U.S. Fish and Wildlife Service Resource Publication 167.

Gustafson, E. W. 1989. The Mexican waterfowl harvest. International Waterfowl Symposium 6:168–173.

Hall, D. L. 1987. Impacts of hunting on duck populations. Proceedings of the Southeastern Association of Fish and Wildlife Agencies 41:447–460.

Hall, D. L., G. J. Bonnaffons, and R. M. Jackson. 1989. The relationship of enforcement, courts and sentencing to compliance with waterfowl hunting regulations. Transactions of the North American Wildlife and Natural Resources Conference 54:341–354.

Hansen, W. R., S. E. Brown, S. W. Nashold, and D. L. Knudson. 1999. Identification of duck plague virus by polymerase chain reaction. Avian Diseases 43:106–115.

Hanson, H. C., H. G. Lumsden, J. J. Lynch, and H. W. Norton. 1972. Population characteristics of three mainland colonies of Blue and Lesser Snow Geese nesting in the southern Hudson Bay region. Ontario Ministry of Natural Resources Research Report (Wildlife) 92.

Haramis, G. M., E. L. Derleth, and W. A. Link. 1994. Flock sizes and sex ratios of Canvasbacks in Chesapeake Bay and North Carolina. Journal of Wildlife Management 58:123–131.

Haramis, G. M., J. R. Goldsberry, D. G. McAuley, and E. L. Derleth. 1985. An aerial photographic census of Chesapeake Bay and North Carolina Canvasbacks. Journal of Wildlife Management 49:449–454.

Hario, M. 1998. Recent trends and research results for four archipelago bird species — Common Eider, Velvet Scoter, Herring Gull and Lesser Black-backed Gull. Pages 12–24 *in* T. Solonen and E. Lammi, editors. The yearbook of the Linnut magazine. Bird Life Finland, Kuopio, Finland.

Harrison, J. 1963. Heavy mortality of Mute Swans from electrocution. Wildfowl Trust Annual Report 14:164–165.

Hartung, R. 1967. Energy metabolism in oil-covered ducks. Journal of Wildlife Management 31:798–804.

Hartung, R., and G. S. Hunt. 1966. Toxicity of some oils to waterfowl. Journal of Wildlife Management 30:564–570.

Havera, S. P., R. M. Whitton, and R. T. Shealy. 1992. Blood lead and ingested and embedded shot in diving ducks during spring. Journal of Wildlife Management 56:539–545.

Hay, K. G. 1975. The status of oiled wildlife: research and planning. Pages 249–253 *in* Proceedings on Prevention and Control of Oil Spills. American Petroleum Institute, Washington, D.C.

Heberlein, T. A. 1991. Changing attitudes and funding for wildlife — preserving the sport hunter. Wildlife Society Bulletin 19:528–534.

Heinz, G. L. 1976. Methylmercury: second-year feeding effects on Mallard reproduction and duckling behavior. Journal of Wildlife Management 40:82–90.

Heitmeyer, M. E., L. H. Fredrickson, and D. D. Humburg. 1993. Further evidence of biases associated with hunter-killed Mallards. Journal of Wildlife Management 57:733–740.

Henny, C. J., D. R. Anderson, and R. S. Pospahala. 1972. Aerial surveys of waterfowl production in North America, 1955–71. U.S. Fish and Wildlife Service Special Scientific Report Wildlife 160.

Hepp, G. R., and J. D. Hair 1984. Dominance in wintering waterfowl (Anatini): effects on distribution of sexes. Condor 86:251–257.

Heusmann, H W. 1991. The history and status of the Mallard in the Atlantic Flyway. Wildlife Society Bulletin 19:14–22.

Heusmann, H W., and J. E. McDonald. 2002. Distribution of Wood Duck harvest in the Atlantic and Mississippi Flyways in relation to hunting season length. Wildlife Society Bulletin 30:666–674.

Hickey, J. J. 1952. Survival studies of banded birds. U.S. Fish and Wildlife Service Special Scientific Report Wildlife 15.

Higgins, K. F., and M. A. Johnson. 1978. Avian mortality caused by a September wind and hail storm. Prairie Naturalist 10:43–48.

Hindman L. J., W. F. Harvey, IV, and V. D. Stotts. 1992. Harvest and band recovery of captive-reared Mallards released by the State of Maryland. Proceedings of the Southeastern Association of Fish and Wildlife Agencies 46:215–222.

Hochbaum, G. S., and C. J. Walters. 1984. Components of hunting mortality in ducks: a management analysis. Canadian Wildlife Service Occasional Paper 52.

Hochbaum, H. A. 1944. The Canvasback on a prairie marsh. Stackpole Books, Harrisburg, Pennsylvania, and the Wildlife Management Institute, Washington, D.C.

Hochbaum, H. A. 1947. The effect of concentrated hunting pressure on waterfowl breeding stock. Transactions of the North American Wildlife Conference 12:53–62.

Hochbaum, H. A. 1955. Travels and traditions of waterfowl. Charles T. Branford, Newton, Massachusetts.

Hoffman, D. J., and W. C. Eastin. 1982. Effects of lindane, paraquat, toxaphene, and 2,4,5–trichlorophenoxyacetic acid on Mallard embryo development. Archives of Environmental Contamination and Toxicology 11:79–86.

Hoffman, D. J., H. M. Ohlendorf, and T. W. Aldrich. 1988. Selinium teratogenesis in natural populations of aquatic birds. Archives of Environmental Contamination and Toxicology 17:519–525.

Hohman, W. L., J. L. Moore, and J. C. Franson. 1985. Winter survival of immature Canvasbacks in inland Louisiana. Journal of Wildlife Management 59:384–392.

Hollmén, T., J. C. Franson, D. E. Docherty, M. Kilpi, M. Hario, L. H. Creekmore, and M. R. Petersen. 2000. Infectious bursal disease virus antibodies in eider ducks and Herring Gulls. Condor 102:688–691.

Hopper, R. M., A. D. Geis, J. R. Grieb, and L. Nelson, Jr. 1975. Experimental duck hunting seasons, San Luis Valley, Colorado, 1963–1970. Wildlife Monographs 46.

Hudson, R. H., R. K. Tucker, and M. A. Haegele. 1984. Handbook of toxicity of pesticides to wildlife. U.S. Fish and Wildlife Service Resource Publication 153.

Huffman, J. E., and B. Fried. 1983. Trematodes from Goniobasis virginica (Gastropoda: Pleuroceridae) in Lake Musconetcong, New Jersey. Journal of Parasitology 69:429.

Humburg, D. D., D. Graber, S. Sheriff, and T. Miller. 1983. Estimating autumn-spring waterfowl nonhunting mortality in north Missouri. Transactions of the North American Wildlife and Natural Resources Conference 48:241–245.

Hunt, G. S. 1961. Waterfowl losses on the Lower Detroit River due to oil pollution. Proceedings of the Great Lakes Research Conference 4:10–26.

Hunt, G. S., and A. B. Cowan. 1963. Causes of deaths of waterfowl on the Lower Detroit River — winter 1960. Transactions of the North American Wildlife and Natural Resources Conference 28:150–163.

Hunt, R. A., L. R. Jahn, R. C. Hopkins, and G. H. Amelong. 1958. An evaluation of artificial Mallard propagation in Wisconsin. Wisconsin Conservation Department Wildlife Technical Bulletin 16.

Hunt, R. A., and C. F. Smith. 1966. An evaluation of hand-reared Wood Ducks at Goose Island, Mississippi River, Wisconsin. Pages 132–140 in L. R. Jahn, B. T. Crawford, H. H. Dill, A. S. Hawkins, E. J. Mikula, and H. K. Nelson, editors. Wood Duck management and research: a symposium. Wildlife Management Institute, Washington, D.C.

Hunter, B., and G. Wobeser. 1980. Pathology of experimental avian cholera in Mallard ducks. Avian Diseases 24:403–414.

Hunter, B. F., W. Clark, P. Perkins, and P. Coleman. 1970. Applied botulism research, including management recommendations. Unpublished report, California Department of Fish and Game, Sacramento, California.

Jackson, R., R. Norton, and R. Anderson. 1979. Improving ethical behavior in hunters. Transactions of the North American Wildlife and Natural Resources Conference 44:306–318.

Jansen, J. H. 1968. Duck plague. Journal of the Veterinary Medical Association 152:1009–1016.

Jarvis, R. L. 1976. Soybean impaction in Canada Geese. Wildlife Society Bulletin 4:175–179.

Jefferies, R. L., R. F. Rockwell, and K. F. Abraham. 2003. The embarrassment of riches: agricultural food subsidies, high goose numbers, and loss of arctic wetlands — a continuing saga. Environmental Review 11:193–232.

Jensen, W. I., and C. S. Williams. 1964. Botulism and fowl cholera Pages 333–341 in J.P. Linduska, editor. Waterfowl tomorrow. U.S. Government Printing Office, Washington, D.C.

Jenssen, B. M., and M. Ekker. 1991. Effects of plumage contamination with crude oil dispersant mixtures on thermoregulation in Common Eiders and Mallards. Archives of Environmental Contamination and Toxicology 20:398–403.

Jessen, R. L. 1970. Mallard population trends and hunting losses in Minnesota. Journal of Wildlife Management 34:93–105.

Johnsgard, P. A. 1960. Hybridization in the Anatidae and its taxonomic implications. Condor 62:25–33.

Johnson, C. S. 1947. Canada goose management, Seney National Wildlife Refuge. Journal of Wildlife Management 11:21–24.

Johnson, D. H., and A. B. Sargeant. 1977. Impact of red fox predation on the sex ratio of prairie Mallards. U.S. Fish and Wildlife Service Research Report 6.

Johnson, D. H., and T. L. Shaffer. 1987. Are Mallards declining in North America? Wildlife Society Bulletin 15:340–345.

Johnson, F. A., and D. J. Case. 2000. Adaptive regulation of waterfowl harvests: lessens learned and prospects for the future. Transactions of the North American Wildlife and Natural Resources Conference 65:94–108.

Johnson, F. A., J. E. Hines, F. Montalbano, III, and J. D. Nichols. 1986. Effects of liberalized harvest regulations on Wood Ducks in the Atlantic Flyway. Wildlife Society Bulletin 14:383–388.

Johnson, F. A., W. L. Kendall, and J. A. Dubovsky. 2002. Conditions and limitations on learning in the adaptive management of Mallard harvests. Wildlife Society Bulletin 30:176–185.

Johnson, F. A., and C. T. Moore. 1996. Harvesting multiple stocks of ducks. Journal of Wildlife Management 60:551–559.

Johnson, M. A. 2003. Alternative strategies to increase light goose harvest in the United States and Canada. Pages 23–42 in M.A. Johnson and C. D. Ankney, editors. Direct control and alternative harvest strategies for North American light geese: report of the Direct Control and Alternative Harvest Measures Working Group, Arctic Goose Joint Venture Special Publication. U.S. Fish and Wildlife Service, Washington, D.C., and Canadian Wildlife Service, Ottawa.

Johnson, M. A., and C. D. Ankney, editors. 2003. Direct control and alternative harvest strategies for North American light geese: report of the Direct Control and Alternative Harvest Measures Working Group. Arctic Goose Joint Venture Special Publication. U.S. Fish and Wildlife Service, Washington, D.C., and Canadian Wildlife Service, Ottawa.

Jordan, J. S., and F. C. Bellrose. 1951. Lead poisoning in wild waterfowl. Illinois Natural History Survey Biological Notes 26.

Kadlec, J. A. 2002. Avian botulism in Great Salt Lake marshes: perspectives and possible mechanisms. Wildlife Society Bulletin 30:983–989.

Kalmbach, E. R. 1930. Western duck sickness produced experimentally. Science 72:658–660.

Kalmbach, E.R. 1968. Type C botulism among wild birds: a historical sketch. U.S. Fish and Wildlife Service Special Scientific Report Wildlife 110.

Kalmbach, E. R., and M. F. Gunderson. 1934. Western duck sickness: a form of botulism. U.S. Department of Agriculture Technical Bulletin 411.

Kaminski, R. M., and E. A. Gluesing. 1987. Density- and habitat-related recruitment in Mallards. Journal of Wildlife Management 51:141–148.

Kaufmann, O. W., and L. D. Fay. 1964. Clostridium botulinum Type E toxin in tissues of dead loon and gulls. Michigan State University Experiment Station Quarterly Bulletin 47:236–242.

Kautz, J. E., and R. A. Malecki. 1990. Effects of harvest on feral Rock Dove survival, nest success, and population size. U.S. Fish and Wildlife Service Technical Report 31.

Kear, J., and A. J. Berger. 1980. The Hawaiian Goose, an experiment in conservation. Buteo Books, Vermillion, South Dakota.

Kear, J., and M. Brown. 1976. A pox-like condition in the Hawaiian Goose. International Zoo Yearbook 16:133–134.

Kerbes, R. H., P. M. Kotanen, and R. L. Jefferies. 1990. Destruction of wetland habitats by Lesser Snow Geese; a keystone species on the west coast of Hudson Bay. Journal of Applied Ecology 27:242–258.

Kiel, W. H., Jr. 1970. A release of hand-reared Mallards in south Texas. Texas Agricultural Experiment Station Publication MP-968.

Kirby, R. E., J. E. Hines, and J. D. Nichols. 1983. Afternoon closure of hunting and recovery rates of Mallards banded in Minnesota. Journal of Wildlife Management 47:209–213.

Klukas, R. W., and L. N. Locke. 1970. An outbreak of fowl cholera in Everglades National Park. Bulletin of the Wildlife Disease Society 6:77–79.

Korschgen, C. E., H. C. Gibbs, and H. L. Mendall. 1978. Avian cholera in eider ducks in Maine. Journal of Wildlife Diseases 14:254–258.

Kotanen, P. M., and R. L. Jefferies. 1997. Long-term destruction of sub-arctic wetland vegetation by Lesser Snow Geese. EcoScience 4:179–182.

Krapu, G. L., G. A. Swanson, and H. K. Nelson. 1973. Mercury residues in pintails breeding in North Dakota. Journal of Wildlife Management 37:395–399.

Krementz, D. G., M. J. Conroy, J. E. Hines, and H. F. Percival. 1988. The effects of hunting on survival rates of American Black Ducks. Journal of Wildlife Management 52:214–226.

Krueger, D. M., and R. J. Whyte. 1978. Lesser Scaup collides with fence in south Texas. Bulletin of the Texas Ornithological Society 11:19.

Kwon, Y. K., and M. I. Kang. 2003. Outbreak of fowl cholera in Baikal Teals in Korea. Avian diseases 47:1491–1495.

Ladd, W. N., Jr., J. C. Bartonek, K. E. Gamble, and J. R. Serie. 1989. Experiences with special harvest management strategies for ducks. Transactions of the North American Wildlife and Natural Resources Conference 54:552–565.

Lagler, K. F. 1956. The pike, *Esox lucius*, Linnaeus, in relation to waterfowl on the Seney National Wildlife Refuge, Michigan. Journal of Wildlife Management 20:114–124.

Lance, B. K., D. B. Irons, S. J. Kendall, and L. L. MacDonald. 2001. An evaluation of marine bird population trends following the *Exxon Valdez* oil spill, Prince William Sound, Alaska. Marine Pollution Bulletin 42:298–309.

Lancia, R. A., C. E. Braun, M. W. Collopy, R. D. Dueser, J. G. Kie, C. J. Martinka, J. D. Nichols, T. D. Nudds, W. R. Porath, and N. G. Tilghman. 1996. ARM! For the future: adaptive resource management in the wildlife profession. Wildlife Society Bulletin 24:436–442.

Lanctot, R., B. Goatcher, K. Scribner, S. Talbot, B. Pierson, D. Esler, and D. Zwiefelhofer. 1999. Harlequin Duck recovery from the *Exxon Valdez* oil spill: a population genetics perspective. Auk 116:781–791.

Laycock, G. 1966. The alien animals. Natural History Press, Garden City, New York.

Lebret, T. 1950. The sex-ratios and the proportion of adult drakes of teal, pintail, shoveler and wigeon in the Netherlands, based on field counts made during autumn, winter and spring. Ardea 38:1–18.

Lee, F. B., and H. K. Nelson. 1966. The role of artificial propagation in Wood Duck management. Pages 140–150 *in* L. R. Jahn, B. T. Crawford, H. H. Dill, A. S. Hawkins, E. J. Mikula, and H. K. Nelson, editors. Wood Duck management and research: a symposium. Wildlife Management Institute, Washington, D.C.

Leibovitz, L., and J. Hwang. 1968. Duck plague on the American continent. Avian Diseases 12:361–378.

Lincoln, F. C. 1932. Do drakes outnumber susies? American Game 21:3–4, 16–17.

Locke, L. N., and M. Friend. 1987. Avian botulism. Pages 83–93 *in* M. Friend, editor. Field guide to wildlife diseases. Vol. 1. General field procedures and diseases of migratory birds. U.S. Fish and Wildlife Service Resource Publication 167.

Longcore, J. R., R. Andrews, L. N. Locke, G. E. Bagley, and L. T. Young. 1974. Toxicity of lead and proposed substitute shot to Mallards. U.S. Fish and Wildlife Service Special Scientific Report Wildlife 183.

Longcore, J. R., D. G. McAuley, D.A. Clugston, C. M. Bunck, J-F. Giroux, C. Ouellet, G. R. Parker, P. Dupuis, D. B. Stotts, and J. R. Goldsberry. 2000. Survival of American Black Ducks radiomarked in Quebec, Nova Scotia, and Vermont. Journal of Wildlife Management 64:238–252.

Longcore, J. R., D. G. McAuley, and C. Frazer. 1991. Survival of postfledging female American Black Ducks. Journal of Wildlife Management 55:573–580.

Lynch, J. 1984. Escape from mediocrity: a new approach to American waterfowl hunting regulations. Wildfowl 35:5–13.

Macy, R. W. 1973. Acquired resistance in ducks to infection with the psilostome trematode *phaeridiotrema globulus* (Rudulphi, 1814). Journal of Wildlife Diseases 9:44–46.

Macy, R. W., A. K. Berntzen, and M. Benz. 1968. In vitro excystation of *Sphaeridiotrema globulus metacercariae*, structure of cyst, and the relationship to host specificity. Journal of Parasitology 54:28–38.

Maier, A., N. Clark, and M. A. Johnson. 2003. Human food, processing, marketing, food programs, and other products. Pages 105–117 *in* M. A. Johnson and C. D. Ankney, editors. Direct control and alternative harvest strategies for North American light geese: report of the Di-rect Control and Alternative Harvest Measures Working Group. Arctic Goose Joint Venture Special Publication. U.S. Fish and Wildlife Service, Washington, D.C., and Canadian Wildlife Service, Ottawa.

Malcolm, J. M. 1982. Bird collisions with a power transmission line and their relation to botulism at a Montana wetland. Wildlife Society Bulletin 10:297–304.

Mañosa, S., R. Mateo, and R. Guitart. 2001. A review of the effects of agricultural and industrial contamination on the Ebro Delta biota and wildlife. Environmental Monitoring and Assessment 71:187–205.

Marra, P. P., S. Griffing, C. Caffrey, A. M. Kilpatrick, R. McLean, C. Brand, E. Saito, A. P. Dupuis, L. Kramer, and R. Novak. 2004. West Nile virus and wildlife. BioScience 54:393–402.

Martin, E. M., and S. M. Carney. 1977. Population ecology of the Mallard. IV. A review of duck hunting regulations, activity, and success, with special reference to the Mallard. U.S. Fish and Wildlife Service Resource Publication 130.

Martinson, R. K., A. D. Geis, and R. I. Smith. 1968. Black Duck harvest and population dynamics in eastern Canada and the Atlantic Flyway. Pages 21–52 *in* P. Barske, editor. The Black Duck. Evaluation, management, and research: a symposium. Wildlife Management Institute, Washington, D.C.

Martinson, R. K., M. E. Rosasco, E. M. Martin, M. G. Smart, S. M. Carney, C. F. Kaczynski, and A. D. Geis. 1966. 1965 experimental September hunting season on teal. U.S. Fish and Wildlife Service Special Scientific Report Wildlife 95.

Mateo, R., R. Cadenas, M. Mañez, and R. Guitart. 2001. Lead shot in two raptor species from Doñana, Spain. Ecotoxicology and Environmental Safety 48:6–10.

Mateo, R., J. C. Dolz, J. M. Aguilar Serrano, J. Belliure, and R. Guitart. 1997. An epizootic of lead poisoning in Greater Flamingos (*Phoenicopterus ruber ruber*) in Spain. Journal of Wildlife Diseases 33:131–134.

Mateo, R., A. J. Green, C. W. Jeske, V. Urios, and C. Gerique. 2001. Lead poisoning in the globally threatened Marbled Teal and White-headed Duck in Spain. Environmental Toxicology and Chemistry 20:2860–2868.

Mateo, R., A. Martínez-Vilalta, and R. Guitart. 1997. Lead shot pellets in the Ebro Delta, Spain: densities in sediments and prevalence of exposure in waterfowl. Environmental Pollution 96:335–341.

McAtee, W. L. 1908. Lead poisoning in ducks. Auk 25:472.

McGilvrey, F. B. 1969. Survival in Wood Duck broods. Journal of Wildlife Management 33:73–76.

McIlhenny, E. A. 1940. Sex ratio in wild birds. Auk 57:85–93.

McLean, R. G. 2002a. Wildlife diseases: crying wolf or crying shame? Opening remarks. Transactions of the North American Wildlife and Natural Resources Conference 67:37–39.

McLean, R. G. 2002b. West Nile virus: a threat to North American avian species. Transactions of the North American Wildlife and Natural Resources Conference 67:62–74.

McMahan, C. A., and R. L. Fritz. 1967. Mortality to ducks from trotlines in Lower Laguna Madre, Texas. Journal of Wildlife Management 31:783–787.

Mendall, H. L. 1958. The Ring-necked Duck in the northeast. University of Maine Studies, Second Series, 73.

Mendall, H. L. 1968. An inventory of Maine's breeding Eider ducks. Transactions of the Northeast Fish and Wildlife Conference 25:95–104.

Metz, K. J., and C. D. Ankney. 1991. Are brightly colored male ducks selectively shot by hunters? Canadian Journal of Zoology 69:279–282.

Migoya, R., and G. A. Baldassarre. 1993. Harvest and food habits of waterfowl wintering in Sinaloa, Mexico. Southwestern Naturalist 38:168–171.

Mikula, E. J., G. F. Martz, and C. L. Bennett, Jr. 1972. Field evaluation of three types of waterfowl hunting regulations. Journal of Wildlife Management 36:441–459.

Miller, M. R., and D. C. Duncan. 1999. Northern Pintail in North America: status and conservation needs of a struggling population. Wildlife Society Bulletin 27:788–800.

Miner, J. 1925. Jack Miner and the birds, and some things I know about nature. Ryerson Press, Toronto.

Miner, M. F. 1931. Migration of Canada Geese from the Jack Miner Sanctuary and banding operations. Wilson Bulletin 43:29–34.

Mitchell, R. R., S. D. Fitzgerald, R. J. Aulerich, R. J. Balander, D. C. Powell, R. J. Tempelman, R. L. Stickle, W. Stevens, and S. J. Bursian. 2001. Health effects following chronic dosing with tungsten-iron and tungsten-polymer shot in adult game-farm Mallards. Journal of Wildlife Diseases 37:451–458.

Moore, J. L., W. L. Hohman, T. M. Stark, and G. A. Weisbrich. 1998. Shot prevalences and diets of diving ducks five years after ban on use of lead shotshells at Catahoula Lake, Louisiana. Journal of Wildlife Management 62:564–569.

Moore, R. L., and C. D. Simpson. 1981. Disease mortality of waterfowl on Texas playa lakes. Southwestern Naturalist 25:566–568.

Mudge, G. P. 1983. The incidence and significance of ingested lead pellet poisoning in British waterfowl. Biological Conservation 27:333–372.

Murray, B. G., Jr. 1979. Population dynamics: alternative models. Academic Press, New York.

Murray, B. G., Jr. 1982. On the meaning of density dependence. Oecologia 53:370–373.

Neff, J. A. 1955. Outbreak of aspergillosis in Mallards. Journal of Wildlife Management 19:415–416.

Nelson, H. K. 1963. Restoration of breeding Canada Goose flocks in the north central states. Transactions of the North American Wildlife and Natural Resources Conference 28:133–150.

Nelson, L., Jr., and J. B. Low. 1977. Acceptance of the 1970–71 point system season by duck hunters. Wildlife Society Bulletin 5:52–55.

Nichols, J. D. 1991. Science, population ecology, and the management of the American Black Duck. Journal of Wildlife Management 55:790–799.

Nichols, J. D. 2000. Evolution of harvest management for North American waterfowl: selective pressures and preadaptations for adaptive harvest management. Transactions of the North American Wildlife and Natural Resources Conference 65:65–77.

Nichols, J. D., M. J. Conroy, D. R. Anderson, and K. P. Burnham. 1984. Compensatory mortality in waterfowl populations: a review of the evidence and implications for research and management. Transactions of the North American Wildlife and Natural Resources Conference 49:535–554.

Nichols, J. D., and G. M. Haramis. 1980a. Inferences regarding survival and recovery rates of winter-banded Canvasbacks. Journal of Wildlife Management 44:164–173.

Nichols, J. D., and G. M. Haramis. 1980b. Sex-specific differences in winter distribution patterns of Canvasbacks. Condor 82:406–416.

Nichols, J. D., and J. E. Hines. 1983. The relationship between harvest and survival rates of Mallards: a straightforward approach with partitioned data sets. Journal of Wildlife Management 47:334–348.

Nichols, J. D., and F. A. Johnson. 1989. Evaluation and experimentation with duck management strategies. Transactions of the North American Wildlife and Natural Resources Conference 54:566–593.

Nichols, J. D., F. A. Johnson, and B. K. Williams. 1995. Managing North American waterfowl in the face of uncertainty. Annual Review of Ecology and Systematics 26:177–199.

Nilsson, L. 1970. Local and seasonal variation in sex ratios of diving ducks in south Sweden during the non-breeding season. Ornis Scandinavica 1:115–128.

Norman, F. I., J. S. Garnham, and K. W. Lowe. 1993. Further notes on lead concentrations in tissues of waterfowl in Victoria. Wildlife Research 20:621–624.

Nudds, T. D., and R. W. Cole. 1991. Changes in populations and breeding success of boreal forest ducks. Journal of Wildlife Management 55:569–573.

Ochiai, K., K. Hoshiko, K. Jin, T. Tsuzuki, and C. Itakura. 1993. A survey of lead poisoning in wild waterfowl in Japan. Journal of Wildlife Diseases 29:349–352.

Ochiai, K., T. Kimura, K. Uematsu, T. Umemura, and C. Itakura. 1999. Lead poisoning in wild waterfowl in Japan. Journal of Wildlife Diseases 35:766–769.

Ogilvie, M. A. 1967. Population changes and mortality of the Mute Swan in Britain. Wildfowl Trust Annual Report 18:64–73.

Ogilvie, M. A. 1972. Distribution, numbers and migration. Pages 29–55 in P. Scott, editor. The swans. Houghton Mifflin, Boston.

Olson, D. P. 1965. Differential vulnerability of male and female Canvasbacks to hunting. Transactions of the North American Wildlife and Natural Resources Conference 30:121–134.

Olson, R. E., and A. D. Afton. 2000. Vulnerability of Lesser Snow Geese to hunting with electronic calling devices. Journal of Wildlife Management 64:983–993.

Owen, M., and M. Dix. 1986. Sex ratios in some common British wintering ducks. Wildfowl 37:104–112.

Pain, D. J. 1990. Lead shot ingestion by waterbird in the Camargue, France: an investigation of levels and interspecific differences. Environmental Pollution 66:273–285.

Pain, D. J. 1991. Lead shot densities and settlement rates in Camargue marshes, France. Biological Conservation 57:273–286.

Palmer, R. S., editor. 1976. Handbook of North American birds. Waterfowl. Volume 3. Yale University Press, New Haven, Connecticut.

Parker, G. R. 1991. Survival of juvenile American Black Ducks on a managed wetland in New Brunswick. Journal of Wildlife Management 55:466–470.

Pattee, O. H., and S. K. Hennes. 1983. Bald Eagles and waterfowl: the lead shot connection. Transactions of the North American Wildlife and Natural Resources Conference 48:230–237.

Pearson, G. L., and D. R. Cassidy. 1997. Perspectives on the diagnosis, epizootiology, and control of the 1973 duck plague epizootic in wild waterfowl at Lake Andes, South Dakota. Journal of Wildlife Diseases 33:681–705.

Perrins, C. M., G. Cousquer, and J. Waine. 2003. A survey of blood lead levels in Mute Swans *Cygnus olor*. Avian Pathology 32:205–212.

Perrins, C. M., and J. Sears. 1991. Collisions with overhead wires as a cause of mortality in Mute Swans *Cygnus olor*. Wildfowl 42:5–11.

Perry, M. C., F. Ferrigno, and F. H. Settle. 1978. Rehabilitation of birds oiled on two mid-Atlantic estuaries. Proceedings of the Southeastern Association of Fish and Wildlife Agencies 32:318–325.

Peters, M. S. 1992. Effects of deep tillage on redistribution of lead shot and chufa tuber biomass at Catahoula Lake, Louisiana. Thesis, Louisiana State University, Baton Rouge.

Petersen, M. R., and D. C. Douglas. 2004. Winter ecology of Spectacled Eiders: environmental characteristics and population change. Condor 106:79–94.

Peterson, C. A., S. L. Lee, and J. E. Elliott. 2001. Scavenging of waterfowl carcasses by birds in agricultural fields of British Columbia. Journal of Field Ornithology 72:150–159.

Peterson, S. R., and R. S. Ellarson. 1977. Food habits of Oldsquaws wintering on Lake Michigan. Wilson Bulletin 89:81–91.

Petrides, G. A. 1944. Sex ratios in ducks. Auk 61:564–571.

Petrides, G. A., and C. R. Byrant. 1951. An analysis of the 1949–50 fowl cholera epizootic in Texas Panhandle waterfowl. Transactions of the North American Wildlife Conference 16:193–216.

Piatt, J. F., C. J. Lensink, W. Butler, M. Kendziorek, and D. R. Nysewander. 1990. Immediate impact of the "*Exxon Valdez*" oil spill on marine birds. Auk 107:387–397.

Pirnie, M. D. 1935. Michigan waterfowl management. Michigan Department of Conservation, Game Division Report, Lansing.

Pokras, M., and R. Chafel. 1992. Lead toxicosis from ingested fishing sinkers in adult Common Loons (*Gavia immer*) in New England. Journal of Zoo and Wildlife Medicine 23:92–97.

Price, J. I. 1985. Immunizing Canada Geese against avian cholera. Wildlife Society Bulletin 13:508–515.

Price, J. I., and C. J. Brand. 1984. Persistence of *Pasturella multocida* in Nebraska wetlands under epizootic conditions. Journal of Wildlife Diseases 20:90–94.

Price, J. I., B. S. Yandell, and W. P. Porter. 1992. Chemical ions affect survival of avian cholera organisms in pondwater. Journal of Wildlife Management 56:274–278.

Price, P. W. 1991. Foreword. Pages v–vii *in* J. E. Loye and M. Zuk, editors. Bird-parasite interactions: ecology, evolution and behaviour. Oxford University Press, Oxford.

Pursglove, S. R., Jr., D. F. Holland, F. H. Settle, and D. C. Gnegy. 1976. Control of a fowl cholera outbreak among Coots in Virginia. Proceedings of the Southeastern Association of Fish and Wildlife Agencies 30:602–609.

Quortrup, E. R., F. B. Queen, and L. J. Merovka. 1946. An outbreak of pasteurellosis in wild ducks. Journal of the American Veterinary Medical Association 108:94–100.

Quortrup, E. R., and R. L. Sudheimer. 1943. Detection of botulinum toxin in the bloodstream of wild ducks, Journal of the American Vererinary Association 102:264–266.

Ramo, C., C. Sánchez, and L. Hernández Saint-Aubin. 1992. Lead poisoning of Greater Flamingos *Phoenicopterus ruber*. Wildfowl 43:220–222.

Rate, H. 1957. Redheads killed by a downdraft. Auk 74:391.

Raveling, D. G., and M. E. Heitmeyer. 1989. Relationships of population size and recruitment of Pintails to habitat conditions and harvest. Journal of Wildlife Management 53:1088–1103.

Reed, T. M., and T. E. Rocke. 1992. The role of avian carcasses in botulism epizootics. Wildlife Society Bulletin 20:175–182.

Reinecke, K. J., C. W. Shaiffer, and D. Delnicki. 1987. Winter survival of female Mallards in the Lower Mississippi Valley. Transactions of the North American Wildlife and Natural Resources Conference 52:258–263.

Rexstad, E. A. 1992. Effect of hunting on annual survival of Canada Geese in Utah. Journal of Wildlife Management 56:297–305.

Rexstad, E. A., and D. R. Anderson. 1988. Effect of the point system on redistributing hunting pressure on Mallards. Journal of Wildlife Management 52:89–94.

Rexstad, E. A., D. R. Anderson, and K. P. Burnham. 1991. Lack of sex-selectivity in harvest of Mallards under the point system. Journal of Wildlife Management 55:586–592.

Rhodes, R. 2004. John James Audubon. Alfred A. Knopf, New York.

Richkus, K. 2004. Are you HIP certified? A closer look at the Harvest Information Program. Delta Waterfowl 5:54–59.

Rimler, R. B., P. A. Rebers, and M. Phillips. 1984. Lipopolysaccharides of the Heddleston serotypes of *Pasturella multocida*. American Journal of Veterinary Research 45:759–763.

Rocke, T. E., N. H. Euliss, Jr., and M. D. Samuel. 1999. Environmental characteristics associated with the occurrence of avian botulism in wetlands of a northern California refuge. Journal of Wildlife Management 63:358–368.

Rocke, T. E., and M. D. Samuel. 1999. Water and sediment characteristics associated with avian botulism outbreaks in wetlands. Journal of Wildlife Management 63:1249–1260.

Rocke, T. E., S. R. Smith, A. Miyamoto, and D. J. Shadduck. 2002. A serotype-specific polymerase chain reaction for isolation of *Pasturella multocida*. Avian Diseases 46:370–377.

Rocke, T. E., S. R. Smith, and S. W. Nashold. 1998. Preliminary evaluation of a simple *in vitro* test for the diagnosis of Type C botulism in wild birds. Journal of Wildlife Diseases 34:744–751.

Rogers, J. P., J. D. Nichols, F. W. Martin, C. F. Kimball, and R. S. Pospahala. 1979. An examination of harvest and survival rates of ducks in relation to hunting. Transactions of the North American Wildlife and Natural Resources Conference 44:114–126.

Roscoe, D. E., and J. E. Huffman. 1982. Trematode (*Sphaeridiotrema globulus*)-induced ulcerative hemorrhagic enteritis in wild Mute Swans (*Cygnus olor*). Avian Diseases 26:214–224.

Roscoe, D. E., and J. E. Huffman. 1983. Fatal enteritis caused by *Sphaeridiotrema globulus* (Trematoda: Psilostomidae) in a Whistling Swan. Journal of Wildlife Diseases 19:370–371.

Roscoe, D. E., S. W. Nielsen, A. A. Lamola, and D. Zuckerman. 1979. A simple, quantitative test for erythrocytic protoporphyrin in lead-poisoned ducks. Journal of Wildlife Diseases 15:127–136.

Rosen, M. N. 1969. Species susceptibility to avian cholera. Bulletin of the Wildlife Disease Association 5:195–2000.

Rosen, M. N. 1971a. Botulism. Pages 100–117 *in* J. W. Davis, R. C. Anderson, L. Karstad, and D. O. Trainer, editors. Infectious and parasitic diseases of wild birds. Iowa State University Press, Ames.

Rosen, M. N. 1971b. Avian cholera. Pages 59–74 *in* J. W. Davis, R. C. Anderson, L. Karstad, and D. O. Trainer, editors. Infectious and parasitic diseases of wild birds. Iowa State University Press, Ames.

Rosen, M. N., and A. I. Bischoff. 1949. The 1948–49 outbreak of fowl cholera in birds in the San Francisco Bay area and surrounding counties. California Fish and Game 35:185–192.

Rosen, M. N., and A. I. Bischoff. 1950. The epidemiology of fowl cholera as it occurs in the wild. Transactions of the North American Wildlife Conference 15:147–153.

Rosen, M. N., and E. E. Morse. 1959. A interspecies chain in a fowl cholera epizootic. California Fish and Game 45:51–56.

Rydzewski, W. 1951. A historical review of bird marking. Dansk Ornitologisk Forenings Tidsskrift 45:61–95.

Samuel, M. D., and E. F. Bowers. 2000. Lead exposure in American Black Ducks after implementation of non-toxic shot. Journal of Wildlife Management 64:947–953.

Samuel, M. D., D. J. Shadduck, and D. R. Goldberg. 2004. Are wetlands the reservoir for avian cholera? Journal of Wildlife Diseases 40:377–382.

Samuel, M. D., D. J. Shadduck, D. R. Goldberg, and W. P. Johnson. 2003. Comparison of methods to detect *Pasturella multocida* in carrier waterfowl. Journal of Wildlife Diseases 39:125–135.

Samuel, M. D., D. J. Shadduck, D. R. Goldberg, M. A. Wilson, D. O. Joly, and M. A. Lehr. 2003. Characterization of *Pasturella multocida* isolates from wetland ecosystems during 1996 to 1999. Journal of Wildlife Diseases 39:798–807.

Samuel, M. D., and J. Y. Takekawa, G. Samelius, and D. R. Goldberg. 1999. Avian cholera mortality in Lesser Snow Geese nesting on Banks Island, Northwest Territories. Wildlife Society Bulletin 27:780–787.

Sanderson, G. C., and F. C. Bellrose. 1986. A review of the problem of lead poisoning in waterfowl. Illinois Natural History Survey Special Publication 4.

Sandler, R. J., T. E. Rocke, M. D. Samuel, and T. M. Yuill. 1993. Seasonal prevalence of *Clostridium botulinum* Type C in sediments of a northern California wetland. Journal of Wildlife Diseases 29:533–539.

Sargeant, A. B. 1981. Road casualties of prairie nesting ducks. Wildlife Society Bulletin 9:65–69.

Schladweiler, J. L., and J. R. Tester. 1972. Survival and behavior of hand-reared Mallards released in the wild. Journal of Wildlife Management 36:1118–1127.

Schmitz, R. A., A. A. Aguirre, R. S. Cook, and G. A. Baldassarre. 1990. Lead poisoning of Caribbean Flamingos in Yucatan, Mexico. Wildlife Society Bulletin 18:399–404.

Sears, J. 1988. Regional and seasonal variation in lead poisoning in Mute Swans *Cygnus olor* in relation to the distribution of lead and lead weights in the Thames area, England. Biological Conservation 46:115–134.

Sears, J. 1989. A review of lead poisoning among the River Thames Mute Swan *Cygnus cygnus* population. Wildfowl 40:151–152.

Sedinger, J. S., and E. A. Rexstad. 1994. Do restrictive harvest regulations result in higher survival rates in Mallards? A comment. Journal of Wildlife Management 58:571–577.

Sellers, R. A. 1973. Mallard releases in understocked prairie pothole habitat. Journal of Wildlife Management 37:10–22.

Shawky, S. A., and T. S. Sandhu. 1997. Inactivated vaccine for protection against duck viral enteritis. Avian Diseases 41:461–468.

Siegfried, W. R. 1972. Ruddy Ducks colliding with wires. Wilson Bulletin 84:486–487.

Simpson, V. R.., A. E. Hunt, and M. C. French. 1979. Chronic lead poisoning in a herd of Mute Swans. Environmental Pollution 18:187–202.

Smith, A. E., S. R. Craven, and P. D. Curtis. 1999. Managing Canada Geese in urban environments. Jack H. Berryman Institute Publication 16, Utah State University, Logan.

Smith, A. G., and H. R. Webster. 1955. Effects of hail storms on waterfowl populations in Alberta, Canada — 1953. Journal of Wildlife Management 19:368–374.

Smith, B. J., and K. F. Higgins. 1990. Avian cholera and temporal changes in wetland numbers and densities in Nebraska's Rainwater Basin area. Wetlands 10:1–5.

Smith, B. J., K. F. Higgins, and W. L. Tucker. 1991. Precipitation, waterfowl densities and mycotoxins: their potential effect on avian cholera epizootics in the Nebraska Rainwater Basin area. Transactions of the North American Wildlife and Natural Resources Conference 55:269–282.

Smith, D. B. 2000. Survival, behavior, and movements of captive-reared Mallards in Dorchester County, Maryland. Dissertation, Louisiana State University, Baton Rouge.

Smith, D. B., and F. C. Rohwer. 1997. Perceptions of releases of captive-reared Mallards, with emphasis on an intensive program in Maryland. Transactions of the North American Wildlife and Natural Resources Conference 62:403–411.

Smith, G. R., J. C. Oliphant, and W. R. White. 1982. *Clostridium botulinum* Type C in the Mersey Estuary. Journal of Hygiene 89:507–511.

Smith, G. W., and J. A. Dubovsky. 1998. The Point System and duck-harvest management. Wildlife Society Bulletin 26:333–341.

Smith, G. W., and R. E. Reynolds. 1992. Hunting and Mallard survival, 1979–88. Journal of Wildlife Management 56:306–316.

Smith, G. W., and R. E. Reynolds. 1994. Hunting and Mallard survival: a reply. Journal of Wildlife Management 58:578–581.

Smith, R. I., R. J. Blohm, S. T. Kelly, R. E. Reynolds, and F. D. Caswell. 1989. Review of data bases for managing duck harvests. Transactions of the North American Wildlife and Natural Resources Conference 54:537–551.

Smoot, L. A., and M. D. Pierson. 1979. Effect of oxidation-reduction potential on the outgrowth and chemical inhibition of *Clostridium botulinum* 10755A spores. Journal of Food Science 44:700–704.

Solman, V. E. F. 1945. The ecological relations of pike, *Esox lucius* L., and waterfowl. Ecology 26:157–170.

Sowls, L. K. 1955. Prairie ducks: a study of their behavior, ecology and management. Stackpole Books, Harrisburg, Pennsylvania.

Spieker, J. O., T. M. Yuill, and E. C. Burgess. 1996. Virulence of six strains of duck plague virus in eight waterfowl species. Journal of Wildlife Diseases 32:453–460.

Stehn, R. A., C. P. Dau, B. Conant, and W. I. Butler, Jr. 1993. Decline of Spectacled Eiders nesting in western Alaska. Arctic 46:264–277.

Stone, W. B., and J. C. Okoniewski. 2001. Necropsy findings and environmental contaminants in Common Loons from New York. Journal of Wildlife Diseases 37:178–184.

Stout, I. J., and G. W. Cornwell. 1976. Nonhunting mortality of fledged North American waterfowl. Journal of Wildlife Management 40:681–693.

Surrendi, D. C. 1970. The mortality, behavior, and homing of transplanted juvenile Canada Geese. Journal of Wildlife Management 34:719–733.

Swennen, C., P. Duiven, and L. A. Reyrink. 1979. Notes on the sex ration of the Common Eider, *Somateria molllissima* (L.). Ardea 67:54–61.

Tamisier, A. 1976. Diurnal activities of Green–winged Teal and Pintail wintering in Louisiana. Wildfowl 27:19–32.

Taylor, T. T., and D. B. Pence. 1981. Avian cholera in Common Crows, *Corvus brachyrhynchos*, from the central Texas panhandle. Journal of Wildlife Diseases 17:511–514.

Thill, J. 2001. Lake Erie botulism outbreak. The Prothonotory 67:24, 27.

Thomas, N. J., and others (editors). 2007. Infectious and parasitic diseases of wild birds. Iowa State University Press, Ames, Iowa, USA. (in press).

Thompson, J. D., and G. A. Baldassarre. 1988. Postbreeding survival estimates for Wood Ducks in northern Alabama. Journal of Wildlife Management 52:424–425.

Thompson, J. D., and G. A. Baldassarre. 1989. Postbreeding dispersal by Wood Ducks in northern Alabama with reference to early hunting seasons. Wildlife Society Bulletin 17:142–146.

Thompson, J. D., B. J. Sheffer, and G. A. Baldassarre. 1989. Incidence of ingested lead shot in waterfowl harvested in Yucatan, Mexico. Wildlife Society Bulletin 17:189–191.

Thul, J. E. 1990. Proportion of northern Wood Ducks in southern harvests: application of a biological tag model. Pages 335–339 *in* L. H. Fredrickson, G. V. Burger, S. P. Havera, D. A. Graber, R. E. Kirby, and T. S. Taylor, editors. Proceedings of the 1988 North American Wood Duck Symposium, St. Louis.

Tirelli, E., N. Maestrini, S. Govoni, E. Catelli, and R. Serra. 1996. Lead contamination in the Mallard (*Anas platyrhynchos*) in Italy. Bulletin of Environmental Contamination and Toxicology 56:729–753.

Todd, C. S., L. S. Young, R. B. Owen, Jr., and F. J. Gramlich. 1982. Food habits of Bald Eagles in Maine. Journal of Wildlife Management 46:636–645.

Trauger, D. L., and J. H. Stoudt. 1978. Trends in waterfowl populations and habitats on study areas in Canadian parklands. Transactions of the North American Wildlife and Natural Resources Conference 43:187–205.

Trost, R. E. 1987. Mallard survival and harvest rates: a reexamination of relationships. Transactions of the North American Wildlife and Natural Resources Conference 52:264–284.

Trost, R. E. 1989. Measuring the waterfowl harvest. International Waterfowl Symposium 6:134–147.

Turnbull, R. E., D. H. Brakhage, and F. A. Johnson. 1986. Lesser Scaup mortality from commercial trotlines on Lake Okeechobee, Florida. Proceedings of the Southeastern Association of Fish and Wildlife Agencies 40:465–469.

Twiss, M., and V. G. Thomas. 1998. Preventing fishing-sinker-induced lead poisoning of Common Loons through Canadian policy and regulative reform. Journal of Environmental Management 53:49–59.

U.S. Department of the Interior. 2002. Draft Environmental Impact Statement: resident Canada Goose management. U.S. Fish and Wildlife Service, Washington, D.C.

U.S. Fish and Wildlife Service. 1976. Final environmental statement: proposed use of steel shot for hunting waterfowl in the United States. U.S. Fish and Wildlife Service, Washington, D.C.

U.S. Fish and Wildlife Service. 1977. Environmental assessment: proposed shooting hours regulations. U.S. Fish and Wildlife Service, Washington, D.C.

U.S. Fish and Wildlife Service. 2004a. Waterfowl population status, 2004. U.S. Department of Interior, Washington, D.C.

U.S. Fish and Wildlife Service. 2004b. Adaptive harvest management. 2004 duck hunting season. U.S. Department of Interior, Washington, D.C.

U.S. Fish and Wildlife Service. 2004c. North American Waterfowl Management Plan: strengthening the biological foundation. 2004 strategic guide. U.S. Fish and Wildlife Service, Washington, D.C.

U.S. Fish and Wildlife Service. 2005. Waterfowl status report, 2005. U.S. Fish and Wildlife Service, Wasington, D.C.

U.S. Fish and Wildlife Service and Canadian Wildlife Service. 1991. North American bird banding. Volume 1. Canadian Wildlife Service, Ottawa.

Vangilder, L. D., L. M. Smith, and R. K. Lawrence. 1986. Nutrient reserves of premigratory Brant during spring. Auk 103:237–241.

Vaught, R. W., and L. L. Kirsch. 1966. Canada Geese of the Eastern Prairie Population, with special reference to the Swan Lake flock. Missouri Department of Conservation Technical Bulletin 3.

Vaught, R. W., H. C. McDougle, and H. H. Burgess. 1967. Fowl cholera in waterfowl at Squaw Creek National Wildlife Refuge, Missouri. Journal of Wildlife Management 31:248–253.

Ver Steeg, J. M., and R. C. Elden, compilers. 2002. Harvest Information Program: evaluation and recommendations. International Association of Fish and Wildlife Agencies, Migratory Shore and Upland Game Bird Working Group, Ad Hoc Committee on HIP, Washington, D.C.

Walker, J. W., C. J. Pfow, S. S. Newcomb, W. D. Urban, H. E. Nadler, and L. N. Locke. 1969. Status of duck virus enteritis (duck plague) in the USA. Proceedings of the United States Animal Health Association 1969:254–279.

Walters, C. J. 1986. Adaptive management of renewable resources. Macmillan, New York.

Warner, R. E. 1968. The role of introduced diseases in the extinction of the endemic Hawaiian avifauna. Condor 70:101–120.

Wayland, M., E. Neugebauer, and T. Bollinger. 1999. Concentrations of lead in liver, kidney, and bone of Bald and Golden Eagles. Archives of Environmental Contamination and Toxicology 37:267–272.

Wayland, M., L. K. Wilson, J. E. Elliott, M. J. R. Miller, T. Bollinger, M. McAdie, K. Langelier, J. Keating, and J. M. W. Froese. 2003. Mortality, morbidity, and lead poisoning of eagles in western Canada, 1968–98. Journal of Raptor Research 37:8–18.

Weller, M. W. 1969. Potential dangers of exotic waterfowl introductions. Wildfowl 20:55–58.

Wendt, J. S., and J. A. Kennedy. 1991. Policy considerations regarding the use of lead pellets for waterfowl hunting in Canada. Pages 61–67 in D. J. Pain, editor. Lead poisoning in waterfowl. International Waterfowl and Wetlands Research Bureau Special Publication 16.

Wetmore, A. 1915. Mortality among waterfowl around Great Salt Lake, Utah. U.S. Department of Agriculture Bulletin 217.

Wetmore, A. 1918. The duck sickness in Utah. U.S. Department of Agriculture Bulletin 672.

White, D. H., and J. T. Seginak. 1994. Dioxins and furans linked to reproductive impairment in Wood Ducks. Journal of Wildlife Management 58:100–106.

Williams, B. K., and F. A. Johnson. 1995. Adaptive management and the regulation of waterfowl harvests. Wildlife Society Bulletin 23:430–436.

Williams, B. K., F. A. Johnson, and K. Wilkins. 1996. Uncertainty and the adaptive management of waterfowl harvests. Journal of Wildlife Management 60:223–232.

Williams, B. K., J. D. Nichols, and M. J. Conroy. 2001. Analysis and management of animal populations. Academic Press, New York.

Williamson, J. L., T. E. Rocke, and J. M. Aiken. 1999. In situ detection of Clostridium botulinum Type C in wetland sediments with a nested PCR assay. Applied and Environmental Microbiology 65:3240–3243.

Wilson, S. S. 1979. A bibliography of references to avian cholera. U.S. Fish and Wildlife Service Special Scientific Report Wildlife 217.

Wilson, S. S., and L. N. Locke. 1982. Bibliography of references to avian botulism: update. U.S. Fish and Wildlife Service Special Scientific Report Wildlife 243.

Windingstad, R. M., R. M. Duncan, and D. Thornburg. 1983. Outbreak of avian cholera on the wintering grounds of the Mississippi Valley Canada Goose flock. Journal of Wildlife Diseases 19:95–97.

Windingstad, R. M., S. M. Kerr, R. M. Duncan, and C. J. Brand. 1988. Characterization of an avian cholera epizootic in wild birds in western Nebraska. Avian Diseases 32:124–131.

Wishart, R. A., R. M. Kaminski, and D. W. Soprovich. 1981. Further evidence of Marsh Hawks feeding on ducks. Prairie Naturalist 13:23–25.

Wobeser, G. 1992. Avian cholera and waterfowl biology. Journal of Wildlife Diseases 28:674–682.

Wobeser, G. 1997a. Diseases of wild waterfowl. Second edition. Plenum Press, New York.

Wobeser, G. 1997b. Avian botulism — another perspective. Journal of Wildlife Diseases 33:181–186.

Wobeser, G., and T. Bollinger. 2002. Type C avian botulism — management dilemma. Transactions of the North American Wildlife and Natural Resources Conference 67:40–50.

Wolfe, D. A., M. J. Hameedi, J. A. Galt, G. Watabayashi, J. Short, C. O'Clair, S. Rice, J. Michel, J. R. Payne, J. Braddock, S. Hanna, and D. Sale. 1994. The fate of the oil spilled from the *Exxon Valdez*. Environmental Science and Technology 28:561–568.

Wooten, W. A. 1954. Waterfowl losses in the surf along the northern California coast. Journal of Wildlife Management 18:140–141.

Wright, B. S. 1954. High tide and an east wind: the story of the Black Duck. Stackpole, Harrisburg, Pennsylvania, and the Wildlife Management Institute, Washington, D.C.

Yerkes, T., and C. Bluhm. 1998. Return rates and reproductive output of captive-reared Mallards. Journal of Wildlife Management 62:192–198.

York, D. L., J. L. Cummings, R. M. Engemen, K. L. Wedemeyer. 2000. Hazing and movements of Canada Geese near Elmendorf Air Force Base in Anchorage, Alaska. International Biodeterioration and Biodegradation 45:103–110.

Zinkl, J. G., N. Dey, J. M. Hyland, J. J. Hurt, and K. L. Heddleston. 1977. An epornitic of avian cholera in waterfowl and Common Crows in Phelps County, Nebraska, in the spring. Journal of Wildlife Diseases 13:194–198.

Zinkl, J. G., J. Rathert, and R. R. Hudson. 1978. Diazinon poisoning in wild Canada Geese. Journal of Wildlife Management 42:406–409.

Zwank, P. J., V. L. Wright, P. M. Shealy, and J. D. Newsom. 1985. Lead toxicosis in waterfowl on two major wintering areas in Louisiana. Wildlife Society Bulletin 13:17–26.

Chapter 9
MAJOR WATERFOWL HABITATS

The abundance and availability of suitable habitat is unquestionably the greatest limitation confronting waterfowl. Other factors fade to virtual insignificance when compared with the chronic loss and deterioration of habitats on which waterfowl depend. Indeed, the precipitous decline in waterfowl populations in North America and elsewhere is the direct result of habitat loss. Moreover, these losses have fallen across the entire spectrum of breeding, wintering, and migration areas so essential for waterfowl and many other kinds of wildlife.

Leopold (1933) defined habitat as the sum of those environmental factors a species requires for its survival and reproduction; in common terms, these are suitable food, cover, and water. For waterfowl, however, the concept of habitat is especially complex because of the well-developed migratory behavior of most species. To illustrate, Blue-winged Teal breeding in the Prairie Pothole Region of Manitoba may overwinter on the coastal marshes of Venezuela, stopping at numerous wetlands while en route between these far-flung destinations. Thus, the survival and reproduction of Blue-winged Teal requires the availability and protection of suitable habitat in several states and provinces within at least three countries on two continents. Management on such a scale is scarcely an easy task — state/provincial, national, and international cooperation is required to achieve realistic goals (see Chapter 11). Coordinated protection for habitat may be even more difficult in Europe where migrating waterfowl often cross a dozen or more international boundaries each year.

We have repeatedly stressed the importance of waterfowl habitat in relation to the annual cycle of waterfowl. That is, spatial protection of only breeding and wintering habitat is ineffective without the availability of intermittent stopping points during migration. Likewise, the timing of habitat manipulations should coincide with the life-history features of targeted species (see Chapter 10).

Despite extensive loss, North America and other areas of the world still possesses a rich assortment of productive wetlands, many of which are of great consequence for the welfare of waterfowl populations. In North America, these habitats span the continent, some providing breeding habitat, whereas others primarily benefit wintering or migrating waterfowl; some may serve each of these functions. This chapter accordingly describes the key features and functional roles of major wetland systems of importance to waterfowl and other wetland-related

wildlife. Our emphasis is on North America, but we also include brief descriptions of representative wetlands of international importance to waterfowl based on information available from the Secretariat of the Ramsar Convention

MAJOR WETLAND HABITATS IMPORTANT TO WATERFOWL IN NORTH AMERICA

Several major habitats important to breeding, wintering, and migrating waterfowl occur across the breadth of North America, 67 of which have been recognized in the United States, Canada, and Mexico by the U.S. Fish and Wildlife Service (Fig. 9-1). Space does not permit review of the function, characteristics, and waterfowl populations for each of these areas. Hence, we instead shall focus on a selection of sites we believe are generally recognized as being of particular significance to North America's waterfowl. Specific management scenarios for many of these areas are presented on a flyway-by-flyway basis in Smith et al. (1989); thus, we shall limit our treatment of wetland management to more general considerations, drawing examples from the wetland habitats described here. Readers also are directed to a brief, but thorough, summary of important waterfowl habitats appearing in Linduska (1964) as well as other habitat information reviewed in Bellrose (1980).

The Prairie Potholes and Allied Areas

Known popularly as the "duck factory," the Prairie Pothole Region (PPR) on the northern Great Plains of North America is the greatest duck production habitat in the world. The PPR may produce 50–80% of the primary species of game ducks on the continent (Batt et al. 1989), and yet the area contains only 10% of the breeding habitat in North America (Smith et al. 1964). From 1955 to 1974, Bellrose (1979) estimated that the PPR contained about 50% of all the breeding dabbling ducks on the continent. Densities of breeding pairs can approach 30/km^2 (Stewart and Kantrud 1974), which are the highest reported anywhere in North America. Twelve of the 34 species of ducks in North America are common to the PPR, and during a 30-year period more than 50% of the populations of eight species occurred in the area (Batt et al. 1989). As examples, averages for Gadwall were 94%, Blue-winged Teal 88%, Redhead 81%, Ruddy Duck 87%, Canvasback 64%, Mallard 67%, and Northern Pintail 62%.

The PPR also provides habitat for migrating and, to a much lesser extent, for wintering waterfowl

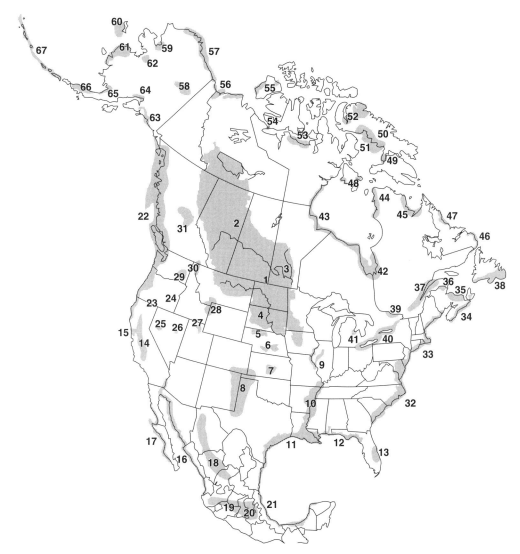

Figure 9-1. Major waterfowl habitats in North America identified by the U.S. Fish and Wildlife Service: 1 = Prairie Pothole Region, 2 = Western Boreal Forest, 3 = South Interlakes Marshes, 4 = Northern Great Plains, 5 = Sandhills, 6 = Rainwater Basin, 7 = Central Kansas Marshes, 8 = Playa Lakes, 9 = Central Mississippi and Illinois River, 10 = Lower Mississippi Alluvial Valley, 11 = Gulf Coastal Prairie, 12 = East Gulf Coast, 13 = St. John's River, 14 = Central Valley, 15 = San Francisco Bay, 16 = Pacific Coast of Mexico, 17 = Baja California, 18 = Northern Highlands of Mexico, 19 = Central Lakes and Lagoons of Mexico, 20 = Wetlands of the Valley of Mexico, 21 = Gulf Coast of Mexico, 22 = Pacific Coast, 23 = Klamath Basin, 24 = Malheur Basin, 25 = Carson Sink, 26 = Ruby Lake, 27 = Great Salt Lake and Bear River Marshes, 28 = Yellowstone–Intermountain Wetlands, 29 = Columbia Basin, 30 = Bitterroot Intermountain, 31 = British Columbia Central Plateau, 32 = Mid-Atlantic Coast, 33 = Northeast Atlantic Coast, 34 = Nova Scotian Coast, 35 = Prince Edward Island, 36 = Chaleur Bay, 37 = Gulf of St. Lawrence, 38 = Coastal Newfoundland, 39 = Ottawa Valley, 40 = Lower Great Lakes, 41 = Saginaw Bay, 42 = James Bay Lowlands, 43 = West Coast of Hudson Bay, 44 = West Ungava Peninsula, 45 = East Ungava Peninsula, 46 = South Labrador Coast, 47 = North Labrador Coast, 48 = East Bay–Harry Gibbons, 49 = Dewey Soper, 50 = Central Baffin–Spicer–Prince Charles–Airforce Islands Complex, 51 = Bylot Island–Northwest Baffin Island, 52 = Arctic Bay–Northwest Baffin Island, 53 = Queen Maud Gulf, 54 = Lambert Channel Polynya, 55 = Banks Island, 56 = Old Crow Flats–Anderson River Delta–Bathurst Polynya, 57 = North Slope–Beaufort Sea, 58 = Yukon Flats, 59 = Selawik National Wildlife Refuge, 60 = Bering Sea Ice Lead, 61 = Yukon–Kuskokwim Delta, 62 = Innoka National Wildlife Refuge, 63 = Copper River Delta, 64 = Upper Cook Inlet, 65 = Bristol Bay–Kvichak Bay, 66 = Izembek Lagoon–Alaska Peninsula, 67 = Aleutian Islands. Map is from North American Waterfowl Management Plan (2004:15).

(Pederson et al. 1989). It is especially important as a major migration corridor during fall and spring. Van der Valk (1989) provides excellent coverage for the vegetation and other ecological features of these important wetlands.

The PPR extends along a northwest–southeast arc some 480 km wide and 1,600 km long from North and South Dakota, western Minnesota, northwest Iowa, and parts of northern Montana north to the edge of the boreal forest in Saskatchewan, Alberta, and Manitoba. This area covers about 78 million ha (777,000 km²) and is divided into two major zones: (1) the aspen parklands, which cover the northern one-third; and (2) the grasslands, which cover the lower two-thirds (Fig. 9-2). In essence, the parklands form a 22-million-ha ecotone between the grasslands to the south and the boreal forest to the north. Grasslands cover 26 million ha in Canada but only 15 million of the original 30 million ha remain in the United States (Bellrose 1980). Before settlement, the PPR contained an estimated 8 million ha of potholes, and in some areas, potholes covered as much as 40–60%

of the landscape (Hewes and Frandson 1952, Frayer et al. 1983). The potholes themselves were formed during the Wisconsin glacial advance about 12,000 years ago.

The density of potholes varies from about 4/km² in some parts of the Dakotas to 38/km² in southeastern Saskatchewan; the average for the entire PPR is about 11.6 potholes/km² (Smith et al. 1964). Near Melfort, Saskatchewan, the density of potholes was 36/km² or 12.5 ha/km², which was some 12.5% of the total area (Millar 1969). Estimates vary, but there may be as many 10 million potholes in Prairie Canada (Gollop 1965) and at least 1.2 million in the United States (Bellrose 1980). Most potholes are small; 82–88% of the basins in Saskatchewan were 0.4 ha or less and together occupied 29–44% of the total coverage of potholes (Millar 1969). In contrast, only 13–18% of the basins were greater than 0.4 ha on the same study areas and, in some places, only 6--9% of all potholes were greater than 2 ha in size (Table 9-1).

Melting snow is the major source of water for

Figure 9-2. A complex of prairie potholes near Minnedosa, Manitoba. Photo courtesy of Karen J. Bataille, Missouri Department of Conservation.

Table 9-1. The size distribution of wetlands in the Prairie Pothole Region as determined at three areas in Saskatchewan. Modified from Millar (1969:77).

Basin size (hectares)[a]	Percentage of basins in each study area			
	Melfort (n = 2447)	Saskatoon (n = 1,138)	Swift Current (n = 1,931)	Overall (n = 5,516)
≤0.10	46.7	43.1	44.4	45.1
0.11–0.20	14.9	25.9	19.5	18.8
0.21–0.41	20.4	18.5	20.7	20.1
0.41–1.01	12.7	9.3	11.5	11.6
1.02–2.03	3.3	1.8	2.4	2.7
2.03–4.05	1.2	0.8	1.0	1.0
4.05–8.10	0.4	0.3	0.4	0.4
8.10–16.20	0.2	0.3	0.1	0.2
>16.20	0.2	0.0	0.0	0.1

[a]Categories did not overlap in original data, which were reported in acres.

prairie potholes, although widely scattered and infrequent rains also fill some basins. Potholes store about 72% of the runoff resulting from a 2-year-frequency flood (Ludden et al. 1983), but precipitation varies markedly between years, and droughts are common events. This pattern produces a "boom or bust" system in which highly productive waterfowl habitat occurs only about 3 years in 10. The impact of drought was clear during a study in southern Saskatchewan where water-filled potholes averaged 39/km² in 1955, 19/km² in 1956, and less than 1.2/km² during severe drought in 1961 (Fig. 9-3; Smith et al. 1964). Over a broad area in northern North Dakota, the number of potholes present in Stratum 45 of the Breeding Waterfowl and Habitat Survey (see Chapter 8) between 1980 and 2000 varied from 59,100 in 1991 to 895,000 in 1999 (Niemuth and Solberg 2003). Ducks use the prairie potholes in direct proportion to the extent of drought as measured by the number of ponds containing water in May (Batt et al. 1989; Fig. 9-4). Production also declines, as revealed in North and South Dakota, where Duebbert and Frank (1984) recorded only 23 broods in a drought year (1961) compared with 557 broods when good water conditions returned in 1969.

During drought, the lack of breeding habitat displaces many ducks from grassland areas into the parklands where water conditions are generally more stable. But when drought strikes the entire PPR, ducks move even farther north into boreal forests and tundra (Crissey 1969). However, even though water may be more available farther north, breeding productivity is generally much less than normal and duck populations accordingly decline. Northern

Figure 9-3. Drought, which is a regularly occurring feature in the Prairie Pothole Region, produces dramatic reductions in duck populations. During years of severe drought, many prairie-nesting ducks move farther north to breed. Photo courtesy of Henry R. Murkin, Ducks Unlimited Canada.

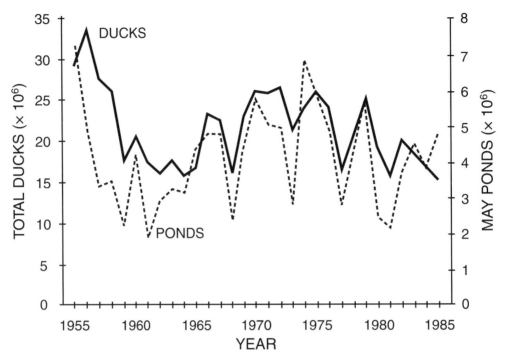

Figure 9-4. A strong relationship exists between the number of May ponds and duck numbers in the Prairie Pothole Region. From Batt et al. (1989:215). With mermission from Blackwell Publishing Professional.

Pintails illustrate this situation; in dry years the proportion of the population moving north of the prairie grasslands is strongly, but inversely, related to the number of potholes with water (r = -0.91). The relationship between the young–adult age ratio and the ratio of north–south Northern Pintail populations is also strongly negative (r = -0.92), thereby providing evidence that the reproductive output of Northern Pintails is diminished when the birds do not nest in the prairie grasslands (Smith 1970a). Importantly, however, this does not imply that Northern Pintails fail to breed when moving to subarctic areas. For example, data collected in subarctic areas of Alaska revealed that Northern Pintails did breed and that sex ratios approached normal, although production was stifled by low nest success (Flint and Grand 1996). The influence of drought also appears to be somewhat species-specific. Ruwaldt et al. (1979) found that Northern Pintails, Blue-winged Teal, and Northern Shovelers were most sensitive to drought, whereas Mallards, Gadwall, and American Wigeon were less sensitive. Nonetheless, 59% fewer pairs of ducks of all species nested on their study area in response to drought conditions.

Even with so-called normal weather patterns, however, potholes containing water in April and May are often dry later in the summer. In North Dakota,

for example, water-filled potholes declined in number by 58% — a reduction of 395,000 basins or 502,000 ha — from spring to late summer (Bellrose 1980). In some years 80% of the smaller basins and 35–45% of the larger basins often dry out between spring and mid-summer. Hence, the flora and the fauna of potholes thereafter changes dramatically in response to the regular occurrence of wet–dry cycles; the ensuing vegetation is strongly influenced by the nature of the seed bank (Kantrud et al. 1989a).

Vegetation in prairie potholes develops in distinctive zones, which became a means for classifying these wetlands (Stewart and Kantrud 1971). The zones are (1) wetland–low prairie, (2) wet meadow, (3) shallow marsh, (4) deep marsh, (5) permanent open water, (6) intermittent alkali, and (7) fen (alkaline bog). Thereafter seven major classes of potholes were distinguished based largely on the vegetational zone occurring in the center of a pothole (Fig. 9-5). Within each class are five subclasses based on vegetational differences and their correlations with salinity: (1) fresh, (2) slightly brackish, (3) moderately brackish, (4) brackish, and (5) subsaline. Each pothole then is assigned to one of four cover types.

Temporary, seasonal, and semipermanent potholes are by far the most important to breeding waterfowl (Stewart and Kantrud 1973, Kantrud and

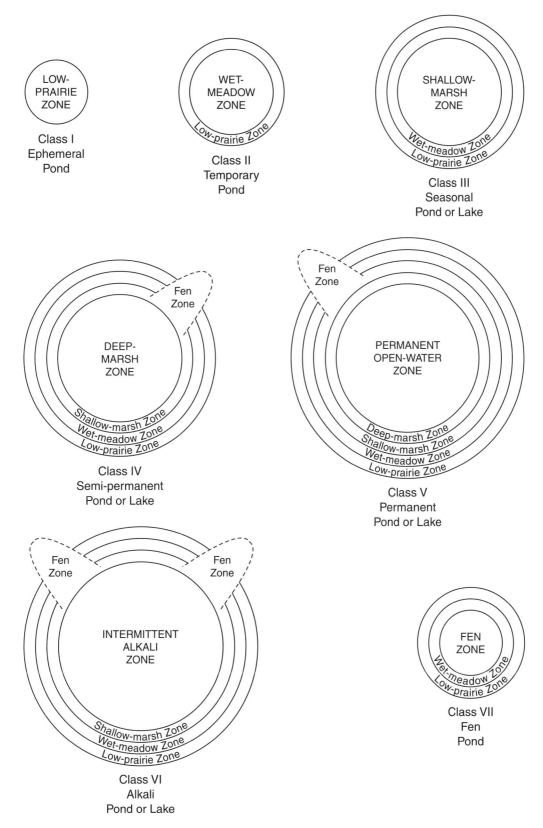

Figure 9-5. Spatial arrangement for zones of wetland vegetation associated with the seven major classes of prairie potholes. From Stewart and Kantrud (1971:8).

Stewart 1977). Temporary wetlands hold water for only a few weeks after snowmelt and occasionally for a few days following heavy rainstorms in late spring, summer, and fall. Seasonal wetlands maintain water in spring and early summer but normally are dry by late summer and early fall, whereas semipermanent wetlands ordinarily maintain water through spring and summer and frequently into fall and winter.

Temporary basins are especially important because they provide isolation and spacing for pairs of breeding waterfowl. Further, because their shallow waters warm rapidly, temporary wetlands also provide the first invertebrate food resources in spring (Swanson et al. 1974). Temporary wetlands are particularly important breeding habitat for early-nesting species such as Mallards and Northern Pintails, but they also serve as habitat for migrating waterfowl. In North Dakota, Ruwaldt et al. (1979) recorded 1–13% of the breeding population of nine species of ducks on temporary wetlands (Table 9-2).

Seasonal wetlands provide abundant invertebrate foods and other components of breeding habi-

tat, including nesting cover for those species of ducks that nest over water (Kantrud et al. 1989b). In North Dakota, for example, 55% of the breeding population of 12 species of ducks selected seasonal wetlands, and 60% of all dabbling ducks occurred here (Kantrud and Stewart 1977). Also in North Dakota, Stewart and Kantrud (1973) determined that 48% of the total breeding duck population used seasonal wetlands (also see Krapu et al. 2000). Seasonal wetlands, especially those dominated by whitetop rivergrass (*Scolochloa festucacea*), were highly favored as brood cover for Mallards during years of favorable water conditions in North Dakota (Talent et al. 1982). During a 20-year period in North and South Dakota, 24% of all brood use occurred on seasonal wetlands (Duebbert and Frank 1984).

Again in North Dakota, semipermanent wetlands received 36% of all duck use, but for pochards the figure reached 75% (Kantrud and Stewart 1977). Semipermanent potholes thus are the principal habitats for breeding pochards, although these wetlands remain especially important for dabbling ducks in years when drought limits the availability of tempo-

Table 9-2. Use of natural and man-made wetlands in the Prairie Pothole Region as determined by the percentage of duck pairs using these various wetland classes in South Dakota. Number in parentheses is sample size. From Ruwaldt et al. (1979:378).

Wetland class	Blue-winged Teal (846)	Mallard (383)	Northern Pintail (245)	Gadwall (146)	Northern Shoveler (71)	American Wigeon (22)	Green-winged Teal (35)	Redhead (46)	Ruddy Duck (36)
Potholes/lakes									
Ephemeral	0.5	0.7			1.4				
Temporary	7.6	3.8	7.6	2.7	12.5		12.1		
Seasonal	16.8	12.8	17.7	18.4	14.7	7.4	10.5	10.7	9.9
Semipermanent	40.1	22.0	28.9	39.6	35.0	15.5	35.0	89.3	72.2
Permanent	1.7	0.7	0.3	0.7					8.0
Total	66.7	40.0	54.5	61.4	63.6	22.9	57.6	100.0	90.1
Streams									
Intermittent	3.1	13.6	6.6	2.1	1.4	4.6	7.3		
Permanent	<0.5	1.9	<0.5	0.6					
Man-made wetlands									
Dug outs	7.3	8.9	13.3	10.8	6.8	3.4	5.2		
Stock ponds	18.5	33.2	22.1	20.9	22.8	65.1	27.5		9.9
Others[a]	4.3	2.4	3.2	4.2	5.4	4.0	2.4		

[a]Primarily tillage ponds and roadside ditches.

rary and seasonal potholes. During drought conditions in North Dakota, Mallard broods occurred only on semipermanent wetlands (Talent et al. 1982), and more duck broods (58%) were recorded using semipermanent potholes in comparison with other types of wetlands in North and South Dakota (Duebbert and Frank 1984). Other species of wetland birds also find valuable habitat in prairie potholes; excluding waterfowl, 26% of the 223 birds breeding in North Dakota are wetland-associated species (Kantrud and Stewart 1984).

Across a broad area of North Dakota, the average density and size of pothole types/km² were as follows: ephemeral (2.5, 0.04 ha), temporary (2.9, 0.25 ha), seasonal (5.6, 1.15 ha), semipermanent (0.8, 9.34 ha), permanent (0.02, 32.92 ha), alkali (0.02, 48.04 ha), and fen (0.02, 3.63 ha); others that were altered by agriculture and could not be assigned to a particular class averaged 12.7/km² and 0.21 ha (Kantrud and Stewart 1977). In Prairie Canada, Lynch et al. (1963) classified potholes as permanent (3.8%), semipermanent (7.7%), ephemeral/seasonal (23.3%), and temporary (56.1%); 9.1% were classified as unsuitable habitat for waterfowl. Ruwaldt et al. (1979) summarized similar data based on a sample of 476 65-ha plots across South Dakota and reported an average of 290 prairie pothole wetlands covering 441 ha per plot. Some 69% of all wetlands in the plots were prairie potholes, while the remainder were dugouts and stock ponds.

Waterfowl take advantage of this complex of wetlands, exploiting several types of potholes, each of which may serve various roles in fulfilling the life-history requirements of a given species during the breeding season. For example, during a radio-telemetry study of Mallards nesting in North Dakota, eight females used 7–22 different wetlands during the breeding period, preferring temporary, seasonal and, to a lesser extent, semipermanent potholes (Dwyer et al. 1979). For both sexes, feeding occurred most often on seasonal wetlands. For females, the home range averaged 468 ha, which underscores that ducks exploit an array of wetland habitats in a semiarid environment such as the prairies. Mallard broods in North Dakota used up to 11 different wetlands, which again emphasizes the importance of maintaining a complex of wetlands as a prerequisite for good waterfowl production (Talent et al. 1982).

The PPR in both the United States and Canada has experienced a long history of destruction, primarily from agricultural drainage. In North and South Dakota, potholes originally covered 2.8 mil-lion ha, but little more than 1.2 million ha remain (Tiner 1984). Iowa has lost almost all of its original wetlands, and 3.6 million ha have been drained in Minnesota. The situation in Canada is only slightly better, but the losses continue. Losses of upland nesting cover and the associated increases in nest predation likewise pose serious problems for waterfowl in the PPR (see Chapter 6). However, in the United States legislation such as the Food Security Act of 1985 (and subsequent reauthorizations), as well as other public and private initiatives for the protection and restoration of wetlands in both the United States and Canada, seemingly herald a new era for the conservation of prairie potholes. In the United States, the Conservation Reserve Program and Wetlands Reserve Program are paramount to this process (see Chapter 11).

Overall, the future for waterfowl on the PPR clearly depends on the ability of the conservation community to maintain nesting habitat and prairie pothole wetlands. However, despite the notable successes associated with the Farm Bill, severe setbacks still occur. In 2001, a court decision in favor of the Solid Waste Agency of Northern Cook County (SWANCC) removed most prairie pothole wetlands in the United States from federal protection under Section 404 of the Clean Water Act (see Chapter 11). Hence, the Swampbuster provision of the 1985 Farm Bill remains as the only major law protecting prairie potholes in the United States. In North Dakota, state law prohibits nonprofit groups from purchasing lands beyond a token acreage that has largely been acquired. Indeed, when the Elkhorn Ranch once owned by former President Teddy Roosevelt was up for sale in 2004, the owners — recognizing the historic significance of the ranch — offered it at reduced price to become part of Theodore Roosevelt National Park, but the state attempted to block the sale. Lastly, development of genetically modified soybeans, which are unaffected by glyphosate herbicides, allows farmers to convert some of the remaining grassland habitats in the PPR into cropland (Krapu et al. 2004; also see Chapter 5). All told — despite heroic efforts of the conservation community — no more than a vestige of the potholes and grasslands once common in midcontinent North America exists today, yet the region is still the most significant production area for many species of ducks.

Rainwater Basin

Two adjacent areas in south-central Nebraska once contained nearly 4,000 wetlands, but because of drainage and filling in the years following settlement, only 445 marshes remained by 1981, which represent 11% of their former numbers and about 30% of the original wetland area (Smith and Higgins 1990). Most of these wetlands lie within the Tallgrass Prairie Region that is now a landscape dedicated to agricultural production. The wetlands, which occupy irregularly shaped basins oriented on a northwest–southeast axis, originated 20,000–25,000 years ago as wind-deflated depressions in the deep surface deposits of Pleistocene loess. They fill from snow melt and rainwater runoff —hence the region's name — which cannot percolate downward because of underlying pans of impervious clay. Water is lost by evaporation; thus, the wetland vegetation is adapted to alternating periods of wet and dry conditions (see Erickson and Leslie 1987 for soil and vegetation relationships in the Rainwater Basin). In addition to outright drainage, siltation has also degraded many of the wetlands as have pits designed to collect and store water for irrigation. Smith and Higgins (1990) estimated that only 19% of the remaining wetlands were in a natural condition, with the balance affected by drainage ditches. The basins are vegetated with smartweeds (*Polygonum* spp.), cattail (*Typha* spp.), and bulrushes (*Scripus* spp.), but in dry years many basins are farmed (Evans and Wolfe 1967). In comparison with the western part of the Rainwater Basin, wetlands in the eastern part are deeper, more permanent, and contain clearer water (Smith et al. 1989, 1990).

The Rainwater Basin provides key habitat for spectacular numbers of waterfowl migrating across the interior of North America. Figuratively, the location of the Rainwater Basin represents the constricted part of an hourglass whose north and south ends extend across the middle of North America. Estimates indicate 5–9 million ducks and several hundred thousand geese use the basin during spring migration (Windingstad et al. 1984), as do large numbers of shorebirds. In particular, 90% of the midcontinent population of White-fronted Geese, 50% of the midcontinent population of Mallards, and 30% of the Northern Pintail population stop each spring in the Rainwater Basin. These wetlands thus represent a major site where waterfowl and other birds obtain the nutrient reserves necessary to continue migration and to prepare for the forthcoming breeding season (e.g., see Gordon et al. 1990 concerning the aquatic invertebrate fauna in the Rainwater Basin, including taxa important as waterfowl foods). Nesting ducks, primarily Blue-winged Teal, Mallards, and Northern

Pintails, experience limited success (about 11%) because of predation and farming operations (Evans and Wolfe 1967).

The importance of the Rainwater Basin to migrating White-fronted Geese triggered a study of their spring staging ecology (Krapu et al. 1995). Corn and the shoots of winter wheat dominated their diet, and the birds typically made two flights per day — midmorning and late afternoon — from the wetlands to forage in the surrounding farmland. Geese of both sexes steadily increased their fat deposits while in the staging area, and adult females added more protein. Whereas the geese flourished on a diet of agricultural foods, and therefore likely arrive on their arctic breeding grounds in exceptional condition, the availability and distribution of suitable wetlands as roosting habitat in the Rainwater Basin allows the birds to take advantage of food supplies over a large area. Similarly, the availability of widely distributed wetlands disperses the goose population, which likely lessens the opportunities for disease transmission (see following).

Unfortunately, the reduced numbers of wetlands within the Rainwater Basin further concentrate the large numbers of waterfowl using the area, thereby enhancing conditions for diseases. Indeed, since 1975, when an estimated 25,000 ducks and geese died, severe epizootics of avian cholera (*Pasteurella multocida*) have occurred in the Rainwater Basin (Zinkl et al. 1977, Windingstad et al. 1984); the largest die-off killed between 72,000 and 80,000 ducks and geese in 1980 (Smith et al. 1989). Smith and Higgins (1990) confirmed the idea that epizootics of avian cholera varied inversely with the densities of the semipermanent wetlands remaining in the Rainwater Basin, which underscores the importance of conserving these wetland habitats. The severest epizootics of avian cholera usually occur in the western region of the Rainwater Basin where the wetlands are less permanent and shallower than those in the eastern region. Infected birds apparently transmit the disease from one wetland to another, instead of the pathogen spreading from place to place in surface water; hence, the spring migration of waterfowl moving northward from the playa lakes in Texas may carry the disease to the Rainwater Basin (Smith et al. 1989). See Oates (1989) for details concerning the incidence of expended lead shot in the substrate of Rainwater Basin wetlands.

Several thousand hectares of wetlands and their associated upland habitats within the Rainwater Basin are now owned and managed by state and federal wildlife agencies. The area also is designated as a joint venture in the North American Waterfowl Management Plan, which will direct conservation efforts to those wetlands on private property. See Novacek (1989) for further treatment on the ecology of the Nebraska Sandhills, and Pederson et al. (1989) for an outline of waterfowl use of the Northern Great Plains in general, including the Rainwater Basin.

The Platte River is a significant component in this region; it drains about 75% of the Sandhills and provides migration habitat for waterfowl as well as for about 80% of the continent's population of Lesser Sandhill Cranes (*Grus canadensis canadensis*; U.S. Fish and Wildlife Service 1981, Davis 2003). In most years, the Platte River remains unfrozen and provides open water habitat suitable for wintering waterfowl. Indeed, the river has long been important to wintering Canada Geese (Vrtiska and Lyman 2004). Johnson et al. (1996) recorded an average of 7,040 waterfowl (of 19 species) wintering on a 10-km portion of the South Platte River in Colorado.

All is not well in the Platte's watershed, however, as diversions for agricultural and municipal uses have captured nearly 70% of the river's water. These conditions have significantly diminished the Platte's flow and channel width, which in turn produced ecological setbacks for waterfowl, cranes and other wildlife (U.S. Fish and Wildlife Service 1981). In response, the Platte River now is a focus of conservation efforts designed to restore and manage wildlife and other resources within its watershed (see Currier 1991, Jenkins 1999, U.S. Fish and Wildlife Service 2001).

Northern Tundra, Forests, and River Deltas

North, and then east and west, of the prairie potholes lies an immense area of nearly 1 billion ha, which covers more than two-thirds of Canada, most of Alaska, and parts of the northeastern United States; river deltas cover about 14,437,000 ha of this area (Sanderson 1980; Fig. 9-6). Except for the productive river deltas, the soil in this region is poor; hence, duck populations average only 0.4–2.0 birds/km². However, because the northern forests and tundra cover such a large area and include wetlands largely free from either drought or drainage, the region produces a dependable crop of waterfowl each year. Wetlands in this area also provide nesting habitat for ducks in years when drought strikes the Prairie Pothole Region. Whereas the prairies produce more ducks per unit area, a good argument nevertheless can be made that habitat in the northern

tundra and forests is critical for North America's duck populations. Except for some subpopulations of Canada Geese, this region also provides breeding habitat for most of the continent's populations of geese, Tundra Swans, and Trumpeter Swans (Bellrose 1980).

In Canada, the region includes the northern edges of the southern tier of provinces (e.g., Ontario and Alberta) and all of the Yukon and Northwest Territories. However, in 1999, a new territory — Nunavut ("Our Land") — was carved out of the Northwest Territories to recognize the traditional homeland of Inuit, the native people who now are guaranteed seats on those boards that administer wildlife resources and other areas of government. Nunavut comprises about 2 million km² or 21% of Canada's total area, and includes two-thirds of Canada's coastline. Essentially all of Nunavut lies above "tree line"; hence the new territory is a vast area of tundra.

The major life zones in this region are, from north to south, tundra, open boreal forest, closed boreal forest, and mixed forest (Wellein and Lumsden 1964). As a transition zone into tundra, the open boreal forest features thin stands of black spruce (*Picea mariana*) and extensive areas of bog and muskeg. The closed boreal forest consists of conifers interspersed with willow (*Salix* spp.), aspen (*Populus* spp.), and birch (*Betula* spp.) and a dominant ground cover of sphagnum moss (*Sphagnum* spp.), whereas the mixed forest is combination of conifers and deciduous hardwoods.

Tundra environments are quite arid, averaging only 10–25 cm/yr of rainfall, and permafrost results in poor drainage of surface water. Hence, much of the land is soggy underfoot during the brief growing season (Wellein and Lumsden 1964). The tundra well away from the coastal areas is the least productive but is important breeding habitat for Long-tailed Ducks, Black Scoters, and Canada Geese. In the forests south of the tundra are breeding Trumpeter Swans, Surf and White-winged Scoters, Red-breasted and Common Mergansers, Common and Barrow's Goldeneyes, Buffleheads, Lesser Scaup, and a scattered variety of other species (Bellrose 1980).

In contrast, coastal tundra is highly productive habitat for ducks and geese, which may occur there in high densities. The western coastal tundra supports high populations of Lesser Snow Geese, Black Brant, Greater White-fronted Geese, and Cackling Canada Geese as well as King Eiders, Common Eiders, Northern Pintails, and Greater Scaup, among other ducks. The coastal tundra of Alaska also sup-

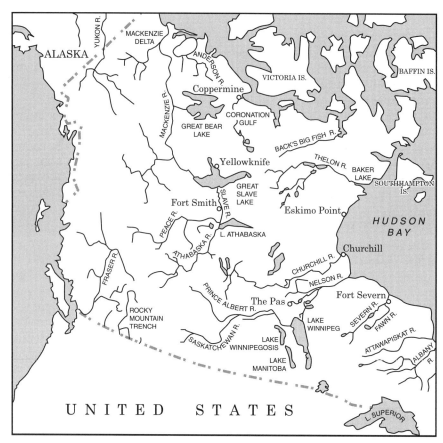

Figure 9-6. Major lakes and connecting river systems in western Canada provide important habitat for breeding waterfowl. After Hawkins et al. (1984:370).

ports some unique species, namely Spectacled Eiders, Steller's Eiders, and Emperor Geese. In the east, coastal tundra covers about 7,770 km² in the lowlands of Hudson Bay, particularly near Cape Henrietta Maria and Cape Churchill. A far lesser area of tundra occurs along James Bay. These sites are famous as breeding areas for Canada Geese and as staging areas for Snow Geese, Common Eiders, Greater Scaup, and Long-tailed Ducks, all of which also nest here. Unfortunately, excessive numbers of Lesser Snow Geese and other "white geese" are destroying large areas of coastal tundra on the western shore of Hudson Bay and elsewhere in the Canadian Arctic (Batt 1997, Johnson and Ankney 2003; see Chapter 8).

By far the most productive areas in the coastal tundra occur along the river deltas, whose significance as waterfowl habitat is summarized here based on Smith et al. (1964). The most southerly of the northern river deltas is the Saskatchewan, which flows eastward into Lake Winnipeg and exits as the Nelson River before terminating in Hudson Bay. The

Saskatchewan River Delta originally covered 9,065 km², but about 75% of this area has been claimed by dikes, drainage, and hydroelectric dams. The MacKenzie River system is a complex of rivers converging at Great Slave Lake, where the MacKenzie River itself forms the outlet and flows 1,770 km to the Beaufort Sea. The delta here is about 12,950 km² and supports large breeding duck populations, depending on water conditions on the prairies. The Athabaska River forms a delta where it enters Lake Athabaska and merges with the Peace River; beyond the junction, they combine to form the Slave River, which flows northward into Great Slave Lake. Breeding duck populations on the Slave River Delta and associated parklands fluctuate but tend to be higher when drought forces the ducks northward from the prairies.

In Alaska, the spectacular 67,340-km² Yukon-Kuskokwim Delta is a major breeding site for much of the continental populations of Cackling Canada Geese, Emperor Geese, Black Brant, a large segment of Tundra Swans, and an array of dabbling ducks, pochards, and sea ducks, especially Greater Scaup, Northern Pintails, Black Scoters, Long-tailed Ducks, and Mallards; the breeding population of ducks approaches 750,000, and geese have numbered 500,000. In interior Alaska, the Yukon Flats form a 5,180-km^2 basin dotted by small lakes and ponds; the area has up to 40,000 wetland and lowland lakes, most of which are concentrated near the Yukon River and associated tributaries (Lanctot and Quang 1992). The Yukon Flats, together with the Yukon-Kuskokwim Delta, produce about half of the ducks in Alaska. The Old Crow Flats in the Yukon Territories of Canada is among the other large delta systems in the far north. Several of these environments, while still quite pristine, nonetheless face the constant threat of hydroelectric and petrochemical development.

Coastal Marshes of Louisiana and Texas

The coastal wetlands of Louisiana and Texas represent the quintessential wintering grounds in the Mississippi and Central Flyways. In Louisiana, marshes extend inland along the coastline for 24–32 km, encompassing a belt of about 9,840 km^2 (Chabreck 1972, West 1977). In Texas, coastal wetlands cover about 1,920 km^2 (Alexander et al. 1986). Collectively, these areas constitute about 50% of the coastal marshes in the United States, excluding Alaska (Chabreck 1988). Louisiana alone contains 41% of the coastal marshes in the continental United States (Turner and Gosselink 1975). In addition to its coastal marshes, Louisiana also contains some 0.89 million ha of bays and 0.73 million ha of ponds and lakes (Chabreck 1972).

The numbers of ducks and geese wintering in Texas and Louisiana often are described in legendary terms. Specifically, coastal Louisiana provides wintering habitat for about 4 million ducks, which is about two-thirds of the wintering population in the Mississippi Flyway (Bellrose 1980). Indeed, in some years as much as 25% of the entire continental population of dabbling ducks winters in Louisiana (Palmisano 1973). Of these, Louisiana's coastal marshes provide habitat for more than 60% of the Blue-winged Teal and Gadwalls wintering in the United States (Michot 1996). Louisiana also is the winter home for about 400,000 geese and 1.5 million American Coots (*Fulica americana*; Chabreck et al. 1989). Moreover, the coastal marshes in Louisiana also serve as year-round habitat for 50% of the continental population of the nonmigratory Mottled Duck.

The Texas Gulf Coast is the primary site for ducks wintering in the Central Flyway, with an average 1.3–4.5 million birds, or 30–71% of the total flyway population (Stutzenbaker and Weller 1989). This area also winters 90% of the Snow, Canada, and Greater White-fronted Geese in the Central Flyway (Buller 1964). Embayments on the Texas coast, especially the Laguna Madre, are especially important for the continental population of Redheads (Weller 1964). About 125 km inland from the upper coast of Texas is an extensive "rice belt," where large areas of coastal prairie have been converted to rice production; these so-called rice prairies now exceed the coastal marshes in importance as wintering habitat for geese. Four rice prairies, totaling about 9,000 km^2, are noteworthy: Beaumont, Katy, Lissie, and Garwood. Hobaugh et al. (1989) describe the rice prairies and their management for waterfowl.

As might be expected, water salinity exerts a major influence on the plant and animal communities in coastal areas. The salinity of ocean water is 35–36 ppt; hence, Chabreck (1982) noted a landward gradient in salinity ranging from salt marsh (18 ppt), brackish marsh (8 ppt), intermediate marsh (3 ppt), to freshwater marsh (1 ppt); a similar but much steeper gradient occurs along the Texas coast. According to Chabreck et al. (1989), the extent of each type in Louisiana is salt marsh (27%), brackish marsh (30%), intermediate marsh (15%), and freshwater marsh (28%). Each of these communities displays a characteristic pattern and composition of plants (Table 9-3). Following Cowardin et al. (1979), most of the coastal wetlands in Louisiana represent persistent or nonpersistent emergent within the estuarine intertidal or palustrine systems.

These marshes vary in function as habitat for waterfowl. Palmisano (1973) ranked freshwater and intermediate marshes as first and second, respectively, in importance in the Louisiana coastal zone, each providing feeding and resting sites during the winter for nearly all migratory species. Freshwater and intermediate marshes are also crucial for Mottled Ducks, a nonmigratory species whose broods experience high mortality in marshes where the salinity exceeds 9–12 ppt (Moorman et al. 1991). Brackish marshes rank highest as habitat for wintering Lesser Snow Geese but are of lesser significance to ducks.

The functional roles of these marshes also vary by species. Green-winged Teal wintering at the Rockefeller Wildlife Refuge in coastal Louisiana fed most often in freshwater marsh, intermediate marsh, and on brackish tidal flats, and rested most commonly in brackish marshes (Rave and Baldassarre

Table 9-3. Plant species composition (%) of the marsh types in coastal Louisiana marshes. Modified from Chabreck et al. (1989:252).

Plant species	Marsh type			
	Saline	Brackish	Intermediate	Fresh
Batis maritima	4.4	0.0	0.0	0.0
Distichlis spicata	14.3	13.3	0.4	0.1
Juncus roemerianus	10.1	3.9	0.7	0.6
Spartina alterniflora	62.1	4.8	0.9	0.0
Eleocharis parvula	0.0	2.5	0.5	0.5
Ruppia maritima	0.0	3.8	0.6	0.0
Scirpus olneyi	0.0	5.0	3.3	0.5
Scirpus robustus	0.7	1.8	0.7	0.0
Spartina patens	6.0	55.2	34.0	3.7
Bacopa monnieri	0.0	0.9	4.8	1.4
Cyperus odoratus	0.0	0.8	2.2	1.6
Echinochloa walteri	0.0	0.4	2.7	0.8
Paspalum vaginatum	0.0	1.4	4.5	0.4
Phragmites communis	0.0	0.3	6.6	2.5
Alternanthera philoxeroides	0.0	0.0	2.5	5.3
Eleocharis spp.	0.0	0.8	3.3	10.7
Hydrocotyle spp.	0.0	0.0	0.0	1.9
Panicum hemitomon	0.0	0.0	0.8	25.6
Sagittaria falcata	0.0	0.0	6.5	15.2
Other species	2.4	5.1	25.3	29.1

1989). Similarly, Paulus (1984, 1988) showed that wintering Gadwalls and Mottled Ducks differentially used wetland habitats in Louisiana. Hence, as is true of the breeding season, these studies illustrate how wintering waterfowl depend on a complex of wetland types — a requisite for meeting both the inter- and intraspecific needs of waterfowl and many other species.

Wetland complexes can be formed by the creation and management of impoundments (Chabreck and Junkin 1989; Fig. 9-7). However, impoundments may interfere with the migratory patterns of fish and crustaceans, and they may not prevent wetland loss in coastal areas (Herke and Rogers 1989). Moreover, marsh communities in these impoundments sometimes disappear, probably because sediment supplies are cut off and the deposition of organic matter does not keep pace with subsidence, although these conditions may not occur in impoundments where water is controlled by pumps or other means (Gosselink 1984). Bolduc and Afton (2004) compared several variables, including salinity and water depth, in ponds within coastal marshes subject to levees and other types of water-control structures with those in open, unimpounded marshes on the coast of southwestern Louisiana. The structures were constructed as a means of halting saltwater intrusion. Salinities indeed were reduced in ponds within the impounded marshes, which presumably favor populations of insect larvae and other invertebrates useful as foods for waterfowl and other wetland birds. On the other hand, these same ponds were deeper and thus restrict those birds that forage in shallow water, whereas water depths in ponds in open marshes varied considerably and offered a variety of opportunities for a more diverse assemblage of birds.

Paradoxically, just as the waterfowl populations wintering along the Gulf Coast are legendary, so too

Figure 9-7. The coastal wetlands of Louisiana and Texas are beset by saltwater intrusion, which necessitates control of both water and salinity in managed waterfowl impoundments. These flap-gate structures, when opened, passively allow fresh water to leave the impoundment at low tide, but keep out salt water when the tide rises and naturally closes the flaps. Management of coastal impoundments is not without controversy, however, as some biologists argue that control structures inhibit movements of fish, shrimp, and other organisms into and out of the impoundment. Photo courtesy of Guy A. Baldassarre.

are the large-scale losses of wetlands. These conditions are most severe in Louisiana where Barras et al. (2003) reported a net loss of 1,704 km², or 77.4 km² per year, of coastal marsh between 1978 and 2000. Shoreline erosion and pond expansion caused by subsidence were the primary reasons for the large-scale conversion of marsh to open water. The projections for the period 2000–2050 are less severe, but nonetheless indicate a net loss of 1,329 km², or 26.6 km² of marsh per year. In response, the Coastal Wetlands Planning, Protection, and Restoration Act (1990) funded research and management designed to end the damage.

In 2000, large areas of coastal marsh, primarily in Louisiana, were afflicted with what is sometimes called the "brown marsh phenomenon" — the rapid browning and dieback of smooth cordgrass (*Spartina alterniflora*; Stewart et al. 2001). By March 2001, aerial surveys revealed the damage had covered 51,000 ha marsh; although all types of marsh were affected, most (95%) of the dieback occurred in sa-

line marsh (Michot et al. 2004; see also Smith 1970b, Mendelssohn and McKee 1988, and Webb et al. 1995 for reports of dieback on smaller areas). By late 2003, however, all but 6,880 ha of affected marsh had recovered. The implications of such events on waterfowl ecology are not clear, but the initial breakup of thick, unbroken marsh to include some openings and small ponds may yield some short-term benefits by providing additional food production and feeding opportunities (Michot 1996). In fact, an analysis did not reveal any significant changes in the numbers of waterfowl wintering in coastal Louisiana between 1969 and 1994, but this may mean that (1) although the quantity of habitat has diminished, quality — thanks to management efforts — has not; or (2) the extent of wetland loss has not yet reached a threshold where food production can no longer maintain vast numbers of birds (Michot 1996). In the long-run, however, healthy marsh vegetation remains the vital source of primary productivity and, without it, the entire wetland community — ducks included —

rapidly declines.

Texas has fared somewhat better, although large areas of coastal wetland either have been converted to rice culture or degraded by the Intracoastal Waterway, diversion of inflows, real-estate development, and urban and industrial encroachment (Stutzenbacker and Weller 1989). Moreover, agricultural chemicals, petroleum hydrocarbons, heavy metals, and other pollutants contaminate much of the wetland habitat on the Texas coast (Cain 1988).

Gosselink (1984) described the geological processes at work on the Louisiana coast. Basically, coastal wetlands have disappeared for millennia, a result of natural causes such as erosion from waves and storms, deterioration of abandoned river deltas, and the geologically incurred subsidence of underlying substrates (Morgan 1973). In pristine times, however, wetland losses in one area normally were offset by the accretion of marshes in another so that, although dynamic, the net area remained more or less the same. But in the last century, the balance between loss and gain has changed dramatically.

Navigation canals and channels, flood-control levees, and reservoirs along the Mississippi River eliminated much of the overbank flooding that once carried river-borne sediments into existing marshes. Today an extensive levee system extends fully 97 km south of New Orleans, and most river sediments now flow downstream into the Gulf of Mexico, with grave consequences for the integrity of the coastal wetlands (Chabreck 1982). The sediment load is immense: The Mississippi River, draining an area of 3,344,560 km², discharges about 2.4 × 1,011 kg of sediment annually (Coleman 1976). Thus, in large measure because of this man-made interruption in hydrology, the marsh floor is submerging at a rate of about 1.35 cm/yr but only accreting at slightly more than 0.8 cm/yr (DeLaune et al. 1983). Canals and channels, which occupy only about 2.4% of Louisiana's coastal marshes, directly or indirectly account for as much as 90% of the lost area (Turner et al. 1982). The canals enhance access, especially for petrochemical development, but direct losses of marsh occur when spoil dredged from the canals is deposited on the marshes and when boat wakes erode the adjacent banks. Indeed, in areas with heavy boat traffic, the canals may expand in width at a rate of 2.5 m/yr (Johnson and Gosselink 1982).

Despite these conditions, the indirect loss of marsh is much more serious, particularly as a result of saltwater intrusion. This damage occurs at low tide, when the canals flush fresh water from the marshes, and at high tides, when the same canals move salt water far inland into areas where the salinity readily kills the intolerant vegetation (i.e., freshwater marsh). With the death of the root systems, organic materials are no longer held in place, and the affected wetland is now vulnerable to complete destruction. Thereafter, the deteriorating marsh is swept away by tidal action well before salt-tolerant species can take root; the marsh simply degrades to a depth where it is impossible to establish new forms of emergent vegetation. The result is a virtually irreplaceable loss of marsh and an open expanse of saline water (Chabreck 1982).

Both extensive and intensive management options are required to stem the continuing loss of wetland habitat along the Gulf Coast. On an extensive scale, vital new wetlands will build once again along the coast if sediments from the Mississippi River are returned to their original course. As a case in point, in 1983 a deliberate breach was made in a levee at Octave Pass on the lower Mississippi River Delta. By spring 1985, a new wetland of 30,000 m² was established from the rerouted sediments, which accumulated at an average rate of 6.9 cm/yr; the area had expanded to 60,000 m² by the summer of 1988 (White 1989). The new mudflats were vegetated with 62 species of plants representing 21 families, for which the above- and below-ground biomasses were 1,194 and 1,212 g/m², respectively. Elsewhere in Louisiana, the U.S. Army Corps of Engineers diverts about 30% of the Mississippi River's flow into the Atchafalaya River, where an estimated 48,600 ha of marsh eventually will accrue (Louisiana State University 1983). These results demonstrate the dramatic and rapid formation of quality wetland habitat that can occur when river-borne sediments are returned to their original course — a clear indication of effective management.

Intensive management is directed primarily toward the construction, maintenance, and management of impoundments and canals, the specifics of which are described by Boesch (1982), Gosselink (1984), Chabreck et al. (1989), and Stutzenbacker and Weller (1989). However, the effects of Hurricane Katrina, which struck New Orleans and the Gulf Coast on 29 August 2005 will undoubtedly influence future wetland management in the region.

The Mississippi Alluvial Valley and Associated Drainages

The floodplain of the Mississippi River, also known as the Mississippi Alluvial Valley (MAV), is a huge area about 800 km long and 32–128 km wide that extends from southern Illinois to Louisiana; in all, the area includes about 10 million ha in 7 states (Reinecke et al. 1989). In elevation, the MAV increases about 0.1 m/km from sea level at its lower end in Louisiana to about 100 m above sea level near its upper end in southeastern Missouri. Rainfall averages 115 cm/yr in the north to 150 cm/yr in the south, with late summer and early fall normally being dry periods. Historically, the wet–dry cycle produced periods of overbank flooding, and the vast areas of inundated forest formed quality habitat for waterfowl. To the north but hydrologically connected to the MAV, the upper Mississippi River, as well as the Ohio, Illinois, and Missouri Rivers, provide additional wetland habitat that forms a major migration corridor for the midcontinental population of waterfowl (Reid et al. 1989).

The bottomland hardwood forests of the MAV are famous for their winter populations of Mallards, which at times may number 2.5 million birds (Tiner 1984). Indeed, the MAV is the most important wintering area for Mallards in North America (Reinecke and Baxter 1996). The MAV also provides breeding and wintering habitat for a large Wood Duck population, which although difficult to census, may easily exceed 1 million birds in winter (Bellrose 1980). A variety of other dabbling ducks occur here, but in much lesser numbers than Wood Ducks or Mallards. Interestingly, commercial catfish ponds offer manmade habitat for wintering ducks in parts of the MAV (Fig. 9-8) — of the 43,000 ha of catfish ponds in the region, 70% occurs in Mississippi (Dubovsky and Kaminski 1987). Overall, 27 species of waterfowl used catfish ponds in Mississippi, but most were Northern Shovelers, Ruddy Ducks, and Lesser and Greater Scaup. Indeed, during dry winters, about half of the waterfowl surveyed in the MAV of Mississippi occurred on catfish ponds (Christopher et al. 1988).

Characteristic vegetation in the MAV consists of bottomland hardwood forests arranged in distinct zones; these are classified based on the frequency and duration of flooding, which decreases with distance from the river channel. Whereas the forest communities are distinctive and occur along a moisture gradient, the sequence may vary in keeping with the uneven elevation of the floodplain. Larson et al. (1981) provide a checklist of trees and shrubs characteristic of each zone, in which species diversity generally increases with distance from the river (Zone I). Thus, the community closest to the river channel (Zone II) is usually composed of only highly flood-tolerant trees such as baldcypress (*Taxodium distichum*), water tupelo (*Nyssa aquatica*), and black willow (*Salix nigra*), and shrubs such as buttonbush (*Cephalanthus occidentalis*). Zone III may include these same species, but also those somewhat less tolerant of flooding such as red maple (*Acer rubrum*), swamp privet (*Forestiera acuminata*), river birch (*Betula nigra*), and some species of oaks such as laurel oak (*Quercus laurifolia*) and overcup oak (*Q. lyrata*) that produce important acorn crops used by wintering waterfowl. Zone IV contains many of the species of Zone III as well as additional species such as sweetgum (*Liquidambar styraciflua*), boxelder (*Acer negundo*), sycamore (*Plantanus occidentalis*), American elm (*Ulmus americana*), and oaks such as Nuttall oak (*Q. nuttallii*), live oak (*Q. virginiana*), and water oak (*Q. nigra*). Characteristic shrubs include common alder (*Alnus serrulata*), blue beech (*Carpinus caroliniana*), privet (*Ligustrum sinense*), and wax myrtle (*Myrica cerifiera*). Zone V is the highest elevation within the floodplain still regarded as a wetland (Mitsch and Gosselink 2000). The species may include many of the same plants from Zone IV and a few from Zone III, but none from Zone II. The trees here can tolerate occasional flooding and include oaks such as chestnut oak (*Q. michauxii*), white oak (*Q. alba*), and cherrybark oak (*Q. pagoda*) as well as blackgum (*Nyssa sylvatica*), spruce pine (*Pinus glabra*), American beech (*Fagus grandifolia*), southern magnolia (*Magnolia grandiflora*), and several hickories (*Caraya* spp.). Characteristic shrubs include flowering dogwood (*Cornus florida*), strawberry bush (*Euonymus americanus*), American beautyberry (*Callicarpa americana*), and dwarf pawpaw (*Asimina parviflora*). Zone VI contains upland trees and shrubs no longer representative of wetland vegetation.

The flooded forests of the MAV provide waterfowl with a variety of needs. Acorns, as well as seeds and tubers from wetland plants growing in forested openings, are especially important foods (see Kaminski et al. 2003). Leaf litter on the forest floor furnishes a rich substrate for invertebrates, which can be a significant component of waterfowl diets during winter (Heitmeyer 1988). Elsewhere within the floodplain, the river's continual meandering creates oxbow lakes and sloughs, adding to the diversity of wetland types in the MAV. Oxbows are horseshoe-shaped lakes of permanent water formed when the river shifts course at a bend and cuts off the old channel, whereas sloughs are usually less permanent wetlands that develop where the river has traveled over the floodplain (Mitsch and Gosselink 2000). The forest also affords waterfowl shelter, protection from predators, and lessens human disturbances.

Figure 9-8. Significant waterfowl habitat develops along the Mississippi River when overbank flooding inundates the surrounding bottomland hardwood forest in the Mississippi Alluvial Valley or MAV (*top*). Unfortunately, much of the forest has been cleared for agriculture and catfish ponds (*bottom*). Photos courtesy of Richard M. Kaminski (*top*) and Stephen J. Dinsmore (*left*), Mississippi State University.

Huge losses of wetlands have occurred in the MAV, and continued at an annual rate of 2% into the 1980s (Tiner 1984). Perhaps no more than 2 million ha — or just 20% — of the original 10 million ha of bottomland hardwood forests remain in the MAV (MacDonald et al. 1979, Forsythe 1985, Hefner et al. 1994). Much of the area was cleared for agriculture, and by 1977 croplands claimed more than 5.7 million ha of land once covered by bottomland forests (MacDonald et al. 1979). The frequency and duration of the flooding in the MAV also have been reduced dramatically by flood control and agricultural development. In Mississippi alone, the cumulative impacts of the levee systems bordering the Mississippi River have reduced the 2-year flood by about 88% (Reinecke et al. 1989).

Nevertheless, protection, restoration, and acquisition of wetland habitat in the MAV is a high priority of federal, state, and private conservation groups. Indeed, responses to a 1993 survey revealed that approximately 324,000 ha of forested wetlands on more than 80 sites are in public ownership, and about 65% of that habitat floods regularly, potentially providing food for about 500,000 ducks during an average winter (Reinecke and Baxter 1996; also see Forsythe and Gard 1980). Efforts to restore bottomland hardwood forests are also a focus of conservation and management in the MAV (Allen et al. 2000, Stanturf et al. 2000).

In addition, harvested rice and soybean fields

provide important food sources for wintering water-fowl when they are naturally or deliberately flooded (see Uihlein 2000, Manley et al. 2004). For example, the area of harvested ricefields in the MAV from 1999 to 2003 averaged 612,000 ha in Arkansas, 99,000 ha in Mississippi, 33,000 in Louisiana, and 43,000 ha in Missouri, which collectively accounted for 63% of the U.S. rice harvest (National Agricultural Statistics Service 1999–2003). Private landowners managed about 81,000 ha (10%) of the harvested ricefields to provide habitat for wintering waterfowl, as well about 43,000 ha of harvested soybean fields, 12,000 ha of forested wetlands, and 6,000 ha of moist-soil wet-lands (Uihlein 2000). However, Manley et al. (2004) determined that 79–99% of the waste rice in the MAV was lost between harvest and early winter, which may overestimate the carrying capacity for ducks by 52–83% (Stafford et al. 2005). Thus, management efforts and land-acquisition programs in the MAV must be accelerated to maintain the integrity of the area as a major wintering area for waterfowl, especially Mallards.

Some of the first sites acquired for waterfowl habitat in the MAV include Reelfoot National Wild-life Refuge in Tennessee, Yazoo National Wildlife Refuge in Mississippi, and both the Mingo National Wildlife Refuge and state-owned Duck Creek Water-fowl Area in Missouri. National wildlife refuges ac-quired largely in the 1980s include Panther Swamp, Tensas River, Cache River, and Chickasaw. Further, the Lower Mississippi Valley Joint Venture of the North American Waterfowl Management Plan (see Chapter 11) calls for protecting and securing some 165,000 additional hectares of wetlands in the MAV, and enhancing/restoring another 830,000 ha. Hence, the status and management of waterfowl habitat is steadily improving in the MAV, but more must be accomplished to offset the staggering losses of the past.

Playa Lakes

Playa lakes are shallow, circular, semipermanent wetlands occurring in arid or semiarid regions throughout the world. However, this discussion will focus on playas in the Great Plains of North America and primarily on those 25,000 playas dotting the Southern High Plains of Texas, eastern New Mexico, the Oklahoma Panhandle, and parts of Kansas and Colorado where they cover 152,000–168,000 ha, or 1% of the land area in this region (Fig. 9-9). Of these, in excess of 19,000 occur in Texas (Guthery and Bryant 1982; see also Bolen et al. 1989a). Each basin

Figure 9-9. Playa lakes on the Southern High Plains of Texas provide crucial habitat for millions of wintering and migrating waterfowl; a few species also breed on these shallow wetlands. The playas provide an oasis of wetland habitat within a large, semiarid expanse of the southwestern United States. Photo courtesy of the High Plains Underground Water Conservation District No. 1, Lubbock, Texas.

represents a closed watershed and, under pristine conditions, fills exclusively from stormwater runoff; hence, vegetational development in one playa may, at a given time, be unlike others. In the recent past, significant amounts of irrigation tailwater also en-tered playa basins (Bolen and Guthery 1982), but changing agricultural practices and economic condi-tions have reduced this influence. Playas on the Southern High Plains occur at a density of about 0.4/km^2 and average 6.3 ha in size (Guthery and Bryant 1982); each drains a watershed with an aver-age area of 56 ha (Guthery et al. 1982). Most playas would be palustrine/emergent or lacustrine/littoral, based on the widely accepted classification devised by Cowardin et al. (1979).

The appellation "playa," meaning "beach" in Span-ish, has obscure origins and does little to reflect the physical appearance of the basins. Their geological origins and development also are not fully clear but are acknowledged to include — to some degree — dissolution, which causes subsidence from subsur-face chemical reactions (Wood and Osterkamp 1987) and wind erosion, which deflates the land surface (Sabin and Holliday 1995, Reeves and Reeves 1996). A common but largely fanciful explanation suggests playas originated as "buffalo wallows," but it seems likely that a number of factors in fact contributed to their formation (see Gustavson et al. 1995).

Originally set in a sea of shortgrass prairie, playas now exist as islands of wetland habitat in one of the most intensively farmed regions in the Western Hemisphere. Corn, cotton, winter wheat, and sorghum are the dominant crops. The High Plains sit about 915 m above sea level on a broad, exceptionally flat landscape regionally known in Spanish as the Llano Estacado. Because of uncertain precipitation in the semiarid Llano, playa basins may not receive surface runoff and rapidly dry until visited by another storm. Based on Curtis and Beierman (1980), playas in Texas are 27–53% perennial (contain water at least 9 months/yr), 9–34% intermittent (contain water 3–9 months/yr), and 29–64% ephemeral (contain water less than 3 months/yr). Nonetheless, playas are second only to the Texas Gulf Coast as habitat for waterfowl wintering in the Central Flyway (Buller 1964). About 2 million ducks may winter on the Southern High Plains, most of which are Mallards, Northern Pintails, Green-winged Teal, and American Wigeon (Bolen et al. 1989b). Green-winged Teal banded on the Southern High Plains were recovered on the Gulf Coast or central highlands of Mexico, thereby underscoring the importance of playas as habitat for migrating waterfowl (Baldassarre et al. 1988). Several hundred thousand Canada Geese and Snow Geese also use playa lakes during the winter.

Waterfowl wintering on playas are concentrated on relatively small areas of wetland, especially during the dry winter months; between December and February, precipitation averages only 3.0–4.6 cm. Based on a census of large plots, for example, Guthery et al. (1984) recorded 50% of the duck use on just three permanent playas, which formed only 2% of the available water area. Thus concentrated, waterfowl are highly susceptible to epizootics of botulism and avian cholera. Indeed, the first documented case of avian cholera in North America was recorded on the Southern High Plains (Quortrup et al. 1946). Such die-offs may claim large numbers of birds; 60,000 ducks died from cholera on playa lakes at Muleshoe National Wildlife Refuge in Texas during the winter of 1956–57 (Jensen and Williams 1964), and perhaps 35,000 died from cholera and botulism in Castro County, Texas, during the winter of 1978–79 (Moore and Simpson 1981). Unfortunately, die-offs from these diseases may worsen if the availability of surface water declines in the playa lake region and ducks become even more concentrated on the remaining habitat.

Playas also host breeding waterfowl, primarily Mallards, Blue-winged Teal, Cinnamon Teal, and a few Redheads (Bolen et al. 1989b) but, because of the extended nesting period (April–August) in this region, surveys on which to base production estimates are not as feasible in comparison with samples obtained from nesting areas farther north (i.e., where the length of the nesting season is more restricted). Nonetheless, Smith (2003) concluded that 50,000–100,000 ducks may be produced from playa habitat in years with average precipitation, but production may reach as many as 250,000 in "wet" years.

In semiarid environments, landforms that collect water (i.e., wetlands) become an asset instead of a liability. Consequently, playa basins may be "modified" to collect and conserve surface water. Thus farmers traditionally excavated deep pits on the edges of playa basins that would concentrate runoff water and reduce evaporation of surface water (Fig. 9-10). In this way, excess irrigation water, which originally was pumped at considerable expense from the underlying aquifer, collects in the pits and can be pumped a second time at much less cost (i.e., pumping from a pit lifts water only a few meters and therefore costs less when compared with the costs of pumping from a deep well). Rainwater also collects in the pits, all of which can be stored with little evaporation until needed for irrigation. As a result, 69% of those playas larger than 4 ha were modified and, regardless of size, 33% of all playas were modified with pits (Guthery and Bryant 1982). However, as a consequence of modification, the pits often drain the littoral zones in playa basins and thereby diminish much of the food and cover that otherwise might be available for waterfowl (Bolen and Guthery 1982). Rollo and Bolen (1969) determined that natural playas, in comparison with those that were modified with pits, offered Blue and Green-winged Teal better choices of seeds from smartweeds and other wetland food plants. Similarly, unmodified playas harbored greater densities and more taxa of aquatic insects, and provided more emergent cover, than playas with pits (Rhodes and Garcia 1981).

When undisturbed by agriculture, playas feature distinct concentric zones of vegetation, which fall into 14 physiognomic types; of these, open water, wet-meadow, and broad-leaved emergent are most common (Guthery et al. 1982). Vegetation in open water areas is dominated by pondweeds (*Potamogeton* spp.) and, secondarily, by arrowhead (*Sagittaria longiloba*). The wet-meadow vegetation consists mostly of barnyard grass (*Echinochloa crusgalli*) and red spangletop (*Leptochloa filiformis*); smartweeds, spike rushes (*Eleocharis* spp.), occur in the broad-leaved emergent zone. Narrow-leaved

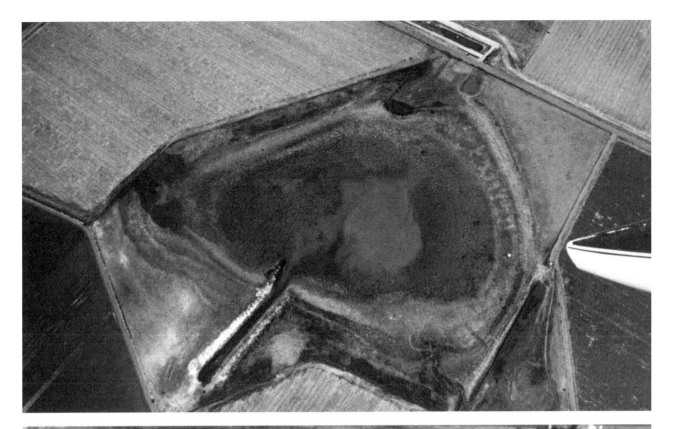

Figure 9-10. A playa lake modified by the excavation of a steep-sided pit (*top*). The pit (*bottom*) drains and concentrates water from the shallow basin, thereby forming a pumping site for irrigation of the surrounding cropland. Photos courtesy of Fred S. Guthery, Oklahoma State University (*top*), and Paul N. Gray, Audubon of Florida (*bottom*).

emergent vegetation is less common, but where it occurs, cattail (*Typha domingensis*) and bulrushes are the principal species. Seed banks in playas are dominated by annuals and, as might be expected, include seeds of species representing all moisture regimes (i.e., dry, moist, and flooded) regardless of the actual vegetation present at a given time (Haukos and Smith 1993a). See Rowell (1971), Hoagland and Collins (1997), and Haukos and Smith (1997) for the aquatic flora associated with playas. See also Smith and Haukos (2002) for influences of wetland area and disturbance on the floral diversity of playa lakes.

Early studies of the foods and feeding behavior of dabbling ducks wintering on the Southern High Plains emphasized the importance of waste corn derived from field feeding, but they also noted that critical nutrients — calcium and protein — not found in a corn-dominated diet were supplied by the natural foods found in playas (Baldassarre et al. 1983, Baldassarre and Bolen 1984). As indicated by a study of Mallards, lipid reserves and other measures of body condition varied during the course of the winter, presumably reflecting changes in the availability of waste corn (Whyte and Bolen 1984a, 1984b; Whyte et al. 1986). These results suggested that wintering waterfowl might face reduced fitness, which could lead to poorer winter survival and diminished breeding success the following spring, if farmers moved away (because of lowered water tables and increased pumping costs) from the irrigation necessary to produce corn. Subsequent research determined that the contents in the esophagi and stomachs of Northern Pintails varied according to the method by which the samples were obtained, so that the presence of natural foods in comparison with agricultural grains might be understated in some analyses (Sheeley and Smith 1989), which again stressed that foods besides corn were important to meet the nutritional needs of wintering waterfowl (Baldassarre et al. 1983). Hence, the role of playa lakes, and not only cornfields, remains of considerable importance as a source of nutritionally balanced diet for waterfowl wintering on the Southern High Plains. Other work considered methods to increase the output of seed-producing plants in playa environments (e.g., Guthery and Stormer 1984, Merendino and Smith 1991). Haukos and Smith (1993b) studied moist-soil management in playas by experimentally manipulating water levels in some basins and not in others, which resulted in significant increases in the biomass of both seeds and aboveground parts for two species of smartweed that are valuable duck food plants (see also Whyte and

Bolen 1985 for other details about seed production of smartweeds in playa lakes and Haukos and Smith 1996 for the effects of moist-soil management on playa soils). Dabbling ducks also rely on playa lakes as an exclusive source of invertebrates, apparently because these protein-rich foods are required to meet the nutritional demands associated with midwinter molting (Anderson and Smith 1999, Anderson et al. 2000).

Earlier, Gray and Bolen (1987) developed a management technique that addressed the design of pits constructed in playa lakes; instead of excavating the traditional steep-sided pits, at least one side is constructed with a series of terraces, thereby establishing artificial littoral zones consistent with changes in water levels as the pits either fill with runoff or dry (Fig. 9-11). The terraces provide habitat for both smartweeds and other seed-producing plants as well as for numerous invertebrates, and they attracted larger numbers of wintering waterfowl and shorebirds than unterraced pits (Bolen and Gray 1988). Likewise, Rhodes and Garcia (1981) reported significantly more waterfowl broods on playas where pits had not affected the development and function of littoral zones.

Because almost all playas occur on privately owned land, the fate of these wetlands as waterfowl habitat rests on programs of benefit to both ducks and local residents. Toward that end, fee-lease hunting — for waterfowl as well as Ring-necked Pheasants (*Phasianus colchicus*) — may offer significant financial rewards for landowners. Indeed, wildlife-related income may prove especially attractive as dry-land farming replaces irrigation and incentives for practicing long-term habitat management take hold (Bolen and Guthery 1982). Playa lakes are specifically identified for a joint venture in the current North American Waterfowl Management Plan (see Chapter 11). Smith (2003) includes a fuller look at conservation and management strategies in his book-length treatment, *Playas of the Great Basin*.

The Central Valley of California

Extending for 640 km on a north–south axis and averaging 64 km in width, the Central Valley of California covers 41,440 km² between the foothills of the Sierra Nevada to the east and the Coast Ranges to the west (Gilmer et al. 1982). The Central Valley is actually composed of two valleys: (1) the Sacramento Valley, which is drained southward by the Sacramento River; and (2) the San Joaquin Valley, which is drained northward by the San Joaquin River. Both rivers empty into San Francisco Bay at the Sacra-

Figure 9-11. A sterile, steep-sided pit in a playa basin was managed for waterfowl by constructing terraces along one side (*left*). Productive zones of emergent vegetation soon developed on the terraces (*top*), yet the pit remained otherwise suitable as a site for collecting and pumping irrigation water. Compare with Figure 9-10. Photos courtesy of Paul N. Gray, Audubon of Florida.

mento-San Joaquin River Delta (the Delta) and the Suisun Marsh. To the south of the Central Valley are the extremely arid Imperial and Coachella Valleys, where about 4,000 ha of man-made wetlands also provide wintering waterfowl habitat (Heitmeyer et al. 1989). Historically, these areas combined to create one of the world's most spectacular wetland systems and, as a result, as many as 50 million ducks

and geese may have wintered in California as recently as the 1940s (Arend 1967).

California also is both the nation's leader in agricultural production and the most populated state. These factors have placed intensive pressures on both water and wetlands, and a long history of wetland destruction and water diversion has followed (Heitmeyer et al. 1989). As a result, about 95% of the Central Valley's original 1.6 million ha of wetlands are gone, along with more than 90% of the riparian corridors (Gilmer et al. 1982). Rice, cotton, and a variety of other crops replaced the wetlands.

Nevertheless, the Central Valley of California still witnesses spectacular concentrations — 10–12 million strong — of migrating and wintering ducks and geese each year (Gilmer et al. 1982; Fig. 9-12). Midwinter Surveys for the area report more than 70% of the Pacific Flyway populations of Tundra Swans, Greater White-fronted Geese, Lesser Snow Geese, Cackling Canada Geese, and Northern Pintails. Most of North America's Ross's Geese, Tule White-fronted Geese, and Aleutian Canada Geese also winter here. Overall, the Central, Coachella, and Imperial Valleys have wintered more than 60% of all the wintering waterfowl in the Pacific Flyway and about 20% of the wintering waterfowl population in the United States (Heitmeyer et al. 1989). The Central Valley also contains a significant breeding population of waterfowl, especially Mallards, but also Cinnamon Teal, Gadwalls, Northern Shovelers, Ruddy Ducks, Redheads, Wood Ducks, and Great Basin Canada Geese (Anderson 1957, 1960; Heitmeyer 1989, Thompson and Simmons 1990). As of 1990, however, the waterfowl population was crowded onto just 56,700 ha of wetlands still remaining in the Central Valley; of this area, 66% was privately owned and 33% was held in state or federal ownership (Heitmeyer et al. 1989). In the following sections, we summarize the wetland environments in the Central Valley as described by Heitmeyer et al. (1989).

In the Sacramento Valley, the original wetland acreage probably covered more than 600,000 ha and consisted largely of riparian forests and semipermanent tule (= bulrush) marshes. This area contains the famous Butte Sink, which is the largest area of riparian habitat remaining in the Central Valley. Of the 32,000 ha still present in 1987, 65% was privately owned, 26% was federally owned, and 9% was in state ownership. Annual rainfall averages only 60 cm, most of which falls between November and February; winters thus are wet and the summers are hot and dry. During wet winters, overbank flooding may inundate an additional 162,000 ha of agricultural lands, which thereby become seasonally available as waterfowl habitat. Almost all the rice grown in the Central Valley occurs in the Sacramento Valley, and about 70% is flooded after harvest to provide waterfowl habitat and hunting opportunities. Within the natural wetlands still remaining in the Sacramento Valley, the vegetation in permanent and semipermanent wetlands is dominated by emergent communities, whereas the more ephemeral wetlands are dominated by moist-soil annuals and perennials.

In contrast to the Sacramento Valley, the San Joaquin Valley is arid. Mean annual rainfall is less than 23 cm, most of which falls between October and February. The Valley consists of two major basins: (1) the San Joaquin, which covers the northern two-thirds; and (2) the Tulare Basin on the southern

Figure 9-12. The Central Valley of California is known for its spectacular concentrations of wintering waterfowl such as these Lesser Snow Geese near the Tule Lake National Wildlife Refuge. However, because wetland habitat is limited, crowding has made disease a chronic threat in this area of the Pacific Flyway. Photo courtesy of Mickey E. Heitmeyer, Gaylord Memorial Laboratory, University of Missouri.

one-third. The Tulare Basin has no outlet, having been isolated by an uplifting of alluvial fans. Historically, wetlands in the San Joaquin Basin probably exceeded 400,000 ha, most of which were seasonally flooded grasslands. Wetlands within the Tulare Basin were associated with Tulare, Kern, Goose, and Buena Vista Lakes, which during wet years formed bands of tule marsh up to 16 km wide. Only 36,500 ha of wetlands remain in the San Joaquin Basin, and nearly all of the wetlands in the Tulare Basin have been drained and converted to agriculture.

At the confluence of the drainages of the San Joaquin and Sacramento Valleys lie the Delta and Suisun Marsh. The Delta is largely a freshwater network of wetlands, tidal and tule marshes, riparian forests, and islands originally estimated at 284,000 ha, but only about 3,000 ha of wetlands remain in the eastern Delta, along with 12,000 ha of winter-flooded agricultural crops. The Suisun Marsh is an estuarine system, and the high soil salinity has precluded developing the area for cropland; hence, some 22,000 ha remain of the original 24,300 ha. Wetlands follow a gradient dominated by California bulrush (*Scirpus californicus*) on sites below mean low-tide levels to those where hardstem bulrush (*S. acutus*), alkali (= salt marsh) bulrush (*S. robustus*), Olney three-square bulrush (*S. olneyi*), California bulrush, and cattails occur between mean low and mean high tide. Salt-tolerant species dominate the communities at higher elevations.

The major difficulty facing waterfowl habitat in the Central Valley of California is the quantity and quality of available water. Agriculture currently consumes 80% of the available water, but increasing population growth and urban development will further exacerbate competition for water—often at the expense of the water requirements for fish and wildlife. Passage of the Central Valley Project Improvement Act in 1992 helped assure adequate water supplies for wildlife conservation on areas such as state and federal refuges, but more water must be secured for adequate management of other areas, especially private lands. Water draining from irrigated croplands also is often contaminated with toxic amounts of selenium (Paveglio et al. 1992). In fact, selenium contamination has reached a point where managers intentionally discourage waterfowl from using wetlands on the Kesterson National Wildlife Refuge (see Zahm 1986). Pesticide contamination is another concern; California accounts for about 17% of all the pesticides applied in the United States. In 1981, 55 million kg were used in California, of which 55% was applied in the Central Valley.

Finally, overcrowding by both humans and waterfowl will undoubtedly affect wetland habitats in the California Valley. Waterfowl crowding on the remaining habitat encourages epizootics; avian botulism and avian cholera have occurred in the Central Valley since at least the 1940s (McLean 1946). Some 250,000 birds died from botulism in the Tulare Basin in 1941, and both diseases still kill thousands of waterfowl in the Central Valley each year (see Chapter 8). Relative to humans, increased population growth in the Central Valley almost certainly will affect wetland habitat. The human population in California is predicted to double by 2040, with much of this growth occurring in the Central Valley. As a consequence, existing patterns of land use likely will change by converting irrigated agricultural areas to urban development.

The problems besetting waterfowl and wetlands in California are being met head-on, however, by the U.S. Fish and Wildlife Service, California Fish and Game Department, and private groups such as Ducks Unlimited, the California Waterfowl Association, and the Nature Conservancy. In 1976, California passed the California Wetlands Preservation Act, which recognized the importance of the state's wetlands. In the 1980s, a $60-million bond issue enabled the purchase and management of wetlands.

The U.S. Fish and Wildlife Service also targeted the Central Valley as a priority area under the auspices of the North American Waterfowl Management Plan with the designation as the Central Valley Joint Venture. Numerical goals for the Central Valley seek to sustain peak wintering populations of about 6 million ducks and 1 million geese, with a further goal that at least 50% of their energetic needs will be provided by wetland habitats. Toward that goal, some 24,000 ha of additional wetlands were restored and protected between 1990 and 2003, which represents half of the targeted 48,600 ha. In addition, more than 23,000 ha of existing wetlands have received long-term protection, which equals 70% of a 32,400-ha goal. The Joint Venture also calls for annual enhancement of 10,400 ha of public and privately owned wetlands, as well as securing additional water for national wildlife refuges, state wildlife management areas, and private lands. Another goal calls for enhancement of 134,400 ha of grain fields to help meet the energy demands of wintering waterfowl, as well as enhancement of 45,100 ha of uplands to provide nesting habitat for breeding waterfowl. By 2004, more than 142,000 ha of ricefields were deliberately flooded to provide habitat for wintering waterfowl. However, meeting these ambitious objectives will not be easy, and to do so will require an unprecedented level of cooperation among agricultural, municipal, and wetland–waterfowl conservation interests, as well as a continued base of strong public support.

The Great Basin Marshes

The Great Basin lies within the vast Intermountain Region, which is west of the Rocky Mountains and east of the Sierras and Cascades. The Great Basin proper encompasses nearly all of Nevada and Utah, parts of California east of the Sierras, and southeastern Oregon. The Basin, true to its name, lacks an outlet to the sea (Fig. 9-13). This shrubby semi-desert region receives less than 15 cm of rainfall/yr; it is a land of sagebrush (*Artemisia* spp.), saltbush (*Atriplex nuttallii*), and greasewood (*Sarcobatus vermiculatus*). Because the availability of water is greatest after snow melt, most of the annual growth of native vegetation occurs during the spring (see Kadlec and Smith 1989).

Marshes in this arid environment are few and far between, and thus they concentrate spectacular numbers of waterfowl. Water for many of these wetlands depends largely on snowmelt from the adjacent mountain ranges rather than the sparse rainfall occurring within the basin itself, although some Great Basin marshes are spring-fed (Bolen 1964). The Great Basin is not heavily populated, but wetlands nonetheless remain in serious competition with agriculture for the sparse amounts of available water. Water rights are legally bought and sold in the Great Basin, and wildlife habitat often receives last priority. In fact, in extraordinarily dry years, nearly the entire supply of fresh water may be diverted for irrigation before reaching wetlands farther downstream (Christiansen and Low 1970). In all, wetlands in the Great Basin experience dramatic extremes in moisture regimes. Moreover, fluctuating water levels, together with warm temperatures and high soil pH, create conditions favorable for frequent epizootics of avian botulism. Infestations of carp (*Cyprinus carpio*) impair desirable aquatic vegetation at some wetlands in the Great Basin to the point of requiring management responses (see Ivey et al. 1998).

The ecological significance of the Great Basin wetlands lies in their use as migration habitat for a large segment of the waterfowl population in the Pacific Flyway (Bellrose 1980). These wetlands also offer crucial breeding habitat for a variety of waterfowl. Few ducks winter in the Great Basin, although the area does include some important wintering

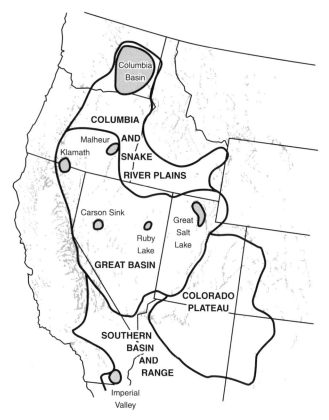

Figure 9-13. Wetland areas of significance in the Great Basin and adjacent areas. From Kadlec and Smith. (1989:452). With permission from Texas Tech University Press, Lubbock, Texas.

habitat for Canada Geese, Mallards, and Trumpeter Swans. Tundra Swans also overwinter in the Great Basin, where they are especially numerous in mild winters (Sherwood 1960). The most significant waterfowl habitats in the area are the Bear River and Ogden Bay marshes along the eastern edge of Great Salt Lake in Utah, Malheur and Summer Lakes in Oregon, the Tule and Klamath Basins in California and Oregon, and Carson Sink and Ruby Lake in Nevada; these and other areas are now state or federal wildlife refuges (see following).

Because many of their watersheds are closed, wetlands in the Great Basin are often brackish to saline, although marshes formed from impounded waters may be fresh. In keeping with the high levels of salinity, many wetland plants in the basin are the same as those found in coastal marshes; these include alkali bulrush (*Scirpus maritimus*), Olney three-square bulrush, pickelweed (*Salicornia* spp.), and widgeongrass (*Ruppia maritima*). The plants most commonly managed for waterfowl are sago pondweed (*Potamogeton pectinatus*), alkali bulrush, Olney three-square bulrush, hardstem bulrush, pickelweed, widgeongrass, horned pondweed (*Zannichellia palustris*), and, to a lesser extent, red goosefoot (*Chenopodium rubrum*) and smartweeds (Kadlec and Smith 1989). Of the various management scenarios, most focus on the acquisition and manipulation of water and reducing the levels of soil salinity.

Early explorers were understandably impressed with the "millions" of waterfowl they encountered along the rim of Great Salt Lake, a resource that was later exploited by market hunters (Williams and Marshall 1938, van den Akker and Wilson 1951). Waterfowl surveys often have tallied autumn populations in excess of 1 million birds (Nelson 1954). Additionally, wetlands bordering the lake have produced as many as 100,000 ducklings annually, mostly Gadwalls, Cinnamon Teal, Redheads, and Mallards (Sanderson 1980). As a result, these marshes received the early attention of waterfowl biologists not only because of the great concentrations of birds, but also because some of the first-known and most extensive reports of botulism in North America occurred here (Wetmore 1918). In 1932, for example, a major epizootic of botulism killed 250,000 ducks along Great Salt Lake (Jensen and Williams 1964). Botulism continues to plague this area; 84,000 dead birds were retrieved in 1997, with the overall loss estimated at 400,000 birds (Kadlec 2002). Early studies of waterfowl food habits also originated on the Bear River Marshes (Wetmore 1921).

Because of the hypersaline Great Salt Lake, the wetland vegetation originally was restricted to the deltas of the Bear, Weber, and Jordan Rivers. Then, in the 1920s and 1930s, state and federal refuges were established to manage these areas by conserving supplies of fresh water, stabilizing water levels, and reducing botulism (Smith and Kadlec 1986). With the construction of diked impoundments, large areas on these refuges could be inundated with fresh water, which reduced the soil salinity and thereby promoted the growth of desirable food plants such as sago pondweed, curly-leaved pondweed (*Potamogeton crispus*), widgeongrass, and alkali bulrush (Smith and Kadlec 1986; see also Kadlec and Smith 1984). Macroinvertebrate production also increased in this management regime, and expanding stands of bulrushes and cattails provided nesting and brood-rearing cover. See Cox and Kadlec (1995) for details about the dynamics of plant and animal waterfowl foods in these wetlands.

Foremost among these areas were the 4,761-ha state-owned Public Shooting Grounds initiated in 1923, the 3,534-ha Farmington Bay, and 6,755-ha Ogden Bay Refuges established in 1935 and 1937, respectively, and the 26,283-ha federally owned Bear River Migratory Bird Refuge opened in 1928. The beneficial effects of these refuges were almost immediate: (1) losses from botulism diminished, (2) nesting populations increased, and (3) quality habitat stabilized (Nelson 1954).

As a consequence of the stabilized water levels, however, cattails and common reed (*Phragmites australis*) eventually proliferated, and dense stands of this vegetation rendered the refuges less attractive to waterfowl (Smith and Kadlec 1986). In response, significant research was initiated in the 1960s, 1970s, and 1980s to identify methods of improving the habitat conditions on these once-productive wetlands (see Kadlec and Smith 1989). The management scenarios include manipulating water levels, burning, mowing, and grazing, each designed to promote desirable vegetation.

Unfortunately, Great Salt Lake rose 3 m between 1983 and 1986, thereby inundating 90% (more than 162,000 ha) of the adjacent wetlands, including many of the managed impoundments (Smith and Kadlec 1986). In addition to inflicting overwhelming physical and ecological damage to the refuges, the flooding displaced some 20,000 nesting waterfowl, which did not relocate on unaffected marshes within 100 km and instead left the Great Basin to nest elsewhere (Foote 1989). The lake later subsided, but years of extensive repairs awaited. Besides restoring the original dikes, new cross dikes and water-control structures were added at Bear River Migratory Bird Refuge, and about 3,600 ha of additional upland and wetland habitat were acquired. Nonetheless, upland-nesting waterfowl have been slow to reestablish their preflood populations, and for those that did nest, predation took a significant toll. In 2001, the refuge initiated predator control, which improved nesting success in 2004 to about 30%, or about a four-fold increase (Olson et al. 2004). Regrettably, migrating waterfowl stopping at the refuge — where they once numbered in the hundreds of thousands — still remain at no more than half of their preflood populations, although local drought conditions may be a contributing factor. See Olson et al. (2004) for more about the current status of Bear River Migratory Bird Refuge.

The 74,000-ha Malheur National Wildlife Refuge in Oregon was established by President Theodore Roosevelt in 1908 to protect habitat for migrating and breeding waterfowl, for which Duebbert (1969) and Cornely (1982) are sources for the following summary. Malheur is a closed basin, but it is among the largest freshwater marshes in the West. The marsh varies, however, from 4,050 to 24,360 ha, depending on rainfall, which annually averages only 23 cm. Hardstem bulrush and sago pondweed, respectively, form the dominant emergent and submergent vegetation. Trumpeter Swans, Canada Geese, and 14 species of ducks nest on the refuge, including a major breeding population of Redheads. Duck production at Malheur once (1942–50) exceeded 100,000, but this has diminished to about 33,000 annually. Nearby is Summer Lake, a 7,316-ha state-owned area also important to breeding waterfowl. Both Summer and Malheur provide migration habitat for hundreds of thousands of ducks and geese each year. Malheur and nearby private lands are also an important nesting area for Greater Sandhill Cranes (*Grus canadensis tabida*; Littlefield 2003).

If jewels adorn the crown of waterfowl refuges in North America, they may be the wetlands in the Klamath Basin on the California–Oregon border. Drainage associated with agriculture and competition for water have extracted their toll in the Klamath Basin, but some 8,680 ha of wetlands remain in Lower Klamath National Wildlife Refuge and another 15,230 ha at Tule Lake National Wildlife Refuge. Lower Klamath, established in 1908, was the first of the nation's waterfowl refuges. During migration, the numbers of ducks and geese on the refuges — including large flocks of Greater White-fronted Geese, Lesser Snow Geese, and Cackling Canada Geese — often exceeded 5 million and peaked at 7 million in 1955 (O'Neill 1979). Both refuges also provide nesting habitat for Redheads, Mallards, and Gadwalls (Miller and Collins 1954); 50,000 ducklings are fledged in some years (Jensen and Chattin 1964).

Elsewhere in the Great Basin lies Carson Sink, where the 9,800-ha Stillwater National Wildlife Refuge protects the largest wetland complex in Nevada. Nearby is a state-owned marsh of 58,320 ha, which provides additional habitat for nesting Mallards, Redheads, and Cinnamon Teal (Jensen and Chattin 1964). Agricultural development in this region began in the early 1900s and soon reduced the once vast Stillwater, Carson Sink, and Carson Lake marshes to a fraction of their former size. Although today just a remnant of a much larger area, the Stillwater wetlands nevertheless provide refuge for as many as 200,000 ducks during migration. Each year the area also produces up to 15,000 ducklings, mostly Cinnamon Teal, Redheads, and Gadwalls. Securing adequate quantities of suitable water remains the most serious long-term concern for the

Stillwater wetlands, as indeed it does for marshes throughout the Great Basin.

Chesapeake Bay

Chesapeake Bay — at 6,500 km^2 in area the largest estuary in the United States — is home to about 2,700 species of plants and animals. The 290-km-long Bay varies in width from 8 to 48 km, with an average depth of 8.4 m in open water (Hindman and Stotts 1989). The total system, inclusive of tributaries, covers 11,500 km^2 and drains an area of 165,760 km^2 in six states as well as Washington, D.C. The Bay's shoreline extends for 13,033 km, divided almost equally between Maryland and Virginia. Winters in this area are cool, and annual precipitation averages about 115 cm.

The salinity gradient in Chesapeake Bay runs from 0–5 ppt at the head of the estuary to 25–30 ppt at its mouth (Hindman and Stotts 1989). Wetlands associated with the Bay cover 172,000 ha, again divided almost equally between Maryland and Virginia. The major wetland types include many of those described by Cowardin et al. (1979); see also Stewart (1962) and Hindman and Stotts (1989). South of Chesapeake Bay are other major sites for waterfowl in the Atlantic Flyway, namely Back Bay in Virginia, and Lake Mattamuskeet, and Currituck, Pamlico, and Albemarle Sounds in North Carolina (Hindman and Stotts 1989).

The immense numbers of waterfowl once overwintering on Chesapeake Bay nurtured the most extensive market hunting enterprise in history (Kimball and Kimball 1969, Walsh 1971). Indeed, the Bay was renowned for its winter populations of Tundra Swans, Canvasbacks, Redheads, American Wigeon, and American Black Ducks, among others, that were attracted by the seemingly inexhaustible beds of aquatic vegetation. More recently, the numbers of both Canada Geese and Snow Geese have escalated dramatically on the Eastern Shore of the Bay. The geese previously selected a diet of native aquatic plants (Stewart 1962), but the birds now thrive on waste corn and the weeds associated with agriculture. According to Perry (1987), an average of about 1 million ducks and geese — about 35% of the winter population in the Atlantic Flyway — spend the winter months on Chesapeake Bay (see also Perry et al. 1981). American Black Ducks and Mallards are common breeding species, although the reproductive success of Black Ducks is at times poor in salt marshes bordering islands in the Bay (Haramis et al. 2002; see also Perry 2002 for more about Black Ducks in Chesapeake Bay). Hundreds of Mute Swans — an invasive species — reside in Chesapeake Bay where, among other disruptions, they remove large amounts of native vegetation (Perry 2004; see also Infobox 5-1).

Historically, the Bay furnished an extraordinarily rich environment for wintering waterfowl, including luxuriant beds of submergent vegetation comprised of redhead grass (*Potamogeton perfoliatus*), widgeongrass, Eurasian water milfoil (*Myriophyllum spicatum*), eelgrass (*Zostera marina*), horned pondweed, wild celery (*Vallisneria americana*), waterweed (*Elodea canadensis*), muskgrass (*Chara* spp.), coontail (*Ceratophyllum demersum*), naiads (*Najas* spp.), and sago pondweed (Stevenson and Confer 1978). Moreover, aquatic invertebrates of importance as waterfowl foods flourished in this vegetation. Stewart (1962) determined that three submergent species — redhead grass, widgeongrass, and wild celery — were major foods for the majority of waterfowl in the Bay, whereas Olney three-square bulrush was among the important emergent food plants. Much of the Chesapeake's wetlands already has been destroyed or altered, especially to control mosquitoes, and preventing further deterioration of the habitat —particularly the underwater vegetation — remains the primary focus for future management.

Submersed aquatic vegetation in Chesapeake Bay began declining in the 1960s, and today only a token of its former abundance remains available as waterfowl habitat. Extensive beds of aquatic plants on the Susquehanna Flats, for example, once provided food for spectacular concentrations of Canvasbacks and other pochards, but by the early 1970s the Flats were a resting area for only a few birds (Hindman and Stotts 1989). In Maryland alone, the aquatic vegetation declined 65% between 1971 and 1978 (Stevenson et al. 1979). A variety of factors were involved: (1) increased water turbidity from agricultural and urban expansion, (2) excessive nutrient loads, (3) agrochemical pollution, and (4) contamination from heavy metals and other toxic materials (Stevenson and Confer 1978, Kemp et al. 1983, Hurley 1991). Further harm occurred in 1972 when runoff from Hurricane Agnes concurrently increased the sediment load and reduced the water's salinity. Whereas none of these factors can be held totally accountable, the decline of the Bay's aquatic vegetation nonetheless forced an equally dramatic reduction in the numbers of waterfowl wintering on Chesapeake Bay (Steiner 1984). Today, estimates suggest that just 10–15% remains of the area once occupied by submerged aquatic vegetation (for his-

torical reviews, see Orth and Moore 1981, 1984). In 2003, about 25,000 ha of submerged aquatic vegetation remained in Chesapeake Bay and its tributaries, which represented a 30% reduction from the previous year (Orth et al. 2004). Much of the change was attributed to substantial reductions of widgeongrass. An aggressive exotic, hydrilla (*Hydrilla verticillata*), now dominates the submerged aquatic vegetation in the freshwater tidal areas of the Potomac River and other locations in Chesapeake Bay (Steward et al. 1984, Carter and Rybicki 1986, Moore et al. 2000).

In particular, Canvasback and Redhead populations suffered from this loss of aquatic vegetation. Wild celery and sago pondweed once formed much of the winter diet for Canvasbacks, but when these foods were no longer abundant in Chesapeake Bay, Canvasbacks turned to the Baltic clam (*Macoma balthica*), whereas Redheads continued feeding on the other species of aquatic plants (Stewart 1962, Perry and Uhler 1988, Haramis et al. 2001). Winter populations of Canvasbacks in the Bay declined from about 250,000 birds — about half of their total population — in the 1950s to only 50,000 in the following decades (Haramis 1991). Overall, Perry et al. (1981) considered the loss of aquatic vegetation in Chesapeake Bay as the most important change affecting the number of pochards.

Like other degraded wetland systems in North America, Chesapeake Bay is the target of major efforts for reversing these conditions. In 1985, Maryland initiated the Chesapeake Bay Critical Areas Program, and Virginia followed suit in 1988 with its Chesapeake Bay Preservation Program. Maryland's initiative protects lands within 300 m of tidal waters, tidal wetlands, and tributary streams. In 1982, several federal agencies concluded a joint 7-year, $27-million study of the Bay and its ecology. By 2004, the nongovernmental Chesapeake Bay Foundation boasted a membership of 116,500 and a staff of 165, whose slogan "Save the Bay" is a rallying cry of grassroots support. Today, although still sick, the Bay is far from dead and in fact is showing strong signs of recovery at several locations.

Mexico

Large numbers of several species of North American waterfowl overwinter each year in the expansive coastal and interior marshes of Mexico. Blue-winged Teal, Cinnamon Teal, Northern Pintails, Northern Shovelers, Redheads, Lesser Scaup, and Black Brant are noteworthy in this regard. Blue-winged Teal also winter well south of Mexico, reaching Central America and northern South America (Botero and Rusch 1988), but the wetlands of Mexico remain foremost in their importance to the waterfowl of North America.

Mexico is richly endowed with wetland resources, some of which are among the largest and most spectacular in the Western Hemisphere (e.g., Tabasco Lagoons). Overall, Mexico contains about 3.3 million ha of wetlands, of which 1.5 million ha are coastal wetlands and estuaries and 1.8 million ha occur inland (see Olmsted 1993, Carrera and de la Fuente 2003). Most significantly, Mexico has taken major steps toward safeguarding this rich natural heritage. Mexico lists 51 Ramsar sites, 34 of which were added on World Wetlands Day in 2004 — the greatest number of Ramsar sites ever designated in a single day (see Perez-Arteaga et al. 2002). Also, the North American Wetlands Conservation Act (NAWCA; see Chapter 11) has been enormously active in Mexico as evidenced by 163 projects from 1991 to 2004 that collectively involved $20.7 million of NAWCA funds that were matched by $30.5 million in partner funds. (see Wilson and Ryan 1997).

Mexico's wetlands gained notice in the late 1930s when the U.S. Fish and Wildlife Service, in cooperation with conservation agencies in Mexico, extended the Midwinter Survey across the border, including associated surveys of habitat conditions. Overall, however, wetland environments in Mexico remain poorly studied in comparison with those elsewhere in North America. Geographically, Mexico is partitioned by the peaks of the Sierra Madre Occidental on the west and the Sierra Madre Oriental to the east and south. Hence, most of the country's wetlands occur in three major areas: (1) the Caribbean and Gulf Coastal Plain, which has a 2,970-km coastline; (2) the Pacific Coastal Plain, which has a 6,760-km coastline including 2,900 km along Baja California; and (3) the Interior or Central Highlands, which form a tableland between the mountains. Many of Mexico's wetlands have been degraded by human activities, especially in the Central Highlands, but those on the coasts are still essentially pristine. Saunders and Saunders (1981) describe each region, including tallies from the 1937–64 Midwinter Surveys.

Waterfowl habitat and populations from 1970 to 1988 on Mexico's east and west coasts were reviewed, respectively, by Baldassarre et al. (1989) and Kramer and Migoya (1989). Much less is known about waterfowl populations in the Central Highlands, although

fewer waterfowl winter here than along the coasts. Wetlands in the Highlands also are much smaller than coastal systems, and many were destroyed years ago by drainage and human encroachment associated with agricultural activities. The Mexican government has identified 32 priority wetlands in Mexico, although all do not provide important waterfowl habitat (Fig. 9-14). However, in the early 1990s, Ducks Unlimited de México began an inventory of the 28 wetlands in Mexico deemed most important to North American waterfowl. This work produced a detailed evaluation of the Laguna Madre on the east coast, the coastal wetlands of Sinaloa and Sonora on the west coast, the Marismas Nacionales in Nayarit, and four major bays on the Baja Peninsula (San Quintin, Scammon's Lagoon, San Ignacio, Bahia Magdalena; see Carrera and de la Fuente 2003); a second volume is underway.

Along the east coast, seven major wetland complexes serve as important waterfowl habitat (Baldassarre et al. 1989); in descending order in terms of importance these are (1) the 2,030-km^2 Lower Laguna Madre, (2) the 20,000-km^2 Tabasco Lagoons, (3) the 5,380-km^2 Alvarado Lagoons, (4) the Yucatan Lagoons, (5) the 2,000-km^2 Rio Grande Delta, (6) the 4,035-km^2 Tampico Lagoons, and (7) the 1,050- km^2 Tamiahua Lagoon. The most important area, the Lower Laguna Madre, is a brackish embayment with extensive beds of submerged vegetation (e.g., shoalgrass, *Halodule wrightii*) and large populations of small mollusks. Just inland along the Laguna's coast, heavy rainfall periodically forms numerous freshwater ponds, which offer additional wetland habitat for such species as Redheads. A major part of the continental Redhead population (Weller 1964) and a significant number of Northern Pintails annually winter on the Lower Laguna Madre during some years.

Farther south along the eastern coast, the Tabasco Lagoons form the largest and commercially most important wetland complex in Mexico — a massive system about the size of Lake Ontario. These wetlands occur primarily on the deltas of the Usumacinta and Grijalva Rivers, which converge with some lesser rivers in the vicinity of Villahermosa, Tabasco. At least nine major wetland communities occur in the Tabasco Lagoons, ranging from mangrove forest to open savannas, and emergent freshwater marshes to gallery forests along the river channels (Scott and Carbonell 1986). In addition to habitat for resident and migratory waterfowl, this area also harbors large populations of wading

Figure 9-14. Location of priority wetlands in Mexico designated by the Director General for Aprovechamiento Ecológico de los Recursos Naturales. 1 = Ensenada Pabellón, 2 = Complejo Lagunar Topolobampo, 3 = Laguna Santiaguillo, 4 = Laguna Madre, 5 = Pantanos de Centla, 6 = Marismas Nacionales, 7 = Ría Lagartos, 8 = La Encrucijada, 9 = Complejo Lagunar Alvarado, 10 = Laguna de Babícora, 11 = Laguna los Mexicanos, 12 = Zona de Húmedas de Guanajuato, 13 = Bahía San Quintín, 14 = Laguna Cuitzeo, 15 = Lago de Chapala, 16 = Delta del Río Colorado, 17 = Laguna de Términos, 18 = Ciénaga de Tláhuac, 19 = Bahía de Santa María, 20 = Laguna Bustillos, 21 = Lagunas Fierro and Redonda, 22 = Ría Celestún, 23 = Laguna Ojo de Liebre, 24 = Laguna San Ignacio, 25 = Bahía Magdalena, 26 = Presa Guadalupe Victoria, 27 = Laguna de Tamiahua, 28 = Zonas Húmedas Sian Ka'an; 29 = Estero El Soldado, 30 = Valle de Cuatrociénagas, 31 = El Palmar, and 32 = Yalahua. From Wilson and Ryan (1997:60). With permission from The Wildlife Society.

birds and many other species of vertebrates; additionally, the lagoons serve as the nursery for the most important shrimp fishery in Mexico. The Tabasco system is largely pristine, but huge oil reserves underlie much of the area, and extraction activities already have seriously degraded some areas. Proposed upriver dams and chronic deforestation pose other threats.

Along the Pacific Coast of mainland Mexico are nine major sites of brackish and freshwater wetlands, which from north to south are (1) the 960-km^2

Tiburon, (2) the 600-km^2 Obregon, (3) the 300-km^2 Agiabampo, (4) the 400-km^2 Topolobampo, (5) the 1,330-km^2 Santa Maria, (6) the 800-km^2 Pabellón, (7) the 120-km^2 Dimas, (8) the 300-km^2 Caimanero, and (9) the expansive 1,920-km^2 Marismas Nacionales (Kramer and Migoya 1989). Pabellón, Topolobampo, and the Marismas Nacionales are especially important sites for wintering waterfowl. Large areas in these systems remain in pristine condition, but dams and water diversions have reduced freshwater inflows, increased nutrient loads, and likely added harmful burdens of pesticides. More recently, aquacultural impoundments have altered the habitat in some of these wetlands.

Major wetland areas on the coastline of Baja California are the 43-km² Bahia San Quintin, the 295-km² Scammon's Lagoon, the 202-km² Laguna San Ignacio, and the 240-km² Bahia Magdalena; some of these areas also serve as calving grounds for gray whales (*Eschrichtius robustus*). Together these wetlands overwinter nearly the entire continental population of Black Brant, and are also important habitat for several species of ducks as well as shorebirds (Page et al. 1997). The Baja wetlands are shallow coastal lagoons vegetated with extensive beds of eelgrass (*Zostera marina*) and sea lettuce (*Ulva* spp.), which attract large numbers of Black Brant each winter.

Other Important Habitats

It is not possible to mention all habitats of importance to waterfowl in North America, not only because of limited space but also because of the difficulty of deciding which are "important." Indeed, the North American Waterfowl Management Plan identifies some 67 important waterfowl habitats across Canada, the United States, and Mexico (North American Waterfowl Management Plan 2004; see Chapter 11). Nevertheless, the following briefly describes some additional areas that we believe represent significant waterfowl habitat.

North of the Brooks Range, the Alaska Coastal Plain stretches from the Canadian border about 900 km along the coasts of the Beaufort and Chukchi Seas. King (1970) identified this area as an important breeding site for Greater White-fronted Geese and Black Brant. Tundra Swans also breed here, as do a variety of ducks. Within the plain, Teshekpuk Lake is one of several lakes serving as important molting areas for geese and brant (Derksen et al. 1982). Hobbie (1984) has described the area in greater detail.

On the Alaska Peninsula, the majority of the Black Brant population concentrates at Izembek Lagoon each autumn before departing for Mexico; along with other species, as many as 250,000 Black Brant gather at the Izembek National Wildlife Refuge (Bellrose 1980). In spring, the same area also serves as a major resting stop for ducks and geese migrating to breeding areas elsewhere in Alaska. In southeast Alaska, the Copper River Delta is famous as habitat for migrating shorebirds, but waterfowl occur here as well.

The wetlands bordering the Great Lakes sustain large numbers of migrating waterfowl, with as many as 3 million ducks and geese using these marshes annually (Bookhout et al. 1989). Most of the larger marshes occur along the shores of Lake Erie (including Lake St. Clair) and Lake Ontario, but even these are only remnants of much larger wetlands that once existed here. The ecology of wetlands associated with Lake St. Clair and western Lake Erie is summarized in Herdendorf et al. (1986) and Herdendorf (1987), respectively. The marshes on western Lake Erie alone originally covered 121,500 ha, but today only about 13,000 ha remain along all of Lakes Erie, St. Clair, and Ontario (Bednarik 1984, Bookhout et al. 1989). Many of these marshes also suffer from both point and nonpoint pollution, thereby accelerating sedimentation and eutrophication (Crowder and Bristow 1988). See Bookhout et al. (1989) for a full account of the extent, management, and waterfowl use of the Great Lakes marshes.

To some extent, waterfowl habitat includes the 33,670-km² Everglades and Big Cypress Swamp in southern Florida, although Lake Okeechobee immediately to the north probably overwinters more ducks. On the Florida–Georgia border lies the 1,760-km² Okefenokee Swamp, and in northeastern North Carolina is Lake Matamuskeet, once a wintering area for large numbers of Canada Geese but more recently important winter habitat for some 50,000 Tundra Swans (see Gordon et al. 1989, Hindman and Stotts 1989). Along the border between North Carolina and Virginia lies the Great Dismal Swamp. In New York, south of Lake Ontario, are inland wetlands serving as breeding and migration habitat; however, much of the wetland area once existing between the Finger Lakes and Lake Ontario has been drained for agriculture. East of Lake Ontario, the Great Lakes–St. Lawrence River Basin has been recognized as a priority area since the inception of the North American Waterfowl Management Plan.

Elsewhere in the Atlantic Flyway are sites where large numbers of waterfowl concentrate each winter. Among the more notable is Long Island Sound, where Lesser Scaup, American Black Ducks, Mallards, and Atlantic Brant are particularly numerous. The U.S. National Park Service operates the Jamaica Bay Refuge as part of the Gateway National Recreational Area on the south shore of western Long Island. The bay is a shallow tidal lagoon filled with salt-marsh islands, which offers sanctuary for Canada Geese, Atlantic Brant, and a large number of other wetland birds well within sight of New York City's skyline (Burger et al. 1983).

Barnegat Bay on the New Jersey coast is a principal wintering area for Atlantic Brant, although the winter range of the species extends southward to North Carolina. Several national wildlife refuges in the mid-Atlantic states are managed for waterfowl; Edwin B. Forsythe (Brigantine) in New Jersey and Bombay Hook and Prime Hook, both in Delaware, are among the more prominent of these. The latter two refuges are important wintering sites for Greater Snow Geese.

Westward, the Great Kankakee Marsh in northwestern Indiana and northeastern Illinois once encompassed nearly 405,000 ha, but almost all of this area was drained by 1938. The Illinois and Detroit Rivers still provide habitat for migrating waterfowl, but again much has been lost or degraded. Cheyenne Bottoms in central Kansas provides key migration habitat for both waterfowl and shorebirds; the area is among those designated by the United States as a Wetland of International Importance under terms of the Ramsar Convention. For descriptions of other waterfowl habitats in North America,

Bellrose (1980) contains the best summary of nearly all the state and federally owned wetland areas.

Specialized Habitats: Beaver Ponds, Sewage Lagoons, Stock Ponds, Dugouts, Farm Ponds, and Reservoirs

Across much of North America are "specialized" wetlands and aquatic areas where waterfowl often find suitable habitat. In addition to beaver ponds, artificial environments such as sewage lagoons, stock ponds, and reservoirs are of growing interest to managers; as natural wetlands decline, these areas take on greater importance as waterfowl habitat.

Beaver Ponds: With a distribution covering much of North America south of the arctic tundra, beaver (*Castor canadensis*) create wetlands long recognized as desirable habitat for breeding, wintering, and migrating waterfowl, especially in heavily forested areas (Fig. 9-15). In southern Ontario, Collins (1974) noted a strong relationship between the number of beaver ponds and the size of the breeding waterfowl population, and Merendino et al. (1995) determined

Figure 9-15. Beaver ponds create quality waterfowl habitat, but they also provide habitats for other kinds of wildlife, including many nongame species. Photo courtesy of the Montezuma National Wildlife Refuge.

that beaver ponds were selected by Wood Ducks and received high overall use by dabbling ducks. Beaver ponds also provide important waterfowl habitat in northern Ontario (Ross et al. 2002). Beaver ponds serve the needs of American Black Ducks nesting in Maine (Hodgdon and Hunt 1966). In northern New York, the most common species using beaver ponds were Wood Ducks, American Black Ducks, Hooded Mergansers, and Mallards (Brown and Parsons 1979). In Alabama, Wood Ducks and Mallards comprised 94% of the ducks recorded on beaver ponds (Speake 1955). Green-winged Teal and Ring-necked Ducks are among the other species commonly associated with beaver ponds.

At the Seney National Wildlife Refuge in Michigan, nine species of ducks selected beaver ponds as breeding habitat; production ranged from 4.2 to 11.4 ducklings/ha (Beard 1953). In New Brunswick, Renouf (1972) recorded 0.27-1.85 broods/ha for six species on beaver ponds, but the ponds were especially important for American Black Ducks. In Maine, Boettger (1967) estimated that 8,570 active beaver ponds produced 46,000 ducklings, about half of which were American Black Ducks.

In regions where beaver ponds are of various ages, depths, sizes, and juxtapositions and vary in vegetational structure and composition, waterfowl may find habitat suitable for many segments of their life history. For example, in Michigan, waterfowl used beaver ponds to fulfill several functions: (1) courtship activities and territories, (2) food and cover for breeding adults and broods, (3) escape cover during flightless periods, and (4) feeding and resting sites during spring and fall migration (Beard 1953; see also Arner et al. 1969, Johnson et al. 1975, Arner and Hepp 1989). Those beaver ponds with overhead cover formed by a well-developed layer of shrubs are especially favored by Wood Ducks as roost sites (Bellrose 1980). In South Carolina, pond size and vegetation interspersion where important factors influencing the abundance of waterfowl and other birds occurring on beaver ponds (Edwards and Otis 1999).

Management of beaver ponds usually involves manipulating water levels for desirable aquatic vegetation. Because beaver ponds usually are created within a forested environment, wetland plants may not be abundant in the local seed bank. In Mississippi, Arner et al. (1969) reported that many beaver ponds, although flooded with shallow water, lacked much emergent vegetation. Hence, such sites may require sowing commercially available seed. On beaver ponds in Alabama, for example, Japanese millet (*Echinochloa crusgalli*) planted at a rate of about 22

kg/ha later produced seed crops ranging from 1,570–2,260 kg/ha (Arner 1963). Where seed banks are adequate, however, techniques similar to those used for moist-soil management (see Chapter 10) may be effective in encouraging desirable vegetation in beaver ponds. Manipulation of water levels in beaver ponds usually involves breaking the dam or installing three-log drains or perforated pipes, which are removed once the vegetation is established (Arner and Hepp 1989).

Sewage Lagoons: Municipalities construct sewage lagoons for treating raw sewage and other waterborne wastes. Whereas they usually lack wetland vegetation, sewage lagoons are phosphorus- and nitrogen-enriched environments with superabundant populations of midges and other invertebrates, which in turn attract waterfowl (Uhler 1964). Midges are particularly abundant in these environments, with numbers at times exceeding $16/cm^2$ (Kimerle and Enns 1968). Swanson (1977) reported midge larvae and cladocerans as each accounting for 44% of the diets of dabbling ducks feeding in sewage lagoons in North Dakota, and the sites provided habitat for migrants, breeding adults, and ducklings. On a 263-ha sewage lagoon in North Dakota, Maxson (1981) listed 24 species of waterfowl, of which eight species accounted for 90% of the use. Brood density on 36 sewage lagoons in South Dakota averaged 14/ha, which was twice that on natural wetlands nearby (Dornbush and Anderson 1964).

In Arizona, a 19-ha sewage lagoon was managed for waterfowl by constructing 14 nesting islands and fencing 100 ha around the area to keep out livestock (Piest and Sowls 1985). Dramatic results soon followed: In 3 years, the lagoon supported 380 duck nests with a hatching success of 94%; breeding-pair densities peaked at 10/ha, and duckling production reached 148/ha! Moreover, ducks in this study were not highly infected with contaminants, although mortality on sewage lagoons elsewhere has occurred from microbial diseases and contaminants (e.g., Moulton et al. 1976, Choules et al. 1978). Accordingly, research is needed to determine the pathogenic environment in sewage lagoons for a full assessment of their suitability as waterfowl habitat (Friend 1981). This and related research gains significance in light of the 10,000 or more sewage lagoons operating in the United States (Middlebrooks et al. 1978).

Additionally, stormwater retention basins often are constructed in urban developments; hence, these structures offer another type of man-made wetland with potential for waterfowl management. Mallards are among the species most often using these sites (Figley and VanDruff 1982). In Columbia, Maryland, 94% of the residents responding to a survey favored including wildlife habitat in the design of retention basins (Adams et al. 1984). Fully 98% of the respondents enjoyed viewing wildlife associated with neighborhood stormwater basins, and 92% considered seeing ducks as outweighing any nuisances the birds might cause.

Stock Ponds, Dugouts, and Farm Ponds: Stock ponds and dugouts are common features on western rangelands, where they hold drinking water for livestock. In arid areas on the northern Great Plains, the density of stock ponds may reach 1–2 ponds per 2.6 km^2, each varying in size from 0.3 to 16 ha, but dugouts, while designed for the same purpose, seldom exceed 50 × 20 m (Bue et al. 1964). Stock ponds are formed by damming natural watercourses, whereas dugouts are excavated. Both are used by waterfowl, but stock ponds generally offer better habitat because they more closely resemble natural ponds than do dugouts (Fig. 9-16). More than 85% of the stock ponds in South Dakota are found in the western half of the state, where there are few natural wetlands (Ruwaldt et al. 1979). In contrast, dugouts are often constructed in seasonal wetlands so as to accumulate water, but this often destroys the natural vegetation, hence lessening their attractiveness to ducks. Dugouts thus attract more ducks when they are constructed adjacent to a complex of natural wetlands. Estimates are difficult, but by 1964 some 230,000 stock ponds and 225,000 dugouts dotted the north-central United States and prairie provinces of Canada, with perhaps 10,000 more stock ponds or dugouts added each year (Bue et al. 1964). By 1979, there were more than 88,000 stock ponds in South Dakota alone (Ruwaldt et al. 1979).

During a 7-year study in western South Dakota, waterfowl logged an average of 32,018 use-days each year on 12 stock ponds, and duckling production varied from 10 to 24/pond (Evans and Kerbs 1977). Generally, dabbling ducks use stock ponds far more than pochards, but use is affected by variables such as pond size, water depth, wetland vegetation, surrounding wetlands, and adjacent upland nesting cover. Of these, size and vegetation exert the greatest influence on the use of stock ponds by breeding pairs and their broods (Lokemoen 1973, Flake et al. 1977). In Montana, brood densities were highest on ponds characterized by intermediate size (0.51–1.50 ha), an irregular shoreline, a water depth less than 61

Figure 9-16. Both dugouts (*top*) and stock ponds (*bottom*) provide important habitat for breeding waterfowl in arid areas. These were built in South Dakota. Note the fencing around the stock pond, which is important in preventing overgrazing and hence loss of nesting cover. Photos courtesy of Lester D. Flake, South Dakota State University.

cm, more than 30% coverage of emergent vegetation, less than 20% coverage by submerged vegetation, and less than 10% bare shoreline, but the desired vegetation did not develop for at least 5 years following construction (Hudson 1983). Shallow water and dense emergent vegetation were important features attracting broods to 36 stock ponds in South Dakota (Rumble and Flake 1983). In North Dakota, ponds created by dams that impounded more than 0.4 ha constituted only 29% of all ponds, but these were used by 65% of the pairs and 87% of the broods (Lokemoen 1973). Mack and Flake (1980) discovered at least one brood — all were dabbling ducks — on 83% of the 276 stock ponds they studied in South Dakota. Stock ponds also provide suitable habitat for other wildlife, especially shorebirds (Evans and Kerbs 1977).

Elsewhere in the United States, stock ponds often are known as farm or fish ponds. Many such ponds were constructed by private landowners in consultation with the U.S. Soil Conservation Service (now the Natural Resources Conservation Service), often following guidelines that included features for attracting waterfowl (e.g., Addy and MacNamara 1948). About 1.3 million ha of these habitats occurred in the United States by the mid-1980s (Tiner 1984).

Management recommendations for stock ponds include a size of >0.5 ha with an irregular shoreline and more than 40% of the area covered by a water depth of <61 cm (Hudson 1983). It is also important not to overgraze adjacent upland nesting cover (Mundinger 1976) or emergent vegetation (Whyte and Cain 1981) because this will decrease both duck use and production (Bue et al. 1952). Grazing, in fact, should be curtailed altogether around ponds managed primarily for waterfowl, as nest success may be twice as high on ungrazed compared to grazed ponds (Kirsch 1969). In Montana, ponds protected from grazing for just 1 year increased pair use by 42% and brood production by 50% (Mundinger 1976). Lokemoen (1973) noted how fencing prevented overgrazing on stock ponds where waterfowl nested. Bue et al. (1952) found that a grazing rate of 37 cattle days/ha/yr maintained suitable vegetation for waterfowl production. Other guidelines for managing stock ponds for waterfowl appear in Eng et al. (1979) and Rumble and Flake (1983).

Reservoirs: Large bodies of water are impounded for a variety of reasons, among them irrigation, municipal needs, and hydroelectric power, or for boat and barge traffic along major river courses. "Reservoir" is a somewhat arbitrary term, but was defined by Ringelman et al. (1989) as a man-made wetland of more than 200 ha. Reservoirs increased by 566,800 ha from the mid–1950s to mid–1970s, thus representing one of the few wetland types that are actually increasing in North America (Tiner 1984). In eastern Texas alone, for example, 90 reservoir projects were finished by the late 1970s and another 50 were proposed for completion before the year 2030 (Johnson and Swank 1981). Many of the larger reservoirs do not freeze in winter and may offer waterfowl some escape from hunting and other disturbances (Ringelman et al. 1989). At times, however, excessive recreational boat traffic may disrupt waterfowl in some areas (Korschgen et al. 1985).

Reservoirs provide habitat for waterfowl in two general ways: (1) they contain significant aquatic vegetation and/or benthic invertebrates; and (2) if they do not contain much plant or animal food, they occur where food is available on agricultural lands nearby. An example of the first type of reservoir concerns the famous Keokuk Navigation Pool on the Mississippi River in Iowa, where a standing crop of fingernail clams (*Sphaerium transversum*) has generated 20 million duck-use days annually (Thompson 1973). Keokuk, along with Navigation Pools 5, 7, 8, and 9, forms the most important migration corridor for pochards along the Mississippi River (Korschgen 1989). The second type of reservoir is evident on the High Plains of the United States where water has been impounded for irrigation. However, because of their widely fluctuating water levels, reservoirs of this kind may not develop emergent vegetation, and submergent vegetation may be limited by wave action and unstable bottom materials (Ringelman et al. 1989). Such reservoirs nonetheless may attract Mallards and Canada Geese because both species are particularly adept at field-feeding on waste grains. In some cases, migration patterns and winter distributions have shifted under the combined influence of open water and agriculture; some populations of waterfowl now remain well north of their traditional wintering grounds (Jorde et al. 1983).

The Fish and Wildlife Coordination Act of 1934 gave the U.S. Fish and Wildlife Service authority to manage migratory birds on reservoirs constructed with federal funds. Hence, several national wildlife refuges are associated with reservoirs. These include the Wheeler on the Tennessee River in northern Alabama, the Santee in South Carolina, the Eufaula along the Chattahoochee River on the Alabama–Georgia border, and the Columbia in Washington. Despite such benefits, however, waterfowl habitat is not the prime reason for building reservoirs; thus, amenable plans for waterfowl management should be developed during the design and construction phases of reservoir projects (Johnson and Swank 1981). One technique is to include impoundments adjacent to reservoirs, in which waterfowl foods may be managed intensively. Following construction, those agencies responsible for manipulating water levels in reservoirs should coordinate their activities in the best interests of waterfowl management. Further information on the importance of reservoirs as habitat for waterfowl is discussed in greater depth by White and Malaher (1964), Ball et al. (1989), Johnson and Montalbano (1989), Korschgen (1989), and Ringelman et al. (1989).

GLOBAL HABITATS OF SIGNIFICANCE TO WATERFOWL POPULATIONS

In addition to describing most of the major wetlands of importance to waterfowl in North America, we follow here with a sampling of wetlands of importance to waterfowl elsewhere in the world. Our intention is to present, albeit briefly, a more global view of habitats available to waterfowl, thereby providing a focus on wetland landscapes that are often unlike those in North America (e.g., Okavango Delta in Botswana and Laguna Colorada in Bolivia). Waterfowl indeed are a global resource, and many species range widely across continental boundaries in the course of their annual cycle, and some annually traverse obstacles unmatched in the geography of North America (e.g., Sahara Desert and Himalaya Mountains).

Several dozens of sites might be noted from among the hundreds listed under the imprimatur of the Ramsar Convention (see Chapter 11). The United Kingdom alone lists 145 wetlands, Australia 64, and even the desert nation of Algeria lists 26 (Table 9-4). Not all of these, of course, serve as important waterfowl habitat; most in fact are listed for other reasons (e.g., as habitat for other kinds of birds, rare or endemic plants, key areas for fishes or aquatic mammals). Nonetheless, the constraints of space limit our selection to just a few for each of the regions recognized through Ramsar. For the most part, these were chosen, often with the counsel of local authorities, because of their ecological settings as well as for the kinds of waterfowl found therein. Fact sheets are available on line for Ramsar-listed wetlands. Two other sources also were consulted for descriptions of wetlands in Asia (Scott 1989) and the Neotropical region (Scott and Carbonell 1986).

Europe

Ouse Washes (United Kingdom): Under a charter granted by Charles I in 1630, the mouth of Great Ouse River was modified into two channels as a means of flood control. A "wash" or floodplain of some 2,470 ha between the new "rivers" developed into a wet grassland where about 27% of the Bewick's Swans in the flyway now spend the winter, as do Whooper Swans and thousands of ducks of several species (e.g., nearly 30,000 Eurasian Wigeon). The site is the largest example of its wetland type in Britain and is managed with water-control structures and grazing under supervision of the Royal Society for the Protection of Birds.

Martin Mere (United Kingdom): Once part of a lake and mire, this 120-ha site is now a damp grassland and rush pasture mixed with open water and seasonally flooded marsh. The area provides grazing and roosting habitat for wintering waterfowl, including nearly 26,000 Pink-footed Geese — about 12% of the world population — along with Bewick's Swans and various pochards and dabbling ducks. The Wildfowl and Wetlands Trust manages the site.

Doñana (Spain): The mouth of the Guadalquivir River, which enters the Atlantic Ocean south of Seville, is partially blocked by a huge system of dunes and sandbars. About 50,700 ha of wetlands form behind this natural barrier, but this is only the remnant of a once larger area that later was drained for farmland. In 1969, the wetland — one of the largest and best-known in Europe — became part of a national park. It lies on a major flyway for birds migrating between western Europe and western Africa. Some 500,000 waterfowl utilize the wetland, including large numbers of Greylag Geese, Eurasian Green-winged Teal, and Eurasian Wigeon. Breeding species include the Marbled Duck and the endangered White-headed Duck. The park also protects Iberian lynx (*Felis pardina*), one of the world's rarest mammals.

Wadden Sea (The Netherlands): This 249,998-ha marine zone — the largest unbroken stretch of intertidal mudflats in the world — is associated with Ramsar sites in Germany and Denmark; the three nations signed a joint declaration for protecting the Wadden Sea in 1982. Salt marshes and wet meadows provide other habitat at the site, which is utilized each year by an average of 10 million birds, many of which pass through while migrating between their breeding areas in Siberia, Greenland, and North America to wintering areas in Europe and Africa. It is an important wintering and staging area for Barnacle Geese, Common Eiders, and Greater Scaup; other waterfowl include Black Brant, Common Shelducks, and several species of dabbling ducks.

Volga Delta (Russian Federation): The largest inland delta in Europe lies at the mouth of the longest river in Europe where it empties into the Caspian Sea. The habitat is predominately a freshwater riverine wetland complex of floodplains and permanent and seasonal lakes in which more than 400 species of plants from 256 genera and 82 families occur. In mild winters, the Volga Delta supports up to 750,000

Table 9-4. Number and total area of Ramsar-listed wetlands in selected nations within each of six regions recognized by the Ramsar Secretariat. All data as of August 2004.

Region and nation		Number of Ramsar-listed wetlands	Area (ha)
Africa	Algeria	26	2,791,992
	Botswana	1	6,864,000
	Egypt	2	105,700
	Ghana	6	178,410
	Kenya	4	90,969
	Morocco	4	14,350
	Senegal	4	99,720
	South Africa	17	498,721
	Uganda	2	37,000
Asia	Cambodia	3	54,600
	China	21	2,547,763
	India	19	648,507
	Japan	13	84,089
	Malaysia	4	48,745
	Mongolia	11	1,439,530
	Pakistan	19	1,343,627
Neotropics	Argentina	13	3,582,589
	Bolivia	8	6,518,073
	Brazil	8	6,434,086
	Chile	6	94,811
	Costa Rica	11	509,600
	Guatemala	4	502,707
	Panama	4	159,903
	Peru	10	2,777,414
	Venezuela	5	263,636
Europe	Austria	16	137,285
	Bulgaria	9	17,406
	Czech Republic	10	41,861
	Denmark	25	702,533
	France	19	566,951
	Germany	32	816,827
	Italy	45	55,507
	Netherlands	41	806,048
	Norway	32	155,919
	Poland	8	90,455
	Russian Federation	35	10,323,967
	Spain	39	173,126
	United Kingdom	145	746,745
North America	Canada	36	13,051,501
	Mexico	51	5,101,433
	United States	19	1,192,730
Oceania	Australia	64	7,368,698
	Marshall Islands	1	69,000
	New Zealand	5	38,868

waterbirds, including several kinds of ducks (*Anas, Aythya,* and *Mergus* spp.) and Greylag Geese. In the summer months, as many as 400,000 ducks, mainly Garganey, Northern Pintails, Northern Shovelers, and Eurasian Green-winged Teal, molt in this wetland, which is also breeding habitat for about 10,000 pairs of Mute Swans.

Thjorsarver (Iceland): This 37,500-ha site encloses the upper Thjorsa River. The habitat consists of tundra meadows dissected by numerous glacial streams, a few spring-fed streams, marshes, and many ponds and shallow lakes. In effect, the site is a wetland oasis within a desert of lava gravel where about 20,000 Pink-footed Geese breed each summer. Scott and Fisher (1954) described the discovery of this important colony — the species' largest — but, if approved, construction of a hydroelectric facility may inundate key parts of this crucial area.

Africa

Okavango Delta (Botswana): The Okavango River rises in the highlands of Angola, then makes its way across Nambia to the Kalahari Desert, where it fans out along fault lines to form the world's largest inland delta (15,000 km²). A vast network of reed-dominated channels develops from floodwaters during the rainy season from October to March, but it returns to an arid landscape during the subsequent dry period when 90% of the water evaporates. In season, the delta teems with waterfowl, including interesting species such as Spur-winged Geese, Black-sided Comb Ducks, African Pygmy-Geese, Hottentot Teal, Egyptian Sheldgeese, and White-backed Ducks. This habitat also serves the endangered Wattled Crane (*Grus carunculatus*).

Doudj Bird Sanctuary (Senegal): Located in the delta of the Senegal River, this 16,000-ha site consists of a large lake surrounded by streams, ponds and backwaters, supplemented by dikes that help retain floodwater runoff. The wetland is one of the first freshwater areas available to migrating birds after crossing 200 km of Sahara Desert. Some 3 million migrant birds, including large numbers of Garganey, Northern Shovelers, and Northern Pintails, stop here each year between September and April. Nesting species include both White-faced and Fulvous Whistling-Ducks and Spur-winged Geese.

De Hoop Vlei (South Africa): This 750-ha coastal lake lacks an outlet; hence, the water experiences widely fluctuating salinities as the winter influx of freshwater steadily evaporates during the summer months. These conditions favor development of extensive beds of sago pondweed, a major food plant for waterfowl as well as habitat for large numbers of invertebrates. Each year up to 15% of the world population of Cape Shovelers use the site as a molting refuge, where they feed on the teeming invertebrate life. Yellow-billed Ducks also visit the lake, as do Egyptian Sheldgeese. Breeding birds notably include Greater Flamingoes (*Phoenicopterus ruber roseus*).

Lac Fitri (Chad): This freshwater wetland is a normally permanent lake fed by seasonal rainfall and runoff from a 70,000-km² catchment basin in the Sahelian region of north-central Africa. The protected area extends for 195,000 ha within which the lake itself covers 50,000 ha at its maximum extent. During severe droughts, the lake may dry. Large numbers of Palearctic waterbirds winter at this site; these include Northern Pintails (35,000) and Garganey (21,600). The lake also serves as a drought refuge for White-faced and Fulvous Whistling-Ducks (35,800), as well as other species of waterfowl and waterbirds.

Oceania

Lake Pinaroo (Australia): The Freckled Duck is among the waterfowl found at this 800-ha terminal basin located in the driest region of New South Wales. The basin fills when intense local rains produce an overflow from an adjacent swamp, then may take up to 6 years to dry again, becoming increasingly more saline as the water evaporates. These conditions support little vegetation, but large numbers of waterbirds, including Pink-eared Ducks, Gray Teal, and Maned Ducks are common whenever water is available. Archaeological evidence indicates that a large Aboriginal population once occupied the location, which is now a nature conservation area within Sturt National Park.

Moulting Lagoon Nature Reserve (Australia): A large estuary on the east coast of Tasmania formed about 10,000 years ago when the mouths the Apsley and Swan Rivers almost closed. The blockage flooded the nearby low ground and produced a lagoon that offers year-round habitat, including nesting cover, for about 8,000 Black Swans. The 4,580-site also serves as a major staging area for large concentrations of Australian Shelducks and Chestnut Teal.

Kakadu National Park (Australia): This immense area of 683,000 ha in the Northwest Territory represents an outstanding example of floodplain communities occurring within the monsoon tropics. The vegetation mainly consists of grasses and sedges, with freshwater mangroves bordering stream and lagoon edges. Between August and October, about 1 million waterbirds visit the area, including large numbers of Magpie Geese and Wandering Whistling-Ducks that breed on site. Radjah Selducks also occur here.

Neotropics

Banados del Este y Franja Costera (Uruguay): This 407,400-ha coastal area is Uruguay's only Ramsar-listed wetland; similar habitat continues northward into Brazil but is not currently listed. In addition to Laguna Merin, the site includes a vast complex of coastal wetlands, including freshwater marshes, flooded grasslands, peat bogs, and sections of several rivers. Waterfowl utilizing the area include Black-necked Swans, Coscoroba Swans, Rosy-billed Pochards, Silver Teal, and White-faced and Fulvous Whistling-Ducks.

Laguna de Llancanelo (Argentina): This saline lake lies at the foot of the central Andes; water also accumulates in semipermanent ponds on clay soils in areas around the lake. At its maximum, the lake covers 65,000 ha, but it is now about a third of this size because reduced snow accumulations in the surrounding mountains no longer provide enough meltwater to balance evaporation from the lake basin. About 1,500 Black-necked Swans nest at the site; thereafter some 24,000 of the same species and 8,000 Coscoroba Swans seek refuge on the lake during the flightless period of their postbreeding molt.

Palo Verde (Costa Rica): Located in a tropical dry forest, a 24,500-ha wetland complex of marshes, mangrove swamps, lakes, coastal lagoons, tidal flats, rivers, and streams on the floodplain of the Rio Tempisque forms one of Central America's most important areas for waterfowl. Peak counts of resident species include 20,000 Black-bellied Whistling-Ducks and 400 Muscovy Ducks and, in season, Northern Pintails and Northern Shovelers are among the common Nearctic species utilizing the area. Blue-winged Teal are especially numerous in winter and during migration.

Laguna Colorada (Bolivia): This saline lake lies 4,278 m above sea level in the Antiplano ("High Plateau") of the Andes; the lake and surrounding area comprise 51,300 ha within the Eduardo Avaroa National Reserve for Andean Fauna. In addition of the flow of glacial meltwater from streams and rivers, the shallow lake is fed by thermal springs, but there is no outflow from the basin and evaporation leaves behind high concentrations of salts. Small islands of ice float in the lake (Hurlbert and Chang 1984). Andean Sheldgoose, Crested Ducks, Brown Pintails, and Speckled Teal occur at this interesting wetland. Laguna Colorada also is the most important nesting site for the James Flamingo (*Phoenicoparrus jamesi*) in South America (Valqui et al. 2000).

Asia

Keoladeo Ghana National Park (India): The 1,500 ha of inundated land inside this park — often known simply as Bharatpur — is the most famous wetland in India. It was once the private shooting reserve of a maharajah who developed the site into a series of lagoons that were managed to attract waterfowl, but the area is now also a sanctuary for many other kinds of waterbirds (e.g., cranes). Water supplies depend heavily on monsoons and are therefore variable. Thousands of common puddle ducks (e.g., Eurasian Wigeon) winter at Bharatpur, as do lesser numbers of Indonesian Spot-billed Ducks and Red-crested Pochards. Other waterfowl include Bar-headed Geese, Ruddy Shelducks, and Black-sided Comb Ducks. Lesser Whistling-Ducks are among the waterfowl nesting at Bharatpur.

Ogii Nuur (Mongolia): Three rivers flow through marshes into the western border of this shallow freshwater lake; together with associated alluvial areas, the site covers 2,500 ha. Much of the lake's shoreline is gravel, but zones of aquatic plants lie immediately offshore. The wetland habitats serve as a major breeding and staging area for anatids, which may include 1,000 Swan Geese and lesser numbers of Greylag Geese, Bar-headed Geese, and Whooper Swans. A variety of ducks (e.g., *Anas, Aythya, Tadorna, and Bucephala*) also occur at the site.

Yancheng National Nature Reserve (People's Republic of China): This 453,000-ha area stretches along 300 km of coastline and includes a complex of freshwater and brackish ponds and marshes, together with wet grasslands, reed beds, and tidal flats. Nearly two dozen species of waterfowl overwinter at the site, some which occur in large numbers: Swan Geese (35,000), Bean Geese (*20,000*), Indonesian Spot-billed Ducks (113,000), Northern Shovelers (20,700), and Mallards (157,000). As many as 750 Baer's Pochards (listed as vulnerable by IUCN) have been recorded in these wetlands, which also include areas where the extremely rare Pere David's deer (*Elaphurus davidianus*) have been reintroduced.

Candaba Swamp (Philippines): This area, a mix of freshwater ponds, marshes, and swamps, is flooded in the wet season, then dries when the rains subsist. Some 32,000 ha are included, but because of rice cultivation and aquaculture, only a small part of the site serves as undisturbed waterfowl habitat. Nonetheless, as many as 100,000 ducks have been counted at this staging and wintering area. Garganey and Philippine Ducks are the most abundant species; others include Wandering Whistling-Ducks, Northern Pintails, Eurasian Wigeon, Common Pochards, and Tufted Ducks.

LITERATURE CITED

Adams, L. W., L. E. Dove, and D. L. Leedy. 1984. Public attitudes toward urban wetlands for stormwater control and wildlife enhancement. Wildlife Society Bulletin 12:299–303.

Addy, C. E., and L. G. MacNamara. 1948. Waterfowl management on small areas. Wildlife Management Institute, Washington, D.C.

Alexander, C. E., M. A. Boutman, and D. W. Field. 1986. An inventory of coastal wetlands of the USA. U.S. Department of Commerce, Washington, D.C.

Allen, J. A., B. D. Keeland, J. A. Stanturf, A. F. Clewell, and H. E. Kennedy. 2000. A guide to bottomland hardwood restoration. U.S. Forest Service Information and Technology Report USGS/BRD/ITR–2000–0011. General Technical Report SRS–40.

Anderson, J. T., and L. M. Smith. 1999. Carrying capacity and diel use of managed playa wetlands by nonbreeding waterbirds. Wildlife Society Bulletin 27:281–291.

Anderson, J. T., and L. M. Smith. 2000. Invertebrate response to moist-soil management of playa wetlands. Ecological Applications 10:550–558.

Anderson, J. T., L. M. Smith, and D. A. Haukos. 2000. Food selection and feather molt by nonbreeding American Green-winged Teal in Texas playas. Journal of Wildlife Management 64:222–230.

Anderson, W. 1957. A waterfowl nesting study in the Sacramento Valley, California, 1955. California Fish and Game 43:71–90.

Anderson, W. 1960. A study of waterfowl nesting in the Suisun marshes. California Fish and Game 46:217–226.

Arend, P. H. 1967. Water requirements for the waterfowl of Butte Basin, California. California Department of Fish and Game, Water Project Branch Report 6.

Arner, D. H. 1963. Production of duck foods in beaver ponds. Journal of Wildlife Management 27:76–81.

Arner, D. H., J. Baker, D. Wesley, and B. Herring. 1969. An inventory of beaver impounded water in Mississippi. Proceedings of the Southeastern Association of Game and Fish Commissioners 23:110–128.

Arner, D. H., and G. R. Hepp. 1989. Beaver pond wetlands: a southern perspective. Pages 117–128 *in* L. M. Smith, R. L. Pederson, and R. M. Kaminski, editors. Habitat management for migrating and wintering waterfowl in North America. Texas Tech University Press, Lubbock.

Baldassarre, G. A., and E. G. Bolen. 1984. Field-feeding ecology of waterfowl wintering on the Southern High Plains of Texas. Journal of Wildlife Management 48:63–71.

Baldassarre, G. A., A. R. Brazda, and E. Rangel Woodyard. 1989. The east coast of Mexico. Pages 407–425 *in* L. M. Smith, R. L. Pederson, and R. M. Kaminski, editors. Habitat management for migrating and wintering waterfowl in North America. Texas Tech University Press, Lubbock.

Baldassarre, G. A., R. J. Whyte, E. E. Quinlan, and E. G. Bolen. 1983. Dynamics and quality of waste corn available to postbreeding waterfowl in Texas. Wildlife Society Bulletin 11:25–31.

Baldassarre, G. A., E. E. Quinlan, and E. G. Bolen. 1988. Mobility and site fidelity of Green-winged Teal wintering on the Southern High Plains of Texas. Pages 483–493 *in* M. W. Weller, editor. Waterfowl in winter. University of Minnesota Press, Minneapolis.

Ball, I. J., R. D. Bauer, K. Vermeer, and M. J. Rabenberg. 1989. Northwest riverine and Pacific Coast. Pages 429–449 *in* L. M. Smith, R. L. Pederson, and R. M. Kaminski, editors. Habitat management for migrating and wintering waterfowl in North America. Texas Tech University Press, Lubbock.

Barras, J., S. Beville, D. Britsch, S. Hartley, S. Hawes, J. Johnston, P. Kemp, Q. Kinler, A. Martucci, J. Porthouse, D. Reed, K. Roy, S. Sapkota, and J. Suhayda. 2003. Historical and projected coastal Louisiana land changes: 1978–2050. U.S. Geological Survey Open File Report 03–334. (Revised 2004).

Batt, B. D. J., editor. 1997. Arctic ecosystems in peril: report of the Arctic Goose Habitat Working Group. Arctic Goose Joint Venture Special Publication. U.S. Fish and Wildlife Service, Washington, D.C., and Canadian Wildlife Service, Ottawa.

Batt, B. D. J., M. G. Anderson, C. D. Anderson, and F. D. Caswell. 1989. The use of prairie potholes by North American ducks. Pages 204–227 in A. van der Valk, editor. Northern prairie wetlands. Iowa State University Press, Ames.

Beard, E. B. 1953. The importance of beaver in waterfowl management at the Seney National Wildlife Refuge. Journal of Wildlife Management 17:398–436.

Bednarik, K. E. 1984. Saga of the Lake Erie marshes. Pages 423–430 in A. S. Hawkins, R. C. Hanson, H. K. Nelson, and H. M. Reeves, editors. Flyways. U.S. Government Printing Office, Washington, D.C.

Bellrose, F. C. 1979. Species distribution, habitats, and characteristics of breeding dabbling ducks in North America. Pages 1–15 in T. A. Bookhout, editor. Waterfowl and wetlands — an integrated review. La Crosse Printing Company, La Crosse, Wisconsin.

Bellrose, F. C. 1980. Ducks, geese and swans of North America. Stackpole Books, Harrisburg, Pennsylvania.

Boesch, D. F., editor. 1982. Proceedings of the conference on coastal erosion and wetland modification in Louisiana: causes, consequences, and options. U.S. Fish and Wildlife Service FWS/OBS–82/59.

Boettger, R. W. 1967. Management of beaver to benefit waterfowl in Maine. Transactions of the Northeast Fish and Wildlife Conference 24:46–51.

Bolduc, F, and A. D. Afton. 2004. Hydrologic aspects of marsh ponds during winter on the Gulf Coast Chenier Plain, USA: effects of structural marsh management. Marine Ecology Progress Series 266:35–42.

Bolen, E. G. 1964. Plant ecology of spring-fed salt marshes in western Utah. Ecological Monographs 34:143–166.

Bolen, E. G., G. A. Baldassarre, and F. S. Guthery. 1989b. Playa lakes. Pages 341–365 in L. M. Smith, R. L. Pederson, and R. M. Kaminski, editors. Habitat management for migrating and wintering waterfowl in North America. Texas Tech University Press, Lubbock.

Bolen, E. G., and P. N. Gray. 1988. Playa lakes: natural impoundments and waterfowl management of the Southern High Plains. Pages 115–129 in J. L. Thames and C. D. Ziebell, editors, Small water impoundments in semi-arid regions. University of New Mexico Press, Albuquerque.

Bolen, E. G., and F. S. Guthery. 1982. Playas, irrigation, and wildlife in west Texas. Transactions of the North American Wildlife and Natural Resources Conference 47:528–541.

Bolen, E. G., L. M. Smith, and H. L. Schramm, Jr. 1989a. Playa lakes: prairie wetlands of the Southern High Plains. BioScience 39:615–623.

Bookhout, T. A., K. E. Bednarik, and R. W. Kroll. 1989. The Great Lakes marshes. Pages 131–156 in L. M. Smith, R. L. Pederson, and R. M. Kaminski, editors. Habitat management for migrating and wintering waterfowl in North America. Texas Tech University Press, Lubbock.

Botero, J. E., and D. H. Rusch. 1988. Recoveries of North American waterfowl in the Neotropics. Pages 469–482 in M. W. Weller, editor. Waterfowl in winter. University of Minnesota Press, Minneapolis.

Brown, M. K., and G. R. Parsons. 1979. Waterfowl production on beaver flowages in a part of northern New York. New York Fish and Game Journal 26:142–153.

Bue, I. G., L. Blankenship, and W. H. Marshall. 1952. The relationship of grazing practices to waterfowl breeding populations and production on stock ponds in western South Dakota. Transactions of the North American Wildlife Conference 17:396–414.

Bue, I. G., H. G. Uhlig, and J. D. Smith. 1964. Stock ponds and dugouts. Pages 391–398 in J. P. Linduska, editor. Waterfowl tomorrow. U.S. Government Printing Office, Washington, D.C.

Buller, R. F. 1964. Central Flyway. Pages 209–232 in J. P. Linduska, editor. Waterfowl tomorrow. U.S. Government Printing Office, Washington, D.C.

Burger, J., R. Trout, W. Wander, and G. Ritter. 1983. Jamaica Bay studies: IV. Abiotic factors affecting abundance of Brant and Canada Geese on an east coast estuary. Wilson Bulletin 95:384–403.

Cain, B. W. 1988. Wintering waterfowl habitat in Texas: shrinking and contaminated. Pages 583–596 in M. W. Weller, editor. Waterfowl in winter. University of Minnesota Press, Minneapolis.

Carrera, E., and G. de la Fuente. 2003. Inventario y clasificación de humedales en México. Parte I. Ducks Unlimited de México, A.C., Monterrey, Nuevo Leon, Mexico.

Carter, V., and N. B. Rybicki. 1986. Resurgence of submersed aquatic macrophytes in the tidal Potomac River, Maryland, Virginia, and the District of Columbia. Estuaries 9:368–375.

Chabreck, R. H. 1972. Vegetation, water and soil characteristics of the Louisiana coastal region. Louisiana Agricultural Experiment Station Bulletin 664.

Chabreck, R. H. 1982. The effect of coastal alteration on marsh plants. Pages 92–98 in D. F. Boesch, editor. Proceedings of the conference on coastal erosion and wetland modification in Louisiana: causes, consequences, and options. U.S. Fish and Wildlife Service, FWS/OBS– 8 2 / 59.

Chabreck, R. H. 1988. Coastal marshes. University of Minnesota Press, Minneapolis.

Chabreck, R. H., T. Joanen, and S. L. Paulus. 1989. Southern coastal marshes and lakes. Pages 249–277 in L. M. Smith, R. L. Pederson, and R. M. Kaminski, editors. Habitat management for migrating and wintering waterfowl in North America. Texas Tech University Press, Lubbock.

Chabreck, R. H., and G. M. Junkin. 1989. Marsh impoundments for the management of wildlife and plants in Louisiana. Pages 112–119 in W. G. Duffy and D. Clark, editors. Marsh management in coastal Louisiana: effects and issues — proceedings of a symposium. U.S. Fish and Wildlife Service Biological Report 89(22).

Choules, G. L., W. C. Russell, and D. A. Gauthier. 1978. Duck mortality from detergent-polluted water. Journal of Wildlife Management 42:410–414.

Christiansen, J. E., and J. B. Low. 1970. Water requirements of waterfowl marshlands in northern Utah. Utah Division of Fish and Game Publication 69–12.

Christopher, M. W., E. P. Hill, and D. E. Steffen. 1988. Use of catfish ponds by waterfowl wintering in Mississippi. Pages 413–418 in M. W. Weller, editor. Waterfowl in winter. University of Minnesota Press, Minneapolis.

Coleman, J. M. 1976. Deltas: processes of deposition and models for exploration. Continuing Education Publishing Company, Champaign, Illinois.

Collins, J. M. 1974. The relative abundance of ducks breeding in southern Ontario in 1951 and 1971. Pages 32–44 in H. Boyd, editor. Canadian Wildlife Service waterfowl studies in eastern Canada, 1969–1973. Canadian Wildlife Service Report Series 29.

Cornely, J. E. 1982. Waterfowl production at Malheur National Wildlife Refuge, 1942–80. Transactions of the North American Wildlife and Natural Resources Conference 47:559–571.

Cowardin, L. M., V. Carter, F. C. Golet, and E. T. LaRoe, 1979. Classification of wetlands and deepwater habitats of the United States. U.S. Fish and Wildlife Service, FWS/OBS–79/31.

Cox, R. R., Jr., and J. A. Kadlec. 1995. Dynamics of potential waterfowl foods in Great Salt Lake marshes during summer. Wetlands 15:1–8.

Crissey, W. F. 1969. Prairie potholes from a continental viewpoint. Pages 161–171 in Saskatoon wetlands seminar. Canadian Wildlife Service Report Series 6.

Crowder, A. A., and J. M. Bristow. 1988. The future of waterfowl habitats in the Canadian lower Great Lakes marshes. Journal of Great Lakes Research 14:115–127.

Currier, P. J. 1991. Reclamation of crane roosting habitat on the Platte River and restoration of riverine wetlands. Pages 403–407 in J. Harris, editor. Proceedings of the 1987 International Crane Workshop. International Crane Foundation, Baraboo, Wisconsin.

Curtis, D., and H. Beierman. 1980. Playa lakes characterization study. Ecological Services, U.S. Fish and Wildlife Service, Ft. Worth, Texas.

Davis, C. A. 2003. Habitat use and migration patterns of Sandhill Cranes along the Platte River, 1998–2001. Great Plains Research 13:199–216.

DeLaune, R. D., R. H. Baumann, and J. G. Gosselink. 1983. Relationships among vertical accretion, coastal submergence, and erosion in a Louisiana Gulf Coast marsh. Journal of Sedimentary Petrology 53:147–157.

Derksen, D. V., W. D. Eldridge, and M. W. Weller. 1982. Habitat ecology of Pacific Black Brant and other geese moulting near Teshekpuk Lake, Alaska. Wildfowl 33:39–57.

Dornbush, J. N., and J. R. Anderson. 1964. Ducks on the wastewater pond. Water and Sewage Works 111:271–276.

Dubovsky, J. A., and R. M. Kaminski. 1987. Estimates and chronology of waterfowl use of Mississippi catfish ponds. Proceedings of the Southeastern Association of Fish and Wildlife Agencies 41:257–265.

Duebbert, H. F. 1969. The ecology of Malheur Lake and management implications. U.S. Fish and Wildlife Service Refuge Leaflet 412.

Duebbert, H. F., and A. M. Frank. 1984. Value of prairie wetlands to duck broods. Wildlife Society Bulletin 12:27–34.

Dwyer, T. J., G. L. Krapu, and D. M. Janke. 1979. Use of prairie pothole habitat by breeding Mallards. Journal of Wildlife Management 43:526–531.

Edwards, N. T., and D. L. Otis. 1999. Avian communities and habitat relationships in South Carolina Piedmont beaver ponds. American Midland Naturalist 141:158–171.

Eng, R. L., J. D. Jones, and F. M. Gjersing. 1979. Construction and management of stockponds for waterfowl. U.S. Bureau of Land Management Technical Note TN-327.

Erickson, N. W., and D. M. Leslie. 1987. Soil–vegetation correlations in the Sandhills and Rainwater Basin wetlands of Nebraska. U.S. Fish and Wildlife Service Biological Report 87-11.

Evans, K. E., and R. R. Kerbs. 1977. Avian use of livestock watering ponds in western South Dakota. U.S. Forest Service General Technical Report RM-35.

Evans, R. D., and C. W. Wolfe. 1967. Waterfowl production in the Rainwater Basin area of Nebraska. Journal of Wildlife Management 31:788–794.

Figley, W. K., and L. W. VanDruff. 1982. The ecology of urban Mallards. Wildlife Monographs 81.

Flake, L. D., G. L. Petersen, and W. L. Tucker. 1977. Habitat relationships of breeding waterfowl on stock ponds in northwestern South Dakota. Proceedings of the South Dakota Academy of Science 56:135–151.

Flint, P. L., and J. B. Grand. 1996. Nest success of Northern Pintails on the coastal Yukon-Kuskokwim Delta, Alaska. Condor 98:54–60.

Foote, A. L. 1989. Response of nesting waterfowl to flooding in Great Salt Lake wetlands. Great Basin Naturalist 49:614–617.

Forsythe, S. W. 1985. The protection of bottomland hardwood wetlands of the lower Mississippi Valley. Transactions of the North American Wildlife and Natural Resources Conference 50:566–572.

Forsythe, S. W., and S. W. Gard. 1980. Status of bottomland hardwoods along the lower Mississippi River. Transactions of the North American Wildlife and Natural Resources Conference 45:333–340.

Frayer, W. E., T. J. Monahan, D. C. Bowden, and F. A. Graybill. 1983. Status and trends of wetlands and deepwater habitats in the conterminous United States, 1950's to 1970's. Department of Forest and Wood Sciences, Colorado State University, Ft. Collins.

Friend, M. 1981. Waterfowl management and waterfowl disease: independent or cause and effect relationships? Transactions of the North American Wildlife and Natural Resources Conference 46:94–103.

Gilmer, D. S., M. R. Miller, R. D. Bauer, and J. R. LeDonne. 1982. California's Central Valley wintering waterfowl: concerns and challenges. Transactions of the North American Wildlife and Natural Resources Conference 47:441–452.

Gollop, J. B. 1965. Wetland inventories in western Canada. Transactions of the International Union of Game Biologists 6:249–264.

Gordon, C. C., L. D. Flake, and K. F. Higgins. 1990. Aquatic invertebrates of the Rainwater Basin area of Nebraska. Prairie Naturalist 22:191–200.

Gordon, D. H., B. T. Gray, R. D. Perry, M. B. Prevost, T. H. Strange, and R. K. Williams. 1989. South Atlantic Coastal Wetlands. Pages 57–92 in L. M. Smith, R. L. Pederson, and R. M. Kaminski, editors. Habitat management for migrating and wintering waterfowl in North America. Texas Tech University Press, Lubbock.

Gosselink, J. G. 1984. The ecology of delta marshes of coastal Louisiana: a community profile. U.S. Fish and Wildlife Service, FWS/OBS-84/09.

Gray, P. N., and E. G. Bolen. 1987. Seed reserves in the tailwater pits of playa lakes in relation to waterfowl management. Wetlands 7:11–23.

Gustavson, T. C., V. T. Holliday, and S. D. Hovorka. 1995. Origin and development of playa basins, sources of recharge to the Ogallala Aquifer, Southern High Plains, Texas and New Mexico. Bureau of Economic Geology Report of Investigations 229. University of Texas, Austin.

Guthery, F. S., and F. C. Bryant. 1982. Status of playas in the southern Great Plains. Wildlife Society Bulletin 10:309–317.

Guthery, F. S., S. M. Obenberger, and F. A. Stormer. 1984. Predictors of site use by ducks on the Texas High Plains. Wildlife Society Bulletin 12:35–40.

Guthery, F. S., J. M. Pates, and F. A. Stormer. 1982. Characterization of playas of the north-central Llano Estacado in Texas. Transactions of the North American Wildlife and Natural Resources Conference 47:516–527.

Guthery, F. S., and F. A. Stormer. 1984. Wildlife management scenarios for playa vegetation. Wildlife Society Bulletin 12:227–234.

Haramis, G. M. 1991. Canvasback *Aythya valisineria*. Pages 17–1 to 17–10 *in* S. L. Funderburk, S. J. Jordan, J. A. Mihursky, and D. Riley, editors. Habitat requirements for Chesapeake Bay living resources. Second edition. NOAA, Maryland Department of Natural Resources, U.S. Environmental Protection Agency, U.S. Fish and Wildlife Service, Washington, D.C.

Haramis, G. M., D. G. Jorde, S. A. Macko, and J. L. Walker. 2001. Stable-isotope analysis of Canvasback winter diet in Upper Chesapeake Bay. Auk 118:1008–1017.

Haramis, G. M., D. G. Jorde, G. H. Olsen, and D. B. Stotts. 2002. Breeding productivity of Smith Island Black Ducks. Pages 22–30 *in* M. C. Perry, editor. Black Ducks and their Chesapeake Bay habitats: proceedings of a symposium. U.S. Geological Survey, Biological Resources Discipline Information and Technology Report USGS/BRD/ITR — 2002–0005.

Haukos, D. A., and L. M. Smith. 1993a. Seed-bank composition and predictive ability of field vegetation in playa lakes. Wetlands 13:32–40.

Haukos, D. A., and L. M. Smith. 1993b. Moist-soil management of playa lakes for migrating and wintering ducks. Wildlife Society Bulletin 21:288–298.

Haukos, D. A., and L. M. Smith. 1996. Effects of moist-soil management on playa wetland soils. Wetlands 16:143–149.

Haukos, D. A., and L. M. Smith. 1997. Common flora of the playa lakes. Texas Tech University Press, Lubbock.

Hawkins, A. S., R. C. Hanson, H. K. Nelson, and H. M. Reeves, editors. 1984. Flyways. U.S. Fish and Wildlife Service, Washington, D.C.

Hefner, J. M., B. O. Wilen, T. E. Dahl, and W. E. Frayer. 1994. Southeast wetlands: status and trends, mid 1970's to mid 1980's. U.S. Fish and Wildlife Service, Atlanta, Georgia.

Heitmeyer, M. E. 1988. Protein costs of the prebasic molt of female Mallards. Condor 90:263–266.

Heitmeyer, M. E. 1989. Agriculture/wildlife enhancement in California: the Central Valley habitat joint venture. Transactions of the North American Wildlife and Natural Resources Conference 54:391–402.

Heitmeyer, M. E., D. P. Connelly, and R. L. Pederson. 1989. The Central, Imperial, and Coachella Valleys of California. Pages 475–505 *in* L. M. Smith. R. L. Pederson, and R. M. Kaminski, editors. Habitat management for migrating and wintering waterfowl in North America. Texas Tech University Press, Lubbock.

Herdendorf, C. E. 1987. The ecology of the coastal marshes of western Lake Erie: a community profile. U.S. Fish and Wildlife Service Biological Report 85(7.9).

Herdendorf, C. E., C. N. Raphael, and E. Jaworski. 1986. The ecology of Lake St. Clair wetlands: a community profile. U.S. Fish and Wildlife Service Biological Report 85(7.7).

Herke, W. H., and B. D. Rogers. 1989. Threats to coastal fisheries. Pages 196–212 *in* W. G. Duffy and D. Clark, editors. Marsh management in coastal Louisiana: effects and issues — proceedings of a symposium. U.S. Fish and Wildlife Service Biological Report 89(22).

Hewes, L., and P. E. Frandson. 1952. Occupying the wet prairie: the role of artificial drainage in Story County, Iowa. Annals of the Association of American Geographers 42:24–50.

Hindman, L. J., and V. D. Stotts. 1989. Chesapeake Bay and North Carolina sounds. Pages 27–55 *in* L. M. Smith, R. L. Pederson, and R. M. Kaminski, editors. Habitat management for migrating and wintering waterfowl in North America. Texas Tech University Press, Lubbock.

Hoagland, B. W., and S. L. Collins. 1997. Heterogeneity in shortgrass prairie vegetation: the role of playa lakes. Journal of Vegetation Science 8:277–286.

Hobaugh, W. C., C. D. Stutzenbaker, and E. L. Flickinger. 1989. The rice prairies. Pages 367–383 *in* L. M. Smith, R. L. Pederson, and R. M. Kaminski, editors. Habitat management for migrating and wintering waterfowl in North America. Texas Tech University Press, Lubbock.

Hobbie, J. E. 1984. The ecology of tundra ponds of the Arctic Coastal Plain: a community profile. U.S. Fish and Wildlife Service, FWS/OBS–83/25.

Hodgdon, K. W., and J. H. Hunt. 1966. Beaver management in Maine. Maine Department of Inland Fisheries and Game, Game Division Bulletin 3.

Hudson, M. S. 1983. Waterfowl production on three age-classes of stock ponds in Montana. Journal of Wildlife Management 47:112–117.

Hurlbert, S. H., and C. C. Y. Chang. 1984. Ancient ice islands in salt lakes of the central Andes. Science 224:299–302.

Hurley, L. M. 1991. Submerged aquatic vegetation. Pages 2–1 to 2–19 *in* S. L. Funderburk, S. J. Jordan, J. A. Mihursky, and D. Riley, editors. Habitat requirements for Chesapeake Bay living resources. Second edition. NOAA, Maryland Department of Natural Resources, U.S. Environmental Protection Agency, U.S. Fish and Wildlife Service, Washington, D.C.

Ivey, G. L., J. E. Cornely, and B. D. Ehlers. 1998. Carp impacts on waterfowl at Malheur National Wildlife Refuge, Oregon. Transactions of the North American Wildlife and Natural Resources Conference 63:66–74.

Jenkins, A. 1999. The Platte River Cooperative Agreement: a basinwide approach to endangered species issues. Great Plains Research 9:95–113.

Jensen, G. H., and J. E. Chattin. 1964. Western production areas. Pages 79–88 *in* J. P. Linduska, editor. Waterfowl tomorrow. U.S. Government Printing Office, Washington, D.C.

Jensen, W. I., and C. S. Williams. 1964. Botulism and fowl cholera. Pages 333–341 *in* J. P. Linduska, editor. Waterfowl tomorrow. U.S. Government Printing Office, Washington, D.C.

Johnson, F. A., and F. Montalbano, III. 1989. Southern reservoirs and lakes. Pages 93–116 *in* L. M. Smith, R. L. Pederson, R. M. Kaminski, editors. Habitat management for migrating and wintering waterfowl in North America. Texas Tech University Press, Lubbock.

Johnson, F. A., and W. G. Swank. 1981. Waterfowl habitat selection on a multipurpose reservoir in east Texas. Proceedings of the Southeastern Association of Fish and Wildlife Agencies 35:38–48.

Johnson, G. D., D. P. Young, Jr., W. P. Erickson, M. D. Stickland, and L. L. McDonald. 1996. Assessing river habitat selection by waterfowl wintering in the South Platte River, Colorado. Wetlands 16:542–547.

Johnson, M. A., and C. D. Ankney, editors. 2003. Direct control and alternative harvest strategies for North American light geese. Report of the Direct Control and Alternative Harvest Measures Working Group. Arctic Goose Joint Venture special publication. U.S. Fish and Wildlife Service, Washington, D. C., and Canadian Wildlife Service, Ottawa.

Johnson, R. C., J. W. Preacher, J. R. Gwaltney, and J. E. Kennamer. 1975. Evaluation of habitat manipulation for ducks in an Alabama beaver pond complex. Proceedings of the Southeastern Association of Game and Fish Commissioners 29:512–518.

Johnson, W. B., and J. G. Gosselink. 1982. Wetland loss directly associated with canal dredging in the Louisiana coastal zone. Pages 60–72 *in* D. F. Boesch, editor. Proceedings of the conference on coastal erosion and wetland modification in Louisiana: causes, consequences, and options. U.S. Fish and Wildlife Service, FWS/OBS-82/59.

Jorde, D. G., G. L. Krapu, and R. D. Crawford. 1983. Feeding ecology of Mallards wintering in Nebraska. Journal of Wildlife Management 47:1044–1053.

Kadlec, J. A. 2002. Avian botulism in Great Salt Lake marshes: perspectives and possible mechanisms. Wildlife Society Bulletin 30:983–989.

Kadlec, J. A., and L. M. Smith. 1984. Marsh plant establishment on newly flooded salt flats. Wildlife Society Bulletin 12:388–394.

Kadlec, J. A., and L. M. Smith. 1989. The Great Basin marshes. Pages 451–474 *in* L. M. Smith, R. L. Pederson, and R. M. Kaminski, editors. Habitat management for migrating and wintering waterfowl in North America. Texas Tech University Press, Lubbock.

Kaminski, R. M., J. B. Davis, H. W. Essig, P. D. Gerard, and K. J. Reinecke. 2003. True metabolizable energy for Wood Ducks from acorns compared to other waterfowl foods. Journal of Wildlife Management 67:542–550.

Kantrud, H. A., G. L. Krapu, and G. A. Swanson. 1989b. Prairie basin wetlands of the Dakotas: a community profile. U.S. Fish and Wildlife Service Biological Report 85(7.28).

Kantrud, H. A., J. B. Millar, and A. G. van der Valk. 1989a. Vegetation of wetlands of the prairie pothole region. Pages 132–187 in A. van der Valk, editor. Northern prairie wetlands. Iowa State University Press, Ames.

Kantrud, H. A., and R. E. Stewart. 1977. Use of natural basin wetlands by breeding waterfowl in North Dakota. Journal of Wildlife Management 41:243–253.

Kantrud, H. A., and R. E. Stewart. 1984. Ecological distribution and crude density of breeding birds on prairie wetlands. Journal of Wildlife Management 48:426–437.

Kemp, W. M., R. R. Twilley, J. C. Stevenson, W. R. Boynton, and J. C. Means. 1983. The decline of submerged vascular plants in upper Chesapeake Bay: summary of results concerning possible causes. Marine Technology Society Journal 17:78–89.

Kimball, D., and J. Kimball. 1969. The market gunner. Dillon Press, Minneapolis, Minnesota.

Kimerle, R. A., and W. R. Enns. 1968. Aquatic insects associated with midwestern waste stabilization lagoons. Journal of Water Pollutution Control Federal 40:R31–R41.

King, J. G. 1970. The swans and geese of Alaska's arctic slope. Wildfowl 21:11–17.

Kirsch, L. M. 1969. Waterfowl production in relation to grazing. Journal of Wildlife Management 33:821–828.

Korschgen, C. E. 1989. Riverine and deepwater habitats for diving ducks. Pages 157–180 in L. M. Smith, R. L. Pederson, and R. M.Kaminski, editors. Habitat management for migrating and wintering waterfowl in North America. Texas Tech University Press, Lubbock.

Korschgen, C. E., L. S. George, and W. L. Green.1985. Disturbance of diving ducks by boaters on a migrational staging area. Wildlife Society Bulletin 13:290–296.

Kramer, G. W., and R. Migoya. 1989. The Pacific coast of Mexico. Pages 507–528 in L. M. Smith, R. L. Pederson, and R. M. Kaminski, editors. Habitat management for migrating and wintering waterfowl in North America. Texas Tech University Press, Lubbock.

Krapu, G. L., D. A. Brandt, and R. R. Cox, Jr. 2004. Less waste corn, more land in soybeans, and the switch to genetically modified crops: trends with important implications for wildlife management. Wildlife Society Bulletin 32:127–136.

Krapu, G. L., P. J. Pietz, D. A. Brandt, and R. R. Cox, Jr. 2000. Factors limiting Mallard brood survival in prairie pothole landscapes. Journal of Wildlife Management 64:553–561.

Krapu, G. L., K. J. Reinecke, D. G. Jorde, and S. G. Simpson. 1995. Spring-staging ecology of midcontinent Greater White–fronted Geese. Journal of Wildlife Management 59:736–746.

Lanctot, R. B., and P. X. Quang. 1992. Density of loons in central Alaska. Condor 94:282–280.

Larson, J. S., M. S. Bedinger, C. F. Bryan, S. Brown, R. T. Huffman, E. L. Miller, D. G. Rhodes, and B. A. Touchet. 1981. Transition from wetlands to uplands in southeastern bottomland hardwood forests. Pages 225–273 in J. R. Clark and J. Benforado, editors. Wetlands of bottomland hardwood forests. Elsevier Science, Amsterdam, The Netherlands.

Leopold, A. 1933. Game management. Charles Scribner's Sons, New York.

Linduska, J. P., editor. 1964. Waterfowl tomorrow. U.S. Government Printing Office, Washington, D.C.

Littlefield, C. D. 2003. Sandhill Crane nesting success and productivity in relation to predator removal in southeastern Oregon. Wilson Bulletin 115:263–269.

Lokemoen, J. T. 1973. Waterfowl production on stock-watering ponds in the northern Great Plains. Journal of Range Management 26:179–184.

Louisiana State University. 1983. Exploring the Atchafalaya Delta. Aquanotes 12:1–4.

Ludden, A. P., D. L. Frink, and D. H. Johnson. 1983. Water storage capacity of natural wetland depressions in the Devils Lake Basin of North Dakota. Journal of Soil and Water Conservation 38:45–48.

Lynch, J. J., C. D. Evans, and V. C. Conover. 1963. Inventory of waterfowl environments of prairie Canada. Transactions of the North American Wildlife Conference 28:93–108.

MacDonald, P. O., W. E. Frayer, and J. K. Clauser. 1979. Documentation, chronology, and future projections of bottomland hardwood habitat loss in the Lower Mississippi Alluvial Plain. Volume I: basic report. U.S. Fish and Wildlife Service, Ecological Services, Vicksburg, Mississippi.

Mack, G. D., and L. D. Flake. 1980. Habitat relationships of waterfowl broods on South Dakota stock ponds. Journal of Wildlife Management 44:695–700.

Manley, S. W., R. M. Kaminski, K. J. Reinecke, and P. D. Gerard. 2004. Waterbird foods in winter-managed ricefields in Mississippi. Journal of Wildlife Management 68:74–83.

Maxson, G-A. D. 1981. Waterfowl use of a municipal sewage lagoon. Prairie Naturalist 13:1–12.

McLean, D. D. 1946. Duck disease at Tulare Lake. California Fish and Game 32:71–80.

Mendelssohn, I. A., and K. L. McKee. 1988. *Spartina alterniflora* dieback in Louisiana: time-course investigation of soil waterlogging effects. Journal of Ecology 76:509–521.

Merendino, M. T., G. B. McCullough, and N. R. North. 1995. Wetland availability and use by breeding waterfowl in southern Ontario. Journal of Wildlife Management 59:527–532.

Merendino, M. T., and L. M. Smith. 1991. Influence of drawdown date and reflood depth on wetland vegetation establishment. Wildlife Society Bulletin 19:143–150.

Michot, T. C. 1996. Marsh loss in coastal Louisiana: implications for management of North American Anatidae. Gibier Faune Sauvage 13:941–957.

Michot, T. C., C. J. Wells, and R. S. Kemmerer. 2004. Spatial and temporal distribution of coastal marsh dieback in Louisiana, 2000–2003, as determined from aerial surveys. Unpublished report, Task III.8, U.S. Geological Survey, National Wetlands Research Center, Lafayette, Louisiana.

Middlebrooks, E. J., N. B. Jones, J. H. Reynolds, M. F. Torpy, and R. P. Bishop. 1978. Lagoon information sourcebook. Ann Arbor Science, Ann Arbor, Michigan.

Millar, J. B. 1969. Some characteristics of wetland basins in central and southwestern Saskatchewan. Pages 73–101 *in* Saskatoon wetlands seminar. Canadian Wildlife Service Report Series 6.

Miller, A. W., and B. D. Collins. 1954. A nesting study of ducks and Coots on Tule Lake and Lower Klamath National Wildlife Refuges. California Fish and Game 40:17–37.

Mitsch, W. J., and J. G. Gosselink. 2000. Wetlands. Third edition. John Wiley & Sons, New York.

Moore, K. A., D. J. Wilcox, and R. J. Orth. 2000. Analysis of the abundance of submersed aquatic vegetation communities in the Chesapeake Bay. Estuaries 23:115–127.

Moore, R. L., and C. D. Simpson. 1981. Disease mortality of waterfowl on Texas playa lakes. Southwestern Naturalist 25:566–568.

Moorman, A. M., T. E. Moorman, G. A. Baldassarre, and D. M. Richard. 1991. Effects of saline drinking water on growth and survival of Mottled Duck ducklings in Louisiana. Journal of Wildlife Management 55:471–476.

Morgan, J. P. 1973. Impact of subsidence and erosion on Louisiana coastal marshes and estuaries. Pages 217–233 *in* R. H. Chabreck, editor. Proceedings of the second coastal marsh and estuary management symposium. Division of Continuing Education, Louisiana State University, Baton Rouge, Louisiana.

Moulton, D. W., W. I. Jensen, and J. B. Low. 1976. Avian botulism epizootiology on sewage oxidation ponds in Utah. Journal of Wildlife Management 40:735–742.

Mundinger, J. G. 1976. Waterfowl responses to rest-rotation grazing. Journal of Wildlife Management 40:60–68.

National Agricultural Statistics Service. 1999–2003. Crop production summaries, 1999–2003. U.S. Department of Agriculture, National Agricultural Statistics Service, Agricultural Statistics Board, Washington, D.C.

Nelson, N. F. 1954. Factors in the development and restoration of waterfowl habitat at Ogden Bay Refuge. Utah Department of Fish and Game Publication 6.

Niemuth, N. D., and J. W. Solberg. 2003. Response of waterbirds to number of wetlands in the Prairie Pothole Region of North Dakota, U.S.A. Waterbirds 26:233–238.

North American Waterfowl Management Plan, Plan Committee. 2004. North American Waterfowl Management Plan 2004. Strategic guidance: strengthening the biological foundation. Canadian Wildlife Service, U.S. Fish and Wildlife Service, and Secretaria de Medio Ambiente y Recursos Naturales.

Novacek, J. M. 1989. The water and wetland resources of the Nebraska Sandhills. Pages 340–384 *in* A. van der Valk, editor. Northern prairie wetlands. Iowa State University Press, Ames.

Oates, D. W. 1989. Incidence of lead shot in the Rainwater Basins of south central Nebraska. Prairie Naturalist 21:137–146.

Olmsted, I. 1993. Wetlands of Mexico. Pages 637–678 *in* D. F. Whigham, D. Dykyjová, and S. Henjý, editors. Wetlands of the world: inventory, ecology and management. Volume I. Kluwer Academic, Dordrecht, The Netherlands.

Olson, B. E., K. Lindsey, and V. Hirschboeck. 2004. Bear River Migratory Bird Refuge, habitat management plan. Unpublished report, U.S. Fish and Wildlife Service, Brigham City, Utah.

O'Neill, E. J. 1979. Fourteen years of goose populations and trends at Klamath Basin refuges. Pages 316–321 *in* R. L. Jarvis and J. C. Bartonek, editors. Management and biology of Pacific Flyway geese — a symposium. OSU Book Stores, Corvallis, Oregon.

Orth, R. J., and K. A. Moore. 1981. Submerged aquatic vegetation in the Chesapeake Bay: past, present, and future. Transactions of the North American Wildlife and Natural Resources Conference 46:271–283.

Orth, R. J., and K. A. Moore. 1984. Distribution and abundance of submerged aquatic vegetation in Chesapeake Bay: an historical perspective. Estuaries 7:531–540.

Orth, R. J., D. J. Wilcox, L. S. Nagey, A. L. Owens, J. R. Whiting, and A. Serio. 2004. 2003 distribution of submerged aquatic vegetation in Chesapeake Bay and coastal bays. Virginia Institute of Marine Science Special Scientific Report 144.

Osterkamp, W. R., and W. W. Wood. 1987. Playa-lake basins on the Southern High Plains of Texas and New Mexico: Part I. Hydrologic, geomorphic, and geologic evidence for their development. Geological Society of America Bulletin 99:215–223.

Page, G. W., E. Palacios, L. Alfaro, S. Gonzalez, L. E. Stenzel, and M. Jungers. 1997. Numbers of wintering shorebirds in coastal wetlands of Baja California, Mexico. Journal of Field Ornithology 68:562–574.

Palmisano, A. W. 1973. Habitat preference of waterfowl and fur animals in the northern Gulf Coast marshes. Pages 163–190 *in* R. H. Chabreck, editor. Proceedings of the second coastal marsh and estuary management symposium. Division of Continuing Education, Louisiana State University, Baton Rouge.

Paulus, S. L. 1984. Activity budgets of nonbreeding Gadwalls in Louisiana. Journal of Wildlife Management 48:371–380.

Paulus, S. L. 1988. Time–activity budgets of Mottled Ducks in Louisiana in winter. Journal of Wildlife Management 52:711–718.

Paveglio, F. L., C. M. Bunck, and G. H. Heinz. 1992. Selenium and boron in aquatic birds from central California. Journal of Wildlife Management 56:31–42.

Pederson, R. L., D. G. Jorde, and S. G. Simpson. 1989. Northern Great Plains. Pages 281–310 *in* L. M. Smith, R. L. Pederson, and R. M. Kaminski, editors. Habitat management for migrating and wintering waterfowl in North America. Texas Tech University Press, Lubbock.

Perez-Arteaga, A., K. J. Gaston, and M. Kershaw. 2002. Undesignated sites in Mexico qualifying as wetlands of international importance. Biological Conservation 107:47–57.

Perry, M. C. 1987. Waterfowl of Chesapeake Bay. Pages 94–114 *in* S. K. Majumdar, L. W. Hall, Jr., and H. M. Austin, editors. Contaminant problems and management of living Chesapeake Bay resources. Pennsylvania Academy of Science, Easton, Pennsylvania.

Perry, M. C., editor. 2002. Black Ducks and their Chesapeake Bay habitats: proceedings of a symposium. U.S. Geological Survey, Biological Resources Discipline Information and Technology Report USGS/BRD/ITR — 2002–0005.

Perry, M. C., editor. 2004. Mute Swans and their Chesapeake Bay habitats: proceedings of a symposium. U.S. Geological Survey, Biological Resources Discipline Information and Technology Report USGS/BRD/ITR — 2004–0005.

Perry, M. C., R. E. Munro, and G. M. Haramis. 1981. Twenty-five year trends in diving duck populations in Chesapeake Bay. Transactions of the North American Wildlife and Natural Resources Conference 46:299–310.

Perry, M. C., and F. M. Uhler. 1988. Food habits and distribution of wintering Canvasbacks, *Aythya valisineria*, on Chesapeake Bay. Estuaries 11:57–67.

Piest, L. A., and L. K. Sowls. 1985. Breeding duck use of a sewage marsh in Arizona. Journal of Wildlife Management 49:580–585.

Quortrup, E. R., F. B. Queen, and L. J. Merovka. 1946. An outbreak of pasteurellosis in wild ducks. Journal of the American Veterinary Medical Association 108:94–100.

Rave, D. P., and G. A. Baldassarre. 1989. Activity budget of Green-winged Teal wintering in coastal wetlands of Louisiana. Journal of Wildlife Management 53:753–759.

Reeves, C. C., Jr., and J. A. Reeves. 1996. The Ogallala Aquifer (of the Southern High Plains). Estacado Books, Lubbock, Texas.

Reid, F. A., J. R. Kelley, Jr., T. S. Taylor, and L. H. Fredrickson. 1989. Upper Mississippi Valley wetlands — refuges and moist-soil impoundments. Pages 181–202 in L. M. Smith, R. L. Pederson, and R. M. Kaminski, editors. Habitat management for migrating and wintering waterfowl in North America. Texas Tech University Press, Lubbock.

Reinecke, K. J., and C. K. Baxter. 1996. Waterfowl habitat management in the Mississippi Alluvial Valley. International Waterfowl Symposium 7:159–167.

Reinecke, K. J., R. M. Kaminski, D. J. Moorhead, J. H. Hodges, and J. R. Nassar. 1989. Mississippi Alluvial Valley. Pages 203–247 in L. M. Smith, R. L. Pederson, and R. M. Kaminski, editors. Habitat management for migrating and wintering waterfowl in North America. Texas Tech University Press, Lubbock.

Renouf, R. N. 1972. Waterfowl utilization of beaver ponds in New Brunswick. Journal of Wildlife Management 36:740–744.

Rhodes, M. J., and J. D. Garcia. 1981. Characteristics of playa lakes related to summer waterfowl use. Southwestern Naturalist 26:231–235.

Ringelman, J. K., W. R. Eddleman, and H. W. Miller. 1989. High Plains reservoirs and sloughs. Pages 311–340 in L. M. Smith, R. L. Pederson, and R. M. Kaminski, editors. Habitat management for migrating and wintering waterfowl in North America. Texas Tech University Press, Lubbock.

Rollo, J. D., and E. G. Bolen. 1969. Ecological relationships of Blue and Green-winged Teal on the High Plains of Texas in early fall. Southwestern Naturalist 14:171–188.

Ross, R. K., K. F. Abraham, T. R. Gadawski, R. S Rempel, S. T. Gabor, and R. Maher. 2002. Abundance and distribution of breeding waterfowl in the Great Clay Belt of northern Ontario. Canadian Field-Naturalist 116:4–50.

Rowell, C. M., Jr. 1971. Vascular plants of the playa lakes of the Texas Panhandle and South Plains. Southwestern Naturalist 5:407–417.

Rumble, M. A., and L. D. Flake. 1983. Management considerations to enhance use of stock ponds by waterfowl broods. Journal of Range Management 36:691–694.

Ruwaldt, J. J., Jr., L. D. Flake, and J. M. Gates. 1979. Waterfowl pair use of natural and man-made wetlands in South Dakota. Journal of Wildlife Management 43:375–83.

Sabin, T. J., and V. T. Holliday. 1995. Playas and lunettes on the Southern High Plains: morphometric and spatial relationships. Annals of the Association of American Geographers 85:286–305.

Sanderson, G. C. 1980. Conservation of waterfowl. Pages 43–58 in F. C. Bellrose. Ducks, geese and swans of North America. Stackpole Books, Harrisburg, Pennsylvania.

Saunders, G. B., and D. C. Saunders. 1981. Waterfowl and their wintering grounds in Mexico, 1937–64. U.S. Fish and Wildlife Service Resource Publication 138.

Scott, D. A., editor. 1989. A directory of Asian wetlands. IUCN Gland, Switzerland, and Cambridge.

Scott, D. A., and M. Carbonell. 1986. A directory of Neotropical wetlands. IUCN Cambridge and IWRB Slimbridge, United Kingdom.

Scott, P., and J. Fisher. 1954. A thousand geese. Houghton Mifflin, Boston.

Sheeley, D. G., and L. M. Smith. 1989. Tests of the diet and condition bias in hunter-killed Northern Pintails. Journal of Wildlife Management 53:765–769.

Sherwood, G. A. 1960. The Whistling Swan in the west with particular reference to the Great Salt Lake Valley, Utah. Condor 62:370–377.

Smith, A. G., J. H. Stoudt, and J. B. Gollop. 1964. Prairie potholes and marshes. Pages 39–50 in J. P. Linduska, editor. Waterfowl tomorrow. U.S. Government Printing Office, Washington, D.C.

Smith, B. J., and K. F. Higgins. 1990. Avian cholera and temporal changes in wetland numbers and densities in Nebraska's Rainwater Basin area. Wetlands 10:1–5.

Smith, B. J., K. F. Higgins, and C. F. Gritzner. 1989. Land use relationships to avian cholera outbreaks in the Nebraska Rainwater Basin area. Prairie Naturalist 21:125–136.

Smith, B. J., K. F. Higgins, and W. L. Tucker. 1990. Precipitation, waterfowl densities, and mycotoxins: their potential effect on avian cholera epizootics in the Nebraska Rainwater Basin area. Transactions of the North American Wildlife and Natural Resources Conference 55:269–282.

Smith. L. M. 2003. Playas of the Great Plains. University of Texas Press, Austin.

Smith, L. M., and D. A. Haukos. 2002. Floral diversity in relation to playa wetland area and watershed disturbance. Conservation Biology 16:964–974.

Smith, L. M., and J. A. Kadlec. 1986. Habitat management for wildlife in marshes of Great Salt Lake. Transactions of the North American Wildlife and Natural Resources Conference 51:222–231.

Smith, L. M., R. L. Pederson, and R. M. Kaminski, editors. 1989. Habitat management for migrating and wintering waterfowl in North America. Texas Tech Univeristy Press, Lubbock, Texas.

Smith, R. H., F. Dufresne, and H. A. Hansen. 1964. Northern watersheds and deltas. Pages 51–66 in J. P. Linduska, editor. Waterfowl tomorrow. U.S. Government Printing Office, Washington, D.C.

Smith, R. I. 1970a. Response of Pintail breeding populations to drought. Journal of Wildlife Management 34:943–946.

Smith, W. G. 1970b. Spartina "die–back" in Louisiana marshlands. Coastal Studies Bulletin 5:89–96.

Speake, D. W. 1955. Waterfowl use of creeks, beaver swamps, and small impoundments in Lee County, Alabama. Proceedings of the Southeastern Association of Game and Fish Commissioners 9:178–185.

Stafford, J. D., R. M. Kaminski, K. J. Reinecke, and S. W. Manley. 2006. Waste rice for waterfowl in the Mississippi Alluvial Valley. Journal of Wildlife Management 70:in press.

Stanturf, J. A., E. S. Gardiner, P. B. Hamel, M. S. Devall, T. D. Leininger, and M. E. Warren, Jr. 2000. Restoring bottomland hardwood ecosystems in the Lower Mississippi Alluvial Valley. Journal of Forestry 98:10–16.

Steiner, A. J. 1984. Mid-winter waterfowl inventory, Atlantic Flyway, 1954–84 trend analysis. U.S. Fish and Wildlife Service, Newton Corner, Massachusetts.

Stevenson, J. C., and N. M. Confer. 1978. Summary of available information on Chesapeake Bay submerged vegetation. U.S. Fish and Wildlife Service, FWS/OBS-78/66.

Stevenson, J. C., N. M. Confer, and C. B. Pieper. 1979. The decline of submerged aquatic plants in Chesapeake Bay. U.S. Fish and Wildlife Service, FWS/OBS-79/24.

Steward, K. K., T. K. Van, V. Carter, and A. H. Pieterse. 1984. Hydrilla invades Washington, D.C. and the Potomac. American Journal of Botany 71:162–163.

Stewart, R. E. 1962. Waterfowl populations in the upper Chesapeake region. U.S. Fish and Wildlife Service Special Scientific Report Wildlife 65.

Stewart, R. E., and H. A. Kantrud. 1971. Classification of natural ponds and lakes in the glaciated prairie region. U.S. Fish and Wildlife Service Resource Publication 92.

Stewart, R. E., and H. A. Kantrud. 1973. Ecological distribution of breeding waterfowl populations in North Dakota. Journal of Wildlife Management 37:39–50.

Stewart, R. E., and H. A. Kantrud. 1974. Breeding waterfowl populations in the prairie pothole region of North Dakota. Condor 76:70–79.

Stewart, R. E., C. E. Proffitt, and T. M. Charron. 2001. Coastal marsh dieback in the northern Gulf of Mexico: extent, causes, consequences, and remedies. U.S. Geological Survey Information and Technical Report USGS/BRD/ITR-2001 0003. U.S. Geological Survey, National Wetlands Research Center, Lafayette, Louisiana.

Stutzenbaker, C. D., and M. W. Weller. 1989. The Texas coast. Pages 385–405 in L. M. Smith, R. L. Pederson, and R. M. Kaminski, editors. Habitat management for migrating and wintering waterfowl in North America. Texas Tech Uni=versity Press, Lubbock.

Swanson, G. A. 1977. Diel food selection by Anatinae on a waste-stabilization system. Journal of Wildlife Management 41:226–231.

Swanson, G. A., M. I. Meyer, and J. R. Serie. 1974. Feeding ecology of breeding Blue-winged Teals. Journal of Wildlife Management 38:396–407.

Talent, L. G., G. L. Krapu, and R. L. Jarvis. 1982. Habitat use by Mallard broods in south central North Dakota. Journal of Wildlife Management 46:629–635.

Thompson, D. 1973. Feeding ecology of diving ducks on Keokuk Pool, Mississippi River. Journal of Wildlife Management 37:367–381.

Thompson, S. C., and S. B. Simmons. 1990. Characteristics of second clutches in California Wood Ducks. Pages 171–177 in L. H. Fredrickson, G. V. Burger, S. P. Havera, D. A. Graber, R. Kirby, and T. S. Taylor, editors. Proceedings of the 1988 North American Wood Duck Symposium, St. Louis.

Tiner, R. W., Jr. 1984. Wetlands of the United States: current status and recent trends. National Wetlands Inventory, U.S. Fish and Wildlife Service,

Turner, R. E., R. Costanza, and W. Scaife. 1982. Canals and wetland erosion rates in coastal Louisiana. Pages 73–84 in D. F. Boesch, editor. Proceedings of the conference on coastal erosion and wetland modification in Louisiana: causes, consequences, and options. U.S. Fish and Wildlife Service, FWS/OBS-82/59.

Turner, R. E., and J. G. Gosselink. 1975. A note on standing crops of Spartina alterniflora in Texas and Florida. University of Texas Contributions in Marine Science 19:113–118.

Uhler, F. M. 1964. Bonus from waste places. Pages 643–653 in J. P. Linduska, editor. Waterfowl tomorrow. U.S. Government Printing Office, Washington, D.C.

Uihlein, W. B. 2000. Estimates of private lands managed for waterfowl in the Mississippi Alluvial Valley. Dissertation, Mississippi State University, Mississippi State.

U.S. Fish and Wildlife Service. 1981. The Platte River ecology study. U.S. Fish and Wildlife Service Special Research Report, Jamestown, North Dakota.

U.S. Fish and Wildlife Service. 2001. North Platte National Wildlife Refuge: comprehensive conservation plan. U.S. Fish and Wildlife Service, North Platte National Wildlife Refuge, Scottsbluff, Nebraska.

Valqui, M., S. M. Caziani, O. Rocha-O, and E. Rodriguez-R. 2000. Abundance and distribution of the South American altiplano flamingos. Waterbirds 23 (Special Publication 1):110–113.

van den Akker, J. B., and V. T. Wilson. 1951. Public hunting on the Bear River Migratory Bird Refuge, Utah. Journal of Wildlife Management 15:367–381.

van der Valk, A., editor. 1989. Northern prairie wetlands. Iowa State University Press, Ames.

Vrtiska, M. P., and N. Lyman. 2004. Wintering Canada Geese along the Platte Rivers of Nebraska, 1960–2000. Great Plains Research 14:115–128.

Walsh, H. M. 1971. The outlaw gunner. Tidewater Publishers, Centreville, Maryland.

Webb, E. C., I. A. Mendelssohn, and B. J. Wilsey. 1995. Causes for vegetation dieback in a Louisiana salt marsh: a bioassay approach. Aquatic Botany 51:281–289.

Wellein, E. G., and H. G. Lumsden. 1964. Northern forests and tundra. Pages 67–76 in J. P. Linduska, editor. Waterfowl tomorrow. U.S. Government Printing Office, Washington, D.C.

Weller, M. W. 1964. Distribution and migration of the Redhead. Journal of Wildlife Management 28:64–103.

West, R. C. 1977. Tidal salt-marsh and mangal formations of Middle and South America. Pages 193–213 in V. J. Chapman, editor. Ecosystems of the world. I. Wet coastal environments. Elsevier Scientific, New York.

Wetmore, A. 1918. The duck sickness in Utah. U.S. Department of Agriculture Bulletin 672.

Wetmore, A. 1921. Wild ducks and duck foods of the Bear River Marshes, Utah. U.S. Department of Agriculture Bulletin 936.

White, D. A. 1989. Accreting mudflats at the Mississippi River Delta: sedimentation rates and vascular plant succession. Pages 49–57 in Marsh management in coastal Louisiana: effects and issues — proceedings of a symposium. U.S. Fish and Wildlife Service Biological Report 89(22).

White, W. M., and G. W. Malaher. 1964. Reservoirs. Pages 381–389 in J. P. Linduska, editor. Waterfowl tomorrow. U.S. Government Printing Office, Washington, D.C.

Whyte, R. J., G. A. Baldassarre, and E. G. Bolen. 1986. Winter condition of Mallards on the Southern High Plains of Texas. Journal of Wildlife Management 50:52–57.

Whyte, R. J., and E. G. Bolen. 1984a. Variation in winter fat deposits and condition indices of Mallards. Journal of Wildlife Management 48:1370–1373.

Whyte, R. J., and E. G. Bolen. 1984b. Impact of winter stress on Mallard body composition. Condor 86:477–482.

Whyte, R. J., and E. G. Bolen. 1985. Seed production and morphology of two smartweeds associated with playa lakes in Texas. Southwestern Naturalist 30:605–607.

Whyte, R. J., and B. W. Cain. 1981. Wildlife habitat on grazed or ungrazed small pond shorelines in south Texas. Journal of Range Wildlife Management 34:64–68.

Williams, C. S., and W. H. Marshall. 1938. Duck nesting studies, Bear River Migratory Bird Refuge, Utah, 1937. Journal of Wildlife Management 2:29–48.

Wilson, M. H., and D. A. Ryan. 1997. Conservation of Mexican wetlands: role of the North American Wetlands Conservation Act. Wildlife Society Bulletin 25:57–64.

Windingstad, R. M., J. J. Hurt, A. K. Trout, and J. Cary. 1984. Avian cholera in Nebraska's Rainwater Basin. Transactions of the North American Wildlife and Natural Resources Conference 49:576–583.

Wood, W. W., and W. R. Osterkamp. 1987. Playa-lake basins on the Southern High Plains of Texas and New Mexico, Part 2. A hydrologic model and mass-balance arguments for their development. Geological Society of America Bulletin 99:224–230.

Zahm, G. R. 1986. Kesterson Reservoir and Kesterson National Wildlife Refuge: history, current problems and management alternatives. Transactions of the North American Wildlife and Natural Resources Conference 51:324–329.

Zinkl, J. G., N. Dey, J. M. Hyland, J. J. Hunt, and K. L. Heddleston. 1977. An epornitic of avian cholera in waterfowl and Common Crows in Phelps County, Nebraska, in the spring, 1975. Journal of Wildlife Diseases 13:194–198.

Chapter 10
WETLANDS AND WETLAND MANAGEMENT

Wetlands form the primary natural habitat for waterfowl, but unlike most other land forms, the variety of wetlands is immense. In fact, the hierarchial classification scheme developed by the U.S. Fish and Wildlife Service potentially identifies thousands of wetland types in the United States alone (Cowardin et al. 1979). Such diversity obviously precludes discussions of each type, and that level of detail is not necessary here (for greater coverage, see Mitsch and Gosselink 2000). Instead, we focus on a general understanding of the basic biological features of wetland habitats — an approach that provides the basis for management, which we discuss in comparatively greater detail. The functional values of wetlands important to waterfowl in North America and elsewhere appeared in Chapter 9.

Less than a century ago, North America's wetland resources were largely unspoiled by human negligence. This foundation of pristine habitat supported an unmeasured but certainly enormous population of waterfowl in comparison with the present time. Eventually, however, settlement, plows, and industry extracted a staggering toll (Fig. 10-1). Prairies vanished wholesale, as did wetlands of every description, and with them, populations of water-

fowl and other species plummeted in an ecological freefall. We may lament this history of waste — and there are indeed lessons to be learned from the past — but our actions necessarily should focus on current and future issues befalling waterfowl management.

Regrettably, wetland losses throughout North America have been staggering, and the remaining wetlands continue to be lost or steadily degraded under the attack of acid rain, exotic plants, impaired hydrology, chemical contamination, sedimentation, and other forms of pollution. Ducks no longer flourish on the prairies, where drainage and intensive cultivation have claimed much of the original landscape formerly so productive as nesting habitat. In the Central Valley of California, wintering waterfowl crowd onto the few remaining wetlands, under conditions where disease and death are regular events. Each day wetlands in coastal Louisiana disappear, and only a fraction remains of the once vast forested wetlands of the Mississippi Alluvial Valley.

In the face of these and similar circumstances, one might ask how waterfowl have persisted at all, much less how the numbers of some species actually have increased! The answer is unequivocally simple: ***MANAGEMENT***. Waterfowl management

Figure 10-1. The arrival of settlers to the continent's midsection produced major consequences for the future of waterfowl habitat. These farmers are breaking virgin prairie sod in North Dakota in the early 1900s. Photo courtesy of the North Dakota Game and Fish Department.

Figure 10-2. Every year millions of people enjoy waterfowl at wildlife refuges. These observers are viewing sea ducks at the Parker River National Wildlife Refuge in Massachusetts. Photo courtesy of Evan Rehm, SUNY College of Environmental Science and Forestry.

in North America flowed from the Migratory Bird Treaty, which forms the legal backbone of harvest regulations across the continent (see Chapter 11), and management concepts adopted in the United States created a National Wildlife Refuge System unrivaled in the world. Indeed, we may expect the presence of some form of management wherever we encounter wildlife and wildlife habitat. This action may be land acquisition, harvest or land-use regulations, habitat manipulations, or public education, but whether singly or in combination, these activities signify management.

Leopold (1933:3) long ago defined management as the "art of making land produce sustained annual crops of wild game for recreational use." In time, the somewhat limited concept of "game" broadened into a fuller, more appropriate category "wildlife," but the remaining elements of Leopold's definition still hold, especially the notion that waterfowl and other wildlife are usable, sustainable products of the land and its waters. Furthermore, "recreational use"

encompasses more than hunting and other consumptive uses of wildlife — many millions of nonhunters regularly seek an outdoor experience, not the least of which is to enjoy viewing waterfowl (Fig. 10-2).

The forms of waterfowl management are many, but they fall under two basic categories: (1) population management, by regulating harvest and controlling diseases and other types of mortality, as discussed in Chapter 8; and (2) the preservation and/or manipulation of habitat— the "land" of Leopold and the basis of this chapter. We begin by defining wetlands and their attributes as the basis for our discussion of general principles of wetlands management.

DEFINITION AND FEATURES OF WETLANDS

A definition that differentiates wetlands from other ecosystems is of obvious importance to protection and management activities. The formulation of such a definition is difficult, however, because wetlands represent transitional zones between upland and aquatic ecosystems, and wetlands therefore exhibit some characteristics of each. A useful definition should identify where in this continuum the wetland ends and the upland begins, as well as identify wetlands under a variety of conditions and across a broad geographic area. To these ends, various definitions use a common theme: Wetlands are areas where hydric soils and hydrophytic vegetation predominate (Table 10-1).

"Hydric soils," a term coined in the 1970s, are defined formally by the U.S. Department of Agriculture as, "soils that formed under conditions of saturation, flooding or ponding long enough (about 7–10 days) during the growing season to develop anaerobic conditions in the upper part" (Natural Resources Conservation Service 2003). These soils normally support hydrophytes, which are plants adapted for growth under the anaerobic conditions typical of wet soils. Hydric soils are especially useful in identifying wetland boundaries, particularly where topographical and hydrological changes are gradual or where wetlands occur on perturbed sites.

Wetland soils can be classified as organic or mineral, for which distinguishing criteria appear in *Field Indicators of Hydric Soils in the United* States (Natural Resources Conservation Service 2003). The identification and familiarization with the array of hydric soils requires specific training and lies beyond

Table 10-1. The definitions of wetlands as promulgated by federal management and regulatory agencies in the United States.

U.S. Fish and Wildlife Service definition developed for inventory of all United States wetlands (Cowardin et al. 1979:3):

> Wetlands are lands transitional between terrestrial and aquatic systems where the water table is usually at or near the surface or the land is covered by shallow water. For purposes of this classification wetlands must have one or more of the following three attributes: (1) at least periodically, the land supports predominantly hydrophytes; (2) the substrate is predominantly undrained hydric soil; and (3) the substrate is nonsoil and is saturated with water or covered by shallow water at some time during the growing season of each year.

U.S. Army Corps of Engineers and U.S. Environmental Protection Agency definition for administering the dredge-and-fill permit system required by Section 404 of the Clean Water Act of 1977:

> The term "wetlands" means those areas that are inundated or saturated by surface or ground water at a frequency and duration sufficient to support, and that under normal circumstances do support, a prevalence of vegetation typically adapted for life in saturated soil conditions. Wetlands generally include swamps, marshes, bogs, and similar areas.

U.S. Department of Agriculture, Soil Conservation Service (now the Natural Resources Conservation Service) definition for implementation of the "Swampbuster" provision in the Food Security Act of 1985:

> Wetlands are defined as areas that have a predominance of hydric soils that are inundated or saturated by surface or ground water at a frequency and duration sufficient to support, and under normal circumstances do support, a prevalence of hydrophytic vegetation typically adapted for life in saturated soil conditions, except in lands in Alaska identified as having high potential for agricultural development and a predominance of permafrost soils.

Mandatory Technical Criteria for Wetland Identification as agreed upon by the U.S. Fish and Wildlife Service, Soil Conservation Service, U.S. Army Corps of Engineers, and U.S. Environmental Protection Agency (Wetland Training Institute 1989:7):

> Wetlands possess three essential characteristics: (1) hydrophytic vegetation; (2) hydric soils; and (3) wetland hydrology, which is the driving force creating all wetlands. These characteristics and their technical criteria for identification purposes are described in the following sections. The three technical criteria specified are mandatory and must all be met for an area to be identified as wetland. Therefore, areas that meet these criteria are wetlands.

our scope, but the differences between organic and mineral hydric soils are fundamental and should be understood to appreciate the biological values of wetlands to waterfowl and many other forms of wildlife.

To begin, an organic soil contains organic carbon (by weight) of about 12–18%, depending on the amount of clay (Natural Resources Conservation Service 2003). For wetlands, organic soils known as Histosols are among the more easily identified hydric soils. These soils develop under anaerobic conditions in which partially decomposed plant materials accumulate as peat or muck. Organic soils generally contain at least 40 cm of organic matter in their upper layers and, except for Folists, all organic soils are considered hydric soils (Tiner and Veneman 1989, Natural Resources Conservation Service 2003).

Mineral hydric soils generally contain much less organic matter than organic hydric soils (less than 20–35%), although their surface layers may include a thick profile of organic material. When covered or saturated with water during the growing season, they are regarded as mineral hydric soils, for which gleying and mottling are the two most common indicators (Tiner and Veneman 1989, Mitsch and Gosselink 2000, Natural Resources Conservation Service 2003). Gleyed soils are usually neutral gray, but on occasion may be colored greenish or bluish gray. The distinctive colors result when prolonged anaerobic conditions reduce iron, manganese, and other minerals to states in which they may be completely leached from the soil. In contrast, mottled soils feature spots differing in color from the remainder of the soil. The length of time mineral soils are saturated has much to do with these characteris-tics. Therefore, the profiles of mineral soils subject to permanent saturation normally are uniformly gray, whereas those saturated for lesser periods of time are typically marked with orange/reddish brown (iron) or black (manganese) mottling within 15 cm of the surface. The abundance, size, color, and depth of the spots indicate the length of time mottled soils are saturated (Fig. 10-3).

Because of the anaerobic conditions occurring in hydric soils, many plants cannot experience normal root respiration or gain full access to soil nutrients. Hydrophytes, however, are adapted to anaerobic conditions, primarily by the presence of aerenchyma (air spaces) in the roots and stems. This anatomical feature permits the transport of oxygen from the aerial part of the plant to their roots. When oxygen transported in this fashion contacts the reduced ferrous ions of wetland soils, iron and manganese deposits form a characteristic brown color along the root channels. The presence of these oxidized rhizospheres or oxidized pore linings apparently helps to detoxify and reoxidize the reduced ions in the soil, which then become available for plant uptake and growth (see Mitsch and Gosselink 2000).

Hydrophytes and other plants associated with wetlands were first listed in the publication entitled *National List of Plant Species that Occur in Wetlands*; the list is further subdivided into regional and state inventories (e.g., Reed 1988). Nationally, nearly 7,000 vascular plants are listed, but about 27% of these occur exclusively in wetlands, with the remainder occurring in other habitats as well (Table 10-2). The U.S. Fish and Wildlife Service twice updated (in 1996 and 1998) the list, which was finally approved for use by federal agencies in 2005. In general, an

Table 10-2. Wetland indicator status of vascular plants found in wetlands of the United States. From Reed (1988:9).

Obligate Wetland Plants (OBL)   occur >99% of the time in wetlands
Facultative Wetland Plants (FACW)   occur 67–99% of the time in wetlands
Facultative Plants (FAC)   occur 34–66% of the time in wetlands
Facultative Upland Plants (FACU)   occur only 1–33% of the time in wetlands
Obligate Upland Plants (UPL)   occur >99% of the time in nonwetlands

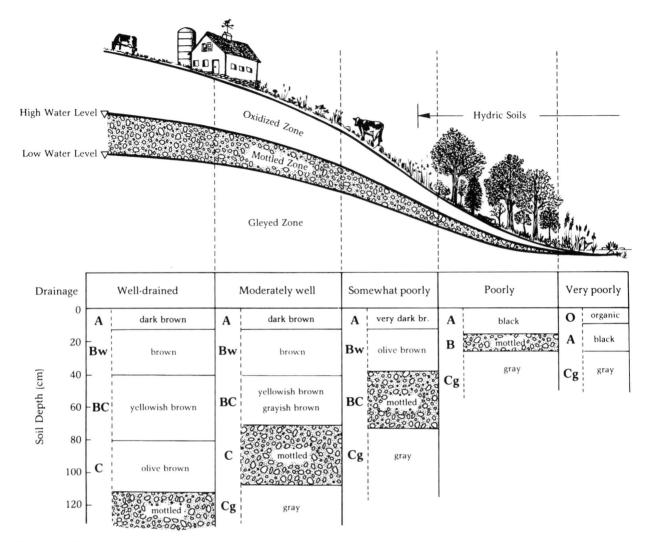

Figure 10-3. A schematic illustration of the relationship between changes in slope and soil morphology, and hence the occurrence of hydric soils. The upland boundary of a wetland usually occurs at the lower end of somewhat poorly drained soils. From Tiner and Veneman (1989:7).

area is considered to have hydrophytic vegetation if more than 50% of the composition of the dominant plants from all strata (e.g., tree, shrub, herbaceous) are obligate wetland species, facultative wetland species, or facultative species, although more detailed criteria are used in some cases (Wetland Training Institute 1989).

Hydrology is the third major characteristic of wetlands. This feature "is probably the single most important determinant of the establishment and maintenance of specific types of wetlands and wetland processes" (Mitsch and Gosselink 2000:108). Hydrology reflects the pathways by which water arrives and departs (e.g., precipitation, runoff, tides), which affects nutrient and energy fluxes resulting

from such movements. The frequency and duration of flooding (hydroperiod), salinity, and nutrient availability are major influences, which in turn affect soil biochemistry and, ultimately, the plants and animals occurring in each wetland system. Hence, hydrological perturbations may produce dramatic changes in wetland biota as seen, for example, where human-induced intrusions of salt water have caused major changes in the plant and animal communities in much of coastal Louisiana (see Chapter 9).

Evidence of wetland hydrology is a useful criterion for the identification of wetlands. In spring, such evidence may be as obvious as the presence of wet or saturated soil. Other signs of wetland hydrology, especially where standing water is absent for much of the growing season, include (1) soggy or peaty soils, (2) water-stained or silt-covered leaves, (3) water-carried debris accumulated about trees or other vegetation, (4) water or silt-stained tree trunks, (5) water-carried debris deposited above ground in trees or shrubs, (6) recent deposits of sand or silt, (7) swollen (buttressed) tree bases, (8) exposed plant roots, and (9) periodically flooded channels through the area (Tiner 1988, 1999).

WETLAND CLASSIFICATION SYSTEMS

A classification system is essential before an effective protection program for wetlands can be implemented; these systems developed with one of two basic approaches. The first is based on ecological attributes such as vegetation, salinity, water depth, and soil type. The second classifies wetlands based on their perceived values to society — fish and wildlife habitat, floodwater storage and control, open space, recreational opportunities, water quality improvement, timber and fiber production, and educational/research opportunities (Kusler 1983). In sum, an ideal wetland classification system will (1) describe ecological units that have certain homogeneous natural attributes, (2) arrange these units in a system that will aid decisions about resource management, (3) furnish units for inventory and mapping, and (4) provide uniform concepts and terminology (Cowardin et al. 1979). An example of the ecological type of classification was developed in the 1950s by the U.S. Fish and Wildlife Service (Martin et al. 1953). The purpose of the system was to inventory the extent and distribution of the nation's wetlands in relation to their value as wildlife habitat, especially for waterfowl. The system recognized 20 different wetland types grouped into four major categories: (1) inland freshwater areas, (2) inland saline areas, (3) coastal freshwater areas, and (4) coastal saline areas. Within each group, sites were classified according to water depth and hydroperiod. Later republished with illustrated descriptions by Shaw and Fredine (1956), this simple scheme remained widely used until the mid-1970s — and is sometimes mentioned even today.

The U.S. Fish and Wildlife Service began a new inventory of the nation's wetlands in 1974, the National Wetlands Inventory. By then, the shortcomings of the earlier system were apparent, and a substantial amount of new knowledge about wetland science had accumulated during the intervening decades. What followed was a movement to replace the previous structure with a comprehensive system of wetland classification. In the interim, several sound regional schemes were produced (e.g., Stewart and Kantrud [1971] for prairie potholes, and Golet and Larson [1974] for northeastern wetlands), but none of these could be expanded into a national system.

This newer classification scheme generated scientific information on the characteristics and extent of the nation's wetland resources, but at the same time Cowardin et al. (1979) recognized that wetlands were continuous with deepwater systems. They accordingly developed a system capable of classifying all the aquatic and semiaquatic habitats in the United States on an ecological basis even though deepwater habitats themselves were not considered wetlands. Their system uses a hierarchial approach not unlike that used in plant and animal taxonomy. The first division places all wetlands and deepwater habitats into one of five systems (Table 10-3), within which are subsystems and classes, then subclasses, dominance types, and modifiers (Fig. 10-4). This system is currently used by the U.S. Fish and Wildlife Service to identify all of the nation's wetlands, with the results entered on National Wetlands Inventory Maps. By 2001, the Inventory had produced draft or final maps for more than 90% of the conterminous United States and 35% of Alaska. Importantly, these maps are widely used by the public; since 1994, more than 1.2 million digital maps have been downloaded from the Inventory's website (U.S. Fish and Wildlife Service 2002).

Below the level of subsystem, classes describe the general appearance of wetlands in terms of their dominant vegetation or substrate; these can be further divided into subclasses. Dominance types refer to the prominent plant or animal forms and constitute the lowest level of the classification scheme. Modifying terms can be applied to levels from class and below and refer to characteristics such as flooding regimes, soils, and water chemistry. Thus, the user of this classification system can categorize a wetland in great detail, depending on the information available at a given site.

The second approach to developing a wetland classification scheme is based on the values that wetlands provide to society, which after all, is the primary reason wetlands have been targeted for protection. Inherent in such a classification scheme is the realization that not all wetlands are "equal" in their perceived value to people. For example, some wetlands have high capacities for floodwater retention, but otherwise may offer poor habitat for wildlife. Overall, the degree to which a wetland system

Table 10-3. The five major systems recognized in the wetland classification scheme developed by the U.S. Fish and Wildlife Service (Cowardin et al. 1979). This classification system is widely used in the United States, especially for the National Wetlands Inventory.

---

1. MARINE SYSTEM — open ocean overlying the continental shelf and its associated high-energy coastline. The Marine System extends from the outer edge of the continental shelf shoreward to (1) the landward limit of tidal inundation, (2) the seaward limit of wetland vegetation, or (3) the seaward limit of the Estuarine System. The Marine System has two subsystems: (1) subtidal, and (2) intertidal.

2. ESTUARINE SYSTEM — deepwater tidal habitats and adjacent tidal wetlands that are usually semi-enclosed by land but have open, partially obstructed, or sporadic access to the ocean and in which ocean water is at least occasionally diluted by freshwater runoff from land. The Estuarine System extends (1) upstream to where ocean-derived salts are <0.5% during average annual flow; (2) to an imaginary line closing the mouth of a river, bay, or sound; and (3) to the seaward limit of wetland emergents not included under (2) above. The Estuarine System has two subsystems: (1) subtidal, and (2) intertidal.

3. RIVERINE SYSTEM — wetland and deepwater habitats contained within a channel with two exceptions: (1) wetlands dominated by trees, shrubs, persistent emergents, emergent mosses, or lichens, and (2) habitats with water containing ocean-derived salts in excess of 0.5%. The Riverine System is bound on the landward side by upland, the channel bank, or wetlands, and terminates downstream where the concentration of ocean-derived salts is >0.5% during average annual flow. Riverine Systems terminate upstream where the tributary streams originate or the channel leaves a lake. The Riverine System has four subsystems: (1) tidal, (2) lower perennial, (3) upper perennial, and (4) intermittent.

4. LACUSTRINE SYSTEM — wetlands and deepwater habitats with all of the following characteristics: (1) situated in a topographic depression or a dammed river channel; (2) lacking trees, shrubs, persistent emergents, emergent mosses, or lichens with >30% areal coverage; and (3) total area >8 ha (20 acres). Similar wetland and deepwater habitats totaling <8 ha are also included in the Lacustrine System if an active wave-formed or bedrock shoreline feature makes up all or part of the boundary, or if the depth in the deepest part of the basin exceeds 2 m at low water. Lacustrine Systems are bounded by uplands or wetlands. Lacustrine Systems typically are extensive areas of deepwater where there is considerable wave action. The Lacustrine System has two subsystems: (1) limnetic, and (2) littoral.

5. PALUSTRINE SYSTEM — all nontidal wetlands dominated by trees, shrubs, persistent emergents, emergent mosses or lichens, and all such wetlands that occur in tidal areas where salinity due to ocean-derived salts is below 5%. It also includes wetlands lacking such vegetation, but with all of the following characteristics: (1) area <8 ha, (2) active wave-formed or bedrock shoreline feature lacking, (3) water depth in the deepest part of the basin <2 m at low water, and (4) salinity due to ocean-derived salts is <0.5%. Palustrine Systems are bounded by uplands or any of the other four systems. The Palustrine System has no subsystems.

---

supplies services or values to society depends on a complex of factors. Nonetheless, a classification scheme based on societal values can help people to apply protective regulations differentially (i.e., those with higher values can be protected more stringently). As an additional advantage, a value-driven classification scheme can be superimposed over an ecological scheme such as the current federal system. In the 1970s, New York developed a value-driven classification scheme in response to legislation enacted for the protection of the state's wetland resources (Department of Environmental Conserva-

tion 1980). The scheme classifies all wetlands into one of just four major classes (Table 10-4).

A widely available methodology for assessing wetland functions is WET — Wetland Evaluation Technique — which evaluates an array of functions for which each is assigned a high, moderate, or low value (Adamus et al. 1987). The WET technique was developed to provide a rapid, initial judgment of wetland functions, and hence should not be considered a substitute for a more detailed assessment.

A more recent evaluation technique is the hydrogeomorphic (HGM) classification, which quan-

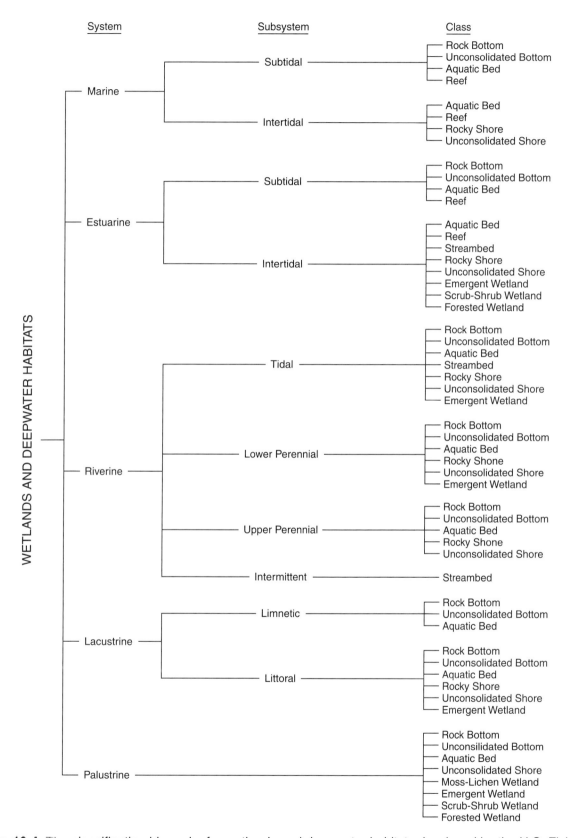

Figure 10-4. The classification hierarchy for wetlands and deepwater habitats developed by the U.S. Fish and Wildlife Service. The system is used widely throughout the United States. From Cowardin et al. (1979:5).

Table 10-4. New York State's wetland classification system, which was developed to implement that state's wetland protection laws (Department of Environmental Conservation 1980).

(A) CLASS I WETLANDS — are wetlands having any of the following seven characteristics:

    (1) It is a classic kettlehole bog.
    (2) It is resident habitat of a state or federal threatened or endangered animal.
    (3) It is resident habitat of a state or federal threatened or endangered plant.
    (4) It supports an animal species in abundance or diversity unusual for the state or for the major region of the state in which it is found.
    (5) It is a tributary to a body of water which could subject a substantially developed area to significant damage from flooding or from additional flooding should the wetland be modified, filled, or drained.
    (6) It is adjacent or contiguous to a reservoir or other body of water that is used primarily for public water supply or is hydrologically connected to an aquifer which is used for public water supply.
    (7) It contains four or more of the enumerated Class II wetland characteristics.

(B) CLASS II WETLANDS — are wetlands that contain any of 17 characteristics, examples of which are:

    (1) It is contiguous to a tidal wetland.
    (2) It is resident habitat of an animal vulnerable in the state.
    (3) It supports an animal species in abundance or diversity unusual for the county in which it is found.
    (4) It is within an urbanized area.
    (5) It acts in a tertiary treatment capacity for a sewage disposal system.

(C) CLASS III WETLANDS — are wetlands that contain any of 15 characteristics, examples of which are:

    (1) It is resident habitat of an animal species vulnerable in the major region of the state in which it is found, or it is traditional migration habitat of an animal species vulnerable in the state or major region of the state within which it is found.
    (2) It is one of the three largest wetlands of the same cover type within a town.
    (3) It is a deciduous swamp.
    (4) Is visible from an interstate highway, a parkway, a designated scenic highway, or a passenger railroad and serves a valuable aesthetic or open space function.

(D) CLASS IV WETLANDS — are wetlands that do not have any of the characteristics of a Class I, II, or III wetland. Class IV wetlands include wet meadows and coniferous swamps that lack other characteristics justifying a higher classification.

---

tifies wetland functions (Brinson 1993). HGM assesses wetland values independently of the known or perceived values by society by comparing the wetland under evaluation to a reference site from the same hydrogeomorphic class. The results generate quantitative data that then can be used in the decision-making process (e.g., mitigation) for the wetland in question.

STATUS OF WETLANDS IN THE UNITED STATES AND ELSEWHERE

After classification schemes are established, the next step is to inventory the types, extent, and geographic location of wetlands. Such inventories are essential for identifying trends and problems. For example,

an inventory can identify areas where all types of wetlands are being rapidly lost or places where a particular type of wetland is threatened, thus allowing management efforts to be focused accordingly. Inventories also can document the recovery of wetlands in the wake of new policies and restoration activities.

Unfortunately, wetland resources in the United States, like elsewhere around the world, initially were regarded as "waste places" in need of becoming "useful." Sweeping legislation toward that end began with the Swamp Land Acts of 1849, 1850, and 1860, which gave federally owned wetlands back to the states for "reclamation." By the mid-1950s, these programs had transferred about 26 million ha of wetlands from federal to state control, most of which

Figure 10-5. The percentage of wetlands lost per state in the United States from the 1780s to 1980s. Data from Dahl (1990:6).

ultimately fell into private ownership (Shaw and Fredine 1956). Today, 22 states have lost 50% or more of their original wetlands, and 11 states (Arkansas, Arizona, California, Connecticut, Illinois, Indiana, Iowa, Kentucky, Maryland, Missouri, and Ohio) have lost more than 70% (Dahl 1990; Fig. 10-5).

Estimating the original extent of the nation's wetlands is difficult because so many sites were drained or filled before inventory started. The most recent "best estimate" is that at the time of colonial America there were 89.5 million ha of wetlands in the lower 48 states, with another 69 million ha in Alaska and 24,000 ha in Hawaii; 21 states originally contained at least 1.2 million ha of wetlands (Dahl 1990). Historical documentation is useful, but greater focus should be placed on the current status of wetlands using modern techniques such as remote sensing and satellite imagery, especially as a measure of wetland conservation programs. National trends are summarized here, and regional data appear later in the chapter.

By the mid-1980s, about 42 million ha of wetlands remained in the lower 48 states; hence,

wetland losses during the past 200 years proceeded at a rate of *24 ha/hr* (Dahl 1990). The remaining wetlands represented about 5% of the area in the lower 48 states — about equal to the size of California — but nevertheless embody a loss of 53% of the original wetland habitat. About 40 million ha of the remaining wetlands were fresh water and 2.4 million ha were estuarine (Dahl and Johnson 1991). Elsewhere, Alaska lost only 0.1% and Hawaii 12% of their original wetland areas; thus, the nation contained about 111 million ha of wetlands in the 1980s.

The most recent estimate of wetlands remaining in the conterminous United States was completed for the period 1986 to 1997 (Dahl 2000). This survey reported 42.7 million ha in the lower 48 states, of which 95% were inland freshwater wetlands. Significantly, the net loss during this period was 260,700 ha or 23,700 ha/yr, which represents an 80% reduction in the annual rate of 117,400 ha/yr reported by Dahl and Johnson (1991) from the mid-1970s to the mid 1980s. From the mid-1950s to the mid-1970s, some 3.6 million ha of wetlands — an area equal in size to the state of New Jersey — were lost at the rate of 185,500 ha/yr (Frayer et al. 1983).

Agricultural activities caused 87% of the wetland losses recorded from the mid-1950s to the mid-1970s (Frayer et al. 1983), compared with 54% from the same cause during the following decade (Dahl and Johnson 1991). From 1986 to 1997, however, urban development emerged as the leading cause (30%) of wetland loss in the United States; agriculture ranked second (26%), followed by forest management (23%) and rural development (21%; Dahl 2000).

Fortunately, the results of the current inventory indicate that the long-standing plague of wetland destruction is finally lessening. Certainly the estimated loss of 2.5% from 1974 to 1983 contrasts dramatically with the 53% loss estimated from the time of settlement to the mid-1980s! Equally encouraging is that restoration has added literally thousands of hectares of wetlands to the nation's inventory, much of which stemmed from the "Swampbuster" provisions of the 1985 Food Security Act and other federal initiatives (e.g., the "Partners" program of the U.S. Fish and Wildlife Service; see Chapter 11). Perhaps the United States is on a path toward a national goal of "no net loss of wetlands," a pledge invoked in 1989 by then President George H. W. Bush (see Bush 1989).

Globally, wetland loss may be as much as 50% (Dugan 1993), although loss is more severe in some regions than others. Based on a summary appearing in Mitsch and Gosselink (2000:38), losses exceed 90% in Europe and New Zealand, 60% in China, and more than 50% in Australia. Within nations, certain regions or types of wetlands may be particularly affected. For example, about 67% of all mangrove swamps in the Philippines are gone, as are an estimated 80% of the Pacific coastal estuarine wetlands and 71% of the prairie potholes in Canada.

WETLAND SUCCESSION

Actions that manipulate wetland vegetation are a central focus of waterfowl management for the simple reason that some plants are desirable for food and cover, whereas others are of lesser or even negative value. Vegetation is not static, however, and a beneficial plant community can in time give way to another, less desirable type of vegetation. The basic concepts of wetland succession thus represent an essential foundation for habitat management. Once the basic forces driving succession are understood, the appropriate manipulations of the wetland environment can be initiated to meet management objectives. In contrast, without such an understanding, management efforts are doomed to hit-or-miss propositions.

The classical approach to plant succession stemmed from the persuasive arguments of Clements (1916), whose concept championed three major elements: (1) succession is an orderly process of community change that is directional, and thus communities are recognizable and changes predictable; (2) changes in the community are autogenic (i.e., brought about by the biota itself); and (3) succession culminates in a stable, climax community (Odum 1971). In this view, wetlands are regarded as seral stages lying between the extremes of deepwater habitats (e.g., lakes) and terrestrial communities (e.g., upland forests). Clementsian ecologists used the term "hydrarch succession" to indicate the autogenic and orderly progression of vegetational changes occurring in wetland communities.

Bogs are often cited as illustrations of hydrarch succession. In this example, sedges and other plants at the edge of open water form thick mats that extend outward and gradually cover the water's surface. In time, the mats offer conditions suitable for the establishment of plants such as ericaceous shrubs. Detritus from the bog community slowly accumulates in the form of peat, which steadily fills the pond, with the eventual result that a climax community of upland forest occupies the same site that was once a wetland.

The Clementsian view of autogenic succession was challenged almost immediately by Gleason (1917), although the latter's arguments did not gain much support until the continuum concept of succession was developed some time later. Advocates of the continuum concept believe that the distribution of a species reflects its response to external geophysical forces; thus, they espouse a conception of succession as an allogenic — rather than autogenic — process (Whittaker 1967, McIntosh 1980).

The differences between these two viewpoints — Clementsian versus Gleasonian succession — cannot be completely resolved, as autogenic as well as allogenic factors influence the flora and fauna of wetlands. For example, herbivory by muskrats (*Ondatra zibethicus*) and Lesser Snow Geese may remove large quantities of vegetation in Gulf Coast marshes (Lynch et al. 1947); muskrats also may reduce or even eliminate emergent vegetation in freshwater prairie marshes (Weller and Spatcher 1965). In these cases, herbivory is autogenic, yet subsequent events such as storms and high water

Figure 10-6. High populations of muskrats often produce major autogenic impacts on wetland vegetation and successional patterns. Shown here is a large muskrat "eat-out" in a coastal Louisiana marsh. Photo courtesy of Greg Linscombe, Louisiana Department of Fisheries and Wildlife.

represent allogenic influences that may wash away these "eat-outs" and dramatically affect the marsh ecosystem (Lynch et al. 1947; Fig. 10-6). Along the McConnell River on the western coast of Hudson Bay, extensive grubbing for vegetation by Lesser Snow Geese has uncovered 1–5-m² areas of peat where erosion subsequently exposed the underlying glacial gravels (see Fig. 8-12). In fact, where the colonies of Lesser Snow Geese are large enough, Kerbes et al. (1990:242) concluded that, "the geese determine the structure and species composition of the coastal plant communities." Thus, regardless of the label autogenic or allogenic, a factor of either type can profoundly affect wetland ecosystems.

Overall, a general breakdown of the allogenic and autogenic factors controlling the composition of wetland plant communities reveals (1) losses of some or all of the existing plants by pathogens, herbivores, or humans; (2) changes in physical or chemical characteristics; (3) competition and allelopathy among the plants; and (4) invasion and establishment of new species (van der Valk 1981).

SEED BANKS AND VEGETATION DYNAMICS

The impact of allogenic factors depends largely on each wetland's seed bank, which is defined as the amount of viable seed in the substrate at a given time (van der Valk and Davis 1976). Because wetlands may experience both prolonged drought and flooding, the seeds and other propagules of wetland plants have evolved to survive long periods when conditions are not favorable for germination. Whereas only those seeds present in the upper few centimeters of the soil normally germinate (Galinato and van der Valk 1986), the propagules of the various species within a wetland's seed bank nonetheless germinate differentially in response to current habitat conditions. Waterfowl managers thus should clearly understand the ecology of seed banks because each management regime (e.g., deep or shallow flooding) will favor or repress the various species of plants present in the seed bank.

Seed banks can be quite rich — those in some prairie marshes in Iowa contain more than 25 spe-

Table 10-5. An example of the size and diversity of seed banks as determined from substrate samples taken at Eagle Lake marsh in north-central Iowa. Modified from van der Valk and Davis (1978:325).

Species	Sites (mean number of seeds/m²)					
	Open water	*Scirpus validus*	*Sparganium*	*Typha*	*Scirpus fluviatilis*	*Carex*
Bidens cernua	690	764	5	144	4	19
Ceratophyllum demersum	0	107	0	0	0	5
Chara globularis	329	176	829	269	23	412
Leersia oryzoides	23	23	0	111	0	143
Lemna minor	1,019	352	125	1,514	46	121
Lemna trisulca	0	0	28	5	0	5
Najas flexilis	176	227	0	14	79	0
Polygonum lapathifolium	148	65	0	111	176	199
Potamogeton pectinatus	23	0	0	0	0	0
Riccia fluitans	0	0	33	0	5	5
Sagittaria latifolia	56	125	287	102	48	144
Scirpus validus	565	1,380	1,746	1,760	2,083	856
Sium suave	5	0	56	19	0	5
Spirodela polyrhiza	0	47	42	1,162	842	19
Typha glauca	116	84	324	616	139	186
Utrucularia vulgaris	0	5	5	0	0	0

Note: Four species found at a frequency of <5% are not included.

cies and as many as 21,445–42,615 seeds/m² in the upper 5 cm of soil (van der Valk and Davis 1976, 1978; Table 10-5). Further, because the seeds of most wetland plants are dispersed by wind or water, virtually every zone within a given marsh contains a similar seed bank (i.e., seeds from all species at the site occur in all zones). Accordingly, seed banks from different zones within a single wetland are more alike than a seed bank from the same zone in a different marsh (van der Valk and Davis 1976).

Van der Valk and Davis (1978) expanded these ideas for prairie marshes in Iowa, noting that variability in water levels differentially affected germination of seeds within the seed bank. They described four basic phases in the cycle of prairie marsh vegetation: (1) dry marsh, (2) regenerating marsh, (3) degenerating marsh, and (4) lake marsh (Fig. 10-7). Each type developed in response to current water levels, with a complete cycle requiring 5 to more than 30 years. Dry marsh developed during years of drought when all or part of the marsh lacks water, which causes the germination of seeds that required exposed mudflats. Regenerating marsh occurred

when the drought ended, which eliminated the emergent mudflat species and stopped the germination of new emergents, but favored germination of free-floating and submergent plants. The resulting marsh developed into a mix of emergents and submergents, which added their propagules to the seed bank. During the degenerating marsh phase, emergent vegetation declined rapidly from a variety of physical and biological factors such as prolonged high water and herbivory. In the final phase, most of the emergent vegetation was lost, and the marsh — now lake-like in appearance — was dominated by submergent and floating plants. Overall, the successional phase within each marsh was a function of water level, but the actual species composition was a function of the seed bank. Further, because of their characteristic seed banks, prairie marshes jumped from one successional stage to another depending on the water conditions prevailing on the seed bank. Thus, contrary to the claims of Clements, succession in these wetlands lacked a fixed, directional pattern (van der Valk and Davis 1976).

Van der Valk (1981) later developed a model us-

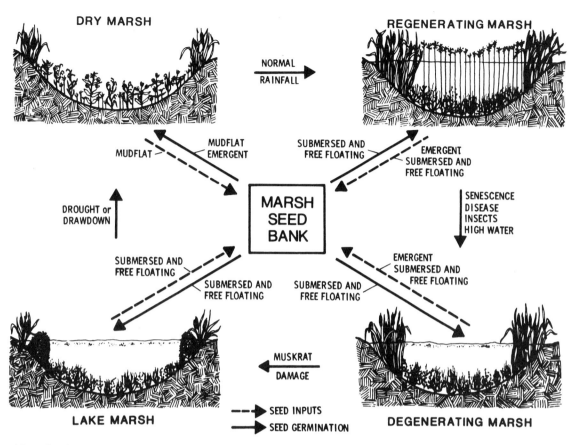

Figure 10-7. A schematic representation of the vegetational dynamics for a prairie glacial marsh in Iowa. Fluctuating water levels, as a result of alternating periods of drought and precipitation, dictate the inputs and outputs from the seed bank and hence the resulting vegetation. From van der Valk and Davis (1978:333). With permission from the Ecological Society of America.

ing the continuum (allogenic) approach to describe succession in freshwater wetlands. His model is of importance, and reviewed at length here, because it can aid managers in predicting the vegetation that will result from their manipulations of wetland environments. The model characterizes all species of wetland plants into one of two categories: (1) species with long-lived propagules that persist in the seed bank — these remain viable until environmental conditions are suitable for their germination; and (2) species with short-lived propagules — these germinate only if they experience immediately favorable conditions. In either case, the environment also must favor establishment of the seedlings. Thus, to predict the outcome of management, the model requires knowledge of only three key features about the life history of each species present or reaching the site: (1) life span, (2) propagule longevity, and (3) establishment requirements for seedlings.

Relative to life span, all wetland plants can be

characterized as annuals, perennials, or vegetatively reproducing perennials. Annuals occur only in the absence of standing water (i.e., mudflat species), whereas perennials thrive with or without vegetative reproduction but have a limited life span. In contrast, vegetatively reproducing perennials have an indefinite life span. Based on an extensive catalog of aquatic plants, 86% are perennials and 14% are annuals (Kadlec and Wentz 1974, van der Valk 1981).

In terms of longevity, the propagules for wetland plants are either (1) those from dispersal-dependent species, which have short-lived seeds and/or vegetative propagules; or (2) those from seed-bank species, which have long-lived seeds and/or vegetative propagules. Seed-bank species can be established whenever conditions are suitable, even in the absence of mature seed-bearing plants. In contrast, a dispersal-dependent species can be established only if seeds from a nearby source reach the site at a time coincident with the occurrence of favorable environmental conditions.

Ducks can be significant dispersers of seeds, as shown by Mueller and van der Valk (2002). In captive Mallards, 7% of all ingested seeds were still viable when evacuated after a mean passage time of 7.6 hr. Further, estimates indicate that Mallards easily transport seeds for distances of 20–30 km, and up to 1,400 km. Although a single duck may carry only few viable seeds, the millions of ducks migrating across North America each year undoubtedly serve as a potent agent of seed dispersal.

Regardless of whether seeds are dispersed or originate from a seed bank, the requirements for establishing propagules fall into two categories: (1) species that can establish only when and where there is no standing water (Type I), and (2) species that can establish when and where there is standing water (Type II). Type I species are typically emergent species or mudflat annuals, whereas Type II species are submergent, free-floating, or rooted, floating-leaved plants. These basic categories can be further subdivided into shade-tolerant and shade-intolerant species. The former can establish themselves within stands of existing vegetation, whereas the latter cannot. Most mudflat and emergent plants are shade-intolerant species that establish themselves in the absence of standing water. Van der Valk (1981) then combined the three life-history features — life span, propagule longevity, and establishment requirements — into a scheme that classified all wetland plants into one of 12 life-history types. Each type is unique in character, which provides the basis for predicting its response to changing environmental conditions (e.g., drawdown). Hence, the model functions as a "sieve" that determines the presence or absence of each species. The information required for such predictions is (1) the potential flora for the wetland, and (2) the life-history characteristics of those species. The former can be obtained by inventorying the visible species and by conducting a seed-bank study to determine those species present only as propagules in the substrate. Life-history information can be gleaned from the literature or inferred from the morphology of each species.

These models of vegetation dynamics in prairie wetlands were tested at the Delta Waterfowl and Wetlands Research Station in Manitoba (see Infobox 10-1), in a large-scale multidisciplinary effort known as the Marsh Ecology Research Program (MERP). MERP, initiated in 1979, relied on 10 experimental wetlands manipulated to simulate wet–dry cycles. After 10 years (1980–89), a wealth of new informa-

tion appeared in a comprehensive book, *Prairie Wetland Ecology, The Contribution of the Marsh Ecology Research Program* (Murkin et al. 2000a). The primary objective of MERP was to document changes that occur in response to a simulated wet-dry cycle, but the results also provided insights for wetland management, which are addressed here.

Consider, for example, the changes in marsh vegetation that occurred during the wet–dry cycle simulated by MERP, as reviewed by van der Valk (2000). During the lake-marsh stage, which was established by raising the water level by 1 m for 2 years, the mean aboveground biomass of the emergent plants declined from 400 g/m² to 75 g/m² after 1 year of flooding, and 77 g/m² after 2 years (van der Valk 2000; Table 10-6). For some emergents, the results were even more dramatic: The biomass of both whitetop (*Scolochloa festucacea*) and bulrush (*Scirpus lacustris*) was reduced to only 1 g/m² following 1 year of flooding. In contrast, the biomass of submergent vegetation, which was nearly nonexistent 1 year after flooding, increased to 33% of total biomass by year 2.

Flooding also produced dramatic changes belowground. In the spring of the second year of flooding, for example, the belowground biomass of emergent vegetation declined to only 38 g/m² compared with 460 g/m² the previous fall, yet the roots and rhizomes of common reed (*Phragmites australis*), cattail (*Typha glauca*), and bulrush remained dormant but alive. All told, 2 years of deep flooding were required before these species exhausted their carbon reserves and disappeared.

When water was removed (drawdown) for 1–2 years, the four dominant emergents were reestablished, as were mudflat annuals, especially atriplex (*Atriplex patula*), aster (*Aster laurentianus*), and goosefoot (*Chenopodium rubrum*). Total aboveground biomass during the drawdown years (about 325 g/m²) was only about 20% less than the baseline year, but the annuals contributed 50% or more of the biomass.

During the reflooding period (5 years), changes in aboveground biomass of the dominant emergents exhibited three distinct responses. Bulrush declined steadily during the 5-year period, although the two subspecies of bulrush in the impoundments varied in their respective tolerance to flooding. In contrast, whitetop and common reed increased in biomass for the first 3 years, then declined in the last 2 years. Cattail biomass increased steadily during the period, except for a small decline in year 4. The increase in cattail powered the steadily increas-

Infobox 10-1

Delta Waterfowl and Wetlands Research Station — Research on the Canadian Prairies

A site on a 14,000-ha marsh at the southern end of Lake Manitoba evolved from a hunting lodge to a research center dedicated to studies of prairie waterfowl and wetlands. The locale was known as Delta, one of a series of isolated construction depots used during the completion of the railroad across Canada. James Ford Bell, the wealthy founder of General Mills, owned a large tract of marsh at Delta where he maintained a hunting lodge and hatchery from which he vowed to produce two ducks for every one he shot. In the 1930s, artificial propagation represented a prevailing concept in wildlife management, but three pioneers of wildlife management — Aldo Leopold, William Rowan, and Miles Pirnie — joined forces with Bell in seeking a broader approach to waterfowl ecology and management. In 1938, the hatch-

ery and other facilities thus were transformed into the Delta Waterfowl Research Station, whose name later was expanded to include wetland research. Today the station includes living quarters for students and visiting scientists, a well-stocked library, a hall for seminars, laboratories, pens, and modern hatchery facilities. The Delta marsh and associated wet-prairie meadows became a Ramsar-listed wetland in 1982, famed not only as a nesting grounds for pochards and puddle ducks but also as major staging area where peak autumn populations have at times exceeded 2 million ducks and geese.

The station's first director was H. Albert Hochbaum, who at the time of his appointment was studying for a graduate degree under Aldo Leopold at the University

of Wisconsin. Following the lead of Hochbaum's own research, the station has since helped more than 350 graduate students from 75 universities to complete their theses and dissertations that in turn produced in excess of 730 publications in the scientific literature. A book-length publication featuring the renesting behavior of puddle ducks (Sowls 1955) was among the major studies to appear after the program was firmly established. In addition to the marsh itself, Delta offers a system of 10 experimental 5 ha-wetland cells, each with independent water-level control. Between 1980 and 1989, these cells were manipulated in ways designed to match the phases in the wet–dry cycle of prairie marshes in what was known as the Marsh Ecology Research Program (MERP). The MERP included numerous disciplines (e.g., nutrient cycling, invertebrate

and vertebrate ecology, hydrology, and plant ecology), with the results appearing in Murkin et al. (2000a). Delta also maintains a permanent field station in the Minnedosa parklands of southwestern Manitoba, where there is access to thousands of prairie potholes on privately owned farmlands.

Graduate students receive support from the Delta Waterfowl Foundation, a private organization whose mission is to assist in the education of those professionals who will help conserve waterfowl and wetland resources in North America — a process that also yields the discovery of new basic and applied information. See Bell and Ward (1984) for a more complete history of Delta. Photo courtesy of Fred Greenslade, Delta Waterfowl Foundation.

---

ing belowground biomass that occurred during the 5-year reflooding period. Overall, the lowest aboveground biomass (about 75 g/m²) occurred during the second year of deep flooding (lake marsh stage), compared with a maximum of 400 g/m² that occurred during the earlier reflooding years (regenerating marsh stage).

Based on these and other data from MERP, van der Valk (2000) added the tolerance of each species to water-depth as a factor in his original model for the establishment and growth of wetland vegetation. His revision recognized four types of plants in relation to water depth: (1) annuals, (2) wet-meadow species, (3) emergents, and (4) submergents. The mudflat species do not tolerate flooding and therefore occur only when sediments are exposed, whereas wet-meadow species can tolerate short intervals of standing water but not long-term inundation. Emergents can tolerate permanent flooding as well as a year or so without standing water, whereas submergents require permanent water but can survive brief periods of exposure. Other MERP projects revealed discrepancies between the predicted and actual recruitment of species from the seed bank, wherein germination was significantly less than the predictions of the life-history model. The discrepancies resulted from the strong influences of soil moisture, temperature, and salinity (see van der Valk 2000).

MERP led to more sophisticated models of vegetation dynamics in prairie wetlands (Seabloom 1997); the new models were based on the original idea of environmental filters (e.g., water levels) developed by van der Valk (1981). Acting together, these

filters determine which species become established, which persist, and which are extirpated on the wetland landscape. For managers, the duration and depth of water (hydroperiod) remain the major tools to manipulate wetland vegetation, but their effect is modified by subtleties of soil moisture, temperature, and salinity. When these tools are used in association with an understanding of the life-history requirements of plants, managers can successfully manipulate wetland vegetation and thereby improve the value of wetlands as habitat for waterfowl and other wildlife.

The combinations of the life-history types adapted to particular wetland conditions can be assembled into biotic communities, which are assemblages of interdependent plants and animals coexisting in a common environment. In wetlands, communities establish along a water-depth gradient and are recognized as submergent, rooted floating-leaved, free-floating, and emergent (Weller 1981), whereas communities established along a salinity gradient are recognizable as salt marsh, brackish marsh, intermediate marsh, and freshwater marsh (Chabreck 1988). Beyond these are communities of lowland shrubs and, ultimately, trees.

For the most part, the structure of each community determines the responses of birds and other wildlife and, as described above, structure changes during the wet–dry cycle. Murkin and Caldwell (2000) summarized such a response during the MERP project. In this case, the absence of water during the dry-marsh stage eliminated invertebrates and submergent vegetation, although invertebrates and

Table 10-6. Mean aboveground maximum biomass (g/m²) for dominant emergent species and other plant groups, and mean belowground spring and fall biomass (g/m²) over the entire simulated wet–dry cycle during MERP. From van der Valk (2000:132).

	Baseline year	Deep flooding		Drawdown		Reflooding				
		First	Second	First	Second	1985	1986	1987	1988	1989
Aboveground biomass										
Algae	0	0	12	0	0	8	1	2	1	0
Submersed aquatics	2	1	26	0	6	0	17	39	14	11
Scirpus lacustris	61	1	1	23	14	100	47	46	18	21
Typha glauca	160	45	17	5	6	7	18	87	74	160
Scolochloa festucacea	29	1	1	4	16	66	86	150	83	56
Phragmites australis	85	19	10	17	25	18	44	47	37	42
Annuals	11	0	1	200	160	11	3	2	1	2
Total	400	75	77	330	320	310	250	400	240	300
Belowground biomass										
Spring	840	680	510	38	110	130	200	360	320	420
Fall	870	570	460	100	240	250	390	450	670	490
Production	+30	-110	-50	+62	+130	120	190	90	370	70

fish concentrate as the water recedes, which creates pockets of highly available food sources for many kinds of wetland birds. However, once the dry marsh stage is fully realized, avian use largely involves upland species. When water is returned during the regenerating marsh stage, the abundant supply of seed deposited by mudflat annuals becomes readily available to waterfowl, and geese and American Wigeon feed on newly germinated emergents, particularly grasses such as whitetop. Aquatic invertebrates also quickly reappear and are readily available to foraging waterfowl. With continued flooding and the resulting dieback of emergent vegetation as the degenerating marsh stage begins, the invertebrate community again changes because flooding eliminates those species whose life cycles require a dry marsh. At this point, amphipods and chironomids dominate the invertebrate fauna. At the lake marsh stage, food resources are generally at a low point for waterfowl and other wetland birds, although fish and benthic invertebrates now may be abundant. In the following section, we profile several of the more typical wetland communities that develop during the wet–dry cycle and the value of each as waterfowl habitat.

WETLAND PLANT COMMUNITIES

Submerged Plant Communities

The submerged plant community serves as a direct source of waterfowl foods (e.g., seeds and tubers) and, indirectly, as a rich environment for aquatic macroinvertebrates, which provide seasonally important foods for laying females and broods (see Chapter 5). Krull (1970) determined that the abundance of aquatic macroinvertebrates was directly related to the surface area and mass of 12 species of submerged plants. Coontail (*Ceratophyllum demersum*), for example, harbored more than 1.5 g or 161 macroinvertebrates per 100 g of vegetation. The fauna also was diverse within stands of submerged vegetation, with some 45 macroinvertebrate taxa occurring in waterweed (*Elodea canadensis*) and 18 occurring in coontail. Indirectly, then, many of these species ranked highly as desirable vegetation for waterfowl even though the same plants often ranked poorly as direct producers of edible seeds (Table 10-7). Based on MERP, Murkin and Ross (2000) also highlighted the importance of submerged vegetation as a substrate for aquatic macroinvertebrates.

Light penetration and turbidity are the most important abiotic factors affecting the establishment and maintenance of submerged vegetation. Water depth limits light penetration even in clear water, but any prolonged interruption of light will inhibit photosynthetic activity, even in shallow water. Turbidity, whether from erosion or other disturbances, directly affects the establishment and growth of plants in submerged plant communities by inhibiting light penetration. Robel (1961a) documented a significant negative correlation ($r = -0.91$) between water turbidity and submerged vegetation. In other instances, however, submerged vegetation can moderate the influence of wind as a cause of water turbidity (Chamberlain 1948).

The activities of carp (*Cyprinus carpio*) may damage submerged vegetation. In 1877, carp from Germany were introduced and thereafter (1889–1897) distributed widely in the United States by the U.S. Bureau of Fisheries. Carp have been adversely affecting waterfowl habitat ever since. Indeed, a recent survey of 162 national wildlife refuges in the United States disclosed that more than 80% of those with wetland impoundments were experiencing problems with carp (Ivey et al. 1998). At the Malheur National Wildlife Refuge in Oregon, where control measures began in 1955, reductions in carp populations increased diving duck numbers by 50–70% and dabbling duck numbers by as much as 116% in some areas (Ivey et al. 1998). Rotenone was the control agent of choice in these efforts.

Carp affect submerged vegetation in two ways: (1) directly by consuming the plants as food, and (2) indirectly by increasing turbidity as a result of their foraging activities (Fig. 10-8). Carp rooting and digging in the substrate of experimental pens decreased submerged vegetation long before these same activities adversely increased water turbidity (Robel 1961b). King and Hunt (1967) determined that feeding carp badly damaged the rooted algae, muskgrass (*Chara* spp.), but once the numbers of carp were reduced, muskgrass and other submerged vegetation rapidly recovered. In waterfowl habitat in North Carolina, water transparency increased from 15 cm to more than 1 m after carp were removed (Cahoon 1953). Soil types may influence the relationship between water turbidity and carp; clay or silt soils infested with carp populations are particularly susceptible to turbidity problems (Chamberlain 1948). In general, it appears that carp densities of 225 kg/ha or more can severely inhibit the growth of aquatic

Table 10-7. An example of the relationships between submergent plants and macroinvertebrate abundance as determined in central New York. Modified from Krull (1970:716).

Plant species	Food value rank[a]	Macroinvertebrates		
		Taxa/species	Mass (g)/100 g of plant	Rank
Lemna trisulca	6	46	2.1	1
Heteranthera dubia	29	30	1.5	2
Ceratophyllum demersum	20	18	1.5	3
Elodea canadensis	37	45	1.1	4
Chara and *Najas*[b]	10	30	0.8	7
Potamogeton spp.	1	30	0.7	9
Algae	18	32	0.3	11
Myriophyllum spicatum	27	18	0.07	12

[a]Rank as determined from Martin and Uhler (1939).
[b]*Chara vulgaris* and *Najas flexilis*.

Figure 10-8. The feeding activities of carp may destroy desirable wetland vegetation, thereby requiring constant control in impoundments managed for waterfowl. A drawdown has concentrated these carp (*top*) for removal from a large impoundment on a wildlife refuge in New York (*bottom*). Photos courtesy of the Montezuma National Wildlife Refuge.

plants. Moreover, ducks may be incessantly disturbed and unable to rest where carp are active, but this behavior changes quickly after the fish are controlled (Weier and Starr 1950).

Within the submerged plant community, pondweeds (*Potamogeton* spp.) form an important source of foods for waterfowl throughout much of the United States and Canada. For example, in their extensive examination of waterfowl food plants, Martin and Uhler (1939) found that pondweeds ranked first, by volume, as food consumed by 18 species of ducks. In fact, pondweeds occurred in about twice the volume as the next ranked food plant. Seed and tuber production of an important species in this group, sago pondweed (*P. pectinatus*), varies with habitat condi-

tions such as water depth and turbidity (Low and Bellrose 1944, Robel 1961a) and salinity (Teeter 1965). Under favorable conditions, sago pondweed produces large quantities of desirable seed. Further, the finely dissected leaves of sago pondweed harbor diverse and abundant populations of aquatic invertebrates, especially chironomids (Wrubleski and Rosenberg 1990). Another important species, curly-leaved pondweed (*P. crispus*), yielded an average of 140 kg/ha of seed, or enough to sustain 2,470 Mallards per hectare per day (Hunt and Lutz 1959).

Other plants within the submerged community of importance to waterfowl include wild celery (*Vallisneria americana*), the winter buds of which are among the most important foods of pochards (Perry and Uhler 1982, Schloesser and Manny 1990). In coastal saline habitats, eelgrass (*Zostera marina*), widgeongrass (*Ruppia maritima*), and shoalgrass (*Halodule wrightii*) are major waterfowl foods; the last is a crucial food for Redheads and Northern Pintails wintering in the Laguna Madre of Texas and adjacent Tamaulipas, Mexico. Eelgrass is an especially important food for Brant wintering on both the Atlantic and Pacific Coasts of North America. In the 1930s, a disease associated with the mycetozoan *Labyrinthula* caused immense damage to eelgrass beds along the entire Atlantic Coast, where the Atlantic Brant population thereafter declined precipitously before the birds turned to sea lettuce (*Ulva* sp.) as a principal food (Cottam et al. 1944).

Although many species of submerged plants provide valuable waterfowl habitat, management conflicts occur when dense, monotypic stands of certain species inhibit human recreational opportunities. Perhaps the best example concerns hydrilla (*Hydrilla verticillata*), which may be "the most controversial of all aquatic macrophytes in the United States" (Johnson and Montalbano 1987:466). An African species, hydrilla was introduced in Florida around 1960 and now infests wetlands, waterways, and managed waterfowl impoundments in all of the southeastern states as well as in Texas and California. Indeed, hydrilla is regarded as a noxious aquatic plant throughout much of the world because it (1) outcompetes native plant communities; (2) impedes water flow; (3) interferes with fishing, boating and swimming; and (4) is aesthetically unappealing to waterfront residents (Haller 1978). The competitive advantage of hydrilla stems from its broad tolerance for levels of pH, salinity, and water turbidity (Tarver et al. 1979) as well as its ability to produce several million vegetative propagules per hectare (Haller and Sutton 1975).

However, hydrilla is an important plant for several species of ducks. At Lake Okeechobee in Florida, hydrilla harbored a greater diversity of birds and was used by more species of waterfowl than any of six other plant communities (Johnson and Montalbano 1984). Similarly, Esler (1990) found that aquatic birds in Texas made considerable use of hydrilla stands. The opposing views on outdoor values — recreation or waterfowl habitat — thus present a challenging dilemma for managing hydrilla in much of its new range in the United States and elsewhere.

To conclude, the importance of the submerged community to waterfowl lies in its value as a source of food. Directly, the seeds, tubers, and leafy materials of some plants in this community represent major foods for several species of waterfowl. Indirectly, even plants lacking much value as food often provide crucial habitat for macroinvertebrates, which in turn are seasonally important to waterfowl as sources of protein. The open water areas above this community also can provide habitat for resting and courtship activities of waterfowl.

Floating-leaved Communities

The floating-leafed community often overlaps spatially with the submergent community, although the latter usually extends into deeper water. Nevertheless, the floating-leafed community is distinctive because of the location and availability of the plants, at least in part, at the water's surface. The family Nymphaeaceae typifies the vegetation in this community; representatives include such familiar species as the white water lily (*Nymphaea odorata*), yellow water lily (*Nuphar luteum*), water shield (*Brasenia schreberi*), and American lotus (*Nelumbo lutea*). Most of the Nymphaeaceae have large rootstocks with fleshy rhizomes well anchored to the wetland bottom.

Lotus is unlike most other species of floating aquatic plants in that it projects erect stems and elevated umbrella-like leaves well above the water instead of lying flush on the surface. Dense stands of lotus also can limit submergent vegetation by preventing sunlight from reaching the underlying biota (Bolen et al. 1975). Indeed, Bellrose (1941) noted that the rapid spread of lotus reduced a submergent community of coontail from 40 ha to less than 1.2 ha in only 2 years, which, as mentioned earlier, may correspond with a reduction of habitat for macroinvertebrates. Conversely, the dense overhead cover provided by lotus served as the preferred roosting habitat for Wood Ducks in northern Alabama during early fall (Fig. 10-9); when the lotus later became senescent, Wood Ducks moved to other roosting habitats (Thompson and Baldassarre 1988).

Overall, only a few species of floating-leaved plants produce waterfowl foods of much value. A few smartweeds (*Polygonum* spp.) and a few floating-leafed pondweeds (e.g., *Potamogeton natans*) are seed producers of fair to good quality, but these species usually do not develop into stands of extensive size.

Unrooted, free-floating aquatic plants also are included in this community, although these may occur virtually anywhere in the wetland landscape (e.g., within emergent vegetation). The duckweed family, Lemnaceae, is a prominent group of free-floating plants in many wetland systems. Duckweeds are among the smallest of flowering plants; these include the genera *Wolffiella* (bog-mat), *Wolffia* (water meal), *Lemna* (duckweed), and *Spirodela* (giant duckweed). The winter bud stage of duckweeds, the turion, is readily transported on the exterior of ducks and other animals, which act as important dispersal agents for the plant (Jacobs 1947).

Contrary to their common name, duckweeds are not important foods for waterfowl. Martin and Uhler (1939) ranked duckweeds 14th in their list of food plants. However, duckweeds are significant as habitat for aquatic macroinvertebrates. Krull (1970) recorded a biomass of 2.1 g of macroinvertebrates per 100 g of plant material, thereby ranking duckweed first among 12 species examined for value as macroinvertebrate habitat (Table 10-7). No doubt much of the duckweed discovered in duck stomachs has been ingested incidentally to the primary consumption of macroinvertebrates.

At the other extreme, free-floating species such as water lettuce (*Pistia stratiotes*), water hyacinth (*Eichhornia crassipes*), water chestnut (*Trapa natans*), and alligator weed (*Alternanthera philoxeroides*) are far less desirable and, indeed, are generally regarded as noxious vegetation. These species, all of which were introduced into North America, often form dense mats of monotypic vegetation. The unwanted mats spread across large areas, steadily replacing native vegetation as they expand. When unchecked, extensive growths of these plants often reduce or eliminate boating, fishing, and swimming, as well as offer little value as food or habitat for waterfowl. Because these species transpire tremendous amounts of water during the growing season, they also can become especially troublesome in reservoirs.

Figure 10-9. American lotus (*Nelumbo lutea*) provides Wood Ducks with desirable roosting habitat in early fall at the Wheeler National Wildlife Refuge in Alabama (*top*), but senescence renders this habitat unsuitable for roosting later in the year (*bottom*). Photos courtesy of John D. Thompson, U.S. Geological Survey.

Figure 10-10. According to some studies, wetlands with a water-to-vegetation ratio of 50:50 — a condition known as "hemi-marsh" — may support the greatest diversity of bird species. Photo courtesy of Henry R. Murkin, Ducks Unlimited Canada.

Interestingly, floating-leafed vegetation — either free-floating or rooted — is characteristically absent from saline habitats. Plants forming this community are not found in coastal saline marshes, in saline marshes bordering Great Salt Lake (Nelson 1954), or in wetlands fed by saline springs (Bolen 1964), but the reasons for their absence remain obscure.

Emergent Communities

Emergent vegetation, perhaps more than any other, signifies the physiognomy of a wetland. In terms of function, the structure created by emergent vegetation is an essential feature of wetland habitats. Weller and Spatcher (1965) recorded maximum diversity and abundance of birds on marshes in Iowa where the ratio of emergent vegetation to water was 50:50 and

referred to this form of wetland physiognomy as "hemi-marsh" (Fig. 10-10).

Bulrushes and especially cattails are among the most common plants in emergent communities, which create a life zone sometimes known as a "reed swamp." Overall, about 40 species of bulrushes and four species of cattails occur in the United States. These plants are primarily important as cover, although alkali bulrush (*Scirpus maritimus*) of some western marshes and other bulrushes of the leafy, triangular-stemmed type are key food producers. A second major group of bulrushes (hardstem, *S. acutus*; softstem, *S. validus*; and California, *S. californicus*) has tall, round, whip-like stems and produces desirable nutlets, although not always in great volume. A third group, known as the "three-square bulrushes," has triangular stems but lacks leaves. Of these, the tubers of Olney three-square bulrush (*S. olneyi*) are a major winter food for Lesser Snow Geese (Lynch et al. 1947, Alisauskas et al. 1988).

Cattails are of little value as duck food, but wintering geese sometimes feed on the underground stems (Martin et al. 1951). Broad-leaved cattail (*Typha latifolia*) and narrow-leaved cattail (*T. angustifolia*) are easily recognized and commonplace across large areas of North America. Cattails are especially important for escape and loafing cover and also provide nesting cover for some species of waterfowl. However, when unchecked, cattail stands often expand rapidly to the exclusion of other vegetation and open water; such conditions severely restrict waterfowl use (Kaminski et al. 1985). A case in point occurred at the Horicon Marsh in Wisconsin, where sedge-marsh communities were dominant and cattails covered only 30% of the vegetated areas in 1967. By 1971, however, monotypic stands of cattail accounted for 80% of all emergent vegetation, and waterfowl use of the marsh declined (Beule 1979). Hence, if useful waterfowl habitat is desired, cattail-dominated wetlands require the intervention of active management. Keith (1961) thus recorded three times as many ducks after cattail was partially removed from the shorelines of prairie potholes. He attributed this response to (1) greater accessibility to loafing areas; (2) unobstructed view of adjacent terrain and, to a lesser degree; (3) better accessibility to shallow-water food plants; and (4) an overall increase in the abundance of food plants.

Grasses and sedges are another group of common emergent plants. Their structure generally forms low to moderately high communities in shallow water, although a few species such as the common reed may reach heights of several meters. Each of these groups contains numerous species, many of which are difficult to identify, but Martin and Uhler (1939) provide useful descriptions, range maps, and photographs of grasses and sedges of importance to waterfowl management.

Among the grasses, wild rice (*Zizania aquatica*), which is actually a barley, is an excellent duck food in the northeastern and north-central states. Other grasses important as waterfowl foods include manna grasses (*Glyceria* spp.), wild millets (*Echinochloa* spp.), rice cutgrass (*Leersia oryzoides*), sprangletop (*Leptochloa fascicularis*), paspalums (*Paspalum* spp.), and panic grasses (*Panicum* spp.); in the United States, wetland representatives of the last two genera are largely restricted to the southeastern states.

Among the sedges, tubers and seeds of species in the genus *Cyperus* are important duck foods, as are seeds of spike rushes (*Eleocharis* spp.) and some

sedges (*Carex* spp.). Spike rushes are especially prominent duck foods in many areas (Martin and Uhler 1939, Singleton 1951). Most rushes (Juncaceae) are not highly valued as waterfowl foods, although the seeds of plants in this group are used when available.

Landscapes of low-growing emergent vegetation often are referred to as sedge meadows. These habitats, while still part of the emergent community, usually form on the somewhat drier sites at the edges of large wetlands or occur seasonally at sites holding water for only a short time. A variety of forbs, some of which may have colorful flowers, often enrich this vegetation. Cattails or bulrushes may occupy small areas where water-filled depressions occur in a sedge meadow.

The emergent zone also contains such broad-leaved plants as pickerelweed (*Pontederia cordata*), water plantain (*Alisma plantago-aquatica*), and arrowhead or duck potato (*Sagittaria latifolia*); the tubers of the last-named are an especially important food. Many species of smartweed occur in the emergent zone, but several of these are so adaptable that classification of their life form is difficult (i.e., plants of the same species exhibit various postures, some standing erect with others lying decumbent in the water). However, several species (*Polygonum lapathifolium*, *P. amphibium*, *P. pensylvanicum*, *P. punctatum*, *P. hydropiperoides*) are widespread and produce good crops of small nutlets, which are highly sought by ducks. The seeds of burreeds (*Sparganium* spp.) also serve as food for waterfowl.

As expected, marked changes occur in the species that dominate marshes transcending a salinity gradient, but the life form of the communities remains unchanged. Thus, in a coastal Louisiana marsh, maidencane (*Panicum hemitomon*) and bull tongue (*Sagittaria falcata*) may characterize a freshwater marsh, whereas brackish and intermediate marshes are characterized by marsh hay cordgrass (*Spartina patens*), and salt marsh is dominated by smooth cordgrass (*S. alterniflora*) and saltgrass (*Distichlis spicata*; Chabreck 1972). The diversity of the coastal vegetation varied in keeping with the salinity gradient; the salt marsh contained just 17 species of plants, but the composition of the freshwater marsh reached a high of 93 species.

Bottomland Hardwood Forests

Bottomland hardwood forests are periodically flooded stands of mature river-bottom trees. Some eight species of waterfowl regularly use bottomland hardwood forests, which are especially important for wintering Mallards and breeding and wintering Wood Ducks (Fredrickson and Heitmeyer 1988). The most expansive bottomland hardwood forests occur in the southern United States, especially along the Mississippi River and its tributaries.

The major factor affecting the distribution of vegetation in bottomland hardwood forests is the frequency and duration of floodwater from the adjacent river. Accordingly, as distance from the river increases, frequency and duration of flooding decreases and more flood-intolerant species can become established. Further, slight elevational changes in the floodplain interact with the frequency and duration of floods to produce a diverse mosaic of vegetation that renders bottomland hardwood forests among the highest-quality wildlife habitats.

Within this community, various oaks (*Quercus* spp.) provide sizable crops of acorns, which are preferred foods in the diets of wintering waterfowl. Pin oak (*Q. palustris*) is a particularly desirable food source because of the abundance and size of its acorns. However, aside from its specialized uses for food and cover, the bottomland hardwood forest serves a major function in filtering nutrients and sediments. For example, in an agricultural area adjacent to the Chesapeake Bay in Maryland, a 50-m strip of bottomland forest was estimated to remove some 80–90% of the phosphorus and nitrogen runoff (Peterjohn and Correll 1984). Unfortunately, large areas of bottomland hardwood forest have been cleared — most often for agricultural purposes — with the result that runoff from soil erosion has increased dramatically in much of North America.

Our discussion of this community type and its functional value to waterfowl is brief here because these topics are addressed in Chapter 9 under the section "The Mississippi Alluvial Valley and Associated Drainages." Readers also are referred to *Ecology and Management of Bottomland Hardwood Forests: the State of Our Understanding* (Fredrickson et al. 2005), which provides a comprehensive treatment of all aspects of bottomland hardwood forest ecology and management.

THE NEED AND BASIS FOR MANAGEMENT

Resource managers sometimes assume that acquisition, easement, or legal designations may be adequate to endow wetlands with lasting benefits as wildlife habitat when, in fact, active management is almost always necessary to sustain the ecological structure and function of wetlands. Left alone, plant succession may alter wetlands to the point where the habitat may no longer be suitable for the very species that prompted an area's protection in the first place! Exotic plants and animals also may invade protected wetlands, thereby wreaking ecological havoc on native communities. Activities (e.g., intensive farming, logging, or urban development) that alter the cover on nearby uplands also may diminish the value of wetlands as habitat for waterfowl and other species. Various kinds of surface or subsurface pollution elsewhere in a watershed also can severely damage protected wetlands. Additional examples might be cited, but the following point must be emphasized: Although a wetland may enjoy legal protection, constant assessments of habitat conditions are needed, including awareness as to when management actions are and are not warranted.

Overall, quality habitat — abundant and available — is unequivocally the most important ecological component affecting populations of waterfowl and other wetland-dependent biota. Habitat encompasses the essential elements of food, cover, and water, each of which has qualitative and quantitative elements, although many of these remain unmeasured in total or in part. Waterfowl, however, further complicate considerations of habitat because most species are migratory. Thus, habitat protection and management must occur on spatial scales large enough to accommodate the needs of species as they move across a landscape that may be continental in scope.

However, whenever the abundance or availability of habitat is reduced, the quality and availability of the remaining habitat gains increased significance. This idea is based on a canon of wildlife management that, within limits, some lesser amount of quality habitat is more important than a greater amount of poorer-quality habitat. Thus, management has evolved as an unequivocal necessity resulting from the direct loss of an immense amount of habitat. Furthermore, with those losses comes the improbable likelihood that nature can compensate by providing high-quality habitats at the right time and place to meet the life-history requirements of waterfowl. Lacking such compensation and conservation, one can scarcely expect to sustain both viable and harvestable populations of waterfowl in North America or elsewhere in the world.

Management, of course, cannot alter features in the life history of waterfowl, most of which are inherently fixed by genetic patterns without regard to human influences; similarly, a threshold exists for the specific physiological and nutritional requirements that ensure survival and reproduction. Management can, however, be especially effective in synchronizing the abundance, availability, and spatial distribution of food, cover, and water resources to coincide with specific events in the life history of waterfowl. Such "where and when" decisions are relatively simple considerations in the practice of waterfowl management. Most species of waterfowl in North America are migratory, and their schedules, while often species-specific, are rather well known, as are those places where ducks and geese breed, rest, and winter. Hence, the timing of specific management practices to coincide temporally and spatially with waterfowl movements and life-history events can affect the success of those events, paramount of which are survival and reproduction.

In contrast, "how" is more complicated because such questions encompass many dimensions in which current knowledge is far less complete. For instance, how do managers decide on what habitats to protect, as well as where and how much should be protected? How do managers reconcile issues of habitat patch size, habitat diversity, and habitat juxtaposition for waterfowl and integrate these with the requirements for other kinds of wildlife? How can managers best provide requisite nutrients amid many physical and economic constraints? How might cover and patch size be managed to produce more successful nests? How are diseases related to habitat? The list is endless, but adequate amounts of quality habitat clearly remain the preeminent and lasting key to effective management of waterfowl.

However, waterfowl biologists can no longer achieve sound management decisions about wetland habitats based solely on benefits accrued by relatively few game species of waterfowl. Responsible management also must acknowledge biodiversity and the welfare of other wetland-dependent biota (e.g., wading birds, shorebirds, amphibians, rare plants, and invertebrates). Thus, biologists constantly face decisions about what species and areas should be protected and managed, knowing full well that other wetland-dependent elements may suffer to some degree. Waterfowl and wetland managers may wish away such complex decisions, but the 21st century nonetheless will be troubled by expanding human populations and continuing habitat destruction. Hence, despite desires to the contrary, the urgency for hard decisions will not conveniently disappear — it represents an integral part of the management landscape.

Therefore, given that significant amounts of wetland habitat have been lost or degraded, we be-

gin with the recognition that protection of the remaining wetlands — by some combination of regulation, acquisition, or active management — is the best way to ensure the continued existence of waterfowl populations and other wetland-dependent species. Yet conservationists will never have enough money to purchase all important wetlands, which are still lost daily despite a plethora of local, state, and federal laws. Hence, hard decisions on where to focus scarce dollars and management efforts are challenging but not insurmountable obstacles to waterfowl and wetland managers.

In the next sections, we review some of the science currently guiding management of waterfowl and other wetland wildlife, including a few general principles from conservation biology (see Soulé and Wilcox 1980, Wilson 1988, Primack 2004) and integrated wetland management (Parsons et al. 2002) as a guide for waterfowl and wetland managers in the 21st century.

WATERFOWL MANAGEMENT AND CONSERVATION BIOLOGY

Habitat Size, Isolation, and Species Richness The Value of Wetland Complexes

The theory about species richness — the number of species in an area — in relation to habitat size and isolation stems from MacArthur and Wilson (1967), whose concepts of "island biogeography" examined why some islands contained more bird species than others. They concluded that an island's size and proximity to the mainland were major determinants of species richness, which is reflected in the species–area curves now familiar to every student of conservation biology. Size is a particularly important consideration in habitat protection because as area increases, so does the number of species contained therein. The equation for this relationship is $S = CA^z$, where S = number of species, A = area, and C and z are constants that must be fitted for each set of species–area data (Wilcox 1980). Because the curve is a power function, a logarithmic transformation produces a linear equation of the form $\log S = C + z \log A$, where z is the slope of the line and C is the intercept.

The relationship between area, isolation, and species richness appears unequivocal on islands or other insular habitats such as woodlots, prairie remnants, and wetlands. In New Jersey, for example, a strong positive correlation ($r = 0.92$) existed between the size of 30 woodlots and the number of bird species (Galli et al. 1976). Based on an even more extensive study of 469 sites ranging in size from 0.1 to more than 3,000 ha in the deciduous forest of the eastern United States, Robbins et al. (1989) determined that area and isolation were the most significant of the 28 variables tested as predictors of species richness for birds.

The potential management applicability of the species–area equation ($S = CA^z$) is seen in an example from Shaw (1985). Assuming $z = 0.30$ and $C = 1.0$ for a proposed biological reserve of 250 km², $S = 1 \times 250^{0.30} = 5.24$; expanding the reserve to 2,500 km² means $S = 1 \times 2,500^{0.30} = 10.46$. In other words, a 10-fold increase in area is needed to double the estimated number of species contained therein. An application of a species–area curve in this fashion quickly leads to the idea that "bigger is better," and that biologists interested in protecting biodiversity should strive to preserve the largest contiguous tract of habitat possible. However, this rationale is not always true.

To begin, groups of smaller areas (fragments) may contain as many species as a single area of the same size (Simberloff and Abele 1982). This finding is significant because large tracts of habitat seldom remain today; thus, most opportunities to establish large reserves already have been lost. Also, the original ideas about island biogeography (MacArthur and Wilson 1967) always included a species-rich continent as a source of organisms for colonizing outlying islands, the equivalent of today's habitat fragments. A functional "continent" often does not exist today, simply because humans have fragmented landscapes and the surrounding habitat may be too inhospitable to act as a source of colonizing organisms. Accordingly, a debate known as SLOSS — "single large or several small" — often dominates discussions about the protection of important habitat (see Primack 2004). This debate in turn leads to the question of whether fragments isolated from a larger area of the same habitat are as effective as clusters of small areas, each with similar habitat. Indeed, most studies of species–area relationships include isolation as an important factor affecting species richness.

What About Wetlands?: Wetlands are among the most diminished insular habitats in North America, yet relatively few studies have addressed the influence of habitat size and isolation on the species richness of wetland birds. Nevertheless, these studies have provided important guidance on wetland management issues — especially from a wetland com-

plex perspective — and hence warrant detailed review.

The first major study occurred in 1983–84 when Brown and Dinsmore (1986) addressed the influence of size and isolation on the diversity of breeding birds in Iowa wetlands, a state where wetlands have been drained since settlement. Their study examined 30 prairie pothole wetlands that were either seasonal or semipermanent, ranged in size from 0.2 to 182.0 ha, and were evenly distributed in size classes of less than 1 to more than 20 ha; 15 were isolated and 15 occurred in complexes.

During 2 years, 25 species of birds nested in the wetlands, with an average of 9.9–10.0/wetland/yr and a range of 2–17 species/wetland (Fig. 10-11). Data for both years yielded a significant correlation between the number of species and wetland area ($r = 0.82$, slope = 0.23). Hence, wetland area explained 68% of the variation in species richness, which increased by 1.0 for each 4.3 units of additional area. However, when wetlands were separated by size class, the species–area relationship was significant for the 14 smallest sites (0.2–5.5 ha) but not the 14 largest (8.3–182.0 ha). Also, the three richest wetlands (16 species) were smaller (14, 19, 28 ha) than the three largest sites (84, 123, 182 ha), which averaged 13 species.

Gibbs et al. (1991) examined 87 wetlands in eastern and central Maine for the presence of 15 species of breeding waterbirds and likewise found that area was positively correlated ($r = 0.66$) with species richness. Similarly, Grover and Baldassarre (1995), after surveying 70 active and inactive beaver (*Castor canadensis*) ponds in south-central New York, determined that wetland area was correlated ($r = 0.65–0.67$) with species richness of obligate wetland birds.

In another study in Maine, Gibbs (1993) simulated the impact from loss of small wetlands (i.e., less than 4.05 ha) on a 600-km² area that contained 354 wetlands ranging in size from 0.05 to 105.3 ha. Loss of small wetlands reduced total wetland area by only 19%, but decreased the total wetland number by 62%, and increased the interwetland distance by 67%. The simulation predicted that local populations of turtles, small birds, and small mammals faced significant risk of extinction with the loss of small wetlands. This study thereby underscored the value of small wetlands as a means of maintaining many kinds of wildlife. Unfortunately, small wetlands often receive the least legal protection, are easy to drain or fill, and, because of their ephemeral nature, often are ignored by biologists. Hence, small

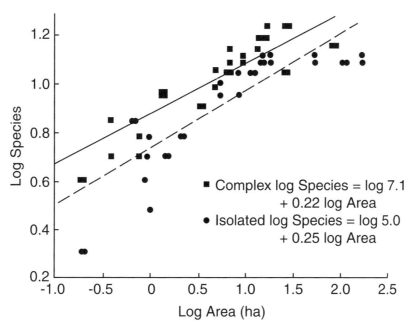

Figure 10-11. Log-transformed species–area curves for wetland birds in Iowa. Two relationships are illustrated: one for wetlands that occurred in complexes (e.g., sites where the area of wetlands within 5 km was greater than 55 ha) and another for wetlands that were isolated (e.g., wetland area within 5 km was less than 55 ha). From Brown and Dinsmore (1986:395). With permission from The Wildlife Society.

wetlands are often the first to disappear from wetland complexes despite their importance.

Relative to isolation, Brown and Dinsmore (1986) found that total area of wetlands within 5 km of each wetland explained the most variation in species richness ($r = 0.42$); in fact, area was the only significant factor among 12 isolation variables examined. Generally, wetlands within complexes held more species (11) despite being half as large (14 ha) as isolated wetlands (30 ha, 9 species). Gibbs et al. (1991) found that isolation was weakly correlated ($r = 0.24$) with the species richness of birds. In a two-variable model, wetland size and isolation explained 74% of the variation associated with species richness in Iowa and 43% in Maine. Fairbairn and Dinsmore (2001) later determined that the total wetland area within 3 km of a given wetland complex, and the percentage of wetland area covered by emergent vegetation, were significant predictors of species richness on wetlands in Iowa. Although these and other studies highlight the importance of habitat size and isolation relative to the diversity of wetland birds, they do not provide an unequivocal formula for making management decisions.

For example, relative to the question of how much habitat might be needed to protect the diversity of birds in Iowa's wetlands, Brown and Dinsmore

(1986) began by using two recognized methods. The first extrapolates a simple species–area curve from the data, while the second cumulatively tallies species as one proceeds from the smallest to largest habitat until the desired number of species is reached (McCoy 1983). The first method predicted that a 379-ha marsh was needed in Iowa to support 24 species of birds, whereas the second method predicted 236 ha (40% less area). Finally, by selectively picking among the sites, 24 species were included in four wetlands totaling only 62 ha. Thus, as these results demonstrate — even with sound empirical data at hand — the techniques currently available provide little more than guidelines, which deny biologists the luxury of reaching black-and-white management decisions. Nevertheless, it is a starting point for making more informed decisions.

As a case in point, Brown and Dinsmore (1986) concluded that wetlands of 20–30 ha were more efficient than larger marshes for preserving rich avifaunas, but they also recommended that biologists ponder other considerations. First, while one large marsh may be less costly to manage, a complex of several smaller wetlands increases habitat heterogeneity, which is important to waterfowl and other species because life-history requirements typically demand various types of wetlands (Leitch and

Kaminski 1985). Fairbairn and Dinsmore (2001) argued that wetland complexes of various sizes and types indeed provided, at any given time, the highest probability that life-history needs would be satisfied for the greatest array of wetland birds. Similarly, Murkin et al. (1997) and Murkin and Caldwell (2000), based on nearly 95,000 sightings of birds during a 10-year period, concluded that wetland complexes provide the various water depths and hydroperiods characteristic of prairie wetlands during a wet–dry cycle — conditions that ensure the greatest variety of habitat types for waterfowl and other waterbirds.

As an example of how wetland complexes satisfy the life-history requirements of individual species, consider the requirements of dabbling ducks breeding in the Prairie Pothole Region of North America. In early spring, breeding females may feed on the macroinvertebrates that are often abundant in temporary and seasonal wetlands (Swanson et al. 1974). By early summer, however, these wetlands often dry, and semipermanent wetlands thereafter provide females and their broods with food and cover. By late summer, both adults and juveniles may concentrate on permanent water potholes before departing for wintering areas. Hence, although species richness is often a focal point for protecting wetland complexes, they also should be protected to enable a single species to fulfill its life-history requirements (Murkin et al. 1997).

Although a wetland complex may contain more species than a single large site, wetland complexes nonetheless may exclude area-dependent species. For example, in Iowa, 10 of the 25 species did not occur in wetlands less than 5 ha in size (Brown and Dinsmore 1986). Other studies have started to unravel the complexities associated with area-dependent species. Naugle et al. (1999) determined that Pied-billed Grebes (*Podilymbus podiceps*) and Yellow-headed Blackbirds (*Xanthocephalus xanthocephalus*) are area-dependent species, but they rarely exploited habitat outside the immediate vicinity of their nesting areas. In contrast, the area requirements for Black Terns (*Chlidonias niger*) fluctuated in response to landscape structure — terns were more likely to occur in landscapes that contained grasslands instead of agricultural fields. Significantly, this study empirically documented that characteristics of the entire landscape can affect habitat suitability rather than individual patches.

Overall, these studies suggest that the best strategy for protecting marsh birds is to enhance existing wetland complexes by adding additional areas.

In doing so, a good rule-of-thumb is to add and protect the as much heterogeneity as possible, in terms of both size and types of communities. At the regional level, this strategy also protects biodiversity. For breeding ducks, heterogeneity remains important because pairs, broods, and fledged juveniles select different habitats within a diverse array of wetland types (Patterson 1976, Nelson and Wishart 1988, Murkin et al. 1997, Murkin and Caldwell 2000).

Managers must recognize, however, that habitat protection is a complex decision-making process that involves consideration of many factors not unrelated to the goals and objectives associated with each decision. For example, regardless of species–area considerations or area-dependent species, limited dollars may mandate that habitat for an endangered or threatened species takes priority, regardless of how many other species might be protected if those same dollars were spent elsewhere. In other cases, the objective may be to protect habitat simply to increase the numbers of a few target species, even though they may not be rare. Finally, political considerations may influence when, where, and how much effort and money will be directed toward conservation efforts. As important as conservation politics may be, we shall leave political science to other sources and instead focus on science-based conservation. However, mastery of the latter provides the requisite credibility within the political arenas in which biologists inevitably operate. Relative to that credibility, our next topic — integrated management — represents a critical advance in the focus of managing wetlands for waterfowl as well as other wetland wildlife.

WETLAND MANAGEMENT

Integrated Management for Waterfowl and Waterbirds

Integrated wetland management came of age in 1993, when the North American Wildlife and Natural Resources Conference featured a session titled, "Wetland Management for Shorebirds and Other Species." As discussed in the previous section, waterfowl biologists recognized that wetland management for ducks and geese often benefited other kinds of wildlife, but the 1993 conference formalized these concepts and proposed new initiatives. These ideas were expanded in 2000 when the Waterbird Society sponsored a symposium entitled *Managing Wetlands for Waterbirds: Integrated Approaches* (see Parsons et al. 2002).

In general, reductions in area, distribution, connectivity, and types of wetlands, as well as an increased appreciation for all wetland-dependent species, complicate wetland management — as a result, managers face working with a large number of species on a reduced base of habitat. Indeed, the term "waterbird" describes habitat use more than a taxonomic category, and thus nearly 800 species of birds can be described as waterbirds (Reid 1993). Laubhan and Fredrickson (1993:323) recognized this diversity and coined the term "integrated wetland management," which they defined as "management to maximize benefits for a community of species associated with a wetland complex." Their concept emphasized that integrated wetland management was complex and needed to incorporate principles of wetland dynamics with life-history information for selected species, annual cycle events, and spatial and temporal considerations of habitats. They later considered other dimensions of integrated wetland management, especially the importance of protecting wetland complexes (Fredrickson and Laubhan 1996). Erwin (2002) then developed a philosophy of integrated management that considered five major elements: (1) taxonomic, (2) spatial, (3) temporal, (4) population–habitat, and (5) multiple-use management objectives. We review his work because of its value as a framework for the management of waterfowl as well as other waterbirds.

Taxonomic integration addresses the growing concerns for birds besides waterfowl, which is reflected in the emergence of the North American Partners in Flight program in 1990 and the North American Bird Conservation Initiative in 1999. The latter group is a coalition of government and private groups in the United States, Canada, and Mexico whose goal is to address the conservation issues confronting *all species of birds* in North America. Spatial integration recognizes that management of waterbirds depends on activities conducted at several scales, of which the regional scales may be of greatest significance and require coordination among landowners, government agencies and nongovernment groups, as well as states and countries. Temporal integration recognizes that wetlands are used for agricultural purposes but can and are managed to benefit waterbirds after crops are harvested. For example, rice, catfish, and crawfish cultures benefit wading birds and shorebirds as well as waterfowl (Dubovsky and Kaminski 1987, Twedt and Nelms 1999, Huner et al. 2002, Tourenq et al. 2004), and commercial salt extraction operations simultaneously benefit Caribbean Flamin-

gos (*Phoenicopterus ruber ruber*; Baldassarre and Arengo 1998). In many agricultural regions in the Northern Hemisphere, croplands lay fallow in fall and winter, providing waste grains, native plant seeds, and invertebrates as food for waterfowl, shorebirds, and wading birds.

Population and habitat integration recognizes habitats as "sources" or "sinks" (sensu Pulliam 1988), and thus requires assessment of habitat values throughout the annual cycle for a single species or group of species, and to relate those values to demographics. Lastly, the concept of multiple use recognizes that wetland birds are managed on a landscape subject to many kinds of commercial, agricultural, and other uses. In addition to birds, wetland management now includes concerns for amphibians (see Semlitsch 2000).

In summary of the discussion of waterfowl management and conservation biology, we conclude with seven general principles to bear in mind relative to wetland conservation: (1) protect wetland complexes that include various hydroperiods and thus sizes of wetlands, thereby providing habitat for the greatest diversity of waterbirds and other wetland wildlife such as amphibians and reptiles; (2) protect small wetlands, especially when they add diversity to existing wetland complexes, because small wetlands are often the most vulnerable to loss; (3) consider all wetland-dependent wildlife when actively managing a given wetland or wetland complex; (4) recognize that large wetlands are needed to maintain area-dependent species; (5) recognize that wetland complexes likely enable a given species to fulfill its life-history requirements, in addition to protecting biodiversity; (6) recognize that protected sites will likely require direct management intervention to maintain their value as wildlife habitat; and (7) protect or restore upland habitats, especially grasslands, that are contiguous with wetlands.

In the following sections, we highlight some basic approaches to wetland management, which fall under two general categories: natural and artificial (Weller 1981). The former takes advantage of natural attributes of wetlands to achieve desired habitat-related objectives (e.g., seed banks, plant succession, water-level fluctuations, herbivores), whereas the latter focuses more on human-induced activities (e.g., planting, ditching, island building). We have not presented specific techniques at length because these topics are treated elsewhere (Linde 1969, Atlantic Waterfowl Council 1972, Fredrickson and Taylor 1982, Knighton 1985, Smith et al. 1989, Payne 1992, Whitman et al. 1995, Fredrickson and Laubhan

1996). Instead, we structured our discussion on the attributes of wetlands and the life-history requirements of waterfowl and other waterbirds; both components form the basis of all wetland management. In this way, we draw attention to how wetlands naturally function and *why* manipulations benefit wetland birds. The specific techniques are of secondary importance — the manager who does not understand *why* is doomed to more failures than successes.

Drawdowns, Decomposition, and Nutrient Cycling

By the late 1940s and early 1950s, waterfowl biologists recognized the importance of creating small impoundments or restoring small wetlands as a means for improving waterfowl habitat. The most extensive program was initiated in New York, where biologists created hundreds of small marshes (80% were 1–4 ha in size). Early evaluations of 559 of the new marshes revealed that more than 80% had attracted breeding ducks and nearly 70% had served as brood habitat (Benson and Foley 1956). Perhaps of greater significance, however, was the realization that waterfowl use, by both pairs and broods, declined after the third season of flooding. Thus began wide-ranging studies of wetland ecology, the results of which formed the basis for many management principles used today.

First and foremost among these principles was the necessity for a deliberate, partial or complete removal of water as a fundamental means for maintaining wetland productivity — management known as a "drawdown." Drawdowns are necessary because the comparatively high levels of productivity usually witnessed during the first few years after flooding stem from the initial release of soluble nutrients from newly inundated soil, as well as from decomposition of flooded vegetation. This process results from the store of nutrients released from the soil and decomposing vegetation under the aerobic conditions that characterize a drawdown; in the presence of oxygen, microbial activity readily decomposes organic matter into oxidized and soluble states. Nitrogenous compounds, for example, decompose under aerobic conditions into nitrates, the chemical form of nitrogen most available to plants. Hence, when terrestrial soils are inundated, the site becomes an aquatic environment enriched by a flush of water-soluble nutrients (see Whitman 1976, Kadlec et al. 2000, Mitsch and Gosselink 2000; Murkin et al. 2000b, 2000c).

Researchers quickly recognized that stable wa-

ter conditions produced anaerobic soils, where decomposition is not only slower but also may be completely arrested at various intermediate stages. Indeed, rates of anaerobic decomposition may be only 10% of the activity under aerobic conditions (Hammer 1992), largely because anaerobic bacteria extract much less energy from the substrate and only attack the more readily decomposed types of organic matter. Thus, anaerobic decomposition results in an accumulation of partially decomposed organic matter, as well as reduced and less available forms of nutrients such as methane, ammonia, and hydrogen sulfide (see Phillips 1970, Mitsch and Gosselink 2000). Kadlec (1962:279) noted that the reduced availability of soil nutrients "goes on inexorably, as long as water levels remain stable," wherein the shift from a productive to a less productive condition is rapid. The key issue associated with stable water levels is that wetland soils remain flooded and anaerobic conditions prevail. Moreover, the colloidal fraction of the soil increases with continuous flooding and steadily absorbs the flow of nutrient ions, which further decreases productivity the longer water levels remain stabilized. Such accumulations also may lower pH and produce concentrations of iron and manganese potentially toxic to plants (Cook and Powers 1958, Mitsch and Gosselink 2000).

Not all of the soil profile in wetlands becomes anaerobic, however, as aerobic conditions usually occur in a layer a few millimeters in thickness at the soil–water interface; this thin layer is of crucial importance to the nutrient cycles occurring in wetlands (Mitsch and Gosselink 2000; see also Phillips 1970). In this zone, the substances released by anaerobic decomposition deeper in the soil undergo further transformation and enter the water column where they are absorbed by plants. However, this zone is not capable of releasing nutrients at the same magnitude as occurs when the soil is again exposed during a drawdown.

During drawdown, most of the accumulated organic matter is exposed to aerobic decomposition, which may be surprisingly rapid and complete. To illustrate, 70% of the organic matter was decomposed in 63 days after drawdown on an impoundment continuously inundated for 20 years (Cook and Powers 1958). Rates of decomposition are also affected by pH, temperature, and moisture. In general, warm, moist, and alkaline conditions promote rapid decay by microorganisms, especially important nitrifying bacteria such as *Nitrosomonas* and *Nitrobacter*, along with certain types of fungi. At a site where the organic matter remained moist after drawdown, soil nitrates increased from 2.7 ppm before drawdown to 15.9 afterward (Kadlec 1962). In contrast, nitrates are greatly diminished in the soils of bogs and other areas where the low pH often precludes nitrifying bacteria (Moore and Bellamy 1974).

Early studies did not recommend annual drawdowns because many of the nutrients from the previous year's drawdown remained in the water column and could be flushed out of the system (Cook and Powers 1958). For example, experimental MERP cells at the Delta Marsh in Manitoba lost 10% of their nitrogen and 25% of their phosphorus in a drawdown after 2 years of deep flooding. However, a significant pool of nitrogen and phosphorus remained in the sediments and litter; hence, nutrients lost through the water column likely did not affect fu-

ture marsh productivity (see Murkin et al. 2000c). Further, only small amounts of these nutrient pools (0.01–5.0%) are needed to satisfy the needs of plants during the growing season (see Murkin et al. 2000c, Kadlec et al. 2000). Overall, the nutrient budgets generated from MERP provide significant new data, which we review here (Fig. 10-12).

During the dry-marsh (drawdown) phase, nutrients (nitrogen and phosphorus) previously locked in sediments and pore water (water in the pores of the sediment) during the lake-marsh stage (permanent water) are rapidly incorporated into plant biomass (Murkin et al. 2000c). Pore water is of great interest to a discussion of nutrient cycling in wetlands because it can influence microbial metabolic processes by restricting oxygen penetration and nutrient trans-

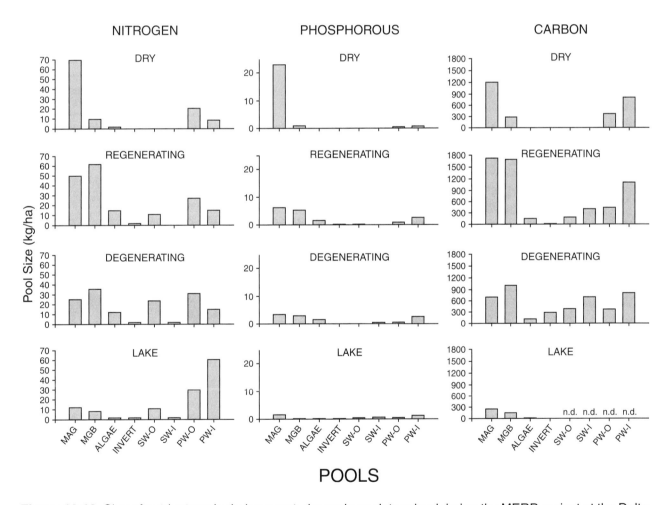

Figure 10-12. Size of nutrient pools during a wet–dry cycle as determined during the MERP project at the Delta Waterfowl and Wetlands Research Station, Manitoba, Canada. MAG = aboveground macrophytes; MBG = belowground macrophytes; SW-O = surface water organic; SW-I = surface water inorganic; PW-O = pore water organic; PW-I = pore water inorganic; n. d. = no data. From Murkin et al. (2000c:104). With permission from Blackwell Publishing Professional.

port. During the dry-marsh stage, however, major nutrient fluxes associated with macrophytes are restored, particularly nutrient uptake, leaching, and litter-fall. Indeed, the aboveground biomass of annuals during the dry-marsh stage can equal or exceed the biomass of emergent vegetation during the regenerating marsh cycle (see Murkin et al. 2000c; Fig. 10-13). The most important nutrient pathway restored during the dry-marsh stage is the uptake of nitrogen and phosphorus by annual plants from sediments and pore water. In contrast, nutrient pools (e.g., invertebrates and algae) that depend on standing water become much reduced during the dry-marsh stage. Algae at this time largely occur as epipelon associated with moist soil (see Robinson et al. 2000), and aquatic invertebrates enter dormant

phases awaiting the return of water (see Murkin and Ross 2000).

When water was returned (regenerating marsh), annual plants were immediately killed and their biomass entered the aboveground litter pool of nutrients (Murkin et al. 2000c). However, the return of water also leaches, often quite rapidly, large amounts of nutrients from this litter, especially nitrogen and phosphorus, which then enter the water (Wrubleski et al. 1997). For instance, 30% of the nutrients in the litter were released by leaching within 2 days of inundation, and these are quickly absorbed by algae, particularly the epiphyton and metaphyton (Robinson et al. 2000). Indeed, based on the nutrient budget developed in the MERP studies, the uptake of nutrients by algae was similar to the

Figure 10-13. Drawdowns increase nutrient cycling as well as affect germination within the seed bank. These photos highlight vegetation changes associated with the drawdown of an emergent marsh in central New York. After prolonged flooding the emergent vegetation has died back and open water dominates (lake-marsh stage, *top*). A drawdown in early spring exposes mudflats and the seed bank (*bottom left*), which responds with germination and growth of annuals (*bottom right*). Photos courtesy of Matt Kaminski, Ducks Unlimited.

loss from the aboveground litter during the early flooding years (Kadlec et al. 2000). Hence, although the increase in productivity after a drawdown had been known for many years, the MERP studies suggested that the increase resulted largely from nutrients leached from the aboveground litter, the uptake of these nutrients by algae, and the abundant surfaces on submersed litter that provided sites for algal colonization and the subsequent microbial and invertebrate productivity (see Murkin et al. 2000c). The productivity of the regenerating stage is generally maintained until prolonged inundation causes the dieback of long-lived emergent vegetation, thereby "locking" nutrient pools in sediments and litter again is subject to anaerobic decomposition. The marsh then enters the degenerating stage.

During the regenerating stage in the MERP studies, macrophyte production and litter availability combined to support several kinds of primary producers and secondary consumers. For example, litter availability and nutrient leaching early in this phase maintain significant algal production in the water column (see Robinson et al. 2000). The litter also provides a substrate for algal growth, and the loss of emergent vegetation increases light penetration that benefits photosynthesis within the water column. Indeed, algal populations remained fairly high even after 5 years of flooding (see Murkin et al. 2000c, Robinson et al. 2000). The rate that a wetland progresses though the degenerating phase seems influenced, at least in part, by water depth — medium or deeply flooded experimental units proceeded more quickly through this phase than shallow-water units.

By the lake-marsh stage, the experimental units typically reached their lowest level of productivity; emergent vegetation was nearly absent and wave action often increased the turbidity of standing water. Low productivity occurs at this point because nutrient cycling in the system occurs only in the sediments, and few fluxes are available to move nutrients among pools such as the macrophytes. Wetland productivity at this point remains low until fluxes are restored, as occurs during the dry-marsh stage (e.g., drawdown).

Drawdowns for Moist-Soil Management

In addition to stimulating decomposition and nutrient cycling, drawdowns produce habitats with food resources of special value for waterfowl and other wildlife. "Moist-soil management" is the term referring to these manipulations — even though water is actually removed during the process — because many desirable plants germinate on mudflats (i.e., moist soils). Such plants generally include those providing cover, energy, or specific nutrients. "Moist-soil" habitats thus are defined as seasonally flooded wetlands dominated by annual and perennial plants (van der Valk 1981).

Bellrose (1941) and Low and Bellrose (1944) pioneered moist-soil management in their studies of wetland plants along the Illinois River in the north-central United States. Thereafter, overviews of moist-soil management appeared in Fredrickson and Taylor (1982), Smith et al. (1989), Reinecke et al. (1989), and Reid et al. (1989); see also Murkin et al. (2000b) for results obtained by MERP at the Delta Marsh in Manitoba. Fredrickson (1996) nonetheless provided the most thorough review of the history and development of moist-soil management. These studies and reviews collectively recognized several major factors that determine plant composition following drawdown, foremost of which are (1) the seed bank, (2) seasonal timing of drawdowns (e.g., spring or summer), (3) type of drawdown (partial or complete), (4) rate of drawdown (fast or slow), and (4) number of years since the previous drawdown or soil disturbance. Our review draws heavily from these studies.

To begin, drawdowns were initially designed to promote the growth of waterfowl food plants (see Linde 1969, Atlantic Waterfowl Council 1972). The timing of drawdowns varies with latitude, but early spring drawdowns generally allow a longer growth period for emergent plants, thereby enhancing their numbers, diversity, and survival. As discussed earlier, drawdowns mimic the dry-marsh stage of the wetland cycle, which promotes the growth of annuals that, unlike vegetatively reproducing perennials, produce tremendous quantities of seeds under favorable conditions (Table 10-8). For example, on playa lakes managed to produce moist-soil vegetation, five species of plants produced a total of 2,907 kg of seed per hectare (Haukos and Smith 1993). Seed production from moist-soil management on marshes in the Upper Mississippi River Valley ranged from 660 kg/ha (Fredrickson and Taylor 1982) to 1,344 kg/ha (Reid et al. 1989). Timing also influences the germination of propagules in the seed bank. During the MERP studies, the seed bank from a May drawdown yielded a total stem density of about $1,400/m^2$ compared with about 900 from a drawdown initiated in July (Murkin et al. 2000b; Table 10-9).

Drawdown areas are reflooded in autumn to depths of 10–25 cm so that seeds and other foods

Table 10-8. Dried seed biomass and standing crop (kg/ha) for plant species in playa wetlands managed for most-soil plants compared to unmanaged playas on the Southern High Plains, Texas. Modified from Haukos and Smith (1993:294).

Species	Managed (n = 4)		Unmanaged (n = 4)	
	Seed	Standing crop	Seed	Standing crop
Persicaria lapathifolia	730	11,487	55	1,074
Persicaria pensylvanica	532	6,492	105	1,378
Echinochloa crusgalli	346	2,635	45	376
Rumex crispus	1,233	3,274	703	1,582
Eleocharis spp.	66	1,228	28	986

Table 10-9. Seedling density (m²) at the end of August for drawdown treatments initiated in mid-May, June, July, and August during MERP at the Delta Marsh, Manitoba. Modified from Murkin et al. (2000b:331)

Species	May	June	July	August
Emergents				
Phragmites australis	16	21	11	0
Scirpus lacustris	300	220	130	0
Scirpus maritimus	620	110	70	0
Schlocholoa festucacea	10	39	58	0
Typha spp.	140	500	310	18
Lythrum salicaria	71	180	120	22
Annuals				
Aster brachyactis	29	27	13	0
Chenopodium rubrum	94	120	140	27
Rumex crispus	9	17	20	8
Others	27	48	15	0
Total	1,316	1,282	887	75

become available to waterfowl, although shallower depths or even exposed mudflats are needed for shorebirds. We emphasize that integrated wetland management does not propose a certain water depth as an infallible rule; wetland birds rely on several depths to meet their needs. Early spring drawdowns create ideal feeding habitat on mudflats for migrating shorebirds because most of the residual vegetation lies flat at that season and therefore seldom interferes with foraging activities. Green-winged Teal also readily forage in shallow water, as do Northern Pintails. Hence, to achieve maximum benefits, managers should schedule spring drawdowns to coincide with the occurrence of greatest diversity of migrants present, yet still consider the water depths preferred by each species.

Early spring drawdowns also increase the availability of seeds, invertebrates, and fishes as food for waterbirds. In particular, the drawdowns concentrate invertebrates and fish in small pools and thereby increase their availability as food (Swanson and Meyer 1977). On unproductive wetlands in central Wisconsin, for example, the density of breeding waterfowl was correspondingly reduced, but a late-May drawdown on one impoundment attracted 350 Mallards, 150 Blue-winged Teal, and 125 Great Blue

Herons (*Ardea herodias*), whereas no more than 20 ducks/day visited six nearby impoundments (Baldassarre 1980). Thus, although management generally emphasizes abundance of waterfowl foods, high levels of abundance are not always possible in areas of low biological productivity. In these areas, however, drawdowns may enhance the *availability* of food for waterfowl and other birds, thereby partially offsetting the reduced abundance of food resources. In essence, all drawdowns increase the availability of food for some species, but benefits of this approach in nutrient-poor wetlands should not be overlooked by managers.

For delayed or late-spring drawdowns, Fredrickson and Taylor (1982) recommend that water initially be lowered just 5–15 cm and maintained at that level until seed germination begins on exposed mudflats, and then proceed with a full drawdown. Initial phases of a late-spring drawdown can be timed to coincide with the arrival of shorebirds, herons, and rails. Ideally, managers also coordinate early- and late-spring drawdowns within a complex of wetlands. For example, a complete drawdown of all wetlands in early spring might attract migrant shorebirds, but little water would be available later for other wetland-associated wildlife. Reflooding takes place when the desired vegetation can tolerate deeper water, which is usually when the plants are 10–15 cm high, although reflooding may decrease seed production for some species.

In contrast to spring drawdowns, little research has examined the effects of winter drawdowns as a management tool. However, Taft et al. (2002) examined winter drawdowns in the Central Valley of California, where the maximum abundance and diversity of waterbirds occurred on sites with average water depths of 10–20 cm and where the topographical gradient differed by 30–40 cm between the deepest and shallowest ends of the marsh.

Other techniques (mowing, disking, tilling) during the autumn may enhance the responses of moist-soil plants during the following growing season. At the Noxubee National Wildlife Refuge in Mississippi, sites that were tilled or disked produced more seed biomass than other locations (Gray et al. 1999). Plant diversity also was greater on tilled plots. In contrast, the greatest biomass of macroinvertebrates (up to 31.2 kg/ha) occurred without treatment or on sites that were mowed. Autumn tilling also retarded succession and enhanced plant productivity and diversity during the following growing season (see Gray et al. 1999 for other benefits). In Texas, Smith et al. (2004) disked playa lake basins to create different

cover–water ratios and noted high seed production from moist-soil plants.

Managers attempting moist-soil management in marshes of the Great Basin in the western United States also must consider whether underlying soil sediments are fresh or saline before conducting drawdowns. In saline wetlands, flooding with fresh water reduces salinity in the sediments whereby aquatic plants may become established, but sediment salinity increases rapidly with drawdown, which precludes traditional moist-soil management scenarios (Smith and Kadlec 1985a). In general, the germination of moist-soil plants is restricted at salinities greater than 7 ppt (Fredrickson 1996). Smith and Kadlec (1983) accordingly recommended that drawdowns maintain a water depth of a few centimeters, which prevented the establishment of undesirable salt-tolerant plants, yet promoted preferred species such as hardstem bulrush, alkali bulrush, and sago pondweed. Kadlec and Smith (1989) provide further details on water-level manipulations and plant growth relationships on saline soils.

Overall — regardless of geographical location — moist-soil management becomes an excellent technique where several wetlands are available for water-level manipulations. In these cases, a wetland complex can be managed to maximize the availability of habitat for a variety of waterfowl and other wetland wildlife throughout the annual cycle (Fig. 10-14). For example, if species such as grebes (Podicipedidae), pochards, and muskrats are management targets, then water levels will be maintained at fairly high levels (lake marsh). At the other end of the spectrum, shorebirds require mudflats and shallow water with sparse vegetation, whereas rails require both shallow water and dense emergent vegetation (regenerating marsh). These few examples amply underline the complexity of moist-soil management, even without the added factor of controlling undesirable vegetation. Indeed, there are no "rules" for scheduling the timing and type of drawdowns for all wetlands — moist-soil management certainly remains both a local art and science. Nevertheless, we can summarize a few major principles as reported by Fredrickson and Taylor (1982) and Fredrickson (1996:174).

(1). Initiate water-level manipulations based on the phenology of the plants and animals of the area and not on calendar dates, but also recognize that there is no ideal hydrologic regime or frequency of disturbance.

(2). Implement management for the benefit of several species. For example, if a deeply flooded

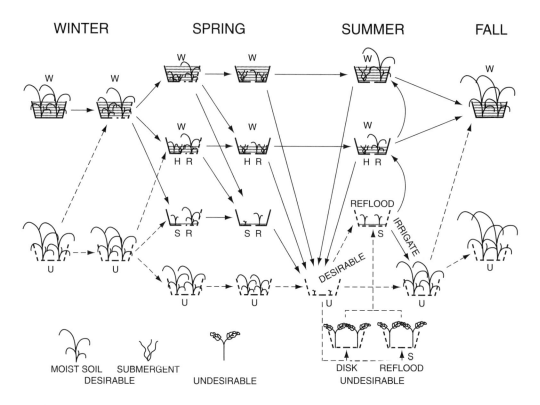

Figure 10-14. A schematic illustration of the relationships between the manipulation of wetland habitat and the responses of waterbirds and upland wildlife (W = waterfowl, H = herons, R = rails, S = shorebirds, U = upland wildlife). Shading depicts water depths (full = deep flooding of greater than 15 cm; half-full = shallow flooding of less than 15 cm; empty = mudflats). Dashed arrows depict flooding, with the results indicated by dashes in the basin outline. Solid arrows and basins represent manipulations and results under continuous flooding. The robustness of the vegetation is indicated by relative size of the plants within the basins. From Fredrickson and Taylor (1982:17).

impoundment is gradually drawn down in spring, shorebirds can be accommodated, yet the deeper areas still will provide habitat for pochards. The moist-soil vegetation produced by such a regime will be established at different times, which will increase habitat diversity.

(3). Consider management within the context of a wetland complex, thereby maximizing habitat quality for several species and over their annual cycles. Little is accomplished, for example, if drawdowns attract pairs of breeding ducks but management does not provided brood habitat later in the season. In this regard, a drawdown does not always have to be complete, but instead may be partial and therefore maintain core areas of open water.

(4). Continually monitor activities during water-level manipulations so that corrective actions may be initiated if undesirable situations occur.

(5). Maintain records of responses by both plants and animals as a guide for future drawdowns; a per-

manent record also becomes essential when new personnel take charge of established management areas. These data, faithfully kept over the years, will prove especially helpful for determining the frequency of drawdowns for each site.

Management for Macroinvertebrates

Nearly all of the principles discussed thus far have concerned either plant communities or individual species of plants. Aquatic macroinvertebrates, however, are important waterfowl foods, especially because of the protein they supply for functions such as egg production, growth of ducklings, and molting (see Chapter 6); they also represent an integral component in the ecology of freshwater wetland ecosystems (see Murkin and Ross 2000). Macroinvertebrates also contain several amino acids and minerals fundamental for a balanced diet (see Chapter 5). The MERP at the Delta Marsh generated significant new information about the ecology of macroinvertebrate in prairie wetlands (Murkin and Ross 2000). Batzer et al. (1999) also contains numerous studies of invertebrates in freshwater wetlands. We relied heavily on these sources for the following discussion.

Macroinvertebrates occur in four basic wetland habitats: (1) the water surface, (2) the water column, (3) submersed surfaces (e.g., plant parts) within the water column, and (4) the bottom substrate (Murkin and Ross 2000). They are especially abundant in areas of shallow water dominated by dense vegetation (Swanson et al. 1974), and shallow water also renders macroinvertebrates available to dabbling ducks. At the Delta Marsh in Manitoba, for example, positive correlations exist at normal water levels between macroinvertebrates and the presence of dabbling ducks, but these correlations no longer occurred when the water depth was elevated 1 m above normal (Murkin and Kadlec 1986).

Macroinvertebrates also can be abundant on submerged vegetation, in benthic areas, and in open water. As noted earlier in this chapter, submerged vegetation offers important macroinvertebrate habitat, and several studies have demonstrated that submerged plants with finely dissected leaves harbor the largest standing crops of macroinvertebrates (Krull 1970). At the Delta Marsh, Wrubleski and Rosenberg (1990) reported the greatest diversity and abundance of chironomids from areas dominated by sago pondweed, a plant with an abundance of finely dissected leaves. In Mississippi, the greatest biomass of macroinvertebrates (231 kg/ha) occurred in stands of coontail and fanwort (*Cabomba caroliniana*; Teels et al. 1976). At the Noxubee National Wildlife Refuge in Mississippi, coontail also had the highest macroinvertebrate biomass (213 kg/ha) of any plant community sampled, as well as the most favorable ratio (1:49, in grams) of macroinvertebrate to plant biomass (Arner et al. 1974). Krull (1970) recorded more aquatic macroinvertebrates in vegetated than in unvegetated areas of marshes in New York. His work determined that about 1 g of animal material was associated with every 100 g of submerged vegetation, and that plants with greater amounts of surface area harbored more macroinvertebrates. In Texas, both diversity and abundance of macroinvertebrate taxa were greater on playa lake wetlands managed for moist-soil vegetation compared to unmanaged playa wetlands (Anderson and Smith 2000).

The variability in macroinvertebrate abundance and distribution within wetlands was illustrated in an early study of four prairie marshes in Iowa (Voigts 1976). Although isopods (mainly *Asellus* spp.), planorbid snails (*Gyraulus* spp.), and physid snails (mainly *Physa* spp.) were greatest in shallow-water areas with emergent and dead vegetation, midge larvae and amphipods (mostly *Hyallela* spp.) were most numerous in submerged vegetation protected from the wind; cladocerans and copepods were most abundant in open water. Overall, the greatest numbers of macroinvertebrates occurred where open-water habitats of submerged vegetation were interspersed with emergent vegetation.

These results support the contention that habitats with a balanced mix of emergent plants and open water — hemi-marsh — attract the largest diversity of breeding birds (Weller and Spatcher 1965, Weller and Fredrickson 1973, Murkin and Caldwell 2000), perhaps because birds recognize the structural features of wetland habitats where macroinvertebrate food supplies may be greatest (Voigts 1976, Kaminski and Prince 1981). Indeed, in two of the major experimental studies conducted thus far, the response of breeding dabbling ducks to the structure of marsh habitat has been greatest where cover-to-water ratios were 50:50 (Kaminski and Prince 1981, Murkin et al. 1982).

An especially revealing study took place at the Delta Marsh in Manitoba where wetlands dominated by whitetop rivergrass (*Scolochloa festucacea*) were manipulated for 2 years (Kaminski and Prince 1981). The abundance, biomass, and number of macroinvertebrate families were not significantly different among three artificially created treatments of emergent vegetation–water ratios of 30:70, 50:50, and 70:30, although the highest macroinvertebrate biomass occurred at a 50:50 (hemi-marsh) ratio. Macroinvertebrates were most abundant in unmanipulated open-water areas (controls), which were dominated by large numbers of midge larvae (Chironomidae) and water fleas (Daphnidae). However, macroinvertebrate biomass increased between years on plots that were either mowed or rototilled; the most diverse communities of macroinvertebrates occurred in mowed plots. The rich community and high number of macroinvertebrates in mowed plots were attributed to the abundance of detritus. Hence, mowing and shallow flooding were recommended as effective ways for enhancing the ratio of cover to water interspersion and thus aquatic macroinvertebrates. Mowing in late summer, followed by reflooding the next spring, produced macroinvertebrate densities averaging 8,000–11,000/m^3 and a biomass of 0.47–0.91 g/m^3. Later research also demonstrated that mowing and flooding emergent vegetation enhances invertebrate populations in wetlands (Gray et al. 1999). Disking areas of robust emergent vegetation promotes decomposition and invertebrate populations (Fredrickson and Reid 1990).

Nelson and Kadlec (1984) synthesized a great deal of information to develop a conceptual approach toward understanding the relationships among habitat structure, macroinvertebrate populations, and breeding dabbling ducks, which was subsequently supported by empirical data from the MERP studies (Murkin and Ross 1999). Basically, the spring growth of submergent vegetation is not extensive and thus does not form an important substrate for the subsistence of macroinvertebrate populations. Instead, flooded litter from the previous growing season provides highly desirable, heterogeneous habitat for macroinvertebrates. Temperatures are comparatively warm in these areas of shallow water, and epiphytic algae readily colonize the litter, which in turn stimulates development of an expanding community of grazing and predatory macroinvertebrates. By summer, however, various environmental conditions — mainly high temperatures, anoxia, and reduced litter — may begin restricting the macroinvertebrate populations harbored in the dead vegetation. By this time, however, submerged plants and their associated algal epiphytes are well established, and macroinvertebrates are afforded a new and more benign environment where their populations might flourish. Further, some of the fine particulate matter resulting from the continuing microbial decomposition of the litter is trapped by collector macroinvertebrates, thereby becoming assimilated into the food web of the invertebrate community.

Results from the MERP studies demonstrated that invertebrate abundance and diversity peak when wetlands shift from regenerating marsh to degenerating marsh (the hemi-marsh stage), which coincides with the peak in the plant biomass and diversity of vegetation types (Murkin and Ross 1999). However, Murkin et al. (1992) concluded that the high numbers and diversity of macroinvertebrates in hemi-marsh wetlands likely were related to the diversity of habitat types rather than to the interspersion of cover and water per se. This situation occurred because each habitat type differentially contributed to macroinvertebrate abundance throughout summer; hence, macroinvertebrates always were abundant somewhere in the wetland. Also, only during the hemi-marsh stage are emergent vegetation and open water at their maximum proportions.

Significantly, the MERP studies also documented the responses of invertebrates throughout the wet–dry cycle of prairie wetlands (Murkin and Ross 2000). During the dry-marsh stage, for example, aquatic invertebrates occur as dormant forms in the substrate or flying adults from nearby wetlands still containing water. In contrast, during the regenerating stage — as water returns — the invertebrate fauna is dominated initially by the dormant species and mobile forms that arrive from other wetlands. Cladocerans, ostracods, and copepods all appeared quickly in the water column after the dry basins were flooded. In the litter, invertebrates known as shredders and grazers start breaking down coarse organic matter into finer materials that are then available to another set of invertebrate consumers, the filter feeders (see Murkin and Ross 2000:204). Mosquito larvae also appeared about this time, followed by snails and several other groups immigrating from other wetlands. With continued flooding, however, decomposition reduces the litter, which is replaced by emergent vegetation, in turn changing the invertebrate community. A turnover occurred, for example, in the chironomid community: Those species that depend on flooded litter declined, whereas those species that depend on emergent vegetation increased. Invertebrate communities changed again as litter developed within the stands of emergent vegetation.

As already mentioned, the early degenerating marsh stage represents the period of maximum invertebrate abundance and diversity, the result of an abundant supply of plant and detrital material in the substrate and the matrix of wetland types. As the degenerating phase continues, however, emergent vegetation dies, litter decomposes, phytoplankton levels decline, and open-water expands. Invertebrate communities thereafter become dominated by benthic species, and loss of submersed structure increases the vulnerability of the remaining invertebrates to predators (e.g., fish, carnivorous invertebrates, and vertebrates such as salamanders). During the lake-marsh stage, invertebrate habitat is greatly reduced, and large benthic chironomids become the dominant taxa.

However, although invertebrate populations and avian diversity and density are often greatest during the hemi-marsh stage, that phase of wetland development cannot meet the ecological requirements of every species for all seasons. Indeed, during the MERP studies, few avian species occurred in equal abundance across the stages of the wet–dry marsh cycle (Murkin and Caldwell 2000). MERP aptly demonstrated that the wet–dry cycle provides a mix of habitat types over time, as well as ensuring marsh productivity. So, once again we emphasize that management must strive to maintain wetland complexes as the best way to ensure functioning ecosystems that benefit waterbirds and other forms of wildlife.

As a final note, wintering waterfowl apparently also respond to 50:50 cover-to-water ratios, as documented during experimental manipulation of playa lake wetlands on the Southern High Plains of Texas (Smith et al. 2004). Highest waterfowl densities and avian species richness occurred at sites with 50:50 cover-to-water ratios compared to ratios of 75:25 and 25:75, but the density of other birds did not differ among the three treatments. Food resources were similarly available at each site, so the response of waterfowl to the 50:50 treatment may be related to the optimal amount of edge and visual isolation the birds desire for forming and maintaining pairs.

Management of Greentree Reservoirs

Bottomland hardwood forests, especially along the Mississippi River and its tributaries in the southern United States, provide excellent habitat when shallow flooding makes acorns and other food resources (e.g., invertebrates) available for wintering and migrating waterfowl. Managers quickly recognized that they could enhance waterfowl habitat by manipulating water levels to mimic the naturally occurring hydroperiod (Rudolph and Hunter 1964). Furthermore, because the trees are alive, these areas can serve the dual purpose of timber production because the flooding regime, by design, does not kill the trees (Reinecke et al. 1989). Such managed sites are called "greentree reservoirs" or GTRs (Fig. 10-15), most of which are located in the southeastern United States where they are typically uneven-aged stands of oaks that deliberately are flooded (Wigley and Filer 1989). Acorns are especially important waterfowl foods in GTRs, where production on good sites can reach 8,400 kg/ha (Fredrickson and Batema 1992). GTRs can also produce substantial invertebrate populations. In Mississippi, for example, Wehrle et al. (1995) reported invertebrate densities of 10.3 kg/ha on GTRs compared with 60.3 kg/ha in naturally flooded forests nearby. In Missouri, invertebrate densities reached 13.7 kg/ha on GTRs (White 1985). Managers usually flood GTRs from late fall and winter to early spring to provide habitat for migrating and wintering waterfowl, especially Mallards and Wood Ducks.

The general principles for managing GTRs are similar in many ways to moist-soil management, except that most species of trees and shrubs characteristic of bottomland hardwood forests are adversely affected by permanent flooding. In the southern states, consistent flooding does not mimic the natural hydroperiod and thus can change the forest composition from pin oak (*Quercus palustris*) and Nuttall oak (*Q. nuttalli*) to more water tolerant but less desirable overcup oak (*Q. lyrata*; Fredrickson and Batema 1992). Cherrybark oak (*Q. pagoda*) can be killed within 1 year when permanently flooded at a depth of less than 30 cm (Broadfoot and Williston 1973). At the Noxubee National Wildlife Refuge in Mississippi, Young et al. (1995) evaluated winter flooding at two GTRs constructed in the 1950s. Except for 1 year, the GTRs were flooded annually through 1985, after which flooding occurred every 2 years. The flood-tolerant overcup oak was the dominant species in both of the managed GTRs, but this species ranked fourth in a control area with a more natural hydroperiod. Willow oak (*Q. phellos*), a less flood-tolerant species, ranked first in the control area but fifth and sixth in the GTRs. Seedlings of overcup oak were abundant in the GTRs, whereas Nuttall oak seedlings in the control area decreased 90% after 1 year of flooding.

At the Montezuma National Wildlife Refuge in New York, studies of two GTRs constructed in 1965 provided significant insight into the long-term effects of flooding; the sites were evaluated before they were impounded as well as during the following a 30-year period. Comparative information was gathered at a control site (Reed 1968, Thompson et al. 1968, Malecki et al. 1983, Deller and Baldassarre 1998). The GTRs were flooded annually until 1977, but flooding was terminated because of the crown dieback in the overstory (Malecki et al. 1983). Another evaluation occurred in 1995, 18 years after flooding ended (Deller and Baldassarre 1998). Red maple (*Acer rubrum*) and green ash (*Fraxinus pennsylvanica*) remained as the dominant overstory species, but flooding had changed the density of green ash saplings in the control area to 300/ha compared with 30–90/ha in the GTRs. Shrub density was similar 18 years postflooding and preflooding, but several species in the GTRs occurred at significantly lower densities than in the control area. Richness of the herbaceous species was similar at all sites (29–31 species), but two species of ferns were less dense in the GTRs. Elsewhere on the refuge, 2 years of permanent flooding of bottomland hardwood areas resulted in

Figure 10-15. Well-managed greentree reservoirs (GTRs) mimic the natural hydroperiod of a bottomland hardwood forest, as depicted here at the Noxubee National Wildlife Refuge in Mississippi. These sites are dry during the spring and summer (*top*), thus enabling the continued growth of trees and, in open areas, the temporary development of moist-soil plants. The scene is dramatically different when flooded in winter to attract wintering waterfowl (*bottom*). Photos courtesy of Richard M. Kaminski, Mississippi State University.

the loss of most trees and the associated understory (Cowardin 1969).

As mentioned earlier, GTRs also produce abundant populations of macroinvertebrates (Fredrickson and Batema 1992) which may differ greatly from macroinvertebrates occurring in other types of wetlands. For instance, fingernail clams (*Sphaerium* and *Musculium*) are common in the flooded forests along the upper Mississippi River and at the Montezuma National Wildlife Refuge in New York (Krull 1969, Eckblad et al. 1977), but these desirable waterfowl foods are not typical of marshes dominated by emergent vegetation. Isopods (*Asellus forbesi*) and amphipods (*Crangonyx forbesi*) were abundant in a GTR in Tennessee (Hubert and Krull 1973).

As with moist-soil management, flooding must be monitored closely on GTRs to prevent changes in species composition, retardation of tree growth and vigor, and acorn production. Reinecke et al. (1989) recommended that fall flooding not commence until trees were dormant (as evidenced by autumn coloration), and that flooding terminate in spring by the time leaf growth begins. They also recommended that GTRs not be flooded annually, which may more closely simulate the natural hydroperiod. Indeed, Fredrickson and Batema (1992) noted that after 10 or more years of annual flooding, GTRs exhibited declining use by waterfowl as well as decreased acorn production, tree growth, and plant diversity. They advised managers to mimic the natural hydroperiod as the best way to provide desirable foraging habitat for waterfowl and to maintain the long-term health and productivity of tree species.

Overall, management of forested wetlands is highly desirable, especially within the context of wetland complexes. Further, GTRs are not only important for waterfowl, but also afford key habitat for various reptiles, amphibians, birds of prey, Neotropical migrants (e.g., wood warblers, Parulidae), Wild Turkey (*Meleagris gallopavo*), and white-tailed deer (*Odocoileus virginianus*), among others. For more information on GTRs, see Wigley and Filer (1989) for a description of their distribution and habitat characteristics, and Fredrickson and Batema (1992) for management techniques.

Management of Agricultural Wetlands (Ricefields)

Agricultural activities occupy about one third of the Earth's land surface, of which rice culture is one of the most dominant endeavors. Indeed, rice is the primary staple for more than half the world's popu-

lation. Worldwide, about 154 million ha of rice were planted in 2000, primarily (90%) in Asia (Aselmann and Crutzen 1989). Some 1.4 million ha of rice were planted in the United States in 2004, particularly in Arkansas, Louisiana, Mississippi, and California. The amount of rice remaining in these fields after harvest is often substantial, with estimates in the Mississippi Alluvial Valley ranging from 140 to 490 kg/ha (Reinecke et al. 1989, Huitink and Siebenmorgen 1996, Manley et al. 2004; Fig. 10-16). Across the United States, an average of 344–491 kg/ha of residual rice remains after harvest (see Manley et al. 2004). Ricefields also contain seeds from moist-soil plants, as well as aquatic macroinvertebrates. In Arkansas, for example, Reinecke et al. (1989) reported 12–37 kg/ha of moist-soil plant seeds in harvested ricefields. Invertebrate densities averaged 6.3 kg/ha and reached a maximum of 21.1–31.7 kg/ha in ricefields in Mississippi (Manley et al. 2004) and 22.0 kg/ha in Louisiana (Hohman et al. 1996).

In winter, large concentrations of waterfowl feed in flooded ricefields, and they have done so for many years (Horn and Glasgow 1964). The "rice prairies" along the Gulf Coast of Texas are particularly famous as feeding habitat for millions of wintering ducks and geese (Hobaugh et al. 1989). In the Mississippi Alluvial Valley, 29–39% of all Mallards monitored in aerial surveys were in ricefields, most of which were managed to retain water (Reinecke et al. 1992). Three species of whistling-ducks in Venezuela make extensive use of ricefields in the Llanos area (Dallmeier 1991). Ricefields also provide important habitat for shorebirds (Hands et al. 1991, Shuford et al. 1998, Twedt and Nelms 1999) and rails (Meanley 1956). In the Mississippi Alluvial Valley, Twedt and Nelms (1998) found large densities of shorebirds in soybean fields, but shorebirds occurred more frequently (51%) in ricefields than soybean fields (32%). In the Central Valley of California, ricefields held more (23–30%) shorebirds during winter than other croplands, managed moist-soil areas, and evaporation ponds (Shuford et al. 1998). Harvested ricefields in Louisiana are used to for commercial production of crayfish (*Procambarus* spp.), which greatly increased the number of waterbirds occurring in the state during winter (Fleury and Sherry 1995). Use of such ricefields peaks during drawdown, which concentrates crayfish and therefore increases their availability to wading birds.

When flooded, ricefields thus provide important habitat for many kinds of waterbirds, and deliberate flooding of harvested ricefields is occurring more often worldwide. Rice seeds also resist decomposi-

Figure 10-16. Waste remaining in ricefields after harvest offers an important food for wintering waterfowl provided that the leftover grain is made available by either natural or deliberate flooding of the fields. Such postharvest flooding of ricefields is an integral component of waterfowl management in parts of the Mississippi Alluvial Valley (above) and the Central Valley of California. Photo courtesy of Stephen J. Dinsmore, Mississippi State University.

tion better than corn or soybeans. In field experiments in the Mississippi Alluvial Valley, 74% of rice seeds persisted after 120 days of submersion compared with soybeans, which almost completely disappeared after 90 days; about 50% of the corn persisted after 100 days (Nelms and Twedt 1996). Rice is also nutritionally superior to soybeans, with a metabolizable energy content of 13.8 kJ compared with 11.3 kJ for soybeans (Loesch and Kaminski 1989, Kaminski et al. 2003). Raw soybeans contain a trypsin inhibitor that renders most of the protein unavailable to young broiler chickens (McNaughton et al. 1981). Furthermore, because rice is grown in an aquatic setting, the associated water-control systems facilitate habitat management (Manley et al. 2004). Thus, to some degree, the management of ricefields for waterfowl and other waterbirds can offset the loss of natural wetlands by providing waste

grain, invertebrates, and seeds from moist-soil plants.

Indeed, deliberate flooding of harvested ricefields is gaining ground as a tool for managing waterbird habitat, but the practice also produces other benefits. In California, waterfowl foraging in flooded ricefields increased the decomposition of residual surface straw by 78% and reduced nitrogen concentrations (Bird et al. 2000). Winter flooding also can improve the quality of runoff water and retard the growth of winter weeds in ricefields (Manley 1999, Manley et al. 2004). Waterfowl concentrating in flooded ricefields also offer landowners opportunities to reap revenues from fee-lease hunting (see Grado et al. 2001). All told, landowners are recognizing the collective benefits of flooding their harvested ricefields as a practice of waterfowl management (Zekor and Kaminski 1987, Miller et al. 1989).

In the Mississippi Alluvial Valley of the United States, a major rice-growing region, about 10% of the harvested ricefields are managed to retain water for wintering and migrating waterbirds, especially waterfowl (Uihlein 2000). In the Central Valley of California, another key rice-growing region in North America, about 60,000 ha of ricefields were intentionally flooded during the winters of 1992–95 (Shuford et al. 1998). In the eastern portion of the Camargue of southern France, ricefields provide important waterfowl habitat as well as hunting opportunities (Mesleard et al. 1995, Mathevet et al. 2002). Ricefields also have been flooded for wintering waterfowl in central Japan (Yamamoto and Oohata 2003).

Management for Shorebirds and Wading Birds

As mentioned continually throughout this section, shorebirds and wading birds use many of the same wetlands that attract waterfowl. Accordingly, biologists and managers concerned with these groups of waterbirds share a common interest in wetland management. Hence, this section summarizes some basic approaches that illustrate how waterfowl managers can consider other species of waterbirds when implementing habitat management techniques. We also hope to show that emphasizing management of one group of waterbirds (i.e., waterfowl) rarely, if ever, excludes management of the others.

Shorebirds occur throughout the world, with about 50 species occurring in North America; hence, management can potentially benefit a large group of species. In Europe, the term "waders" typically designates shorebirds in the order Charadriiformes, especially the Scolopacidae (88 species of sandpipers) and Charadriidae (86 species of plovers). From a management perspective, shorebirds exploit shallow water ranging from 0 to 18 cm, but about 70% of all species prefer depths less than 10 cm (Helmers 1992, Collazo et al. 2002). Most species also prefer areas where vegetative cover is less than 25% (see Helmers 1993). Within these habitats, macroinvertebrates are a key food source, but shorebirds also consume the seeds of aquatic plants (Baldassarre and Fisher 1984, Davis and Smith 1998).

Most shorebird management targets migration habitat because the majority of the species breed in arctic habitats, which are generally less threatened than nonbreeding sites. Hence, protection of key winter and migration habitat is the strategy of the Western Hemisphere Shorebird Reserve Network

(see Myers et al. 1987) Begun in 1985, the Network included 57 sites in seven countries by May 2004. The program's operations are carried out by more than 250 organizations and agencies in these countries. Shorebirds often gather in great concentrations at such traditional stopover or staging areas. For example, nearly the entire global population of Red Knots (*Calidris canutus*) stops at Delaware Bay during their migrations along the Atlantic Coast (Myers 1986). A major component of shorebird management at these sites is to keep the birds free from human disturbances (Kate et al. 2003).

More specifically, habitat management for shorebirds focuses on seasonally flooded impoundments traditionally managed for waterfowl, as well as on the management of flooded agricultural fields (Helmers 1993). At these sites, effective management requires knowledge of migration schedules, as well as the foraging and niche requirements for the respective guilds of shorebirds (Rundle and Fredrickson 1981, Helmers 1992, Fredrickson 1996). Accordingly, several approaches are used to provide quality habitat for shorebirds (e.g., Helmers 1992).

The compatibility of waterfowl and shorebird management is evident in the North American Waterfowl Management Plan (see Chapter 11), which has expended funds to secure critical shorebird habitat in areas such as the Bay of Fundy in New Brunswick. The Plan also funded management and restoration activities at Cheyenne Bottoms in central Kansas, a stopover site for more than 45% of the North American shorebird population — and 90% for each of five species — east of the Rocky Mountains (Streeter et al. 1993).

Wading birds include the order Ciconiiformes, in which Ardeidae (65 species of herons, egrets, and bitterns), Threskiornithidae (33 species of ibises and spoonbills), and Ciconiidae (19 species of storks) represent important families. Other important wetland birds are in the order Gruiformes (215 species of cranes, rails, and allies), of which Rallidae (144 species of rails, gallinules, and coots) is by far the largest family. All species in these orders share habitat with waterfowl. However, little is known about managing habitat for rails, beyond protecting wetlands in general and emergent vegetation in particular (but see Tacha and Braun 1994).

Overall, habitat acquisition represents the major thrust in the conservation of wading birds. As with waterfowl, wetland complexes that provide a range of water depths are key components for managing waterbirds (see Reid 1993). Drawdowns scheduled during the breeding season for wading birds concentrate their prey, thereby increasing the foraging opportunities for adult birds to feed their nestlings (see Parsons 2002). Habitat protection at nesting colonies ("rookeries") of herons and other wading birds is also an obvious and critical component of management.

Control of Noxious and Exotic Vegetation

One means for controlling undesirable vegetation in managed wetlands is achieved using the same methods that encourage the growth of desirable species: (1) the timing and duration of drawdowns, and (2) the depth of reflooding. For example, a winter-long drawdown, which exposes plants to freezing and desiccation, may control undesirable submergent and floating-leaved vegetation (Nichols 1974). Other examples might be cited, but the crucial requirement is to understand the life history of the problem plant so that seasonally vulnerable points might be determined. At Horicon Marsh in Wisconsin, for example, detailed life-history studies of broad-leaved cattails determined that the plants' carbohydrate reserves were lowest in late June; hence, that period was the time cattails were most vulnerable to control measures (Linde et al. 1976).

An essential skill concerns the ability to identify plants in the seedling stage when control methods often are particularly effective. Indeed, submergence of seedlings for even 2–3 days may retard growth and even kill plants (Fredrickson and Taylor 1982). Flooding is not a cure-all, however, because the seedlings of desirable species also may be killed along with those of less desirable vegetation. Nonetheless, drawdowns followed by flooding are an effective means of controlling some kinds of woody plants that often diminish the value of wetlands as wildlife habitat.

For some undesirable woody plants (e.g., willows, *Salix* spp.; ashes, *Fraxinus* spp.; and cottonwoods, *Populus* spp.) control can be achieved with a drawdown followed by mowing, disking, or chopping. The remaining stubble then should be flooded to create anaerobic conditions, all of which may be necessary to completely rid a site of the unwanted vegetation. In contrast, shallow flooding of mature plants actually may stimulate growth and worsen the problem (Fredrickson and Taylor 1982). Cattle can provide an effective means of browsing and trampling vegetation, which can create openings as well as expose the seed bank of more desirable plants (Severson and Boldt 1978, Duncan and d'Herbes 1982).

Controlled burning is another useful tool for managing undesirable vegetation (see Kirby et al. 1988, Nyman and Chabreck 1995). Burning also may stimulate growth of desirable species, and because fires consume dense litter, previously unavailable food resources may be exposed. In the brackish marshes of coastal Louisiana, for example, fall and winter burning of Olney three-square bulrush is a major management practice; fire may stimulate new growth and increases the availability of the rhizomes for wintering Lesser Snow Geese by removing the thick litter accumulated during the previous growing season (Perkins 1968). In fact, Snow Geese react so quickly to the increased availability of the rhizomes that the birds may begin feeding in still-smoking areas of the burned marsh (Yancey 1964; Fig. 10-17). However, other studies in the coastal marshes of Louisiana concluded that fire may not play a strong role in the establishment of Olney three-square bulrush; also, the vegetative characteristics in marshes burned during winter did not differ from unburned marshes by the end of the following summer (Gabrey et al. 2001). Marsh birds responded to the dramatic change in habitat structure immediately after a burn, but the response was short lived because of the rapid recovery of the vegetation (Gabrey et al. 1999). These studies recommended that burning should create a patchy distribution at both the local and landscape level to achieve management objectives for waterfowl yet still provide habitat for nontarget species. In northeast Minnesota, shearing followed by burning effectively controlled shrubs and concurrently promoted emergent vegetation, but bird communities were altered accordingly (Hanowski et al. 1999).

Generally, burns made during late summer and early fall produce the best kills of woody vegetation; fires at these times are especially hot, and the substrate may be dry enough to extend the damage to root systems. Nonetheless, a slow, hot burn during winter killed 75% of the paper birch (*Betula papyrifera*) and willows on the Germania Marsh Wildlife Management Area in southern Wisconsin (Linde 1969). In the Okefenokee Swamp of Georgia, a hot burn reportedly killed most shrubs (Anderson and Best 1982). However, in marshes along Great Salt Lake in Utah, fires were not hot enough to burn into sediments and kill broad-leaved cattail, alkali bulrush, or hardstem bulrush (Smith and Kadlec 1985b). If a hot burn cannot be achieved, repeated annual burns of lesser intensity may control invading woody vegetation, but the rule-of-thumb is to burn when the fuel supply and weather conditions

Figure 10-17. Burning, an effective management technique widely used in the coastal wetlands of Louisiana, enhances plant growth and increases the availability of tubers and rhizomes for Lesser Snow Geese. Photo courtesy of the Rockefeller Wildlife Refuge.

will produce a hot, killing fire. Lastly, in wetlands with accumulations of peat, hot fires set during prolonged dry periods often burn out kettle-like depressions and other openings, some of which may reach depths of about 45 cm and later fill with water. Many of these sites subsequently produce desirable waterfowl food plants (Lynch 1941, Ward 1968, Linde 1969).

Komarek (1965) long ago demonstrated that fire increases the mineral and protein content of terrestrial grasses, and fire also may affect the nutritive quality of wetland plants. Potassium, calcium, phosphorus, magnesium, and chlorides in ash deposits become available for wetland plants after fires (Yancy 1964). At Ogden Bay Waterfowl Management Area on the east shore of Great Salt Lake, controlled burning increased the protein content of cattails, saltgrass, and hardstem bulrush (Smith et al. 1984). Waterfowl and muskrats later grazed some of the burned areas in preference to unburned sites, responding either to the increased nutritional quality of the food

plants or better foraging conditions such as increased food availability (Smith and Kadlec 1985c). Fire can also increase seed production of some wetland plants (Linde 1969).

Fire is not a cure-all, however, but should be seen as a management option that can be very effective under the right circumstances. Fire can greatly enhance wetland habitat, but it can have the opposite effect if done incorrectly. Overall, managers do best to (1) consider all possible consequences of each potential burn, (2) consult with experienced personnel beforehand, and (3) obtain a general background in fire ecology and management (see Wright and Bailey 1982).

Potholes also can be blasted in wetlands overgrown with dense, impenetrable, and often monotypic vegetation. Dynamite was initially used for this purpose, but an ammonium nitrate-fuel oil mixture (ANFO) now is preferred; ANFO produces the same results as dynamite, but it is about 90% cheaper and

Figure 10-18. Explosives offer an effective means for diversifying wetland habitat, especially where dense stands of monotypic emergent vegetation dominate the plant community. Photo courtesy of U.S. Forest Service.

much safer to store. A 23-kg charge of ANFO produces a depression 6–11 m in diameter and at least 0.8–1.8 m deep (Mathiak 1965). Such blasting can create the open-water areas necessary for a hemi-marsh (Fig. 10-18), thereby providing habitat for breeding ducks and muskrats, especially during winter in shallow marshes (Strohmeyer and Fredrickson 1967). However, in one of the few studies evaluating the response of waterfowl to blasted potholes, Hoffman (1970) found that 86% of the use at 25 such potholes at the Delta Marsh in Manitoba occurred on the elevated spoil bank surrounding the ponds; the ponds also received little use after initial arrival of waterfowl in early spring. Thus, ponds functioned more as loafing sites and areas where pairs — especially Blue-winged Teal and Northern Shovelers — could isolate themselves early in the breeding season; pochards rarely used the ponds. Hence, the benefits seem limited in blasting ponds in thick stands of vegetation to create open water.

Other fairly common management techniques are level ditching and mowing. Level ditches are ungraded ditches closed at both ends. They are established to improve cover–water ratios in dense vegetation, which can increase the quality of brood-rearing and courtship habitat for waterfowl as well as increase furbearer production and aquatic plant growth (Atlantic Waterfowl Council 1972, Broschart and Linder 1986). However, the utility of level ditching may be limited because it often creates deep,

open water areas subjected to the same habitat limitations as blasted potholes. Mowing is another technique sometimes used in coordination with drawdown to control undesirable emergent vegetation, especially bulrushes and cattails; mowing also can stimulate production of aquatic macroinvertebrates (see below).

Undesirable plants may occur locally or be restricted to unique areas, but others are spread over much larger regions or even across the continent. Control methods for some of these species are well known and effective, but other species remain especially troublesome because no effective means of control have been discovered. Unfortunately, some of these plants establish dense, monotypic stands that exclude vegetation more valuable as food and cover for wildlife. Moreover, they also thrive in a wide range of environmental conditions and spread prolifically by both vegetative and sexual reproduction; such adaptability further hinders effective controls. A few of these species are native plants, but most are exotic species. Whether native or exotic, however, they are highly competitive species capable of displacing other vegetation. We consider here some of these species more fully; they were selected because (1) they represent plants wetland managers are most likely to encounter, and (2) they provide examples of how detailed life-history information is necessary in order to initiate effective management.

Cattail: Cattails are distributed worldwide and often dominate wetlands. Cattails serve as a major food of muskrats and as important resting, nesting, and escape cover for several species of waterfowl and other marsh birds. Conversely, dense, monotypic stands of cattails markedly reduce habitat diversity; other plants — and much of the wildlife — are scarce or eliminated from cattail-choked wetlands.

In the 1970s, extensive studies of cattails were undertaken at the Horicon Marsh in Wisconsin, where expansive, monotypic stands had developed over much of the 12,150-ha wetland. Our summary is based on this research, primarily from the works of Linde et al. (1976) on phenology and Beule (1979) on methods of control.

Cattails largely spread during summer when sprouts are produced on new rhizomes; the sprouts continue growing until late fall. After overwintering in a dormant condition, the sprouts again become active the following spring, growing at a rate of nearly 0.6 cm/day. Leaves emerge from these shoots in early spring; a single shoot may produce 10–15 leaves, which grow for 17–26 days. Maximum leaf growth — up to 18.5 cm/day — is achieved by early summer and, remarkably, the total biomass may reach 33,600 kg/ha (Weller 1975). Cattail seeds also germinate on mudflats, and a single pistillate spike is capable of producing 125,000 new plants; the seeds remain 70% viable after 5.5 years of dry storage. Thus, with such aggressive reproductive capabilities as well as the capacity of mature plants to tolerate various water depths, soil types, salinities, and pH, cattails may dominate a wetland community.

Rhizomes are an important part of cattail anatomy. These structures tie several plants together in an underground network in which clones are reproduced vegetatively; these clones spread outwardly, invading new areas. Rhizomes also serve as the principal storage area for carbohydrates, which are essential for renewed plant growth in spring. Carbohydrate storage peaks by late summer (more than 60% dry mass), but reaches a low (less than 10% dry mass) late in June, which corresponds with the emergence and shedding of the pistillate spathe (see Linde et al. 1976). Another important feature is that the rhizome exists under largely anaerobic conditions; hence, aerenchyma cells in its tissues are connected to similar cells in the aerial shoot. This adaptation allows the rhizomes to receive some oxygen even during winter.

As we have stressed, control methods should focus on points in the life cycle where plants are particularly vulnerable. For cattails, one control method is to cut plants during late fall or winter (i.e., when plants are dormant), a procedure readily accomplished by mowing on top of ice. Winter mowing is effective because the oxygen supply reaching the rhizomes is reduced, weakening the plants for killing if the stand is flooded with 18 cm of water the following spring and summer. Cutting in summer, after leaf growth is complete and when carbohydrate storage is minimal, also is effective if water floods the cut stubble throughout the next growing season (see Weller 1975, Beule 1979, Kaminski et al. 1985). Murkin and Ward (1980) determined that cutting and flooding stems in spring killed cattail effectively. Permanent flooding to depths greater than 30 cm also will control cattails by reducing the number of shoots produced from rhizomes. In Saskatchewan and Manitoba, cutting followed by flooding decreased the shoot density of cattail as well as two species of bulrushes by some 50–97% (Kaminski et al. 1985). At Agassiz National Wildlife Refuge in Minnesota, cattails were eliminated after 4–5 years of continuous flooding at a depth of 30–38 cm (Harris and Marshall 1963). Similarly, van der Valk (2000) reported significant control when cattail was flooded with 1 m of water for 2 years. High water levels also make cattails more accessible to muskrats, whose use of the plants for food and house construction may markedly reduce cattail stands (Mathiak 1971). As discussed earlier in this chapter, muskrat herbivory may remove significant amounts of vegetation to the point of creating the lake-marsh stage of wetland development.

Mechanical or chemical treatments also can control cattails under some circumstances, particularly with glyphosate herbicides (Solberg and Higgins 1993, Linz et al. 1997, Homan et al. 2003), but herbicides largely are recommended only after other measures have been exhausted. Dead plants remain standing for at least 1 year after chemical treatment and, in Iowa, effective treatment with the herbicide Dalpon was achieved only where cattails had been previously cut underwater (Weller 1975). Burning in the fall or spring will reduce the aboveground biomass of cattail in the following growing season (Saenz and Smith 1995), and cattail can be killed when the burned stalks are completely flooded (Ball 1985).

Purple Loosestrife: Purple loosestrife (*Lythrum salicaria*) is an erect, colorful, herbaceous perennial native to Eurasia. The plant was established in the late 1880s in North America, where it first appeared in estuaries of the Northeast. Today, purple loosestrife is widespread in freshwater wetlands of the northeastern United States and southeastern Canada, and it continues spreading from scattered locations in the Midwest, Pacific Northwest, California, and south-central Canada (Hight and Drea 1991). The steady spread of this plant has seriously contributed to the decline of native plants and wildlife values in many wetlands (see Thompson et al. 1987, Blossey et al. 2001).

Purple loosestrife is extremely prolific. One mature plant may produce 2.7 million seeds, which remain viable for at least 3 years and probably longer; seeds disperse by drifting in moving water (Thompson et al. 1987). The plants also spread from adventitious buds on lateral roots, and both the plants and their seeds thrive over a wide range of environmental and soil conditions. Germination is best on soils of neutral pH, but seeds also germinate from a low of pH 4.0 to a high of pH 9.1 (Shamsi and Whitehead 1974, Thompson et al. 1987).

Purple loosestrife generally prefers disturbed moist-soil areas where its aggressive growth habits and prolific reproductive capacity readily establish dense monotypic stands that often replace native communities of wetland plants. In these cases, wetland quality is markedly diminished by the loss of diversity in plants and animals. Some loosestrife stands have remained viable for more than 20 years and replaced 50% or more of the biomass in those wetland plant communities (Thompson et al. 1987). Monotypic stands of loosestrife have contributed to the dramatic decline of several wetland plants such as an inland population of dwarf spike rush (*Eleocharis parvula*) in New York (Malecki and Rawinski 1985). Diminished numbers of vertebrates such as the bog turtle (*Clemmys muhlenbergi*) and Black Tern also have been linked with invasions of purple loosestrife (Thompson et al. 1987). In fact, based on an intensive study at Montezuma National Wildlife Refuge in New York, only Red-winged Blackbirds (*Agelaius phoeniceus*) commonly used sites dominated by purple loosestrife (Rawinski and Malecki 1984). Bird density was high in stands of purple loosestrife growing in wetlands on Saginaw Bay on Lake Huron, Michigan, but avian diversity, as measured by the Shannon-Weaver Index, was low (0.22) in comparison to seven other types of wetland vegetation (Whitt et al. 1999). Purple loosestrife also is of low palatability for white-tailed deer, muskrats, cattle, and other herbivorous mammals.

Management of purple loosestrife is difficult, but some control may be accomplished by chemical,

cultural, and biological means; however, the effect is seldom long-lasting (Blossey et al. 2001). Chemically, a systemic herbicide, glyphosate (*N*-[phosphonomethyl] glycine), proved effective against loosestrife in the 1970s. Glyphosate is especially useful because it is effective at low concentrations, offers little risk of bioaccumulation, and can achieve nearly 100% control when applied to late-flowering plants at rates as low as 1.7 kg/ha; spraying in mid to late summer largely eliminates seedlings the following growing season (Malecki and Rawinski 1985). In 1982, the formulation of glyphosate was modified for use over water and marketed under the trade name of Rodeo, which has proved effective for controlling both loosestrife and other troublesome aquatic plants (e.g., cattails; see Solberg and Higgins 1993). In Minnesota, the herbicide 2,4-D reduced the density of purple loosestrife seedlings by 94% (Welling and Becker 1993).

Cultural controls emphasize cutting loosestrife plants in late summer and then flooding the stubble to a depth greater than 50 cm, but these measures may be hard to implement because of the difficulty of sustaining high water levels. Also, stabilized deep water may adversely affect desirable species of emergent vegetation and, in fact, may facilitate transport and spread of loosestrife propagules (Malecki and Rawinski 1985). Hence, although water-level manipulations are potentially effective, managers often do not have such an option available on many loosestrife-infested areas; even if they do, such a "cure" actually may eliminate some wetland plant diversity already present. However, in southern Ontario, Haworth-Brockman et al. (1991) found little effect in cutting plants 10 cm below water level during varying times over the summer and then flooding them to a depth of 40–50 cm. Elsewhere, seedlings cut 21 days after germination following a drawdown reduced seedling density to 8 plants/treatment compared with 60 plants in an unclipped control; this method also prevented reestablishment of sprouts (Gabor and Murkin 1990).

Purple loosestrife also may be controlled effectively by disking and then planting infected areas with a replacement species, or by seeding exposed mudflats. In New York, Japanese millet (*Echinochloa crusgalli*) and reed canary grass (*Phalaris arundinacea*) were most successful, but the latter species is itself a problem plant in most wetlands where it occurs (Paveglio and Kilbride 2000). Japanese millet was especially useful on mudflats because its seedlings effectively overshadow loosestrife seedlings (Rawinski 1982). In Minnesota experimental plantings of Italian ryegrass (*Lolium perenne*) reduced the density of purple loosestrife by 72%, but Japanese millet produced similar results (Welling and Becker 1993). As with chemical controls or water-level manipulations, however, establishing replacement vegetation is an expensive means of controlling loosestrife and may not be possible on many infested areas. Hence, wherever possible, a good management strategy is to aggressively control recently established populations of purple loosestrife before scattered groups of plants can begin to dominate existing herbaceous communities.

However, biological control emerged as the method of choice for dealing with purple loosestrife. This method relies on identifying and introducing controlling agents from the plant's native habitat in Eurasia. Studies in Europe identified 15 species of insects that are host-specific to loosestrife, none of which occur in North America (Hight and Drea 1991, Manguin et al. 1993). The U.S. Fish and Wildlife Service, in cooperation with the U.S. Department of Agriculture, then tested several of these insects and determined that a root-mining weevil (*Hylobius transversovittatus*) and two leaf-eating beetles (*Galerucella calmariensis* and *G. pusilla*) were potentially suitable for introduction. In 1992, populations of these three insects were released in seven states (Malecki et al. 1993); subsequent evaluations revealed the efficacy of these beetles as a means to control purple loosestrife (Blossey et al. 1994a, 1994b; Blossey et al. 2001). Management involves (1) rearing the beetles en masse in captivity and (2) transporting and releasing the beetles in areas where loosestrife requires control (Blossey and Hunt 1999, Blossey et al. 2000). The two species of *Galerucella* now have been released in more than 1,500 wetlands in 33 states (Blossey et al. 2001), and subsequent evaluations demonstrate the efficacy of these beetles for controlling purple loosestrife. However, this or other biological controls are not likely to eliminate purple loosestrife, but instead should reduce the occurrence and dominance of this unwanted plant in the wetland communities of North America (see Blossey et al. 2001 for a full review).

Common Reed or Phragmites: Common reed is a tall perennial grass that may be the most widespread flowering plant in the world. As with cattail and purple loosestrife, phragmites can establish dense monotypic stands that radically reduce the quality of wetlands as habitat for wildlife and other plants.

Phragmites has been controlled by cutting the stems underwater (Martin 1953, Husak 1978), but this method is not feasible in many areas because phragmites grows well on unflooded soils and in a wide range of water depths. Control has been achieved in coastal areas where phragmites can be flooded with highly saline water (25–35 ppt). Burning phragmites in late summer is effective because fires at that time often kill the roots, whereas spring burning usually only removes dead growth from the previous year (Ward 1942, Ward 1968). Late-summer burns also can create holes in the peat layer, and thus increase cover–water ratios.

The herbicide Rodeo also is a widely applied and useful means for control of phragmites. In Delaware, an initial application over a broad range of wetland habitats achieved reductions of 80-99% when Rodeo was applied at a rate of 4.7 L/ha during late September. A second spraying at 2.4 L/ha prevented regrowth before more desirable vegetation could be established on the sprayed sites (Jones and Lehman 1987). Helicopter application for the two treatments cost $221/ha. Winter burning of the phragmites killed by the first treatment also was recommended to keep the dense litter from inhibiting the growth of other vegetation.

Researchers later explored the feasibility for treating phragmites with a biological control (Tewksbury et al. 2002). In Europe, more than 170 herbivores feed on phragmites, some which cause significant damage. In contrast, only 26 species are known to feed on phragmites in North America, and only five of those species are native. Perhaps because of the damage caused by such a large number of herbivores, phragmites communities in Europe may be held in check wherein they are often regarded as important wildlife habitat (see Hudec and Stastny 1978, Bibby and Lunn 1982). In North America, however, phragmites often forms dense monotypic stands that generally are not good wildlife habitat, certainly not for waterfowl and most other waterbirds (see Benoit and Askins 1999).

In Europe, the rhizomes of phragmites are significantly damaged by several species of Lepidoptera, one of which (*Rhizedra lutosa*) already occurs in North America. The chloropid fly, *Platycephala planifrons*, also damages phragmites. Hence, Tewksbury et al. (2002) proposed that these and associated species be evaluated as potential agents for biological control of phragmites in North America, and that research is currently underway.

Reed Canary Grass: Reed canary grass (hereafter, canarygrass) was introduced into North America by Euro-American settlers and now occurs throughout the continental United States and Canada (Anderson 1961). Canarygrass grows under a variety of conditions, but optimal growth occurs on moist soils; hence, canarygrass is a significant threat to wetland habitat. Infestations of canarygrass occur quickly and expand rapidly because the plants produce vigorous rhizome growth within one growing season, and the seeds of canarygrass are capable of germination immediately upon ripening (Kilbride and Paveglio 1999). As a result, extensive monotypic stands of canarygrass are quickly established and persist for decades, which obviously decreases the diversity of other wetland species (see Paveglio and Kilbride 2000).

On seasonal wetlands in Minnesota, applications of the herbicide Rodeo achieved complete control (100%) of canarygrass, but seedlings germinated the following year (Lyford 1993). In Washington, Rodeo, followed by disking, controlled canarygrass, but a second application of herbicide was necessary in the next growing season to suppress new plants that emerged from viable rhizomes (Kilbride and Paveglio 1999). However, the follow-up herbicide applications were not necessary if water levels could be raised. Moreover, if high water levels can be maintained throughout late winter and early spring, re-infestation of canarygrass can be prevented and more desirable species of wetland plants can be established after a drawdown in late spring–early summer. Based on these results, Paveglio and Kilbride (2000) advocate treating canarygrass only on wetlands where managers can control water levels.

Other Exotic Wetland Vegetation: Many other species of exotic plants are widely established in aquatic environments in North America and elsewhere around the world, and it would be impossible to address each species here. Generally, however, submerged and floating-leaved species are especially troublesome, including hydrilla from Africa, water hyacinth from Central and South America, Eurasian watermilfoil (*Myriophyllum spicatum*) from its namesake range, water chestnut from Asia, and alligator weed and Brazilian elodea (*Egeria densa*), both from South America. Unfortunately, control of these and similar plants so far has largely been possible only with herbicides, especially Rodeo (Hammer 1992), or by mechanical harvests and removal of the plants themselves. As we have already discussed, a few of these species (e.g., hydrilla) harbor high populations of macroinvertebrates and thus may be useful to waterfowl, but most are subject to control where wildlife is managed. Moreover, these plants commonly impede sport and commercial boat traffic, decrease recreation, diminish overall plant diversity, increase transpiration, and reduce the aesthetic value of waterways. Various agencies (e.g., transportation) therefore may share with wildlife managers a mutual interest in the control of exotic wetland vegetation.

Waterfowl managers often express their concern when grass carp (*Ctenopharyngodon idella*) are introduced to control exotic vegetation because the fish also reduce the biomass and diversity of native aquatic plants. For example, after grass carp were released in Guntersville Reservoir in Alabama, the native macrophytes were virtually eliminated, but the exotic Eurasian watermilfoil remained unaffected (McKnight and Hepp 1995, Benedict and Hepp 2000). Grass carp have been introduced elsewhere in the world (e.g., New Zealand), where they are also likely to adversely affect waterfowl habitats (Williams 1985).

As with phragmites and other emergent species, insects represent a potential means for controlling unwanted submerged vegetation. For example, the aquatic weevil, *Euhrychiopsis lecontei*, from Europe is a potential agent for the biological control of Eurasian watermilfoil in North America (Mazzei et al. 1999). Several other pathogens may control hydrilla (Shabana et al. 2003), including a fly larvae that effectively reduces photosynthesis and therefore seems likely kill the plants (Doyle et al. 2002). Indeed, literally hundreds of potential plant pathogens might be harnessed as agents to control undesirable aquatic plants (Joye 1990). Worldwide, more than 350 species of insects and other pathogens have been deployed in about 1,200 programs to control some 135 species of plants (Julien and Griffiths 1998).

CONCLUDING STATEMENT

Wetland management has emerged as a science-guided discipline whose complexity becomes increasingly apparent with each new study. Perceptions associated with management changed when new information about the importance of wetlands became available in the 1970s and 1980s. Wetland scientists and, perhaps more importantly, society at large now recognize the values and functions of wetlands for biodiversity, flood control, recreation, aesthetics, and water quality — in addition to their long-recognized importance as habitat for waterfowl and other waterbirds (see Mitsch and Gosselink 2000). The implications of this information for human welfare — as well as for wildlife — helped promulgate the spectrum of local, state, national, and international regulations and treaties now protecting wetland ecosystems.

Hands-off protection is not always enough, however, as many wetlands eventually will require various forms of proactive management, whether these concern habitat manipulations or governance under new policies and regulations. Unwanted vegetation may require vigorous control, whereas more desirable species or communities may flourish with careful manipulations, especially of water levels. In the future, science-guided and experiential management may create new and better patterns of vegetation and water in wetland environments.

We emphasize that there are seldom step-by-step "rules" or consistently "right" answers governing many situations, perhaps excepting the recognition that wetland protection without management is too often the wrong approach. Our goal in this chapter has been to set forth some guiding principles for wetland management in the hope that these might stimulate deeper familiarity with the many sources offering more specific management prescriptions. If a common thread has appeared in the fabric of this chapter, it is one that stresses the importance of providing and managing wetland complexes — those landscapes with various sizes and types of wetlands. Therein lies the cornerstone of wetland conservation everywhere.

LITERATURE CITED

Adamus, P. R., E. J. Clairain, Jr., R. D. Smith, and R. E. Young. 1987. Wetland evaluation technique (WET). Volume II: methodology. U.S. Army Corps of Engineers, Vicksburg, Mississippi.

Alisauskas, R. T., C. D. Ankney, and E. E. Klaas. 1988. Winter diets and nutrition of midcontinental Lesser Snow Geese. Journal of Wildlife Management 52:403–414.

Anderson, D. E. 1961. Taxonomy and distribution of the genus *Phalaris*. Iowa State Journal of Science 36:1–96.

Anderson, J. T., and L. M. Smith. 2000. Invertebrate response to moist-soil management of playa wetlands. Ecological Applications 10:550–558.

Anderson, P. B., and G. R. Best. 1982. Fire in Okefenokee Swamp: successional response of a young cypress community. Bulletin of the Ecological Society of America 63:205.

Arner, D. H., E. D. Norwood, and B. M. Teels. 1974. Comparison of aquatic ecosystems in two national waterfowl refuges. Proceedings of the Southeastern Association of Game and Fish Commissioners 28:456–467.

Aselmann, I., and P. J. Crutzen. 1989. Global distribution of natural freshwater wetlands and rice paddies, their net primary productivity, seasonality and possible methane emissions. Journal of Atmospheric Chemistry 8:307–358.

Atlantic Waterfowl Council. 1972. Techniques handbook of waterfowl habitat development and management. Atlantic Waterfowl Council, Bethany Beach, Delaware.

Baldassarre, G. A. 1980. Residual seeds as potential spring waterfowl foods in small, man-made impoundments. Prairie Naturalist 12:1–8.

Baldassarre, G. A., and F. Arengo. 1998. A review of the ecology and conservation of Caribbean Flamingos in Yucatan, Mexico. Waterbirds 23 (Special Publication 1):70–79.

Baldassarre, G. A., and D. H. Fisher. 1984. Food habits of fall migrant shorebirds on the Texas High Plains. Journal of Field Ornithology 55:220–229.

Ball, J. P. 1985. Marsh management by water level manipulation or other natural techniques: a community approach. Pages 263–277 *in* H. H. Prince and F. M. D'Itri, editors. Coastal wetlands. Lewis Publishing, Chelsea, Michigan.

Batzer, D., R. D. Rader, and S. A. Wissinger, editors. 1999. Invertebrates in freshwater wetlands. John Wiley & Sons, New York.

Bell, C. H., and P. Ward. 1984. Delta Waterfowl Research Station. Pages 321–328 *in* A. S. Hawkins, R. C. Hanson, H. K. Nelson, and M. M. Reeves, editors. Flyways: pioneering waterfowl management in North America. U.S. Fish and Wildlife Service, Washington, D.C.

Bellrose, F. C. 1941. Duck food plants of the Illinois River Valley. Illinois Natural History Survey Bulletin 21:237–280.

Benedict, R. J., and G. R. Hepp. 2000. Wintering waterbird use of two aquatic plant habitats in a southern reservoir. Journal of Wildlife Management 64:269–278.

Benoit, L. K., and R. A. Askins. 1999. Impact of the spread of *Phragmites* on the distribution of birds in Connecticut tidal marshes. Wetlands 19:194–208.

Benson, D., and D. Foley. 1956. Waterfowl use of small, man-made wildlife marshes in New York State. New York Fish and Game Journal 3:217–224.

Beule, J. D. 1979. Control and management of cattails in southeastern Wisconsin wetlands. Wisconsin Department of Natural Resources Technical Bulletin 112.

Bibby, C. J., and J. Lunn. 1982. Conservation of reed beds and their avifauna in England and Wales. Biological Conservation 23:167–186.

Bird, J. A., G. S. Pettygrove, and J. M. Eadie. 2000. The impact of waterfowl foraging on the decomposition of rice straw: mutual benefits for rice growers and waterfowl. Journal of Applied Ecology 37:728–741.

Blossey, B., D. Eberts, E. Morrison, and T. R. Hunt. 2000. Mass rearing the weevil *Hylobius transversovittatus* (Coleoptera: Curculionidae), biological control agent of *Lythrum salicaria* on semiartificial diet. Journal of Economic Entomology 93:1644–1656.

Blossey, B., and T. R. Hunt. 1999. Mass rearing methods for *Galerucella calmariensis* and *G. pusilla* (Coleoptera: Chrysomelidae), biological control agents of *Lythrum salicaria* (Lythraceae). Journal of Economic Entomology 92:325–334.

Blossey, B., D. Schroeder, S. D. Hight, and R. A. Malecki. 1994a. Host specificity and environmental impact of the weevil *Hylobius transversovittatus*, a biological control agent of purple loosestrife. Weed Science 42:128–133.

Blossey, B., D. Schroeder, S. D. Hight, and R. A. Malecki. 1994b. Host specificity and environmental impact of two leaf beetles (*Galerucella calmariensis* and *G. pusilla*) for biological control of purple loosestrife. Weed Science 42:134–140.

Blossey, B., L. C. Skinner, and J. Taylor. 2001. Impact and management of purple loosestrife (*Lythrum salicaria*) in North America. Biodiversity and Conservation 10:1787–1807.

Bolen, E. G. 1964. Plant ecology of spring-fed salt marshes in western Utah. Ecological Monographs 34:143–166.

Bolen, E. G., J. W. Bennett, and C. Cottam. 1975. Some ecological effects of lotus on submersed vegetation in southern Texas. Southwestern Naturalist 20:205–214.

Brinson, M. M. 1993. A hydrogeomorphic classification for wetlands. U.S. Army Corps of Engineers, Wetlands Research Program Technical Report WRP-DE-4.

Broadfoot, W. M., and H. L. Williston. 1973. Flooding effects on southern forests. Journal of Forestry 71:584–587.

Broschart, M. R., and R. L. Linder. 1986. Aquatic invertebrates in level ditches and adjacent emergent marsh in a South Dakota wetland. Prairie Naturalist 18:167–178.

Brown, M., and J. J. Dinsmore. 1986. Implications of marsh size and isolation for marsh bird management. Journal of Wildlife Management 50:392–397.

Bush, G. 1989. Presidential address. International Waterfowl Symposium 6:6–9.

Cahoon, W. G. 1953. Commercial carp removal at Lake Mattamuskeet, North Carolina. Journal of Wildlife Management 17:312–317.

Chabreck, R. H. 1972. Vegetation, water and soil characteristics of the Louisiana coastal region. Louisiana Agricultural Experiment Station Bulletin 664.

Chabreck, R. H. 1988. Coastal marshes. University of Minnesota Press, Minneapolis.

Chamberlain, E. B., Jr. 1948. Ecological factors influencing the growth and management of certain waterfowl food plants on Back Bay National Wildlife Refuge. Transactions of the North American Wildlife Conference 13:347–355.

Clements, F. E. 1916. Plant succession. Carnegie Institute of Washington, Publication 242.

Collazo, J. A., D. A. O'Harra, and C. A. Kelly. 2002. Accessible habitat for shorebirds: factors influencing its availability and conservation implications. Waterbirds 25 (Special Publication 2):13–24.

Cook, A. H., and C. F. Powers. 1958. Early biochemical changes in the soils and waters of artificially created marshes in New York. New York Fish and Game Journal 5:9–65.

Cottam, C., J. J. Lynch, and A. L. Nelson. 1944. Food habits and management of American Sea Brant. Journal of Wildlife Management 8:36–56.

Cowardin, L. M. 1969. Use of flooded timber by waterfowl at the Montezuma National Wildlife Refuge. Journal of Wildlife Management 33:829–842.

Cowardin, L. M., V. Carter, F. C. Golet, and E. T. LaRoe. 1979. Classification of wetlands and deepwater habitats of the United States. U.S. Fish and Wildlife Service, FWS/OBS-79/31.

Dahl, T. E. 1990. Wetlands losses in the United States, 1780's to 1980's. U.S. Fish and Wildlife Service, Washington, D.C.

Dahl, T. E. 2000. Status and trends of wetlands in the conterminous United States, 1986 to 1997. U.S. Fish and Wildlife Service, Washington, D.C.

Dahl, T. E., and C. E. Johnson. 1991. Status and trends of wetlands in the conterminous United States, mid-1970's to mid-1980's. U.S. Fish and Wildlife Service, Washington, D.C.

Dallmeier, F. 1991. Whistling-ducks as a manageable and sustainable resource in Venezuela: balancing economic costs and benefits. Pages 266–287 *in* J. G. Robinson and K. H. Redford, editors. Neotropical wildlife use and conservation. University of Chicago Press, Chicago.

Davis, C. A., and L. M. Smith. 1998. Ecology and management of migrant shorebirds in thePlaya Lakes Region of Texas. Wildlife Monographs 140.

Deller, A. S., and G. A. Baldassarre. 1998. Effects of flooding on the forest community in a greentree reservoir 18 years after flood cessation. Wetlands 18:90–99.

Department of Environmental Conservation. 1980. Freshwater wetlands maps and classification regulations. New York State Department of Environmental Conservation, Albany, New York.

Doyle, R. D., M. Grodowitz, R. M. Smart, and C. Owens. 2002. Impact of herbivory by *Hydrellia pakistanae* (Diptera: Ephydridae) on growth and photosynthetic potential of *Hydrilla verticillata*. Biological Control: Theory and Applications in Pest Management 24:221–229.

Dubovsky, J. A., and R. M. Kaminski. 1987. Estimates and chronology of waterfowl use of Mississippi catfish ponds. Proceedings of the Southeastern Association of Fish and Wildlife Agencies 41:247–265.

Dugan, P. 1993. Wetlands in danger. Reed International Books, London.

Duncan, P., and J. M. d'Herbes. 1982. The use of domestic herbivores in the management of wetlands for waterbirds in Camargue, France. Pages 51–66 *in* D. A. Scott, editor. Management of wetlands and their birds: a manual of wetland and waterfowl management. IWRB, Slimbridge, United Kingdom.

Eckblad, J. W., N. L. Peterson, K. Ostlie, and A. Temte. 1977. The morphometry, benthos, and sedimentation rates of a floodplain lake in pool 9 of the upper Mississippi River. American Midland Naturalist 97:433–443.

Erwin, R. M. 2002. Integrated management of waterbirds: beyond the conventional. Waterbirds 25 (Special Publication 2):5–12.

Esler, D. 1990. Avian community responses to hydrilla invasion. Wilson Bulletin 102:427–440.

Fairbairn, S. E., and J. J. Dinsmore. 2001. Local and landscape-level influences on wetland bird communities of the Prairie Pothole Region of Iowa, USA. Wetlands 21:41–47.

Fleury, B. E., and T. W. Sherry. 1995. Long-term population trends of colonial wading birds in the southern United States: the impact of crayfish aquaculture on Louisiana populations. Auk 112:613–632.

Frayer, W. E., T. J. Monahan, D. C. Bowden, and F. A. Graybill. 1983. Status and trends of wetlands and deepwater habitats in the conterminous United States, 1950's to 1970's. Department of Forest and Wood Sciences, Colorado State University, Ft. Collins.

Fredrickson, L. H. 1996. Moist-soil management, 30 years of field experimentation. International Waterfowl Symposium 7:168–177.

Fredrickson, L. H., and D. L. Batema. 1992. Greentree reservoir management handbook. Gaylord Memorial Laboratory, Wetland Management Series 1.

Fredrickson, L. H., and M. E. Heitmeyer. 1988. Waterfowl use of forested wetlands of the southern United States: an overview. Pages 307–323 *in* M. W. Weller, editor Waterfowl in winter. University of Minnesota Press, Minneapolis.

Fredrickson, L. H., S. L. King, and R. M. Kaminski. 2005. Ecology and management of bottomland hardwood systems: the state of our understanding. Gaylord Memorial Laboratory Publication 10.

Fredrickson, L. H., and M. K. Laubhan. 1996. Managing wetlands for wildlife. Pages 623–647 *in* T. A. Bookhout, editor. Research and management techniques for wildlife and habitats. Fifth edition. The Wildlife Society, Bethesda, Maryland.

Fredrickson, L. H., and F. A. Reid. 1990. Impacts of hydrologic alteration on management of freshwater wetlands. Pages 71–90 *in* J. M. Sweeney, editor. Management of dynamic ecosystems. North Central Section of The Wildlife Society, West Lafayette, Indiana.

Fredrickson, L. H., and T. S. Taylor. 1982. Management of seasonally flooded impoundments for wildlife. U.S. Fish and Wildlife Service Resource Publication 148.

Gabor, T. S., and H. R. Murkin. 1990. Effects of clipping purple loosestrife seedlings during a simulated wetland drawdown. Journal of Aquatic Plant Management 28:98–100.

Gabrey, S. W., A. D. Afton, and B. C. Wilson. 1999. Effects of winter burning and structural marsh management on vegetation and winter bird abundance in the Gulf Coast Chenier Plain, USA. Wetlands 19:594–606.

Gabrey, S. W., A. D. Afton, and B. C. Wilson. 2001. Effects of structural marsh management and winter burning on plant and bird communities during summer in the Gulf Coast Chenier Plain. Wildlife Society Bulletin 29:218–231.

Galinato, M. I., and A. G. van der Valk. 1986. Seed germination traits of annuals and emergents recruited during drawdowns in the Delta Marsh, Manitoba, Canada. Aquatic Botany 26:89–102.

Galli, A. E., C. F. Leck, and R. T. T. Forman. 1976. Avian distribution patterns in forest islands of different sizes in central New Jersey. Auk 93:356–364.

Gibbs, J. P. 1993. Importance of small wetlands for the persistence of local populations of wetland-associated animals. Wetlands 13:25–31.

Gibbs, J. P., J. R. Longcore, D. G. McAuley, and J. K. Ringelman. 1991. Use of wetland habitats by selected nongame water birds in Maine. U.S. Fish and Wildlife Service, Fish and Wildlife Research 9.

Gleason, H. A. 1917. The structure and development of the plant association. Bulletin of the Torrey Botanical Club 44:463–481.

Golet, F. C., and J. S. Larson. 1974. Classification of freshwater wetlands in the glaciated northeast. U.S. Fish and Wildlife Service Resource Publication 116.

Grado, S. C., R. M. Kaminski, I. A. Munn, and T. A. Tullos. 2001. Economic impacts of waterfowl hunting on public lands and at private lodges in the Mississippi Delta. Wildlife Society Bulletin 29:846–855.

Gray, M. J., R. M. Kaminski, G. Weerakkody, B. D. Leopold, and K. C. Jensen. 1999. Aquatic invertebrate and plant responses following mechanical manipulations of moist-soil habitat. Wildlife Society Bulletin 27:770–779.

Grover, A. M., and G. A. Baldassarre. 1995. Bird species richness within beaver ponds in south-central New York. Wetlands 15:108–118.

Haller, W. T. 1978. Hydrilla: a new and rapidly spreading aquatic weed problem. University of Florida Agricultural Experiment Station, Institute of Food and Agriculture Science Circular S-245.

Haller, W. T., and D. L. Sutton. 1975. Community structure and competition between hydrilla and vallisneria. Hyacinth Control Journal 13:48–50.

Hammer, D. A. 1992. Creating freshwater wetlands. Lewis Publishers, Chelsea, Michigan.

Hands, H. M., M. R. Ryan, and J. W. Smith. 1991. Migrant shorebird use of marsh, moist-soil, and flooded agricultural habitats. Wildlife Society Bulletin 19:457–464.

Hanowski, J. M., D. P. Christian, and M. C. Nelson. 1999. Response of breeding birds to shearing and burning in wetland brush ecosystems. Wetlands 19:584–593.

Harris, S. W., and W. H. Marshall. 1963. Ecology of water-level manipulations on a northern marsh. Ecology 44:331–343.

Haukos, D. A., and L. M. Smith. 1993. Moist-soil management of playa lakes for migrating and wintering ducks. Wildlife Society Bulletin 21:288–298.

Haworth-Brockman, M. J., H. R. Murkin, R. T. Clay, and E. Armson. 1991. Effects of underwater clipping of purple loosestrife in a southern Ontario wetland. Journal of Aquatic Plant Management 29:117–118.

Helmers, D. L. 1992. Shorebird management manual. Western Hemisphere Shorebird Reserve Network, Manomet, Massachusetts.

Helmers, D. L. 1993. Enhancing the management of wetlands for migrant shorebirds. Transactions of the North American Wildlife and Natural Resources Conference 58:335–344.

Hight, S. D., and J. J. Drea, Jr. 1991. Prospects for a classical biological control project against purple loosestrife (Lythrum salicaria). Natural Areas Journal 11:151–157.

Hobaugh, W. C., C. D. Stutzenbaker, and E. L. Flickinger. 1989. The rice prairies. Pages 367–383 in L. M. Smith, R. L. Pederson, and R. M. Kaminski, editors. Habitat management for migrating and wintering waterfowl in North America. Texas Tech University Press, Lubbock.

Hoffman, R. H. 1970. Waterfowl utilization of ponds blasted at Delta, Manitoba. Journal of Wildlife Management 34:586–593.

Hohman, W. L., T. M. Stark, and J. L. Moore. 1996. Food availability and feeding preferences of Fulvous Whistling-Ducks in Louisiana ricefields. Wilson Bulletin 108:137–150.

Homan, H. J., G. M. Linz, R. C. Carlson, and W. J. Bleier. 2003. Spring distribution of Ring-necked Pheasants (*Phasianus colchicus*) following a cattail reduction with glyphosate herbicide. Wildlife Research 30:159–166.

Horn, E. E., and L. L. Glasgow. 1964. Rice and waterfowl. Pages 435–443 *in* J. P. Linduska, editor. Waterfowl tomorrow. U.S. Government Printing Office, Washington, D.C.

Hubert, W. A., and J. N. Krull. 1973. Seasonal fluctuations of aquatic macroinvertebrates in Oakwood Bottoms greentree reservoir. American Midland Naturalist 90:177–185.

Hudec, K., and K. Stastny. 1978. Birds in the reedswamp ecosystem. Pages 366–372 *in* D. Dykyjova and J. Kvet, editors. Pond littoral ecosystems. Springer–Verlag, Berlin, Germany.

Huitink, G., and T. Siebenmorgen. 1996. Maintaining yield and grain quality. Pages 79–85 *in* R. S. Helms, editor. Rice production handbook. University of Arkansas Cooperative Extension Service Publication MP-192.

Huner, J. V., C. W. Jeske, and W. Norling. 2002. Managing agricultural wetlands for waterbirds in the coastal regions of Louisiana, U.S.A. Waterbirds 25 (Special Publication 2):66–78.

Hunt, G. S., and R. W. Lutz. 1959. Seed production by curly-leaved pondweed and its significance to waterfowl. Journal of Wildlife Management 23:405–408.

Husak, S. 1978. Control of reed and reed mace stands by cutting. Pages 404–408 *in* D. Dykyjova and J. Kvet, editors. Pond littoral ecosystems. Structure and functioning. Methods and results of quantitative ecosystem research in the Czechoslovakian IBP wetland project. Springer-Verlag, New York.

Ivey, G. L., J. E. Cornely, and B. D. Ehlers. 1998. Carp impacts on waterfowl at the Malheur National Wildlife Refuge, Oregon. Transactions of the North American Wildlife and Natural Resources Conference 63:66–74.

Jacobs, D. L. 1947. An ecological life-history of *Spirodela polyrhiza* (greater duckweed) with emphasis on the turion phase. Ecological Monographs 17:438–469.

Johnson, F. A., and F. Montalbano, III. 1984. Selection of plant communities by wintering waterfowl on Lake Okeechobee, Florida. Journal of Wildlife Management 48:174–178.

Johnson, F. A., and F. Montalbano, III. 1987. Considering waterfowl habitat in hydrilla control policies. Wildlife Society Bulletin 15:466–469.

Jones, W. L., and W. C. Lehman. 1987. Phragmites control and revegetation following aerial applications of glyphosate in Delaware. Pages 185–196 *in* W. R. Whitman and W. H. Meredith, editors. Proceedings of a symposium on waterfowl and wetlands management in the coastal zone of the Atlantic Flyway. Delaware Department of Natural Resources and Environmental Control and Delaware Coastal Management Program, Dover, Delaware.

Joye, G. F. 1990. Biological control of aquatic weeds with plant pathogens. American Chemical Society Symposium Series 439:155–174.

Julien, M. H., and M. W. Griffiths. 1998. Biological control of weeds. A world catalogue of agents and their target weeds. Fourth edition. CABI Publishing, Wallingford, United Kingdom.

Kadlec, J. A. 1962. Effects of a drawdown on a waterfowl impoundment. Ecology 43:267–281.

Kadlec, J. A., and L. M. Smith. 1989. The Great Basin marshes. Pages 451–474 *in* L. M. Smith, R. L. Pederson, and R. M. Kaminski, editors. Habitat management for migrating and wintering waterfowl in North America. Texas Tech University Press, Lubbock.

Kadlec, J. A., A. G. van der Valk, and H. R. Murkin. 2000. The MERP nutrient budgets. Pages 37–54 *in* H. R. Murkin, A. G. van der Valk, and W. R. Clark, editors. Prairie wetland ecology: the contribution of the Marsh Ecology Research Program. Iowa State University Press, Ames.

Kadlec, J. A., and W. A. Wentz. 1974. State-of-the-art survey and evaluation of marsh plant establishment techniques: induced and natural. School of Natural Resources, University of Michigan, Ann Arbor.

Kaminski, R. M., B. J. Davis, H. W. Essig, P. D. Gerard, and K. J. Reinecke. 2003. True metabolizable energy for Wood Ducks from acorns compared to other waterfowl foods. Journal of Wildlife Management 67:542–550.

Kaminski, R. M., H. R. Murkin, and C. E. Smith. 1985. Control of cattail and bulrush by cutting and flooding. Pages 253–262 *in* H. H. Prince and F. M. D'Itri, editors. Coastal wetlands. Lewis Publishers, Chelsea, Michigan.

Kaminski, R. M., and H. H. Prince. 1981. Dabbling duck and aquatic macroinvertebrate responses to manipulated wetland habitat. Journal of Wildlife Management 45:1–15.

Kate, T., R. G. Kvitek, and C. Bretz. 2003. Effects of human activity on the foraging behavior of Sanderlings *Calidris alba*. Biological Conservation 109:67–71.

Keith, L. B. 1961. A study of waterfowl ecology on small impoundments in southeastern Alberta. Wildlife Monographs 6.

Kerbes, R. H., P. M. Kotanen, and R. L. Jefferies. 1990. Destruction of wetland habitats by Lesser Snow Geese: a keystone species on the west coast of Hudson Bay. Journal of Applied Ecology 27:242–258.

Kilbride, K. M., and F. L. Paveglio. 1999. Integrated pest management to control reed canarygrass in seasonal wetlands of southwestern Washington. Wildlife Society Bulletin 27:292–297.

King, D. R., and G. S. Hunt. 1967. Effects of carp on vegetation in a Lake Erie marsh. Journal of Wildlife Management 31:181–188.

Kirby, R. E., S. J. Lewis, and T. N. Sexson. 1988. Fire in North American wetland ecosystems and fire–wildlife relations: an annotated bibliography. U.S. Fish and Wildlife Service Biological Report 88(1).

Knighton, N. D., compiler. 1985. Water impoundments for wildlife: a habitat management workshop. U.S. Forest Service, North Central Forest Experiment Station Technical Report NC-100.

Komarek, E. V., Sr. 1965. Fire ecology — grasslands and man. Proceedings of the Tall Timbers Fire Ecology Conference 4:169–220.

Krull, J. N. 1969. Seasonal occurrence of macroinvertebrates in a green-tree reservoir. New York Fish and Game Journal 16:119–124.

Krull, J. N. 1970. Aquatic plant–macroinvertebrate associations and waterfowl. Journal of Wildlife Management 34:707–718.

Kusler, J. A. 1983. Our national wetland heritage: a protection guidebook. Environmental Law Institute, Washington, D.C.

Laubhan, M. K., and L. H. Fredrickson. 1993. Integrated wetland management: concepts and opportunities. Transactions of the North American Wildlife and Natural Resources Conference 58:323–334.

Leitch, W. G., and R. M. Kaminski. 1985. Long-term wetland–waterfowl trends in Saskatchewan grassland. Journal of Wildlife Management 49:212–222.

Leopold, A. 1933. Game management. Charles Scribner's Sons, New York.

Linde, A. F. 1969. Techniques for wetland management. Wisconsin Department of Natural Resources Research Report 45.

Linde, A. F., T. Janisch, and D. Smith. 1976. Cattail — the significance of its growth, phenology and carbohydrate storage to its control and management. Wisconsin Department of Natural Resources Technical Bulletin 94.

Linz, G. M., D. L. Bergman, D. C. Blixt, and C. McMurl. 1997. Response of American Coots and Soras to herbicide-induced vegetation changes in wetlands. Journal of Field Ornithology 68:450–457.

Loesch, C. R., and R. M. Kaminski. 1989. Winter body-weight patterns of female Mallards fed agricultural seeds. Journal of Wildlife Management 53:1081–1087.

Low, J. B., and F. C. Bellrose, Jr. 1944. The seed and vegetative yield of waterfowl food plants in the Illinois River Valley. Journal of Wildlife Management 8:7–22.

Lyford, M. 1993. Reed canary grass controls tested (Minnesota). Restoration and Management Notes 11:169.

Lynch, J. J. 1941. The place of burning in management of the Gulf Coast wildlife refuges. Journal of Wildlife Management 5:454–457.

Lynch, J. J., T. O'Neil, and D. W. Lay. 1947. Management significance of damage by geese and muskrats to Gulf Coast marshes. Journal of Wildlife Management 11:50–72.

MacArthur, R. H., and E. O. Wilson. 1967. The theory of island biogeography. Princeton University Press, Princeton, New Jersey.

Malecki, R. A., B. Blossey, S. D. Hight, D. Schroeder, L. T. Kok, and J. R. Coulson. 1993. Biological control of purple loosestrife. BioScience 43:680–686.

Malecki, R. A., J. R. Lassoie, E. Rieger, and T. Seamans. 1983. Effects of long-term artificial flooding on a northern bottomland hardwood forest community. Forest Science 29:535–544.

Malecki, R. A., and T. J. Rawinski. 1985. New methods for controlling purple loosestrife. New York Fish and Game Journal 32:9–19.

Manguin, S., R. White, B. Blossey, and S. D. Hight. 1993. Genetics, taxonomy, and ecology of certain species of *Galerucella* (Coleopters: Chrysomelidae). Annals of the Entomological Society of America 86:397–410.

Manley, S. W. 1999. Ecological and agricultural values of winter-flooded ricefields in Mississippi. Dissertation, Mississippi State University, Mississippi State.

Manley, S. W., R. M. Kaminski, K. J. Reinecke, and P. D. Gerard. 2004. Waterbird foods in winter-managed ricefields in Mississippi. Journal of Wildlife Management 68:74–83.

Martin, A. C. 1953. Improving duck marshes by weed control. U.S. Fish and Wildlife Service Circular 19.

Martin, A. C., N. Hotchkiss, F. M. Uhler, and W. S. Bourn. 1953. Classification of wetlands of the United States. U.S. Fish and Wildlife Service Special Scientific Report Wildlife 20.

Martin, A. C., and F. M. Uhler. 1939. Food of game ducks in the United States and Canada. U.S. Department of Agriculture Technical Bulletin 634.

Martin, A. C., H. S. Zim, and A. L. Nelson. 1951. American wildlife and plants. McGraw-Hill, New York.

Mathevet, R., and A. Tamisier. 2002. Creation of a nature reserve, its effects on hunting management and waterfowl distribution in the Camargue (southern France). Biodiversity and Conservation 11:509–519.

Mathiak, H. A. 1965. Pothole blasting for wildlife. Wisconsin Department of Conservation Publication 352.

Mathiak, H. A. 1971. Observations on changes in the status of cattails at Horicon Marsh, Wisconsin. Wisconsin Department of Natural Resources Research Report 66.

Mazzei, K. C., R. M. Newman, A. Loos, and D. W. Ragsdale. 1999. Developmental rates of the native milfoil weevil, *Euhrychiopsis lecontei*, and damage to Eurasian watermilfoil at constant temperatures. Biological Control: Theory and Applications in Pest Management 16:139–143.

McCoy, E. D. 1983. The application of island-biogeographic theory to patches of habitat: how much land is enough? Biological Conservation 25:53–61.

McIntosh, R. P. 1980. The background and some current problems of theoretical ecology. Synthese 43:195–255.

McKnight, S. K., and G. R. Hepp. 1995. Potential effects of grass carp herbivory on waterfowl foods. Journal of Wildlife Management 59:720–727.

McNaughton, J. L., F. N. Reece, and J. W. Deaton. 1981. Relationships between color, trypsin inhibitor contents, and urease index of soybean meal and effects on broiler performance. Poultry Science 60:393–400.

Meanley, B. 1956. Food habits of the King Rail in Arkansas rice fields. Auk 73:252–258.

Mesleard, F., P. Grillas, and L. T. Ham. 1995. Restoration of seasonally-flooded marshes in abandoned ricefields in the Camargue (southern France) — preliminary results on vegetation and use by ducks. Ecological Engineering 5:95–106.

Miller, M. R., D. E. Sharp, D. S. Gilmer, and W. R. Mulvaney. 1989. Rice available to waterfowl in harvested fields in the Sacramento Valley, California. California Fish and Game 75:113–123.

Mitsch, W. J., and J. G. Gosselink. 2000. Wetlands. Third edition. John Wiley & Sons, New York.

Moore, P. D., and D. J. Bellamy. 1974. Peatlands. Springer-Verlag, New York.

Mueller, M. H., and A. G. van der Valk. 2002. The potential role of ducks in wetland seed dispersal. Wetlands 22:170–178.

Murkin, E. J., H. R. Murkin, and R. D. Titman. 1992. Nektonic invertebrate abundance and distribution at the emergent–open water interface in the Delta Marsh, Manitoba, Canada. Wetlands 12:45–52.

Murkin, H. R., and P. J. Caldwell. 2000. Avian use of prairie wetlands. Pages 249–286 *in* H. R. Murkin, A. G. van der Valk, and W. R. Clark, editors. Prairie wetland ecology: the contribution of the Marsh Ecology Research Program. Iowa State University Press, Ames.

Murkin, H. R., and J. A. Kadlec. 1986. Relationships between waterfowl and macroinvertebrate densities in a northern prairie marsh. Journal of Wildlife Management 50:212–217.

Murkin, H. R., R. M. Kaminski, and R. D. Titman. 1982. Responses by dabbling ducks and aquatic invertebrates to an experimentally manipulated cattail marsh. Canadian Journal of Zoology 60:2324–2332.

Murkin, H. R., E. J. Murkin, and J. P. Ball. 1997. Avian habitat selection and prairie wetland dynamics: a 10-year experiment. Ecological Applications 7:1144–1159

Murkin, H. R., E. J. Murkin, and R. D. Titman. 1992. Nektonic invertebrate abundance and distribution at the emergent vegetation–open water interface in the Delta Marsh, Manitoba, Canada. Wetlands 10:45–52.

Murkin, H. R., and L. C. M. Ross. 1999. Northern prairie marshes (Delta Marsh, Manitoba): macroinvertebrate responses to a simulated wet–dry cycle. Pages 543–569 in D. Batzer, R. D. Rader, and S. A. Wissinger, editors. Invertebrates in freshwater wetlands of North America: ecology and management. John Wiley & Sons, New York.

Murkin, H. R., and L. C. M. Ross. 2000. Invertebrates in prairie wetlands. Pages 201–247 in H. R. Murkin, A. G. van der Valk, and W. R. Clark, editors. Prairie wetland ecology: the contribution of the Marsh Ecology Research Program. Iowa State University Press, Ames.

Murkin, H. R., A. G. van der Valk, and W. R. Clark, editors. 2000a. Prairie wetland ecology: the contribution of the Marsh Ecology Research Program. Iowa State University Press, Ames.

Murkin, H. R., A. G. van der Valk, W. R. Clark, L. G. Goldsborough, D. A. Wrubleski, and J. A. Kadlec. 2000b. Marsh Ecology Research Program: management implications for prairie wetlands. Pages 317–344 in H. R. Murkin, A. G. van der Valk, and W. R. Clark, editors. Prairie wetland ecology: the contribution of the Marsh Ecology Research Program. Iowa State University Press, Ames.

Murkin, H. R., A. G. van der Valk, and J. A. Kadlec. 2000c. Nutrient budgets and the wet–dry cycle of prairie wetlands. Pages 99–121 in H. R. Murkin, A. G. van der Valk, and W. R. Clark, editors. Prairie wetland ecology: the contribution of the Marsh Ecology Research Program. Iowa State University Press, Ames.

Murkin, H. R., and P. Ward. 1980. Early spring cutting to control cattail in a northern marsh. Wildlife Society Bulletin 8:254–256.

Myers, J. P. 1986. Sex and gluttony on Delaware Bay. Natural History 95:68–77.

Myers, J. P., P. D. McLain, R. I. G. Morrsion, P. Z. Antas, P. Canevari, B. A. Harrington, T. E. Lovejoy, V. Pulido, M. Sallaberry, and S. E. Senner. 1987. The Western Hemisphere Shorebird Reserve Network. Pages 122–124 in N. C. Davidson and M. W. Pienkowski, editors. The conservation of international flyway populations of waders. Wader Study Group Bulletin 49, and IWRB Special Publication 7.

Natural Resources Conservation Service (NRCS). 2003. Field indicators of hydric soils in the United States, version 5.01. G. W. Hurt, P. M. Whited, and R. F. Pringle, editors. U.S. Department of Agriculture, NRCS, in cooperation with the National Technical Committee for Hydric Soils, Ft. Worth, Texas.

Naugle, D. E., K. F. Higgins, S. M. Nusser, and W. C. Johnson. 1999. Scale-dependent habitat use in three species of prairie wetland birds. Landscape Ecology 14:267–276.

Nelms, C. O., and D. J. Twedt. 1996. Seed deterioration in flooded agricultural fields during winter. Wildlife Society Bulletin 24:85–88.

Nelson, J. W., and J. A. Kadlec. 1984. A conceptual approach to relating habitat structure and macroinvertebrate production in freshwater wetlands. Transactions of the North American Wildlife and Natural Resources Conference 49:262–270.

Nelson, J. W., and R. A. Wishart. 1988. Management of wetland complexes for waterfowl production: planning for the prairie habitat joint venture. Transactions of the North American Wildlife and Natural Resources Conference 53:444–453.

Nelson, N. F. 1954. Factors in the development and restoration of waterfowl habitat at Ogden Bay Refuge, Weber County, Utah. Utah Department of Fish and Game Publication 6.

Nichols, S. A. 1974. Mechanical and habitat manipulation for aquatic plant management. Wisconsin Department of Natural Resources Technical Bulletin 77.

Nyman, J. A., and R. H. Chabreck. 1995. Fire in coastal marshes: history and recent concerns. Proceedings of the Tall Timbers Fire Ecology Conference 19:134–141.

Odum, E. P. 1971. Fundamentals of ecology. Third edition W.B. Saunders, Philadelphia.

Parsons, K. C. 2002. Integrated management of waterbird habitats at impounded wetlands in Delaware Bay, U.S.A. Waterbirds 25 (Special Publication 2):25–41.

Parsons, K. C., S. C. Brown, R. M. Erwin, H. A. Czech, and J. C. Coulson, editors. 2002. Managing wetlands for waterbirds: integrated approaches. Waterbirds 25 (Special Publication 2).

Patterson, J. H. 1976. The role of environmental heterogeneity in the regulation of duck populations. Journal of Wildlife Management 40:22–32.

Paveglio, F. L., and K. M. Kilbride. 2000. Response of vegetation to control of reed canarygrass in seasonally managed wetlands of southwestern Washington. Wildlife Society Bulletin 28:730–740.

Payne, N. F. 1992. Techniques for wildlife habitat management of wetlands. McGraw-Hill, New York.

Perkins, C. J. 1968. Controlled burning in the management of muskrats and waterfowl in Louisiana coastal marshes. Proceedings of the Tall Timbers Fire Ecology Conference 8:269–280.

Perry, M. C., and F. M. Uhler. 1982. Food habits of diving ducks in the Carolinas. Proceedings of the Southeastern Association of Fish and Wildlife Agencies 36:492–504.

Peterjohn, W. T., and D. L. Correll. 1984. Nutrient dynamics in an agricultural watershed: observations on the role of a riparian forest. Ecology 65:1466–1475.

Phillips, J. 1970. Wisconsin's wetland soils. Wisconsin Department of Natural Resources Research Report 57.

Primack, R. B. 2004. Essentials of conservation biology. Third edition. Sinauer Associates, Sunderland, Massachusetts.

Pulliam, H. R. 1988. Sources, sinks, and population regulation. American Naturalist 132:652–661.

Rawinski, T. J. 1982. The ecology and management of purple loosestrife (Lythrum salicaria L.) in central New York. Thesis, Cornell University, Ithaca, New York.

Rawinski, T. J., and R. A. Malecki. 1984. Ecological relationships among purple loosestrife, cattail and wildlife at the Montezuma National Wildlife Refuge. New York Fish and Game Journal 31:81–87.

Reed, P. B., Jr. 1968. Preliminary study of green-timber impoundment. Thesis, Cornell University, Ithaca, New York.

Reed, P. B., Jr. 1988. National list of plant species that occur in wetlands: Northeast (Region 1). U.S. Fish and Wildlife Service Biological Report 88(26.1).

Reid, F. A. 1993. Managing wetlands for waterbirds. Transactions of the North American Wildlife and Natural Resources Conference 58:345–350.

Reid, F. A., J. R. Kelley, Jr., T. S. Taylor, and L. H. Fredrickson. 1989. Upper Mississippi Valley wetlands — refuges and moist-soil impoundments. Pages 181–202 in L. M. Smith, R. L. Pederson, and R. M. Kaminski, editors. Habitat management for migrating and wintering waterfowl in North America. Texas Tech University Press, Lubbock.

Reinecke, K. J., M. W. Brown, and J. R. Nassar. 1992. Evaluation of aerial transects for counting wintering Mallards. Journal of Wildlife Management 53:515–525.

Reinecke, K. J., R. M. Kaminski, D. J. Moorhead, J. D. Hodges, and J. R. Nassar. 1989. Mississippi Alluvial Valley. Pages 203–247 in L. M. Smith, R. L. Pederson, and R. M. Kaminski, editors. Habitat management for migrating and wintering waterfowl in North America. Texas Tech University Press, Lubbock.

Robbins, C. S., D. K. Dawson, and B. A. Dowell. 1989. Habitat area requirements of breeding forest birds of the middle Atlantic states. Wildlife Monographs 103.

Robel, R. J. 1961a. Water depth and turbidity in relation to growth of sago pondweed. Journal of Wildlife Management 25:436–438.

Robel, R. J. 1961b. The effects of carp populations on the production of waterfowl food plants on a western waterfowl marsh. Transactions of the North American Wildlife and Natural Resources Conference 26:147–159.

Robinson, G. G. C., S. E. Gurney, and L. G. Goldsborough. 2000. Algae in prairie wetlands. Pages 163–199 in H. R. Murkin, A. G. van der Valk, and W. R. Clark, editors. Prairie wetland ecology: the contribution of the Marsh Ecology Research Program. Iowa State University Press, Ames.

Rudolph, R. R., and C. G. Hunter. 1964. Green trees and greenheads. Pages 611–618 in J. P. Linduska, editor. Waterfowl tomorrow. U.S. Government Printing Office, Washington, D.C.

Rundle, W. D., and L. H. Fredrickson. 1981. Managing seasonally flooded impoundments for migrant rails and shorebirds. Wildlife Society Bulletin 9:80–87.

Saenz, J. H., Jr., and L. M. Smith. 1995. Effects of spring and fall burning on cattail in South Dakota. Proceedings of the Tall Timbers Fire Ecology Conference 19:151–157.

Schloesser, D. W., and B. A. Manny. 1990. Decline of wildcelery buds in the Lower Detroit River, 1950–85. Journal of Wildlife Management 54:72–76.

Seabloom, E. W. 1997. Vegetation dynamics in prairie wetlands. Dissertation, Iowa State University, Ames.

Semlitsch, R. D. 2000. Principles for management of aquatic-breeding amphibians. Journal of Wildlife Management 64:615–631.

Severson, K. E., and C. E. Boldt. 1978. Cattle, wildlife, and riparian habitat in the western Dakotas. Pages 94–103 in Management and use of northern plains rangeland. Regional Rangeland Symposium, Bismark, North Dakota.

Shabana, Y. M., J. P. Cuda, and R. Charudattan. 2003. Evaluation of pathogens as potential biological agents of hydrilla. Journal of Phytopathology 151:607–613.

Shamsi, S. R. A., and F. H. Whitehead. 1974. Comparative eco-physiology of Epilobium hirsutum L. and Lythrum salicaria L. I. General biology, distribution and germination. Journal of Ecology 62:279–290.

Shaw, J. H. 1985. Introduction to wildlife management. McGraw-Hill, New York.

Shaw, S. P., and C. G. Fredine. 1956. Wetlands of the United States, their extent and their value to waterfowl and other wildlife. U.S. Fish and Wildlife Service Circular 39.

Shuford, W. D., G. W. Page, and J. E. Kjelmyr. 1998. Patterns and dynamics of shorebird use of California's Central Valley. Condor 100:227–244.

Simberloff, D., and L. G. Abele. 1982. Refuge design and island biogeographic theory: effects of fragmentation. American Naturalist 120:41–50.

Singleton, J. R. 1951. Production and utilization of waterfowl food plants on the east Texas Gulf Coast. Journal of Wildlife Management 15:46–56.

Smith, L. M., D. A. Haukos, and R. M. Prather. 2004. Avian response to vegetative pattern in playa lake wetlands during winter. Wildlife Society Bulletin 32:474–480.

Smith, L. M., and J. A. Kadlec. 1983. Seed banks and their role during drawdown of a North American marsh. Journal of Applied Ecology 20:673–684.

Smith, L. M., and J. A. Kadlec. 1985a. Predictions of vegetation change following fire in a Great Salt Lake marsh. Aquatic Botany 21:43–51.

Smith, L. M., and J. A. Kadlec. 1985b. Comparisons of prescribed burning and cutting of Utah marsh plants. Great Basin Naturalist 45:462–466.

Smith, L. M., and J. A. Kadlec. 1985c. Fire and herbivory in a Great Salt Lake marsh. Ecology 66:259–265.

Smith, L. M., J. A. Kadlec, and P. V. Fonnesbeck. 1984. Effects of prescribed burning on nutritive quality of marsh plants in Utah. Journal of Wildlife Management 48:285–288.

Smith, L. M., R. L. Pederson, and R. M. Kaminski, editors. 1989. Habitat management for migrating and wintering waterfowl in North America. Texas Tech University Press, Lubbock.

Solberg, K. L., and K. F. Higgins. 1993. Effects of glyphosate herbicide on cattails, invertebrates, and waterfowl in South Dakota wetlands. Wildlife Society Bulletin 21:299–307.

Soulé, M. E., and B. A. Wilcox, editors. 1980. Conservation biology. Sinauer Associates, Sunderland, Massachusetts.

Stewart, R. E., and H. A. Kantrud. 1971. Classification of natural ponds and lakes in the glaciated prairie region. U.S. Fish and Wildlife Service Resource Publication 92.

Streeter, R. G., M. W. Tome, and D. K. Weaver. 1993. North American Waterfowl Management Plan: shorebird benefits. Transactions of the North American Wildlife and Natural Resources Conference 58:363–369.

Strohmeyer, D. L., and L. H. Fredrickson. 1967. An evaluation of dynamited potholes in northwest Iowa. Journal of Wildlife Management 31:525–532.

Swanson, G. A., and M. I. Meyer. 1977. Impact of fluctuating water levels on feeding ecology of breeding Blue-winged Teal. Journal of Wildlife Management 41:426–433.

Swanson, G. A., M. I. Meyer, and J. R. Serie. 1974. Feeding ecology of breeding Blue-winged Teals. Journal of Wildlife Management 38:396–407.

Tacha, T. C., and C. E. Braun, editors. 1994. Migratory shore and upland game bird management in North America. International Association of Fish and Wildlife Agencies, Washington, D.C.

Taft, O., M. A. Colwell, C. R. Isola, and R. J. Saffran. 2002. Waterbird response to experimental drawdown: implications for multispecies management. Journal of Applied Ecology 39:987–1001.

Tarver, D. P., J. A. Rodgers, M. J. Mahler, and R. L. Lazor. 1979. Aquatic and wetland plants of Florida. Florida Department of Natural Resources, Tallahassee, Florida.

Teels, B. M., G. Anding, D. H. Arner, E. D. Norwood, and D. E. Wesley. 1976. Aquatic plant-invertebrate and waterfowl associations in Mississippi. Proceedings of the Southeastern Association of Game and Fish Commissioners 30:610–616.

Teeter, J. W. 1965. Effects of sodium chloride on the sago pondweed. Journal of Wildlife Management 29:838–845.

Tewksbury, L., R. Casagrande, B. Blossey, P. Hafliger, and M. Schwarzlander. 2002. Potential for biological control of *Phragmites australis* in North America. Biological Control: Theory and Applications in Pest Management 23:191–212.

Thompson, D. Q., P. B. Reed, Jr., G. E. Cummings, E. Kivisalu. 1968. Muck hardwoods as green-timber impoundments for waterfowl. Transactions of the North American Wildlife and Natural Resources Conference 33:142–159.

Thompson, D. Q., R. L. Stuckey, and E. B. Thompson. 1987. Spread, impact, and control of purple loosestrife (*Lythrum salicaria*) in North American wetlands. U.S. Fish and Wildlife Service Fish and Wildlife Research 2.

Thompson, J. D., and G. A. Baldassarre. 1988. Postbreeding habitat preference of Wood Ducks in northern Alabama. Journal of Wildlife Management 52:80–85.

Tiner, R. W., Jr. 1988. Field guide to nontidal wetland identification. Maryland Department of Natural Resources, Annapolis, Maryland, and U.S. Fish and Wildlife Service, Newton Corner, Massachusetts.

Tiner, R. W., Jr. 1999. Wetland indicators: a guide to wetland identification, delineation, classification, and mapping. Lewis Publishers, Boca Raton, Florida.

Tiner, R. W., Jr., and P. L. M. Veneman. 1989. Hydric soils of New England. University of Massachusetts Cooperative Extension Revised Bulletin C-183R.

Tourenq, C., S. Benhamou, N. Sadoul, A. Sandoz, F. Mesléard, J-L. Martin, and H. Hafner. 2004. Spatial relationships between tree-nesting heron colonies and rice fields in the Camargue, France. Auk 121:192–202.

Twedt, D. J., and C. O. Nelms. 1998. Shorebird use of managed wetlands in the Mississippi Alluvial Valley. American Midland Naturalist 140:140–152.

Twedt, D. J., and C. O. Nelms. 1999. Waterfowl density on agricultural fields managed to retain water in winter. Wildlife Society Bulletin 27:924–930.

Uihlein, W. B. 2000. Estimates of private lands managed for waterfowl in the Mississippi Alluvial Valley. Dissertation, Mississippi State University, Mississippi State.

U.S. Fish and Wildlife Service. 2002. National wetlands inventory: a strategy for the 21st century. U.S. Fish and Wildlife Service, Washington, D.C.

van der Valk, A. G. 1981. Succession in wetlands: a Gleasonian approach. Ecology 62:688–696.

van der Valk, A. G. 2000. Vegetation dynamics and models. Pages 125–161 *in* H. R. Murkin, A. G. van der Valk, and W. R. Clark, editors. Prairie wet-land ecology: the contribution of the Marsh Ecology Research Program. Iowa State University Press, Ames.

van der Valk, A. G., and C. B. Davis. 1976. The seed banks of prairie glacial marshes. Canadian Journal of Botany 54:1832–1838.

van der Valk, A. G., and C. B. Davis. 1978. The role of seed banks in the vegetation dynamics of prairie glacial marshes. Ecology 59:322–335.

Voigts, D. K. 1976. Aquatic invertebrate abundance in relation to changing marsh vegetation. American Midland Naturalist 95:313-322.

Ward, E. 1942. Phragmites management. Transactions of the North American Wildlife Conference 7:294–298.

Ward, P. 1968. Fire in relation to waterfowl habitat of the Delta Marshes. Proceedings of the Tall Timbers Fire Ecology Conference 8:255–267.

Wehrle, B. W., R. M. Kaminski, B. D. Leopold, and W. P. Smith. 1995. Aquatic invertebrate resources in Mississippi forested wetlands during winter. Wildlife Society Bulletin 23:774–783.

Weier, J. L., and D. F. Starr. 1950. The use of rotenone to remove rough fish for the purpose of improving migratory waterfowl refuge areas. Journal of Wildlife Management 14:203–205.

Weller, M. W. 1975. Studies of cattail in relation to management for marsh wildlife. Iowa State Journal of Research 49:383–412.

Weller, M. W. 1981. Freshwater marshes, ecology and wildlife management. University of Minnesota Press, Minneapolis.

Weller, M. W., and L. H. Fredrickson. 1973. Avian ecology of a managed glacial marsh. Living Bird 12:269–291.

Weller, M. W., and C. E. Spatcher. 1965. Role of habitat in the distribution and abundance of marsh birds. Iowa State Agricultural Home and Economics Experiment Station Special Report 43.

Welling, C. H., and R. L. Becker. 1993. Reduction of purple loosestrife establishment in Minnesota wetlands. Wildlife Society Bulletin 21:56–64.

Wetland Training Institute. 1989. Field guide for delineating wetlands: unified federal method. Wetland Training Institute 89-1. Poolesville, Maryland.

Whigham, D., D. Dykyjová, and S. Hejný. 1993. Wetlands of the world: inventory, ecology and management. Volume I. Kluwer Academic, Dordrecht, The Netherlands.

White, D. C. 1985. Lowland hardwood wetland invertebrate community and production in Missouri. Archives for Hydrobiologia 103:509–533.

Whitman, W. R. 1976. Impoundments for waterfowl. Canadian Wildlife Service Occasional Paper 22.

Whitman, W. R., T. Strange, L. Widjeskog, R. Whittemore, P. Kehoe, and L. Roberts, editors. 1995. Waterfowl habitat restoration, enhancement and management in the Atlantic Flyway. Third edition. Delaware Division of Fish and Wildlife, Dover, Delaware.

Whitt, M. B., H. H. Prince, and R. R. Cox, Jr. 1999. Avian use of purple loosestrife dominated habitat relative to other vegetation types in a Lake Huron wetland complex. Wilson Bulletin 111:105–114.

Whittaker, R. H. 1967. Gradient analysis of vegetation. Biological Reviews 42:207–264.

Wigley, T. B., Jr., and T. H. Filer, Jr. 1989. Characteristics of greentree reservoirs: a survey of managers. Wildlife Society Bulletin 17:136–142.

Wilcox, B. A. 1980. Insular ecology and conservation. Pages 95–117 in M. E. Soulé and B. A. Wilcox, editors. Conservation biology. Sinauer Associates, Sunderland, Massachusetts.

Williams, M. 1985. Fish v. fowl: the likely impact on waterfowl of the introduction of grass carp into New Zealand waterways. New Zealand Journal of Ecology 8:144.

Wilson, E. O., editor. 1988. Biodiversity. National Academy Press, Washington, D.C.

Wright, H. A., and A. W. Bailey. 1982. Fire ecology — United States and southern Canada. John Wiley & Sons, New York.

Wrubleski, D. A., H. R. Murkin, A. G. van der Valk, and C. B. Davis. 1997. Decomposition of litter of three mudflat annual species in a northern prairie marsh during drawdown. Plant Ecology 129:141–148.

Wrubleski, D. A., and D. M. Rosenberg. 1990. The Chironomidae of Bone Pile Pond, Delta Marsh, Manitoba, Canada. Wetlands 11:1–16.

Yamamoto, H., and K. Oohata. 2003. The effects of water flooding and provision of the food for wintering ducks on rice fields — a preliminary study for establishing a stable wintering duck population at Katano-kamoike. III. Strix 21:111–123.

Yancey, R. K. 1964. Matches and marshes. Pages 619–626 in J. P. Linduska, editor. Waterfowl tomorrow. U.S. Government Printing Office, Washington, D.C.

Young, G. L., B. L. Karr, B. D. Leopold, and J. D. Hodges. 1995. Effect of greentree reservoir management on Mississippi bottomland hardwoods. Wildlife Society Bulletin 23:525–531.

Zekor, D. T., and R. M. Kaminski. 1987. Attitudes of Mississippi Delta farmers toward private-land waterfowl management. Wildlife Society Bulletin 15:346–354.

Chapter 11
WATERFOWL POLICY AND ADMINISTRATION

EXPAND the VISION

NORTH AMERICAN

WATERFOWL

MANAGEMENT PLAN

North American Waterfowl
Management Plan

Plan nord-américain de
gestion de la sauvagine

Plan de Manejo de Aves
Acuáticas de Norteamérica

With ratification of the Migratory Bird Treaty between the United States and Great Britain (acting on behalf of Canada), waterfowl became subject to federal jurisdiction in the United States and Canada. The Treaty removed the primary responsibility for waterfowl management from the states and provinces where, previously, policies often ignored the obvious fact that waterfowl were migratory, and thus represented a natural resource superseding the jurisdictional boundaries of individual states, provinces, or nations. To be sure, state and provincial governments still influenced waterfowl management in many ways, but their role was subordinated to national authority after 1916.

Beginning with a look at the state of affairs before the passage of the Migratory Bird Treaty, this chapter traces the evolution of the policies and administration of waterfowl resources in the United States initiated by that landmark event. The track of this history has not always lacked controversies or complications, but the framework resulting from these events gradually formed a model of resource management on an international basis.

EARLY DAYS

Simply stated, waterfowl resources in North America experienced harsh exploitation in the years preceding passage of the Migratory Bird Treaty. Market hunting was commonplace, taking untold numbers of birds at any time and by any means, events that are discussed here in some detail (see also Chapter 1). Nowhere was market hunting more widespread than on the eastern seaboard, where burgeoning cities were the outlets for fresh meat and immense flocks of waterfowl existed in fabled places such as Chesapeake Bay and Long Island Sound. Many market hunters used "punt guns," which were little more than homemade cannons mounted on the bows of small, flat-bottomed boats (see Fig. 1-8). The bores of the punt guns varied in size according to the fortitude of their makers, but each was capable of holding large amounts of shot. Indeed, amounts equivalent to 10 or more modern shotgun shells were loaded as a single charge in the larger punt guns. One firing of such a weapon into a flock of ducks easily killed or wounded scores of birds, which often were attracted to the site with bait. With two or more guns per boat, market hunters might launch a deadly fusillade, firing first on a flock on the water, and then unloosing a second salvo as the remaining birds took flight. Pochards such as the Canvasback were

particularly vulnerable to attacks of this sort because they run across the water before taking flight and hence presented highly susceptible targets. The only factors limiting market hunting were the skill of the operator, his supply of powder and shot, and the seasonal availability of waterfowl — neither regulations nor any tinge of conservation ethics curtailed the unchecked slaughter (Fig. 11-1).

Day (1949) summarized some of the excesses of the era, including one dealer's shipment from Virginia of as many as 1,000 ducks at a time throughout a 6-month season each year — and his marketing career spanned 30 years. Waterfowl shot on Currituck Sound, North Carolina, provided at least $100,000 each year to the local economy of duck hunters between 1903 and 1909. Among these transactions was the sale, for $1,700, of 2,300 Ruddy Ducks killed in a single month by four hunters. One hunter's daily bag once reached 282 Ruddy Ducks.

The slaughter by no means was limited to the eastern seaboard. A market hunter in Louisiana boasted of a day's kill of 430 ducks, and two others in California killed 218 geese in an hour, taking a total of about 450 geese for the day. Similar tallies are known from choice hunting areas on the Mississippi River, including 122 Wood Ducks shot by a lone hunter before 0900 hr. In Iowa, Musgrove (1949) reported that one group of market hunters shot an average of 1,000 ducks/week, or 14,000 ducks and shorebirds during a season. The ducks sold for $6–$15/dozen, depending on the species, but others sometimes sold for only 10 cents apiece. Another operation in Iowa coupled market hunting with the hardware business; in some seasons, 75,000 ducks were marketed and ammunition sales reached 250,000 shells.

The last-known Labrador Duck fell to a hunter during the autumn of 1875 on Long Island Sound (Fuller 2000). The extinction of this species can be blamed, in part, on market hunting within its limited range on the northern coastline of North America. Despite allegations of their poor-tasting flesh, Labrador Ducks appeared in the markets of New York, New Jersey, Maryland, and most likely, in other eastern states. Without the modern-day convenience of refrigeration, however, shipments of Labrador Ducks and other waterfowl often spoiled before reaching the marketplace. A full explanation for the Labrador Duck's disappearance remains uncertain, but whatever the reasons were, the extinction of this species occurred during an era of exploitation and utter disregard for the welfare of waterfowl populations.

Figure 11-1. Market hunters, unchecked by either regulations or conservation ethics, often killed hundreds of ducks and geese in a single day of shooting. Shown here is a day's bag on display at A. C. Ward's General Store in the marketplace at Norfolk, Virginia, circa 1910. Photo courtesy of J. A. "Archie" Johnson.

Spring hunting also was legal, or at least it was not illegal to shoot waterfowl en route to their breeding grounds. Only nine states protected waterfowl from spring hunting in 1900. Bag limits also were either nonexistent or so liberal as to be meaningless, thereby abetting the carnage of market hunting.

Plume hunting was another activity of the day, wantonly supporting the needs of a lucrative millinery trade with the slaughter of herons and egrets (Ardeidae) as well as other waterbirds. The demand for feathers led to the decimation of entire colonies of nesting waterbirds. Nonetheless, waterfowl also were part of the feather trade. The skins of more than 17,500 swans, mostly Trumpeter Swans, were sold for their plumage between 1853 and 1877, bringing a drastic reduction to the population; only 57 skins were sold between 1888 and 1897 as the availability of swans diminished over much of their

former range (Banko 1960). More than 100,000 swan skins had been marketed by the Hudson's Bay Company by the time overhunting forced trade to a close (Banko and Mackay 1964). Regrettably, most of the market hunting took place in Canada, where swan colonies were accessible during the nesting season; hence, plume hunting claimed large numbers of breeding birds.

However, although this early trade in swan skins is well known, the trade is swan and goose quills was equally substantial. Houston et al. (2003) provide a succinct documentary of this trade, noting that swan and goose quills sold from Hudson Bay increased from 58,000 in 1799 to a peak of 1.2 million in 1834, when a grand total of 18.7 million quills were sold in London. Houston et al. (2003:194) also cite an entry in the 1942 edition of *Encyclopedia Britannica* under "feather," which further underscores the nuances of the quill-pen industry of this era: "Only the five outer wing feathers of the goose are useful for writing, and of these the second and third are the best, while left-wing quills are more esteemed than those of the right as they curve outward and away from the [right handed] writer using them . . . Swan quills indeed are better than those from the goose." Indeed, "Hudson's Bay quills" were the most preferred in the world at that time, with sales during the peak years of the 1830s commanding as much as 63 shillings per 100 compared to 15 shillings for domestic goose quills. Swan quills were especially prized because they were much more durable than goose quills. By 1822 there were at least 27 quill and pen manufacturers and dealers in London to process into pens the swan and goose quills arriving from Canada. Further, although metal pens were available by the 1820s, most writers and almost all lawyers still preferred quill pens. The last quill-pen manufacturer in London closed in 1954 (see Houston et al. 2003).

The colorful plumage of male Wood Ducks also added a bonus to their value as table fare, thereby increasing the impetus for overshooting Wood Ducks throughout their range in the eastern United States. Indeed, naturalists of the day predicted that Wood Ducks easily might follow the Labrador Duck into extinction because of relentless year-long hunting pressure (see Bellrose 1976).

In addition to waterfowl, other birds were diminishing rapidly under unacceptable levels of market hunting. Traps and nets, as well as guns, steadily eroded wildlife populations. During the slaughter of Passenger Pigeons (*Ectopistes migratorius*), as many as 3,500 birds were captured with the snap of a single trap, and netters in Michigan marketed more than 1 billion pigeons within the space of a few weeks, destroying forever one of the last great nesting colonies of that now-extinct species (Trefethen 1975). Greater Prairie Chickens (*Tympanuchus cupido pinnatus*) also were killed wholesale by market hunters; Swift and Lawrence (1966) reported that one poultry dealer in New York City received 20 tons of Prairie Chicken meat in a single shipment. Unremitting exploitation of wildlife — with little thought of conservation — clearly prevailed until the dawn of the 20th century.

INITIAL LEGISLATION

The Lacey Act of 1900

An awareness gradually prevailed that legal means were needed to protect waterfowl and other wildlife from market hunting. The initial response by the federal government to the commercial abuse of wildlife came from Congressman John F. Lacey in legislation entitled the Game and Wild Birds Preservation and Disposition Act of 1900. Popularly known as the Lacey Act, its provisions regulated introductions of some harmful species of exotic wildlife and, more central to our interests, forbade interstate transport of wildlife and wildlife products secured in violation of state laws. In short, it now was a federal offense to ship wildlife obtained illegally from one state to another. Previously, market hunters might transport for sale wildlife killed in a state that protected wildlife into another state where there were no restrictions, thereby thwarting any threat of apprehension or prosecution. Henceforth, the weight of federal authority prevailed in such cases, but for all of its good intentions the Lacey Act unfortunately lacked a viable enforcement arm to impede interstate trafficking in wildlife. Regardless, the Lacey Act represented the first federal involvement with wildlife management, including a small measure of regulating the kill of waterfowl destined for the marketplace.

Strictly speaking, the Yellowstone Park Protection Act of 1884, another bill sponsored by Congressman Lacey, the "father of conservation legislation," was the first federal measure protecting wildlife. Since its establishment in 1872, Yellowstone National Park had been governed solely by military law, which failed to include any protection for wildlife inside the Park's boundaries. In comparison, the Lacey Act established jurisdiction for its provisions across the United States, not just for a single site of publicly owned land. Thus, for all practical purposes, the Lacey Act represented the first widespread involvement of the federal government in wildlife conservation.

The Migratory Bird Act of 1913 (Weeks-McLean Act)

Several attempts to unify the status of migratory game birds — particularly hunting regulations for waterfowl — under federal control were thwarted between 1900 and 1913. Bills for this purpose were introduced as early as 1904, but these failed, usually because of the prevailing view that hunting regulations properly remained in the jurisdictional realm of the individual states. Long-standing traditions, if not the tenets of common law, were difficult obstacles in the legislative paths of lawmakers wishing to mandate federal authority over hunting. Nevertheless, the idea of federal regulation of migratory birds did not vanish; sportsmen's and ornithological organizations continually pressed for action.

After almost a decade of failure, bills proposed by Congressman John W. Weeks of Massachusetts and Senator George P. McLean of Connecticut finally gained approval, becoming the Migratory Bird Act with the signature of President William Howard Taft on 4 March 1913. The Act conferred federal jurisdiction on all waterfowl and other migratory birds, which then closed the seasons for nearly all migratory species of nongame birds and ended spring waterfowl hunting once and for all. Further, the Secretary of Agriculture was empowered to set legal hunting seasons for migratory birds, overriding the former jurisdiction of state authority in such matters.

Conservationists, including the majority of hunters, welcomed the new legislation, but advocates of states' rights were less than enthusiastic about another intrusion of the federal government into the province of state authority. The issue transcended the immediate subject of wildlife conservation and instead focused on theory and practice of legal governance. Perhaps it was a vestige remaining from the Civil War, or perhaps not, but the champions of states' rights nonetheless introduced a bill for repeal of the Weeks-McLean Act and initiated a test of its constitutionality in the Supreme Court. The subject of migratory bird management suddenly emerged as the focal point of a hotly debated issue within the very pinnacles of government.

Attacks on the Weeks-McLean Act faded when Senator McLean successfully proposed a resolution authorizing the President of the United States to initiate international conventions for the protection of migratory birds. In fact, however, Senator Elihu Root, a winner of the Nobel Peace Prize and former Secretary of State, earlier proposed a resolution for the same purpose, but his ideas languished when Congress rushed to adjourn. Nonetheless, it was Root's skilled diplomacy that provided the substance of McLean's successful resolution when Congress reconvened. McLean's action, in short, established a means for preparing treaties that, if ratified, seemingly would remove the subject of federal jurisdiction from further constitutional challenges. In other words, what could not be accomplished by law might be achieved by treaty. World War I slowed progress toward completion of the convention, but steady work by dedicated officials in Canada and the United States finally produced a treaty 3 years after McLean's resolution was adopted by the Senate.

President Woodrow Wilson signed the Migratory Bird Treaty for the United States on 18 August 1916, 2 days after similar action by Great Britain acting on behalf of Canada. The beleaguered Weeks-McLean Act now was superseded, as was any further test of federal authority for regulating migratory birds — or so it seemed.

The Migratory Bird Treaty of 1916

Ratification of the Migratory Bird Treaty heralded a new era for waterfowl and other migratory birds. These birds now were afforded international status and a good measure of much-needed protection. No less important was the unification of waterfowl management under the mantle of federal responsibility. In brief, the provisions of the Treaty included

(1) A definition of migratory birds, including those classified as (1) waterfowl, (2) insectivorous, and (3) nongame.

(2) A closed season each year between 10 March and 1 September with hunting seasons no longer than 3.5 months in length at other times of the year. Insectivorous birds were protected throughout the year as were nongame birds, although certain exceptions were permitted for specific areas and for certain species of waterfowl and nongame birds required as subsistence food and clothing by Indians and Inuit. Among waterfowl, scoters were designated specifically as subsistance food for Indians.

(3) Initiation of a 10-year closed season for swans and a variety of other migratory birds, including Whooping Cranes (*Grus americana*). American Woodcock (*Scolopax minor*) and some other abundant species of shorebirds were exempted from this moratorium.

(4) Initiation of a 5-year closed season for Wood Ducks and eiders (*Polysticta* and *Somateria*).

(5) Protection of nests and eggs of migratory birds.

(6) Prohibition from shipping or export of migratory birds or their eggs from any state or province during the closed season. Shipments of these items at other times must be marked appropriately.

(7) Authorization of a permit system for killing migratory birds seriously damaging private property.

(8) Agreement between each nation to seek separate enactment of legislation ensuring the execution of the convention and this Treaty.

(9) Establishment of a means for ratification of the convention and this Treaty, including its enforcement for 15 years and thereafter on a yearly basis unless either nation provided notice 12 months in advance of its intention to terminate the agreement.

The Migratory Bird Treaty Act of 1918

The Migratory Bird Treaty of 1916 required ratification by the legislative branches of both the United States and Great Britain (Canada), which resulted in the Migratory Birds Convention Act in Canada in 1917 and the Migratory Bird Treaty Act (MBTA) in the United States in 1918. Both acts enabled the respective governments of each nation to protect migratory birds with police powers and penalties. Furthermore, each government was empowered with regulatory and administrative authorities.

The MBTA came under attack just as had its predecessor, the Weeks-McLean Act of 1913, again on constitutional grounds. The enabling legislation in Canada likewise was attacked in court. However, the constitutionality of both measures was upheld in 1920, respectively, by the Supreme Court of the United States and by the Supreme Court of Prince Edward Island in Canada. The U.S. Supreme Court's action stemming from this challenge deserves further mention as it indeed was a landmark decision widely cited by political scientists and jurists (see Swisher 1943, Cushman 1958, Woll 1981). The State of Missouri led the challenge to federal intervention and soon more or less arranged a test case when that state's attorney general was arrested by Federal Warden Ray P. Holland. The decision reached in *Missouri v. Holland* dealt a stunning blow to the doctrine that state ownership barred regulation of wildlife by federal authority (Bean 1977). The Court's opinion, delivered by Justice Oliver Wendell Holmes, clearly disposed of Missouri's claim to ownership, to wit:

"The treaty in question does not contravene any prohibitory words to be found in the Constitution. The only question is whether it is forbidden by some invisible radiation from the general terms of the Tenth Amendment . . . The state, as we have intimated, founds its claim of exclusive authority upon an assertion of title to migratory birds — an assertion that is embodied in statute. No doubt it is true that, as between a state and its inhabitants, the state

may regulate the killing and sale of such birds, but it does not follow that its authority is exclusive of paramount powers. Wild birds are not in the possession of anyone; and possession is the beginning of ownership. The whole foundation of the state's rights is the presence within their jurisdiction of birds that yesterday had not arrived, tomorrow may be in another state, and in a week a thousand miles away . . . But for the treaty and the statute there soon might be no birds for any powers to deal with. . . . It is not sufficient to rely upon the states . . . The reliance is vain . . . We are of the opinion that the treaty and the statute must be upheld."

In accordance with the MBTA, state governments were authorized to adopt and enforce laws or regulations protecting migratory birds, as long as these were not inconsistent with those of the federal government. That is, state authority may be more restrictive than the federal regulations, but not more liberal. For example, if the federal bag limit was set at five ducks per day, a state might set a limit of only four, but not six. The first regulations issued under authority of the MBTA prescribed

(1) Open seasons for migratory game birds.
(2) The means by which migratory birds may be hunted legally.
(3) Rules for possession and shipment of migratory birds legally secured.
(4) Bag limits.
(5) Rules for the propagation of migratory birds and for their sale.
(6) Prohibition of sale of migratory birds except waterfowl propagated under permit.
(7) Special permits for collecting migratory birds for purposes of scientific study or other needs.

The provisions of the MBTA and its Canadian counterpart understandably have been modified many times in the years following 1918. But with these first steps, waterfowl management gained a foothold for the future.

Amendments to the Migratory Bird Treaty

Since 1918, two amendments were added to the MBTA that are especially significant to waterfowl management. The Migratory Bird Treaty Reform Act of 1998 made it unlawful to use bait to harvest migratory game birds if the person knows or reasonably should know that an area is baited, which had long been a controversial enforcement issue in waterfowl (see "Other Issues" later in this chapter).

The second amendment, the Migratory Bird Treaty Reform Act of 2004, specifically stated that the MBTA applied only to species native to the United States and its territories, and defined native birds as those present as a result of natural biological or ecological processes. This amendment stemmed from the controversy surrounding control measures implemented by the Maryland Department of Natural Resources to control Mute Swans (see Infobox 5-2). Historically, authority to manage Mute Swans was granted to the states because the U.S. Fish and Wildlife Service interpreted the original MBTA to exclude exotic species; hence, Maryland started controlling Mute Swans in 1993. However, in December 2001, the U.S. District Court of Appeals in Washington, D.C. (*Hill v. Norton*) ruled that Mute Swans were indeed protected under the MBTA, which halted Maryland's control efforts. The U.S. Fish and Wildlife Service then issued depredation permits to individual states, but this approach also incurred lawsuits. Likewise, a draft Environmental Assessment that addressed the issue was challenged in court, which ruled against empowering the states to use lethal measures. The 2004 amendment thus ends this controversy by excluding all exotic birds from protection of the MBTA. In March 2005, the U.S. Fish and Wildlife Service published a list of 125 exotic species — including the Mute Swan — that are no longer protected by the MBTA, of which 17 have established self-sustaining populations in the United States. The decision to include the Mute Swan was immediately challenged in court, but that petition was denied by the U.S. Court of Appeals on 21 June 2005.

Other Treaties

The success of the 1916 treaty with Great Britain (Canada) later prompted similar treaties with Mexico (1936), Japan (1972), and the Soviet Union (1978). The details of these treaties varied somewhat (see Bean 1977), but each clearly provided protection for migratory birds, although the Mexico treaty also included "game mammals." In particular, the treaty with Mexico is noteworthy — with its ratification, the United States joined with its southern neighbor, as it had earlier with Canada, thereby consolidating the protection and management of migratory birds across all of North America.

As one example of their importance, these treaties collectively bear on the severely diminished population of the Aleutian Canada Goose. The breeding range of these birds once included islands in the possession of the former Soviet Union as well as those belonging to the United States. Furthermore, Aleutian Canada Geese formerly wintered in Japan, and still do on the western coasts of Canada, the United States, and, occasionally, Mexico. Hence, the historical and current distribution of a single race of goose touches all nations now in treaty with the United States for the protection of migratory birds (see "Endangered Species" later in this chapter for more about Aleutian Canada Geese).

Migratory Bird Conservation Act of 1929

Protection of waterfowl was assured by the Migratory Bird Treaty Act of 1918, but protection of the birds alone represented only half of the equation if crucial habitats also were not preserved and managed for migratory birds. An attempt in 1921 known as the Public Shooting Grounds-Game Refuge Bill failed when its opponents balked at a provision for a $1 federal hunting license. At least 60% of the license fees were designated for the acquisition of lands serving as refuges and public hunting areas. Not more than 40% of the fees were allocated for enforcement of the measure's provisions. Despite repeated introduction for several years, the bill failed in Congress, largely because it featured public shooting areas and a federal hunting license. However, in 1929, when the objectionable features were dropped, a new bill known as the Migratory Bird Conservation Act was adopted.

The Act provided funding — $1 million by 1933 and for each year thereafter until 1940 — for the acquisition of refuges for migratory game birds. Whereas a few waterfowl refuges had been established previously (e.g., the Bear River marshes in Utah and marshes along the upper Mississippi River), these were each the result of specific legislation and not a general commitment to a national effort for habitat preservation. Thus, enactment of the Migratory Bird Conservation Act emerged as the beginning of a national thrust for the steady acquisition of waterfowl habitat. Unfortunately, the flow of funding promised by Congress proved less than reliable, compromised in part by the Great Depression of the next decade.

An important feature of the Migratory Bird Conservation Act concerned the administration of habitat acquisition. The Act established a Migratory Bird Conservation Commission for the purpose of approving proposals for renting or purchasing habitat. The Commission consists of the Secretaries of Interior, Agriculture, and Transportation and two members each from the Senate and House of Representatives. An officer of the wildlife agency in any state where habitat acquisition is under consideration also serves as an ex-officio member of the Commission. Most notably, no acquisition could be completed without the consent of the state where the habitat was located (Bean 1977). This provision, as we shall see, was the genesis of a troublesome regulation affecting later legislation designed to acquire wetland habitats for waterfowl.

FEDERAL FUNDING BEGINS

Jay N. "Ding" Darling and the "Duck Stamp"

A dynamic personality entered the conservation scene early in the administration of President Franklin D. Roosevelt. Jay N. Darling was a skilled cartoonist with a rapier pen who signed his drawings with the pseudonym "J. N. Ding" (see Infobox 11-1). His cartoons covered the spectrum of political life, but Darling also drew poignant characterizations of human abuse of the landscape; waterfowl often highlighted his clever drawings (Fig. 11-2). Darling sketched for the *Des Moines Register* in Iowa, but he answered the call to Washington in 1934, taking over duties as Chief of the U.S. Bureau of Biological Survey, which in 1940 became the U.S. Fish and Wildlife Service. His tenure was brief — about 18 months — but his imprint on wildlife management has endured far into the future. Darling's ideas and spirited leadership brought many new programs to fruition, among them the formation of Cooperative Wildlife Research Units, but we shall focus on the "Duck Stamp" and its influence on the preservation of waterfowl habitat.

A few weeks after Darling's appointment, a bill introduced earlier by Senator Frederic Walcott of Connecticut and Congressman Richard Kleberg of Texas became law. This law was the Migratory Bird Hunting Stamp Act, approved on 16 March 1934. The idea for a Duck Stamp scarcely was new, however, as the chief of the federal warden corps, George Lawyer, had proposed selling a federal stamp at the end of World War I. However, attempts to pass such a

Figure 11-2. J. N. "Ding" Darling's skillful drawings of wildlife often featured the plight of waterfowl, especially when poor land management was at fault. Leaving his career as a political cartoonist in Iowa in 1934, Darling went to Washington, D.C. to become the Chief of the U.S. Bureau of Biological Survey, the precursor of the U.S. Fish and Wildlife Service. Photo courtesy of the J. N. "Ding" Darling Foundation.

InfoBox 11-1

Jay N. "Ding" Darling
Artist and Conservationist
(1878–1962)

Darling's clever cartoons propelled him into national prominence early in the 20th century. Most of his drawings were political in nature, but others focused on conservation and often called attention to the plight of waterfowl from drought and poaching. His cartoons originated with the *Des Moines Daily Register* but, as his work gained notice, they were later syndicated through the *New York Herald Tribune* and eventually appeared in 130 daily newspapers. He received Pulitzer Prizes in 1923 and 1942. With a flourish, Darling signed his drawings with "Ding"— a contraction of his last name — a pen name that later became an enduring appellation in the annals of wildlife conservation.

During the early days of the 1930s, the ravages of the Dust Bowl on soil and water resources, along with

the drought's effect on waterfowl and other wildlife, were common topics of his drawings. At the same time, his political cartoons often poked fun at the depression-era programs of President Franklin D. Roosevelt. In 1934, Roosevelt responded by appointing Darling as Chief of the Bureau of Biological Survey, predecessor to the present-day U.S. Fish and Wildlife Service. In a stroke, Roosevelt had chosen a nationally known conservationist to head the Bureau while also slyly ending Darling's political attacks on the president's New Deal.

Darling was scarcely a do-nothing government appointee. He used his administrative skills to successfully expand the national wildlife refuge system, which he made sure included an ever-larger number of sites devoted to waterfowl and wetland protection. In 1934, he personally drew the design for the first Duck Stamp (Fig. 11-3) and thereby initiated a new and much-needed source of funds devoted exclusively for waterfowl management. Darling also designed the "Blue Goose" icon that appears on signs marking the boundaries of national wildlife refuges and, indeed, is the hallmark symbol of the refuge system itself. In 1935, Darling established a source of college-trained field biologists when he created a series of Cooperative Wildlife Research Units on university campuses across the nation. Darling's energy was contagious and brought new vigor to the Bureau across the breadth of its conservation activities, but waterfowl management remained of special importance to him. His tenure in office was brief — just 18 months — but during that time he became a national voice for wildlife conservation as well as an administrative leader who got things done when they needed doing. After leaving government, Darling organized the National Wildlife Federation, which has become the largest citizen-based conservation organization in the United States; he served as the Federation's first president. The J. N. (Ding) Darling National Wildlife Refuge at Sanibel Island, Florida, is named in his honor, as is a foundation dedicated, in part, to conservation education in grade schools. See Lendt (2001) for a full biography. Photo courtesy of the J. N. "Ding" Darling Foundation.

bill failed repeatedly, beginning with one proposed in 1921 by Senator Harry New of Indiana and Congressman Dan Anthony of Kansas. Had the New-Anthony Bill passed, it would have given conservationists more than a decade's head start toward the acquisition of waterfowl habitat, no doubt saving vast areas of wetlands for the future (Trefethen 1975). Nonetheless, with enactment of the Migratory Bird Hunting Stamp Act in 1934, the belated work of wetland acquisition gained a sorely needed source of funds. This legislation was a crucial step as Congress had not always appropriated the money committed earlier by the Migratory Bird Conservation Act. Now, however, revenues from duck hunters and others who bought the stamps provided an independent source of funds dedicated to a single mission; the Migratory Bird Conservation Fund was the formal name given to these revenues.

Thus, two forces merged in the midst of the greatest drought ever known in the United States. The long drought had begun in 1930, and together with the abusive treatment of Midwestern farmland, wetland habitats in the nation's interior withered and shrunk as the Dust Bowl continued unabated. Waterfowl populations followed suit — their numbers plunged to levels never before imagined. "Ding" Darling's pen drew the design for the first

Duck Stamp, which was issued in 1934, sold for $1, and produced revenues of $635,000 (Fig. 11-3). Programs protecting waterfowl habitat now began in earnest.

Whereas the stamp originally was correctly identified as the Migratory Bird Hunting Stamp, it is required only of hunters 16 years or more of age who hunted waterfowl. The stamp is not required for hunters of doves (Columbidae), cranes (Gruidae), or other migratory birds; hence the popular name "Duck Stamp" emerged as a reflection of this distinction. In 1976, the stamp was renamed the Migratory Bird Hunting and Conservation Stamp, in part reflecting the additional commitment of nonhunters who also purchased these stamps for the purpose of contributing to wetland preservation.

The legacy of the Duck Stamp continues today. Until 1949, wildlife artists commissioned by the U.S. Fish and Wildlife Service designed each year's Duck Stamp. Since then, artists have competed in an annual contest, with the winners gaining wide recognition for their work. No direct remuneration is involved, but winning artists later are rewarded financially from sales of enlarged prints of their designs to private collectors of wildlife artwork. Many hundreds of artists enter the competition each year.

The first Duck Stamp sold for $1, but it steadily

Figure 11-3. The first Duck Stamp featured the artwork of J. N. "Ding" Darling. Funds from the sale of these stamps are committed to the acquisition of waterfowl habitat. Initially selling for $1 in 1934, the stamps reached $15 by 1991, but the price has scarcely kept pace with inflated land values. Photo courtesy of the U.S. Fish and Wildlife Service.

rose in price to $5 in 1972, $10 in 1987, and the current (2004–05) price of $15 in 1991 — the increases reflect the increasing cost of land acquired by the program. In fact, the increased price of Duck Stamps actually added only a few cents of purchasing power compared with the original $1 price of the stamps, whereas the average value of farmland rose by as much as 2,600% (Poole 1982). By the end of 2004, some 1,616,093 Duck Stamps had been sold, which generated $696 million used to purchase 2.1 million ha of wetland habitat for waterfowl. Peak sales exceeded 2.4 million stamps for the 1970–71 waterfowl season; 1.6 million were sold in 2003–04.

Federal Aid in Wildlife Restoration Act of 1937

In terms of general support for wildlife management, the Federal Aid in Wildlife Restoration Act of 1937 remains paramount in the logbook of legislation dealing with wildlife resources and their conservation. Like many other bills, earlier versions had failed several times before an acceptable bill was enacted in 1937 under the sponsorship of Senator Key Pittman of Nevada and Congressman A. Willis Robertson of Virginia. This landmark legislation accordingly is known popularly as "P-R" for the initials of its sponsors.

P-R established a far-reaching means of funding management programs at the state level. Previously, each state agency responsible for wildlife management remained largely at the mercy of its annual legislative appropriation. Some years, wildlife management fared well; in others, it starved for lack of adequate funding. Political considerations, as well as economic influences, often governed the appropriation of funds for wildlife management. Furthermore, revenues derived from the sales of hunting licenses commonly disappeared into the coffers of other state agencies instead of remaining available to wildlife departments. The result was predictable for its uncertainty; wildlife management was little more than an on-again, off-again affair with each state's legislature. This situation changed dramatically under the provisions of the new law.

P-R levied a 10% federal excise tax on most types of arms and ammunition (the tax later was increased to 11% and expanded to include sales of handguns in 1971 and archery equipment in 1975). The pool of tax revenues then was reallocated to each state based on a formula considering the size of the state and the number of licensed hunters therein. To qualify for its allocation, each state had to match the fed-

eral contribution with its own funds on a 1 to 3 ratio. That is, every $3 of federal money had to be matched with $1 of state money. The attractiveness of this windfall proved too great to ignore, and the states quickly saw to it that matching funds became available. The states also agreed to stop diverting license fees from their wildlife departments; each state soon adapted its laws to meet this fundamental requirement of the new federal legislation (Bean 1977). P-R thus assured state wildlife programs a steady financial footing never before possible; nearly $3 million became available in the first year alone (see Kallman 1987).

Projects supported by P-R funds are by no means limited to waterfowl management, however, and a breakdown of these into convenient categories is a task beyond our means. Nevertheless, scores of waterfowl projects receive P-R funds each year, and the list would be lengthy indeed if those of the past were tallied in full. Suffice it to highlight the unequivocal assertion that waterfowl management prospered from the vision of this legislation. Nearly every aspect of wildlife management, including habitat acquisition and research, has been touched by P-R in dimensions unequaled by other legislation. Indeed, the success of P-R led to the enactment of similar legislation in 1950 for the support of fisheries management. Overall, P-R has distributed over $4 billion dollars back to the states from 1937 to 2004, and land purchases alone now total some 1.6 million ha of wildlife habitat.

FLYWAYS AS ADMINISTRATIVE UNITS

North American Flyways

Humans have been fascinated by the movements of birds since the beginnings of recorded history. Biblical references include those in Exodus 16:13, Numbers 11:31, Job 39:26, and Jeremiah 8:7, and ancient Persians apparently derived parts of their calendars based on the predictable movements of birds (Lincoln 1939, Dorst 1962). Many myths originated because of the seasonal disappearances of waterfowl and other birds. One proposed by Aristotle concluded that some birds hibernated, thus explaining why they were not observed in winter. Another myth was the belief that certain European geese turned into sea creatures each spring, thereby initiating the still-used name Barnacle Goose to account for their disappearance at winter's end.

Migratory behavior no longer is the fantasy of earlier times, although much still is unknown. Routes and destinations were discovered after years of banding. An analysis of many thousands of band recoveries eventually gave rise to the concept of four discernible flyways spanning North America (Lincoln 1935, 1939): Atlantic, Mississippi, Central, and Pacific (Fig. 11-4). Three decades later, Bellrose (1968) carefully refined the movements of waterfowl with radar and recognized the existence of lesser routes known as "migration corridors" within and across the major flyways. For example, Serie et al. (1983) determined that Canvasbacks staging in Wisconsin during their autumn migration later separated into discrete populations and overwintered in different areas of three flyways. Nonetheless, the flyways reflect the general nature of waterfowl migrations in North America, and despite certain inconsistencies, these became the functional units employed to manage waterfowl.

The administrative convenience of the flyway concept first gained significance during the Dust Bowl years (Lincoln 1939). Duck and goose populations diminished in all flyways, but particularly in the Central and Pacific Flyways. The birds adhered to these ancestral routes of migration so that, even for species distributed across North America, those in one flyway might be so diminished as to be jeopardized, whereas the same species in another flyway might be relatively abundant. However, hunting regulations for waterfowl were not based on the flyway concept until 1948.

Flyway Councils: Using the funding available from P-R, state wildlife agencies quickly launched numerous studies of wildlife, including large-scale banding programs for waterfowl. As a result, the states learned much about their respective roles in the distribution and harvest of waterfowl. This information, in turn, brought greater — and continuing — impetus for each state to voice its opinions about waterfowl management, particularly on the subject of hunting regulations. Whereas the states participated in gathering field information, they seldom could use these data for management decisions because, as a result of the Migratory Bird Treaty Act,

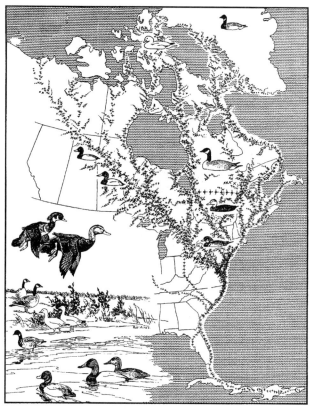

Atlantic Flyway

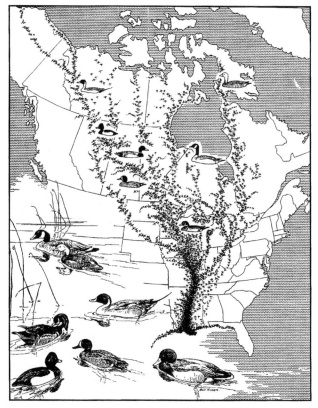

Mississippi Flyway

Figure 11-4. Long years of banding waterfowl and other birds revealed the presence of four flyways crossing North America, although some species and populations regularly cross from one flyway to another. The flyways today provide the administrative units for managing migratory waterfowl. Drawings courtesy of the U.S. Fish and Wildlife Service.

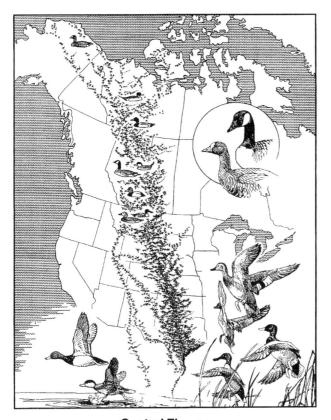

Central Flyway

Pacific Flyway

regulatory authority rested with the federal government. Each state accordingly made separate recommendations to the U.S. Fish and Wildlife Service for bag limits and season lengths. These proposals often conflicted with those of other states and usually lacked coordination within the flyway.

By 1947 it was clear that other means were needed to coordinate waterfowl management within each flyway, and the topic emerged at the annual meeting of the Western Association of Game and Fish Commissioners in that same year. In the following year, the directors of state wildlife agencies in the Pacific and Central Flyways held their first meetings. The latter called themselves the Central Flyway Council, thereby formally establishing a new era of administration and intra-flyway cooperation.

The idea of waterfowl councils in each flyway gained momentum when the International Association of Game, Fish, and Conservation Commissioners adopted Resolution 10 at their meeting in 1951. The resolution included two recommendations. First, that a council be established in each of the four flyways and second, that a National Waterfowl Council also be formed. Two members from each flyway council were to form the body of the national council. Further, representatives of the U.S. Fish and Wildlife Service — one per flyway — were to join the council as liaison officers for coordination of state and federal programs. The resolution led to the formal organization of councils for all flyways in 1952 and to a national council in 1953. This framework continues today except for minor adjustments in voting privileges for those states encompassing two flyways. In some instances, the flyway councils include representatives from Canadian provinces, although they do not vote on matters concerning harvest regulations in the United States. The councils also support investigations with funds obtained from member states or other sources and set overall policy for these activities. Much of the field work thereafter falls into the hands of flyway technical committees.

Flyway Technical Committees: Membership of the flyway councils usually consists of each state wildlife agency's chief administrator or a designated representative. Whereas these persons are authorized to act on behalf of their state governments, it was clear that they required current technical advice from practicing biologists for developing policies and regulations. This situation led to the formulation of flyway technical committees, which consist of state biologists involved with waterfowl management and research, sometimes complemented by associate members from private conservation organizations, universities, or federal wildlife agencies. The committees supply and analyze data concerning the status of waterfowl populations, habitat requirements, and other matters influencing waterfowl management in each flyway.

In addition to the routine collection and analysis of population, production, and harvest survey data each year, the technical committees also initiate, usually at the request or recommendation of the flyway councils, management-oriented research projects. Some of these initiatives produced important techniques that soon became universally accepted well beyond the sphere of the flyway where they were developed originally. Among these is a now widely applied method for aging duck broods under field conditions (Gollop and Marshall 1954; see Chapter 5). Other contributions of the flyway technical committees include support for large-scale banding programs or investigations of breeding biology designed to answer specific questions. For example, after the Mississippi Flyway Technical Committee recommended that the feasibility of helicopter and ground searches for goose nests be assessed, Raveling and Lumsden (1977) and Malecki et al. (1980, 1981), respectively, surveyed two populations of Canada Geese nesting in northern Manitoba. Similarly, more than 25,000 geese were captured and marked in the first year of a 2-year study of Snow Goose populations in the eastern Arctic, a cooperative effort involving the Mississippi and Central Flyways as well as federal agencies in Canada and the United States (Brace et al. 1978).

How Regulations are Developed: Each year, regulations for waterfowl hunting in the United States are established by the U.S. Fish and Wildlife Service working in cooperation with the states, which work through their respective Flyway Councils. The Canadian Wildlife Service has similar statutory authority to establish hunting seasons for migratory birds in Canada. The Migratory Bird Treaty grants this authority to both countries, wherein hunting seasons are closed each year unless these two agencies annually take specific action to establish seasons. In the United States, the process of establishing annual hunting regulations is thorough, involving the states, Flyway Councils, nongovernment organizations, and the public. The final product results in two types of regulations: basic and annual. The basic regulations are those associated with methods of harvest, transport, and possession limits, and

usually are unchanged from year-to-year. Annual regulations are reviewed each year and adjusted in accordance with projected levels of harvest and harvest rates. The early-season regulations are for those seasons that begin on or before 1 October, and include other migratory game birds in addition to waterfowl (e.g., doves and American Woodcock). The late-season regulations are those generally associated with the regular waterfowl hunting seasons. The entire process begins in January and moves through a series of steps before the final hunting regulations are issued. The sequence and substance of these events can be summarized as follows:

(1) January — Important issues and potential major changes to the previous year's regulations are discussed among the Service Regulations Committee (SRC), which is comprised of five high-level U.S. Fish and Wildlife Service officials (four Regional Directors and the Assistant Director for Migratory Birds) and two designated Flyway Consultants from each flyway (Council members or their designees). The Service then publishes the "first rulemaking" or "Notice of Intent to Establish Open Seasons" in the *Federal Register*, within which they present these issues and potential major changes to the previous year's regulations, as well as describe the regulation development process.

(2) February/March — The Flyway Technical Committees meet to consider changes in hunting regulations for migratory shore and upland game birds as well as some waterfowl seasons, primarily the early seasons. The recommendations are then forwarded to the Flyway Councils which send approved recommendations to the SRC. The regulatory proposals under Adaptive Harvest Management (see Chapter 8) are also considered; all alternatives are published in the *Federal Register*.

(3) June — The SRC, including Flyway Consultants, meets to develop the early-season frameworks based upon the recommendations of their technical staffs and Flyway Councils.

(4) July — The U.S. Fish and Wildlife Service publishes the specific proposals for the early seasons in the *Federal Register* and accepts public comments. The Flyway Technical Committees and Flyway Councils also meet to consider "late seasons," which include the regular duck and goose seasons, and forward those recommendations to the SRC. The SRC, including Flyway Consultants, meets to develop the late-season

frameworks based upon recommendations of their technical staffs and Flyway Councils.

(5) August — The U.S. Fish and Wildlife Service publishes a "Final Rule" in the *Federal Register,* which describes the early seasons from which the states then select their early season hunting dates. The Service then publishes these season selections and bag limits in the *Federal Register*, along with the proposed rules for the late season. Public comment is then accepted, and a Final Rule on late seasons is published in September, which includes the actual seasons selected by each state.

(6) September — The U.S. Fish and Wildlife Service finalizes the late-season frameworks and publishes the "Final Rule" in the *Federal Register*. The states then select their hunting dates for the late season from the "Final Rule," and the Service publishes those selections and bag limits in the *Federal Register*.

In summary, the development of hunting seasons and associated regulations has evolved over many years into a highly collaborative process involving federal, state/provincial, and private entities. The high-level personnel comprising the SRC also attests to the importance of this process to the U.S. Fish and Wildlife Service. Overall, this approach ensures ample opportunity for all interested parties to participate in the process and provide input. The collective efforts are guided at every step by the waterfowl management community to achieve and maintain desired population levels while sustaining recreational hunting opportunities.

LAND-MANAGEMENT POLICIES

The Wetlands Loan Act of 1961

As noted in Chapter 10, wetlands in the United States experienced immense losses, especially in the years following World War II, and the funds derived from the sales of Duck Stamps alone could not stem this destructive tide. Congress responded to this alarming situation in 1961 with the Wetlands Loan Act introduced by Congressman John D. Dingell of Michigan. A 7-year loan of $105 million was granted to the U.S. Fish and Wildlife Service for accelerated acquisition of crucial wetlands. These funds were merged with Duck Stamp receipts in the Migratory Bird Conservation Fund. Future revenues from the sales of Duck Stamps were pledged for repayment of the loan. Congress reauthorized the Act in 1967, extending

the loan for another 8 years. In 1976, the loan was increased to $200 million and extended again until 1983, although only $144 million of the authorization had been released by 1982. Eventually all but about $2.5 million was appropriated, and most importantly, the loan was forgiven in its entirety, thereby making repayment unnecessary from the future sales of Duck Stamps. Also, the language in the last reauthorization extended the life of the loan until all funds have been appropriated and expended (i.e., no date of expiration was specified). This means that, until the last dollar is spent, the door is open for the Wetlands Loan Act to receive further funding from Congress without the need of introducing new enabling legislation.

As mentioned earlier, an innocuous provision in the Migratory Bird Conservation Act of 1929 required state approval for the acquisition of habitat proposed from within that state. With the Wetlands Loan Act, however, the requirement was given formal emphasis: The governor *or* the head of the appropriate state agency was given special authority to approve these acquisitions (Bean 1977). Between 1961 and 1977, successive governors of North Dakota — a state in the heartland of the prairie breeding grounds — approved acquisitions of about 600,000 ha, of which about half had been completed by 1977 (Wildlife Management Institute 1983). Then an issue developed when North Dakota enacted state laws limiting approval *only* to the governor and which altered the guidelines for acquiring wetlands. Armed with these measures, the governor at the time would not consent to additional acquisitions and, in fact, challenged the status of wetlands already acquired in North Dakota (see review in Sidle and Harmon 1987). In brief, North Dakota limited the terms under which landowners might enter into agreements with the U.S. Fish and Wildlife Service and mandated ways that previous agreements might be thwarted. The federal government accordingly sued North Dakota, winning its case in a U.S. District Court, although North Dakota appealed the decision. The issue was settled by the U.S. Supreme Court in 1983 with the ruling that, "The consent required by the Wetlands Act of 1961 cannot be revoked at the will of an incumbent governor. To hold otherwise would be inconsistent with the Act's purpose of facilitating the acquisition of wetlands . . . Nothing in the statute authorizes withdrawal of approval previously given." Hence, North Dakota's effort to thwart the Act was declared unconstitutional.

Emergency Wetlands Resources Act of 1986

The Emergency Wetlands Resources Act is an often overlooked but nonetheless major piece of legislation affecting wetlands and waterfowl conservation. The legislation authorized purchase of wetlands with monies from the Land and Water Conservation Fund, which was modified to permit such expenditures. The Act also extended the Wetlands Loan Act through 1988 and forgave repayment of funds Congress had advanced to that program. The Act additionally directed the Secretary of Interior to continue the National Wetlands Inventory and to report to Congress by 1990 (and at 10-year intervals thereafter) on the status of the Nation's wetlands (see Dahl 1990, Dahl 2000). This legislation approved entrance fees at national wildlife refuges, with 70% of these funds going to the Migratory Bird Conservation Fund and 30% dedicated to the maintenance and operation of refuges. Finally, the Act increased the price of the Migratory Bird Conservation Stamp (Duck Stamp) from $7.50 to $10.

Waterfowl Production Areas

Not all wetlands were of a size to warrant protection as a federal refuge. Many small areas, even isolated potholes and sloughs no more than a few hectares in size, remained available as valuable habitat for waterfowl. An efficient means was needed to acquire such areas, particularly on the breeding grounds in the northern prairies.

In 1958, the Migratory Bird Hunting Stamp Act of 1934 was amended to provide for acquisitions of small marshes and potholes. These wetlands might be leased, exchanged, or received as gifts and were to be designated as Waterfowl Production Areas (WPAs). Most WPAs, however, were acquired by direct purchase or easement, and the necessary monies were derived from the Migratory Bird Conservation Fund.

WPAs acquired by purchase become federal property and taxes, if any, are paid by the government to the county in which the wetland is located. On easement areas, the owner retains title to the property but, in return for a lump sum, agrees not to damage the wetland; burning, leveling, drainage, and filling are prohibited, but the landowner retains all other property rights including hunting, trapping, farming, and grazing. The long-term goal of the WPA program is to acquire more than 1 million ha of small wetlands.

North American Wetlands Conservation Act

Another effort directed toward the dwindling availability of wetlands was enacted in December 1989, in part as support for the North American Waterfowl Management Plan described later in this Chapter. Known as the North American Wetlands Conservation Act, the measure supplies federal funds as matching monies for state and private agencies proposing sites for wetland protection. Congress initially authorized $15 million for the North American Wetlands Conservation Fund established by the Act, but the money has not always been supplied in full. The mainstay of the Act originates with the interest earned by funds held in the Pittman-Robertson account, but other sources at times become available (e.g., $11 million in fines from the *Exxon Valdez* oil spill). The Act received increased funding in subsequent years, with the 2002 reauthorization increasing funding from $55 million in 2003 to $75 million in 2007.

The federal funds are matched in a ratio of at least 1:1 by monies from organizations such as The Nature Conservancy and Ducks Unlimited, as well as from state wildlife agencies, but in practice the partners have matched at least $2 for every $1 of the federal contribution. Proposals are submitted to a nine-member North American Wetlands Conservation Council, which then submits its recommendations to the Migratory Bird Conservation Commission for final action. At least 50% of the money must support wetland conservation in Canada and Mexico.

Agriculture and Waterfowl

National policies commonly bear direct or indirect influences on the welfare of wildlife populations. Regrettably, few farm policies are enacted with much concern for wildlife, but because many programs focus on land management, both the quality and quantity of wildlife habitat may be affected. Of these, policies designed to reduce crop surpluses typically include incentives for removing large areas of cropland from further production. Such programs in turn offer enormous management potentials for waterfowl and other wildlife (Harmon and Nelson 1973).

One of the more prominent policies was initiated with the Agricultural Act of 1956, popularly known as the "Soil Bank." Farmers entered into 5- or 10-year agreements with the government that retired land from continued crop production. These agreements further required that the idled land remain protected by adequate plant cover. Ring-necked Pheasants (*Phasianus colchicus*) responded dramatically to the favorable habitat on the retired croplands (Erickson and Wiebe 1973). Waterfowl, too, benefited from the tracts of new cover. For example, Benson (1964) reported finding more duck nests on lands idled by the Soil Bank than in other cover types, and of these, more hatched successfully than elsewhere in his Minnesota study area. However, agreements idling croplands under the auspices of the Soil Bank expired in 1969.

Another policy, the Food and Agriculture Act of 1965, established the Cropland Adjustment Program (CAP). Under the CAP, about 16 million ha could be deferred from crop production and instead be planted in grasses and legumes (Jaenke 1966). Dense cover suitable as nesting habitat for many species of ducks thus replaced crops on an area equivalent to all of Ohio and half of Pennsylvania. The availability of this habitat produced impressive results in the heavily farmed Prairie Pothole Region. Duebbert (1969) recorded 61 duck nests of seven species on little more than 50 ha of CAP land in South Dakota. Nearly 80% of these nests hatched successfully, compared with only 30% hatching success on nearby land still in crop production. About eight ducklings were produced per hectare of CAP land. By extrapolation of these data, all CAP land in the county where the study was conducted could have produced 15,000 ducks as a by-product of the diverted cropland. Additional study later determined nest densities of 77 nests/km^2 on CAP lands compared with 25 nests/km^2 on adjacent agricultural lands (Duebbert and Lokemoen 1976). Similarly, ducklings hatched at a rate of 4 ducks/ha on CAP lands, whereas only 0.5 ducklings/ha hatched on nearby farmland (Duebbert and Kantrud 1974).

Other efforts to curtail agricultural production have not been as beneficial for wildlife. Harmon and Nelson (1973) described the aftermath of the Wheat and Feed Grain Program, one of several other programs encouraging idled lands for reduced crop production. Unlike the expectations raised by the Soil Bank, however, land idled by this and some related programs seldom attained a cover of protective vegetation. Instead, 40–50% of the idled lands in Minnesota lacked any cover and remained exposed to severe soil erosion throughout the year. Another 30–35% contained sparse stands of seedling oats that later were plowed under. No more than 25% of the idled land was covered with vegetation useful to wildlife. Similar results emerged when the survey was expanded to a 13-state area; up to 75% of the idled lands had inadequate cover for either wildlife or soil protection.

The Conservation Reserve Program: The Food Security Act of 1985 extended federal programs to stem the tide of crop surpluses and soil erosion. Under one of the Act's provisions, the Conservation Reserve Program (CRP), farmers voluntarily remove highly erodible land from further crop production for 10 years in return for annual payments, as determined by a bid system, from the U.S. Department of Agriculture. For wildlife, however, the importance of CRP lies in the requirement that permanent cover be established and maintained on the idled land. Grasses and legumes have been among the choices available for the cover; hence, CRP lands often have established prime nesting habitat for many species of waterfowl and other ground-nesting birds. Moreover, mowing and grazing are prohibited on CRP lands. In addition to the annual payments, the government shares with the farmer up to 50% of the cost of establishing the cover on CRP lands.

By 2003, the CRP program had enrolled 14 million ha, which benefited grassland-nesting birds in general, as well as waterfowl. In the Prairie Pothole Region of North Dakota, South Dakota, and northeastern Montana, about 1.9 million ha of cropland was converted to grassland cover by 1992, the effect of which was evaluated during the 1990s (Reynolds et al. 2001). Survival rates of duck nests were higher in all habitats examined during the CRP period compared with the pre-CRP period. Further, estimated nest success was 46% higher and recruitment rate 30% higher with CRP cover on the landscape compared with a simulated replacement with cropland. An overall model estimated an additional 12.4 million ducks were recruited to the fall population as a consequence of the CRP program from 1992 to 1997. Similarly, Kantrud (1993) recorded high rates of nest success on CRP lands in the Prairie Pothole Region planted to dense nesting cover (23%) compared with planted areas on U.S. Fish and Wildlife Service Waterfowl Production Areas (8%). CRP fields (64 ha) also were about twice the size of fields on Waterfowl Production Areas (32 ha).

CRP is also of great benefit to grassland nesting birds other than waterfowl. Johnson and Schwartz (1993), for example, reported 73 species of birds using CRP fields on their study areas in the Prairie Pothole Region. In a further comparison involving 20 species, only the Horned Lark (*Eremophila alpestris*) occurred in appreciably higher densities on croplands compared with CRP fields. In contrast, densities of 16 species were 7 times greater (median) on CRP fields compared with croplands, and 6 of these species were characterized by declining populations. Similarly, CRP lands provided important nesting habitat for nongame birds on the Southern High Plains of Texas (Berthelsen and Smith 1995). In Missouri, CRP fields have contributed to the conservation of several grassland bird species (McCoy et al. 1999; see also Ryan et al. 1998). However, CRP fields planted to dense nesting cover will change in structure and plant composition with age (current contracts require that enrolled cropland be idle for 10–15 years), producing corresponding changes in the avifauna that may require further management (Millenbah et al. 1996).

In addition to benefits as grassland bird habitat, Dunn et al. (1993) noted unintentional benefits of the CRP program, including mitigation of landscape and habitat fragmentation, maintenance of regional biodiversity, and changes in regional carbon flux. CRP unquestionably can influence habitat diversity at the landscape level (Weber et al. 2002), but CRP was first and foremost established to reduce soil erosion, improve water quality, and retire crops from production. Nonetheless, the program has and will continue to afford benefits to grassland-nesting birds and other wildlife.

A similar crop retirement program was established in Canada in 1989 under the administration of Agriculture and Agrifood Canada — the Permanent Cover Program (PCP). Landowners in the program agree to maintain the land in permanent cover for a 10- or 21-year period. Unlike CRP, however, farmers can use the forage from PCP sites. Enrollment currently exceeds 500,000 ha on more than 13,000 sites. McMaster and Davis (2001) provided an extensive review PCP in relation to grassland-nesting birds, noting high avian use and diversity on PCP sites in comparison with croplands.

The Wetlands Reserve Program: The 1985 Farm Bill contained a provision popularly known as "Swampbuster," which remains of major importance to waterfowl and other wetland-related wildlife. This measure prohibited farmers from receiving the benefits of federal subsidies such as price supports, low-interest loans, and crop insurance if they drain wetlands. Swampbuster thus simultaneously curtails both bringing additional land into crop production and draining valuable wetland habitat. Still another feature of the Act enables the Secretary of Agriculture to acquire easements on wetlands and other

lands for periods of at least 50 years. In return, farmers with loans held by the Farmers Home Administration have part of their debts canceled. Also, when lands held by the Farmers Home Administration are sold to private interests, the deeds are restricted in ways that will preserve or restore wetlands on the properties. In 1996, participants were granted greater flexibility to comply with the conservation provisions of the Swampbuster program, thereby increasing the overall area of wetlands subject to some form of management and protection.

However, a newer approach to wetland conservation emerged in the Food, Agriculture, Conservation, and Trade Act of 1990, conveniently known as the "1990 Farm Bill." This is the Wetlands Reserve Program (WRP), which offers farmers payments for restoring and preserving wetlands on their property. Congress appropriated more than $46 million in fiscal year 1992 to enroll about 20,200 ha in the first phase of the program, nearly all of which was achieved.

Like the CRP, WRP is entirely voluntary and provides cost-sharing payments for wetland restoration, but wetlands can be protected for more than the 10 years specified in CRP agreements, and wetlands can be protected in perpetuity. Landowners wishing to enroll in the program may select one of three options: (1) a minimal 10-year restoration–cost share agreement that does not include an easement but pays 75% of restoration costs, (2) a 30-year easement that includes an easement payment and 75% of the restoration cost, and (3) a permanent easement that pays the landowner 100% of the appraised agricultural value of the wetland and pays 100% of the restoration cost. In all instances, the landowner retains ownership. Each agreement also specifies the acceptable uses of the wetland, which may include hunting, fishing, haying, or grazing; the plans are prepared jointly by the landowner with the USDA Natural Resources Conservation Service and the U.S. Fish and Wildlife Service. The 2002 renewal of the Farm Bill, the Farm Security and Rural Investment Act, reauthorized the WRP program up to an enrollment of 0.9 million ha. By 2003, WRP had enrolled 7,831 projects affecting some 0.6 million ha.

Partners for Wildlife

In 1987, the U. S. Fish and Wildlife Service instituted its Partners for Wildlife program, which is a voluntary program that helps private (non-federal) landowners restore wetlands and other fish and wildlife habitats on their property. The program is usually a dollar-for-dollar cost share between the U.S. Fish and Wildlife Service and the landowner, but the Fish and Wildlife Service has the flexibility to pay more of the restoration cost. The landowner agrees to retain the restoration project for the life of a signed agreement, which is at least 10 years. The program is immensely popular with landowners, with whom the Fish and Wildlife Service has signed some 35,000 agreements from 1987 to 2004. These agreements have led to restoration of 293,000 ha of wetlands and 637,000 ha of prairie, native grasslands, and other uplands.

NATIONAL ENVIRONMENTAL POLICIES

The National Environmental Policy Act

For nearly 200 years, public policy in the United States largely ignored the inimical influences of human encroachment on environmental quality. Indeed, early legislation expressly enhanced the settlement and development of a young nation richly endowed with natural resources (e.g., the Homestead Act of 1862). Tax incentives later encouraged expansion of commerce and industry. Technology advanced rapidly under these influences, but these developments often added environmental disruptions never before envisioned. By the 1960s, however, a national awareness developed for environmental quality, undoubtedly stimulated in large measure by the disturbing message of *Silent Spring* (Carson 1962). Enactment of the National Environmental Policy Act (NEPA) in 1969 brought dramatic pause to unimpeded development and instead charged federal agencies to assess the environmental consequences of their actions (Skillern 1981).

Environmental Impact Statements (EIS) and related documents became the heart of NEPA's powerful mandate for maintaining safe, healthful, productive, and aesthetically and culturally pleasing surroundings. Wildlife resources, including waterfowl, often played a primary role in fulfilling that mandate. The events at Ruby Lake National Wildlife Refuge in Nevada illustrate, in part, the influence of NEPA.

Ruby Lake became a federal refuge in 1938 in recognition of its importance as a major nesting area for Canvasbacks in the western United States; up to 3,500 Canvasback ducklings are fledged at Ruby Lake each year. A sizable population of Redheads also nests at the refuge. However, Ruby Lake is one of the few areas in Nevada with sufficient water for outdoor recreation. Fishing and waterskiing highlight these

activities, but with them have come boats equipped with outboard motors averaging more than 90 horsepower. The Refuge Recreation Act of 1962 authorized public use of wildlife refuges, but only as a function secondary to the primary purpose of refuges. Unfortunately, the majority of the boating occurred between May and September, at the same time waterfowl were engaged with breeding activities. Ducks involved with courtship were interrupted by boats, as were incubation duties later in the season. Incubating females flushed by the noise of outboard motors seldom covered their nests, thus exposing their eggs to adverse temperatures or to predators (Bouffard 1982). Field studies conducted as part of NEPA requirements determined that motorboats reduced the sizes of Canvasback broods by as much as 30% when areas with heavy boating and no boating were compared (U.S. Fish and Wildlife Service 1976a, 1976b). Further, boating unfavorably altered the habitat as propellers cut aquatic vegetation, reducing its biomass by 77% in some areas of the marshes and altering its composition in others (Bouffard 1982). Bank erosion and siltation followed the loss of aquatic vegetation, particularly in waterskiing areas. In all, the studies concluded that boating interfered with waterfowl production at Ruby Lake.

The stage now was set for a confrontation. Whereas the public clearly favored continued boating at Ruby Lake, the Defenders of Wildlife — a private organization — successfully stopped the boating with a court order. The findings contained in the federal impact statements provided clear evidence of the harm boating was inflicting on the waterfowl resources at the refuge. After several thwarted attempts to modify boating regulations at Ruby Lake, the U.S. Fish and Wildlife Service completely prohibited waterskiing and regulated the size and type of outboard motors. The refuge also was zoned to minimize boating disturbances at times when waterfowl production was underway (Bouffard 1982).

Clean Water Act: Section 404

Enactment of the Clean Water Act in 1977 strengthened the national commitment to a clean and productive environment. The Act replaced an earlier law, the Federal Water Pollution Control Act of 1972. Measures in both acts controlled pollution and other forms of degradation in those aquatic systems known as "navigable waters." However, Congress did not define its meaning of navigable waters in terms of physical features (e.g., rates of flow, volume, width or depth, ebb and flow of tides, and high- and low-water marks) or in the literal sense of transportation. Instead, Congress intended to restore and maintain the chemical, physical, and biological integrity of waters in the United States.

This interpretation is reflected further in the report of the Committee on Public Works that accompanied the presentation of the Act to the House of Representatives. The report defined "integrity" as a condition in which the natural structure and function of ecosystems are maintained (*House Report* 92-911, 1977). Hence, the Clean Water Act intended (1) to extend federal jurisdiction to the fullest constitutional limits possible, (2) to bring broad protection to the full hydrological cycle, and (3) to protect and maintain wildlife resources and recreational activities dependent on aquatic ecosystems. In short, under weight of language in the U.S. Code, "navigable waters means the waters of the United States, including the territorial seas" (U.S. Code, Section 1362c, 7). Left unstated, however, is the legally sound definition for those parts of water systems popularly known as "wetlands." Indeed, wetlands are not even mentioned directly in the original Section 404 legislation, which was then interpreted narrowly by the U.S. Army Corps of Engineers to apply only to navigable waterways. The fortunes of waterfowl and other wetland wildlife thus became tied directly to the outcomes of subsequent legal battles balancing on such a determination.

Section 404 of the Clean Water Act, in simple terms, requires that the U.S. Army Corps of Engineers issue permits for any discharge of dredged and fill materials into the waters of the United States that alters and modifies the course, condition, and capacity of those waters. (Additional forms of aquatic degradation — pollution, for example — are covered in other sections of the Act, but, in fact, wetlands most often are damaged by one or more forms of dredging and filling.) Accordingly, whether some sites scheduled for development indeed require permits rests largely on their designation as a "true" wetland under the meaning and intent of the Clean Water Act. The modifications allowed when a permit is issued are a related concern. In keeping with the ecosystem concept of the Act, for example, development taking place in a watershed eventually may prove as degrading to the integrity of an aquatic system as much as an action taken directly within a streambed. As illustrated in the following case history, these matters often are charged with controversy and subject to the decisions of judges instead of biologists.

Lake Ophelia is one of several sites in a complex backwater system associated with the Red River and its tributaries in Louisiana, where the rich soils originally supported a luxuriant bottomland forest of baldcypress (*Taxodium distichum*) and other species. Logging of these forests promoted some clearing of the land, but soybean production became the primary reason for wholesale clearing of the bottomlands, and in the process, the degradation of Lake Ophelia. Of prime concern was a threatened tract of 8,000 ha of forest lying between two state-owned wildlife management areas. The state, however, did not challenge the clearing of this prime habitat; instead, citizen conservation organizations such as the Environmental Defense Fund brought suit alleging that clearing of the Lake Ophelia system was subject to the jurisdiction of Section 404 and other federal statues. The defendants included not only the developers who intended to clear the land, but also the U.S. Army Corps of Engineers and the U.S. Environmental Protection Agency.

The foremost questions before the federal court hearing the case were (1) to determine the activities permitted on wetlands; and (2) to rule on whether Lake Ophelia and its immediate environment indeed represented "waters of the United States," or more precisely, whether they were "wetlands" and therefore subject to Section 404 of the Clean Water Act. These questions bore important implications for waterfowl management because most of the forested wetlands in the southern United States already had been converted to row crops; hence, those that remained were especially valuable for Wood Ducks and other waterfowl (e.g., Heitmeyer and Fredrickson 1981). On the other hand, because the bottomland habitat at Lake Ophelia attained its character largely from seasonal overflow and complex drainage patterns, the defendants purported that it was neither navigable water nor a wetland.

In court, the testimony of expert witnesses described the seasonal flooding regime and topographic features of the site and verified the water-tolerant nature of the vegetation in the Lake Ophelia forest. More importantly, features of the seasonally saturated soils in the bottomlands were entered into the legal record, thereby providing the court with clear evidence of a wetland regime. The fact that these soils could produce crops once they were deforested and drained was dismissed by the court as an inappropriate criterion to determine what is or is not a wetland environment.

The court accepted the evidence and ruled that Lake Ophelia's forested bottomlands were wetlands subject to the regulatory authority of Section 404. Furthermore, the opinion addressed four important points concerning the legality of certain activities in wetlands: (1) land clearing, ditching, and disking produced point sources of pollution; (2) sheared trees and other vegetation, scraped soil, and leaf litter constituted dredged material that filled or partially filled wetlands; (3) land clearing was not a normal farming practice since the machinery required was not farming equipment, and (4) clearing for soybean production definitely altered the land use because removal of the native vegetation destroyed the wetland and impaired the circulation and flow of water. Hence, along with a second opinion, these decisions halted further clearing and ditching at Lake Ophelia unless a permit was secured from the U.S. Army Corps of Engineers. They stressed that the ecological goals sought by the Clean Water Act could not be achieved when such traditional criteria as high-water marks alone were applied to the determination of wetlands. Indeed, the revised regulations of the Army Corps of Engineers stated that wetlands adjacent to or bordering other, more clearly defined waters of the United States *must* remain within the jurisdiction of Section 404 (*Federal Register* 42:37128, 1977).

The significance of the Lake Ophelia decision seems clear. First, the court recognized the full range of ecological features of the site in reaching its decision. Soils, vegetation, and drainage patterns were accepted as valid evidence of a wetland environment. Second, the decision, by implication, recognized the complex hydrological relationships existing between easily defined "navigable waters" and the more obscure nature of associated "wetlands." Whereas the court recognized that wetlands may not be a term of pure science, the ruling accepted that wetlands could be defined in ways that satisfied social and political needs for the jurisdictional goals of Section 404. According to the ruling, the definition of wetlands should be interpreted with that purpose in mind. Most importantly, the rulings firmly established that land-clearing activities converting wetlands to agriculture require a Section 404 permit. The decision held that the Clean Water Act was a legitimate national policy reflecting the public interest.

In 1983, the Fifth Circuit Court of Appeals heard the Lake Ophelia case and upheld the requirement for a permit, a decision of considerable importance: Clearing wetlands for agriculture is regulated by Section 404. The ruling thus gave legal protection to wetlands that otherwise might be saved only by outright purchase or other types of expensive intervention.

Section 404 and the SWANCC Decision

A major change to Section 404 began when the Solid Waste Agency of Northern Cook County (SWANCC) proposed to develop a nonhazardous solid waste facility on the site of an abandoned sand and gravel pit. The proposal requested a permit to fill 7.2 ha of small ponds and wetlands within the 215-ha site. However, the U.S. Army Corps of Engineers denied the permit because more than 100 species of migratory birds used the wetlands. A subsequent legal challenge upheld the Corps' decision in lower courts, but SWANCC eventually appealed to the U.S. Supreme Court. On 9 January 2001, the U.S. Supreme Court issued its decision for *Solid Waste Agency of Northern Cook County v. United States Army Corps of Engineers*, now popularly known as the SWANCC decision. The Court ruled that jurisdiction by the U.S. Army Corps of Engineers did not extend to isolated wetlands if they are not adjacent to navigable waters, and that the Corps lacks authority over the wetlands based solely on the use of those "nonnavigable, isolated, intrastate" waters by migratory birds, the so-called "Migratory Bird Rule." With this decision, the Supreme Court ruled that the U.S. Army Corps of Engineers could regulate isolated wetlands only if those wetlands bore some relationship to interstate commerce besides use by migratory birds. In essence, the Supreme Court ruling eliminated the "Migratory Bird Rule" that the Corps had used to assert control over isolated wetlands (see Freeman and Rasband 2002, Downing et al. 2003). Hence, Section 404 no longer affords protection for many thousands of wetlands important to waterfowl and other waterbirds. Indeed, the SWANCC decision removes protection for most prairie pothole wetlands, although they still receive protection under the Swampbuster provisions of the Food Security Act of 1985 (van der Valk and Pederson 2003). The SWANCC decision also has major ramifications for amphibians, which often breed in isolated wetlands such as vernal pools (see Zedler 2003).

Endangered Species

Legislation expressly concerning species threatened with extinction was enacted in 1966. Supplemental legislation followed, including the Endangered Species Act of 1973 and later amendments, further defining the national commitment to the preservation and management of threatened and endangered biota (see Bean 1977; Johnson 1979, 1980). The 1973 Act clarified a troubling problem with the legal (but not necessarily scientific) definition of a "species," as only full species had received protection under the original 1966 legislation. After 1973, however, subspecies or subpopulations of an otherwise secure species were protected by federal jurisdiction when these were in jeopardy of continued existence. This welcome distinction thereby included a number of waterfowl populations that otherwise may have fallen into further neglect.

Additionally, the International Union for the Conservation of Nature and Natural Resources (IUCN) maintains a worldwide watch on species whose populations are no longer secure; these are listed in Red Data Books issued periodically by IUCN. Unfortunately, the IUCN categories used to define the status of these organisms do not coincide fully with the categories declared in the United States under the current definitions of the Endangered Species Act. Regardless, in 2004 the IUCN (2004) listed six species as critically endangered, nine as endangered, and 11 as vulnerable (see Table 2-3), whereas six taxa have been listed by the U.S. Fish and Wildlife Service as threatened or endangered in the United States.

Recovery plans have been developed for each of the taxa of American waterfowl currently listed by the U.S. Fish and Wildlife Service under auspices of the Endangered Species Act, although the results of these efforts are not yet clear in all cases. Some of the plans call for captive breeding programs from which new stocks were reintroduced into former range (e.g., Hawaiian Goose). However, other measures such as habitat protection and the control of predators or competitors often are required to assure the success of the stocking programs.

The Aleutian Canada Goose, for example, was listed as an endangered species in 1967, with an estimated population of only 800. The original nesting range of the Aleutian Canada Goose is not well known, but historical records suggest that most of the larger Aleutian Islands to the Kuril Islands in Asia were once within its historic distribution. The demise of the Aleutian Canada Goose occurred when both arctic foxes (*Alopex lagopus*) and red foxes (*Vulpes vulpes*) were introduced on about 190 islands in Alaska during the height of the fur trade from 1915 to 1936, although some introductions occurred as early as 1750. The foxes subsequently decimated the goose population wherein

none was seen from 1938 to 1962, until a small population (200–300) was discovered on remote Buldir Island in the Aleutians. A second wild population of no more than 200 birds was later discovered on Chaulak Island (Bailey and Trapp 1984). The population began to recover following efforts that eliminated foxes from 35 nesting islands, to which family groups of Aleutian Canada Geese were translocated from the population on Buldir Island. Reduced hunting pressure on selected wintering areas in California also increased the number of Aleutian Canada Geese (Woolington et al. 1979, Yparraguirre 1982) — 790 birds were counted in 1975 on their principal wintering grounds in California (Springer et al. 1978), and about 2,700 were counted in California in the early 1980s (U.S. Fish and Wildlife Service (1982a, 1992). The Aleutian Canada Goose was subsequently downlisted to threatened in 1991, when the population had reached 7,000. The population has now increased some 12% per year in the last decade to an estimated 69,900 in 2003–04, and was delisted in 2001 (see Murie 1959, Jones 1963, Byrd and Wollington 1983, Byrd et al. 1991, Balogh 2000).

Restoration of the pitifully diminished population of Hawaiian Geese actually began well before enactment of formal legislation. The long history of that effort has been chronicled fully by Kear and Berger (1980) and need not be repeated here in detail. Their recovery is remarkable, however, considering that the wild population late in the 18th century probably numbered 25,000 but fell to some 50 birds by 1944 and perhaps to as few as 30 by 1951 (Baldwin 1945, Smith 1952). Restoration involved intensive captive rearing efforts and releases of some 2,000 birds back into the wild. Nonetheless, many populations still are not self-sustaining, wherein current recommendations call for addressing habitat issues rather than further reintroductions (see Kear and Burger 1980, Black et al. 1997, Black 1998, Banko et al. 1999).

The Hawaiian Duck, or Koloa Maoli is another endangered species, presumably having reached its precarious status from wetland drainage (for sugarcane production) and from the introduction of the Indian mongoose (*Herpestes auropunctatus*) and other exotic predators. Originally common on the main Hawaiian Islands, the Hawaiian Duck was extirpated from all but three islands by the 1950s. By 1962 the population was only about 500 birds and had become restricted to only two islands (see Engilis et al. 2002). The Hawaiian Duck was listed as endangered in 1978. The most significant threat now confronting the Hawaiian Duck is introgressive hybridization with the nonnative Mallard (see Chapter 2), wherein only about 2,200 genetically pure Hawaiian Ducks remain in the wild. Indeed, above and beyond habitat protection and other management, current recommendations call for eradication of Mallards and hybrid swarms of Mallards and Hawaiian Ducks (see Engilis et al. 2002).

The status of the Laysan Duck is less comforting than the present situation for either of the other Hawaiian species. Virtually all of the perils peculiar to island-dwelling birds have befallen this small-bodied duck: exotic introductions, habitat destruction, highly limited distribution, poor abilities for coexisting with humans, and, presumably, overhunting. The vulnerability of Laysan Ducks to any of these factors was clear early in the 20th century. Fisher (1903) noted that, of all the birds on Laysan, these ducks were most likely to be exterminated; at the time he estimated that no more than 100 ducks still remained on the island. No other living duck is as restricted in distribution as the Laysan Duck — the sole surviving population is confined to a single, approximately 370-ha island in the Hawaiian Archipelago, Laysan Island.

Laysan Ducks are quite tame and show little fear of humans; although able to fly, they more often swim or walk. Hence, a single encounter in the past with the crew of a fishing vessel easily might have decimated half of the population in one day (U.S. Fish and Wildlife Service 1982b). Even today, the possibility remains for rats (*Rattus* spp.) to escape from a shipwreck, thereby introducing a potentially harmful predator of eggs and ducklings (Moulton and Weller 1984). The release of European rabbits (*Oryctolagus cuniculus*) on the island in 1903 caused the most serious threat to these birds, as the exotic rabbit population exploded and rapidly devegetated the island. As a result, Laysan Ducks were brought to the verge of extinction, with only 6–12 counted in 1911–12 (see Berger 1972, Moulton and Marshall 1996). By the time the rabbits were eliminated in 1923, Wetmore (1925) estimated that only 20 Laysan Ducks still survived, and censuses of the population have varied since then. Brock (1951), for instance, counted 33 in 1950, but other estimates shortly thereafter suggested as many as 700 birds might exist; about 450 birds were banded in 1979 from a total population of perhaps 500 (Weller 1980). The carrying capacity of the island is perhaps no more than 500 (Moulton and Marshall 1996).

Laysan Island is now part of the Hawaiian Islands National Wildlife Refuge and represents the entire ecosystem used by a wild population of Laysan Ducks. The island contains a central, hypersaline lagoon that represents the principal feeding area where brine flies (*Neoscatella sexnotata*) comprise much of the Laysan Teal's diet (Caspers 1981, Moulton and Weller 1984, Moulton and Marshall 1996). However, drifting sand and past changes in water level have reduced the lagoon to about 30% of its capacity, which has increased the vulnerability of Laysan Ducks (Warner 1963, Moulton and Weller 1984). Indeed, a severe drought in 1993–94, coupled with proventricular infections from the nematode *Echinuria uncinata*, reduced the population to less than 100.

The initial recovery plan stresses the importance of a propagation program using captive birds. At least four separate breeding locations, each with a minimum of 20 birds, were recommended (U.S. Fish and Wildlife Service 1982b). Fossil and subfossil remains now indicate that the Laysan Duck occurred on the main islands in the archipelagos, so potential reintroduction sites probably exist. However, as with the Hawaiian Duck, hybridization with the Mallard is a likely threat to any reintroduction plans. On Laysan Island, management actions include use of snow fences to stabilize dunes and prevent sand from filling the lake, as well as strict control to prevent introductions of exotic plants or animals. Nonetheless, the persistence of a wild population of Laysan Ducks is clearly tenuous and will require intensive monitoring and management. Fortunately, however, at least 45 zoos and other facilities have Laysan Ducks in captivity.

The Spectacled Eider was added to the U.S. Endangered Species List in 1993, where it was listed as threatened. This species, restricted in range to coastal Alaska and easternmost Russia, persists in three major populations: western Alaska, northern Alaska, and arctic Russia. The population in western Alaska declined 96% between 1957 and 1992 to less than 4,000 nesting females (Stehn et al. 1993). The other populations are declining or thought to be declining (see Petersen et al. 2000). Recovery efforts include intensive research on their biology and ecology, and the curtailment of harvest.

The Steller's Eider is the latest addition to the U.S. Endangered Species List, where the population breeding in Alaska was listed as threatened in 1997. The Steller's Eider — the smallest of the four species of eiders — occurs in two main populations: (1) a small Atlantic population that breeds in western Russia and winters in Europe; and (2) a larger Pacific population found primarily in eastern Siberia but also in the United States, principally on the Arctic Coastal Plain near Barrow, Alaska. The species is all but gone from the Yukon-Kuskokwim Delta. In Alaska, Steller's Eiders have plummeted from 400,000–500,000 tallied on winter surveys in the 1960s to less than 200,000 in the 1990s. The cause for the decline is unknown but likely includes overharvest, predation, lead shot ingestion, and climate change. Recovery efforts will be difficult, however, because much of the basic biology remains unknown about Steller's Eiders, and this species occurs in remote areas (see Fredrickson 2001, U.S. Fish and Wildlife Service 2002). As with the Spectacled Eider, recovery efforts focus on research and the curtailment of harvest. Also, the Alaska Migratory Bird Co-Management Council (see Subsistence Hunting and Native Peoples below), in cooperation with the U.S. Fish and Wildlife Service, has protected both the Steller's and Spectacled Eider from harvest and egg collecting by subsistence hunters, which automatically removes both species from sport hunting throughout Alaska.

STATE AND PRIVATE SECTORS

State Waterfowl Stamps

As already presented, requirements for a federal migratory bird hunting stamp began in 1934. However, several states copied that idea and require a supplementary stamp as part of a valid license for legal waterfowl hunting within their jurisdictional territories. As with the federal stamp, the state stamps are popularly known as Duck Stamps.

The first state Duck Stamp, priced at $1, was issued by the California Fish and Game Department in 1971. At least 80% of the revenues were expended on waterfowl habitat in Canada under the auspices of Ducks Unlimited Canada. In 1978, the California stamp began selling for $5, with resulting revenues averaging more than $500,000 each year thereafter; at least 45% of these funds again were spent on habitat programs in Canada, but the balance (after deducting administrative costs) was spent on waterfowl breeding habitat in California.

The idea of state Duck Stamps spread rapidly after 1971, often being introduced in legislatures with the strong support of Ducks Unlimited. Some 49 states now have issued stamps, which are required to hunt waterfowl in most instances. The result is that additional millions of dollars are raised each year for wetland preservation, thereby complementing the funds originating from P-R excise taxes, sales

of federal Duck Stamps, and the donations of private organizations.

The revenues reported for the sales of state Duck Stamps are not limited to the purchases of hunters. Additional sales to stamp collectors can generate even more income with appropriate marketing techniques. In 1982, for example, hunters in Ohio expended $220,000 for 40,000 stamps, but collectors purchased another 10,000 stamps, thereby adding another $55,000 to waterfowl management (Denney 1983). Prior to 1979, states did not retain any rights to revenues produced from sales of artwork based on the colorful stamps. Since 1980, however, states initiating stamp programs have retained partial or full rights to sales of limited-edition prints of the stamps, thus producing additional revenues. Texas realized $587,000 from its share of the sales of prints of its first (in 1981) Duck Stamp (Denney 1983).

The success of the stamp programs initiated some controversy about the ways states might expend their new-found revenues. As might be expected, waterfowl management varies among the states in relation to the perceptions of each for their needs and problems. For its part, Ducks Unlimited believes at least some of the state funds should be spent furthering its mission of habitat development in Canada, and most states indeed provide a part of their revenues for habitat programs in Canada. Many states contribute 50% or more, after deducting the administrative costs (commonly 10% of the total revenue) associated with printing and issuing the stamps.

In all, state Duck Stamps have become a major source of revenue for waterfowl management. Further, like the receipts from federal stamps, these funds represent the overwhelming financial commitment of hunters for the perpetuation of waterfowl and waterfowl hunting.

Private Organizations

Several private organizations influence the development and implementation of policies affecting waterfowl conservation and management. Among these are the National Audubon Society, the Wildlife Management Institute, The Nature Conservancy, and the National Wildlife Federation. Each group has made important and long-standing contributions, but few private organizations maintain a focus exclusively on waterfowl. Ducks Unlimited is an important and well-known exception that has been involved with waterfowl management for nearly 70 years (see Infobox 11-2).

Infobox 11-2

Ducks Unlimited — Waterfowl Conservation in the Private Sector

Ducks Unlimited (DU) was triggered by the Dust Bowl, the prolonged drought of the 1930s that caused widespread losses of waterfowl habitat. In response, a group of American businessmen and conservationists formed DU in 1937 as a nonprofit organization committed to raising private funds to expend on nesting areas in Canada, particularly in the vital Prairie Pothole Region. DU later expanded its mission to include the United States and Mexico; hence, it now addresses the conservation, restoration, and management of wetlands and associated habitats of importance to waterfowl across the breath of North America.

In some instances, landowners enter into long-term easements (up to 99 years) with DU, thereby agreeing not to alter their wetlands (and uplands) in ways that diminish their value as waterfowl habitat. A staff of engineers and biologists then designs a development plan, which may require construction of dams, levees, channels, and other water-control structures. At times DU may also purchase key sites for waterfowl conservation and management.

In addition to wetlands, DU programs include uplands where critical nesting habitat is besieged by both urban development and intensive agriculture. Partnerships with farmers promote land-management practices of mutual benefit to agricultural production and wildlife (e.g., minimum tillage). DU also works closely with lawmakers to develop agricultural policies that encourage — often with economic incentives — wildlife management on farmland. On wintering areas, DU focuses on wetlands where large numbers of waterfowl can thrive in relatively confined areas, with a goal of providing food and other conditions that ensure high survival rates and adequate fitness for spring migration and successful breeding.

Between 1937 and the end of 2003, DU had raised nearly $2 billion for about 14,000 wetland-related projects of all kinds (e. g., land acquisition, restoration, development, research, and protection). In completing these projects, DU typically works closely with other groups such as nonprofit organizations, state and federal agencies, and Indian tribes, as well as with individuals; these

partnerships highlight DU's operations and approach to conservation. DU also conducts surveys of nesting conditions, at times engages in banding operations, and cooperates with the research activities of other agencies. DU periodically sponsors an International Waterfowl Symposium and publishes the proceedings.

In 1991, DU formed its own research arm in Canada, the Institute for Waterfowl and Wetlands Research (IWWR), which provides scientific evaluations for existing conservation programs and helps guide and integrate the development of new activities. A current IWWR project in Canada addresses the role of wetlands in

sequestering carbon, which may reduce the amount of carbon dioxide and methane naturally entering the atmosphere (i.e., lessen the total output of these "greenhouse gasses" and therefore help curtail global warming). Thus, if wetlands function as "biological sinks" by slowing the release of carbon, the relationship reveals yet another reason for wetland conservation.

DU maintains a current (2004) membership of nearly 500,000 hunters and conservationists, who are organized in 3,800 chapters. The national headquarters is located in Memphis, Tennessee. Photo courtesy of Ducks Unlimited.

Another private organization is The Trumpeter Swan Society (TTSS), founded in 1968 to nurture and secure the recovery of North America's largest species of waterfowl. Market and subsistence hunting nearly caused the extinction of the Trumpeter Swan before enactment of the Migratory Bird Treaty Act in 1918. Creation of Red Rock Lakes National Wildlife Refuge, Montana, in 1935 added further protection for Trumpeter Swans nesting in the "lower" United States. These safeguards helped increase the number of swans, but the birds — which are not strong pioneers — did not reoccupy much of their former range. Moreover, other threats continued to undermine the security of their populations. Hence TTSS was founded to assure the security of Trumpeter Swan populations and to restore the species to its original range in North America (see Gillette and Shea 1995, Shea et al. 2001). To fulfill this mission, the organization promotes research into the ecology and management of Trumpeter Swans and, through its bulletin *North American Swans* and newsletter *Trumpetings*, provides a framework for exchanging information about the species. It also hosts and publishes the proceedings of the Trumpeter Swan Society Conference, which is held biannually in either a breeding or wintering area. TTSS operates from its headquarters in Maple Plain, Minnesota.

Currently, TTSS is concerned with such issues as lead poisoning in the border area between Washington state and British Columbia, where more than 1,350 wintering Trumpeter Swans died between 1999 and 2004. At present, the source of the lead shot contamination is unclear, as is an effective means of halting further losses. TTSS also is focusing on the restoration of the numbers of Trumpeter Swans breeding in the western United States, where only

64 nesting pairs were recorded in 2004. Most of this remnant breeding population is restricted to the Greater Yellowstone region of Montana, Idaho, and Wyoming. Restoration efforts center on encouraging this population to reoccupy long-vacant breeding and wintering habitat, but the results have been hindered by legal hunting for Tundra Swans in adjacent states. Hunters mistakenly shoot the similar Trumpeter Swans on those occasions when the birds in fact pioneer into these areas. Conflicts concerning the hunt thus have prevented key habitats from being used in the effort to expand the nesting range of Trumpeter Swans. A long-standing winter feeding program at Red Rock Lakes ended in 1992 and translocations of Trumpeter Swans were made thereafter to disperse the concentrated population, but the effectiveness of this program also was diminished by the impact of otherwise legal swan hunting. See Shea (2000, 2004) for fuller discussions of these and other issues central to the restoration of Trumpeter Swans and the TTSS agenda.

Hunter-based waterfowl associations also occur in several states, among them New Jersey, South Carolina, Colorado, Arkansas, Michigan, and Alabama, each with similar missions: to conserve waterfowl, wetlands, and the tradition of sport hunting. The first such group was established in California in 1945. Today, the California Waterfowl Association (CWA) has more than 19,000 members who support programs involved with waterfowl biology, habitat restoration and enhancement, education, and public policy. Financial support for CWA programs originates from donations, fund-raising events, grants, contracts, and membership dues.

A core philosophy of CWA is that the perpetuation of waterfowl hunting is essential to waterfowl and wetland conservation. Consequently, CWA's programs focus on goals that support sustainable hunting opportunities. The "Hunting Heritage" program includes activities that focus on public policy associated with wetland conservation, protection of hunters' rights and opportunities, education efforts to improve the understanding of hunting's benefits to California's wetland environments, and encouragement of others, especially youngsters and minorities, to become hunters. CWA has actively defended hunters from legislative attempts to restrict firearms. Each year CWA also comments on the regulations proposed for waterfowl hunting in California. In recent years these comments included requests to reduce the bag limit for Mallards, and a recommendation designed to recognize the distinction between Mallards produced from breeding areas in California from those produced in midcontinental North America. Another activity in the realm of government affairs concerns water allocations for the Upper Kalmath Basin where the needs of waterfowl are strongly linked with those for agriculture.

CWA's biological programs focus on enhancing waterfowl and wetlands of significance to hunters or those that present unique opportunities for conservation. For example, the "Mallard Legacy Program" secures and increases habitat for ducks nesting in California. Northern Pintails represent another species-specific target, which in this case concerns the enhancement of winter habitat and staging areas in California; it also includes political activities that assist efforts leading to the recovery of Northern Pintails on nesting grounds outside the state. These programs often mesh with federal efforts (e.g., Conservation Reserve Program, Wetland Reserve Program) and, in concert with its partners, CWA has restored or enhanced more than 48,500 ha of habitat in the past decade. CWA biologists and staff also offer landowners advice and technical assistance for wetland improvement and management.

CWA actively promotes conservation education by providing grade schools with kits that inform children about the benefits of wetland ecosystems, sponsoring field trips known as "Marsh Madness Youth Days," and setting up "Wetland Wizard" games at fairs and festivals in which youngsters identify animal tracks, feathers, and similar items. CWA also organizes events where older children build, erect, and monitor nest boxes for Wood Ducks; about 30,000 ducklings are reared each year in nest boxes provided by CWA. The organization administers the Dennis Raveling Scholarship that aids college students who plan a career in waterfowl and wetland ecology. CWA publishes the *Sprig Tales Newsletter*

for children, *California Waterfowl Magazine*, and distributes monthly e-news and legislative *News Alerts* from its headquarters in Sacramento. The organization operates with 45 full-time employees.

OTHER ISSUES

Subsistence Hunting and Native Peoples

The Migratory Bird Treaty of 1916 prohibited hunting of waterfowl and other migratory birds between 10 March and 1 September. However, the Treaty gave year-round hunting rights to Inuit and other native peoples for some seabirds, shorebirds, and scoters in recognition of human needs for those resources. These provisions of the Treaty were determined largely without any direct involvement of those native peoples who traditionally exploited waterfowl — especially geese — for food and other uses after the birds arrived on their northern nesting grounds. For decades, however, little concern was expressed about the technical illegality of subsistence hunting under terms of the Migratory Bird Treaty.

Inevitably, research began revealing the magnitude of waterfowl harvests by native peoples, especially for some goose populations (Hanson and Currie 1957, Hanson and Gagnon 1964, Klein 1966). These reports demonstrated the economic and cultural importance of geese to native peoples, but they also revealed a substantial harvest rate per hunter — kills were made increasingly easy by the availability of modern weapons. In the early 1960s, for example, Inuit living on the Yukon-Kuskokwim Delta of Alaska — a population then of about 9,500 people — may have harvested as many as 83,000 geese of five species each year, including as much as 15% of the spring populations of Cackling Canada Geese and Pacific White-fronted Geese (Klein 1966).

In Canada at the southern end of Hudson Bay, James Bay represents a major staging area for migrating geese and Atlantic Brant where Reed (1991) reported Cree hunters claim an annual harvest of 90,200 geese; 58% of the harvest occurred in the spring. The meat — about 200,000 kg — provided about 25% of the total consumption of wild animal food. The Cree harvest represented about 13% of the total kill of Canada Geese in the Mid-Atlantic Population and an estimated 22% of the Atlantic Brant in the Atlantic Flyway. However, while the Cree harvest must be included in the management of these populations, subsistence hunting of this magnitude has occurred for many decades and thus should not be regarded as the emergence of a new factor. In fact, the impact of these harvests was unknowingly reflected for years in the annual winter assessments of population size (Reed 1991).

Other data indicate smaller harvests. A survey conducted between 1995 and 1999 of villages in the Yukon-Kuskokwim Delta in Alaska revealed an annual waterfowl harvest of 13 geese, 13 ducks, and 2 swans per household (Wentworth and Wong 2001). Most of the harvest occurs in spring, just after the birds return to the tundra and when waterfowl represent a desirable source of fresh meat after a winter diet of dried and frozen fish. However, waterfowl comprised just 2–6%, by weight, of the year-round subsistence diet in most villages. The harvest then decreases sharply in early summer when the nesting birds are less accessible and native people turn to commercial and subsistence fishing. Nonetheless, duck and goose eggs are harvested, especially in coastal areas where nest densities are highest. Women are primarily responsible for gathering eggs, which is often done in conjunction with gathering edible greens; both activities are of nutritional importance and offer women a welcome change after a long winter inside their homes. Overall, the survey estimated that villagers collectively harvested an average of about 4,500 goose, 2,250 duck, and 820 swan eggs each year.

In Cree culture, goose hunting is a structured activity that includes the entire community (e.g., school schedules are adjusted to allow children to accompany their parents on the spring and fall hunts). The coastline is divided into hunting territories, each of which is governed by an experienced hunter (the "goose boss"). Hunting is subject to long-standing rules, including rotating hunting pressure among several locations to minimize disturbing the main flock. For generations, Cree hunters also have constructed dikes that catch run-off water to create both hunting areas and lush sites where geese and other migratory birds find additional food (see Reed 1991 for more about Cree subsistence hunting).

Recognition of these spring harvests along with more intensive management of goose populations created needs for more information (e.g., Timm and Dau 1979, Reed 1991). However, collecting reliable data about spring hunting is difficult because native peoples (1) live in remote and scattered villages, (2) commonly are overlooked in government surveys of licensed hunters, and (3) are aware that white people consider their spring hunting illegal. To illustrate the difficulty in assessing the situation, the subsistence kill of geese in the James–Hudson Bay region

of Ontario probably doubled or tripled during a 20-year period, with spring harvests averaging 20–63 geese/hunter in different villages. Yet during the same period, the Mississippi Valley and Tennessee Valley Populations of Interior Canada Geese and others of Lesser Snow Geese were increasing (Prevett et al. 1983; see also Boyd 1977 and Finney 1979 for additional data). On the other hand, winter populations of Cackling Canada Geese and White-fronted Geese each diminished from more than 300,000–400,000 to less than 100,000 birds (O'Neill 1979). Goose hunting was restricted in California in response to those reductions. Whereas some other goose populations in California increased as a result of the new regulations, Pacific White-fronted Geese did not respond in kind, nor was the dramatic decline of Cackling Canada Geese halted (Raveling 1984).

As long as waterfowl populations were expanding or at least seemed undiminished, government agencies experienced little pressure to enforce the provisions of the Migratory Bird Treaty. The violations were ignored for practical reasons. In some instances, the Migratory Bird Treaty may conflict with other treaties negotiated with native peoples, thereby forming legal clouds for the issues at hand. Native peoples nonetheless still voiced their concerns about their cultural heritage, which include their needs and, in their view, their *rights* for subsistence hunting (Klein 1966, Kelso 1982). Indeed, the issue has larger connotations in terms of minority rights in modern society and produced at least one instance of physical turbulence when native peoples were confronted by federal agents (Klein 1966). For many years these political, cultural, and legal difficulties produced little direct action from conservation agencies responsible for administration of the Migratory Bird Treaty.

More recently, however, the pressing issue of subsistence hunting stimulated renegotiation of the Treaty between Canada and the United States. These deliberations resulted in Protocols that were formally approved in 1997; the amendments allow permanent residents of villages within designated areas in Alaska to continue harvesting waterfowl and other migratory birds between 10 March and 1 September as has been the case for many centuries. However, the amendments are not intended to produce significant increases in the harvests of migratory birds. Indeed, management-based conservation remains a central theme in the amended treaty, highlighted by a role played by Inuit as equal partners with representatives from state and federal wildlife agencies. The

Alaska Migratory Bird Co-Management Council is the result of this partnership. In 2003, the council issued its first set of recommendations for season and bag limits, hunting methods, law-enforcement policies, population and harvest monitoring, as well as for education programs, habitat protection, and the role of traditional knowledge in managing migratory birds. In the interest of conservation, Trumpeter Swans were among the nine species removed from the harvest list. These recommendations later were incorporated into Spring and Summer Subsistence Harvest Regulations approved for Alaska.

Baiting and Waterfowl Hunting

Simply stated, baiting is the practice of attracting game into gun range with enticements such as salt, cereal grains or other foods. The first recorded baiting of waterfowl in the United States dates to about 1894 in Maryland, after which the practice gradually increased until it became commonplace following World War I. By the 1920s, baiting became particularly widespread in the Illinois River Valley and along the eastern shore of Maryland. Baiting expanded even more as the abundance of waterfowl declined during the severe drought of the 1930s.

In response, federal biologists Clarence Cottam and Francis Uhler investigated the impacts of baiting along the Atlantic Coast and in the Mississippi Valley during the 1933–34 waterfowl season. In their unpublished reports (e.g., Cottam 1934), the two biologists emphasized that bait, as intended, indeed lured large concentrations of birds within shooting range. Baiting typically began a week or two before the hunting season opened and stopped shortly before the season ended, although in Maryland, about 20% of the hunting clubs continued feeding waterfowl after the season closed as an alternate form of "habitat management."

About 4,500 metric tons of grain were used as bait along the Atlantic Coast in the 1933–34 waterfowl season. In the Illinois River Valley, where baiting was more extensive, more than 16,000 metric tons of grain were scattered in front of blinds — enough to feed more than 2 million waterfowl each day for the duration of the 70-day hunting season! Thus, in 1933 alone, hunters at 584 clubs in the Illinois River Valley killed an estimated 926,000 ducks, most of which were Mallards. Income stemming from the sales of bait, plus some 60,000 live decoys, bolstered the local economy. Baiting clearly found strong supporters among both hunters and merchants.

The findings of Cottam and Uhler, in part, led to a new regulation in 1935 that prohibited baiting, which was defined as the artificial placement of grain or other foods for the purpose of luring, attracting, or enticing migratory birds on or over any area where they might be shot. The rationale for the regulation stems from the conviction that baiting significantly increases the vulnerability of waterfowl to shooting, thereby adversely affecting waterfowl populations and the sport of waterfowl hunting (Rogers 1981); since its inception, the regulation has provoked numerous challenges in court.

The controversial aspects of the baiting regulation largely involve the legitimate activity of feeding birds. Thousands of people feed birds legally every day, and neither the 1935 regulation nor any other federal rule prohibits feeding birds at any time of the year. The issue is *hunting* in association with baiting, which, under terms of the 1935 regulation, places liability on the hunter and not on the person providing the food. Moreover, a violation occurs even if the hunter was unaware of the bait. In short, it remains the responsibility of the hunter to determine, or try to determine, whether bait is present (Rogers 1981).

Key elements in the interpretation and application of the 1935 regulation concern the definition of baiting as a hunting practice. Namely, it is illegal to hunt or shoot migratory birds while they feed on bait *and* while they are being lured or attracted to the baited site. Unfortunately, the regulation did not specify clearly defined criteria for determining either the legal existence of "lure or attraction" or the boundaries of a baited area. Further complications arise because of the behavioral differences among the species of waterfowl and from the various kinds of field conditions that may be encountered; these variables normally require that the arresting officer testify as an expert witness (Rogers 1981).

In sum, the controversial points about baiting are (1) that the regulation is inequitable since it places all liability on the hunter and/or gives insufficient consideration to a hunter who is unaware of a baited site, and (2) that the ambiguous and indefinite wording of the regulation makes it difficult or impossible for hunters to determine what is legal or illegal in particular situations. Nonetheless, the courts generally have supported the baiting regulation despite the controversial points outlined above, although the distance between bait and hunter remains at issue. In one case, *United States v. Olesen,* the defendant was found not guilty because he was hunting at a distance of more than 200 m from a baited area in California. Conversely, in *Yandell v.*

United States, the court upheld the arrest of a hunter for shooting ducks some 1,120 m from a site he had baited.

The long-standing controversy over baiting finally saw resolution with passage of the Migratory Bird Treaty Reform Act of 1998, which made it unlawful to use bait to harvest migratory game birds, if the person knows or reasonably should know that an area is baited. A baited area remains off limits to hunters for 10 days after all bait has been completely removed. This legislation replaced the "strict liability" standard then in use to enforce federal baiting regulations, replacing it with a "know or should have known"standard (see U.S. Fish and Wildlife Service 2004).

INTERNATIONAL PROTECTION OF WETLANDS

Ramsar Convention

In 1971, an international forum gathered at Ramsar, Iran, on the southern shores of the Caspian Sea. There delegates from 23 nations adopted a convention popularly known as the "Ramsar Treaty." The thrust of the agreement is evident in the full name: *Convention on Wetlands of International Importance, Especially as Waterfowl Habitat*. Waterfowl, for purposes of this treaty, are birds ecologically dependent on wetlands; thus Charadiiformes (shorebirds, gulls, and allied families), Ciconiiformes (herons, ibises, storks), and other orders of waterbirds are included as well as Anseriformes.

The Ramsar Convention became the first treaty in which signatory countries agreed to modify their national land-use planning, in this instance specifically for the protection of selected wetlands within their respective boundaries; no other treaty concerning wildlife conservation focuses on the protection of habitat (King 1983; see also Anonymous 1971, Nivid 1984, for the full text of the Convention and an overview of its provisions). By 2004, about 140 nations are party to the Convention; the United States joined in 1987 after several years of deferral. Initial opposition within the United States stemmed from the fears of several state governments that joining the treaty might compromise the traditional management and enforcement rights of state wildlife agencies (King 1983).

Nations joining the Convention promote the conservation of wetlands in general, but under provisions of Article 2, they also specifically declare the international importance of at least one wetland within their territories for inclusion on an official list. The United States initially declared four federal wildlife refuges for listing, including the Edwin B. Forsythe National Wildlife Refuge in New Jersey noted for its winter populations of Atlantic Brant. By 2004, Canada had listed 36 sites, Mexico 51, and the United States 19. The treaty lacks penalties but instead presents a strong moral obligation for the protection of crucial wetlands throughout the world.

Structurally, the treaty is managed by the Ramsar Secretariat, whose duties include convening conferences, the latest of which was held in Spain in 2002; the next will meet in Uganda in 2005. The Secretariat is housed within the IUCN — the World Conservation Union in Gland, Switzerland. Its functions include listing the wetlands officially recognized by the treaty and recording any ecological or territorial changes for wetlands on the list. The Ramsar Secretariat also promotes World Wetlands Day, which has been held each year since 1997 on 2 February to commemorate the treaty's signing date in 1971. Many nations choose this occasion to announce their new listings of Ramsar-approved wetlands. Each nation organizes its own activities for World Wetlands Day, which typically involves the participation of both governmental and private organizations; reports originating from these events are later publicized by the Secretariat.

Criteria for listing wetlands were expanded in the years following the 1971 conference and now include the following, of which one or more must apply:

(1) contain a representative, rare, or unique wetland type.

(2) protect a vulnerable, threatened or endangered species or ecosystem to maintain biological diversity.

(3) support plants and/or animals during a critical stage in their life cycle or provide refuge during times of adverse conditions.

(4) support 20,000 or more waterbirds.

(5) regularly support 1% of a population of a species or subspecies of waterbird.

(6) support a significant population of a subspecies, species or families of indigenous fishes.

(7) for fishes, provide important sources of food or serve as spawning grounds, nursery areas, and/or migration paths or habitat for indigenous species.

Braakhekke and Drijver (1984) noted that the "1% rule" helps establish national priorities since a small but exclusive segment of a large waterfowl population might mistakenly overshadow the needs of other species. For example, about 8,000 Common Eiders represent all the eiders breeding in Holland but, overall, that number is less than 1% of a total population of about 2 million birds. In this instance, what seems to be a scarcity of Common Eiders in Holland is misleading and might divert attention from other waterfowl in far greater need of protected habitat. Hence, for the Dutch, Common Eider habitat actually is of less priority than other wetlands.

Under one or more of these criteria, more than 1,370 areas exceeding 120 million ha were listed officially as important wetlands by 2004 in six administrative regions recognized by the Ramsar Secretariat: Africa, Asia, the Neotropics, Europe, North America, and Oceana (see Table 9-4). A few Ramsar wetlands of importance to waterfowl are described in Chapter 9.

North American Waterfowl Management Plan

A landmark endeavor for protection of key wetland habitats in North America made its formal debut in 1986. This initiative is the North American Waterfowl Management Plan (NAWMP), an intensive effort to protect the continent's wetlands and associated waterfowl populations. The NAWMP initially was the mutual undertaking of Canada and the United States, but Mexico joined the program in 1994, thereby enlarging the program to a truly continental scope and perspective. The goals were ambitious: a continental population of 62 million breeding waterfowl, with specific population targets set for each of 10 species of ducks, 27 goose populations, and 5 swan populations, and protection of 2.4 million ha of important wetlands. The intent was to achieve an average fall flight in excess of 100 million waterfowl.

To accomplish these ends, biologists identified 34 areas of distinct importance to waterfowl in North America. Each area or groups of areas then could potentially become the focus of a Joint Venture, which is a regional partnership of public and private organizations and individuals working in concert for waterfowl and wetland conservation and management (Fig. 11-5). Each Joint Venture deals with administration and planning, raising funds, and coordination within the specified region. Quill Lakes, a major staging area for ducks and geese in Saskatchewan, became the NAWMP's first joint venture. Other Joint Ventures quickly followed: the Prairie Pothole Region, Lower Mississippi Valley, Central Valley of

California, Gulf Coast, Great Lakes–St. Lawrence River Valley, and Atlantic Coast. Overall coordination of NAWMP is provided by an 18-member committee of which six are appointed, respectively, by the Director General of the Canadian Wildlife Service, the Director of the U.S. Fish and Wildlife Service, and the Director General de Vida Silvestre in SEMARNAT (Mexico's Ministry of the Environment and Natural Resources).

The NAWMP uses any of several methods to protect and restore wetlands; these include purchase, leases, and easements, as well as providing landowners with economic incentives for soil and water management that benefit waterfowl. Where needed, drainage ditches are removed, and in bottomland areas, cleared land is being reforested. In rice-producing regions, fields are reflooded after harvest, thereby increasing the habitat available for wintering waterfowl. As with other wetland conservation programs, not only waterfowl but also a multitude of other wildlife benefits from the recovery of these vital habitats. Moreover, MacMillan (1998) linked the NAWMP with benefits for the rural economy in Manitoba.

The original plan was first updated in 1994 and reported that more than $500 million had been spent in pursuit of the plan's goals, including the purchase, lease, restoration, and protection of more than 800,000 ha of habitat. Twelve habitat Joint Ventures were in place and two other Joint Ventures targeted individual species or suites of species: American Black Ducks and arctic-nesting geese. The 1994 update increased the goals for habitat conservation to 10.1 million ha, which by then included 32 priority wetlands in Mexico (see Fig. 9-14). The update also connected the NAWMP with other conservation activities (e.g., the Ramsar Treaty and initiatives for protecting biodiversity).

A second update appeared in 1998, when expenditures had reached $1.5 billion. By then, several populations of waterfowl had attained or exceeded the plan's goals, thanks not only to habitat conservation, but also to changing agricultural practices and the blessing of increased precipitation in the midcontinent of North America (see Ankney 1996a). Nonetheless, other species, including Northern Pintails and Tule White-fronted Geese, had not increased to the desired levels. Conversely, the midcontinent population of Lesser Snow Geese had exploded far beyond the carrying capacity of their nesting grounds along the western rim of Hudson Bay, where their grubbing was rapidly turning feeding areas into salt-caked mudflats (Kotanen and Jefferies 1997). The

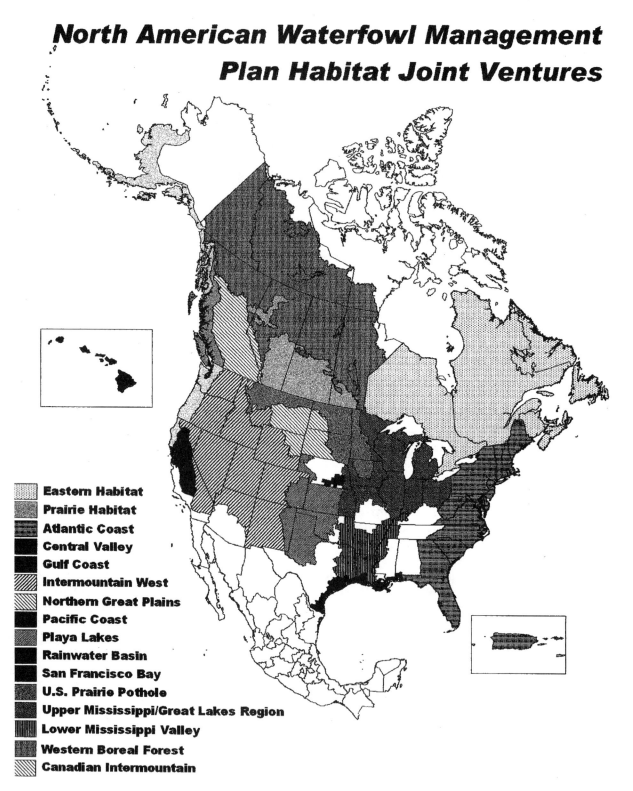

North American Waterfowl Management Plan Habitat Joint Ventures

Eastern Habitat
Prairie Habitat
Atlantic Coast
Central Valley
Gulf Coast
Intermountain West
Northern Great Plains
Pacific Coast
Playa Lakes
Rainwater Basin
San Francisco Bay
U.S. Prairie Pothole
Upper Mississippi/Great Lakes Region
Lower Mississippi Valley
Western Boreal Forest
Canadian Intermountain

Figure 11-5. Implementation of the North American Waterfowl Management Plan relies on a cooperative approach to conservation by means of partnerships called Joint Ventures. The partners then work collaboratively to accomplish goals often difficult or even impossible to achieve individually. Shown here are the habitat Joint Ventures in the United States and Canada as of 2004. Other joint ventures target species or groups of species. Map courtesy of U.S. Fish and Wildlife Service.

Table 11-1. Joint Venture habitat objectives and accomplishments associated with the 2004 North American Waterfowl Management Plan.

| Joint Venture | Objectives[a] (2004) | | Accomplishments[b] (1986–2002) | |
	Protect/Secure (ha)	Restore/Enhance (ha)	Total Area (ha)	Expenditure (dollars)
Atlantic Coast	382,428	84,899	510,676	360,036,000
Central Valley Habitat	80,937	297,264	232,772	248,831,000
Eastern Habitat	580,817	494,344	318,823	266,692,200
Gulf Coast	457,283	372,722	439,849	205,328,000
Intermountain West	607,029	404,686	66,365	14,819,000
Lower Mississippi Valley	167,707	827,987	412,273	204,945,000
Pacific Coast (U.S)	100,767	43,706	88,589	433,909,000
Pacific Coast (Canada)	158,109	42,555	50,270	45,642,196
Playa Lakes	161,874	485,623	42,873	50,425,399
Prairie Habitat	2,700,160	-	1,403,851	687,711,938
Prairie Pothole	765,388	1,784,420	1,526,484	455,130,842
Rainwater Basin	20,234	15,513	7,409	12,776,984
San Francisco Bay	43,301	52,205	14,801	148,828,393
Upper Mississippi/Great Lakes	306,983	-	199,197	123,382,783
Total	6,533,017	4,905,924	5,314,232	3,258,458,735

[a]Data from North American Waterfowl Management Plan (2004:13).
[b]Data courtesy of U.S. Fish and Wildlife Service. Total area includes purchases, restoration, and enhancement of habitats.

situation — an "embarrassment of riches" (Ankney 1996b) — quickly dominated the agenda for the Arctic Goose Joint Venture (see Batt 1997; also see Chapter 8). The 1998 update also highlighted needs to strengthen the biological foundation of the NAWMP in terms of better understanding the links between habitat management and waterfowl populations (see Williams et al. 1999 for more on this subject; also Norton and Thomas 1994). It also advocated a landscape approach that would benefit a parade of wetland species in addition to sustaining waterfowl.

Another update appeared in 2004 and reported the investment of more than $3 billion in the conservation and management of some 5.3 million ha of waterfowl habitat associated with 14 Joint Ventures (Table 11-1) covering all or parts of 67 important waterfowl habitats identified across North America (see Fig. 9-1). Known as the 2004 update, it extends NAWMP's commitment for an additional 15 years "to sustain abundant waterfowl populations by

conserving landscapes, through partnerships, guided by sound science" — a clear thrust to continue waterfowl conservation into the 21st century (Table 11-2). In particular, the theme of the 2004 update emphasizes refining and improving the biological foundation for the plan, including continent-wide assessments of the conservation actions taken since 1986. An appendix establishes regional priorities for addressing threats to the habitat of individual species. Reduced production of Northern Pintails remains a concern, as do the continuing threats to American Black Ducks. A Sea Duck Joint Venture, begun in 1999, addresses declines and restoration of Spectacled and Steller's Eiders in Alaska, concerns for Harlequin Ducks and Barrow's Goldeneyes in eastern Canada, and the uncertain status of Long-tailed Ducks and other species of sea ducks in North America. Of particular note, the 2004 update advocates the use of adaptive management strategies to assess the NAWMP's effectiveness (see Walters 1986

Table 11-2. Breeding population objectives, recent status, and long-term trends for ducks (in thousands) as outlined in the 2004 North American Waterfowl Management Plan. Data from U.S. Fish and Wildlife Service (2004:7).

Species/species group	Population objective	Average popultion size (1994–2003)	Long-term trend (1970–2003)
Mallard	8,200	8,640	No trend
Northern Pintail	5,600	2,815	Decreasing
American Black Duck	640	533	Decreasing
Mottled Duck, Florida subspecies	9.4	11	Increasing
Gadwall	1,500	2,963	Increasing
American Wigeon	3,000	2,628	No trend
Green-winged Teal	1,900	2,485	Increasing
Blue-winged and Cinnamon Teal	4,700	5,875	No trend
Northern Shoveler	2,000	3,318	Increasing
Hawaiian duck	5	2.5	No trend
Laysan Duck	10.5	0.3	No trend
Redhead	640	811	No trend
Canvasback	540	657	No trend
Lesser and Greater Scaup	6,300	4,017	Decreasing

for the theory and practice of adaptive management in relation to natural resources). That is, by employing iterative cycles of planning, implementation, evaluation, and modification, adaptive management steadily improves the beneficial impacts of the plan for waterfowl and wetland resources in North America.

LITERATURE CITED

Ankney, C. D. 1996a. Why did ducks come back in 1994 and 1995: was Johnny Lynch right? International Waterfowl Symposium 7:40–44.

Ankney, C. D. 1996b. An embarrassment of riches: too many geese. Journal of Wildlife Management 60:217–223.

Anonymous. 1971. International conference on the conservation of wetlands and waterfowl, Ramsar, Iran. Wildfowl 22:122–125.

Bailey, E. P., and J. L. Trapp. 1984. A second wild breeding population of the Aleutian Canada Goose. American Birds 38:284–286.

Baldwin, P. H. 1945. The Hawaiian Goose, its distribution and reduction in numbers. Condor 47:27–37.

Balogh, G. 2000. Wild goose chase helps save wild goose. Endangered Species Bulletin 25:20–21.

Banko, W. E. 1960. The Trumpeter Swan. North American Fauna 63. U. S. Fish and Wildlife Service, Washington, D.C.

Banko, P. C., J. M. Black, and W. E. Banko. 1999. Hawaiian Goose (Nene; *Branta sandvicensis*). The birds of North America, 434. The American Ornithologists' Union, Washington, D.C., and The Academy of Natural Sciences, Philadelphia, Pennsylvania.

Banko, W. E., and R. H. Mackay. 1964. Our native swans. Pages 155–164 *in* J. P. Linduska, editor. Waterfowl tomorrow. U.S. Government Printing Office, Washington, D.C.

Batt, B. D. J., editor. 1997. Arctic ecosystems in peril: report of the Arctic Goose Habitat Working Group. Arctic Goose Joint Venture special publication, U.S. Fish and Wildlife Service, Washington, D.C., and Canadian Wildlife Service, Ottawa.

Bean, M. J. 1977. The evolution of national wildlife law. Report to the Council on Environmental Quality. U. S. Government Printing Office, Washington, D.C.

Bellrose, F. C. 1968. Waterfowl migration corridors east of the Rocky Mountains in the United States. Illinois Natural History Survey Biological Notes 61.

Bellrose, F. C. 1976. The comeback of the Wood Duck. Wildlife Society Bulletin 4:107–110.

Benson, R. I. 1964. A study of duck nesting and production as related to land use in Pope County, Minnesota. Pages 107–126 in J. B. Moyle, editor. Ducks and land use in Minnesota. Minnesota Department of Conservation Technical Bulletin 8.

Berger, A. J. 1972. Hawaiian birdlife. University of Hawaii Press, Honolulu.

Berthelsen, P. S., and L. M. Smith. 1995. Nongame bird nesting on CRP lands in the Texas Southern High Plains. Journal of Soil and Water Conservation 50:672–675.

Black, J. M. 1998. Threatened waterfowl: priorities and reintroduction potential with special reference to the Hawaiian Goose. Pages 125–140 in J. M. Marzluff and R. Shallabanks, editors. Avian conservation: research and management. Island Press, Washington, D.C.

Black, J. M., A. P. Marshall, A. Gilburn, N. Santos, H. Hoshide, J. Medeiros, J. Mello, C. N. Hodges, and L. Katahira. 1997. Survival, movements, and breeding of released Hawaiian Geese: an assessment of the reintroduction program. Journal of Wildlife Management 61:1161–1173.

Bouffard, S. H. 1982. Wildlife values versus human recreation: Ruby Lake National Wildlife Refuge. Transactions of the North American Wildlife and Natural Resources Conference 47:553–558.

Boyd, H. 1977. Waterfowl hunting by native people in Canada: the case of James Bay and northern Quebec. International Congress of Game Biologists 13:463–473.

Braakhekke, W. G., and C. A. Drijver. 1984. Wetlands: importance, threats and protection. Dutch Society for the Protection of Birds, Zeist, The Netherlands.

Brace, R. K., R. H. Kerbes, A. X. Dzubin, and G. W. Beyersbergen. 1978. International arctic Snow Goose study. Report to the Mississippi and Central Flyway Council Technical Sections. Canadian Wildlife Service, Saskatoon, Saskatchewan.

Brock, V. E. 1951. Some observations on the Laysan Duck, Anas wyvilliana laysanensis. Auk 68:371–372.

Byrd, G. V., K. Durdin, T. Rothe, D. Yparraguirre, F. Lee, P. Springer, and F. Zeillemaker. 1991. Aleutian Canada Goose (Branta canadensis leucopareia) recovery plan. Second revision. U.S. Fish and Wildlife Service, Anchorage, Alaska.

Byrd, G. V., and D. W. Woolington. 1983. Ecology of Aleutian Canada Geese at Buldir Island, Alaska. U.S. Fish and Wildlife Service Special Scientific Report Wildlife 253.

Carson, R. 1962. Silent spring. Houghton Mifflin, Boston.

Caspers, H. 1981. On the ecology of hypersaline lagoons on Laysan Atoll and Kauai Island, Hawaii, with special reference to the Laysan Duck, Anas laysanensis Rothschild. Hydrobiologia 82:261–270.

Cottam, C. 1934. Baiting and gunning practices from Maine to Virginia. Unpublished report, Office of Migratory Bird Management, U.S. Fish and Wildlife Service, Washington, D.C.

Cushman, R. E. 1958. Leading constitutional decisions. Eleventh edition. Appleton-Century-Crofts, New York.

Dahl, T. E. 1990. Wetlands losses in the United States, 1780's to 1980's. U.S. Fish and Wildlife Service, Washington, D.C..

Dahl, T. E. 2000. Status and trends of wetlands in the conterminous Unite States, 1986 to 1997. U.S. Fish and Wildlife Service, Washington, D.C.

Day, A. M. 1949. North American waterfowl. Stackpole and Heck, New York.

Denney, R. R. 1983. Waterfowl stamp and print history — discussion — staff recommendations. Unpublished report, Oregon Wildlife Division, Portland, Oregon.

Dorst, J. 1962. The migrations of birds. Houghton Mifflin, Boston.

Downing, D. M., C. Winer, and L. D. Wood. 2003. Navigating through Clean Water Act jurisdiction: a legal review. Wetlands 23:475–493.

Duebbert, H. F. 1969. High nest density and hatching success of ducks on South Dakota CAP land. Transactions of the North American Wildlife and Natural Resources Conference 34:218–228.

Duebbert, H. F., and H. A. Kantrud. 1974. Upland duck nesting related to land use and predator reduction. Journal of Wildlife Management 38:257–265.

Duebbert, H. F., and J. T. Lokemoen. 1976. Duck nesting in fields of undisturbed grass–legume cover. Journal of Wildlife Management 40:39–49.

Dunn, C. P., F. Stearns, G. R. Guntenspergen, and D. M. Sharp. 1993. Ecological benefits of the Conservation Reserve Program. Conservation Biology 7:132–139.

Engilis, A., Jr., K. J. Uyehara, and J. G. Giffin. 2002. Hawaiian Duck (*Anas wyvilliana*). The birds of North America, 694. The American Ornithologists' Union, Washington, D.C., and The Academy of Natural Sciences, Philadelphia, Pennsylvania.

Erickson, R. E., and J. E. Wiebe. 1973. Pheasants, economics and land retirement programs in South Dakota. Wildlife Society Bulletin 1:22–27.

Finney, G. H. 1979. Some aspects of the native harvest of wildlife in Canada. Transactions of the North American Wildlife and Natural Resources Conference 44:573–582.

Fisher, W. K. 1903. Birds of Laysan and the Leeward islands, Hawaiian Group. U.S. Fish Commission Bulletin 23:767–807.

Fredrickson, L. H.. 2001. Steller's Eider (*Polysticta stelleri*). The birds of North America, 571. The American Ornithologists' Union, Washington, D.C., and The Academy of Natural Sciences, Philadelphia, Pennsylvania.

Freeman, G. E., and J. R. Rasband. 2002. Federal regulation of wetlands in aftermath of the Supreme Court's decision in *SWANCC v. United States*. Journal of Hydraulic Engineering 128:806–810.

Fuller, E. 2000. Extinct birds. Oxford University Press, Oxford.

Gillette, L. N., and R. Shea. 1995. An evaluation of Trumpeter Swan management today and a vision for the future. Transactions of the North American Wildlife and Natural Resources Conference 60:258–265.

Gollop, J. B., and W. H. Marshall. 1954. A guide for aging duck broods in the field. Mississippi Flyway Council Technical Section (unpublished mimeo).

Hanson, H. C., and C. Currie. 1957. The kill of wild geese by the natives of the Hudson–James Bay region. Arctic 10:211–229.

Hanson, H. C., and A. Gagnon. 1964. The hunting and utilization of wild geese by Indians of the Hudson Bay Lowlands of northern Ontario. Ontario Fish and Wildlife Review 3:2–11.

Harmon, K. W., and M. M. Nelson. 1973. Wildlife and soil considerations in land retirement programs. Wildlife Society Bulletin 1:28–38.

Heitmeyer, M. E., and L. H. Fredrickson. 1981. Do wetland conditions in the Mississippi Delta hardwoods influence Mallard recruitment? Transactions of the North American Wildlife and Natural Resources Conference 46:44–57.

Houston, S., T. Ball, and M. Houston. 2003. Eighteenth-century naturalists of Hudson Bay. McGill-Queen's University Press, Montreal.

International Union for the Conservation of Nature and Natural Resources (IUCN). 2004. IUCN Red List of threatened species. Gland, Switzerland.

Jaenke, E. A. 1966. Opportunities under the Cropland Adjustment Program. Transactions of the North American Wildlife and Natural Resources Conference 31:323–327.

Johnson, D. H., and M. D. Schwartz. 1993. The Conservation Reserve Program and grassland birds. Conservation Biology 7:934–937.

Johnson, M. K. 1979. Review of endangered species: policies and legislation. Wildlife Society Bulletin 7:79–93.

Johnson, M. K. 1980. Management involvement lacking at recent international meeting. Wildlife Society Bulletin 8:65–69.

Jones, R. D., Jr. 1963. Buldir Island, site of a remnant breeding population of Aleutian Canada Geese. Wildfowl 14:80–84.

Kallman, H., editor. 1987. Restoring America's wildlife. U.S. Fish and Wildlife Service, Washington, D.C.

Kantrud, H. A. 1993. Duck nest success of Conservation Reserve Program land in the Prairie Pothole Region. Journal of Soil and Water Conservation 48:238–242.

Kear, J., and A. J. Berger. 1980. The Hawaiian Goose: an experiment in conservation. Buteo Books, Vermillion, South Dakota.

Kelso, D. D. 1982. Subsistence use of fish and game resources in Alaska: considerations in formulating effective management policies. Transactions of the North American Wildlife and Natural Resources Conference 47:630–640.

King, W. B. 1983. Ramsar Convention. Bird Conservation 1:106–108.

Klein, D. R. 1966. Waterfowl in the economy of the Eskimos on the Yukon-Kuskokwim Delta, Alaska. Arctic 19:319–336.

Kotanen, P., and R. L. Jefferies. 1997. Long-term destruction of sub-arctic wetland vegetation by Lesser Snow Geese. EcoScience 4:179–182.

Lendt. D. L. 2001. Ding, the life of Jay Norwood Darling. Fourth edition. Maecenas Press, Mt. Pleasant, South Carolina.

Lincoln, F. C. 1935. The waterfowl flyways of North America. U.S. Department of Agriculture Circular 342.

Lincoln, F. C. 1939. The migration of American birds. Doubleday, Doran & Company, New York.

MacMillan, J. A. 1998. Regional economic impacts of sustainable development activities: the North American Waterfowl Management Plan introduction. Canadian Journal of Agricultural Economics 46:17–35.

Malecki, R. A., F. D. Caswell, K. M. Babcock, R. A. Bishop, and R. K. Brace. 1980. Major nesting range of the Eastern Prairie Population of Canada Geese. Journal of Wildlife Management 44:229–232.

Malecki, R. A., F. D. Caswell, R. A. Bishop, K. M. Babcock, and M. M. Gillespie. 1981. A breeding-ground survey of EPP Canada Geese in northern Manitoba. Journal of Wildlife Management 45:46–53.

McCoy, T. D., M. R. Ryan, E. W. Kurzejeski, and L. W. Burger, Jr. 1999. Conservation Reserve Program: source or sink habitat for grasslands birds in Missouri. Journal of Wildlife Management 63:530–538.

McMaster, D. G., and S. K. Davis. 2001. An evaluation of Canada's Permanent Cover Program: habitat for grasslands birds. Journal of Field Ornithology 72:195–210.

Millenbah, K. F., S. R. Winterstein, H. Campa III, L. T. Furrow, and R. B. Minnis. 1996. Effects of Conservation Reserve Program field age on avian relative abundance, diversity, and productivity. Wilson Bulletin 108:76–770.

Moulton, D. W., and A. P. Marshall. 1996. Laysan Duck (*Anas laysanensis*). The birds of North America, 242. The American Ornithologists' Union, Washington, D.C., and The Academy of Natural Sciences, Philadelphia, Pennsylvania.

Moulton, D. W., and M. W. Weller. 1984. Biology and conservation of the Laysan Duck (*Anas laysanensis*). Condor 86:105–117.

Murie, O. J. 1959. Fauna of the Aleutian Islands and Alaska Peninsula. North American Fauna 61.

Musgrove, J. W. 1949. Iowa. Pages 193–223 *in* E. V. Connett, editor. Wildfowling in the Mississippi Flyway. Van Nostrand, New York.

Nivid, D. 1984. International cooperation for wetland conservation: the Ramsar Convention. Transactions of the North American Wildlife and Natural Resources Conference 49:33–41.

North American Waterfowl Management Plan, Plan Committee. 2004. Strategic guidance: strength_ening the biological foundation. Canadian Wildlife Service, U.S. Fish and Wildlife Service, and Secretaria de Medio Ambiente y Recursos Naturales.

Norton, M. R., and V. G. Thomas. 1996. Economic analysis of "crippling losses" of North American waterfowl and their policy implications for management. Environmental Conservation 21:347–353.

O'Neill, E. J. 1979. Fourteen years of goose populations and trends at Klamath Basin refuges. Pages 316–321 *in* R. L. Jarvis and J. C. Bartonek, editors. Management and biology of Pacific Flyway geese. OSU Book Stores, Corvallis, Oregon.

Petersen, M. R., J. B. Grand, and C. P. Dau. 2000. Spectacled Eider (*Somateria fischeri*). The birds of North America, 547. The American Ornithologists' Union, Washington, D.C., and The Academy of Natural Sciences, Philadelphia, Pennsylvania.

Poole, D. A. 1982. Where have all the dollars gone? Ducks Unlimited Magazine 46:17–18.

Prevett, J. P., H. G. Lumsden, and F. C. Johnson. 1983. Waterfowl kill by Cree hunters of the Hudson Bay Lowland, Ontario. Arctic 36:185–192.

Raveling, D. G. 1984. Geese and hunters of Alaska's Yukon Delta: management problems and political dilemmas. Transactions of the North American Wildlife and Natural Resources Conference 49:555–575.

Raveling, D. G., and H. G. Lumsden. 1977. Nesting ecology of Canada Geese in the Hudson Bay Lowlands of Ontario: evolution and population regulation. Ontario Ministry of Natural Resources Fish and Wildlife Research Report 98.

Reed, A. 1991. Subsistence harvesting of waterfowl in northern Quebec: goose hunting and the James Bay Cree. Transactions of the North American Wildlife and Natural Resources Conference 56:344–349.

Reynolds, R. E., T. L. Shaffer, R. W. Renner, W. E. Newton, and B. D. J. Batt. 2001. Impact of the Conservation Reserve Program on duck recruitment in the U.S. Prairie Pothole Region. Journal of Wildlife Management 65:765–780.

Rogers, J. P. 1981. Waterfowl baiting regulations — a government view. International Waterfowl Symposium 4:100–103.

Ryan, M. R., L. W. Burger, and E. W. Kurzejski. 1998. The impact of CPR on avian wildlife: a review. Journal of Production Agriculture 11:61–66.

Serie, J. R., D. L. Trauger, and D. E. Sharp. 1983. Migration and winter distributions of Canvasbacks staging on the upper Mississippi River. Journal of Wildlife Management 47:741–753.

Shea, R. E. 2000. Rocky Mountain Trumpeter Swans: current vulnerability and restoration potential. North American Swans 29:73–80.

Shea, R. E. 2004. Status of Trumpeter Swans nesting in the western United States and management issues. North American Swans 32:85–94.

Shea, R. E., H. K. Nelson, L. N. Gillette, J. G. King, and D. K. Weaver. 2001. Restoration of Trumpeter Swans in North America: a century of progress and challenges. Waterbirds 25 (Special Publication 1):296–300.

Sidle, J. G., and K. W. Harmon. 1987. Prairie pothole politics. Wildlife Society Bulletin 15:355–362.

Skillern, F. F. 1981. Environmental protection: the legal framework. Shepard's/McGraw-Hill, Colorado Springs, Colorado.

Smith, J. D. 1952. The Hawaiian Goose (Nene) restoration program. Journal of Wildlife Management 16:1–9.

Springer, P. F., G. V. Byrd, and D. W. Woolington. 1978. Reestablishing Aleutian Canada Geese. Pages 331–338 in S. A. Temple, editor. Endangered birds: management techniques for preserving threatened species. University of Wisconsin Press, Madison.

Stehn, R. A., C. P. Dau, B. Conant, and W. I. Butler, Jr. 1993. Decline of Spectacled Eiders nesting in western Alaska. Arctic 46:264–277.

Swift, E., and C. H. Lawrence. 1966. Laws that protect. Pages 468–475 in A. Stefferud, editor. Birds in our lives. U. S. Fish and Wildlife Service, Washington, D.C.

Swisher, C. B. 1943. American constitutional development. Houghton Mifflin, Boston.

Timm, D. E., and C. P. Dau. 1979. Productivity, mortality, distribution and population status of Pacific Flyway White-fronted Geese. Pages 280–298 in R. L. Jarvis and J. C. Bartonek, editors. Management and biology of Pacific Flyway geese. OSU Book Stores, Corvallis, Oregon.

Trefethen, J. B. 1975. An American crusade for wildlife. Winchester Press, New York.

U.S. Fish and Wildlife Service. 1976a. Final environmental statement: operation of the National Wildlife Refuge System. U.S. Fish and Wildlife Service, Washington, D.C.

U.S. Fish and Wildlife Service. 1976b. Environmental impact assessment: effect of boating on management of the Ruby Lake National Wildlife Refuge, Nevada. U.S. Fish and Wildlife Service, Portland, Oregon.

U.S. Fish and Wildlife Service. 1982a. Aleutian Canada Goose recovery plan. U.S. Fish and Wildlife Service, Denver, Colorado.

U.S. Fish and Wildlife Service. 1982b. The Laysan Duck recovery plan. U.S. Fish and Wildlife Service, Portland, Oregon.

U.S. Fish and Wildlife Service. 1992. Aleutian Canada Goose recovery plan. U.S. Fish and Wildlife Service, Anchorage, Alaska.

U.S. Fish and Wildlife Service. 2002. Steller's Eider recovery plan. U.S. Fish and Wildlife Service, Fairbanks, Alaska.

U.S. Fish and Wildlife Service. 2004. Waterfowl hunting and baiting. U.S. Fish and Wildlife Service, Washington, D.C.

van der Valk, A. G., and R. L. Pederson. 2003. The SWANCC decision and its implications for prairie potholes. Wetlands 23:590–596.

Walters, C. J. 1986. Adaptive Resource Management. Macmillan, New York.

Warner, R. E. 1963. Recent history and ecology of the Laysan Duck. Condor 65:3–23.

Weber, W. L., J. L. Roseberry, and A. Woolf. 2002. Influence of the Conservation Reserve Program on landscape structure and potential upland wildlife habitat. Wildlife Society Bulletin 30:888–898.

Weller, M. W. 1980. The island waterfowl. Iowa State University Press, Ames.

Wentworth, C., and D. Wong. 2001. Subsistence waterfowl harvest survey, Yukon-Kuskokwim Delta, 1995–1999. U. S. Fish and Wildlife Service, Anchorage, Alaska.

Wetmore, A. 1925. Bird life among lava rock and coral sand. National Geographic Magazine 48:77–108.

Wildlife Management Institute. 1983. Court rules for wetland program. Outdoor News Bulletin 37:1.

Williams, B. K., M. D. Koneff, and D. A. Smith. 1999. Evaluation of waterfowl conservation under the North American Waterfowl Management Plan. Journal of Wildlife Management 63:417–440.

Woll, P. 1981. Constitutional law, cases and comments. Prentice-Hall, Englewood Cliffs, New Jersey.

Woolington, D. W., P. F. Springer, and D. R. Yparraguirre. 1979. Migration and wintering distribution of Aleutian Canada Geese. Pages 299–309 *in* R. L. Jarvis and J. C. Bartonek, editors. Management and biology of Pacific Flyway geese. OSU Book Stores, Corvallis, Oregon.

Yparraguirre, D. R. 1982. Annual survival and wintering distribution of Aleutian Canada Geese. 1976–1981. Thesis, Humboldt State University, Arcata, California.

Zedler, P. H. 2003. Vernal pools and the concept of "isolated wetlands." Wetlands 23:597–607.

Chapter 12
CONCLUSION

The preceding chapters have spanned the development of waterfowl biology from investigations of "alkali disease" and the propagation of food plants early in the 20th century to the dawn of wetland conservation and the search for better ways to regulate harvests. In charting the course of these and other events, we described a well-grounded and modern classification of waterfowl, some features of courtship behavior and nesting ecology, important aspects of the nonbreeding season, and both natural and hunting mortality. We then followed with an overview of wetlands and their management and a digest of the policies that influence and govern waterfowl management. In all, we believe these subjects offer a fair characterization of our central topic.

The steady march indeed has produced some significant milestones but other goals remain, whether they concern the rush to preserve the dwindling reserve of wetlands or to rid waterfowl of botulism and avian cholera. Solutions also must be reached within the appropriate social and biological contexts for dealing with subsistence hunting by native peoples.

Still other concerns have come to the fore in recent decades, each of which affect far more than waterfowl alone. These include global issues, such as the quickening pace of biological extinctions and the growing evidence of excessive warming within our planet's thin biosphere. We also face increasing public sentiment against hunting as well as the ultimate threat to the health of global ecosystems — the burgeoning growth of human populations. We thus close with some brief remarks about each of these subjects as they affect waterfowl, leaving to others the burden of describing the broader implications to other organisms, including our own species. First, however, we address concerns about the training and availability of waterfowl biologists in the decades ahead.

The Next Generation of Waterfowl Biologists

Kaminski (2002) expressed concerns about the future sources of professional training for students wishing to study waterfowl ecology and management. In effect, will universities in North America have available the coursework and faculty to produce another generation of passionate biologists like those of the past (see Hawkins et al. 1984)? Curricula dealing with natural resources changed markedly toward the end of the 20th century (e.g., Krausman 2000, Porter and Baldassarre 2000), thereby raising questions about the future training of waterfowl biologists. Kaminski (2002) accordingly surveyed administrators at 76 universities in Canada and the United States with programs in biology or natural resources to determine the current and future status of waterfowl science at their institutions and received responses from 71 (93%). Of these, 65% reported that they currently employed at least one faculty member with expertise in waterfowl, but the majority of these instructors were more than 45 years old with a modal age class of 56–60 years in the year 2000. Moreover, when these positions are vacated, only 53% of the administrators in the sample indicated they would seek replacements with similar expertise. These data indicate that the availability of college-level training, including research opportunities, for aspiring waterfowl biologists will be halved within a decade; subsequent monitoring in the wake of recently vacated waterfowl positions support this inference (Kaminski, personal communication). The results further suggest these reductions will be greater in Canada than in the United States.

This emerging situation, if realized, seems sure to create unhealthy conditions for the best stewardship of waterfowl resources. For example, long-term programs already in place will require a steady flow of trained biologists with specific knowledge and understanding of the needs of waterfowl. The North American Waterfowl Management Plan, arguably the most far-reaching ecosystem plan ever implemented, is a prime example. Other programs and organizations — public and private — concerned with waterfowl resources also will need well-trained personnel if they are to flourish as intended. Otherwise, persons lacking the appropriate educational background may be entrusted, by default, with responsibilities beyond their immediate expertise and, likely, their impassioned commitment. Worse yet, without strong advocates and proper guidance, efforts designed to protect waterfowl and their habitats may simply wither and vanish.

Similarly, while the societal values of wetlands (e.g., for flood control and as groundwater filters) are now generally accepted, much still remains unknown about wetland functions — an area of research commonly explored by those professionals who study waterfowl habitats. Wetlands are among the yardsticks for monitoring changes in global climate, a subject that already has captured the attention of waterfowl biologists (see following). Thus, if universities discontinue their programs in waterfowl ecology, the output of wetland scientists may be reduced and thereby short-circuit future contributions to an important field of knowledge.

What might be done to keep waterfowl ecology and management alive and well in university curricula? Kaminski (2002) offered several ideas, which we consolidate and reiterate. First, economic engines should be brought to bear. Waterfowl hunting and observation represent a significant component of outdoor recreation, which turns a powerful economic wheel of expenditures for equipment and travel. In Mississippi, for example, waterfowl hunting generates an annual economic impact of at least $27.4 million (Grado et al. 2001). Universities should respond to these economic forces in the design of their curricula, and those who reap benefits (e.g., hunter-based conservation organizations; manufacturers and retailers of sporting goods; outfitters; private hunting clubs) should provide tangible assistance with endowments, scholarships, and research funding. Second, those public and private organizations having special interests in waterfowl and wetlands should let their concerns be known in the halls of academia as well as in the legislative bodies governing higher education. Many universities seek the guidance of advisory boards, which should include persons familiar with the management of waterfowl, wetlands, and other natural resources. Third, existing programs must continue their productivity and maintenance of high-profile programs. Nothing is more persuasive than the steady output of high quality students who make sound contributions — whether in basic or applied science — and publish their work in leading journals. Faculty who specialize in waterfowl ecology and management also should regularly engage in those forums that inform the public about the significance of the research efforts they direct. Finally, waterfowl and wetlands are a public resource with esthetic, economic, and ecological values, which university curricula should acknowledge with the same commitment as they invest in other disciplines, whether art, geology, philosophy, or physics.

Biodiversity

Extinctions once were measured in terms of millennia, but no longer. Indeed, the recent extinction rates from well-known, taxonomically diverse groups are 100 to 1,000 times greater than prehuman levels; more alarmingly, future rates could climb to 10 times the current rate (Pimm et al. 1995). Some estimates suggest that species may be vanishing at a rate of one per day or even one per hour (Myers 1979). Geological history records five episodes of massive extinctions, of which the departure of dinosaurs at the Cretaceous–Tertiary boundary is the best known, but instead of expanding glaciation or the collision of a meteor, human activities today are the causative agents for a sixth era of extinctions. Indeed, according to Wilson (1992), perhaps as much as 20% of the Earth's biota will disappear by the year 2020 — a rate of extinction exceeding any of the previous episodes by several orders of magnitude.

In the last century, the Labrador Duck was lost forever, an extinction not fully understood, but which likely included the heavy toll of market hunting. Most evidence also suggests the extinction of the Pink-headed Duck, although slim hope remains that a few birds of this species may yet exist in some remote corner of India, Myanmar (Burma), or Nepal; none remains in captivity. These, of course, are a few of the better-known examples; no one knows for sure just how many inconspicuous wetland species have vanished unnoticed. Fortunately, the Hawaiian Goose, once a prime candidate for extinction, has responded exceptionally well to management (Kear and Berger 1980), as has the Wood Duck and other species.

The case for diminished biodiversity usually is rooted in examples from tropical rain forests or ravaged islands such as Madagascar. But we also suggest the importance of wetlands as sites of biodiversity. Food webs in wetlands are no less intricately assembled than those of terrestrial environments, and when human activities eliminate links in wetland food chains, alternate pathways may not always be available. Regrettably, inventories for many species of aquatic organisms are so fragmentary as to preclude precise estimates. Even so, currently available data are not particularly encouraging. For example, fully 325 (40%) of the 820 species of mollusks occurring in the freshwater systems of the United States are endangered or candidates for federal protection (Williams and Neves 1992).

As we have emphasized throughout this book, diversity also applies to wetland types. Waterfowl often require various kinds of wetlands, some of which are seasonal, but these are of no less ecological importance than those of greater permanence. As stated by Weller (1981:17), the "diversity produced by clusters of wetlands will gain importance as we examine habitat use by various species of wildlife. It is important that we maintain this diversity of land forms and vegetative types in a natural state and with a balance characteristic of what existed in pristine times."

Drainage obviously represents one way wetlands

and their biotas are diminished, but there are more subtle ways that wetlands lose their biodiversity. A single example will suffice: Wetlands in some regions are vulnerable to the effects of acid rain, which commonly extirpates many types of invertebrates (see Bell 1971, Haines 1981, and Eilers et al. 1984). Invertebrate foods, as we have seen in Chapter 5, are crucial sources of protein for ducklings; hence, abnormally high levels of acidity threaten the reproductive success of waterfowl (Reinecke 1979, DesGranges and Hunter 1987, Longcore et al. 1987). Many species of fishes also are intolerant of increased acidity; hence, not only are fish populations eliminated from acid-damaged aquatic systems, but so are mergansers and other fish-eating birds.

Our point is simple: Continued degradation of wetlands poses a significant threat to the biological diversity of our planet. We again emphasize that wetland conservation executed under the aegis of waterfowl management benefits far more than ducks — or duck hunters. Moreover, were it not largely for the impetus of waterfowl management, literally hundreds of plants and animals depending on wetland habitats might have faced the perils of human indifference to natural environments and their biota.

Global Warming

After years of debate, the scientific community has reached a consensus seldom achieved: global temperatures indeed are rising (Kennedy 2001, IPCC 2001), perhaps with greater warming than previously anticipated (Kerr 2004). Simply put, human activities beginning with the Industrial Revolution have accelerated the production of so-called "greenhouse gases — chiefly carbon dioxide — with the result that a greater-than-normal proportion of the sun's radiation is trapped on the Earth's surface. Under this blanket, Earth steadily warms in a fashion not unlike the microcosm of a greenhouse. The phenomenon has already produced a number of responses, including changing patterns in polar ice, shrinking glaciers, and rising sea levels. Other impacts concern animals from frogs to bears (see Pounds et al. 1999, Stirling et al. 1999).

Climatologists have constructed various models for the future, each with its own set of outcomes and predictions. However, virtually all of the models predict a decrease in precipitation and soil moisture, especially on the Great Plains of North America. The aridity associated with global warming will subject water resources to even greater demands (e.g., increased irrigation), very likely at the expense of

wetlands. Global warming thus portends significant reductions in the remaining potholes and other wetlands in what is today the heartland of waterfowl production. Models developed by Larson (1995) indicate that a 3 °C increase in temperature will reduce wetlands in prairies by 22% and those in parklands by 56%. Moderate drought, which is predicted to represent average conditions by the 2050s, may reduce wetlands numbers in the northern Great Plains by 38% (Sorenson et al. 1998). Moreover, large areas of coastal marsh will be inundated as the ice caps melt and the oceans rise — with no promise of equal replacement along the new shorelines.

Sorenson et al. (1998) assessed the usefulness of the Palmer Drought Severity Index as an indication of wetland availability and the numbers of ducks breeding in the northern Great Plains. This analysis suggested a strong positive relationship in both cases; hence, the index represents a way to create future scenarios under various temperature regimes produced by global warming (the importance of precipitation in making predictions is negated by higher rates of evapotranspiration resulting from the warmer temperatures).

More than wetland numbers will be affected by a changing climate. Global warming will influence salinity, hydroperiod, and depth and area of surface water, as well as impact basic ecological relationships such as aquatic food webs and the vegetation available for food and cover (see Anderson and Sorenson 2001 for numerous sources). One example of how wetland quality may change concerns the mix of open water to emergent vegetation, an important aspect of nesting habitat (Weller and Spatcher 1965). Ducks typically favor a 50:50 ratio (see Chapter 10), but a warmer climate seems likely to shift the balance toward wetlands essentially closed in by vegetation, thereby diminishing the value of those wetlands still available to nesting ducks in the decades ahead (Poiani and Johnson 1991).

Detailed models also offer predictions about waterfowl production in the wake of global warming. Anderson and Sorenson (2001) projected a range of 9–69% fewer ducks by 2080, depending on the scenarios used in their models. Some parts of the Prairie Pothole Region undoubtedly will prove less vulnerable than others to climate change, but, overall, the duck population breeding in this region seems sure to diminish as a result of global warming. Unfortunately, ducks displaced northward by drought conditions in the Prairie Pothole Region typically experience lower productivity when they nest in either boreal forest or tundra habitat (Rogers 1964,

Smith 1970, Hestbeck 1995). Hence, the nesting efforts by drought-displaced ducks cannot compensate for the loss of production in high-quality nesting areas elsewhere.

Such results project a bleak future for waterfowl. In the interior of North America, conditions may mirror the great but temporary droughts of the past, replete with plummeting waterfowl populations. Many, even most, of the refuges and other areas managed for waterfowl may no longer function in keeping with their intended purpose if the birds move elsewhere. Waterfowl may alter their migration patterns and overwinter in new areas well north of their current wintering grounds. However, there is no assurance that wildlife can adapt new strategies that match the pace of global warming, although Babcock et al. (2002) noted that Tundra Swans advanced their nesting chronology in keeping with recent changes in snow-melt phenology in Alaska (see also Crick and Sparks 1999). A future with fewer ducks and wetlands means more than a loss of aesthetics and outdoor recreation. Hundreds of millions of dollars generated each year by duck hunters also are at risk. Such funds are important to local economies, but they also gird a number of established conservation programs (e.g., taxes on arms and ammunition sales help fund wildlife refuges).

Given these circumstances, resource managers must face the challenges of the worst-case scenario (i.e., the reality of global warming on top of other, more traditional stresses such as urbanization and industrial expansion). Thus, wetland conservation should accelerate in those regions where global warming may expand agriculture, because longer growing seasons will place ever-greater demands on water resources. Moreover, global warming will create even greater stresses on those wetlands already compromised by human development (e.g., ditching and drainage); hence, remaining habitats must be protected immediately from further anthropogenic influences. For more recommendations concerning policies and research, see Bethke and Nudds (1995), Sorenson et al. (1998), and Anderson and Sorenson (2001). All told, global warming places a heavy burden on the next generation of wildlife managers.

A Look at Hunting

Mounting condemnation of sport hunting demands a response, and we shall do so by blending our own convictions with those published by the Wildlife Management Institute (n.d.). The issue of hunting separates the public into three segments: (1) antihunters, (2) hunters, and (3) nonhunters. Antihunters maintain that hunting is both cruel and unnecessary, and they actively work for its abolishment (e.g., Grandy et al. 1992). Nonhunters, the largest of the three groups, form an important audience for the doctrines of the other two groups. Hunting, of course, is not for everyone anymore than opera or football is universally enjoyed, but for those people who do, hunting represents a deep-seated tradition and an outdoor heritage.

Unregulated gunning provided the catalyst for wildlife management, which applied scientific principles to the harvest of waterfowl and other game. Indeed, the very basis of wildlife management is to assure the welfare of animal *populations,* including in some cases an annual harvest of *individuals* of selected species (i.e., those designated as "game"). As we have seen, waterfowl harvests have been thoughtfully governed by equipment limitations and various types of bag limits, each of which is designed to assure the lasting welfare of the population. In other cases, now including Snow Geese (see Ankney 1996) as well as ungulates (see Brown et al. 2000), hunting itself is a management tool for controlling burgeoning wildlife populations, without which habitats may be seriously degraded by the demands of too many animals (e.g., overbrowsing, loss of plant diversity, and soil erosion).

Overall, the modern era of regulated hunting has never jeopardized a single species of wildlife. On the contrary, sport hunting has seldom been a contributing factor to the plight of species today facing the threat of extinction in North America (e.g., freshwater mussels, amphibians, and songbirds). Hunting also may play a role in keeping wild animals wild and wary (Geist et al. 2001), without which Canada Geese often become tame and an urban nuisance — as may other species such as black bears (*Ursus americanus*). Pursuing geese from a hunting blind in a cornfield is far different from watching a flock roam on a golf course or city park, where they resemble little more than domestic stock at risk of becoming devalued as creatures of nature (Seng et al. 2001).

Nonetheless, according to data summarized by Heberlein (1991), we must realize that (1) at least half of the citizens of the United States were opposed to hunting by the mid-1970s, and (2) women and urban residents have the most negative attitudes toward hunting. Significantly, women are becoming more influential in public life (e.g., composition of the U.S. Senate), and the typical father-to-son transfer of the hunting tradition has diminished as more women become single parents and the sole heads of households. Moreover, instead of hunting, many hunting-age youngsters engage in sports and other organized activities or spend their leisure time with computers.

Because of these and other sociological changes, hunters have declined (as a percentage of the U.S. population), but the number of hunters has held fairly steady at 13 million in 2001 compared with 14.1 million in 1991; during this same period, waterfowl hunters dropped from 3.9 million to 2.6 million. Regardless of these trends, however, hunting is increasingly viewed in an antisocial context. The dilemma thus arises about the future: Waterfowl and other kinds of hunting face social retribution, yet hunters provide significant fiscal support for the very programs that conserve wildlife and their habitat (see Williamson et al. 2001). True, general tax revenues also support various wildlife programs, and private agencies such as The Nature Conservancy make significant contributions for the protection of wildlife habitat, but for the present, the funding provided by hunters — particularly at the state level — represents a source that cannot be forsaken (Southwick et al. 2001). Hunter-generated funding via the Pittman-Robetrson Act (see Chapter 11) has been a long-standing source of revenue for state wildlife programs (see Kallman 1987). The most current figures (for 2001) indicate that U.S. hunters expended $21.6 billion, which represents a 29% increase since 1991 (U.S. Fish and Wildlife Service 2002). Nonetheless, with the notable exception of state income tax check-offs, efforts to broaden funding for wildlife conservation to include nonhunters seldom receive legislative support (e.g., proposals to levy excise taxes on birdseed).

Hunters, as they have for many years, also remain among the foremost champions for the protection of wildlife and their habitat. They have, with millions of dollars expended on licenses, excise taxes, and Duck Stamps, as well as personal contributions and memberships, protected wetlands and other habitats that would have long since disappeared — and hunters represent only about 6% of the population of the United States. At the state level, hunters thus pay a disproportionately large part of the costs associated with the management and protection of *all* wildlife, not just game species. Moreover, each year hunters spend nearly $1 billion for hunting privileges (e.g., leases), and because of these expenditures, land that otherwise might be developed is maintained as wildlife habitat. All told, hunting protects the integrity of about 10 million ha of wildlife habitat — an area about the size of Texas, New York, Illinois, and South Carolina combined. Nearly 6 million ha of wetlands are included in this total (Wildlife Management Institute n. d.).

Hunters also have played key roles in the political arena, urging, for example, enactment of various treaties and legislation for the protection of wildlife (see Chapter 11). In short, hunters often provided the primary catalyst for wildlife conservation, a movement dating to the presidency of hunter–naturalist Theodore Roosevelt and continuing today. Most notably in the case of waterfowl, Wood Ducks have fully recovered from their dire status early in the 20th century (see Bellrose and Holm 1994:107–121).

Recall also that hunting is just *one* of several mortality factors acting on wildlife populations. Diseases, accidents, and predation confront animals every day, and in combination with food and water shortages, these events extract an annual toll of natural mortality. Although the mechanics of these processes still are not fully resolved, hunting represents yet another form of mortality that, to some degree, may compensate for other types of losses (see Chapter 8).

Few hunters depend on their sport solely for table fare. Hunting, in fact, is a relatively expensive form of recreation; hence, most hunters would be far better off buying meat at a supermarket than trying to subsist on game. Nonetheless, wild meat amounting to some 341 million kg — the equivalent of 2 million head of cattle — is consumed each year in the United States. Hence, hunters consume what they kill, quite often taking considerable pride in the way their game is prepared for the table. Moreover, it is illegal to wantonly discard game in the field (i.e., game laws throughout the land require appropriate, noncommercial use of harvested animals).

We also wish to repeat, for well-deserved emphasis, that habitats managed primarily for game species also harbor large numbers of nongame species. Some 1,150 species of birds and mammals occur in North America, yet only about 145 of these — just 12.5% — are hunted. That is, habitat managed for one game species, on average, concurrently serves as habitat for seven other species of birds and mammals, to say nothing of fishes, reptiles, amphibians, invertebrates, and plants. As a matter of fact, because of rising concerns for threatened and endangered species and other nongame, state wildlife agencies, on average, currently expend only about one-third of their budgets specifically for the management of huntable species of wildlife. Note, too, that hunting occurs for only a few weeks per year, whereas the same habitat harbors a much greater number of species *year-round*. Good management also may improve diversity; in South Carolina, 76 species of birds use tidal wetlands managed for waterfowl, but only 56 species use the unmanaged wetlands nearby (Epstein and Joyner 1988).

Seng et al. (2001) proposed that it would be difficult to identify any human endeavor with more impact — whether utilitarian, philosophical, or spiritual — on culture and social fabric than hunting. The association transcends both time and political boundaries, being as prevalent in Asia, Europe, Africa, and Australia as in North or South America. In the case of art, for example, consider the remarkable drawings of Ice Age cave dwellers or those of George Catlin, John James Audubon, or Frederick Remington; for literature, the works of James Fenimore Cooper, Washington Irving, Jack London, or Ernest Hemingway. Hunting provides benefits for family and personal relationships. The growing number of women hunters has strengthened bonds within families, as well as improved their own self-esteem and confidence (Lueck and Thomas 1997, Stange and Oyster 2000). Decker et al. (1986) recorded that parents used hunting to teach ethics to their children who were learning to hunt. An appreciation of fairness, self-discipline, and responsibility likewise were included in the transmission of values from one generation to the next. Perhaps of greater significance, however, is that hunting forms strong connections between humans and the land. This relationship provides a fundamental appreciation for conservation, as heralded in the scripture of Leopold's (1949) now famous Land Ethic. By no means are hunters the only conservationists, but virtually all hunters are indeed conservationists; they have experienced first hand how landscapes, whether marsh, field, or forest, define the existence of wildlife communities. See Seng et al. (2001) for a fuller discussion about these and other influences that hunting has instilled into society and culture.

Finally, a word about the so-called "blood thirst" of hunters, a notion we spiritedly reject. We know of no person worthy of the designation of sportsman — and we happily use the term generically to include both men and women — who wishes for anything but a clean kill. Those who "sky bust" at waterfowl far out of killing range have no place in the marshes, nor do those who seek an unfair advantage by ignoring any of the laws designed to promote sportsmanship (e.g., baiting and live decoys). True sportsmen indeed honor a time-honored code, both legal and ethical, of respect for nature. Early in the 20th century, for example, hunter-naturalists successfully lobbied for the end of market hunting and even earlier (in 1887) organized the Boone and Crockett Club. Hunters today continue their role as guardians of wildlife (e.g., Ducks Unlimited, Pheasants Forever, Rocky Mountain Elk Foundation, and National Wild Turkey Federation, among others). True enough, hunters kill, but hunting is not just killing — if it were, the tangible rewards would be so few that most would-be hunters would stay home! Hunting instead is a long-standing tradition that sometimes — but certainly not always — ends with the harvest of individual animals. As stated by Ortega y Gasset (1985:96-97), ". . . one does not hunt in order to kill; on the contrary, one kills in order to have hunted." Hunting thus engenders an outdoor experience, an exposure to things wild and, for some, offers a visceral contact with their ancestral roots. Eaton (1986) offered both an analogy and explanation:

> The people who most love roses, who spend hours pruning them, kill them . . . The men who most love waterfowl . . . who invest in their habitat and protection, also kill and eat them. This is a paradox only to men and women who suffer from centuries of separation from nature, and thus from their true nature.

We thus share the concerns expressed by Heberlein (1991): As hunting and hunters decline in their influence, the funding and infrastructure gained on behalf of waterfowl and other wildlife during most of the last century will be lost. Without the time-proven husbandry of sport hunters — whose existence provided the very genesis of wildlife management — wildlife of all kinds surely will suffer from neglect. Not unexpectedly, sentiments embedded in the writings of Aldo Leopold (1949, 1953) touch at the soul of the issue: The instinct of hunting is almost physiological in the fiber of humans, and those without it have become so supercivilized as to risk losing a wild poem and the music of geese.

Human Populations

The ultimate issue befalling the management of waterfowl and other wildlife deals with the human condition: the size of the human population and the quality of life resulting from its unchecked growth. Ask a person 50 years of age or older about the residential and commercial development they have witnessed in their lifetime; then project a change of the same magnitude for the next generation. The result is an image of ever more urban sprawl and a steady loss of habitat for wildlife. More specifically, what will waterfowl populations and the recreation derived from them — whether consumptive or nonconsumptive — be like if the number of humans continues its geometrical rate of growth?

Currently available statistics describing the growth of human populations are not encouraging (U.S. Bureau of the Census 2003). In 1995, just after the first edition of this book appeared, the world population numbered 5.686 billion and reached 6.229 billion by 2002. For 2010, the world population is projected to reach 6.812 billion and climb to 7.172 in 2015. These data reflect an increase of more than 70 million each year. For the nations of North America, the data (in millions) are

	1990	2001	2010
Canada	27.791	31.593	34.253
United States	250.132	285.024	309.163
Mexico	84.914	101.247	112.469

With the exception of Europe, populations throughout the world will continue to expand, the result of high birth rates (e.g., 2.8 children per woman worldwide, 2.0 in the United States, but only 1.4 in Europe, as reported by the Population Reference Bureau 2004). Moreover, most population growth in the years ahead will occur in developing nations, including those in Latin America. These sobering statistics must be weighed against the environmental pressures of continuing the unrelenting growth of a single, domineering species. Hence, because of what are sure to be worldwide declines in habitat quality and quantity, the numbers of most animals — whether butterflies or dabbling ducks — per human clearly will diminish. Of greater importance, extinctions — permanent losses in the richness of life — will continue, likely at an ever-increasing rate. Of the world's 10,000 or so species of birds, about one in eight, or 1,200, may face extinction during the next 100 years (how many will be waterfowl?). Of these, about 180 already are critically endangered and thus could disappear within 10 years (BirdLife International 2000).

The demands of an ever-larger human population for food and shelter beg additional questions about sources of energy and the per capita acquisition of those trappings representing the modern, technological society desired by most humans (e.g., cars are rapidly replacing bicycles in China's cities). That is, peoples of many nations desire the same stan-dard of living as is currently available to most Americans, yet can the world's resources provide a two-car garage attached to an air-conditioned home for the masses of China, India, or Brazil? Clearly, human populations must be balanced against the finite supply of Earth's natural resources. Waterfowl and their habitats, we trust, will remain among those resources evaluated in that crucial equation.

LITERATURE CITED

Anderson, M. G., and L. G. Sorenson. 2001. Global climate change and waterfowl: adaptation in the face of uncertainty. Transactions of the North American Wildlife and Natural Resources Conference 66:300–319.

Ankney, C. D. 1996. An embarrassment of riches: too many geese. Journal of Wildlife Management 60:217–223.

Babcock, C. A., A. C. Fowler, and C. R. Ely. 2002. Nesting ecology of Tundra Swans on the coastal Yukon-Kuskokwim Delta, Alaska. Waterbirds 25 (Special Publication 1):236–240.

Bell, H. L. 1971. Effects of low pH on the survival and emergence of aquatic insects. Water Research 5:313–319.

Bellrose, F. C., and D. J. Holm. 1994. Ecology and management of the Wood Duck. Stackpole Books, Mechanicsburg, Pennsylvania.

Bethke, R. W., and T. D. Nudds. 1995. Effects of climate change and land use on duck abundance in Canadian prairie-parkland. Ecological Applications 5:588–600.

BirdLife International. 2000. Threatened birds of the world. Lynx Edicions, Barcelona.

Brown, T. L., D. J. Decker, S. J. Riley, J. W. Enck, T. B. Lauber, P. D. Curtis, and G. F. Mattfeld. 2000. The future of hunting as a mechanism to control white-tailed deer populations. Wildlife Society Bulletin 28:797–807.

Crick, H. Q. P., and T. H. Sparks. 1999. Climate change related to egg–laying trends. Nature 399:423–424.

Decker, D. J., K. G. Purdy, and T. L. Brown. 1986. Early hunting experiences: insights into the role of hunting "apprenticeship" from perspectives of youths and adults. New York Fish and Game Journal 33:51–54.

DesGranges, J-L., and M. L. Hunter, Jr. 1987. Duckling response to lake acidification. Transactions of the North American Wildlife and Natural Resources Conference 52:636–644.

Eaton, R. L. 1986. Zen and the art of hunting: a personal search for environmental values. Carnivore Press, Reno, Nevada.

Eilers, J. M., G. J. Lien, and R. G. Berg. 1984. Aquatic organisms in acidic environments: a literature review. Wisconsin Department of Natural Resources Technical Bulletin 150.

Epstein, M. B., and R. L. Joyner. 1988. Waterbird use of brackish wetlands managed for waterfowl. Proceedings of the Southeastern Association of of Fish and Wildlife Agencies 42:476–490.

Geist, V., S. P. Mahoney, and J. F. Organ. 2001. Why hunting has defined the North American model of wildlife conservation. Transactions of the North American Wildlife and Natural Resources Conference 66:175–185.

Grado, S. C., R. M. Kaminski, I. A. Munn, and T. A. Tullos. 2001. Economic impacts of waterfowl hunting on public lands and at private lodges in the Mississippi Delta. Wildlife Society Bulletin 29:846–855.

Grandy, J. W., S. Hagood, and K. Berger. 1992. Alternatives to hunting in wildlife management programs on national wildlife refuges. Transactions of the North American Wildlife and Natural Resources Conference 57:586–591.

Haines, T. A. 1981. Acidic precipitation and its consequences for aquatic ecosystems: a review. Transactions of the American Fisheries Society 110:669–707.

Hawkins, A. S., R. C. Hanson, H. K. Nelson, and H. M. Reeves, editors. 1984. Flyways: pioneering waterfowl management in North America. U.S. Fish and Wildlife Service, Washington, D.C.

Heberlein, T. A. 1991. Changing attitudes and funding for wildlife — preserving the sport hunter. Wildlife Society Bulletin 19:528–534.

Hestbeck, J. B. 1995. Response of Northern Pintail breeding populations to drought, 1961–92. Journal of Wildlife Management 59:9–15.

Intergovernmental Panel on Climate Change (IPCC). 2001. Climate change 2001: the scientific basis. Cambridge University Press, New York.

Kallman, H., editor. 1987. Restoring America's wildlife, 1937–1987. The first 50 years of the Federal Aid in Wildlife Restoration (Pittman-Robertson) Act. U.S. Fish and Wildlife Service, Washington, D.C.

Kaminski, R. M. 2002. Status of waterfowl science and management programs in United States and Canadian universities. Wildlife Society Bulletin 30:616–622.

Kear, J., and A. J. Berger. 1980. The Hawaiian Goose: an experiment in conservation. Buteo Books, Vermillion, South Dakota.

Kennedy, D. 2001. An unfortunate U–turn on carbon. Science 291:2515.

Kerr, R. A. 2004. Three degrees of consensus. Science 305:932–934.

Krausman, P. R. 2000. Wildlife management in the twenty-first century: educated predictions. Wildlife Society Bulletin 28:490–495.

Larson, D. L. 1995. Effects of climate on numbers of northern prairie wetlands. Climate Change 30:169–180.

Leopold, A. 1949. A sand county almanac and sketches here and there. Oxford University Press, New York.

Leopold, L. B., editor. 1953. Round river: from the journals of Aldo Leopold. Oxford University Press, New York.

Longcore, J. R., R. K. Ross, and K. L. Fisher. 1987. Wildlife resources at risk through acidification of wetlands. Transactions of the North American Wildlife and Natural Resources Conference 52:608–618.

Lueck, D., and C. L. Thomas. 1997. Effect of the Becoming an Outdoors-Woman program on attitudes and activities. Women in Natural Resources 19:4–8.

Myers, N. 1979. The sinking ark: a new look at the problem of disappearing species. Pergamon Press, New York.

Ortega y Gasset, J. 1985. Meditations on hunting. Charles Scribners' Sons, New York.

Pimm, S. L., G. J. Russell, J. L. Gitttleman, and T. M. Brooks. 1995. The future of biodiversity. Science 269:347–350.

Poiani, K. A., and W. C. Johnson. 1991. Prairie wetlands: potential consequences for waterfowl habitat. BioScience 41:611–618.

Porter, W. F., and G. A. Baldassarre. 2000. Future directions for the graduate curriculum in wildlife biology: building on our strengths. Wildlife Society Bulletin 28:508–513.

Pounds, J. A., M. P. L. Fogden, and J. H. Campbell. 1999. Biological response to climate change on a tropical mountain. Nature 398:611–615.

Reinecke, K. J. 1979. Feeding ecology and development of juvenile Black Ducks in Maine. Auk 96:737–745.

Rogers, J. P. 1964. Effect of drought on reproduction of the Lesser Scaup. Journal of Wildlife Management 28:213–222.

Seng, P. T., D. J. Case, M. Conover, D. J. Decker, J. Enck, S. N. Frey, M. Z. Stange, B. Staton, R. Stedman, C. Thomas, and D. Thorne. 2001. Contributions of hunting to North American society and cultures. Transactions of the North American Wildlife and Natural Resources Conference 66:202–231.

Smith, R. I. 1970. Response of Pintail breeding populations to drought. Journal of Wildlife Management 34:943–946.

Sorenson, L. G., R. Goldberg, T. L. Root, and M. G. Anderson. 1998. Potential effects of global warming on waterfowl populations breeding in the northern Great Plains. Climatic Change 40:343–369.

Southwick, R., M. Teisl, and M. Gable. 2001. Economics: how it can assist hunting and wildlife management. Transactions of the North American Wildlife and Natural Resources Conference 66:232–242.

Stange, M. Z., and C. K. Oyster. 2000. Gun women: firearms and feminism in contemporary America. New York University Press, New York.

Stirling, I., N. J. Lunn, and J. Iacozza. 1999. Long-term trends in the population ecology of polar bears in western Hudson Bay in relation to climate change. Arctic 52:294–306.

U.S. Bureau of the Census. 2003. Statistical abstract of the United States: 2003. 123rd edition. U.S. Department of Commerce, Washington, D.C.

U.S. Fish and Wildlife Service. 2002. National survey of hunting, fishing, and wildlife-associated recreation for 2001. U.S. Fish and Wildlife Service, Washington, D.C.

Weller, M. W. 1981. Freshwater marshes: ecology and wildlife management. University of Minnesota Press, Minneapolis.

Weller, M. W., and C. E. Spatcher. 1965. Role of habitat in the distribution and abundance of marsh birds. Iowa State University Agricultural and Home Economics Experiment Station Special Report 43.

Wildlife Management Institute. n. d. Placing hunting in perspective. Wildlife Management Institute, Washington, D.C.

Williams, J. E., and R. J. Neves. 1992. Introducing the elements of biological diversity in the aquatic environment. Transactions of the North American Wildlife and Natural Resources Conference 57:345–354.

Williamson, S. J., S. Adair, K. L. Borwn, and J. Turner. 2001. Contributions made by hunters toward conservation of the North American landscape. Transactions of the North American Wildlife and Natural Resources Conference 66:255–269.

Wilson, E. O. 1992. The diversity of life. The Belknap Press of Harvard University Press, Cambridge.

INDEX

Note: Page numbers followed by "f" refer to a figure; "t" refers to a table; "i" refers to an infobox.